T0180750

Lecture Notes in Computer Science 13691

More information about this series at https://link.springer.com/bookseries/558

Shai Avidan · Gabriel Brostow ·
Moustapha Cissé · Giovanni Maria Farinella ·
Tal Hassner (Eds.)

Computer Vision – ECCV 2022

17th European Conference
Tel Aviv, Israel, October 23–27, 2022
Proceedings, Part XXXI

 Springer

Editors
Shai Avidan
Tel Aviv University
Tel Aviv, Israel

Gabriel Brostow ⓘ
University College London
London, UK

Moustapha Cissé
Google AI
Accra, Ghana

Giovanni Maria Farinella ⓘ
University of Catania
Catania, Italy

Tal Hassner ⓘ
Facebook (United States)
Menlo Park, CA, USA

ISSN 0302-9743   ISSN 1611-3349 (electronic)
Lecture Notes in Computer Science
ISBN 978-3-031-19820-5   ISBN 978-3-031-19821-2 (eBook)
https://doi.org/10.1007/978-3-031-19821-2

This Springer imprint is published by the registered company Springer Nature Switzerland AG
The registered company address is: Gewerbestrasse 11, 6330 Cham, Switzerland

Foreword

Organizing the European Conference on Computer Vision (ECCV 2022) in Tel-Aviv during a global pandemic was no easy feat. The uncertainty level was extremely high, and decisions had to be postponed to the last minute. Still, we managed to plan things just in time for ECCV 2022 to be held in person. Participation in physical events is crucial to stimulating collaborations and nurturing the culture of the Computer Vision community.

There were many people who worked hard to ensure attendees enjoyed the best science at the 16th edition of ECCV. We are grateful to the Program Chairs Gabriel Brostow and Tal Hassner, who went above and beyond to ensure the ECCV reviewing process ran smoothly. The scientific program includes dozens of workshops and tutorials in addition to the main conference and we would like to thank Leonid Karlinsky and Tomer Michaeli for their hard work. Finally, special thanks to the web chairs Lorenzo Baraldi and Kosta Derpanis, who put in extra hours to transfer information fast and efficiently to the ECCV community.

We would like to express gratitude to our generous sponsors and the Industry Chairs, Dimosthenis Karatzas and Chen Sagiv, who oversaw industry relations and proposed new ways for academia-industry collaboration and technology transfer. It's great to see so much industrial interest in what we're doing!

Authors' draft versions of the papers appeared online with open access on both the Computer Vision Foundation (CVF) and the European Computer Vision Association (ECVA) websites as with previous ECCVs. Springer, the publisher of the proceedings, has arranged for archival publication. The final version of the papers is hosted by SpringerLink, with active references and supplementary materials. It benefits all potential readers that we offer both a free and citeable version for all researchers, as well as an authoritative, citeable version for SpringerLink readers. Our thanks go to Ronan Nugent from Springer, who helped us negotiate this agreement. Last but not least, we wish to thank Eric Mortensen, our publication chair, whose expertise made the process smooth.

October 2022

Rita Cucchiara
Jiří Matas
Amnon Shashua
Lihi Zelnik-Manor

Preface

Welcome to the proceedings of the European Conference on Computer Vision (ECCV 2022). This was a hybrid edition of ECCV as we made our way out of the COVID-19 pandemic. The conference received 5804 valid paper submissions, compared to 5150 submissions to ECCV 2020 (a 12.7% increase) and 2439 in ECCV 2018. 1645 submissions were accepted for publication (28%) and, of those, 157 (2.7% overall) as orals.

846 of the submissions were desk-rejected for various reasons. Many of them because they revealed author identity, thus violating the double-blind policy. This violation came in many forms: some had author names with the title, others added acknowledgments to specific grants, yet others had links to their github account where their name was visible. Tampering with the LaTeX template was another reason for automatic desk rejection.

ECCV 2022 used the traditional CMT system to manage the entire double-blind reviewing process. Authors did not know the names of the reviewers and vice versa. Each paper received at least 3 reviews (except 6 papers that received only 2 reviews), totalling more than 15,000 reviews.

Handling the review process at this scale was a significant challenge. To ensure that each submission received as fair and high-quality reviews as possible, we recruited more than 4719 reviewers (in the end, 4719 reviewers did at least one review). Similarly we recruited more than 276 area chairs (eventually, only 276 area chairs handled a batch of papers). The area chairs were selected based on their technical expertise and reputation, largely among people who served as area chairs in previous top computer vision and machine learning conferences (ECCV, ICCV, CVPR, NeurIPS, etc.).

Reviewers were similarly invited from previous conferences, and also from the pool of authors. We also encouraged experienced area chairs to suggest additional chairs and reviewers in the initial phase of recruiting. The median reviewer load was five papers per reviewer, while the average load was about four papers, because of the emergency reviewers. The area chair load was 35 papers, on average.

Conflicts of interest between authors, area chairs, and reviewers were handled largely automatically by the CMT platform, with some manual help from the Program Chairs. Reviewers were allowed to describe themselves as senior reviewer (load of 8 papers to review) or junior reviewers (load of 4 papers). Papers were matched to area chairs based on a subject-area affinity score computed in CMT and an affinity score computed by the Toronto Paper Matching System (TPMS). TPMS is based on the paper's full text. An area chair handling each submission would bid for preferred expert reviewers, and we balanced load and prevented conflicts.

The assignment of submissions to area chairs was relatively smooth, as was the assignment of submissions to reviewers. A small percentage of reviewers were not happy with their assignments in terms of subjects and self-reported expertise. This is an area for improvement, although it's interesting that many of these cases were reviewers hand-picked by AC's. We made a later round of reviewer recruiting, targeted at the list of authors of papers submitted to the conference, and had an excellent response which helped provide enough emergency reviewers. In the end, all but six papers received at least 3 reviews.

The challenges of the reviewing process are in line with past experiences at ECCV 2020. As the community grows, and the number of submissions increases, it becomes ever more challenging to recruit enough reviewers and ensure a high enough quality of reviews. Enlisting authors by default as reviewers might be one step to address this challenge.

Authors were given a week to rebut the initial reviews, and address reviewers' concerns. Each rebuttal was limited to a single pdf page with a fixed template.

The Area Chairs then led discussions with the reviewers on the merits of each submission. The goal was to reach consensus, but, ultimately, it was up to the Area Chair to make a decision. The decision was then discussed with a buddy Area Chair to make sure decisions were fair and informative. The entire process was conducted virtually with no in-person meetings taking place.

The Program Chairs were informed in cases where the Area Chairs overturned a decisive consensus reached by the reviewers, and pushed for the meta-reviews to contain details that explained the reasoning for such decisions. Obviously these were the most contentious cases, where reviewer inexperience was the most common reported factor.

Once the list of accepted papers was finalized and released, we went through the laborious process of plagiarism (including self-plagiarism) detection. A total of 4 accepted papers were rejected because of that.

Finally, we would like to thank our Technical Program Chair, Pavel Lifshits, who did tremendous work behind the scenes, and we thank the tireless CMT team.

October 2022

Gabriel Brostow
Giovanni Maria Farinella
Moustapha Cissé
Shai Avidan
Tal Hassner

Organization

General Chairs

Rita Cucchiara   University of Modena and Reggio Emilia, Italy
Jiří Matas   Czech Technical University in Prague, Czech Republic
Amnon Shashua   Hebrew University of Jerusalem, Israel
Lihi Zelnik-Manor   Technion – Israel Institute of Technology, Israel

Program Chairs

Shai Avidan   Tel-Aviv University, Israel
Gabriel Brostow   University College London, UK
Moustapha Cissé   Google AI, Ghana
Giovanni Maria Farinella   University of Catania, Italy
Tal Hassner   Facebook AI, USA

Program Technical Chair

Pavel Lifshits   Technion – Israel Institute of Technology, Israel

Workshops Chairs

Leonid Karlinsky   IBM Research, Israel
Tomer Michaeli   Technion – Israel Institute of Technology, Israel
Ko Nishino   Kyoto University, Japan

Tutorial Chairs

Thomas Pock   Graz University of Technology, Austria
Natalia Neverova   Facebook AI Research, UK

Demo Chair

Bohyung Han   Seoul National University, Korea

Social and Student Activities Chairs

Tatiana Tommasi	Italian Institute of Technology, Italy
Sagie Benaim	University of Copenhagen, Denmark

Diversity and Inclusion Chairs

Xi Yin	Facebook AI Research, USA
Bryan Russell	Adobe, USA

Communications Chairs

Lorenzo Baraldi	University of Modena and Reggio Emilia, Italy
Kosta Derpanis	York University & Samsung AI Centre Toronto, Canada

Industrial Liaison Chairs

Dimosthenis Karatzas	Universitat Autònoma de Barcelona, Spain
Chen Sagiv	SagivTech, Israel

Finance Chair

Gerard Medioni	University of Southern California & Amazon, USA

Publication Chair

Eric Mortensen	MiCROTEC, USA

Area Chairs

Lourdes Agapito	University College London, UK
Zeynep Akata	University of Tübingen, Germany
Naveed Akhtar	University of Western Australia, Australia
Karteek Alahari	Inria Grenoble Rhône-Alpes, France
Alexandre Alahi	École polytechnique fédérale de Lausanne, Switzerland
Pablo Arbelaez	Universidad de Los Andes, Columbia
Antonis A. Argyros	University of Crete & Foundation for Research and Technology-Hellas, Crete
Yuki M. Asano	University of Amsterdam, The Netherlands
Kalle Åström	Lund University, Sweden
Hadar Averbuch-Elor	Cornell University, USA

Hossein Azizpour	KTH Royal Institute of Technology, Sweden
Vineeth N. Balasubramanian	Indian Institute of Technology, Hyderabad, India
Lamberto Ballan	University of Padova, Italy
Adrien Bartoli	Université Clermont Auvergne, France
Horst Bischof	Graz University of Technology, Austria
Matthew B. Blaschko	KU Leuven, Belgium
Federica Bogo	Meta Reality Labs Research, Switzerland
Katherine Bouman	California Institute of Technology, USA
Edmond Boyer	Inria Grenoble Rhône-Alpes, France
Michael S. Brown	York University, Canada
Vittorio Caggiano	Meta AI Research, USA
Neill Campbell	University of Bath, UK
Octavia Camps	Northeastern University, USA
Duygu Ceylan	Adobe Research, USA
Ayan Chakrabarti	Google Research, USA
Tat-Jen Cham	Nanyang Technological University, Singapore
Antoni Chan	City University of Hong Kong, Hong Kong, China
Manmohan Chandraker	NEC Labs America, USA
Xinlei Chen	Facebook AI Research, USA
Xilin Chen	Institute of Computing Technology, Chinese Academy of Sciences, China
Dongdong Chen	Microsoft Cloud AI, USA
Chen Chen	University of Central Florida, USA
Ondrej Chum	Vision Recognition Group, Czech Technical University in Prague, Czech Republic
John Collomosse	Adobe Research & University of Surrey, UK
Camille Couprie	Facebook, France
David Crandall	Indiana University, USA
Daniel Cremers	Technical University of Munich, Germany
Marco Cristani	University of Verona, Italy
Canton Cristian	Facebook AI Research, USA
Dengxin Dai	ETH Zurich, Switzerland
Dima Damen	University of Bristol, UK
Kostas Daniilidis	University of Pennsylvania, USA
Trevor Darrell	University of California, Berkeley, USA
Andrew Davison	Imperial College London, UK
Tali Dekel	Weizmann Institute of Science, Israel
Alessio Del Bue	Istituto Italiano di Tecnologia, Italy
Weihong Deng	Beijing University of Posts and Telecommunications, China
Konstantinos Derpanis	Ryerson University, Canada
Carl Doersch	DeepMind, UK

Matthijs Douze	Facebook AI Research, USA
Mohamed Elhoseiny	King Abdullah University of Science and Technology, Saudi Arabia
Sergio Escalera	University of Barcelona, Spain
Yi Fang	New York University, USA
Ryan Farrell	Brigham Young University, USA
Alireza Fathi	Google, USA
Christoph Feichtenhofer	Facebook AI Research, USA
Basura Fernando	Agency for Science, Technology and Research (A*STAR), Singapore
Vittorio Ferrari	Google Research, Switzerland
Andrew W. Fitzgibbon	Graphcore, UK
David J. Fleet	University of Toronto, Canada
David Forsyth	University of Illinois at Urbana-Champaign, USA
David Fouhey	University of Michigan, USA
Katerina Fragkiadaki	Carnegie Mellon University, USA
Friedrich Fraundorfer	Graz University of Technology, Austria
Oren Freifeld	Ben-Gurion University, Israel
Thomas Funkhouser	Google Research & Princeton University, USA
Yasutaka Furukawa	Simon Fraser University, Canada
Fabio Galasso	Sapienza University of Rome, Italy
Jürgen Gall	University of Bonn, Germany
Chuang Gan	Massachusetts Institute of Technology, USA
Zhe Gan	Microsoft, USA
Animesh Garg	University of Toronto, Vector Institute, Nvidia, Canada
Efstratios Gavves	University of Amsterdam, The Netherlands
Peter Gehler	Amazon, Germany
Theo Gevers	University of Amsterdam, The Netherlands
Bernard Ghanem	King Abdullah University of Science and Technology, Saudi Arabia
Ross B. Girshick	Facebook AI Research, USA
Georgia Gkioxari	Facebook AI Research, USA
Albert Gordo	Facebook, USA
Stephen Gould	Australian National University, Australia
Venu Madhav Govindu	Indian Institute of Science, India
Kristen Grauman	Facebook AI Research & UT Austin, USA
Abhinav Gupta	Carnegie Mellon University & Facebook AI Research, USA
Mohit Gupta	University of Wisconsin-Madison, USA
Hu Han	Institute of Computing Technology, Chinese Academy of Sciences, China

Bohyung Han	Seoul National University, Korea
Tian Han	Stevens Institute of Technology, USA
Emily Hand	University of Nevada, Reno, USA
Bharath Hariharan	Cornell University, USA
Ran He	Institute of Automation, Chinese Academy of Sciences, China
Otmar Hilliges	ETH Zurich, Switzerland
Adrian Hilton	University of Surrey, UK
Minh Hoai	Stony Brook University, USA
Yedid Hoshen	Hebrew University of Jerusalem, Israel
Timothy Hospedales	University of Edinburgh, UK
Gang Hua	Wormpex AI Research, USA
Di Huang	Beihang University, China
Jing Huang	Facebook, USA
Jia-Bin Huang	Facebook, USA
Nathan Jacobs	Washington University in St. Louis, USA
C.V. Jawahar	International Institute of Information Technology, Hyderabad, India
Herve Jegou	Facebook AI Research, France
Neel Joshi	Microsoft Research, USA
Armand Joulin	Facebook AI Research, France
Frederic Jurie	University of Caen Normandie, France
Fredrik Kahl	Chalmers University of Technology, Sweden
Yannis Kalantidis	NAVER LABS Europe, France
Evangelos Kalogerakis	University of Massachusetts, Amherst, USA
Sing Bing Kang	Zillow Group, USA
Yosi Keller	Bar Ilan University, Israel
Margret Keuper	University of Mannheim, Germany
Tae-Kyun Kim	Imperial College London, UK
Benjamin Kimia	Brown University, USA
Alexander Kirillov	Facebook AI Research, USA
Kris Kitani	Carnegie Mellon University, USA
Iasonas Kokkinos	Snap Inc. & University College London, UK
Vladlen Koltun	Apple, USA
Nikos Komodakis	University of Crete, Crete
Piotr Koniusz	Australian National University, Australia
Philipp Kraehenbuehl	University of Texas at Austin, USA
Dilip Krishnan	Google, USA
Ajay Kumar	Hong Kong Polytechnic University, Hong Kong, China
Junseok Kwon	Chung-Ang University, Korea
Jean-Francois Lalonde	Université Laval, Canada

Ivan Laptev   Inria Paris, France
Laura Leal-Taixé   Technical University of Munich, Germany
Erik Learned-Miller   University of Massachusetts, Amherst, USA
Gim Hee Lee   National University of Singapore, Singapore
Seungyong Lee   Pohang University of Science and Technology,
                                       Korea
Zhen Lei   Institute of Automation, Chinese Academy of
                                       Sciences, China
Bastian Leibe   RWTH Aachen University, Germany
Hongdong Li   Australian National University, Australia
Fuxin Li   Oregon State University, USA
Bo Li   University of Illinois at Urbana-Champaign, USA
Yin Li   University of Wisconsin-Madison, USA
Ser-Nam Lim   Meta AI Research, USA
Joseph Lim   University of Southern California, USA
Stephen Lin   Microsoft Research Asia, China
Dahua Lin   The Chinese University of Hong Kong,
                                       Hong Kong, China
Si Liu   Beihang University, China
Xiaoming Liu   Michigan State University, USA
Ce Liu   Microsoft, USA
Zicheng Liu   Microsoft, USA
Yanxi Liu   Pennsylvania State University, USA
Feng Liu   Portland State University, USA
Yebin Liu   Tsinghua University, China
Chen Change Loy   Nanyang Technological University, Singapore
Huchuan Lu   Dalian University of Technology, China
Cewu Lu   Shanghai Jiao Tong University, China
Oisin Mac Aodha   University of Edinburgh, UK
Dhruv Mahajan   Facebook, USA
Subhransu Maji   University of Massachusetts, Amherst, USA
Atsuto Maki   KTH Royal Institute of Technology, Sweden
Arun Mallya   NVIDIA, USA
R. Manmatha   Amazon, USA
Iacopo Masi   Sapienza University of Rome, Italy
Dimitris N. Metaxas   Rutgers University, USA
Ajmal Mian   University of Western Australia, Australia
Christian Micheloni   University of Udine, Italy
Krystian Mikolajczyk   Imperial College London, UK
Anurag Mittal   Indian Institute of Technology, Madras, India
Philippos Mordohai   Stevens Institute of Technology, USA
Greg Mori   Simon Fraser University & Borealis AI, Canada

Vittorio Murino	Istituto Italiano di Tecnologia, Italy
P. J. Narayanan	International Institute of Information Technology, Hyderabad, India
Ram Nevatia	University of Southern California, USA
Natalia Neverova	Facebook AI Research, UK
Richard Newcombe	Facebook, USA
Cuong V. Nguyen	Florida International University, USA
Bingbing Ni	Shanghai Jiao Tong University, China
Juan Carlos Niebles	Salesforce & Stanford University, USA
Ko Nishino	Kyoto University, Japan
Jean-Marc Odobez	Idiap Research Institute, École polytechnique fédérale de Lausanne, Switzerland
Francesca Odone	University of Genova, Italy
Takayuki Okatani	Tohoku University & RIKEN Center for Advanced Intelligence Project, Japan
Manohar Paluri	Facebook, USA
Guan Pang	Facebook, USA
Maja Pantic	Imperial College London, UK
Sylvain Paris	Adobe Research, USA
Jaesik Park	Pohang University of Science and Technology, Korea
Hyun Soo Park	The University of Minnesota, USA
Omkar M. Parkhi	Facebook, USA
Deepak Pathak	Carnegie Mellon University, USA
Georgios Pavlakos	University of California, Berkeley, USA
Marcello Pelillo	University of Venice, Italy
Marc Pollefeys	ETH Zurich & Microsoft, Switzerland
Jean Ponce	Inria, France
Gerard Pons-Moll	University of Tübingen, Germany
Fatih Porikli	Qualcomm, USA
Victor Adrian Prisacariu	University of Oxford, UK
Petia Radeva	University of Barcelona, Spain
Ravi Ramamoorthi	University of California, San Diego, USA
Deva Ramanan	Carnegie Mellon University, USA
Vignesh Ramanathan	Facebook, USA
Nalini Ratha	State University of New York at Buffalo, USA
Tammy Riklin Raviv	Ben-Gurion University, Israel
Tobias Ritschel	University College London, UK
Emanuele Rodola	Sapienza University of Rome, Italy
Amit K. Roy-Chowdhury	University of California, Riverside, USA
Michael Rubinstein	Google, USA
Olga Russakovsky	Princeton University, USA

Mathieu Salzmann	École polytechnique fédérale de Lausanne, Switzerland
Dimitris Samaras	Stony Brook University, USA
Aswin Sankaranarayanan	Carnegie Mellon University, USA
Imari Sato	National Institute of Informatics, Japan
Yoichi Sato	University of Tokyo, Japan
Shin'ichi Satoh	National Institute of Informatics, Japan
Walter Scheirer	University of Notre Dame, USA
Bernt Schiele	Max Planck Institute for Informatics, Germany
Konrad Schindler	ETH Zurich, Switzerland
Cordelia Schmid	Inria & Google, France
Alexander Schwing	University of Illinois at Urbana-Champaign, USA
Nicu Sebe	University of Trento, Italy
Greg Shakhnarovich	Toyota Technological Institute at Chicago, USA
Eli Shechtman	Adobe Research, USA
Humphrey Shi	University of Oregon & University of Illinois at Urbana-Champaign & Picsart AI Research, USA
Jianbo Shi	University of Pennsylvania, USA
Roy Shilkrot	Massachusetts Institute of Technology, USA
Mike Zheng Shou	National University of Singapore, Singapore
Kaleem Siddiqi	McGill University, Canada
Richa Singh	Indian Institute of Technology Jodhpur, India
Greg Slabaugh	Queen Mary University of London, UK
Cees Snoek	University of Amsterdam, The Netherlands
Yale Song	Facebook AI Research, USA
Yi-Zhe Song	University of Surrey, UK
Bjorn Stenger	Rakuten Institute of Technology
Abby Stylianou	Saint Louis University, USA
Akihiro Sugimoto	National Institute of Informatics, Japan
Chen Sun	Brown University, USA
Deqing Sun	Google, USA
Kalyan Sunkavalli	Adobe Research, USA
Ying Tai	Tencent YouTu Lab, China
Ayellet Tal	Technion – Israel Institute of Technology, Israel
Ping Tan	Simon Fraser University, Canada
Siyu Tang	ETH Zurich, Switzerland
Chi-Keung Tang	Hong Kong University of Science and Technology, Hong Kong, China
Radu Timofte	University of Würzburg, Germany & ETH Zurich, Switzerland
Federico Tombari	Google, Switzerland & Technical University of Munich, Germany

James Tompkin   Brown University, USA
Lorenzo Torresani   Dartmouth College, USA
Alexander Toshev   Apple, USA
Du Tran   Facebook AI Research, USA
Anh T. Tran   VinAI, Vietnam
Zhuowen Tu   University of California, San Diego, USA
Georgios Tzimiropoulos   Queen Mary University of London, UK
Jasper Uijlings   Google Research, Switzerland
Jan C. van Gemert   Delft University of Technology, The Netherlands
Gul Varol   Ecole des Ponts ParisTech, France
Nuno Vasconcelos   University of California, San Diego, USA
Mayank Vatsa   Indian Institute of Technology Jodhpur, India
Ashok Veeraraghavan   Rice University, USA
Jakob Verbeek   Facebook AI Research, France
Carl Vondrick   Columbia University, USA
Ruiping Wang   Institute of Computing Technology, Chinese
                               Academy of Sciences, China
Xinchao Wang   National University of Singapore, Singapore
Liwei Wang   The Chinese University of Hong Kong,
                               Hong Kong, China
Chaohui Wang   Université Paris-Est, France
Xiaolong Wang   University of California, San Diego, USA
Christian Wolf   NAVER LABS Europe, France
Tao Xiang   University of Surrey, UK
Saining Xie   Facebook AI Research, USA
Cihang Xie   University of California, Santa Cruz, USA
Zeki Yalniz   Facebook, USA
Ming-Hsuan Yang   University of California, Merced, USA
Angela Yao   National University of Singapore, Singapore
Shaodi You   University of Amsterdam, The Netherlands
Stella X. Yu   University of California, Berkeley, USA
Junsong Yuan   State University of New York at Buffalo, USA
Stefanos Zafeiriou   Imperial College London, UK
Amir Zamir   École polytechnique fédérale de Lausanne,
                               Switzerland
Lei Zhang   Alibaba & Hong Kong Polytechnic University,
                               Hong Kong, China
Lei Zhang   International Digital Economy Academy (IDEA),
                               China
Pengchuan Zhang   Meta AI, USA
Bolei Zhou   University of California, Los Angeles, USA
Yuke Zhu   University of Texas at Austin, USA

Todd Zickler   Harvard University, USA
Wangmeng Zuo   Harbin Institute of Technology, China

Technical Program Committee

Davide Abati
Soroush Abbasi
  Koohpayegani
Amos L. Abbott
Rameen Abdal
Rabab Abdelfattah
Sahar Abdelnabi
Hassan Abu Alhaija
Abulikemu Abuduweili
Ron Abutbul
Hanno Ackermann
Aikaterini Adam
Kamil Adamczewski
Ehsan Adeli
Vida Adeli
Donald Adjeroh
Arman Afrasiyabi
Akshay Agarwal
Sameer Agarwal
Abhinav Agarwalla
Vaibhav Aggarwal
Sara Aghajanzadeh
Susmit Agrawal
Antonio Agudo
Touqeer Ahmad
Sk Miraj Ahmed
Chaitanya Ahuja
Nilesh A. Ahuja
Abhishek Aich
Shubhra Aich
Noam Aigerman
Arash Akbarinia
Peri Akiva
Derya Akkaynak
Emre Aksan
Arjun R. Akula
Yuval Alaluf
Stephan Alaniz
Paul Albert
Cenek Albl

Filippo Aleotti
Konstantinos P.
  Alexandridis
Motasem Alfarra
Mohsen Ali
Thiemo Alldieck
Hadi Alzayer
Liang An
Shan An
Yi An
Zhulin An
Dongsheng An
Jie An
Xiang An
Saket Anand
Cosmin Ancuti
Juan Andrade-Cetto
Alexander Andreopoulos
Bjoern Andres
Jerone T. A. Andrews
Shivangi Aneja
Anelia Angelova
Dragomir Anguelov
Rushil Anirudh
Oron Anschel
Rao Muhammad Anwer
Djamila Aouada
Evlampios Apostolidis
Srikar Appalaraju
Nikita Araslanov
Andre Araujo
Eric Arazo
Dawit Mureja Argaw
Anurag Arnab
Aditya Arora
Chetan Arora
Sunpreet S. Arora
Alexey Artemov
Muhammad Asad
Kumar Ashutosh

Sinem Aslan
Vishal Asnani
Mahmoud Assran
Amir Atapour-Abarghouei
Nikos Athanasiou
Ali Athar
ShahRukh Athar
Sara Atito
Souhaib Attaiki
Matan Atzmon
Mathieu Aubry
Nicolas Audebert
Tristan T.
  Aumentado-Armstrong
Melinos Averkiou
Yannis Avrithis
Stephane Ayache
Mehmet Aygün
Seyed Mehdi
  Ayyoubzadeh
Hossein Azizpour
George Azzopardi
Mallikarjun B. R.
Yunhao Ba
Abhishek Badki
Seung-Hwan Bae
Seung-Hwan Baek
Seungryul Baek
Piyush Nitin Bagad
Shai Bagon
Gaetan Bahl
Shikhar Bahl
Sherwin Bahmani
Haoran Bai
Lei Bai
Jiawang Bai
Haoyue Bai
Jinbin Bai
Xiang Bai
Xuyang Bai

Yang Bai
Yuanchao Bai
Ziqian Bai
Sungyong Baik
Kevin Bailly
Max Bain
Federico Baldassarre
Wele Gedara Chaminda
  Bandara
Biplab Banerjee
Pratyay Banerjee
Sandipan Banerjee
Jihwan Bang
Antyanta Bangunharcana
Aayush Bansal
Ankan Bansal
Siddhant Bansal
Wentao Bao
Zhipeng Bao
Amir Bar
Manel Baradad Jurjo
Lorenzo Baraldi
Danny Barash
Daniel Barath
Connelly Barnes
Ioan Andrei Bârsan
Steven Basart
Dina Bashkirova
Chaim Baskin
Peyman Bateni
Anil Batra
Sebastiano Battiato
Ardhendu Behera
Harkirat Behl
Jens Behley
Vasileios Belagiannis
Boulbaba Ben Amor
Emanuel Ben Baruch
Abdessamad Ben Hamza
Gil Ben-Artzi
Assia Benbihi
Fabian Benitez-Quiroz
Guy Ben-Yosef
Philipp Benz
Alexander W. Bergman

Urs Bergmann
Jesus Bermudez-Cameo
Stefano Berretti
Gedas Bertasius
Zachary Bessinger
Petra Bevandić
Matthew Beveridge
Lucas Beyer
Yash Bhalgat
Suvaansh Bhambri
Samarth Bharadwaj
Gaurav Bharaj
Aparna Bharati
Bharat Lal Bhatnagar
Uttaran Bhattacharya
Apratim Bhattacharyya
Brojeshwar Bhowmick
Ankan Kumar Bhunia
Ayan Kumar Bhunia
Qi Bi
Sai Bi
Michael Bi Mi
Gui-Bin Bian
Jia-Wang Bian
Shaojun Bian
Pia Bideau
Mario Bijelic
Hakan Bilen
Guillaume-Alexandre
  Bilodeau
Alexander Binder
Tolga Birdal
Vighnesh N. Birodkar
Sandika Biswas
Andreas Blattmann
Janusz Bobulski
Giuseppe Boccignone
Vishnu Boddeti
Navaneeth Bodla
Moritz Böhle
Aleksei Bokhovkin
Sam Bond-Taylor
Vivek Boominathan
Shubhankar Borse
Mark Boss

Andrea Bottino
Adnane Boukhayma
Fadi Boutros
Nicolas C. Boutry
Richard S. Bowen
Ivaylo Boyadzhiev
Aidan Boyd
Yuri Boykov
Aljaz Bozic
Behzad Bozorgtabar
Eric Brachmann
Samarth Brahmbhatt
Gustav Bredell
Francois Bremond
Joel Brogan
Andrew Brown
Thomas Brox
Marcus A. Brubaker
Robert-Jan Bruintjes
Yuqi Bu
Anders G. Buch
Himanshu Buckchash
Mateusz Buda
Ignas Budvytis
José M. Buenaposada
Marcel C. Bühler
Tu Bui
Adrian Bulat
Hannah Bull
Evgeny Burnaev
Andrei Bursuc
Benjamin Busam
Sergey N. Buzykanov
Wonmin Byeon
Fabian Caba
Martin Cadik
Guanyu Cai
Minjie Cai
Qing Cai
Zhongang Cai
Qi Cai
Yancheng Cai
Shen Cai
Han Cai
Jiarui Cai

Bowen Cai
Mu Cai
Qin Cai
Ruojin Cai
Weidong Cai
Weiwei Cai
Yi Cai
Yujun Cai
Zhiping Cai
Akin Caliskan
Lilian Calvet
Baris Can Cam
Necati Cihan Camgoz
Tommaso Campari
Dylan Campbell
Ziang Cao
Ang Cao
Xu Cao
Zhiwen Cao
Shengcao Cao
Song Cao
Weipeng Cao
Xiangyong Cao
Xiaochun Cao
Yue Cao
Yunhao Cao
Zhangjie Cao
Jiale Cao
Yang Cao
Jiajiong Cao
Jie Cao
Jinkun Cao
Lele Cao
Yulong Cao
Zhiguo Cao
Chen Cao
Razvan Caramalau
Marlène Careil
Gustavo Carneiro
Joao Carreira
Dan Casas
Paola Cascante-Bonilla
Angela Castillo
Francisco M. Castro
Pedro Castro

Luca Cavalli
George J. Cazenavette
Oya Celiktutan
Hakan Cevikalp
Sri Harsha C. H.
Sungmin Cha
Geonho Cha
Menglei Chai
Lucy Chai
Yuning Chai
Zenghao Chai
Anirban Chakraborty
Deep Chakraborty
Rudrasis Chakraborty
Souradeep Chakraborty
Kelvin C. K. Chan
Chee Seng Chan
Paramanand Chandramouli
Arjun Chandrasekaran
Kenneth Chaney
Dongliang Chang
Huiwen Chang
Peng Chang
Xiaojun Chang
Jia-Ren Chang
Hyung Jin Chang
Hyun Sung Chang
Ju Yong Chang
Li-Jen Chang
Qi Chang
Wei-Yi Chang
Yi Chang
Nadine Chang
Hanqing Chao
Pradyumna Chari
Dibyadip Chatterjee
Chiranjoy Chattopadhyay
Siddhartha Chaudhuri
Zhengping Che
Gal Chechik
Lianggangxu Chen
Qi Alfred Chen
Brian Chen
Bor-Chun Chen
Bo-Hao Chen

Bohong Chen
Bin Chen
Ziliang Chen
Cheng Chen
Chen Chen
Chaofeng Chen
Xi Chen
Haoyu Chen
Xuanhong Chen
Wei Chen
Qiang Chen
Shi Chen
Xianyu Chen
Chang Chen
Changhuai Chen
Hao Chen
Jie Chen
Jianbo Chen
Jingjing Chen
Jun Chen
Kejiang Chen
Mingcai Chen
Nenglun Chen
Qifeng Chen
Ruoyu Chen
Shu-Yu Chen
Weidong Chen
Weijie Chen
Weikai Chen
Xiang Chen
Xiuyi Chen
Xingyu Chen
Yaofo Chen
Yueting Chen
Yu Chen
Yunjin Chen
Yuntao Chen
Yun Chen
Zhenfang Chen
Zhuangzhuang Chen
Chu-Song Chen
Xiangyu Chen
Zhuo Chen
Chaoqi Chen
Shizhe Chen

Xiaotong Chen
Xiaozhi Chen
Dian Chen
Defang Chen
Dingfan Chen
Ding-Jie Chen
Ee Heng Chen
Tao Chen
Yixin Chen
Wei-Ting Chen
Lin Chen
Guang Chen
Guangyi Chen
Guanying Chen
Guangyao Chen
Hwann-Tzong Chen
Junwen Chen
Jiacheng Chen
Jianxu Chen
Hui Chen
Kai Chen
Kan Chen
Kevin Chen
Kuan-Wen Chen
Weihua Chen
Zhang Chen
Liang-Chieh Chen
Lele Chen
Liang Chen
Fanglin Chen
Zehui Chen
Minghui Chen
Minghao Chen
Xiaokang Chen
Qian Chen
Jun-Cheng Chen
Qi Chen
Qingcai Chen
Richard J. Chen
Runnan Chen
Rui Chen
Shuo Chen
Sentao Chen
Shaoyu Chen
Shixing Chen

Shuai Chen
Shuya Chen
Sizhe Chen
Simin Chen
Shaoxiang Chen
Zitian Chen
Tianlong Chen
Tianshui Chen
Min-Hung Chen
Xiangning Chen
Xin Chen
Xinghao Chen
Xuejin Chen
Xu Chen
Xuxi Chen
Yunlu Chen
Yanbei Chen
Yuxiao Chen
Yun-Chun Chen
Yi-Ting Chen
Yi-Wen Chen
Yinbo Chen
Yiran Chen
Yuanhong Chen
Yubei Chen
Yuefeng Chen
Yuhua Chen
Yukang Chen
Zerui Chen
Zhaoyu Chen
Zhen Chen
Zhenyu Chen
Zhi Chen
Zhiwei Chen
Zhixiang Chen
Long Chen
Bowen Cheng
Jun Cheng
Yi Cheng
Jingchun Cheng
Lechao Cheng
Xi Cheng
Yuan Cheng
Ho Kei Cheng
Kevin Ho Man Cheng

Jiacheng Cheng
Kelvin B. Cheng
Li Cheng
Mengjun Cheng
Zhen Cheng
Qingrong Cheng
Tianheng Cheng
Harry Cheng
Yihua Cheng
Yu Cheng
Ziheng Cheng
Soon Yau Cheong
Anoop Cherian
Manuela Chessa
Zhixiang Chi
Naoki Chiba
Julian Chibane
Kashyap Chitta
Tai-Yin Chiu
Hsu-kuang Chiu
Wei-Chen Chiu
Sungmin Cho
Donghyeon Cho
Hyeon Cho
Yooshin Cho
Gyusang Cho
Jang Hyun Cho
Seungju Cho
Nam Ik Cho
Sunghyun Cho
Hanbyel Cho
Jaesung Choe
Jooyoung Choi
Chiho Choi
Changwoon Choi
Jongwon Choi
Myungsub Choi
Dooseop Choi
Jonghyun Choi
Jinwoo Choi
Jun Won Choi
Min-Kook Choi
Hongsuk Choi
Janghoon Choi
Yoon-Ho Choi

Yukyung Choi
Jaegul Choo
Ayush Chopra
Siddharth Choudhary
Subhabrata Choudhury
Vasileios Choutas
Ka-Ho Chow
Pinaki Nath Chowdhury
Sammy Christen
Anders Christensen
Grigorios Chrysos
Hang Chu
Wen-Hsuan Chu
Peng Chu
Qi Chu
Ruihang Chu
Wei-Ta Chu
Yung-Yu Chuang
Sanghyuk Chun
Se Young Chun
Antonio Cinà
Ramazan Gokberk Cinbis
Javier Civera
Albert Clapés
Ronald Clark
Brian S. Clipp
Felipe Codevilla
Daniel Coelho de Castro
Niv Cohen
Forrester Cole
Maxwell D. Collins
Robert T. Collins
Marc Comino Trinidad
Runmin Cong
Wenyan Cong
Maxime Cordy
Marcella Cornia
Enric Corona
Huseyin Coskun
Luca Cosmo
Dragos Costea
Davide Cozzolino
Arun C. S. Kumar
Aiyu Cui
Qiongjie Cui

Quan Cui
Shuhao Cui
Yiming Cui
Ying Cui
Zijun Cui
Jiali Cui
Jiequan Cui
Yawen Cui
Zhen Cui
Zhaopeng Cui
Jack Culpepper
Xiaodong Cun
Ross Cutler
Adam Czajka
Ali Dabouei
Konstantinos M. Dafnis
Manuel Dahnert
Tao Dai
Yuchao Dai
Bo Dai
Mengyu Dai
Hang Dai
Haixing Dai
Peng Dai
Pingyang Dai
Qi Dai
Qiyu Dai
Yutong Dai
Naser Damer
Zhiyuan Dang
Mohamed Daoudi
Ayan Das
Abir Das
Debasmit Das
Deepayan Das
Partha Das
Sagnik Das
Soumi Das
Srijan Das
Swagatam Das
Avijit Dasgupta
Jim Davis
Adrian K. Davison
Homa Davoudi
Laura Daza

Matthias De Lange
Shalini De Mello
Marco De Nadai
Christophe De
    Vleeschouwer
Alp Dener
Boyang Deng
Congyue Deng
Bailin Deng
Yong Deng
Ye Deng
Zhuo Deng
Zhijie Deng
Xiaoming Deng
Jiankang Deng
Jinhong Deng
Jingjing Deng
Liang-Jian Deng
Siqi Deng
Xiang Deng
Xueqing Deng
Zhongying Deng
Karan Desai
Jean-Emmanuel Deschaud
Aniket Anand Deshmukh
Neel Dey
Helisa Dhamo
Prithviraj Dhar
Amaya Dharmasiri
Yan Di
Xing Di
Ousmane A. Dia
Haiwen Diao
Xiaolei Diao
Gonçalo José Dias Pais
Abdallah Dib
Anastasios Dimou
Changxing Ding
Henghui Ding
Guodong Ding
Yaqing Ding
Shuangrui Ding
Yuhang Ding
Yikang Ding
Shouhong Ding

Haisong Ding
Hui Ding
Jiahao Ding
Jian Ding
Jian-Jiun Ding
Shuxiao Ding
Tianyu Ding
Wenhao Ding
Yuqi Ding
Yi Ding
Yuzhen Ding
Zhengming Ding
Tan Minh Dinh
Vu Dinh
Christos Diou
Mandar Dixit
Bao Gia Doan
Khoa D. Doan
Dzung Anh Doan
Debi Prosad Dogra
Nehal Doiphode
Chengdong Dong
Bowen Dong
Zhenxing Dong
Hang Dong
Xiaoyi Dong
Haoye Dong
Jiangxin Dong
Shichao Dong
Xuan Dong
Zhen Dong
Shuting Dong
Jing Dong
Li Dong
Ming Dong
Nanqing Dong
Qiulei Dong
Runpei Dong
Siyan Dong
Tian Dong
Wei Dong
Xiaomeng Dong
Xin Dong
Xingbo Dong
Yuan Dong

Samuel Dooley
Gianfranco Doretto
Michael Dorkenwald
Keval Doshi
Zhaopeng Dou
Xiaotian Dou
Hazel Doughty
Ahmad Droby
Iddo Drori
Jie Du
Yong Du
Dawei Du
Dong Du
Ruoyi Du
Yuntao Du
Xuefeng Du
Yilun Du
Yuming Du
Radhika Dua
Haodong Duan
Jiafei Duan
Kaiwen Duan
Peiqi Duan
Ye Duan
Haoran Duan
Jiali Duan
Amanda Duarte
Abhimanyu Dubey
Shiv Ram Dubey
Florian Dubost
Lukasz Dudziak
Shivam Duggal
Justin M. Dulay
Matteo Dunnhofer
Chi Nhan Duong
Thibaut Durand
Mihai Dusmanu
Ujjal Kr Dutta
Debidatta Dwibedi
Isht Dwivedi
Sai Kumar Dwivedi
Takeharu Eda
Mark Edmonds
Alexei A. Efros
Thibaud Ehret

Max Ehrlich
Mahsa Ehsanpour
Iván Eichhardt
Farshad Einabadi
Marvin Eisenberger
Hazim Kemal Ekenel
Mohamed El Banani
Ismail Elezi
Moshe Eliasof
Alaa El-Nouby
Ian Endres
Francis Engelmann
Deniz Engin
Chanho Eom
Dave Epstein
Maria C. Escobar
Victor A. Escorcia
Carlos Esteves
Sungmin Eum
Bernard J. E. Evans
Ivan Evtimov
Fevziye Irem Eyiokur
  Yaman
Matteo Fabbri
Sébastien Fabbro
Gabriele Facciolo
Masud Fahim
Bin Fan
Hehe Fan
Deng-Ping Fan
Aoxiang Fan
Chen-Chen Fan
Qi Fan
Zhaoxin Fan
Haoqi Fan
Heng Fan
Hongyi Fan
Linxi Fan
Baojie Fan
Jiayuan Fan
Lei Fan
Quanfu Fan
Yonghui Fan
Yingruo Fan
Zhiwen Fan

Zhengyang Geng
Kyle A. Genova
Georgios Georgakis
Markos Georgopoulos
Marcel Geppert
Shabnam Ghadar
Mina Ghadimi Atigh
Deepti Ghadiyaram
Maani Ghaffari Jadidi
Sedigh Ghamari
Zahra Gharaee
Michaël Gharbi
Golnaz Ghiasi
Reza Ghoddoosian
Soumya Suvra Ghosal
Adhiraj Ghosh
Arthita Ghosh
Pallabi Ghosh
Soumyadeep Ghosh
Andrew Gilbert
Igor Gilitschenski
Jhony H. Giraldo
Andreu Girbau Xalabarder
Rohit Girdhar
Sharath Girish
Xavier Giro-i-Nieto
Raja Giryes
Thomas Gittings
Nikolaos Gkanatsios
Ioannis Gkioulekas
Abhiram
    Gnanasambandam
Aurele T. Gnanha
Clement L. J. C. Godard
Arushi Goel
Vidit Goel
Shubham Goel
Zan Gojcic
Aaron K. Gokaslan
Tejas Gokhale
S. Alireza Golestaneh
Thiago L. Gomes
Nuno Goncalves
Boqing Gong
Chen Gong

Yuanhao Gong
Guoqiang Gong
Jingyu Gong
Rui Gong
Yu Gong
Mingming Gong
Neil Zhenqiang Gong
Xun Gong
Yunye Gong
Yihong Gong
Cristina I. González
Nithin Gopalakrishnan
    Nair
Gaurav Goswami
Jianping Gou
Shreyank N. Gowda
Ankit Goyal
Helmut Grabner
Patrick L. Grady
Ben Graham
Eric Granger
Douglas R. Gray
Matej Grcić
David Griffiths
Jinjin Gu
Yun Gu
Shuyang Gu
Jianyang Gu
Fuqiang Gu
Jiatao Gu
Jindong Gu
Jiaqi Gu
Jinwei Gu
Jiaxin Gu
Geonmo Gu
Xiao Gu
Xinqian Gu
Xiuye Gu
Yuming Gu
Zhangxuan Gu
Dayan Guan
Junfeng Guan
Qingji Guan
Tianrui Guan
Shanyan Guan

Denis A. Gudovskiy
Ricardo Guerrero
Pierre-Louis Guhur
Jie Gui
Liangyan Gui
Liangke Gui
Benoit Guillard
Erhan Gundogdu
Manuel Günther
Jingcai Guo
Yuanfang Guo
Junfeng Guo
Chenqi Guo
Dan Guo
Hongji Guo
Jia Guo
Jie Guo
Minghao Guo
Shi Guo
Yanhui Guo
Yangyang Guo
Yuan-Chen Guo
Yilu Guo
Yiluan Guo
Yong Guo
Guangyu Guo
Haiyun Guo
Jinyang Guo
Jianyuan Guo
Pengsheng Guo
Pengfei Guo
Shuxuan Guo
Song Guo
Tianyu Guo
Qing Guo
Qiushan Guo
Wen Guo
Xiefan Guo
Xiaohu Guo
Xiaoqing Guo
Yufei Guo
Yuhui Guo
Yuliang Guo
Yunhui Guo
Yanwen Guo

Akshita Gupta
Ankush Gupta
Kamal Gupta
Kartik Gupta
Ritwik Gupta
Rohit Gupta
Siddharth Gururani
Fredrik K. Gustafsson
Abner Guzman Rivera
Vladimir Guzov
Matthew A. Gwilliam
Jung-Woo Ha
Marc Habermann
Isma Hadji
Christian Haene
Martin Hahner
Levente Hajder
Alexandros Haliassos
Emanuela Haller
Bumsub Ham
Abdullah J. Hamdi
Shreyas Hampali
Dongyoon Han
Chunrui Han
Dong-Jun Han
Dong-Sig Han
Guangxing Han
Zhizhong Han
Ruize Han
Jiaming Han
Jin Han
Ligong Han
Xian-Hua Han
Xiaoguang Han
Yizeng Han
Zhi Han
Zhenjun Han
Zhongyi Han
Jungong Han
Junlin Han
Kai Han
Kun Han
Sungwon Han
Songfang Han
Wei Han

Xiao Han
Xintong Han
Xinzhe Han
Yahong Han
Yan Han
Zongbo Han
Nicolai Hani
Rana Hanocka
Niklas Hanselmann
Nicklas A. Hansen
Hong Hanyu
Fusheng Hao
Yanbin Hao
Shijie Hao
Udith Haputhanthri
Mehrtash Harandi
Josh Harguess
Adam Harley
David M. Hart
Atsushi Hashimoto
Ali Hassani
Mohammed Hassanin
Yana Hasson
Joakim Bruslund Haurum
Bo He
Kun He
Chen He
Xin He
Fazhi He
Gaoqi He
Hao He
Haoyu He
Jiangpeng He
Hongliang He
Qian He
Xiangteng He
Xuming He
Yannan He
Yuhang He
Yang He
Xiangyu He
Nanjun He
Pan He
Sen He
Shengfeng He

Songtao He
Tao He
Tong He
Wei He
Xuehai He
Xiaoxiao He
Ying He
Yisheng He
Ziwen He
Peter Hedman
Felix Heide
Yacov Hel-Or
Paul Henderson
Philipp Henzler
Byeongho Heo
Jae-Pil Heo
Miran Heo
Sachini A. Herath
Stephane Herbin
Pedro Hermosilla Casajus
Monica Hernandez
Charles Herrmann
Roei Herzig
Mauricio Hess-Flores
Carlos Hinojosa
Tobias Hinz
Tsubasa Hirakawa
Chih-Hui Ho
Lam Si Tung Ho
Jennifer Hobbs
Derek Hoiem
Yannick Hold-Geoffroy
Aleksander Holynski
Cheeun Hong
Fa-Ting Hong
Hanbin Hong
Guan Zhe Hong
Danfeng Hong
Lanqing Hong
Xiaopeng Hong
Xin Hong
Jie Hong
Seungbum Hong
Cheng-Yao Hong
Seunghoon Hong

Yi Hong
Yuan Hong
Yuchen Hong
Anthony Hoogs
Maxwell C. Horton
Kazuhiro Hotta
Qibin Hou
Tingbo Hou
Junhui Hou
Ji Hou
Qiqi Hou
Rui Hou
Ruibing Hou
Zhi Hou
Henry Howard-Jenkins
Lukas Hoyer
Wei-Lin Hsiao
Chiou-Ting Hsu
Anthony Hu
Brian Hu
Yusong Hu
Hexiang Hu
Haoji Hu
Di Hu
Hengtong Hu
Haigen Hu
Lianyu Hu
Hanzhe Hu
Jie Hu
Junlin Hu
Shizhe Hu
Jian Hu
Zhiming Hu
Juhua Hu
Peng Hu
Ping Hu
Ronghang Hu
MengShun Hu
Tao Hu
Vincent Tao Hu
Xiaoling Hu
Xinting Hu
Xiaolin Hu
Xuefeng Hu
Xiaowei Hu

Yang Hu
Yueyu Hu
Zeyu Hu
Zhongyun Hu
Binh-Son Hua
Guoliang Hua
Yi Hua
Linzhi Huang
Qiusheng Huang
Bo Huang
Chen Huang
Hsin-Ping Huang
Ye Huang
Shuangping Huang
Zeng Huang
Buzhen Huang
Cong Huang
Heng Huang
Hao Huang
Qidong Huang
Huaibo Huang
Chaoqin Huang
Feihu Huang
Jiahui Huang
Jingjia Huang
Kun Huang
Lei Huang
Sheng Huang
Shuaiyi Huang
Siyu Huang
Xiaoshui Huang
Xiaoyang Huang
Yan Huang
Yihao Huang
Ying Huang
Ziling Huang
Xiaoke Huang
Yifei Huang
Haiyang Huang
Zhewei Huang
Jin Huang
Haibin Huang
Jiaxing Huang
Junjie Huang
Keli Huang

Lang Huang
Lin Huang
Luojie Huang
Mingzhen Huang
Shijia Huang
Shengyu Huang
Siyuan Huang
He Huang
Xiuyu Huang
Lianghua Huang
Yue Huang
Yaping Huang
Yuge Huang
Zehao Huang
Zeyi Huang
Zhiqi Huang
Zhongzhan Huang
Zilong Huang
Ziyuan Huang
Tianrui Hui
Zhuo Hui
Le Hui
Jing Huo
Junhwa Hur
Shehzeen S. Hussain
Chuong Minh Huynh
Seunghyun Hwang
Jaehui Hwang
Jyh-Jing Hwang
Sukjun Hwang
Soonmin Hwang
Wonjun Hwang
Rakib Hyder
Sangeek Hyun
Sarah Ibrahimi
Tomoki Ichikawa
Yerlan Idelbayev
A. S. M. Iftekhar
Masaaki Iiyama
Satoshi Ikehata
Sunghoon Im
Atul N. Ingle
Eldar Insafutdinov
Yani A. Ioannou
Radu Tudor Ionescu

Umar Iqbal
Go Irie
Muhammad Zubair Irshad
Ahmet Iscen
Berivan Isik
Ashraful Islam
Md Amirul Islam
Syed Islam
Mariko Isogawa
Vamsi Krishna K. Ithapu
Boris Ivanovic
Darshan Iyer
Sarah Jabbour
Ayush Jain
Nishant Jain
Samyak Jain
Vidit Jain
Vineet Jain
Priyank Jaini
Tomas Jakab
Mohammad A. A. K.
    Jalwana
Muhammad Abdullah
    Jamal
Hadi Jamali-Rad
Stuart James
Varun Jampani
Young Kyun Jang
YeongJun Jang
Yunseok Jang
Ronnachai Jaroensri
Bhavan Jasani
Krishna Murthy
    Jatavallabhula
Mojan Javaheripi
Syed A. Javed
Guillaume Jeanneret
Pranav Jeevan
Herve Jegou
Rohit Jena
Tomas Jenicek
Porter Jenkins
Simon Jenni
Hae-Gon Jeon
Sangryul Jeon

Boseung Jeong
Yoonwoo Jeong
Seong-Gyun Jeong
Jisoo Jeong
Allan D. Jepson
Ankit Jha
Sumit K. Jha
I-Hong Jhuo
Ge-Peng Ji
Chaonan Ji
Deyi Ji
Jingwei Ji
Wei Ji
Zhong Ji
Jiayi Ji
Pengliang Ji
Hui Ji
Mingi Ji
Xiaopeng Ji
Yuzhu Ji
Baoxiong Jia
Songhao Jia
Dan Jia
Shan Jia
Xiaojun Jia
Xiuyi Jia
Xu Jia
Menglin Jia
Wenqi Jia
Boyuan Jiang
Wenhao Jiang
Huaizu Jiang
Hanwen Jiang
Haiyong Jiang
Hao Jiang
Huajie Jiang
Huiqin Jiang
Haojun Jiang
Haobo Jiang
Junjun Jiang
Xingyu Jiang
Yangbangyan Jiang
Yu Jiang
Jianmin Jiang
Jiaxi Jiang

Jing Jiang
Kui Jiang
Li Jiang
Liming Jiang
Chiyu Jiang
Meirui Jiang
Chen Jiang
Peng Jiang
Tai-Xiang Jiang
Wen Jiang
Xinyang Jiang
Yifan Jiang
Yuming Jiang
Yingying Jiang
Zeren Jiang
ZhengKai Jiang
Zhenyu Jiang
Shuming Jiao
Jianbo Jiao
Licheng Jiao
Dongkwon Jin
Yeying Jin
Cheng Jin
Linyi Jin
Qing Jin
Taisong Jin
Xiao Jin
Xin Jin
Sheng Jin
Kyong Hwan Jin
Ruibing Jin
SouYoung Jin
Yueming Jin
Chenchen Jing
Longlong Jing
Taotao Jing
Yongcheng Jing
Younghyun Jo
Joakim Johnander
Jeff Johnson
Michael J. Jones
R. Kenny Jones
Rico Jonschkowski
Ameya Joshi
Sunghun Joung

Felix Juefei-Xu
Claudio R. Jung
Steffen Jung
Hari Chandana K.
Rahul Vigneswaran K.
Prajwal K. R.
Abhishek Kadian
Jhony Kaesemodel Pontes
Kumara Kahatapitiya
Anmol Kalia
Sinan Kalkan
Tarun Kalluri
Jaewon Kam
Sandesh Kamath
Meina Kan
Menelaos Kanakis
Takuhiro Kaneko
Di Kang
Guoliang Kang
Hao Kang
Jaeyeon Kang
Kyoungkook Kang
Li-Wei Kang
MinGuk Kang
Suk-Ju Kang
Zhao Kang
Yash Mukund Kant
Yueying Kao
Aupendu Kar
Konstantinos Karantzalos
Sezer Karaoglu
Navid Kardan
Sanjay Kariyappa
Leonid Karlinsky
Animesh Karnewar
Shyamgopal Karthik
Hirak J. Kashyap
Marc A. Kastner
Hirokatsu Kataoka
Angelos Katharopoulos
Hiroharu Kato
Kai Katsumata
Manuel Kaufmann
Chaitanya Kaul
Prakhar Kaushik

Yuki Kawana
Lei Ke
Lipeng Ke
Tsung-Wei Ke
Wei Ke
Petr Kellnhofer
Aniruddha Kembhavi
John Kender
Corentin Kervadec
Leonid Keselman
Daniel Keysers
Nima Khademi Kalantari
Taras Khakhulin
Samir Khaki
Muhammad Haris Khan
Qadeer Khan
Salman Khan
Subash Khanal
Vaishnavi M. Khindkar
Rawal Khirodkar
Saeed Khorram
Pirazh Khorramshahi
Kourosh Khoshelham
Ansh Khurana
Benjamin Kiefer
Jae Myung Kim
Junho Kim
Boah Kim
Hyeonseong Kim
Dong-Jin Kim
Dongwan Kim
Donghyun Kim
Doyeon Kim
Yonghyun Kim
Hyung-Il Kim
Hyunwoo Kim
Hyeongwoo Kim
Hyo Jin Kim
Hyunwoo J. Kim
Taehoon Kim
Jaeha Kim
Jiwon Kim
Jung Uk Kim
Kangyeol Kim
Eunji Kim

Daeha Kim
Dongwon Kim
Kunhee Kim
Kyungmin Kim
Junsik Kim
Min H. Kim
Namil Kim
Kookhoi Kim
Sanghyun Kim
Seongyeop Kim
Seungryong Kim
Saehoon Kim
Euyoung Kim
Guisik Kim
Sungyeon Kim
Sunnie S. Y. Kim
Taehun Kim
Tae Oh Kim
Won Hwa Kim
Seungwook Kim
YoungBin Kim
Youngeun Kim
Akisato Kimura
Furkan Osman Kınlı
Zsolt Kira
Hedvig Kjellström
Florian Kleber
Jan P. Klopp
Florian Kluger
Laurent Kneip
Byungsoo Ko
Muhammed Kocabas
A. Sophia Koepke
Kevin Koeser
Nick Kolkin
Nikos Kolotouros
Wai-Kin Adams Kong
Deying Kong
Caihua Kong
Youyong Kong
Shuyu Kong
Shu Kong
Tao Kong
Yajing Kong
Yu Kong

Zishang Kong
Theodora Kontogianni
Anton S. Konushin
Julian F. P. Kooij
Bruno Korbar
Giorgos Kordopatis-Zilos
Jari Korhonen
Adam Kortylewski
Denis Korzhenkov
Divya Kothandaraman
Suraj Kothawade
Iuliia Kotseruba
Satwik Kottur
Shashank Kotyan
Alexandros Kouris
Petros Koutras
Anna Kreshuk
Ranjay Krishna
Dilip Krishnan
Andrey Kuehlkamp
Hilde Kuehne
Jason Kuen
David Kügler
Arjan Kuijper
Anna Kukleva
Sumith Kulal
Viveka Kulharia
Akshay R. Kulkarni
Nilesh Kulkarni
Dominik Kulon
Abhinav Kumar
Akash Kumar
Suryansh Kumar
B. V. K. Vijaya Kumar
Pulkit Kumar
Ratnesh Kumar
Sateesh Kumar
Satish Kumar
Vijay Kumar B. G.
Nupur Kumari
Sudhakar Kumawat
Jogendra Nath Kundu
Hsien-Kai Kuo
Meng-Yu Jennifer Kuo
Vinod Kumar Kurmi

Yusuke Kurose
Keerthy Kusumam
Alina Kuznetsova
Henry Kvinge
Ho Man Kwan
Hyeokjun Kweon
Heeseung Kwon
Gihyun Kwon
Myung-Joon Kwon
Taesung Kwon
YoungJoong Kwon
Christos Kyrkou
Jorma Laaksonen
Yann Labbe
Zorah Laehner
Florent Lafarge
Hamid Laga
Manuel Lagunas
Shenqi Lai
Jian-Huang Lai
Zihang Lai
Mohamed I. Lakhal
Mohit Lamba
Meng Lan
Loic Landrieu
Zhiqiang Lang
Natalie Lang
Dong Lao
Yizhen Lao
Yingjie Lao
Issam Hadj Laradji
Gustav Larsson
Viktor Larsson
Zakaria Laskar
Stéphane Lathuilière
Chun Pong Lau
Rynson W. H. Lau
Hei Law
Justin Lazarow
Verica Lazova
Eric-Tuan Le
Hieu Le
Trung-Nghia Le
Mathias Lechner
Byeong-Uk Lee

Chen-Yu Lee
Che-Rung Lee
Chul Lee
Hong Joo Lee
Dongsoo Lee
Jiyoung Lee
Eugene Eu Tzuan Lee
Daeun Lee
Saehyung Lee
Jewook Lee
Hyungtae Lee
Hyunmin Lee
Jungbeom Lee
Joon-Young Lee
Jong-Seok Lee
Joonseok Lee
Junha Lee
Kibok Lee
Byung-Kwan Lee
Jangwon Lee
Jinho Lee
Jongmin Lee
Seunghyun Lee
Sohyun Lee
Minsik Lee
Dogyoon Lee
Seungmin Lee
Min Jun Lee
Sangho Lee
Sangmin Lee
Seungeun Lee
Seon-Ho Lee
Sungmin Lee
Sungho Lee
Sangyoun Lee
Vincent C. S. S. Lee
Jaeseong Lee
Yong Jae Lee
Chenyang Lei
Chenyi Lei
Jiahui Lei
Xinyu Lei
Yinjie Lei
Jiaxu Leng
Luziwei Leng

Jan E. Lenssen
Vincent Lepetit
Thomas Leung
María Leyva-Vallina
Xin Li
Yikang Li
Baoxin Li
Bin Li
Bing Li
Bowen Li
Changlin Li
Chao Li
Chongyi Li
Guanyue Li
Shuai Li
Jin Li
Dingquan Li
Dongxu Li
Yiting Li
Gang Li
Dian Li
Guohao Li
Haoang Li
Haoliang Li
Haoran Li
Hengduo Li
Huafeng Li
Xiaoming Li
Hanao Li
Hongwei Li
Ziqiang Li
Jisheng Li
Jiacheng Li
Jia Li
Jiachen Li
Jiahao Li
Jianwei Li
Jiazhi Li
Jie Li
Jing Li
Jingjing Li
Jingtao Li
Jun Li
Junxuan Li
Kai Li

Kailin Li
Kenneth Li
Kun Li
Kunpeng Li
Aoxue Li
Chenglong Li
Chenglin Li
Changsheng Li
Zhichao Li
Qiang Li
Yanyu Li
Zuoyue Li
Xiang Li
Xuelong Li
Fangda Li
Ailin Li
Liang Li
Chun-Guang Li
Daiqing Li
Dong Li
Guanbin Li
Guorong Li
Haifeng Li
Jianan Li
Jianing Li
Jiaxin Li
Ke Li
Lei Li
Lincheng Li
Liulei Li
Lujun Li
Linjie Li
Lin Li
Pengyu Li
Ping Li
Qiufu Li
Qingyong Li
Rui Li
Siyuan Li
Wei Li
Wenbin Li
Xiangyang Li
Xinyu Li
Xiujun Li
Xiu Li

Xu Li
Ya-Li Li
Yao Li
Yongjie Li
Yijun Li
Yiming Li
Yuezun Li
Yu Li
Yunheng Li
Yuqi Li
Zhe Li
Zeming Li
Zhen Li
Zhengqin Li
Zhimin Li
Jiefeng Li
Jinpeng Li
Chengze Li
Jianwu Li
Lerenhan Li
Shan Li
Suichan Li
Xiangtai Li
Yanjie Li
Yandong Li
Zhuoling Li
Zhenqiang Li
Manyi Li
Maosen Li
Ji Li
Minjun Li
Mingrui Li
Mengtian Li
Junyi Li
Nianyi Li
Bo Li
Xiao Li
Peihua Li
Peike Li
Peizhao Li
Peiliang Li
Qi Li
Ren Li
Runze Li
Shile Li

Sheng Li
Shigang Li
Shiyu Li
Shuang Li
Shasha Li
Shichao Li
Tianye Li
Yuexiang Li
Wei-Hong Li
Wanhua Li
Weihao Li
Weiming Li
Weixin Li
Wenbo Li
Wenshuo Li
Weijian Li
Yunan Li
Xirong Li
Xianhang Li
Xiaoyu Li
Xueqian Li
Xuanlin Li
Xianzhi Li
Yunqiang Li
Yanjing Li
Yansheng Li
Yawei Li
Yi Li
Yong Li
Yong-Lu Li
Yuhang Li
Yu-Jhe Li
Yuxi Li
Yunsheng Li
Yanwei Li
Zechao Li
Zejian Li
Zeju Li
Zekun Li
Zhaowen Li
Zheng Li
Zhenyu Li
Zhiheng Li
Zhi Li
Zhong Li

Zhuowei Li
Zhuowan Li
Zhuohang Li
Zizhang Li
Chen Li
Yuan-Fang Li
Dongze Lian
Xiaochen Lian
Zhouhui Lian
Long Lian
Qing Lian
Jin Lianbao
Jinxiu S. Liang
Dingkang Liang
Jiahao Liang
Jianming Liang
Jingyun Liang
Kevin J. Liang
Kaizhao Liang
Chen Liang
Jie Liang
Senwei Liang
Ding Liang
Jiajun Liang
Jian Liang
Kongming Liang
Siyuan Liang
Yuanzhi Liang
Zhengfa Liang
Mingfu Liang
Xiaodan Liang
Xuefeng Liang
Yuxuan Liang
Kang Liao
Liang Liao
Hong-Yuan Mark Liao
Wentong Liao
Haofu Liao
Yue Liao
Minghui Liao
Shengcai Liao
Ting-Hsuan Liao
Xin Liao
Yinghong Liao
Teck Yian Lim

Che-Tsung Lin
Chung-Ching Lin
Chen-Hsuan Lin
Cheng Lin
Chuming Lin
Chunyu Lin
Dahua Lin
Wei Lin
Zheng Lin
Huaijia Lin
Jason Lin
Jierui Lin
Jiaying Lin
Jie Lin
Kai-En Lin
Kevin Lin
Guangfeng Lin
Jiehong Lin
Feng Lin
Hang Lin
Kwan-Yee Lin
Ke Lin
Luojun Lin
Qinghong Lin
Xiangbo Lin
Yi Lin
Zudi Lin
Shijie Lin
Yiqun Lin
Tzu-Heng Lin
Ming Lin
Shaohui Lin
SongNan Lin
Ji Lin
Tsung-Yu Lin
Xudong Lin
Yancong Lin
Yen-Chen Lin
Yiming Lin
Yuewei Lin
Zhiqiu Lin
Zinan Lin
Zhe Lin
David B. Lindell
Zhixin Ling

Zhan Ling
Alexander Liniger
Venice Erin B. Liong
Joey Litalien
Or Litany
Roee Litman
Ron Litman
Jim Little
Dor Litvak
Shaoteng Liu
Shuaicheng Liu
Andrew Liu
Xian Liu
Shaohui Liu
Bei Liu
Bo Liu
Yong Liu
Ming Liu
Yanbin Liu
Chenxi Liu
Daqi Liu
Di Liu
Difan Liu
Dong Liu
Dongfang Liu
Daizong Liu
Xiao Liu
Fangyi Liu
Fengbei Liu
Fenglin Liu
Bin Liu
Yuang Liu
Ao Liu
Hong Liu
Hongfu Liu
Huidong Liu
Ziyi Liu
Feng Liu
Hao Liu
Jie Liu
Jialun Liu
Jiang Liu
Jing Liu
Jingya Liu
Jiaming Liu

Jun Liu
Juncheng Liu
Jiawei Liu
Hongyu Liu
Chuanbin Liu
Haotian Liu
Lingqiao Liu
Chang Liu
Han Liu
Liu Liu
Min Liu
Yingqi Liu
Aishan Liu
Bingyu Liu
Benlin Liu
Boxiao Liu
Chenchen Liu
Chuanjian Liu
Daqing Liu
Huan Liu
Haozhe Liu
Jiaheng Liu
Wei Liu
Jingzhou Liu
Jiyuan Liu
Lingbo Liu
Nian Liu
Peiye Liu
Qiankun Liu
Shenglan Liu
Shilong Liu
Wen Liu
Wenyu Liu
Weifeng Liu
Wu Liu
Xiaolong Liu
Yang Liu
Yanwei Liu
Yingcheng Liu
Yongfei Liu
Yihao Liu
Yu Liu
Yunze Liu
Ze Liu
Zhenhua Liu

Zhenguang Liu
Lin Liu
Lihao Liu
Pengju Liu
Xinhai Liu
Yunfei Liu
Meng Liu
Minghua Liu
Mingyuan Liu
Miao Liu
Peirong Liu
Ping Liu
Qingjie Liu
Ruoshi Liu
Risheng Liu
Songtao Liu
Xing Liu
Shikun Liu
Shuming Liu
Sheng Liu
Songhua Liu
Tongliang Liu
Weibo Liu
Weide Liu
Weizhe Liu
Wenxi Liu
Weiyang Liu
Xin Liu
Xiaobin Liu
Xudong Liu
Xiaoyi Liu
Xihui Liu
Xinchen Liu
Xingtong Liu
Xinpeng Liu
Xinyu Liu
Xianpeng Liu
Xu Liu
Xingyu Liu
Yongtuo Liu
Yahui Liu
Yangxin Liu
Yaoyao Liu
Yaojie Liu
Yuliang Liu

Yongcheng Liu
Yuan Liu
Yufan Liu
Yu-Lun Liu
Yun Liu
Yunfan Liu
Yuanzhong Liu
Zhuoran Liu
Zhen Liu
Zheng Liu
Zhijian Liu
Zhisong Liu
Ziquan Liu
Ziyu Liu
Zhihua Liu
Zechun Liu
Zhaoyang Liu
Zhengzhe Liu
Stephan Liwicki
Shao-Yuan Lo
Sylvain Lobry
Suhas Lohit
Vishnu Suresh Lokhande
Vincenzo Lomonaco
Chengjiang Long
Guodong Long
Fuchen Long
Shangbang Long
Yang Long
Zijun Long
Vasco Lopes
Antonio M. Lopez
Roberto Javier
    Lopez-Sastre
Tobias Lorenz
Javier Lorenzo-Navarro
Yujing Lou
Qian Lou
Xiankai Lu
Changsheng Lu
Huimin Lu
Yongxi Lu
Hao Lu
Hong Lu
Jiasen Lu

Juwei Lu
Fan Lu
Guangming Lu
Jiwen Lu
Shun Lu
Tao Lu
Xiaonan Lu
Yang Lu
Yao Lu
Yongchun Lu
Zhiwu Lu
Cheng Lu
Liying Lu
Guo Lu
Xuequan Lu
Yanye Lu
Yantao Lu
Yuhang Lu
Fujun Luan
Jonathon Luiten
Jovita Lukasik
Alan Lukezic
Jonathan Samuel Lumentut
Mayank Lunayach
Ao Luo
Canjie Luo
Chong Luo
Xu Luo
Grace Luo
Jun Luo
Katie Z. Luo
Tao Luo
Cheng Luo
Fangzhou Luo
Gen Luo
Lei Luo
Sihui Luo
Weixin Luo
Yan Luo
Xiaoyan Luo
Yong Luo
Yadan Luo
Hao Luo
Ruotian Luo
Mi Luo

Tiange Luo
Wenjie Luo
Wenhan Luo
Xiao Luo
Zhiming Luo
Zhipeng Luo
Zhengyi Luo
Diogo C. Luvizon
Zhaoyang Lv
Gengyu Lyu
Lingjuan Lyu
Jun Lyu
Yuanyuan Lyu
Youwei Lyu
Yueming Lyu
Bingpeng Ma
Chao Ma
Chongyang Ma
Congbo Ma
Chih-Yao Ma
Fan Ma
Lin Ma
Haoyu Ma
Hengbo Ma
Jianqi Ma
Jiawei Ma
Jiayi Ma
Kede Ma
Kai Ma
Lingni Ma
Lei Ma
Xu Ma
Ning Ma
Benteng Ma
Cheng Ma
Andy J. Ma
Long Ma
Zhanyu Ma
Zhiheng Ma
Qianli Ma
Shiqiang Ma
Sizhuo Ma
Shiqing Ma
Xiaolong Ma
Xinzhu Ma

Gautam B. Machiraju
Spandan Madan
Mathew Magimai-Doss
Luca Magri
Behrooz Mahasseni
Upal Mahbub
Siddharth Mahendran
Paridhi Maheshwari
Rishabh Maheshwary
Mohammed Mahmoud
Shishira R. R. Maiya
Sylwia Majchrowska
Arjun Majumdar
Puspita Majumdar
Orchid Majumder
Sagnik Majumder
Ilya Makarov
Farkhod F.
   Makhmudkhujaev
Yasushi Makihara
Ankur Mali
Mateusz Malinowski
Utkarsh Mall
Srikanth Malla
Clement Mallet
Dimitrios Mallis
Yunze Man
Dipu Manandhar
Massimiliano Mancini
Murari Mandal
Raunak Manekar
Karttikeya Mangalam
Puneet Mangla
Fabian Manhardt
Sivabalan Manivasagam
Fahim Mannan
Chengzhi Mao
Hanzi Mao
Jiayuan Mao
Junhua Mao
Zhiyuan Mao
Jiageng Mao
Yunyao Mao
Zhendong Mao
Alberto Marchisio

Diego Marcos
Riccardo Marin
Aram Markosyan
Renaud Marlet
Ricardo Marques
Miquel Martí i Rabadán
Diego Martin Arroyo
Niki Martinel
Brais Martinez
Julieta Martinez
Marc Masana
Tomohiro Mashita
Timothée Masquelier
Minesh Mathew
Tetsu Matsukawa
Marwan Mattar
Bruce A. Maxwell
Christoph Mayer
Mantas Mazeika
Pratik Mazumder
Scott McCloskey
Steven McDonagh
Ishit Mehta
Jie Mei
Kangfu Mei
Jieru Mei
Xiaoguang Mei
Givi Meishvili
Luke Melas-Kyriazi
Iaroslav Melekhov
Andres Mendez-Vazquez
Heydi Mendez-Vazquez
Matias Mendieta
Ricardo A. Mendoza-León
Chenlin Meng
Depu Meng
Rang Meng
Zibo Meng
Qingjie Meng
Qier Meng
Yanda Meng
Zihang Meng
Thomas Mensink
Fabian Mentzer
Christopher Metzler

Gregory P. Meyer
Vasileios Mezaris
Liang Mi
Lu Mi
Bo Miao
Changtao Miao
Zichen Miao
Qiguang Miao
Xin Miao
Zhongqi Miao
Frank Michel
Simone Milani
Ben Mildenhall
Roy V. Miles
Juhong Min
Kyle Min
Hyun-Seok Min
Weiqing Min
Yuecong Min
Zhixiang Min
Qi Ming
David Minnen
Aymen Mir
Deepak Mishra
Anand Mishra
Shlok K. Mishra
Niluthpol Mithun
Gaurav Mittal
Trisha Mittal
Daisuke Miyazaki
Kaichun Mo
Hong Mo
Zhipeng Mo
Davide Modolo
Abduallah A. Mohamed
Mohamed Afham
   Mohamed Aflal
Ron Mokady
Pavlo Molchanov
Davide Moltisanti
Liliane Momeni
Gianluca Monaci
Pascal Monasse
Ajoy Mondal
Tom Monnier

Aron Monszpart
Gyeongsik Moon
Suhong Moon
Taesup Moon
Sean Moran
Daniel Moreira
Pietro Morerio
Alexandre Morgand
Lia Morra
Ali Mosleh
Inbar Mosseri
Sayed Mohammad
    Mostafavi Isfahani
Saman Motamed
Ramy A. Mounir
Fangzhou Mu
Jiteng Mu
Norman Mu
Yasuhiro Mukaigawa
Ryan Mukherjee
Tanmoy Mukherjee
Yusuke Mukuta
Ravi Teja Mullapudi
Lea Müller
Matthias Müller
Martin Mundt
Nils Murrugarra-Llerena
Damien Muselet
Armin Mustafa
Muhammad Ferjad Naeem
Sauradip Nag
Hajime Nagahara
Pravin Nagar
Rajendra Nagar
Naveen Shankar Nagaraja
Varun Nagaraja
Tushar Nagarajan
Seungjun Nah
Gaku Nakano
Yuta Nakashima
Giljoo Nam
Seonghyeon Nam
Liangliang Nan
Yuesong Nan
Yeshwanth Napolean

Dinesh Reddy
    Narapureddy
Medhini Narasimhan
Supreeth
    Narasimhaswamy
Sriram Narayanan
Erickson R. Nascimento
Varun Nasery
K. L. Navaneet
Pablo Navarrete Michelini
Shant Navasardyan
Shah Nawaz
Nihal Nayak
Farhood Negin
Lukáš Neumann
Alejandro Newell
Evonne Ng
Kam Woh Ng
Tony Ng
Anh Nguyen
Tuan Anh Nguyen
Cuong Cao Nguyen
Ngoc Cuong Nguyen
Thanh Nguyen
Khoi Nguyen
Phi Le Nguyen
Phong Ha Nguyen
Tam Nguyen
Truong Nguyen
Anh Tuan Nguyen
Rang Nguyen
Thao Thi Phuong Nguyen
Van Nguyen Nguyen
Zhen-Liang Ni
Yao Ni
Shijie Nie
Xuecheng Nie
Yongwei Nie
Weizhi Nie
Ying Nie
Yinyu Nie
Kshitij N. Nikhal
Simon Niklaus
Xuefei Ning
Jifeng Ning

Yotam Nitzan
Di Niu
Shuaicheng Niu
Li Niu
Wei Niu
Yulei Niu
Zhenxing Niu
Albert No
Shohei Nobuhara
Nicoletta Noceti
Junhyug Noh
Sotiris Nousias
Slawomir Nowaczyk
Ewa M. Nowara
Valsamis Ntouskos
Gilberto Ochoa-Ruiz
Ferda Ofli
Jihyong Oh
Sangyun Oh
Youngtaek Oh
Hiroki Ohashi
Takahiro Okabe
Kemal Oksuz
Fumio Okura
Daniel Olmeda Reino
Matthew Olson
Carl Olsson
Roy Or-El
Alessandro Ortis
Guillermo Ortiz-Jimenez
Magnus Oskarsson
Ahmed A. A. Osman
Martin R. Oswald
Mayu Otani
Naima Otberdout
Cheng Ouyang
Jiahong Ouyang
Wanli Ouyang
Andrew Owens
Poojan B. Oza
Mete Ozay
A. Cengiz Oztireli
Gautam Pai
Tomas Pajdla
Umapada Pal

Simone Palazzo
Luca Palmieri
Bowen Pan
Hao Pan
Lili Pan
Tai-Yu Pan
Liang Pan
Chengwei Pan
Yingwei Pan
Xuran Pan
Jinshan Pan
Xinyu Pan
Liyuan Pan
Xingang Pan
Xingjia Pan
Zhihong Pan
Zizheng Pan
Priyadarshini Panda
Rameswar Panda
Rohit Pandey
Kaiyue Pang
Bo Pang
Guansong Pang
Jiangmiao Pang
Meng Pang
Tianyu Pang
Ziqi Pang
Omiros Pantazis
Andreas Panteli
Maja Pantic
Marina Paolanti
Joao P. Papa
Samuele Papa
Mike Papadakis
Dim P. Papadopoulos
George Papandreou
Constantin Pape
Toufiq Parag
Chethan Parameshwara
Shaifali Parashar
Alejandro Pardo
Rishubh Parihar
Sarah Parisot
JaeYoo Park
Gyeong-Moon Park

Hyojin Park
Hyoungseob Park
Jongchan Park
Jae Sung Park
Kiru Park
Chunghyun Park
Kwanyong Park
Sunghyun Park
Sungrae Park
Seongsik Park
Sanghyun Park
Sungjune Park
Taesung Park
Gaurav Parmar
Paritosh Parmar
Alvaro Parra
Despoina Paschalidou
Or Patashnik
Shivansh Patel
Pushpak Pati
Prashant W. Patil
Vaishakh Patil
Suvam Patra
Jay Patravali
Badri Narayana Patro
Angshuman Paul
Sudipta Paul
Rémi Pautrat
Nick E. Pears
Adithya Pediredla
Wenjie Pei
Shmuel Peleg
Latha Pemula
Bo Peng
Houwen Peng
Yue Peng
Liangzu Peng
Baoyun Peng
Jun Peng
Pai Peng
Sida Peng
Xi Peng
Yuxin Peng
Songyou Peng
Wei Peng

Weiqi Peng
Wen-Hsiao Peng
Pramuditha Perera
Juan C. Perez
Eduardo Pérez Pellitero
Juan-Manuel Perez-Rua
Federico Pernici
Marco Pesavento
Stavros Petridis
Ilya A. Petrov
Vladan Petrovic
Mathis Petrovich
Suzanne Petryk
Hieu Pham
Quang Pham
Khoi Pham
Tung Pham
Huy Phan
Stephen Phillips
Cheng Perng Phoo
David Picard
Marco Piccirilli
Georg Pichler
A. J. Piergiovanni
Vipin Pillai
Silvia L. Pintea
Giovanni Pintore
Robinson Piramuthu
Fiora Pirri
Theodoros Pissas
Fabio Pizzati
Benjamin Planche
Bryan Plummer
Matteo Poggi
Ashwini Pokle
Georgy E. Ponimatkin
Adrian Popescu
Stefan Popov
Nikola Popović
Ronald Poppe
Angelo Porrello
Michael Potter
Charalambos Poullis
Hadi Pouransari
Omid Poursaeed

Shraman Pramanick
Mantini Pranav
Dilip K. Prasad
Meghshyam Prasad
B. H. Pawan Prasad
Shitala Prasad
Prateek Prasanna
Ekta Prashnani
Derek S. Prijatelj
Luke Y. Prince
Véronique Prinet
Victor Adrian Prisacariu
James Pritts
Thomas Probst
Sergey Prokudin
Rita Pucci
Chi-Man Pun
Matthew Purri
Haozhi Qi
Lu Qi
Lei Qi
Xianbiao Qi
Yonggang Qi
Yuankai Qi
Siyuan Qi
Guocheng Qian
Hangwei Qian
Qi Qian
Deheng Qian
Shengsheng Qian
Wen Qian
Rui Qian
Yiming Qian
Shengju Qian
Shengyi Qian
Xuelin Qian
Zhenxing Qian
Nan Qiao
Xiaotian Qiao
Jing Qin
Can Qin
Siyang Qin
Hongwei Qin
Jie Qin
Minghai Qin

Yipeng Qin
Yongqiang Qin
Wenda Qin
Xuebin Qin
Yuzhe Qin
Yao Qin
Zhenyue Qin
Zhiwu Qing
Heqian Qiu
Jiayan Qiu
Jielin Qiu
Yue Qiu
Jiaxiong Qiu
Zhongxi Qiu
Shi Qiu
Zhaofan Qiu
Zhongnan Qu
Yanyun Qu
Kha Gia Quach
Yuhui Quan
Ruijie Quan
Mike Rabbat
Rahul Shekhar Rade
Filip Radenovic
Gorjan Radevski
Bogdan Raducanu
Francesco Ragusa
Shafin Rahman
Md Mahfuzur Rahman
    Siddiquee
Hossein Rahmani
Kiran Raja
Sivaramakrishnan
    Rajaraman
Jathushan Rajasegaran
Adnan Siraj Rakin
Michaël Ramamonjisoa
Chirag A. Raman
Shanmuganathan Raman
Vignesh Ramanathan
Vasili Ramanishka
Vikram V. Ramaswamy
Merey Ramazanova
Jason Rambach
Sai Saketh Rambhatla

Clément Rambour
Ashwin Ramesh Babu
Adín Ramírez Rivera
Arianna Rampini
Haoxi Ran
Aakanksha Rana
Aayush Jung Bahadur
    Rana
Kanchana N. Ranasinghe
Aneesh Rangnekar
Samrudhdhi B. Rangrej
Harsh Rangwani
Viresh Ranjan
Anyi Rao
Yongming Rao
Carolina Raposo
Michalis Raptis
Amir Rasouli
Vivek Rathod
Adepu Ravi Sankar
Avinash Ravichandran
Bharadwaj Ravichandran
Dripta S. Raychaudhuri
Adria Recasens
Simon Reiß
Davis Rempe
Daxuan Ren
Jiawei Ren
Jimmy Ren
Sucheng Ren
Dayong Ren
Zhile Ren
Dongwei Ren
Qibing Ren
Pengfei Ren
Zhenwen Ren
Xuqian Ren
Yixuan Ren
Zhongzheng Ren
Ambareesh Revanur
Hamed Rezazadegan
    Tavakoli
Rafael S. Rezende
Wonjong Rhee
Alexander Richard

Christian Richardt
Stephan R. Richter
Benjamin Riggan
Dominik Rivoir
Mamshad Nayeem Rizve
Joshua D. Robinson
Joseph Robinson
Chris Rockwell
Ranga Rodrigo
Andres C. Rodriguez
Carlos Rodriguez-Pardo
Marcus Rohrbach
Gemma Roig
Yu Rong
David A. Ross
Mohammad Rostami
Edward Rosten
Karsten Roth
Anirban Roy
Debaditya Roy
Shuvendu Roy
Ahana Roy Choudhury
Aruni Roy Chowdhury
Denys Rozumnyi
Shulan Ruan
Wenjie Ruan
Patrick Ruhkamp
Danila Rukhovich
Anian Ruoss
Chris Russell
Dan Ruta
Dawid Damian Rymarczyk
DongHun Ryu
Hyeonggon Ryu
Kwonyoung Ryu
Balasubramanian S.
Alexandre Sablayrolles
Mohammad Sabokrou
Arka Sadhu
Aniruddha Saha
Oindrila Saha
Pritish Sahu
Aneeshan Sain
Nirat Saini
Saurabh Saini

Takeshi Saitoh
Christos Sakaridis
Fumihiko Sakaue
Dimitrios Sakkos
Ken Sakurada
Parikshit V. Sakurikar
Rohit Saluja
Nermin Samet
Leo Sampaio Ferraz
    Ribeiro
Jorge Sanchez
Enrique Sanchez
Shengtian Sang
Anush Sankaran
Soubhik Sanyal
Nikolaos Sarafianos
Vishwanath Saragadam
István Sárándi
Saquib Sarfraz
Mert Bulent Sariyildiz
Anindya Sarkar
Pritam Sarkar
Paul-Edouard Sarlin
Hiroshi Sasaki
Takami Sato
Torsten Sattler
Ravi Kumar Satzoda
Axel Sauer
Stefano Savian
Artem Savkin
Manolis Savva
Gerald Schaefer
Simone Schaub-Meyer
Yoni Schirris
Samuel Schulter
Katja Schwarz
Jesse Scott
Sinisa Segvic
Constantin Marc Seibold
Lorenzo Seidenari
Matan Sela
Fadime Sener
Paul Hongsuck Seo
Kwanggyoon Seo
Hongje Seong

Dario Serez
Francesco Setti
Bryan Seybold
Mohamad Shahbazi
Shima Shahfar
Xinxin Shan
Caifeng Shan
Dandan Shan
Shawn Shan
Wei Shang
Jinghuan Shang
Jiaxiang Shang
Lei Shang
Sukrit Shankar
Ken Shao
Rui Shao
Jie Shao
Mingwen Shao
Aashish Sharma
Gaurav Sharma
Vivek Sharma
Abhishek Sharma
Yoli Shavit
Shashank Shekhar
Sumit Shekhar
Zhijie Shen
Fengyi Shen
Furao Shen
Jialie Shen
Jingjing Shen
Ziyi Shen
Linlin Shen
Guangyu Shen
Biluo Shen
Falong Shen
Jiajun Shen
Qiu Shen
Qiuhong Shen
Shuai Shen
Wang Shen
Yiqing Shen
Yunhang Shen
Siqi Shen
Bin Shen
Tianwei Shen

Xi Shen
Yilin Shen
Yuming Shen
Yucong Shen
Zhiqiang Shen
Lu Sheng
Yichen Sheng
Shivanand Venkanna
    Sheshappanavar
Shelly Sheynin
Baifeng Shi
Ruoxi Shi
Botian Shi
Hailin Shi
Jia Shi
Jing Shi
Shaoshuai Shi
Baoguang Shi
Boxin Shi
Hengcan Shi
Tianyang Shi
Xiaodan Shi
Yongjie Shi
Zhensheng Shi
Yinghuan Shi
Weiqi Shi
Wu Shi
Xuepeng Shi
Xiaoshuang Shi
Yujiao Shi
Zenglin Shi
Zhenmei Shi
Takashi Shibata
Meng-Li Shih
Yichang Shih
Hyunjung Shim
Dongseok Shim
Soshi Shimada
Inkyu Shin
Jinwoo Shin
Seungjoo Shin
Seungjae Shin
Koichi Shinoda
Suprosanna Shit

Palaiahnakote
    Shivakumara
Eli Shlizerman
Gaurav Shrivastava
Xiao Shu
Xiangbo Shu
Xiujun Shu
Yang Shu
Tianmin Shu
Jun Shu
Zhixin Shu
Bing Shuai
Maria Shugrina
Ivan Shugurov
Satya Narayan Shukla
Pranjay Shyam
Jianlou Si
Yawar Siddiqui
Alberto Signoroni
Pedro Silva
Jae-Young Sim
Oriane Siméoni
Martin Simon
Andrea Simonelli
Abhishek Singh
Ashish Singh
Dinesh Singh
Gurkirt Singh
Krishna Kumar Singh
Mannat Singh
Pravendra Singh
Rajat Vikram Singh
Utkarsh Singhal
Dipika Singhania
Vasu Singla
Harsh Sinha
Sudipta Sinha
Josef Sivic
Elena Sizikova
Geri Skenderi
Ivan Skorokhodov
Dmitriy Smirnov
Cameron Y. Smith
James S. Smith
Patrick Snape

Mattia Soldan
Hyeongseok Son
Sanghyun Son
Chuanbiao Song
Chen Song
Chunfeng Song
Dan Song
Dongjin Song
Hwanjun Song
Guoxian Song
Jiaming Song
Jie Song
Liangchen Song
Ran Song
Luchuan Song
Xibin Song
Li Song
Fenglong Song
Guoli Song
Guanglu Song
Zhenbo Song
Lin Song
Xinhang Song
Yang Song
Yibing Song
Rajiv Soundararajan
Hossein Souri
Cristovao Sousa
Riccardo Spezialetti
Leonidas Spinoulas
Michael W. Spratling
Deepak Sridhar
Srinath Sridhar
Gaurang Sriramanan
Vinkle Kumar Srivastav
Themos Stafylakis
Serban Stan
Anastasis Stathopoulos
Markus Steinberger
Jan Steinbrener
Sinisa Stekovic
Alexandros Stergiou
Gleb Sterkin
Rainer Stiefelhagen
Pierre Stock

Ombretta Strafforello
Julian Straub
Yannick Strümpler
Joerg Stueckler
Hang Su
Weijie Su
Jong-Chyi Su
Bing Su
Haisheng Su
Jinming Su
Yiyang Su
Yukun Su
Yuxin Su
Zhuo Su
Zhaoqi Su
Xiu Su
Yu-Chuan Su
Zhixun Su
Arulkumar Subramaniam
Akshayvarun Subramanya
A. Subramanyam
Swathikiran Sudhakaran
Yusuke Sugano
Masanori Suganuma
Yumin Suh
Yang Sui
Baochen Sun
Cheng Sun
Long Sun
Guolei Sun
Haoliang Sun
Haomiao Sun
He Sun
Hanqing Sun
Hao Sun
Lichao Sun
Jiachen Sun
Jiaming Sun
Jian Sun
Jin Sun
Jennifer J. Sun
Tiancheng Sun
Libo Sun
Peize Sun
Qianru Sun

Shanlin Sun
Yu Sun
Zhun Sun
Che Sun
Lin Sun
Tao Sun
Yiyou Sun
Chunyi Sun
Chong Sun
Weiwei Sun
Weixuan Sun
Xiuyu Sun
Yanan Sun
Zeren Sun
Zhaodong Sun
Zhiqing Sun
Minhyuk Sung
Jinli Suo
Simon Suo
Abhijit Suprem
Anshuman Suri
Saksham Suri
Joshua M. Susskind
Roman Suvorov
Gurumurthy Swaminathan
Robin Swanson
Paul Swoboda
Tabish A. Syed
Richard Szeliski
Fariborz Taherkhani
Yu-Wing Tai
Keita Takahashi
Walter Talbott
Gary Tam
Masato Tamura
Feitong Tan
Fuwen Tan
Shuhan Tan
Andong Tan
Bin Tan
Cheng Tan
Jianchao Tan
Lei Tan
Mingxing Tan
Xin Tan

Zichang Tan
Zhentao Tan
Kenichiro Tanaka
Masayuki Tanaka
Yushun Tang
Hao Tang
Jingqun Tang
Jinhui Tang
Kaihua Tang
Luming Tang
Lv Tang
Sheyang Tang
Shitao Tang
Siliang Tang
Shixiang Tang
Yansong Tang
Keke Tang
Chang Tang
Chenwei Tang
Jie Tang
Junshu Tang
Ming Tang
Peng Tang
Xu Tang
Yao Tang
Chen Tang
Fan Tang
Haoran Tang
Shengeng Tang
Yehui Tang
Zhipeng Tang
Ugo Tanielian
Chaofan Tao
Jiale Tao
Junli Tao
Renshuai Tao
An Tao
Guanhong Tao
Zhiqiang Tao
Makarand Tapaswi
Jean-Philippe G. Tarel
Juan J. Tarrio
Enzo Tartaglione
Keisuke Tateno
Zachary Teed

Ajinkya B. Tejankar
Bugra Tekin
Purva Tendulkar
Damien Teney
Minggui Teng
Chris Tensmeyer
Andrew Beng Jin Teoh
Philipp Terhörst
Kartik Thakral
Nupur Thakur
Kevin Thandiackal
Spyridon Thermos
Diego Thomas
William Thong
Yuesong Tian
Guanzhong Tian
Lin Tian
Shiqi Tian
Kai Tian
Meng Tian
Tai-Peng Tian
Zhuotao Tian
Shangxuan Tian
Tian Tian
Yapeng Tian
Yu Tian
Yuxin Tian
Leslie Ching Ow Tiong
Praveen Tirupattur
Garvita Tiwari
George Toderici
Antoine Toisoul
Aysim Toker
Tatiana Tommasi
Zhan Tong
Alessio Tonioni
Alessandro Torcinovich
Fabio Tosi
Matteo Toso
Hugo Touvron
Quan Hung Tran
Son Tran
Hung Tran
Ngoc-Trung Tran
Vinh Tran

Phong Tran
Giovanni Trappolini
Edith Tretschk
Subarna Tripathi
Shubhendu Trivedi
Eduard Trulls
Prune Truong
Thanh-Dat Truong
Tomasz Trzcinski
Sam Tsai
Yi-Hsuan Tsai
Ethan Tseng
Yu-Chee Tseng
Shahar Tsiper
Stavros Tsogkas
Shikui Tu
Zhigang Tu
Zhengzhong Tu
Richard Tucker
Sergey Tulyakov
Cigdem Turan
Daniyar Turmukhambetov
Victor G. Turrisi da Costa
Bartlomiej Twardowski
Christopher D. Twigg
Radim Tylecek
Mostofa Rafid Uddin
Md. Zasim Uddin
Kohei Uehara
Nicolas Ugrinovic
Youngjung Uh
Norimichi Ukita
Anwaar Ulhaq
Devesh Upadhyay
Paul Upchurch
Yoshitaka Ushiku
Yuzuko Utsumi
Mikaela Angelina Uy
Mohit Vaishnav
Pratik Vaishnavi
Jeya Maria Jose Valanarasu
Matias A. Valdenegro Toro
Diego Valsesia
Wouter Van Gansbeke
Nanne van Noord

Simon Vandenhende
Farshid Varno
Cristina Vasconcelos
Francisco Vasconcelos
Alex Vasilescu
Subeesh Vasu
Arun Balajee Vasudevan
Kanav Vats
Vaibhav S. Vavilala
Sagar Vaze
Javier Vazquez-Corral
Andrea Vedaldi
Olga Veksler
Andreas Velten
Sai H. Vemprala
Raviteja Vemulapalli
Shashanka
   Venkataramanan
Dor Verbin
Luisa Verdoliva
Manisha Verma
Yashaswi Verma
Constantin Vertan
Eli Verwimp
Deepak Vijaykeerthy
Pablo Villanueva
Ruben Villegas
Markus Vincze
Vibhav Vineet
Minh P. Vo
Huy V. Vo
Duc Minh Vo
Tomas Vojir
Igor Vozniak
Nicholas Vretos
Vibashan VS
Tuan-Anh Vu
Thang Vu
Mårten Wadenbäck
Neal Wadhwa
Aaron T. Walsman
Steven Walton
Jin Wan
Alvin Wan
Jia Wan

Jun Wan
Xiaoyue Wan
Fang Wan
Guowei Wan
Renjie Wan
Zhiqiang Wan
Ziyu Wan
Bastian Wandt
Dongdong Wang
Limin Wang
Haiyang Wang
Xiaobing Wang
Angtian Wang
Angelina Wang
Bing Wang
Bo Wang
Boyu Wang
Binghui Wang
Chen Wang
Chien-Yi Wang
Congli Wang
Qi Wang
Chengrui Wang
Rui Wang
Yiqun Wang
Cong Wang
Wenjing Wang
Dongkai Wang
Di Wang
Xiaogang Wang
Kai Wang
Zhizhong Wang
Fangjinhua Wang
Feng Wang
Hang Wang
Gaoang Wang
Guoqing Wang
Guangcong Wang
Guangzhi Wang
Hanqing Wang
Hao Wang
Haohan Wang
Haoran Wang
Hong Wang
Haotao Wang

Hu Wang
Huan Wang
Hua Wang
Hui-Po Wang
Hengli Wang
Hanyu Wang
Hongxing Wang
Jingwen Wang
Jialiang Wang
Jian Wang
Jianyi Wang
Jiashun Wang
Jiahao Wang
Tsun-Hsuan Wang
Xiaoqian Wang
Jinqiao Wang
Jun Wang
Jianzong Wang
Kaihong Wang
Ke Wang
Lei Wang
Lingjing Wang
Linnan Wang
Lin Wang
Liansheng Wang
Mengjiao Wang
Manning Wang
Nannan Wang
Peihao Wang
Jiayun Wang
Pu Wang
Qiang Wang
Qiufeng Wang
Qilong Wang
Qiangchang Wang
Qin Wang
Qing Wang
Ruocheng Wang
Ruibin Wang
Ruisheng Wang
Ruizhe Wang
Runqi Wang
Runzhong Wang
Wenxuan Wang
Sen Wang

Shangfei Wang
Shaofei Wang
Shijie Wang
Shiqi Wang
Zhibo Wang
Song Wang
Xinjiang Wang
Tai Wang
Tao Wang
Teng Wang
Xiang Wang
Tianren Wang
Tiantian Wang
Tianyi Wang
Fengjiao Wang
Wei Wang
Miaohui Wang
Suchen Wang
Siyue Wang
Yaoming Wang
Xiao Wang
Ze Wang
Biao Wang
Chaofei Wang
Dong Wang
Gu Wang
Guangrun Wang
Guangming Wang
Guo-Hua Wang
Haoqing Wang
Hesheng Wang
Huafeng Wang
Jinghua Wang
Jingdong Wang
Jingjing Wang
Jingya Wang
Jingkang Wang
Jiakai Wang
Junke Wang
Kuo Wang
Lichen Wang
Lizhi Wang
Longguang Wang
Mang Wang
Mei Wang

Min Wang
Peng-Shuai Wang
Run Wang
Shaoru Wang
Shuhui Wang
Tan Wang
Tiancai Wang
Tianqi Wang
Wenhai Wang
Wenzhe Wang
Xiaobo Wang
Xiudong Wang
Xu Wang
Yajie Wang
Yan Wang
Yuan-Gen Wang
Yingqian Wang
Yizhi Wang
Yulin Wang
Yu Wang
Yujie Wang
Yunhe Wang
Yuxi Wang
Yaowei Wang
Yiwei Wang
Zezheng Wang
Hongzhi Wang
Zhiqiang Wang
Ziteng Wang
Ziwei Wang
Zheng Wang
Zhenyu Wang
Binglu Wang
Zhongdao Wang
Ce Wang
Weining Wang
Weiyao Wang
Wenbin Wang
Wenguan Wang
Guangting Wang
Haolin Wang
Haiyan Wang
Huiyu Wang
Naiyan Wang
Jingbo Wang

Jinpeng Wang
Jiaqi Wang
Liyuan Wang
Lizhen Wang
Ning Wang
Wenqian Wang
Sheng-Yu Wang
Weimin Wang
Xiaohan Wang
Yifan Wang
Yi Wang
Yongtao Wang
Yizhou Wang
Zhuo Wang
Zhe Wang
Xudong Wang
Xiaofang Wang
Xinggang Wang
Xiaosen Wang
Xiaosong Wang
Xiaoyang Wang
Lijun Wang
Xinlong Wang
Xuan Wang
Xue Wang
Yangang Wang
Yaohui Wang
Yu-Chiang Frank Wang
Yida Wang
Yilin Wang
Yi Ru Wang
Yali Wang
Yinglong Wang
Yufu Wang
Yujiang Wang
Yuwang Wang
Yuting Wang
Yang Wang
Yu-Xiong Wang
Yixu Wang
Ziqi Wang
Zhicheng Wang
Zeyu Wang
Zhaowen Wang
Zhenyi Wang

Zhenzhi Wang
Zhijie Wang
Zhiyong Wang
Zhongling Wang
Zhuowei Wang
Zian Wang
Zifu Wang
Zihao Wang
Zirui Wang
Ziyan Wang
Wenxiao Wang
Zhen Wang
Zhepeng Wang
Zi Wang
Zihao W. Wang
Steven L. Waslander
Olivia Watkins
Daniel Watson
Silvan Weder
Dongyoon Wee
Dongming Wei
Tianyi Wei
Jia Wei
Dong Wei
Fangyun Wei
Longhui Wei
Mingqiang Wei
Xinyue Wei
Chen Wei
Donglai Wei
Pengxu Wei
Xing Wei
Xiu-Shen Wei
Wenqi Wei
Guoqiang Wei
Wei Wei
XingKui Wei
Xian Wei
Xingxing Wei
Yake Wei
Yuxiang Wei
Yi Wei
Luca Weihs
Michael Weinmann
Martin Weinmann

Congcong Wen
Chuan Wen
Jie Wen
Sijia Wen
Song Wen
Chao Wen
Xiang Wen
Zeyi Wen
Xin Wen
Yilin Wen
Yijia Weng
Shuchen Weng
Junwu Weng
Wenming Weng
Renliang Weng
Zhenyu Weng
Xinshuo Weng
Nicholas J. Westlake
Gordon Wetzstein
Lena M. Widin Klasén
Rick Wildes
Bryan M. Williams
Williem Williem
Ole Winther
Scott Wisdom
Alex Wong
Chau-Wai Wong
Kwan-Yee K. Wong
Yongkang Wong
Scott Workman
Marcel Worring
Michael Wray
Safwan Wshah
Xiang Wu
Aming Wu
Chongruo Wu
Cho-Ying Wu
Chunpeng Wu
Chenyan Wu
Ziyi Wu
Fuxiang Wu
Gang Wu
Haiping Wu
Huisi Wu
Jane Wu

Jialian Wu
Jing Wu
Jinjian Wu
Jianlong Wu
Xian Wu
Lifang Wu
Lifan Wu
Minye Wu
Qianyi Wu
Rongliang Wu
Rui Wu
Shiqian Wu
Shuzhe Wu
Shangzhe Wu
Tsung-Han Wu
Tz-Ying Wu
Ting-Wei Wu
Jiannan Wu
Zhiliang Wu
Yu Wu
Chenyun Wu
Dayan Wu
Dongxian Wu
Fei Wu
Hefeng Wu
Jianxin Wu
Weibin Wu
Wenxuan Wu
Wenhao Wu
Xiao Wu
Yicheng Wu
Yuanwei Wu
Yu-Huan Wu
Zhenxin Wu
Zhenyu Wu
Wei Wu
Peng Wu
Xiaohe Wu
Xindi Wu
Xinxing Wu
Xinyi Wu
Xingjiao Wu
Xiongwei Wu
Yangzheng Wu
Yanzhao Wu

Yawen Wu
Yong Wu
Yi Wu
Ying Nian Wu
Zhenyao Wu
Zhonghua Wu
Zongze Wu
Zuxuan Wu
Stefanie Wuhrer
Teng Xi
Jianing Xi
Fei Xia
Haifeng Xia
Menghan Xia
Yuanqing Xia
Zhihua Xia
Xiaobo Xia
Weihao Xia
Shihong Xia
Yan Xia
Yong Xia
Zhaoyang Xia
Zhihao Xia
Chuhua Xian
Yongqin Xian
Wangmeng Xiang
Fanbo Xiang
Tiange Xiang
Tao Xiang
Liuyu Xiang
Xiaoyu Xiang
Zhiyu Xiang
Aoran Xiao
Chunxia Xiao
Fanyi Xiao
Jimin Xiao
Jun Xiao
Taihong Xiao
Anqi Xiao
Junfei Xiao
Jing Xiao
Liang Xiao
Yang Xiao
Yuting Xiao
Yijun Xiao

Yao Xiao

Zeyu Xiao

Zhisheng Xiao

Zihao Xiao

Binhui Xie

Christopher Xie

Haozhe Xie

Jin Xie

Guo-Sen Xie

Hongtao Xie

Ming-Kun Xie

Tingting Xie

Chaohao Xie

Weicheng Xie

Xudong Xie

Jiyang Xie

Xiaohua Xie

Yuan Xie

Zhenyu Xie

Ning Xie

Xianghui Xie

Xiufeng Xie

You Xie

Yutong Xie

Fuyong Xing

Yifan Xing

Zhen Xing

Yuanjun Xiong

Jinhui Xiong

Weihua Xiong

Hongkai Xiong

Zhitong Xiong

Yuanhao Xiong

Yunyang Xiong

Yuwen Xiong

Zhiwei Xiong

Yuliang Xiu

An Xu

Chang Xu

Chenliang Xu

Chengming Xu

Chenshu Xu

Xiang Xu

Huijuan Xu

Zhe Xu

Jie Xu

Jingyi Xu

Jiarui Xu

Yinghao Xu

Kele Xu

Ke Xu

Li Xu

Linchuan Xu

Linning Xu

Mengde Xu

Mengmeng Frost Xu

Min Xu

Mingye Xu

Jun Xu

Ning Xu

Peng Xu

Runsheng Xu

Sheng Xu

Wenqiang Xu

Xiaogang Xu

Renzhe Xu

Kaidi Xu

Yi Xu

Chi Xu

Qiuling Xu

Baobei Xu

Feng Xu

Haohang Xu

Haofei Xu

Lan Xu

Mingze Xu

Songcen Xu

Weipeng Xu

Wenjia Xu

Wenju Xu

Xiangyu Xu

Xin Xu

Yinshuang Xu

Yixing Xu

Yuting Xu

Yanyu Xu

Zhenbo Xu

Zhiliang Xu

Zhiyuan Xu

Xiaohao Xu

Yanwu Xu

Yan Xu

Yiran Xu

Yifan Xu

Yufei Xu

Yong Xu

Zichuan Xu

Zenglin Xu

Zexiang Xu

Zhan Xu

Zheng Xu

Zhiwei Xu

Ziyue Xu

Shiyu Xuan

Hanyu Xuan

Fei Xue

Jianru Xue

Mingfu Xue

Qinghan Xue

Tianfan Xue

Chao Xue

Chuhui Xue

Nan Xue

Zhou Xue

Xiangyang Xue

Yuan Xue

Abhay Yadav

Ravindra Yadav

Kota Yamaguchi

Toshihiko Yamasaki

Kohei Yamashita

Chaochao Yan

Feng Yan

Kun Yan

Qingsen Yan

Qixin Yan

Rui Yan

Siming Yan

Xinchen Yan

Yaping Yan

Bin Yan

Qingan Yan

Shen Yan

Shipeng Yan

Xu Yan

Yan Yan
Yichao Yan
Zhaoyi Yan
Zike Yan
Zhiqiang Yan
Hongliang Yan
Zizheng Yan
Jiewen Yang
Anqi Joyce Yang
Shan Yang
Anqi Yang
Antoine Yang
Bo Yang
Baoyao Yang
Chenhongyi Yang
Dingkang Yang
De-Nian Yang
Dong Yang
David Yang
Fan Yang
Fengyu Yang
Fengting Yang
Fei Yang
Gengshan Yang
Heng Yang
Han Yang
Huan Yang
Yibo Yang
Jiancheng Yang
Jihan Yang
Jiawei Yang
Jiayu Yang
Jie Yang
Jinfa Yang
Jingkang Yang
Jinyu Yang
Cheng-Fu Yang
Ji Yang
Jianyu Yang
Kailun Yang
Tian Yang
Luyu Yang
Liang Yang
Li Yang
Michael Ying Yang

Yang Yang
Muli Yang
Le Yang
Qiushi Yang
Ren Yang
Ruihan Yang
Shuang Yang
Siyuan Yang
Su Yang
Shiqi Yang
Taojiannan Yang
Tianyu Yang
Lei Yang
Wanzhao Yang
Shuai Yang
William Yang
Wei Yang
Xiaofeng Yang
Xiaoshan Yang
Xin Yang
Xuan Yang
Xu Yang
Xingyi Yang
Xitong Yang
Jing Yang
Yanchao Yang
Wenming Yang
Yujiu Yang
Herb Yang
Jianfei Yang
Jinhui Yang
Chuanguang Yang
Guanglei Yang
Haitao Yang
Kewei Yang
Linlin Yang
Lijin Yang
Longrong Yang
Meng Yang
MingKun Yang
Sibei Yang
Shicai Yang
Tong Yang
Wen Yang
Xi Yang

Xiaolong Yang
Xue Yang
Yubin Yang
Ze Yang
Ziyi Yang
Yi Yang
Linjie Yang
Yuzhe Yang
Yiding Yang
Zhenpei Yang
Zhaohui Yang
Zhengyuan Yang
Zhibo Yang
Zongxin Yang
Hantao Yao
Mingde Yao
Rui Yao
Taiping Yao
Ting Yao
Cong Yao
Qingsong Yao
Quanming Yao
Xu Yao
Yuan Yao
Yao Yao
Yazhou Yao
Jiawen Yao
Shunyu Yao
Pew-Thian Yap
Sudhir Yarram
Rajeev Yasarla
Peng Ye
Botao Ye
Mao Ye
Fei Ye
Hanrong Ye
Jingwen Ye
Jinwei Ye
Jiarong Ye
Mang Ye
Meng Ye
Qi Ye
Qian Ye
Qixiang Ye
Junjie Ye

Sheng Ye
Nanyang Ye
Yufei Ye
Xiaoqing Ye
Ruolin Ye
Yousef Yeganeh
Chun-Hsiao Yeh
Raymond A. Yeh
Yu-Ying Yeh
Kai Yi
Chang Yi
Renjiao Yi
Xinping Yi
Peng Yi
Alper Yilmaz
Junho Yim
Hui Yin
Bangjie Yin
Jia-Li Yin
Miao Yin
Wenzhe Yin
Xuwang Yin
Ming Yin
Yu Yin
Aoxiong Yin
Kangxue Yin
Tianwei Yin
Wei Yin
Xianghua Ying
Rio Yokota
Tatsuya Yokota
Naoto Yokoya
Ryo Yonetani
Ki Yoon Yoo
Jinsu Yoo
Sunjae Yoon
Jae Shin Yoon
Jihun Yoon
Sung-Hoon Yoon
Ryota Yoshihashi
Yusuke Yoshiyasu
Chenyu You
Haoran You
Haoxuan You
Yang You

Quanzeng You
Tackgeun You
Kaichao You
Shan You
Xinge You
Yurong You
Baosheng Yu
Bei Yu
Haichao Yu
Hao Yu
Chaohui Yu
Fisher Yu
Jin-Gang Yu
Jiyang Yu
Jason J. Yu
Jiashuo Yu
Hong-Xing Yu
Lei Yu
Mulin Yu
Ning Yu
Peilin Yu
Qi Yu
Qian Yu
Rui Yu
Shuzhi Yu
Gang Yu
Tan Yu
Weijiang Yu
Xin Yu
Bingyao Yu
Ye Yu
Hanchao Yu
Yingchen Yu
Tao Yu
Xiaotian Yu
Qing Yu
Houjian Yu
Changqian Yu
Jing Yu
Jun Yu
Shujian Yu
Xiang Yu
Zhaofei Yu
Zhenbo Yu
Yinfeng Yu

Zhuoran Yu
Zitong Yu
Bo Yuan
Jiangbo Yuan
Liangzhe Yuan
Weihao Yuan
Jianbo Yuan
Xiaoyun Yuan
Ye Yuan
Li Yuan
Geng Yuan
Jialin Yuan
Maoxun Yuan
Peng Yuan
Xin Yuan
Yuan Yuan
Yuhui Yuan
Yixuan Yuan
Zheng Yuan
Mehmet Kerim Yücel
Kaiyu Yue
Haixiao Yue
Heeseung Yun
Sangdoo Yun
Tian Yun
Mahmut Yurt
Ekim Yurtsever
Ahmet Yüzügüler
Edouard Yvinec
Eloi Zablocki
Christopher Zach
Muhammad Zaigham
    Zaheer
Pierluigi Zama Ramirez
Yuhang Zang
Pietro Zanuttigh
Alexey Zaytsev
Bernhard Zeisl
Haitian Zeng
Pengpeng Zeng
Jiabei Zeng
Runhao Zeng
Wei Zeng
Yawen Zeng
Yi Zeng

Yiming Zeng
Tieyong Zeng
Huanqiang Zeng
Dan Zeng
Yu Zeng
Wei Zhai
Yuanhao Zhai
Fangneng Zhan
Kun Zhan
Xiong Zhang
Jingdong Zhang
Jiangning Zhang
Zhilu Zhang
Gengwei Zhang
Dongsu Zhang
Hui Zhang
Binjie Zhang
Bo Zhang
Tianhao Zhang
Cecilia Zhang
Jing Zhang
Chaoning Zhang
Chenxu Zhang
Chi Zhang
Chris Zhang
Yabin Zhang
Zhao Zhang
Rufeng Zhang
Chaoyi Zhang
Zheng Zhang
Da Zhang
Yi Zhang
Edward Zhang
Xin Zhang
Feifei Zhang
Feilong Zhang
Yuqi Zhang
GuiXuan Zhang
Hanlin Zhang
Hanwang Zhang
Hanzhen Zhang
Haotian Zhang
He Zhang
Haokui Zhang
Hongyuan Zhang

Hengrui Zhang
Hongming Zhang
Mingfang Zhang
Jianpeng Zhang
Jiaming Zhang
Jichao Zhang
Jie Zhang
Jingfeng Zhang
Jingyi Zhang
Jinnian Zhang
David Junhao Zhang
Junjie Zhang
Junzhe Zhang
Jiawan Zhang
Jingyang Zhang
Kai Zhang
Lei Zhang
Lihua Zhang
Lu Zhang
Miao Zhang
Minjia Zhang
Mingjin Zhang
Qi Zhang
Qian Zhang
Qilong Zhang
Qiming Zhang
Qiang Zhang
Richard Zhang
Ruimao Zhang
Ruisi Zhang
Ruixin Zhang
Runze Zhang
Qilin Zhang
Shan Zhang
Shanshan Zhang
Xi Sheryl Zhang
Song-Hai Zhang
Chongyang Zhang
Kaihao Zhang
Songyang Zhang
Shu Zhang
Siwei Zhang
Shujian Zhang
Tianyun Zhang
Tong Zhang

Tao Zhang
Wenwei Zhang
Wenqiang Zhang
Wen Zhang
Xiaolin Zhang
Xingchen Zhang
Xingxuan Zhang
Xiuming Zhang
Xiaoshuai Zhang
Xuanmeng Zhang
Xuanyang Zhang
Xucong Zhang
Xingxing Zhang
Xikun Zhang
Xiaohan Zhang
Yahui Zhang
Yunhua Zhang
Yan Zhang
Yanghao Zhang
Yifei Zhang
Yifan Zhang
Yi-Fan Zhang
Yihao Zhang
Yingliang Zhang
Youshan Zhang
Yulun Zhang
Yushu Zhang
Yixiao Zhang
Yide Zhang
Zhongwen Zhang
Bowen Zhang
Chen-Lin Zhang
Zehua Zhang
Zekun Zhang
Zeyu Zhang
Xiaowei Zhang
Yifeng Zhang
Cheng Zhang
Hongguang Zhang
Yuexi Zhang
Fa Zhang
Guofeng Zhang
Hao Zhang
Haofeng Zhang
Hongwen Zhang

Hua Zhang
Jiaxin Zhang
Zhenyu Zhang
Jian Zhang
Jianfeng Zhang
Jiao Zhang
Jiakai Zhang
Lefei Zhang
Le Zhang
Mi Zhang
Min Zhang
Ning Zhang
Pan Zhang
Pu Zhang
Qing Zhang
Renrui Zhang
Shifeng Zhang
Shuo Zhang
Shaoxiong Zhang
Weizhong Zhang
Xi Zhang
Xiaomei Zhang
Xinyu Zhang
Yin Zhang
Zicheng Zhang
Zihao Zhang
Ziqi Zhang
Zhaoxiang Zhang
Zhen Zhang
Zhipeng Zhang
Zhixing Zhang
Zhizheng Zhang
Jiawei Zhang
Zhong Zhang
Pingping Zhang
Yixin Zhang
Kui Zhang
Lingzhi Zhang
Huaiwen Zhang
Quanshi Zhang
Zhoutong Zhang
Yuhang Zhang
Yuting Zhang
Zhang Zhang
Ziming Zhang

Zhizhong Zhang
Qilong Zhangli
Bingyin Zhao
Bin Zhao
Chenglong Zhao
Lei Zhao
Feng Zhao
Gangming Zhao
Haiyan Zhao
Hao Zhao
Handong Zhao
Hengshuang Zhao
Yinan Zhao
Jiaojiao Zhao
Jiaqi Zhao
Jing Zhao
Kaili Zhao
Haojie Zhao
Yucheng Zhao
Longjiao Zhao
Long Zhao
Qingsong Zhao
Qingyu Zhao
Rui Zhao
Rui-Wei Zhao
Sicheng Zhao
Shuang Zhao
Siyan Zhao
Zelin Zhao
Shiyu Zhao
Wang Zhao
Tiesong Zhao
Qian Zhao
Wangbo Zhao
Xi-Le Zhao
Xu Zhao
Yajie Zhao
Yang Zhao
Ying Zhao
Yin Zhao
Yizhou Zhao
Yunhan Zhao
Yuyang Zhao
Yue Zhao
Yuzhi Zhao

Bowen Zhao
Pu Zhao
Bingchen Zhao
Borui Zhao
Fuqiang Zhao
Hanbin Zhao
Jian Zhao
Mingyang Zhao
Na Zhao
Rongchang Zhao
Ruiqi Zhao
Shuai Zhao
Wenda Zhao
Wenliang Zhao
Xiangyun Zhao
Yifan Zhao
Yaping Zhao
Zhou Zhao
He Zhao
Jie Zhao
Xibin Zhao
Xiaoqi Zhao
Zhengyu Zhao
Jin Zhe
Chuanxia Zheng
Huan Zheng
Hao Zheng
Jia Zheng
Jian-Qing Zheng
Shuai Zheng
Meng Zheng
Mingkai Zheng
Qian Zheng
Qi Zheng
Wu Zheng
Yinqiang Zheng
Yufeng Zheng
Yutong Zheng
Yalin Zheng
Yu Zheng
Feng Zheng
Zhaoheng Zheng
Haitian Zheng
Kang Zheng
Bolun Zheng

Haiyong Zheng
Mingwu Zheng
Sipeng Zheng
Tu Zheng
Wenzhao Zheng
Xiawu Zheng
Yinglin Zheng
Zhuo Zheng
Zilong Zheng
Kecheng Zheng
Zerong Zheng
Shuaifeng Zhi
Tiancheng Zhi
Jia-Xing Zhong
Yiwu Zhong
Fangwei Zhong
Zhihang Zhong
Yaoyao Zhong
Yiran Zhong
Zhun Zhong
Zichun Zhong
Bo Zhou
Boyao Zhou
Brady Zhou
Mo Zhou
Chunluan Zhou
Dingfu Zhou
Fan Zhou
Jingkai Zhou
Honglu Zhou
Jiaming Zhou
Jiahuan Zhou
Jun Zhou
Kaiyang Zhou
Keyang Zhou
Kuangqi Zhou
Lei Zhou
Lihua Zhou
Man Zhou
Mingyi Zhou
Mingyuan Zhou
Ning Zhou
Peng Zhou
Penghao Zhou
Qianyi Zhou

Shuigeng Zhou
Shangchen Zhou
Huayi Zhou
Zhize Zhou
Sanping Zhou
Qin Zhou
Tao Zhou
Wenbo Zhou
Xiangdong Zhou
Xiao-Yun Zhou
Xiao Zhou
Yang Zhou
Yipin Zhou
Zhenyu Zhou
Hao Zhou
Chu Zhou
Daquan Zhou
Da-Wei Zhou
Hang Zhou
Kang Zhou
Qianyu Zhou
Sheng Zhou
Wenhui Zhou
Xingyi Zhou
Yan-Jie Zhou
Yiyi Zhou
Yu Zhou
Yuan Zhou
Yuqian Zhou
Yuxuan Zhou
Zixiang Zhou
Wengang Zhou
Shuchang Zhou
Tianfei Zhou
Yichao Zhou
Alex Zhu
Chenchen Zhu
Deyao Zhu
Xiatian Zhu
Guibo Zhu
Haidong Zhu
Hao Zhu
Hongzi Zhu
Rui Zhu
Jing Zhu

Jianke Zhu
Junchen Zhu
Lei Zhu
Lingyu Zhu
Luyang Zhu
Menglong Zhu
Peihao Zhu
Hui Zhu
Xiaofeng Zhu
Tyler (Lixuan) Zhu
Wentao Zhu
Xiangyu Zhu
Xinqi Zhu
Xinxin Zhu
Xinliang Zhu
Yangguang Zhu
Yichen Zhu
Yixin Zhu
Yanjun Zhu
Yousong Zhu
Yuhao Zhu
Ye Zhu
Feng Zhu
Zhen Zhu
Fangrui Zhu
Jinjing Zhu
Linchao Zhu
Pengfei Zhu
Sijie Zhu
Xiaobin Zhu
Xiaoguang Zhu
Zezhou Zhu
Zhenyao Zhu
Kai Zhu
Pengkai Zhu
Bingbing Zhuang
Chengyuan Zhuang
Liansheng Zhuang
Peiye Zhuang
Yixin Zhuang
Yihong Zhuang
Junbao Zhuo
Andrea Ziani
Bartosz Zieliński
Primo Zingaretti

Nikolaos Zioulis
Andrew Zisserman
Yael Ziv
Liu Ziyin
Xingxing Zou
Danping Zou
Qi Zou

Shihao Zou
Xueyan Zou
Yang Zou
Yuliang Zou
Zihang Zou
Chuhang Zou
Dongqing Zou

Xu Zou
Zhiming Zou
Maria A. Zuluaga
Xinxin Zuo
Zhiwen Zuo
Reyer Zwiggelaar

Contents – Part XXXI

GOCA: Guided Online Cluster Assignment for Self-supervised Video Representation Learning

Huseyin Coskun[1,2]([✉]), Alireza Zareian[1], Joshua L. Moore[1], Federico Tombari[2,3], and Chen Wang[1]

[1] Snap Inc., Santa Monica, USA
hcoskun@snap.com
[2] TU Munich, Munich, Germany
[3] Google, Menlo Park, USA

Abstract. Clustering is a ubiquitous tool in unsupervised learning. Most of the existing self-supervised representation learning methods typically cluster samples based on visually dominant features. While this works well for image-based self-supervision, it often fails for videos, which require understanding motion rather than focusing on background. Using optical flow as complementary information to RGB can alleviate this problem. However, we observe that a naïve combination of the two views does not provide meaningful gains. In this paper, we propose a principled way to combine two views. Specifically, we propose a novel clustering strategy where we use the initial cluster assignment of each view as prior to guide the final cluster assignment of the other view. This idea will enforce similar cluster structures for both views, and the formed clusters will be semantically abstract and robust to noisy inputs coming from each individual view. Additionally, we propose a novel regularization strategy to address the feature collapse problem, which is common in cluster-based self-supervised learning methods. Our extensive evaluation shows the effectiveness of our learned representations on downstream tasks, e.g., video retrieval and action recognition. Specifically, we outperform the state of the art by 7% on UCF and 4% on HMDB for video retrieval, and 5% on UCF and 6% on HMDB for video classification (Code available at https://github.com/Seleucia/goca).

Keywords: Clustering · Self-supervised learning · Action recognition

1 Introduction

The pursuit of understanding human activities in videos is a fundamental problem in computer vision. Representation learning methods with supervised training strategies showed promising results on various tasks, such as action understanding [12,20,28,43,54], action detection and localization [13,95], and action

---

H. Coskun—Work done during internship at Snap Inc.

S. Avidan et al. (Eds.): ECCV 2022, LNCS 13691, pp. 1–22, 2022.
https://doi.org/10.1007/978-3-031-19821-2_1

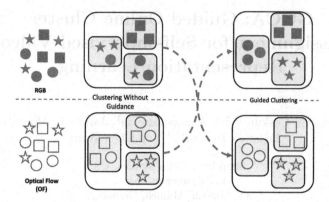

Fig. 1. An abstract illustration of the proposed idea. The filled and empty shapes represent RGB and OF views respectively. Each shape represents a different type of activity, while colors represent intra-class variations. In this toy example, the initial clustering is wrong for both views. RGB fails because it clusters based on color (e.g. irrelevant background information), while OF fails since it confuses square with circle (due to the lower resolution of details). By combining the two types of information, clustering can be achieved correctly on both views.

proposal [32,56]. It is fair to say that large-scale, manually labeled video datasets such as Kinetics [45], AVA [35], and Epic [22] substantially contributed to that success. In spite of those promising results, these algorithms can usually only recognise activities if they have access to a semantically labelled dataset. The cost and challenges of collecting large-scale, manually labelled videos hinder further improvements in activity understanding. On the other hand, the internet is a virtually unlimited source of unlabeled videos (e.g. YouTube). Therefore, designing a representation learning strategy that does not rely on manual labelling is fundamentally important.

Self-supervised learning (SSL) aims to address this issue, by designing pretext tasks that only rely on input, and training networks to solve those tasks. Recent advances in SSL for image understanding [11,15,34,36,38,70,79,96] have achieved excellent performance in various downstream tasks. Motivated by this success, several papers brought these ideas to the video domain [23,29,68,76]. Although these methods show promising results to some extent, they rely solely on an RGB stream. As demonstrated by [4,6,37], this is not sufficient to learn a strong temporal representation.

Johansson's classical psychology work [44] shows that humans can recognize activities by only watching a few bright dots depicting the movement of the main body joints. This intuitive work motivated researchers to use optical flow as a representation of motion for activity understanding [12,30,71,72], and they have achieved significant improvements over RGB-only models in the supervised learning literature. Inspired by this success, many recent SSL works [33,37,80] have explored using optical flow (OF) to advance SSL beyond RGB-only baselines. Han *et al.* (CoCLR) [37] used OF to retrieve positive samples for the infoNCA [63], which led to significant improvements. Nevertheless, CoCLR did not utilize OF for training the backbone and hence may not have realized the full potential of learning motion representations. VICC [80] adopted the online cluster assignment [11] to videos by considering OF as another view of RGB, and minimized the distance between RGB and OF features during online clustering. This method obtained SOTA results on various datasets. However, enforcing similarity between RGB and OF features can be detrimental, especially if one information source is noisy, as is usually the case for OF due to camera motion. Furthermore, these models [37,80] require a complicated training strategy that successively updates one model while freezing the parameters of the other model, which prevents end-to-end training.

In this paper, we introduce the guided online cluster assignment algorithm (GOCA) to address the aforementioned problems. Specifically, for a given video with RGB and OF representations, we first compute initial cluster assignments for only using RGB or OF separately, and then we use these assignments as priors for each other to compute a final assignment that is guided by both views, as illustrated in Fig. 1. After we obtain our final assignment, we train a backbone network by minimizing a cross entropy loss between the final cluster assignment of different augmentations of the same video (as used in [11]). The proposed idea has several benefits compared to the state of the art [11,37,80]. First, it constructs more robust clusters during training due to prior information, which is particularly important when one information source is noisy. Second, allowing RGB and OF to share information by means of sharing cluster assignment encourages the two views to form similar cluster structure, which leads to more semantically abstract representations. Third, both RGB and OF backbones are trained jointly and information flows both ways during training, which is beneficial for both backbones due to the complementary nature of these views. Fourth, compared to the CoCLR method [37], OF is utilized more explicitly in our formulation, which leads to stronger spatio-temporal representations. Finally, the proposed approach circumvents complicated training strategies [33,37,80] and allows simple and end to end training.

We also propose a novel prototype regularization method to address the feature collapse problem, where all features are mapped to a single point. This is a common problem in SSL and was partially addressed in SwAV [11] via equipartition constraint. However, it requires careful tuning[1] of the parameter λ (See Eq. 5) of the Sinkhorn algorithm, which makes it hard used in practice [9, 16,17,69]. We address this problem by constructing cluster prototypes which are maximally distant from each other. We achieve this by locating the N prototypes in the Φ dimensional space such that they divide the space equally. Despite the simplicity of the proposed idea, it yields consistent performance improvements.

To sum up, our contributions are: 1) we introduce a novel Guided Online Cluster Assignment (GOCA) algorithm that aims to learn stronger spatio-temporal representations by utilizing the complementary information of RGB and OF; 2) we mathematically prove that guidance based clustering can be

---

[1] https://github.com/facebookresearch/swav#common-issues.

achieved efficiently with the Sinkhorn algorithm; 3) we propose a prototype regularization strategy that addresses the common feature collapse problem; 4) we perform extensive evaluations of our method using two backbones (S3D [85] and R(2+1)D [81]) on four different evaluation regimes (See Sect. 4). The proposed model outperforms the state of the art in almost all experiments. Furthermore, we present ablation studies to show the effect of each contribution and the key parameters of our method.

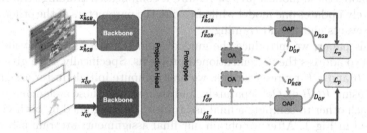

Fig. 2. An overview of the proposed GOCA algorithm. The *RGB* and Optical Flow (*OF*) views have the same backbone architectures and share the projection head and prototypes. Optimal assignment (OA) and optimal assignment with prior (OAP) are defined in Eq. (6) and Eq. (7), respectively. $\mathcal{L}_p$ is defined for a batch of videos in Eq. (13)

2   Related Works

Self-supervised Representation Learning. The success of image-based SSL methods [25,26,38,48,62,70,79,94,96] has inspired their application in the video domain, resulting in several recently proposed methods in that domain. Early approaches for video representation learning [1,24,75,82] typically relied on the idea of predicting the future frames given the past frames, which requires carefully training a deep generative model. Other works focus on designing proxy tasks to exploit temporal information. In a pioneering work, Misra *et al.* [60] designed a pretext task that predicts whether the order of video frames is correct or wrong. Follow-up methods achieved better performance by designing new pretext tasks such as predicting clip order [31,49,60,86], pace [8,18,83,88], or the arrow of time [66,84]. To achieve better generalization, aside from designing novel pretext tasks, some recent works focus on using instance-based contrastive learning approaches [23,29,39,52,64,68]. Since videos often contain multi-modal data, many recent works used audio [2–6,46,65] or language [2,3,59,77] as complementary information to improve results. Unlike those works, we focus on learning representations purely on visual input, namely *RGB* and optical flow (*OF*). Note that we compute *OF* from *RGB* videos in an unsupervised way.

Clustering Based Self-supervised Learning. Early works in this direction adopted clustering to representation learning by simply applying clustering to obtain pseudo-labels [4,10,87]. The common approach has two alternating steps, as it performs clustering offline, rather than concurrently with training as described in Sect. 3.1. One of the main limitations of that approach is that such naive implementations may form degenerate clusters where all samples are clustered to the same point. Asano *et al.* [6,7] tackle this problem by adding an equipartition constraint on the number of samples per cluster and converting the pseudo-label generation step into an optimal assignment problem. They solve the resulting problem using the Sinkhorn-Knopp algorithm [21]. Although the equipartition constraint achieves promising results, it is still inefficient due to the offline clustering. Recently, Caron *et al.* [11] (closest work to ours) eliminated offline label generation via an online clustering algorithm which allows them to train end-to-end on large-scale datasets. Although it works well for images, we observe that adapting this idea to videos is not as effective as with images. As seen in [4,6] and our results, RGB alone is not sufficient to form representative clusters for videos. We tackle this problem by using *OF* as complementary information to guide clustering.

3   Method

Figure 2 shows an overview of the proposed method. For a given video with *RGB* and *OF* views, we first compute two different augmentations for each view, and then pass them through the *RGB* and *OF* backbones, followed by a shared projection head and a shared prototype layer in order to compute cluster assignments.

3.1   Preliminaries

State-of-the-art clustering based SSL methods (SwAV [11], VICC [80], Sela [90], Selavi [7]) are built on top of the Cuturi *et al.* [21] formulation. The Cuturi *et al.* [21] formulation is used to find optimal assignments from samples to cluster centers (or prototypes) under constraints.

Formally, consider a given minibatch of M videos $X = \{x_1, ..., x_M\}$, and N prototypes $P = \{p_1, ..., p_N\}$ represented by trainable vectors. The idea of [11] is to compute two random augmentations X^t and X^s, and compute their feature vectors $F^t = \{f_1^t, ..., f_i^t\}$ and $F^s = \{f_1^s, ..., f_i^s\}$ using an encoder network θ. Next, optimal assignments $D^t = \{d_1^t, ..., d_M^t\}$ and $D^s = \{d_1^s, ..., d_M^s\}$ are computed from features F^t and F^s to prototypes P, as described in the following paragraph. $d_i^t \in D^t$ and $d_i^s \in D^s$ vectors represent assignment values from f_i^s and f_i^t to prototypes, respectively. Finally, θ is trained with the following loss function:

$$\mathcal{L}(F^t, F^s) = \sum_i^M \left(l(d_i^t, g_i^s) + l(d_i^s, g_i^t) \right), \tag{1}$$

where

$$l(d^t, g^s) = - \sum_n^N d_n^t log(g_n^s), \quad g_n^s = \frac{exp((f^s)^\top p_n)}{\sum_{n'} exp((f^s)^\top p_{n'})} \quad (2)$$

This loss function minimizes the distance of two different augmentations by comparing them according to their assignment. Ideally, the two augmentations should be assigned to the same prototype, due to identical semantic content.

Computing Optimal Assignment: The optimal assignment (OA) D can be found by solving the following optimization:

$$d_C(F, P) := \min_{D \in U} \langle D, C \rangle, \quad (3)$$

where $C \in R^{M \times N}$ is a distance matrix from a batch of feature vectors to prototypes and $\langle D, C \rangle = tr(C^\top D)$. U represents all possible assignments from our features F to prototypes P. Formally:

$$U := \{D \in R_+^{M \times N} \mid D1_N = \psi, D^\top 1_M = \omega\}, \quad (4)$$

where $\psi = \frac{1}{M} * \vec{1}_M$ and $\omega = \frac{1}{N} * \vec{1}_N$, and $\vec{1}_M \in R^M$ and $\vec{1}_N \in R^N$ are ones vectors. The constraint on U ensures all the prototypes are selected. Equation (3) can be solved with linear programming. Since this is computationally expensive, it is infeasible to carry it out during training for every batch. Cuturi *et al..* [21] address this issue by adding entropy regularization and solving the resulting problem with the Sinkhorn algorithm:

$$d_C(F, P) := \min_{D \in U} \left(\langle D, C \rangle - \lambda_1 h(D) \right). \quad (5)$$

where h represents the entropy. The above formulation is a strictly convex and smoothed version of Eq. (3). This allows us to efficiently approximate D. Specifically, D has a unique solution for any given λ_1, which is in the form of: $D^{\lambda_1} = diag(u) K diag(v)$ where $K = e^{\lambda_1 C}$, and u, v are non-negative unique vectors. The proof of this statement can be found in [21]. According to the Sinkhorn theorem [27], if K has only positive elements, the unknowns u and v can be determined via the Sinkhorn algorithm.

There are two main problems with this conventional formulation: First, it does not allow utilizing the complementary information, which is particularly important in the video, since it has been shown that using RGB alone encourages the model to focus on the background and ignore motion cues [6]. We address this problem by rewriting Eq. (3) such that we can fuse two information sources to obtain the cluster assignment. Second, in the conventional formulation [11, 80], the prototypes are randomly initialized and trained with the rest of the model without any restriction, which can lead to a degenerate solution where all prototypes collapse into a single point, and consequently the feature vectors too [9,16,17,69]. To overcome this problem, we propose to use a novel prototype regularizer, which encourages prototypes to be maximally far apart.

3.2 Guided Online Cluster Assignment (GOCA)

Our goal is to train backbone networks θ_{RGB} and θ_{OF} while sharing information between the two views. The single-view approach of [10,11,90] does not allow combining the two information sources. A straightforward way is to concatenate the F_{RGB} and F_{OF} features, but we have observed that this approach yields a very small improvement over RGB-only training on various downstream tasks (see Experiments Sect. 4.1). Another way is to force the similarity of OF and RGB features as in [80]. Even though this idea obtains better results on downstream tasks, it leads to a loss of information by forcing each view to only maintain mutual information. Hence, it does not reach the maximum potential performance of correctly combining the two views (Table 1).

In contrast, we propose a principled way to combine two information sources. We use each information source as a prior to the other. We assign D'_{OF} and D'_{RGB} as the initial prototype assignment (computed based on Eq. (5)), and D_{OF} and D_{RGB} as the final. To this end, we use the D'_{OF} as the prior to D_{RGB}, and D'_{RGB} as the prior to D_{OF}

We implement this idea by modifying Eq. (5) in a way that it takes the prior into account. Our optimal assignment with prior (OAP) optimization problems for D_{RGB} and D_{OF} takes this form:

$$d_{C_{\text{RGB}}}(F_{\text{RGB}}, P) := \min_{D_{\text{RGB}} \in U} \left(\langle D_{\text{RGB}}, C_{\text{RGB}} \rangle - \lambda_1 h(D_{\text{RGB}}) + \lambda_2 \text{KL}(D_{\text{RGB}}|D'_{\text{OF}}) \right), \quad (6)$$

and

$$d_{C_{\text{OF}}}(F_{\text{OF}}, P) := \min_{D_{\text{OF}} \in U} \left(\langle D_{\text{OF}}, C_{\text{OF}} \rangle - \lambda_1 h(D_{\text{OF}}) + \lambda_2 \text{KL}(D_{\text{OF}}|D'_{\text{RGB}}) \right). \quad (7)$$

where C_{RGB} and C_{OF} are distance matrices from RGB and OF features to prototypes, $\text{KL}(\cdot|\cdot)$ represents the Kullback Leibler divergence between two assignment matrices, λ_1 and λ_2 are hyper-parameters. Note that we use the same prototypes P for OF and RGB features. These two optimization problems can be solved via the following lemma:

Lemma 1. D_{RGB} and D_{OF} have a unique solution for λ_1 and λ_2 in the form of:

$$D_b^{\lambda_1, \lambda_2} = diag(u_b) K_b diag(v_b) \qquad b \in \{RGB, OF\} \quad (8)$$

Proof. We will prove only for D_{RGB}, but the same proof can be used for OF as well. Let $\mathcal{L}(D_{\text{RGB}}, \alpha, \beta)$ be the Lagrangian form of the Eq. (6) with dual variables $\alpha \in R^M$ and $\beta \in R^N$ for the two equality constraints in U (see Eq. (4)):

$$\mathcal{L}(D_{\text{RGB}}, \alpha, \beta) = \sum_{i,j} \lambda_1 d_{\text{RGB}_{ij}} log(d_{\text{RGB}_{ij}}) + \sum_{i,j} d_{\text{RGB}_{ij}} c_{\text{RGB}_{ij}} + \sum_{i,j} \lambda_2 d_{\text{RGB}_{ij}} log\left(\frac{d_{\text{RGB}_{ij}}}{d'_{\text{OF}_{ij}}}\right) \quad (9)$$
$$+ \alpha(D_{RGB} 1_M - \psi) + \beta(D_{RGB}^\top 1_N - \omega)$$

for all (i, j) we set $(\partial \mathcal{L}/\partial d_{\text{RGB}_{ij}} = 0)$ and solve for $d_{\text{RGB}_{ij}}$

$$d_{\text{RGB}_{ij}} = \exp\left(-0.5 - \frac{\alpha_i}{\lambda_1 + \lambda_2}\right) \exp\left(\frac{-c_{\text{RGB}_{ij}} + \lambda_2 log(d'_{\text{OF}_{ij}})}{\lambda_1 + \lambda_2}\right) \exp\left(-0.5 - \frac{\beta_j}{\lambda_1 + \lambda_2}\right). \quad (10)$$

When we choose $K_{\mathrm{RGB}} = exp(\frac{-c_{\mathrm{RGB}_{ij}} + \lambda_2 log(d'_{\mathrm{OF}_{ij}})}{\lambda_1 + \lambda_2})$, we can see that it is strictly positive since it is the element-wise exponential, therefore according the Sinkhorn's theorem [73], $D_{\mathrm{RGB}}^{\lambda_1, \lambda_2}$ has unique solution for any given λ_1 and λ_2. Thus, u_{RGB} and v_{RGB} vectors in Eq. (8) can be computed with Sinkhorn algorithm. In our formulation, since the final cluster assignment relies on both views, formed clusters will be robust to noise and semantically abstract. The supplemental includes the details of the proof.

3.3 Prototype Regularization

It has been shown that SSL models suffer from feature collapse, i.e. when all features are mapped to the same representation [14,34,70,93]. Even though this problem was partially addressed in [11] by using equipartition constraint as in Eq. (3), in practice, λ needs to be carefully tuned [9,16,17,69]. More specifically, we observe that a higher λ leads to numerical issues, and lower values tend to cause feature collapse.

Alternatively, we introduce a regularization term that encourages prototypes to be maximally far apart. We achieve this by utilizing the idea of hyperspherical prototypes [58]. Formally, we divide the Φ-dimensional hyperspherical space equally into N prototypes. For instance, for a 2-dimensional hyperspherical space (circle), this can be easily done by placing N prototypes with a $\frac{2\pi}{N}$ angle difference. Even though this is easy to do for a 2-dimensional space, there is no exact solution for 3 or more dimensions [78]. We solve this problem by finding an approximate solution using gradient descent. Specifically, consider the N prototypes that are represented with a linear layer, $W \in R^{N \times \Phi}$ in our network (Fig. 2). Instead of training W with the rest of the network end-to-end, we train it separately, once before the main training phase, by minimizing the following loss under the following constraint:

$$\mathcal{L}_{reg} = \frac{1}{N} \sum_i^N max(\Omega_{i,.}), \quad \Omega = WW^\top - 2I \quad s.t. \quad \forall_i \|\mathbf{w_i}\| = 1, \quad (11)$$

where I and w_i represents the identity matrix and i-th row in W, respectively. This loss minimizes the similarity of maximally similar prototypes. To apply the constraint, we continuously re-project our prototypes to the hypersphere during training via $l2$ normalization. This can be seen as a simple and quick initialization step, which takes only 5 min on a Nvidia GTX 1060 GPU.

3.4 Training Procedure

After initializing (and fixing) the prototype layer as described in Eq. (11), we train the network by minimizing the following loss function:

$$\mathcal{L}_{final} = \mathcal{L}_p(F_{\mathrm{RGB}}^t, F_{\mathrm{RGB}}^s) + \mathcal{L}_p(F_{\mathrm{OF}}^t, F_{\mathrm{OF}}^s), \quad (12)$$

where

$$\mathcal{L}_p(F_{\mathrm{b}}^t, F_{\mathrm{b}}^s) = \sum_i^M l(d_{\mathrm{b}_i}^t, g_{\mathrm{b}_i}^s) + l(d_{\mathrm{b}_i}^s, g_{\mathrm{b}_i}^t) \tag{13}$$

Here $b \in \{RGB, OF\}$ and d_{b_i} i-th row in D_{b}. D_{b} represents optimal assignment matrix. We compute these matrices using *Lemma 1*, while our prototypes are obtained as described in Sect. 3.3. Note that l and g are defined in Eq. (2). Since RGB and OF features only interact when computing optimal assignment, this formulation encourages cluster similarity without enforcing RGB and OF features to be strictly similar, hence, not leading to information loss.

4   Experimental Results

In this section, we first describe datasets, metrics, and training details. We present our ablation results to show the importance of our method design choices in Sect. 4.1. Then, we compare our approach with SOTA in Sect. 4.2 for retrieval task. Then, we show our cluster analysis results in Sect. 4.3. Finally, we show classification results in Sect. 4.4.

Datasets: We conduct our experiments on four different datasets: Kinetics (K400) [45], UCF [74], HMDB [47], and Diving-48 [51]. We follow the same training protocols as other self-supervised learning approaches [6,37,68,80]. K400 training set contains 240k videos. UCF, HMDB, and Diving-48 contain 13k, 7k, and 17k videos respectively.

Evaluation Metrics: We evaluate our model performance on the action retrieval and action classification tasks. To evaluate action retrieval, we compute *Recall* at $K \in \{1, 5, 10, 20\}$, similar to earlier works [6,37,68,80]. More specifically, if the correct class is within the K nearest neighbours we consider it a correct result. For action classification, we consider top-1 accuracy for *Linear Classification* and *Fine Tuning* experimental setups (See Sect. 4.4). We report all numbers in terms of percentage.

Data Augmentations: Following [37,68,80], we use horizontal flipping, random cropping, Gaussian blurring, and color jittering for augmentation. We also use a *multi-temporal-resolution* idea which is analogous to multi-crop in SwAV [11]. In this augmentation strategy, we sample shorter length clips alongside longer ones. We observe this makes convergence faster, but does not affect the final accuracy.

Backbones and Training Details: We conduct our experiments with two widely used backbones: S3D [85] and R(2+1)D+18 [81]. We use two datasets (K400 [45] and UCF [74]) for self-supervised training. Optical flow (OF) is computed using the TV-L1 algorithm [92] and pre-processed as in [12,37,80]. We follow earlier works [29,68,80] and use SGD+LARS [91] optimizer with a learning rate of 4.8 that is increased during the first 10 warm-up epochs and then is decreased to 0.0048 with cosine learning rate decay. All models are pre-trained on 64 V100 GPUs (10 samples per GPU) for 500 epochs as in [6,29,68,80]. Each clip contains 32 consecutive frames. During the test, we turn off all augmentations and use a standard 3 (spatial) × 10 (temporal). We always denote with a "+" suffix the case of RGB and OF being used during testing. Following the earlier works [37,67,80] and we use 32 and 16 frames for S3D and R(2+1)D, respectively during the training of fine-tuning and linear-classification experiments.

4.1   Ablation Study

In these experiments, we demonstrate the effectiveness of each proposed component in terms of recall values. All models pre-trained on the UCF training set and evaluated on the UCF and HMDB test sets with S3D backbone.

Effect of View Merging Strategies. For a better understanding of the effectiveness of the proposed approach, we design 3 different baselines: **SView**, **Avg**, and **Sep**. **SView**: We train OF and RGB separately with identical but independent backbones, projection heads, and prototypes. This baseline can be considered a trivial extension of SwAV [11] to videos. **Avg**: We train OF and RGB jointly, by passing OF and RGB from different backbones and then feeding their average into the projection head and prototypes. **Sep**: We train the model jointly but this time OF and RGB information do not interact. We use separate backbones but share the projection head and prototypes. Our model differentiates from this only at the assignment computing stage. We train all our baselines by minimizing the loss described in Eq. (1). Finally, to better compare our method (**GOCA**) with the single-view (**SView**) baseline, we also evaluate it in single-view settings by only using one of the backbones during the test. To combine RGB and OF representations during the test, we simply take the average of the two.

Table 1 shows our results on the UCF and HMDB test sets. In single-view settings (first 6 rows), **SView** with RGB obtains very poor results, which can be attributed to an over-emphasis on the background scene and ignoring the motion, which is common for RGB-only models. Our results confirm that motion-only models can perform better than RGB, as observed in [37,80]. Furthermore, GOCA outperforms both baselines even in single-view testing, which confirms that the proposed joint training approach is beneficial for each individual backbone as well. We can also see that enforcing the similarity of the two views as in VICC does not improve OF results compared to single-view training. In contrast, **GOCA** significantly improves the results for both views, by aligning the two representations in a smarter, more implicit manner.

Table 1. Comparison of *RGB* (R) and *OF* (F) merging strategies

Method	Train	Test	UCF R@1	UCF R@5	HMDB R@1	HMDB R@5
SView	R	R	41.3	58.9	17.9	43.2
SView	F	F	62.0	75.8	28.2	53.3
VICC [8	R+F	R	62.1	77.1	25.5	49.6
VICC [8	R+F	F	59.7	77.3	27.7	53.3
GOCA	R+F	R	63.4	76.3	26.3	50.2
GOCA	R+F	F	67.9	79.5	31.8	56.3
SView+	-	R+F	63.6	76.8	28.6	54.1
Avg	R+F	R+F	50.8	63.0	22.8	46.3
Sep	R+F	R+F	65.0	78.2	29.5	54.8
GOCA	R+F	R+F	70.8	81.4	33.7	58.7

Table 2. The effect of lambda parameters on recall values on the UCF RGB-only val.

		λ_1			
		0.01	0.02	0.03	0.04
	0.01	56.4	57.6	55.1	54.1
λ_2	0.02	57.3	58.7	**60.1**	58.9
	0.03	58.1	**60.9**	**60.5**	57.5
	0.04	55.8	58.5	**59.0**	55.2

When we combine *RGB* and *OF* during testing (last 4 rows), we observe that naively merging features at training (**Avg**) performs better than *RGB*-only by 3.5% while significantly worse than *OF*-only training (-11.2%). This might be due to the fact that during training, *RGB* information dominates the gradients, and the *OF* backbone can not be fully trained. The performance of **Sep** indicates that joint training for *RGB* and *OF* can improve the results when we do not naively merge features. Finally, the proposed model, **GOCA**, further improves the results, which verifies the efficacy of the proposed guided cluster assignment idea.

Effect of λ_1 and λ_2. Our next ablation study is observing the impact of the λ_1 and λ_2 parameter values in Eq. (6) and Eq. (7). These parameters control the effect of the uniformity assumption and prior distribution. Table 2 shows how recall at 1 varies depending on the λ_1 and λ_2 parameters. We train GOCA for 200 epochs and evaluate it on the UCF dataset. We can observe that the proposed approach is robust to λ_1 and λ_2, especially in the range of $[0.02, 0.03]$. For all other experiments, we set $\lambda_1 = 0.02$ and $\lambda_2 = 0.03$.

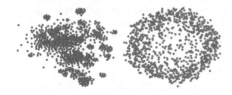

Fig. 3. The t-SNE plot of 1000 prototypes in 2D without regularization (left) and with regularization (right)

Table 3. Effect of prototype regularization on recall values

Method	Use ProtReg	Train	Test	UCF R@1	UCF R@5	HMDB R@1	HMDB R@5
SView	No	R	R	40.9	57.4	17.1	42.7
SView	Yes	R	R	42.3	58.9	17.9	43.2
GOCA+	No	R+F	R+F	69.1	79.4	32.9	58.6
GOCA+	Yes	R+F	R+F	70.8	81.4	33.6	58.7

Effect of Prototype Regularizer. Our prototype regularizer idea guarantees that prototypes are maximally far apart from each other. Figure 3 shows t-SNE plot of 1000 prototypes with and without regularization. As we can see, the proposed method locates the prototypes maximally far apart from each other, on the other hand, in the unregularized case, prototypes are quite closely grouped. As we discuss in Sect. 3.3, maximally far apart prototypes prevent the feature collapse and allow us stable training. Another benefit is that clusters formed around prototypes are also will be far apart from each other which is particularly important for retrieval tasks. We verify this benefit by comparing the recall accuracy with and without using prototype regularization. Table 3 shows the consistent effectiveness of the proposed method for both models on both datasets.

Table 4. Video retrieval results on UCF [74] and HMDB51 [47] datasets. *DS*, *Res*, and *Modl* represent training dataset, input resolution, and input modality respectively. Rows above the double line are trained on Kinetics and the rest use UCF. Light grey colored methods (MCL [50]) use 2 times more input resolution (224). Time-Equ* [41] uses various additional loss functions that used in earlier works (speed [8,89], direction [66], order [86]). These loss functions can be combined with our loss functions as well.

Method	DS	Backbone	Res	Modl	UCF				HMDB			
					R@1	R@5	R@10	R@20	R@1	R@5	R@10	R@20
Selavi [6]	K400	R(2+1)D+18	112	V+A	52.0	68.6	-	84.5	24.8	47.6	-	75.5
Rbst-xID [61]	K400	R(2+1)D+18	112	V+A	60.9	79.4	-	**90.8**	30.8	55.8	-	79.7
TCGL [55]	K400	R(2+1)D+18	112	V	21.5	39.3	49.3	59.5	10.5	27.6	39.7	55.63
MotionFit [33]	K400	R(2+1)D+18	112	V	61.6	75.6	-	85.5	29.4	46.5	-	66.7
ASCNet [40]	K400	R3D-18	112	V	58.9	76.3	82.2	87.5	-	-	-	-
Enhenced [67]	K400	R3D-18	112	V	41.5	60.6	71.2	80.1	20.7	40.8	55.2	68.3
MCN [52]	K400	R(2+1)D-18	128	V	52.5	69.5	77.9	83.1	23.7	46.5	58.9	72.4
Zhang [53]	K400	R3D-18	112	V	46.7	63.1	69.7	78.0	-	-	-	-
CoCLR [37]	K400	S3D	128	V	45.6	63.9	75.4	81.7	-	-	-	-
GOCA	K400	S3D	128	V	67.3	79.1	84.9	89.9	32.7	55.1	68.5	79.5
GOCA+	K400	S3D	128	V	**68.6**	**80.7**	**86.6**	**90.1**	**33.2**	**56.3**	**68.5**	**80.2**
VCOP [86]	UCF	R(2+1)D+18	112	V	14.1	30.3	40.4	51.1	7.6	22.9	34.4	48.8
Var. PSP [19]	UCF	R(2+1)D+18	112	V	24.6	41.9	51.3	62.7	-	-	-	-
RTT [42]	UCF	R(2+1)D+18	112	V	26.1	48.5	59.1	69.6	-	-	-	-
MemDPC [36]	UCF	R2D3D-18	112	V	20.2	40.4	52.4	64.7	7.7	25.7	40.6	57.7
VCP [57]	UCF	R(2+1)D+18	112	V	19.9	33.7	42.0	50.5	6.7	21.3	32.7	49.2
TCLR [23]	UCF	R(2+1)D+18	112	V	56.9	72.2	79.0	84.6	24.1	45.8	58.3	75.3
Enhenced [67]	UCF	R3D-18	112	V	39.6	57.6	69.2	78.0	18.8	39.2	51.0	63.7
GOCA	UCF	R(2+1)D+18	112	V	62.8	77.7	82.0	**87.0**	22.3	47.2	60.1	73.3
GOCA+	UCF	R(2+1)D+18	112	V	**63.4**	**78.6**	**82.5**	86.2	**28.5**	**54.4**	**66.2**	**76.6**
MCL+ [50]	UCF	S3D	224	V	67.0	80.8	86.3	90.8	26.7	52.5	67.0	79.3
Time-Equ* [41]	UCF	R3D-18	128	V	62.1	-	-	-	31.5	-	-	-
CoCLR [37]	UCF	S3D	128	V	53.3	69.4	76.6	82.0	23.2	43.2	53.5	65.5
CoCLR+ [37]	UCF	S3D	128	V	55.9	70.8	76.9	82.5	26.1	45.8	57.9	69.7
ViCC [80]	UCF	S3D	128	V	62.1	77.1	83.7	87.9	25.5	49.6	61.9	72.5
ViCC+ [80]	UCF	S3D	128	V	65.1	80.2	**85.4**	**89.8**	29.7	54.6	66.0	76.2
GOCA	UCF	S3D	128	V	63.4	76.3	81.3	86.5	26.3	50.2	62.6	77.0
GOCA+	UCF	S3D	128	V	**70.8**	**81.4**	85.3	89.5	**33.7**	**58.5**	**70.0**	**80.6**

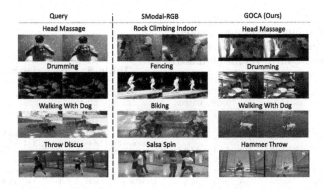

Fig. 4. Retrieval comparison between SView-RGB and GOCA representations on UCF dataset. Query videos (left) are selected from test set and top-1 nearest neighbour videos are retrieved from the training set. Ground truth labels are reported on top of each query.

Comparison with the State-of-the-Art. Given the large body of self-supervised video understanding works published thus far, we only selected recent (from 2019) publications. To the best of our ability, we conducted a fair comparison. However, we still observe small variations in terms of input resolution and fine-tuning details in the literature, which makes it extremely hard to perform perfectly fair comparisons. Furthermore, we encourage the readers to study the supplementary material for more in-depth experimental results. As noted in [29],

Table 5. Retrieval results on Diving-48 [51] with S3D backbone(pre-trained on UCF)

Method	R@1	R@5	R@10	R@20
CoCLR [37]	6.7	23.6	37.4	55.2
VICC [80]	7.2	24.4	38.1	54.5
GOCA	**8.1**	**24.8**	**38.3**	55.1

Table 6. Cluster quality results on UCF test set with S3D backbone. All models are trained on UCF training set.

Method	Acc	NMI	F1
SView-RGB	42.1	65.1	40.3
CoCLR [37]	44.3	65.4	41.9
CoCLR+ [37]	46.1	68.6	43.1
VICC [80]	51.1	70.4	50.0
VICC+ [80]	51.9	72.9	53.7
GOCA	57.3	75.8	57.4
GOCA+	**61.2**	**78.7**	**61.3**

Table 7. Fine tuning. Light grey colored methods use much higher input resolution. MoCo* and CVRL* results obtained from [53] and [23], respectively.

Method	DS	Backbone	Res	UCF	HMDB
CVRL [68]	K400	R3D-50	224	92.9	67.9
MoCo [29]	K400	R-50	224	93.2	70.5
ASCNet[67]	K400	R3D-18	112	80.5	52.3
Enhanced[67]	K400	R3D-18	112	79.1	47.6
CoCLR [37]	K400	S3D	128	87.9	54.6
CoCLR+ [37]	K400	S3D	128	90.6	62.9
GOCA	K400	S3D	128	89.3	63.2
GOCA+	K400	S3D	128	**91.1**	**65.8**
MoCo* [29]	UCF	R(2+1)D+18	112	77.6	45.7
CVRL* [68]	UCF	R3D+18	112	75.8	44.6
TCLR [23]	UCF	R(2+1)D+18	112	82.4	52.9
TCLR [23]	UCF	R(2+1)D+18	112	82.8	55.6
Var. PSP [19]	UCF	R3D+18	112	74.8	36.8
PacePred [88]	UCF	R(2+1)D+18	112	75.9	35.9
VCP [57]	UCF	R(2+1)D+18	112	66.3	32.2
PRP [89]	UCF1	R(2+1)D+18	112	72.1	35.0
RTT [42]	UCF	R(2+1)D+18	112	81.6	46.4
Enhanced [6]	UCF	R3D+18	112	76.2	41.1
Zhang [53]	UCF	R(2+1)D+18	112	79.0	45.4
GOCA	UCF	R(2+1)D+18	112	82.1	54.7
GOCA+	UCF	R(2+1)D+18	112	**88.7**	**60.1**
CoCLR [37]	UCF	S3D	128	81.4	52.1
CoCLR+ [37]	UCF	S3D	128	87.3	58.7
ViCC [80]	UCF	S3D	128	84.3	47.9
ViCC+ [80]	UCF	S3D	128	90.5	62.2
GOCA	UCF	S3D	128	83.4	53.5
GOCA+	UCF	S3D	128	90.2	**64.8**

Table 8. Linear classification.

Method	DS	Backbone	Res	UCF	HMDB
MemDPC [39]	K400	R-2D3D	224	54.1	30.5
CVRL [68]	K400	R3D-50	224	89.8	58.3
TCLR [23]	UC	R3D+18	112	69.9	52.8
Enhanced[67]	K40	R3D+18	112	63.2	33.4
CoCLR [37]	K40	S3D	128	74.5	46.1
CoCLR+ [37]	K40	S3D	128	77.8	52.4
GOCA	K40	S3D	128	78.9	50.5
GOCA+	K40	S3D	128	**82.8**	**58.7**
MCL+ [50]	UC	S3D	224	79.8	52.7
Time-Equ [41]	UC	R3D-18	128	74.1	47.5
CoCLR [37]	UC	S3D	128	70.2	39.1
CoCLR+ [37]	UC	S3D	128	72.1	40.2
ViCC [80]	UC	S3D	128	72.2	38.5
ViCC+ [80]	UC	S3D	128	78.0	47.9
GOCA	UC	S3D	128	69.2	38.6
GOCA+	UC	S3D	128	**81.1**	**50.0**

we observe that during the *Fine-Tuning* experiment, backbone networks tend to overfit validation datasets (UCF and HMDB), therefore we perform extensive retrieval and cluster analysis experiments to show our contributions' influence (On these experiments there is no supervised training on validation datasets).

4.2   Retrieval Results

Table 4 and Table 5 show the retrieval results for *Recall@K* (*R@K*). In this experiment, we follow the standard protocol defined in [23,36,37,42,57,67,80] and perform the evaluation on the frozen features that were computed from a pre-trained model. At Table 4, the first part of the table (above the double line) includes models that are all pre-trained on K400 [45], while evaluated on the UCF and HMDB datasets. We can see a significant improvement (5% and 8% on UCF and HMDB respectively, averaged over all K values). Surprisingly, the proposed approach even outperforms models [6,61] that use an additional view (Audio) by a large margin. Below the double line, we show models that are pre-trained on the UCF training set, using two different backbone architectures, S3D and $R(2+1)D$, separated by a horizontal line. On the S3D, we achieve an improvement of 5.7% on UCF and 4.0% on HMDB at $K = 1$. On the $R(2 + 1)D$, we can see a nearly 6% increase across all recall values for UCF and 5% for HMDB. Our RGB-only model also achieves state-of-the-art results and outperforms baselines by a large margin on both datasets for both backbones. These findings verify our intuition that effectively utilizing OF can result in strong spatio-temporal representations. We observe that Time-Equ* [41] method also performs well however, this work uses speed [8,89], direction [66], and order [86] as auxiliary loss as well. These loss functions can be combined with our method also. Time-Equ* [41] obtains 52.1% and 21.4% at $K = 1$ on UCF and HMDB respectively, without these auxiliary loss function. We also evaluate our pre-trained model on motion centric dataset [51]. Table 5 show our result for Diving-48 [51]. We can see that proposed model improves the baselines for the motion centric dataset as well and obtain SOTA results. Figure 4 shows our retrievals results. GOCA retrieves videos from the same semantic categories and it fails only for one case where it confuses *Disk Throwing* with *Hammer Throwing*. This is a quite hard example because these two activities have very similar motions and the only difference is the quite small object in the person's hand. Higher resolution input images would help to solve this problem. We can see that SModel-RGB fails to retrieve relevant videos and consistently retrieves based on the background.

4.3   Cluster Analysis

Ideally, video representations should form semantic clusters in order to facilitate activity recognition. To evaluate the clustering quality of our learned representations, we use two metrics that measure the correlation between clusters and semantic labels (ground truth). To this end, we perform K-means clustering on the our representations that are extracted from the UCF101 test set. Then we use the given labels of the test set to determine a label for each cluster via majority voting. We assign each cluster's label to all its members and compare those assigned labels to given labels. Specifically, we compute the accuracy of the assigned labels (Acc), as well as the F_1 score, which is the harmonic mean of recall and precision. We also compute the Normalized Mutual Information (NMI), which measures the mutual information between clusters and ground truth labels, divided by the sum of their entropy. Due to the randomness of K-means, we repeat experiments 50 times and take the average for each metric. As shown in Table 6, GOCA significantly improves the cluster quality in terms of all metrics, both with and without *OF*. This verifies the high quality semantic clustering ability of our method.

4.4   Classification Tasks

Linear Classification. We follow the earlier works of [37,67,80] for the linear classification experiments. After the self-supervised training on the K400 dataset, we discard the projection head and prototypes and replace them with a linear layer. Then we train the linear layer on the training set of each downstream dataset (UCF and HMDB) with frozen backbone. The results are shown in the first section of Table 7, and demonstrate that the proposed model significantly outperforms CoCLR [37] on both datasets by 5% and 6%, respectively. Notably, when we combine *RGB* and *OF*, we achieve state-of-the-art results on the HMDB dataset, even though the other methods [36,68] benefit from a higher input resolution. For the case of UCF dataset, our model with the S3D marginally outperforms the other methods, achieving 80.1% on UCF and 50.0% on HMDB.

Fine-Tuning. We follow the standard protocol from [37,67,80], where we train the full backbone on the downstream tasks. We summarize the results in the second section of Table 8. On the S3D backbone, our method improves CoCLR+ [37] by 0.5% and 2.9%, respectively. In addition, when using only *RGB* as input, we achieve improvements of 1.4% and 8.8% on both datasets. Moving to the UCF dataset, our approach obtains state-of-art results with R(2+1)D; while, with S3D, we are slightly worse than ViCC+ [80]. However, on the HMDB dataset, our results outperform ViCC+ [80] by a large margin of 6.6% and 2.6% when using *RGB* and *RGB+OF*. Note that CVRL [68] and ρ BYOL [29] use higher input resolution (224) than ours (112), which leads to better performance, but needs significantly more computation. In fact, when we compare to CVRL at a resolution of 112, we significantly outperform CVRL [68].

5   Conclusion

In this paper, we presented a novel self-supervised learning approach for videos. We showed that the proposed guided online clustering idea and the prototype regularization approach both substantially improve the performance of our learned representations on both activity retrieval and action classification tasks. We believe that our work establishes a new direction for SSL research on multi-view and multi-modal data. Although we conduct our experiments using *RGB* and optical flow, the proposed idea can be applied to fuse other modalities such as *RGB+Audio* or *RGB+Text*, which we will explore in our future work. Furthermore, our method simplifies the training procedure for multi-modal SSL on videos (CoCLR and VICC require multi-stage training).

References

1. Ahsan, U., Sun, C., Essa, I.: DiscrimNet: semi-supervised action recognition from videos using generative adversarial networks. arXiv preprint arXiv:1801.07230 (2018)
2. Akbari, H., et al.: VATT: transformers for multimodal self-supervised learning from raw video, audio and text. In: Advances in Neural Information Processing Systems (2021)
3. Alayrac, J.B., et al.: Self-supervised multimodal versatile networks. In: NeurIPS, vol. 2, no. 6, p. 7 (2020)

4. Alwassel, H., Mahajan, D., Korbar, B., Torresani, L., Ghanem, B., Tran, D.: Self-supervised learning by cross-modal audio-video clustering. In: Advances in Neural Information Processing Systems 33 (2020)

5. Alwassel, H., Mahajan, D., Korbar, B., Torresani, L., Ghanem, B., Tran, D.: Self-supervised learning by cross-modal audio-video clustering. In: Advances in Neural Information Processing Systems (NeurIPS) (2020)

6. Asano, Y.M., Patrick, M., Rupprecht, C., Vedaldi, A.: Labelling unlabelled videos from scratch with multi-modal self-supervision. In: Advances in Neural Information Processing Systems (2020)

7. Asano, Y.M., Rupprecht, C., Vedaldi, A.: Self-labelling via simultaneous clustering and representation learning. In: International Conference on Learning Representations (ICLR) (2020)

8. Benaim, S., et al.: SpeedNet: learning the speediness in videos. in: Proceedings of the IEEE/CVF Conference on Computer Vision and Pattern Recognition, pp. 9922–9931 (2020)

9. Cai, T., Gao, R., Lee, J.D., Lei, Q.: A theory of label propagation for subpopulation shift. arXiv preprint arXiv:2102.11203 (2021)

10. Caron, M., Bojanowski, P., Joulin, A., Douze, M.: Deep clustering for unsupervised learning of visual features. In: Ferrari, V., Hebert, M., Sminchisescu, C., Weiss, Y. (eds.) Computer Vision – ECCV 2018. LNCS, vol. 11218, pp. 139–156. Springer, Cham (2018). https://doi.org/10.1007/978-3-030-01264-9_9

11. Caron, M., Misra, I., Mairal, J., Goyal, P., Bojanowski, P., Joulin, A.: Unsupervised learning of visual features by contrasting cluster assignments. In: Advances in Neural Information Processing Systems (2020)

12. Carreira, J., Zisserman, A.: Quo Vadis, action recognition? A new model and the kinetics dataset. In: Proceedings of the IEEE Conference on Computer Vision and Pattern Recognition, pp. 6299–6308 (2017)

13. Chao, Y.W., Vijayanarasimhan, S., Seybold, B., Ross, D.A., Deng, J., Sukthankar, R.: Rethinking the faster R-CNN architecture for temporal action localization. In: Proceedings of the IEEE Conference on Computer Vision and Pattern Recognition, pp. 1130–1139 (2018)

14. Chen, S., Tian, Y., Wen, F., Xu, Y., Tang, X.: EasyToon: an easy and quick tool to personalize a cartoon storyboard using family photo album. In: El-Saddik, A., Vuong, S., Griwodz, C., Bimbo, A.D., Candan, K.S., Jaimes, A. (eds.) Proceedings of the 16th International Conference on Multimedia 2008, Vancouver, British Columbia, Canada, 26–31 October 2008, pp. 499–508. ACM (2008). https://doi.org/10.1145/1459359.1459426

15. Chen, T., Kornblith, S., Norouzi, M., Hinton, G.: A simple framework for contrastive learning of visual representations. In: International Conference on Machine Learning, pp. 1597–1607. PMLR (2020)

16. Chen, X., He, K.: Exploring simple Siamese representation learning. In: Proceedings of the IEEE/CVF Conference on Computer Vision and Pattern Recognition, pp. 15750–15758 (2021)

17. Chen, X., Xie, S., He, K.: An empirical study of training self-supervised vision transformers. arXiv preprint arXiv:2104.02057 (2021)

18. Cho, H., Kim, T., Chang, H.J., Hwang, W.: Self-supervised spatio-temporal representation learning using variable playback speed prediction. arXiv preprint arXiv:2003.02692 (2020)

19. Cho, H., Kim, T., Chang, H.J., Hwang, W.: Self-supervised visual learning by variable playback speeds prediction of a video. IEEE Access **9**, 79562–79571 (2021)

20. Coskun, H., et al.: Domain-specific priors and meta learning for low-shot first-person action recognition. IEEE Trans. Pattern Anal. Mach. Intell. (2021)
21. Cuturi, M.: Sinkhorn distances: lightspeed computation of optimal transport. In: Advances in Neural Information Processing Systems 26, pp. 2292–2300 (2013)
22. Damen, D., et al.: Scaling egocentric vision: the EPIC-KITCHENS dataset. In: Ferrari, V., Hebert, M., Sminchisescu, C., Weiss, Y. (eds.) ECCV 2018. LNCS, vol. 11208, pp. 753–771. Springer, Cham (2018). https://doi.org/10.1007/978-3-030-01225-0_44
23. Dave, I., Gupta, R., Rizve, M.N., Shah, M.: TCLR: temporal contrastive learning for video representation. arXiv preprint arXiv:2101.07974 (2021)
24. Diba, A., Sharma, V., Gool, L.V., Stiefelhagen, R.: DynamoNet: dynamic action and motion network. In: Proceedings of the IEEE/CVF International Conference on Computer Vision, pp. 6192–6201 (2019)
25. Doersch, C., Gupta, A., Efros, A.A.: Unsupervised visual representation learning by context prediction. In: Proceedings of the IEEE International Conference on Computer Vision, pp. 1422–1430 (2015)
26. Dosovitskiy, A., Fischer, P., Springenberg, J.T., Riedmiller, M., Brox, T.: Discriminative unsupervised feature learning with exemplar convolutional neural networks. IEEE Trans. Pattern Anal. Mach. Intell. $38(9)$, 1734–1747 (2015)
27. Erlander, S., Stewart, N.F.: The Gravity Model in Transportation Analysis: Theory and Extensions, vol. 3. VSP, Utrecht (1990)
28. Feichtenhofer, C., Fan, H., Malik, J., He, K.: SlowFast networks for video recognition. In: Proceedings of the IEEE/CVF International Conference on Computer Vision, pp. 6202–6211 (2019)
29. Feichtenhofer, C., Fan, H., Xiong, B., Girshick, R., He, K.: A large-scale study on unsupervised spatiotemporal representation learning. In: Proceedings of the IEEE/CVF Conference on Computer Vision and Pattern Recognition, pp. 3299–3309 (2021)
30. Feichtenhofer, C., Pinz, A., Zisserman, A.: Convolutional two-stream network fusion for video action recognition. In: Proceedings of the IEEE Conference on Computer Vision and Pattern Recognition, pp. 1933–1941 (2016)
31. Fernando, B., Bilen, H., Gavves, E., Gould, S.: Self-supervised video representation learning with odd-one-out networks. In: Proceedings of the IEEE Conference on Computer Vision and Pattern Recognition, pp. 3636–3645 (2017)
32. Gao, J., Chen, K., Nevatia, R.: CTAP: complementary temporal action proposal generation. In: Ferrari, V., Hebert, M., Sminchisescu, C., Weiss, Y. (eds.) ECCV 2018. LNCS, vol. 11206, pp. 70–85. Springer, Cham (2018). https://doi.org/10.1007/978-3-030-01216-8_5
33. Gavrilyuk, K., Jain, M., Karmanov, I., Snoek, C.G.M.: Motion-augmented self-training for video recognition at smaller scale. In: Proceedings of the IEEE/CVF International Conference on Computer Vision (ICCV), pp. 10429–10438, October 2021
34. Grill, J.B., et al.: Bootstrap your own latent - a new approach to self-supervised learning. In: Larochelle, H., Ranzato, M., Hadsell, R., Balcan, M.F., Lin, H. (eds.) Advances in Neural Information Processing Systems, vol. 33, pp. 21271–21284. Curran Associates, Inc. (2020). https://proceedings.neurips.cc/paper/2020/file/f3ada80d5c4ee70142b17b8192b2958e-Paper.pdf
35. Gu, C., et al.: AVA: a video dataset of spatio-temporally localized atomic visual actions. In: Proceedings of the IEEE Conference on Computer Vision and Pattern Recognition, pp. 6047–6056 (2018)

36. Han, T., Xie, W., Zisserman, A.: Memory-augmented dense predictive coding for video representation learning. In: Vedaldi, A., Bischof, H., Brox, T., Frahm, J.-M. (eds.) ECCV 2020. LNCS, vol. 12348, pp. 312–329. Springer, Cham (2020). https://doi.org/10.1007/978-3-030-58580-8_19

37. Han, T., Xie, W., Zisserman, A.: Self-supervised co-training for video representation learning. In: NeurIPS (2020)

38. He, K., Fan, H., Wu, Y., Xie, S., Girshick, R.: Momentum contrast for unsupervised visual representation learning. In: Proceedings of the IEEE/CVF Conference on Computer Vision and Pattern Recognition, pp. 9729–9738 (2020)

39. Hu, K., Shao, J., Liu, Y., Raj, B., Savvides, M., Shen, Z.: Contrast and order representations for video self-supervised learning. In: Proceedings of the IEEE/CVF International Conference on Computer Vision (ICCV), pp. 7939–7949, October 2021

40. Huang, D., et al.: ASCNet: self-supervised video representation learning with appearance-speed consistency. In: Proceedings of the IEEE/CVF International Conference on Computer Vision (ICCV), pp. 8096–8105, October 2021

41. Jenni, S., Jin, H.: Time-equivariant contrastive video representation learning. In: Proceedings of the IEEE/CVF International Conference on Computer Vision, pp. 9970–9980 (2021)

42. Jenni, S., Meishvili, G., Favaro, P.: Video representation learning by recognizing temporal transformations. In: Vedaldi, A., Bischof, H., Brox, T., Frahm, J.-M. (eds.) ECCV 2020. LNCS, vol. 12373, pp. 425–442. Springer, Cham (2020). https://doi.org/10.1007/978-3-030-58604-1_26

43. Jiang, Y.G., Dai, Q., Liu, W., Xue, X., Ngo, C.W.: Human action recognition in unconstrained videos by explicit motion modeling. IEEE Trans. Image Process. **24**(11), 3781–3795 (2015)

44. Johansson, G.: Visual perception of biological motion and a model for its analysis. Percept. Psychophys. **14**(2), 201–211 (1973)

45. Kay, W., et al.: The kinetics human action video dataset. arXiv preprint arXiv:1705.06950 (2017)

46. Korbar, B., Tran, D., Torresani, L.: Cooperative learning of audio and video models from self-supervised synchronization. In: Bengio, S., Wallach, H., Larochelle, H., Grauman, K., Cesa-Bianchi, N., Garnett, R. (eds.) Advances in Neural Information Processing Systems, vol. 31. Curran Associates, Inc. (2018). https://proceedings.neurips.cc/paper/2018/file/c4616f5a24a66668f11ca4fa80525dc4-Paper.pdf

47. Kuehne, H., Jhuang, H., Garrote, E., Poggio, T., Serre, T.: HMDB: a large video database for human motion recognition. In: 2011 International Conference on Computer Vision, pp. 2556–2563 (2011). https://doi.org/10.1109/ICCV.2011.6126543

48. Larsson, G., Maire, M., Shakhnarovich, G.: Learning representations for automatic colorization. In: Leibe, B., Matas, J., Sebe, N., Welling, M. (eds.) ECCV 2016. LNCS, vol. 9908, pp. 577–593. Springer, Cham (2016). https://doi.org/10.1007/978-3-319-46493-0_35

49. Lee, H.Y., Huang, J.B., Singh, M., Yang, M.H.: Unsupervised representation learning by sorting sequences. In: Proceedings of the IEEE International Conference on Computer Vision, pp. 667–676 (2017)

50. Li, R., Zhang, Y., Qiu, Z., Yao, T., Liu, D., Mei, T.: Motion-focused contrastive learning of video representations. In: Proceedings of the IEEE/CVF International Conference on Computer Vision, pp. 2105–2114 (2021)

51. Li, Y., Li, Y., Vasconcelos, N.: RESOUND: towards action recognition without representation bias. In: Ferrari, V., Hebert, M., Sminchisescu, C., Weiss, Y. (eds.)

ECCV 2018. LNCS, vol. 11210, pp. 520–535. Springer, Cham (2018). https://doi.org/10.1007/978-3-030-01231-1_32

52. Lin, Y., Guo, X., Lu, Y.: Self-supervised video representation learning with meta-contrastive network. In: Proceedings of the IEEE/CVF International Conference on Computer Vision, pp. 8239–8249 (2021)

53. Lin, Z., Qi, S., Zhengyang, S., Changhu, W.: Inter-intra variant dual representations for self-supervised video recognition. In: BMVC (2021)

54. Liu, J., Chen, C., Zhu, Y., Liu, W., Metaxas, D.N.: Video classification via weakly supervised sequence modeling. Comput. Vis. Image Underst. **152**, 79–87 (2016)

55. Liu, Y., Wang, K., Liu, L., Lan, H., Lin, L.: TCGL: temporal contrastive graph for self-supervised video representation learning. IEEE Trans. Image Process. **31**, 1978–1993 (2022). https://doi.org/10.1109/TIP.2022.3147032

56. Liu, Y., Ma, L., Zhang, Y., Liu, W., Chang, S.F.: Multi-granularity generator for temporal action proposal. In: Proceedings of the IEEE/CVF Conference on Computer Vision and Pattern Recognition, pp. 3604–3613 (2019)

57. Luo, D., et al.: Video cloze procedure for self-supervised spatio-temporal learning. In: Proceedings of the AAAI Conference on Artificial Intelligence, vol. 34, pp. 11701–11708 (2020)

58. Mettes, P., van der Pol, E., Snoek, C.: Hyperspherical prototype networks. In: Advances in Neural Information Processing Systems 32, pp. 1487–1497 (2019)

59. Miech, A., Alayrac, J.B., Smaira, L., Laptev, I., Sivic, J., Zisserman, A.: End-to-end learning of visual representations from uncurated instructional videos. In: Proceedings of the IEEE/CVF Conference on Computer Vision and Pattern Recognition, pp. 9879–9889 (2020)

60. Misra, I., Zitnick, C.L., Hebert, M.: Shuffle and learn: unsupervised learning using temporal order verification. In: Leibe, B., Matas, J., Sebe, N., Welling, M. (eds.) ECCV 2016. LNCS, vol. 9905, pp. 527–544. Springer, Cham (2016). https://doi.org/10.1007/978-3-319-46448-0_32

61. Morgado, P., Misra, I., Vasconcelos, N.: Robust audio-visual instance discrimination. In: Proceedings of the IEEE/CVF Conference on Computer Vision and Pattern Recognition, pp. 12934–12945 (2021)

62. Noroozi, M., Favaro, P.: Unsupervised learning of visual representations by solving jigsaw puzzles. In: Leibe, B., Matas, J., Sebe, N., Welling, M. (eds.) ECCV 2016. LNCS, vol. 9910, pp. 69–84. Springer, Cham (2016). https://doi.org/10.1007/978-3-319-46466-4_5

63. Oord, A.v.d., Li, Y., Vinyals, O.: Representation learning with contrastive predictive coding. arXiv preprint arXiv:1807.03748 (2018)

64. Pan, T., Song, Y., Yang, T., Jiang, W., Liu, W.: VideoMoCo: contrastive video representation learning with temporally adversarial examples. In: Proceedings of the IEEE/CVF Conference on Computer Vision and Pattern Recognition, pp. 11205–11214 (2021)

65. Patrick, M., et al.: Multi-modal self-supervision from generalized data transformations (2021)

66. Pickup, L.C., et al.: Seeing the arrow of time. In: Proceedings of the IEEE Conference on Computer Vision and Pattern Recognition, pp. 2035–2042 (2014)

67. Qian, R., et al.: Enhancing self-supervised video representation learning via multi-level feature optimization. In: Proceedings of the IEEE/CVF International Conference on Computer Vision (ICCV), pp. 7990–8001, October 2021

68. Qian, R., et al.: Spatiotemporal contrastive video representation learning. In: Proceedings of the IEEE/CVF Conference on Computer Vision and Pattern Recognition, pp. 6964–6974 (2021)

69. Regatti, J.R., Deshmukh, A.A., Manavoglu, E., Dogan, U.: Consensus clustering with unsupervised representation learning. In: 2021 International Joint Conference on Neural Networks (IJCNN), pp. 1–9. IEEE (2021)

70. Richemond, P.H., et al.: BYOL works even without batch statistics. CoRR abs/2010.10241 (2020). https://arxiv.org/abs/2010.10241

71. Sevilla-Lara, L., Liao, Y., Güney, F., Jampani, V., Geiger, A., Black, M.J.: On the integration of optical flow and action recognition. In: Brox, T., Bruhn, A., Fritz, M. (eds.) GCPR 2018. LNCS, vol. 11269, pp. 281–297. Springer, Cham (2019). https://doi.org/10.1007/978-3-030-12939-2_20

72. Simonyan, K., Zisserman, A.: Two-stream convolutional networks for action recognition in videos. In: Advances in Neural Information Processing Systems, pp. 568–576 (2014)

73. Sinkhorn, R.: Diagonal equivalence to matrices with prescribed row and column sums. Am. Math. Mon. **74**(4), 402–405 (1967)

74. Soomro, K., Zamir, A.R., Shah, M.: UCF101: a dataset of 101 human actions classes from videos in the wild. CoRR abs/1212.0402 (2012). http://arxiv.org/abs/1212.0402

75. Srivastava, N., Mansimov, E., Salakhudinov, R.: Unsupervised learning of video representations using LSTMs. In: International Conference on Machine Learning, pp. 843–852. PMLR (2015)

76. Sun, C., Baradel, F., Murphy, K., Schmid, C.: Learning video representations using contrastive bidirectional transformer. arXiv preprint arXiv:1906.05743 (2019)

77. Sun, C., Myers, A., Vondrick, C., Murphy, K., Schmid, C.: VideoBERT: a joint model for video and language representation learning. In: Proceedings of the IEEE/CVF International Conference on Computer Vision, pp. 7464–7473 (2019)

78. Tammes, P.M.L.: On the origin of number and arrangement of the places of exit on the surface of pollen-grains. Recueil des travaux botaniques néerlandais **27**(1), 1–84 (1930)

79. Tian, Y., Krishnan, D., Isola, P.: Contrastive multiview coding. In: Vedaldi, A., Bischof, H., Brox, T., Frahm, J.-M. (eds.) ECCV 2020. LNCS, vol. 12356, pp. 776–794. Springer, Cham (2020). https://doi.org/10.1007/978-3-030-58621-8_45

80. Toering, M., Gatopoulos, I., Stol, M., Hu, V.T.: Self-supervised video representation learning with cross-stream prototypical contrasting. Proceedings of the IEEE/CVF Winter Conference on Applications of Computer Vision (WACV), January 2022

81. Tran, D., Wang, H., Torresani, L., Ray, J., LeCun, Y., Paluri, M.: A closer look at spatiotemporal convolutions for action recognition. In: Proceedings of the IEEE conference on Computer Vision and Pattern Recognition, pp. 6450–6459 (2018)

82. Vondrick, C., Pirsiavash, H., Torralba, A.: Generating videos with scene dynamics. In: Advances in Neural Information Processing Systems 29, pp. 613–621 (2016)

83. Wang, J., Jiao, J., Liu, Y.-H.: Self-supervised video representation learning by pace prediction. In: Vedaldi, A., Bischof, H., Brox, T., Frahm, J.-M. (eds.) ECCV 2020. LNCS, vol. 12362, pp. 504–521. Springer, Cham (2020). https://doi.org/10.1007/978-3-030-58520-4_30

84. Wei, D., Lim, J.J., Zisserman, A., Freeman, W.T.: Learning and using the arrow of time. In: Proceedings of the IEEE Conference on Computer Vision and Pattern Recognition, pp. 8052–8060 (2018)

85. Xie, S., Sun, C., Huang, J., Tu, Z., Murphy, K.: Rethinking spatiotemporal feature learning: speed-accuracy trade-offs in video classification. In: Ferrari, V., Hebert, M., Sminchisescu, C., Weiss, Y. (eds.) ECCV 2018. LNCS, vol. 11219, pp. 318–335. Springer, Cham (2018). https://doi.org/10.1007/978-3-030-01267-0_19

86. Xu, D., Xiao, J., Zhao, Z., Shao, J., Xie, D., Zhuang, Y.: Self-supervised spatiotem-poral learning via video clip order prediction. In: Proceedings of the IEEE/CVF Conference on Computer Vision and Pattern Recognition, pp. 10334–10343 (2019)
87. Yang, J., Parikh, D., Batra, D.: Joint unsupervised learning of deep representations and image clusters. In: Proceedings of the IEEE Conference on Computer Vision and Pattern Recognition, pp. 5147–5156 (2016)
88. Yao, Y., Liu, C., Luo, D., Zhou, Y., Ye, Q.: Video playback rate perception for self-supervised spatio-temporal representation learning. In: Proceedings of the IEEE/CVF Conference on Computer Vision and Pattern Recognition, pp. 6548–6557 (2020)
89. Yao, Y., Liu, C., Luo, D., Zhou, Y., Ye, Q.: Video playback rate perception for self-supervised spatio-temporal representation learning. In: Proceedings of the IEEE/CVF Conference on Computer Vision and Pattern Recognition (CVPR), June 2020
90. Asano, Y.M., Rupprecht, C., Vedaldi, A.: Self-labelling via simultaneous clustering and representation learning. In: International Conference on Learning Representa-tions (2020). https://openreview.net/forum?id=Hyx-jyBFPr
91. You, Y., Gitman, I., Ginsburg, B.: Large batch training of convolutional networks. arXiv preprint arXiv:1708.03888 (2017)
92. Zach, C., Pock, T., Bischof, H.: A duality based approach for realtime TV-L^1 opti-cal flow. In: Hamprecht, F.A., Schnörr, C., Jähne, B. (eds.) DAGM 2007. LNCS, vol. 4713, pp. 214–223. Springer, Heidelberg (2007). https://doi.org/10.1007/978-3-540-74936-3_22
93. Zbontar, J., Jing, L., Misra, I., LeCun, Y., Deny, S.: Barlow twins: self-supervised learning via redundancy reduction. In: ICML (2021)
94. Zhang, R., Isola, P., Efros, A.A.: Colorful image colorization. In: Leibe, B., Matas, J., Sebe, N., Welling, M. (eds.) ECCV 2016. LNCS, vol. 9907, pp. 649–666. Springer, Cham (2016). https://doi.org/10.1007/978-3-319-46487-9_40
95. Zhao, Y., Xiong, Y., Wang, L., Wu, Z., Tang, X., Lin, D.: Temporal action detec-tion with structured segment networks. In: Proceedings of the IEEE International Conference on Computer Vision, pp. 2914–2923 (2017)
96. Zhuang, C., Zhai, A.L., Yamins, D.: Local aggregation for unsupervised learning of visual embeddings. In: Proceedings of the IEEE/CVF International Conference on Computer Vision, pp. 6002–6012 (2019)

Constrained Mean Shift Using Distant yet Related Neighbors for Representation Learning

K. L. Navaneet[1(✉)], Soroush Abbasi Koohpayegani[1], Ajinkya Tejankar[1], Kossar Pourahmadi[1], Akshayvarun Subramanya[2], and Hamed Pirsiavash[1]

[1] University of California, Davis, Davis, USA
nkadur@ucdavis.edu
[2] University of Maryland, Baltimore County, Baltimore, USA

Abstract. We are interested in representation learning in self-supervised, supervised, and semi-supervised settings. Some recent self-supervised learning methods like mean-shift (MSF) cluster images by pulling the embedding of a query image to be closer to its nearest neighbors (NNs). Since most NNs are close to the query by design, the averaging may not affect the embedding of the query much. On the other hand, far away NNs may not be semantically related to the query. We generalize the mean-shift idea by constraining the search space of NNs using another source of knowledge so that NNs are far from the query while still being semantically related. We show that our method (1) outperforms MSF in SSL setting when the constraint utilizes a different augmentation of an image from the previous epoch, and (2) outperforms PAWS in semi-supervised setting with less training resources when the constraint ensures that the NNs have the same pseudo-label as the query. Our code is available here: https://github.com/UCDvision/CMSF.

1 Introduction

Recently, we have seen great progress in self-supervised learning (SSL) methods that learn rich representations from unlabeled data. Such methods are important since they do not rely on manual annotation of data, which can be costly, biased, or ambiguous. Hence, SSL representations may perform better than supervised ones in transferring to downstream visual recognition tasks.

Most recent SSL methods, *e.g.*, MoCo [29] and BYOL [27], pull the embedding of a query image to be closer to its own augmentation compared to some other random images. Follow-up works have focused on improving the positive pairs through generating better augmentations [41,51,62] and the negative set by

---

K. L. Navaneet, S. Abbasi Koohpayegani and A. Tejankar—Equal contribution.

Supplementary Information The online version contains supplementary material available at https://doi.org/10.1007/978-3-031-19821-2_2.

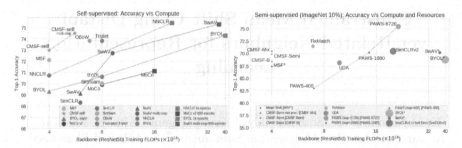

Fig. 1. Accuracy vs. training compute on ImageNet with ResNet50: We report the total training FLOPs for forward and backward passes through the CNN backbone. **(Left) Self-supervised:** All methods are for 200 epochs. CMSF$_{self}$ achieves competitive accuracy with considerably lower compute. **(Right) Semi-supervised:** Circle radius is proportional to the number of GPUs/TPUs used. The results are on ImageNet with 10% labels. In addition to being compute efficient, CMSF is trained with an order of magnitude lower resources, making it more practical and accessible. * methods use self-supervised pre-training and finetuning on the labeled set.

increasing the set size [29] or mining effective samples [34,35,67], but have largely ignored possibility of utilizing additional positive images. More recently, [5,21,37] expand the positive set using nearest neighbors. Inspired by classic mean-shift algorithm, MSF [37] generalizes BYOL to group similar images together. MSF pulls a query image to be close to not only its augmentation, but also the top-k nearest neighbors (NNs) of its augmentation.

We argue that the top-k neighbors are close to the query image by construction, and thus may not provide a strong supervision signal. We are interested in choosing far away (non-top) neighbors that are still semantically related to the query image. This cannot be trivially achieved by increasing the number of NNs since the *purity* of retrieved neighbors decreases with increasing k (See Fig. 4 and Fig. 5). Purity is defined as the percentage of the NNs belonging to the same category as the query image.

We generalize MSF [37] method by simply limiting the NN search to a smaller subset that we believe is reasonably far from the query but still semantically related to it. We define this constraint to be (1) the nearest neighbors of another augmentation of the query in SSL setting and (2) images sharing the same label or pseudo-label as the query in supervised and semi-supervised settings. While we aim to obtain distant samples of the same category, note that we group only a few neighbors (k in our method) from the constrained subset instead of grouping the whole subset together. This is in contrast to cross-entropy supervised learning, where we pull all images of a category to form a cluster or be on the same side of a hyper-plane. Our method can benefit from this relaxation by preserving the latent structure of the categories and also being robust to noisy labels.

Our experiments show that the method outperforms the various baselines in all three settings with same or less amount of computation in training (refer Fig. 1). It outperforms MSF [37] in SSL, cross-entropy in supervised (with clean or noisy labels), and PAWS [4] in semi-supervised settings. Our main novelty is in developing a simple but effective method for searching for far away but

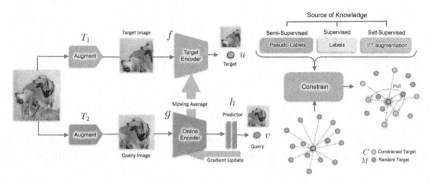

Fig. 2. Our method (CMSF): We augment an image twice and pass them through online and target encoders followed by ℓ_2 normalization to get u and v. Mean-shift [37] encourages v to be close to both u and its nearest neighbors (NN). To make NNs diverse, we constrain the NN search space based on additional knowledge in the form of NNs of the previous augmentation in self-supervised setting or the labels or pseudo-labels in semi or fully supervised settings. These constraints encourages the query to be pulled towards semantically related NNs that are farther away from the target embedding. See Fig. 3 for constructing the constrained set.

semantically related NNs and in generalizing it to work across the board from self-supervised to semi-supervised and fully supervised settings. To summarize,

1. We propose constrained mean-shift (CMSF), a generalization of MSF [37], to utilize additional sources of knowledge to constrain the NN search space (Fig. 2).
2. We develop methods to select the constraint set in self-, semi- and fully supervised settings. The retrieved samples are empirically shown to be far away in the embedding space but semantically related to the query image, providing a stronger training signal compared to MSF.
3. CMSF achieves non-trivial gains in performance over self-supervised MSF and a direct extension of MSF to semi-supervised version. CMSF outperforms SOTA methods with comparable compute in self- and semi-supervised settings.

2   Method

Similar to MSF [37], given a query image, we are interested in pulling its embedding closer to the mean of the embeddings of its nearest neighbors (NNs). However, since top NNs are close to the target itself, they may not provide a strong supervision signal. On the other hand, far away (non-top) NNs may not be semantically similar to the target image. Hence, we constrain the NN search space to include mostly far away points with high purity. The purity is defined as the percentage of the selected NNs being from the same ground truth category as the query image. We use different constraint selection techniques to analyze our method in supervised, self- and semi-supervised settings.

Following MSF and BYOL, we use two embedding networks: a target encoder $f(.)$ with parameters θ_f and an online encoder $g(.)$ with parameters

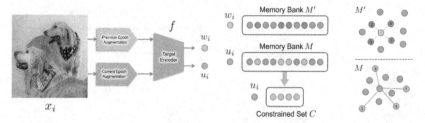

Fig. 3. CMSF$_{\text{self}}$: The indices of the NNs of the previous epoch's memory bank M' are used to construct the constrained set C from the current memory bank M.

θ_g. The online encoder is directly updated using backpropagation while the target encoder is updated as a slowly moving average of the online encoder: $\theta_f \leftarrow m\theta_f + (1 - m)\theta_g$ where m is close to 1. We add a predictor head $h(.)$ [27] to the end of the online encoder so that pulling the embeddings together encourages one embedding to be predictable by the other one and not necessarily encouraging the two embeddings to be equal. In the experiments, we use a two-layer MLP for $h(.)$.

Given a query image x_i, we augment it twice with transformations $T_1(.)$ and $T_2(.)$, feed them to the two encoders, and normalize them with their ℓ_2 norm to get $u_i = \frac{f(T_1(x_i))}{||f(T_1(x_i))||_2}$ and $v_i = \frac{h(g(T_2(x_i)))}{||h(g(T_2(x_i)))||_2}$. We add u_i to the memory bank M and remove the oldest entries to maintain a fixed size M. We select the constraint set C_i as a subset of M. Constraint set selection is explained in detail in Sects. 2.1, 2.2, and 2.3. We then find the set S_i of top-k nearest neighbors of u_i in C_i including u_i itself. Finally, we update $g(.)$ by minimizing:

$$L = \sum_{i=1}^{n} \frac{1}{|S_i|} \sum_{z \in S_i} v_i^T z$$

where n is the size of mini-batch and $|S_i|$ is the size of set S_i, e.g., k in top-k. Finally, we update $f(.)$ with the momentum update. In the top-*all* variation of our method, number of neighbors k is set equal to the size of C_i, i.e., $S_i = C_i$. Note that since u_i itself is included in the nearest neighbor search, the method will be identical to BYOL [27] when $k = 1$ and to self-supervised mean-shift [37] when the constraint is fully relaxed ($C_i = M$). Our method covers a larger spectrum of algorithms by defining the constrained set. Below we discuss the selection of constrained set in various settings.

2.1   Self-supervised Setting

In addition to M, we maintain a second memory bank M' that is exactly the same as M but contains features from a different (3rd) augmentation of the image x_i fed through target encoder $f(.)$. We assume $w_i \in M'$ and $u_i \in M$ are two embeddings corresponding to the same image x_i. Then, we find NNs of w_i in M' and use their indices to construct the search space C_i from M (See Fig. 3). Note that although the NNs of w_i in M' are already close to each other, their corresponding elements in M may not be close to each other since M contains different augmentations u_i of the same images. As a result, C_i will maintain good purity while containing distant NNs (refer to Table 1-Right and Fig. 5).

Since it is expensive to embed a 3rd augmentation of each image, we embed only two augmentations as in MSF and BYOL and cache the embeddings from the previous epoch, keeping the most recent embedding for each image. The cached embedding will be still valid after one epoch since the target encoder is updated slowly using the momentum update rule (similar to MoCo). Since cache size is equal to the dataset size, we store it in the CPU memory and maintain the auxiliary memory bank M' by loading the corresponding part of it to the GPU memory for each mini-batch. Caching of features is not essential for CMSF to work and is only used to reduce computational cost. We performed experiments with an actual 3rd augmentation instead and found the results to be similar to our method except that it was nearly 30% slower due to forwarding an additional augmentation. Table 1-Right shows that in the intermediate stages of learning, the top elements of C_i are spread apart in M with higher median ranks, and get closer to the top elements of M as the learning progresses. Note that we use w_i instead of u_i in finding the NNs in M' since both w_i and M' use an older target model, so are more comparable.

Since CMSF adds farther NNs only for stronger supervision, we additionally employ MSF loss calculated on the unconstrained M. Then, in the self-supervised setting, the total loss is an equally weighted sum of MSF and CMSF losses.

Our method can be extended to cross-modal self-supervised setting where the constraint can use NNs in a different modality rather than the 3rd augmentation of the same modality. We report the details and some preliminary experiments on this setting in the supplementary.

2.2   Supervised Setting

While supervised setting is not our primary novelty or motivation, we study it to provide more insights into our constrained mean-shift framework. With access to the labels of each image, we can simply construct C_i as the subset of M that shares the same label as the query x_i. This guarantees 100% purity for NNs.

Note that most supervised methods, including cross-entropy loss, try to group all examples of a category together on the same side of a hyper-plane while remaining categories are on the other side. However, our method pulls the target to be close to only those examples of the same category that are already close to the target. This results in a supervised algorithm that may keep the latent structure of each category which can be useful for pre-training on coarse-grained labels. Moreover, as shown in the experiments (Fig. 6), our method is more robust to label noise since most mis-labeled images will be far from the target embedding, thus ignored in learning. This motivates applying our method to semi-supervised setting where the limited supervision provides noisy labels.

2.3   Semi-supervised Setting

In this setting, we assume access to a dataset with a small labeled and a large unlabeled subset. We train a simple classifier using the current embeddings of the labeled data and use the classifier to pseudo-label the unlabeled data. Then, similar to the supervised setting, we construct C_i to be the elements of M that share the pseudo-label with the target embedding. Again, this method increases the diversity of C_i while maintaining high purity. To keep the purity high, we enforce the constraint only when the pseudo-label is very confident (the probability is above a threshold.) For the samples with non-confident pseudo-label, we relax the constraint resulting in regular MSF loss (*i.e.*, $C_i = M$.) Moreover to reduce the computational overhead of pseudo-labeling, we cache the embeddings of labeled examples throughout the epoch and train a 2-layer MLP classifier using the frozen cached features and their groundtruth labels in the middle and end of each epoch.

3   Experiments

Implementation Details: We use PyTorch for all our experiments. Unless specified, we use the same hyper-parameter values in self-, semi- and fully supervised settings. All models are trained on ImageNet-1k (IN-1k) for 200 epochs with ResNet-50 [30] backbone and SGD optimizer (learning rate $= 0.05$, batch size $= 256$, momentum $= 0.9$, and weight decay $= 1e-4$) with cosine scheduling for learning rate. While we focus on single crop setting in most of our experiments, we also report the results for multiple crop inputs in the SSL setting. Following SwAV [11], we use four additional crops of 96×96 resolution as input. These are used as inputs only to the online encoder and not the target encoder. The momentum value of CMSF for the moving average key encoder is 0.99. The 2-layer MLP architecture for CMSF$_{semi}$ is as follows: (linear (2048×4096), batch norm, ReLU, linear (4096×512)). The default memory bank size is 128k. Top-k is set to 10 in the semi- and fully supervised settings and 5 in the self-supervised setting. Additional details are provided in the supplementary. Our main CMSF experiment with 200 epochs takes nearly 6 d on four NVIDIA-2080TI GPUs. The overhead in training time due to NN search is negligible compared to the forward and backward passes through the network (that is also done in BYOL): the increase in time is 0.7% for MSF [37] and 2.1% for CMSF$_{self}$.

Recent SSL methods are usually computationally expensive leading to worse environmental impact and exclusion of smaller research labs. While our experiments are more efficient and accessible than most SOTA methods, *e.g.*, PAWS, we limit our training length to 200 epochs due to resource constraints. We do not empirically verify whether the improvements observed over SOTA approaches at lower epochs (200) are persistent with longer training (*e.g.*, 800 or 1000 epochs).

Evaluation: We evaluate the pre-trained models using linear evaluation (*Linear IN-1k*) in both ImageNet classification and transfer settings. The model backbone parameters are fixed and a single linear layer is trained atop them following the setting in CompRess [2]. Additionally, we report k-nearest neighbor ($k = 1, 20$) evaluation for the SSL setting as in [2]. The transfer performance is evaluated on the following datasets: Food101 [8], SUN397 [73], CIFAR10 [39], CIFAR100 [39], Cars196 [38], Aircraft [43], Flowers (Flwrs102) [46], Pets [49],

Caltech-101 (Calt101) [22], and DTD [18] (additional details in supplementary material.)

3.1 Self-supervised Learning (CMSF$_{self}$)

To reduce the GPU memory footprint, we cache the previous augmentation embedding of each sample in the dataset in the CPU. The cached features corresponding to the current mini-batch are retrieved from CPU memory to maintain

Table 1. Left: Evaluation on full ImageNet: We compare our model with other SOTA methods in Linear (Top-1 Linear) and Nearest Neighbor (1-NN, 20-NN) evaluation. We use a memory bank of size 128K for CMSF and provide comparison with both 256K and 1M memory bank versions of MSF. Since CMSF$_{self}$ uses NNs from two memory banks, it is comparable to MSF (256K) in memory and computation overhead. Both single crop and multi-crop versions of our method outperform other SOTA methods, including MSF, with similar compute. **Right: Histogram of constrained sample ranks:** We consider the 5th NN in the constrained set C and obtain its rank in the unconstrained memory bank M. The histogram of these ranks are shown up to rank 100 for different train stages of CMSF$_{self}$. Also, the median of these ranks are shown in Fig. 5. A large number of distant neighbors are included in the constrained set in the early stages of training while there is a higher overlap between constrained and unconstrained NN sets towards the end of training.

Method	Ref.	Batch Size	Epochs	Sym. Loss 2x FLOPS	Multi-Crop Training	Top-1 Linear	NN	20-NN
Supervised	[1]	256	100	-	-	76.2	71.4	74.8
Random-init	-	-	-	-	-	5.1	1.5	2.0
SeLa-v2 [76]	[11]	4096	400	✓	✗	67.2	-	-
SimCLR[13]	[13]	4096	1000	✓	✗	69.3	-	-
SwAV [11]	[11]	4096	400	✓	✗	70.1	-	-
DeepCluster-v2 [10]	[11]	4096	400	✓	✗	70.2	-	-
SimSiam [16]	[16]	256	400	✓	✗	70.8	-	-
MoCo v2 [29]	[15]	256	800	✗	✗	71.1	57.3	61.0
CompRess [2]	[2]	256	1K+130	✗	✗	71.9	63.3	66.8
InvP [66]	[66]	256	800	✗	✗	71.3	-	-
BYOL [27]	[27]	4096	1000	✓	✗	74.3	62.8	66.9
SwAV [11]	[11]	4096	800	✓	✓	75.3	-	-
NNCLR	[21]	4096	1000	✗	✗	75.4	-	-
SimCLR[13]	[16]	4096	200	✓	✗	68.3	-	-
SwAV [11]	[16]	4096	200	✓	✗	69.1	-	-
MoCo v2 [29]	[16]	256	200	✓	✗	69.9	-	-
SimSiam [16]	[16]	256	200	✓	✗	70.0	-	-
NNCLR[21]	[21]	4096	200	✗	✗	70.7	-	-
BYOL [27]	[16]	4096	200	✓	✗	70.6	-	-
SwAV [11]	[16]	256	200	✓	✓	72.7	-	-
Truncated Triplet [67]	[67]	832	200	✓	✗	73.8	-	-
OBoW [24]	[24]	256	200	✗	✓	73.8	-	-
CMSF$_{self}$ (128K)	-	256	200	✗	✓	**74.4**	**62.3**	**66.2**
MoCo v2 [29]	[15]	256	200	✗	✗	67.5	50.9	54.3
CO2 [69]	[69]	256	200	✗	✗	68.0	-	-
BYOL-asym [27]	[37]	256	200	✗	✗	69.3	55.0	59.2
ISD [60]	[60]	256	200	✗	✗	69.8	59.2	62.0
MSF (1M) [37]	[37]	256	200	✗	✗	72.4	62.0	64.9
MSF (256K)[37]	[37]	256	200	✗	✗	72.2	62.1	65.1
CMSF$_{self}$ (128K)	-	256	200	✗	✗	**73.0**	**63.2**	**66.4**

Histograms (right): Epoch 10, Epoch 20, Epoch 40, Epoch 80, Epoch 200.

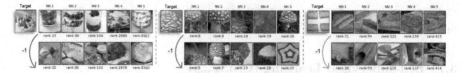

Fig. 4. Nearest neighbor selection on constrained memory bank: First row shows top-5 NNs of target in constrained set C and their corresponding rank in the unconstrained memory bank M obtained using an intermediate checkpoint (epoch 100). While they are not the closest samples to the target (higher rank index), they are semantically similar to the target. This shows that the constraint can capture far away samples with similar semantic as the target. The second row depicts images from memory bank with one rank lower than the corresponding image in the first row. These images contain incorrect category retrievals. Distant neighbors cannot be trivially obtained by increasing the number of NNs. Examples are chosen randomly.

memory bank M' with previous augmentations. This cache is updated using the oldest features in M that we remove from M after each iteration.

Results on ImageNet: Results of CMSF$_\text{self}$ are shown in Table 1. CMSF$_\text{self}$ outperforms MSF baseline with a larger memory bank, which we believe is due to pulling together far yet semantically similar samples (Fig. 4). We use MSF with $2x$ larger memory bank for fair comparison. CMSF$_\text{self}$ also achieves state-of-the-art performance on both NN and Linear metrics when compared with approaches with similar computational budget. We compare our method to other state-of-the-art approaches with 200 epochs of training in Fig. 1. We observe a good trade-off in terms of accuracy and compute for CMSF$_\text{self}$. Our best performance is obtained with the multi-crop version but at the cost of increased compute.

Evaluation on ImageNet Subsets: Following [13,31], we evaluate the pretrained models on the ImageNet classification task with limited labels. We report results with 1% and 10% labeled subsets of ImageNet (Table 4). CMSF$_\text{self}$ outperforms MSF on top-1 accuracy in both 1% and 10% settings and is comparable to existing approaches that require significantly higher training time.

Transfer Learning: We follow the procedure in [13,27] for transfer evaluation (refer to Table 2). Hyperparameters for each dataset are tuned independently based on the validation set accuracy and final accuracy is reported on the held-out test set (more details in supplementary). CMSF$_\text{self}$ achieves SOTA average performance among methods trained for 200 epochs.

Purity of Constrained Samples: In CMSF$_\text{self}$, we depend on information from previous augmentations to constrain NN search in the current memory bank. Our goal is to improve learning by using distant samples with a good purity. We observe that the top-k samples from constrained memory bank C have higher rank in M, so are far neighbors of the target (see Table 1-Right and Fig. 5). Also, as shown in Fig. 5, those samples maintain almost the same purity as the top-k samples from unconstrained memory bank M. As a result, C maintains good purity while being diverse.

Table 2. Transfer learning evaluation: Our supervised CMSF model at just 200 epochs outperforms all supervised baselines on transfer learning evaluation. Our SSL model outperforms MSF, the comparable state-of-the-art approach, by 1.2 points on average over 10 datasets. We get the results for MoCo v2, MSF, and BYOL-asym from [37], SimCLR and Xent (1000 epoch) from [13], and BYOL from [27].

Method	Epoch	Food 101	CIFAR 10	CIFAR 100	SUN 397	Cars 196	Air-craft	DTD	Pets	Calt. 101	Flwr 102	Mean Trans	Linear IN-1k
				Supervised Models								
Xent	200	67.7	89.8	72.5	57.5	43.7	39.8	67.9	91.8	91.1	88.0	71.0	77.2
Xent	90	72.8	91.0	74.0	59.5	56.8	48.4	70.7	92.0	90.8	93.0	74.9	76.2
ProtoNW	200	73.3	93.2	78.3	61.5	65.0	57.6	73.7	92.2	94.3	93.7	78.3	76.0
SupCon	200	72.5	93.8	77.7	61.5	64.8	58.6	74.6	**92.5**	93.6	94.1	78.4	**77.5**
Xent	1000	72.3	93.6	78.3	61.9	66.7	61.0	**74.9**	91.5	94.5	94.7	78.9	76.3
CMSF$_{sup}$ top-all	200	73.7	94.2	**78.7**	62.1	**71.7**	**64.1**	73.4	**92.5**	94.5	**95.8**	**80.1**	75.7
CMSF$_{sup}$ top-10	200	**74.9**	**94.4**	**78.7**	**62.7**	70.8	63.4	73.8	92.2	**94.9**	95.6	**80.1**	76.4
				Self-Supervised Models								
SimCLR	1000	72.8	90.5	74.4	60.6	49.3	49.8	**75.7**	84.6	89.3	92.6	74.0	69.3
MoCo v2	800	72.5	**92.2**	74.6	59.6	50.5	53.2	74.4	84.6	90.0	90.5	74.2	71.1
BYOL	1000	**75.3**	91.3	**78.4**	**62.2**	**67.8**	**60.6**	75.5	**90.4**	**94.2**	**96.1**	**79.2**	**74.3**
MoCo v2	200	70.4	91.0	73.5	57.5	47.7	51.2	73.9	81.3	88.7	91.1	72.6	67.5
BYOL-asym	200	70.2	91.5	74.2	59.0	54.0	52.1	73.4	86.2	90.4	92.1	74.3	69.3
MSF	200	72.3	**92.7**	76.3	60.2	59.4	56.3	71.7	89.8	90.9	93.7	76.3	72.1
CMSF$_{self}$	200	**73.0**	92.2	**77.2**	**61.0**	**60.6**	**58.4**	74.1	**91.1**	**92.0**	**94.5**	**77.4**	**73.0**

Table 3. Effect of k' in sampling NN from M': In CMSF$_{self}$, we constrain top-k NN search space in M with top-k' samples from M'. **(Left)** Increasing k' results in a drop in accuracy. The k in top-k is set to 5 for all values of k'. **(Right)** Histogram of the constrained sample ranks at epoch 50. The histogram shifts left, *i.e.*, overlap between constrained and unconstrained NN sets increases with increasing value of k'.

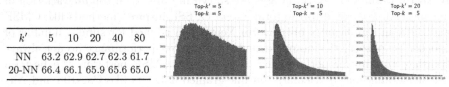

k'	5	10	20	40	80
NN	63.2	62.9	62.7	62.3	61.7
20-NN	66.4	66.1	65.9	65.6	65.0

Effect of k': In CMSF$_{self}$, we first calculate top-k' samples (the first k' NNs of the target) from the secondary memory bank M'. We then use those indices to constrain NN search space in the primary memory bank M and select top-k for optimization. We varied the value of k' in CMSF$_{self}$ to explore its effect, keeping k fixed to 5. We observe that increasing k' (relaxing the constraint) will decrease the accuracy of the model. As observed in Table 3-right, the overlap between constrained and unconstrained NN set increases with increasing value of k'. Note that in a case where $k' = \infty$, CMSF$_{self}$ will be identical to the MSF baseline.

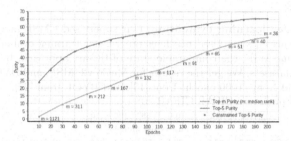

Fig. 5. Purity of constrained samples: During training of CMSF$_{self}$, we plot purity of the top-5 samples in unconstrained set M (in black) and that of the top-5 samples in constrained set C (in red). The red curve is not significantly below the black one suggesting that the purity is not dropped by increasing the distance of the NNs. To show that elements in C may be far from the target u, we choose the 5th element in C and find its rank in the set M. We calculate the median of this rank as m. The purity of the top-m elements of set M (green curve) is consistently lower than that of top-5 elements of the constrained set C (red curve). This suggests that one cannot maintain high purity by simply considering more NNs using a larger k. (Color figure online)

3.2   Supervised Learning

Evaluation: Unlike cross-entropy (Xent [7,42,52]) baseline, SupCon [36], ProtoNW [55] and CMSF do not train a linear classifier during the pre-training stage. Thus, we use the pre-training dataset ImageNet-1k (IN-1k) for linear evaluation of the frozen features as done in SSL. For Xent, we use the linear classifier trained during pre-training. We use the same settings and datasets as self-supervised for transfer learning evaluation.

Results: Results on IN-1k dataset are shown in Table 2. In top-*all* variation of our method, k is equal to the total size of C. SSL inspired methods like CMSF and SupCon significantly outperform Xent when trained for similar number of epochs. We observe that improvements in ImageNet performance do not always translate to transfer performance. Interestingly, CMSF performs the best on transfer evaluation, particularly on fine-grained datasets like Cars196 and Aircraft. We believe that the absence of explicit cross-entropy based optimization using the supervised labels preserves the multi-modal distribution of categories improving fine-grained performance. Supervised CMSF uses class labels only as a constraint for MSF during pre-training and does not explicitly optimize on the classification task. Superior performance of CMSF$_{sup}$ top-10 demonstrates the importance of using distant yet semantically related neighbors as positives.

Noisy Labels: In the noisy setting, we use random i.i.d. noise to corrupt the labels (change the label randomly) of a percentage of images. We consider, 5%, 10%, 25%, and 50% label corruption (noise) rates. For faster experiments, we report results on the ImageNet-100 dataset [61] (Fig. 6). We observe a significantly higher degradation in performance of Xent baseline and CMSF$_{sup}$ top-*all* compared to CMSF$_{sup}$ top-10 at high noise levels. The gap between the approaches is larger on transfer learning. These observations indicate that NN based methods like CMSF are better suited for noisy constraint settings com-

Table 4. Evaluation on small labeled ImageNet: We compare our model to MSF and other baselines on ImageNet 1% and 10% linear evaluation benchmarks. "Fine-tuned" refers to fine-tuning the entire backbone network instead of a single linear layer. $CMSF_{self}$ outperforms MSF on top-1 metric in both 1% and 10% settings.

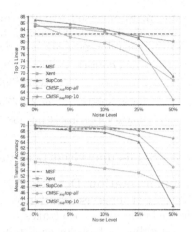

Fig. 6. Noisy supervised setting on ImageNet-100: Our method is more robust to noisy annotation compared to Xent and SupCon. Also, using top-*all* degrades the results since all images from a single category are not guaranteed to be semantically related due to noisy labels. Mean Transfer Accuracy is the average over 10 transfer datasets.

Method	Fine-tuned	Epochs	Top-1 1%	Top-1 10%	Top-5 1%	Top-5 10%
Supervised	✓		25.4	56.4	48.4	80.4
PIRL [44]	✓	800	-	-	57.2	83.8
CO2 [69]	✓	200	-	-	71.0	85.7
SimCLR [13]	✓	1000	48.3	65.6	75.5	87.8
InvP [66]	✓	800	-	-	78.2	88.7
BYOL [27]	✓	1000	53.2	68.8	78.4	89.0
SwAV [11]	✓	800	**53.9**	**70.2**	**78.5**	**89.9**
MoCo v2 [15]	✗	800	51.5	63.6	77.6	86.1
BYOL [27]	✗	1000	55.7	**68.6**	80.0	**88.6**
CompRess [2]	✗	1K+130	**59.7**	67.0	**82.3**	87.5
MoCo v2 [15]	✗	200	43.6	58.4	71.2	82.9
BYOL-asym	✗	200	47.9	61.3	74.6	84.7
ISD [60]	✗	200	53.4	63.0	78.8	85.9
MSF [37]	✗	200	55.5	66.5	**79.9**	87.6
$CMSF_{self}$	✗	200	**56.4**	**67.5**	79.8	**87.7**

pared to approaches utilizing all samples of a class as positives. This robustness to label noise motivates our application of CMSF to self- and semi-supervised settings where pseudo-labels or the NNs of previous augmentations may be noisy.

Coarse-Grained ImageNet: CMSF groups together only top-k neighbors and thus can help in preserving the latent structure of the data compared to top-*all*. To verify this, we consider a dataset with coarse-grained labels where this difference is pronounced. Based on the WordNet hierarchy, we merge each category in the ImageNet dataset to its parent class. We further ensure that no two classes are in the same path in the graph by merging the descendant into the ancestor class. The total number of classes is thus reduced from 1000 in ImageNet-1k to 93 in our ImageNet-coarse. We train CMSF and the baseline approaches in a supervised manner using the coarse labels and then evaluate on the fine-grained/original labels on ImageNet-1k validation set. In Table 5 we compare the top-*all* and top-k variants on the coarse grained version of ImageNet. $CMSF_{sup}$ top-k sees a minor drop in performance compared to training on ImageNet-1k. However, methods in which all samples in a class are explicitly brought closer - $CMSF_{sup}$ top-*all*, cross-entropy and supervised contrastive - see a huge drop in accuracy. More details on coarse-grained ImageNet are in the supplementary.

Table 5. Supervised learning on coarse grained ImageNet: We train on the coarse grained version of ImageNet (93 super categories) and perform linear evaluation on the original ImageNet-1k validation set with fine-grained labels (1000 categories).

Train dataset	ImageNet-1k Validation Set			
	Xent	SupCon	$CMSF_{sup}$ top-*all*	$CMSF_{sup}$ top-10
ImageNet-1k	77.2	**77.5**	75.7	76.4
ImageNet-coarse	61.4	58.7	67.0	**74.2**

3.3   Semi-supervised Learning

Implementation Details: We train a 2-layer MLP atop the cached target features of supervised set for pseudo-labeling. The pseudo-label training is performed twice per epoch (takes 40 s per training) and the label assignment is done in an online fashion for each mini-batch. The confidence threshold for pseudo-labeling is set to 0.85. We use the same optimizer settings as in self-supervised CMSF for the pre-training stage. Similar to S4L [78], we perform two stages of fine-tuning with supervised and pseudo-labels. We fine-tune the backbone network with two MLPs (as in PAWS [4]) on the 10% labeled set for 20 epochs and pseudo-label the train set. Samples above confidence threshold (nearly 30% of dataset) are combined with supervised set to fine-tune again for 20 epochs (more details in suppl.). The second fine-tuning is equivalent to 5 epochs with full data and is a small increase in our total compute. This is needed since we do not directly optimize cross-entropy loss in pre-training as in [50,57,74].

Evaluation: The final epoch parameters are used to perform evaluation. We report top-1 accuracy on the ImageNet validation set. We additionally report the total number of FLOPs for forward and backward passes (backward is 2× forward) through ResNet-50 backbone and the number of GPUs/TPUs used by each method in the pre-training stage (more details in suppl.).

Baselines: We compare the proposed approach ($CMSF_{semi}$) with self- and semi-supervised approaches. $CMSF_{semi}$-*basic* minimizes unconstrained MSF loss on the unlabeled examples (no pseudo-labeling) and CMSF loss on the labeled examples only. We provide comparison of PAWS method with different support set sizes. We train PAWS on 4x 16 GB GPUs with maximum possible support set size (200 classes, 2 images/class) using code provided by the authors. We also report results using mixed precision training ($CMSF_{semi}$-*mix precision*) as in PAWS [4] with a higher batch size of 768 since it has lower memory requirement.

Results: $CMSF_{semi}$-mix precision achieves comparable performance to most methods with significantly less training and without the use of stronger augmentation schemes like RandAugment [19] (Table 6, Fig. 1). PAWS with a support set size of 6720 outperforms other approaches. However, this requires significantly higher compute (4.8× FLOPs) and resources (64 GPUs) compared to $CMSF_{semi}$-mix precision (4 GPUs). Since PAWS requires a large support set, it does not scale well to lower resource (4/8 GPUs) settings even if the total compute remains the same. When trained on only 4 GPUs, CMSF outper-

Table 6. Semi-supervised learning on ImageNet dataset with 10% labels: FLOPs denotes the total number of FLOPS for forward and backward passes through ResNet-50 backbone while batch size denotes the sum of labeled and unlabeled samples in a batch. CMSF$_{semi}$-mix precision is compute and resource efficient, achieving SOTA performance at comparable compute. PAWS requires large number of GPUs to be compute efficient and its performance drastically drops with 4/8 GPUs. [†] Trained with stronger augmentations like RandAugment [19]. [*] TPUs are used.

Method	Epochs	Batch Size	GPUs	FLOPs $(x10^{18})$	Top-1
Self-supervised Pre-training					
Mean Shift [37]	200	256	4	4	67.4
BYOL [27]	1000	4096	512*	40	68.8
SwAV [11]	800	4096	64	37	70.2
SimCLRv2 [14]	800	4096	128*	16	68.4
Semi-supervised Pre-training					
SimCLRv2 (+Self Dist) [14]	1200	4096	128*	20	70.5
UDA† [74]	800	15872	64*	10	68.1
FixMatch† [57]	300	6144	32*	7	71.5
MPL† [50]	800	2048	-	30	73.9
PAWS (support=6720) [4]	300	4096	64	21	75.5
PAWS (support=1680) [4]	100	256	8	15	70.2
PAWS (support=400) [4]	100	256	4	7	62.9
CMSF$_{semi}$-basic	200	256	4	4	68.6
CMSF$_{semi}$	200	256	4	4	69.9
CMSF$_{semi}$-mix precision	200	768	4	4	70.5

forms PAWS by **7.6%** points. Additional ablations and results on ImageNet-100 dataset are in supplementary.

4   Related Work

Self-supervised Learning (SSL): Earlier works on SSL focused on solving a pretext task that does not require additional labeling. Examples of pretext tasks include colorization [80], jigsaw puzzle [47], counting [48], and rotation prediction [25]. Another class of SSL methods is based on instance discrimination [20]. The idea is to classify each image as its own class. Some methods adopt the idea of contrastive learning for instance discrimination [10–13,29]. BYOL [27] proposes a non-contrastive approach by removing the negative set and simply regressing one view of an image from another.

Several recent works aim to find a larger positive sample set to improve learning. In LA [82], samples are clustered using k-means and samples within a cluster are brought closer together compared to cross-cluster samples. MSF [37] and

MYOW [5] generalize BYOL by regressing target view and its NNs. NNCLR [21] extends SimCLR to use NNs as positives. CLD [68] integrates grouping using instance-group discrimination. Affinity diffusion [33] uses strongly connected nodes in a graph constructed using embeddings to find positive samples. Unlike these methods, we focus on grouping together far away neighbors that are semantically similar. We show quantitatively and qualitatively the diversity and purity of retrieved neighbors and improved performance over MSF. We generalize the idea in MSF [37] to use an additional source of knowledge to constrain the NN search space for the target view. CoCLR [28] and Cl-InfoNCE [64] also use additional information sources in the form of additional modality and auxiliary labels respectively to improve performance. However, we focus on self- and semi-supervised classification settings and design methods to obtain and use the additional information as a constraint in NN search space.

Supervised Learning: A drawback of Cross-entropy is its lack of robustness to noisy labels [58,81]. [45,59,63,75] address the issue of hard labeling, *e.g.*, (one-hot labels) with label smoothing, [6,23,32] replace hard labels with prediction of pre-trained teacher, and [77,79] propose an augmentation strategy to train on combination of instances and their labels. Another line of work [26,53] is to learn representations with good kNN performance. SupCon [36] and [72] improve upon [26] by changing the distance to inner product on ℓ_2 normalized embeddings. We include the supervised setting to better understand the effect of using constrained NNs, particularly in the noisy label setting.

Semi-supervised Learning: Several methods combine self-supervised and supervised learning to form semi-supervised methods. S4L [78] uses rotation prediction based loss on the unlabeled set along with cross-entropy loss on the labeled set. Similarly, SuNCEt [3] combines SimCLR [13] and SwAV [11] methods with supervised contrastive loss. Pseudo-labeling is frequently used in semi-supervised learning. In Pseudo-Label [40], the network is trained with cross-entropy loss using supervised data on the labeled examples and pseudo-labels on the unlabeled ones. In SimCLR-v2 [14], a teacher network is pre-trained using SimCLR [13] and fine-tuned with supervised labels. The teacher is then distilled to a student network using pseudo-labels on the unlabeled set. FixMatch [57] uses pseudo-labels obtained using a weakly augmented image to train a strongly augmented version of the same image. UDA [74] leverages strong data augmentation techniques in enforcing this consistency in pseudo-labels across augmentations. MPL [50] optimizes a student network using pseudo-labels from a teacher network, while the teacher is optimized to maximize the student's performance on the labeled set. PAWS [4] uses consistency based loss on soft pseudo-labels obtained in a non-parametric manner. Our method too uses pseudo-labels to train the unlabeled samples. However, we use the labels as a constraint in MSF [37] and do not directly optimize samples using cross-entropy loss.

Metric Learning: The goal of metric learning is to train a representation that puts two instances close in the embedding space if they are semantically close. Two important methods in metric learning are: triplet loss [17,54,70] and contrastive loss [9,56]. Metric learning methods perform well on tasks like image retrieval [71] and few-shot learning [55,65]. Prototypical networks [55] is similar to a contrastive version of our method with top-*all*.

5   Conclusion

MSF is a recent SSL method that pulls an image towards its nearest neighbors. We argue that the model can benefit from more diverse yet pure neighbors. Hence, we generalize MSF method by constraining the NN search. This opens the door to using the mean-shift idea to various settings of self-supervised, supervised, and semi-supervised. To construct the constraint, our SSL method uses cached augmentations from the previous epoch while the supervised and semi-supervised settings use labels or pseudo-labels. We show that our method outperforms SOTA approaches like MSF in SSL, PAWS in semi-supervised, and supervised contrastive in transfer-learning evaluation of supervised settings.

Acknowledgments. This material is based upon work partially supported by DARPA under Contract No. HR00112190135, the United States Air Force under Contract No. FA8750?19?C?0098, funding from SAP SE, and NSF grants 1845216 and 1920079. Any opinions, findings, and conclusions or recommendations expressed in this material are those of the authors and do not necessarily reflect the views of the United States Air Force, DARPA, or other funding agencies.

References

1. Torchvision models. https://pytorch.org/docs/stable/torchvision/models.html
2. Abbasi Koohpayegani, S., Tejankar, A., Pirsiavash, H.: CompRess: self-supervised learning by compressing representations. In: Advances in Neural Information Processing Systems 33 (2020)
3. Assran, M., Ballas, N., Castrejon, L., Rabbat, M.: Supervision accelerates pretraining in contrastive semi-supervised learning of visual representations. arXiv preprint arXiv:2006.10803 (2020)
4. Assran, M., Caron, M., Misra, I., Bojanowski, P., Joulin, A., Ballas, N., Rabbat, M.: Semi-supervised learning of visual features by non-parametrically predicting view assignments with support samples. In: ICCV (2021)
5. Azabou, M., et al.: Mine your own view: self-supervised learning through across-sample prediction. arXiv preprint arXiv:2102.10106 (2021)
6. Bagherinezhad, H., Horton, M., Rastegari, M., Farhadi, A.: Label refinery: improving ImageNet classification through label progression. arXiv preprint arXiv:1805.02641 (2018)
7. Baum, E., Wilczek, F.: Supervised learning of probability distributions by neural networks. In: Anderson, D. (ed.) Neural Information Processing Systems. American Institute of Physics (1988). https://proceedings.neurips.cc/paper/1987/file/eccbc87e4b5ce2fe28308fd9f2a7baf3-Paper.pdf
8. Bossard, L., Guillaumin, M., Van Gool, L.: Food-101 – mining discriminative components with random forests. In: Fleet, D., Pajdla, T., Schiele, B., Tuytelaars, T. (eds.) ECCV 2014. LNCS, vol. 8694, pp. 446–461. Springer, Cham (2014). https://doi.org/10.1007/978-3-319-10599-4_29

9. Bromley, J., Guyon, I., LeCun, Y., Säckinger, E., Shah, R.: Signature verification using a "Siamese" time delay neural network. In: Advances in neural information processing systems 6, pp. 737–744 (1993)
10. Caron, M., Bojanowski, P., Joulin, A., Douze, M.: Deep Clustering for Unsupervised Learning of Visual Features. In: Ferrari, V., Hebert, M., Sminchisescu, C., Weiss, Y. (eds.) Computer Vision – ECCV 2018. LNCS, vol. 11218, pp. 139–156. Springer, Cham (2018). https://doi.org/10.1007/978-3-030-01264-9_9
11. Caron, M., Misra, I., Mairal, J., Goyal, P., Bojanowski, P., Joulin, A.: Unsupervised learning of visual features by contrasting cluster assignments. In: Advances in Neural Information Processing Systems, pp. 9912–9924. Curran Associates, Inc. (2020). https://proceedings.neurips.cc/paper/2020/file/70feb62b69f16e0238f741fab228fec2-Paper.pdf
12. Caron, M., et al.: Emerging properties in self-supervised vision transformers (2021)
13. Chen, T., Kornblith, S., Norouzi, M., Hinton, G.: A simple framework for contrastive learning of visual representations. In: International Conference on Machine Learning, pp. 1597–1607. PMLR (2020)
14. Chen, T., Kornblith, S., Swersky, K., Norouzi, M., Hinton, G.E.: Big self-supervised models are strong semi-supervised learners. In: Advances in Neural Information Processing Systems 33, pp. 22243–22255 (2020)
15. Chen, X., Fan, H., Girshick, R., He, K.: Improved baselines with momentum contrastive learning. arXiv preprint arXiv:2003.04297 (2020)
16. Chen, X., He, K.: Exploring simple Siamese representation learning. arXiv preprint arXiv:2011.10566 (2020)
17. Chopra, S., Hadsell, R., LeCun, Y.: Learning a similarity metric discriminatively, with application to face verification. In: 2005 IEEE Computer Society Conference on Computer Vision and Pattern Recognition (CVPR 2005), vol. 1, pp. 539–546. IEEE (2005)
18. Cimpoi, M., Maji, S., Kokkinos, I., Mohamed, S., Vedaldi, A.: Describing textures in the wild. In: Computer Vision and Pattern Recognition (2014)
19. Cubuk, E.D., Zoph, B., Shlens, J., Le, Q.: RandAugment: practical automated data augmentation with a reduced search space. In: Larochelle, H., Ranzato, M., Hadsell, R., Balcan, M.F., Lin, H. (eds.) Advances in Neural Information Processing Systems, vol. 33, pp. 18613–18624. Curran Associates, Inc. (2020). https://proceedings.neurips.cc/paper/2020/file/d85b63ef0ccb114d0a3bb7b7d808028f-Paper.pdf
20. Dosovitskiy, A., Springenberg, J.T., Riedmiller, M., Brox, T.: Discriminative unsupervised feature learning with convolutional neural networks. In: Advances in Neural Information Processing Systems, pp. 766–774 (2014)
21. Dwibedi, D., Aytar, Y., Tompson, J., Sermanet, P., Zisserman, A.: With a little help from my friends: nearest-neighbor contrastive learning of visual representations (2021)
22. Fei-Fei, L., Fergus, R., Perona, P.: Learning generative visual models from few training examples: an incremental Bayesian approach tested on 101 object categories. In: Computer Vision and Pattern Recognition Workshop (2004)
23. Furlanello, T., Lipton, Z.C., Tschannen, M., Itti, L., Anandkumar, A.: Born again neural networks (2018)
24. Gidaris, S., Bursuc, A., Puy, G., Komodakis, N., Cord, M., Perez, P.: OBoW: online bag-of-visual-words generation for self-supervised learning. In: Proceedings of the IEEE/CVF Conference on Computer Vision and Pattern Recognition (CVPR), pp. 6830–6840, June 2021

25. Gidaris, S., Singh, P., Komodakis, N.: Unsupervised representation learning by predicting image rotations. In: International Conference on Learning Representations (2018). https://openreview.net/forum?id=S1v4N2l0-
26. Goldberger, J., Hinton, G.E., Roweis, S., Salakhutdinov, R.R.: Neighbourhood components analysis. In: Advances in Neural Information Processing Systems 17, pp. 513–520 (2004)
27. Grill, J.B., et al.: Bootstrap your own latent: a new approach to self-supervised learning. arXiv preprint arXiv:2006.07733 (2020)
28. Han, T., Xie, W., Zisserman, A.: Self-supervised co-training for video representation learning (2021)
29. He, K., Fan, H., Wu, Y., Xie, S., Girshick, R.: Momentum contrast for unsupervised visual representation learning. In: Proceedings of the IEEE/CVF Conference on Computer Vision and Pattern Recognition, pp. 9729–9738 (2020)
30. He, K., Zhang, X., Ren, S., Sun, J.: Deep residual learning for image recognition. In: Proceedings of the IEEE Conference on Computer Vision and Pattern Recognition, pp. 770–778 (2016)
31. Hénaff, O.J., et al.: Data-efficient image recognition with contrastive predictive coding. arXiv preprint arXiv:1905.09272 (2019)
32. Hinton, G., Vinyals, O., Dean, J.: Distilling the knowledge in a neural network. arXiv preprint arXiv:1503.02531 (2015)
33. Huang, J., Dong, Q., Gong, S., Zhu, X.: Unsupervised deep learning via affinity diffusion. In: Proceedings of the AAAI Conference on Artificial Intelligence, vol. 34, pp. 11029–11036 (2020)
34. Huynh, T., Kornblith, S., Walter, M.R., Maire, M., Khademi, M.: Boosting contrastive self-supervised learning with false negative cancellation. arXiv preprint arXiv:2011.11765 (2020)
35. Kalantidis, Y., Sariyildiz, M.B., Pion, N., Weinzaepfel, P., Larlus, D.: Hard negative mixing for contrastive learning. In: Advances in Neural Information Processing Systems (2020)
36. Khosla, P., et al.: Supervised contrastive learning. In: Advances in Neural Information Processing Systems 33 (2020)
37. Koohpayegani, S.A., Tejankar, A., Pirsiavash, H.: Mean shift for self-supervised learning. In: Proceedings of the IEEE/CVF International Conference on Computer Vision (ICCV), pp. 10326–10335, October 2021
38. Krause, J., Stark, M., Deng, J., Fei-Fei, L.: 3D object representations for fine-grained categorization. In: Workshop on 3D Representation and Recognition, Sydney, Australia (2013)
39. Krizhevsky, A.: Learning multiple layers of features from tiny images. Technical report, University of Toronto (2009)
40. Lee, D.H., et al.: Pseudo-label: the simple and efficient semi-supervised learning method for deep neural networks. In: Workshop on challenges in representation learning, ICML, vol. 3, p. 896 (2013)
41. Lee, K., Zhu, Y., Sohn, K., Li, C.L., Shin, J., Lee, H.: i-mix: a domain-agnostic strategy for contrastive representation learning. In: International Conference on Learning Representations (2020)
42. Levin, E., Fleisher, M.: Accelerated learning in layered neural networks. Complex Syst. **2**(625–640), 3 (1988)
43. Maji, S., Rahtu, E., Kannala, J., Blaschko, M.B., Vedaldi, A.: Fine-grained visual classification of aircraft. arXiv preprint arXiv:1306.5151 (2013)
44. Misra, I., van der Maaten, L.: Self-supervised learning of pretext-invariant representations. arXiv preprint arXiv:1912.01991 (2019)

45. Müller, R., Kornblith, S., Hinton, G.: When does label smoothing help? (2020)
46. Nilsback, M.E., Zisserman, A.: Automated flower classification over a large number of classes. In: Indian Conference on Computer Vision, Graphics and Image Processing (2008)
47. Noroozi, M., Favaro, P.: Unsupervised learning of visual representations by solving jigsaw puzzles. In: Leibe, B., Matas, J., Sebe, N., Welling, M. (eds.) ECCV 2016. LNCS, vol. 9910, pp. 69–84. Springer, Cham (2016). https://doi.org/10.1007/978-3-319-46466-4_5
48. Noroozi, M., Pirsiavash, H., Favaro, P.: Representation learning by learning to count. In: Proceedings of the IEEE International Conference on Computer Vision, pp. 5898–5906 (2017)
49. Parkhi, O.M., Vedaldi, A., Zisserman, A., Jawahar, C.V.: Cats and dogs. In: Computer Vision and Pattern Recognition (2012)
50. Pham, H., Dai, Z., Xie, Q., Le, Q.V.: Meta pseudo labels. In: Proceedings of the IEEE/CVF Conference on Computer Vision and Pattern Recognition, pp. 11557–11568 (2021)
51. Reed, C.J., Metzger, S., Srinivas, A., Darrell, T., Keutzer, K.: SelfAugment: automatic augmentation policies for self-supervised learning. In: Proceedings of the IEEE/CVF Conference on Computer Vision and Pattern Recognition, pp. 2674–2683 (2021)
52. Rumelhart, D.E., Hinton, G.E., Williams, R.J.: Learning representations by back-propagating errors. Nature **323**(6088), 533–536 (1986)
53. Salakhutdinov, R., Hinton, G.: Learning a nonlinear embedding by preserving class neighbourhood structure. In: Artificial Intelligence and Statistics, pp. 412–419. PMLR (2007)
54. Schroff, F., Kalenichenko, D., Philbin, J.: FaceNet: a unified embedding for face recognition and clustering. In: Proceedings of the IEEE Conference on Computer Vision and Pattern Recognition, pp. 815–823 (2015)
55. Snell, J., Swersky, K., Zemel, R.S.: Prototypical networks for few-shot learning. arXiv preprint arXiv:1703.05175 (2017)
56. Sohn, K.: Improved deep metric learning with multi-class n-pair loss objective. In: Proceedings of the 30th International Conference on Neural Information Processing Systems, pp. 1857–1865 (2016)
57. Sohn, K., et al.: FixMatch: simplifying semi-supervised learning with consistency and confidence. In: Advances in Neural Information Processing Systems 33 (2020)
58. Sukhbaatar, S., Bruna, J., Paluri, M., Bourdev, L., Fergus, R.: Training convolutional networks with noisy labels (2015)
59. Szegedy, C., Vanhoucke, V., Ioffe, S., Shlens, J., Wojna, Z.: Rethinking the inception architecture for computer vision (2015)
60. Tejankar, A., Koohpayegani, S.A., Pillai, V., Favaro, P., Pirsiavash, H.: ISD: self-supervised learning by iterative similarity distillation. In: Proceedings of the IEEE/CVF International Conference on Computer Vision (ICCV), pp. 9609–9618, October 2021
61. Tian, Y., Krishnan, D., Isola, P.: Contrastive multiview coding. arXiv preprint arXiv:1906.05849 (2019)
62. Tian, Y., Sun, C., Poole, B., Krishnan, D., Schmid, C., Isola, P.: What makes for good views for contrastive learning? In: Advances in Neural Information Processing Systems, vol. 33, pp. 6827–6839. Curran Associates, Inc. (2020). https://proceedings.neurips.cc/paper/2020/file/4c2e5eaae9152079b9e95845750bb9ab-Paper.pdf

63. Touvron, H., Sablayrolles, A., Douze, M., Cord, M., Jégou, H.: Grafit: learning fine-grained image representations with coarse labels (2020)
64. Tsai, Y.H.H., Li, T., Liu, W., Liao, P., Salakhutdinov, R., Morency, L.P.: Integrating auxiliary information in self-supervised learning (2021)
65. Vinyals, O., Blundell, C., Lillicrap, T., Kavukcuoglu, K., Wierstra, D.: Matching networks for one shot learning (2017)
66. Wang, F., Liu, H., Guo, D., Fuchun, S.: Unsupervised representation learning by invariance propagation. In: Advances in Neural Information Processing Systems, vol. 33, pp. 3510–3520. Curran Associates, Inc. (2020). https://proceedings.neurips.cc/paper/2020/file/23af4b45f1e166141a790d1a3126e77a-Paper.pdf
67. Wang, G., Wang, K., Wang, G., Torr, P.H.S., Lin, L.: Solving inefficiency of self-supervised representation learning (2021)
68. Wang, X., Liu, Z., Yu, S.X.: Unsupervised feature learning by cross-level instance-group discrimination. In: Proceedings of the IEEE/CVF Conference on Computer Vision and Pattern Recognition (CVPR), pp. 12586–12595, June 2021
69. Wei, C., Wang, H., Shen, W., Yuille, A.: CO2: consistent contrast for unsupervised visual representation learning. arXiv preprint arXiv:2010.02217 (2020)
70. Weinberger, K.Q., Blitzer, J., Saul, L.K.: Distance metric learning for large margin nearest neighbor classification. In: Advances in Neural Information Processing Systems, pp. 1473–1480 (2006)
71. Wu, C.Y., Manmatha, R., Smola, A.J., Krahenbuhl, P.: Sampling matters in deep embedding learning. In: Proceedings of the IEEE International Conference on Computer Vision (ICCV), October 2017
72. Wu, Z., Efros, A.A., Yu, S.X.: Improving generalization via scalable neighborhood component analysis (2018)
73. Xiao, J., Hays, J., Ehinger, K.A., Oliva, A., Torralba, A.: Sun database: large-scale scene recognition from abbey to zoo. In: Computer Vision and Pattern Recognition (2010)
74. Xie, Q., Dai, Z., Hovy, E., Luong, M.T., Le, Q.V.: Unsupervised data augmentation for consistency training. In: NeurIPS (2020)
75. Xu, Y., Qian, Q., Li, H., Jin, R., Hu, J.: Weakly supervised representation learning with coarse labels (2021)
76. Asano, Y.M., Rupprecht, C., Vedaldi, A.: Self-labelling via simultaneous clustering and representation learning. In: International Conference on Learning Representations (2020). https://openreview.net/forum?id=Hyx-jyBFPr
77. Yun, S., Han, D., Oh, S.J., Chun, S., Choe, J., Yoo, Y.: CutMix: regularization strategy to train strong classifiers with localizable features (2019)
78. Zhai, X., Oliver, A., Kolesnikov, A., Beyer, L.: S4L: self-supervised semi-supervised learning. In: The IEEE International Conference on Computer Vision (ICCV), October 2019
79. Zhang, H., Cisse, M., Dauphin, Y.N., Lopez-Paz, D.: mixup: beyond empirical risk minimization (2018)
80. Zhang, R., Isola, P., Efros, A.A.: Colorful image colorization. In: Leibe, B., Matas, J., Sebe, N., Welling, M. (eds.) ECCV 2016. LNCS, vol. 9907, pp. 649–666. Springer, Cham (2016). https://doi.org/10.1007/978-3-319-46487-9_40
81. Zhang, Z., Sabuncu, M.R.: Generalized cross entropy loss for training deep neural networks with noisy labels. arXiv preprint arXiv:1805.07836 (2018)
82. Zhuang, C., Zhai, A.L., Yamins, D.: Local aggregation for unsupervised learning of visual embeddings. In: Proceedings of the IEEE/CVF International Conference on Computer Vision, pp. 6002–6012 (2019)

Revisiting the Critical Factors of Augmentation-Invariant Representation Learning

Junqiang Huang, Xiangwen Kong, and Xiangyu Zhang$^{(\boxtimes)}$

MEGVII Technology, Beijing, China
{huangjunqiang,kongxiangwen,zhangxiangyu}@megvii.com

Abstract. We focus on better understanding the critical factors of augmentation-invariant representation learning. We revisit MoCo v2 and BYOL and try to prove the authenticity of the following assumption: different frameworks bring about representations of different characteristics even with the same pretext task. We establish the first benchmark for fair comparisons between MoCo v2 and BYOL, and observe: (i) sophisticated model configurations enable better adaptation to pre-training dataset; (ii) mismatched optimization strategies of pre-training and fine-tuning hinder model from achieving competitive transfer performances. Given the fair benchmark, we make further investigation and find asymmetry of network structure endows contrastive frameworks to work well under the linear evaluation protocol, while may hurt the transfer performances on long-tailed classification tasks. Moreover, negative samples do not make models more sensible to the choice of data augmentations, nor does the asymmetric network structure. We believe our findings provide useful information for future work.

1 Introduction

Recently, with the advancement of research on pretext tasks [11,12,16,29,30,40], self-supervised learning (SSL) presents extraordinary potential in computer vision, pushing the frontier of transfer learning. The effectiveness of self-supervised learned representations has been empirically verified. Compared to supervised pre-training counterparts, MoCo series [7,9,20] achieves comparable or even better performances on object detection, semantic segmentation, etc. Moreover, under the linear evaluation protocol on ImageNet [34] (an often used evaluation metric for SSL), BYOL [18] and SwAV [3] have largely shrunk the gap with supervised learning.

J. Huang and X. Kong—Equal Contribution.
Code: https://github.com/megvii-research/revisitAIRL.

Supplementary Information The online version contains supplementary material available at https://doi.org/10.1007/978-3-031-19821-2_3.

S. Avidan et al. (Eds.): ECCV 2022, LNCS 13691, pp. 42–58, 2022.
https://doi.org/10.1007/978-3-031-19821-2_3

Among various pretext tasks, one of the most promising ways is to pull together the positive sample pairs (different augmented views of the same image), which enables the model to learn augmentation-invariant representations. The simplicity of this pretext task also brings about a notorious problem: without careful design, the model will collapse to a trivial solution that all images are mapped to a constant vector, resulting in useless representations. To avoid this collapse, contrastive methods like MoCo impose regularization by pushing away the negative sample pairs (different images), while BYOL develops the asymmetric siamese network with a stop-gradient operation. Though sharing the same pretext task, MoCo v2 and BYOL show different results of linear classification and transfer learning. As reported in [8,18], BYOL has higher linear accuracy, while MoCo v2 presents better transferability. Given this observation, it is natural to assume different frameworks bring about representations of different characteristics.

To prove or disprove the above assumption, it is essential to build the benchmark for fair comparison between contrastive frameworks and BYOL. Since MoCo v2 shares many similarities with BYOL, which is convenient to perform controlled experiments, we choose it as the representative of contrastive methods. We aim to study the experimental impact of the following variables on augmentation-invariant representation learning: model configurations (i.e., network architecture, symmetry of training loss, etc.), combination of data augmentations, and optimization strategies. The evaluation criteria consist of linear classification accuracy and transfer performances of typical downstream tasks. Our efforts and contributions will be described next.

We challenge the opinion arising from previous experimental observations of [8,18] that the superiority of linear evaluation is unique to SSL frameworks without negative sample pairs (e.g., BYOL [18], SimSiam [8]). We ablate the differences in model configurations between MoCo v2 and BYOL, including network architecture, rule of momentum update, and symmetry of training loss. The differences are iteratively removed based on MoCo v2. Without searching pre-training hyper-parameters, the linear accuracy of MoCo v2 on ImageNet consistently benefits from the sophisticated model configurations (72.0% top-1 accuracy for 200-epoch pre-training). On top of this, we reformulate MoCo v2 into a more effective version as shown in Fig. 1c (MoCo v2+ for short). Moreover, when pre-training with more complex data augmentations, MoCo v2+ receives further improvement (72.4%). Our study suggests that the sophisticated design of model configurations affects a lot on the pretext task's performance.

Second, we try to uncover the mystery of BYOL's poor transferability. It seems that practitioners struggle to fully unleash the potential of BYOL even with heavy computation to search fine-tuning learning rates [8]. We tackle this issue by investigating the optimization strategy (e.g., optimizer, learning rate, etc.) of pre-training and fine-tuning. By delving into the original implementation of BYOL and its LARS optimizer [42], we find the distribution of LARS-trained representations is different from that of SGD-trained representations. The currently used fine-tuning optimization strategy best selected for SGD-

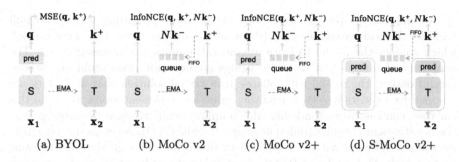

Fig. 1. This figure compares the structures of four SSL frameworks discussed in our paper. All of them are siamese network along with the stop-gradient operation and momentum update. For convenient reference, we name the encoder updated by gradients as student encoder, and the encoder with stop-gradient operation as the teacher encoder. They are represented by the capital letter, **S** and **T** respectively. Note that the backbones of both student and teacher encoder include a projector that is a non-linear 2-layer MLP (not shown in the picture). **pred** in the green box represents the predictor (also a non-linear 2-layer MLP). The only difference between MoCo v2+ and S-MoCo v2+ lies in the existence of teacher encoder's predictor (Color figure online)

trained features is not suitable for LARS-trained features. We therefore can conclude that the mismatched optimizer choices (LARS for pre-training and SGD for fine-tuning) cause the sub-optimal performances of BYOL. Obviously, using matched optimizers or searching optimization hyper-parameters for fine-tuning can circumvent this issue. In this paper, we also propose one simple yet effective technique NormRescale to solve this problem. NormRescale rescales the weight norm of LARS-trained model by the SGD-trained counterpart. NormRescale works well across many downstream tasks and significantly outperforms the baseline, which proves its capability to recover BYOL's transferability.

Thus far, a fair benchmark has been established. We can make a robust argument that it is not the frameworks but the training details that determine the characteristics of learned representations.

Thanks to the unified training details, we are able to quest for the experimental impact of the asymmetric network structure. Previous work [8,9,18] has verified the effectiveness of asymmetric network structure for linear classification. The influences on transfer learning are yet to be examined. To this goal, we symmetrize the network structure of MoCo v2+, which gives us the Symmetric MoCo v2+ (abbreviated as S-MoCo v2+, the structure can be seen in Fig. 1d). Based on the comparison among MoCo v2+, S-MoCo v2+, and BYOL, our findings are threefold: (i) asymmetric network structure leads to better adaptation on the pre-training datasets but does not mean higher transferability; (ii) the performances of long-tailed classification datasets are more outstanding for contrastive methods, and will be further improved by the symmetric network structure; (iii) contrary to the claim in [18,43], contrastive methods with or without symmetry of network structure are not more susceptible to data augmentations than BYOL.

Compared to the current literature, our findings are surprising and challenge existing understanding of self-supervised learning. The extensive experiments convey a main idea that *training details determine the characteristics of learned representations*. As long as we align the model configurations, combination of data augmentations and optimization strategy of MoCo v2 and BYOL, they show similar performances in linear evaluation and transferring to other downstream tasks. We hope the fair benchmark and our observations will motivate future research.

2   Related Work

Augmentation-Invariant Representation Learning. There have been a great deal of pretext task [2–4, 6, 11, 12, 14, 16, 18, 20, 23, 28–31, 35, 37, 39–41, 43] proposed in self-supervised learning. Amongst them, augmentation-invariant representation learning shines brightly. The core idea of augmentation-invariant representation learning is to attract different augmented views of the same image as closely as possible. Many research branches are derived from the creative endeavor of the community. Contrastive methods [6, 20, 23, 30, 37, 39, 41] follow the idea proposed in [19] to pull together the positive sample pairs and push away the negative sample pairs. BYOL [18] and SimSiam [8] directly minimize the distance of positive sample pairs, along with an asymmetric siamese network. W-MSE [14] attracts the positive pairs based on the whitening features. SwAV [3] first performs online clustering and then classification according to the clustering label generated by its positive sample. DINO [4] optimizes the distribution distances of positive sample pairs along with the "centering" and "sharpening" operations. BarlowTwins [43] maximizes the correlation of positive sample pairs and decorrelates the features of different images. Research on augmentation-invariant representation learning has sprung up, which also illustrates the advantages of augmentation-invariant representation learning as a pretext task for self-supervised learning.

Impact of Training Details. Discussion about the impact of training details on representation quality is not new to the community. Previous work has explored which factors enable performance promotion for their algorithms. For example, in order to boost the accuracy of linear evaluation, MoCo series [7, 9, 20] and SimCLR [6] search for optimization hyper-parameters (e.g., learning rate, learning rate decay schedule, batch size, etc.), the combination of data augmentations, and the number of negative samples. BYOL [18, 33] and SimSiam [8] ablates the coefficients of momentum update and the choice of batch normalization. Due to the lack of a fair benchmark, the successes of these methods seem to be binding together with their unique framework. We are not aware of whether future work can learn from their successes.

Other work like [44] makes a contribution to better understanding the transfer performance of instance discrimination. But the scope of their study is narrowed down to MoCo v2. SimSiam [8] pays more attention to what the optimization problem for frameworks without using negative samples is. [13] focuses on the fine-tuning results based on frozen pre-trained weights. Unlike them, we provide extensive experiments based on MoCo v2 and BYOL that are pre-trained given various training details. The standard evaluation protocol includes linear evaluation on pre-training datasets and transfer performance of some typical downstream tasks. Our goal is to build the first fair benchmark to compare MoCo v2 and BYOL, two influential frameworks in augmentation-invariant representation learning.

Asymmetric Network Structure. The notorious problem of augmentation-invariant representation learning is that without careful design, all input images are mapped to a constant vector. The solution of contrastive frameworks is simple and intuitive—repulsing the negative sample pairs. Likewise, feature decorrelation methods [4,14,24] separate the features according to the specific rules to avoid the collapse. BYOL [18] and SimSiam [8] rely on the asymmetric network structure and the stop-gradient operation. To study the optimization problem based on asymmetric network structure, SimSiam ablates many hyper-parameters of pre-training. Later work [38] concentrates on the theoretical influence of the asymmetric network structures.

It should be noted that the focus of this work is not on advancing the development of SSL by proposing a new algorithm. On the opposite, we aim to present a fair and comprehensive investigation based on existing algorithms to gain better understanding.

3   Experimental Setup

3.1   Framework

In this section, we briefly review two well-known frameworks of augmentation-invariant representation learning: MoCo v2 [7] and BYOL [18]. Both of them adopt the design of teacher-student siamese network with momentum update rule [36], where the teacher encoder is updated by the exponential moving average of the student encoder. This unity of network structure is convenient for us to perform controlled experiments. It is worth noting that other self-supervised learning frameworks pre-training with different pretext tasks are beyond the scope of our paper.

MoCo v2. By optimizing the contrastive loss [19], MoCo v2 learns to pull the features of positive sample pairs (different augmented views of the same image) together and to push the features of negative sample pairs (different images) away. Different from other contrastive frameworks [6,28,30,37,40], MoCo v2 designs a memory queue (first-in, first-out) to store features computed in previous training iterations. Meanwhile, the rule of momentum update helps maintain the feature consistency. In practice, a batch of input images will be independently transformed twice, resulting in a batch of positive sample pairs. The teacher-student siamese network then encodes them as features respectively. The mini-batch contrastive loss is described as follow:

$$L = -\frac{1}{N} \sum_{\mathbf{q}} \log \left(\frac{\exp(\mathbf{q}^\mathsf{T} \mathbf{k}^+/\tau)}{\exp(\mathbf{q}^\mathsf{T} \mathbf{k}^+/\tau) + \sum_{\mathbf{k}^-} \exp(\mathbf{q}^\mathsf{T} \mathbf{k}^-/\tau)} \right) \tag{1}$$

$\mathbf{q}$ and $\mathbf{k}^+$ stand for the student feature and teacher feature that are encoded from the positive sample pair by the siamese network respectively. $\mathbf{k}^-$ is the negative feature stored in the memory queue. N is the batch size and τ is the temperature (for the following experiments of our paper, we use 0.2 by default). After back-propagating the contrastive loss, all the teacher features $\{\mathbf{k}^+\}$ are enqueued and the "oldest" of the memory queue features are dequeued.

BYOL. Similar to contrastive methods, BYOL learns to attract the positive sample pairs as close as possible in feature space without regularization of negative sample pairs. Previous work [8,18] have stated the asymmetric structure of siamese network and the stop-gradient operation (no gradient will flow to the teacher encoder) are critical to avoiding trivial solution in BYOL. The asymmetric structure refers to that the student branch of siamese network is followed by a predictor (a non-linear two-layer MLP), yielding the asymmetry between student and teacher branches. The mini-batch training loss of BYOL is symmetric:

$$L = \frac{1}{N} \left(\sum_{\mathbf{q_1}} \|\mathbf{q_1} - \mathbf{k_1}\|^2 + \sum_{\mathbf{q_2}} \|\mathbf{q_2} - \mathbf{k_2}\|^2 \right) \tag{2}$$

The samples from a positive pair are mapped to $\mathbf{q_1}$ and $\mathbf{q_2}$ by the student encoder, and mapped to $\mathbf{k_1}$ and $\mathbf{k_2}$ by the teacher encoder. $\|\cdot\|$ is the Euclidean distance.

3.2   Pre-training and Evaluation

In this section, we provide the required information on pre-training and fine-tuning for our experiments. The backbone of siamese network is ResNet-50 [22], and the pre-training dataset is ImageNet [34]. The details about data augmentations can be found in Supplementary Materials.

Pre-training. To re-implement MoCo v2 efficiently, we make the following adjustments: increasing the training batch size to 1024, linearly scaling up the learning rate to 0.12 according to [17], and introducing a 10-epoch linear warm-up schedule before the decay of learning rate. Note that these modifications do not change the performance of MoCo v2. To reproduce BYOL, we faithfully follow the training settings in [18]. There are two combinations of data augmentations mentioned in BYOL. We use the symmetric one for our experiments. In the crossover study of Sect. 4.2, when training MoCo v2+ with LARS [42] optimizer, the training hyper-parameters are copied from the implementation of the original BYOL. Likewise, when training BYOL with SGD optimizer, we adopt the same hyper-parameters used in MoCo v2+.

Linear Evaluation. The common practice of linear evaluation is to freeze the backbone and train a linear classifier based on the fixed representations. Here, we provide two settings for the training phase of linear evaluation. For models pre-trained with SGD optimizer, we use SGD optimizer to train for 100 epochs. The batch size is 256, and the initial learning rate is 30 which is decayed by a factor of 10 at the 60 and 80-th epoch. For models pre-trained with LARS optimizer, we follow the hyper-parameters adopted in BYOL. We use SGD optimizer with Nesterov to train for 80 epochs. The batch size is 1024, and the initial learning rate is 0.8 and is decayed to 0 by the cosine schedule. Both training settings use a momentum of 0.9 and no weight decay. After training, we report the single-crop classification accuracy on ImageNet validation set.

PASCAL VOC Object Detection. We transfer the pre-trained models on PASCAL VOC [15] for object detection. We strictly follow the training details in [20], which uses a Faster R-CNN [32] detector with a backbone of ResNet50-C4. It takes 9k iterations to fine-tune on `trainval2007` set and 24k iterations to fine-tune on `trainval07+12` set. We report the results evaluated on `test2007` set.

COCO Object Detection and Instance Segmentation. We fine-tune the pre-trained models on COCO [27] for object detection and instance segmentation. We adopt Mask R-CNN [21] as the detector with two kinds of backbone, ResNet50-C4 and ResNet50-FPN. For a fair comparison, the training settings are exactly the same used in [20]. Following the 1× optimization setting, it takes 90k iterations to fine-tune on `train2017` set. Finally, we report the results evaluated on `val2017` set.

CityScapes Semantic Segmentation. We train on CityScapes [10] to evaluate the performance on semantic segmentation. For easy re-implementation, we use DeepLab-v3 architecture [5]. The backbone is ResNet50 with a stride of 8. The crop size is 512×1024 for training, and 1024×2048 for testing. It takes 40k iterations to fine-tune on `train_fine` set, and finally we report the results evaluated on `val` set.

4   Experiments and Analyses

4.1   What Matters in Linear Evaluations?

In the light of previous work, SSL methods without negative sample pairs (e.g., BYOL [18], SimSiam [8], DINO [4]) have higher accuracy in linear evaluation, compared to contrastive methods. What on earth hinders contrastive methods like MoCo v2 from better adapting to the pre-training dataset to achieve better performance in linear evaluation, the negative sample pairs or other previously ignored factors?

   In this subsection, we seek to answer the question by exploring how to elevate MoCo v2 to achieve higher accuracy in linear evaluation. Given this goal, it

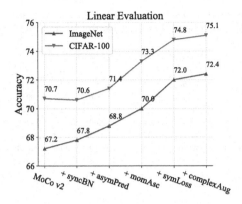

Fig. 2. Top-1 accuracy of linear evaluation on ImageNet and CIFAR-100. The x-axis represents the modifications of model configurations. We use MoCo v2 as our baseline. All models are trained for 200 epochs. The trend of these two curves indicates that the linear accuracy consistently benefits from the sophisticated model configurations

is desirable to improve linear accuracy under modifications to model configurations. With reference to BYOL, we make the following adjustment on MoCo v2. First, we replace the ShufflingBN with synchronized BN (SyncBN). However, this direct replacement does not bring the expected performance improvement. Hence we insert a BN to the hidden layer of the projector (a non-linear two-layer MLP after the backbone) as BYOL does. Second, we add a predictor (an MLP similar to projector) at the end of student encoder, yielding asymmetry between student encoder and teacher encoder. Third, the coefficient of momentum update no longer stays still, but increases from 0.99 to 1 according to a cosine schedule. Forth, we symmetrize the contrastive loss, as has been done in [3,6,8,18]. For convenient reference, we name this enhanced framework as MoCo v2+, which is an extension of MoCo v2. Last, we train MoCo v2+ with more complex data augmentations (introducing solarization to the combination)[1].

The results of linear evaluation on ImageNet are in Fig. 2. Surprisingly, the linear accuracy consistently benefits from the modifications even without searching hyper-parameters. When training with more complex augmentations, MoCo v2+ finally catches up to BYOL in terms of linear accuracy (72.4% top-1 accuracy). Among these changes, the symmetrization of contrastive loss brings the most obvious improvement (2.0% accuracy increment). To validate the effectiveness of representations with high linear accuracy on ImageNet, we train a linear classifier on CIFAR-100 [26]. The accuracy curve is in Fig. 2. Similarly, we observe distinct promotions for linear evaluation on CIFAR-100 compared to baseline.

Table 1 presents the transfer performances on downstream tasks. The promotions (about 0.5% improvement) in transfer learning are not as obvious as

---

[1] The detailed information about the combination of data augmentations can be found in Supplementary Materials.

Table 1. The results of transfer learning on detection and segmentation tasks. All models are trained for 200 epochs. The best results are marked as bold

	VOC07	VOC07+12	COCO					CityScapes
	AP_{50}	AP_{50}	AP_{box}^{C4}	AP_{seg}^{C4}	AP_{box}^{FPN}	AP_{seg}^{FPN}		mIoU
MoCo v2	76.5	82.2	38.8	34.0	39.5	35.8		77.4
+ SyncBN	76.7	82.0	38.6	33.7	39.7	35.8		76.9
+ Asymmetric Predictor	76.7	82.1	39.0	34.1	39.8	35.9		77.3
+ Momentum Ascending	77.0	82.3	39.0	34.3	39.7	35.8		77.4
+ Symmetric Loss (MoCo v2+)	77.1	**82.7**	**39.4**	**34.5**	40.3	36.5		**77.6**
+ More Complex Augmentations	**77.3**	**82.7**	39.2	34.4	**40.4**	**36.7**		**77.6**
BYOL	71.7	79.1	35.3	31.1	40.8	36.9		76.4

in linear evaluation. One possible explanation for this contradiction is that better adaptation to pre-training dataset is more helpful to those datasets whose distribution are similar to the pre-training dataset. As we can see in Fig. 2, the trends of two curves in Fig. 2 are accordant. In a nutshell, *sophisticated design of model configurations affects a lot on the pretext task's performance.*

4.2 How to Improve Transfer Performances?

Despite BYOL being one of the significant frameworks in SSL, its capability on typical downstream tasks like object detection on VOC [15] and COCO [27] have not received enough attention. From one of only a few studies concerning this problem, we find MoCo v2 outperforms BYOL on VOC and COCO detection and instance segmentation [8]. Table 1 also reflects this issue. We notice these comparisons are based on misaligned optimization strategies. Specifically, BYOL utilizes LARS optimizer [42] to train with large batch size, while MoCo v2+ uses SGD optimizer. In this case, it remains an open question whether BYOL has innately poor transferability on those challenging downstream tasks given the same optimization strategy.

In this subsection, we investigate how to improve transfer performances of BYOL from the perspective of optimization. To understand how optimization strategy influences the transferability of learned representations, we provide a crossover study of SGD and LARS optimizers for pre-training. The results of downstream tasks are in Table 2. Both frameworks are less competitive on most downstream tasks when pre-trained with LARS. It seems that the poor results may originate from the pre-training optimization strategy. There is one exception, though, that LARS-trained models show comparable or even better results for the downstream tasks adopting ResNet50-FPN as backbone. We, therefore, infer that the LARS optimizer does not compromise the quality of learned representations.

By examining the implementation details of BYOL, we find that, unlike SGD, the LARS optimizer does not impose L2-regularization on the parameters of batch normalization layers. As training goes on, the weight norm becomes larger. We can see the clear contrast in Fig. 3a that the weight norms of the LARS-trained model are significantly larger. In other words, the distribution of learned representations is different from those trained by SGD. Fine-tuning LARS-trained models with the hyper-parameters best suited for SGD-trained models naturally yields sub-optimal performances. Thus, we can conclude that *mismatched optimizer used in pre-training and fine-tuning is the reason for performance degeneration in BYOL, but not the framework itself.*

Table 2. The results of crossover study involving SGD and LARS optimizer. All models are trained for 200 epochs. The best results are marked bold

	Optimizer	ImageNet	VOC07	VOC07+12	COCO				CityScapes
		Acc	AP_{50}	AP_{50}	AP_{box}^{C4}	AP_{seg}^{C4}	AP_{box}^{FPN}	AP_{seg}^{FPN}	mIoU
MoCo v2+	SGD	72.0	**77.1**	**82.7**	**39.4**	**34.5**	40.3	36.5	**77.7**
	LARS	**72.5**	62.9	74.4	32.1	28.9	40.0	36.2	73.2
BYOL	SGD	72.1	76.2	82.4	38.8	33.9	39.9	36.1	77.5
	LARS	72.4	71.7	79.1	35.3	31.1	**40.8**	**36.9**	75.2

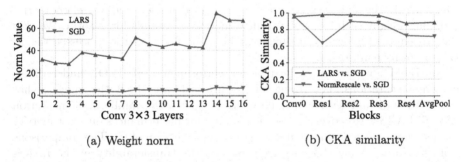

(a) Weight norm

(b) CKA similarity

Fig. 3. (**a**): Weight norms of all conv3 × 3 layers from LARS-trained and SGD-trained models. (**b**): CKA similarities of LARS-trained and SGD-trained representations across all stages of ResNet-50. Best viewed in color (Color figure online)

Table 2 points out a solution to circumvent this issue—using SGD optimizer for pre-training. This solution, however, is not universally effective, since it does not apply to large batch size training where LARS is more popularly used. To alleviate this issue, [8] searches learning rates for fine-tuning LARS-trained models, inevitably inducing heavy computation. Next, we describe two findings that lead us to a flexible approach.

First, we utilize the CKA similarity [25] to measure how similar the representations learned by LARS and SGD are. The blue line of Fig. 3b indicates these representations are sufficiently similar although they follow different distributions. Second, as described in [20], the features for the region proposal are normalized by the newly initialized BN in ResNet50-FPN, while not in ResNet50-C4. We argue the rescale operation in newly initialized BN helps LARS-trained models to adapt to optimization of fine-tuning driven by SGD. Motivated by

Table 3. The downstream performances of BYOL under various implementations. "NR" stands for NormRescale. All models are trained for 200 epochs. The best results are marked bold

	VOC07			VOC07+12			COCO detection			COCO instance seg.		
	AP_{50}	AP	AP_{75}	AP_{50}	AP	AP_{75}	AP_{50}	AP	AP_{75}	AP_{50}^M	AP^M	AP_{75}^M
BYOL-SGD	76.2	**48.1**	**52.9**	**82.4**	56.5	**63.6**	58.5	38.8	42.1	55.2	34.0	36.2
BYOL-LARS	71.7	38.8	37.0	79.1	48.7	51.7	56.2	35.3	37.5	52.3	31.1	32.2
BYOL in [8]	**77.1**	47.0	49.9	81.4	55.3	61.1	57.8	37.9	40.9	54.3	33.2	35.0
BYOL-NR	76.6	**48.1**	51.6	82.1	**56.7**	62.9	**59.3**	**39.3**	**42.6**	**56.0**	**34.5**	**36.7**

the analyses above, we present a simple yet effective technique, NormRescale, to address this issue. Assume we have a well-trained model that is pre-trained by SGD[2]. For any weight of the LARS-trained model, we rescale its norm as follows:

$$\mathbf{w}^* = \|\mathbf{w}_S\| \cdot \frac{\mathbf{w}_L}{\|\mathbf{w}_L\|}, \tag{3}$$

where $\mathbf{w}_L$ is the weight vector of LARS-trained model, and $\mathbf{w}_S$ is the corresponding weight vector of SGD-trained model. $\|\cdot\|$ stands for 2-norm. We skip the procedure of hyper-parameters searching and fine-tune the processed weight $\mathbf{w}^*$ on downstream tasks.

In Table 3, we compare the transfer performances of BYOL under different implementations. The results of NormRescale are about the same as that of BYOL-SGD and significantly better than that of the vanilla implementation (BYOL-LARS). Moreover, it also shows superior performances on most metrics for detection and segmentation against the reproduction of [8]. The comparisons confirm NormRescale can effectively recover the transferability of the LARS-trained model. We also plot the CKA similarities between the representations of BYOL-SGD and NormRescale in Fig. 3 (red line). It can be seen that Norm-Rescale retains the characteristics of LARS-trained representations. Apart from using BYOL-SGD as the anchor weight, we also explore other anchor choices for NormRescale. The detailed comparison can be found in Supplementary Materials.

These results suggest that optimization strategy is the key to the transferability of BYOL. For efficient comparison, we adopt SGD as our default optimizer for all the below experiments. Without confusing references, we continue to use BYOL to stand for SGD-trained BYOL.

Thus far, we have presented the first fair benchmark to compare two important frameworks of SSL, namely MoCo and BYOL. Our extensive experiments show that the performances of linear evaluation and transfer learning are similar in MoCo v2+ and BYOL given the aligned training details, leading to an authentic argument that *the training details determine the characteristics of learned representations.*

---

[2] In default, we choose the 200-epoch SGD-trained BYOL.

Table 4. Results on ImageNet and downstream tasks of BYOL, MoCo v2+, S-MoCo v2+. All models are trained for 200 epochs. The best results are marked bold

	Asymmetry	ImageNet	VOC07	VOC07+12	COCO				CityScapes
		Acc	AP_{50}	AP_{50}	AP^{C4}_{box}	AP^{C4}_{seg}	AP^{FPN}_{box}	AP^{FPN}_{seg}	mIoU
BYOL	✓	72.1	77.2	**82.7**	**39.3**	**34.5**	**40.6**	36.6	77.1
MoCo v2+	✓	**72.4**	**77.3**	**82.7**	39.2	34.4	40.4	**36.7**	**77.6**
S-MoCo v2+		71.2	77.1	82.4	39.1	34.2	**40.6**	**36.7**	77.2

4.3 What Is the Impact of Asymmetric Network Structure?

The asymmetric network structure first proposed in BYOL plays an important role in avoiding model collapse for augmentation-invariant representation learning. There are follow-up studies on the asymmetric structure that are mainly about the theoretical understanding [8,38] and the effectiveness for linear classification [8,9]. Here, we explore the experimental impact of asymmetric structure in transfer learning and its comparison to symmetric one. We symmetrize the network structure of MoCo v2+ by adding an extra predictor to the teacher encoder. We call it Symmetric MoCo v2+ (abbreviated as S-MoCo v2+). We refer to Fig. 1d for visual description. In this subsection, the experiments are mainly about the following three parts.

Standard Evaluation Tasks. We first provide a direct comparison amongst MoCo v2+, S-MoCo v2+, and BYOL on the typical datasets. The results of linear evaluation and transfer learning are listed in Table 4. As shown in the third column (ImageNet Acc), S-MoCo v2 is inferior in linear evaluation, indicating that models with asymmetric structure may better fit pretext tasks. The performances of transfer learning, in contrast, are similarly good on many downstream tasks. The biggest gap between the best and the worst is within 0.4. We conclude that the transferability for these regular downstream tasks may be neutral to the symmetry of network structure.

Long-Tailed Classification Task. We next study the effects on two long-tailed classification tasks (CIFAR-10-LT and CIFAR-100-LT [1]). The effectiveness of pre-trained models is measured in two aspects: linear evaluation and fine-tuning. For solid comparisons, we provide models pre-trained with different hyper-parameters (e.g., learning rate, training epochs, etc.). As plotted in Fig. 4, the horizontal coordinate for each point represents the pre-trained model's linear accuracy on ImageNet and the vertical coordinate stands for linear or fine-tuning accuracy on long-tailed datasets. Our findings can be summarized as follows:

(i) Model with higher linear accuracy on ImageNet shows better performance on CIFAR-10/100-LT under the linear evaluation protocol. But the situation is different for fine-tuning. We do not see a clear trend between linear accuracy on ImageNet and fine-tuning accuracy.

(ii) In all four sub-figures, we can observe a clear ranking result that S-MoCo v2+ has the best effect, followed by MoCo v2+, and finally BYOL. The superiority of contrastive methods in linear evaluation and fine-tuning implies that the regularization imposed by pushing away negative sample pairs which renders a more uniform representation space is conducive to long-tailed classification. Besides, we point out the strength of symmetric network structure, as it provides the best performances of S-MoCo v2+ (see Fig. 4).

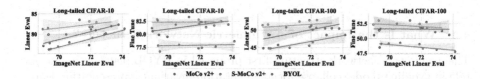

Fig. 4. Linear evaluation and fine-tuning results of BYOL, MoCo v2+ and S-MoCo v2+. The regression lines describe the correlation between linear accuracy on ImageNet and linear or fine-tuning accuracy on long-tailed classification datasets, with confidence intervals in shaded areas. Best viewed in color (Color figure online)

Data Augmentations. We make an attempt to investigate the sensitivity of contrastive methods and BYOL to data augmentations, which has been discussed in [18,43]. The conclusions about this problem are consistent in their work—contrastive methods are more sensitive to the variation of data augmentations. Following our above analyses, we are sceptical about the validity of this conclusion where a fair benchmark is absent. To get a clear picture of it, we ablate data augmentations based on MoCo v2+, S-MoCo v2+, and BYOL. The baseline combination of data augmentations includes random cropping and resizing to 224×224, horizontal flipping, color jittering, gray scale converting, Gaussian blur, and solarization. The specific parameters of augmentations can be found in Supplementary Materials. Likewise, we iteratively remove the data augmentations involving color transformations. The order goes solarization, Gaussian blur, gray scale converting, and color jittering. After removing all color transformations, the combination is the same as used in supervised training. The results are depicted in Fig. 5.

Interestingly, the obvious accuracy gap between contrastive methods and BYOL reported in [18,43] vanishes; instead, we observe similar results of linear accuracy on ImageNet for contrastive methods and BYOL. The comparison of contrastive methods (MoCo v2+ vs. S-MoCo v2+) demonstrates that it is not the asymmetric head that causes these similarities. Therefore, we can present a convincing and empirically verified conclusion that a sufficiently complex combination of data augmentation is equally important for contrastive methods and BYOL. In turn, the consistency of effects between MoCo v2+, S-MoCo v2+ and BYOL suggests that ignoring training details can give misperceptions in SSL.

In addition to the linear accuracy on ImageNet, we also report the transfer performances across various downstream tasks. As clearly shown in Fig. 5, similar phenomena can be found in the results of different downstream tasks that

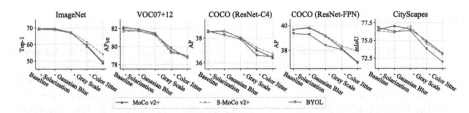

Fig. 5. The results of linear evaluation and downstream tasks under different combinations of data augmentations. Best viewed in color (Color figure online)

transferability is positively correlated to the complexity of data augmentation combinations. Through careful observation, we find that most models meet significant performance degeneration if gray scale converting is cancelled. Strictly speaking, it is biased to believe gray scale converting is so important that SSL methods would face degradation without it. A more likely explanation is that the combination of data augmentations lacks complexity when cancelling out gray scale converting, inducing less competitive representations.

5 Conclusion

In summary, the extensive experiments throughout the paper revolve around the idea that training details determine the characteristics of learned representations in augmentation-invariant representation learning. In the process of verifying the idea, we observe the following:

(i) Sophisticated design of model configurations helps representations better adapt to the pre-training dataset, which in turn improves the linear accuracy on datasets with similar distribution to pre-training dataset.

(ii) What truly prevents BYOL from achieving competitive performances on typical downstream tasks is the mismatched optimization strategy for pre-training and fine-tuning. Using matched optimizers can remedy the performances drop. We also propose one simple yet effective technique to do the same, and it can apply to the situation where using mismatched optimizers is inevitable.

(iii) Asymmetric network structure leads to higher linear accuracy on pre-training dataset, while symmetric one has more competitive results on long-tailed classification tasks. Based on the fair comparisons among MoCo v2+, S-MoCo v2+ and BYOL, we confirm that contrastive methods and BYOL are equally sensitive to data augmentations.

We hope the fair benchmark and our observations will shed light on the understanding of MoCo v2 and BYOL, and help motivate future research to push forward the frontier of SSL.

Acknowledgements. This research was supported by National Key R&D Program of China (No. 2017YFA0700800) and Beijing Academy of Artificial Intelligence (BAAI).

References

1. Cao, K., Wei, C., Gaidon, A., Aréchiga, N., Ma, T.: Learning imbalanced datasets with label-distribution-aware margin loss. In: NeurIPS, pp. 1565–1576 (2019)
2. Caron, M., Bojanowski, P., Joulin, A., Douze, M.: Deep clustering for unsupervised learning of visual features. In: Ferrari, V., Hebert, M., Sminchisescu, C., Weiss, Y. (eds.) Computer Vision – ECCV 2018. LNCS, vol. 11218, pp. 139–156. Springer, Cham (2018). https://doi.org/10.1007/978-3-030-01264-9_9
3. Caron, M., Misra, I., Mairal, J., Goyal, P., Bojanowski, P., Joulin, A.: Unsupervised learning of visual features by contrasting cluster assignments. In: Larochelle, H., Ranzato, M., Hadsell, R., Balcan, M., Lin, H. (eds.) Advances in Neural Information Processing Systems 33: Annual Conference on Neural Information Processing Systems 2020, NeurIPS 2020, Virtual, 6–12 December 2020 (2020)
4. Caron, M., et al.: Emerging properties in self-supervised vision transformers. In: Proceedings of the IEEE/CVF International Conference on Computer Vision, pp. 9650–9660 (2021)
5. Chen, L.C., Papandreou, G., Schroff, F., Adam, H.: Rethinking atrous convolution for semantic image segmentation. arXiv preprint arXiv:1706.05587 (2017)
6. Chen, T., Kornblith, S., Norouzi, M., Hinton, G.E.: A simple framework for contrastive learning of visual representations. In: Proceedings of the 37th International Conference on Machine Learning, ICML 2020, Virtual Event, 13–18 July 2020. Proceedings of Machine Learning Research, vol. 119, pp. 1597–1607. PMLR (2020)
7. Chen, X., Fan, H., Girshick, R., He, K.: Improved baselines with momentum contrastive learning. arXiv preprint arXiv:2003.04297 (2020)
8. Chen, X., He, K.: Exploring simple siamese representation learning. arXiv preprint arXiv:2011.10566 (2020)
9. Chen, X., Xie, S., He, K.: An empirical study of training self-supervised vision transformers. arXiv preprint arXiv:2104.02057 (2021)
10. Cordts, M., et al.: The cityscapes dataset for semantic urban scene understanding. In: 2016 IEEE Conference on Computer Vision and Pattern Recognition, CVPR 2016, Las Vegas, NV, USA, 27–30 June 2016, pp. 3213–3223. IEEE Computer Society (2016). https://doi.org/10.1109/CVPR.2016.350
11. Doersch, C., Gupta, A., Efros, A.A.: Unsupervised visual representation learning by context prediction. In: 2015 IEEE International Conference on Computer Vision, ICCV 2015, Santiago, Chile, 7–13 December 2015, pp. 1422–1430. IEEE Computer Society (2015). https://doi.org/10.1109/ICCV.2015.167
12. Dosovitskiy, A., Springenberg, J.T., Riedmiller, M., Brox, T.: Discriminative unsupervised feature learning with convolutional neural networks. In: Ghahramani, Z., Welling, M., Cortes, C., Lawrence, N., Weinberger, K.Q. (eds.) Advances in Neural Information Processing Systems, vol. 27. Curran Associates, Inc. (2014)
13. Ericsson, L., Gouk, H., Hospedales, T.M.: How well do self-supervised models transfer? In: Proceedings of the IEEE/CVF Conference on Computer Vision and Pattern Recognition, pp. 5414–5423 (2021)
14. Ermolov, A., Siarohin, A., Sangineto, E., Sebe, N.: Whitening for self-supervised representation learning. arXiv preprint arXiv:2007.06346 (2020)
15. Everingham, M., Eslami, S.M.A., Van Gool, L., Williams, C.K.I., Winn, J., Zisserman, A.: The pascal visual object classes challenge: a retrospective. Int. J. Comput. Vis. 111(1), 98–136 (2015)

16. Gidaris, S., Singh, P., Komodakis, N.: Unsupervised representation learning by predicting image rotations. In: 6th International Conference on Learning Representations, ICLR 2018, Vancouver, BC, Canada, 30 April–3 May 2018. Conference Track Proceedings. OpenReview.net (2018)

17. Goyal, P., et al.: Accurate, large minibatch SGD: training ImageNet in 1 hour. arXiv preprint arXiv:1706.02677 (2017)

18. Grill, J.B., et al.: Bootstrap your own latent-a new approach to self-supervised learning. In: Advances in Neural Information Processing Systems 33, pp. 21271–21284 (2020)

19. Hadsell, R., Chopra, S., LeCun, Y.: Dimensionality reduction by learning an invariant mapping. In: Proceedings of CVPR. IEEE (2006)

20. He, K., Fan, H., Wu, Y., Xie, S., Girshick, R.: Momentum contrast for unsupervised visual representation learning. In: Proceedings of the IEEE/CVF Conference on Computer Vision and Pattern Recognition, pp. 9729–9738 (2020)

21. He, K., Gkioxari, G., Dollár, P., Girshick, R.B.: Mask R-CNN. In: IEEE International Conference on Computer Vision, ICCV 2017, Venice, Italy, 22–29 October 2017, pp. 2980–2988. IEEE Computer Society (2017). https://doi.org/10.1109/ICCV.2017.322

22. He, K., Zhang, X., Ren, S., Sun, J.: Deep residual learning for image recognition. In: 2016 IEEE Conference on Computer Vision and Pattern Recognition, CVPR 2016, Las Vegas, NV, USA, 27–30 June 2016, pp. 770–778. IEEE Computer Society (2016). https://doi.org/10.1109/CVPR.2016.90

23. Hu, Q., Wang, X., Hu, W., Qi, G.J.: ADCO: adversarial contrast for efficient learning of unsupervised representations from self-trained negative adversaries. In: Proceedings of the IEEE/CVF Conference on Computer Vision and Pattern Recognition, pp. 1074–1083 (2021)

24. Hua, T., Wang, W., Xue, Z., Ren, S., Wang, Y., Zhao, H.: On feature decorrelation in self-supervised learning. In: Proceedings of the IEEE/CVF International Conference on Computer Vision, pp. 9598–9608 (2021)

25. Kornblith, S., Norouzi, M., Lee, H., Hinton, G.: Similarity of neural network representations revisited. In: International Conference on Machine Learning, pp. 3519–3529. PMLR (2019)

26. Krizhevsky, A., Hinton, G.: Learning multiple layers of features from tiny images. Master's thesis, Department of Computer Science, University of Toronto (2009)

27. Lin, T.-Y., et al.: Microsoft COCO: common objects in context. In: Fleet, D., Pajdla, T., Schiele, B., Tuytelaars, T. (eds.) ECCV 2014. LNCS, vol. 8693, pp. 740–755. Springer, Cham (2014). https://doi.org/10.1007/978-3-319-10602-1_48

28. Misra, I., van der Maaten, L.: Self-supervised learning of pretext-invariant representations. In: 2020 IEEE/CVF Conference on Computer Vision and Pattern Recognition, CVPR 2020, Seattle, WA, USA, 13–19 June 2020, pp. 6706–6716. IEEE (2020). https://doi.org/10.1109/CVPR42600.2020.00674

29. Noroozi, M., Favaro, P.: Unsupervised learning of visual representations by solving jigsaw puzzles. In: Leibe, B., Matas, J., Sebe, N., Welling, M. (eds.) ECCV 2016. LNCS, vol. 9910, pp. 69–84. Springer, Cham (2016). https://doi.org/10.1007/978-3-319-46466-4_5

30. Oord, A.v.d., Li, Y., Vinyals, O.: Representation learning with contrastive predictive coding. arXiv preprint arXiv:1807.03748 (2018)

31. Pathak, D., Krahenbuhl, P., Donahue, J., Darrell, T., Efros, A.A.: Context encoders: feature learning by inpainting. In: Proceedings of the IEEE Conference on Computer Vision and Pattern Recognition, pp. 2536–2544 (2016)

32. Ren, S., He, K., Girshick, R.B., Sun, J.: Faster R-CNN: towards real-time object detection with region proposal networks. In: Cortes, C., Lawrence, N.D., Lee, D.D., Sugiyama, M., Garnett, R. (eds.) Advances in Neural Information Processing Systems 28: Annual Conference on Neural Information Processing Systems 2015, Montreal, Quebec, Canada, 7–12 December 2015, pp. 91–99 (2015)
33. Richemond, P.H., et al.: BYOL works even without batch statistics. arXiv preprint arXiv:2010.10241 (2020)
34. Russakovsky, O., et al.: ImageNet large scale visual recognition challenge. Int. J. Comput. Vis. **115**(3), 211–252 (2015). https://doi.org/10.1007/s11263-015-0816-y
35. Tao, C., et al.: Exploring the equivalence of Siamese self-supervised learning via a unified gradient framework. In: Proceedings of the IEEE/CVF Conference on Computer Vision and Pattern Recognition, pp. 14431–14440 (2022)
36. Tarvainen, A., Valpola, H.: Mean teachers are better role models: weight-averaged consistency targets improve semi-supervised deep learning results. In: Guyon, I., et al. (eds.) Advances in Neural Information Processing Systems 30: Annual Conference on Neural Information Processing Systems 2017, 4–9 December 2017, Long Beach, CA, USA, pp. 1195–1204 (2017)
37. Tian, Y., Krishnan, D., Isola, P.: Contrastive multiview coding. arXiv preprint arXiv:1906.05849 (2019)
38. Tian, Y., Chen, X., Ganguli, S.: Understanding self-supervised learning dynamics without contrastive pairs. In: International Conference on Machine Learning, pp. 10268–10278. PMLR (2021)
39. Wang, X., Zhang, R., Shen, C., Kong, T., Li, L.: Dense contrastive learning for self-supervised visual pre-training. In: Proceedings of the IEEE/CVF Conference on Computer Vision and Pattern Recognition, pp. 3024–3033 (2021)
40. Wu, Z., Xiong, Y., Yu, S.X., Lin, D.: Unsupervised feature learning via non-parametric instance discrimination. In: 2018 IEEE Conference on Computer Vision and Pattern Recognition, CVPR 2018, Salt Lake City, UT, USA, 18–22 June 2018, pp. 3733–3742. IEEE Computer Society (2018). https://doi.org/10.1109/CVPR.2018.00393
41. Xie, Z., Lin, Y., Zhang, Z., Cao, Y., Lin, S., Hu, H.: Propagate yourself: exploring pixel-level consistency for unsupervised visual representation learning. arXiv preprint arXiv:2011.10043 (2020)
42. You, Y., Gitman, I., Ginsburg, B.: Large batch training of convolutional networks. arXiv preprint arXiv:1708.03888 (2017)
43. Zbontar, J., Jing, L., Misra, I., LeCun, Y., Deny, S.: Barlow twins: self-supervised learning via redundancy reduction. arXiv preprint arXiv:2103.03230 (2021)
44. Zhao, N., Wu, Z., Lau, R.W., Lin, S.: What makes instance discrimination good for transfer learning? arXiv preprint arXiv:2006.06606 (2020)

CA-SSL: Class-Agnostic Semi-Supervised Learning for Detection and Segmentation

Lu Qi[1,3], Jason Kuen[2], Zhe Lin[2], Jiuxiang Gu[2], Fengyun Rao[1], Dian Li[1],
Weidong Guo[1(✉)], Zhen Wen[1], Ming-Hsuan Yang[3], and Jiaya Jia[4]

[1] QQ Browser Lab, Tencent, Shenzhen, China
weidongguo@tencent.com
[2] Adobe Research, San Jose, USA
[3] The University of California, Merced, Merced, USA
[4] The Chinese University of Hong Kong, Shatin, Hong Kong

Abstract. To improve instance-level detection/segmentation performance, existing self-supervised and semi-supervised methods extract either task-unrelated or task-specific training signals from unlabeled data. We show that these two approaches, at the two extreme ends of the task-specificity spectrum, are suboptimal for the task performance. Utilizing too little task-specific training signals causes underfitting to the ground-truth labels of downstream tasks, while the opposite causes overfitting to the ground-truth labels. To this end, we propose a novel **C**lass-**A**gnostic **S**emi-**S**upervised **L**earning (CA-SSL) framework to achieve a more favorable task-specificity balance in extracting training signals from unlabeled data. CA-SSL has three training stages that act on either ground-truth labels (labeled data) or pseudo labels (unlabeled data). This decoupling strategy avoids the complicated scheme in traditional SSL methods that balances the contributions from both data types. Especially, we introduce a warmup training stage to achieve a more optimal balance in task specificity by ignoring class information in the pseudo labels, while preserving localization training signals. As a result, our warmup model can better avoid underfitting/overfitting when fine-tuned on the ground-truth labels in detection and segmentation tasks. Using 3.6M unlabeled data, we achieve a significant performance gain of 4.7% over ImageNet-pretrained baseline on FCOS object detection. In addition, our warmup model demonstrates excellent transferability to other detection and segmentation frameworks.

Keywords: Semi-supervised · Class-agnostic · Instance-level detection

Supplementary Information The online version contains supplementary material available at https://doi.org/10.1007/978-3-031-19821-2_4.

1   Introduction

Deep learning [20,22,23,28,48,51–53] has enabled instance-level detection (object detection [16,17,45], instance segmentation [19,35], *etc.*) methods to achieve previously unattainable performance. Such success cannot be achieved without large datasets with instance annotations such as COCO [34], Cityscapes [12] and Open Images [27]. However, annotating instances is laboriously expensive due to the great intricateness needed for annotating instance-level bounding boxes, masks, and/or semantic classes. Due to such a limitation, the datasets in instance-level detection domain are relatively small in scale, compared to other domains. As such, instance-level detection models generally have degraded generalization performance in real-world applications [11,37,39,47].

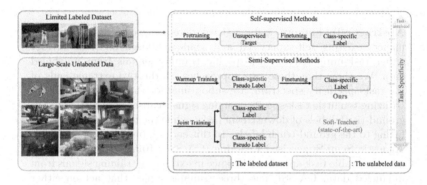

Fig. 1. Schematic comparison between existing semi-supervised methods and CA-SSL. Instead of joint training with labeled and unlabeled data, we train on unlabeled and labeled dataset in different stages: **pseudo labeler training**, **warmup training**, and **finetuning**. Furthermore, we use class-agnostic pseudo labels during warmup training.

To alleviate the heavy cost of data annotation, numerous methods have been developed to leverage unlabeled images for instance-level detection [12,34]. Unlike labeled data that can provide explicit and indisputable supervision signals, the extraction of training signals from unlabeled data remains as an open issue. Two widely-adopted approaches for learning from unlabeled data are self-supervised and semi-supervised learning. Self-supervised methods [8,14,18,21,44,59,62] usually rely on training signals like the relative distances between the augmented samples of a positive/negative pair, while semi-supervised strategies [24,30,43,49,54,57,64,68] directly leverage the pseudo labels generated by a detector pretrained on ground-truth labels. In terms of task specificity, these two approaches are at the two extreme ends of the spectrum – self-supervised learning utilizes hardly any task-specific training signals from unlabeled data, whilst semi-supervised learning utilizes too much of them. Consequently, the model tends to underfit/overfit (depending on the amount of task specificity in the training signals) the ground-truth labels of downsteam task during the finetuning or final-training stage. This motivates us – *is there a good middle ground between the two extremes that has a more optimal amount of task specificity?*

In instance-level detection/segmentation tasks, the datasets usually have two types of annotations: localization-based annotations (*e.g.,* boxes, masks) and class labels for those annotations. While semi-supervised methods utilize the information from both kinds of annotations to do pseudo labeling on unlabeled data, we show that such a practice is not optimal for training and would hurt the final performance. Given the pseudo labels that closely mimic ground-truth labels, the model is likely to take an easier optimization path and potentially arrive at a less-favorable local optimum at the period of training. To mitigate the issue, we can disregard either one of the annotation types for the purpose of pseudo labeling. A related example is the conventional practice of pretraining the model on ImageNet [15] with just image-level class labels. Conversely, the approach of using localization-based annotations (while ignoring class labels) has not been explored previously, which we believe is a promising direction given the nature of detection/segmentation tasks.

In this work, we propose a novel Class-Agnostic Semi-Supervised Learning (CA-SSL) framework for instance-level detection and segmentation. CA-SSL is a framework consisting of three cascaded training stages (pseudo labeler training, warmup training, and finetuning) with two detector types (pseudo labeler and target detector). Each stage employs a specific type of training data and a type of detector. Concretely, we first train a pseudo labeler on the labeled dataset with class-agnostic annotations and then use it to generate pseudo labels on unlabeled images. After that, we perform warmup training for the target detector on the unlabeled data with class-agnostic pseudo labels. Finally, we finetune the warmed-up target detector on class-specific ground-truth annotations for a particular instance-level task. Unlike existing state-of-the-art SSL method Soft-Teacher [64] that jointly uses labeled and unlabeled data within its single training stage, these two data types are assigned separately to the different stages of CA-SSL, as shown in Fig. 1. This decoupling strategy provides the warmup model with a good initial solution (learned from unlabeled data) that guides it to maintain a good generalization performance during finetuning.

In our experiments, we carry out evaluations by considering upper-bound model performance on multiple large-scale unlabeled data splits that have different dataset scales, consisting of images from COCO unlabeled [34], Open Images [29] and Places365 [66]. Through extensive experiments, we demonstrate that our method can obtain consistent performance gains when using different unlabeled splits ranging from 0.12M to 3.6M images. Owing to the superior effectiveness of our method at consuming large-scale unlabeled data, we are the first successful attempt to improve task performance using an unlabeled dataset with an enormous amount of 3.6M images, in the history of semi-supervised object detection. Moreover, our class-agnostic warmup model trained with warmup training demonstrates excellent transferability to other instance-level detection and segmentation frameworks. The contributions for this paper are threefold:

- We propose a novel class-agnostic semi-supervised learning framework for instance-level detection/segmentation tasks. By leveraging cascaded training stages and class-agnostic pseudo labels, it achieves a more optimal amount of task specificity in the training signals extracted from unlabeled data.
- We conduct extensive ablative and comparative experiments on object detection, demonstrating the effectiveness of our method. To the best of our knowledge, we are the first to use unlabeled data at an unprecedented scale of 3.6M for semi-supervised object detection.
- We demonstrate that our class-agnostic warmup model trained with warmup training can significantly improve the performance on other instance-level detection/segmentation tasks (instance segmentation, keypoint detection, entity segmentation, panoptic segmentation) and frameworks.

2   Related Work

Instance-Level Detection/Segmentation. Instance-level detection tasks, including object detection [13,16,17,32,33,40,45,56], instance segmentation [7, 19,35,42,63,65], and key point detection [19,50,61,67], require detecting objects with different instance-level representations such as bounding box, pixelwise mask, and keypoints. Recently, numerous class-specific panoptic segmentation [3,10,31] and class-agnostic entity segmentation [41] methods have been developed to perform dense image segmentation by treating all segmentation masks as instances. Most of instance-level detection research works generally focus on designing more advanced architectures or detection methods that work well on existing labeled datasets. Instead, we aim to design a training framework that better utilizes unlabeled images, without modifying the underlying architecture or method. This facilitates better understanding of how far current methods can scale with the help of large-scale unlabeled data.

Semi-supervised Detection. Semi-supervised learning approaches mainly focus on two directions for instance-level detection. One is concerned with the consistency-based methods [24,54], which are closely related to self-supervised approaches. They usually construct a regularization loss by designing some contrastive pretext task [8,18,21,44,59,62]. Another direction is on pseudo labeling [30,43,49,57,64,68]. As the name implies, they leverage a pretrained detector to generate pseudo labels on unlabeled images. The pseudo labels are usually almost identical to the ground-truth labels. Thus, both two types of labels can be used for joint training with similar losses. Our framework is also based on pseudo labeling, but we decouple the semi-supervised pipeline into three cascaded training stages, where each stage employs a specific type of training data (labeled dataset or unlabeled data). Such a design avoids the complicated and careful weighting strategy required to balance unlabeled and labeled data in the joint training scheme of semi-supervised methods [64], where the common issue is to effectively balance the contributions of noisy pseudo labels and ground-truth annotations.

Class-Agnostic Detection and Segmentation. Class-Agnostic localization [25,41,45,46,58] has been widely used in detection and segmentation. One
of the most prominent examples is the two-stage detector [45]. It mainly has a
class-agnostic region proposal network (RPN) and a detection head. RPN predicts numerous high-quality class-agnostic proposals for further classification and
localization refinement. Inspired by this design, our method use class-agnostic
pseudo labels on unlabeled data for warming up class-specific target detector. As
demonstrated by recent works on open-world detection/segmentation [25,41,46],
it can improve the model's generalization on unseen objects. Aside from the benefits shown by existing works, in this paper, we present the first evidence that
class-agnostic training can significantly bridge the quality gap between pseudo
labels and human (ground-truth) labels. This is important because the quality of
pseudo labels directly impacts the effectiveness of learning from unlabeled data.

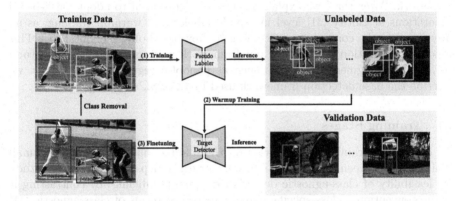

Fig. 2. Illustration of CA-SSL framework. The numbered texts indicate the three cascade stages of our framework. It mainly involves two detectors, namely *pseudo labeler*
and *target* detector. The bridge between these two detectors is the unlabeled images.
We use the pseudo labeler to predict class-agnostic pseudo labels on the unlabeled
images, which are then used as training data for warmup training of target detector.

3   Methodology

Figure 2 provides an overview of the proposed **C**lass-**a**gnostic **S**emi-**S**upervised
Learning (CA-SSL) framework. The framework consists of three stages, including
pseudo labeler training, warmup training, and finetuning. In the first stage, we
use the labeled data but with only class-agnostic annotations to train a pseudo
labeler. This labeling detector then predicts class-agnostic pseudo labels on unlabeled images. In warmup training, these numerous unlabeled images with their
pseudo labels are used to train a target detector. This process is akin to pre-
training in self-supervised learning with unlabeled data. We refer to it as warmup

Table 1. COCO `val2017` validation results from training on ground-truth and pseudo labels, across class-specific (AP^{det}) and -agnostic (AP^{det-a}) tasks. 'Num' is the number of training images. AP^{det} and AP^{det-a} indicate the class-specific and -agnostic object detection mAPs respectively.

Train data	Annotation	Num	AP^{det}	AP^{det-a}
COCO `train2017`	Ground-truth	118k	41.0	41.9
COCO `unlabeled`	Pseudo labels	123k	35.9	40.0

training because only localization-based pseudo labels are used as training data, while class labels are ignored. Finally, we fine-tune the warmed-up target detector on the labeled dataset with class-specific annotations.

In the following sections, we first introduce the entire process of our training framework. After that, we explain in detail our proposal to adopt mask-based annotations at Entity [41] level in pseudo labeler and warmup training, as an alternative to the common practice of using box-based object annotations. This annotation adoption is to enable our framework work more effectively beyond instance-level segmentation tasks such as panoptic segmentation. Finally, we describe the base detection framework used by CA-SSL's training stages.

3.1 Training Stages

We design our training stages based on the finding that there is only a small quality gap between class-agnostic ground-truth and pseudo labels. We study the feasibility of class-agnostic detection for pseudo labeling, by contrasting it to the conventional class-specific detection task, in terms of class-agnostic [41] and class-specific [34] AP metrics respectively. Table 1 shows that the validation performance gap between training on either ground-truth data (COCO `train2017`) or pseudo labels (COCO `unlabeled`), for both class-specific and -agnostic settings[1] on COCO validation set [34]. The groundtruth-unlabeled AP gaps of class-specific and class-agnostic models are 5.1% (41.0–35.9) and 1.9% (41.9–40.0) respectively. The much smaller gap indicates that the class-agnostic pseudo labels have much a better quality than the class-specific ones, thus enabling the model to closely approach the AP of training on ground-truth labels. In many cases, class-agnostic pseudo labels can eliminate the ambiguities caused by confusing predefined classes such as *cyclist* and *person*, while generalizing well to other kinds of objects unseen, which have been well studied in $\mathcal{D}^t$ [41]. The class-agnostic model with stronger generalization ability provides a greater variety of proposals which help localize objects better during finetuning. We show that such properties of class-agnostic pseudo labels are more useful for

---

[1] We use FCOS [56] with ResNet50 backbone, a widely-used one-stage detector, to explore the performance gap between using class-specific and -agnostic labels. We follow its 36 epoch training setting widely adopted in detectron2 [60] or mmdetection [5].

warmup training of the class-specific model, compared to prematurely learning classification-aware features through the class-specific ground-truth annotations of downstream task.

Similar to other semi-supervised learning frameworks [24,30,43,49,54,57,64, 68], our CA-SSL framework is largely based on the conventional object detection training process which we first briefly introduce here. Conventionally, given the input images I and their ground-truth annotations Y from the human-labeled training dataset $\mathcal{D}^t$, the detection model denoted as h_* is trained with the composite detection loss: $\mathcal{L}_{\text{det}} = \mathcal{L}_{\text{cls}}$ (classification loss) + $\mathcal{L}_{\text{loc}}$ (localization loss). The detection model h_* is learned through a function $\mathcal{H}(*)$ that determines the neural network hypothesis spaces, depending on the task at hand. Next, we provide the details of the three stages of CA-SSL framework.

Pseudo Labeler Training. The goal of this stage is to train a pseudo labeler on $\mathcal{D}^t$ to generate high-quality class-agnostic pseudo labels $\mathcal{D}^p$ from the unlabeled dataset split $\mathcal{D}^u$. To keep the training and inference consistent, we train the pseudo labeler on the class-agnostic annotations obtained from $\mathcal{D}^t$. We directly remove class information from the annotations in $\mathcal{D}^t$ using the class-agnostic conversion function $\alpha(\cdot)$ and regard each label as a class-free "object". To train the pseudo labeler, we use a recent class-specific detection framework (see Sect. 3.3) and replace its multi-class classifier with a binary classifier. Given the labeled dataset $\mathcal{D}^t$, the pseudo labeler h_{L} is trained as follows:

$$h_{\text{L}} = \underset{h \in \mathcal{H}(\text{L})}{\text{argmin}} \sum_{\{I_i, Y_i\} \in \mathcal{D}^t} \mathcal{L}_{\text{det}}^a(h(I_i), \alpha(Y_i)), \tag{1}$$

where $\mathcal{L}_{\text{det}}^a$ representation the class-agnostic version of $\mathcal{L}_{\text{det}}$ and $\mathcal{H}(\text{L})$ indicates the neural network hypotheses conditioned on the labeling detection task.

Once the training is done, we apply the pseudo labeler to the unlabeled images and then filter the prediction results using merely a single (constant) score threshold δ. Without semantic class labels in the prediction results, class-agnostic pseudo labels avoid the long-tail problem suffered by in class-specific predictions. Some related ablations are in the supplementary file. As a result, there is no need for a complicated strategy that applies class-dynamic score thresholds as in existing works [30,43,49,57,64,68]. Given the pseudo labeler h_{L} and score threshold δ, our class-agnostic pseudo labeling process to obtain the pseudo labels Y^p and pseudo-label dataset $\mathcal{D}^p$ is represented by the following:

$$Y_i^p = \{y_j \in h_{\text{L}}(I_i^u) | \textbf{score}(y_j) > \delta\} \quad \forall I_i^u \in \mathcal{D}^u, \tag{2}$$

$$\mathcal{D}^p = \{(I_i^u \in \mathcal{D}^u, Y_i^p \in Y^p) | Y_i^p \neq \emptyset\}, \tag{3}$$

where 'p' indicates the association with pseudo labels and $\textbf{score}(\cdot)$ returns the objectness score of any prediction.

Warmup Training. We perform warmup training of the target detector only on the pseudo-label dataset $\mathcal{D}^p$. We do not make use of any ground-truth dataset in this stage, which is different from the state-of-the-art semi-supervised approach

Soft-Teacher [64] that carries out joint training on ground-truth and unlabeled dataset splits. Given that, we do not require a divide-and-conquer strategy to handle different dataset splits, such as applying different loss weights to noisy pseudo labels and clean ground-truth labels [1,2]. To obtain the warmed-up target 'T' detection model h_T, we perform warmup training as follows:

$$h_T = \underset{h \in \mathcal{H}(T)}{\operatorname{argmin}} \sum_{\{I_i^p, Y_i^p\} \in \mathcal{D}^p} \mathcal{L}_{\det}^a(h(I_i^p), \lceil Y_i^p \rceil), \tag{4}$$

where $\lceil \cdot \rceil$ transforms Y^p to binary training targets. Note that warmup training is related to the pretraining step of self-supervised learning. The weights of the model are well-initialized for better adaptation to downstream tasks. Compared to self-supervised methods [6,21,44,59,62], the unlabeled data with class-agnostic pseudo labels provides relatively more informative and task-specific supervision signals (class-agnostic localization) that significantly facilitate instance-level detection and segmentation tasks.

Finetuning. After obtaining the warmup model h_T from warmup training, we finetune it for the downstream task using the class-specific ground-truth annotations of $\mathcal{D}^t$. Instance-level detection/segmentation tasks are typically class-specific tasks. Thus, the output channel of target detector's semantic classifier should be adapted to the number of pre-defined classes for the downstream task at hand. There are two ways to initialize multi-class classification layer: (1) random initialization; (2) initialize each output channel with the one from the classification layer of h_T. We empirically find these two strategies produce similar results. The finetuning process to obtain the final 'F' downstream-task model h_F is represented by:

$$h_F = \underset{h \in \mathcal{H}(F; h_T)}{\operatorname{argmin}} \sum_{\{I_i, Y_i\} \in \mathcal{D}^t} \mathcal{L}_{\det}(h(I_i), Y_i), \tag{5}$$

where $\mathcal{H}(F; h_T)$ indicates that the neural network hypotheses are conditioned on both the task 'F' and pretrained model h_T. Our approach of warming up the target detector with only unlabeled data guarantees it less prone to overfitting to the downstream task's images and ground-truth labels, since they have not been exposed to the model in the warmup training stage.

3.2 Switching from Objects to Entities

Warmup training with large-scale unlabeled data is a costly process. Thus, it is desirable to design our CA-SSL framework such that the trained class-agnostic model can serve a good range of tasks that expand to detection and also include segmentation. Instance segmentation and panoptic segmentation are two widely-used instance-level segmentation tasks that require more fine-grained visual information for predicting pixelwise masks for each instance.

We draw inspiration from Entity Segmentation [41] on how to boost the applicability and usefulness of our CA-SSL framework. Instead of just focusing on objects, we propose to perform warmup training for the target detector

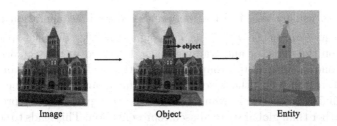

Fig. 3. An example showing that switching from *box-based object* annotations to *mask-based Entity* [41] annotations results in a more substantial set of labels for pseudo labeler and warmup training.

based on the semantically-coherent and class-agnostic mask regions known as Entities. Entities include not just object regions but also stuff regions such as *sky* and *road* which come with the panoptic segmentation task in mainstream datasets (*e.g.,* COCO [34]). With this, even the unlabeled images with little-to-no object regions can still provide substantial pseudo-label training signals through the stuff regions. In Fig. 3, there is only a single object (*clock*), while multiple Entities like *building* and *sky* are present. Furthermore, stuff regions have close relationships with objects, and thus we hypothesize that the training on stuff pseudo labels strongly benefits the downstream task even if it is an object-based task [38].

3.3 Base Detector

We adopt the CondInst [55], a widely-used instance segmentation framework, as our base detector for the pseudo labeler and target detector. Different from Mask R-CNN [19], the Condinst is in fully convolutional manner with two parts: a dense one-stage detector FCOS for detection and a segmentation head for mask prediction. The FCOS has a backbone, FPN neck, and a detection head. The detection head has three output branches: the classification, regression, and kernel branch. The first two branches perform instance-level classification and regression to achieve object detection. Whereas, the kernel branch generates dynamic convolution weights which are used to convolve with high-res feature maps to generate binary instance masks within the segmentation head. Such a network architecture keeps the detection and segmentation parts fairly independent, making it easy to transfer its arbitrary parts to other networks and tasks for finetuning, as proved by our ablation study in Table 9 and Table 10. *E.g.,* we can easily initialize the backbone and FPN neck of Mask R-CNN with our CondInst target detector without any modifications. Overall, the CondInst base detector is trained with the following:

$$\mathcal{L}^e = \mathcal{L}_{\det}^{\{a,c\}} + \mathcal{L}_{\text{seg}}, \tag{6}$$

where $\mathcal{L}_{seg}$ is usually the dice loss between predicted segmentation mask and ground truth. We choose $\mathcal{L}_{det}^{\{a,c\}}$ as class-agnostic $\mathcal{L}_{det}^{a}$ or class-specific $\mathcal{L}_{det}^{c}$ depending on the detector and training stage described in Subsect. 3.1.

Also, CondInst learns to group the pixels that belong to the same semantic/instance region, and otherwise push them far apart. This can be seen as a form of implicit contrastive learning which focuses on spatial-level representation learning, rather than global vector-based representation. This leads to segregated features which are useful for detection and segmentation tasks.

4   Experiments

Datasets. MS-COCO [34] is used as the main evaluation dataset. In addition to MS-COCO `train2017` and `val2017` splits, we curate 3.6 million unlabeled images from COCO `unlabeled` [34], Places365 [66], and Open Images [29]. To better demonstrate the data scalability of CA-SSL, we construct four unlabeled data subsets (`tiny`, `small`, `base`, `large`) with 120K, 660K, 1.74M, and 3.66M images respectively. Unless specified, we report the experimental results from using `tiny` as the unlabeled subset, which is from COCO `unlabeled` and has nearly the same scale as `train2017` as shown in Table 1.

Training Setup. For fair comparisons with other methods (some may require less training time), we train all models to reach their respectively upper-bound performances, by increasing the number of training epochs accordingly. Unless specified, we train with 60 and 36 epochs in warmup training and finetuning respectively for CA-SSL to achieve the upper-bound performance. Upper-bound performance evaluation is the preferred way to gauge the true performance of different methods that may require different training costs. We apply either *weak* data augmentation (conventional multi-scale training) or *strong* data augmentation (jittering of scale, brightness, contrast, etc. [9,64]) to the unlabeled images before generating pseudo labels.

Implementation. We adopt the Condinst [55] framework with Swin Transformer Tiny (T) backbone [36] as our base model. Please refer to our supplementary file for the hyper-parameter settings in the warmup training and finetuning.

4.1   Experimental Results

Warmup Training Data. Table 2 shows the impact of the choice of warmup training data on the downstream task performances after the finetuning stage. From the first two rows, we observe that ImageNet supervised-pretrained model and the warmup model trained on class-agnostic ground-truth labels suffer from the worst downstream performances. Whereas, in the last three rows, the models that leverage pseudo labels 'P' for training consistently achieve stronger downstream performances. It can also be clearly seen that using class-agnostic labels 'A' during warmup training is better than using class-specific labels 'S', resulting in a downstream AP^{det} gap of 1.0% (48.1–47.1). Class-Agnostic warmup training

Table 2. Effect of warmup training data choice. AP^{det} and AP^{seg} indicate the APs for class-specific object detection and instance segmentation tasks. Their class-agnostic counterparts have names appended with '-a'. AP^e and PQ are the evaluation metrics of class-agnostic Entity detection [41] and panoptic segmentation. 'G' and 'P' indicate whether ground-truth (COCO `train2017` with 118K images) or pseudo labels (COCO unlabeled data with 123K images) are used. They are different datasets but with comparable numbers of images. 'A' and 'S' indicate whether class-agnostic or class-specific labels are used. Note that all the results here are obtained via COCO `val2017`.

Warmup training data	Warmed-up model				Finetuned model		
	$AP^{det\text{-}a}$	$AP^{seg\text{-}a}$	AP^{det}	AP^e	AP^{det}	AP^{seg}	PQ
ImageNet	–	–	–	–	46.8	43.0	41.4
Objects(G, A)	41.9	35.3	–	–	46.9	–	–
Objects(P, S)	–	–	35.9	–	47.1	–	–
Objects(P, A)	40.0	33.4	–	–	48.1	45.0	42.5
Entities(P, A)	–	–	–	40.2	**48.2**	**45.2**	**43.7**

Table 3. Performances of pretrained model with different number of warmup training epochs. The AP^e_{50} and AP^e_{75} are APs of the Entity detection task based on 0.5 and 0.75 IoU thresholds. The AP^e_s, AP^e_m and AP^e_l indicate the mAP performance on small, middle, and large entities.

Epochs	AP^e	AP^e_{50}	AP^e_{75}	AP^e_s	AP^e_m	AP^e_l
12 (1×)	38.4	59.6	40.5	14.5	35.0	52.6
24 (2×)	39.6	60.5	41.9	15.0	36.3	54.1
36 (3×)	39.9	60.8	42.4	15.1	36.9	54.6
48 (4×)	40.2	60.8	42.7	15.4	37.1	54.8
60 (5×)	**40.2**	**60.9**	**42.8**	**15.4**	**37.0**	**54.9**

helps to prevent the model from overfitting to the ground-truth labels during finetuning. In particular, Entity-based warmup training data provides the best overall downstream task performance, while strongly raising the downstream PQ performance by 1.2% (43.7–42.5) due to the inclusion of both object and stuff elements. Note that the last two rows of Table 2 use identical COCO `unlabeled` images but with different annotation types: box-based objects and mask-based entities [41] (objects & stuffs), as illustrated in Sect. 3.2.

Upper-Bound Performance. We investigate the number of training epochs required to achieve the upper-bound performance in both the warmup training and finetuning stages. Table 3 shows the class-agnostic performance under different numbers of warmup training epochs. When increasing the number of epochs from 12 to 48, the performance of trained model improves from 38.4 to 40.2 in terms of class-agnostic AP^e. The improvement saturates after 40 epochs. Table 4 shows the the downstream class-specific object detection performance under different combinations of warmup training and finetuning epochs. With 60 epochs (5×) in the warmup training and 36 epochs (3×) in finetuning stages, we obtain the best performance of 48.2 AP^{det}. Therefore, we adopt this particular setting in the rest of the experiments.

Table 4. Exploration to the best training epoch combination in the warmup training and finetuning stages on downstream object detection performance AP^{det}. E× indicates the E×12 training epochs. *E.g.*, 1× and 5× represent 12 and 60 training epochs, respectively. 'F' and 'W' represent the **F**inetuning and **W**armup training stages.

F	W				
	1×	2×	3×	4×	5×
1×	45.3	46.3	46.4	46.8	47.1
2×	47.0	47.4	47.7	47.3	47.7
3×	47.2	47.7	47.6	47.9	**48.2**
4×	47.3	47.6	47.7	47.9	48.0
5×	47.5	47.7	47.9	47.9	48.0

Table 5. Relationship between the performance of pseudo labeler and the performance of the warmed-up target detector right after warmup training. The different columns correspond to the various backbones (ResNet-101, Swin-Tiny, Swin-Small, Swin-Base, and Swin-Large.) used by the pseudo labeler. The warmup target detector is always based on **Tiny** backbone.

Pseudo labeler (AP^e)	38.0	39.1	40.6	41.4	**42.1**
Warmed-up target detector (AP^e)	36.1	37.3	38.8	39.6	**40.2**

Pseudo Labeler. We investigate the impact of pseudo labeler in the first training stage. Table 5 shows how the performance of pseudo labeler affects the performance of the target detector (after warmup training is performed) on the class-agnostic entity detection task. The results here conclude that a stronger pseudo labeler consistently leads to a stronger target detector in warmup training.

Data Augmentation. Table 6 shows the impact of data augmentation scheme adopted in the warmup training and finetuning stages, on the intermediate and final detection performances. Using strong data augmentation independently for any of the two stages brings some performance improvement, while combining the two provides the largest AP^{det} improvement of 0.9% (49.1–48.2).

Table 6. Ablation study on data augmentation. 'W' and 'F' represent the warmup training and finetuning stages, while 'weak' and 'strong' refer to weak and strong data augmentation. (A, B) indicate the class-agnostic AP^e and class-specific AP^{det} in warmup training and finetuning.

F	W	
	Weak	Strong
Weak	(40.2, 48.2)	(**40.6**, 48.6)
Strong	(40.2, 48.6)	(**40.6**, **49.1**)

Table 7. Ablation study on unlabeled splits with different dataset scales.

Setting	Num	Warmup model (AP^e)	Fine-tuned model (AP^{det})
Tiny	123K	40.2	48.2
Small	660k	40.7	48.8
Base	1.74M	41.4	49.7
Large	3.66M	**42.0**	**50.6**

Table 8. Comparison with the state-of-the-arts under the setting of `train2017` set with 118k images. The 'unlabeled images' means the number of unlabeled images we use. In the column of 'AP^{det}', the left part is the baseline performance of using only `train2017`, and the right part is the performance of using both `train2017` and unlabeled dataset. → indicates the performance gain. The symbols [§](ImageNet), [*](COCO), [†] [‡](our curated sets described in Sect. 4) refer to the same respective sets of unlabeled images.

Type	Method	Unlabeled images	Model	AP^{det}
Self-supervised	MoCo-v2 [6]	1.28M	R-50-FPN	39.7 $\xrightarrow{+0.1}$ 39.8
	DenseCL [59]	1.28M	R-50-FPN	39.7 $\xrightarrow{+0.6}$ 40.3
	DetCo [62]	1.28M	R-50-MaskRCNN	38.9 $\xrightarrow{+1.2}$ 40.1
	DetCon [21]	1.28M	R-50-FPN	41.6 $\xrightarrow{+1.8}$ 42.7
	PreDet [44]	50.00M	R-50-MaskRCNN	44.9 $\xrightarrow{+2.2}$ 47.1
Semi-supervised	Proposal learning [54]	0.12M	R-50-FPN	37.4 $\xrightarrow{+1.0}$ 38.4
	STAC [49]	0.12M	R-50-FPN	39.5 $\xrightarrow{-0.3}$ 39.2
	Self-training [68]	2.90M	R-50-FPN (SimCLR)	41.1 $\xrightarrow{+0.8}$ 41.9
	Soft Teacher [64]	1.74M[†]	Swin-T-FCOS	46.8 $\xrightarrow{+2.5}$ 49.3
		3.66M[‡]	Swin-L-HTC++	58.2 $\xrightarrow{+1.7}$ 59.9
	CA-SSL (ours)	1.74M[†]	Swin-T-FCOS	46.8 $\xrightarrow{+4.0}$ 50.8
		3.66M[‡]		46.8 $\xrightarrow{+4.7}$ 51.5
			Swin-L-HTC++	58.2 $\xrightarrow{+2.7}$ 60.9

Scale of Unlabeled Dataset. Table 7 shows how the performance varies by training the model on different unlabeled dataset splits. With the increase of unlabeled dataset scale, the performances of the models from the warmup training and finetuning stages improve consistently. We also notice that the class-agnostic performance of the warmup model correlates well with the performance of the finetuning model. This is expected as the substantial task similarity between those two training stages.

State-of-the-Art Comparison. In Table 8, we compare the performance of CA-SSL on the downstream object detection task with those of state-of-the-art methods in strong data augmentation. Our method achieves the most significant performance gains even though our model is based on an already strong baseline with the powerful Swin-Tiny backbone. With 1.74M unlabeled images, we obtain 50.8 AP^{det} with 4.0% improvement over the ImageNet-pretrained baseline. Furthermore, by increasing the number of unlabeled images to 3.66M, we observe an even bigger performance gain of 4.7% that leads to 51.5 AP^{det}. Since there is no obvious sign of performance saturation, we believe that using a super-scale unlabeled dataset (larger than our 3.66M one) can potentially improve model performance significantly.

Table 9. Ablation study on the initialization strategy. The pretrained model is divided into four parts here. ○ indicates the particular part's pretrained weights are not being used, while ✓ indicates otherwise.

Backbone	Neck	Head	Classifier	AP^{det}	AP^{det}_{50}	AP^{det}_{75}
○	○	○	○	46.8	66.2	50.8
✓	○	○	○	50.6	69.2	55.2
✓	✓	○	○	50.8	69.4	55.5
✓	✓	✓	○	**51.5**	69.5	55.3
✓	✓	✓	✓	**51.5**	**69.6**	**55.4**

Moreover, using a stronger detector Swin-Large-HTC++ [4] with CA-SSL still provides a meaningful 2.7% improvement (58.2 → 60.9 AP^{det}), suggesting that CA-SSL is compatible with advanced detectors. With the same detector and similar unlabeled images, Soft Teacher [64] merely achieves a 2.5 % (Swin-Tiny-FCOS) and 1.7 % (Swin-Large-HTC++) gain, despite its relatively significant 3.6% gain with R-50-FPN backbone and 120K unlabeled images. The reasons are twofold. Unlike CA-SSL that decouples the usage of different source data into three stages, Soft Teacher performs joint training and that requires it to be particular about the scale of unlabeled data, in order to achieve a good balance between the contributions from labeled and unlabeled data. Using an unlabeled dataset larger than expected can spoil such a balance. On the other hand, Self-training [68] performs much worse than ours, even with a large amount of 2.9M unlabeled images. This is due to the premature use of class/downstream-specific labels in the pseudo-labeling stage, potentially causing the model overfit easily to ground-truth labels during finetuning. Whereas, CA-SSL mitigates such a problem by not allowing the model to train on labeled images and class-specific labels during warmup training.

Note that the performance improvements of our proposed semi-supervised learning do not come from Transformer architecture. With R-50-FPN detector and similar 0.12M unlabeled images, CA-SSL improves the performance at a much larger margin than other semi-supervised methods.

Initialization Strategy. We study the effects of including/excluding the multiple parts (backbone, neck, head, and classifier) of the pretrained model from the warmup training stage for initializing the finetuning model. Table 9 shows that the main source of improvement (+3.8%) comes from backbone initialization, while the other parts make smaller improvements. This ablation study motivates us to transfer our pretrained model to other instance-level detection/segmentation tasks that may not use the downstream frameworks as ours.

Table 10. Evaluation on representative instance-level detection/segmentation tasks with Swin-Tiny backbone. "E" and "P" indicate initializing the framework with *entire* or *part(s) of* our pretrained model. "ImageNet" and "Ours" refer to ImageNet and our weights trained in the warmup stage. "Task Perf" refers to the task-specific evaluation metrics, including AP for object detection, instance segmentation and key-point detetcion, AP^e for entity segmentation, and PQ for panoptic segmentation.

Task	Type	Framework	Pretrained w/	Task perf.	
DET	E	FCOS [56]	ImageNet	46.8	
			Ours	51.5	(+4.7)
	P	RetinaNet [33]	ImageNet	42.8	
			Ours	47.9	(+5.1)
		FPN [32]	ImageNet	44.0	
			Ours	46.5	(+2.5)
INS	E	CondInst [55]	ImageNet	41.9	
			Ours	44.9	(+3.0)
	P	Mask R-CNN [19]	ImageNet	42.8	
			Ours	45.5	(+2.7)
Entity	E	CondInst [55]	ImageNet	35.1	
			Ours	38.2	(+3.1)
Point	P	Mask R-CNN [19]	ImageNet	66.8	
			Ours	67.8	(+1.0)
Panop	P	PanopticFPN [26]	ImageNet	39.5	
			Ours	41.5	(+2.0)

Generalization to Other Frameworks/Tasks. Table 10 shows the strong performance improvements resulted from initializing the downstream models with a single model h_T pretrained with CA-SSL, on various instance-level detection and segmentation tasks. Some frameworks like Mask R-CNN have heads that are incompatible with those of our Condinst base detector. Using just our FPN backbone pretrained weights to initialize Mask R-CNN, we achieve 2.7 AP^{seg} and 1.0 AP^{point} improvements on instance segmentation and keypoint detection. This demonstrates the strong generalization ability of our semi-supervised learning method.

5   Conclusion

In this work, we propose a class-agnostic semi-supervised learning framework to improve instance-level detection/segmentation performance with unlabeled data. To extract the training signals with a more optimal amount of task specificity, the framework adopts class-agnostic pseudo labels and includes three cascaded training stages, where each stage uses a specific type of data. By performing warmup training on a large amount of class-agnostic pseudo labels on unlabeled data, the class-agnostic model has strong generalization ability and is equipped with the right amount task-specific knowledge. When finetuned on different downstream tasks, the model can better avoid overfitting to the ground-truth labels and thus can achieve better downstream performance. Our extensive experiments show the effectiveness of our framework on object detection with different unlabeled splits. Moreover, the pretrained class-agnostic model demonstrates excellent transferability to other instance-level detection frameworks and tasks.

References

1. Berthelot, D., et al.: MixMatch: a holistic approach to semi-supervised learning. In: NeurIPS (2019)
2. et al, R.: Not all unlabeled data are equal: learning to weight data in semi-supervised learning. In: NeurIPS (2020)
3. Carion, N., Massa, F., Synnaeve, G., Usunier, N., Kirillov, A., Zagoruyko, S.: End-to-end object detection with transformers. In: Vedaldi, A., Bischof, H., Brox, T., Frahm, J.-M. (eds.) ECCV 2020. LNCS, vol. 12346, pp. 213–229. Springer, Cham (2020). https://doi.org/10.1007/978-3-030-58452-8_13
4. Chen, K., et al.: Hybrid task cascade for instance segmentation. In: CVPR (2019)
5. Chen, K., et al.: MMDetection: open MMLab detection toolbox and benchmark (2019)
6. Chen, X., Fan, H., Girshick, R., He, K.: Improved baselines with momentum contrastive learning. arXiv (2020)
7. Chen, X., Girshick, R., He, K., Dollár, P.: Tensormask: A foundation for dense object segmentation. In: ICCV (2019)
8. Chen, X., He, K.: Exploring simple Siamese representation learning. In: CVPR (2021)
9. Chen, Y., et al.: Scale-aware automatic augmentation for object detection. In: CVPR (2021)
10. Cheng, B., Schwing, A.G., Kirillov, A.: Per-pixel classification is not all you need for semantic segmentation. In: NeurIPS (2021)
11. Chu, R., Sun, Y., Li, Y., Liu, Z., Zhang, C., Wei, Y.: Vehicle re-identification with viewpoint-aware metric learning. In: ICCV (2019)

12. Cordts, M., et al.: The cityscapes dataset for semantic urban scene understanding. In: CVPR (2016)
13. Dai, J., Li, Y., He, K., Sun, J.: R-FCN: object detection via region-based fully convolutional networks. In: NeurIPS (2016)
14. Dai, Z., Cai, B., Lin, Y., Chen, J.: UP-DETR: unsupervised pre-training for object detection with transformers. In: CVPR (2021)
15. Deng, J., Dong, W., Socher, R., Li, L.J., Li, K., Fei-Fei, L.: ImageNet: a large-scale hierarchical image database. In: CVPR (2009)
16. Dollár, P., Zitnick, C.L.: Fast edge detection using structured forests. PAMI **37**, 1558–1570 (2015)
17. Girshick, R., Donahue, J., Darrell, T., Malik, J.: Rich feature hierarchies for accurate object detection and semantic segmentation. In: CVPR (2014)
18. He, K., Fan, H., Wu, Y., Xie, S., Girshick, R.: Momentum contrast for unsupervised visual representation learning. In: CVPR (2020)
19. He, K., Gkioxari, G., Dollár, P., Girshick, R.B.: Mask R-CNN. In: ICCV (2017)
20. He, K., Zhang, X., Ren, S., Sun, J.: Deep residual learning for image recognition. In: CVPR (2016)
21. Hénaff, O.J., Koppula, S., Alayrac, J.B., van den Oord, A., Vinyals, O., Carreira, J.: Efficient visual pretraining with contrastive detection. In: ICCV (2021)
22. Hu, J., Shen, L., Sun, G.: Squeeze-and-excitation networks. In: CVPR (2018)
23. Huang, G., Liu, Z., Van Der Maaten, L., Weinberger, K.Q.: Densely connected convolutional networks. In: CVPR (2017)
24. Jeong, J., Lee, S., Kim, J., Kwak, N.: Consistency-based semi-supervised learning for object detection (2019)
25. Kim, D., Lin, T.Y., Angelova, A., Kweon, I.S., Kuo, W.: Learning open-world object proposals without learning to classify. arXiv (2021)
26. Kirillov, A., Girshick, R., He, K., Dollár, P.: Panoptic feature pyramid networks. In: CVPR (2019)
27. Krasin, I., et al.: OpenImages: a public dataset for large-scale multi-label and multi-class image classification. Dataset (2016). http://github.com/openimages
28. Krizhevsky, A., Sutskever, I., Hinton, G.E.: ImageNet classification with deep convolutional neural networks. In: NeurIPS (2012)
29. Kuznetsova, A., et al.: The open images dataset V4: unified image classification, object detection, and visual relationship detection at scale. IJCV **128**, 1956–1981 (2020). https://doi.org/10.1007/s11263-020-01316-z
30. Li, Y., Huang, D., Qin, D., Wang, L., Gong, B.: Improving object detection with *Selective* self-supervised self-training. In: Vedaldi, A., Bischof, H., Brox, T., Frahm, J.-M. (eds.) ECCV 2020. LNCS, vol. 12374, pp. 589–607. Springer, Cham (2020). https://doi.org/10.1007/978-3-030-58526-6_35
31. Li, Y., et al.: Fully convolutional networks for panoptic segmentation with point-based supervision. arXiv (2021)
32. Lin, T., Dollár, P., Girshick, R.B., He, K., Hariharan, B., Belongie, S.J.: Feature pyramid networks for object detection. In: CVPR (2017)
33. Lin, T.Y., Goyal, P., Girshick, R., He, K., Dollár, P.: Focal loss for dense object detection. In: ICCV (2017)
34. Lin, T.-Y., et al.: Microsoft COCO: common objects in context. In: Fleet, D., Pajdla, T., Schiele, B., Tuytelaars, T. (eds.) ECCV 2014. LNCS, vol. 8693, pp. 740–755. Springer, Cham (2014). https://doi.org/10.1007/978-3-319-10602-1_48
35. Liu, S., Qi, L., Qin, H., Shi, J., Jia, J.: Path aggregation network for instance segmentation. In: CVPR (2018)

36. Liu, Z., et al.: Swin transformer: hierarchical vision transformer using shifted windows. In: ICCV (2021)
37. Morrison, D., et al.: Cartman: the low-cost cartesian manipulator that won the amazon robotics challenge. In: ICRA (2018)
38. Mottaghi, R., et al.: The role of context for object detection and semantic segmentation in the wild. In: CVPR (2014)
39. Qi, L., Jiang, L., Liu, S., Shen, X., Jia, J.: Amodal instance segmentation with KINS dataset. In: CVPR (2019)
40. Qi, L., et al.: Multi-scale aligned distillation for low-resolution detection. In: CVPR (2021)
41. Qi, L., et al.: Open-world entity segmentation. arXiv (2021)
42. Qi, L., Zhang, X., Chen, Y., Chen, Y., Sun, J., Jia, J.: PointINS: point-based instance segmentation. arXiv (2020)
43. Radosavovic, I., Dollár, P., Girshick, R., Gkioxari, G., He, K.: Data distillation: towards omni-supervised learning. In: CVPR (2018)
44. Ramanathan, V., Wang, R., Mahajan, D.: PreDet: large-scale weakly supervised pre-training for detection. In: ICCV (2021)
45. Ren, S., He, K., Girshick, R.B., Sun, J.: Faster R-CNN: towards real-time object detection with region proposal networks. In: NeurIPS (2015)
46. Sharma, A., Khan, N., Mubashar, M., Sundaramoorthi, G., Torr, P.: Class-agnostic segmentation loss and its application to salient object detection and segmentation. In: ICCV (2021)
47. Shu, G.: Human detection, tracking and segmentation in surveillance video (2014)
48. Simonyan, K., Zisserman, A.: Very deep convolutional networks for large-scale image recognition. In: ICLR (2015)
49. Sohn, K., Zhang, Z., Li, C.L., Zhang, H., Lee, C.Y., Pfister, T.: A simple semi-supervised learning framework for object detection. arXiv (2020)
50. Sun, K., Xiao, B., Liu, D., Wang, J.: Deep high-resolution representation learning for human pose estimation. In: CVPR (2019)
51. Szegedy, C., Ioffe, S., Vanhoucke, V., Alemi, A.: Inception-v4, inception-ResNet and the impact of residual connections on learning. arXiv (2016)
52. Szegedy, C., et al.: Going deeper with convolutions. In: CVPR (2015)
53. Szegedy, C., Vanhoucke, V., Ioffe, S., Shlens, J., Wojna, Z.: Rethinking the inception architecture for computer vision. In: CVPR (2016)
54. Tang, P., Ramaiah, C., Wang, Y., Xu, R., Xiong, C.: Proposal learning for semi-supervised object detection. In: WACV (2021)
55. Tian, Z., Shen, C., Chen, H.: Conditional convolutions for instance segmentation. In: Vedaldi, A., Bischof, H., Brox, T., Frahm, J.-M. (eds.) ECCV 2020. LNCS, vol. 12346, pp. 282–298. Springer, Cham (2020). https://doi.org/10.1007/978-3-030-58452-8_17
56. Tian, Z., Shen, C., Chen, H., He, T.: FCOS: fully convolutional one-stage object detection. In: ICCV (2019)
57. Wang, K., Yan, X., Zhang, D., Zhang, L., Lin, L.: Towards human-machine cooperation: self-supervised sample mining for object detection. In: CVPR (2018)
58. Wang, W., Feiszli, M., Wang, H., Tran, D.: Unidentified video objects: a benchmark for dense, open-world segmentation. arXiv (2021)
59. Wang, X., Zhang, R., Shen, C., Kong, T., Li, L.: Dense contrastive learning for self-supervised visual pre-training. In: CVPR (2021)
60. Wu, Y., Kirillov, A., Massa, F., Lo, W.Y., Girshick, R.: Detectron2 (2019). http://github.com/facebookresearch/detectron2

61. Xiao, B., Wu, H., Wei, Y.: Simple baselines for human pose estimation and tracking. In: Ferrari, V., Hebert, M., Sminchisescu, C., Weiss, Y. (eds.) ECCV 2018. LNCS, vol. 11210, pp. 472–487. Springer, Cham (2018). https://doi.org/10.1007/978-3-030-01231-1_29
62. Xie, E., et al.: DetCo: unsupervised contrastive learning for object detection. In: ICCV (2021)
63. Xie, E., et al.: PolarMask: single shot instance segmentation with polar representation. In: CVPR (2020)
64. Xu, M., et al.: End-to-end semi-supervised object detection with soft teacher. In: ICCV (2021)
65. Zhang, R., Tian, Z., Shen, C., You, M., Yan, Y.: Mask encoding for single shot instance segmentation. In: CVPR (2020)
66. Zhou, B., Lapedriza, A., Khosla, A., Oliva, A., Torralba, A.: Places: a 10 million image database for scene recognition. TPAMI **40**, 1452–1464 (2017)
67. Zhou, X., Wang, D., Krähenbühl, P.: Objects as points (2019)
68. Zoph, B., et al.: Rethinking pre-training and self-training. In: NeurIPS (2020)

Dual Adaptive Transformations for Weakly Supervised Point Cloud Segmentation

Zhonghua Wu[1,2], Yicheng Wu[3], Guosheng Lin[1,2(✉)], Jianfei Cai[2,3], and Chen Qian[4]

[1] S-Lab, Nanyang Technological University, Singapore, Singapore
zhonghua001@e.ntu.edu.sg, gslin@ntu.edu.sg
[2] School of Computer Science and Engineering, Nanyang Technological University, Singapore, Singapore
[3] Department of Data Science and AI, Monash University, Melbourne, Australia
[4] SenseTime Research, Shanghai, China

Abstract. Weakly supervised point cloud segmentation, i.e. semantically segmenting a point cloud with only a few labeled points in the whole 3D scene, is highly desirable due to the heavy burden of collecting abundant dense annotations for the model training. However, existing methods remain challenging to accurately segment 3D point clouds since limited annotated data may lead to insufficient guidance for label propagation to unlabeled data. Considering the smoothness-based methods have achieved promising progress, in this paper, we advocate applying the consistency constraint under various perturbations to effectively regularize unlabeled 3D points. Specifically, we propose a novel DAT (**D**ual **A**daptive **T**ransformations) model for weakly supervised point cloud segmentation, where the dual adaptive transformations are performed via an adversarial strategy at both point-level and region-level, aiming at enforcing the local and structural smoothness constraints on 3D point clouds. We evaluate our proposed DAT model with two popular backbones on the large-scale S3DIS and ScanNet-V2 datasets. Extensive experiments demonstrate that our model can effectively leverage the unlabeled 3D points and achieve significant performance gains on both datasets, setting new state-of-the-art performance for weakly supervised point cloud segmentation.

Keywords: Weakly supervised segmentation · Point cloud segmentation · Dual adaptive transformations

1 Introduction

Recently, the deep learning (DL)-based methods have achieved significant performance gains for the point cloud segmentation task, which is a fundamental

Supplementary Information The online version contains supplementary material available at https://doi.org/10.1007/978-3-031-19821-2_5.

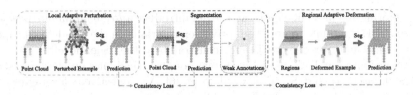

Fig. 1. Illustration of the proposed Dual Adaptive Transformation (DAT) model. We encourage DAT to produce consistent predictions under local and regional adaptive transformations. Note that, there are only few labeled points inside the whole scene to train our model. During testing, only segmentation module (blue) is used to generate the segmentation prediction. (Color figure online)

and critical step to understand realistic scenes [13] and analyze 3D geometric data [59]. However, it is extremely costly and labor-consuming to collect abundant dense annotations of 3D point clouds for model training. Thus, it is highly desirable to develop effective algorithms that can well segment point cloud data with only weak annotations of point clouds.

For semantic image segmentation tasks, there are different types of weak annotations including image-level labels [31,41,55], scribbles [22,48], or partially labeled samples [23,28,49]. For the point cloud segmentation task, following the recent work [24], we consider partially labeled samples as weak annotations for the model training, i.e., only a few sparse points inside the whole scene are labeled and all other points are unlabeled. The latest model 1T1C [24] attempts to train a segmentation model with limited labeled points and then propagate the labels to the unlabeled points as the pseudo labels for iteratively refining the model. However, such a training strategy is time-consuming and is often affected by unreliable pseudo labels, resulting in sub-optimal segmentation performance. Here, we hypothesize that the weakly supervised segmentation performance can be further improved by adding more constraints on the unlabeled 3D points.

To exploit the unlabeled data, the consistency-based learning methods have shown promising progress in natural image classification and segmentation. For example, [2,8,34] encouraged the model to produce invariant results under various strong data augmentations. However, it is non-trivial to apply these image-based strong data augmentation techniques to point cloud processing, and point cloud-specific augmentations are still under early exploration [4,19]. This motivates us to investigate an effective transformation method to leverage large amounts of unlabeled 3D points by applying sufficient smoothness constraints for weakly supervised point cloud segmentation.

Specifically, in this paper, we propose a **Dual Adaptive Transformation (DAT)** model, where we encourage consistent predictions between original and local/regional adaptively transformed point clouds data. As shown in Fig. 1, we first design a *Local Adaptive Perturbation (LAP)* module that computes the adaptive perturbations for both point coordinates and their associate features. Meanwhile, considering the feature distributions are quite different between different classes, we further embed the class-aware information into the LAP module to generate class-aware adaptive feature perturbations. Then, to capture more structural information in point clouds, we further introduce a *Regional Adaptive Deformation (RAD)* module to apply adaptive deformations on the pre-defined superpoints, which enforces the consistency constraints at the region level.

We evaluate our DAT model with two popular backbones on the large-scale S3DIS dataset [1] and ScanNet-v2 dataset [6]. Via effectively leveraging the unlabeled point clouds, our DAT model is able to segment point cloud data with very few annotations, setting new state-of-the-art (SOTA) performance for the weakly supervised point cloud segmentation task. For example, on S3DIS dataset [1], the DAT model outperforms the previous SOTA model 1T1C [24] by 6.5% under the "One Thing One Click" annotation setting. Note that our proposed strategy can be easily combined with other frameworks. For instance, based on our design, the segmentation performance of 1T1C [24] model can be further improved by 2.9%/3.0% on the ScanNet-v2 test/validation set [6], respectively.

Overall, our main contributions are three-fold:

- We propose a novel Dual Adaptive Transformation (DAT) model for weakly supervised point cloud segmentation, with the key insight that applying the consistency constraint under local and regional adaptive transformations can effectively leverage a large amount of unlabeled 3D points and facilitate a better model training.
- We introduce the Local Adaptive Perturbation (LAP) module, where we inject the adaptive perturbations to point coordinates and the associate feature inputs separately. Meanwhile, we embed the information of the class-aware point feature distribution into the generation of the local adaptive feature perturbations, which leads to better performance.
- We introduce the Regional Adaptive Deformation (RAD) module, where we generate structural adaptive deformations at the region-level, i.e. adaptive deformations such as shifting, scaling, and rotation for the superpoint regions. Such regional deformations introduce another level of the consistency constraint, which is a complement to LAP.

2   Related Work

2.1   Deep Learning on Point Clouds

DL-based methods have achieved great progress to process point cloud data. For example, PointNet model [32] used permutation-invariant operators such as pooling layers to aggregate the features from all points. Then, PointNet++ model [33] further designed a hierarchical spatial structure to extract local geometric features. Furthermore, the graph-based methods [17,18,42] built a graph for all points and applied the message passing mechanism on the graph. For instance, DGCNN [42] used a kNN graph to perform graph convolutions. To capture contextual relationships, SPG [17] constructed a graph on the sub-regions, i.e. the superpoints. DeepGCNs [18] explored the depth information in graph convolutional networks. Afterwards, [26,35,38,54] further improved the performance by directly applying continuous convolutions on the points without any quantization. Spider-CNN [54] used polynomial functions to generate the kernel weights and the spherical convolution [35] was used to address the 3D rotation equivariance problem in Spherical CNN. KPConv [38] constructed the kernel weights based on the input coordinates and achieved good performance. Similarly, InterpCNN [26] interpolated point-wise kernel weights by utilizing the coordinate information. Different from point convolution networks, the voxel-based methods [5] firstly quantized all the points and map the points to the regular voxels and then applied 3D convolutions on the regular voxels to obtain point features.

In this paper, we adopt the point-based KPConv model [38] as our backbone, where the model is trained via encouraging the dual adaptive transformation consistency for weakly supervised point cloud segmentation. Furthermore, in Sect. 4.2, we also extend our method to the voxel-based framework MinkowiNet [5] so as to demonstrate the generalization ability of our training strategy.

2.2 Weakly Supervised Point Cloud Segmentation

There are some DL-based methods being proposed recently for the weakly supervised point cloud segmentation task [7,9,10,12,20,27,30,36,40,51,56,60]. For example, Wang et al. [39] proposed to generate point cloud segmentation labels by back-projecting 2D image annotations to 3D spaces. However, annotating large-scale image semantic segmentation datasets is extremely labor-consuming. To reduce the labeling costs, Wei et al. [44] used the Class Activation Map (CAM) [50,58] to generate pseudo segmentation masks with sub-cloud level annotations. However, its performance is limited due to the lack of localization information in labels. To address the issue, Xu et al. [53] further labeled 10% points in the whole point cloud, which is able to achieve a good performance comparable to the fully-supervised references. Then, the 1T1C method [24] under the "One Thing One Click" setting was introduced to tackle this task, which uses fewer labeled points, i.e. only labeling one point per thing in each scene.

Here, we follow the 1T1C method [24] to conduct experiments. Different from the iterative refinement mechanism used in 1T1C which brings in significant computational cost, we propose an end-to-end training strategy to train a model in the identical weakly supervised manner while without the need for any iterative refinement.

2.3 Consistency-Based Semi-supervised Learning

Our work is closely related to the consistency based semi-supervised learning (SSL) [45,46], where the basic idea is to leverage the unlabeled data based on the smoothness assumptions, i.e. deep models under various small perturbations or augmentations should output consistent results. For example, Bortsova et al. [3] enforced the model to produce invariant predictions for unlabeled images under different transformations. For semi-supervised image classification task, the VAT model [29] designed an adversarial perturbation and then encouraged the consistency between the original data and its adversarial one. Temporal ensembling [16] and mean teacher [37] generated similar distributions for the perturbed inputs. Meanwhile, the mutual learning strategy has been studied for semi-supervised learning [47,57]. For instance, the dual-student model [14] enforced two sub-networks learn from each other via constraining the consistent predictions. FixMatch [34] further explicitly generated the pseudo labels from the data with weak augmentations and used them to guide the prediction from the strongly augmented samples.

Motivated by the consistency-based semi-supervised learning methods which encourage the model to produce consistent results under various perturbations, we propose the DAT model for the weakly supervised point cloud segmentation task with two major novel designs, i.e. the LAP and RAD modules.

3   Methods

Figure 2 gives an overview of the proposed Dual Adaptive Transformation (DAT) model, which consists of three main modules: the class-aware Local Adaptive Perturbation (LAP) module, the Regional Adaptive Deformation (RAD) module, and the original SEGmentation (SEG) module. LAP contains a novel Class-aware Perturbation Generator (CPG) to produce semantic perturbations at the point level. RAD generates structural augmented examples by applying various deformations at the region level. SEG contains a conventional point cloud segmentation backbone.

3.1   Segmentation Module

We first define a set of notations for the weakly supervised point cloud segmentation task. Specifically, consider a set of points $X = [C, F] \in \mathbb{R}^{N \times 3 + D_f}$ with point coordinates $C \in \mathbb{R}^{N \times 3}$ and the corresponding features $F \in \mathbb{R}^{N \times D_f}$ as the model input, and denote $Y \in \mathbb{R}^{N \times 1}$ as the groundtruth label, which is a very sparse one with only M known entries, $M << N$. The output of SEG module is the predicted segmentation mask $\hat{Y}$. The segmentation module aims to train the backbone model with few labeled points in Y. Here, we adopt a popular segmentation framework KPConv [38] as our backbone. With the kernel parameters denoted as θ, the model prediction is given by $p(\hat{y}_i | c_i, f_i; \theta)$, $i \in \{1, ..., N\}$, where c_i and f_i are respectively the point coordinates and features of point x_i. We train the segmentation module by applying a cross-entropy loss $\mathcal{L}_{seg}$ on the few labels in Y and the corresponding predictions in $\hat{Y}$.

3.2   Local Adaptive Perturbation Module

We design a Local Adaptive Perturbation (LAP) module to generate perturbed examples X^{lap} by applying the adaptive perturbations on the point coordinates and the corresponding features. In particular, the input to LAP is the point cloud X and the output is the perturbed examples X^{lap} with the injection of the adaptive perturbations R^{ada}. Inspired by VAT [29], which is proposed for

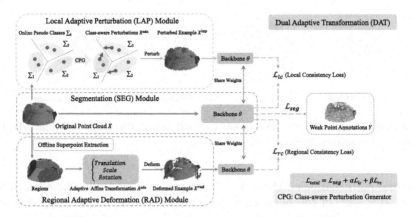

Fig. 2. Overall pipeline of our proposed Dual Adaptive Transformation (DAT) model, which consists of three main modules: the segmentation (SEG) module (blue), the Local Adaptive Perturbation (LAP) module (yellow), and the Regional Adaptive Deformation (RAD) Module (green). SEG module adopts KPConv backbone to train the model with few labeled points. LAP module is to generate class-aware perturbed examples on each point. RAD module generates structural deformed data by applying the adaptive affine transformations on each region. Note that, during testing, we only employ SEG module to process point cloud data. (Color figure online)

semi-supervised image classification, to achieve local distributional smoothness (LDS) as a smoothness constrain to regularize unlabeled data, we encourage our model to generate consistent outputs between each input point $x \in X$ and its perturbed version $x + r^{ada}$, where $r^{ada} \in R^{ada}$ is the corresponding adaptive perturbation:

$$\mathcal{LDS}(x; \theta) = D\left[p(\hat{y}|x; \theta), p(\hat{y}|x + r^{ada}; \theta)\right]. \tag{1}$$

Here D is a non-negative loss function to measure the divergence between x and $x + r^{ada}$. Then, we compute r^{ada} by estimating a gradient g of $\mathcal{LDS}$ with a random input vector d as

$$g = \nabla_R D\left[p(\hat{y}|x, \theta), p(\hat{y}|x + r, \theta)\right]\Big|_{r=\xi d}$$
$$r^{ada} = \epsilon \times g/\|g\|_2, \tag{2}$$

where ξ and ϵ are two hyper-parameters to control the magnitude of the perturbation, and g can be efficiently computed by applying the back-propagation on the network.

Considering the input point coordinates and features are two different types of inputs, we generate their perturbations separately. In other words, for an input point x consisting of its coordinates c and features f, we generate the adaptive perturbation data $c + r_c^{ada}$ and $f + r_f^{ada}$ with the initial random unit vectors d_c and d_f, respectively.

Class-Aware Perturbation Generator. Note that many existing perturbation based semi-supervised image classification methods [29] usually generate

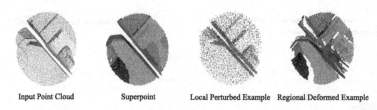

Input Point Cloud   Superpoint   Local Perturbed Example   Regional Deformed Example

Fig. 3. Visual results for the superpoint estimation and the generated dual adaptive transformed examples during the training stage.

the initial perturbations d through sampling them from an iid Gaussian distribution. However, in the point cloud segmentation task, directly applying this to generate d_f might not be optimal. This is because, for different classes, their input point feature distributions are quite different across different dimensions. A class-agnostic iid Gaussian sampling might generate unrealistic perturbations.

Therefore, we propose a Class-aware Perturbation Generator (CPG) to obtain d_f for each point. Specifically, in each training iteration, we generate the pseudo labels $\hat{y}$ for all the points with the current model parameter $\hat{\theta}$, where $\hat{y} \in \{1, ..., K_c\}$ with K_c being the number of classes. Based on that, we establish a zero-mean multivariate normal distribution $\mathbb{N}(0, \sum_k)$. Here $\sum_k$ is the class-conditional covariance matrix estimated from all the input point features (e.g. rgbh for KPConv) that belong to the pseudo-class k. Afterward, we update the covariance matrix in an online manner [43] with the statistics of the features from each mini-batch. In this way, at each iteration, d_f is then generated by sampling from the up-to-date class-aware multivariate Gaussian distribution. For d_c, we adopt the conventional way i.e. sampling the initial input vectors from an iid Gaussian distribution, since the point clouds are unordered and the individual coordinates alone are not closely related to the class of the points. This is also observed in the PointNet model [32].

With the generated d_c and d_f, our LDS loss for point clouds now becomes:

$$\begin{aligned}
\mathcal{LDS}(x;\theta) &= D\left[p(\hat{y}|c, f; \theta), p(\hat{y}|c + \xi_c d_c, f + \xi_f d_f; \theta)\right] \\
g_c &= \nabla_{\xi_c d_c} \mathcal{LDS}(x, \theta) \\
g_f &= \nabla_{\xi_f d_f} \mathcal{LDS}(x, \theta),
\end{aligned} \tag{3}$$

where we use the Kullback-Leibler divergence (KL-div) for D. Finally, we obtain the r_c^{ada} and r_f^{ada} by

$$\begin{aligned}
r_c^{\mathrm{ada}} &= \epsilon_c g_c / \|g_c\|_2 \\
r_f^{\mathrm{ada}} &= \epsilon_f g_f / \|g_f\|_2.
\end{aligned} \tag{4}$$

In this way, the perturbed examples X^{lap} is obtained by point-wise adding the perturbations r_c^{ada} and r_f^{ada} on the coordinates c and the features f, respectively. One example is visualized in the third column of Fig. 3.

3.3   Regional Adaptive Deformation Module

In addition to the local adaptive perturbations, considering point clouds often contain various structural local deformations such as region shift, rotation, and scaling, we further design a regional adaptive deformation (RAD) module to generate structural local deformations. RAD module takes point cloud X as input and outputs region-level augmented examples X^{rad} by deforming each region with adaptive affine transformations A^{ada}. As shown in Fig. 2, we firstly over-segment point cloud X into a set of superpoints $S_i, i \in \{1, ..., K_s\}$ via [6,17]. For each superpoint S_i, we generate the adaptive deformed example S_i^{ada}. Combing all $S_i^{ada}, i \in \{1, ..., K_s\}$, we obtain X^{rad}.

For each superpoint S_i, we firstly generate the initial affine transformation matrices $A_{i,j}$, whose parameters are randomly sampled from an iid Gaussian distribution. Then, we deform each superpoint as

$$S_i^{int} = S_i \cdot \prod_{j=1}^{K_a} \xi_A A_{i,j}, \tag{5}$$

where $A_{i,j}, j \in \{1, ..., K_a\}$, corresponds to the j-th type of deformations. Combining all $S_i^{int}, i \in \{1, ..., K_s\}$, we obtain the initial deformed point cloud X^{int}. The $\mathcal{LDS}$ loss becomes

$$\mathcal{LDS}(X; \theta) = D\left[p(\hat{y}|x; \theta), p(\hat{y}|x^{int}; \theta)\right]$$
$$g_{A_{i,j}} = \nabla_{\xi_A A_{i,j}} \mathcal{LDS}(x; \theta). \tag{6}$$

Then, we obtain the $A_{i,j}^{ada}$ by

$$A_{i,j}^{ada} = \epsilon_A g_{A_{i,j}} / \|g_{A_{i,j}}\|_2. \tag{7}$$

Finally, the regional deformed examples X^{rad} is obtained by combining all the deformed superpoints S_i^{ada}, which is computed as

$$S_i^{ada} = S_i * \prod_{j=1}^{K_a} A_{i,j}^{ada}. \tag{8}$$

Specifically, we use the following three types of affine transformations: translation, scale and rotation.

One RAD example is given in the fourth column of Fig. 3. Algorithm 1 summarizes the process of generating the adversarial examples under both LAP and RAD.

3.4   Training Losses

The overall training loss can be written as

$$\mathcal{L}_{total} = \mathcal{L}_{seg} + \alpha \mathcal{L}_{lc} + \beta \mathcal{L}_{rc} \tag{9}$$

Algorithm 1. Generating adaptive transformed examples (LAP/RAD)

Input: Training Point Cloud X

Output: Local perturbed examples X^{lap}/ Regional deformed examples X^{rad}

1. Generate initial R/A for initial transformation.
2. Compute the gradient of D with respective to R/A

   $g_R/g_A \leftarrow \nabla_r D\left[p(\hat{y}|x;\theta), p(\hat{y}|x \odot R;\theta)\right]\Big|_{r=\xi(R/A)}$ where $\odot$: $\oplus/\otimes$ for LAP/RAD,
   respectively.
3. Normalize the gradient to generate adaptive perturbations R^{ada}/A^{ada}.
   $R^{ada} \leftarrow \epsilon \cdot g_R/\|g_R\|_2$ or $A^{ada} \leftarrow \epsilon \cdot g_A/\|g_A\|_2$
4. Generate the adversarial examples X^{lap} / X^{rad} by injecting the R^{ada} / A^{ada} to
   Point Cloud X.

---

where $\mathcal{L}_{seg}$, $\mathcal{L}_{lc}$ and $\mathcal{L}_{rc}$ are *Segmentation Loss*, *Local Consistency Loss* and *Regional Consistency Loss*, respectively, and α and β are trade-off weights, both set as 2 to balance the losses. Segmentation Loss $\mathcal{L}_{seg}$ is to guide the segmentation prediction with the limited annotations in Y. Specifically, we follow the KPConv [38] by using the cross entropy loss for $\mathcal{L}_{seg}$ to train the segmentation prediction $\hat{Y}$. Local Consistency Loss $\mathcal{L}_{lc}$ encourages the consistency and penalizes the prediction difference between the original point cloud X and the local perturbed examples X^{lap}. Regional Consistency Loss $\mathcal{L}_{rc}$ ensures the consistency between X and its regional deformed examples X^{rad}. $\mathcal{L}_{pc}$ and $\mathcal{L}_{rc}$ are defined as

$$\mathcal{L}_{pc} = D\left[p(\hat{y}|x;\theta), p(\hat{y}|x^{lap};\theta)\right]$$
$$\mathcal{L}_{rc} = D\left[p(\hat{y}|x;\theta), p(\hat{y}|x^{rad};\theta)\right] \tag{10}$$

where D is the KL-div loss.

4   Experiments and Results

4.1   Implementation Details

Datasets. Following the 1T1C [24] model, we conduct experiments on two large-scale point cloud datasets - the S3DIS [1] and ScanNet-v2 [6]. The S3DIS dataset consists of 3D scans of 271 rooms with 13 categories belonging to 6 areas. For fair comparisons, we train the segmentation model on Area 1, 2, 3, 4, 6 and test on Area 5 as [24]. The ScanNet-v2 dataset contains 1201, 312, and 100 3D scans for training, validation, and testing, respectively.

Weak Annotation Scheme. For fair comparisons, on the S3DIS dataset, we label the data under the "One Thing One Click" (OTOC) setting as in 1T1C [24]. We randomly select a point in each object with the identical probability as the labeled points. Therefore, only 0.02% of points have annotations inside the whole point cloud. On the ScanNet-v2 dataset, we evaluate our DAT model on the "3D Semantic label with Limited Annotations" benchmark [6]. In this benchmark, only 20 points are labeled in each room scene.

Table 1. Comparison of our DAT with several existing methods on the S3DIS Area-5 set. Note that, we report the performance as final results based on the KPConv [38] backbone.

Method	Supervision (%)	mIoU (%)
PointNet [32]	100%	41.1
PointCNN [21]	100%	57.3
Xu et al. [53]	0.2%	44.5
Xu et al. [53]	10%	48.0
GPFN [39]	16.7% 2D	50.8
GPFN [39]	100% 2D	52.5
1T1C [24]	0.02% (OTOC)	50.1
1T1C [24]	0.06% (OTTC)	55.3
Our DAT	0.02% (OTOC)	**56.5**
Our DAT	0.06% (OTTC)	**58.5**
Our upper bound	100%	65.4

Table 2. Comparison of our DAT with its variant methods with the KPConv framework. Note that, all experiments are conducted under the OTOC setting on the S3DIS dataset

Method	Random noises		LAP	RAD	mIoU (%)
	Features	Coordinates			
Our baseline					50.1
Ours w/ Noise	✓				49.1
Ours w/ Noise		✓			52.9
Ours w/ Noise	✓	✓			52.6
Ours w/ PAP			✓		53.9
Ours w/ RAD				✓	54.8
Our DAT			✓	✓	**56.5**

Experiment Setting. If there is no special declaration, we implement our proposed DAT training method based on the KPConv *rigid* model. We use SGD to train the model with learning rate of 0.01 and batch size of 2. Following 1T1C [24], we use the geometrical partition results [17] and mesh segment results [6] as the superpoints for S3DIS and ScanNet-v2 datasets, respectively. We set the hyper-parameters $\xi_c = 10$, $\xi_f = 0.1$, $\xi_A = 0.1$, $\epsilon_c = 1$, $\epsilon_f = 0.05$, $\epsilon_A = 0.05$. During the model training, to reduce the GPU memory consumption, we employ the segmentation loss $\mathcal{L}_{seg}$ at all iterations and randomly apply local consistency loss $\mathcal{L}_{lc}$ or regional consistency loss $\mathcal{L}_{rc}$ with an equal probability of 0.5 to train our model. All of our experiments are conducted on a single NVIDIA RTX 3090 GPU with PyTorch 1.7.0 and CUDA 11.0.

Table 3. Ablation studies of our DAT about the Class-aware Perturbation Generator (CPG) used in our LAP module under the OTOC setting on the S3DIS dataset.

Method	LAP			RAD	mIoU (%)
	Feat. w/o CPG	Feat. w/ CPG	Coordinates		
Ours w/o RAD	✓				51.3
Ours w/o RAD		✓			**51.7**
Ours w/o RAD	✓		✓		53.3
Ours w/o RAD		✓	✓		**53.9**
Our DAT	✓		✓	✓	55.1
Our DAT		✓	✓	✓	**56.5**

4.2 Evaluations on S3DIS Dataset

Comparing with State-of-the-Art Methods. Table 1 shows the results of our DAT and several SOTA methods on the S3DIS Area 5 dataset. Via effectively exploiting the unlabeled data, the DAT model with few labeled points training achieves comparable results with the upper bound (i.e. the fully-supervised KPConv model with 100% labeled data training). Furthermore, under the "OTOC" setting, the DAT model significantly outperforms the second-best 1T1C method by 6.4% mIOU gains on the S3DIS dataset. In addition, we further perform the "One Thing Three clicks" (OTTC) setting, where we annotate three points for each target. Our model outperforms the corresponding second-best method 1T1C [24] by 3.2%.

Ablation Studies Comparisons with Baselines. We perform the ablation studies on the S3DIS dataset, to show the effectiveness of our proposed DAT. The first baseline is that we only use the segmentation loss $\mathcal{L}_{seg}$ on a few labeled points to train the segmentation model, which is denoted as "Our Baseline" in Table 2. Our proposed DAT outperforms "Our baseline" by 6.4%. Another baseline is that we apply random noises to all the points to generate perturbed examples. Then we use KL-div loss to encourage the prediction consistency between the original point cloud and the perturbed examples. Specifically, similar to our designed LAP, we are able to apply random noises to point coordinates, point features, or both, which is denoted as "Ours w/ Noise". As Table 2 shows, the DAT significantly outperforms two baseline methods, which suggests that our adaptive perturbations achieve better regularization to the unlabeled data compared to the random noises.

Effects of LAP and RAD. To demonstrate the effects of two novel modules, as shown in Table 2, with separately applying consistency loss on the transformed examples generated by LAP (Ours w/ LAP) or RAD (Ours w/ RAD), we are able to significantly improve mIoU results compared with the "Our Baseline". This suggests that enforcing the consistency between the prediction of transformed

	R	G	B	H		R	G	B	H		R	G	B	H
R	0.0711	0.0698	0.0635	-0.0036	R	0.0683	0.0720	0.0724	-0.0154	R	0.0700	0.0515	0.0383	0.0147
G	0.0698	0.0698	0.0646	-0.0081	G	0.0720	0.0807	0.0860	-0.0430	G	0.0515	0.0441	0.0353	0.0113
B	0.0635	0.0646	0.0622	-0.0084	B	0.0724	0.0860	0.0991	-0.0689	B	0.0383	0.0353	0.0309	0.0095
H	-0.0036	-0.0081	-0.0084	0.8208	H	-0.0154	-0.0430	-0.0689	0.7161	H	0.0147	0.0113	0.0095	0.0820
		Wall					Window					Sofa		

Fig. 4. Three covariance matrices estimated via our designed CPG module under the OTOC setting on the S3DIS datasets.

Table 4. Ablation studies of our DAT on different affine transformations used in RAD module under the OTOC setting on the S3DIS dataset.

Method	LAP	RAD			mIoU (%)
		Translation	Scale	Rotation	
Ours w/ RAD		✓			54.1
Ours w/ RAD			✓		54.6
Ours w/ RAD				✓	53.9
Ours w/ RAD		✓	✓		**54.8**
Ours w/ RAD		✓		✓	54.6
Ours w/ RAD		✓	✓	✓	54.5
Our DAT	✓	✓			55.5
Our DAT	✓		✓		55.9
Our DAT	✓			✓	55.2
Our DAT	✓	✓	✓		56.0
Our DAT	✓	✓		✓	55.2
Our DAT	✓	✓	✓	✓	**56.5**

examples and the original point clouds can predict better segmentation masks. "Our DAT" denotes that we apply the consistency loss on both LAP and RAD. Table 2 shows combining both modules can further improve mIoU by 2.6% and 1.7% compared with only using LAP or RAD, respectively.

Effects of CPG. We further verify the effectiveness of our designed CPG used in the LAP module. "Feat. w/o CPG" denotes that we generate the initial perturbation d_f from the iid Gaussian distribution, instead of the class-aware multivariate Gaussian distribution. Table 3 shows that our class-aware perturbation generator is able to boost segmentation performance under all settings, which suggests that the class-aware information is critical in the point cloud segmentation task.

Besides, Fig. 4 gives three examples of the computed covariance matrices in the CPG, where we randomly select them from all 13 covariance matrices. We can observe that different classes have different covariance matrices.

Different Affine Transformations in RAD. Table 4 shows the mIoU results for our DAT with different affine transformations. "Ours w/ RAD" indicates that we only apply the consistency loss on the deformed examples generated by RAD, and "Our DAT" indicates that we make use of all the transformed examples generated by LAP and RAD to train the model. As Table 4 shows, "Our DAT" achieves the best performance by using all three affine transformation methods (i.e. translation, scale and rotation).

Generalization Ability. To verify the generalization ability, we further use our training strategy to train a voxel-based segmentation framework (i.e. Minkowski-iNet [5]). Unlike the point-based methods, the voxel-based methods firstly project the point cloud into regular voxels and then apply 3D sparse convolution on it. Since the projecting operation is non-differentiable and cannot back-propagate the gradients to point coordinates, we only employ the LAP

Table 5. To show the generalization ability, we further show the results with Minkowski-iNet32 [5] backbone on the S3DIS Area-5 set. "Our DAT*" denotes we only use our LAP module to train the backbone.

Method	Supervision (%)	mIoU (%)
Our Baseline	0.02% (OTOC)	48.7
Our Baseline	0.06% (OTTC)	55.0
Our DAT*	0.02% (OTOC)	**54.6**
Our DAT*	0.06% (OTTC)	**58.2**
Our Upper bound	100%	65.4

Table 6. Comparison of our DAT model with several existing methods on the ScanNet-v2 test set. "Our DAT†" denotes that our DAT is built upon the 1T1C [24] model.

Method	Supervision	mIoU (%)
Pointnet++ [33]	100%	33.9
PointCNN [21]	100%	45.8
MinkowskiNet [5]	100%	73.6
Virtual MVFusion [15]	100%+2D	74.6
MPRM [44]	Scene-level	24.4
MPRM [44]	Subcloud-level	41.1
MPRM+CRF [44]	Subcloud-level	43.2
CSC_LA_SEM [11]	20 points	53.1
Viewpoint_BN_LA_AIR [25]	20 points	54.8
PointContrast_LA_SEM [52]	20 points	55.0
1T1C [24]	20 points	59.4
Our Baseline	20 points	51.6
Our DAT	20 points	55.2
Our DAT†	20 points	**62.3**
Our Upper Bound	100%	68.4

module to add adaptive perturbations on the input features with the CPG module (labeled as "Our DAT*" in Table 5). Table 5 shows, under the OTOC/OTTC setting, our model improves the mIoU results by 5.9%/3.2% compared to their respective "Our Baseline", which demonstrates that such novel training strategy is general and effective, and can be easily applied to various point cloud frameworks.

4.3   Evaluations on ScanNet-v2 Dataset

Tables 6 and 7 respectively give the results on the test and validation set of ScanNet-v2 dataset in the "3D Semantic label with Limited Annotations" benchmark. We use the officially given 20 points annotations as the sparse labels to train the model. Compared with "Our Baseline", our DAT (denoted as "Our DAT") with the KPConv backbone can achieve impressive performance gains of 3.2% and 3.9% mIoU on ScanNet-v2 test and validation sets, respectively.

Meanwhile, such a training strategy can be easily combined with existing models for point cloud segmentation. For example, on the ScanNet-v2 dataset, we build our DAT upon the 1T1C model, which is used to generate the pseudo labels for all training data. Then we use the pseudo labels to train our DAT. Based on the 1T1C model (denoted as "Our DAT †" in Tables 6 and 7), our DAT can further improve the mIoU results by 2.9% and 3.0% on the ScanNet-v2 test and validation set compared with 1T1C, respectively. This suggests that our training strategy can further improve the performance of other SOTA models.

Table 7. Comparison of our DAT model with several existing methods on the ScanNet-v2 validation set. "Our DAT†" denotes that our DAT is built upon the 1T1C [24] model.

Method	Supervision	mIoU (%)
1T1C [24]	20 points	61.4
Our Baseline	20 points	54.6
Our DAT	20 points	58.9
Our DAT†	20 points	**64.4**
Our Upper Bound	100%	68.5

Fig. 5. Two results of our DAT on the S3DIS (first two rows, under the "OTOC" setting) and ScanNet-v2 datasets (last two rows, under the "20 points" setting).

4.4   Qualitative Results

Figure 5 shows the segmentation results obtained by our proposed DAT model on the S3DIS and ScanNet-v2 dataset. It reveals that the DAT model can successfully preserve most of the object structures and segment the 3D point clouds accurately, only with the weak annotation training.

5   Conclusion

In this paper, we have presented a Dual Adaptive Transformations (DAT) model for the weakly supervised point cloud segmentation task, with two novel designs, i.e. the LAP and RAD module. First, the LAP module generates point-wise adaptive coordinate perturbations and class-aware adaptive feature perturbations based on the online estimated class distribution. Second, we propose the RAD module to generate regional adaptive deformations by applying a set of adaptive affine transformations on the superpoint regions. Extensive experimental results under multiple weakly supervised settings have demonstrated that our proposed DAT model achieves new SOTA segmentation performance on the S3DIS and ScanNet-v2 datasets.

Acknowledgments. This study is supported under the RIE2020 Industry Alignment Fund - Industry Collaboration Projects (IAF-ICP) Funding Initiative, as well as cash and in-kind contribution from the industry partner(s). This research is partly supported by the National Research Foundation, Singapore under its AI Singapore Programme (AISG Award No: AISG-RP-2018-003), the Ministry of Education, Singapore, under its Academic Research Fund Tier 2 (MOE-T2EP20220-0007) and Tier 1 (RG95/20). This research is also partially supported by Monash FIT Start-up Grant and SenseTime Gift Fund.

References

1. Armeni, I., et al.: 3D semantic parsing of large-scale indoor spaces. In: Proceedings of the IEEE Conference on Computer Vision and Pattern Recognition, pp. 1534–1543 (2016)
2. Berthelot, D., Carlini, N., Goodfellow, I., Papernot, N., Oliver, A., Raffel, C.A.: MixMatch: a holistic approach to semi-supervised learning. In: Advances in Neural Information Processing Systems 32 (2019)
3. Bortsova, G., Dubost, F., Hogeweg, L., Katramados, I., de Bruijne, M.: Semi-supervised medical image segmentation via learning consistency under transformations. In: Shen, D., Liu, T., Peters, T.M., Staib, L.H., Essert, C., Zhou, S., Yap, P.-T., Khan, A. (eds.) MICCAI 2019. LNCS, vol. 11769, pp. 810–818. Springer, Cham (2019). https://doi.org/10.1007/978-3-030-32226-7_90
4. Chen, Y., et al.: PointMixup: augmentation for point clouds. In: Vedaldi, A., Bischof, H., Brox, T., Frahm, J.-M. (eds.) ECCV 2020. LNCS, vol. 12348, pp. 330–345. Springer, Cham (2020). https://doi.org/10.1007/978-3-030-58580-8_20
5. Choy, C., Gwak, J., Savarese, S.: 4D spatio-temporal convnets: Minkowski convolutional neural networks. In: Proceedings of the IEEE Conference on Computer Vision and Pattern Recognition, pp. 3075–3084 (2019)

6. Dai, A., Chang, A.X., Savva, M., Halber, M., Funkhouser, T., Nießner, M.: Scan-Net: richly-annotated 3d reconstructions of indoor scenes. In: Proceedings of the IEEE Conference on Computer Vision and Pattern Recognition, pp. 5828–5839 (2017)
7. Deng, S., Dong, Q., Liu, B., Hu, Z.: Superpoint-guided semi-supervised semantic segmentation of 3D point clouds. arXiv preprint arXiv:2107.03601 (2021)
8. French, G., Laine, S., Aila, T., Mackiewicz, M., Finlayson, G.: Semi-supervised semantic segmentation needs strong, varied perturbations. arXiv preprint arXiv:1906.01916 (2019)
9. Gao, B., Pan, Y., Li, C., Geng, S., Zhao, H.: Are we hungry for 3D LiDAR data for semantic segmentation? arXiv preprint arXiv:2006.04307 3, 20 (2020)
10. Hamdi, A., Rojas, S., Thabet, A., Ghanem, B.: AdvPC: transferable adversarial perturbations on 3D point clouds. In: Vedaldi, A., Bischof, H., Brox, T., Frahm, J.-M. (eds.) ECCV 2020. LNCS, vol. 12357, pp. 241–257. Springer, Cham (2020). https://doi.org/10.1007/978-3-030-58610-2_15
11. Hou, J., Graham, B., Nießner, M., Xie, S.: Exploring data-efficient 3D scene understanding with contrastive scene contexts. In: Proceedings of the IEEE/CVF Conference on Computer Vision and Pattern Recognition, pp. 15587–15597 (2021)
12. Hu, Q., et al.: SQN: weakly-supervised semantic segmentation of large-scale 3D point clouds with 1000x fewer labels. arXiv preprint arXiv:2104.04891 (2021)
13. Jaritz, M., Gu, J., Su, H.: Multi-view PointNet for 3D scene understanding. In: Proceedings of the IEEE/CVF International Conference on Computer Vision Workshops (2019)
14. Ke, Z., Wang, D., Yan, Q., Ren, J., Lau, R.W.: Dual student: breaking the limits of the teacher in semi-supervised learning. In: Proceedings of the IEEE/CVF International Conference on Computer Vision, pp. 6728–6736 (2019)
15. Kundu, A., et al.: Virtual multi-view fusion for 3D semantic segmentation. In: Vedaldi, A., Bischof, H., Brox, T., Frahm, J.-M. (eds.) ECCV 2020. LNCS, vol. 12369, pp. 518–535. Springer, Cham (2020). https://doi.org/10.1007/978-3-030-58586-0_31
16. Laine, S., Aila, T.: Temporal ensembling for semi-supervised learning. arXiv preprint arXiv:1610.02242 (2016)
17. Landrieu, L., Simonovsky, M.: Large-scale point cloud semantic segmentation with superpoint graphs. In: Proceedings of the IEEE Conference on Computer Vision and Pattern Recognition, pp. 4558–4567 (2018)
18. Li, G., Muller, M., Thabet, A., Ghanem, B.: DeepGCNs: can GCNs go as deep as CNNs? In: Proceedings of the IEEE/CVF International Conference on Computer Vision, pp. 9267–9276 (2019)
19. Li, R., Li, X., Heng, P.A., Fu, C.W.: PointAugment: an auto-augmentation framework for point cloud classification. In: Proceedings of the IEEE/CVF Conference on Computer Vision and Pattern Recognition, pp. 6378–6387 (2020)
20. Li, X.: SnapshotNet: self-supervised feature learning for point cloud data segmentation using minimal labeled data. Ph.D. thesis, City University of New York (2021)
21. Li, Y., Bu, R., Sun, M., Wu, W., Di, X., Chen, B.: PointCNN: convolution on X-transformed points. In: Advances in Neural Information Processing Systems 31, pp. 820–830 (2018)
22. Lin, D., Dai, J., Jia, J., He, K., Sun, J.: ScribbleSup: scribble-supervised convolutional networks for semantic segmentation. In: Proceedings of the IEEE Conference on Computer Vision and Pattern Recognition, pp. 3159–3167 (2016)
23. Liu, W., Wu, Z., Ding, H., Liu, F., Lin, J., Lin, G.: Few-shot segmentation with global and local contrastive learning. arXiv preprint arXiv:2108.05293 (2021)

24. Liu, Z., Qi, X., Fu, C.W.: One thing one click: a self-training approach for weakly supervised 3d semantic segmentation. In: Proceedings of the IEEE/CVF Conference on Computer Vision and Pattern Recognition, pp. 1726–1736 (2021)
25. Luo, L., Tian, B., Zhao, H., Zhou, G.: Pointly-supervised 3D scene parsing with viewpoint bottleneck. arXiv preprint arXiv:2109.08553 (2021)
26. Mao, J., Wang, X., Li, H.: Interpolated convolutional networks for 3D point cloud understanding. In: Proceedings of the IEEE/CVF International Conference on Computer Vision, pp. 1578–1587 (2019)
27. Meng, Q., Wang, W., Zhou, T., Shen, J., Jia, Y., Van Gool, L.: Towards a weakly supervised framework for 3D point cloud object detection and annotation. IEEE Trans. Pattern Anal. Mach. Intell. **44**, 4454–4468 (2021)
28. Mittal, S., Tatarchenko, M., Brox, T.: Semi-supervised semantic segmentation with high- and low-level consistency. IEEE Trans. Pattern Anal. Mach. Intell. **43**(4), 1369–1379 (2021). https://doi.org/10.1109/TPAMI.2019.2960224
29. Miyato, T., Maeda, S., Koyama, M., Ishii, S.: Virtual adversarial training: a regularization method for supervised and semi-supervised learning. IEEE Trans. Pattern Anal. Mach. Intell. **41**(8), 1979–1993 (2018)
30. Nekrasov, A., Schult, J., Litany, O., Leibe, B., Engelmann, F.: Mix3D: out-of-context data augmentation for 3D scenes. In: 2021 International Conference on 3D Vision (3DV), pp. 116–125. IEEE (2021)
31. Oh, S.J., Benenson, R., Khoreva, A., Akata, Z., Fritz, M., Schiele, B.: Exploiting saliency for object segmentation from image level labels. In: Proceedings of the IEEE Conference on Computer Vision and Pattern Recognition, pp. 5038–5047. IEEE (2017)
32. Qi, C.R., Su, H., Mo, K., Guibas, L.J.: PointNet: deep learning on point sets for 3D classification and segmentation. In: Proceedings of the IEEE Conference on Computer Vision and Pattern Recognition, pp. 652–660 (2017)
33. Qi, C.R., Yi, L., Su, H., Guibas, L.J.: PointNet++: deep hierarchical feature learning on point sets in a metric space. arXiv preprint arXiv:1706.02413 (2017)
34. Sohn, K., et al.: FixMatch: simplifying semi-supervised learning with consistency and confidence. arXiv preprint arXiv:2001.07685 (2020)
35. Su, Y.C., Grauman, K.: Learning spherical convolution for fast features from 360 imagery. In: Advances in Neural Information Processing Systems 30, pp. 529–539 (2017)
36. Tao, A., Duan, Y., Wei, Y., Lu, J., Zhou, J.: SegGroup: seg-level supervision for 3D instance and semantic segmentation. arXiv preprint arXiv:2012.10217 (2020)
37. Tarvainen, A., Valpola, H.: Mean teachers are better role models: weight-averaged consistency targets improve semi-supervised deep learning results. arXiv preprint arXiv:1703.01780 (2017)
38. Thomas, H., Qi, C.R., Deschaud, J.E., Marcotegui, B., Goulette, F., Guibas, L.J.: KPConv: flexible and deformable convolution for point clouds. In: Proceedings of the IEEE/CVF International Conference on Computer Vision, pp. 6411–6420 (2019)
39. Wang, H., Rong, X., Yang, L., Feng, J., Xiao, J., Tian, Y.: Weakly supervised semantic segmentation in 3D graph-structured point clouds of wild scenes. arXiv preprint arXiv:2004.12498 (2020)
40. Wang, P., Yao, W.: A new weakly supervised approach for ALS point cloud semantic segmentation. arXiv preprint arXiv:2110.01462 (2021)
41. Wang, X., You, S., Li, X., Ma, H.: Weakly-supervised semantic segmentation by iteratively mining common object features. In: Proceedings of the IEEE Conference on Computer Vision and Pattern Recognition, pp. 1354–1362 (2018)

42. Wang, Y., Sun, Y., Liu, Z., Sarma, S.E., Bronstein, M.M., Solomon, J.M.: Dynamic graph CNN for learning on point clouds. ACM Trans. Graph. (TOG) **38**(5), 1–12 (2019)

43. Wang, Y., Huang, G., Song, S., Pan, X., Xia, Y., Wu, C.: Regularizing deep networks with semantic data augmentation. IEEE Trans. Pattern Anal. Mach. Intell. **44**, 3733–3748 (2021)

44. Wei, J., Lin, G., Yap, K.H., Hung, T.Y., Xie, L.: Multi-path region mining for weakly supervised 3D semantic segmentation on point clouds. In: Proceedings of the IEEE/CVF Conference on Computer Vision and Pattern Recognition, pp. 4384–4393 (2020)

45. Wu, Y., et al.: Mutual consistency learning for semi-supervised medical image segmentation. Med. Image Anal. **81**, 102530 (2022)

46. Wu, Y., Wu, Z., Wu, Q., Ge, Z., Cai, J.: Exploring smoothness and class-separation for semi-supervised medical image segmentation. arXiv preprint arXiv:2203.01324 (2022)

47. Wu, Y., Xu, M., Ge, Z., Cai, J., Zhang, L.: Semi-supervised left atrium segmentation with mutual consistency training. In: de Bruijne, M., et al. (eds.) MICCAI 2021. LNCS, vol. 12902, pp. 297–306. Springer, Cham (2021). https://doi.org/10.1007/978-3-030-87196-3_28

48. Wu, Z., Lin, G., Cai, J.: Keypoint based weakly supervised human parsing. Image Vis. Comput. **91**, 103801 (2019)

49. Wu, Z., Shi, X., Lin, G., Cai, J.: Learning meta-class memory for few-shot semantic segmentation. In: Proceedings of the IEEE/CVF International Conference on Computer Vision, pp. 517–526 (2021)

50. Wu, Z., Tao, Q., Lin, G., Cai, J.: Exploring bottom-up and top-down cues with attentive learning for webly supervised object detection. In: Proceedings of the IEEE/CVF Conference on Computer Vision and Pattern Recognition, pp. 12936–12945 (2020)

51. Xiang, C., Qi, C.R., Li, B.: Generating 3D adversarial point clouds. In: Proceedings of the IEEE/CVF Conference on Computer Vision and Pattern Recognition, pp. 9136–9144 (2019)

52. Xie, S., Gu, J., Guo, D., Qi, C.R., Guibas, L., Litany, O.: PointContrast: unsupervised pre-training for 3D point cloud understanding. In: Vedaldi, A., Bischof, H., Brox, T., Frahm, J.-M. (eds.) ECCV 2020. LNCS, vol. 12348, pp. 574–591. Springer, Cham (2020). https://doi.org/10.1007/978-3-030-58580-8_34

53. Xu, X., Lee, G.H.: Weakly supervised semantic point cloud segmentation: towards 10x fewer labels. In: Proceedings of the IEEE/CVF Conference on Computer Vision and Pattern Recognition, pp. 13706–13715 (2020)

54. Xu, Y., Fan, T., Xu, M., Zeng, L., Qiao, Yu.: SpiderCNN: deep learning on point sets with parameterized convolutional filters. In: Ferrari, V., Hebert, M., Sminchisescu, C., Weiss, Y. (eds.) ECCV 2018. LNCS, vol. 11212, pp. 90–105. Springer, Cham (2018). https://doi.org/10.1007/978-3-030-01237-3_6

55. Zhang, T., Lin, G., Liu, W., Cai, J., Kot, A.: Splitting vs. merging: mining object regions with discrepancy and intersection loss for weakly supervised semantic segmentation. In: Vedaldi, A., Bischof, H., Brox, T., Frahm, J.-M. (eds.) ECCV 2020. LNCS, vol. 12367, pp. 663–679. Springer, Cham (2020). https://doi.org/10.1007/978-3-030-58542-6_40

56. Zhang, Y., Qu, Y., Xie, Y., Li, Z., Zheng, S., Li, C.: Perturbed self-distillation: weakly supervised large-scale point cloud semantic segmentation. In: Proceedings of the IEEE/CVF International Conference on Computer Vision, pp. 15520–15528 (2021)

57. Zhang, Y., Xiang, T., Hospedales, T.M., Lu, H.: Deep mutual learning. In: Proceedings of the IEEE Conference on Computer Vision and Pattern Recognition, pp. 4320–4328 (2018)
58. Zhou, B., Khosla, A., Lapedriza, A., Oliva, A., Torralba, A.: Learning deep features for discriminative localization. In: Proceedings of the IEEE Conference on Computer Vision and Pattern Recognition, pp. 2921–2929 (2016)
59. Zhou, Y., Tuzel, O.: VoxelNet: end-to-end learning for point cloud based 3D object detection. In: Proceedings of the IEEE Conference on Computer Vision and Pattern Recognition, pp. 4490–4499 (2018)
60. Zhu, X., et al.: Weakly supervised 3D semantic segmentation using cross-image consensus and inter-voxel affinity relations. In: Proceedings of the IEEE/CVF International Conference on Computer Vision, pp. 2834–2844 (2021)

Semantic-Aware Fine-Grained Correspondence

Yingdong Hu[1], Renhao Wang[1], Kaifeng Zhang[1], and Yang Gao[1,2(✉)]

[1] Tsinghua University, Beijing, China
{huyd21,wangrh21,zhangkf19}@mails.tsinghua.edu.cn,
gaoyangiiis@tsinghua.edu.cn
[2] Shanghai Qi Zhi Institute, Shanghai, China

Abstract. Establishing visual correspondence across images is a challenging and essential task. Recently, an influx of self-supervised methods have been proposed to better learn representations for visual correspondence. However, we find that these methods often fail to leverage semantic information and over-rely on the matching of low-level features. In contrast, human vision is capable of distinguishing between distinct objects as a pretext to tracking. Inspired by this paradigm, we propose to learn semantic-aware fine-grained correspondence. Firstly, we demonstrate that semantic correspondence is implicitly available through a rich set of image-level self-supervised methods. We further design a pixel-level self-supervised learning objective which specifically targets fine-grained correspondence. For downstream tasks, we fuse these two kinds of complementary correspondence representations together, demonstrating that they boost performance synergistically. Our method surpasses previous state-of-the-art self-supervised methods using convolutional networks on a variety of visual correspondence tasks, including video object segmentation, human pose tracking, and human part tracking.

Keywords: Self-supervised learning · Representation learning · Visual correspondence · Tracking

1 Introduction

Correspondence is considered one of the most fundamental problems in computer vision. At their core, many tasks require learning visual correspondence across space and time, such as video object segmentation [14,45,69], object tracking [4,28,36,38], and optical flow estimation [17,30,51,57,58]. Despite its importance, prior art in visual correspondence has largely relied on supervised learning [26,61,67], which requires costly human annotations that are difficult to obtain at scale. Other works rely on weak supervision from methods like off-the-shelf optical flow

---

Supplementary Information The online version contains supplementary material available at https://doi.org/10.1007/978-3-031-19821-2_6.

S. Avidan et al. (Eds.): ECCV 2022, LNCS 13691, pp. 97–115, 2022.
https://doi.org/10.1007/978-3-031-19821-2_6

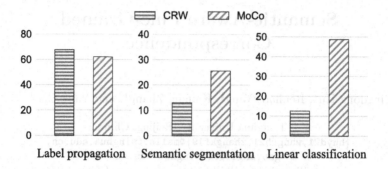

Fig. 1. We compare Contrastive Random Walk (CRW) [32] and MoCo [24] on three different downstream tasks. CRW surpasses MoCo on the label propagation task, but is dramatically outperformed by MoCo on semantic segmentation and image classification (more details are in the appendix).

estimators, or synthetic training data, which lead to generalization issues when confronted with the long-tailed distribution of real world images.

Recognizing these limitations, many recent works [32,34,35,37,66,70,75] are exploring self-supervision to learn robust representations of spatiotemporal visual correspondence. Aside from creatively leveraging self-supervisory signals across space and time, these works generally share a critical tenet: evaluation on label propagation as an indication of representation quality. Given label information, such as segmentation labels or object keypoints, within an initial frame, the goal is to propagate these labels to subsequent frames based on correspondence.

Let us briefly consider the human visual system and how it performs tracking. Many works have argued that our ability to track objects is rooted in our ability to distinguish and understand differences between said objects [19,20]. We have rough internal models of different objects, which we adjust by attending more closely to local locations that require fine-grained matching [3,78]. In other words, both high-level semantic information and low-level fined-grained information play an important role in correspondence for real visual systems.

However, when we examine current self-supervised correspondence learning methods, we find them lacking under this paradigm. These methods often overprioritize performance on the label propagation task, and fail to leverage semantic information as well as humans can. In particular, when representations obtained under these methods are transferred to other downstream tasks which require a deeper semantic understanding of images, performance noticeably suffers (see Fig. 1). We show that label propagation and tracking-style tasks rely on frame-to-frame differentiation of low-level features, a kind of "shortcut" exploited by the contrastive-based self-supervised algorithms developed so far. Thus, representations learned via these tasks contain limited semantic information, and underperform drastically when used in alternative tasks.

To this end, we propose Semantic-aware Fine-grained Correspondence (SFC), which simultaneously takes into account semantic correspondence and fine-grained correspondence. Firstly, we find that current image-level self-supervised representation learning methods e.g. MoCo [24] force the mid-level convolutional features to implicitly capture correspondences between similar objects or parts. Second, we design an objective which learns high-fidelity representations of fine-grained correspondence (FC). We do this by extending prior image-level loss functions in self-supervised representation learning to a dense paradigm, thereby encouraging local feature consistency. Crucially, FC does not use temporal information to learn this low-level correspondence, but our ablations show that this extension alone makes our model competitive with previous methods relying on temporal signals in large video datasets for pretraining.

Prior works [71, 74] have shown that image-level self-supervision can further facilitate the dense self-supervision in a multitask framework. However, we surprisingly find that our fine-grained training objective and image-level semantic training objectives are inconsistent: each of them requires the model to encode conflicting information about the image, leading to degradation in performance when used in conjunction. We hypothesize that it is necessary to have two independent models, and propose a late fusion operation to combine separately pretrained semantic correspondence and fine-grained correspondence feature vectors. Figure 2 overviews the proposed method. Through our ablations, we categorically verify that low-level fine-grained correspondence and high-level semantic correspondence are complementary, and indeed orthogonal, in the benefits they bring to self-supervised representation learning. The main contributions of our work are as follows:

- We propose to learn semantic-aware fine-grained correspondence (SFC), while most previous works consider and improve the two kinds of correspondence separately.
- We design a simple and effective self-supervised learning method tailored for low-level fine-grained correspondence. Despite using static images and discarding temporal information, we outperform previous methods trained on large-scale video datasets.
- Late fusion is an effective mechanism to prevent conflicting image-level and fine-grained training objectives from interfering with each other.
- Our full model (SFC) sets the new state-of-the-art for self-supervised approaches using convolutional networks on various video label propagation tasks, including video object segmentation, human pose tracking, and human part tracking.

2 Related Work

Self-supervised Representation Learning.   Self-supervised representation learning has gained popularity because of its ability to avoid the cost of annotating large-scale datasets. Specifically, methods using instance-level pretext tasks have recently become dominant components in self-supervised learning for computer vision [1, 6, 9, 11, 18, 24, 27, 44, 46, 50, 59, 72]. Instance-level discrimination aims to pull embeddings of augmented views of the same image (positive pairs) close to each other, while trying to push away embeddings from different images

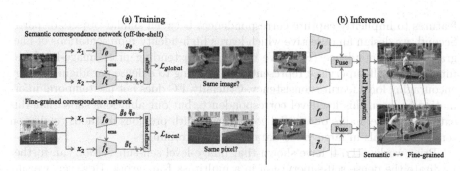

Fig. 2. Overview of semantic-aware fine-grained correspondence learning framework. By maximizing agreement between positive (similar) image pairs, convolutional representations capture semantic correspondences between similar objects implicitly. By encouraging the spatially close local feature vectors to be consistent, model can learn fine-grained correspondence explicitly. For downstream task, we utilize two kinds of correspondence together to achieve complementary effects.

(negative pairs). Recently, some works [12,21] have discovered that even without negative pairs, self-supervised learning can exhibit strong performance.

To obtain better transfer performance to dense prediction tasks such as object detection and semantic segmentation, other works [48,71,74] explore pretext tasks at the pixel level for representation learning. But empirically, we find that these methods fail to leverage fine-grained information well. Our fine-grained correspondence network (FC) is most closely related to PixPro [74] which obtains positive pairs by extracting features from the same pixel through two asymmetric pipelines. Both FC and PixPro can be seen as dense versions of BYOL [21], but the two methods have completely different goals. FC has many design choices tailored for correspondence learning: FC preserves spatial sensitivity by avoiding entirely a pixel propagation module which introduces a certain smoothing effect. Furthermore, we discard color augmentation and use higher resolution feature maps, as we find both modifications are beneficial to the fine-grained correspondence task. Finally, FC can achieve competitive performance to predominant approaches, with compelling computational and data efficiency. In contrast, the transfer performance of PixPro on the correspondence task is far behind its instance-level counterpart [21] and our FC.

We note that DINO [7], a self-supervised Vision Transformer (ViT) [16], exhibits surprisingly strong correspondence properties and competitive performance on DAVIS-2017 benchmark. We speculate that the success of DINO on this task is attributed to the architecture of ViT and much more computation.

Self-supervised Correspondence Learning. Recently, numerous approaches have also been developed for correspondence learning in a self-supervised manner [32,34,35,37,66,68,70,75]. The key idea behind a number of these methods [34,35,66] is to propagate the color of one frame in a video to future frames. TimeCycle [70] relies on a cycle-consistent tracking pretext task. Along this line, CRW [32] cast correspondence as pathfinding on a space-time graph, also using cycle-consistency as a self-supervisory signal. VFS [75] propose to learn correspondence implicitly by performing image-level similarity learning. Despite the success of these methods, they all rely heavily on temporal information from videos as the core form of self-supervision signal. In our work, we demonstrate that representations with good space-time correspondence can be learned even without videos. Moreover, our framework is an entirely alternative perspective on correspondence learning, which can be flexibly adapted with other video-based methods to further improve performance.

Semantic Correspondence. We borrow the notion of semantic correspondence from literature [39,41–43,52–54,60], which aim to establish dense correspondences across images depicting different instances of the same object categories. Evaluation of these methods exists solely on image datasets with keypoint annotations, which can be more forgiving and translates poorly to the real world. Our semantic correspondence is evaluated on video, which we argue is a much more realistic setting for correspondence. In addition, many supervised semantic correspondence approaches [13,29,39,42] adopt a CNN pre-trained on image classification as their frozen backbone, but we explore a self-supervised pre-trained backbone as an alternative.

3   Method

While our framework is compatible with a wide array of contemporary self-supervised representation methods, we demonstrate its efficacy with two recent approaches: MoCo [24] and BYOL [21], which are reviewed in Sect. 3.1. Next, in Sect. 3.2, we argue that image-level methods implicitly learn high-level semantic correspondence. In Sect. 3.3, we propose our framework to improve fine-grained correspondence learning. Finally, in Sect. 3.4, we show how to unify these two complementary forms of correspondence to improve performance on video label propagation tasks.

3.1   Background

In image-level self-supervised representation learning, we seek to minimize a distance metric between two random augmentations x_1 and x_2 of a single image x. One popular framework for doing this is contrastive learning [22].

Formally, two augmented views x_1 and x_2 are fed into an online encoder and target encoder respectively, where each encoder consists of a backbone f (e.g. ResNet), and a projection MLP head g. The l_2-normalized output global feature vectors for x_1 and x_2 can be represented as $z_1 \triangleq g_\theta(f_\theta(x_1))$ and $z_2 \triangleq g_\xi(f_\xi(x_2))$, where θ and ξ are parameters of the two respective networks. Let the negative features obtained from K different images be represented by the set $\mathcal{S} = \{s_1, s_2, \ldots, s_K\}$. Then contrastive learning uses the InfoNCE [46] to pull z_1 close to z_2 while pushing it away from negative features:

$$\mathcal{L}_{\text{InfoNCE}} = -\log \frac{\exp(z_1 \cdot z_2 / \tau)}{\exp(z_1 \cdot z_2 / \tau) + \sum_{k=1}^{K} \exp(z_1 \cdot s_k / \tau)} \qquad (1)$$

where τ is the temperature hyperparameter. While numerous methods have been explored to construct the set of negative samples $\mathcal{S}$, we choose MoCo [24] for obtaining semantic correspondence representations, which achieves this goal via a momentum-updated queue. In particular, the target encoder's parameters $\boldsymbol{\xi}$ are the exponential moving average of the online parameters $\boldsymbol{\theta}$:

$$\boldsymbol{\xi} \leftarrow m\boldsymbol{\xi} + (1 - m)\boldsymbol{\theta}, \qquad m \in [0, 1] \tag{2}$$

where m is the exponential moving average parameter.

Some recent works [12,21] show that it is not necessary to use negative pairs to perform self-supervised representation learning. One such method, BYOL [21], relies on an additional prediction MLP head $\mathbf{q}_\theta$ to transform the output of online encoder $\mathbf{p}_1 \triangleq \mathbf{q}_\theta(\mathbf{z}_1)$. The contrastive objective then reduces to simply minimizing the negative cosine distance between the predicted features $\mathbf{p}_1$ and the features obtained from the target encoder $\mathbf{z}_2$ (l_2-normalized):

$$\mathcal{L}_{\text{global}} = -\frac{\langle \mathbf{p}_1, \mathbf{z}_2 \rangle}{\|\mathbf{p}_1\|_2 \cdot \|\mathbf{z}_2\|_2} \tag{3}$$

Note again that MoCo and BYOL bear striking similarities in their formulation and training objectives. In the following section, we hypothesize that such similarities in frameworks lead to similarities in types of features learned. In particular, we claim that image-level representations in general contain information about semantic correspondences.

3.2   Semantic Correspondence Learning

Representations learned by current self-supervised correspondence learning methods may contain limited semantic information. To make the representations more neurophysiologically intuitive, we add the crucially missing semantic correspondence learning into our method. Recent image-level self-supervised methods learn representations by imposing invariances to various data augmentations. Two random crops sampled from the same image, followed by strong color augmentation [9] are considered as positive pairs. The augmentation significantly changes the visual appearance of the image but keeps the semantic meaning unchanged. The model can match positive pairs by attending only to the essential part of the representation, while ignoring other non-essential variations. As a result, different images with similar visual concepts are grouped together, inducing a latent space with rich semantic information [10,62,63]. This is evidenced by the results shown in Fig. 1, where MoCo [24] achieve high performance on tasks that require a deeper semantic understanding of images. Moreover, previous works [40,75] demonstrate that correspondence naturally emerges in the middle-level convolutional features. Thus we conclude that current self-supervised representation methods can implicitly learn semantic correspondence well.

We utilize one approach, MoCo [24], in our downstream correspondence task. In particular, only the pre-trained online backbone $\mathbf{f}_\theta$ is retained, while all other parts of the network, including the online projection head $\mathbf{g}_\theta$ and target encoder

$\mathbf{f}_\xi, \mathbf{g}_\xi$, are discarded. We use $\mathbf{f}_\theta$ to encode each image as a semantic correspondence feature map: $\mathbf{F} = \mathbf{f}_\theta(\mathbf{x}) \in \mathbb{R}^{H \times W \times C_s}$, where H and W are spatial dimensions. Note also that we can adjust the size of the feature map by changing the stride of residual blocks, offering additional flexibility in the scale of semantic information we wish to imbue our representations with.

Finally, we comment that the emergent mid-level feature behavior extends readily to MoCo, and moreover also to other self-supervised methods like BYOL [21] and SimCLR [9], as the encoders for all such methods are based on ResNet-style architectures. We can thus flexibly swap out the semantic correspondence backbone for any of these image-level self-supervised representations.

3.3   Fine-Grained Correspondence Learning

Only considering semantic information is not enough for correspondence learning, which often requires analyzing low-level variables such as object edge, pose, articulation, precise location and so on. Like most previous self-supervised methods, we also incorporate low-level fine-grained correspondence in our approach. BYOL-style methods [21] learn their representations by directly maximizing the similarity of two views of one image (positive pairs) in the feature space. This paradigm naturally connects with our intuitive understanding of correspondence: similar objects, parts and pixels should have similar representations. We are thus inspired to generalize this framework to a dense paradigm to learn fine-grained correspondence specifically.

At a high level, we learn our embedding space by pulling local feature vectors belonging to the same spatial region close together. Specifically, given two augmented views $\mathbf{x}_1$ and $\mathbf{x}_2$ of one image, we extract their dense feature maps $\mathbf{F}_1 \triangleq \tilde{\mathbf{f}}_\theta(\mathbf{x}_1) \in \mathbb{R}^{H \times W \times C_f}$ and $\mathbf{F}_2 \triangleq \tilde{\mathbf{f}}_\xi(\mathbf{x}_2) \in \mathbb{R}^{H \times W \times C_f}$ by removing the global pooling layer in the encoders. We adopt a ResNet-style backbone, and we can thus reduce the stride of some residual blocks in order to obtain a higher resolution feature map. In addition, to maintain dense 2D feature vectors, we replace the MLPs in the projection head and prediction head with 1×1 convolution layers. Then we can get dense prediction feature vectors $\mathbf{P}_1 \triangleq \tilde{\mathbf{q}}_\theta(\tilde{\mathbf{g}}_\theta(\mathbf{F}_1)) \in \mathbb{R}^{H \times W \times D}$ and dense projection feature vectors $\mathbf{Z}_2 \triangleq \tilde{\mathbf{g}}_\xi(\mathbf{F}_2) \in \mathbb{R}^{H \times W \times D}$. $\mathbf{P}_1^i$ denotes the local feature vector at the i-th position of $\mathbf{P}_1$. Now, a significant question remains: for a given local feature vector $\mathbf{P}_1^i$, how can we find its positive correspondence local feature vector in $\mathbf{Z}_2$?

Positive Correspondence Pairs.   Note that after we apply different spatial augmentations (random crop) to the two views, the local feature vectors on the two feature maps are no longer aligned. An object corresponding to a local feature vector in one view may even be cropped in another view. Thus, we only consider feature vectors corresponding to the same cropped region (overlapped areas of two views) and define a small spatial neighborhood around each local feature vector. All the local feature vectors in the spatial neighborhood are designated positive samples.

Specifically, we construct a binary positive mask $\mathbf{M} \in \mathbb{R}^{H \cdot W \times H \cdot W}$ by computing the spatial distance between all pairs of local feature vectors with:

$$\mathbf{M}_{ij} = \begin{cases} 1 & \text{dist}(\Phi(\mathbf{P}_1^i), \Phi(\mathbf{Z}_2^j)) \leqslant r \\ 0 & \text{dist}(\Phi(\mathbf{P}_1^i), \Phi(\mathbf{Z}_2^j)) > r \end{cases} \quad (4)$$

Φ denotes an operation that translates the coordinates of the local feature vector to the original image space. dist denotes the distance between coordinates of local feature vectors $\mathbf{P}_1^i$ and $\mathbf{Z}_2^j$ in the original image space. r is positive radius, which controls a notion of locality. As we show in the experiment, this is a very important hyperparameter. In summary, all 1s in the i-th row of $\mathbf{M}$ represent the local feature vectors in $\mathbf{Z}_2$ which are positive samples of the i-th vector in $\mathbf{P}_1$. This process is illustrated in Fig. 3.

Learning Objectives. We construct a pairwise similarity matrix $\mathbf{S}$, where $\mathbf{S} \in \mathbb{R}^{H \cdot W \times H \cdot W}$ with:

$$\mathbf{S}_{ij} = \text{sim}(\mathbf{P}_1^i, \mathbf{Z}_2^j) \quad (5)$$

$\text{sim}(\mathbf{u}, \mathbf{v}) = \frac{\langle \mathbf{u}, \mathbf{v} \rangle}{\|\mathbf{u}\|_2 \cdot \|\mathbf{v}\|_2}$ denotes the cosine similarity between two vectors. We multiply the similarity matrix $\mathbf{S}$ and the positive mask $\mathbf{M}$ to get the masked similarity matrix $\widetilde{\mathbf{S}} = \mathbf{S} \odot \mathbf{M}$. Finally, the loss function seeks to maximize each element in the masked similarity matrix $\widetilde{\mathbf{S}}$:

$$\mathcal{L}_{\text{local}} = -\frac{\sum_{i=1}^{H \cdot W} \sum_{j=1}^{H \cdot W} \widetilde{\mathbf{S}}_{ij}}{\sum_{i=1}^{H \cdot W} \sum_{j=1}^{H \cdot W} \mathbf{M}_{ij}} \quad (6)$$

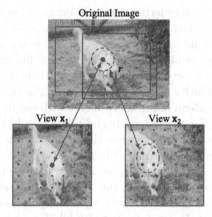

Fig. 3. For a feature vector in one view $\mathbf{x}_1$, we designate all the feature vectors in view $\mathbf{x}_2$ which belonging to the same spatial region as positive pairs.

3.4 Fusion of Correspondence Signals

To combine semantic correspondence (Sect. 3.2) and fine-grained correspondence (Sect. 3.3) representations, one intuitive approach is simultaneously train with both semantic-level and fine-grained level losses, like [2,71,74]. However, our investigations reveal that jointly using both these objectives may not be sensible, as the representations fundamentally conflict, in two main ways. 1)*receptive fields*. We find that fine-grained correspondence relies heavily on a higher resolution feature map (see the appendix). But trivially increasing the feature resolution of a semantic-level method like MoCo [24] during training causes performance on the label propagation task to drop a lot. This is because low-level fine-grained information needs small receptive fields while relatively large receptive fields are necessary to encode global high-level semantic information. 2)*data augmentation*. Similar to VFS [75], we find that color augmentation (e.g. color distortion and grayscale conversion) is harmful to learning fine-grained correspondence, since fine-grained correspondence heavily relies on low-level color and texture details. In contrast, image-level self-supervised learning methods learn semantic representations by imposing invariances on various data transformations. For example, as seen in the augmentations ablation for SimCLR (Fig. 5 in [9]), removing color augmentation leads to severe performance issues.

We conclude that an end-to-end framework utilizing multiple levels of supervision does not always work, especially when these modes of supervision have different requirements on both the model and data sides (see Sect. 4.4 for experimental evidence). We argue it is necessary to decouple the two models, which is consistent with how humans also attend very differently when re-identifying an object's main body versus its accurate pixel boundary. Inspired by Two-Stream ConvNets [55], which use a late fusion to combine two kinds of complementary information, and hypercolumns [23], which effectively leverage information across different layers of CNNs, we implement a similar mechanism to fuse our orthogonal correspondences.

For a given image, suppose we have two networks, one which produces a semantic correspondence feature map $\mathbf{F}_s \triangleq \mathbf{f}_\theta(\mathbf{x}) \in \mathbb{R}^{H \times W \times C_s}$ and one which produces a fine-grained correspondence feature map $\mathbf{F}_f \triangleq \tilde{\mathbf{f}}_\theta(\mathbf{x}) \in \mathbb{R}^{H \times W \times C_f}$. Note that these two feature maps can have different channel dimensions. We consider channel-wise concatenation as a simple and intuitive way to fuse these feature maps:

$$\mathbf{F} = [\text{L2Norm}(\mathbf{F}_s), \lambda \cdot \text{L2Norm}(\mathbf{F}_f)] \tag{7}$$

where L2Norm denotes an l_2 normalization of local feature vectors in every spatial location. This ameliorates issues of scale, considering that the two feature maps are obtained under different training objectives which attend to features of different scales. λ is a hyperparameter to balance two feature maps. Note that $\mathbf{F}$ also needs to be re-normalized when it is employed in downstream tasks, like label propagation.

3.5 Implementation Details

Any off-the-shelf image-level self-supervised pre-trained network can serve as our semantic correspondence backbone. In our implementation, we use MoCo as the default network, with ResNet-50 [25] as the base architecture and pre-trained on the 1000-class ImageNet [15] training set with strong data augmentation.

As for our fine-grained correspondence network, we use YouTube-VOS [76] as our pre-training dataset for direct comparison with previous works [34]. It contains 3471 videos totalling 5.58 h of playtime, much smaller than Kinetics400 [8] (800 h). Although Youtube-VOS is a video dataset, we treat it as a conventional image dataset and randomly sample individual frames during training (equivalent to 95k images). Crucially, this discards temporal information and correspondence signals our model would otherwise be able to exploit. We use *cropping-only* augmentation. Following [32,37,70], we adopt ResNet-18 as the backbone. Please see the appendix for augmentation, architecture and optimization details.

4   Experiments

We evaluate the learned representation without fine-tuning on several challenging video propagation tasks involving objects, human pose and parts. We will first introduce our detailed evaluation settings and baselines, then we conduct the comparison with the state-of-the-art self-supervised algorithms. Finally, we perform extensive ablations on different elements for SFC.

4.1   Experimental Settings

Label Propagation. Ideally, a model with good space-time correspondence should be able to track an arbitrary user-annotated target object throughout a video. Previous works formulate this kind of tracking task as video label propagation [32,37,70,75]. We follow the same evaluation protocol as prior art [32] for consistency and equitable comparison. At a high level, we use the representation from our pre-trained model as a similarity function. Given the ground-truth labels in the first frame, a recurrent inference strategy is applied to propagate the labels to the rest of the frames. See the appendix for detailed description.

We compare with state-of-the-art algorithms on DAVIS-2017 [49], a widely-used publicly-available benchmark for video object segmentation. To see whether our method can generalize to more visual correspondence tasks, we further evaluate our method on JHMDB benchmark [33], which involves tracking 15 human pose keypoints, and on the Video Instance Parsing (VIP) benchmark [79], which involves propagating 20 parts of the human body. We use the same settings as [32,37] and report the standard metrics, namely region-based similarity $\mathcal{J}$ and contour-based accuracy $\mathcal{F}$ [47] for DAVIS, probability of a correct pose (PCK) metric [77] for JHMDB and mean intersection-over-union (IoU) for VIP.

Baselines. We compare with the following baselines:
Instance-Level Pre-Trained Representations: We consider supervised and self-supervised pre-trained models (MoCo, BYOL, SimSiam, etc.) on ImageNet. We also compare with two recent video-based self-supervised representation learning baselines: VINCE [18] and VFS [75]. We evaluate VFS pre-trained model using our label propagation implementation (official CRW [32] evaluation code).
Pixel-Level Pre-Trained Representations: We evaluate representations trained with pixel-level self-supervised proxy tasks: PixPro[74], DetCo[73], DenseCL[71].
Task-Specific Temporal Correspondence Representations: There are many self-supervised methods designed specifically for visual correspondence learning and evaluated on label propagation. We include these for a more comprehensive analysis: Colorization [66], CorrFlow [35], MAST [34], TimeCycle [70], UVC [37], CRW [32].

4.2   Comparison with State-of-the-Art

We compare our method against previous self-supervised methods in Table 1. In summary, our results strongly validate the design choices in our model. In particular, the full semantic-aware fine-grained correspondence network (SFC), achieves state-of-the-art performance on all tasks investigated. SFC significantly

Table 1. Video object segmentation results on the DAVIS-2017 val set. *Dataset* indicates dataset(s) used for pre-training, including: I=ImageNet, V=ImageNet-VID, C=COCO, D=DAVIS-2017, P=PASCAL-VOC, J=JHMDB. ⋆ indicates that the method uses its own label propagation algorithm.

Method	Supervised	Dataset (Size)	DAVIS			JHMDB		VIP
			$\mathcal{J}\&\mathcal{F}_m$	$\mathcal{J}_m$	$\mathcal{F}_m$	PCK@0.1	PCK@0.2	mIoU
Rand.Init	✗	–	32.5	32.4	32.6	50.8	72.3	18.6
Supervised [25]	✓	I (1.28 M)	66.9	64.5	69.4	59.7	81.2	38.6
InstDis [72]	✗	I (1.28 M)	66.4	63.9	68.9	58.5	80.2	32.5
MoCo [24]	✗	I (1.28 M)	65.9	63.4	68.4	59.4	80.9	33.1
SimCLR [9]	✗	I (1.28 M)	66.9	64.4	69.4	59.0	80.8	35.3
BYOL [21]	✗	I (1.28 M)	66.5	64.0	69.0	58.8	80.9	34.8
SimSiam [12]	✗	I (1.28 M)	67.2	64.8	68.8	59.9	81.6	33.8
VINCE [18]	✗	Kinetics (800 h)	65.2	62.5	67.8	58.8	80.4	35.3
VFS⋆ [75]	✗	Kinetics (800 h)	68.9	66.5	71.3	60.9	80.7	43.2
DetCo [73]	✗	I (1.28 M)	65.7	63.3	68.1	57.1	79.3	35.5
DenseCL [71]	✗	I (1.28 M)	61.4	60.0	62.9	58.7	81.4	32.9
PixPro [74]	✗	I (1.28 M)	57.5	56.6	58.3	57.8	80.8	29.6
Colorization⋆ [66]	✗	Kinetics (800 h)	34.0	34.6	32.7	45.2	69.6	–
CorrFlow⋆ [35]	✗	OxUvA (14 h)	50.3	48.4	52.2	58.5	78.8	–
MAST⋆ [34]	✗	YT-VOS (5.58 h)	65.5	63.3	67.6	–	–	–
TimeCycle [70]	✗	VLOG (344 h)	48.7	46.4	50.0	57.3	78.1	28.9
UVC [37]	✗	Kinetics (800 h)	60.9	59.3	62.7	58.6	79.6	34.1
CRW [32]	✗	Kinetics (800 h)	67.6	64.8	70.2	58.8	80.3	37.6
FC(Ours)	✗	YT-VOS (5.58 h)	67.7	64.7	70.5	59.3	80.8	34.0
SFC(Ours)	✗	YT-VOS, I(5.58 h + 1.28 M)	**71.2**	**68.3**	**74.0**	**61.9**	**83.0**	38.4
OSVOS [5]	✓	I/D (1.28 M + 10k)	60.3	56.6	63.9	–	–	–
OnAVOS [65]	✓	I/C/P/D (1.28 M + 517k)	65.4	61.6	69.1	–	–	–
FEELVOS [64]	✓	I/C/D/YT-VOS (1.28M + 663k)	71.5	69.1	74.0	–	–	–
PAAP [31]	✓	I/J (1.28 M + 32K)	-	–	–	51.6	73.8	–
Thin-Slicing [56]	✓	I/J (1.28 M + 32K)	–	–	–	68.7	92.1	–
ATEN [79]	✓	VIP (20k)	–	–	–	–	–	37.9

outperforms other methods that learn only semantic correspondence (MoCo, 65.9 → 71.2 on DAVIS-2017) or only fine-grained correspondence (FC, 67.7 → 71.2 on DAVIS-2017). SFC even outperforms several supervised baselines specially designed for video object segmentation and human part tracking.

Note also that our fine-grained correspondence network (FC) can achieve comparable performance on DAVIS and JHMDB with methods like CRW, despite training with far less data and discarding temporal information. The performance of FC on VIP is lower, but it may be further improved by exploiting more inductive bias, e.g., temporal context or viewpoint changes in videos.

We show the results on DAVIS-2017 of FC using different pre-training datasets in the appendix. FC achieves 67.9 $\mathcal{J}\&\mathcal{F}_m$ when pre-trained on ImageNet. This suggests that a larger dataset offers marginal benefits for fine-grained correspondence learning, which is largely different from learning semantic correspondence. When replacing YouTube-VOS pre-trained FC with ImageNet pre-trained one, SFC still achieves 71.3 $\mathcal{J}\&\mathcal{F}_m$. This indicates that the performance gain of SFC doesn't come from the extra YouTube-VOS dataset. We use YouTube-VOS for faster training and fair comparisons of other correspondence learning methods.

We also report results of SFC on *semantic segmentation* and ImageNet-1K *linear probing* in the appendix. Our SFC achieves improved results on all con-

Fig. 4. Qualitative results for label propagation. Given ground-truth labels in the first frame (outlined in blue), our method can propagate them to the rest of frames. For more results, please refer to the appendix. (Color figure online)

sidered tasks, showing strong generalization ability and the flexibility of our core contribution.

4.3 Visualization

Figure 4 shows samples of video label propagation results. We further visualize the learned correspondences of our model in Fig. 5, compared with its components, MoCo and FC. We notice that the correspondence map of MoCo tends to scatter across the entire visual object, indicating that it focuses more on object-level semantics instead of low-level fine-grained features. On the contrary, the correspondence map of FC is highly concentrated, but sometimes loses track of the source pixel, indicating a failure to capture high-level semantics. By balancing semantics and fine-grained correspondences, our proposed method SFC is able to overcome their respective drawbacks and give the most accurate correspondence.

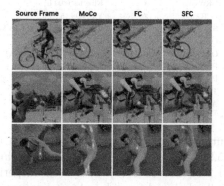

Fig. 5. Correspondence map of SFC, compared with MoCo and FC. Given the source frame with one pixel highlighted in red, we calculate the feature similarity between the target frame and this pixel. Red regions indicate high similarity. (Color figure online)

4.4 Ablative Analysis

In this section, we investigate our results on video object segmentation using DAVIS-2017 in more detail, and outline several ablations on important design choices throughout our model architectures and pipelines.

Fusion Strategy. We perform experiments by combing the FC training objective with a global image-level loss, resulting in an end-to-end multi-task framework. But we find the two losses fail to boost performance synergistically. For example, when we add a BYOL loss to FC for joint optimization (see the appendix for details), the performance on DAVIS-2017 drops a little ($67.7 \rightarrow 67.2$). The reason is that the two losses need different receptive fields and augmentations. The optimal configuration of FC model will induce a sub-optimal solution under the image-level loss, and vice versa. Thus, it is sensible to train two independent models and use concatenation to fuse the two different kinds of representations.

One may expect the concatenation operation is some form of model ensemble. Does combining an arbitrary two networks lead to any reasonable improvement in performance? To answer this, we conduct experiments on two sets of models: in the first set, all models have two semantic correspondence networks; while in the second set, all models have two fine-grained correspondence networks. Results are shown in Table 2. We observe that if two networks have the same type of correspondence, their combination leads to unremarkable increases in performance.

Table 2. Fusion of two networks with the same kind of correspondence. FC denotes our fine-grained correspondence network, it achieves 67.7 $\mathcal{J}\&\mathcal{F}_m$ on DAVIS-2017. Other single model results can be found in Table 1.

Type	Combination	$\mathcal{J}\&\mathcal{F}_m$	$\mathcal{J}_m$	$\mathcal{F}_m$
Semantic correspondence	InstDis + MoCo	67.4	65.0	69.7
	SimCLR + MoCo	67.2	64.7	69.6
	BYOL + MoCo	67.5	65.0	70.0
	Simsiam + MoCo	67.4	65.1	69.6
	VINCE + MoCo	66.7	64.2	69.2
	VFS + MoCo	68.1	66.1	70.2
Fine-grained correspondence	TimeCycle + FC	67.8	65.2	70.5
	UVC + FC	61.5	59.8	63.3
	CRW + FC	68.8	65.7	71.9

In the appendix, we show that we can flexibly replace semantic correspondence backbone (MoCo $\rightarrow$ InstDis, SimCLR, BYOL, etc.) and still maintain strong performance on DAVIS. This strongly confirms our hypothesis that image-level self-supervised representations in general contain information about semantic correspondence. It also supports our framing of semantic correspondence and fine-grained correspondence as orthogonal sources of information.

Next, we mainly conduct a series of ablation studies on our fine-grained network (FC).

Crop Size and Positive Radius. When we apply cropping for an image, a random patch is selected, with an area uniformly sampled between γ_1 (lower bound) and γ_2 (upper bound) of that of the original image. In Figure 6, we plot FC model performance on different ratios of crop size area, by varying γ_1: $\{0, 0.08, 0.2, 0.3\}$ and fixing γ_2 to 1. Simultaneously, for every lower bound γ_1, we investigate how different positive radii r can also affect performance on correspondence learning.

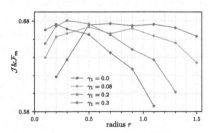

Fig. 6. Effect of random crop size and positive radius.

We find that as the lower bound γ_1 increases, mode performance worsens. $\gamma_1 = 0$ yields relatively strong performance under a wide range of positive radius r. We conjecture that using a small lower bound γ_1 results in larger scale and translation variations between two views of one image, which induces strong spatial augmentation and thus allows our correspondence learning to rely on scale-invariant representations. We also observe that an appropriate positive radius r is crucial for fine-grained correspondence learning. On the DAVIS dataset, we show that a large (smooth) or small (sharp) r is demonstrably harmful to performance. Finally, for different γ_1, the optimal value of r is different.

Data Augmentation. VFS [75] has pointed out that color augmentation jeopardizes fine-grained correspondence learning. To systematically study the effects of individual data augmentations, we investigate the performance of our FC model on DAVIS when applying random cropping and another common augmentation (random flip, color jittering, etc.). We report the results in Table 3. Among

Table 3. Effect of data augmentation. The augmentation strategy follows MoCo v2 [11].

Augmentation	$\mathcal{J}\&\mathcal{F}_m$	$\mathcal{J}_m$	$\mathcal{F}_m$
Random crop	67.6	64.7	70.5
Random crop & Random flip	67.7	64.8	70.6
Random crop & Color jittering	65.5	62.6	68.4
Random crop & Gaussian blur	65.9	63.2	68.6
Random crop & Color dropping	61.9	58.9	64.9

all color data augmentations, the one that has the greatest negative impact on fine-grained correspondence learning is actually color dropping (grayscale conversion). This is in contrast to image-level self-supervised learning, where strong color augmentation [9] is crucial for learning good representations. We adopt random crop as the only augmentation in our best-performing models.

5   Conclusion and Discussions

We have developed a novel framework to learn both semantic and fine-grained correspondence from still images alone. We demonstrate that these two forms of correspondence offer complementary information, thereby facilitating a simple yet intuitive fusion scheme which leads to state-of-the-art results on a number of downstream correspondence tasks. In this work, we mainly explore the correspondence properties of ConvNet. Whether ViT [16] also benefits from dense fine-grained self-supervision and combination of two kinds of correspondence is an interesting open question left to future exploration.

Acknowledgements. This work is supported by the Ministry of Science and Technology of the People's Republic of China, the 2030 Innovation Megaprojects "Program on New Generation Artificial Intelligence" (Grant No. 2021AAA0150000). This work is also supported by a grant from the Guoqiang Institute, Tsinghua University.

References

1. Bachman, P., Hjelm, R.D., Buchwalter, W.: Learning representations by maximizing mutual information across views. arXiv preprint arXiv:1906.00910 (2019)
2. Bai, Y., Chen, X., Kirillov, A., Yuille, A., Berg, A.C.: Point-level region contrast for object detection pre-training. arXiv preprint arXiv:2202.04639 (2022)
3. Ballard, D.H., Zhang, R.: The hierarchical evolution in human vision modeling. Top. Cogn. Sci. **13**(2), 309–328 (2021)
4. Bertinetto, L., Valmadre, J., Henriques, J.F., Vedaldi, A., Torr, P.H.S.: Fully-convolutional siamese networks for object tracking. In: Hua, G., Jégou, H. (eds.) ECCV 2016. LNCS, vol. 9914, pp. 850–865. Springer, Cham (2016). https://doi.org/10.1007/978-3-319-48881-3_56
5. Caelles, S., Maninis, K.K., Pont-Tuset, J., Leal-Taixé, L., Cremers, D., Van Gool, L.: One-shot video object segmentation. In: Proceedings of the IEEE Conference on Computer Vision and Pattern Recognition, pp. 221–230 (2017)
6. Caron, M., Misra, I., Mairal, J., Goyal, P., Bojanowski, P., Joulin, A.: Unsupervised learning of visual features by contrasting cluster assignments. arXiv preprint arXiv:2006.09882 (2020)
7. Caron, M., Touvron, H., Misra, I., Jégou, H., Mairal, J., Bojanowski, P., Joulin, A.: Emerging properties in self-supervised vision transformers. In: Proceedings of the IEEE/CVF International Conference on Computer Vision, pp. 9650–9660 (2021)
8. Carreira, J., Zisserman, A.: Quo vadis, action recognition? a new model and the kinetics dataset. In: proceedings of the IEEE Conference on Computer Vision and Pattern Recognition, pp. 6299–6308 (2017)
9. Chen, T., Kornblith, S., Norouzi, M., Hinton, G.: A simple framework for contrastive learning of visual representations. In: International Conference on Machine Learning PMLR, pp. 1597–1607 (2020)
10. Chen, T., Luo, C., Li, L.: Intriguing properties of contrastive losses. arXiv preprint arXiv:2011.02803 (2020)
11. Chen, X., Fan, H., Girshick, R., He, K.: Improved baselines with momentum contrastive learning. arXiv preprint arXiv:2003.04297 (2020)
12. Chen, X., He, K.: Exploring simple siamese representation learning. In: Proceedings of the IEEE/CVF Conference on Computer Vision and Pattern Recognition, pp. 15750–15758 (2021)
13. Chen, Y.C., et al.: Deep semantic matching with foreground detection and cycle-consistency. In: Jawahar, C.V., Li, H., Mori, G., Schindler, K. (eds.) ACCV 2018. LNCS, vol. 11363, pp. 347–362. Springer, Cham (2019). https://doi.org/10.1007/978-3-030-20893-6_22
14. Cheng, H.K., Tai, Y.W., Tang, C.K.: Rethinking space-time networks with improved memory coverage for efficient video object segmentation. arXiv preprint arXiv:2106.05210 (2021)
15. Deng, J., Dong, W., Socher, R., Li, L.J., Li, K., Fei-Fei, L.: Imagenet: a large-scale hierarchical image database. In: 2009 IEEE Conference on Computer Vision and Pattern Recognition, pp. 248–255. IEEE (2009)
16. Dosovitskiy, A., et al.: An image is worth 16 × 16 words: Transformers for image recognition at scale. arXiv preprint arXiv:2010.11929 (2020)
17. Dosovitskiy, Aet al.: Flownet: Learning optical flow with convolutional networks. In: Proceedings of the IEEE International Conference on Computer Vision, pp. 2758–2766 (2015)

18. Gordon, D., Ehsani, K., Fox, D., Farhadi, A.: Watching the world go by: Representation learning from unlabeled videos. arXiv preprint arXiv:2003.07990 (2020)
19. Gould, S., et al.: Peripheral-foveal vision for real-time object recognition and tracking in video. In: IJCAI, vol. 7, pp. 2115–2121 (2007)
20. Grabner, H., Matas, J., Van Gool, L., Cattin, P.: Tracking the invisible: learning where the object might be. In: 2010 IEEE Computer Society Conference on Computer Vision and Pattern Recognition, pp. 1285–1292. IEEE (2010)
21. Grill, J.B., et al.: Bootstrap your own latent: a new approach to self-supervised learning. arXiv preprint arXiv:2006.07733 (2020)
22. Hadsell, R., Chopra, S., LeCun, Y.: Dimensionality reduction by learning an invariant mapping. In: 2006 IEEE Computer Society Conference on Computer Vision and Pattern Recognition (CVPR 2006), vol. 2, pp. 1735–1742. IEEE (2006)
23. Hariharan, B., Arbeláez, P., Girshick, R., Malik, J.: Hypercolumns for object segmentation and fine-grained localization. In: Proceedings of the IEEE Conference on Computer Vision and Pattern Recognition, pp. 447–456 (2015)
24. He, K., Fan, H., Wu, Y., Xie, S., Girshick, R.: Momentum contrast for unsupervised visual representation learning. In: Proceedings of the IEEE/CVF Conference on Computer Vision and Pattern Recognition, pp. 9729–9738 (2020)
25. He, K., Zhang, X., Ren, S., Sun, J.: Deep residual learning for image recognition. In: Proceedings of the IEEE Conference on Computer Vision and Pattern Recognition, pp. 770–778 (2016)
26. Held, D., Thrun, S., Savarese, S.: Learning to track at 100 FPS with deep regression networks. In: Leibe, B., Matas, J., Sebe, N., Welling, M. (eds.) ECCV 2016. LNCS, vol. 9905, pp. 749–765. Springer, Cham (2016). https://doi.org/10.1007/978-3-319-46448-0_45
27. Henaff, O.: Data-efficient image recognition with contrastive predictive coding. In: International Conference on Machine Learning PMLR, pp. 4182–4192 (2020)
28. Henriques, J.F., Caseiro, R., Martins, P., Batista, J.: High-speed tracking with kernelized correlation filters. IEEE Trans. Pattern Anal. Mach. Intell. **37**(3), 583–596 (2014)
29. Huang, S., Wang, Q., Zhang, S., Yan, S., He, X.: Dynamic context correspondence network for semantic alignment. In: Proceedings of the IEEE/CVF International Conference on Computer Vision, pp. 2010–2019 (2019)
30. Ilg, E., Mayer, N., Saikia, T., Keuper, M., Dosovitskiy, A., Brox, T.: Flownet 2.0: evolution of optical flow estimation with deep networks. In: Proceedings of the IEEE Conference on Computer Vision and Pattern Recognition, pp. 2462–2470 (2017)
31. Iqbal, U., Garbade, M., Gall, J.: Pose for action-action for pose. In: 2017 12th IEEE International Conference on Automatic Face & Gesture Recognition (FG 2017), pp. 438–445. IEEE (2017)
32. Jabri, A., Owens, A., Efros, A.A.: Space-time correspondence as a contrastive random walk. Adv. Neural Inf. Process. Syst. **33**, 19545–19560 (2020)
33. Jhuang, H., Gall, J., Zuffi, S., Schmid, C., Black, M.J.: Towards understanding action recognition. In: Proceedings of the IEEE International Conference on Computer Vision, pp. 3192–3199 (2013)
34. Lai, Z., Lu, E., Xie, W.: Mast: a memory-augmented self-supervised tracker. In: Proceedings of the IEEE/CVF Conference on Computer Vision and Pattern Recognition, pp. 6479–6488 (2020)
35. Lai, Z., Xie, W.: Self-supervised learning for video correspondence flow. arXiv preprint arXiv:1905.00875 (2019)

36. Li, B., Yan, J., Wu, W., Zhu, Z., Hu, X.: High performance visual tracking with siamese region proposal network. In: Proceedings of the IEEE Conference on Computer Vision and Pattern Recognition, pp. 8971–8980 (2018)

37. Li, X., Liu, S., De Mello, S., Wang, X., Kautz, J., Yang, M.H.: Joint-task self-supervised learning for temporal correspondence. arXiv preprint arXiv:1909.11895 (2019)

38. Liu, C., Yuen, J., Torralba, A., Sivic, J., Freeman, W.T.: SIFT flow: dense correspondence across different scenes. In: Forsyth, D., Torr, P., Zisserman, A. (eds.) ECCV 2008. LNCS, vol. 5304, pp. 28–42. Springer, Heidelberg (2008). https://doi.org/10.1007/978-3-540-88690-7_3

39. Liu, Y., Zhu, L., Yamada, M., Yang, Y.: Semantic correspondence as an optimal transport problem. In: Proceedings of the IEEE/CVF Conference on Computer Vision and Pattern Recognition, pp. 4463–4472 (2020)

40. Long, J.L., Zhang, N., Darrell, T.: Do convnets learn correspondence? Adv. Neural Inf. Process. Syst. **27**, 1601–1609 (2014)

41. Min, J., Cho, M.: Convolutional hough matching networks. In: Proceedings of the IEEE/CVF Conference on Computer Vision and Pattern Recognition, pp. 2940–2950 (2021)

42. Min, J., Lee, J., Ponce, J., Cho, M.: Hyperpixel flow: semantic correspondence with multi-layer neural features. In: Proceedings of the IEEE/CVF International Conference on Computer Vision, pp. 3395–3404 (2019)

43. Min, J., Lee, J., Ponce, J., Cho, M.: Learning to compose hypercolumns for visual correspondence. In: Vedaldi, A., Bischof, H., Brox, T., Frahm, J.-M. (eds.) ECCV 2020. LNCS, vol. 12360, pp. 346–363. Springer, Cham (2020). https://doi.org/10.1007/978-3-030-58555-6_21

44. Misra, I., Maaten, L.V.D.: Self-supervised learning of pretext-invariant representations. In: Proceedings of the IEEE/CVF Conference on Computer Vision and Pattern Recognition, pp. 6707–6717 (2020)

45. Oh, S.W., Lee, J.Y., Xu, N., Kim, S.J.: Video object segmentation using space-time memory networks. In: Proceedings of the IEEE/CVF International Conference on Computer Vision, pp. 9226–9235 (2019)

46. Oord, A.v.d., Li, Y., Vinyals, O.: Representation learning with contrastive predictive coding. arXiv preprint arXiv:1807.03748 (2018)

47. Perazzi, F., Pont-Tuset, J., McWilliams, B., Van Gool, L., Gross, M., Sorkine-Hornung, A.: a benchmark dataset and evaluation methodology for video object segmentation. In: Proceedings of the IEEE Conference on Computer Vision and Pattern Recognition, pp. 724–732 (2016)

48. Pinheiro, P.O., Almahairi, A., Benmalek, R.Y., Golemo, F., Courville, A.: Unsupervised learning of dense visual representations. arXiv preprint arXiv:2011.05499 (2020)

49. Pont-Tuset, J., Perazzi, F., Caelles, S., Arbeláez, P., Sorkine-Hornung, A., Van Gool, L.: The 2017 davis challenge on video object segmentation. arXiv preprint arXiv:1704.00675 (2017)

50. Purushwalkam, S., Gupta, A.: Demystifying contrastive self-supervised learning: Invariances, augmentations and dataset biases. arXiv preprint arXiv:2007.13916 (2020)

51. Ranjan, A., Black, M.J.: Optical flow estimation using a spatial pyramid network. In: Proceedings of the IEEE Conference on Computer Vision and Pattern Recognition, pp. 4161–4170 (2017)

52. Rocco, I., Arandjelovic, R., Sivic, J.: Convolutional neural network architecture for geometric matching. In: Proceedings of the IEEE Conference on Computer Vision and Pattern Recognition, pp. 6148–6157 (2017)

53. Rocco, I., Arandjelović, R., Sivic, J.: End-to-end weakly-supervised semantic alignment. In: Proceedings of the IEEE Conference on Computer Vision and Pattern Recognition, pp. 6917–6925 (2018)

54. Rocco, I., Cimpoi, M., Arandjelović, R., Torii, A., Pajdla, T., Sivic, J.: Neighbourhood consensus networks. arXiv preprint arXiv:1810.10510 (2018)

55. Simonyan, K., Zisserman, A.: Two-stream convolutional networks for action recognition in videos. Adv. Neural Inf. Process. Syst. **27** (2014)

56. Song, J., Wang, L., Van Gool, L., Hilliges, O.: Thin-slicing network: a deep structured model for pose estimation in videos. In: Proceedings of the IEEE Conference on Computer Vision and Pattern Recognition, pp. 4220–4229 (2017)

57. Sun, D., Yang, X., Liu, M.Y., Kautz, J.: Pwc-net: Cnns for optical flow using pyramid, warping, and cost volume. In: Proceedings of the IEEE Conference on Computer Vision and Pattern Recognition, pp. 8934–8943 (2018)

58. Teed, Z., Deng, J.: RAFT: recurrent all-pairs field transforms for optical flow. In: Vedaldi, A., Bischof, H., Brox, T., Frahm, J.-M. (eds.) ECCV 2020. LNCS, vol. 12347, pp. 402–419. Springer, Cham (2020). https://doi.org/10.1007/978-3-030-58536-5_24

59. Tian, Y., Krishnan, D., Isola, P.: Contrastive multiview coding. In: Vedaldi, A., Bischof, H., Brox, T., Frahm, J.-M. (eds.) ECCV 2020. LNCS, vol. 12356, pp. 776–794. Springer, Cham (2020). https://doi.org/10.1007/978-3-030-58621-8_45

60. Truong, P., Danelljan, M., Timofte, R.: GLU-net: global-local universal network for dense flow and correspondences. In: Proceedings of the IEEE/CVF Conference on Computer Vision and Pattern Recognition, pp. 6258–6268 (2020)

61. Valmadre, J., Bertinetto, L., Henriques, J., Vedaldi, A., Torr, P.H.: End-to-end representation learning for correlation filter based tracking. In: Proceedings of the IEEE Conference on Computer Vision and Pattern Recognition, pp. 2805–2813 (2017)

62. Van Gansbeke, W., Vandenhende, S., Georgoulis, S., Proesmans, M., Van Gool, L.: SCAN: learning to classify images without labels. In: Vedaldi, A., Bischof, H., Brox, T., Frahm, J.-M. (eds.) ECCV 2020. LNCS, vol. 12355, pp. 268–285. Springer, Cham (2020). https://doi.org/10.1007/978-3-030-58607-2_16

63. Van Gansbeke, W., Vandenhende, S., Georgoulis, S., Van Gool, L.: Revisiting contrastive methods for unsupervised learning of visual representations. arXiv preprint arXiv:2106.05967 (2021)

64. Voigtlaender, P., Chai, Y., Schroff, F., Adam, H., Leibe, B., Chen, L.C.: Feelvos: fast end-to-end embedding learning for video object segmentation. In: Proceedings of the IEEE/CVF Conference on Computer Vision and Pattern Recognition, pp. 9481–9490 (2019)

65. Voigtlaender, P., Leibe, B.: Online adaptation of convolutional neural networks for video object segmentation. arXiv preprint arXiv:1706.09364 (2017)

66. Vondrick, C., Shrivastava, A., Fathi, A., Guadarrama, S., Murphy, K.: Tracking emerges by colorizing videos. In: Proceedings of the European Conference on Computer Vision (ECCV), pp. 391–408 (2018)

67. Wang, N., Yeung, D.Y.: Learning a deep compact image representation for visual tracking. Adv. Neural Inf. Process. Syst. (2013)

68. Wang, N., Song, Y., Ma, C., Zhou, W., Liu, W., Li, H.: Unsupervised deep tracking. In: Proceedings of the IEEE/CVF Conference on Computer Vision and Pattern Recognition, pp. 1308–1317 (2019)

69. Wang, Q., Zhang, L., Bertinetto, L., Hu, W., Torr, P.H.: Fast online object tracking and segmentation: a unifying approach. In: Proceedings of the IEEE/CVF Conference on Computer Vision and Pattern Recognition, pp. 1328–1338 (2019)

70. Wang, X., Jabri, A., Efros, A.A.: Learning correspondence from the cycle-consistency of time. In: Proceedings of the IEEE/CVF Conference on Computer Vision and Pattern Recognition, pp. 2566–2576 (2019)

71. Wang, X., Zhang, R., Shen, C., Kong, T., Li, L.: Dense contrastive learning for self-supervised visual pre-training. In: Proceedings of the IEEE/CVF Conference on Computer Vision and Pattern Recognition, pp. 3024–3033 (2021)

72. Wu, Z., Xiong, Y., Yu, S., Lin, D.: Unsupervised feature learning via non-parametric instance-level discrimination. arXiv preprint arXiv:1805.01978 (2018)

73. Xie, E., et al.: Detco: unsupervised contrastive learning for object detection. In: Proceedings of the IEEE/CVF International Conference on Computer Vision, pp. 8392–8401 (2021)

74. Xie, Z., Lin, Y., Zhang, Z., Cao, Y., Lin, S., Hu, H.: Propagate yourself: exploring pixel-level consistency for unsupervised visual representation learning. In: Proceedings of the IEEE/CVF Conference on Computer Vision and Pattern Recognition, pp. 16684–16693 (2021)

75. Xu, J., Wang, X.: Rethinking self-supervised correspondence learning: a video frame-level similarity perspective. arXiv preprint arXiv:2103.17263 (2021)

76. Xu, N., et al.: Youtube-vos: a large-scale video object segmentation benchmark. arXiv preprint arXiv:1809.03327 (2018)

77. Yang, Y., Ramanan, D.: Articulated pose estimation with flexible mixtures-of-parts. In: CVPR 2011, pp. 1385–1392. IEEE (2011)

78. Zhang, R., et al.: Human gaze assisted artificial intelligence: a review. In: IJCAI: Proceedings of the Conference. vol. 2020, p. 4951. NIH Public Access (2020)

79. Zhou, Q., Liang, X., Gong, K., Lin, L.: Adaptive temporal encoding network for video instance-level human parsing. In: Proceedings of the 26th ACM International Conference on Multimedia, pp. 1527–1535 (2018)

Self-Supervised Classification Network

Elad Amrani[1,3]([✉]), Leonid Karlinsky[2], and Alex Bronstein[3]

[1] IBM Research-AI, Haifa, Israel
[2] MIT-IBM Watson AI Lab, Cambridge, US
[3] Technion, Haifa, Israel
elad.amrani@ibm.com

Abstract. We present Self-Classifier – a novel self-supervised end-to-end classification learning approach. Self-Classifier learns labels and representations simultaneously in a single-stage end-to-end manner by optimizing for same-class prediction of two augmented views of the same sample. To guarantee non-degenerate solutions (i.e., solutions where all labels are assigned to the same class) we propose a mathematically motivated variant of the cross-entropy loss that has a uniform prior asserted on the predicted labels. In our theoretical analysis, we prove that degenerate solutions are not in the set of optimal solutions of our approach. Self-Classifier is simple to implement and scalable. Unlike other popular unsupervised classification and contrastive representation learning approaches, it does not require any form of pre-training, expectation-maximization, pseudo-labeling, external clustering, a second network, stop-gradient operation, or negative pairs. Despite its simplicity, our approach sets a new state of the art for unsupervised classification of ImageNet; and even achieves comparable to state-of-the-art results for unsupervised representation learning. Code is available at https://github.com/elad-amrani/self-classifier.

Keywords: Self-supervised classification · Representation learning

1 Introduction

Self-supervised visual representation learning has gained increasing interest over the past few years [2,5–7,10,18,23,29]. The main idea is to define and solve a pretext task such that semantically meaningful representations can be learned without any human-annotated labels. The learned representations are later transferred to downstream tasks, e.g., by fine-tuning on a smaller dataset. Current state-of-the-art self-supervised models are based on contrastive learning (Sect. 2.1). These models maximize the similarity between two different augmentations of the same image while simultaneously minimizing the similarity between different images, subject to different conditions. Although they attain impressive

---

Supplementary Information The online version contains supplementary material available at https://doi.org/10.1007/978-3-031-19821-2_7.

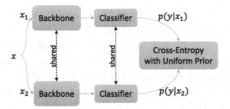

Fig. 1. *Self-Classifier* **architecture.** Two augmented views of the same image are processed by a shared network comprised of a backbone (e.g. CNN) and a classifier (e.g. projection MLP + linear classification head). The cross-entropy of the two views is minimized to promote same class prediction while avoiding degenerate solutions by asserting a uniform prior on class predictions. The resulting model learns representations and discovers the underlying classes in a single-stage end-to-end unsupervised manner.

overall performance, for some downstream tasks, such as unsupervised classification (Sect. 6.1), the objective of the various proposed pretext tasks might not be sufficiently well aligned. For example, instance discrimination methods, such as [7,18] used for pre-training in the current state-of-the-art unsupervised classification method [28], decrease similarity between all instances, even between those that belong to the same (unknown during training) class, thus potentially working against the set task. In contrast, in this paper we propose a classification-based pretext task whose objective is directly aligned with the end goal in this case. Knowing only the number of classes C we learn an unsupervised classifier (*Self-Classifier*) such that two different augmentations of the same image are classified similarly. In practice, such a task is prone to degenerate solutions, where all samples assigned to the same class. To avoid them, we assert a uniform prior on the standard cross-entropy loss function, such that a solution with an equipartition of the data is an optimal solution. In fact, we show that the set of optimal solutions no longer includes degenerate ones.

Our approach can also be viewed as a form of deep unsupervised clustering (Sect. 2.2) [1,4,17,20,28,30–32] combined with contrastive learning. Similarly to deep clustering methods, we learn the parameters of a neural network and cluster (class) assignments simultaneously. Recently, clustering has been combined with contrastive learning in [2,32] with great success, yet in both studies clustering was employed as a separate step used for pseudo-labeling. In contrast, in this work we learn representations and cluster labels in a single-stage end-to-end manner, using only minibatch SGD.

The key contributions of this paper are:

1. A simple yet effective self-supervised single-stage end-to-end classification and representation learning approach. Unlike previous unsupervised classification works, our approach does not require any form of pre-training, expectation-maximization algorithm, pseudo-labeling, or external clustering. Unlike previous unsupervised representation learning works, our approach does not

require a memory bank, a second network (momentum), external clustering, stop-gradient operation, or negative pairs.

2. Although simple, our approach sets a new state of the art for unsupervised classification on ImageNet with 41.1% top-1 accuracy, achieves results comparable to state of the art for unsupervised representation learning, and attains a significant –2% AP) improvement in transfer to COCO det/seg compared to other self. sup. methods.

3. We are the first to provide quantitative analysis of self-supervised classification predictions alignment to a set of different class hierarchies (defined on ImageNet and its subpopulations), and show significant (up to 3.4% AMI) improvement over previous state of the art in this new metric.

2   Related Work

2.1   Self-Supervised Learning

Self-supervised learning methods learn compact semantic data representations by defining and solving a pretext task. In such tasks, naturally existing supervision signals are utilized for training. Many pretext tasks were proposed in recent years in the domain of computer vision, including colorization [35], jigsaw puzzle [24], image inpainting [25], context prediction [9], rotation prediction [14], and contrastive learning [2,5–7,10,18,23,29] just to mention a few.

Contrastive learning has shown great promise and has become a *de facto* standard for self-supervised learning. Two of the earliest studies of contrastive learning are Exemplar CNN [10], and Non-Parametric Instance Discrimination (NPID) [29]. Exemplar CNN [10], learns to discriminate between instances using a convolutional neural network classifier, where each class represents a single instance and its augmentations. While highly simple and effective, it does not scale to arbitrarily large amounts of unlabeled data since it requires a classification layer (softmax) the size of the dataset. NPID [29] tackles this problem by approximating the full softmax distribution with noise-contrastive estimation (NCE) [16] and utilizing a memory bank to store the recent representation of each instance to avoid computing the representations of the entire dataset at each time step of the learning process. Such approximation is effective since, unlike Exemplar CNN, it allows training with large amounts of unlabeled data. However, the proposed memory bank by NPID introduces a new problem - lack of consistency across representations stored in the memory bank, i.e., the representations of different samples in the memory bank are computed at multiple different time steps. Nonetheless, Exemplar CNN and NPID have inspired a line of studies of contrastive learning [2,5–7,18,21].

One such recent study is SwAV [2] which resembles the present work the most. SwAV takes advantage of contrastive methods without requiring to compute pairwise comparisons. More specifically, it simultaneously clusters the data while enforcing consistency between cluster assignments produced for different augmentations (or "views") of the same image, instead of comparing features directly. To avoid a trivial solution where all samples collapse into a single cluster, SwAV alternates between representation learning using back propagation, and a separate clustering step using the Sinkhorn-Knopp algorithm. In contrast to SwAV, in this work we propose a model that allows learning both representations and cluster assignments in a single-stage end-to-end manner.

2.2 Deep Unsupervised Clustering

Deep unsupervised clustering methods simultaneously learn the parameters of a neural network and the cluster assignments of the resulting features using unlabeled data [1,4,17,20,28,30–32]. Such a task is understandably vulnerable to degenerate solutions, where all samples are assigned to a single cluster. Many different solutions that were proposed to avoid the trivial outcome are based on one or few of the following: a) pre-training mechanism; b) Expectation-Maximization (EM) algorithm (i.e., alternating between representation learning and cluster assignment); c) pseudo-labeling; and d) external clustering algorithm such as k-means.

Two of the earliest studies of deep clustering are DEC [30] and JULE [31]. DEC [30] initializes the parameters of its network using a deep autoencoder, and its cluster centroids using standard k-means clustering in the feature space. It then uses a form of EM algorithm, where it iterates between pseudo-labeling and learning from its own high confidence predictions. JULE [30], similarly to DEC, alternates between pseudo-labeling and learning from its own predictions. However, unlike DEC, JULE avoids a pre-training step and instead utilizes the prior on the input signal given by a randomly initialized ConvNet together with agglomerative clustering.

More recent approaches are SeLa [32] and IIC [20]. SeLa [32] uses a form of EM algorithm, where it iterates between minimization of the cross entropy loss and pseudo-labeling by solving efficiently an instance of the *optimal transport problem* using the Sinkhorn-Knopp algorithm. IIC [20] is a single-stage end-to-end deep clustering model conceptually similar to the approach presented in this paper. IIC maximizes the mutual information between predictions of two augmented views of the same sample. The two entropy terms constituting mutual information – the entropy of a sample and its negative conditional entropy given the other sample compete with each other, with the entropy being maximal when the labels are uniformly distributed over the clusters, and the negative conditional entropy being maximal for sharp one-hot instance assignments.

In this work, we follow a similar rationale for single-stage end-to-end classification without the use of any pseudo-labeling. Unlike IIC, our proposed loss is equivalent to the cross-entropy classification loss under a uniform label prior that guarantees non-degenerate, uniformly distributed optimal solution as explained in Sect. 3. Although many deep clustering approaches were proposed over the years, only two of them (SCAN [28] and SeLa [32]) have demonstrated scalability to large-scale datasets such as ImageNet. In fact, the task of unsupervised classification of large-scale datasets remains an open challenge.

3 Self-Classifier

Let x_1, x_2 denote two different augmented views of the same image sample x. Our goal is to learn a classifier $y \triangleq f(x_i) \in [C]$, where C is the given number of classes, such that two augmented views of the same sample are classified similarly, while avoiding degenerate solutions. A naive approach to this would be minimizing the following cross-entropy loss:

$$\tilde{\ell}(x_1, x_2) = - \sum_{y \in [C]} p(y|x_2) \log p(y|x_1), \tag{1}$$

where $p(y|x)$ is a row softmax with temperature τ_{row} [29] of the matrix of logits S produced by our model (backbone + classifier) for all classes (columns) and batch samples (rows). However, without additional regularization, an attempt to minimize (1) will quickly converge to a degenerate solution in which the network predicts a constant y regardless of the x. In order to remedy this, we propose to invoke Bayes and total probability laws, obtaining:

$$p(y|x_2) = \frac{p(y)p(x_2|y)}{p(x_2)} = \frac{p(y)p(x_2|y)}{\sum_{\tilde{y} \in [C]} p(x_2|\tilde{y})p(\tilde{y})}, \tag{2}$$

$$p(y|x_1) = \frac{p(y)p(y|x_1)}{p(y)} = \frac{p(y)p(y|x_1)}{\sum_{\tilde{x}_1 \in B_1} p(y|\tilde{x}_1)p(\tilde{x}_1)}, \tag{3}$$

where B is a batch of N samples (B_1 are the first augmentations of samples of B), and $p(x|y)$ is a column softmax of the aforementioned matrix of logits S with the temperature τ_{col}. Now, assuming that $p(x_1)$ is uniform (under the reasonable assumption that the training samples are equi-probable), and, since we would like all classes to be used, assuming (an intuitive) uniform prior for $p(y)$, we obtain:

$$\ell(x_1, x_2) = - \sum_{y \in [C]} \frac{p(x_2|y)}{\sum_{\tilde{y}} p(x_2|\tilde{y})} \log \left(\frac{N}{C} \frac{p(y|x_1)}{\sum_{\tilde{x}_1} p(y|\tilde{x}_1)} \right), \tag{4}$$

where $p(y)$ and $p(\tilde{y})$ cancel out in (2), and $p(y)/p(\tilde{x}_1)$ becomes N/C in (3). In practice, we use a symmetric variant of this loss (that we empirically noticed to be better):

$$\mathcal{L} = \frac{1}{2} \left(\ell(x_1, x_2) + \ell(x_2, x_1) \right). \tag{5}$$

Note that the naive cross entropy in (1) is in fact mathematically equivalent to our proposed loss function in (4), under the assumption that $p(y)$ and $p(x)$ are uniform. Finally, despite being very simple (only few lines of PyTorch-like pseudocode in Algorithm 1) our method sets a new state of the art in self-supervised classification (Sect. 6.1).

Algorithm 1. *Self-Classifier* PyTorch-like Pseudocode

```
# N: number of samples in batch
# C: number of classes
# t_r / t_c: row / column softmax temperatures
# aug(): random augmentations
# softmaxX(): softmax over dimension X
# normX(): L1 normalization over dimension X
for x in loader:
    s1, s2 = model(aug(x)), model(aug(x))
    log_y_x1 = log(N/C * norm0(softmax1(s1/t_r)))
    log_y_x2 = log(N/C * norm0(softmax1(s2/t_r)))
    y_x1 = norm1(softmax0(s1/t_c))
    y_x2 = norm1(softmax0(s2/t_c))
    l1 = - sum(y_x2 * log_y_x1) / N
    l2 = - sum(y_x1 * log_y_x2) / N
    L = (l1 + l2) / 2
    L.backward()
    optimizer.step()
```

---

4   Theoretical Analysis

In this section, we show mathematically how *Self-Classifier* avoids trivial solutions by design, i.e., a collapsing solution is not in the set of optimal solutions of our proposed loss function (4). Proofs are provided in Supplementary.

Theorem 1 (Non-Zero Posterior Probability). *Let B be a batch of N samples with two views per sample, $(x_1, x_2) \in B$. Let $p(y)$ and $p(x)$ be the class and sample distributions, respectively, where $y \in [C]$. Let (5) be the loss function. Then, each class $y \in [C]$ will have at least one sample $y \in [C]$ with non-zero posterior probability $p(x|y) > 0$ assigned into it, and each sample $x \in [N]$ will have at least one class $y \in [C]$ with $p(x|y) > 0$.*

Theorem 2 (Optimal Solution With Uniform Prior). *Let B be a batch of N samples with two views per sample, $(x_1, x_2) \in B$. Let $p(y)$ and $p(x)$ be the class and sample distribution, respectively, where $y \in [C]$. Then, the uniform probabilities $p(y) = \frac{1}{C}$, $p(x) = \frac{1}{N}$ constitute a global minimizer of the loss (4).*

5   Implementation Details

5.1   Architecture

In all our experiments, we used ResNet-50 [19] backbone (as customary for all compared SSL works) initialized randomly. Following previous work, for our projection heads we used an MLP with 2 layers (of sizes 4096 and 128) with BN, leaky-ReLU activations, and ℓ_2 normalization after the last layer. On top of the projection head MLP we had 4 classification heads into $1K, 2K, 4K$ and $8K$

classes respectively. Each classification head was a simple linear layer without additive bias term. Row-softmax temperature τ_{row} was set to 0.1, while column-softmax temperature τ_{col} – to 0.05. Unless mentioned otherwise, evaluation for unsupervised classification (Sect. 6.1) was done strictly using the $1K$-classes classification head. For linear evaluation (Sect. 6.2) the MLP was dropped and replaced with a single linear layer of $1K$ classes.

5.2   Image Augmentations

We followed the data augmentations of BYOL [15] (color jittering, Gaussian blur and solarization), multi-crop [2] (two global views of 224×224 and six local views of 96×96) and nearest neighbor augmentation [11] (queue for nearest neighbor augmentation was set to $256K$). We refer to Table 8 in Sect. 7 for performance results without multi-crop and nearest neighbor.

5.3   Optimization

Unsupervised Pre-Training/Classification.   Most of our training hyper-parameters are directly taken from SwAV [2]. We used a LARS optimizer [33] with a learning rate of 4.8 and weight decay of 10^{-6}. The learning rate was linearly ramped up (starting from 0.3) over the first 10 epochs, and then decreased using a cosine scheduler for 790 epochs with a final value of 0.0048 (for a total of 800 epochs). We used a batch size of 4096 distributed across 64 NVIDIA V100 GPUs.

Linear Evaluation.   Similarly to [8] we used a LARS optimizer [33] with a learning rate of 0.8 and no weight decay. The learning rate was decreased using a cosine scheduler for 100 epochs. We used a batch size of 4096 distributed across 16 NVIDIA V100 GPUs. We have also tried the SGD optimizer in [18] with a batch size of 256, which gives similar results.

6   Results

6.1   Unsupervised Image Classification

We evaluate our approach on the task of unsupervised image classification using the large-scale ImageNet dataset (Tables. 1 to 3). We report the standard clustering metrics: Normalized Mutual Information (NMI), Adjusted Normalized Mutual Information (AMI), Adjusted Rand-Index (ARI), and Clustering Accuracy (ACC).

Our approach sets a new state-of-the-art performance for unsupervised image classification using ImageNet, on all four metrics (NMI, AMI, ARI and ACC), even when trained for a substantial lower number of epochs (Table 1). We compare our approach to the latest large-scale deep clustering methods [28,32] that have been explicitly evaluated on ImageNet. Additionally, we also compare our

Table 1. ImageNet unsupervised image classification using ResNet-50. NMI: Normalized Mutual Information, AMI: Adjusted Normalized Mutual Information, ARI: Adjusted Rand-Index, ACC: Clustering accuracy. †: produced by fitting a k-means classifier on the learned representations of the training set (models from official repositories were used), and then running inference on the validation set (results for SimCLRv2 and InfoMin are taken from [36]). SimSiam provide only 100-epoch model in their official repository. *: best result taken from the paper's official repository. Top-3 best methods per-metric are underlined. Best in bold

Method	Epochs	NMI	AMI	ARI	ACC
Representation learning methods					
SimCLRv2† [6]	1000	61.5	34.9	11.0	22.4
SimSiam† [8]	100	62.2	34.9	11.6	24.9
SwAV† [2]	800	64.1	38.8	13.4	28.1
MoCoV2† [7]	800	66.6	45.3	12.0	30.6
DINO† [3]	800	66.2	42.3	15.6	30.7
OBoW† [13]	200	66.5	42.0	16.9	31.1
InfoMin† [27]	800	68.8	48.3	14.7	33.2
BarlowT† [34]	1000	67.1	43.6	17.6	34.2
Clustering based methods					
SeLa* [32]	280	65.7	42.0	16.2	30.5
SCAN [28]	800+125	72.0	51.2	27.5	_39.9_
Self-Classifier	100	71.2	49.2	26.1	37.3
Self-Classifier	200	_72.5_	_51.6_	_28.1_	39.4
Self-Classifier	400	_72.9_	_52.3_	_28.8_	_40.2_
Self-Classifier	800	**73.3**	**53.1**	**29.5**	**41.1**

approach to the latest self-supervised representation learning methods (using ImageNet-pretrained models provided in their respective official repositories) after fitting a k-means classifier to the learned representations computed on the training set. For all methods we run inference on the validation set (unseen during training).

The current state-of-the-art approach, SCAN [28], is a multi-stage algorithm that involves: 1) pre-training (800 epochs); 2) offline k-nearest neighbor mining; 3) clustering (100 epochs); and 4) self-labeling and fine-tuning (25 epochs). In contrast, *Self-Classifier* is a single-stage simple-to-implement model (Algorithm 1) that is trained only with minibatch SGD. At only 200 epochs *Self-Classifier* already outperforms SCAN with 925 epochs.

SCAN provided an interesting qualitative analysis of alignment of its unsupervised class predictions to a certain (single) level of the default (WordNet) ImageNet semantic hierarchy. In contrast, here we propose a more diverse set of

Table 2. ImageNet-superclasses unsupervised image classification accuracy using ResNet-50. We define new datasets that contain broad classes which each subsume several of the original ImageNet classes. See Supplementary for details of each superclass. †: produced by fitting a k-means classifier on the learned representations of the training set (models from official repositories were used), and then running inference on the validation set. Results for SCAN and SeLa were produced using ImageNet-pretrained models provided in their respective official repositories

Method	Number of ImageNet superclasses					
	10	29	128	466	591	1000
Representation learning methods						
SwAV† [2]	79.1	69.4	58.0	46.3	34.5	28.1
MoCoV2† [7]	80.0	72.8	63.8	51.4	36.8	30.6
DINO† [3]	79.7	71.3	60.7	49.2	37.8	30.7
OBoW† [13]	83.9	76.5	67.4	53.5	35.7	31.1
BarlowT† [34]	80.2	72.1	62.7	52.7	40.9	34.2
Clustering based methods						
SeLa [32]	55.2	44.9	40.6	36.6	37.8	30.5
SCAN [28]	85.3	79.3	71.2	59.6	44.7	39.9
Self-Classifier	**85.7**	**79.7**	**71.8**	**60.0**	**46.7**	**41.1**

quantitative metrics to evaluate the performance of self-supervised classification methods on various levels of the default ImageNet hierarchy, as well as on several hierarchies of carefully curated ImageNet subpopulations (BREEDS [26]). We believe that this new set of hierarchical alignment metrics expanding on the leaf-only metric used so far, will allow deeper investigation of how self-supervised classification approaches perceive the internal taxonomy of classes of unlabeled data they are applied to, exposing their strength and weaknesses in a new and interesting light. We use these new metrics to compare our proposed approach to previous unsupervised clustering work [28,32], as well as state-of-the-art representation learning work [2,3,6–8,13,27,34].

In Table 2 we report results for different numbers of ImageNet superclasses (10, 29, 128, 466 and 591) resulting from cutting the default (WordNet) ImageNet hierarchy on different levels. See Supplementary for details of each superclass. The results in this table, that are significantly higher then the result for leaf (1000) classes for any hierarchy level, indicate that examples misclassified on the leaf level tend to be assigned to other clusters from within the same superclass. Furthermore, we see that *Self-Classifier* consistently outperforms previous work on all hierarchy levels.

In Table 3 we report the results on four ImageNet subpopulation datasets of BREEDS [26]. These datasets are accompanied by class hierarchies re-calibrated by [26] such that classes on same hierarchy level are of the same visual granular-

Table 3. ImageNet-subsets (BREEDS) unsupervised image classification using ResNet-50. The four BREEDS datasets are: Entity13, Entity30, Living17 and Nonliving26. NMI: Normalized Mutual Information, AMI: Adjusted Normalized Mutual Information, ARI: Adjusted Rand-Index, ACC: Clustering accuracy. †: produced by fitting a k-means classifier on the learned representations of the training set (models from official repositories were used), and then running inference on the validation set. Results for SCAN and SeLa were produced using ImageNet-pretrained models provided in their respective official repositories

Method	Entity13				Entity30				Living17				Nonliving26			
	NMI	AMI	ARI	ACC	NMI	AMI	ARI	ACC	NMI	AMI	ARI	ACC	NMI	AMI	ARI	ACC
Representation learning methods																
SwAV† [2]	64.8	39.9	15.2	75.6	64.6	39.4	15.1	70.5	61.0	40.3	15.7	85.2	62.0	41.1	19.2	63.1
MoCoV2† [7]	67.3	46.6	14.7	79.0	66.4	45.8	15.1	74.6	61.2	45.7	16.3	89.7	63.3	46.2	19.3	66.2
DINO† [3]	67.2	43.7	18.0	78.2	66.8	43.2	18.1	73.7	63.8	45.1	19.6	88.2	63.8	43.9	21.8	66.7
OBoW† [13]	66.4	42.3	17.5	82.2	64.9	40.7	16.4	77.6	53.8	34.0	12.0	91.1	64.8	45.4	22.9	67.9
BarlowT† [34]	68.2	45.5	20.5	77.7	67.7	45.1	20.7	73.0	64.7	47.2	22.2	88.0	64.8	45.7	24.9	66.7
Clustering based methods																
SeLa [32]	67.6	44.8	19.4	50.7	68.2	45.7	21.2	52.6	**71.8**	**53.9**	**29.7**	80.8	68.9	46.6	24.6	67.1
SCAN [28]	72.4	52.3	29.2	83.7	71.3	50.8	27.8	80.0	65.2	49.4	25.3	**92.5**	70.0	53.6	33.4	74.4
Self-Classifier	**73.6**	**54.1**	**30.7**	**84.4**	**72.9**	**53.4**	**29.8**	**81.0**	67.2	51.8	26.4	90.8	**72.2**	**57.0**	**36.8**	**76.7**

ity. Each dataset contains a specific subpopulation of ImageNet, such as 'Entities', 'Living' things and 'Non-living' things, allowing for a more fine-grained evaluation of hierarchical alignment of self-supervised classification predictions. Again, we see consistent improvement of *Self-Classifier* over previous work and self-supervised representation baselines.

6.2 Image Classification with Linear Models

We evaluate the quality of our unsupervised features using the standard linear classification protocol. Following the self-supervised pre-training stage, we freeze the features and train on top of it a supervised linear classifier (a single fully-connected layer). This classifier operates on the global average pooling features of a ResNet. Table 4 summarizes the results and comparison to the state-of-the-art methods for various number of training budgets (100 to 800 epochs).

In addition to good results for unsupervised classification (Sect. 6.1), *Self-Classifier* additionally achieves results comparable to state of the art for linear classification evaluation using ImageNet. Specifically, as detailed in Table 4, it is one of the top-3 result for 3 out of 4 of the training budgets reported, and top-1 in the 100 epochs category.

6.3 Transfer Learning

We further evaluate the quality of our unsupervised features by transferring them to other tasks - object detection and instance segmentation. Table 5 reports results for VOC07+12 [12] and COCO [22] datasets. We fine-tune our pre-trained model end-to-end in the target datasets using the public codebase from MoCo [18]. We obtain significant (–2%) improvements in the more challenging COCO det/seg over all the self-supervised baselines.

Table 4. ImageNet linear classification using ResNet-50. Top-1 accuracy vs. number of training epochs. Top-3 best methods per-category are underlined

Method	Number of training epochs			
	100	200	400	800
Supervised	76.5	–	–	–
SimCLR [5]	66.5	68.3	69.8	70.4
MoCoV2 [7]	67.4	67.5	71.0	71.1
SimSiam [8]	68.1	70.0	70.8	71.3
SimCLRv2 [6]	–	–	–	71.7
InfoMin [27]	–	–	–	73.0
BarlowT [34]	–	–	–	73.2
OBoW [13]	–	<u>73.8</u>	–	–
BYOL [15]	66.5	70.6	73.2	74.3
NNCLR [11]	<u>69.4</u>	70.7	<u>74.2</u>	<u>74.9</u>
DINO [3]	–	–	–	**<u>75.3</u>**
SwAV [2]	<u>72.1</u>	**<u>73.9</u>**	**<u>74.6</u>**	**<u>75.3</u>**
Self-Classifier	**<u>72.4</u>**	<u>73.5</u>	<u>74.2</u>	74.1

Table 5. Transfer learning: object detection and instance segmentation. Results for other methods are taken from [34]

Method	VOC07+12 det			COCO det			COCO seg		
	AP	AP_{50}	AP_{75}	AP	AP_{50}	AP_{75}	AP	AP_{50}	AP_{75}
Supervised	53.5	81.3	58.8	38.2	58.2	41.2	33.3	54.7	35.2
MoCo-v2[7]	**57.4**	82.5	**64.0**	39.3	58.9	42.5	34.4	55.8	36.5
SwAV[2]	56.1	**82.6**	62.7	38.4	58.6	41.3	33.8	55.2	35.9
SimSiam[8]	57.0	82.4	63.7	39.2	59.3	42.1	34.4	56.0	36.7
BarlowT[34]	56.8	**82.6**	63.4	39.2	59.0	42.5	34.3	56.0	36.5
Self-Classifier	56.6	82.4	62.6	**41.5**	**61.3**	**45.0**	**36.1**	**58.1**	**38.7**

6.4 Qualitative Results

In Supplementary, we visualize and analyse a subset of high/low accuracy classes predicted by *Self-Classifier* on **unseen data** (ImageNet validation).

7 Ablation Study

In this section, we evaluate the impact of the design choices of *Self-Classifier*. Namely, the loss function, the number of classes (C), number of classification heads, fixed vs learnable classifier, MLP architecture, Softmax temperatures (row and column), batch-size, some of the augmentations choices, and NN queue length. We evaluate the different models after 100 self-supervised epochs and

Table 6. Ablation: loss function generality. For column definitions see Table 1. SCAN + Eq. (5) is SCAN with clustering step loss replaced with ours.

Method	NMI	AMI	ARI	ACC
SCAN [28]	72.0	51.2	27.5	39.9
SCAN + our loss (Eq. (5))	**72.7**	**52.2**	**29.0**	**40.4**

report results on ImageNet validation set. We report both the K-NN (K=20) classifier accuracy (evaluating the learned representations) and the unsupervised clustering accuracy (evaluating unsupervised classification performance).

Loss Function. For both illustrating the generality of our proposed loss function and making more direct comparison with the unsupervised classification state-of-the-art (SCAN [28]), in Table 6 we report the results of running SCAN official code, while replacing their loss function (in the clustering step) with ours (Eq. (5)) and keeping everything else (e.g. classification heads and augmentations) same as in SCAN. As we can see, our proposed loss generalizes well and improves SCAN result (e.g. by 1.5% ARI and 0.5% ACC). Further results improvements are obtained using our full method (as shown in Table 1).

Number of Classes and Classification Heads. Table 7a reports the results for various number of classes and classification heads. Very interestingly, and somewhat contrary to the intuition of previous unsupervised classification works [28,32] who used the same number of classes for all heads, we found that using a different number of classes for each head while still keeping the total number of parameters constant (e.g. $15 \times 1k$ vs. $1k+2k+4k+8k$) improves results on both metrics. We believe that such a learning objective forces the model to learn a representation that is more invariant to the number of classes, thus improving its generalization performance.

Fixed/Learnable Classifier. As expected, we found that a learnable classifier performs better than a fixed one (Table 7d).

MLP Architecture. Table 7c reports the results for various sizes of hidden/output layers. Surprisingly, we found that decreasing the number of hidden layers and their size improves both metrics. As a result, our best model (4096/128 MLP) has 30% less parameters than the model used in SCAN [28] (that used 2048 sized input to its cls. heads). In addition, we verified there is no peak performance difference between ReLU and leaky-ReLU activation in the MLP.

Softmax Temperature. Table 7b reports the results for a range of Row/-Column softmax temperatures. We found that the ratio between the two temperatures is important for performance (specifically clustering accuracy). The model is robust to ratios (row over column) in the range of 2.0 - 3.5.

Batch Size. Table 7f reports the results for a range of batch size values (256 to 4096). Similarly to previous self-supervised work (and specifically clustering-based), performance improves as we increase batch size.

Table 7. Ablation study. After 100 epochs, reporting performance for ImageNet as accuracy of <'k-NN' | 'unsupervised clustering'> in each experiment.

(a) Classification heads. $(2k)$ $(4k)$ $(8k)$: 2k, 4k and 8k over-clustering accuracy.

	1 × 1k	5 × 1k	10 × 1k	15 × 1k	1 × 2k	1 × 4k	1k+2k+4k+8k
Acc. (%)	59.6|34.1	58.7|34.0	58.6|33.5	58.8|33.9	59.3|38.8$^{(2k)}$	57.0|42.9$^{(4k)}$	**61.7|37.3**,40.6$^{(2k)}$,44.2$^{(4k)}$,48.0$^{(8k)}$

(b) Softmax temperature

τ_{column}	τ_{row} 0.07	0.1
0.03	59.9|36.9	59.2|36.9
0.05	58.9|29.2	**61.7|37.3**

(l) MLP architecture

MLP hidden layer(s)	MLP output layer 128	256
1 × 4096	**61.7|37.3**	61.3|33.5
2 × 4096	60.9|36.4	60.4|33.6
2 × 8192	60.0|36.9	59.6|36.7

(d) Fixed/Learnable classifier

	Fixed	Learnable
Acc. (%)	57.6|32.2	**61.7|37.3**

(e) Nearest neighbor queue length

Queue len.	128K	256K	512K	1M
Acc. (%)	59.2|36.8	**61.7|37.3**	60.3|36.9	56.8|35.5

(f) Batch size

Batch size	256	512	1024	2048	4096
Acc. (%)	49.0|20.9	52.2|23.1	54.5|26.8	57.0|35.1	**61.7|37.3**

Multi-crop and Nearest Neighbor Augmentations. Table 8 reports the impact of removing multi-crop [2] and nearest neighbor augmentations [11] on linear classification accuracy and compares to other state-of-the-art methods.

Nearest Neighbor Queue Length. The model is somewhat robust to a queue length in the range of 128K - 512K (Table 7e), while increasing it further decreases performance. Most likely due to stale embeddings (as noted by [11] as well).

8 Comparative Analysis

A common and critical element of all self-supervised learning methods is collapse prevention. In this section, we discuss the various approaches of state-of-the-art models for preventing collapse. The approaches can be categorized into two categories: 1) negative samples; and 2) stop-grad operation. Where in practice, stop-grad operation includes two more sub-categories: 2.a) external clustering; and 2.b) momentum encoder. In this paper, we propose a third and completely new approach for collapse prevention - a non-collapsing loss function, i.e., a loss function without degenerate optimal solutions.

Negative Samples. SimCLR [5] and Moco [18] prevent collapse by utilizing negative pairs to explicitly force dissimilarity.

Table 8. Performance without multi-crop and without nearest neighbor augmentations. ImageNet Top-1 linear classification accuracy after 100 epochs. [2,5,7,15] are taken from [8]

	SimCLR [5]	BYOL [15]	SwAV [2]	MoCoV2 [7]	SimSiam [8]	**Ours**
Acc. (%)	66.5	66.5	66.5	67.4	**68.1**	**68.1**

External Clustering. SwAV [2], SeLa [32] and SCAN [28] prevent collapse by utilizing external clustering algorithm such as K-Means (SCAN) or Sinkhorn-Knopp (SwAV/SeLa) for generating pseudo-labels.

Momentum Encoder. MoCo [18], BYOL [15] and DINO [3] prevent collapse by utilizing the momentum encoder proposed by MoCo. The momentum encoder generates a different yet fixed pseudo target in every iteration.

Stop-grad Operation. SimSiam [8] prevent collapse by applying a stop-grad operation on one of the views, which acts as a fixed pseudo label. In fact, except for SimCLR, all of the above methods can be simply differentiated by where exactly a stop-grad operation is used. SwAV/SeLa/SCAN apply a stop-grad operation on the clustering phase, while MoCo/BYOL/DINO apply a stop-grad operation on a second network that is used for generating assignments.

Non-Collapsing Loss Function. In contrast, we show mathematically (Sec. 4) and empirically (Sect. 6) that *Self-Classifier* prevents collapse with a novel loss function (4) and without the use of external clustering, pseudo-labels, momentum encoder, stop-grad nor negative pairs. More specifically, a collapsing solution is simply not in the set of optimal solutions of our proposed loss, which makes it possible to train *Self-Classifier* using just a single network and a simple SGD.

9   Conclusions and Limitations

We introduced *Self-Classifier*, a new approach for unsupervised end-to-end classification and self-supervised representation learning. Our approach is mathematically justified and simple to implement. It sets a new state-of-the-art performance for unsupervised classification on ImageNet and achieves comparable to state of the art results for unsupervised representation learning. We provide a thorough investigation of our method in a series of ablation studies. Furthermore, we propose a new hierarchical alignment quantitative metric for self-supervised classification establishing baseline performance for a wide range of methods and showing advantages of our proposed approach in this new task. *Limitations* of this paper include: (i) our method relies on knowledge of the number of classes, but in some cases it might not be optimal as the true number of classes should really be dictated by the data itself. In this paper we relax this potential weakness by introducing the notion of multiple classification heads, but we believe further investigation would be an interesting future work direction; (ii) one of the most common sources of error we observed is merging of nearby classes (e.g. different breeds of cat), introducing additional regularization for reducing this artifact is also an interesting direction of future work.

References

1. Caron, M., Bojanowski, P., Joulin, A., Douze, M.: Deep clustering for unsupervised learning of visual features. In: Proceedings of the European Conference on Computer Vision (ECCV), pp. 132–149 (2018)
2. Caron, M., Misra, I., Mairal, J., Goyal, P., Bojanowski, P., Joulin, A.: Unsupervised learning of visual features by contrasting cluster assignments. Adv. Neural Inf. Process. Syst. **33**, 9912–9924 (2020)
3. Caron, M., Touvron, H., Misra, I., Jégou, H., Mairal, J., Bojanowski, P., Joulin, A.: Emerging properties in self-supervised vision transformers. In: Proceedings of the International Conference on Computer Vision (ICCV), pp. 9650–9660 (2021)
4. Chang, J., Wang, L., Meng, G., Xiang, S., Pan, C.: Deep adaptive image clustering. In: Proceedings of the IEEE International Conference on Computer Vision, pp. 5879–5887 (2017)
5. Chen, T., Kornblith, S., Norouzi, M., Hinton, G.E.: A simple framework for contrastive learning of visual representations. In: International Conference on Machine Learning, ICML, pp. 1597–1607 (2020)
6. Chen, T., Kornblith, S., Swersky, K., Norouzi, M., Hinton, G.E.: Big self-supervised models are strong semi-supervised learners. Adv. Neural Inf. Process. Syst.**33**, 22243–22255 (2020)
7. Chen, X., Fan, H., Girshick, R., He, K.: Improved baselines with momentum contrastive learning. In: arXiv preprint arXiv:2003.04297 (2020)
8. Chen, X., He, K.: Exploring simple siamese representation learning. In: Proceedings of the IEEE/CVF Conference on Computer Vision and Pattern Recognition, pp. 15750–15758 (2021)
9. Doersch, C., Gupta, A., Efros, A.A.: Unsupervised visual representation learning by context prediction. In: Proceedings of the IEEE International Conference on Computer Vision, pp. 1422–1430 (2015)
10. Dosovitskiy, A., Springenberg, J.T., Riedmiller, M., Brox, T.: Discriminative unsupervised feature learning with convolutional neural networks. In: Advances in Neural Information Processing Systems, pp. 766–774 (2014)
11. Dwibedi, D., Aytar, Y., Tompson, J., Sermanet, P., Zisserman, A.: With a little help from my friends: Nearest-neighbor contrastive learning of visual representations. In: Proceedings of the IEEE/CVF International Conference on Computer Vision (ICCV), pp. 9588–9597 (2021)
12. Everingham, M., Van Gool, L., Williams, C.K., Winn, J., Zisserman, A.: The pascal visual object classes (voc) challenge. Int. J. Comput. Vis. **88**(2), 303–338 (2010)
13. Gidaris, S., Bursuc, A., Puy, G., Komodakis, N., Cord, M., Perez, P.: Obow: online bag-of-visual-words generation for self-supervised learning. In: Proceedings of the IEEE/CVF Conference on Computer Vision and Pattern Recognition, pp. 6830–6840 (2021)
14. Gidaris, S., Singh, P., Komodakis, N.: Unsupervised representation learning by predicting image rotations. In: International Conference on Learning Representations, ICLR (2018)

15. Grill, J.B., et al.: Bootstrap your own latent - a new approach to self-supervised learning. Adv. Neural Inf. Process. Syst. **33**, 21271–21284 (2020)
16. Gutmann, M., Hyvärinen, A.: Noise-contrastive estimation: a new estimation principle for unnormalized statistical models. In: Proceedings of the Thirteenth International Conference on Artificial Intelligence and Statistics, pp. 297–304 (2010)
17. Haeusser, P., Plapp, J., Golkov, V., Aljalbout, E., Cremers, D.: Associative deep clustering: training a classification network with no labels. In: Brox, T., Bruhn, A., Fritz, M. (eds.) GCPR 2018. LNCS, vol. 11269, pp. 18–32. Springer, Cham (2019). https://doi.org/10.1007/978-3-030-12939-2_2
18. He, K., Fan, H., Wu, Y., Xie, S., Girshick, R.: Momentum contrast for unsupervised visual representation learning. In: Proceedings of the IEEE/CVF Conference on Computer Vision and Pattern Recognition, pp. 9729–9738 (2020)
19. He, K., Zhang, X., Ren, S., Sun, J.: Deep residual learning for image recognition. In: Proceedings of the IEEE Conference on Computer Vision and Pattern Recognition, pp. 770–778 (2016)
20. Ji, X., Henriques, J.F., Vedaldi, A.: Invariant information clustering for unsupervised image classification and segmentation. In: Proceedings of the IEEE/CVF International Conference on Computer Vision, pp. 9865–9874 (2019)
21. Li, J., Zhou, P., Xiong, C., Hoi, S.: Prototypical contrastive learning of unsupervised representations. In: International Conference on Learning Representations, pp. 9475–9484 (2021)
22. Lin, T.-Y., Maire, M., Belongie, S., Hays, J., Perona, P., Ramanan, D., Dollár, P., Zitnick, C.L.: Microsoft COCO: common objects in context. In: Fleet, D., Pajdla, T., Schiele, B., Tuytelaars, T. (eds.) ECCV 2014. LNCS, vol. 8693, pp. 740–755. Springer, Cham (2014). https://doi.org/10.1007/978-3-319-10602-1_48
23. Misra, I., Maaten, L.V.D.: Self-supervised learning of pretext-invariant representations. In: Proceedings of the IEEE/CVF Conference on Computer Vision and Pattern Recognition, pp. 6707–6717 (2020)
24. Noroozi, M., Favaro, P.: Unsupervised learning of visual representations by solving jigsaw puzzles. In: Leibe, B., Matas, J., Sebe, N., Welling, M. (eds.) ECCV 2016. LNCS, vol. 9910, pp. 69–84. Springer, Cham (2016). https://doi.org/10.1007/978-3-319-46466-4_5
25. Pathak, D., Krahenbuhl, P., Donahue, J., Darrell, T., Efros, A.A.: Context encoders: feature learning by inpainting. In: Proceedings of the IEEE Conference on Computer Vision and Pattern Recognition, pp. 2536–2544 (2016)
26. Santurkar, S., Tsipras, D., Madry, A.: Breeds: Benchmarks for subpopulation shift. arXiv preprint arXiv:2008.04859 (2020)
27. Tian, Y., Sun, C., Poole, B., Krishnan, D., Schmid, C., Isola, P.: What makes for good views for contrastive learning? Adv. Neural Inf. Process. Syst. (2020)
28. Van Gansbeke, W., Vandenhende, S., Georgoulis, S., Proesmans, M., Van Gool, L.: SCAN: learning to classify images without labels. In: Vedaldi, A., Bischof, H., Brox, T., Frahm, J.-M. (eds.) ECCV 2020. LNCS, vol. 12355, pp. 268–285. Springer, Cham (2020). https://doi.org/10.1007/978-3-030-58607-2_16
29. Wu, Z., Xiong, Y., Yu, S.X., Lin, D.: Unsupervised feature learning via non-parametric instance discrimination. In: Proceedings of the IEEE Conference on Computer Vision and Pattern Recognition, pp. 3733–3742 (2018)
30. Xie, J., Girshick, R., Farhadi, A.: Unsupervised deep embedding for clustering analysis. In: International Conference on Machine Learning, pp. 478–487. PMLR (2016)

31. Yang, J., Parikh, D., Batra, D.: Joint unsupervised learning of deep representations and image clusters. In: Proceedings of the IEEE Conference on Computer Vision and Pattern Recognition, pp. 5147–5156 (2016)
32. YM., A., C., R., A., V.: Self-labelling via simultaneous clustering and representation learning. In: International Conference on Learning Representations (2020)
33. You, Y., Gitman, I., Ginsburg, B.: Large batch training of convolutional networks. arXiv preprint arXiv:1708.03888 (2017)
34. Zbontar, J., Jing, L., Misra, I., LeCun, Y., Deny, S.: Barlow twins: Self-supervised learning via redundancy reduction. In: Meila, M., Zhang, T. (eds.) Proceedings of the 38th International Conference on Machine Learning, ICML 2021, 18–24 July 2021, Virtual Event. Proceedings of Machine Learning Research, vol. 139, pp. 12310–12320. PMLR (2021)
35. Zhang, R., Isola, P., Efros, A.A.: Colorful image colorization. In: Leibe, B., Matas, J., Sebe, N., Welling, M. (eds.) ECCV 2016. LNCS, vol. 9907, pp. 649–666. Springer, Cham (2016). https://doi.org/10.1007/978-3-319-46487-9_40
36. Zheltonozhskii, E., Baskin, C., Bronstein, A.M., Mendelson, A.: Self-supervised learning for large-scale unsupervised image clustering. arXiv preprint arXiv:2008.10312 (2020)

Data Invariants to Understand Unsupervised Out-of-Distribution Detection

Lars Doorenbos[✉][iD], Raphael Sznitman[iD], and Pablo Márquez-Neila[iD]

University of Bern, Bern, Switzerland
{lars.doorenbos,raphael.sznitman,pablo.marquez}@unibe.ch

Abstract. Unsupervised out-of-distribution (U-OOD) detection has recently attracted much attention due to its importance in mission-critical systems and broader applicability over its supervised counterpart. Despite this increased attention, U-OOD methods suffer from important shortcomings. By performing a large-scale evaluation on different benchmarks and image modalities, we show in this work that most popular state-of-the-art methods are unable to consistently outperform a simple anomaly detector based on pre-trained features and the Mahalanobis distance (MahaAD). A key reason for the inconsistencies of these methods is the lack of a formal description of U-OOD. Motivated by a simple thought experiment, we propose a characterization of U-OOD based on the invariants of the training dataset. We show how this characterization is unknowingly embodied in the top-scoring MahaAD method, thereby explaining its quality. Furthermore, our approach can be used to interpret predictions of U-OOD detectors and provides insights into good practices for evaluating future U-OOD methods.

Keywords: Out-of-distribution detection · Unsupervised learning

1 Introduction

The use of deep learning (DL) models for mission-critical systems, such as in autonomous driving or medicine, is one of the most active research areas in computer vision. Yet, despite impressive performances in recent methods, their ability to extrapolate beyond their training data remains limited. For trained and deployed models, this is particularly problematic when processing images that are corrupted or whose content differs from their expectation. Predictions for unexpected images are often incorrect with high confidence and cannot be identified as such [4]. Ultimately, these silent failures deeply impact the reliability of machine learning systems in mission-critical applications and can have fatal consequences.

Supplementary Information The online version contains supplementary material available at https://doi.org/10.1007/978-3-031-19821-2_8.

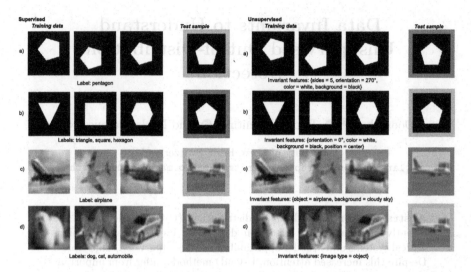

Fig. 1. The difference between supervised and unsupervised OOD. For the unsupervised case, invariants in the training data rather than class labels define what should be considered as OOD: in (a) a pentagon at a different angle leads to an OOD test sample, while (b) shows variants in shapes in the training set such that a pentagon is in-distribution at test time. While the train and test data are the same in each row, the interpretation of OOD differs in the supervised and unsupervised cases. Green and red boxes denote in- and out-of-distribution samples, respectively. (Color figure online)

To mitigate these limitations, numerous *out-of-distribution* (OOD) detection methods have emerged in the recent past. Closely related to anomaly detection [44] and one-class learning [38], OOD detection aims to spot samples at inference time that do not belong to the training distribution and should not be processed by subsequent machine learning models. At their core, OOD detection methods learn scoring functions that measure the level of anomaly, or *out-of-distributionness*, in test samples with respect to a training data distribution.

Broadly, OOD methods are categorized into supervised and unsupervised, as illustrated in Fig. 1. Supervised OOD methods compute an OOD score by using the labels of the training dataset or by knowing the trained downstream network [19,22,23]. Conversely, unsupervised OOD (U-OOD) methods are agnostic to the downstream task or data labels, and learn tractable representations of the training images to compute OOD scores [7,12,15,45], which makes them more general than supervised methods and applicable to a larger range of scenarios.

Considering its significance and generality, the recent emergence of U-OOD methods is unsurprising. Yet with many methods reporting state-of-the-art performance [18,21,25,34,40,48,53,54,56], the overwhelming majority of these only validate their approach on one or two tasks. Given the broadness of U-OOD, these limited experimental validations have produced an inconsistent state-of-the-art, while simultaneously establishing an unclear sense of progress in the field. For instance, [20] showed excellent results for one-class tasks using CIFAR10 and ImageNet, only to be contradicted 8 months later in [6] using different data. More alarmingly, this trend of inconsistencies is being perpetuated with evaluation protocols remaining unchanged [5,21,32].

For this reason, we first aim to explore and assess the performance and robustness of existing U-OOD detectors by establishing a wide and varied panel of experiments using different datasets and setups. Not only do we show that U-OOD state-of-the-art methods perform erratically when evaluated over a wide and varied range of datasets and tasks (*i.e.* methods that perform extremely well on some datasets, frequently perform poorly on others), but that the relatively unnoticed MahaAD method [43] consistently outperforms all considered methods by remarkable margins in addition to being extremely simple, stable, and easy to train.

More fundamentally however, we hypothesize that despite the large number of recently proposed U-OOD methods, the main reason for this lack of overall consistency is that the fundamental concept of U-OOD remains vague and ill-defined. In fact, the vast majority of works fail to clearly define U-OOD, let alone provide an intuition to their approach's functioning. This subsequently leads to brittle methods and weak evaluation protocols.

Intuitively, a test sample should be considered OOD if it *looks different* from training samples. While this intuition seems straightforward, it is unclear how to characterize a training dataset or identify what makes a test sample similar or not to training samples. Yet, characterizing OOD is a fundamental necessity to not only produce reasonable U-OOD detectors, but also to properly evaluate and understand their behavior. Previous works have overlooked this important step and devised OOD detectors following more or less reasonable heuristics with limited formal justification. For example, using the observation that blurred images are assigned higher likelihoods compared to their original counterparts, SVD-RND [13] leveraged this property to characterize OOD by directly optimizing for it. Similarly, [42,54] identified OOD samples by correcting for their input complexity and the number of background pixels. Other examples include Puzzle-AE [47], which relied on solving puzzles of OOD images worse than their in-distribution counterparts, and MHRot [20] assumed that geometric transformations of OOD samples will be predicted incorrectly.

We also address here this apparent lack of a proper U-OOD definition by proposing a characterization based on identifying and leveraging image *invariants* of the training set. Following this idea, we formulate the general problem of finding dataset invariants and show that, when constrained to a linear setting, this formulation reduces to the MahaAD method, which unknowingly embodies a dataset invariant characterization. Importantly, we show that the invariants found within a training set are more relevant for U-OOD detection than its variant counterparts.

In summary, the contributions of this paper include (1) a thorough evaluation of numerous state-of-the-art U-OOD methods on different tasks and datasets, whereby highlighting that most methods perform erratically and inconsistently, (2) a novel interpretation of U-OOD using training set invariants, which allows for an appropriate definition of U-OOD and (3) a new U-OOD benchmark derived from our novel interpretation with invariants. A consequence of these contributions is that we shed light on why most recent methods do not perform well across datasets and, importantly, why the relatively unknown MahaAD method, that has been disregarded so far by most recent works in the field, is an excellent off-the-shelf U-OOD detector that should be included as a competitive baseline in future comparisons.

2   Related Works

Methods such as one-class support vector machines [52], isolation forest [30], and local outlier factor [10] have traditionally been used for OOD detection in classical machine learning. However these methods suffer greatly when applied to high-dimensional spaces (*i.e.* images). Unsurprisingly, DL based methods have come to replace these more recently. Summarized here are some of the most relevant works on OOD detection using DL, while comprehensive surveys can be found in [11,60].

Supervised OOD detection approaches require either an explicitly trained classifier or a labelled dataset to work. One line of works uses a classifier's maximum softmax probability output as the OOD score [19,22,29]. Another, more closely related to U-OOD, exploits deep features of the task-specific trained classifiers [23,27,50]. However, as all these methods exploit relations between network predictions and the path taken to arrive at those predictions in some way, they are simply incompatible with the U-OOD setting.

On the other hand, U-OOD detection methods rely only on a set of *in-distribution* images to learn the characteristics of the in-distribution data. That is, they do not assume, or have access to, a trained downstream deep network or labeled dataset. Broadly, two families of methods are found in the literature. The first are generative models while the second are based on representation learning.

Generative Models: These learn the distribution of images in high-dimensional spaces. However, most generative models are known to perform poorly in OOD detection [12,35], and many augmentations and improvements have been proposed to increase their performances. [54] showed that the likelihoods obtained by models such as Glow [24] or PixelCNN++ [49] are heavily influenced by the input complexity, and propose a likelihood ratio to correct for this. Interestingly, the work in [42] showed that background pixels dominate test sample likelihood scores, and attempt to correct for these by using the likelihood of a second model that tries to capture the population level background information. Similarly, Schirrmeister *et al.* [51] use the likelihood ratio with respect to a second model trained on a general, large scale dataset.

Representation Learning: Instead of working in the image space, most U-OOD methods aim to learn a low-dimensional image embedding. Here, many works have opted for self-supervised learning strategies to simulate classification problems and train DL models to representative image features. One popular approach is predicting geometric transformations, such as image rotations, translations, scales, flips, or patch re-arrangements [7,15,20,58]. Other self-supervised approaches rely on auto-encoders and optionally perturb the input in some way to create more robust feature descriptions. Example perturbations include adding noise [46] or shuffling patches [47]. Further extensions propose to fit an auto-regressive model to the latent space [1] or to add a memory module [16]. Most recently, approaches based on contrastive learning have been advantageous [41,53,56].

However, various papers showed that learning features on the target domain is not necessary to reach high performance [6,36,43,59]. Bergman et al. [6] find that scoring samples by the distance to their k-nearest neighbours in the space of pre-trained ImageNet features outperformed all previous self-supervised methods. Xiao et al. [59] showed that exploiting features obtained from self-supervised— rather than supervised—training on ImageNet can lead to high performance. Finally, Rippel et al. [43] combined Mahalanobis distances in the space of ImageNet features for state-of-the-art results on the MVTec dataset.

3   Invariants for Unsupervised OOD

In the supervised setting, similar to the problem of zero-shot learning, a sample is considered OOD if it cannot be assigned to one of the training set classes. In the unsupervised setting, however, defining OOD is more challenging as we do not know *a-priori* what and if any classes are present at all. As done in anomaly detection [44], one potential approach to define U-OOD could be to measure if a sample lies in a low-density region of the training data. But doing so would be inappropriate because whether few or many image examples of a specific class appear in a training set may only be a reflection of their natural prevalence, rather than being a real OOD sample. For instance, if one had a training set of dogs, the Norwegian Lundehund (*i.e.* a rare dog breed) would most likely appear in low-density regions of the training distribution, in contrast to German Shepherds (*i.e.* very common bread). Yet both should still be considered dogs. Instead, we propose to use *invariants* as a way to characterize U-OOD. Specifically, our idea is to first determine image invariants in the training set, and then detect OOD test samples by identifying if they keep the invariants of the training set.

To illustrate this, consider the toy examples in Fig. 1, where four different combinations of training sets and test examples are given. Recall that for the unsupervised case, no labels in the training data are available thus losing context as to what is or is not semantically OOD. However, the necessity to leverage context to disentangle relevant and irrelevant aspects of images remains key for U-OOD detection, since it is too broad to be meaning-ful without it (as stated in [2]). Hence, we assume that this necessary con-text is provided by a set of general features that we have at our disposal, that can describe the input images $\mathbf{x}$. For instance, these features could be $\mathbf{f}(\mathbf{x}) = \{\text{sides}(\mathbf{x}), \text{orientation}(\mathbf{x}), \text{color}(\mathbf{x}), ...\}$, or features coming from a net-work pre-trained on a general dataset. Given this, we want to summarize a training set by the *union* of features that are invariant over the entire train-ing set. For example, Fig. 1(a) would use the combination of invariant features $\{\text{sides} = 5, \text{orientation} = 270°, \text{color} = \text{white}, \text{background} = \text{black}\}$, and simi-larly $\{\text{orientation} = 0°, \text{color} = \text{white}, \text{background} = \text{black}, \text{position} = \text{center}\}$ for Fig. 1(b). At inference time then, a test sample described by this union of invariant features would be OOD if these features are no longer invariant with respect to the training set. In this sense, variant features from a dataset are in fact irrelevant for U-OOD detection, which stands in contrast to many previous methods that focused on learning a representation of the training distribution (*e.g.*, [13,31,61]).

In the remainder of this section, we begin by formalizing the above-mentioned idea and propose an approach to identifying these invariants for the general case. We then show how this is related to the MahaAD method [51]. In the experimental section, we demonstrate how MahaAD performs in comparison to recent methods and how it behaves in light of image invariants.

3.1 Formalization

Given a training set $\{\mathbf{x}_i\}_{i=1}^{N}$, with corresponding feature vectors, $\mathbf{f}(\mathbf{x}_i) \equiv \mathbf{f}_i \in \mathcal{F}$, we define an invariant as a non-constant function $g : \mathcal{F} \to \mathbb{R}$, such that $g(\mathbf{f}_i) = 0, \forall i$. That is, g is an invariant if it computes a constant value (*i.e.*, $g(\mathbf{f}_i) = 0$) for the elements of the training set, but in general may not compute the same constant value for other elements (*e.g.*, elements of a test set). Our goal then is to find a set of invariants, $G = \{g_1, \ldots, g_K\}$, over the set of training feature vectors. While doing so in one global optimization is challenging, we propose to solve this by solving a sequence of K problems, one per invariant,

$$g_k(\mathbf{f}_i) = 0 \quad \forall i, \tag{1}$$
$$\|\nabla g_k(\mathbf{f}_i)\|_2 \neq 0 \quad \forall i,$$
$$\nabla g_k(\mathbf{f}_i) \cdot \nabla g_j(\mathbf{f}_i) = 0 \quad \forall i, j < k,$$

where the first equality makes g_k zero for all training samples, the second equality prevents g_k from becoming a projection (*i.e.*, effectively making it non-constant) and the third equality requires that new invariants are different from all previ-ously found invariants by making their gradients mutually orthogonal. After finding G, a test feature vector $\mathbf{f}$ will be considered OOD if $g_k(\mathbf{f}) \neq 0$ for any invariant k.

As noisy real-world data rarely lies in an exact manifold, solving Eq. (1) is unfeasible in practice even for a small number of invariants K. Instead, we relax

Eq. (1) and express it as a minimization problem to find a set of soft invariants,

$$\min_{g_k} \frac{1}{N} \sum_i g_k(\mathbf{f}_i)^2,$$

(2)

$$\text{s.t.} \quad \|\nabla g_k(\mathbf{f}_i)\|_2 = 1 \quad \forall i,$$
$$\nabla g_k(\mathbf{f}_i) \cdot \nabla g_j(\mathbf{f}_i) = 0 \quad \forall i, j < k,$$

where we constrain the magnitude of the gradient to 1 to prevent g_k from arbitrarily compressing its output and minimizing the loss artificially.

Once $G = \{g_1, \ldots, g_K\}$ is established, any test vector $\mathbf{f}$ can be scored by computing the ratios between the test error and the average training error,

$$s^2(\mathbf{f}) = \sum_k \frac{g_k(\mathbf{f})^2}{e_k},$$

(3)

where e_k is the training MSE of the soft invariant g_k,

$$e_k = \frac{1}{N} \sum_i g_k(\mathbf{f}_i)^2.$$

(4)

Intuitively, tight invariants with low e_k values will have a high influence in the final score, while weak invariants with large e_k values will essentially be ignored. Given that the contribution of weak invariants is negligible in s^2, we can circumvent the problem of setting an optimal number of invariants K and safely set K to the dimensionality of the feature space.

We can further simplify the optimization problem of Eq. (2) by constraining the invariants to the family of affine functions $g_k(\mathbf{f}) = \mathbf{a}_k^T \mathbf{f} + b_k$ with unitary $\mathbf{a}_k$. Under these conditions, Eq. (2) reduces to a PCA problem. Its solution sets $\mathbf{a}_k$ to the k-th smallest principal component and the squared error e_k is set to its corresponding eigenvalue. Moreover, the score function Eq. (3) can be re-written as the square of the Mahalanobis distance using the mean and the covariance of the training feature vectors. Ultimately, computing Mahalanobis distances properly weighs and exploits the linear invariants in the training dataset, which, in turn, suggests that the Mahalanobis distance could lead to good OOD detectors despite its simplicity.

Given that the invariants are computed, in practice, from a collection of feature vectors describing the training set, the performance of an invariant-based U-OOD detection method is contingent on the chosen pre-trained feature extractor. We experimentally found that this is not an important limitation and that general ImageNet-based features lead to descriptive invariants for U-OOD detection even for image modalities that are very different from ImageNet, such as medical images.

3.2 The Mahalanobis Anomaly Detector

Given the above, we briefly revisit the the Mahalanobis anomaly detector (MahaAD) from Rippel et al. [43] as it embodies the invariant feature learning we propose. Figure 2 illustrates the approach.

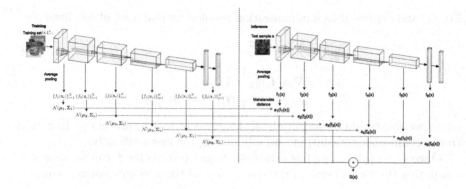

Fig. 2. Training and inference stages of the MahaAD method.

MahaAD uses the spatial pooling of the feature maps of a pre-trained CNN to define feature descriptors $\mathbf{f}$. Instead of choosing a specific CNN layer for $\mathbf{f}$, MahaAD works in a multi-layered manner describing each input image $\mathbf{x}$ with a collection of feature vectors $\{\mathbf{f}_\ell(\mathbf{x})\}_{\ell=1}^L$ computed at L different layers.

At training time, MahaAD computes the mean and the covariance of the descriptor vectors of the images in the training dataset $\{\mathbf{x}_i\}_{i=1}^N$. Specifically, for each layer ℓ, the mean is computed as,

$$\boldsymbol{\mu}_\ell = \frac{1}{N} \sum_{i=1}^N \mathbf{f}_\ell(\mathbf{x}_i), \tag{5}$$

while the corresponding covariance matrix is,

$$\boldsymbol{\Sigma}_\ell = \frac{1}{N} \sum_{i=1}^N (\mathbf{f}_\ell(\mathbf{x}_i) - \boldsymbol{\mu}_l)(\mathbf{f}_\ell(\mathbf{x}_i) - \boldsymbol{\mu}_l)^\mathsf{T}. \tag{6}$$

To avoid singular covariance matrices in high-dimensional or low-data regimes, shrinkage is applied using the standard hyperparameter-free method of [26], although we empirically found that the shrinkage has limited impact on the overall performance of MahaAD. By using multi-layer feature vectors, MahaAD is able to find linear invariants at different image scales.

Importantly, the CNN from which the features are computed is not trained or tuned to the training set whereby making this training phase simple and extremely fast. In practice, it makes the approach more stable and robust across a larger number of datasets. This differs from most recent U-OOD methods that opt to fine-tune their DL models to the training set [40,53,56].

At test time, MahaAD computes the layer-wise Mahalanobis distances between the descriptor vectors of the test image $\mathbf{x}$ and the means $\{\boldsymbol{\mu}_\ell\}_\ell$,

$$s_\ell(\mathbf{f}) = \sqrt{(\mathbf{f} - \boldsymbol{\mu}_\ell)^\mathsf{T} \boldsymbol{\Sigma}_\ell^{-1} (\mathbf{f} - \boldsymbol{\mu}_\ell)}, \tag{7}$$

which is equivalent to the square root of Eq. (3). The final OOD score is the sum of the scores over all layers,

$$S(\mathbf{x}) = \sum_{\ell=1}^{L} s_\ell(\mathbf{f}_\ell(\mathbf{x})). \tag{8}$$

4 Experiments

To explore the current state of U-OOD detection, we design a benchmark comparing the performance of several state-of-the-art U-OOD methods over a broad collection of 73 experiments that involve different image modalities, sizes, perturbations, and different criteria for the in- and out-distributions. These experiments aim to identify in what scenarios different methods may be effective and which may not be. Our benchmark is organized in five tasks (see Fig. 3):

Unimodal CIFAR (*uni-class*). Similar to most works [20,21,25,41,48,53,56], we perform 10 experiments using the CIFAR10 dataset, where each experiment takes one of the 10 classes as in-distribution and uses the remaining 9 as OOD. We also use CIFAR100 for 20 experiments, where each of the 20 semantic superclasses of CIFAR100 are used as in-distribution and treat all remaining 19 superclasses as OOD [6,15,41,56].

Unimodal Anomaly (*uni-ano*). We use the MVTec dataset [8] which contains 15 classes of images of both normal and defect objects. As in [14,28,41,43,55], we perform one experiment per class, where the defect-free images are used for the in-distribution and defect test images are considered OOD samples.

Unimodal Anomaly Medical (*uni-med*). We perform 7 experiments with different medical image modalities. The first 2 experiments use optical coherence tomography (OCT) scans and chest X-rays as training in-distributions and corrupted images as OOD samples. The 3rd experiment trains the models with healthy chest X-rays and uses pathological chest X-rays as OOD. In the remaining 4 experiments, healthy retinal fundus photographs are used for the in-distribution and pathological fundus photographs of four increasing severity levels are used for the OOD images [9,31,36,57].

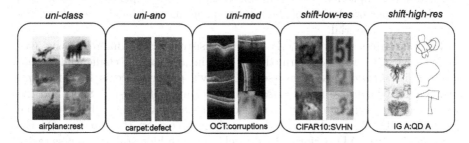

Fig. 3. Example in-distribution and OOD images for each task in our proposed benchmark. IG stands for infograph, QD for quickdraw.

Low-Resolution Domain Shift (*shift-low-res*). 1 experiment using CIFAR10 as the in-distribution and SVHN as OOD [33,34,53,54,56]. In contrast to previous works, we do not consider CIFAR100 as OOD.

High-Resolution Domain Shift (*shift-high-res*). An extended version of the experiments on the dataset DomainNet presented by Hsu et al. [22]. We run 20 experiments separated into two groups: 10 experiments with Real-A as the in-distribution and 10 experiments with Infograph-A as the in-distribution. We avoid using Real-B and Infograph-B as OOD in the first and the second group of experiments respectively.

We refer to a specific experiment by the notation in-dataset:out-dataset.

Evaluated Methods: We evaluate a selection of top-performing U-OOD detection methods, which we selected if they were among the top-performing methods in at least one of the above tasks. These are: **MSCL** [41], **DN2** [6], **SSD** [53], **MHRot** [20], **DDV** [31], **Glow** [24], **IC** [54], **HierAD**[51] and **CFlow** [17].

All methods are used with their default hyperparameters as given in their official implementations, with (where applicable) the same backbone architecture. More details can be found in the supplementary material. No hyperparameter search was performed, given that no validation metrics exist. Specifically, **Glow**, **HierAD** and **IC** models are based on the same Glow network. All other methods use a ResNet-101. All methods resize the input images to 224×224, with the exception of the Glow-based and **SSD** models, where we found that resizing images to 32×32 worked better.

Additionally, we show results when using **MahaAD** with an EfficientNet-b4. As **MahaAD** requires no neural network training and thus, unlike all other methods except **DN2**, the additional computational cost for this is minimal. Note that using a pre-trained CNN to extract image features is not a major limitation in practice, as all standard deep learning libraries offer tools to load and use such models in very few steps.

4.1   Results

The evaluated methods were compared in terms of performance, training times and training complexity. We detail the results of our experiments below and provide a deeper breakdown of the results, including additional methods, in the supplementary material.

Performance. Most methods were inconsistent across different tasks (see Table 1). **MSCL**, which performed very well in *uni-class*, is challenged in *uni-ano* and in *shift-low-res*. Conversely, **CFlow**'s performance is high for *uni-ano*, but heavily drops in *uni-class* and especially *shift-low-res*. **SSD** had the best results on *shift-low-res* but struggled with tasks involving high-dimensional images, and **DN2** scored very well on average except on *shift-low-res*. On the other hand, **MahaAD** performed very well and with high stability across tasks. Specifically, it performed among the top three methods in all tasks but in the low resolution domain shift task, for which it still beats **MSCL**, **DN2** and **DDV** by

Table 1. Performance summary in AUC over three runs on our U-OOD benchmark. We report performances for each task, as well as the mean over tasks and over experiments. No standard deviation is reported for **MahaAD** and **DN2** as they are deterministic. (*) Taken from original publication; ($^+$) taken from [41]; ($^-$) taken from [56]; (†) taken from [51]

Method	Architecture	uni-class	uni-ano	uni-med	shift-low-res	shift-high-res	Task Mean	Experiment Mean
Glow	K = 32, L = 3	53.8±0.1	82.0±2.5	55.8±0.8	8.8 †	34.5±0.1	47.0	53.9
IC	K = 32, L = 3	55.7±0.1	73.6±2.6	65.1±0.5	95.0†	65.8±0.1	71.0	63.6
HierAD	K = 32, L = 3	63.0±0.4	81.6±2.1	72.5±0.6	93.9*	75.0±0.3	77.2	71.4
MHRot	ResNet-101	83.4$^+$	70.8±1.0	69.0±0.7	97.8$^-$	73.3±0.9	78.9	76.9
DDV	ResNet-101	65.8±1.4	65.5±0.2	60.3±3.2	47.9±6.6	63.9±4.9	60.7	64.5
MSCL	ResNet-101	**96.3**±0.0	86.4±0.0	75.2±0.1	88.3±0.0	74.4±0.0	84.1	86.1
CFlow	ResNet-101	75.0±0.0	**95.7**±0.1	68.8±0.3	6.6±0.2	61.8±0.3	61.6	74.1
DN2	ResNet-101	91.2	86.2	**76.7**	57.4	76.0	77.5	84.1
SSD	ResNet-101	83.6±0.3	65.8±3.0	64.6±0.6	**99.6***	60.4±0.9	74.8	72.0
MahaAD	ResNet-101	92.4	91.3	75.7	94.3	**78.6**	86.5	86.8
MahaAD	EfficientNet-b4	95.1	94.4	76.8	96.2	83.8	89.3	90.1

large margins. Furthermore, **MahaAD** was the best performing method on average, beating the second-best method, **MSCL**, by more than 2% points across tasks. These performance instabilities were not only observed across the different tasks reported in Table 1, but also within the tasks with fixed in-distribution across different OOD datasets. For example, for the *shift-high-res* task, performance of most methods fluctuated depending on the chosen OOD dataset (see Fig. 4). In contrast, **MahaAD** again is the only method that stands out in terms of stability, as it performs well regardless of the in and the out datasets selected.

Training Times. **MahaAD** was faster to train than its counterparts (see Fig. 5). For example, in the CIFAR10:SVHN experiment (task *shift-low-res*), using two GeForce RTX 3090s, **MahaAD** was the fastest to train, taking roughly 90 s to process the entire CIFAR10 dataset. Other methods with similar performances were orders of magnitude slower: **MSCL** took more than half an hour for airplane:rest and **SSD** took more than 12 h for CIFAR10:SVHN. In addition,

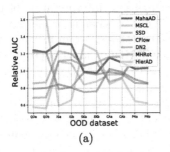
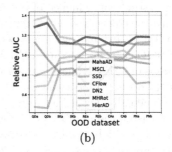

(a)   (b)

Fig. 4. Relative performance (AUC divided by mean AUC on that task) for seven methods on the *shift-high-res* tasks. X-axis indicates the out distribution. (a) `Real-A` as in-distribution. (b) `Infograph-A` as in-distribution.

no method performed consistently better than **MahaAD** on either of these two experiments. This behavior was also observed for the other tasks.

Training Complexity. Furthermore, **MahaAD** was simpler to train, with fewer hyperparameters and more predictable behavior. Predicting the convergence of methods such as **MSCL**, **CFlow** and **DDV** was challenging as there is no apparent correlation between the training loss and OOD performance, as also reported in [41]. It is thus unclear when to stop training before the performance starts degrading. While this lack of obvious stopping criterion is problematic for many methods [37,40,41,45], **MahaAD** is convenient as it avoids this necessity altogether.

4.2   Importance of Data Invariants

We report here additional results that support the importance of data invariants, both for the quality of U-OOD detection and as a tool to analyse U-OOD predictions and evaluation datasets.

In order to assess the importance of data invariants for U-OOD detection, we examined which principal components are most effective at identifying OOD samples. To that end, we measured the AUC score in four experiments by limiting the Mahalanobis score of Eq. (3) to only use the subset of principal components with highest variance, corresponding to the modes of variation of the data. Similarly, we observed the performance with the subset of principal components with the smallest variance, corresponding to data invariants. The latter outperformed the former by a large margin in U-OOD detection (see Fig. 6). Starting from the most variant principal components, the performance slowly increases when adding more components, converging when over 80% of the variance is explained. On the other hand, when starting from the most invariant component, the performance quickly converges when as little as 3% of the variance has been explained, supporting the idea that invariants are more representative to characterize training data and OOD samples. While other works had observed similar findings, they either consider the supervised case [23,39], or frame it in the context of reducing dimensionality [43].

An interesting consequence of our invariant-based interpretation of U-OOD is that, when we considered what to include in our benchmark, some experiments that are valid for evaluating supervised OOD methods, are in fact not suitable for the U-OOD case. For instance, CIFAR10:CIFAR100 [33,34,53] or 9-classes:1-held-out-class of CIFAR10 [3,6] were used in previous U-OOD works even though they do not appear to meet the U-OOD criteria.

More specifically, according to our definition for U-OOD, one would expect that by increasing the number of classes present in a training set, the invariants associated to the high semantic features will decrease, effectively reducing the probability that new classes are considered U-OOD. For example, training with multiple classes from CIFAR10 (*e.g.*, cats, dogs, cars) reduces the probability that an additional class (*e.g.*, plane) from CIFAR10 or CIFAR100 should be considered OOD (Fig. 1(d)), as the class stops being an invariant. However, the

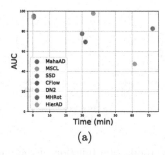
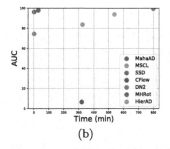

Fig. 5. Training times and performances for different methods on (a) *uni-class*'s `airplane:rest` and (b) *shift-low-res*'s `CIFAR10:SVHN`.

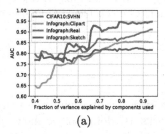
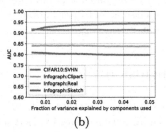

Fig. 6. The OOD AUC for four experiments with a ResNet50 using different sets of principal components. (a) gives result starting from the first principal components, while (b) does so from the last principal components. The x-axis of (a) starts at 0.4 as for Infograph the most variant component of the first layer is responsible for almost 40% of all variance.

number of training classes should not affect the probability that images from a different modality are detected as OOD, as they break other kind of invariants. For instance, when training with images from CIFAR10, the test images from SVHN or MNIST should still be considered OOD regardless of the number of CIFAR10 training classes, as they are clearly distinct in appearance.

In Fig. 7, we investigate this desired behavior experimentally by analyzing the performance of the three best-performing methods when we increased the number of in-distribution CIFAR10 training classes. As expected, all methods consider fewer images from CIFAR100 and one held-out class from CIFAR10 as OOD when the number of training classes increased (Fig. 7(a)). Conversely, increasing the number of training CIFAR10 classes did not affect the predictions for SVHN and MNIST with **MahaAD**, which correctly kept detecting both datasets as OOD (Fig. 7(b)). In contrast, this did negatively affect the predictions of **DN2** and **MSCL**. According to our invariant-based interpretation of U-OOD, **MahaAD**'s behavior is reasonable and consistent in these configurations, yet the unexpected **DN2** and **MSCL** results are hard to justify. To the extent of our knowledge, no previous work on U-OOD detection had provided a similar theoretical tool capable of interpreting and explaining results.

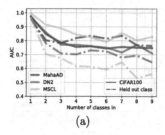 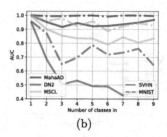

(a)   (b)

Fig. 7. OOD AUC performance for different methods as a function of the number of classes in the training set (CIFAR10), keeping its size constant. (a) Performance on CIFAR100 and a held out CIFAR10 class as out-distribution, which should not be considered U-OOD under our interpretation. (b) Performance on SVHN and a held out MNIST class as out-distribution, which should be considered U-OOD under our interpretation.

5   Conclusion

Our work explores the state of U-OOD detection by observing the behavior of methods on an extensive and varied set of tasks. By doing so, we show a complicated landscape, with most methods being highly inconsistent among and within tasks. **MahaAD** is however an exception to this trend, behaving consistently in a large majority of experimental configurations. Despite being neglected in most recent U-OOD papers, **MahaAD** appears to be the current best off-the-shelf unsupervised OOD detector, as it offers good performance and consistency without requiring time-consuming data pre-processing, careful tuning of the training procedure, or hyperparameter search.

In order to explain these inconsistent results, we introduced a characterization of U-OOD based on training set invariants and showed that the **MahaAD** method embodies a linear version of this concept. We found this framework and the proposed benchmark to be useful to not only qualitatively understand U-OOD detector predictions, but also to assess whether a test dataset is in fact suitable for U-OOD evaluation or not. A key take-away is that we cannot purely rely on semantic labels from datasets to design U-OOD evaluation methods, as done in previous works.

In general, this points to a rather bleak conclusion: at the moment, no method can consistently outperform a simple anomaly detector that uses naively extracted features from a network trained on a different dataset that was optimized for a different task. We believe that with our invariant-based U-OOD characterization, new appropriate methods can be designed and validated in comprehensive ways.

Acknowledgements. This work was funded by the Swiss National Science Foundation (SNSF), research grant 200021_192285 "Image data validation for AI systems".

References

1. Abati, D., Porrello, A., Calderara, S., Cucchiara, R.: Latent space autoregression for novelty detection. In: Proceedings of the IEEE/CVF Conference on Computer Vision and Pattern Recognition, pp. 481–490 (2019)
2. Ahmed, F., Courville, A.: Detecting semantic anomalies. In: Proceedings of the AAAI Conference on Artificial Intelligence, vol. 34, pp. 3154–3162 (2020)
3. Akcay, S., Atapour-Abarghouei, A., Breckon, T.P.: GANomaly: semi-supervised anomaly detection via adversarial training. In: Jawahar, C.V., Li, H., Mori, G., Schindler, K. (eds.) ACCV 2018. LNCS, vol. 11363, pp. 622–637. Springer, Cham (2019). https://doi.org/10.1007/978-3-030-20893-6_39
4. Amodei, D., Olah, C., Steinhardt, J., Christiano, P., Schulman, J., Mané, D.: Concrete problems in AI safety. arXiv preprint arXiv:1606.06565 (2016)
5. Battikh, M.S., Lenskiy, A.A.: Latent-insensitive autoencoders for anomaly detection and class-incremental learning. arXiv preprint arXiv:2110.13101 (2021)
6. Bergman, L., Cohen, N., Hoshen, Y.: Deep nearest neighbor anomaly detection. arXiv preprint arXiv:2002.10445 (2020)
7. Bergman, L., Hoshen, Y.: Classification-based anomaly detection for general data. In: International Conference on Learning Representations (2020)
8. Bergmann, P., Fauser, M., Sattlegger, D., Steger, C.: Mvtec ad - a comprehensive real-world dataset for unsupervised anomaly detection. In: Proceedings of the IEEE/CVF Conference on Computer Vision and Pattern Recognition (CVPR), pp. 9592–9600 (2019)
9. Bozorgtabar, B., Mahapatra, D., Vray, G., Thiran, J.-P.: SALAD: self-supervised aggregation learning for anomaly detection on X-Rays. In: Martel, A.L., et al. (eds.) MICCAI 2020. LNCS, vol. 12261, pp. 468–478. Springer, Cham (2020). https://doi.org/10.1007/978-3-030-59710-8_46
10. Breunig, M.M., Kriegel, H.P., Ng, R.T., Sander, J.: LOF: identifying density-based local outliers. In: Proceedings of the 2000 ACM SIGMOD International Conference on Management of Data, pp. 93–104 (2000)
11. Chalapathy, R., Chawla, S.: Deep learning for anomaly detection: a survey. arXiv preprint arXiv:1901.03407 (2019)
12. Choi, H., Jang, E., Alemi, A.A.: Waic, but why? generative ensembles for robust anomaly detection. arXiv preprint arXiv:1810.01392 (2018)
13. Choi, S., Chung, S.Y.: Novelty detection via blurring. In: International Conference on Learning Representations (2020)
14. Defard, T., Setkov, A., Loesch, A., Audigier, R.: PaDiM: a patch distribution modeling framework for anomaly detection and localization. In: Del Bimbo, A., et al. (eds.) ICPR 2021. LNCS, vol. 12664, pp. 475–489. Springer, Cham (2021). https://doi.org/10.1007/978-3-030-68799-1_35
15. Golan, I., El-Yaniv, R.: Deep anomaly detection using geometric transformations. In: Advances in Neural Information Processing Systems, pp. 9758–9769 (2018)
16. Gong, D., et al.: Memorizing normality to detect anomaly: Memory-augmented deep autoencoder for unsupervised anomaly detection. In: Proceedings of the IEEE/CVF International Conference on Computer Vision, pp. 1705–1714 (2019)
17. Gudovskiy, D., Ishizaka, S., Kozuka, K.: Cflow-ad: Real-time unsupervised anomaly detection with localization via conditional normalizing flows. In: Proceedings of the IEEE/CVF Winter Conference on Applications of Computer Vision, pp. 98–107 (2022)

18. Havtorn, J.D.D., Frellsen, J., Hauberg, S., Maaløe, L.: Hierarchical vaes know what they don't know. In: International Conference on Machine Learning PMLR, pp. 4117–4128 (2021)

19. Hendrycks, D., Gimpel, K.: A baseline for detecting misclassified and out-of-distribution examples in neural networks. International Conference on Learning Representations (2017)

20. Hendrycks, D., Mazeika, M., Kadavath, S., Song, D.: Using self-supervised learning can improve model robustness and uncertainty. Adv. Neural Inf. Process. Syst. **32** (2019)

21. Hou, J., Zhang, Y., Zhong, Q., Xie, D., Pu, S., Zhou, H.: Divide-and-assemble: learning block-wise memory for unsupervised anomaly detection. In: Proceedings of the IEEE/CVF International Conference on Computer Vision, pp. 8791–8800 (2021)

22. Hsu, Y.C., Shen, Y., Jin, H., Kira, Z.: Generalized odin: detecting out-of-distribution image without learning from out-of-distribution data. In: Proceedings of the IEEE/CVF Conference on Computer Vision and Pattern Recognition, pp. 10951–10960 (2020)

23. Kamoi, R., Kobayashi, K.: Why is the mahalanobis distance effective for anomaly detection? arXiv preprint arXiv:2003.00402 (2020)

24. Kingma, D.P., Dhariwal, P.: Glow: generative flow with invertible 1×1 convolutions. Adv. Neural Inf. Process. Syst. **31** (2018)

25. Koner, R., Sinhamahapatra, P., Roscher, K., Günnemann, S., Tresp, V.: Oodformer: Out-of-distribution detection transformer. arXiv preprint arXiv:2107.08976 (2021)

26. Ledoit, O., Wolf, M.: A well-conditioned estimator for large-dimensional covariance matrices. J. Multivariate Anal. **88**(2), 365–411 (2004)

27. Lee, K., Lee, K., Lee, H., Shin, J.: A simple unified framework for detecting out-of-distribution samples and adversarial attacks. Adv. Neural Inf. Process. Syst. **31**, 7167–7177 (2018)

28. Li, C.L., Sohn, K., Yoon, J., Pfister, T.: Cutpaste: self-supervised learning for anomaly detection and localization. In: Proceedings of the IEEE/CVF Conference on Computer Vision and Pattern Recognition, pp. 9664–9674 (2021)

29. Liang, S., Li, Y., Srikant, R.: Enhancing the reliability of out-of-distribution image detection in neural networks. In: International Conference on Learning Representations (2018)

30. Liu, F.T., Ting, K.M., Zhou, Z.H.: Isolation forest. In: 2008 Eighth IEEE International Conference on Data Mining, pp. 413–422. IEEE (2008)

31. Márquez-Neila, P., Sznitman, R.: Image data validation for medical systems. In: Shen, D. (ed.) MICCAI 2019. LNCS, vol. 11767, pp. 329–337. Springer, Cham (2019). https://doi.org/10.1007/978-3-030-32251-9_36

32. Mesarcik, M., Ranguelova, E., Boonstra, A.J., van Nieuwpoort, R.V.: Improving novelty detection using the reconstructions of nearest neighbours. arXiv preprint arXiv:2111.06150 (2021)

33. Mohseni, S., Vahdat, A., Yadawa, J.: Multi-task transformation learning for robust out-of-distribution detection. arXiv preprint arXiv:2106.03899 (2021)

34. Morningstar, W., Ham, C., Gallagher, A., Lakshminarayanan, B., Alemi, A., Dillon, J.: Density of states estimation for out of distribution detection. In: International Conference on Artificial Intelligence and Statistics PMLR, pp. 3232–3240 (2021)

35. Nalisnick, E., Matsukawa, A., Teh, Y.W., Gorur, D., Lakshminarayanan, B.: Do deep generative models know what they don't know? arXiv preprint arXiv:1810.09136 (2018)
36. Ouardini, K., et al.: Towards practical unsupervised anomaly detection on retinal images. In: Wang, Q., et al. (eds.) DART/MIL3ID -2019. LNCS, vol. 11795, pp. 225–234. Springer, Cham (2019). https://doi.org/10.1007/978-3-030-33391-1_26
37. Perera, P., Nallapati, R., Xiang, B.: Ocgan: one-class novelty detection using gans with constrained latent representations. In: Proceedings of the IEEE/CVF Conference on Computer Vision and Pattern Recognition, pp. 2898–2906 (2019)
38. Perera, P., Oza, P., Patel, V.M.: One-class classification: A survey. arXiv preprint arXiv:2101.03064 (2021)
39. Podolskiy, A., Lipin, D., Bout, A., Artemova, E., Piontkovskaya, I.: Revisiting mahalanobis distance for transformer-based out-of-domain detection. arXiv preprint arXiv:2101.03778 (2021)
40. Reiss, T., Cohen, N., Bergman, L., Hoshen, Y.: Panda: adapting pretrained features for anomaly detection and segmentation. In: Proceedings of the IEEE/CVF Conference on Computer Vision and Pattern Recognition, pp. 2806–2814 (2021)
41. Reiss, T., Hoshen, Y.: Mean-shifted contrastive loss for anomaly detection. arXiv preprint arXiv:2106.03844 (2021)
42. Ren, J., et al.: Likelihood ratios for out-of-distribution detection. Adv. Neural Inf. Process. Syst. 14707–14718 (2019)
43. Rippel, O., Mertens, P., Merhof, D.: Modeling the distribution of normal data in pre-trained deep features for anomaly detection. In: 2020 25th International Conference on Pattern Recognition (ICPR), pp. 6726–6733. IEEE (2021)
44. Ruff, L., et al.: A unifying review of deep and shallow anomaly detection. Proc. IEEE 109(5), 756–795 (2021)
45. Ruff, L., et al.: Deep one-class classification. In: International Conference on Machine Learning PMLR, pp. 4393–4402 (2018)
46. Sakurada, M., Yairi, T.: Anomaly detection using autoencoders with nonlinear dimensionality reduction. In: Proceedings of the MLSDA 2014 2nd Workshop on Machine Learning for Sensory Data Analysis, pp. 4–11 (2014)
47. Salehi, M., Eftekhar, A., Sadjadi, N., Rohban, M.H., Rabiee, H.R.: Puzzle-ae: Novelty detection in images through solving puzzles. arXiv preprint arXiv:2008.12959 (2020)
48. Salehi, M., Sadjadi, N., Baselizadeh, S., Rohban, M.H., Rabiee, H.R.: Multiresolution knowledge distillation for anomaly detection. In: Proceedings of the IEEE/CVF Conference on Computer Vision and Pattern Recognition, pp. 14902–14912 (2021)
49. Salimans, T., Karpathy, A., Chen, X., Kingma, D.P.: Pixelcnn++: improving the pixelcnn with discretized logistic mixture likelihood and other modifications. In: International Conference on Learning Representations (2017)
50. Sastry, C.S., Oore, S.: Detecting out-of-distribution examples with gram matrices. In: International Conference on Machine Learning PMLR, pp. 8491–8501 (2020)
51. Schirrmeister, R., Zhou, Y., Ball, T., Zhang, D.: Understanding anomaly detection with deep invertible networks through hierarchies of distributions and features. Adv. Neural Inf. Process. Syst. 33, 21038–21049 (2020)
52. Schölkopf, B., Williamson, R.C., Smola, A.J., Shawe-Taylor, J., Platt, J.C., et al.: Support vector method for novelty detection. In: NIPS, vol. 12, pp. 582–588. Citeseer (1999)
53. Sehwag, V., Chiang, M., Mittal, P.: Ssd: a unified framework for self-supervised outlier detection. In: International Conference on Learning Representations (2021)

54. Serrà, J., Álvarez, D., Gómez, V., Slizovskaia, O., Núñez, J.F., Luque, J.: Input complexity and out-of-distribution detection with likelihood-based generative models. In: International Conference on Learning Representations (2019)
55. Sohn, K., Li, C.L., Yoon, J., Jin, M., Pfister, T.: Learning and evaluating representations for deep one-class classification. In: International Conference on Learning Representations (2021)
56. Tack, J., Mo, S., Jeong, J., Shin, J.: CSI: Novelty detection via contrastive learning on distributionally shifted instances. Adv. Neural Inf. Process. Syst. **33**, 11839–11852 (2020)
57. Tang, Y.X., Tang, Y.B., Han, M., Xiao, J., Summers, R.M.: Abnormal chest x-ray identification with generative adversarial one-class classifier. In: 2019 IEEE 16th International Symposium on Biomedical Imaging (ISBI 2019), pp. 1358–1361. IEEE (2019)
58. Wang, S., et al.: Effective end-to-end unsupervised outlier detection via inlier priority of discriminative network. In: Advances in Neural Information Processing Systems, pp. 5962–5975 (2019)
59. Xiao, Z., Yan, Q., Amit, Y.: Do we really need to learn representations from in-domain data for outlier detection? In: ICML 2021 Workshop on Uncertainty & Robustness in Deep Learning (2021)
60. Yang, J., Zhou, K., Li, Y., Liu, Z.: Generalized out-of-distribution detection: A survey. arXiv preprint arXiv:2110.11334 (2021)
61. Zong, B., Song, Q., Min, M.R., Cheng, W., Lumezanu, C., Cho, D., Chen, H.: Deep autoencoding gaussian mixture model for unsupervised anomaly detection. In: International conference on learning representations (2018)

Domain Invariant Masked Autoencoders for Self-supervised Learning from Multi-domains

Haiyang Yang[1,4], Shixiang Tang[3,4], Meilin Chen[2,4], Yizhou Wang[2,4],
Feng Zhu[4], Lei Bai[3(✉)], Rui Zhao[4,5], and Wanli Ouyang[3]

[1] Nanjing University, Nanjing, China
hyyang@smail.nju.edu.cn
[2] Zhejiang University, Zhejiang, China
{merlinis,yizhouwang}@zju.edu.cn
[3] The University of Sydney, Sydney, Australia
stan3906@uni.sydney.edu.au, baisanshi@gmail.com,
wanli.ouyang@sydney.edu.au
[4] SenseTime Research, Hong Kong, China
{zhufeng,zhaorui}@sensetime.com
[5] Qing Yuan Research Institute, Shanghai Jiao Tong University, Shanghai, China

Abstract. Generalizing learned representations across significantly different visual domains is a fundamental yet crucial ability of the human visual system. While recent self-supervised learning methods have achieved good performances with evaluation set on the same domain as the training set, they will have an undesirable performance decrease when tested on a different domain. Therefore, the self-supervised learning from multiple domains task is proposed to learn domain-invariant features that are not only suitable for evaluation on the same domain as the training set, but also can be generalized to unseen domains. In this paper, we propose a Domain-invariant Masked AutoEncoder (DiMAE) for self-supervised learning from multi-domains, which designs a new pretext task, *i.e.,* the cross-domain reconstruction task, to learn domain-invariant features. The core idea is to augment the input image with style noise from different domains and then reconstruct the image from the embedding of the augmented image, regularizing the encoder to learn domain-invariant features. To accomplish the idea, DiMAE contains two critical designs, 1) content-preserved style mix, which adds style information from other domains to input while persevering the content in a parameter-free manner, and 2) multiple domain-specific decoders, which recovers the corresponding domain style of input to the encoded domain-invariant features for reconstruction. Experiments on PACS and Domain-Net illustrate that DiMAE achieves considerable gains compared with recent state-of-the-art methods.

H. Yang—The work was done during an internship at SenseTime.

Supplementary Information The online version contains supplementary material available at https://doi.org/10.1007/978-3-031-19821-2_9.

1   Introduction

Recent advances on self-supervised learning (SSL) with the contrastive loss [7, 9,19,36] have shown to be effective in easing the burden of manual annotation, and achieved comparable performance with supervised learning methods. When trained on large-scale datasets, *e.g.* ImageNet [12], self-supervised learning methods are capable of learning high-level semantic image representations [14,43,46] that are transferable to various downstream tasks without using expensive annotated labels. However, the great success of existing self-supervised learning methods implicitly relies on the assumption that training and testing sets are identically distributed, and thus these methods will suffer an undesirable performance drop when the trained model is tested on other domains [35,38,50] that do not exist in the training set.

Self-supervised learning from multi-domain data aims at learning domain invariant representations that are not only suitable for domains in the training set, but also can generalize well to other domains missing in the training set. Existing methods can be generally divided into two categories, *i.e,* self-prediction methods and contrastive-based methods. Early methods for self-supervised learning from multi-domain data append self-prediction tasks to learn domain-invariant features. For example, [15] randomly rotates the input image and regularizes the model to predict the rotation angle [16] to increase the model generalization ability. These self-prediction tasks are sub-optimal solutions, because they are not specifically designed to eliminate the domain bias in the dataset. Contrastive-based methods [23,45] explicitly eliminate the domain bias by pulling the sample and its nearest neighbor from a different domain close. However, the positive pair retrieved by the nearest neighbor across the domains is much more noisy than that in a single domain, because semantically similar images from different domains may have a large visual difference.

In this paper, we tackle the self-supervised learning from multi-domain data from a different perspective, *i.e.,* generative self-supervised learning, and propose a new **D**omain invariant **M**asked **A**uto**E**ncoders (**DiMAE**) for learning domain-invariant features from multi-domain data, which is motivated by the recent generative-based self-supervised learning method Masked Auto-Encoders (MAE) [18]. Specifically, MAE eliminates the low-level information by masking large portion of image patches and drives the encoder to extract semantic information by reconstructing pixels from very few neighboring patches [3] with a light-weighted decoder. However, this design does not take the domain gaps into consideration and thus can not generalize well for the self-supervised learning from multi-domain tasks. To close the gap, our proposed DiMAE constructs a cross-domain reconstruction task, which uses *the image with the mixed style from different domains as input for one content encoder to extract domain invariant features and multiple domain-specific decoders to recover the specific domain style for regressing the raw pixel values of masked patches before style mix under an MSE loss*, as shown in Fig. 1. The critical designs and insights behind DiMAE for self-supervised learning from multi-domain data involve:

(1) The **cross-domain reconstruction task** aims at reconstructing the image from the image with other domain styles. DiMAE disentangles the reconstruction into two processes: a content[1] encoder to remove the domain style by extracting domain-invariant features, and a domain-specific decoder to recover the style of the reconstruction target domain. By forcing the decoder to learn specific style information, we regularize the encoder to learn domain-invariant features.

(2) The **content preserved style mixing** aims to add style noise of the other domains to one image while preserving the content information. While there exist some popular mixing methods (*e.g*, mixup [44] and cutmix [42]) able to mix domain styles, they also add content noise to the image. Our experiments find that the content noise will lead to a significant performance decrease in our cross-domain reconstruction task. Therefore, we propose a new non-parametric content preserved style mixing method to take advantage of the cross-domain reconstruction and avoid the undesirable performance decrease by content noise.

(3) The **multiple domain-specific decoders** aim to recover the corresponding domain style of the target image for reconstruction from the encoded domain-irrelevant features. Although the decoder network design, *e.g.*, such as the number of layers, can determine the semantic level of the learned latent representations as pointed out in MAE [18], we find that a single decoder as used in MAE can not help to regularize the encoder to learn domain-invariant features. To reconstruct the image from a specific domain, the encoder will leak the domain information to guide the decoder to reconstruct the image with the input image's style. This prevents the encoder from learning the domain-invariant features. Therefore, multiple domain-specific decoders are proposed to recover different domain styles by domain-corresponding decoders, which regularizes the encoder to only learn domain-invariant features.

To demonstrate the effectiveness of DiMAE, we conduct experiments on the multi-domain dataset PACS [26] and DomainNet [33], observing consistent performance improvements on both in-domain and cross-domain settings. For the in-domain evaluation, DiMAE outperforms state-of-the-art methods by **+0.8%** on the PACS. On cross-domain testing, we achieve considerable gains over the recent state-of-the-art methods in both linear evaluation and full network fine-tuning. Specifically, in linear evaluation, our method improves the recent state-of-the-art by **+8.07%** on PACS with 1% data fine-tuning fraction. In full network fine-tuning with 100% data, we get an averaged **+13.24%** and **+9.87%** performance gains on PACS and DomainNet, respectively.

The contributions of our work are summarized as three-folds: (**1**) We propose a new generative framework which leverages the cross-domain reconstruction as the pretext to learn domain-invariant features from multi-domain data. (**2**) We propose a new non-parametric style-mix method that can preserve the content

---

[1] "content" and "style" are terms widely used in style mix. "content" means domain-invariant information, while "style" means domain-specific information.

information to exploit the cross-domain reconstruction task and avoid performance drop by content noise. **(3)** We modify the single decoder in MAE to multiple domain-specific decoders to regularize the encoder to learn domain-invariant features. We show that our DiMAE outperforms state-of-the-art self-supervised learning baselines on learning representation from multi-domain data.

2   Related Work

2.1   Self-supervised Learning

Self-supervised Learning (SSL) introduces various pretext tasks to learn semantic representations from unlabeled data for a better generalization in downstream tasks. Generally, SSL can be categorized into discriminative [5,7,9,10,16,17,19, 31,43,48] and generative methods [18,24,25,32]. Among the former, some early works try to design auxiliary handcrafted prediction tasks to learn semantic representation, such as jigsaw puzzle [31] and rotation prediction [16]. Recently, contrastive approaches [5,7,9,10,17,19,43] emerge as a promising direction for SSL. They consider each instance a different class and promote the instance discrimination by forcing representation of different views of the same image closer and spreading representation of views from different images apart. Although remarkable progress has been achieved, contrastive methods heavily rely on data augmentation [7,36] and negative sampling [19,40].

Another recent resurgent line of SSL is generative approaches, many of which train an encoder and decoder for pixel reconstruction. Various pretext tasks have been proposed, such as image inpainting [32] and colorization [24,25]. Very recently, since the introduction of ViT [13], masked image modeling (MIM) has re-attracted the attention of the community. iGPT [6] proposes to predict the next pixels of a sequence, and BEiT [2] leverages a variational autoencoder (VAE) to encode masked patches. A very relevant work, MAE [18] proposes to train the autoencoder to capture the semantic representation by recovering the input image from very few neighboring patches. Our proposed method, a novel generative approach for SSL, is devoted into a more common scenario, pretraining from multiple domains. As far as we know, we are the first to propose the generative pretraining method for training from multi domain data.

2.2   Domain Generalization

Domain Generalization (DG) considers the transferability to unseen target domains using labeled data from a single or multiple source domains. A common approach is to minimize the distance between source domains for learning domain-invariant representations, among which are minimizing the KL Divergence [39], minimizing maximum mean discrepancy [28] and adversarial learning [1,30,34]. Several approaches propose to exploit meta-learning [27] or augmentation [4,11,29,47] to promote the transferability for DG.

Despite the promising advances in recent DG methods, they assume that source domains are annotated. To address this issue, Unsupervised DG (UDG)

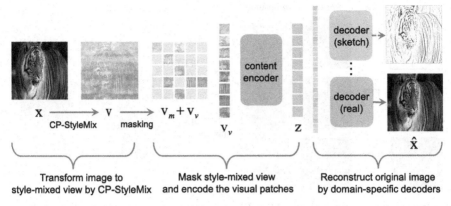

Fig. 1. The pipeline of DiMAE. First, CP-StyleMix transforms the original image **x** to its style-mixed view **v** by adding style information from other domains without introducing content noise. Second, the style-mixed view **v** is divided into visible patches $\mathbf{v}_v$ and masked patches $\mathbf{v}_m$, and the content encoder learns the content representation **z** from visible patches. Third, domain-specific decoders learn to reconstruct $\hat{\mathbf{x}}$ by the corresponding decoder.

is proposed as a more general task of training with unlabeled source domains [15] introduces rotation prediction and mutual information maximization for multi-domain generalization. Derived from contrastive learning, DIUL [45] incorporates domain information into the contrastive loss by a reweighting mechanism considering domain labels. Despite the promising results, these two works carefully design domain-related discriminative pretext tasks and try to strike a compromise between instance and domain discrimination. Our proposed method, in contrast, is a brand new generative approach for self-supervised learning from multi-domain data, showing strong advantages for UDG setting.

3 Domain-Invariant Masked AutoEncoder

3.1 Cross-domain Reconstruction Framework

Different from MAE which learns high-level semantic representations by reconstruction from a highly masked image, our DiMAE learns domain invariant representation by a cross-domain reconstruction task, which aims at recovering images from an image mixed with other domain styles. Specifically, DiMAE consists three modules, including a Content Preserved Style-Mix (CP-StyleMix), a content encoder, and multiple domain-specific decoders. The CP-StyleMix is used to mix the style information from different domains while preserving the domain-irrelevant object content, which generates the input of the cross-domain reconstruction task. The content encoder $\mathcal{F}(*, \theta_{\mathcal{F}})$ are shared by images from all domains, where $\theta_{\mathcal{F}}$ is the parameter of $\mathcal{F}$, and is expected to encode the content and domain-invariant information by denoising the style information.

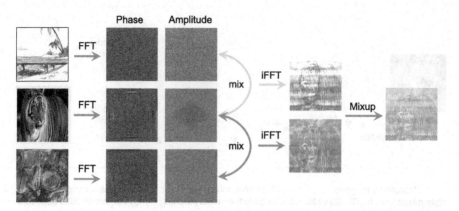

Fig. 2. The pipeline of CP-StyleMix. We mix the Fourier amplitude of the original image **x** and two images from other domains to generate content preserved and style-transferred images, and mix them to generate the style-mixed view **v**.

The domain-specific decoders $\mathcal{G}$ in DiMAE are designed to incorporate the style information to the domain-invariant representation for image reconstruction, where $\mathcal{G} = \{\mathcal{G}_1(*, \phi_1), \mathcal{G}_2(*, \phi_2), ..., \mathcal{G}_{N_d}(*, \phi_{N_d})\}$, ϕ_i is the parameter for the i-th domain-specific decoder and N_d is the number of domains in the training set. As shown in Fig. 1, our DiMAE has the following steps:

Step1: Transform an image $\acute{\mathbf{x}}$ *to its style-mixed view* **v** *by Content Preserved Style-Mix (Sect. 3.2).* Given an image **x**, with Content Preserved Style-Mix, we mix the style from other domains to the image **x** while preserving the content in **x** to generate its style-mixed view **v**.

Step2: Transform the style-mixed view **v** *to content representation* **z** *(Sect. 3.3).* We randomly divides **v** into visible patches $\mathbf{v}_v$ and masked patches $\mathbf{v}_m$, and extract content representation **z** by encoding the visible patches $\mathbf{v}_v$ by $\mathcal{F}(*, \theta_{\mathcal{F}})$.

Step3: Reconstruct the image $\hat{\mathbf{x}}$ *by content representation* **z** *with the domain-specific decoders (Sect. 3.4).* Given content representation **z** and multiple domain-specific decoders $\mathcal{G} = \{\mathcal{G}_1(*, \phi_1), \mathcal{G}_2(*, \phi_2), ..., \mathcal{G}_{N_d}(*, \phi_{N_d})\}$, we reconstruct the image $\hat{\mathbf{x}}$ by $\mathcal{G}_i$, where $\mathcal{G}_i$ is the decoder of the i-th domain.

Step4: Backward propagation using the MSE loss (Sect. 3.5). Given the reconstructed image $\hat{\mathbf{x}}$ and the original image **x**, the parameter $\theta_{\mathcal{F}}$ in $\mathcal{F}(*, \theta_{\mathcal{F}})$ and the parameters $\phi_1, \cdots, \phi_{N_d}$ in $\mathcal{G}(*, \phi_1), ..., \mathcal{G}(*, \phi_{N_d})$ are learned by MSE loss.

3.2   Content Preserved Style-Mix

Content Preserved Style-Mix (CP-StyleMix) aims at mixing styles into an image while preserving the content information. This is a critical part for the cross-domain reconstruction tasks. Inspired by [41], the style information and the content information can be disentangled in the Fourier space. The content information is encoded in the phase of the Fourier signals, and the style information is encoded in the amplitude of the Fourier signals. We propose to first mix the style of the i-th domain to the image $\mathbf{x}$, generating its style views $\{\mathbf{v}_1, \mathbf{v}_2, ..., \mathbf{v}_{N_d}\}$, where N_d is the number of domains. Then we mix these style views by the typical Mixup method [42], generating the final style-mixed view $\mathbf{v}$.

Specifically, for mixing in the Fourier space, given an image $\mathbf{x}$ from j-th domain and a randomly selected image $\mathbf{x}_{aux}$ from the i-th domain ($i \neq j$), the view $\mathbf{v}_i$ of image $\mathbf{x}$ can be formulated as

$$\mathbf{v}_i = \mathcal{K}^{-1}(\mathcal{K}^A_{mix}, \mathcal{K}^P(\mathbf{x})), \qquad (1)$$

where $\mathcal{K}^A_{mix} = \lambda \mathcal{K}^A(\mathbf{x}_{aux}) + (1-\lambda)\mathcal{K}^A(\mathbf{x})$, $\mathcal{K}^{-1}$ is Fourier inversion, and $\mathcal{K}^A$, $\mathcal{K}^P$ returns the amplitude and phase of Fourier transformation, respectively. Then we implement the second step of mix on the image space by Mixup [44] process. Mathematically, the Mixup process can be formulated as

$$\mathbf{v} = \sum_{i=1}^{N_d} \mu_i \mathbf{v}_i, \qquad (2)$$

where μ_i is the weight of different views, $\sum_{i=1}^{N_d} \mu_i = 1$, $\mu_j = 0$. Different from the Fourier style transfer proposed by [41], which do not have style mix, we mix different styles in both Fourier space and image space, leading to more diverse style information.

Discussion. Theoretically, as summarized in Table 1, there are various methods to mix the style information from other domains to the input image, including CutMix [42], MixUp [44], StyleMix [21], and CycleGan+Mix [49]. Our content preserved style mix is better than these methods in two critical aspects. First, our CP-StyleMix can preserve content information compared to CutMix and Mixup, which also mix contents. Detailed experiments and analysis in Sect. 4.3 illustrates that compared with content-pereserved methods, the mixture of content with Mixup and CutMix would significantly decrease the performance in reconstruction tasks by -10.47% and -9.71%, respectively. Second, our CP-StyleMix is non-parametric and does not need extra data. StyleMix [21] and CycleGan+Mix [49] can preserve the content information, but they require to train the transfer module by extra data, which will lead to unfair comparison with existing methods [15, 45].

Method	Venue	Content preserved	No extra training
CutMix [42]	ICCV'2019		✓
MixUp [44]	ICLR'2018		✓
StyleMix [21]	CVPR'2021	✓	
CycleGan+Mix [49]	ICCV'2017	✓	
CP-StyleMix(ours)	–	✓	✓

Table 1. Comparison between existing augmentation methods and CP-StyleMix.

3.3 Content Encoder

The content Encoder, i.e., $\mathcal{F}(*, \theta_{\mathcal{F}})$, is designed to extract the domain-invariant content representations from the style-mixed view $\mathbf{v}$. Similar to MAE [18], our content encoder also follows the vision transformer design, which extracts content representations only by visible patches. Specifically, given a style-mixed view $\mathbf{v}$, we randomly divide the image patches into visible patches $\mathbf{v}_v$ with the probability p, leaving the remaining patches as the masked patches $\mathbf{v}_m$. The content representation $\mathbf{z}$ is then extracted by $\mathbf{v}_v$ using the content encoder, i.e,

$$\mathbf{z} = \mathcal{F}(\mathbf{v}_v, \theta_{\mathcal{F}}). \tag{3}$$

3.4 Domain Specific Decoders

Domain specific decoders are the critical designs in our proposed DiMAE. Besides the target of the decoder in MAE that is to reconstruct the semantic meaning of the masked patches, Domain specific decoders are expected to additionally reconstruct the domain style of the masked patches. To achieve this, we design a domain-specific decoder to each domain in the training set. Specifically, the domain specific decoders are defined as $\mathcal{G} = \{\mathcal{G}_1(*, \phi_1), \mathcal{G}_2(*, \phi_2), ..., \mathcal{G}_{N_d}(*, \phi_{N_d})\}$, where N_d is the number domains in the training set, $\mathcal{G}_1, \mathcal{G}_2, ..., \mathcal{G}_{N_d}$ share the same architectural design, and ϕ_i is the parameter of the i-th domain-specific decoder $\mathcal{G}_i$. Given content representation $\mathbf{z}$, to reconstruct the patches in the i-th domain, we feed both the content representation $\mathbf{z}$ and the learnable masked tokens [18] into the i-th domain specific decoder $\mathcal{G}_i$, i.e.,

$$\hat{\mathbf{v}}_m^i = \mathcal{G}_i(\mathbf{z}, \mathbf{q}_m^i), \tag{4}$$

where $i \in [1, N_d]$ denotes the domain index, and the $\mathbf{q}_m^i$ denotes the masked tokens in the i-th domain-specific decoder.

Discussion. As pointed in MAE [18], the decoder design plays a key role in determining the semantic level of the learnt latent features. However, we argue that the domain-invariant features can not be learnt by changing the single decoder designs probably because of the style conflict in different domains. Instead, we propose to use multiple domain-specific decoders to learn the domain-invariant features. Specifically, we use a shared content encoder to learn the domain-invariant features, and expect the domain-specific decoder to recover the specific style information for the cross-domain reconstruction.

3.5 Objective Function

The objective function constrains the error between predicted patches and target patches, which drives the model to recover the original image $\mathbf{x}$ using very few mixed-styled neighboring patches. Specifically, given the image $\mathbf{x}$ from the j-th domain, the objective function can be formulated as

$$\mathcal{L} = (\hat{\mathbf{v}}^j - \mathbf{x})^2, \tag{5}$$

where $\hat{\mathbf{v}}^j$ is the reconstructed image by $\mathcal{G}_j$, $\mathbf{x}$ is the original image.

4 Experiment

4.1 Experimental Setup

Dataset. To validate our approach, we conduct extensive experiments with two generalization settings, namely in-domain and cross-domain, which detailed in Sect. 4.2. Two benchmark datasets are adopted to carry through these two settings. PACS [26] is a widely used benchmark for domain generalization. It consists of four domains, including Photo (1,670 images), Art Painting (2,048 images), Cartoon (2,344 images), Sketch (3,929 images) and each domain contains seven categories. DomainNet [33] is the largest, most diverse and recent cross-domain benchmark. Six domains are included: Real, Painting, Sketch, Clipart, Infograph and Quickdraw, with 345 object classes and 586, 575 examples.

For In-domain evaluations, we use all training subset in all domains for self-supervised learning, and then use the validation subset of each domain for evaluation. For cross-domain generalization, following DIUL [45], we select Painting, Real, Sketch as source domains and Clipart, Infograph, Quickdraw as target domains for DomainNet [33]. We select 20 classes out of 345 categories for both training and testing, exactly following the setting in [45]. For PACS, we follow the common setting in domain generalization [1, 30, 34] where three domains are selected as source domains, and the remaining domain is target domain.

Implementation Details. In our implementation, we use ViT-small[2] as the backbone unless otherwise specified. The learning rate for pretraining is 0.5×10^{-4} and then decays with a cosine decay schedule. The weight decay is set to 0.05 and the batch size is set to $256 \times N_d$, where N_d is the number of domains in the training set. All methods are pretrained for 1000 epochs, which is consistent with the implementations in [45]. For finetuning, we follow the exact training schedule as that in [45]. Following [23], we use an ImageNet pretraining.

Training domain	(Photo, Art, Cartoon, Sketch)				
Method	Photo	Art	Cartoon	Sketch	Avg.
MoCo V3	70.6	39.4	64.8	54.4	57.3
MAE	83.5	53.4	74.2	**73.8**	71.2
DeepAll+MI,RotNet	81.6	55.5	68.5	63.4	67.3
DeepAll+MI,AET	80.9	56.9	69.6	67.9	68.8
DiMAE (ours)	**84.7**	**57.2**	**76.3**	69.8	**72.0**

Table 2. Results of In-domain top-1 linear evaluation accuracies on PACS dataset. Results style: **best**, second best.

---

[2] We do not use the widely-used ResNet18 [20] as the backbone, because DiMAE is exactly a generative method, in which Convolutaional networks are not applicable. We choose the ViT-small model for comparison because the number of their model parameters is similar.

4.2   Experimental Results

In-Domain Evaluation. In-Domain Evaluation is proposed by [15], and aims to evaluate the performance of the self-supervised learning methods in the domains that appear in the training set. We exactly follow the protocol of [15]. Specifically, we learn the backbone on the training subset of all domains on PACS in a self-supervised manner, and then linearly train a classifier for each domain using the training subset of each domain with the backbone fixed, respectively. We evaluate our model on the validation subset in each domain, and report the averaged results by 10 runs. The experimental results are summarized in Tab. 2. DiMAE outperforms MoCo V3 and MAE by **+14.7%** and **+0.8%**, respectively, showing the superior of in-domain instance discrimination ability against the previous methods. Furthermore, when we compare the baseline generative method, *i.e.*, MAE, with contrastive learning methods, *i.e.*, MoCoV3, we infer that the reconstruction task can learn better representations of the domains that appear in the training set.

Cross-Domain Generalization. Cross-Domain Generalization is firstly proposed by DIUL [45], which evaluates the generalization ability of the self-supervised learning methods to the domains that are missing in the training set. We exactly follow the cross-domain generalization evaluation process in DIUL [45], which is divided into three steps. First, we train our model on source

Method	Label fraction 1%					Label fraction 5%				
	Clipart	Infograph	Quickdraw	Overall	Avg	Clipart	Infograph	Quickdraw	Overall	Avg.
ERM	6.54	2.96	5.00	4.75	4.83	10.21	7.08	5.34	6.81	7.54
MoCo V2 [9]	18.85	10.57	6.32	10.05	11.92	28.13	13.79	9.67	14.56	17.20
SimCLR V2 [8]	23.51	15.42	5.29	11.80	14.74	34.03	17.17	10.88	17.32	20.69
BYOL [17]	6.21	3.48	4.27	4.45	4.65	9.60	5.09	6.02	6.49	6.90
AdCo [22]	16.16	12.26	5.65	9.57	11.36	30.77	18.65	7.75	15.44	19.06
MAE	22.38	12.62	10.50	13.51	15.17	32.60	15.28	13.43	17.85	20.44
DIUL	18.53	10.62	12.65	13.29	13.93	39.32	19.09	10.50	18.73	22.97
DiMAE (ours)	26.52	15.47	15.47	17.72	19.15	42.31	18.87	15.00	21.68	25.39
	Label fraction 10%					Label fraction 100%				
Method	Clipart	Infograph	Quickdraw	Overall	Avg	Clipart	Infograph	Quickdraw	Overall	Avg.
ERM	15.10	9.39	7.11	9.36	10.53	52.79	23.72	19.05	27.19	31.85
MoCo V2	32.46	18.54	8.05	15.92	19.69	64.18	27.44	25.26	33.76	38.96
SimCLR V2	37.11	19.87	12.33	19.45	23.10	68.72	27.60	30.56	37.47	42.29
BYOL	14.55	8.71	5.95	8.46	9.74	54.44	23.70	20.42	28.23	32.86
AdCo	32.25	17.96	11.56	17.53	20.59	62.84	26.69	26.26	33.80	38.60
MAE	51.86	24.81	23.94	29.87	33.54	59.21	28.53	23.27	32.06	37.00
DIUL	35.15	20.88	15.69	21.08	23.91	72.79	32.01	33.75	41.19	46.18
DiMAE (ours)	70.78	38.06	27.39	39.20	45.41	83.87	44.99	39.30	49.96	56.05

Table 3. Results of the cross-domain generalization on DomainNet. All of the models are trained on Painting, Real, Sketch domains of DomainNet and tested on the other three domains. The title of each column indicates the name of the domain used as target. All the models are pretrained for 1000 epochs before finetuned on the labeled data. Results style: **best**, second best.

domains in the unsupervised manner. Then, we will use a small number of labeled training examples of the validation subset in the source domains to finetune the classifier or the whole backbone. In detail, when the fraction of labeled finetuning data is lower than 10% of the whole validation subset in the source domains, we only finetune the linear classifier for all the methods. When the fraction of labeled finetuning data is larger than 10% of the whole validation subset in the source domains, we finetune the whole network, including the backbone and the classifier. Last, we can evaluate the model on the target domains.

The results are presented in Table 3 (DomainNet) and Table 4 (PACS). In this setting, our DiMAE achieves a better performance than previous works on most tasks and gets significant gains over DIUL and other SSL methods on overall and average accuracy[3]. Compared with contrastive learning based methods, such as MoCo V2, SimCLR V2, BYOL, AdCo, our generative based methods improves the cross-domain generalization tasks by +3.98% and +2.42% for DomainNet and +8.07% and +0.23% for PACS on 1% and 5% fraction setting respectively, which is tested by linear evaluation. Our DiMAE also improves other

Method	Label fraction 1%					Label fraction 5%				
	Photo	Art	Cartoon	Sketch	Avg	Photo	Art	Cartoon	Sketch	Avg.
MoCo V2	22.97	15.58	23.65	25.27	21.87	37.39	25.57	28.11	31.16	30.56
SimCLR V2	<u>30.94</u>	17.43	**30.16**	25.20	25.93	**54.67**	35.92	<u>35.31</u>	<u>36.84</u>	40.68
BYOL	11.20	14.53	16.21	10.01	12.99	26.55	17.79	21.87	19.65	21.47
AdCo	26.13	17.11	22.96	23.37	22.39	37.65	28.21	28.52	30.35	31.18
MAE	30.72	<u>23.54</u>	20.78	24.52	24.89	32.69	24.61	27.35	30.44	28.77
DIUL	27.78	19.82	<u>27.51</u>	<u>29.54</u>	<u>26.16</u>	44.61	<u>39.25</u>	**36.41**	36.53	39.20
DiMAE (ours)	**48.86**	**31.73**	25.83	**32.50**	**34.23**	<u>50.00</u>	**41.25**	34.40	**38.00**	40.91
Method	Label fraction 10%					Label fraction 100%				
	Photo	Art	Cartoon	Sketch	Avg	Photo	Art	Cartoon	Sketch	Avg.
MoCo V2	44.19	25.85	33.53	24.97	32.14	59.86	28.58	48.89	34.79	43.03
SimCLR V2	<u>54.65</u>	37.65	46.00	28.25	41.64	67.45	<u>43.60</u>	54.48	34.73	50.06
BYOL	27.01	25.94	20.98	19.69	23.40	41.42	23.73	30.02	18.78	28.49
AdCo	46.51	30.21	31.45	22.96	32.78	58.59	29.81	50.19	30.45	42.26
MAE	35.89	25.59	33.28	<u>32.39</u>	31.79	36.84	25.24	32.25	34.45	32.20
DIUL	53.37	<u>39.91</u>	<u>46.41</u>	30.17	<u>42.47</u>	<u>68.66</u>	41.53	<u>56.89</u>	<u>37.51</u>	<u>51.15</u>
DiMAE (ours)	**77.87**	**59.77**	**57.72**	**39.25**	**58.65**	**78.99**	**63.23**	**59.44**	**55.89**	**64.39**

Table 4. Results of the cross-domain generalization setting on PACS. Given the experiment for each target domain is run respectively, there is no overall accuracy across domains. Thus we report the average accuracy and the accuracy for each domain. The title of each column indicates the name of the domain used as target. All the models are pretrained for 1000 epochs before finetuned on the labeled data. Results style: **best**, <u>second best</u>.

---

[3] Overall and Avg. indicate the overall accuracy of all the test data and the arithmetic mean of the accuracy of 3 domains, respectively. Note that they are different because the capacities of different domains are not equal.

states-of-the-art methods by **+11.87%** and **+9.87%** for DomainNet, **+16.18%** and **+13.24%** for PACS on 10% and 100% fraction setting, respectively, when the whole backbone are finetuned. The significant improvement to contrastive learning based methods illustrate our proposed DiMAE can learn more domain-invariant features in the self-supervised learning from multiple domain data.

4.3   Ablation Study

To investigate the effectiveness of each component of our proposed DiMAE, We ablate our DiMAE on the Cross-Domain Generalization task. Specifically, we train Vit-Tiny [37] for 100 epoches on the combination of Painting, Real, and Sketch training set in DomainNet, and evaluate the model using the linear evaluation protocol on Clipart.

Content-preserved		Content-mix		No aug.
CP-StyleMix	CP-StyleCut	Mixup	CutMix	
48.56	47.21	38.09	37.50	36.85

Table 5. Comparison of using content-preserved methods, content-mix methods, and no augmentation. Aug. is short for augmentation.

Content-preserved augmentation	Top-1
Style transfer [41]	46.11
CP-StyleMix	**48.56**
CP-StyleCut	47.21

Table 6. Comparison of style transfer [41], CP-StyleMix and CP-StyleCut. Aug. is short for augmentation.

Effectiveness of Preserving Contents in Style Mix. To demonstrate the importance of preserving contents in style mix, we ablate the content-preserved and content-mix augmentation methods for DiMAE, which is presented in Table 5. Specifically, we choose CP-StyleMix for content-preserved methods and Mixup and CutMix for content-mixed methods. Additionally, to fairly compare with CutMix, we replace the Mixup step in CP-StyleMix with CutMix, creating a competing method called Content Preserved StyleCut (CP-StyleCut). We conclude that preserving the content information is critical for reconstruction tasks. Specifically, we observe that content-mix methods, *i.e.*, Mixup and CutMix, bring at most **+1.24%** performance improvement compared with no augmentation. However, content preserved style mix methods, *i.e,* CP-StyleMixp and CP-StyleCut, can further improve the content-mix style-mix augmentations, *i.e.,* Mixup and CutMix, by **+10.47%** and **+9.71%**. The large performance gap between content-preserved and content-mix augmentations methods indicates the importance of preserving contents in the reconstruction tasks.

Effectiveness of Mixing Style Information. To illustrate the importance of mixing style information in our proposed DiMAE (Eq. 2), we ablate the mixing step by comparing the experiments where we use the mixed-style view $\mathbf{v}$ in Eq. 2, and the view $\mathbf{v}_i$ before mixing. Here, $\mathbf{v}_i$ is the i-th style view after style transfer (Eq. 1) before Mixup (Eq. 2). As shown in Table 6, after applying Mixup and CutMix on the views after style transfer, the performance further increases by +**2.45**% and +**1.10**%. The consistent improvement indicates that adding more style noise can effectively help the encoder to learn domain-invariant features.

Effectiveness of Multiple Domain-specific Decoders. A novel design of our proposed DiMAE is the domain-specific decoders, which reconstruct corresponding domain-specific images using the encoded latent representation. We ablate this design with all other factors fixed. Experimental results are illustrated in Tab. 7, showing the linear evaluation performance when the single decoder and Domain Specific Decoders are applied. We observe that the methods using domain-specific decoders improve the methods using the single decoder by +**10.47**% and +**9.71**% when images are augmented by CP-StyleMix and CP-StyleCut. The significant performance gap verifies the importance of using domain-specific decodoers in our proposed DiMAE. To explain the performance gap, we argue that this is because domain-specific decoders help to decouple the different style information from different domains to the corresponding decoders, regularizing the encoder to only learn domain-invariant features.

Augmentations	Single decoder	Domain specific decoders
CP-StyleMix	38.09	**48.56**
CP-StyleCut	37.50	**47.21**

Table 7. Comparison of single decoder and domain specific decoders. Domain Specific Decoders achieve significant performance improvement with CP-StyelMix and CP-StyleCut.

Depth	Single decoder	Multi decoders
1	37.46	44.93
2	37.81	45.35
4	38.01	46.62
8	**38.09**	**48.56**
12	37.96	46.11

Table 8. Comparison of different depth of domain specific decoders.

Designs in the Single Decoder and Multiple Domain-Specific Decoders.
Table 8 varies the decoder depth, from which we have two findings. First, we
find the depth of the decoder is also important in our task, because a sufficiently deep decoder can improves the performance by 0.63% and 3.63% in
single and multiple decoders design, respectively. Second, the performance gain
in multi-decoders design (**+3.63%**) is much larger than in single-decoder design
(**+0.63%**), because the depth of decoders can influence the semantic level of
the learned feature, but can not help to regularize the encoder to learn domain-
invariant features, which is crucial in our self-supervised learning from multi-
domain data task.

4.4   Visualization

Feature Distribution Visualization. Qualitatively, Fig. 3 visualizes the feature distribution of MoCo V3, MAE and DiMAE by t-SNE, on the combination
of Painting, Real, and Sketch training set in DomainNet. We observe that the
features of DiMAE between three domains are significantly better mixed than
the others. This suggests that compared with MoCo V3 and MAE, DiMAE is
able to capture better domain-invariant representations.

MoCo V3   MAE   DiMAE

Fig. 3. Visualization of the feature distribution of MoCo V3, MAE and DiMAE.

Reconstruction Visualization. We visualize reconstruction results of DiMAE
using ViT-base in Fig. 4. The results demonstrate that, in our DiMAE, the
encoder removes the domain style and multiple decoders learn specific style
information. Specifically, DiMAE eliminates the style noise on visible patches as
no messy style information appears in reconstructions. Second, DiMAE provides
complete reconstructions with specific domain styles. Third, we also observe that
it is quite hard for DiMAE to recover colors perfectly from sketch inputs.

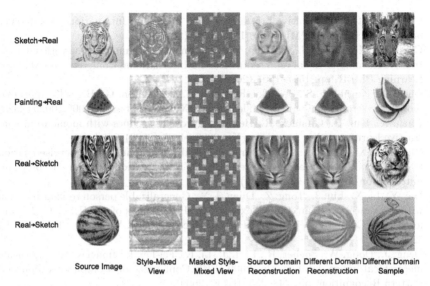

Fig. 4. Reconstruction visualization of different decoders. Sketch→Real denotes using Sketch as source domain and Real as the a different domain to reconstruct.

5   Conclusions

In this paper, we propose a novel Domain invariant Masked AutoEncoder (DiMAE) to tackle the self-supervised learning from multi-domain data. Our DiMAE constructs a new cross-domain reconstruction task with a proposed content preserved style mix and multiple decoder designs to learn domain-invariant features. The content preserved style mix aims to mix style information from different domains, while preserving the image content. The multiple decoders are proposed to regularize the encoder to extract domain-invariant features. Extensive experiments validate the effectiveness of DiMAE.

References

1. Albuquerque, I., Monteiro, J., Darvishi, M., Falk, T.H., Mitliagkas, I.: Generalizing to unseen domains via distribution matching. arXiv preprint arXiv:1911.00804 (2019)
2. Bao, H., Dong, L., Wei, F.: Beit: bert pre-training of image transformers. arXiv preprint arXiv:2106.08254 (2021)
3. Cao, S., Xu, P., Clifton, D.A.: How to understand masked autoencoders. arXiv preprint arXiv:2202.03670 (2022)
4. Carlucci, F.M., D'Innocente, A., Bucci, S., Caputo, B., Tommasi, T.: Domain generalization by solving jigsaw puzzles. In: Proceedings of the IEEE/CVF Conference on Computer Vision and Pattern Recognition, pp. 2229–2238 (2019)
5. Caron, M., et al.: Emerging properties in self-supervised vision transformers. In: Proceedings of the IEEE/CVF International Conference on Computer Vision, pp. 9650–9660 (2021)

6. Chen, M., et al.: Generative pretraining from pixels. In: International Conference on Machine Learning PMLR, pp. 1691–1703 (2020)
7. Chen, T., Kornblith, S., Norouzi, M., Hinton, G.: A simple framework for contrastive learning of visual representations. In: International Conference on Machine Learning PMLR, pp. 1597–1607 (2020)
8. Chen, T., Kornblith, S., Swersky, K., Norouzi, M., Hinton, G.: Big self-supervised models are strong semi-supervised learners. arXiv preprint arXiv:2006.10029 (2020)
9. Chen, X., Fan, H., Girshick, R., He, K.: Improved baselines with momentum contrastive learning. arXiv preprint arXiv:2003.04297 (2020)
10. Chen, X., Xie, S., He, K.: An empirical study of training self-supervised vision transformers. In: Proceedings of the IEEE/CVF International Conference on Computer Vision, pp. 9640–9649 (2021)
11. Dai, Y., Li, X., Liu, J., Tong, Z., Duan, L.Y.: Generalizable person re-identification with relevance-aware mixture of experts. In: Proceedings of the IEEE/CVF Conference on Computer Vision and Pattern Recognition (CVPR), pp. 16145–16154 (2021)
12. Deng, J., Dong, W., Socher, R., Li, L.J., Li, K., Fei-Fei, L.: Imagenet: a large-scale hierarchical image database. In: 2009 IEEE Conference on Computer Vision and Pattern Recognition, pp. 248–255. IEEE (2009)
13. Dosovitskiy, A., et al.: An image is worth 16×16 words: Transformers for image recognition at scale. arXiv preprint arXiv:2010.11929 (2020)
14. Ericsson, L., Gouk, H., Hospedales, T.M.: How well do self-supervised models transfer? In: Proceedings of the IEEE/CVF Conference on Computer Vision and Pattern Recognition, pp. 5414–5423 (2021)
15. Feng, Z., Xu, C., Tao, D.: Self-supervised representation learning from multi-domain data. In: Proceedings of the IEEE/CVF International Conference on Computer Vision, pp. 3245–3255 (2019)
16. Gidaris, S., Singh, P., Komodakis, N.: Unsupervised representation learning by predicting image rotations. arXiv preprint arXiv:1803.07728 (2018)
17. Grill, J.B., et al.: Bootstrap your own latent-a new approach to self-supervised learning. Advances Neural Inf. Process. Syst. **33**, 21271–21284 (2020)
18. He, K., Chen, X., Xie, S., Li, Y., Dollár, P., Girshick, R.: Masked autoencoders are scalable vision learners. arXiv preprint arXiv:2111.06377 (2021)
19. He, K., Fan, H., Wu, Y., Xie, S., Girshick, R.: Momentum contrast for unsupervised visual representation learning. In: Proceedings of the IEEE/CVF Conference on Computer Vision and Pattern Recognition, pp. 9729–9738 (2020)
20. He, K., Zhang, X., Ren, S., Sun, J.: Deep residual learning for image recognition. In: Proceedings of the IEEE Conference on Computer Vision and Pattern Recognition, pp. 770–778 (2016)
21. Hong, M., Choi, J., Kim, G.: Stylemix: separating content and style for enhanced data augmentation. In: Proceedings of the IEEE/CVF Conference on Computer Vision and Pattern Recognition, pp. 14862–14870 (2021)
22. Hu, Q., Wang, X., Hu, W., Qi, G.J.: Adco: adversarial contrast for efficient learning of unsupervised representations from self-trained negative adversaries. In: Proceedings of the IEEE/CVF Conference on Computer Vision and Pattern Recognition, pp. 1074–1083 (2021)
23. Kim, D., Saito, K., Oh, T.H., Plummer, B.A., Sclaroff, S., Saenko, K.: CDS: cross-domain self-supervised pre-training. In: Proceedings of the IEEE/CVF International Conference on Computer Vision, pp. 9123–9132 (2021)

24. Larsson, Gustav, Maire, Michael, Shakhnarovich, Gregory: Learning representations for automatic colorization. In: Leibe, Bastian, Matas, Jiri, Sebe, Nicu, Welling, Max (eds.) ECCV 2016. LNCS, vol. 9908, pp. 577–593. Springer, Cham (2016). https://doi.org/10.1007/978-3-319-46493-0_35

25. Larsson, G., Maire, M., Shakhnarovich, G.: Colorization as a proxy task for visual understanding. In: Proceedings of the IEEE Conference on Computer Vision and Pattern Recognition, pp. 6874–6883 (2017)

26. Li, D., Yang, Y., Song, Y.Z., Hospedales, T.M.: Deeper, broader and artier domain generalization. In: Proceedings of the IEEE International Conference on Computer Vision, pp. 5542–5550 (2017)

27. Li, D., Zhang, J., Yang, Y., Liu, C., Song, Y.Z., Hospedales, T.M.: Episodic training for domain generalization. In: Proceedings of the IEEE/CVF International Conference on Computer Vision, pp. 1446–1455 (2019)

28. Li, H., Pan, S.J., Wang, S., Kot, A.C.: Domain generalization with adversarial feature learning. In: Proceedings of the IEEE Conference on Computer Vision and Pattern Recognition, pp. 5400–5409 (2018)

29. Li, X., Dai, Y., Ge, Y., Liu, J., Shan, Y., Duan, L.: Uncertainty modeling for out-of-distribution generalization. In: International Conference on Learning Representations (2022). https://openreview.net/forum?id=6HN7LHyzGgC

30. Li, Y., et al.: Deep domain generalization via conditional invariant adversarial networks. In: Proceedings of the European Conference on Computer Vision (ECCV), pp. 624–639 (2018)

31. Noroozi, Mehdi, Favaro, Paolo: Unsupervised learning of visual representations by solving Jigsaw puzzles. In: Leibe, Bastian, Matas, Jiri, Sebe, Nicu, Welling, Max (eds.) ECCV 2016. LNCS, vol. 9910, pp. 69–84. Springer, Cham (2016). https://doi.org/10.1007/978-3-319-46466-4_5

32. Pathak, D., Krahenbuhl, P., Donahue, J., Darrell, T., Efros, A.A.: Context encoders: feature learning by inpainting. In: Proceedings of the IEEE Conference on Computer Vision and Pattern Recognition, pp. 2536–2544 (2016)

33. Peng, X., Bai, Q., Xia, X., Huang, Z., Saenko, K., Wang, B.: Moment matching for multi-source domain adaptation. In: Proceedings of the IEEE/CVF International Conference on Computer Vision, pp. 1406–1415 (2019)

34. Rahman, M.M., Fookes, C., Baktashmotlagh, M., Sridharan, S.: Correlation-aware adversarial domain adaptation and generalization. Pattern Recogn. **100**, 107124 (2020)

35. Sariyildiz, M.B., Kalantidis, Y., Larlus, D., Alahari, K.: Concept generalization in visual representation learning. In: Proceedings of the IEEE/CVF International Conference on Computer Vision, pp. 9629–9639 (2021)

36. Tian, Y., Sun, C., Poole, B., Krishnan, D., Schmid, C., Isola, P.: What makes for good views for contrastive learning? arXiv preprint arXiv:2005.10243 (2020)

37. Touvron, H., Cord, M., Douze, M., Massa, F., Sablayrolles, A., Jégou, H.: Training data-efficient image transformers & distillation through attention. In: International Conference on Machine Learning PMLR, pp. 10347–10357 (2021)

38. Wang, Y., et al.: Revisiting the transferability of supervised pretraining: an MLP perspective. arXiv preprint arXiv:2112.00496 (2021)

39. Wang, Z., Loog, M., van Gemert, J.: Respecting domain relations: Hypothesis invariance for domain generalization. In: 2020 25th International Conference on Pattern Recognition (ICPR), pp. 9756–9763. IEEE (2021)

40. Wu, Z., Xiong, Y., Yu, S.X., Lin, D.: Unsupervised feature learning via nonparametric instance discrimination. In: Proceedings of the IEEE Conference on Computer Vision and Pattern Recognition, pp. 3733–3742 (2018)

41. Xu, Q., Zhang, R., Zhang, Y., Wang, Y., Tian, Q.: A fourier-based framework for domain generalization. In: Proceedings of the IEEE/CVF Conference on Computer Vision and Pattern Recognition, pp. 14383–14392 (2021)
42. Yun, S., Han, D., Oh, S.J., Chun, S., Choe, J., Yoo, Y.: Cutmix: regularization strategy to train strong classifiers with localizable features. In: Proceedings of the IEEE/CVF International Conference on Computer Vision, pp. 6023–6032 (2019)
43. Zbontar, J., Jing, L., Misra, I., LeCun, Y., Deny, S.: Barlow twins: self-supervised learning via redundancy reduction. In: International Conference on Machine Learning PMLR, pp. 12310–12320 (2021)
44. Zhang, H., Cisse, M., Dauphin, Y.N., Lopez-Paz, D.: mixup: Beyond empirical risk minimization. In: International Conference on Learning Representations (2018)
45. Zhang, X., Zhou, L., Xu, R., Cui, P., Shen, Z., Liu, H.: Domain-irrelevant representation learning for unsupervised domain generalization. arXiv preprint arXiv:2107.06219 (2021)
46. Zhao, N., Wu, Z., Lau, R.W., Lin, S.: What makes instance discrimination good for transfer learning? arXiv preprint arXiv:2006.06606 (2020)
47. Zhou, K., Yang, Y., Hospedales, T., Xiang, T.: Deep domain-adversarial image generation for domain generalisation. In: Proceedings of the AAAI Conference on Artificial Intelligence, vol. 34, pp. 13025–13032 (2020)
48. Zhu, J., et al.: Complementary relation contrastive distillation. In: 2021 IEEE/CVF Conference on Computer Vision and Pattern Recognition (CVPR), pp. 203–212 (2021)
49. Zhu, J.Y., Park, T., Isola, P., Efros, A.A.: Unpaired image-to-image translation using cycle-consistent adversarial networks. In: Proceedings of the IEEE International Conference on Computer Vision, pp. 2223–2232 (2017)
50. Zhuang, F., et al.: A comprehensive survey on transfer learning. Proc. IEEE **109**(1), 43–76 (2020)

Semi-supervised Object Detection via VC Learning

Changrui Chen[1], Kurt Debattista[1], and Jungong Han[1,2](✉)

[1] University of Warwick, WMG, Coventry, UK
{Changrui.Chen,K.Debattista}@warwick.ac.uk
[2] Computer Science, Aberystwyth University, Wales, UK
juh22@aber.ac.uk

Abstract. Due to the costliness of labelled data in real-world applications, semi-supervised object detectors, underpinned by pseudo labelling, are appealing. However, handling confusing samples is nontrivial: discarding valuable confusing samples would compromise the model generalisation while using them for training would exacerbate the confirmation bias issue caused by inevitable mislabelling. To solve this problem, this paper proposes to use confusing samples proactively without label correction. Specifically, a virtual category (VC) is assigned to each confusing sample such that they can safely contribute to the model optimisation even without a concrete label. It is attributed to specifying the embedding distance between the training sample and the virtual category as the lower bound of the inter-class distance. Moreover, we also modify the localisation loss to allow high-quality boundaries for location regression. Extensive experiments demonstrate that the proposed VC learning significantly surpasses the state-of-the-art, especially with small amounts of available labels.

Keywords: Semi-supervised learning · Object detection

1 Introduction

The Deep Learning community is suffering from the expensive labelling cost of large-scale datasets. Semi-supervised learning, which makes use of limited labelled data combined with large amounts of unlabelled data for training, has shown great potential to reduce the reliance on large amounts of labels [4,22, 25,34]. In particular, this work focuses on object detection, a task that typically requires a significant effort to label, under the semi-supervised setting, especially with extremely small amounts of labelled data.

Pseudo labelling [11], one of the most advanced methods in semi-supervised learning, has been recently introduced to semi-supervised object detection (SSOD) [25,40,41,43]. Unlabelled data are automatically annotated by the detector itself [35] (or an exponential moving average version [25]) and then fed back to re-optimise the detector. Typically, due to the limited diversity of

© The Author(s), under exclusive license to Springer Nature Switzerland AG 2022
S. Avidan et al. (Eds.): ECCV 2022, LNCS 13691, pp. 169–185, 2022.
https://doi.org/10.1007/978-3-031-19821-2_10

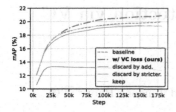
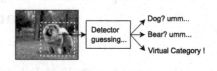

Fig. 1. Left: The mAP of a semi-supervised detector [25] with a preset confidence score filtering on 1% labelled MS COCO [44]. The mAP sees a decrease with all strategies for dealing with confusing samples (*e.g.*, the bear-like dog at the right) except for our VC learning. The additional filtering mechanism (add.) is the temporal stability verification proposed in this paper. Stricter filtering (stricter.) is simply raising the threshold in the score filtering from 0.7 to 0.8. Right: Illustration of the basic idea of our virtual category.

samples in a extremely small available set of labelled data, the detector is usually unable to make a confident decision on some unseen confusing samples when inferring their pseudo labels. Two strategies are usually adopted in SSOD to deal with the confusing samples: a) discarding all of them by a strict filtering mechanism [35], or b) retaining them with all potential labels [41]. However, none of these two options is optimal. Admittedly, the value of confusing hard samples is clear to see, since hard example mining [33] has successfully proven its effectiveness in fully-supervised learning. If all confusing samples are rejected by a strict filtering mechanism in SSOD, their positive contributions will be wasted, while the remaining well-fitted samples only marginally contribute to performance improvements. On the contrary, simply keeping them all does not work either due to the involvement of too many incorrect pseudo labels. Arbitrarily optimising semi-supervised detectors with these noisy labels will lead to the confirmation bias issue [2]. To demonstrate these points, we show in Fig. 1 the mean Average Precision (mAP) of a semi-supervised detector with different strategies on 1% labelled MS COCO [44]. We observe noticeable performance degradations when either choosing one stricter filtering mechanism (orange line) or adding an additional filtering (green line) to reject confusing samples. Likewise, simply keeping all pseudo labels of confusing samples (yellow line) also ends up with a decreased mAP since the unreliable pseudo labels aggravate the confirmation bias issue and even give rise to training collapse.

Therefore, efforts are dedicated to exploring how to correct the biased pseudo labels to utilise the confusing samples without any risks. Existing methods [22,38] initially investigate relatively easy tasks such as classification on CIFAR [18]. However, progress has not yet been made for a complex task, such as object detection with extremely small amounts of labelled data, due to its difficulty in correcting object pseudo labels. Then, a question arises: *what if we do not discard any confusing samples but consider their contributions, which may not necessarily need the concrete label information, during the model training?* This paper answers this question by proposing a novel Virtual Category

(VC) learning, based on an observation that the confusing samples with doubtful pseudo labels can be profitable for training.

Specifically, we discover that building a potential category (PC) set consisting of the possible categories of a confusing sample x, compared to determining the exactly correct label for it, seems more feasible. Therefore, instead of selecting the correct one from the PC set, which is usually hard, we compromise by proposing a virtual category label to *take the place of all unreliable labels in the PC set*. As shown in the example of the right part of Fig. 1, the PC set of this object consists of two categories (*i.e.*, dog and bear). A new modified Cross Entropy loss function, namely VC loss, allows the detector to be optimised with the virtual category label. By doing so, ignoring the categories in the PC set will disable the corresponding output logits, thus avoiding any wrong gradients to mislead the model optimisation. Most importantly, the proposed virtual category specifies a reasonable lower bound for the inter-class distance. Hence, the decision boundary can consistently benefit from the confusing data without suffering from the confirmation bias issue. With regards to the PC set, we investigate multiple methods to build it, including temporal stability verification and cross-model verification. As can be seen in Fig. 1, the mAP of the model armed with the proposed VC loss (dot-dashed line) sees a significant increase due to the effective use of the confusing samples. Furthermore, we also enhance localisation training by decoupling the horizontal and vertical location qualities of a pseudo bounding box, which enables us to use the high-quality boundaries to optimise the bounding box regression head.

We apply our VC learning to a semi-supervised detector and evaluate it on MS COCO [44] and Pascal VOC [13] datasets with extremely low label ratios, including 0.5%, 1%, 2%, 5% and 10%. On MS COCO, our method achieves 19.46 mAP with only 586 labelled images; this outperforms some recently published semi-supervised detectors [35,43] with 1000+ labelled images. The contributions of this paper are summarised as follows:

- We propose VC learning to alleviate the confirmation bias issue caused by confusing samples in SSOD. The proposed method takes the initiative to use confusing samples with unreliable pseudo labels for the first time.
- A detailed explanation of the VC learning is provided to demonstrate the mathematical feasibility and intuitive effect. Our intriguing findings highlight the need to rethink the usage of confusing samples in SSOD tasks.
- We demonstrate how the proposed method surpasses state-of-the-arts by a significant margin on two benchmark datasets with different label ratios.

2   Related Works

Object Detection aims to distinguish foreground objects in images or videos and identify them. Object detectors so far can be divided into three types: 1) Two-stage detectors [7,31], represented by Faster RCNN [31]; 2) One-stage detectors [24,42], such as the YOLO series [6,30]; and 3) Point-based Detectors [12,21,37], such as Center Net [12]. The main difference between two-stage and one-stage detectors lies in whether an additional module is used to generate candidate region proposals. Point-based detectors discard anchor boxes and instead use points and sizes to represent objects. In this paper, Faster RCNN, one of the most widely used detectors, serves as our baseline model.

Semi-supervised Learning is a training scheme that uses only a very small amount of labelled data and a large amount of unlabelled data to train a machine learning model. Recently proposed semi-supervised methods mainly focus on image classification [4,34]. Consistency regularisation is one of the most advanced methods. It requires models to produce consistent outputs when the inputs are perturbed. Image augmentations, such as flipping, Cutout [10], or Gaussian Blurring, are usually applied to perturb inputs [3,20]. Some solutions take advantage of adversarial learning and proposed learnable adversarial augmentations [27]. Inspired by the noisy label learning method [17], negative sampling [8] improved the performance of semi-supervised algorithms by randomly sampling a non-target label for an unlabelled data. Alternatively, Pseudo labelling [11], which is used in this paper, is another semi-supervised technique that has proven successful. It minimises the entropy of the predictions of unlabelled data by generating pseudo labels for them.

Semi-supervised Object Detection (SSOD) originates from semi-supervised classification, where only a small amount of bounding box labelled data and numerous unlabelled data are available for training a detector. Most of the recently proposed SSOD methods can be broadly categorised into two different types: 1) consistency-based and 2) self-supervised (pseudo-labelling) methods. Consistency-based semi-supervised object detectors, such as CSD-SSD [19], when dealing with unlabelled images, apply consistency regularisation on the predicted classification probability vectors and regression vectors of the input image and its mirror version. Alternatively, self-supervised detectors [25,35,41,43] were inspired by the pseudo-labelling classifier. Although the self-supervised detectors show good potential, they are struggling with the confirmation bias when training with confusing samples. This paper alleviates this issue via VC learning.

3   Methodology

In this section, the overall problem is first defined. The VC learning and its explanation are subsequently described.

3.1   Problem Definition

In SSOD, two data subsets $\mathcal{D}^l$ and $\mathcal{D}^u$ are given for model optimisation, where $\mathcal{D}^l = \{(x_n^l, b_n^l)|_{n=0}^{N^l}\}$ is the subset with available ground truth bounding box b^l, $\mathcal{D}^u = \{x_n^u|_{n=0}^{N^u}\}$ is the unlabelled subset. N^l and N^u are the number of labelled and unlabelled data. Usually, $N^u \gg N^l$. $b = [x_1, y_1, x_2, y_2, cls]$ is the label – bounding box, where the first 4 numbers indicate the coordinates of the top-left and bottom-right points and cls is the index of the category label. This

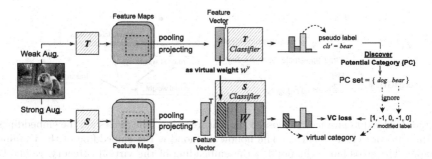

Fig. 2. The pipeline of the VC learning when dealing with a confusing sample. The regression branch is ignored for simplicity. T and S represent the teacher and student model. The black dashed line box on feature maps indicates the pseudo label position. When training the student classifier with a RPN-generated proposal box (pink dashed box in the figure) assigned to this pseudo label, the weight matrix W of the student classifier is extended by a virtual weight w^v, which is transformed from the teacher feature vector $\hat{f}$ of the pseudo label area. (Color figure online)

paper follows the self-supervised framework with a score filtering mechanism [25] to generate pseudo labels b' of x^u. As shown in Fig. 2, two detectors T and S sharing the same architecture are introduced. The parameters of the teacher detector T are updated by the parameters of the student S with a momentum.

3.2   Virtual Category Learning

In Fig. 2, the teacher classifier produces the categorical probability of the candidate object (black dashed box in Fig. 2) according to the pooled and projected feature vector $\hat{f}$ of it. Typically, the category with the highest probability, *e.g.*, $cls' = bear$ here, will then be used as the pseudo label of the candidate proposal box assigned to this instance during the student training. However, incorrect pseudo labels may mislead the training.

In this paper, we propose VC learning which modifies the pseudo category label with an additional virtual category to allow the student model to be optimised safely by confusing samples. Once the initial pseudo label $cls' = bear$ is obtained, a potential category (PC) discovery operation is performed to construct a PC set $\{dog, bear\}$ for this training sample. We find that PC discovery is relatively feasible compared to designing a correction function: $g(cls'|f) = GT$, especially when the labelled subset $\mathcal{D}^l$ is much smaller than $\mathcal{D}^u$. The discovery function will be introduced in the following Sect. 3.3.

If the PC set contains more than one category, it means that this sample is confusing to the detector. In Fig. 2, the bear-like dog is a confusing sample with $PC\,set = \{dog, bear\}$. To allow all the proposal boxes (*e.g.*, pink dashed box in Fig. 2) assigned to this bear-like dog consistently contribute to the optimisation of the student detector S rather than arbitrarily discarding them, the weight matrix W in the student classifier is extended by an additional weight vector w^v

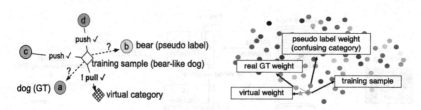

Fig. 3. left) Explanation of VC loss in the feature space. The circles are the embeddings of the category cluster centres. The hollow diamond is the embedding of the training sample. The cross-hatch diamond is the embedding of the virtual category. right) T-SNE visualisation of the virtual weight (star), learned classifier weights (circles), and a training sample (diamond).

named *virtual weight*. The virtual weight w^v is obtained from the feature vector $\hat{f}$, which is the feature of this confusing sample in the teacher model. Thus, the virtual weights for different confusing samples are different. The normalisation and scaling are applied to $\hat{f}$ to ensure the norm of the produced w^v and the norm of the weight vectors in W are in the same range. We investigate two scaling factors, *i.e.*, a constant value and an adaptive factor calculated by averaging the norm of all the weight vectors in W. With the extended weight matrix, the size of the student classifier output (*i.e.*, logits) is therefore increased by 1:

$$f^\top \cdot \overbrace{[w^v, w^{c_0}, ..., w^{c_{N-1}}]}^{1+N} = \overbrace{[l^v, l^{c_0}, ..., l^{c_{N-1}}]}^{1+N}, \tag{1}$$

where N is the number of the predefined categories, l^v and l^{c_i} are the logits of the virtual category and the class c_i respectively. To calculate the loss value of the extended logits, the one-hot label is modified by providing a positive label '1' for the virtual category. Thanks to the virtual category taking on the responsibility of being the target category, the confusing categories in the PC set can be ignored (indicated by '−1' in Fig. 2), thereby avoiding any possible misleading as we can hardly determine which one is the real ground truth.

Explanation. How the proposed VC learning works can be interpreted from both the feature space aspect and the mathematical feasibility.

   In the feature space, as shown in Fig. 3 left, let the circles indicate the centres of the predefined categories. Pulling the training sample (diamond) to the circles a or b is risky since we don't know which one is the real ground truth. Given the virtual category, the decision boundary can still be optimised with VC learning, as the virtual category providing a safe optimising direction: pushing the training sample away from the circles c and d and pulling it closer to the diamond of the virtual category. Although one may suspect that our approach looks similar to the contrastive learning [9,15] in terms of the optimisation target, they differ in several aspects. Firstly, contrastive learning operates before the task-relevant layer (*i.e.*, the classifier). As a result, it only drives the backbone to extract better features but contributes nothing to the task-relevant layer. While our approach acts after the classifier so that the gradient of virtual category can backpropagate to not only the backbone but also the weight vectors in the classifier. Secondly, the weight vectors of the other categories in the classifier naturally constitute negative samples such that there is no need to maintain a negative sample pool, which has been a worrying bottleneck for contrastive learning. Fig. 3 right presents the T-SNE [26] visualisation of the weight vectors w^{c_i} in the trained classifier, and the virtual weight w^v and the feature f of a sample. Our virtual category is clearly a better training target compared to the pseudo labels, which is in line with the feature space aspect explanation.

To explain our method from the mathematical aspect, we first define the VC loss starting from the cross entropy (CE) loss. We abbreviate the category c_i by its index i in the following. Assuming a batch size of 1, the CE loss is:

$$\mathcal{L}_{CE} = -log(\frac{e^{f^\top \cdot w^{i=GT}}}{\sum_{i=0}^{N} e^{f^\top \cdot w^i}}) = log(\sum_{i=0}^{N} e^{l^i - l^{GT}}), \tag{2}$$

where $f \in \mathbb{R}^{channel \times 1}$ is the input feature vector of the last linear layer (*i.e.*, classifier), $w^i \in \mathbb{R}^{channel \times 1}$ is the corresponding weight vector of the category c_i in the last linear layer, $l^i = f^\top \cdot w^i$ is the logit of the category c_i, N is the number of the predefined categories, and GT is the index of the ground truth. Here, we ignore the bias in the last linear layer for simplicity. With Eq. (1), the VC loss can be defined as follows according to Eq. (2):

$$\mathcal{L}_{VC} = log(\sum_{i=0, i \notin PC}^{N+1} e^{l^i - l^v}), \tag{3}$$

where PC is the PC set. $i = N$ indicates the virtual category and $l^{i=N} = l^v$. $i \notin PC$ means the uncertain potential categories in the PC set are ignored.

The intuitive target of minimising CE loss is to get a large logit l^{GT} of the ground truth and small values for the rest of the categories $l^{i \neq GT}$. In a self-supervised scheme, the pseudo classification label cls' of a unlabelled data x_u is generated by the model itself or the EMA (Exponential Moving Average) model. As Eq. (2) can be a smooth approximation of the *max* function [32] (explanation without the approximation and more details are in the supplementary document), the CE loss with the pseudo label cls' can be expressed as:

$$\mathcal{L}_{CE} = log(\sum_{i=0}^{N} e^{l^i - l^{cls'}}) \approx max_{i \in \{0, ..., N-1\}} (l^i - l^{cls'}), \tag{4}$$

minimising Eq. (4) is expected to satisfy:

$$(l^{i \neq cls'} - l^{cls'}) \leq (l^{i=cls'} - l^{cls'}) \triangleq 0, \quad i.e., \quad l^{i \neq cls'} \leq l^{cls'}. \tag{5}$$

Since cls' may not always be correct, when cls' is not equal to the real ground truth GT, satisfying Eq. (5) leads to $l^{GT} \leq l^{cls'}$, thereby aggravating the issue typically termed confirmation bias.

However, for VC loss, following the derivation of Eq. (4), we get:

$$\mathcal{L}_{VC} = log(\sum_{i=0, i \notin PC}^{N+1} e^{l^i - l^v}) \approx max_{i \in \{0,...,N\} \setminus PC}(l^i - l^v). \qquad (6)$$

Similar to Eq. (5), minimising Eq. (6) is expecting:

$$(l^{i \neq v \wedge i \notin PC} - l^v) \leq (l^{i=v} - l^v) \triangleq 0, \quad i.e., \quad l^{i \neq v \wedge i \notin PC} \leq l^v. \qquad (7)$$

Comparing Eq. (7) with Eq. (5) reveals:

1. $\mathcal{L}_{VC}$ firstly ignores the logits $l^{i \in PC}$ of the confusing categories in the PC set when satisfying Eq. (7), thereby avoiding misleading the training.
2. Additionally, it provides an alternative upper bound $l^v = f^\top \cdot w^v$ for all the rest logits $l^{i \notin PC}$. As before-mentioned, w^v is the normalised and scaled feature vector $\hat{f}$ according to the length (norm of the vector) of the weight vectors w^i. The directions of w^v and all the w^i can represent the information of different categories [29]. The $l^v = f^\top \cdot w^v$ should be larger since w^v are obtained by $\hat{f}$ which is the feature in the teacher of the exactly same object of feature f. The shared information between f and $\hat{f}$ should be the most. Thus, l^v can be a meaningful upper bound for all the rest logits $l^{i \notin PC}$.

3.3   Potential Category Set

Two methods are explored in this paper to discover the potential category.

a. Temporal stability

It is observed that the pseudo label set $\mathcal{B}'$ of an image varies at different training iteration steps [41]. As shown in Fig. 4, by comparing $\mathcal{B}'$ at different training steps, those changed pseudo labels reveal the potential categories. We select $\mathcal{B}'$ of the current iteration step and $\mathcal{B}'_{last}$ generated when the model viewed the current image the last time for the comparison. Specifically, for one pseudo label $b' \in \mathcal{B}' \cup \mathcal{B}'_{last}$, if there is any pseudo label $\hat{b}' \in \mathcal{B}' \cup \mathcal{B}'_{last}$ that is close to b' and $b'_{cls} = \hat{b}'_{cls}$, no confusion will be recorded. Otherwise, if there is a nearby $\hat{b}'$ but $b'_{cls} \neq \hat{b}'_{cls}$, $PCset = \{b'_{cls}, \hat{b}'_{cls}\}$. No nearby pseudo label box means that the confusing category is 'background', thus $PCset = \{b'_{cls}, bg\}$. The IoU is adopted to determine whether two pseudo bounding boxes are close enough or not.

b. Cross-model verification

Inspired by the Co-training algorithm [5], comparing the predictions of two conditionally independent models for the same sample can also help to discover the potential category. Two detectors are initialised with different initial parameters. The orders of the training data for these two detectors are also different, ensuring that they will not collapse onto each other. For a pseudo bounding box b'_1 from the detector-1, we use the detector-2 to re-determine the object in the region of b'_1. The decision of the detector-2 is represented by b'_2. Similar to the temporal stability verification, if $b'_{cls_1} = b'_{cls_2}$, the PC set contains only one category b'_{cls_1} (or b'_{cls_2}). Otherwise, $PCset = \{b'_{cls_1}, b'_{cls_2}\}$.

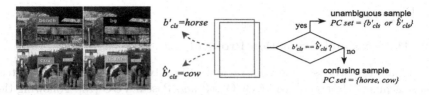

Fig. 4. Left: Examples of the confusing samples found by the temporal stability verification. Right: By comparing the current predictions (blue) with the last predictions (red) of the sample, the PC set should be {horse, cow}. (Color figure online)

In summary, for the classification training, If the size of the PC set is not equal to 1, it means that this sample should be a confusing sample. The VC loss will take over the training of this confusing sample.

3.4 Localisation Loss

Since the classification confidence score is not qualified to indicate the location quality of pseudo labels, some of the previous works [25,35] disabled the localisation loss of unlabelled data. We find that the creating method for the PC set can also measure the location quality of pseudo labels. When we create the PC set for a pseudo box b, we evaluate its location shift with the nearby box $\hat{b}$. We propose to decouple the horizontal and vertical boundary quality instead of using the IoU as a comprehensive metric to filter out the whole bounding box with low IoU value. The reason is that the IoU value can be affected by one biased boundary, even if the remaining boundaries are good. The horizontal quality flag q_{hor} is calculated as:

$$q_{hor} = \begin{cases} 1, \frac{(x_1 - \hat{x}_1)}{w} < t_{loc} \ \& \ \frac{(x_2 - \hat{x}_2)}{w} < t_{loc} \\ 0, otherwise \end{cases} , \quad (8)$$

where $x_1, x_2, \hat{x}_1, \hat{x}_2$ are the coordinates of the left and right boundary of the pseudo box b and the nearby box $\hat{b}$, w is the width of b, t_{loc} is the threshold for high-quality boundaries. q_{ver} is calculated in the same way.

The decoupling allows high-quality boundaries to contribute to the localisation training. For example, the regression of the left and right boundary can be trained when the horizontal boundary quality is satisfied, even the top and bottom boundaries are biased. The localisation loss of four Smooth-L1 [14] terms:

$$\mathcal{L}_{reg^*} = q_{hor}\mathcal{L}^x + q_{ver}\mathcal{L}^y + q_{hor}\mathcal{L}^w + q_{ver}\mathcal{L}^h. \quad (9)$$

In summary, the overall loss function is:

$$\mathcal{L} = \mathcal{L}_{CE}(\mathcal{D}_l) + \mathcal{L}_{reg}(\mathcal{D}_l) + \lambda(\mathcal{L}_{VC}(\mathcal{D}_u) + \mathcal{L}_{reg^*}(\mathcal{D}_u)), \quad (10)$$

where λ is the weight for the loss of the unlabelled data. In the implementation, we also use the VC loss function to handle the unambiguous samples by only ignoring the index of the virtual category.

4   Experiments

4.1   Datasets and Evaluation Protocol

To evaluate the proposed method, we assess it on two well-known object detection benchmark datasets – MS COCO [44] and Pascal VOC [13]. Following the mainstream evaluation setting, we use the subset index provided by Unbiased Teacher [25] to split the *train set* across five different labelled ratios: 0.5%, 1%, 2%, 5% and 10% (each ratio are with five random seeds to get the averaged mAP). We also report the performance on Pascal VOC with *VOC07-trainval* as the labelled subset and *VOC12-trainval* as the unlabelled subset. The performance is evaluated on *VOC07-test*. The evaluation metric of all the experiments reported in this paper is mAP calculated via the COCO evaluation kit [1].

4.2   Implementation

The proposed method is implemented in PyTorch framework [28]. Following the mainstream choice of the community, we adopted Faster-RCNN [31] with FPN [23] and ResNet-50 [16] as the object detector. The weight term in Focal Loss [24] is also integrated into our VC loss to address the class imbalance issue.

The training is operated on 8 GPUs with batch size 1/4 per GPU for labelled/unlabelled data. The training iteration is 180k including a warmup of 2k steps with only the labelled subset. The optimiser is SGD with a constant $lr = 0.01$. The default scaling factor for the virtual weight is a constant 3.5. The location quality threshold t_{loc} in $\mathcal{L}_{reg^*}$ is 0.05. The default PC set creating method is the temporal stability verification. More details are introduced in the supplementary. The code can be found at: https://github.com/GeoffreyChen777/VC.

4.3   Performance

MS COCO. We first evaluate our method on MS COCO with five label ratios. The 5 seeds averaged results are reported in Table 1. 'Ours' is our method with exactly the same settings of the solid baseline Unbiased Teacher for the sake of fairness. 'Ours*' is obtained with some training tricks adopted by Soft Teacher. Results with † are obtained from the available official code. The significant improvements can be summarised as follows:

1) Compared with the supervised baseline, the mAP increases dramatically after training with the unlabelled data via our method.
2) Our method outperforms other state-of-the-art semi-supervised detectors on all the label ratios by a significant margin. The mAP of our method at a small label ratio is close to or even exceeds the mAP of some methods at a large ratio.

Pascal VOC. We also evaluate our method with VOC07 as the labelled subset and VOC12 and COCO* as the unlabelled subsets. We collect the images

Table 1. The performance on MS COCO with different label ratios. Results with †
are obtained from the available official code. Ours is the results of the exactly same
settings of Unbiased Teacher for the sake of fairness. Ours* is the results obtained by
using some training tricks in Soft Teacher.

COCO label ratio	0.5%	1%	2%	5%	10%
Supervised	6.83	9.05	12.70	18.47	23.86
CSD [19]	7.41	10.51	13.93	18.63	22.46
STAC [35]	9.78	13.97	18.25	24.38	28.64
Instant teaching [43]	–	18.05	22.45	26.75	30.40
Interactive [41]	–	18.88	22.43	26.37	30.53
Humble teacher [36]	–	16.96	21.72	27.70	31.61
Combating noise [39]	–	18.41	24.00	28.96	32.43
Soft teacher [40]	15.04†	20.46	25.93†	30.74	34.04
Unbiased teacher [25]	16.94	20.75	24.30	28.27	31.50
Ours	18.12	21.61	25.84	30.31	33.45
Ours*	**19.46**	**23.86**	**27.70**	**32.05**	**34.82**

Table 2. Experiment results on VOC. $\mathcal{D}^l$ and $\mathcal{D}^u$ are the labelled and unlabelled
subset choices. COCO* consists of the images from COCO that contains objects in
VOC categories. Numbers in () are obtained with the VOC-style AP.

Method $\mathcal{D}^l$ $\mathcal{D}^u$	VOC07	
	VOC12	VOC12 + COCO*
STAC [35]	44.64	46.01
Instant teaching [43]	50.00	50.80
Interactive [41]	46.23	49.59
Humble teacher [36]	53.04	54.41
Combating noise [39]	49.30	50.20
Unbiased teacher [25]	48.69	50.34
Ours	**50.40 (55.74)**	**51.44 (56.70)**

that contain objects in VOC predefined categories from MS COCO to build a subset *COCO**. The results are presented in Table 2. Since the source codes of some methods are unavailable, the evaluation styles they used is unclear. *Usually, the Results Based on the VOC-style AP are Higher.* Thus, we evaluate our method with COCO-style mAP and VOC-style AP for the sake of fairness. Our method presents the best performance on these two unlabelled data subsets. Since VOC07 consists of more than 5K labelled images, and it is a relatively easy dataset, Table 2 indicates that our method can effectively further improve the performance, even if there is already sufficient labelled data. The similar conclusion can be drawn when we use the unlabelled COCO-additional and fully-labelled COCO-standard to validate our method (analysised in the supplementary).

4.4   Analysis and Ablation Study

In this section, we choose 1% data of MS COCO as the labelled subset to analyse and validate our method in detail. All the experiments in this section are performed under the exactly same setting of the baseline model Unbiased Teacher except from the batch size. We adopt a smaller batch size to shorten the training time of each ablation study, therefore resulting in slightly decreased mAPs of all experiments compared to Table 1.

Analysis of Virtual Category. Here, we adopt the temporal stability verification to create the PC set for confusing samples. To analyse the effectiveness of the virtual category, we respectively report the mAP of the model under three policies: a) discarding all confusing samples (discard), b) retaining all potential labels for them (keep) and c) assigning our virtual category to replace the potential categories (VC). The baseline model is trained with vanilla pseudo labels (baseline) without the potential category discovery. As shown in Table 3, both discarding and retaining policies decrease the mAP. By analysing the mAP

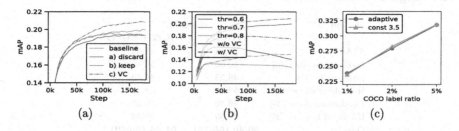

(a)   (b)   (c)

Fig. 5. a) Experiments of different strategies for dealing with confusing samples. As the pseudo labels of the valuable confusing samples are highly unreliable, it is not optimal to either discard or keep them. Our VC learning(dotdashed line) satisfies both demands, thereby resulting in a significant improvement. b) Experiments of different thresholds of the confidence score filtering w/ or w/o our VC learning. c) Comparison of the adaptive and the constant scaling factor. (Color figure online)

during the whole training presented in Fig. 5a, we noticed that rejecting the confusing samples (blue line) results in a low mAP at the very beginning of the training. The reason is that using this policy discards some confusing samples with correct pseudo labels that the model desperately needs. Then, as shown by the green line in Fig. 5a, training with all PCs gives a small performance boost at the early stage of training because more underfitted samples are introduced to the model, but ends up with a low mAP. We believe this is due to the confirmation bias issue caused by incorrect pseudo labels that gradually hurts the performance. Our approach effectively resolves this conflict by providing a virtual category for the confusing sample. The dotdashed line in Fig. 5a demonstrates that these confusing samples consistently benefit the model. The mAP sees a rise of 0.81 with our VC learning. The model with our VC learning exceeds the baseline early in the training and continues to lead until the end of training.

In addition, as can be seen from Fig. 5b, we evaluate our VC learning with different thresholds (indicated by three colours) of the confidence score filtering adopted by our baseline model Unbiased Teacher. The confusing samples always exist, no matter whether the filtering mechanism is strict or not. The model with VC learning (dot-dashed lines) outperforms the baseline (solid lines) on three thresholds. Notably, the slump in the mAP disappears when $thr = 0.6$, meaning that the confirmation bias has been effectively alleviated.

The constant and adaptive scaling factors of the virtual weight are compared in Fig. 5c. The constant 3.5 achieves a mAP which is comparable to the adaptive factor. Interestingly, we discover that $\frac{1}{ada.factor} \approx 3.5$.

Table 3. Validation mAP with different strategies for dealing with the confusing samples.

Strategies	mAP
Baseline	20.00
a) Discard	19.37
b) Keep	19.36
c) VC	**20.81**

Table 4. Ablation study on VC loss and modified localisation loss Reg* Loss. The creating method for the potential category set in VC learning is temporal stability verification.

VC loss	Reg* Loss	mAP
		20.00
√		20.81
√	√	**20.94**

Ablation Study. The overall ablation study is reported in Table 4. The model with VC learning and Reg* Loss performs favourably against the baseline model.

a. Creating methods of potential category set: Sect. 3.3 explored two methods to create the PC set. We validate them and report the results in Table 5b. The cross-model verification achieves the best performance. The reason is that The cross-model verification is similar to the co-training technique which uses two independent models to provide pseudo labels for each other it slightly alleviates the confirmation bias issue, thus resulting in additional improvement. As shown in Table 5b, the co-training can improve the mAP by 0.53 individually. In fairness to other methods without co-training, we use the temporal stability verification in all other experiments, although the cross-model verification performs better.

Table 5. Ablation study: a) different image augmentation for virtual weights generation, b) different methods for creating the PC. We also report the performance with only co-training techniques. c) SC. is the scaling factor of the virtual weight. d) t_{loc} is the threshold of the location quality.

(a)		(b)		(c)		(d)	
Aug.	mAP	Methods	mAP	SC.	mAP	t_{loc}	mAP
none	20.80	baseline	20.00	2.5	20.63	0.03	20.92
flipping	**20.81**	Temporal	20.81	3.5	20.81	0.05	20.94
strong aug.	20.70	Cross	**20.96**	4.5	20.65	0.1	20.31
		co-training only	20.53				

b. Augmentation of the virtual weights: We choose the feature vector from the teacher model to produce the virtual weight. It is natural to validate different augmentations for the input image of the teacher model to generate various virtual weights. We explore three different settings: no augmentation, horizontal flipping, and strong augmentation. The results are reported in Table 5a. No performance gap can be observed between no augmentation and only horizontal flip. Training with the virtual weight generated by the strong augmentation slightly degrades the mAP. The possible reason is that the strong augmentation, especially the cutout, significantly perturbs the input image. Thus, in the feature space, the direction of the virtual weight is far away from the weight vector of the GT category.

c. Hyperparameters: The scaling factor ensures the norm of the virtual weight is in the similar range of the rest weight vectors. In addition to the adaptive version, we investigate the different constant scaling factor values here. The results (w/o $\mathcal{L}_{reg*}$) are reported in Table 5c. $SC. = 3.5$ achieves the best mAP. The ablation study of the location quality threshold t_{loc} in the $\mathcal{L}_{reg*}$ are shown in Table 5d. A higher threshold will retain more unstable boundaries, thereby leading to worse performance.

5   Discussion

In this section, we discuss the limitations and potential of VC learning. The VC loss takes over the optimisation of the confusing samples. Thus, higher quality of the PC set yields more improvement. The proposed creating methods are straightforward and easy to implement. Although a significant increment in mAP was observed already, there is still room to further boost the mAP with a better PC set. The mAP would increase from 20.81 to 24.10 if we were to use the ground truth to create the PC set under the setting of 1% labelled COCO. Generating a better PC set can be worth exploring in the future. Moreover, by comparing the mAP gains of 10% and other small label ratios, the improvement of our method is slightly lower, but still remains first. This phenomenon is expected and reasonable. On the one hand, more labelled data means a better baseline detector. Thus, the room between the baseline and the fully-supervised upper bound is smaller. On the other hand, less unlabelled data and a better detector indicate the confusing samples are fewer. At the extreme, with 100% labelled data, our VC learning will be applied to no sample, thereby resulting in no improvement. Notably, this scenario is not the topic of this paper. We focus on the situation with very few labelled data.

6   Conclusion

This paper proposed VC learning, which exploits the confusing underfitted unlabelled data. We provide a virtual category label to a sample if its pseudo label is unreliable. It allows the model to be safely trained with confusing data for further improvement to achieve state-of-the-art performance. To the best of our knowledge, VC learning is the first method to positively utilise confusing samples in SSOD rather than discarding them. It can also serve as a stepping stone to future work for the community of other semi-supervised learning tasks.

Acknowledgments. We thank China Scholarship Council for the funding. We also thank anonymous reviewers for their comments.

References

1. Coco evaluation kit by facebook detectron2. https://github.com/facebook research/detectron2/blob/main/detectron2/evaluation/coco_evaluation.py
2. Arazo, E., Ortego, D., Albert, P., Connor, N.E.O., McGuinness, K.: Pseudo-labeling and confirmation bias in deep semi-supervised learning. In: 2020 International Joint Conference on Neural Networks (IJCNN), pp. 1–8 (2020)
3. Bachman, P., Alsharif, O., Precup, D.: Learning with pseudo-ensembles. In: NeurIPS **27** (2014)
4. Berthelot, D., Carlini, N., Goodfellow, I.J., Papernot, N., Oliver, A., Raffel, C.: Mixmatch - a holistic approach to semi-supervised learning. In: NeurIPS (2019)
5. Blum, A., Mitchell, T.M.: Combining labeled and unlabeled data with co-training. In: COLT, pp. 92–100 (1998)
6. Bochkovskiy, A., Wang, C.Y., Liao, H.Y.M.: Yolov4 - optimal speed and accuracy of object detection. arXiv (2020)
7. Cai, Z., Vasconcelos, N.: Cascade R-CNN- delving into high quality object detection. In: CVPR, pp. 6154–6162 (2018)
8. Chen, J., Shah, V., Kyrillidis, A.: Negative sampling in semi-supervised learning. In: International Conference on Machine Learning (ICML), pp. 1704–1714 (2020)

9. Chen, T., Kornblith, S., Norouzi, M., Hinton, G.E.: A simple framework for contrastive learning of visual representations. In: ICML, pp. 1597–1607 (2020)
10. DeVries, T., Taylor, G.W.: Improved regularization of convolutional neural networks with cutout. arXiv (2017)
11. Dong-Hyun, L.: Pseudo-label : The simple and efficient semi-supervised learning method for deep neural networks. In: Workshop on Challenges in Representation Learning, ICML, vol. 3, no. 2, p. 896 (2013)
12. Duan, K., Bai, S., Xie, L., Qi, H., Huang, Q., Tian, Q.: Centernet - keypoint triplets for object detection. In: ICCV, pp. 6569–6578 (2019)
13. Everingham, M., et al.: The PASCAL visual object classes challenge: a retrospective. Int. J. Comput. Vis. **111**(1), 98–136 (2014). https://doi.org/10.1007/s11263-014-0733-5
14. Girshick, R.B.: Fast r-CNN. In: IEEE International Conference on Computer Vision (ICCV) (2015)
15. He, K., Fan, H., Wu, Y., Xie, S., Girshick, R.B.: Momentum contrast for unsupervised visual representation learning. In: CVPR, pp. 9729–9738 (2020)
16. He, K., Zhang, X., Ren, S., Sun, J.: Deep residual learning for image recognition. In: CVPR, pp. 770–778 (2016)
17. Kim, Y., Yim, J., Yun, J., Kim, J.: NLNL: negative learning for noisy labels. In: IEEE International Conference on Computer Vision (ICCV), pp. 101–110 (2019)
18. Krizhevsky, A., Hinton, G., et al.: Learning multiple layers of features from tiny images. Citeseer (2009)
19. Jeong, J., Lee, S., Kim, J., Kwak, N.: Consistency-based semi-supervised learning for object detection. In: NeurIPS (2019)
20. Laine, S., Aila, T.: Temporal ensembling for semi-supervised learning. In: ICLR (2017)
21. Law, H., Deng, J.: Cornernet: Detecting objects as paired keypoints. In: Proceedings of the European Conference on Computer Vision (ECCV), pp. 734–750 (2018)
22. Li, J., Xiong, C., Hoi, S.: Comatch - semi-supervised learning with contrastive graph regularization. In: ICCV, pp. 9475–9484 (2020)
23. Lin, T.Y., Dollár, P., Girshick, R.B., He, K., Hariharan, B., Belongie, S.J.: Feature pyramid networks for object detection. In: CVPR, pp. 2117–2125 (2017)
24. Lin, T.Y., Goyal, P., Girshick, R.B., He, K., Dollár, P.: Focal loss for dense object detection. In: TPAMI, pp. 2980–2988 (2020)
25. Liu, Y.C., et al.: Unbiased teacher for semi-supervised object detection. In: ICLR (2021)
26. der Maaten, V., Laurens, Hinton, G.: Visualizing data using t-SNE. J. Mach. Learn. Res. **9**(11) (2008)
27. Miyato, T., ichi Maeda, S., Koyama, M., Ishii, S.: Virtual adversarial training - a regularization method for supervised and semi-supervised learning. TPAMI **41**(8), 1979–1993 (2019)
28. Paszke, A., et al.: Pytorch - an imperative style, high-performance deep learning library. In: NeurIPS (2019)
29. Qi, H., Brown, M., Lowe, D.G.: Low-shot learning with imprinted weights. In: CVPR, pp. 5822–5830 (2018)
30. Redmon, J., Divvala, S.K., Girshick, R.B., Farhadi, A.: You only look once - unified, real-time object detection. In: CVPR, pp. 5822–5830 (2016)
31. Ren, S., He, K., Girshick, R.B., Sun, J.: Faster R-CNN - towards real-time object detection with region proposal networks. In: TPAMI (2017)
32. SP, B., et al.: Convex Optimization, 1st edt., p. 72. Cambridge University Press (2004)

33. Shrivastava, A., Gupta, A., Girshick, R.B.: Training region-based object detectors with online hard example mining. In: CVPR, pp. 761–769 (2016)
34. Sohn, K., et al.: Fixmatch - simplifying semi-supervised learning with consistency and confidence. Adv. Neural Inf. Process. Syst. **33**, 596–608 (2020)
35. Sohn, K., Zhang, Z., Li, C.L., Zhang, H., Lee, C.Y., Pfister, T.: A simple semi-supervised learning framework for object detection. arXiv (2020)
36. Tang, Y., Chen, W., Luo, Y., Zhang, Y.: Humble teachers teach better students for semi-supervised object detection. In: Computer Vision and Pattern Recognition (CVPR), pp. 3132–3141 (2021)
37. Tian, Z., Shen, C., Chen, H., He, T.: Fcos - fully convolutional one-stage object detection. In: ICCV, pp. 9627–9636 (2019)
38. Wang, X., Hua, Y., Kodirov, E., Clifton, D.A., Robertson, N.M.: Proselflc - progressive self label correction for training robust deep neural networks. In: CVPR, pp. 752–761 (2021)
39. Wang, Z., Li, Y., Guo, Y., Wang, S.: Combating noise: semi-supervised learning by region uncertainty quantification. NeurIPS **34**, 9534–9545 (2021)
40. Xu, M., et al.: End-to-end semi-supervised object detection with soft teacher. In: Proceedings of the IEEE/CVF International Conference on Computer Vision, pp. 3060–3069 (2021)
41. Yang, Q., Wei, X., Wang, B., Hua, X.S., Zhang, L.: Interactive self-training with mean teachers for semi-supervised object detection. In: CVPR, pp. 5941–5950 (2021)
42. Carion, N., Massa, F., Synnaeve, G., Usunier, N., Kirillov, A., Zagoruyko, S.: End-to-end object detection with transformers. In: Vedaldi, A., Bischof, H., Brox, T., Frahm, J.-M. (eds.) ECCV 2020. LNCS, vol. 12346, pp. 213–229. Springer, Cham (2020). https://doi.org/10.1007/978-3-030-58452-8_13
43. Zhou, Q., Yu, C., Wang, Z., Qian, Q., Li, H.: Instant-teaching - an end-to-end semi-supervised object detection framework. In: CVPR, pp. 4081–4090 (2021)
44. Lin, T.Y., et al.: Microsoft COCO: common objects in context. In: Fleet, D., Pajdla, T., Schiele, B., Tuytelaars, T. (eds.) ECCV 2014. LNCS, vol. 8693, pp. 740–755. Springer, Cham (2014). https://doi.org/10.1007/978-3-319-10602-1_48

Completely Self-supervised Crowd Counting via Distribution Matching

Deepak Babu Sam[1]($\boxtimes$), Abhinav Agarwalla[1], Jimmy Joseph[1],
Vishwanath A. Sindagi[2], R. Venkatesh Babu[1], and Vishal M. Patel[2]

[1] Indian Institute of Science, Bangalore 560012, India
{deepaksam,venky}@iisc.ac.in
[2] Johns Hopkins University, Baltimore, MD 21218, USA
{vishwanathsindagi,vpatel36}@jhu.edu

Abstract. Dense crowd counting is a challenging task that demands millions of head annotations for training models. Though existing self-supervised approaches could learn good representations, they require some labeled data to map these features to the end task of density estimation. We mitigate this issue with the proposed paradigm of complete self-supervision, which does not need even a single labeled image. The only input required to train, apart from a large set of unlabeled crowd images, is the approximate upper limit of the crowd count for the given dataset. Our method dwells on the idea that natural crowds follow a power law distribution, which could be leveraged to yield error signals for backpropagation. A density regressor is first pretrained with self-supervision and then the distribution of predictions is matched to the prior. Experiments show that this results in effective learning of crowd features and delivers significant counting performance.

Keywords: Self-supervision · Unsupervised learning · Crowd counting

1 Introduction

The ability to estimate head counts of dense crowds effectively and efficiently serves several practical applications. This has motivated deeper research in the field and resulted in a plethora of crowd density regressors. These CNN based models deliver excellent counting performance almost entirely on the support of fully supervised training. Such a data hungry paradigm is limiting the further development of the field as it is practically infeasible to annotate thousands of people in dense crowds for every kind of setting under consideration. The fact that current datasets are relatively small and cover only limited scenarios, accentuates the necessity of a better training regime. Hence, developing methods to leverage the easily available unlabeled data has gained attention recently.

The classic way of performing unsupervised learning revolves around autoencoders [18,26,40,57]. Autoencoders or its variants are optimized to predict back

---

D. Babu Sam and A. Agarwalla—Contributed equally.

S. Avidan et al. (Eds.): ECCV 2022, LNCS 13691, pp. 186–204, 2022.
https://doi.org/10.1007/978-3-031-19821-2_11

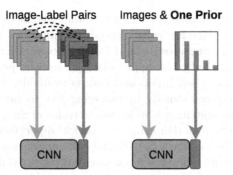

Fig. 1. Though self-supervision methods learn features in an unsupervised manner (in orange), they require labeled training to map these features to the end task (in blue). But complete self-supervision is devoid of any such instance-level supervision, instead relies on matching the statistics of the predictions to a prior distribution (in green). (Color figure online)

their inputs, usually through a representational bottleneck. By doing so, the acquired features are generic enough that they could be employed for solving other tasks of interest. These methods have graduated to the more recent framework of self-supervision, where useful representations are learned by performing some alternate task for which pseudo labels can be easily obtained. For example, in self-supervision with colorization approach [28,29,70], a model is trained to predict the color image given its grayscale version. One can easily generate grayscale inputs from RGB images. Similarly, there are lots of tasks for which labels are freely available like predicting angle of rotation from an image [14,15], solving jumbled scenes [44], inpainting [47] etc. Though self-supervision is effective in learning useful representations, they require a final mapping from the features to the end task of interest. This is thought to be essentially unavoidable as some supervisory signal is necessary to aid the final task. For this, typically a linear layer or a classifier is trained on top of the learned features using supervision from labeled data, defeating the true purpose of self-supervision. In the case of crowd counting, one requires training with annotated data for converting the features to a density map. To reiterate, the current unsupervised approaches could capture the majority of its features from unlabeled data, but demand supervision at the end for them to be made useful for any practical applications.

Our work emerges precisely from the above limitation of the standard self-supervision methods, but narrowed down to the case of crowd density estimation. The objective is to eliminate the mandatory final labeled supervision needed for mapping the learned self-supervised features to a density map output. In other words, we mandate developing a model that can be trained without using any labeled data. Such a problem statement is not only challenging, but also ill-posed. Without providing a supervisory signal, the model cannot recognize the task of interest and how to properly guide the training stands as the prime issue.

We solve this in a novel manner by carefully aiding the model to regress crowd density on the back of making some crucial assumptions. The idea relies on the observation that natural crowds tend to follow certain long tailed statistics and could be approximated to an appropriate parametric prior distribution. If a network trained with a self-supervised task is available, its features can be faithfully mapped to crowd density by enforcing the predictions to match the prior distribution. The matching is measured in terms of Sinkhorn distance [12], which is differentiated to derive error signals for supervision. This proposed framework is contrasted against the normal self-supervision regime in Fig. 1, with the central difference being the replacement of the essential labeled training at the end by supervision through distribution matching. We show that the proposed approach results in effective learning of crowd features and delivers good performance in terms of counting metrics.

2   Related Work

Though there are earlier works like [9] on counting people in sparse crowds, the paradigm of dense crowd counting via density regression plausibly begins with [19]. The initial methods generally employ hand-crafted features and frequency analysis for counting. With the advent of deep learning, many CNN based density regressors have emerged. It ranges from the initial simple models [67] to multi-network/multi-scale architectures designed specifically to address the drastic diversity in crowd images [5,7,8,45,71]. Regressors with better, deeper and recurrent based deep models [24,30,32] are shown to improve counting performance. An alternate line of works enhance density regression by providing auxiliary information through crowd classification [51,52], scene context [2,10,36], perspective data [49,64], attention [35,65,66] and even semantic priors [59]. Models designed to progressively predict density maps and perform refinement is explored in [20,48,54]. Works like [34,53] effectively fuse multi-scale information. Some approaches try to bring flavors of detection to crowd counting [3,4,31,33,38]. Interestingly, all these works, including more recent ones [39,58,60,61], are fully supervised and leverage annotated data to achieve good performance. The issue of annotation has drawn attention of a few works in the field and is mitigated via multiple means. A count ranking loss on unlabeled images is employed in a multi-task formulation along with labeled data by [37]. Wang et al. [62] train using labeled synthetic data and adapt to real crowd scenario. The autoencoder method proposed in [6] optimizes almost 99% of the model parameters with unlabeled data. However, all of these models require some annotated data (either given by humans or obtained through synthetic means) for training.

Our approach is not only new to crowd counting, but also kindles alternate avenues in the area of unsupervised learning as well. Though initial works on the subject employ autoencoders or its variants [18,26,40,57] for learning useful features, the paradigm of self-supervision with pseudo labels stands out to be superior in many aspects. Works like [28,29,70], learn representations through

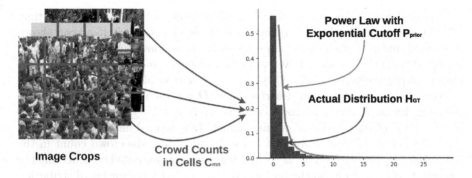

Fig. 2. Computing the distribution of natural crowds: crops from dense crowd images are framed to a spatial grid of cells and crowd counts of all the cells are aggregated to a histogram (obtained on Shanghaitech Part_A dataset [71]). The distribution is certainly long tailed and could be approximated to a power law.

colorizing a grayscale image. Apart from these, pseudo labels for supervision are computed from motion cues [1,22,46], temporal information in videos [41,63], learning to inpaint [47], co-occurrence [21], spatial context [13,43,44], cross-channel prediction [69], spotting artifacts [23], predicting object rotation [14,15] etc. The recent work of Zhang et al. [68] introduce the idea of auto-encoding transformations rather than data. Furthermore, self-supervision is shown effective for unsupervised domain adaptation in [56]. An extensive and rigorous comparison of all major self-supervised methods is available in [27]. All these approaches focus on learning generic features and not the final task. But we extend self-supervision paradigm directly to the downstream task of interest.

3   Our Approach

3.1   Natural Crowds and Density Distribution

As mentioned in Sect. 1, our objective of training a density regressor without using any annotated data is somewhat ill-posed. The main reason being the absence of any supervisory signal to guide the model towards the task of interest, which is the density estimation of crowd images. But this issue could be circumvented by effectively exploiting certain structure or pattern specific to the problem. In the case of crowd images, restricting to only dense ones, we deduce an interesting pattern on the density distribution. They seem to spread out following a power law. To see this, we sample fixed size crops from lots of dense crowd images and divide each crop into a grid of cells as shown in Fig. 2. Then the number people in every cell is computed and accumulated to a histogram. The distribution of these cell counts is quite clearly seen to be long tailed, with regions having low counts forming the head and high counts joining the tail. The number of cell regions with no people has the highest frequency, which then rapidly decays as the crowd density increases. This resembles the way natural crowds are arranged with sparse regions occurring more often than rarely forming highly dense neighborhoods. Coincidentally, it has been shown that many natural phenomena obey a similar power law and is being studied heavily [11]. The dense crowds also appear conforming to this pattern as evident from multiple works [16,17,25,42] etc. on the dynamics of pedestrian gatherings.

Moving to a more formal description, if D represents the density map for the input image I, then the crowd count is given by $C = \sum_{xy} D_{xy}$ (please refer [7,19,71] regarding creation of density maps). D is framed into a grid of $M \times N$ (typically set as $M = N = 3$) cells, with C_{mn} denoting the crowd count in the cell indexed by (m, n). Now let H^{GT} be the histogram computed by collecting the cell counts (C_{mn}s) from all the images. We try to find a parametric distribution that approximately follows H^{GT} with special focus to the long tailed region. The power law with exponential cut-off seems to be better suited (see Fig. 2). Consequently, the crowd counts in cells C_{mn} could be thought as being generated by the following relation,

$$C_{mn} \sim P_{prior}(c) \propto c^\alpha \exp(-\lambda c), \qquad (1)$$

where P_{prior} is the substitute power law distribution. There are two parameters to P_{prior} with α controlling the shape and λ setting the tail length.

Our approach is to fix a prior distribution so that it can be enforced on the model predictions. Studies like [16,42] simulate crowd behaviour dynamics and estimate the exponent of the power law to be around 2. Empirically, we also find that $\alpha = 2$ works in most cases of dense crowds, with the only remaining parameter to fix is the λ. Observe that λ affects the length of the tail and directly determines the maximum number of people in any given cell. If the maximum count C^{max} is specified for the given set of crowd images, then λ could be fixed such that the cumulative probability density (the value of CDF) of P_{prior} at C^{max} is very close to 1. We assume $1/S$ as the probability of finding a cell with count C^{max} out of S images in the given set. Now the CDF value at C^{max} could be set to $1-1/S$, simply the probability for getting values less than the maximum. Note that C^{max} need not be exact as small variations do not change P_{prior} significantly. This makes it practical as the accurate maximum count might not be available in real-world scenarios. Since C^{max} is for the cells, the maximum crowd count of the full image C^{fmax} is related as $C^{max} = C^{fmax}/(MNS_{crop})$, where S_{crop} denotes the average number of crops that make up a full image (and is typically set as 4). Thus, for a given a set of highly dense images, only one parameter, the C^{fmax} is required to fix an appropriate prior distribution.

We make a small modification to the prior distribution P_{prior} as its value range starts from 1. H^{GT} has values from zero with large probability mass concentrated near the low count region. Roughly 30% of the mass is seen to be distributed for counts less than or around 1. So, that much probability mass near the head region of P_{prior} is redistributed to $[0, 1]$ range in a uniform manner. This is found to be better for both training stability and performance.

In short, now we have a prior distribution representing how the crowd density is being allocated among the given set of images. Suppose there exists a CNN

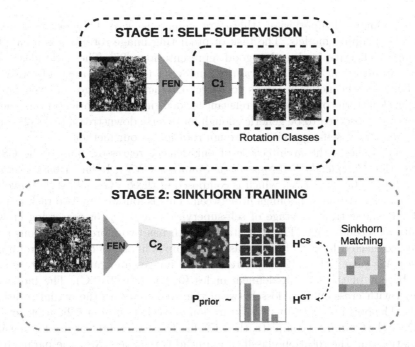

Fig. 3. The architecture of CSS-CCNN is shown. CSS-CCNN has two stages of training: the first trains the base *feature extraction network* in a self-supervised manner with rotation task and the second stage optimizes the model for matching the statistics of the density predictions to that of the prior distribution using optimal transport.

model that can output density maps, then one could try to generate error signals for updating the parameters of the model by matching the statistics of the predictions with that of the prior. But that could be a very weak signal for proper training of the model. It would be helpful if the model has a good initialization to start the supervision by distribution matching, which is precisely what we do by self-supervision in the next section.

3.2   Stage 1: Learning Features with Self-supervision

We rely on training the model with self-supervision to learn effective and generic features that could be useful for the end task of density estimation. That means the model has to be trained in stages, with the first stage acquiring patterns frequently occurring in the input images. Since only dense crowd images are fed, we hope to learn mostly features relevant to crowds. These could be peculiar edges discriminating head-shoulder patterns formed by people to fairly high-level semantics pertaining to crowds. Note that the model is not signaled to pick up representations explicitly pertinent to density estimation, but implicitly culminate in learning crowd patterns as those are the most prominent part of the input data distribution. Hence, the features acquired by self-supervision could serve as a faithful initialization for the second stage of distribution matching.

Regarding self-supervision, there are numerous ways to generate pseudo labels for training models. The task of predicting image rotations is a simple, but highly effective for learning good representations [27]. The basic idea is to randomly rotate an image and train the model to predict the angle of rotation. By doing so, the network learns to detect characteristic edges or even fairly high-level patterns of the objects relevant for determining the orientation. These features are observed to be generic enough for diverse downstream tasks [27] and hence we choose self-supervision through rotation as our method.

Figure 3 shows the architecture of our density regressor, named the CSS-CCNN (for *Completely Self-Supervised Counting CNN*). It has a base *Feature Extraction Network* (FEN), which is composed of three VGG [50] style convolutional blocks with max poolings in-between. This is followed by two task heads: C_1 for the first training stage of self-supervision, and C_2 for regressing crowd density at second stage. The first stage branch has two more convolutions and a fully connected layer to finally classify the input image to one of the rotation classes. We take 112×112 crops from crowd images and randomly rotate the crop by one of the four predefined angles (0, 90, 180, 270 °C). The model is trained with cross-entropy loss between the predicted and the actual rotation labels. The optimization runs till saturation as evaluated on a validation set.

Once the training is complete, the FEN has learned useful features for density estimation and the rotation classification head is removed. Now the parameters of FEN are frozen and is ready to be used in the second stage of training.

3.3   Stage 2: Sinkhorn Training

After the self-supervised training stage, FEN is extended to a density regressor by adding two convolutional layers as shown in Fig. 3. We take features from both second and third convolution blocks for effectively mapping to crowd density. This aggregates features from slightly different receptive fields and is seen to deliver better performance. The layers of FEN are frozen and only a few parameters in the freshly added layers are open for training in the second stage of distribution matching. This particularly helps to prevent over-fitting as the training signal generated could be weak for updating large number of parameters. Now we describe the details of the exact matching process.

The core idea is to compute the distribution of crowd density predicted by CSS-CCNN and optimize the network to match that closely with the prior P_{prior}. For this, a suitable distance metric between the two distributions should be defined with differentiability as a key necessity. Note that the predicted distribution is in the form of an empirical measure (an array of cell count values) and hence it is difficult to formulate an easy analytical expression for the computing similarity. The classic Earth Mover's Distance (EMD) measures the amount of probability mass that needs to be moved if one tries to transform between the distributions (also described as the optimal transport cost). But this is not a differentiable operation and cannot be used directly in our case. Hence, we choose the Sinkhorn distance formulation proposed in [12]. Sinkhorn distance between two empirical measures is proven to be an upper bound for EMD and has a differentiable implementation. Moreover, this method performs favorable in terms of efficiency and speed as well.

Let $\boldsymbol{D}^{CS}$ represent the density map output by CSS-CCNN and $\boldsymbol{C}^{CS}$ hold the cells extracted from the predictions. To make the distribution matching statistically significant, a batch of images are evaluated to get the cell counts ($\boldsymbol{C}^{CS}_{mn}$s), which are then formed into an array H^{CS}. We also sample the prior P_{prior} and create another empirical measure H^{GT} to act as the ground truth. Now the Sinkhorn loss $\mathcal{L}_{sink}$ is computed between H^{GT} and H^{CS}. It is basically a regularized version of optimal transport (OT) distance for the two sample sets. Designate $\boldsymbol{h}^{GT}$ and $\boldsymbol{h}^{CS}$ as the probability vectors (summing to 1) associated with the empirical measures H^{GT} and H^{CS} respectively. Now a transport plan $\boldsymbol{P}$ could be conceived as the joint likelihood of shifting the probability mass from $\boldsymbol{h}^{GT}$ to $\boldsymbol{h}^{CS}$. Define U to be the set of all such valid candidate plans as,

$$U = \{\boldsymbol{P} \in \mathbb{R}^{d \times d}_+ \mid \boldsymbol{P}\mathbf{1} = \boldsymbol{h}^{GT}, \boldsymbol{P}^T\mathbf{1} = \boldsymbol{h}^{CS}\}. \tag{2}$$

There is a cost $\boldsymbol{M}$ associated with any given transport plan, where M_{ij} is the squared difference between the counts of ith sample of H^{GT} and jth of H^{CS}. Closer the two distribution, lower would be the cost for transport. Hence, the Sinkhorn loss $\mathcal{L}_{sink}$ is defined as the cost pertinent to the optimal transportation plan with an additional regularization term. Mathematically,

$$\mathcal{L}_{sink}(H^{GT}, H^{CS}) = \operatorname*{arg\,min}_{\boldsymbol{P} \in U} \langle \boldsymbol{P}, \boldsymbol{M} \rangle_F - \frac{1}{\beta}E(\boldsymbol{P}), \tag{3}$$

where $<>_F$ stands for the Frobenius inner product, $E(\boldsymbol{P})$ is the entropy of the joint distribution $\boldsymbol{P}$ and β is a regularization constant (see [12] for more details). It is evident that minimizing $\mathcal{L}_{sink}$ brings the two distributions closer in terms of how counts are allotted.

The network parameters are updated to optimize $\mathcal{L}_{sink}$, thereby bringing the distribution of predictions close to that of the prior. At every iteration of the training, a batch of crowd images are sampled from the dataset and empirical measures for the predictions as well as prior are constructed to backpropagate the Sinkhorn loss. The value of $\mathcal{L}_{sink}$ on a validation set of images is monitored for convergence and the training is stopped if the average loss does not improve over a certain number of epochs. Note that we do not use any annotated data even for validation. The counting performance is evaluated at the end with the model chosen based on the best mean validation Sinkhorn loss.

Thus, our Sinkhorn training procedure does not rely on instance-level supervision, but exploits matching the statistics computed from a set of inputs to that of the prior. One criticism regarding this method could be that the model need not learn the task of crowd density estimation by optimizing the Sinkhorn loss. It could learn any other arbitrary task that follows a similar distribution. The counter-argument stems from the semantics of the features learned by the base network. Since the initial training mostly captures features related to dense crowds, the Sinkhorn optimization has only limited flexibility in what it can do other than map them through a fairly simple function to crowd density. This

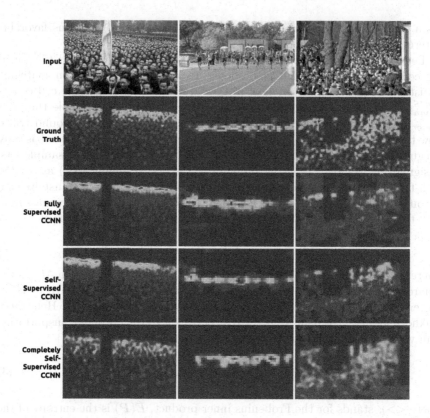

Fig. 4. Density maps estimated by CSS-CCNN along with that of baseline methods. Despite being trained without a single annotated image, CSS-CCNN is seen to be quite good at discriminating the crowd regions as well as regressing the density values.

is especially true as there is only a small set of parameters being trained with Sinkhorn. It is highly likely and straightforward to map the frequent crowd features to its density values, whose distribution is signaled through the prior. Moreover, we show through extensive experiments that CSS-CCNN ends up learning crowd density estimation.

4   Experiments and Analysis

Any crowd density regressor is evaluated mainly for the standard counting metrics. There are two metrics widely being followed by the community. The first is the MAE or Mean Absolute Error, which directly measures the counting performance. It is the absolute difference of the predicted and actual counts averaged over the test set or simply expressed as $\text{MAE} = (1/S_{test}) \sum_{i=1}^{N} |C_i - C_i^{GT}|$, where C_i is the count predicted by the model for ith image and C_i^{GT} denotes the actual count. Note that S_{test} is the number of images in the test set.

Table 1. Performance comparison of CSS-CCNN with other methods. Our model outperforms all the baselines.

Method	ST PartA		UCF-QNRF		UCF-CC-50		JHU-CRWD	
	MAE	MSE	MAE	MSE	MAE	MSE	MAE	MSE
WTA-CCNN [6]	154.7	229.4	–	–	433.7	583.3	–	–
CCNN Self-Super	121.2	197.5	196.8	309.3	348.8	484.3	147.5	436.2
CCNN Random	431.1	559.0	718.7	1036.3	1279.3	1567.9	320.3	793.5
CCNN Mean	282.8	359.9	567.1	752.8	771.2	898.4	316.3	732.3
CCNN P_{prior}	272.2	372.5	535.6	765.9	760.0	949.9	302.3	707.6
CSS-CCNN (*0 labels*)	197.3	295.9	437.0	722.3	564.9	959.4	217.6	651.3

Coming to the second metric, the Mean Squared Error or MSE is defined as $MSE = SQRT((1/S_{test}) \sum_{i=1}^{N} (C_i - C_i^{GT})^2)$, a measure of the variance of count estimation and it represents the robustness of the model.

Our completely self-supervised framework is unique in many ways that the baseline comparisons should be different from the typical supervised methods. It is not fair to compare CSS-CCNN with other approaches as they use the full annotated data for training. Hence, we take a set of solid baselines for our model to demonstrate its performance. The *CCNN Random* experiment refers to the results one would get if only *Stage 1* self-supervision is done without the subsequent Sinkhorn training. This is the random accuracy for our setting and helpful in showing whether the proposed complete self-supervision works. Since our approach takes one parameter, the maximum count value of the dataset (C^{fmax}) as input, *CCNN Mean* baseline indicates the counting performance if the regressor blindly predicts the given value for all the images. We choose mean value as it makes for sense in this setting than the maximum (which anyway has worse performance than mean). Another important validation for our proposed paradigm is the *CCNN* P_{prior} experiment, where the model gives out a value randomly drawn from the prior distribution as its prediction for a given image. The counting performance of this baseline tells us with certainty whether the *Stage 2* training does anything more than that by chance. Note that we do not initialize CCNN with any pretrained weights as is typically done for supervised counting models. *CCNN Self-Super* runs the *Stage 1* training to learn the FEN parameters and is followed by labeled optimization for updating the regressor layers. These self-supervised or fully supervised methods are not directly comparable to our approach as we do not use any annotated data for training, but are shown for completeness. Also note that only the train/validation set images are used for optimizing CSS-CCNN and the ground truth annotations are never used. The counting metrics are computed on the labeled test set.

4.1   Crowd Datasets

The Shanghaitech Part_A [71] is a popular dense crowd counting dataset, containing 482 images randomly crawled from the Internet. It has images with crowd counts as low as 33 to as high as 3139, with an average of 501. The train set has 300 images, out of which 10% is held out for validation. There are 182 images testing. The hyper-parameter used for this is $C^{fmax} = 3000$. We compare the performance of CSS-CCNN with the baselines listed earlier and other competing methods in Table 1. It is clear that CSS-CCNN outperforms all the baselines by a significant margin. This shows that the proposed method works better than any naive strategies that do not consider the input images. Figure 4 visually compares density predictions made by CSS-CCNN and other models. The predictions of our approach are mostly on crowd regions and closely follows the ground truth, emphasizing its ability to discriminate crowds well.

UCF-QNRF dataset [20] is a large and diverse collection of crowd images with 1.2 million annotations. There are 1535 images with crowd count varying from 49 to 12865, resulting in an average of 815 individuals per image. The dataset offers very high-resolution images with an average resolution of 2013 × 2902. The max count hyper-parameter is set to $C^{fmax} = 12000$. We achieve similar performance trends on UCF-QNRF dataset as well. CSS-CCNN outperforms all the unsupervised baselines in terms of MAE and MSE as evident from Table 1.

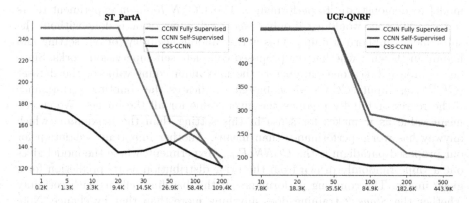

Fig. 5. Comparing our completely self-supervised method to fully supervised and self-supervised approaches under a limited amount of labeled training data. The x-axis denotes the number of training images along with the count (in thousands) of head annotations available for training, while the y-axis represents the MAE thus obtained. At low data scenarios, CSS-CCNN has significantly superior performance.

UCF_CC_50 dataset [19] has just 50 images with extreme variation in crowd density ranging from 94 to 4543. The small size and diversity together makes this dataset the most challenging. We follow the standard 5-fold cross-validation scheme suggested by the creators of the dataset to report the performance metrics. Since the number of images is quite small, the assumption taken for setting the prior distribution gets invalid to certain extent. But a slightly different

Table 2. Evaluating CSS-CCNN in a true practical setting: the model is trained on images crawled from the web, but evaluated on crowd datasets.

Train on web images	MAE	MSE
Test on ST_PartA	208.8	309.5
Test on UCF-QNRF	450.7	755.9
Test on JHU-CROWD++	241.2	706.8

parameter to the prior distribution works. We set $\alpha = 1$ and $C^{fmax} = 4000$. Despite being a small and highly diverse dataset, CSS-CCNN is able to beat all the baselines. The self-supervised MAE is also better than [6]. These results evidence the effectiveness of our method.

JHU-CROWD++ [54,55] is a comprehensive dataset with 1.51 million head annotations spanning 4372 images. The crowd scenes are obtained under various scenarios and weather conditions, making it one of the challenging dataset in terms of diversity. Furthermore, JHU-CROWD++ has a richer set of annotations at head level as well as image level. The maximum count is fixed to $C^{fmax} = 8000$. The performance trends are quite similar to other datasets, with our approach delivering better MAE than the baselines as evident from Table 1. This indicates the generalization ability of CSS-CCNN across different datasets.

4.2 Performance with Limited Data

Here we explore the proposed algorithm along with fully supervised and self-supervised approaches when few annotated images are available for training. The analysis is performed by varying the number of labeled samples and the resultant counting metrics are presented in Fig. 5. For training CSS-CCNN with data, we utilise the available annotated data to compute the optimal Sinkhorn assignments P^* and then optimize the $\mathcal{L}_{sink}$ loss. This way both the labeled as well as unlabeled data can be leveraged for training by alternating respective batches (in a 5:1 ratio). It is clear that, at very low data, scenarios CSS-CCNN beats the supervised as well as self-supervised baselines by a significant margin. The Sinkhorn training shows 13% boost in MAE (for Shanghaitech Part_A) by using just one labeled sample as opposed to no samples. This indicates that CSS-CCNN can perform well in extremely low data regimes. It takes about 20K head annotations for the supervised model to perform as well as CSS-CCNN. Also, CSS-CCNN has significantly less number of parameters to learn using the labeled samples as compared to a fully supervised network. These results suggests that our complete self-supervision is the right paradigm to employ for crowd counting when the amount of available annotated data is less.

4.3 CSS-CCNN in True Practical Setting

The complete self-supervised setting is motivated for scenarios where no labeled images are available for training. But till now we have been using images from

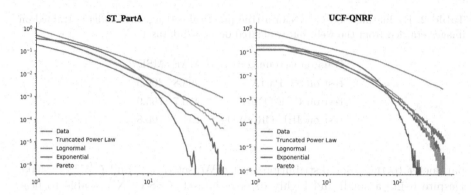

Fig. 6. Double logarithmic representation of maximum likelihood fit for the crowd counts from different datasets.

crowd datasets with the annotations being intentionally ignored. Now consider crawling lots of crowd images from the Internet and employing these unlabeled data for training CSS-CCNN. For this, we use textual tags related to dense crowds and similarity matching with dataset images to collect approximately 5000 dense crowd images. No manual pruning of undesirable images with motion blur, perspective distortion or other artifacts is done. CSS-CCNN is trained on these images with the same hyper-parameters as that of Shanghaitech Part_A and the performance metrics are computed on the datasets with annotations. From Table 2, it is evident that our model achieves very competitive MAE on the crowd datasets (compared to Table 1), despite not using images from those datasets for training. This further demonstrates the generalization ability of CSS-CCNN to learn from less curated data, emphasizing the practical utility.

4.4   Analysis of the Prior Distribution

The proposed Sinkhorn training requires a prior distribution of crowd counts to be defined and the choice of an appropriate prior is essential for the best model performance as seen from Table 3. Here we analyze the crowd data more carefully to see why the truncated power law is the right choice of prior. For this, the counts from crowd images are extracted as described in Sect. 3.1 and a maximum likelihood fit over various parametric distributions is performed. The double logarithmic visualization of the probability distribution of both the data and the priors are available in Fig. 6. Note that the data curve is almost a straight line in the logarithmic plot, a clear marker for power law characteristic. Both truncated power law and lognormal tightly follow the distribution. But on close inspection of the tail regions, we find truncated power law to best represent the prior. This further validates our choice of the prior distribution.

Table 3. Ablating the effect of hyper-parameters on CSS-CCNN. Our model is robust to fairly large change in the maximum count parameter.

Param	MAE	MSE
Uniform prior	261.8	406.0
Pareto prior	248.3	386.2
Lognormal prior	239.5	345.8
Truncated power law prior	197.3	295.9
$C^{fmax} = 2000$	204.2	316.4
$C^{fmax} = 2500$	197.9	304.6
$C^{fmax} = 3000$	197.3	295.9
$C^{fmax} = 3500$	191.9	288.5
$\alpha = 1.9$	202.9	303.3
$\alpha = 2.0$	197.3	295.9
$\alpha = 2.1$	200.7	305.6

4.5 Sensitivity Analysis for the Crowd Parameter

As described in Sect. 3.1, CSS-CCNN requires the maximum crowd count (C^{fmax}) for the given set of images as an input. This is necessary to fix the prior distribution parameter λ. One might not have the exact max value for the crowds in a true practical setting; an approximate estimate is a more reasonable assumption. Hence, we vary C^{fmax} around the actual value and train CSS-CCNN on Shanghaitech PartA [71] and UCF-QNRF [20]. The performance metrics in Table 3 show that changing C^{fmax} to certain extent does not alter the performance significantly. The MAE remained roughly within the same range, even though the max parameter is being changed in the order of 500. These findings indicate that the our approach is insensitive to the exact crowd hyper-parameter value, increasing its practical utility. We also check the sensitivity of our approach on the power law exponent α. Varying α around 2 results in similar performances, in agreement with our design choices (see Sect. 3.1).

5 Conclusions

We show for the first time that a density regressor can be fully trained from scratch without using a single annotated image. This new paradigm of complete self-supervision relies on optimizing the model by matching the statistics of the distribution of predictions to that of a predefined prior. Though the counting performance of the model stands better than other baselines, there is a performance gap compared to fully supervised methods. Addressing this issue could be the prime focus of future works. For now, our work can be considered as a proof of concept that models could be trained directly for solving the downstream task of interest, without providing any instance-level labeled data.

Acknowledgments. This work was supported by MeitY (Ministry of Electronics and Information Technology) project (No. 4(16)2019-ITEA), Govt. of India. VMP was supported by an ARO grant W911NF-21-1-0135.

References

1. Agrawal, P., Carreira, J., Malik, J.: Learning to see by moving. In: Proceedings of the IEEE International Conference on Computer Vision (ICCV) (2015)
2. Babu Sam, D., Babu, R.V.: Top-down feedback for crowd counting convolutional neural network. In: Proceedings of the AAAI Conference on Artificial Intelligence (2018)
3. Babu Sam, D., Peri, S.V., Sundararaman, M.N., Babu, R.V.: Going beyond the regression paradigm with accurate dot prediction for dense crowds. In: Proceedings of the IEEE Winter Conference on Applications of Computer Vision (WACV) (2020)
4. Babu Sam, D., Peri, S.V., Sundararaman, M.N., Kamath, A., Babu, R.V.: Locate, size and count: accurately resolving people in dense crowds via detection. IEEE Trans. Pattern Anal. Mach. Intell. (TPAMI). **43**, 2739–2751 (2020)
5. Babu Sam, D., Sajjan, N.N., Babu, R.V., Srinivasan, M.: Divide and grow: capturing huge diversity in crowd images with incrementally growing CNN. In: Proceedings of the IEEE Conference on Computer Vision and Pattern Recognition (CVPR) (2018)
6. Babu Sam, D., Sajjan, N.N., Maurya, H., Babu, R.V.: Almost unsupervised learning for dense crowd counting. In: Proceedings of the AAAI Conference on Artificial Intelligence (2019)
7. Babu Sam, D., Surya, S., Babu, R.V.: Switching convolutional neural network for crowd counting. In: Proceedings of the IEEE Conference on Computer Vision and Pattern Recognition (CVPR) (2017)
8. Cao, X., Wang, Z., Zhao, Y., Su, F.: Scale aggregation network for accurate and efficient crowd counting. In: Ferrari, V., Hebert, M., Sminchisescu, C., Weiss, Y. (eds.) ECCV 2018. LNCS, vol. 11209, pp. 757–773. Springer, Cham (2018). https://doi.org/10.1007/978-3-030-01228-1_45
9. Chan, A.B., Liang, Z.S.J., Vasconcelos, N.: Privacy preserving crowd monitoring: counting people without people models or tracking. In: IEEE Conference on Computer Vision and Pattern Recognition (2008)
10. Cheng, Z.Q., Li, J.X., Dai, Q., Wu, X., Hauptmann, A.G.: Learning spatial awareness to improve crowd counting. In: Proceedings of the IEEE International Conference on Computer Vision (ICCV) (2019)
11. Clauset, A., Shalizi, C.R., Newman, M.E.: Power-law distributions in empirical data. SIAM Rev. **51**, 661–673 (2009)
12. Cuturi, M.: Sinkhorn distances: Lightspeed computation of optimal transport. In: Advances in Neural Information Processing Systems (NIPS) (2013)
13. Doersch, C., Gupta, A., Efros, A.A.: Unsupervised visual representation learning by context prediction. In: Proceedings of the IEEE International Conference on Computer Vision (ICCV) (2015)
14. Feng, Z., Xu, C., Tao, D.: Self-supervised representation learning by rotation feature decoupling. In: Proceedings of the IEEE Conference on Computer Vision and Pattern Recognition (CVPR) (2019)

15. Gidaris, S., Singh, P., Komodakis, N.: Unsupervised representation learning by predicting image rotations. In: Proceedings of the IEEE Conference on Computer Vision and Pattern Recognition (CVPR) (2018)
16. Helbing, D., Johansson, A., Al-Abideen, H.Z.: Dynamics of crowd disasters: an empirical study. Phys. Rev. E **65**, 046109 (2007)
17. Helbing, D., et al.: Power laws in urban supply networks, social systems, and dense pedestrian crowds. In: Lane, D., Pumain, D., van der Leeuw, S.E., West, G. (eds.) Complexity Perspectives in Innovation and Social Change. Methodos Series, vol. 7, pp. 433–450. Springer, Dordrecht (2009). https://doi.org/10.1007/978-1-4020-9663-1_17
18. Hinton, G.E., Salakhutdinov, R.R.: Reducing the dimensionality of data with neural networks. Science **313**, 504–507 (2006)
19. Idrees, H., Saleemi, I., Seibert, C., Shah, M.: Multi-source multi-scale counting in extremely dense crowd images. In: Proceedings of the IEEE Conference on Computer Vision and Pattern Recognition (CVPR) (2013)
20. Idrees, H., et al.: Composition loss for counting, density map estimation and localization in dense crowds. In: Ferrari, V., Hebert, M., Sminchisescu, C., Weiss, Y. (eds.) ECCV 2018. LNCS, vol. 11206, pp. 544–559. Springer, Cham (2018). https://doi.org/10.1007/978-3-030-01216-8_33
21. Isola, P., Zoran, D., Krishnan, D., Adelson, E.H.: Learning visual groups from co-occurrences in space and time. In: Proceedings of the IEEE Conference on Computer Vision and Pattern Recognition (CVPR) (2016)
22. Jayaraman, D., Grauman, K.: Learning image representations tied to ego-motion. In: Proceedings of the IEEE International Conference on Computer Vision (ICCV) (2015)
23. Jenni, S., Favaro, P.: Self-supervised feature learning by learning to spot artifacts. In: Proceedings of the IEEE Conference on Computer Vision and Pattern Recognition (CVPR) (2018)
24. Jiang, X., et al.: Crowd counting and density estimation by trellis encoder-decoder networks. In: Proceedings of the IEEE Conference on Computer Vision and Pattern Recognition (CVPR) (2019)
25. Karamouzas, I., Skinner, B., Guy, S.J.: A universal power law governing pedestrian interactions. Phys. Rev. Lett. **113**, 238701 (2015)
26. Kingma, D.P., Welling, M.: Auto-encoding variational bayes. In: Proceedings of the International Conference on Learning Representations (ICLR) (2013)
27. Kolesnikov, A., Zhai, X., Beyer, L.: Revisiting self-supervised visual representation learning. In: Proceedings of the IEEE conference on Computer Vision and Pattern Recognition (CVPR) (2019)
28. Larsson, G., Maire, M., Shakhnarovich, G.: Learning representations for automatic colorization. In: Leibe, B., Matas, J., Sebe, N., Welling, M. (eds.) ECCV 2016. LNCS, vol. 9908, pp. 577–593. Springer, Cham (2016). https://doi.org/10.1007/978-3-319-46493-0_35
29. Larsson, G., Maire, M., Shakhnarovich, G.: Colorization as a proxy task for visual understanding. In: Proceedings of the IEEE Conference on Computer Vision and Pattern Recognition (CVPR) (2017)
30. Li, Y., Zhang, X., Chen, D.: CSRNet: dilated convolutional neural networks for understanding the highly congested scenes. In: Proceedings of the IEEE Conference on Computer Vision and Pattern Recognition (CVPR) (2018)
31. Lian, D., Li, J., Zheng, J., Luo, W., Gao, S.: Density map regression guided detection network for RGB-D crowd counting and localization. In: Proceedings of the IEEE Conference on Computer Vision and Pattern Recognition (CVPR) (2019)

32. Liu, C., Weng, X., Mu, Y.: Recurrent attentive zooming for joint crowd counting and precise localization. In: Proceedings of the IEEE Conference on Computer Vision and Pattern Recognition (CVPR) (2019)
33. Liu, J., Gao, C., Meng, D., Hauptmann, A.G.: DecideNet: counting varying density crowds through attention guided detection and density estimation. In: Proceedings of the IEEE Conference on Computer Vision and Pattern Recognition (CVPR) (2018)
34. Liu, L., Qiu, Z., Li, G., Liu, S., Ouyang, W., Lin, L.: Crowd counting with deep structured scale integration network. In: Proceedings of the IEEE International Conference on Computer Vision (ICCV) (2019)
35. Liu, N., Long, Y., Zou, C., Niu, Q., Pan, L., Wu, H.: ADCrowdNet: an attention-injective deformable convolutional network for crowd understanding. In: Proceedings of the IEEE Conference on Computer Vision and Pattern Recognition (CVPR) (2019)
36. Liu, W., Salzmann, M., Fua, P.: Context-aware crowd counting. In: Proceedings of the IEEE Conference on Computer Vision and Pattern Recognition (CVPR) (2019)
37. Liu, X., Van De Weijer, J., Bagdanov, A.D.: Exploiting unlabeled data in CNNs by self-supervised learning to rank. IEEE Trans. Pattern Anal. Mach. Intell. **14**, 1862–1878 (2019)
38. Liu, Y., Shi, M., Zhao, Q., Wang, X.: Point in, box out: Beyond counting persons in crowds. In: Proceedings of the IEEE Conference on Computer Vision and Pattern Recognition (CVPR) (2019)
39. Ma, Z., Wei, X., Hong, X., Gong, Y.: Learning scales from points: A scale-aware probabilistic model for crowd counting. In: Proceedings of the 28th ACM International Conference on Multimedia (2020)
40. Makhzani, A., Frey, B.J.: Winner-take-all autoencoders. In: Advances in Neural Information Processing Systems (NIPS) (2015)
41. Misra, I., Zitnick, C.L., Hebert, M.: Shuffle and learn: unsupervised learning using temporal order verification. In: Leibe, B., Matas, J., Sebe, N., Welling, M. (eds.) ECCV 2016. LNCS, vol. 9905, pp. 527–544. Springer, Cham (2016). https://doi.org/10.1007/978-3-319-46448-0_32
42. Moussaïd, M., Helbing, D., Theraulaz, G.: How simple rules determine pedestrian behavior and crowd disasters. Proc. Natl. Acad. Sci. **108**, 1868–1880 (2011)
43. Nathan Mundhenk, T., Ho, D., Chen, B.Y.: Improvements to context based self-supervised learning. In: Proceedings of the IEEE Conference on Computer Vision and Pattern Recognition (CVPR) (2018)
44. Noroozi, M., Favaro, P.: Unsupervised learning of visual representations by solving jigsaw puzzles. In: Leibe, B., Matas, J., Sebe, N., Welling, M. (eds.) ECCV 2016. LNCS, vol. 9910, pp. 69–84. Springer, Cham (2016). https://doi.org/10.1007/978-3-319-46466-4_5
45. Oñoro-Rubio, D., López-Sastre, R.J.: Towards perspective-free object counting with deep learning. In: Leibe, B., Matas, J., Sebe, N., Welling, M. (eds.) ECCV 2016. LNCS, vol. 9911, pp. 615–629. Springer, Cham (2016). https://doi.org/10.1007/978-3-319-46478-7_38
46. Pathak, D., Girshick, R., Dollár, P., Darrell, T., Hariharan, B.: Learning features by watching objects move. In: Proceedings of the IEEE Conference on Computer Vision and Pattern Recognition (CVPR) (2017)
47. Pathak, D., Krahenbuhl, P., Donahue, J., Darrell, T., Efros, A.A.: Context encoders: Feature learning by inpainting. In: Proceedings of the IEEE Conference on Computer Vision and Pattern Recognition (CVPR) (2016)

48. Ranjan, V., Le, H., Hoai, M.: Iterative crowd counting. In: Ferrari, V., Hebert, M., Sminchisescu, C., Weiss, Y. (eds.) ECCV 2018. LNCS, vol. 11211, pp. 278–293. Springer, Cham (2018). https://doi.org/10.1007/978-3-030-01234-2_17

49. Shi, M., Yang, Z., Xu, C., Chen, Q.: Revisiting perspective information for efficient crowd counting. In: Proceedings of the IEEE Conference on Computer Vision and Pattern Recognition (CVPR) (2019)

50. Simonyan, K., Zisserman, A.: Very deep convolutional networks for large-scale image recognition. arXiv preprint arXiv:1409.1556 (2014)

51. Sindagi, V.A., Patel, V.M.: CNN-based cascaded multi-task learning of high-level prior and density estimation for crowd counting. In: Proceedings of the IEEE International Conference on Advanced Video and Signal Based Surveillance (AVSS) (2017)

52. Sindagi, V.A., Patel, V.M.: Generating high-quality crowd density maps using contextual pyramid CNNs. In: Proceedings of the IEEE International Conference on Computer Vision (ICCV) (2017)

53. Sindagi, V.A., Patel, V.M.: Multi-level bottom-top and top-bottom feature fusion for crowd counting. In: Proceedings of the IEEE International Conference on Computer Vision (ICCV) (2019)

54. Sindagi, V.A., Yasarla, R., Patel, V.M.: Pushing the frontiers of unconstrained crowd counting: new dataset and benchmark method. In: Proceedings of the IEEE International Conference on Computer Vision (ICCV) (2019)

55. Sindagi, V.A., Yasarla, R., Patel, V.M.: JHU-CROWD++: large-scale crowd counting dataset and a benchmark method. Technical report (2020)

56. Sun, Y., Tzeng, E., Darrell, T., Efros, A.A.: Unsupervised domain adaptation through self-supervision. arXiv preprint arXiv:1909.11825 (2019)

57. Vincent, P., Larochelle, H., Bengio, Y., Manzagol, P.A.: Extracting and composing robust features with denoising autoencoders. In: Proceedings of the International Conference on Machine Learning (ICML) (2008)

58. Wan, J., Chan, A.: Modeling noisy annotations for crowd counting. Adv. Neural. Inf. Process. Syst. **33**, 3386–3396 (2020)

59. Wan, J., Luo, W., Wu, B., Chan, A.B., Liu, W.: Residual regression with semantic prior for crowd counting. In: Proceedings of the IEEE Conference on Computer Vision and Pattern Recognition (CVPR) (2019)

60. Wan, J., Wang, Q., Chan, A.B.: Kernel-based density map generation for dense object counting. IEEE Trans. Pattern Anal. Mach. Intell. **44**, 1357–1370 (2020)

61. Wang, Q., Gao, J., Lin, W., Li, X.: NWPU-crowd: a large-scale benchmark for crowd counting and localization. IEEE Trans. Pattern Anal. Mach. Intell. **43**, 2141–2149 (2020)

62. Wang, Q., Gao, J., Lin, W., Yuan, Y.: Learning from synthetic data for crowd counting in the wild. In: Proceedings of the IEEE Conference on Computer Vision and Pattern Recognition (CVPR) (2019)

63. Wang, X., Gupta, A.: Unsupervised learning of visual representations using videos. In: Proceedings of the IEEE International Conference on Computer Vision (ICCV) (2015)

64. Yan, Z., et al.: Perspective-guided convolution networks for crowd counting. In: Proceedings of the IEEE International Conference on Computer Vision (ICCV) (2019)

65. Zhang, A., et al.: Relational attention network for crowd counting. In: Proceedings of the IEEE International Conference on Computer Vision (ICCV) (2019)

66. Zhang, A., et al.: Attentional neural fields for crowd counting. In: Proceedings of the IEEE International Conference on Computer Vision (ICCV) (2019)

67. Zhang, C., Li, H., Wang, X., Yang, X.: Cross-scene crowd counting via deep convolutional neural networks. In: Proceedings of the IEEE Conference on Computer Vision and Pattern Recognition (CVPR) (2015)
68. Zhang, L., Qi, G.J., Wang, L., Luo, J.: AET vs. AED: unsupervised representation learning by auto-encoding transformations rather than data. In: Proceedings of the IEEE Conference on Computer Vision and Pattern Recognition (CVPR) (2019)
69. Zhang, R., Isola, P., Efros, A.: Split-brain autoencoders: unsupervised learning by cross-channel prediction. In: Proceedings of the IEEE Conference on Computer Vision and Pattern Recognition (CVPR) (2017)
70. Zhang, R., Isola, P., Efros, A.A.: Colorful image colorization. In: Leibe, B., Matas, J., Sebe, N., Welling, M. (eds.) ECCV 2016. LNCS, vol. 9907, pp. 649–666. Springer, Cham (2016). https://doi.org/10.1007/978-3-319-46487-9_40
71. Zhang, Y., Zhou, D., Chen, S., Gao, S., Ma, Y.: Single-image crowd counting via multi-column convolutional neural network. In: Proceedings of the IEEE Conference on Computer Vision and Pattern Recognition (CVPR) (2016)

Coarse-To-Fine Incremental Few-Shot Learning

Xiang Xiang[1]([⊠]), Yuwen Tan[1], Qian Wan[1], Jing Ma[1], Alan Yuille[2], and Gregory D. Hager[2]

[1] Key Lab of Image Processing and Intelligent Control, Ministry of Education, School of Artificial Intelligence and Automation, Huazhong University of Science and Technology, Wuhan, China
[2] Department of Computer Science, Johns Hopkins University, Baltimore, USA
`xex@hust.edu.cn`

Abstract. Different from fine-tuning models pre-trained on a large-scale dataset of preset classes, class-incremental learning (CIL) aims to recognize novel classes over time without forgetting pre-trained classes. However, a given model will be challenged by test images with finer-grained classes, e.g., a basenji is at most recognized as a dog. Such images form a new training set (i.e., support set) so that the incremental model is hoped to recognize a basenji (i.e., query) as a basenji next time. This paper formulates such a hybrid natural problem of coarse-to-fine few-shot (C2FS) recognition as a CIL problem named C2FSCIL, and proposes a simple, effective, and theoretically-sound strategy Knowe: to learn, freeze, and normalize a classifier's weights from fine labels, once learning an embedding space contrastively from coarse labels. Besides, as CIL aims at a stability-plasticity balance, new overall performance metrics are proposed. In hat sense, on CIFAR-100, BREEDS, and tieredImageNet, Knowe outperforms all recent relevant CIL or FSCIL methods.

Keywords: Class-incremental learning · Coarse-to-fine · Few shots

1 Introduction

Product visual search is normally driven by a deep model pre-trained on a large-scale private image-set, while at inference it needs to recognize consumer images at a finer granularity. For example, given a tree-like product catalog at Amazon.com, there is a class hierarchy per tree. However, it is rare to add the root-like

---

X. Xiang—Also with China's Belt & Road Joint Lab on Measurement & Control Tech., and National Key Lab of S&T on Multispectral Info Processing.

Supplementary Information The online version contains supplementary material available at https://doi.org/10.1007/978-3-031-19821-2_12.

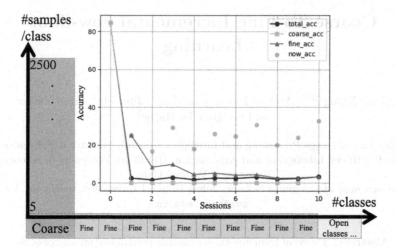

Fig. 1. Catastrophic forgetting when FT-ing a coarsely-trained model on fine samples presently available w/o freezing any weight. We pre-set 10 sessions from CIFAR-100 [21]. There is a fine-class accuracy from the 1st session and yet no coarse-class accuracy as all samples are with fine labels.

categories, such as breads, fruits, meat, *etc.* in the Fresh department and breakfast, snacks, beverages, *etc.* in the Gourmet Food department. That is because such catalogs have set the routine by semantic abstraction and approximate summarization. It is standard to pre-train models at a relatively static scale in such 'super-categories' or coarse levels. Such a model is expected to evolve on-the-fly [30] over time as being used, because fine-tuning (FT) it for specific novel classes induces an increasing number of separate models retrained, and thus is inefficient. In practice, it is common to add leaf-like categories along the use of Amazon, *e.g.*, under Fruits/Snacks, there is a long list that changes daily. Like humans, new labels of an item can be perceived later and then refine models' knowledge. However, it is rare to pre-train models at such dynamic scale. Such expectations of coarse-to-fine knowledge expansion is also valid for vision-driven autonomous systems. Model developers have a lot of coarsely-labeled samples for training but cannot predict what will be input after deploying it. For example, a self-driving car needs to gradually grow its perception capabilities as it runs.

In this paper, we are interested in a coarse-to-fine recognition problem that fits the class-incremental learning (CIL) setting. Moreover, fine classes appear asynchronously, which again fits CIL. It is also a few-shot learning problem, as there is no time to collect abundant samples per new class. We name such an incremental few-shot learning problem Coarse-to-Fine Few-Shot Class-Incremental Learning (C2FSCIL), and aim to propose a method that can evolve a generic model to both avoid catastrophic forgetting of source-blind coarse classes and prevent over-fitting the new few-shot fine-grained classes. However, **what exactly is the knowledge?** Incremental learning (IL) is aimed for the learning model to adapt to new data without forgetting its existing knowledge.

Catastrophic forgetting is a concept in connectionist networks [20,35] and occurs when the new weight vector is completely inappropriate as a solution for the originally learned pattern. In deep learning (DL), knowledge distillation (KD) is one of the most effective approaches to IL, while there lacks a consensus about what exactly the knowledge is in deep networks. Will it be the weight vectors?

Is a Coarsely-Learned Embedding Space Generalizable? We aim to achieve a superior performance at both the coarse and fine granularity. Considering the diversity of fine labels, it is infeasible to train a comprehensive fine-grained model beforehand. Instead, can a model be trained, using coarsely-labeled samples, to classify finely-labeled samples with accuracy comparable to that of a model trained with fine labels [11]? Our hypothesis is yes; then, the next question is how to pre-train a generalizable base model? How to explore a finer embedding space from coarse labels? Namely, what type of knowledge is useful for fine classes and how can we learn and preserve them [7]?

Can We Balance Old Knowledge and Current Learning? (*a.k.a.*, the stability-plasticity dilemma [34,52]). We aim to remember cues of both the pre-trained base classes and fine classes in the previous few-shot sessions. Our hypothesis is yes and our preference is a linear classifier as it is flexible, data in-demanding, and efficient to train as well as simple for derivation. The next question is how a linear classifier evolves the model effectively with a few shots and yet a balanced performance. As presumed, if the knowledge is weights, then freezing weights retains knowledge while updating weights evolves it.

To answer the questions, we propose a new problem for incrementally learning coarse-to-fine with a few shots and a way to measure balanced performance. We theoretically analyze why learning, freezing, and normalizing weights effectively solves the problem with a base model contrastively learned from coarse labels.

2   Related Work

Weak Supervision. Judging from the fine-class stage (Fig. 1 middle to right), if we combine a pre-training set and the support set as a holistic training set, then the few-shot fine-grained recognition using a model pre-trained on coarse samples are similar to the *weakly-supervised learning* and *learning from coarse labels* [6,11,54,55], *e.g.*, C2FS [6]. Ristel *et al.* investigates how coarse labels can be used to recognize sub-categories using random forests [42] (say, NCM [43]).

Open-Set Learning. Judging from the coarse-class stage [5] (see the left side of Fig. 1), CIL [38] can be dated back to the SVM [23] and random forest [42,43], where a new class can be added as a new node, and now seen as a progressive case of *continual/lifelong learning* [8,30], where CF is a challenge as data are hidden. The topology structure is also favored in DL [48,49]. *Few-shot learning* (FSL) measures models' ability to quickly adapt to new tasks [50] and has a flavor of CIL considering novel classes in the support set [10,13,39,49,56].

Incremental Learning (IL). IL allows a model to be continually updated on new data without forgetting, instead of training a model once on all data. There are two settings: class-IL [33] and task-IL [8]. They share main approaches, such as regularization and rehearsal methods. Regularization methods prevent the drift of consolidated weights and optimize network parameters for the current task, e.g., parameter control in EWC [20]. CIL is our focus and aims at learning a classifier that maintains a good performance on all classes seen in different sessions. Li et.al. first introduces KD [12] to IL in LwF [26] by modifying a cross-entropy loss to retain the knowledge. Recent works focus on retaining old-class samples to compute the KD loss. For example, iCaRL [38] learns both features and strong classifiers by combining KD and feature learning, e.g., NME.

Incremental Few-Shot Learning (IFSL). In the IFSL [39] or similarly FSCIL [49] setting, samples in the incremental session are relatively scarce, different from conventional CIL. While IFSL is based on meta learning, IFSL and DFSL [13] both utilize attentions. In FSCIL, a model named TOPIC is proposed, which contains a single neural gas (NG) network to learn feature-space topologies as knowledge, and adjust NG to preserve the stabilization and enhance the adaptation. In [10], Dong et al. propose an exemplar relation KD-IL framework to balance the tasks of old-knowledge preserving and new-knowledge adaptation as done in [53]. CEC [56] is proposed to separate classifier from the embedding learner, and use a graph attention network to propagate context cues between classifiers for adaptation. In [16], Hou et al. address the imbalance between old and new classes by cosine normalization [13,16,51].

Operating Weights for IL. The IL literature since 2017 has seen various weight operations (op. for short) in the sense of consolidation (e.g., EWC [20]), aligning [14,57], normalization [57,58], standardization [4], regularization [20,36], aggregation [28], calibration [47], rectification [46], transfer [25,29], sharing [41], masking [31], imprinting [37], picking [18], scaling [3], merging [24], pruning [32], quantizaton [45], weight importance [19], assignment [17], restricting weights to be positive [57], constraining weight changes [22], and so on.

Different from existing settings [10,49,56] that focus on remembering the pre-trained base classes only, our setting requires remembering the knowledge gained in both the base coarse and previous fine sessions. We add finer classes instead of new classes at the same granularity. Our setting requires a balance between coarse and fine performance unexplored by existing works. C2FS can be seen as going from our Session-0 to Session-1, while our setting has more incremental sessions and is a derived clean one among the **mixed** setups in IIRC [1]. **Different** from exisiting approaches, we do not follow rehearsal methods, namely, our model learns without memorizing samples [9]. However, retaining samples is often infeasible, say, when learning on-the-fly [30]. Even if there is memory for storing previous samples, there often is a budget, buffer, or queue. Thus, we aim to examine the extreme case of knowledge forgetting, and thus design IFSL methods to the upper-bound extent. For example, although in [22] they do not use any base-class training samples and keep the weights of the base classifier frozen, they still use previous samples in their third phase.

3 A New Problem C2FSCIL

Given a model parameterized by Θ and pre-trained on $\mathbb{D} = \{(\mathbf{x}_i, y_i)\}_{i=1}^N$ where $y_i \in \mathbb{Y} = \{\mathcal{Y}_1, \mathcal{Y}_2, ..., \mathcal{Y}_R\}$, a set of R coarse labels $\mathcal{Y}$, we have a stream of C-way K-shot support sets $\mathbb{S}^{(1)}, \mathbb{S}^{(2)}, ..., \mathbb{S}^{(t)}, ..., \mathbb{S}^{(T)}$ where $\mathbb{S}^{(t)} = \{(\mathbf{x}_j^{(t)}, y_j^{(t)})\}_{j=1}^{C \cdot K}$ and $y_j^{(t)} \in \mathbb{Z}^{(t)} = \{\mathcal{Z}_1^{(t)}, ..., \mathcal{Z}_C^{(t)}\}$, a set of C fine-grained labels $\mathcal{Z}$. Then, we adapt our model to $\mathbb{S}^{(1)}, \mathbb{S}^{(2)}, ..., \mathbb{S}^{(t)}$ over time and update the parameter set Θ from $\Theta^{(0)}$ all the way to $\Theta^{(t)}$. For testing, we also have a stream of $(C \cdot t + R)$-way H-shot query sets $\mathbb{Q}^{(1)}, \mathbb{Q}^{(2)}, ..., \mathbb{Q}^{(t)}, ..., \mathbb{Q}^{(T)}$ where $\mathbb{Q}^{(t)} = \{(\mathbf{x}_k^{(t)}, y_k^{(t)})\}_{k=1}^{(Ct+R)H}$ and $y_k^{(t)} \in \cup_{l=1}^t \mathbb{Z}^{(l)} \cup \mathbb{Y}$, which is the generalized union of all label sets till the t-th session. Notably, $\mathbb{Z}^{(t_1)} \cap \mathbb{Z}^{(t_2)} = \varnothing, \forall t_1, t_2$. We assume no sample can be retained (unlike rehearsal methods) and the CIL stage only includes (sub-classes of) base classes. At the t-th session, only the support set $\mathbb{S}^{(t)}$ can be used for training. We set the base of our subsequent theoretical analysis with two definitions [52]. Notably, as we only analyze the last layer, we take off the layer index l therein.

Definition A (Stability). *When the model Θ is being trained in the t-th session, $\Delta\mathbf{w}_{t,s}$ in each session should lie in the null space of the uncentered feature covariance matrix $\bar{\mathcal{X}}_{t-1} = [\mathbf{X}_{1,1}^T, ..., \mathbf{X}_{t-1,t-1}^T]^T$, namely, if $\bar{\mathcal{X}}_{t-1}\Delta\mathbf{w}_{t,s} = 0$ holds, then Θ is stable at the t-th session's s-th step.*

Note $\mathbf{w}$ is the classification-layer's weight vector, $\Delta\mathbf{w}$ is the change of $\mathbf{w}$, t indexes the session, and s indexes the training step. $\mathbf{X}_{p,p}$ where $p < t$ in $\bar{\mathcal{X}}_{t-1}$ is the input features of classification-layer on p-th session using classification-layer's weight trained on p-th session. We call it the absolute stability.

Definition B (Plasticity). *Assume that the network Θ is being trained in the t-th session, and $\mathbf{g}_{t,s} = \{g_{t,s}^1, ..., g_{t,s}^L\}$ denotes the parameter update generated by Gradient Descent for training Θ at step s. If $\langle \Delta\mathbf{w}_{t,s}, \mathbf{g}_{t,s} \rangle > 0$ holds, then Θ preserves plasticity at the t-th session's s-th step.*

If the inequality condition holds, the Θ's loss deceases and thus Θ is learning.

4 A Simple Approach Knowe

4.1 Learning Embedding-Weights Contrastively

Now, we elaborate on how we train a generalizable base embedding space [27,50]. cWe follow ANCOR [6] to use MoCo [15] as the backbone, and keep two network streams each of which contains a backbone network with the last-layer FC replaced by a Multi-Layer Perceptron (MLP). The hidden layer of two streams' MLP outputs intermediate $\mathbf{q}$ and $\mathbf{k}$, respectively. Given coarse labels, the total loss is defined as $\mathcal{L}^c = \mathcal{L}_{Con} + \mathcal{L}_{CE}^c$ where

$$\mathcal{L}_{Con} = -\sum_{n=1}^N \log \frac{exp(\mathbf{q}_n^T \mathbf{k}_n^+ / \tau)}{exp(\mathbf{q}_n^T \mathbf{k}_n^+ / \tau) + \sum_{m \neq n} exp(\mathbf{q}_n^T \mathbf{k}_m^- / \tau)}, \tag{1}$$

and $\mathcal{L}_{CE}^c$ is the standard cross-entropy loss that captures the inter-class cues. We also use angular normalization [6] to improve their synergy.

Note that m, n index samples, τ is a temperature parameter, $\mathbf{k}_m^-$ denotes the intermediate output of the m-th sample, a negative sample, in the same class with the n-th sample, a positive sample, so as to capture intra-class cues (fine cues), and reduce unnecessary noises to the subsequent fine-grained classification [54]. $\mathcal{L}_{Con}$ will be small when $\mathbf{q}_n$ is similar with $\mathbf{k}_n^+$ and different from $\mathbf{k}_m^-$.

4.2 Freezing Memorized Classifier-Weights

In the t-th incremental session, the task is similar to FSL where a support set $\mathbb{S}^{(t)}$ is offered to train a model to be evaluated on a query set $\mathbb{Q}^{(t)}$. However, FSL only evaluates the classification accuracy of the classes appeared in the support set $\mathbb{S}^{(t)}$. In our setting, the query set $\mathbb{Q}^{(t)}$ contains base classes, and all classes in previous support sets. No matter freezing embedding-weights helps or not, it does not hurt. We do so, hoping it to reduce model complexity to avoid over-fitting. As past samples are not retained, we freeze the classifier-weights of past classes to implicitly retain the label information and only train the augmented weight matrix $\mathbf{W}$ where in the t-th session, we have $\mathbf{W}_{[B:E]} = [\mathbf{w}_1^{(t)}|\mathbf{w}_2^{(t)}|...|\mathbf{w}_C^{(t)}]_{d \times C}$ with $B = R + C \cdot (t-1) + 1$, $E = R + C \cdot t$ for $t \geq 1$, except $\mathbf{W}_{[:R]} = [\mathbf{w}_1^{(0)}|\mathbf{w}_2^{(0)}|...|\mathbf{w}_R^{(0)}]_{d \times R}$ where d is the feature dimension.

4.3 Normalizing Classifier-Weights

In the last layer, we set the bias term to 0. For a sample $\mathbf{x}$, once a neuron has its output logit $o = \mathbf{w}^T \mathbf{f}(\mathbf{x})$ ready, then a Softmax activation function $Smx(\cdot)$ is applied to convert o to a probability so that we can classify $\mathbf{x}$. (^{T} is transpose)

However, such an inner-product linear classifier often favors new classes [16]. Instead, we compute the logit using the normalized inner-product [51] (a.k.a., cosine similarity, cosine normalization [13,16]) as $\tilde{o} = \tilde{\mathbf{w}}^T \tilde{\mathbf{f}}(\mathbf{x})$ where $\mathcal{L}_2$-normalized $\tilde{\mathbf{f}}(\mathbf{x}) = \mathbf{f}(\mathbf{x})/\|\mathbf{f}(\mathbf{x})\|_2$ and $\tilde{\mathbf{w}}_i = \mathbf{w}_i/\|\mathbf{w}_i\|_2$, and then apply Softmax to the rescaled logit $\tilde{o}$ as

$$p_i(\mathbf{x}) = Smx(\tilde{o}/\lambda) = \frac{exp(\tilde{\mathbf{w}}_i^T \tilde{\mathbf{f}}(\mathbf{x})/\lambda)}{\sum_j exp(\tilde{\mathbf{w}}_j^T \tilde{\mathbf{f}}(\mathbf{x})/\lambda)} \tag{2}$$

where i is the class index, λ is a temperature parameter that rescales the Softmax distribution, as $\tilde{o}$ is ranged of $[-1, 1]$. In the t-th session, we minimize the following cross-entropy loss on the support set $\mathbb{S}^{(t)}$:

$$\mathcal{L}_{CE}^{\mathbb{S}^{(t)}} = -\frac{1}{C \cdot K} \sum_{n=1}^{C \cdot K} \sum_{i=1}^{R+t*C} \delta_{y_n^{(t)}=i} log[p_i(\mathbf{x}_n^{(t)})] \tag{3}$$

where $\delta_{y_n^{(t)}=i}$ is the indicator function.

5   Theoretical Analysis of Knowe for Stability-Plasticity

In this theory, we decouple the embedding learner and classifier, a linear FC layer, freeze weights of the embedding learner, and use the conventional Softmax cross-entropy loss. Different from the conventional FC layer, we freeze weights of neurons corresponding to previous classes. Now we extend **Def. A** and **B**.

Definition 1 (Stability Decay). *For the same input sample, let* $\tilde{o}_i^{(t)}$ *denote the output of the* i*-th neuron in the last layer in the* t*-th session. After the loss reaches the minimum, we define the decay of stability as* $\mathcal{D} = \sum_i (\frac{\tilde{o}_i^{(T)} - \tilde{o}_i^{(t)}}{\tilde{o}_i^{(t)}})^2$.

Definition 2 (Relative Stability). *Given models* Θ_a *and* Θ_b*, if* $0 \leq \mathcal{D}_a < \mathcal{D}_b$*, then we say* Θ_a *is more stable than* Θ_b.

Assuming embedding-weights are frozen, then we have:

Proposition 1 (Normalizing or freezing weights improves stability; doing both improves the most). *Given* Θ_a*, if we only normalize weights of a linear FC classifier, we obtain* Θ_b*; if we only freeze them, we obtain* Θ_c*; if we do both, we obtain* Θ_d*. Then,* $\mathcal{D}_d < \mathcal{D}_b < \mathcal{D}_a$ *and* $\mathcal{D}_d < \mathcal{D}_c < \mathcal{D}_a$.

Proof. (1) Stability Degree of model Θ_a.

It is assumed that the training for all sessions will reach the minimum loss. For the training sample m in the 0-th session, the probability that m belongs to superclass is one, i.e., $p_{t,c_{super}}^m = 1$ and $p_{t,i}^m = 0 (i \neq c_{super})$. According to $p_i^m = \frac{\exp(o_i^m)}{\sum_{j=1}^I \exp(o_j^m)}$, the following conditions are satisfied,

$$\tilde{o}_{c_{super}}^{(t)} = a(a \in \mathbb{R}), \tilde{o}_i^{(t)}(i \neq c_{super}) = -\infty. \tag{4}$$

After training of T-th session has reached the minimum loss, $\tilde{o}_{c_{sub}}^{(T)} = b(b \in \mathbb{R}), \tilde{o}_i^{(T)}(i \neq c_{sub}) = -\infty$, then,

$$\mathcal{D}_a = \sum_i (\frac{\tilde{o}_i^{(T)} - \tilde{o}_i^{(t)}}{\tilde{o}_i^{(t)}})^2 = (\frac{-\infty - a}{a})^2 + (\frac{b - (-\infty)}{-\infty})^2 = \infty. \tag{5}$$

Similarly, we can analyze the stability degree for Θ_b, Θ_c, Θ_d. Please see the full proof in *Appendix*. Our second claim is about normalization for plasticity.

Proposition 2 (Weights normalized, plasticity remains). *To train our FC classifier, if we denote the loss as* $\mathcal{L}(\mathbf{w})$ *where* $\mathbf{w}$ *is normalized, the weight update at each step as* $\Delta\mathbf{w}$*, and the learning rate as* α*, then we have* $f\mathcal{L}(\mathbf{w} - \alpha\Delta\mathbf{w}) < \mathcal{L}(\mathbf{w})$.

Proof. For a sample m whose feature vector is $\mathbf{x}$, the output of i-th neuron is

$$\mathbf{o}_i = \sigma(\mathbf{x} \cdot \mathbf{w}^i) = \cos\theta_i = \frac{\mathbf{x} \cdot \mathbf{w}^i}{\|\mathbf{x}\|_2 \|\mathbf{w}^i\|_2}. \tag{6}$$

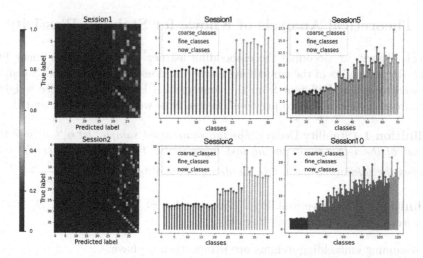

Fig. 2. 10-way 5-shot confusion matrix (left) and visualization of the norm of raw weights (mid-right) in the last layer for old/new classes. As each session can only access labels of the present classes, a linear classifier will have a larger weight for the current classes' neurons, inducing the queries of previous classes to be likely assigned into current classes' region (left) in the embedding space. (CIFAR-100)

The probability of sample m belonging to i-th class is

$$p_i = \frac{\exp(\mathbf{o}_i)}{\sum_{j=1} \exp(\mathbf{o}_j)} \tag{7}$$

And the loss of training is denoted as

$$\mathcal{L}(\mathbf{w}) = -\sum_i y_i log(p_i) \tag{8}$$

where y_i denotes the label of sample m. Denote the weights update of the i-th neuron in linear FC layer as $\Delta \mathbf{w}^i$, then

$$\Delta \mathbf{w}^i = \begin{cases} (p_i - 1)(\dfrac{\mathbf{x}}{\|\mathbf{x}\|_2 \|\mathbf{w}^i\|_2} - \dfrac{\mathbf{w}^i(\mathbf{x} \cdot \mathbf{w}^i)}{\|\mathbf{x}\|_2 \|\mathbf{w}^i\|_2^3}), & i = c \\[3mm] p_i(\dfrac{\mathbf{x}}{\|\mathbf{x}\|_2 \|\mathbf{w}^i\|_2} - \dfrac{\mathbf{w}^i(\mathbf{x} \cdot \mathbf{w}^i)}{\|\mathbf{x}\|_2 \|\mathbf{w}^i\|_2^3}), & i \neq c \end{cases} \tag{9}$$

According to $\hat{\mathbf{w}} = \mathbf{w} - \alpha \Delta \mathbf{w}$, we have

$$\hat{\mathbf{w}}^i = \begin{cases} \mathbf{w}^i + \alpha(1 - p_i)\dfrac{1}{\|\mathbf{w}^i\|_2}(\dfrac{\mathbf{x}}{\|\mathbf{x}\|_2} - \dfrac{\mathbf{w}^i}{\|\mathbf{w}^i\|_2} \cos\theta_i), & i = c \\[3mm] \mathbf{w}^i - \alpha p_i \dfrac{1}{\|\mathbf{w}^i\|_2}(\dfrac{\mathbf{x}}{\|\mathbf{x}\|_2} - \dfrac{\mathbf{w}^i}{\|\mathbf{w}^i\|_2} \cos\theta_i), & i \neq c \end{cases} \tag{10}$$

By denoting $h(\alpha) \triangleq \mathcal{L}(\mathbf{w} - \alpha \Delta \mathbf{w})$, according to Taylor's theorem, we have

$$\mathcal{L}(\mathbf{w} - \alpha \Delta \mathbf{w}) = \mathcal{L}(\mathbf{w}) - \alpha \langle \Delta \mathbf{w}, \mathbf{g} \rangle + o(\alpha) \tag{11}$$

where $\frac{|o(\alpha)|}{\alpha} \to 0$ when $\alpha \to 0$. Therefore, there exists $\bar{\alpha} > 0$ such that

$$|o(\alpha)| < \alpha |\langle \Delta \mathbf{w}, \mathbf{g} \rangle|, \forall \alpha \in (0, \bar{\alpha}) \tag{12}$$

With $\mathbf{g} = \frac{\partial \mathcal{L}(\hat{\mathbf{w}})}{\partial \hat{\mathbf{w}}} = \Delta \hat{\mathbf{w}}$, the calculation leads to the conclusion that $\langle \Delta \mathbf{w}, \mathbf{g} \rangle = \sum_i \Delta \mathbf{w}^i \Delta \hat{\mathbf{w}}^i > 0$, and thus $\mathcal{L}(\mathbf{w} - \alpha \Delta \mathbf{w}) < \mathcal{L}(\mathbf{w})$ for all $\alpha \in (0, \bar{\alpha})$. Weights update $\Delta \mathbf{w}$ is the descent direction.

Notably, freezing the weights does not affect plasticity. As shown in Fig. 2, samples of classes seen in the 1st session are totally classified to classes seen in the 2nd session while only samples of the present classes can be correctly classified. We plot weight norms to find them grow and propose a conjecture implying a need of normalization.

Conjecture 1 (FC weights grow over time). *Let* $\|\mathbf{W}^{(t)}\|_F$ *denotes the Frobenius norm of the weight matrix formed by all weight vectors in the FC layer for new classes in the t-th session. With training converged and norm outliers ignored, it holds that* $\|\mathbf{W}^{(t)}\|_F > \|\mathbf{W}^{(t-1)}\|_F, \forall t \in \{1, ..., T\}$.

Analysis. For a conventional linear FC layer, the output of neural network directly determines the probability of which class the sample belongs to. Thus, we use $\Delta \mathbf{o}_i$ to represent the reward ($\Delta \mathbf{o}_i > 0$) or penalty ($\Delta \mathbf{o}_i < 0$) for different neurons after sample $\mathbf{x}$ with label c is trained, where $\mathbf{o}_i = \mathbf{x} \cdot \mathbf{w}^i$ is the output of the i-th neuron and $\alpha > 0$ is the learning rate. Then, we have

$$\Delta \mathbf{o}_i = \begin{cases} \alpha(1 - p_i) \|\mathbf{x}\|_2^2 \geq 0, & i = c \\ -\alpha p_i \|\mathbf{x}\|_2^2 \leq 0, & i \neq c \end{cases} \tag{13}$$

For a sample m with super-class label c_{super} and sub-class label c_{sub}, when we train sample m only with label c_{super} and reach a relatively good state in the 0-th session, we will get $p^m_{c_{super}} \to 1$ and $p^m_i(i \neq c_{super}) \to 0$. When we train sample m only with label c_{sub} in other sessions and reach a relatively good state, the penalty for superclass of sample m will be much larger than other classes, meanwhile the reward for subclass of sample m will be much larger too. Therefore, if i belongs to previously-seen classes, $i \neq c$ will hold most of the time during training. Thus, previously-seen classes will keep being penalized during the gradient descent. As a result, the weights of previously-seen classes are prone to be smaller than those for the newly added classes. And because we train new classes in stages and reach a relatively good state (say, the training loss converges to small value) for all sessions, the FC weights will piecewisely grow over time. Therefore, the model is consequently biased towards new classes.

As for freezing embedding weights. We have (see the analysis in *Appendix*):

Conjecture 2 (Sufficient & necessary condition of no impact of freezing embedding-weights). $p \vee q \Leftrightarrow \neg r$ *where*

p: *classifier-weights are normalized,*
q: *classifier-weights are frozen,*
r: *freezing embedding-weights improves the performance.*

6   Experiments

6.1   New Overall Performance Measures

In this section, we evaluate the model after each session with the query set $\mathbb{Q}^{(t)}$, and report the Top-1 accuracy. The base session only contains coarse labels, and thus is evaluated by the coarse-grained classification accuracy $\mathcal{A}_c$. We evaluate $\mathcal{A}_c$, the fine-grained accuracy $\mathcal{A}_f$, and the total accuracy $\mathcal{A}_t$ per incremental session, except the last session when only fine labels are available and $\mathcal{A}_c$ is not evaluated. We average $\mathcal{A}_t$ to obtain an overall performance score as

$$\bar{\mathcal{A}} = \frac{1}{T+1} \sum_{i=0}^{T} \mathcal{A}_t^i. \tag{14}$$

Inspired by [3], we define the fine-class forgetting rate

$$\mathcal{F}_f^t = \frac{\mathcal{A}_f^{t-1} - \mathcal{A}_f^t}{\mathcal{A}_f^{t-1}}, \tag{15}$$

and the forgetting rate for the base coarse class as

$$\mathcal{F}_c^t = \frac{\mathcal{A}_c^0 - \mathcal{A}_c^t}{\mathcal{A}_c^0}. \tag{16}$$

With them, we can evaluate the model with an overall measure to represent the catastrophic forgetting rate as

$$\mathcal{F} = \frac{1}{T-1} \left(\sum_{t=2}^{T} \mathcal{F}_f^t * \frac{c_t}{N_f} + \sum_{t=1}^{T-1} \mathcal{F}_c^t * (1 - \frac{c_t}{N_f}) \right) \tag{17}$$

where T is the number of incremental sessions; c_t is the number of appeared fine classes until the t-th session, and N_f is fine-class total number; $\mathcal{A}_c$ and $\mathcal{A}_f$ are the accuracy of coarse and fine classes per session, respectively.

6.2   Datasets and Results

CIFAR-100 contains $60,000$ images from 100 fine classes, each of which has 500 training images and 100 test images [21]. They can be grouped into 20 coarse classes, each of which includes 5 fine classes, *e.g.*, *trees* contains *maple, oak, pine, palm,* and *willow.* The 100 fine classes are divided into 10 10-way 5-shot sessions.

Table 1. Dataset setting and performance. # is class num.

Dataset	Coarse#	Fine#	Total#	Sessions	Way/shot	Queries	$\bar{\mathcal{A}}$	$\mathcal{F}$
CIFAR-100	20	100	120	10	10/5	15	38.50	0.42
Living17	17	68	85	7	10/1	15	54.62	0.33
Nonliving26	26	104	130	11	10/1	15	48.41	0.25
Entity13	13	260	273	13	20/1	15	41.45	0.38
Entity30	30	240	270	8	30/1	15	47.79	0.32
TieredImageNet	20	351	371	10	36/5	15	33.24	0.39

BREEDS is derived from ImageNet with class hierarchy re-calibrated by [44] and contains 4 subsets named living17, nonliving26, entity13, and entity30. They have 17, 26, 13, 30 coarse classes, 4, 4, 20, 8 fine classes per coarse class, 88K, 132K, 334K, 307K training images, 3.4K, 5.2K, 13K, 12K test images.

tieredImageNet (tIN) is a subset of ImageNet and contains 608 classes [40] that are grouped into 34 high-level super-classes to ensure that the training classes are distinct enough from the test classes semantically. The train/val/test set have 20, 6, 8 coarse classes, 351, 97, 160 fine classes, 448K, 124K, 206K images. Table 1 summarizes our performance and Fig. 3 visualizes confusion matrices.

6.3 Implementation Details

We use ResNet-50 on BREEDS, '−12' on CIFAR100 and '−12' on tIN, train $\Theta^{(0)}$ except FC using ANCOR, use SGD with a momentum 0.9, as well as set weight decay to 5e-4, batch size to 256, τ to 0.2, and λ to 0.5. The learning rate is 0.12 for $\Theta^{(0)}$, and is 0.1 for $\Theta^{(1)}, \Theta^{(2)}$, etc. for 200 epochs. Please see also the project page[1].

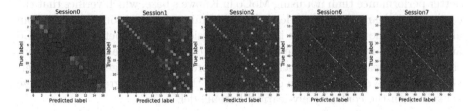

Fig. 3. Confusion matrices of Knowe tested on BREEDS-living17.

---

[1] https://github.com/HAIV-Lab/Knowe.

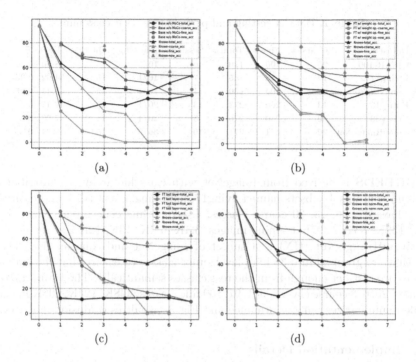

Fig. 4. Ablation study on living17. (a) Contrastive learning? (b) Freezing embedding-weights? (c) Freezing classifier-weights? (d) Normalizing weights?

6.4   Ablation Study

Impact of Base Contrastive Learning. As shown in Fig. 4a, Knowe obtains a better performance than not using MoCo in Knowe's base, which verifies that the contrastively-learned base model helps fine-grained recognition. Starting from almost the same fine accuracy in the 2nd session, the gap between w/ MoCo and w/o MoCo increases, as the former stably outperforms the latter on current classes. It verifies that the former can learn more fine knowledge than the latter. Given there are only a few fine-class samples, the extra fine-grained knowledge is likely from the contrastively-learned base model.

Impact of Freezing Embedding-Weights. Figure 4b illustrates that freezing embedding-weights induces a slightly better performance than not freezing them. *If classifier-weights are normalized and frozen, freezing embedding-weights does not help* ($p \wedge q \Rightarrow \neg r$), which is shown by small changes of $\bar{A}$ and $\mathcal{F}$ in Table 2.

Impact of Freezing Memorized Classifier-Weights. As shown in Fig. 4c, there is severe CF of both fine and coarse knowledge when not freezing the weights of previously-seen classes, which implies that little knowledge is retained. Although embedding-weights are frozen and classifier-weights are normalized, the coarse knowledge is totally forgotten. It implies that, *if classifier-weights are normalized and yet not frozen, freezing the embedding-weights does not help*

$(p \wedge \neg q \Rightarrow \neg r)$. It can be explained that fine-tuning on a few samples normally induces little change to the embedding-weights and yet great change to classifier-weights. Moreover, the model without freezing classifier-weights performs much worse than Knowe that freezes previous weights. The gap of the fine accuracy increases over time and is larger than the gap of the present accuracy. It implies that they also differ in the performance of previous fine classes.

Impact of Normalizing Classifier-Weight. Figure 2 has already shown that, with a linear classifier, the weight norms of new classes totally surpass the weight norms of previous classes, which causes that the linear classifier biases towards new classes (*i.e.*, any sample of previous class can be classified as a new class). That implies a need of normlizing the classifer-weights. As shown in Fig. 4d, when we freeze weights of previous classes and only tune the weights of new classes w/o normalization, the model performs stably worse, which verifies that normalizing classifier-weights plays a positive role.

Table 2. Performance on BREEDS living17 (top) and entity30 (bottom).

Mehtod	Contr. learn.	Decoupled	Frozen	Normalization	Total accuracy per session									$\bar{A}\uparrow$	$\mathcal{F}\downarrow$
					0	1	2	3	4	5	6	7	8		
(a) Base w/o MoCo		✓	✓	✓	93.18	33.04	26.37	31.08	29.51	35.10	34.71	37.84	N/A	40.10	0.50
(b) FT w/ weight op	✓		✓	✓	94.21	63.14	47.45	40.10	41.47	34.80	40.59	43.53	N/A	50.66	0.35
(c) FT last layer	✓	✓		✓	94.21	12.06	11.28	12.26	12.26	12.55	12.65	9.51	N/A	22.09	0.66
(d) Knowe w/o norm	✓	✓	✓		94.50	17.84	14.02	22.26	21.28	24.71	26.77	24.80	N/A	30.77	0.57
LwF+ [26]	✓				**94.50**	*61.47*	*44.61*	27.45	19.12	11.28	6.37	4.22	N/A	33.63	0.51
ScaIL [3]	✓				**94.50**	38.63	25.59	31.08	30.29	35.10	37.84	41.08	N/A	41.76	0.48
Weight Align+ [57]	✓	✓	✓		**94.50**	50.98	37.94	*38.43*	*37.06*	*35.20*	*39.80*	*43.24*	N/A	*47.14*	*0.40*
Subsp. Reg.+ [2]	✓	✓	✓		**94.50**	59.41	39.51	33.43	29.31	25.59	27.84	26.47	N/A	42.01	*0.40*
Knowe (Ours)	✓	✓	✓	✓	*94.21*	**63.63**	**50.88**	**43.82**	**42.84**	**40.29**	**47.75**	**53.53**	N/A	**54.62**	**0.33**
ANCOR [6]	✓				94.50	11.86	11.18	12.35	11.77	12.55	10.78	9.02	N/A	21.75	0.66
Jt. train. (upp. bd.)	✓		✓	✓	94.21	63.63	58.53	52.26	46.28	47.75	36.96	42.75	N/A	55.29	0.25
LwF+ [26]	✓				**89.48**	**65.03**	*48.69*	22.72	9.36	6.03	4.61	2.86	3.33	28.01	0.47
ScaIL [3]	✓				**89.48**	39.25	25.50	22.44	23.69	25.75	30.81	32.08	35.25	36.03	0.48
Weight Align+ [57]	✓	✓	✓		**89.48**	47.36	37.06	*31.72*	*30.56*	*32.28*	*34.11*	*36.39*	*37.06*	*41.78*	*0.42*
Subsp. Reg.+ [2]	✓	✓	✓		**89.48**	42.39	28.94	20.86	16.14	16.44	16.75	16.17	16.06	29.25	0.48
Knowe (Ours)	✓	✓	✓	✓	*87.90*	*63.22*	**49.22**	**37.75**	**34.78**	**36.25**	**38.03**	**40.08**	**42.83**	**47.79**	**0.32**
ANCOR [6]	✓				89.48	8.67	8.28	9.50	6.83	8.75	9.53	8.19	8.69	17.55	0.61
Jt. train. (upp. bd.)	✓		✓	✓	87.90	63.22	56.56	53.72	47.36	44.78	41.61	38.06	36.75	52.22	0.20

More About Freezing Embedding-Weights. We know $\neg p \wedge q \Rightarrow \neg r$. Thus, we have a **Conjecture 3**: $p \vee q \Rightarrow \neg r$, meaning *if classifier-weights are either normalized or frozen, then freezing embedding-weights does not help*. A decent *now_acc* seems a condition for weight freezing and normalization to be effective.

6.5 Performance Comparison and Analysis

Tables 2, 3, 4 and Fig. 5 compare Knowe with SOTA FSCIL or CIL methods including LwF [26], ScaIL [3], Weight Aligning [57] and Subspace Regularizers (Sub. Reg.) [2]. Joint training is non-IL and an *acc* upper bound in principle.

Overall Average *acc* $\bar{A}$ and Forgetting Rate $\mathcal{F}$. As shown in Tables 2, 3, 4, Knowe has the smallest $\mathcal{F}$ and the largest $\bar{A}$ on all datasets. From both metrics,

Table 3. Performance on BREEDS nonliving26 (top) and entity13 (bottom).

Method	Contr. learn.	Decoupled	Frozen	Normalization	0	1	2	3	4	5	6	7	8	9	10	11	12	13	Ā↑	F↓
LwF+ [26]	✓				86.94	65.51	58.14	44.17	22.76	14.36	9.68	6.92	5.19	5.32	3.40	N/A	N/A		27.36	0.38
ScaIL [3]	✓				86.94	36.09	24.10	21.47	23.27	23.65	27.95	31.80	34.23	36.09	37.76	38.14	N/A	N/A	35.12	0.43
Weight Align.+ [57]	✓	✓	✓		86.94	61.41	46.03	40.00	35.77	34.10	35.96	33.81	35.51	36.60	37.56	37.76	N/A	N/A	43.40	0.89
Subsp. Reg.+ [2]	✓	✓	✓		86.94	63.59	52.56	42.95	35.96	31.41	28.01	26.15	23.27	19.68	19.36	20.19	N/A	N/A	37.51	0.25
Knowe (Ours)	✓	✓	✓	✓	86.83	65.90	53.08	46.80	42.82	38.91	41.22	39.10	40.06	41.80	42.44	42.63	N/A	N/A	48.41	0.25
ANCOR [6]	✓				86.94	5.83	6.03	6.92	5.90	6.60	7.63	7.05	7.05	7.50	7.44	2.63	N/A	N/A	13.13	0.61
Jt. train. (upp. bd.)	✓		✓	✓	86.23	65.90	60.51	59.04	53.53	53.85	46.73	46.60	43.85	36.67	37.31	36.80	N/A	N/A	52.25	0.16
LwF+ [26]	✓				92.03	59.10	43.64	18.49	10.49	6.82	3.59	2.54	3.10	2.56	2.10	2.23	1.77	1.54	17.86	0.52
ScaIL [3]	✓				92.03	37.10	13.92	13.36	14.87	18.36	21.72	23.28	24.33	27.62	29.59	31.54	32.36	34.08	29.58	0.49
Weight Align+ [57]	✓	✓	✓		92.03	36.74	24.15	20.51	22.31	24.82	26.41	26.85	27.86	31.49	32.26	35.28	36.72	37.69	33.89	0.46
Subsp. Reg.+ [2]	✓	✓	✓		92.03	52.72	28.95	15.92	12.08	10.82	10.90	11.49	12.05	12.03	11.77	11.72	12.54	14.36	22.10	0.45
Knowe (Ours)	✓	✓	✓	✓	91.35	66.90	45.69	35.54	30.56	29.21	30.10	29.95	30.85	33.74	35.36	38.54	40.26	42.21	41.45	0.38
ANCOR [6]	✓				92.03	5.36	5.67	5.49	5.18	6.51	5.82	4.80	5.39	6.28	5.36	5.13	5.26	5.62	11.71	0.57
Jt. train. (upp. bd.)	✓		✓	✓	91.35	66.90	57.54	49.92	50.59	48.64	47.69	44.41	41.72	39.13	39.62	40.72	38.49	37.26	49.57	0.24

Table 4. Comparison with others on CIFAR-100 (top table) and tieredImageNet.

Method	Contr. learn.	Decoupled	Frozen	Normalization	0	1	2	3	4	5	6	7	8	9	10	Ā↑	F↓
LwF+ [26]	✓				78.39	41.87	28.00	23.80	14.93	10.53	8.00	8.80	6.47	7.33	6.73	21.35	0.51
ScaIL [3]	✓				78.39	14.47	14.13	18.07	21.00	25.20	26.20	31.87	32.60	36.53	38.20	30.61	0.52
Weight Align+ [57]	✓	✓	✓		78.39	13.20	14.13	18.20	21.20	24.60	26.93	32.33	32.60	38.93	38.46	30.82	0.53
Subsp. Reg.+ [2]	✓	✓	✓		78.39	41.47	31.80	32.87	26.73	25.73	25.27	26.73	24.27	25.73	24.00	33.00	0.43
Knowe (Ours)	✓	✓	✓	✓	72.07	36.00	28.13	30.87	32.20	31.20	30.93	36.33	39.27	43.20	43.93	38.50	0.42
ANCOR [6]	✓				78.39	7.93	7.13	8.27	7.80	8.60	6.40	7.53	6.93	8.20	8.33	14.14	0.59
Jt. train. (upp. bd.)	✓		✓	✓	72.07	36.00	37.07	40.27	40.13	41.33	38.60	41.13	40.47	41.40	43.47	42.00	0.33
LwF+ [26]	✓				87.64	69.36	13.88	4.22	4.05	4.03	3.02	2.74	1.44	1.05	1.06	17.50	0.55
ScaIL [3]	✓				87.64	48.51	33.12	26.15	22.66	22.77	23.42	22.72	23.38	25.17	26.65	32.93	0.40
Weight Align+ [57]	✓	✓	✓		87.64	25.13	18.63	18.37	20.08	22.20	24.22	24.73	26.71	29.00	30.45	29.74	0.48
Subsp. Reg.+ [2]	✓	✓	✓		87.64	49.73	32.06	24.35	20.95	20.76	20.84	21.12	21.79	23.15	24.31	31.52	0.42
Knowe (Ours)	✓	✓	✓	✓	76.15	48.24	30.60	25.60	22.34	23.48	24.79	24.69	27.65	30.26	31.87	33.24	0.39
ANCOR [6]	✓				87.64	7.10	6.69	6.55	6.36	6.57	6.42	6.55	6.55	6.40	5.17	13.82	0.61
Jt. train. (upp. bd.)	✓		✓	✓	76.15	48.24	39.89	34.09	32.21	30.85	28.81	29.86	28.57	28.74	29.06	36.95	0.32

Weight Aligning ranks 2nd on BREEDS, Sub. Reg. ranks 2nd on CIFAR-100, and ScaIL ranks 2nd on tIN (consistent across two metrics). LwF has poor numbers, which implies that, with no samples retained, KD does not help.

Total accuracy per session decreases over time yet slower and slower for Knowe and SOTA methods. However, outstanding ones decrease first and then rise, because that the proportion of fine classes in the query set gets higher and their accuracy plays a leading role in the total accuracy. Knowe is the best, with a strong rising trend, which satisfies the aim of CIL the most and envisions Knowe continuing performing well when more sessions are added (Table 3) . Sub. Reg. and Weight Align. often have 2nd-best numbers (both freeze weights); ScaIL and LwF occasionally do.

Coarse class accuracy decreases over time unavoidably (see Fig. 5), while Knowe and SOTA methods slow down the decay, with comparable rates. As IL methods, Weight Aligning, ScaIL, and LwF do not forget knowledge totally although they do not operate weights as done by Knowe. As an non-IL approach, ANCOR totally forgets old knowledge from the 1st session because it fine-tunes on the few fine shots without any extra operation to retain coarse knowledge. The joint training on all fine classes till the present is non-IL, and in principle should bound the fine-class performance. Interestingly, it also suffers less from coarse *acc* decay, the rate of which is much lower (Fig. 5). Differently, the cause can be imbalance between increasing fine classes and coarse classes. Knowe's performance is very competitive and indeed bounded by joint training.

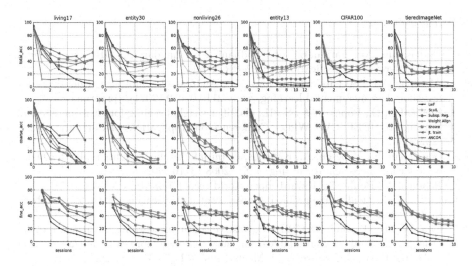

Fig. 5. Accuracy comparison on all datasets. Top-down: total, coarse, fine.

Fine class's total accuracy normally decreases over time yet slower and slower for Knowe and SOTA methods (Fig. 5), and can be maintained in a similar range for most methods, among which Knowe often stays the highest, ScaIl and Weight Aligning are in the middle, Sub Reg. often stays in a low level, and LwF and ANCOR perform stably the worst. Knowe is the most balanced, while Sub. Reg. biases towards stability that is its drawback. Joint training does not bound the accuracy, possibly due to few shots.

Compared Works. All empirically-compared CIL methods and ours are no-rehearsal ones. On the other hand, joint training is rehearsal-based.

7 Conclusion

In this paper, we present a new problem together with new metrics, and theoretically analyze why a simple approach can solve it well in the sense of getting more balanced performance than the SOTA. While it is not new to freeze or normalize weights, we are unaware of them previously being presented as a principled approach (to CIL) that is as simple as fine-tuning. It makes pre-trained big models more useful for finer-grained tasks. For C2FSCIL with a linear classifier, weights seem to be the knowledge. However, how generic are our findings in practice? Can they be applied to general FSCIL? If yes, we are more comfortable with that answer, but then how does a class hierarchy make a difference? Future work will include examining those questions, non-linear classifiers, and so on.

Acknowledgement. This research was supported by National NSFC (62176100), National Key R&D Program of China (2021ZD0201300), HUST Independent Innovation Res. Fund (2021XXJS096), Sichuan Univ. Interdisciplinary Innovation Res. Fund (RD-03-202108), and MoE Key Lab of Image Processing & Inteliigent Control

References

1. Abdelsalam, M., Faramarzi, M., Sodhani, S., Chandar, S.: IIRC: incremental implicitly-refined classification. In: CVPR (2021)
2. Akyürek, A.F., Akyürek, E., Wijaya, D., Andreas, J.: Subspace regularizers for few-shot class incremental learning. arxiv:2110.07059 (2021). (preprint)
3. Belouadah, E., Popescu, A.: ScaIL: classifier weights scaling for class incremental learning. In: IEEE/CVF Winter Conference on Applications of Computer Vision (2020)
4. Belouadah, E., Popescu, A., Kanellos, I.: Initial classifier weights replay for memoryless class incremental learning. arXiv:2008.13710 (2020). (preprint)
5. Bendale, A., Boult, T.: Towards open world recognition. In: CVPR (2015)
6. Bukchin, G., et al.: Fine-grained angular contrastive learning with coarse labels. In: CVPR (2021)
7. Cha, H., Lee, J., Shin, J.: Co2L: contrastive continual learning. In: ICCV (2021)
8. Delange, M., et al.: A continual learning survey: defying forgetting in classification tasks. IEEE Trans. Pattern Anal. Mach. Intell. **44**, 3366–3385 (2021)
9. Dhar, P., Singh, R.V., Peng, K.C., Wu, Z., Chellappa, R.: Learning without memorizing. In: CVPR (2019)
10. Dong, S., Hong, X., Tao, X., Chang, X., Wei, X.: Few-shot class-incremental learning via relation knowledge distillation. In: AAAI (2021)
11. Fotakis, D., Kalavasis, A., Kontonis, V., Tzamos, C.: Efficient algorithms for learning from coarse labels. In: 34th Annual Conference on Learning Theory (2021)
12. Geoffrey, H., Oriol, V., Jeff, D.: Distilling the knowledge in a neural network. In: NeurIPS (2015)
13. Gidaris, S., Komodakis, N.: Dynamic few-shot visual learning without forgetting. In: CVPR (2018)
14. He, C., Wang, R., Chen, X.: A tale of two CILs: the connections between class incremental learning and class imbalanced learning, and beyond. In: CVPR Workshops (2021)
15. He, K., Fan, H., Wu, Y., Xie, S., Girshick, R.: Momentum contrast for unsupervised visual representation learning. In: CVPR (2020)
16. Hou, S., Pan, X., Loy, C.C., Wang, Z., Lin, D.: Learning a unified classifier incrementally via rebalancing. In: CVPR (2019)
17. Hu, X., Tang, K., Miao, C., Hua, X.S., Zhang, H.: Distilling causal effect of data in class-incremental learning. In: CVPR (2021)
18. Hung, S.C.Y., Tu, C.H., Wu, C.E., Chen, C.H., Chan, Y.M., Chen, C.S.: Compacting, picking and growing for unforgetting continual learning. In: NeurIPS (2019)
19. Jung, S., Ahn, H., Cha, S., Moon, T.: Continual learning with node-importance based adaptive group sparse regularization. In: NeurIPS (2020)
20. Kirkpatrick, J., et al.: Overcoming catastrophic forgetting in neural networks. Proc. Natl. Acad. Sci. **114**(13), 3521–3526 (2017)
21. Krizhevsky, A.: Learning multiple layers of features from tiny images. Technical report, Unvieristy of Toronto (2009)
22. Kukleva, A., Kuehne, H., Schiele, B.: Generalized and incremental few-shot learning by explicit learning and calibration without forgetting. In: ICCV (2021)
23. Kuzborskij, I., Orabona, F., Caputo, B.: From n to n+1: multiclass transfer incremental learning. In: CVPR (2013)
24. Lee, J., Hong, H.G., Joo, D., Kim, J.: Continual learning with extended Kronecker-factored approximate curvature. In: CVPR (2020)

25. Lee, S.W., Kim, J.H., Jun, J., Ha, J.W., Zhang, B.T.: Overcoming catastrophic forgetting by incremental moment matching. In: NIPS (2017)
26. Li, Z., Hoiem, D.: Learning without forgetting. In: Leibe, B., Matas, J., Sebe, N., Welling, M. (eds.) ECCV 2016. LNCS, vol. 9908, pp. 614–629. Springer, Cham (2016). https://doi.org/10.1007/978-3-319-46493-0_37
27. Liu, C., et al.: Learning a few-shot embedding model with contrastive learning. In: AAAI (2021)
28. Liu, Y., Schiele, B., Sun, Q.: Adaptive aggregation networks for class-incremental learning. In: CVPR (2021)
29. Liu, Y., Su, Y., Liu, A.A., Schiele, B., Sun, Q.: Mnemonics training: multi-class incremental learning without forgetting. In: CVPR (2020)
30. Mai, Z., Li, R., Jeong, J., Quispe, D., Kim, H., Sanner, S.: Online continual learning in image classification: an empirical survey. arXiv:2101.10423 (2021). (preprint)
31. Mallya, A., Davis, D., Lazebnik, S.: Piggyback: adapting a single network to multiple tasks by learning to mask weights. In: Ferrari, V., Hebert, M., Sminchisescu, C., Weiss, Y. (eds.) ECCV 2018. LNCS, vol. 11208, pp. 72–88. Springer, Cham (2018). https://doi.org/10.1007/978-3-030-01225-0_5
32. Mallya, A., Lazebnik, S.: PackNet: adding multiple tasks to a single network by iterative pruning. In: CVPR (2018)
33. Masana, M., Liu, X., Twardowski, B., Menta, M., Bagdanov, A.D., van de Weijer, J.: Class-incremental learning: survey and performance evaluation on image classification. arXiv:2010.15277 (2020). (preprint)
34. Mermillod, M., Bugaiska, A., Bonin, P.: The stability-plasticity dilemma: investigating the continuum from catastrophic forgetting to age-limited learning effects. Front. Psychol. **4**, 504 (2013)
35. French, R.M.: Catastrophic forgetting in connectionist networks. Trends Cogn. Sci. **3**, 128–135 (1999)
36. Pan, P., Swaroop, S., Immer, A., Eschenhagen, R., Turner, R.E., Khan, M.E.: Continual deep learning by functional regularisation of memorable past. In: NeurIPS (2020)
37. Qi, H., Brown, M., Lowe, D.G.: Low-shot learning with imprinted weights. In: CVPR (2018)
38. Rebuff, S.A., Kolesnikov, A., Sperl, G., Lampert, C.H.: iCaRL: incremental classifier and representation learning. In: CVPR (2017)
39. Ren, M., Liao, R., Fetaya, E., Zemel, R.S.: Incremental few-shot learning with attention attractor networks. In: NeurIPS (2019)
40. Ren, M., et al.: Meta-learning for semi-supervised few-shot classification. In: ICLR (2018)
41. Riemer, M., et al.: Learning to learn without forgetting by maximizing transfer and minimizing interference. In: ICLR (2019)
42. Ristin, M., Gall, J., Guillaumin, M., Gool, L.V.: From categories to subcategories: large-scale image classification with partial class label refinement. In: CVPR (2015)
43. Ristin, M., Guillaumin, M., Gall, J., Gool, L.V.: Incremental learning of NCM forests for large-scale image classification. In: CVPR (2014)
44. Santurkar, S., Tsipras, D., Madry, A.: Breeds: Benchmarks for subpopulation shift arXiv:2008.04859 (2020). (preprint)
45. Shi, Y., Yuan, L., Chen, Y., Feng, J.: Continual learning via bit-level information preserving. In: CVPR (2021)
46. Singh, P., Mazumder, P., Rai, P., Namboodiri, V.P.: Rectification-based knowledge retention for continual learning. In: CVPR (2021)

47. Singh, P., Verma, V.K., Mazumder, P., Carin, L., Rai, P.: Calibrating CNNs for lifelong learning. In: NeurIPS (2020)
48. Tao, X., Chang, X., Hong, X., Wei, X., Gong, Y.: Topology-preserving class-incremental learning. In: Vedaldi, A., Bischof, H., Brox, T., Frahm, J.-M. (eds.) ECCV 2020. LNCS, vol. 12364, pp. 254–270. Springer, Cham (2020). https://doi.org/10.1007/978-3-030-58529-7_16
49. Tao, X., Hong, X., Chang, X., Dong, S., Wei, X., Gong, Y.: Few-shot class-incremental learning. In: CVPR (2020)
50. Tian, Y., Wang, Y., Krishnan, D., Tenenbaum, J.B., Isola, P.: Rethinking few-shot image classification: a good embedding is all you need? In: Vedaldi, A., Bischof, H., Brox, T., Frahm, J.-M. (eds.) ECCV 2020. LNCS, vol. 12359, pp. 266–282. Springer, Cham (2020). https://doi.org/10.1007/978-3-030-58568-6_16
51. Wang, F., Xiang, X., Cheng, J., Yuille, A.L.: NormFace: L2 hypersphere embedding for face verification. In: ACM Conference on Multimedia (2017)
52. Wang, S., Li, X., Sun, J., Xu, Z.: Training networks in null space of feature covariance for continual learning. In: CVPR (2021)
53. Wu, G., Gong, S., Li, P.: Striking a balance between stability and plasticity for class-incremental learning. In: ICCV (2021)
54. Xu, Y., Qian, Q., Li, H., Jin, R., Hu, J.: Weakly supervised representation learning with coarse labels. In: ICCV (2021)
55. Yang, J., Yang, H., Chen, L.: Towards cross-granularity few-shot learning: coarse-to-fine pseudo-labeling with visual-semantic meta-embedding. In: ACM Conference on Multimedia (2021)
56. Zhang, C., Song, N., Lin, G., Zheng, Y., Pan, P., Xu, Y.: Few-shot incremental learning with continually evolved classifiers. In: CVPR (2021)
57. Zhao, B., Xiao, X., Gan, G., Zhang, B., Xia, S.: Maintaining discrimination and fairness in class incremental learning. In: CVPR (2020)
58. Zhu, F., Zhang, X.Y., Wang, C., Yin, F., Liu, C.L.: Prototype augmentation and self-supervision for incremental learning. In: CVPR (2021)

Learning Unbiased Transferability for Domain Adaptation by Uncertainty Modeling

Jian Hu[1]([✉]), Haowen Zhong[2], Fei Yang[2], Shaogang Gong[1], Guile Wu[1], and Junchi Yan[3]

[1] Queen Mary University of London, London, UK
{jian.hu,s.gong}@qmul.ac.uk
[2] Zhejiang Lab, Hangzhou, China
{zhonghw,yangf}@zhejianglab.com
[3] Shanghai Jiao Tong University, Shanghai, China
yanjunchi@sjtu.edu.cn

Abstract. Domain adaptation (DA) aims to transfer knowledge learned from a labeled source domain to an unlabeled or a less labeled but related target domain. Ideally, the source and target distributions should be aligned to each other equally to achieve unbiased knowledge transfer. However, due to the significant imbalance between the amount of annotated data in the source and target domains, usually only the target distribution is aligned to the source domain, leading to adapting unnecessary source specific knowledge to the target domain, i.e., biased domain adaptation. To resolve this problem, in this work, we delve into the transferability estimation problem in domain adaptation and propose a non-intrusive Unbiased Transferability Estimation Plug-in (UTEP) by modeling the uncertainty of a discriminator in adversarial-based DA methods to optimize unbiased transfer. We theoretically analyze the effectiveness of the proposed approach to unbiased transferability learning in DA. Furthermore, to alleviate the impact of imbalanced annotated data, we utilize the estimated uncertainty for pseudo label selection of unlabeled samples in the target domain, which helps achieve better marginal and conditional distribution alignments between domains. Extensive experimental results on a high variety of DA benchmark datasets show that the proposed approach can be readily incorporated into various adversarial-based DA methods, achieving state-of-the-art performance.

Keywords: Unbiased transferability estimation · Domain adaptation · Pseudo labeling

---

J. Hu and H. Zhong: Equal contribution.

Supplementary Information The online version contains supplementary material available at https://doi.org/10.1007/978-3-031-19821-2_13.

1 Introduction

With the rise of deep neural networks, convolutional neural networks (CNNs) [28] and transformers [47], supervised learning based on deep neural networks has shown promising performance in various vision and language tasks. Conventional supervised learning methods mostly assume that the training (source) domain and the test (target) domain are subject to the i.i.d. (independent and identically distributed) hypothesis. As a consequence, they usually show poor generalization in the test domain in the existence of a domain gap [21]. Moreover, deep neural networks have ravenous appetite for a large amount of labeled data, which explores extra linkage between labelled data in a source domain and unlabeled data in a target domain. Domain adaption aims to resolve this quandary by leveraging previously labeled datasets [45,55] to realize effective knowledge transfer across domains. DA can further divide into unsupervised domain adaptation (UDA) and semi-supervised domain adaptation (SSDA) based on the accessibility of labeled data in the target domain.

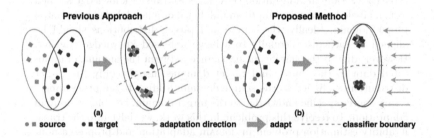

Fig. 1. Motivation for Unbiased Transferability Estimation. The left and right parts in (**a**) (**b**) are distributions of source and target domains before and after adaptation respectively. (**a**) Previous methods [16,41] focus on aligning target samples to source well-clustered classes (distribution), leading to misalignment near the classifier boundary and transferring unnecessary source specific knowledge to the target, and the decision boundaries remain ambiguous for some target samples near the boundaries. (**b**) Our method enforces source and target distributions to align to each other equally, to help unbiased DA to achieve better marginal and conditional distribution alignment. The target decision boundary is further optimized with uncertainty-based pseudo label selection.

Transferability indicates the ability of representations to bridge the discrepancy across domains [8]. Contemporary deep DA methods mainly focus on exploring cross-domain transferability to narrow the gap between domains [51, 61]. There are two typical approaches: 1) High-order moment matching [40,68], which reduces the distribution discrepancy between domains by minimizing the distance between high-dimensional features; 2) Adversarial learning [16,23,54], in which a domain discriminator and a feature extractor play a two-player game to align distributions between domains. Although existing DA methods

Table 1. A comparison of uncertainty modeling methods in DA.

Methods	Online learning	Non-intrusive design	Unbiased transfer	uncertainty usage
CPCS [46]	✓	✗	✗	weighting for calibration
PACET [37]	✓	✗	✗	sample selection
BUM [57]	✓	✗	✗	weighting
TransCal [56]	✗	✓	✗	post-hoc calibration
CADA [33]	✓	✗	✗	weighting for attention
UTEP(Ours)	✓	✓	✓	Weighting + regularization + sample selection

have shown promising performance on resolving domain shift, there remain two major problems. First, most existing methods tend to promote the alignment of domains to encourage transferability, which is evaluated by measuring the distribution discrepancy (estimated transferability) [2,39]. However, even if the distribution discrepancy is completely eliminated, the deviation of the estimated and real transferability still exists, leading to negative transfer (see Fig. 1(a)). Second, existing approaches only consider aligning the overall distributions between domains and tend to assign larger weights to samples that are not sufficiently transferred [39,57]. However, since the number of annotations in the source and target domains is extremely imbalanced, the transferability is usually estimated by the target sample score on the source domain classifier, resulting in a strong bias towards the source domain (see Fig. 1(a)). In other words, under the supervision of source labeled samples, the source domain distribution is well learned and hardly affected by the target one, while the target domain distribution tends to match the source domain instead of encouraging the source to align the target domain. As a consequence, the target domain is not only learning the domain invariant knowledge (features) but also learning domain specific knowledge of the source domain, resulting in *biased domain adaptation*. Therefore, to address these two problems, it is essential to learn unbiased transferability to facilitate knowledge transfer across domains in domain adaptation.

In this work, we focus on the transferability problem in domain adaptation and present a non-intrusive Unbiased Transferability Estimation Plug-in (UTEP) model by uncertainty variance modeling. Specifically, inspired by [56] which uses a post-hoc strategy to re-calibrate existing DA methods, we theoretically analyze the transferability of adversarial-based DA methods and propose to model the uncertainty variance of a discriminator to minimize biased transfer between domains (see Fig. 1(b)). Different from [56], UTEP incorporates unbiased transferability estimation into an online model learning process rather than post-processing, which helps mitigate negative transfer and achieve better alignment between domains for unbiased domain adaptation. Meanwhile, as the estimated uncertainty also reveals the reliability of unlabeled samples from the target domain, we use it for pseudo label selection to achieve better marginal and conditional distribution alignment between source and target domains. The proposed UTEP is plug-and-play and can be easily incorporated into various adversarial based DA methods. An overview of UTEP is depicted in Fig. 2. The **contributions** of this work are in three-fold:

1) To address the transferability bias due to the imbalance between the quantity of labeled data from the source and target domains, unlike prior works [46,56] that model the classifier to obtain better calibrated prediction, which still has a strong bias toward source domain, we propose a novel non-intrusive Unbiased Transferability Estimation Plug-in (UTEP) model for DA by uncertainty variance modeling of a discriminator. 2) To quantify and minimize the bias of transferability, we theoretically analyze the cause of the bias and show that our method can alleviate it by lowering its upper bound. To our best knowledge, this is the first work to explore the unbiased knowledge transfer rather than model calibration via uncertainty modeling in domain adaptation. 3) We plug our technique into various adversarial based DA methods [16,33,66] and show its superiority over the state-of-the-art methods in both UDA and SSDA settings.

2 Related Works

Deep Domain Adaptation. Domain adaptation aims to transfer knowledge between a labeled source domain and an unlabeled or a less labeled target domain. The key challenge of DA is the existence of domain shift [2], the data bias between source and target domains. There have been many distance-based and divergence-based methods proposed in recent years for measuring and resolving the domain shift proposed in DA. These measurement dimensions include Maximum Mean Discrepancy between the feature embeddings of different domains [24,41,68,69], the optimal transmission distance across domains [10], high-dimensional discriminative adversarial learning [16,26,44,54,65], and so on. Although these methods are capable of aligning distribution between domains, they largely ignore the deviation between the estimated transferability and the real one. Our work focuses on learning unbiased transferability by modeling uncertainty variance of a discriminator in adversarial-based domain adaptation.

Uncertainty Estimation. Uncertainty estimation can be used to either measure the uncertainty caused by noise (known as aleatoric uncertainty) or learn the uncertainty of a model (known as epistemic uncertainty) [12,32]. In vision tasks, it is often more challenging and practical to model the epistemic uncertainty, which can be learned by Bayesian neural network [6,42]. Besides, some approximate reasoning methods [48,56] can be used to model the uncertainty based on abundant observation data. Our work employs the MCDropout [15], an efficient method for acquiring Bayesian uncertainty, to model uncertainty variance of a discriminator in adversarial-based domain adaptation.

Uncertainty Modeling in Domain Adaptation. Uncertainty modeling can be used to perform cross-domain calibration and improve the reliability of pseudo labels in DA. CPCS [46] incorporates importance weighting into temperature scaling to cope with the cross-domain calibration. TransCal [56] uses post-hoc transferable calibration to realize more accurate calibration with lower bias and variance. PACET [37] employs uncertainty modeling to describe the cross-domain distribution differences and other intra-domain relationships. BUM [57] uses a Bayesian neural network to quantify prediction uncertainty of a classifier with the aid of a discriminator. CADA [33] utilizes certainty based attention to identify adaptive region on pixel level with Bayesian classifier and discriminator. Besides, uncertainty can also be used to facilitate cross-domain object detection [18] and segmentation [67]. Existing approaches mostly focus more on modeling the classifier to obtain better calibrated prediction. However, due to the extremely unbalanced amount of annotated data in domains, the classifier output is strongly biased to the source, while the discriminator is unbiased. Our work focuses on learning unbiased transferability by uncertainty modeling the discriminator in theory. Table 1 compares representative uncertainty methods.

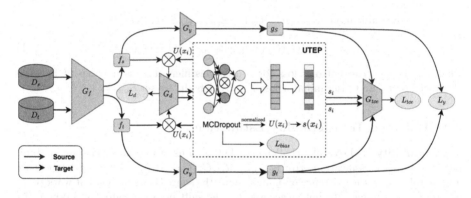

Fig. 2. The proposed UTEP framework. G_f is the feature extractor. G_d is the domain discriminator. G_y is the source classifier. G_{tce} is the pseudo label cluster. f_s and f_t are feature representations defined by $f = G_f(x)$, while g_s and g_t are the classifier prediction obtained from G_y. UTEP is the unbiased transferability estimation plug-in. This module can not only evaluate the unbiased transferability by minimizing $\mathcal{L}_{bias}$ and adding weight $\mu(x)$ on the discriminator with discriminator loss L_d, but also can generate $s(x)$ to evaluate the reliability of pseudo labels to facilitate learning with L_{tce} and L_y.

3 Methodology

3.1 Preliminaries

Problem Definition. Let x_i denote an input of the network, y_i is the corresponding class label of x_i, and d_i is the domain label of x_i. We set $d_i = 1$ when

x_i is from the source domain and $d_i = 0$ when x_i is from the target one. In unsupervised domain adaptation (UDA), the labeled source domain is defined as $\mathcal{D}_s = \{(x_i^s, y_i^s)\}_{i=1}^{n_s}$ with n_s source samples and the unlabeled target domain is defined as $\mathcal{D}_t = \mathcal{D}_{tu} = \{x_i^t\}_{i=1}^{n_{tu}}$ with n_{tu} samples (here, $n_t = n_{tu}$). $\mathcal{D}_s$ and $\mathcal{D}_t$ are sampled from the source $p_s(x)$ and the target $p_t(x)$ distributions. In semi-supervised domain adaptation (SSDA), in addition to the labeled source domain $\mathcal{D}_s$ and the unlabeled target domain $\mathcal{D}_{tu}$, there is an extra target labeled domain $\mathcal{D}_{tl} = \{(x_i^{tl}, y_i^{tl})\}_{i=1}^{n_{tl}}$ with n_{tl} samples, so the whole target domain can be defined as $\mathcal{D}_t = \mathcal{D}_{tl} \cup \mathcal{D}_{tu}$ with $n_t = n_{tl} + n_{tu}$. In our paper, the source label space equals to the target one, there are C categories in both source and target domains.

Classical Adversarial Based UDA. In the classical adversarial based domain adaptation framework, DANN [16], there is a feature extractor and a domain discriminator, where the discriminator tries to find out which domain the features come from while the feature extractor tries to confuse the discriminator. When the discriminator is fully confused, we consider the source classifier can generalize well to the target domains. In this case, the output of the discriminator should be 0.5, $P(d = 0|x) = P(d = 1|x) = 0.5$. Overall, the source classifier G_y, the domain discriminator G_d and the feature extractor G_f can be jointly learned by:

$$\min_{G_y} \min_{G_f} \max_{G_d} \mathcal{L}_{adv}(G_d, G_f, G_y) = \mathbb{E}_{(x,y) \sim p_s}[\mathcal{L}_y(G_y(G_f(x)), y)]$$
$$- \alpha_{adv} \left(\mathbb{E}_{x \sim p_s}[\log(G_d(G_f(x)))] + \mathbb{E}_{x \sim p_t}[\log(1 - G_d(G_f(x)))] \right), \tag{1}$$

where $\mathcal{L}_y$ is the cross-entropy loss for source classifier. α_{adv} is a trade-off between classifier loss $\mathcal{L}_y$ and discriminator loss $\mathcal{L}_d$. By default, we set $\alpha_{adv} = 1$.

3.2   Unbiased Transferability Estimation

Transferability in DA. The challenge of DA is to use the source classifier to minimize the target classification error $\mathbb{E}_{(x,y) \sim p_t}[\mathcal{L}_y(G_y(G_f(x)), y)]$ when target labels are unavailable. Since the existence of domain shift, the source classifier cannot work properly on target samples. To better account for the shift between source and target distributions, density ratio $w(x) = \frac{p_t(x)}{p_s(x)}$ [56,62] can be used as a metric of transferability to measure the discrepancy between domains. In general, the shift will be eliminated when $w(x) = \frac{p_t(x)}{p_s(x)} = 1$. Then, the target classification error can be estimated by the source distribution $p_s(x)$ as:

$$\mathbb{E}_{(x,y) \sim p_t}[\mathcal{L}_y(G_y(G_f(x)), y))] = \int_{D_t} \mathcal{L}_y(G_y(G_f(x)), y) \, p_t(x) dx$$
$$= \int_{D_s} \frac{p_t(x)}{p_s(x)} \mathcal{L}_y(G_y(G_f(x)), y) p_s(x) dx = \mathbb{E}_{(x,y) \sim p_s}[w(x)\mathcal{L}_y(G_y(G_f(x)), y))]. \tag{2}$$

However, the density ratio $w(x)$ is often not accessible in DA, we follow [56] and use estimated $\hat{w}(x)$ to approximate the real $w(x)$. Specifically, LogReg [5,49] is used to estimate the density ratio by Bayesian formula:

$$\hat{w}(x) = \frac{p_t(x)}{p_s(x)} = \frac{m(x|d=0)}{m(x|d=1)} = \frac{P(d=1)P(d=0|x)}{P(d=0)P(d=1|x)} = \frac{n_s}{n_t} \cdot \frac{P(d=0|x)}{P(d=1|x)} = \frac{P(d=0|x)}{P(d=1|x)}, \tag{3}$$

where m is a distribution over $(x, d) \sim X \times (0, 1)$, and $d \sim Bernoulli(0.5)$ is a Bernoulli variable representing which domain x belongs to. Here, $\frac{n_s}{n_t}$ is a constant regarding to sample sizes and the source or the target dataset is randomly up-sampled to ensure $n_s = n_t$. In this way, $\hat{w}(x)$ only depends on $\frac{P(d=0|x)}{P(d=1|x)}$.

In DA, $w(x)$ can be treated as the real transferability, while $\hat{w}(x)$ can be considered as the estimated transferability. Ideally, when $w(x) = \hat{w}(x)$, domain adaptation is unbiased. Previous DA methods [40,68] mainly focus on aligning distributions between source and target domains to encourage $\hat{w}(x) = 1$ but largely ignore the deviation between the estimated $\hat{w}(x)$ and the real $w(x)$, which yields *biased domain adaptation*.

Learning Unbiased Transferability. There have been some DA methods [56,57] employing the classifier output for uncertainty modeling to encourage transferability/-calibration. However, due to the lack of class labels in the target domain, using predictions of unlabeled target samples from the source domain classifier merely describes the alignment of target samples to the source distribution, while not encouraging the source distribution to align to the target one. On the other hand, domain labels are always known for both source and target samples during model learning, which provides abundant label information for measuring the bias between the estimated $\hat{w}(x)$ and the real $w(x)$. In light of this, to account for the deviation between the estimated $\hat{w}(x)$ and the real $w(x)$, *we propose to model the transferability by uncertainty variance estimation of a discriminator in adversarial-based DA.*

Specifically, different from previous classifier-based uncertainty modeling methods, we introduce a novel unbiased transferability estimation method by lowering the variance of the discriminator output $\mathbb{V}ar_{x \sim p_{ds}}(\hat{P}_d(d=1|x))$ and $\mathbb{V}ar_{x \sim p_{dt}}(\hat{P}_d(d=0|x))$. Here, p_{ds} and p_{dt} are the source and target discriminator distributions, an instance is sampled from p_d which equals to be sampled from p_{ds} or p_{dt}. We use MCDropout [15,57] to compute $\mathbb{V}ar_{x \sim p_d}(\hat{P}_d(d|x))$ as:

$$\mathbb{V}ar_{x \sim p_d}(\hat{P}_d(d|x)) \approx \frac{1}{K} \sum_{k=1}^{K} \left((G_d(G_g(x)))_k - \left(\frac{1}{K} \sum_{k=1}^{K} (G_d(G_g(x)))_k \right) \right)^2, \quad (4)$$

where K is the number of times performing stochastic forward passes through the discriminator network. We set $u(x) = \mathbb{V}ar_{x \sim p_{ds}}(\hat{P}_d(d=1|x)) + \mathbb{V}ar_{x \sim p_{dt}}(\hat{P}_d(d=0|x))$, the modeled uncertainty. Here, we set $\mathcal{U} = [u(x_1), ...u(x_i), ...]$, where $u(x_i)$ measures the uncertainty of the ith sample. Since the uncertainty can also be seen as a measurement of the distance between x and the general distribution (initial aligned distribution of source and target samples, which be called $p_{s,t}$ in the following). When a sample x is close to $p_{s,t}$, $u(x)$ is minimized and x possesses better transferability. From this perspective, $u(x)$ can also be seen as a transferability metric. We normalize $u(x)$ by Min-Max Normalization as follows:

$$\mu(x) = \frac{u(x) - \min(\mathcal{U})}{\max(\mathcal{U})}, \quad (5)$$

Then, we set normalized unbiased transferability $\mu(x)$ as the transferability weight in the adversarial learning process (Eq. (1)) to facilitate unbiased DA model learning as:

$$\min_{G_y} \min_{G_f} \max_{G_d} \mathcal{L}_{adv}(G_d, G_f, G_y) = \mathbb{E}_{(x,y) \sim p_s}[\mathcal{L}_y(G_y(G_f(x)), y)]$$
$$- \mathbb{E}_{x \sim p_s}[(1 + \mu(x)) \log(G_d(G_f(x)))] - \mathbb{E}_{x \sim p_t}[(1 + \mu(x)) \log((1 - G_d(G_f(x))))]. \quad (6)$$

Furthermore, based on Eq. (4), we define the L2 regularized $\mathcal{U}$ as the bias loss and minimize the bias loss as:

$$\min \mathcal{L}_{bias} = \min \|\mathcal{U}\|_2^2 = \min_{G_d, G_f} \sum_{i=1}^{n_t + n_s} \left(\mathbb{V}ar_{x_i \sim p_d}(\hat{P}_d(d|x_i)) \right)^2. \tag{7}$$

With each mini-batch, we perform K times stochastic forward passes through the discriminator to estimate the variance in Eq. (7).

Theoretical Analysis. In this section, we theoretically analyze the cause of the bias in transferability and discuss how to lower the upper bound of the bias. With Eqs. (2) and (3), we show how to measure the target classification error and the estimated transferability. Following [56], we can use the difference between the estimated target classification error and the real one to measure the bias of transferability, as:

$$\left| \mathbb{E}_{(x,y) \sim p_t}[\mathcal{L}_y^{\hat{w}(x)}(G_y(G_f(x)), y))] - \mathbb{E}_{(x,y) \sim p_t}[\mathcal{L}_y^{w(x)}(G_y(G_f(x)), y))] \right|$$

$$= \left| \mathbb{E}_{(x,y) \sim p_s}[(\hat{w}(x) - w(x))\mathcal{L}_y(G_y(G_f(x)), y))] \right|$$

$$\leq \frac{1}{2} \left(\mathbb{E}_{x \sim p_s}[(\hat{w}(x) - w(x))^2] + \mathbb{E}_{(x,y) \sim p_s}[(\mathcal{L}_y(G_y(G_f(x)), y))^2] \right). \tag{8}$$

In the above inequality, since the second term is bounded by supervised learning in the labeled source domain, we only need to focus on the first term. We use a discriminator to alleviate the deviation between the estimated $\hat{w}(x)$ and the real $w(x)$. From our unbiased transferability perspective, we further formalize the transferability based on discriminator as $W(x) = \frac{B_t(x|d=0)}{B_s(x|d=1)}$. Here, distribution B is a distribution over $(x, d) \in X(0, 1)$. In this case, $d \sim Bernoulli(0.5)$, if $d = 1$, $x \sim p_s$ or $x \sim p_t$. Furthermore, as the unbiased transferability is derived in the discriminator label space, $W(x)$ and $\hat{W}(x)$ are assumed to be the real and estimated transferability in this space. Assume we have upper bound $N \geq 0$ for $W(x)$ subject to $N \geq W(x) \geq 0$ according to the bounded importance weight assumption [9]. Combined with upper bound N, we have $\frac{1}{N+1} \leq P_d(d = 1|x) \leq 1$ and $P_d(x) = B(d = 1|x) = \frac{1}{1+W(x)}$. Then, the first term of Eq. (8) is bounded by:

$$\mathbb{E}_{x \sim p_s}[(\hat{w}(x_i) - w(x))^2] = \mathbb{E}_{x \sim p_{ds}}\left[(\hat{W}(x) - W(x))^2 * \frac{p_s(x)}{p_{ds}(x)} \right]$$

$$\leq 2\mathbb{E}_{x \sim p_{ds}}[(\hat{W}(x_i) - W(x))^2] = 2\mathbb{E}_{x \sim p_{ds}}\left[\left(\frac{P_d(d = 1|x) - \hat{P}_d(d = 1|x)}{P_d(d = 1|x)\hat{P}_d(d = 1|x)} \right)^2 \right]$$

$$\leq 2(N + 1)^4 \mathbb{E}_{x \sim p_{ds}}\left[\left(P_d(d = 1|x) - \hat{P}_d(d = 1|x) \right)^2 \right]. \tag{9}$$

The first row changes the probability from source label space to source discriminator domain label space. Then, the deviation between the real and the estimated transferability is calculated in the discriminator label space. The second inequality in Eq. (9) can be further rewritten as:

$$2(N + 1)^4 \mathbb{E}_{x \sim p_{ds}} \left[\left(P_d(d = 1|x) - \hat{P}_d(d = 1|x) \right)^2 \right]$$

$$= 2(N + 1)^4 \left(\mathbb{E}_{x \sim p_{ds}}[(P_d(d = 1|x))^2] - (\mathbb{E}_{x \sim p_{ds}}[P_d(d = 1|x)])^2 \right.$$

$$+ (\mathbb{E}_{x \sim p_{ds}}[P_d(d = 1|x)])^2 + \mathbb{E}_{x \sim p_{ds}}[(\hat{P}_d(d = 1|x))^2]$$

$$- (\mathbb{E}_{x \sim p_{ds}}[\hat{P}_d(d = 1|x)])^2 + (\mathbb{E}_{x \sim p_{ds}}[\hat{P}_d(d = 1|x)])^2$$

$$\left. - 2\mathbb{E}_{x \sim p_{ds}}[\hat{P}_d(d = 1|x) P_d(d = 1|x)] \right)$$

$$= 2(N + 1)^4 \left(\mathbb{V}ar_{x \sim p_{ds}}(P_d(d = 1|x)) + \mathbb{V}ar_{x \sim p_{ds}}(\hat{P}_d(d = 1|x)) \right.$$

$$\left. + \left(\mathbb{E}_{x \sim p_{ds}}[P_d(d = 1|x)] - \mathbb{E}_{x \sim p_{ds}}[\hat{P}_d(d = 1|x)] \right)^2 \right), \quad (10)$$

where the variances of outputs under real and estimated probability distributions are $\mathbb{V}ar_{x \sim p_{ds}}(P_d(d = 1|x))$ and $\mathbb{V}ar_{x \sim p_{ds}}(\hat{P}_d(d = 1|x))$ respectively. Ideally, when the source and target domains are aligned, the output of discriminator should be 0.5, then, $\mathbb{V}ar_{x \sim p_{ds}}(P_d(d = 1|x)) = 0$. Hence, the bias of transferability can be formulated as:

$$\mathbb{E}_{x \sim p_{ds}} \left[(\hat{w}(x) - w(x))^2 \right] \leq 2(N + 1)^4 \left[\mathbb{V}ar_{x \sim p_{ds}} \left(\hat{P}_d(d = 1|x) \right) \right.$$

$$\left. + \left(\mathbb{E}_{x \sim p_{ds}}[P_d(d = 1|x)] - \mathbb{E}_{x \sim p_{ds}}[\hat{P}_d(d = 1|x)] \right)^2 \right]. \quad (11)$$

The second term of Eq. (11) is constrained since the domain adaptation process encourages $\mathbb{E}_{x \sim p_{ds}}(P_d(d = 1|x))$ to approximate to $\mathbb{E}_{x \sim p_{ds}}(\hat{P}_d(d = 1|x))$. Therefore, to learn unbiased transferability, we can minimize $\mathbb{V}ar_{x \sim p_{ds}}(\hat{P}_d(d = 1|x))$. Besides, since we need to use the estimated uncertainty of unlabeled samples from the target domain for pseudo label selection (see Sec. 3.3), we also minimize $\mathbb{V}ar_{x \sim p_{dt}}(\hat{P}_d(d = 0|x))$ and use it as a part of the transferability weight. Thus, we set:

$$u(x) = \mathbb{V}ar_{x \sim p_{ds}}(\hat{P}_d(d = 1|x)) + \mathbb{V}ar_{x \sim p_{dt}}(\hat{P}_d(d = 0|x)). \quad (12)$$

In this way, for both the source and target samples, we lower the variance of the discriminator outputs with Eq. (4), and use Eq. (7) to lower the upper bound of the deviation between estimated transferability and the real one to realize unbiased domain adaptation. The details of the theoretical analysis are in the supplementary materials.

3.3 Unbiased Domain Adaptation

Pseudo Label Selection. Originally, pseudo label is introduced to solve the problem of label shortage in unlabeled domain in semi-supervised learning. However, recent works [7,38] implies that when domain shift exists, the pseudo label selection strategies tailored for semi-supervised learning is difficult to be effective. Different from the classifier-based pseudo label evaluation methods [14,50,60], we evaluate pseudo label reliability under domain shift by the normalized unbiased transferability $\mu(x)$ of domain discriminator. Intuitively, the lower $\mu(x)$ indicates the better transferability of x, which is more reliable for pseudo labeling. Denote $s(x)$ as the selected weight for x:

$$s(x) = 1 - \mu(x). \quad (13)$$

Then, pseudo labels are generated with those preliminary refined unlabeled samples of the target domain based on the predefined thresholds. Specifically, suppose $g(x)$ is the C-ways source classifier probability prediction output for sample x, $g(x) = G_y(G_f(x)) = [g^{[1]}(x), ...g^{[c]}(x), ..., g^{[C]}(x)]$. Here, $g^{[c]}(x)$ is the probability of class c for the sample. Only when the $g^{[c]}(x)$ is higher than the threshold β, where $\beta \in (0, 1)$, the positive pseudo label for the sample is selected. Hence, $h(x) = [h^{[1]}(x), ..., h^{[C]}(x)]$ is a binary vector representing the selected positive pseudo label for the sample. When $g^{[c]}(x)$ is selected, $h^{[c]}(x)$ is 1, or $h^{[c]}(x)$ is 0. Here, $h^{[c]}(x)$ is obtained by:

$$h^{[c]}(x) = \mathbb{1}[g^{[c]}(x) \geq \beta]. \tag{14}$$

Then, the selected $g^{[c]}(x)$ is treated as a soft positive pseudo label, so the positive cross-entropy loss is defined as:

$$\mathcal{L}_{pce}(g, h) = -\mathbb{E}_{x \sim p_d} s(x) \sum_{c=1}^{C} h^{[c]}(x) \left[g^{[c]}(x) \cdot \log(g^{[c]}(x)) \right]. \tag{15}$$

Similarly, we pick out those unlikely categories with high probability as negative pseudo labels to further dismiss the interference of noises on training. Only when $g^{[c]}(x) \leq \gamma$, where $\gamma \in (0, 1)$, the negative pseudo label is generated for the sample. Thus, we have:

$$l^{[c]}(x) = \mathbb{1}[g^{[c]}(x) \leq \gamma], \tag{16}$$

where $l(x)$ is corresponding to $h(x)$, representing the selected negative pseudo label for the sample. Then, the selected $g^{[c]}(x)$ is seen as a soft negative pseudo-label, so a negative cross-entropy loss is defined as:

$$\mathcal{L}_{nce}(g, l) = -\mathbb{E}_{x \sim p_d} s(x) \sum_{c=1}^{C} l^{[c]}(x) \left[(1 - g^{[c]}(x)) \cdot \log(1 - g^{[c]}(x)) \right]. \tag{17}$$

Thus, the pseudo label cluster learning loss is modeled as:

$$\mathcal{L}_{tce}(g, h, l) = \mathcal{L}_{pce}(g, h) + \alpha_{nce} \mathcal{L}_{nce}(g, l). \tag{18}$$

By default, $\alpha_{nce} = 1$. Note that this strategy is similar to UPS [50] which presents uncertainty-aware pseudo labeling for semi-supervised learning, but we conjecture that the uncertainty of labels mostly comes from the domain gap between labeled and unlabeled data. Hence, unlike UPS, uncertainty is derived by a variance of the discriminator output and used for pseudo label selection to facilitate unbiased domain adaptation. Such a strategy is not only suitable for DA and SSDA, but also for semi-supervised learning problems. Furthermore, we conducted a comparative experiment in Table 5 to show the effectiveness of our uncertainty-aware pseudo labeling.

Unbiased Domain Adaptation. The proposed UTEP for DA includes three parts, namely unbiased domain alignment with adversarial learning, transferability bias regularization, and pseudo label cluster learning. The overall loss of UTEP is defined as:

$$\mathcal{L} = \mathcal{L}_{adv} + \alpha_{bias} \mathcal{L}_{bias} + \alpha_{tce} \mathcal{L}_{tce}, \tag{19}$$

where $\mathcal{L}_{adv}$ focuses on domain alignment with the adversarial loss and the source classification loss. $\mathcal{L}_{bias}$ is the unbiased transferability estimation loss which is obtained per batch during model training. $\mathcal{L}_{tce}$ is the pseudo label cluster loss. α_{bias} and α_{tce} are the hyper-parameters.

4   Experiments

4.1   Datasets and Protocols

Datasets. To evaluate the effectiveness of the proposed UTEP approach, we conduct extensive experiments on three popular DA datasets: **Office-31**, **Office-Home** and **VisDA-2017**. **Office-31** is the most popular DA dataset, containing 31 classes and 4600 images from three domains, namely Webcam(**W**), Amazon(**A**) and Dslr(**D**). **Office-Home** includes 15,500 images from 65 categories collected from four domains, namely Artistic Images (**Ar**), Clip Art (**Cl**), Product (**Pr**) and Real-World (**Rw**). **VisDA-2017** is a more challenging Simulation-to-Real dataset with more than 280K images in 12 categories.

Protocols. Our experiments are performed under two different settings, namely UDA and SSDA, and are carried out using PyTorch. Our codes are based on [29] and released on Github. We use mini-batch SGD to fine-tune an ImageNet pretrained model (ResNet-50 [20] and ResNet-101 for different DA tasks) as the feature encoder with the learning rate as 0.001 and to learn the new layers (bottleneck layer and classification layer) from scratch with the learning rate is 0.01. In the UDA setting, each training batch consists of 32 source samples and 32 target samples. In the SSDA setting, each training batch consists of 16 source samples, 16 labeled target samples and 32 unlabeled target samples. We conduct the experiment with ResNet-34 as the feature encoder. It is worth noting that only 1% target samples are selected out as the labeled target domain for training. More implementation details are in the supplementary material.

Table 2. Classification accuracy of UDA on *Office-31* with ResNet-50 as backbone model. Best in **bold** and the second best in **bold with underline**.

Method	A→W	D→W	W→D	A→D	D→A	W→A	Avg
MinEnt [17]	89.4	97.5	100.0	90.7	67.1	65.0	85.0
ResNet [20]	75.8	95.5	99.0	79.3	63.6	63.8	79.5
GTA [16]	89.5	97.9	99.8	87.7	72.8	71.4	86.5
CDAN+E [39]	94.2	98.6	100.0	94.5	72.8	72.2	88.7
SAFN [59]	90.1	98.6	99.8	90.7	73.0	70.2	87.1
CAN [31]	94.5	99.1	99.8	95.0	**78.0**	**77.0**	**90.6**
MCC [30]	94.0	98.5	100.0	92.1	74.9	75.3	89.1
BNM [11]	94.0	98.5	100.0	92.2	74.9	75.3	89.2
GSDA [25]	95.7	99.1	100.0	94.8	73.5	74.9	89.7
SRDC [53]	95.7	**99.2**	100.0	**95.8**	76.7	**77.1**	90.8
VAK [22]	91.8	98.7	**99.9**	89.9	73.9	72.0	87.7
DANN [16]	91.4	97.9	100.0	83.6	73.3	70.4	86.1
DANN+UTEP	92.7	98.5	100.0	90.4	73.8	72.7	88.0(+1.9%)
MDD [66]	94.5	98.4	100.0	93.4	74.6	72.2	88.9
MDD+UTEP	94.7	99.0	100.0	94.4	77.0	74.5	89.9(+1.0%)
CADA [33]	**97.0**	99.3	100.0	**95.6**	71.5	73.0	89.5
CADA+UTEP	**97.2**	**99.4**	100.0	95.3	73.5	74.3	90.0(+0.5%)
TransPar [19]	95.5	98.9	100.0	94.2	77.7	72.8	89.9
TransPar+UTEP	95.7	**99.4**	100.0	95.2	**78.6**	75.6	**90.8**(+0.9%)

Table 3. Accuracy of UDA on *Office-Home* with ResNet-50.

Method	Ar→Cl	Ar→Pr	Ar→Rw	Cl→Ar	Cl→Pr	Cl→Rw	Pr→Ar	Pr→Cl	Pr→Rw	Rw→Ar	Rw→Cl	Rw→Pr	Avg
MinEnt [17]	51.0	71.9	77.1	61.2	69.1	70.1	59.3	48.7	77.0	70.4	53.0	81.0	65.8
ResNet [20]	41.1	65.9	73.7	53.1	60.1	63.3	52.2	36.7	71.8	64.8	42.6	75.2	58.4
CDAN+E [39]	54.6	74.1	78.1	63.0	72.2	74.1	61.6	52.3	79.1	72.3	57.3	82.8	68.5
DAN [63]	45.6	67.7	73.9	57.7	63.8	66.0	54.9	40.0	74.5	66.2	49.1	77.9	61.4
SAFN [59]	52.0	71.7	76.3	64.2	69.9	71.9	63.7	51.4	77.1	70.9	57.1	81.5	67.3
TransCal [56]	49.4	68.4	75.5	57.6	70.1	70.4	51.1	50.3	72.4	68.9	54.4	81.2	64.1
ATM [36]	52.4	72.6	78.0	61.1	72.0	72.6	59.5	52.0	79.1	73.3	58.9	83.4	67.9
CKD [43]	54.2	74.1	77.5	64.6	72.2	71.0	64.5	53.4	78.7	72.6	58.4	82.8	68.7
GSDA [27]	**61.3**	76.1	79.4	65.4	73.3	74.3	65.0	53.2	80.0	72.2	60.6	83.1	70.3
SRDC [53]	52.3	76.3	**81.0**	**69.5**	76.2	78.0	68.7	53.8	81.7	76.3	57.1	**85.0**	71.3
DCC [35]	**58.0**	54.1	58.0	74.6	70.6	**77.5**	64.3	**73.6**	74.9	80.9	75.1	80.4	70.2
DANN [16]	53.8	62.6	74.0	55.8	67.3	67.3	55.8	55.1	77.9	71.1	60.7	81.1	65.2
DANN+UTEP	50.7	68.9	77.1	58.7	72.3	71.7	59.3	52.9	79.8	73.5	59.9	83.6	67.3(+2.1%)
MDD [66]	54.9	73.7	77.8	60.0	71.4	71.8	61.2	53.6	78.1	72.5	60.2	82.3	68.1
MDD+UTEP	57.2	75.9	79.6	63.4	72.8	73.7	64.6	**55.4**	79.8	74.0	61.1	84.2	70.1(+2.0%)
CADA [33]	56.9	76.4	80.7	61.3	75.2	75.2	63.2	54.5	80.7	73.9	61.5	84.1	70.2
CADA+UTEP	57.1	**76.5**	**81.1**	61.7	**75.4**	75.2	63.9	54.9	**80.9**	74.2	**61.8**	84.1	**70.6**(+0.4%)
TransPar [19]	55.3	75.9	79.2	63.2	72.4	71.8	61.2	55.1	80.0	74.5	60.9	83.7	69.8
TransPar+UTEP	57.4	76.1	80.2	64.2	73.2	73.7	**64.8**	**55.4**	**80.9**	**74.7**	61.1	**84.6**	**70.6**(+0.8%)

Table 4. Classification accuracy of UDA on *VisDA-2107* using ResNet-101.

Method	Plane	Bicycle	bus	Car	Horse	Knife	Mcycl	Person	Plant	Sktbrd	Train	Truck	Mean
MinEnt [17]	88.6	29.5	82.5	75.8	88.7	16.0	93.2	63.4	94.2	40.1	87.3	12.1	64.3
ResNet [20]	55.1	53.3	61.9	59.1	80.6	17.9	79.7	31.2	81.0	26.5	73.5	8.5	52.4
SAFN [59]	94.2	56.2	81.3	**69.8**	93.0	81.0	**93.0**	74.1	91.7	55.0	**90.6**	18.1	75.0
MixMatch [4]	93.9	71.8	93.5	**82.1**	**95.3**	0.7	90.8	38.1	94.2	96.0	86.3	2.2	70.4
BNM [11]	91.1	69.0	76.7	64.3	89.8	61.2	90.8	74.8	90.9	66.6	88.1	46.1	75.8
MCC [30]	92.2	**82.9**	76.8	66.6	90.9	78.5	87.9	73.8	90.1	76.1	87.1	41.0	78.7
DWL [58]	90.7	**80.2**	86.1	67.6	92.4	81.5	86.8	78.0	90.6	57.1	85.6	28.7	77.1
VAK [22]	**94.3**	79.0	**84.9**	63.6	92.6	92.0	88.4	79.1	92.2	79.8	87.6	43.0	81.4
DANN [16]	90.0	58.9	76.9	56.1	80.3	60.9	89.1	72.5	84.3	73.8	**89.3**	35.8	72.3
DANN+UTEP	93.8	70.7	**85.5**	62.7	91.0	90.7	88.6	76.2	87.2	85.4	84.7	33.8	79.2(+6.9%)
MDD [66]	94.2	71.6	84.3	65.4	91.5	94.9	92.0	**80.3**	90.8	**90.0**	82.4	42.0	81.4
MDD+UTEP	**94.7**	75.4	83.2	60.1	**93.7**	95.3	**93.1**	82.6	**94.3**	**89.8**	84.6	41.1	**82.3**(+0.9%)
CADA [33]	85.1	61.2	84.4	69.0	89.8	**97.1**	93.0	75.8	90.2	84.1	81.4	45.4	79.7
CADA+UTEP	88.9	76.9	82.6	65.6	90.8	**96.9**	90.6	78.5	86.3	86.4	83.8	**48.8**	81.3(+1.6%)
TransPar [19]	84.2	57.7	85.3	62.7	90.0	92.9	92.3	73.9	**95.9**	86.9	84.2	44.7	79.4
TransPar+UTEP	90.0	74.8	82.6	66.2	91.1	95.8	91.3	77.5	89.0	88.3	82.6	**47.2**	**81.5**(+2.1%)

4.2 Experimental Results

Unsupervised DA. To verify the universality of our UTEP, we incorporate it into various adversarial-based UDA methods, including three classical methods (DANN [16], MDD [66] and CADA [33]) and a state-of-the-art method (TransPar [19]). Tables 2, 3 and 4 show experimental results on the small-sized Office-31, the medium-sized Office-Home and the more challenging VisDA-2017, respectively. Overall, our UTEP module can improve the performance of various adversarial-based baseline methods, achieving state-of-the-art performance among UDA methods. On Office-31, for average accuracy, UTEP improves DANN (by 1.9%), MDD (by 1.0%), CADA (by 0.5%) and TransPar (by 0.9%) and TransPar+UTEP achieves 90.8% which is on par with the state-of-the-art. On Office-Home, in terms of average accuracy, UTEP significantly improves DANN, MDD and TransPar by approximately 2.0% and improves CADA by 0.4%, while CADA+UTEP and TransPar+UTEP achieve 70.6% which are the second best results. On VisDA-2017, we can see a notable improvement of UTEP to DANN (by 6.9%) in average accuracy while the improvement of UTEP to MDD, CADA and TransPar are also significant, yielding state-of-the-art performance. In our analysis, the improvement of UTEP to various adversarial-based DA methods can be attributed to learning unbiased transferability by uncertainty variance modeling and uncertainty-based pseudo label selection.

Table 5. Classification accuracy of SSDA with 1% target labeled data on *Office-Home* with ResNet-34 as backbone model (left) and accuracy of 3-shot SSL on *Office-Home* with ResNet-50 as backbone (right).

Methods	SSDA setting				Methods	3-shot SSL setting				
	Ar→Rw	Rw→Pr	Pr→Cl	Avg		Ar	Cl	Pr	Rw	Avg
ADR [64]	70.6	76.6	49.5	65.6	ResNet [20]	48.7	42.1	68.9	66.6	56.6
IRM [1]	71.1	77.6	51.5	66.7	MixMatch [4]	52.2	41.9	73.1	69.1	59.1
MME [52]	72.1	78.1	52.8	67.7	MinEnt [17]	51.7	44.5	72.4	68.9	59.4
CDAN [39]	73.0	79.2	53.1	68.4	MCC [30]	58.9	**47.7**	77.4	74.3	**64.6**
LIRR [34]	**73.6**	**80.2**	53.8	**69.2**	BNM [11]	59.0	**46.0**	**76.5**	71.5	63.2
DANN [16]	72.2	78.1	52.5	67.6	DANN [16]	57.4	41.6	74.5	73.4	61.7
DANN+UPS [50]	73.2	79.6	52.8	68.5	DANN+UPS [50]	**59.1**	42.6	75.3	**76.2**	63.3
DANN+UTEP	**74.4**	**82.1**	**53.3**	**69.9** (+2.3%)	DANN+UTEP	**60.2**	43.6	**77.9**	**78.8**	**65.1**(+3.4%)

Semi-Supervised DA. On SSDA, we follow the setting of the state-of-the-art LIRR [34] and conduct experiments on Office-Home. We randomly select 1% of target samples as the labeled target domain for training and evaluate SSDA methods on unlabeled samples from the target domain. As shown in the left of Table 5, our method significantly improves the mean accuracy of DANN (by 2.3%) and achieves compelling performance against the state-of-the-art SSDA methods. This also examines the efficacy of UTEP for DA under the semi-supervised learning scenario.

4.3   Further Analysis and Discussion

Visualization. In Fig. 3(a)–(b), we use t-SNE [13] to visualize feature embeddings of vanilla ResNet, DANN, DANN+UPS and DANN+UTEP on task **Pr→Ar** (65 classes) on Office-Home. From Figs. 3(a) to 3(c), we can see that the vanilla ResNet has large

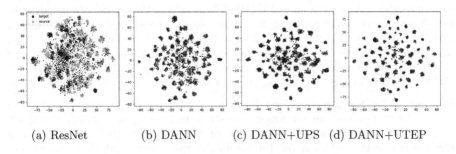

(a) ResNet   (b) DANN   (c) DANN+UPS   (d) DANN+UTEP

Fig. 3. Visualization results for baseline and ours of UDA w/ ResNet-50.

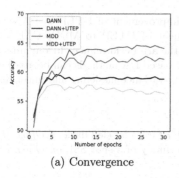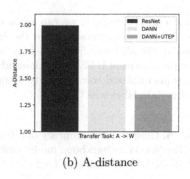

(a) Convergence   (b) A-distance

Fig. 4. (a) Comparison of the training convergence between the two baseline UDA methods(DANN and MDD) and variants equipped with our UTEP with ResNet-50 as backbone; (b) Comparison of the distribution discrepancy measured by A-distance between vanilla ResNet-50, DANN and DANN with our UTEP.

domain discrepancy, while DANN significantly decreases the domain discrepancy. However, the decision boundaries are still not clear in DANN due to the misalignment between the source and target distributions, while DANN+UPS can make the target decision boundary much clearer, but there are still many samples near the boundary are hard to distinguish. By contrast, as shown in Fig. 3(d), DANN+UTEP further resolves this issue and achieves both better marginal and conditional distribution alignments thanks to the effective learning of unbiased transferability.

Convergence and Distribution Discrepancy. In Fig. 4(a), we compare the convergence of DANN, DANN+UTEP, MDD and MDD+UTEP on task $\mathbf{Pr} \rightarrow \mathbf{Ar}$ on Office-Home. We can see that our UTEP can significantly improve the accuracy of DANN and MDD while achieving more stable convergence. Figure 4(b) compares A-distance, a widely used measure for distribution discrepancy in DA [3], of vanilla ResNet, DANN and DANN+UTEP on task $\mathbf{Pr} \rightarrow \mathbf{Ar}$ on Office-Home. It is clearly shown that A-distance of DANN+UTEP on task $\mathbf{A} \rightarrow \mathbf{W}$ is smaller than that of vanilla ResNet and DANN, indicating better distribution alignment and higher accuracies of DANN+UTEP.

Component Effectiveness Evaluation. In Table 6, we study the effectiveness of each component in the proposed UTEP using DANN as the baseline method. In Table 6, the results in the first and seventh rows refer to DANN and DANN+UTEP, respectively. It shows that all the variants perform better than DANN only, showing the effectiveness of each component in the proposed UTEP. The results in the second row are those of DANN using uncertainty modeling for sample weighting and bias loss regularization, which are superior to those of DANN only but inferior to those of DANN+UTEP. The results in the third row shows that without the bias loss, the performance of DANN+UTEP decreases. The results in the fourth, fifth and sixth rows further show that using parts of the proposed components will also lead to performance degradation.

Evaluation on Semi-Supervised Learning. To further study the efficacy of the proposed UTEP, especially compared with semi-supervised pseudo labeling methods (such as UPS [50]), we conduct 3-shot semi-supervised learning (SSL) experiments on Office-Home in the right part of Table 5. In the SSL setting, only three samples of each class are selected as the labeled domain while the rest are used as the unlabeled

Table 6. Ablation study of variants with baseline DANN [16]. SIW and TIW denote using importance weights for samples from source and target domains respectively (Eq. (6)); SBL and TBL represent using the bias loss for samples from source and target domains (Eq. (7)); PCE and NCE indicate using the positive and negative cross-entropy in pseudo label cluster learning (Eq. (18)).

DANN [16]'s variant						Settings on Office-31						
SIW	TIW	SBL	TBL	PCE	NCE	A→W	D→W	W→D	A→D	D→A	W→A	Avg
✗	✗	✗	✗	✗	✗	91.4	97.9	100.0	83.6	73.3	70.4	86.1
✓	✓	✓	✓	✗	✗	92.0	98.2	100.0	85.7	73.0	71.1	86.7
✓	✓	✗	✗	✓	✓	92.2	98.2	100.0	88.5	72.9	71.5	87.2
✓	✓	✓	✓	✓	✗	92.3	98.3	100.0	87.9	73.3	72.0	87.3
✓	✗	✓	✗	✓	✓	91.8	98.2	100.0	88.2	73.5	70.9	87.1
✓	✓	✓	✗	✓	✓	92.0	98.2	100.0	89.0	73.3	71.5	87.3
✓	✓	✓	✓	✓	✓	**92.7**	**98.5**	100.0	**90.4**	**73.8**	**72.7**	**88.0**

domain. For fair comparison between UTEP and UPS, we incorporate both UTEP and UPS into DANN for experiments. From the right part of Table 5, we can see that both UTEP and UPS can improve the performance of DANN, which shows the effectiveness of uncertainty-aware pseudo label selection. Here, DANN+UTEP outperforms DANN+UPS, which further shows the effectiveness of learning unbiased transferability between labeled and unlabeled data for SSL.

5   Conclusion

In this work, we present the Unbiased Transferability Estimation Plug-in (UTEP) to learn unbiased transferability in domain adaptation. The key idea is to model the variance uncertainty of a discriminator in adversarial-based DA method and further exploit the uncertainty for pseudo label selection to achieve better marginal and conditional distribution alignment. Experiments on DA benchmarks show its effectiveness for improving various DA methods with state-of-the-art performance.

Acknowledgement. This work was in part supported by Vision Semantics Limited, Alan Turing Institute, Open Research Projects of Zhejiang Lab (No. 2021KB0AB04), Zhejiang Provincial Natural Science Foundation of China (No. LQ21F020004), Natural Science Foundation of China (No. 61906176), and China Scholarship Council.

References

1. Arjovsky, M., Bottou, L., Gulrajani, I., Lopez-Paz, D.: Invariant risk minimization. arXiv preprint arXiv:1907.02893 (2019)
2. Ben-David, S., Blitzer, J., Crammer, K., Kulesza, A., Pereira, F., Vaughan, J.W.: A theory of learning from different domains. Mach. Learn. **79**, 151–175 (2010)
3. Ben-David, S., Blitzer, J., Crammer, K., Pereira, F.: Analysis of representations for domain adaptation. Adv. Neural Inf. Process. Syst. **19**, 1–8 (2006)
4. Berthelot, D., Carlini, N., Goodfellow, I., Papernot, N., Oliver, A., Raffel, C.A.: Mixmatch: a holistic approach to semi-supervised learning. Adv. Neural Inf. Process. Syst. **32**, 1–11 (2019)

5. Bickel, S., Scheffer, T.: Dirichlet-enhanced spam filtering based on biased samples. In: NIPS (2007)
6. Blundell, C., Cornebise, J., Kavukcuoglu, K., Wierstra, D.: Weight uncertainty in neural network. In: ICML (2015)
7. Chen, C., et al.: Progressive feature alignment for unsupervised domain adaptation. In: Proceedings of the IEEE/CVF Conference on Computer Vision and Pattern Recognition (CVPR), pp. 627–636 (2019)
8. Chen, X., Wang, S., Long, M., Wang, J.: Transferability vs. discriminability: batch spectral penalization for adversarial domain adaptation. In: International Conference on Machine Learning, pp. 1081–1090. PMLR (2019)
9. Cortes, C., Mansour, Y., Mohri, M.: Learning bounds for importance weighting. In: NIPS (2010)
10. Courty, N., Flamary, R., Tuia, D., Rakotomamonjy, A.: Optimal transport for domain adaptation. IEEE Trans. Pattern Anal. Mach. Intell. **39**(9), 1853–1865 (2016)
11. Cui, S., Wang, S., Zhuo, J., Li, L., Huang, Q., Tian, Q.: Towards discriminability and diversity: Batch nuclear-norm maximization under label insufficient situations. In: CVPR (2020)
12. Der Kiureghian, A., Ditlevsen, O.: Aleatory or epistemic? Does it matter? Struct. Saf. **31**(2), 105–112 (2009)
13. Donahue, J., et al.: DeCAF: a deep convolutional activation feature for generic visual recognition. In: International Conference on Machine Learning, pp. 647–655. PMLR (2014)
14. French, G., Mackiewicz, M., Fisher, M.: Self-ensembling for visual domain adaptation. In: International Conference on Learning Representations (ICLR) (2018)
15. Gal, Y., Ghahramani, Z.: Dropout as a Bayesian approximation: representing model uncertainty in deep learning. In: ICML (2016)
16. Ganin, Y., et al.: Domain-adversarial training of neural networks. J. Mach. Learn. Res. **17**, 2096–3000 (2016)
17. Grandvalet, Y., Bengio, Y., et al.: Semi-supervised learning by entropy minimization. CAP **367**, 281–296 (2005)
18. Guan, D., Huang, J., Xiao, A., Lu, S., Cao, Y.: Uncertainty-aware unsupervised domain adaptation in object detection. IEEE Trans. Multimed. **24**, 2502–2514 (2021)
19. Han, Z., Sun, H., Yin, Y.: Learning transferable parameters for unsupervised domain adaptation. arXiv preprint arXiv:2108.06129 (2021)
20. He, K., Zhang, X., Ren, S., Sun, J.: Deep residual learning for image recognition. In: CVPR (2016)
21. Hoffman, J., et al.: CyCADA: cycle-consistent adversarial domain adaptation. In: International Conference on Machine Learning, pp. 1989–1998. PMLR (2018)
22. Hou, Y., Zheng, L.: Visualizing adapted knowledge in domain transfer. In: Proceedings of the IEEE/CVF Conference on Computer Vision and Pattern Recognition (CVPR), pp. 13824–13833, June 2021
23. Hu, J., Tuo, H., Wang, C., Qiao, L., Zhong, H., Jing, Z.: Multi-weight partial domain adaptation. In: BMVC (2019)
24. Hu, J., et al.: Discriminative partial domain adversarial network. In: Vedaldi, A., Bischof, H., Brox, T., Frahm, J.-M. (eds.) ECCV 2020. LNCS, vol. 12372, pp. 632–648. Springer, Cham (2020). https://doi.org/10.1007/978-3-030-58583-9_38
25. Hu, J., Tuo, H., Wang, C., Zhong, H., Pan, H., Jing, Z.: Unsupervised satellite image classification based on partial transfer learning. Aerosp. Syst. **3**(1), 21–28 (2019). https://doi.org/10.1007/s42401-019-00038-6

26. Hu, J., et al.: Self-adaptive partial domain adaptation. arXiv preprint arXiv:2109.08829 (2021)
27. Hu, L., Kan, M., Shan, S., Chen, X.: Unsupervised domain adaptation with hierarchical gradient synchronization. In: Proceedings of the IEEE/CVF Conference on Computer Vision and Pattern Recognition (CVPR), pp. 4043–4052 (2020)
28. Iandola, F.N., Han, S., Moskewicz, M.W., Ashraf, K., Dally, W.J., Keutzer, K.: SqueezeNet: alexnet-level accuracy with 50× fewer parameters and<0.5 mb model size. arXiv preprint arXiv:1602.07360 (2016)
29. Jiang, J., Baixu, C., Bo, F., Mingsheng, L.: Transfer-learning-library. GitHub (2020)
30. Jin, Y., Wang, X., Long, M., Wang, J.: Minimum class confusion for versatile domain adaptation. In: Vedaldi, A., Bischof, H., Brox, T., Frahm, J.-M. (eds.) .: Minimum class confusion for versatile domain adaptation. LNCS, vol. 12366, pp. 464–480. Springer, Cham (2020). https://doi.org/10.1007/978-3-030-58589-1_28
31. Kang, G., Jiang, L., Yang, Y., Hauptmann, A.G.: Contrastive adaptation network for unsupervised domain adaptation. In: CVPR, pp. 4893–4902 (2019)
32. Kendall, A., Gal, Y.: What uncertainties do we need in Bayesian deep learning for computer vision? arXiv preprint arXiv:1703.04977 (2017)
33. Kurmi, V.K., Kumar, S., Namboodiri, V.P.: Attending to discriminative certainty for domain adaptation. In: CVPR, pp. 491–500 (2019)
34. Li, B., Wang, Y., Zhang, S., Li, D., Keutzer, K., Darrell, T., Zhao, H.: Learning invariant representations and risks for semi-supervised domain adaptation. In: CVPR (2021)
35. Li, G., Kang, G., Zhu, Y., Wei, Y., Yang, Y.: Domain consensus clustering for universal domain adaptation. In: Proceedings of the IEEE/CVF Conference on Computer Vision and Pattern Recognition (CVPR), pp. 9757–9766 (June 2021)
36. Li, J., Chen, E., Ding, Z., Zhu, L., Shen, H.T.: Maximum density divergence for domain adaptation. IEEE Trans. Pattern Anal. Mach. Intell. **43**, 3918–3930 (2020)
37. Liang, J., He, R., Sun, Z., Tan, T.: Exploring uncertainty in pseudo-label guided unsupervised domain adaptation. Pattern Recogn. **96**, 106996 (2019)
38. Liu, H., Wang, J., Long, M.: Cycle self-training for domain adaptation. arXiv preprint arXiv:2103.03571 (2021)
39. Long, M., Cao, Z., Wang, J., Jordan, M.I.: Conditional adversarial domain adaptation. In: NeurIPS (2018)
40. Long, M., Cao, Y., Wang, J., Jordan, M.: Learning transferable features with deep adaptation networks. In: ICML (2015)
41. Long, M., Zhu, H., Wang, J., Jordan, M.I.: Unsupervised domain adaptation with residual transfer networks. arXiv preprint arXiv:1602.04433 (2016)
42. Louizos, C., Welling, M.: Multiplicative normalizing flows for variational bayesian neural networks. In: ICML (2017)
43. Luo, Y.W., Ren, C.X.: Conditional bures metric for domain adaptation. In: CVPR (2021)
44. Luo, Z., Zou, Y., Hoffman, J., Fei-Fei, L.: Label efficient learning of transferable representations across domains and tasks. arXiv preprint arXiv:1712.00123 (2017)
45. Pan, Y., Yao, T., Li, Y., Wang, Y., Ngo, C.W., Mei, T.: Transferrable prototypical networks for unsupervised domain adaptation. In: CVPR (2019)
46. Park, S., Bastani, O., Weimer, J., Lee, I.: Calibrated prediction with covariate shift via unsupervised domain adaptation. In: AISTATS (2020)
47. Parmar, N., et al.: Image transformer. In: International Conference on Machine Learning, pp. 4055–4064. PMLR (2018)

48. Pawlowski, N., Brock, A., Lee, M.C.H., Rajchl, M., Glocker, B.: Implicit weight uncertainty in neural networks. arXiv preprint arXiv:1711.01297 (2017)
49. Qin, J.: Inferences for case-control and semiparametric two-sample density ratio models. Biometrika **85**(3), 619–630 (1998)
50. Rizve, M.N., Duarte, K., Rawat, Y.S., Shah, M.: In defense of pseudo-labeling: an uncertainty-aware pseudo-label selection framework for semi-supervised learning. In: ICLR (2020)
51. Saenko, K., Kulis, B., Fritz, M., Darrell, T.: Adapting visual category models to new domains. In: Daniilidis, K., Maragos, P., Paragios, N. (eds.) ECCV 2010. LNCS, vol. 6314, pp. 213–226. Springer, Heidelberg (2010). https://doi.org/10.1007/978-3-642-15561-1_16
52. Saito, K., Kim, D., Sclaroff, S., Darrell, T., Saenko, K.: Semi-supervised domain adaptation via minimax entropy. In: ICCV (2019)
53. Tang, H., Chen, K., Jia, K.: Unsupervised domain adaptation via structurally regularized deep clustering. In: CVPR, pp. 8725–8735 (2020)
54. Tzeng, E., Hoffman, J., Saenko, K., Darrell, T.: Adversarial discriminative domain adaptation. In: CVPR (2017)
55. Wang, X., Li, L., Ye, W., Long, M., Wang, J.: Transferable attention for domain adaptation. In: AAAI (2019)
56. Wang, X., Long, M., Wang, J., Jordan, M.: Transferable calibration with lower bias and variance in domain adaptation. Adv. Neural Inf. Process. Syst. **33**, 19212–19223 (2020)
57. Wen, J., Zheng, N., Yuan, J., Gong, Z., Chen, C.: Bayesian uncertainty matching for unsupervised domain adaptation. arXiv preprint arXiv:1906.09693 (2019)
58. Xiao, N., Zhang, L.: Dynamic weighted learning for unsupervised domain adaptation. In: Proceedings of the IEEE/CVF Conference on Computer Vision and Pattern Recognition (CVPR), pp. 15242–15251, June 2021
59. Xu, R., Li, G., Yang, J., Lin, L.: Larger norm more transferable: an adaptive feature norm approach for unsupervised domain adaptation. In: ICCV, pp. 1426–1435 (2019)
60. Yang, X., Hou, L., Zhou, Y., Wang, W., Yan, J.: Dense label encoding for boundary discontinuity free rotation detection. In: Proceedings of the IEEE/CVF Conference on Computer Vision and Pattern Recognition, pp. 15819–15829 (2021)
61. Yosinski, J., Clune, J., Bengio, Y., Lipson, H.: How transferable are features in deep neural networks? arXiv preprint arXiv:1411.1792 (2014)
62. You, K., Wang, X., Long, M., Jordan, M.: Towards accurate model selection in deep unsupervised domain adaptation. In: International Conference on Machine Learning, pp. 7124–7133. PMLR (2019)
63. Zhang, J., Ding, Z., Li, W., Ogunbona, P.: Importance weighted adversarial nets for partial domain adaptation. In: CVPR (2018)
64. Zhang, S., Wu, G., Costeira, J.P., Moura, J.M.: Understanding traffic density from large-scale web camera data. In: CVPR (2017)
65. Zhang, S., Tuo, H., Hu, J., Jing, Z.: Domain adaptive yolo for one-stage cross-domain detection. arXiv preprint arXiv:2106.13939 (2021)
66. Zhang, Y., Liu, T., Long, M., Jordan, M.: Bridging theory and algorithm for domain adaptation. In: International Conference on Machine Learning, pp. 7404–7413. PMLR (2019)
67. Zheng, Z., Yang, Y.: Rectifying pseudo label learning via uncertainty estimation for domain adaptive semantic segmentation. Int. J. Comput. Vision. **129**, 1106–1120 (2021)

68. Zhong, H., Tuo, H., Wang, C., Ren, X., Hu, J., Qiao, L.: Source-constraint adversarial domain adaptation. In: 2019 IEEE International Conference on Image Processing (ICIP), pp. 2486–2490. IEEE (2019)
69. Zou, Z., Qu, X., Zhou, P., Xu, S., Ye, J.: Coarse to fine: Domain adaptive crowd counting via adversarial scoring network (2021)

Learn2Augment: Learning to Composite Videos for Data Augmentation in Action Recognition

Shreyank N. Gowda[1]([✉]), Marcus Rohrbach[2], Frank Keller[1],
and Laura Sevilla-Lara[1]

[1] University of Edinburgh, Edinburgh, UK
S.Narayana-Gowda@sms.ed.ac.uk
[2] Meta AI, Menlo Park, USA

Abstract. We address the problem of data augmentation for video action recognition. Standard augmentation strategies in video are hand-designed and sample the space of possible augmented data points either at random, without knowing which augmented points will be better, or through heuristics. We propose to learn what makes a "good" video for action recognition and select only high-quality samples for augmentation. In particular, we choose video compositing of a foreground and a background video as the data augmentation process, which results in diverse and realistic new samples. We learn which pairs of videos to augment *without* having to actually composite them. This reduces the space of possible augmentations, which has two advantages: it saves computational cost and increases the accuracy of the final trained classifier, as the augmented pairs are of higher quality than average. We present experimental results on the entire spectrum of training settings: few-shot, semi-supervised and fully supervised. We observe consistent improvements across all of them over prior work and baselines on Kinetics, UCF101, HMDB51, and achieve a new state-of-the-art on settings with limited data. We see improvements of up to 8.6% in the semi-supervised setting. Project Page: https://sites.google.com/view/learn2augment/home.

1 Introduction

Large-scale datasets have played a key role in the progress of research across AI problems. In computer vision, neural networks have existed for decades, but one of the enabling factors for the current revolution was the development of the large ImageNet [8]. In the video domain, manually collecting and annotating data can be a prohibitively expensive process. In video action recognition, for

---

Supplementary Information The online version contains supplementary material available at https://doi.org/10.1007/978-3-031-19821-2_14.

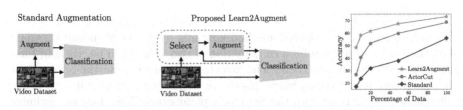

Fig. 1. Standard video augmentation techniques generate data using hand-designed heuristics (left). We propose to learn to select videos for augmentation, based on how effective they will be for learning to classify (middle). Our approach, Learn2Augment, improves classification across datasets and settings, including UCF101 (right).

example, collecting data requires an immense amount of manual labor, as it involves finding suitable videos, trimming them and classifying them.

Recent efforts in video focus on relieving the strong dependency of current methods to the size of labeled datasets. Some of these efforts [33,43] involve increasing the number of data samples through data augmentation. This strategy aims to create new videos in the training set by performing transformations on the original annotated videos, where labels are known. This process adds diversity to the training data, while new videos are still realistic and plausible. In the simplest version of data augmentation in video, new data samples are generated by flipping the input video horizontally, or by cropping a subsection of the video. New methods [38,43] propose more sophisticated processes like combining two videos. VideoMix [38] randomly crops regions of one video and pastes them onto another. ActorCut [43] goes one step further and uses the bounding box detections of humans on one video to paste them onto the background of another video. This increases the diversity of the new videos, and despite the lack of visual realism of the resulting videos, this strategy helps (Fig. 1).

However, as datasets become larger, such data augmentation strategies become computationally expensive. The search space of possible video pairs and transformations is enormous and difficult to explore. The solution is often to sample the space randomly, or to manually design augmentation heuristics. Any exploration process is particularly burdening in the context of video data, where the augmentation process needs to be repeated in every frame, which may be orders of magnitude more expensive than for images.

In this paper we address the problem of sampling for data augmentation, and propose to learn to select pairs of videos. We show that this reduces the search space of augmented data points by orders of magnitude and improves the final accuracy of the classifier significantly. We leverage two observations. First, not all data points are as useful for classification. This idea has been exploited in the context of frame or clip selection [11,16,20]. Second, we can learn to predict which data points will be useful without actually generating them. This is essential, as the space of transformations is huge, and if we needed to create each candidate augmented video, the process would be prohibitively expensive.

More concretely, we propose a data augmentation method which we call Learn2Augment. The proposed method contains a "Selector" network, which predicts a score of how useful a combination of two videos will be, without having to actually composite them. The Selector is trained using the accuracy of the classification as the cue. Since this metric depends on the classifier, it is not differentiable with respect to the Selector's parameters. Therefore we optimize the network using reinforcement learning. Once the Selector network is trained, we use it to choose good pairs of videos, composite them, and train a classification network. In our experiments, for example in the case of the UCF101 dataset, using the Selector reduces the number of augmented videos by 92% while increasing the classification accuracy.

In the proposed method, each augmented video is created from a pair of videos using a composition of the segmented foreground of one video, including actor and objects, onto the background of the other video. This process yields diverse and realistic new data samples, which we demonstrate is important for learning. More concretely, results show an improvement of 4.4% over using a simpler transformation.

The Selector is indeed useful to reduce the number of videos for training the classifier. However, we also need to reduce the space of possible pairs for training the Selector network itself. For example, the number of possible pairs of videos in video datasets can be in the order of millions for small datasets or billions for large datasets. For this, we leverage the natural correlation between the occurrence of foreground activities and background scenes [5]. This is, it is more likely to find someone playing football in a football field than at a restaurant. Instead of sampling at random the pairs of videos to train the Selector on, we sample pairs from classes that are semantically similar. In particular, we use the class names to obtain a semantic embedding, and match each class to their nearest neighbor in this space. Experiments show that this extremely simple design choice of Semantic Matching reduces the space of possible pairs of videos by several orders of magnitude (from quadratic to linear on the number of videos). This yields better results than choosing pairs at random, which may result in non-plausible scenarios, or choosing pairs from the same class, which may not add as much diversity.

In summary, the proposed **Learn2Augment** contains three core components: a Selector that learns to choose good videos to augment, a Semantic Matching method that improves optimization, and a Video Compositing that composites video pairs for augmentation. Experimental results show that all components contribute to the performance of the system in different ways, and the overall method obtains state-of-the-art in all datasets, and in all settings that involve limited training data. In addition, in the setting which considers the full training set, the proposed data augmentation technique improves upon the baseline on all datasets, including UCF101, HMDB51, and the large-scale Kinetics-400.

2   Related Work

Data Augmentation for Video Action Recognition. Standard data augmentation techniques in action recognition include horizontal flip and cropping, where new videos are created by selecting a box at each frame, and then resizing the resulting video to have the same size as the original one. While this strategy helps, generated videos do not add much diversity to the training set. Recent efforts such as ActorCut [43] and VideoMix [38] increase the diversity of new video samples by cutting and pasting the foreground of one video onto another. This general technique of combining two data samples has proven to be quite effective, even in the image domain [37]. However, the resulting videos are not very realistic, and are used for training regardless of their quality. Zhang et al. [42] go one step further and synthesize new samples using GANs, and use "self-paced selection" to train, starting with easy samples and progressively choosing harder samples. Instead, we propose to create realistic data samples by segmenting, inpainting and blending the foreground of one video onto the background of another. Crucially, we learn to discard novel video samples that are not expected to be useful for classification, overall producing a more accurate data augmentation strategy.

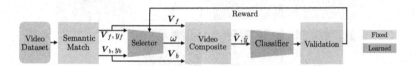

Fig. 2. Overview of the proposed Learn2Augment. Given a pair of videos and their labels, a Selector network gives a score ω of the quality of the potential composited video. At training time, the Selector is trained with the validation loss of the classification network. Once the Selector is trained, pairs of videos are sampled, and only the promising combinations with high score ω are composited and used for training the classifier.

Learning to Augment Data. The idea of learning to augment data has been used in other computer vision problems. In the image classification domain, this strategy has been done using the final classification loss as the training criterion [25], augmenting in feature space [9], and learning data augmentation policies [6]. As in this paper, in the image domain it has been noted that the search space for data samples can be large and thus expensive [7].

Other computer vision domains like low level vision, also struggle with data dependency, as creating ground truth is particularly hard. In optical flow, AutoFlow [33] recently introduced the strategy of learning to generate good training data for a target dataset.

Semi-supervised Video Action Recognition. Semi-supervised learning (SSL) also aims to reduce data dependence by learning from large sets of unlabeled samples and a small set of labeled ones. SSL in images has been widely explored. For example, some strategies include giving pseudo-labels [1,24] to samples where the classifier has high confidence, and adding these to the labeled training data. Other common approaches use consistency regularization [22,23,34]. Approaches that combine consistency regularization and entropy minimization [13] have shown to be very effective in tackling the SSL task in images such as MixMatch [3] and RemixMatch [2].

SSL in videos however, has not been explored as much. One of the early works used extreme learning machines [17] to perform SSL on videos. Recently, VideoSSL [18] and Temporal Contrastive Learning (TCL) [30] leverage SSL in videos. VideoSSL [18] uses pseudo-labels and object cues from unlabeled samples to guide the learning process. TCL [30] use a two-pathway contrastive learning model using unlabeled videos at two different speeds with the intuition that changing video speeds do not change the action being performed.

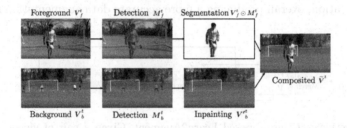

Fig. 3. Pipeline for compositing a single frame. The foreground is from the class "soccer juggling" and the background from the class "soccer penalty", which are semantic class neighbors. We can see objects such as 'person' and 'ball' are detected as objects of interest.

Data augmentation and SSL are two different families of techniques to relieve the dependence on labeled data, and in this paper we experiment with the combination of both, showing that they are actually complementary.

Sample Selection. Recent work [16] has shown that not all data samples are as useful. Selecting a subset of high quality frames or clips at test time shows better results than using the entire video for action recognition. In this spirit, SMART [11] uses an attention and relation network to learn scores for each frame in a video and then select only the high ranked ones for inference. Similarly, SCSampler [20] uses a lightweight clip sampling model to select the salient clips in a video and use only those. Unlike the proposed method, these learn to choose single videos, which are already available, while we learn to choose pairs of videos to be composited, which are not already combined.

The most relevant work to ours is data valuation in the image domain, using RL [36], in the image domain where each sample is given a score of how effective the sample is, and at training time the sample is multiplied by this score. In our work, instead of learning the effectiveness of the training set, we leverage that knowledge for augmentation.

3   Learn2Augment

In this section we describe in detail the architecture of the proposed Learn2Augment. In a nutshell, the goal is to learn to augment novel data points which are realistic and diverse, such that we can train a better classifier with them. For this, we train a Selector network, which predicts a score of how useful a given pair of videos is for augmentation. We pick pairs that have a high score to be augmented. The transformation we use for augmentation is Video Compositing. Training the Selector using the entire dataset is infeasible, and sampling pairs of videos at random will yield unlikely pairs. Thus we sample pairs of videos using Semantic Matching. Figure 2 shows an overview of the proposed method and in Sect. 4 we describe how we train our approach.

3.1   Selector

Given two input videos V_1 and V_2, the goal of the Selector is to predict a weight ω, rating the quality of the potential composited video. Note that the input to the Selector is two putative videos instead of the composited one. This means that at test time, we can predict how useful the composited video will be without having to actually create it.

The architecture of the Selector includes a standard video classification network to extract video features, which is ResNet3D-18 [15] followed by a simple multi-layer perceptron (MLP) with 3 hidden layers of sizes 2048, 1024 and 512. Two videos are input to the Selector at a time, and their features and labels are concatenated and input to the MLP.

Since there is no ground truth of how "good" a video sample is for learning, we train the Selector using the change in validation loss of the classifier. This is, we argue that a "good" training sample is one which, if used for training, improves the validation loss of the classification network. In other words, if we take one optimization step training the classifier, after updating the weights, the validation loss will go down. Section 4.1 describes the training process in detail.

At test time, we use the Selector by sampling pairs of videos, choosing those pairs with high score ω, and input to the Video Compositing module, which we describe in Sect. 3.3. The resulting video is finally used to augment the training set for the classification network.

3.2   Semantic Matching (SM)

The number of pairs in the full dataset can be very large, as it grows with the square of the number of videos. For Kinetics [4], for example, we would encounter 360 billion pairs. Training the classifier using these is clearly infeasible, and thus we use the Selector. But training the Selector itself with all these samples is infeasible too. Sampling uniformly is a reasonable solution, but many video pairs may not be useful for learning. We leverage the observation that all combinations of actions and backgrounds are not equally likely [5]. This natural correlation between actions and backgrounds helps to prune unlikely class combinations.

For this, we make the assumption that classes that are semantically similar are more likely to contain a foreground and a background that are plausible in the real world, and therefore more realistic for our data augmentation purposes. Thus, we use the class names to extract a language embedding using sen2vec [28], and use these embeddings to match each class to its nearest neighbor. We sample videos V_1 and V_2 from class c_1 and its closest neighbor c_2 respectively. This simple decision reduces the number of pairs to grow linearly with the size of the dataset, and furthermore increases the accuracy significantly with respect to sampling video pairs at random. More details on the numerical impact can be found in Sect. 5.3. Semantic class pairs and additional experiments using intra-class augmentation can be found in the supplementary material.

Fig. 4. Sample frames of rendered videos. While the segmentation contains errors, such as missing limbs or portions of the object, the action category remains clear.

3.3 Video Compositing (VC)

The goal of the augmentation process is to composite two videos, to produce realistic, plausible and diverse new videos, that will improve the classification. Figure 3 shows the overall pipeline for compositing a single frame.

Given two videos which will be used for foreground V_f and background V_b, we use a standard object segmentation network (MaskRCNN [14]) to segment out people and objects in every frame of both videos. Objects categories in action datasets are not completely contained in the image dataset COCO [26], which is used for training MaskRCNN. However, we observe that object detections with high confidence tend to correspond to actual objects, even if the category is not correct (boxing bag is often classified as fire hydrant), and therefore are useful to our purpose. We could also have selected only the humans in the video, as action categories tend to be focused on humans. However, we find that the presence of specific objects is highly correlated with action categories (musical instruments in the classes "playing guitar" or "playing violin"). Therefore removing the original objects from the background and adding the ones from the foreground is essential for recognition. See numerical results of the impact of these decisions in the ablation study of Sect. 5.3.

We remove the segmented objects from the background video and fill in the holes using image inpainting [27], to obtain a clean background video V'_b. Finally, we combine the foreground objects and the background at each frame by simple composition, as in:

$$\widetilde{V}^t = V_f^t \odot M_f^t + V'^t_b \odot (1 - M_f^t), \qquad (1)$$

where $\widetilde{V}^t$ is the resulting composited frame at time t, V_f^t and V'^t_b are frames of the foreground and background videos respectively, M_f^t is the binary mask with the union of all detected objects, and $\odot$ is the element-wise multiplication. Figure 4 shows sample frames of the resulting videos.

4   Optimization of Learn2Augment

The optimization of the proposed Learn2Augment method has two stages. In the first stage, we train the Selector network using RL, as described in Sect. 4.1. Once the Selector network is trained, in the second stage, we perform data augmentation to train the classifier. That is, we sample pairs of videos, pass them through the trained Selector, choose the pairs with high score, create new videos with these pairs through Video Compositing, and add them to the training set. We now describe the details of these two training stages.

4.1   Training the Selector

As mentioned before, there is no ground truth to tell us how good an augmented data sample is. Instead, we use the validation loss of the classification network to train the Selector network. This function is not differentiable with respect to the parameters of the Selector. A common solution to dealing with this is to use RL [36].

Specifically, the state s_t at time t is the batch of video pairs sampled using SM. The action a_t is the subset of these video pairs selected for compositing and is represented as a vector of values between 0 and 1. The environment is the classification network and the validation process. This environment is used to compute a reward $R(\theta)$ for choosing a particular action, where θ are the parameters of the Selector.

We calculate the reward in a single step, as the difference between the loss in the current batch and the moving average of losses in the previous S steps (where $S = 5$) denoted as δ, as in Eq. 2:

$$R(\phi) = \left(\frac{1}{|D_{\text{val}}|} \sum_{i=1}^{|D_{\text{val}}|} \mathcal{L}_{\text{cls}}(f_\phi(V_i), y_i) \right) - \delta \qquad (2)$$

where $\mathcal{L}_{\text{cls}}$ is the classification cross-entropy loss, f_ϕ is the classifier network of parameters ϕ, V_i and y_i are an input video and its label respectively, D_{val} is the validation set and $|D_{\text{val}}|$ is the number of samples in D_{val}. The objective function that we want to maximize is the expected value of the reward:

$$J(\theta) = \mathbb{E}(R(\phi)). \tag{3}$$

To find the optimal policy, we would typically differentiate the objective function with respect to the parameters θ. However, the reward function is dependent on the validation loss, calculated with the classifier network, which does not involve θ. Instead, using REINFORCE [35], we approximate the objective function as:

$$\nabla_\theta J(\theta) \approx \frac{1}{M} \sum_{i=1}^{M} R_{\tau^i}(\phi) \left(\sum_{t=0}^{T-1} \nabla_\theta \log \pi_\theta(a_i^t | s_i^t) \right), \tag{4}$$

where, τ^i is the ith state-action trajectory under the policy π_θ, M is the number of sample trajectories and T is the number of actions performed in a trajectory. Note that as we have single-step episodes, we can make several simplifications as $M = 1$, as $T = 1$, and as there is only one trajectory τ^i, and thus $R_{\tau^i}(\phi)$ is just $R(\phi)$. With these simplifications and substituting Eq. 3 in Eq. 4, we obtain:

$$\nabla_\theta J(\theta) \approx R(\phi) \nabla_\theta \log \pi_\theta(D_M | D_B), \tag{5}$$

where D_M corresponds to the subset of pairs of samples to composite and D_B to all the pairs of samples in the batch. The Selector is updated by $\alpha \nabla_\theta J(\theta)$ where α is the learning rate and δ is updated with the last calculated loss as seen in Eq 6.

$$\delta_t = \frac{S-1}{S} \delta_{t-1} + \frac{1}{|D_{\text{val}}|} \sum_{i=1}^{|D_{\text{val}}|} \left(\mathcal{L}_{cls}(f_\theta(\boldsymbol{V}_i), y_i) \right). \tag{6}$$

Note that this training process does involve generating the composited videos for pairs in D_M, to input to the classifier and compute the loss. However, crucially, during training this is a small portion (one order of magnitude smaller) of how many videos would need to be generated if we were to composite all pairs of videos.

Once the Selector is trained, we use it for actually filtering good pairs. At that point, given two videos and their labels, the Selector network predicts a policy π of how likely it is to select the pair. The score ω is the value of π for each pair. We use a threshold on that score to select the pairs of videos to augment. In our experiments, we first determine a budget on the number of videos that we want to augment, and then pick the threshold to select the top-ranked video pairs. We use these selected pairs of videos as input to Video Compositing, add them to the training set, and use them to train the classifier.

4.2   Training the Classifier

Similar to previous work which combines multiple samples for augmentation [37,43], composited/mixed samples should include mixed labels. We adopt the strategy of Cutmix [37], where the foreground label y_f and the background label y_b are combined using a ratio λ, as:

$$\tilde{y} = \lambda y_f + (1 - \lambda) y_b, \tag{7}$$

to obtain the mixed label $\tilde{y}$. A simple way to choose λ is to use the ratio of the foreground mask with respect to the overall video. Given the foreground video V_f of dimensions $T \times H \times W$, and mask at each frame M_f, the foreground ratio would be $\gamma = \sum M_f / (THW)$. Instead of choosing λ to be directly proportional to the foreground ratio γ, we give slightly more weight to the foreground [43], as in Eq. 8, where $\alpha = 4$.

$$\lambda = -(\gamma - 1)^\alpha + 1, \gamma \in [0, 1] \tag{8}$$

We add composited videos $\widetilde{V}$, and their mixed labels $\tilde{y}$ to the training set, and train the classifier network using a standard cross-entropy loss, with stochastic gradient descent.

The choice of classifier is not tied to our method. In our experiments, we choose the widely used 3D ResNet-18 architecture, which allows us to compare directly to other approaches.

5   Experiments

We experiment extensively with Learn2Augment using three data settings, four datasets, and two splits. We also present ablation studies. In this section we first describe the details of the experiments and then discuss our results.

5.1   Experimental Details

Datasets. In order to provide comparison to prior work (e.g. [30,43]), we use standard datasets for evaluation in action recognition, including HMDB51 [21], UCF101 [32], Kinetics-400 [4], and Kinetics-100, which includes the 100 classes with the largest amount of samples in Kinetics, as it is used in prior work [18] and helps us compare directly. For experiments on the effect of pre-training the Selector, we use Kinetics-400. For the semi-supervised setting, we split the datasets following the protocol of VideoSSL [18] and ActorCut [43]. For few-shot we use the standard split [40] and the Truze split [12] which ensures no overlap of novel classes with Kinetics-400.

Problem Settings. We test the proposed method in three different settings. In the *semi-supervised* setting, a portion of the training set is artificially held out, and the rest of the training data is assumed to be available, but unlabeled. Tests are performed on different percentages of held out data. In the *few-shot* setting, some classes (novel classes) are assumed to have a very small number of training samples (one to five instances), while other classes have the full number of samples (seen classes). We effectively change the n-shot learning problem to a $n + k$-shot problem where k is the number of augmented samples. Finally, in the standard *full set* setting, all training data is available.

Training Settings. We use mini-batch stochastic gradient descent, with momentum of 0.9 and weight decay 0.001. For each video, we use an 8-frame clip,
where the frames are uniformly sampled. We use batch size of 8. For UCF101
and Kinetics100 in the SSL setting, we train the model for 400 epochs and for
HMDB51, we train for 500 epochs. The initial learning rate is set to 0.1 and
then decayed using cosine annealing policy. For the SSL setting, we use the data
split proposed in VideoSSL [18]. For the few-shot setting, we use the default
hyperparameters of TRX [29], ARN [40] and C3D-PN [31], respectively. In the
fully supervised setting, we train R(2+1)D for 100 epochs on UCF101, HMDB51
and 50 epochs on Kinetics-400.

5.2   Architectural Changes for Different Settings

We briefly explain the structural adaptations of our approach for each of the
settings.

Table 1. Ablation study to explore the impact of each proposed component. All settings use the same number of samples for training, so that they can be compared fairly.
The # Videos (S) corresponds to the search space in each scenario. As we can see, we
obtain the best accuracy using just 12K instead of the standard scenario which would
have had 10.4M i.e. a reduction of over 1000x.

Pairs selector	Video compositing	Semantic matching	Accuracy in %	#Videos (S)
✓	✓	✓	**58.9**	12K
✗	✓	✓	55.8	99K
✓	✗	✓	54.5	12K
✓	✓	✗	55.2	(1.2M)
✓	✗	✗	52.9	(1.2M)
✗	✓	✗	48.6	(10.4M)
✗	✗	✓	50.8	99K
✗	✗	✗	45.5	(10.4M)

Semi-supervised Learning. Similar to VideoSSL [18], we first train the classifier
on the available labeled data using the categorical cross-entropy loss. Once this
network is trained, we do a forward pass of the unlabeled examples and assign
pseudo-labels to those samples with high confidence. We use these pseudo-labels
as additional data for augmentation. We also add a knowledge distillation loss
inspired by VideoSSL [18]. Details can be found in the supplementary material.

Few-shot Learning. We only augment the novel classes using Learn2Augment. We also do not perform label mixing and simply use the foreground label for the augmented sample. This incorporates our composited samples seamlessly into the meta-learning framework typically followed. We show results on the standard split, as on the recently proposed TruZe [12]. TruZe ensures that the novel classes do not overlap with Kinetics-400.

Fully-Supervised Learning. This is the simplest setting, where the Selector is trained on the full training set, and used for data augmentation to train the classifier. We explore two scenarios: training the classifier from scratch and using a model pre-trained on Sports1M [19].

5.3   Ablation Study

Table 1 shows the ablation study of Learn2Augment, which illustrates the impact of each of the proposed elements in the design. The experiment is done on the UCF101 dataset, using 20% of the data i.e. in a semi-supervised setting. All three contributions (Selector, Semantic Matching and Video Compositing) improve accuracy. Crucially, Semantic Matching and the Selector also reduce greatly the number of possible video combinations, and the overall reduction is around three orders of magnitude. We see that Learn2Augment obtains a 13.4% improvement over the baseline. While there are improvements of up to 7.4% for each component, the combination of all three gives the best results. Further analysis can be found in the supplementary material.

Table 2. Ablation study of compositing components. The version "w/o Inpaint" refers to pasting the foreground without first filling in the holes of removed objects in the background. The version "w/o Segmentation" refers to using bounding boxes instead of object segmentations. "w/o Objects" refers to copying and pasting only the humans in the scene, leaving the objects.

Method	Accuracy
L2A	58.9
L2A w/o Inpaint	57.6
L2A w/o Segmentation	56.8
L2A w/o Objects	55.7
L2A w/o All	54.5

The Video Compositing module also has multiple components. In Table 2, we ablate these components and observe that removing objects is actually essential, and has the most significant impact, followed by using segmentation instead of a bounding box, and finally inpainting.

Although the compositing process is more computationally expensive than previous simpler mixing strategies, it is important to note that 1) the overall accuracy indeed improves, 2) the actual composition for training the classifier is done on a small subset of pairs of videos and 3) the Selector can be trained on a large dataset (e.g.: Kinetics) just once and can be reused for the smaller datasets without the need of fine-tuning (see Table 3).

Table 3. Results on the semi-supervised setting. Results for TCL and ActorCut are obtained by us running the author's code. All methods are run with a 3D ResNet-18 backbone for fair comparison. L2A +Pre-training refers to pre-training the selector and fixing it.

Method	Conference	Kinetics 100				UCF101				HMDB51		
		50%	20%	10%	5%	50%	20%	10%	5%	60%	50%	40%
CutMix [37]	ICCV19	53.7	46.1	43.2	39.9	46.1	36.5	34.6	25.8	33.9	30.8	27.8
MixUp [41]	ICLR18	53.4	45.5	43.0	39.6	45.8	36.1	34.2	25.5	33.7	31.0	27.5
CutOut [10]	Arxiv17	52.8	45.1	42.3	38.8	45.2	35.6	33.9	24.6	33.0	30.5	27.1
ST-VideoMix [38]	Arxiv21	55.3	46.6	43.9	40.4	46.4	36.4	35.2	25.9	34.8	31.3	28.7
PseudoLabel [24]	ICMLW13	59.0	48.0	38.9	27.9	47.5	37.0	24.7	17.6	33.5	32.4	27.3
MeanTeacher [34]	Neurips17	59.3	47.1	36.4	27.8	45.8	36.3	25.6	17.5	32.2	30.4	27.2
S4L [39]	ICCV19	54.6	51.1	43.3	33.0	47.9	37.7	29.1	22.7	35.6	31.0	29.8
VideoSSL [18]	WACV21	65.0	57.7	52.6	47.6	54.3	48.7	42.0	32.4	37.0	36.2	32.7
ActorCut [43]	Arxiv21	68.7	61.2	56.8	52.7	59.9	51.7	40.2	27.0	38.9	38.2	32.9
ActorCut+ID [43]	Arxiv21	72.2	68.7	63.9	59.1	64.7	57.4	53.0	45.1	40.8	39.5	35.7
TCL [30]	ICCV21	70.4	64.7	61.1	58.2	62.1	55.4	52.1	42.8	41.2	40.4	34.8
L2A		**75.9**	**72.1**	**67.5**	**63.7**	72.1	60.3	56.1	48.0	44.5	43.2	37.9
L2A +Pre-training		-	-	-	-	**73.3**	**64.8**	**60.1**	**50.9**	**47.1**	**46.3**	**42.1**

5.4 Augmenting in the Semi-supervised Setting

In this setting we artificially hold out a portion of the training set, with the goal of observing the behavior of different methods as the size of the training set changes. In this setting, we use the remaining part of the dataset by producing pseudo-labels, similar to VideoSSL [18]. Table 3 shows results in this semi-supervised setting. The L2A version of the method uses a Selector and a classifier trained only on the target dataset (in this case UCF101, HMDB51 or Kinetics-100). We observe that Learn2Augment improves on all settings over all previous methods.

The "L2A +Pre-training" row refers to Learn2Augment where the Selector has been pre-trained on Kinetics-400, without fine-tuning on the target dataset. We make two observations: First that pre-training on a large dataset helps, as the results from the pre-trained model are higher for all datasets and settings. Second that the Selector trained on Kinetics generalizes quite well to the smaller datasets without the need for fine-tuning. We do not test on Kinetics-100 with the pre-trained model, as this would mix training and testing sets.

5.5 Augmenting in the Few-shot Setting

We also explore the impact of the proposed method on the more extreme few-shot setting, where there are only a few examples per class. This is interesting because few-shot methods are already designed to address data scarcity.

We compare with the current state of the art in this setting, including CD3-PN [31], ARN [40] and TRX [29], on the UCF101 and HMDB51 datasets. We observe that the proposed Learn2Augment method improves upon all existing approaches, suggesting data augmentation is complementary to few-shot methods. Table 4 shows the results of the experiments.

Table 4. Results on UCF101 for the Few-Shot Learning setting, with different splits. Accuracies are reported for 5-way, 1, 2, 3, 4, 5-shot classification. S corresponds to the split used in [29,40] and T is the TruZe split [12], which avoids overlapping classes with Kinetics.

Method	Split	UCF101					HMDB51				
		1	2	3	4	5	1	2	3	4	5
C3D-PN [31]	S	57.1	66.4	71.7	75.5	78.2	38.1	47.5	50.3	55.6	57.4
C3D-PN + L2A	S	**60.8**	**68.9**	**73.3**	**76.6**	**79.1**	**39.8**	**48.9**	**51.5**	**57.3**	**58.2**
ARN [40]	S	66.3	73.1	77.9	80.4	83.1	45.5	50.1	54.2	58.7	60.6
ARN + L2A	S	**67.7**	**74.2**	**79.6**	**81.1**	**84.4**	**47.3**	**51.7**	**55.5**	**60.1**	**61.8**
TRX [29]	S	77.5	88.8	92.8	94.7	96.1	50.5	62.7	66.9	73.5	75.6
TRX + L2A	S	**79.2**	**89.2**	**93.2**	**95.0**	**96.3**	**51.9**	**63.8**	**68.2**	**74.4**	**77.0**
C3D-PN [31]	T	50.9	61.9	67.5	72.9	75.4	28.8	38.5	43.4	46.7	49.1
C3D-PN + L2A	T	**52.5**	**63.8**	**70.1**	**75.2**	**78.2**	**29.9**	**40.1**	**44.5**	**47.7**	50.8
ARN [40]	T	61.2	70.7	75.2	78.8	80.2	31.9	42.3	46.5	49.8	53.2
ARN + L2A	T	**63.9**	**73.1**	**77.4**	**80.4**	**81.3**	**33.6**	**43.7**	**48.0**	**51.1**	**53.8**
TRX [29]	T	75.2	88.1	91.5	93.1	93.5	33.5	46.7	49.8	57.9	61.5
TRX + L2A	T	**76.8**	**88.9**	**92.7**	**93.8**	**94.1**	**35.0**	**48.1**	**51.1**	**59.2**	**62.1**

Table 5. Augmenting standard datasets improves classification even with a model pre-trained on the largest existing dataset (Sports1M).

Augmentation	Dataset	Pretrained	Top-1
Standard	UCF101	No Pretraining	55.7
ActorCut [43]	UCF101	No Pretraining	68.3
L2A	UCF101	No Pretraining	**73.1**
Standard	HMDB51	No Pretraining	40.8
ActorCut [43]	HMDB51	No Pretraining	44.5
L2A	HMDB51	No Pretraining	**46.4**
Standard	UCF101	Sports1M	93.6
L2A	UCF101	Sports1M	**95.3**
Standard	HMDB51	Sports1M	66.6
L2A	HMDB51	Sports1M	**68.4**
Standard	Kinetics	Sports1M	75.4
L2A	Kinetics	Sports1M	**76.3**

5.6   Augmenting the Full Training Set

We finally explore the effect of augmenting the full dataset, both for smaller datasets, and the large-scale Kinetics. Results can be found on Table 5. Again, Learn2Augment improves the performance on all datasets even for a pre-trained model.

6   Limitations and Future Work

The main area of improvement is the time needed for training. Optimizing the Selector with RL is time-consuming, and so is compositing the initial samples for training it. Future work could address this by parameterizing the composition process and learn these parameters instead of compositing the pairs directly. It could also learn to select particular frames in a video, and avoid the computational cost of temporal redundancy. Finally, another possible direction is to learn what samples to discard from the initial dataset itself.

7   Conclusion

While standard data augmentation strategies in action recognition are hand-crafted, we propose to learn which pairs of videos are good to composite. In order to do this, our approach leverages three components. We train a Selector optimized with RL to choose which pairs of videos are good to composite. We reduce the search space by using samples from semantically similar classes. We perform a clean segmentation for mixing samples and remove actors as well as objects from foreground and background samples. With this, we obtain state-of-the-art results in semi-supervised and few-shot action recognition settings, and improve in the fully supervised setting. In particular, we see gains of up to 8.6% and 3.7% in the semi-supervised and few-shot settings. We also see an improvement of up to 17.4% when compared to standard augmentation in the fully supervised setting when training from scratch.

References

1. Arazo, E., Ortego, D., Albert, P., O'Connor, N.E., McGuinness, K.: Pseudo-labeling and confirmation bias in deep semi-supervised learning. In: 2020 International Joint Conference on Neural Networks (IJCNN), pp. 1–8. IEEE (2020)
2. Berthelot, D., et al.: RemixMatch: semi-supervised learning with distribution matching and augmentation anchoring. In: International Conference on Learning Representations (2019)
3. Berthelot, D., Carlini, N., Goodfellow, I., Papernot, N., Oliver, A., Raffel, C.A.: Mixmatch: a holistic approach to semi-supervised learning. Adv. Neural. Inf. Process. Syst. **32**, 1–11 (2019)
4. Carreira, J., Zisserman, A.: Quo vadis, action recognition? A new model and the kinetics dataset. In: proceedings of the IEEE Conference on Computer Vision and Pattern Recognition, pp. 6299–6308 (2017)
5. Choi, J., Gao, C., Messou, J.C., Huang, J.B.: Why can't I dance in the mall? learning to mitigate scene bias in action recognition. In: NeurIPS (2019)
6. Cubuk, E.D., Zoph, B., Mane, D., Vasudevan, V., Le, Q.V.: Autoaugment: learning augmentation strategies from data. In: Proceedings of the IEEE/CVF Conference on Computer Vision and Pattern Recognition (CVPR), June 2019
7. Cubuk, E.D., Zoph, B., Shlens, J., Le, Q.: Randaugment: Practical automated data augmentation with a reduced search space. In: Larochelle, H., Ranzato, M., Hadsell, R., Balcan, M.F., Lin, H. (eds.) Advances in Neural Information Processing Systems, vol. 33, pp. 18613–18624. Curran Associates, Inc. (2020). https://proceedings.neurips.cc/paper/2020/file/d85b63ef0ccb114d0a3bb7b7d808028f-Paper.pdf
8. Deng, J., Dong, W., Socher, R., Li, L.J., Li, K., Fei-Fei, L.: ImageNet: a large-scale hierarchical image database. In: 2009 IEEE Conference On Computer Vision And Pattern Recognition, pp. 248–255. IEEE (2009)
9. DeVries, T., Taylor, G.W.: Dataset augmentation in feature space. In: ICLR Workshop (2017)
10. DeVries, T., Taylor, G.W.: Improved regularization of convolutional neural networks with cutout. arXiv preprint arXiv:1708.04552 (2017)
11. Gowda, S.N., Rohrbach, M., Sevilla-Lara, L.: Smart frame selection for action recognition. In: Proceedings of the AAAI Conference on Artificial Intelligence, vol. 35(2), pp. 1451–1459, May 2021. https://ojs.aaai.org/index.php/AAAI/article/view/16235
12. Gowda, S.N., Sevilla-Lara, L., Kim, K., Keller, F., Rohrbach, M.: A new split for evaluating true zero-shot action recognition. In: Bauckhage, C., Gall, J., Schwing, A. (eds.) DAGM GCPR 2021. LNCS, vol. 13024, pp. 191–205. Springer, Cham (2021). https://doi.org/10.1007/978-3-030-92659-5_12
13. Grandvalet, Y., Bengio, Y., et al.: Semi-supervised learning by entropy minimization. CAP **367**, 281–296 (2005)

14. He, K., Gkioxari, G., Dollár, P., Girshick, R.: Mask R-CNN. In: ICCV (2017)
15. He, K., Zhang, X., Ren, S., Sun, J.: Identity mappings in deep residual networks. In: Leibe, B., Matas, J., Sebe, N., Welling, M. (eds.) ECCV 2016. LNCS, vol. 9908, pp. 630–645. Springer, Cham (2016). https://doi.org/10.1007/978-3-319-46493-0_38
16. Huang, D.A., et al.: What makes a video a video: analyzing temporal information in video understanding models and datasets, pp. 7366–7375, June 2018. https://doi.org/10.1109/CVPR.2018.00769
17. Iosifidis, A., Tefas, A., Pitas, I.: Semi-supervised classification of human actions based on neural networks. In: 2014 22nd International Conference on Pattern Recognition, pp. 1336–1341. IEEE (2014)
18. Jing, L., Parag, T., Wu, Z., Tian, Y., Wang, H.: VideoSSL: semi-supervised learning for video classification. In: Proceedings of the IEEE/CVF Winter Conference on Applications of Computer Vision (WACV), pp. 1110–1119, January 2021
19. Karpathy, A., Toderici, G., Shetty, S., Leung, T., Sukthankar, R., Fei-Fei, L.: Large-scale video classification with convolutional neural networks. In: Proceedings of the IEEE conference on Computer Vision and Pattern Recognition, pp. 1725–1732 (2014)
20. Korbar, B., Tran, D., Torresani, L.: SCSampler: sampling salient clips from video for efficient action recognition. In: Proceedings of the IEEE International Conference on Computer Vision, pp. 6232–6242 (2019)
21. Kuehne, H., Jhuang, H., Garrote, E., Poggio, T., Serre, T.: HMDB: a large video database for human motion recognition. In: 2011 International Conference on Computer Vision, pp. 2556–2563. IEEE (2011)
22. Kuo, C.-W., Ma, C.-Y., Huang, J.-B., Kira, Z.: FeatMatch: feature-based augmentation for semi-supervised learning. In: Vedaldi, A., Bischof, H., Brox, T., Frahm, J.-M. (eds.) ECCV 2020. LNCS, vol. 12363, pp. 479–495. Springer, Cham (2020). https://doi.org/10.1007/978-3-030-58523-5_28
23. Laine, S., Aila, T.: Temporal ensembling for semi-supervised learning. arXiv preprint arXiv:1610.02242 (2016)
24. Lee, D.H., et al.: Pseudo-label: The simple and efficient semi-supervised learning method for deep neural networks. In: Workshop on Challenges In Representation Learning, ICML, vol. 3, p. 896 (2013)
25. Lemley, J., Bazrafkan, S., Corcoran, P.M.: Smart augmentation learning an optimal data augmentation strategy. IEEE Access 5, 5858–5869 (2017)
26. Lin, T.Y., et al.: Microsoft coco: Common objects in context (2014). http://arxiv.org/abs/1405.0312
27. Liu, G., Reda, F.A., Shih, K.J., Wang, T.-C., Tao, A., Catanzaro, B.: Image inpainting for irregular holes using partial convolutions. In: Ferrari, V., Hebert, M., Sminchisescu, C., Weiss, Y. (eds.) ECCV 2018. LNCS, vol. 11215, pp. 89–105. Springer, Cham (2018). https://doi.org/10.1007/978-3-030-01252-6_6
28. Pagliardini, M., Gupta, P., Jaggi, M.: Unsupervised learning of sentence embeddings using compositional n-gram features. In: NAACL 2018 - Conference of the North American Chapter of the Association for Computational Linguistics (2018)
29. Perrett, T., Masullo, A., Burghardt, T., Mirmehdi, M., Damen, D.: Temporal-relational crosstransformers for few-shot action recognition. arXiv preprint arXiv:2101.06184 (2021)
30. Singh, A., et al.: Semi-supervised action recognition with temporal contrastive learning. In: Proceedings of the IEEE/CVF Conference on Computer Vision and Pattern Recognition, pp. 10389–10399 (2021)
31. Snell, J., Swersky, K., Zemel, R.S.: Prototypical networks for few-shot learning. arXiv preprint arXiv:1703.05175 (2017)

32. Soomro, K., Zamir, A.R., Shah, M.: Ucf101: a dataset of 101 human actions classes from videos in the wild. arXiv preprint arXiv:1212.0402 (2012)
33. Sun, D., et al.: Autoflow: learning a better training set for optical flow. In: CVPR (2021)
34. Tarvainen, A., Valpola, H.: Mean teachers are better role models: weight-averaged consistency targets improve semi-supervised deep learning results. arXiv preprint arXiv:1703.01780 (2017)
35. Williams, R.J.: Simple statistical gradient-following algorithms for connectionist reinforcement learning. Mach. Learn. **8**(3), 229–256 (1992)
36. Yoon, J., Arik, S., Pfister, T.: Data valuation using reinforcement learning. In: International Conference on Machine Learning, pp. 10842–10851. PMLR (2020)
37. Yun, S., Han, D., Oh, S.J., Chun, S., Choe, J., Yoo, Y.: CutMix: regularization strategy to train strong classifiers with localizable features. In: International Conference on Computer Vision (ICCV) (2019)
38. Yun, S., Oh, S.J., Heo, B., Han, D., Kim, J.: VideoMix: rethinking data augmentation for video classification. arXiv preprint arXiv:2012.03457 (2020)
39. Zhai, X., Oliver, A., Kolesnikov, A., Beyer, L.: S4l: self-supervised semi-supervised learning. In: Proceedings of the IEEE/CVF International Conference on Computer Vision, pp. 1476–1485 (2019)
40. Zhang, H., Zhang, L., Qi, X., Li, H., Torr, P.H.S., Koniusz, P.: Few-shot action recognition with permutation-invariant attention. In: Vedaldi, A., Bischof, H., Brox, T., Frahm, J.-M. (eds.) ECCV 2020. LNCS, vol. 12350, pp. 525–542. Springer, Cham (2020). https://doi.org/10.1007/978-3-030-58558-7_31
41. Zhang, H., Cisse, M., Dauphin, Y.N., Lopez-Paz, D.: mixup: Beyond empirical risk minimization. In: International Conference on Learning Representations (2018)
42. Zhang, Y., Jia, G., Chen, L., Zhang, M., Yong, J.: Self-paced video data augmentation by generative adversarial networks with insufficient samples. In: Proceedings of the 28th ACM International Conference on Multimedia, pp. 1652–1660. MM 2020, Association for Computing Machinery, New York, NY, USA (2020). https://doi.org/10.1145/3394171.3414003
43. Zou, Y., Choi, J., Wang, Q., Huang, J.: Learning representational invariances for data-efficient action recognition. CoRR abs/2103.16565 (2021). https://arxiv.org/abs/2103.16565

CYBORGS: Contrastively Bootstrapping Object Representations by Grounding in Segmentation

Renhao Wang[1], Hang Zhao[1,2], and Yang Gao[1,2(✉)]

[1] Tsinghua University, Beijing, China
gaoyangiiis@tsinghua.edu.cn
[2] Shanghai Qi Zhi Institute, Shanghai, China

Abstract. Many recent approaches in contrastive learning have worked to close the gap between pretraining on iconic images like ImageNet and pretraining on complex scenes like COCO. This gap exists largely because commonly used random crop augmentations obtain semantically inconsistent content in crowded scene images of diverse objects. In this work, we propose a framework which tackles this problem via joint learning of representations and segmentation. We leverage segmentation masks to train a model with a mask-dependent contrastive loss, and use the partially trained model to bootstrap better masks. By iterating between these two components, we ground the contrastive updates in segmentation information, and simultaneously improve segmentation throughout pretraining. Experiments show our representations transfer robustly to downstream tasks in classification, detection and segmentation. (Code and pretrained models available at https://github.com/renwang435/CYBORGS).

1 Introduction

Many self-supervised contrastive methods have come to rival and even surpass the performance of fully supervised methods on a number of tasks, including object detection [3,44], semantic segmentation [17,41], video understanding [23,30], and image classification [8,13]. A large portion of these methods rely on random cropping to select positive pairs of image subregions for a self-supervised instance-level discrimination task. Recently, many works have found this random cropping strategy succeeds for iconic image pretraining, but struggles when applied to pretraining on complex scene images. Treating two random crops from the same image as containing semantically similar information works well for images with singular, dominant subjects, like those in ImageNet. But such an

---

H. Zhao and Y. Gao—Equal advising.

Supplementary Information The online version contains supplementary material available at https://doi.org/10.1007/978-3-031-19821-2_15.

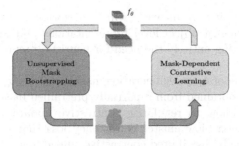

Fig. 1. Mutually improving representation learning and semantic segmentation. In the first stage, we use available segmentation masks to ground contrastive learning. In the second stage, we use representations from the backbone f_θ to bootstrap improved segmentation masks.

assumption inevitably fails due to inconsistent learning signals in scene images full of diverse objects [9,33,40]. To address this issue, prior works have generated random crops in an object-aware manner [3,34,44]. By localizing objects with unsupervised algorithms (e.g. selective search), these works are able to ground random crops around singular objects, validating the assumption that such crops contain similar information about objects.

We argue that utilizing *pixel-level* object information can be even more effective than detection-level boxes. By parsing random crop contents with segmentation masks, we can turn a pair of crops into a diverse wealth of similar and dissimilar object regions, facilitating contrastive self-supervised learning. To fully realize this idea in SSL frameworks, we also need to meet two important criteria. Firstly, these masks should be obtained in an *unsupervised* manner. Secondly, we want to *avoid preprocessing pipelines* to obtain pseudo-segmentations (*e.g.*, graph cut algorithms), which often lack awareness of object-level semantics and require human domain knowledge for good performance [20,50].

To this end, we propose in this work to perform segmentation and concept learning *jointly* (Fig. 1). In the first stage of our framework, we ground self-supervised learning with segmentation information to train a representation backbone. In a periodic second stage, we leverage these representations to bootstrap segmentation masks, which can subsequently be fed back to the first stage to further improve representations. By iterating between these two core stages, we develop representations which strongly generalize to many downstream tasks, and are especially well-aligned with object detection and segmentation. Furthermore, to ameliorate issues of representation collapse, we also optimize a clustering consistency objective during the first stage. We show that the formulation of this loss fits naturally within any contrastive framework, and helps improve masks more reliably between bootstrap cycles. Thus, in ContrastivelY Bootstrapping Object Representations by Grounding in Segmentation (CYBORGS), our contributions are fourfold:

1. We develop the first framework which performs end-to-end, joint self-supervised learning of object-level representations and semantic segmentation, while removing entirely the need for heuristic preprocessing of pseudo-segmentations.
2. We show how to bootstrap segmentation masks robustly by directly clustering on feature maps obtained from a partially pretrained backbone.
3. We demonstrate how to regularize contrastive updates in our framework with an intra-/inter-view cluster consistency loss that is well-aligned with the hyperspherically-distributed contrastive embeddings.
4. With pretraining on complex scene images such as COCO, we demonstrate that grounding in segmentation leads to representations which transfer competitively to a diversity of downstream tasks and real-world, long-tail objects and scene semantics.

2 Related Work

Self-Supervised Representation Learning. SSL methods utilize internal structure as a source of supervision to learn general representations, including auxiliary tasks such as context prediction [13], solving jigsaws [35], inpainting [37], colorization [51], or orientation prediction [27]. Most relevant to our work is contrastive learning, where the goal is to perform instance discrimination, concentrating positive pairs and separating negative pairs of feature embeddings in a latent space [8,15,19,36]. Despite their convincing performance on downstream tasks, the majority of current contrastive-based methods are pretrained on ImageNet, and subject to strong object-centric bias and poor visual grounding [21,34,38,40].

To this end, a number of emerging methods examine self-supervised representation learning on in-the-wild, scene image datasets such as COCO [33,40,45]. CAST improves visual grounding by ensuring crops overlap readily with object regions identified by saliency masks, and guides representation learning using a Grad-CAM loss [39,40]. ORL uses a pretrained self-supervised model to approximate object-level semantic correspondence, thus improving positive-negative identification for contrastive refinement of the pretrained model [45].

Going a step further, CYBORGS and other works obtain object-level semantics through pixel level pseudo-labeling [1,17,20,41,52]. For example, DetCon [20] involves unsupervised preprocessing of images to obtain masks, and uses these masks to aggregate features over object regions for contrastive learning. Crucially, all other previous methods suffer from the disadvantage that mask proposals are generated i) via graph-based algorithms requiring heuristic hyperparameter decisions, and ii) only once before training, with no further learning. In contrast, by integrating object mask proposals and contrastive pretraining into the same loop, CYBORGS iteratively refines and improves both segmentation quality and learned representation quality, jointly.

Unsupervised Segmentation and Clustering. The use of clustering-based approaches in SSL has a long history [5,6,31]. DeepCluster is a seminal work which proposed to train a CNN by alternating between feature clustering to obtain class pseudo-labels, and learning to predict those very labels [5]. PCL and SwAV combine a clustering objective with a contrastive objective, directly encoding semantic structure learned by clustering into a latent representation space [6,31]. Instead of directly improving features by learning to cluster feature prototypes, CYBORGS primarily uses clustering as a mechanism to improve segmentation.

Indeed, clustering-based algorithms have recently found application in a number of unsupervised and self-supervised image segmentation works [11,22,50,52]. Both pixel and region-level contrastive learning methods have been employed to i) improve semantic segmentation for better representation learning [46,52], and ii) vice versa [11,22,26]. To the best of our knowledge, CYBORGS is the first work to consider these two well-studied tasks as complementary, iteratively synergizing them together via a bootstrapping paradigm. Additionally, CYBORGS does not directly optimize for segmentation quality via pixel-level losses, and aims to improve segmentation strictly insofar as it aids in representation learning.

3   CYBORGS

We now describe the details in our proposed framework. In Sect. 3.1, we provide an overview of the abstractions in our work. At its core, we require iteration between two components: a contrastive objective capable of leveraging masks to train an encoder, and an unsupervised method to generate masks from a (partially) trained encoder. In Sect. 3.2 and Sect. 3.3, we describe the particular instantiations of these two components in our demonstration of the framework. Finally, in Sect. 3.4, we show how to construct a self-supervised consistency loss to guide mask generation.

3.1   CYBORGS Framework Abstraction

Following typical contrastive learning frameworks in vision, we begin with a given RGB image $\mathbf{I} \in \mathbb{R}^{3 \times H \times W}$ of height H and width W, and two transformations t, t' independently sampled from data augmentation pipelines $\mathcal{T}, \mathcal{T}'$. For the time being, we assume we also have ground truth semantic segmentation masks $\{\mathbf{M}\} \in [0,1]^{C \times H \times W}$. Each $H \times W$ binary mask $\mathbf{M}$ describes pixel-wise class membership for a particular class, for C total classes. Applying the transformations to $\mathbf{I}, \{\mathbf{M}\}$ yields two augmented views $\mathbf{v} = t(\mathbf{I}), \mathbf{v}' = t'(\mathbf{I})$, and two semantic maps $\{\mathbf{m}\} = t(\{\mathbf{M}\}), \{\mathbf{m}'\} = t'(\{\mathbf{M}\})$. Note that every $\mathbf{m}$ contains object-level assignments spatially aligned with view $\mathbf{v}$, and likewise every $\mathbf{m}'$ aligns with $\mathbf{v}'$. After passing view $\mathbf{v}$ to a (fully) convolutional encoder f_θ for featurization, we can extract a (sub)set of intermediate feature maps $\{\mathbf{F}\} = \{\mathbf{y}^{[1]}, \ldots, \mathbf{y}^{[l]}\}$, where $\mathbf{y}^{[l]} = f_\theta^{[l]}(\mathbf{v})$ for layer l. Doing the same for view $\mathbf{v}'$ yields feature maps $\{\mathbf{F}'\}$.

These feature maps inherently contain spatial and latent information about the image, which we can leverage using the segmentation masks. The core idea is conceptually simple and lightweight: we can sample arbitrary regions in the feature maps and apply the binary masks $\{\mathbf{m}\}, \{\mathbf{m'}\}$ to filter out groups of features which correspond to the same underlying object regions. Applying mean pooling, concatenation, or some other general aggregation operator to these groups yields feature vectors containing similar and dissimilar object-level semantics. These positive-negative pairs allow us to use a flexible class of contrastive objectives to train our encoder f_θ. Note that this naturally requires upsampling or downsampling either the masks or the feature maps to the same spatiality, and our framework is entirely agnostic to these details. But a more immediate problem is obtaining reasonable masks $\{\mathbf{M}\}$ to begin with.

A crucial assumption we have thus maintained is that ground truth segmentation masks are available. Indeed, without specification of how object regions correspond to each other across views, the very notion of positives and negatives for a contrastive formulation becomes ill-defined. Previous works which have relied on such masks in a similar fashion have used simple spatial heuristics such as grid-based masks, or more complex unsupervised algorithms such as graph cut segmentations [1,20,52]. Ultimately, we find that these approaches yield unsatisfactory masks which are semantics-unaware, or require significant hand-tuning, especially when employed on scene images. But composing a learning-based procedure is non-trivial; the contrastive objective cannot backpropagate through the non-differentiable augmentations t, t' and modify a mask $\mathbf{m}$ directly (Fig. 2).

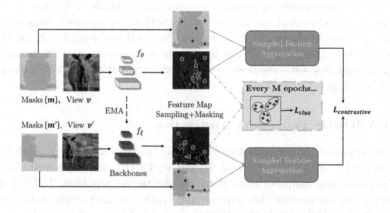

Fig. 2. CYBORGS Training Framework. We sample over the feature maps for different views, using segmentation masks to identify similar and dissimilar object regions. These are aggregated into positive and negative feature vectors, respectively, for the contrastive objective $\mathcal{L}_{mask}$ (Sect. 3.2). Periodically, we also backprop through a clustering consistency loss $\mathcal{L}_{clus}$ (Sect. 3.4).

To this end, our framework bootstraps segmentation masks using representations from the partially trained model f_θ. This idea is motivated by two insights.

Firstly, the contrastive objective directly improves the encoder f_θ, and thus leveraging the features from f_θ can help us obtain semantic-aware masks which correspondingly improve over the course of training. Secondly, recall that the ultimate goal of our framework is to improve representation learning. Since downstream transfer of representations takes places on f_θ, using the representations from f_θ to construct our segmentation masks ensures that representation quality and bootstrapped mask quality are tied together. Implementation-wise, our framework is agnostic to the actual algorithm employed for mask generation, with the only constraint being that the method cannot rely on ground truth supervision. For concreteness, we illustrate in Sect. 3.3 how to generate robust masks using a simple KMeans clustering-based algorithm on the feature maps $\{F\}$. By iterating between contrastive updating of f_θ and unsupervised generation of masks, we mutually improve our representations and segmentations.

3.2   Mask-Dependent Contrastive Learning

To demonstrate the utility of our framework, we first choose the loss function from [20] as the particular instantiation of a mask-based contrastive objective for training our encoder in the first stage. We provide a high level review here.

In [20], $\{F\}$ is a single $2048 \times 7 \times 7$ feature map extracted from the final layer of a standard ResNet-50 encoder processing view $\mathbf{v}$ (before average pooling). The entire feature map is sampled, and the segmentation masks in $\{m\}$ are spatially downsampled accordingly. Aggregation of $\{F\}$ is obtained via mask-based pooling for each $\mathbf{m} \in \{m\}$:

$$\mathbf{h_m} = \frac{1}{\sum_{i,j} \mathbf{m}[i,j]} \sum_{i,j} \mathbf{m}[i,j] \mathbf{F}[i,j] \qquad (1)$$

Feature map $\{F'\}$ is similarly aggregated after processing view $\mathbf{v}'$ with a target encoder f_ξ, yielding $\mathbf{h'_{m'}}$. For additional asymmetry, $\mathbf{h_m}$ is further transformed by an online projector g_θ and predictor q_θ to obtain $\mathbf{v_m} = q_\theta(g_\theta(\mathbf{h_m}))$, and $\mathbf{h_{m'}}$ is transformed by a target projector g_ξ to obtain $\mathbf{v'_{m'}} = g_\xi(h'_{m'})$. The target parameters ξ are updated as an exponential moving average (EMA) of their online counterparts θ. The final mask-based contrastive objective is given by:

$$\mathcal{L}_{contrastive} = \mathbb{E}_{\mathbf{m},\mathbf{m'} \sim \{m\},\{m'\}} \left[-\log \frac{\exp(\mathbf{v_m} \cdot \mathbf{v'_{m'}})}{\exp(\mathbf{v_m} \cdot \mathbf{v'_{m'}}) + \sum_n \exp(\mathbf{v_m} \cdot \mathbf{v_n})} \right] \qquad (2)$$

for negative pooled features $\{\mathbf{v}_n\}$ sampled from different masks and images.

In addition, inspired by prior art demonstrating that different layers within a CNN encode information at different semantic resolutions [18,28,47], we also extract and utilize features from throughout ResNet-50, instead of relying solely on features from the final convolutional map as in [20]. By fusing these features together spatially (after upsampling or downsampling), downstream learning is able to leverage information across the semantic spectrum, from low-level local structure, to high-level global style. Further details are available in the appendix.

3.3   Bootstrapping Segmentation Masks

Recall that our framework is agnostic to the particular algorithm used in the second stage bootstrapping of better segmentation masks. For simplicity, we illustrate the details of this stage using a classic KMeans clustering algorithm.

More formally, we begin by considering a batch of B input RGB images $\{\mathbf{I}\} \in \mathbb{R}^{B \times 3 \times H \times W}$, and a (fully) convolutional backbone f_θ which has been trained in a self-supervised fashion via the objective in (2). We choose a particular layer ℓ, and extract the feature map $\mathbf{y}_\theta^{[\ell]} = f_\theta^{[\ell]}(\{\mathbf{I}\}) \in \mathbb{R}^{B \times D_F \times H_F \times W_F}$. We omit the layer index ℓ and online encoder parameters θ for brevity, so that $\mathbf{y} \triangleq \mathbf{y}_\theta^{[\ell]}$. We then flatten the feature maps and ℓ2-normalize feature-wise, generating a matrix of features $\mathbf{F} \in \mathbb{R}^{(B \cdot H_F \cdot W_F) \times D_F}$. Given

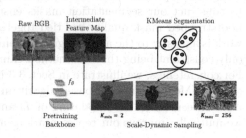

Fig. 3. Bootstrapping Masks. To generate the segmentation masks, we perform simple KMeans clustering on a feature map from the trained backbone, with a dynamic number of clusters.

a hyperparameter K, representing the number of clusters (or unique object classes) within the segmentation mask, we perform spherical K-means clustering on $\mathbf{F}$, ending up with a matrix of feature prototypes $\mathbf{P} = \{\mu_1, \mu_2, \ldots, \mu_K\} \in \mathbb{R}^{D_F \times K}$. We assign to each cell in the original feature map $\mathbf{y}^{[\ell]}$ a cluster label based on their Euclidean distances to the prototypes in $\mathbf{P}$. Finally, we broadcast the class assignments back to the original dimensions of the image $\mathbf{I}$ via nearest neighbor interpolation, akin to [9] (Fig. 3).

Periodic Bootstrapping. Performing such a clustering operation on every epoch to regenerate the segmentations can be expensive. Even if computation was not an issue, we empirically find that representations do not improve monotonically with epochs, so bootstrapping masks too frequently can actually lead to worse masks. Moreover, as a result of an undertrained encoder f_θ at the beginning of training, we obtain poorer early clusterings; noisy masks lead to noisy gradients for updating the encoder, and vice versa. Thus, to avoid representation collapse, we periodically bootstrap the segmentation masks every N epochs, where N is a hyperparameter much greater than 1.

Scale-Dynamic Sampling. The choice of K also merits discussion. Given access to some oracle, a natural choice might be to set K equal to the number of unique object classes within the image. However, as a number of prior works have identified, the semantic context provided by extra "distractor" classes outside of the main object classes can serve as a useful signal for clustering [5,9,24]. But increasing K also requires more images within the bootstrapping batch to perform KMeans reliably on the features, reducing the scalability of our method.

To balance these motivations, for every batch of images where we wish to bootstrap segmentations, we dynamically sample integer K uniformly between $K_{min} = 2$ and $K_{max} = 256$, inclusive. Intuitively, $K_{min} = 2$ represents a mask which imparts the model with simple foreground-background semantics, while the upper bound of $K_{max} = 256$ yields an oversegmentation (COCO offers only 81 labeled object segmentation classes.) By varying K in such a fashion, not only do we maintain efficiency in bootstrapping, but we also reintroduce our model to information of varying semantic scale on every bootstrap cycle. As we show in Sect. 4.4, this technique improves the robustness of our representations.

3.4   Consistency as a Curriculum for Segmentation

Despite the use of periodic bootstrapping and scale-dynamic sampling, we find that the long training schedules employed in contrastive learning can still lead to divergence between our representation learning and semantic segmentation objectives. This is because our framework up to now improves the segmentation only *implicitly*. While we are optimizing on every iteration our contrastive objective in (2), regularly improving our encoded representations, the bootstrapping of masks is optimization-free with respect to the encoder. Without an update signal to explicitly encode the semantics of desirable vs. non-desirable segmentations, the encoder over-prioritizes the goal of representation learning, and can diverge from a feature distribution which yields good segmentations.

Clustering Consistency. To this end, we reuse a universal paradigm in contrastive learning: similar objects across different scenes and different views should have similar labels. We introduce a clustering consistency loss, similar to that employed in [11], which can be applied more regularly every M epochs, where M is more frequent than the every N epochs used per bootstrapping cycle.

Concretely, recall the feature map $\mathbf{y} \in \mathbb{R}^{D_F \times H_F \times W_F}$ and feature prototypes $\mathbf{P} = \{\mu_1, \mu_2, \ldots, \mu_K\} \in \mathbb{R}^{D_F \times K}$ we obtained in Sect. 3.3 after processing view $\mathbf{v}$ using the online encoder f_θ. We obtain a similar map $\mathbf{y}'$ and set of prototypes $\mathbf{P}' = \{\mu'_1, \mu'_2, \ldots, \mu'_K\}$ after featurizing $\mathbf{v}'$ with the target encoder f_ξ. Consider the feature at pixel $[i, j]$ within $\mathbf{y}$, for an arbitrary $1 \le i \le H_F$ and $1 \le j \le W_F$. With a slight abuse of notation, we let $\mu_{[i,j]}$ represent the prototype this feature is assigned to under $\mathbf{P}$ (and similarly, $\mu'_{[i,j]}$ the assignment of $\mathbf{y}'[i,j]$ under $\mathbf{P}'$). Then we define a clustering consistency loss via:

$$\mathcal{L}_{clus} = \frac{1}{H_F W_F} \sum_{i=1}^{H_F} \sum_{j=1}^{W_F} \overbrace{d\left(\mu_{[i,j]}, \mathbf{y}_{[i,j]}\right) + d\left(\mu'_{[i,j]}, \mathbf{y}'_{[i,j]}\right)}^{intra-loss} + \overbrace{d\left(\mu'_{[i,j]}, \mathbf{y}_{[i,j]}\right) + d\left(\mu_{[i,j]}, \mathbf{y}'_{[i,j]}\right)}^{inter-loss}$$

(3)

where $d(\cdot, \cdot)$ is some distance function. Intuitively, intra-cluster consistency enforces that under one scene, object regions with similar features should be clustered into similar prototypes. Similarly, inter-cluster consistency enforces that under different scenes, we still wish for features from different regions corresponding to similar objects to be assigned to the same prototype. This forces our learned prototypes to be invariant to differences between views and generalize to object-centric semantics, which translates readily to higher fidelity segmentation masks during bootstrapping updates.

To formulate $d(\cdot, \cdot)$, we draw inspiration from recent work which demonstrates that the infoNCE objective in contrastive learning promotes a feature space which is uniformly distributed on the unit hypersphere [42]. The von Mises-Fisher (vMF) distribution defines a probability density over a unit hypersphere, making it a natural candidate to characterize the feature space learned by our mask-based contrastive objective in (2). We refer readers to a comprehensive treatment in [14] for details. In our setting, we can assume a vMF mixture model where each feature $\mathbf{y}$ is drawn uniformly from one of K vMF distributions, each parameterized by a feature clustering prototype $\mu_1, \mu_2, \ldots, \mu_K$, and sharing a common concentration hyperparameter κ. Then our clustering consistency loss objective is formulated as maximizing the posterior likelihood of a particular encoded feature $\mathbf{y}$ being assigned to its corresponding cluster c under this mixture, with $1 \leq c \leq K$. That is, we seek to minimize the negative log-likelihood given by:

$$d(\mu_{[i,j]}, \mathbf{y}) = -\log p(\mu_{[i,j]=c} \mid \mathbf{y}, \mu_1, \mu_2, \ldots, \mu_K) = -\log \frac{\exp\left(\kappa \mu_{[i,j]}^T \mathbf{y}\right)}{\sum\limits_{c'=1}^{K} \exp\left(\kappa \mu_{c'}^T \mathbf{y}\right)} \quad (4)$$

The vMF clustering loss objective described in (3) also serves an additional purpose towards the beginning of our pretraining pipeline. In the total absence of reliable masks before the first bootstrapping cycle, we train our encoder f_θ strictly with the loss in (3), setting K to a fixed parameter depending on the median number of objects per scene in our dataset (*e.g.*, for COCO, we use $K = 8$). This *vMF warmup period* of W epochs ($W = 5$ in our work) serves to burn in our encoder. After more reasonable representations have been learned, we immediately bootstrap the masks, and subsequent epochs using a combination of the mask-based contrastive loss in (2) and the vMF clustering loss in (3), as their respective periods N and M dictate. For a comprehensive outlining of our algorithm flow, we refer readers to the pseudocode presented in the appendix.

4   Experiments

In our experiments, we aim to demonstrate that joint learning of general representations and semantic segmentation can be successfully accomplished via our bootstrapping method. We show strong performance on multiple downstream tasks (Sect. 4.2), surprisingly robust segmentation performance over a long-tailed distribution of objects (Sect. 4.3), and a convincing array of ablations which validate our design choices and methodological contributions (Sect. 4.4).

4.1   Experimental Settings

Datasets. Given our primary goal of learning on images in the wild, we follow previous works [33,40,43] and pretrain on the train2017 split of the MS COCO dataset [32]. With ~118k images of natural settings, MS COCO is widely adopted as a benchmark more reflective of real-world scenarios across a breadth of downstream tasks of interest, such as object detection or instance segmentation. For a relevant quantitative comparison, note that the heavily object-dominant ImageNet dataset contains on average 1.1 objects per image, whereas the average scene image in COCO contains 7.3 objects [43]. Crucially, we use no scene-level, object-level, or pixel-level label information in our pretraining pipeline.

Implementation Details. To enable easy comparison to other SSL works in similar settings [33,40,43,45], we use a ResNet-50 backbone in all of our models. Other architectural details such as the dimensionality of projection and prediction MLPs described in Sect. 3.2 follow directly from BYOL [15].

For our mask-based contrastive objective in (2), we aggregate features from res2, res3, res4, downsampling all layers to a spatial resolution of 7×7. This allows us to leverage a lightweight but comprehensive semantic hierarchy. We bootstrap the segmentation masks every $N = 100$ epochs, performing clustering on the feature map from res2.b2 in batches of 16 images (where b2 refers to block 2). We use a vMF warmup period of 5 epochs; outside the warmup period, the vMF clustering loss is employed every 5 epochs with weight $\lambda = 0.1$ and $\kappa = 10$. In pretraining, we use the LARS optimizer [49] with a batch size of 64 across 8 NVIDIA RTX 3090s s for 800 epochs. The initial learning rate is set to 0.1, and the weight decay is $1.5e^{-6}$. Clustering is implemented via GPU-accelerated mini-batch approximation using the FAISS library [25].

Table 1. Transfer Learning on Downstream Tasks. We report strong, state-of-the-art performance across linear classification on VOC07, semi-supervised finetuning on ImageNet-1k, and transfer on VOC object detection and COCO instance segmentation. All methods are pretrained on COCO with a ResNet-50 backbone, and finetuned on the reported datasets.

	Method	VOC07 clf.	IN-1k, 1% Labels		IN-1k, 10% Labels		VOC Detection			COCO instance segmentation					
		mAP	Top-1 acc.	Top-5 acc.	Top-1 acc.	Top-5 acc.	AP^{bb}	AP_{50}^{bb}	AP_{75}^{bb}	AP^{bb}	AP_{50}^{bb}	AP_{75}^{bb}	AP^{mk}	AP_{50}^{mk}	AP_{75}^{mk}
1)	SIMCLR [8]	78.1	23.4	46.4	52.2	77.4	–	–	–	37.0	56.8	40.3	33.7	53.8	36.1
2)	MOCO-V2 [10]	82.2	28.2	54.7	57.1	81.7	54.7	81.0	60.6	38.5	58.1	42.1	34.8	55.3	37.3
3)	BYOL [15]	84.5	28.4	55.9	58.4	82.7	55.5	81.7	61.7	39.5	59.3	43.2	35.6	56.5	38.2
4)	BAI ET AL. [1]	–	–	–	–	–	57.1	82.1	63.8	39.8	59.6	43.7	35.9	56.9	38.6
5)	DENSECL [43]	83.8	–	–	–	–	56.7	81.7	63.0	39.6	59.3	43.3	35.7	56.5	38.4
6)	CAST [40]	73.1	–	–	–	–	54.2	80.1	59.9	36.7	56.7	39.9	33.6	53.6	35.8
7)	ORL [45]	86.7	31.0	58.9	60.5	**84.2**	55.8	82.1	62.3	40.3	60.2	44.4	36.3	57.3	38.9
8)	CYBORGS(ours)	**86.9**	**31.3**	**59.4**	**61.7**	**84.2**	**58.0**	**83.0**	**64.3**	**42.0**	**62.6**	**46.2**	**38.0**	**59.7**	**40.8**

4.2   Main Results: Representation Learning

We follow standard downstream transfer-based protocols to evaluate the strength of representations learned by CYBORGS. In particular, we begin with *frozen* linear evaluation on VOC07 and semi-supervised transfer on ImageNet-1k. In comparison to similar state-of-the-art self-supervised methods pretrained on COCO, we achieve improvements of +0.2 mAP for VOC07 and +0.3%, +1.2% in top-1 accuracy for semi-supervised 1% and 10% on IN-1k, respectively. While these gains are only incremental, image classification requires semantic-level knowledge [2,38,48], whereas we design our method around leveraging pixel-level information, and so even marginal gains are a surprising windfall.

While linear probing has been treated as the gold standard for assessing feature quality, that strong performance in tasks such as detection and segmentation are even more reflective of potent learned representations. We demonstrate convincing state-of-the-art on PASCAL VOC detection and COCO instance segmentation. In comparison to a strong and well-established BYOL baseline, we provide a +2.5 AP improvement on the former, and a +2.5 and +2.4 AP improvement on the latter. Our results on segmentation in particular are noteworthy; while we do not make use of pixel annotations, our bootstrapping scheme clearly aligns with latent information critical to the segmentation task. To further verify this robust segmentation performance, we also perform transfer-based evaluation on CityScapes semantic segmentation [12], as well as LVIS long-tailed instance

(a) Raw RGB   (b) KMeans Mask   (c) CRF-Refined Mask   (d) Ground Truth

Fig. 4. Bootstrapped segmentation masks from a CYBORGS-pretrained encoder on COCO. We show KMeans segmentations on the bilinearly upsampled feature maps for visual quality. During actual bootstrapping, we first segment the feature map, before performing nearest neighbors upsampling, and do not perform CRF refinement on the mask. Colors do not necessarily correspond across images (rows) or between mask types (columns), but are consistent within a single image itself.

segmentation [16], which we detail in the appendix. We achieve state-of-the-art on these datasets amongst all other previous SSL methods pretrained on COCO, with a substantial +3.4 AP and +3.3 AP improvement on LVIS, demonstrating that our framework can also generalize to unseen object structures and semantics.

4.3 Segmentation Quality

We first confirm qualitatively (Fig. 4) that bootstrapped masks generated by CYBORGS are indeed semantically meaningful. Note that our clustering-based segmentations easily extend beyond the original labeled classes of COCO, despite receiving no ground truth information about pixel labels throughout pretraining.

How does CYBORGS *work with such noisy masks?* In addition to the masks generated by clustering on the feature maps from the backbone encoder, we also show the mask resulting from refinement using a fully connected conditional random field (CRF), using the distances to feature prototypes in latent space as priors, following the protocol described in previous works [7,29]. We argue that although the raw masks at a pixel-level appear to be noisy, their easy refinement into masks closely aligned with ground truth masks indicates that the encoded features are quite well aligned with object-level concepts at the semantic level.

Why Bootstrap Masks? To further demonstrate the robustness of our bootstrapping process for mask generation, we retrain CYBORGS using alternative masks. Instead of bootstrapping masks, we employ random cropping masks (i.e. all pixels in the scene belong to the same class), a 5 × 5 spatial grid mask and Felzenszwalb-Huttenlocher (FH) masks used in [1,20], detection-level object

Type of Mask	mIoU
Random Crop	15.9
5x5 Grid	18.7
FH Masks	27.7
Obj. Bounding Boxes	29.0
CYBORGS Masks (ours)	33.6
Ground Truth Masks	35.2

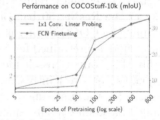

(a) **Importance of bootstrapping.** (b) **Masks** (blue) **and representations** (red) **improve jointly.**

Fig. 5. Using semantic segmentation performance on COCO-Stuff-10k to evaluate bootstrapping value. (a) Replacing our bootstrapping segmentation core with static boxes from other unsupervised heuristics leads to decreased performance. (b) Note a single epoch of using improved masks can lead to significant gains (epoch 100).

masks acquired via selective search pre-processing, and ground truth masks available in COCO. These masks are generated before pretraining and remain fixed, supplanting our bootstrapping algorithm. Given the unsupervised generalization of masks generated under our framework to a long-tailed distribution of objects (c.f. Fig. 4), we evaluate the representations by transferring the trained backbones to a ResNet-50 FCN and finetuning end-to-end on COCO-Stuff-10k semantic segmentation. COCO-Stuff-10k is a *densely* labeled subset of COCO, comprising of 9k images for training and 1k images for testing, across 171 semantic categories [4]. We verify in Fig. 5a that bootstrapping mask-level information through CYBORGS outperforms detection-level boxes obtained from selective search, and nears performance of pretraining with fixed, stable ground truth masks.

Joint Improvement of Masks and Representations. The harmonious interplay between the representation learning and semantic segmentation components of our framework is one of our major contributions. To ascertain that representations and segmentation quality mutually improve over pretraining, we continue to assess semantic segmentation performance on the COCO-Stuff-10k dataset, for saved checkpoints throughout various stages of pretraining. For a batch of input images, we extract frozen feature maps from the same layer we use to bootstrap segmentation masks (`res2.b2`), and bilinearly interpolate to the original image dimensions. We then add a single layer of 1×1 convolutions to predict the pixel labels, yielding a final setup akin to linear probing in transfer-based evaluation.

Because only this last layer is trainable in the resulting model, segmentation performance is heavily dependent on the quality of the extracted feature maps. Since these are exactly the inputs to our KMeans segmentation algorithm, we obtain transfer results which correlate readily with the quality of our bootstrapped masks. To evaluate representation quality in the same pretrained models, we transfer the ResNet-50 backbones, unfreeze all layers, and add an FCN head, finetuning on COCO-Stuff-10k end-to-end. We perform these evaluations for CYBORGS models pretrained for 5, 25, 50, 100, 200, 500 and 800 epochs. As seen in Fig. 5b, this evaluation scheme demonstrates that mask quality and representation quality improve jointly over the course of pretraining. Note that we bootstrap masks for the first time at the *beginning* of epoch 100 using our partially pretrained backbone; a subsequent iteration over the entire dataset is sufficient to improve both mask and representation semantics significantly.

Table 2. Ablations for design choices in CYBORGS. We report average precision (AP) for object detection on PASCAL VOC test2007. Default settings corresp. to Table 1 are highlighted in gray.

N	AP_{all}
0	9.75
10	52.6
50	58.3
100	58.0
200	55.0
400	52.7

(a) Bootstrapping frequency. Mask bootstrapping too often or not enough leads to poor performance.

Case	AP_{all}
CRF	58.6
No CRF	58.0

(b) CRF in bootstrapping. Refining bootstrapped masks with CRFs during pretraining is not necessary.

Layers	AP_{all}
2	55.1
3	55.8
4	52.7
2+4	56.4
2+3+4	58.0

(c) Features in contrastive objective. Leveraging a semantic hierarchy of features is important.

Layers	AP_{all}
2.b2	58.0
2+3	58.2
2+4	54.4
2+3+4	55.0

(d) Features in KMeans. Earlier maps are more amenable to KMeans segmentation.

K	AP_{all}
$K = 2$	22.6
$K = 81$	42.5
$K = 256$	33.2
$K \sim \mathcal{U}[2, 256]$	58.0

(e) Scale-dynamic sampling. Dynamically sampling cluster resolution for KMeans segmentation works best.

Loss	AP_{all}
Euclidean	53.8
vMF	58.0

(f) Clustering loss. Euclidean distance for (4) leads to significant performance degradation.

M	AP_{all}
0	41.8
1	58.6
5	58.0
10	57.8
50	55.6

(g) vMF Loss Frequency. Applying the vMF curriculum more regularly leads to stronger performance.

λ	AP_{all}
0	41.5
0.001	42.3
0.01	57.8
0.1	58.0
1	57.2

(h) vMF Loss Weight. Performance is sensitive to the presence but not weight of the vMF loss.

4.4 Ablations and Discussion

All ablation models are pretrained using a ResNet-50 backbone, and evaluations are performed on PASCAL VOC detection for faster turnaround time.

Bootstrapping Frequency. We perform a sensitivity analysis on the bootstrapping frequency parameter N, where we regenerate the masks on epoch N, $2N$, ..., using feature maps from the improving encoder (Table 2a). Using only the initial masks obtained under vMF warmup for pretraining (*i.e.*, $N = 0$) leads to collapsed performance. Moreover, bootstrapping the masks too frequently ($N = 10$) also leads to a performance drop, consistent with our hypothesis in Sect. 3.3 that unstable masks which are changing too rapidly can lead to representational collapse. Finally, we also note that bootstrapping too *infrequently* (*i.e.*, $N = 400$) is similarly suboptimal, validating our default chosen schedule.

CRF-Refinement of Masks. Given the qualitative improvements of the CRF-refined masks when performing the final evaluation (c.f. Fig. 4), a natural consideration is to apply CRF post-processing to the masks during every bootstrapping cycle. As we show in Table 2b, this brings only incremental improvements to the resulting representations, which we believe do not justify the increase in computational complexity. This result also further validates our claim in Sect. 4.3 that the representations under CYBORGS are already well-aligned in latent space with respect to the semantic segmentation task.

Usage of Multiple Layers of Features. Throughout our method, there are two points where we potentially use feature maps from multiple layers of our encoder backbone. The first is in the aggregation of features for our contrastive objective in (2). We show in Table 2c that using `res2, res3, res4` from our backbone in combination is crucial to performance. This further verifies that leveraging information from across the semantic spectrum learned by the encoder is vital.

The second point is in the bootstrapping of masks, where we use only the feature map from `res2.b2` of our backbone. We show in Table 2d that feature aggregation across multiple layers does not help here. One explanation for this phenomenon is curse of dimensionality; a simple KMeans clustering procedure on extremely high dimensional features aggregated across multiple layers may result in clusters with few or no points.

Scale-Dynamic Sampling. We also perform an ablation on dynamically sampling the semantic resolution of masks during bootstrapping. We compare with a foreground-background masks ($K = 2$), object-level masks ($K = 81$ categories from COCO), and clustering with the same number of unique labels as the default graph-based segmentation algorithm used in [20]. As shown in Table 2e, fixing the KMeans cluster dimension at any level reduces the performance of CYBORGS. This validates our choice to provide the encoder with diverse levels of detail through bootstrapped masks of varying semantic resolution.

vMF Clustering Loss. We verify several properties of the clustering loss in (4). As seen in Table 2f, basing the loss on the vMF distribution, which aligns better with our hyperspherically-distributed embeddings, results in better transfer performance. We also examine the frequency at which the vMF clustering loss is applied, and how sensitive our method is to the weight of this loss. Table 2g validates that applying the loss more frequently increases downstream transfer performance. In combination with Table 2h we note the weight of the loss does not dramatically influence performance, but its presence is important; at $\lambda = 0, 0.001$ or if $M = 0$ (*i.e.*, no application of vMF loss), the performance collapses.

5 Conclusion

We have proposed CYBORGS, a novel self-supervised framework which learns object-level representations and semantic segmentation jointly, in an end-to-end fashion. In pretraining on complex scene images, our representations transfer competitively to a diverse array of downstream tasks, with particularly strong alignment with a long-tailed distribution of object-level segmentation semantics.

Acknowledgements. YG is supported by the Ministry of Science and Technology of the People's Republic of China, the 2030 Innovation Megaprojects "Program on New Generation Artificial Intelligence" (Grant No. 2021AAA0150000). YG is also supported by a grant from the Guoqiang Institute, Tsinghua University. RW would like to thank Yu Sun and Yingdong Hu for valuable edits to the paper, without which this work would not be possible.

References

1. Bai, Y., Chen, X., Kirillov, A., Yuille, A., Berg, A.C.: Point-level region contrast for object detection pre-training. arXiv preprint arXiv:2202.04639 (2022)
2. Ballard, D.H., Zhang, R.: The hierarchical evolution in human vision modeling. Top. Cogn. Sci. **13**(2), 309–328 (2021)
3. Bar, A., et al.: DETReg: unsupervised pretraining with region priors for object detection. arXiv preprint arXiv:2106.04550 (2021)
4. Caesar, H., Uijlings, J., Ferrari, V.: Coco-stuff: Thing and stuff classes in context. In: Proceedings of the IEEE Conference on Computer Vision and Pattern Recognition, pp. 1209–1218 (2018)
5. Caron, M., Bojanowski, P., Joulin, A., Douze, M.: Deep clustering for unsupervised learning of visual features. In: Ferrari, V., Hebert, M., Sminchisescu, C., Weiss, Y. (eds.) Computer Vision – ECCV 2018. LNCS, vol. 11218, pp. 139–156. Springer, Cham (2018). https://doi.org/10.1007/978-3-030-01264-9_9
6. Caron, M., Misra, I., Mairal, J., Goyal, P., Bojanowski, P., Joulin, A.: Unsupervised learning of visual features by contrasting cluster assignments. In: Larochelle, H., Ranzato, M., Hadsell, R., Balcan, M.F., Lin, H. (eds.) Advances in Neural Information Processing Systems, vol. 33, pp. 9912–9924. Curran Associates, Inc. (2020). https://proceedings.neurips.cc/paper/2020/file/70feb62b69f16e0238f741fab228fec2-Paper.pdf
7. Chen, L.C., Papandreou, G., Schroff, F., Adam, H.: Rethinking Atrous convolution for semantic image segmentation. arXiv preprint arXiv:1706.05587 (2017)
8. Chen, T., Kornblith, S., Norouzi, M., Hinton, G.: A simple framework for contrastive learning of visual representations. In: International Conference on Machine Learning, pp. 1597–1607. PMLR (2020)
9. Chen, T., Luo, C., Li, L.: Intriguing properties of contrastive losses. Adv. Neural. Inf. Process. Syst. **34**, 1–9 (2021)
10. Chen, X., Fan, H., Girshick, R., He, K.: Improved baselines with momentum contrastive learning. arXiv preprint arXiv:2003.04297 (2020)
11. Cho, J.H., Mall, U., Bala, K., Hariharan, B.: PiCIE: unsupervised semantic segmentation using invariance and equivariance in clustering. In: Proceedings of the IEEE/CVF Conference on Computer Vision and Pattern Recognition, pp. 16794–16804 (2021)
12. Cordts, M., et al.: The cityscapes dataset for semantic urban scene understanding. In: Proceedings of the IEEE Conference on Computer Vision and Pattern Recognition, pp. 3213–3223 (2016)
13. Doersch, C., Gupta, A., Efros, A.A.: Unsupervised visual representation learning by context prediction. In: Proceedings of the IEEE International Conference on Computer Vision, pp. 1422–1430 (2015)
14. Gopal, S., Yang, Y.: Von mises-fisher clustering models. In: International Conference on Machine Learning, pp. 154–162. PMLR (2014)
15. Grill, J.B., et al.: Bootstrap your own latent - a new approach to self-supervised learning. In: Larochelle, H., Ranzato, M., Hadsell, R., Balcan, M.F., Lin, H. (eds.) Advances in Neural Information Processing Systems, vol. 33, pp. 21271–21284. Curran Associates, Inc. (2020). https://proceedings.neurips.cc/paper/2020/file/f3ada80d5c4ee70142b17b8192b2958e-Paper.pdf
16. Gupta, A., Dollar, P., Girshick, R.: Lvis: a dataset for large vocabulary instance segmentation. In: Proceedings of the IEEE/CVF Conference on Computer Vision and Pattern Recognition, pp. 5356–5364 (2019)

17. Hamilton, M., Zhang, Z., Hariharan, B., Snavely, N., Freeman, W.T.: Unsupervised semantic segmentation by distilling feature correspondences. In: International Conference on Learning Representations (2021)
18. Hariharan, B., Arbeláez, P., Girshick, R., Malik, J.: Hypercolumns for object segmentation and fine-grained localization. In: Proceedings of the IEEE Conference on Computer Vision and Pattern Recognition, pp. 447–456 (2015)
19. He, K., Fan, H., Wu, Y., Xie, S., Girshick, R.: Momentum contrast for unsupervised visual representation learning. In: Proceedings of the IEEE/CVF Conference on Computer Vision and Pattern Recognition, pp. 9729–9738 (2020)
20. Hénaff, O.J., Koppula, S., Alayrac, J.B., Oord, A., Vinyals, O., Carreira, J.: Efficient Visual Pretraining with Contrastive Detection. In: International Conference on Computer Vision (2021)
21. Herranz, L., Jiang, S., Li, X.: Scene recognition with CNNs: objects, scales and dataset bias. In: Proceedings of the IEEE Conference on Computer Vision and Pattern Recognition, pp. 571–579 (2016)
22. Hwang, J.J., Yet al.: SegSort: segmentation by discriminative sorting of segments. In: Proceedings of the IEEE/CVF International Conference on Computer Vision, pp. 7334–7344 (2019)
23. Jabri, A., Owens, A., Efros, A.: Space-time correspondence as a contrastive random walk. Adv. Neural. Inf. Process. Syst. **33**, 19545–19560 (2020)
24. Ji, X., Henriques, J.F., Vedaldi, A.: Invariant information clustering for unsupervised image classification and segmentation. In: Proceedings of the IEEE/CVF International Conference on Computer Vision, pp. 9865–9874 (2019)
25. Johnson, J., Douze, M., Jégou, H.: Billion-scale similarity search with GPUs. IEEE Trans. Big Data. **7**, 537–547 (2019)
26. Ke, T.W., Hwang, J.J., Yu, S.X.: Universal weakly supervised segmentation by pixel-to-segment contrastive learning. In: International Conference on Learning Representations (2021)
27. Komodakis, N., Gidaris, S.: Unsupervised representation learning by predicting image rotations. In: International Conference on Learning Representations (ICLR) (2018)
28. Kornblith, S., Shlens, J., Le, Q.V.: Do better imagenet models transfer better? In: Proceedings of the IEEE/CVF Conference on Computer Vision and Pattern Recognition, pp. 2661–2671 (2019)
29. Krähenbühl, P., Koltun, V.: Efficient inference in fully connected CRFs with gaussian edge potentials. Adv. Neural. Inf. Process. Syst. **24**, 1–11 (2011)
30. Kuang, H., et al.: Video contrastive learning with global context. In: Proceedings of the IEEE/CVF International Conference on Computer Vision, pp. 3195–3204 (2021)
31. Li, J., Zhou, P., Xiong, C., Hoi, S.C.: Prototypical contrastive learning of unsupervised representations. In: ICLR (2021)
32. Lin, T.-Y., et al.: Microsoft COCO: common objects in context. In: Fleet, D., Pajdla, T., Schiele, B., Tuytelaars, T. (eds.) ECCV 2014. LNCS, vol. 8693, pp. 740–755. Springer, Cham (2014). https://doi.org/10.1007/978-3-319-10602-1_48
33. Liu, S., Li, Z., Sun, J.: Self-EMD: self-supervised object detection without imagenet. arXiv preprint arXiv:2011.13677 (2020)
34. Mo, S., Kang, H., Sohn, K., Li, C.L., Shin, J.: Object-aware contrastive learning for debiased scene representation. Adv. Neural. Inf. Process. Syst. **34**, 1–14 (2021)
35. Noroozi, M., Favaro, P.: Unsupervised learning of visual representations by solving jigsaw puzzles. In: Leibe, B., Matas, J., Sebe, N., Welling, M. (eds.) ECCV 2016. LNCS, vol. 9910, pp. 69–84. Springer, Cham (2016). https://doi.org/10.1007/978-3-319-46466-4_5

36. Oord, A.v.d., Li, Y., Vinyals, O.: Representation learning with contrastive predictive coding. arXiv preprint arXiv:1807.03748 (2018)
37. Pathak, D., Krahenbuhl, P., Donahue, J., Darrell, T., Efros, A.A.: Context encoders: feature learning by inpainting. In: Proceedings of the IEEE Conference On Computer Vision and Pattern Recognition, pp. 2536–2544 (2016)
38. Purushwalkam, S., Gupta, A.: Demystifying contrastive self-supervised learning: invariances, augmentations and dataset biases. Adv. Neural. Inf. Process. Syst. **33**, 3407–3418 (2020)
39. Selvaraju, R.R., Cogswell, M., Das, A., Vedantam, R., Parikh, D., Batra, D.: Grad-CAM: visual explanations from deep networks via gradient-based localization. In: Proceedings of the IEEE International Conference on Computer Vision, pp. 618–626 (2017)
40. Selvaraju, R.R., Desai, K., Johnson, J., Naik, N.: Casting your model: learning to localize improves self-supervised representations. In: Proceedings of the IEEE/CVF Conference on Computer Vision and Pattern Recognition, pp. 11058–11067 (2021)
41. Van Gansbeke, W., Vandenhende, S., Georgoulis, S., Van Gool, L.: Unsupervised semantic segmentation by contrasting object mask proposals. In: Proceedings of the IEEE/CVF International Conference on Computer Vision (ICCV), pp. 10052–10062, October 2021
42. Wang, T., Isola, P.: Understanding contrastive representation learning through alignment and uniformity on the hypersphere. In: International Conference on Machine Learning, pp. 9929–9939. PMLR (2020)
43. Wang, X., Zhang, R., Shen, C., Kong, T., Li, L.: Dense contrastive learning for self-supervised visual pre-training. In: Proceedings of the IEEE/CVF Conference on Computer Vision and Pattern Recognition, pp. 3024–3033 (2021)
44. Xiao, T., Reed, C.J., Wang, X., Keutzer, K., Darrell, T.: Region similarity representation learning. arXiv preprint arXiv:2103.12902 (2021)
45. Xie, J., Zhan, X., Liu, Z., Ong, Y.S., Loy, C.C.: Unsupervised object-level representation learning from scene images. arXiv preprint arXiv:2106.11952 (2021)
46. Xiong, Y., Ren, M., Zeng, W., Urtasun, R.: Self-supervised representation learning from flow equivariance. In: Proceedings of the IEEE/CVF International Conference on Computer Vision (ICCV), pp. 10191–10200, October 2021
47. Xu, J., Wang, X.: Rethinking self-supervised correspondence learning: a video frame-level similarity perspective. In: Proceedings of the IEEE/CVF International Conference on Computer Vision (ICCV), pp. 10075–10085, October 2021
48. Yang, C., Wu, Z., Zhou, B., Lin, S.: Instance localization for self-supervised detection pretraining. In: Proceedings of the IEEE/CVF Conference on Computer Vision and Pattern Recognition, pp. 3987–3996 (2021)
49. You, Y.,et al.: Large batch optimization for deep learning: training BERT in 76 minutes. arXiv preprint arXiv:1904.00962 (2019)
50. Zhang, F., Torr, P., Ranftl, R., Richter, S.: Looking beyond single images for contrastive semantic segmentation learning. Adv. Neural. Inf. Process. Syst. **34**, 1–13 (2021)
51. Zhang, R., Isola, P., Efros, A.A.: Colorful image colorization. In: Leibe, B., Matas, J., Sebe, N., Welling, M. (eds.) ECCV 2016. LNCS, vol. 9907, pp. 649–666. Springer, Cham (2016). https://doi.org/10.1007/978-3-319-46487-9_40
52. Zhang, X., Maire, M.: Self-supervised visual representation learning from hierarchical grouping. In: Larochelle, H., Ranzato, M., Hadsell, R., Balcan, M.F., Lin, H. (eds.) Advances in Neural Information Processing Systems, vol. 33, pp. 16579–16590. Curran Associates, Inc. (2020). https://proceedings.neurips.cc/paper/2020/file/c1502ae5a4d514baec129f72948c266e-Paper.pdf

PSS: Progressive Sample Selection for Open-World Visual Representation Learning

Tianyue Cao[ID], Yongxin Wang[✉][ID], Yifan Xing[ID], Tianjun Xiao[ID], Tong He[ID], Zheng Zhang[ID], Hao Zhou[ID], and Joseph Tighe[ID]

Amazon Web Services, Seattle, USA
vanessa @sjtu.edu.cn, {yongxinw, yifax, tianjux, htong, zhnzhe, zhouho, tighej}@amazon.com

Abstract. We propose a practical open-world representation learning setting where the objective is to learn the representations for unseen categories without prior knowledge or access to images associated with these novel categories during training. Existing open-world representation learning methods make assumptions, which are often violated in practice and thus fail to generalize to the proposed setting. We propose a novel progressive approach which does not depend on such assumptions. At each iteration our approach selects unlabeled samples that attain a high homogeneity while belonging to classes that are distant to the current set of known classes in the feature space. Then we use the high-quality pseudo-labels generated via clustering over these selected samples to improve the feature generalization iteratively. Experiments demonstrate that the proposed method consistently outperforms state-of-the-art open-world semi-supervised learning methods and novel class discovery methods over nature species image retrieval and face verification benchmarks. Our training and inference code are released. (https://github.com/dmlc/dgl/tree/master/examples/pytorch/hilander/PSS).

Keywords: Open-world representation learning · Semi-supervised learning · Sample selection · Iterative methods

1 Introduction

Great progress has been made in the past decade to improve the accuracy of computer vision models and they are starting to be used in real-world applications. But one thing that holds back the wide adoption of such models is their restrictive closed universe requirements. Many real-world applications for computer vision do not operate in a fixed set of categories known a priori. Take the

T. Cao—Currently at The Shanghai Jiao Tong University. Work conducted while at AWS.

Supplementary Information The online version contains supplementary material available at https://doi.org/10.1007/978-3-031-19821-2_16.

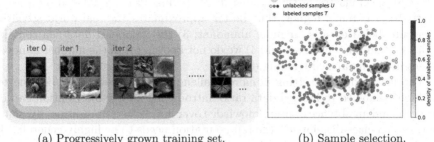

(a) Progressively grown training set.   (b) Sample selection.

Fig. 1. *Progressive Sample Selection* (PSS) approach. (a) shows the progressively grown training set. The training set gradually expands during iterations. (b) shows a toy example of sample selection in one iteration. We select samples that are densely clustered together with high local homogeneity

task of building a fine-grain species recognition system for example. One would start with a large set of annotated images, perhaps with a focus on mammals, for a set of known species and deploy such a system. Its users will expect it to recognize all fine-grain categories of, not only mammals, for which there might already be good coverage, but also birds, reptiles, etc. An effective way to expand to these new user specified fine-grain categories is to pose the problem as a metric learning task that leverages a single visual representation to retrieve examples from an ever expanding pool of labeled data. But learning such a visual representation without knowledge of the complete set of target labels is challenging. To this end, we present a practical open-world representation learning setting to realistically reflect real-world applications. Here, the training procedure has access to both labeled and unlabeled data, with the unlabeled data containing images of both the labeled classes as well as a set of unseen categories. We aim to train a visual representation that can generalize to the open-world setting where new unseen categories are encountered. Thus, the test data comes from labels that are disjoint from both the labeled and unlabeled training sets.

Our formulation is different from semi-supervised learning (SSL) or open-set semi-supervised learning as ours requires learning representations that cover both known and novel classes. Although there have been existing works aiming to discover novel classes and learn representations for them with a partially labeled dataset [10,37], they often assume constraints which are impractical in the real-world. Those include the assumptions that the unlabeled data is only comprised of samples from novel classes and the number test-time unseen classes is known a priori. The closest setting to our is [37]. However, they directly test unseen class recognition performance over the unlabeled dataset that is already accessible in training. They also assume an up-to a 2:1 ratio between the unlabeled and labeled data where in practice the ratio is much larger. Our setting does not assume any of the before-mentioned constraints and thus is more practical: 1) we test over a disjoint set of classes to the known classes in the labeled training data and novel classes in the unlabeled; 2) the unlabeled to labeled data ratio (up-to 10:1) is much higher, thus better approximates the real-world scenario where unlabeled data is far more abundant; 3) the unlabeled data can contain both seen and unseen classes and 4) we do not know a priori the number of novel classes in the unlabeled training data.

The new proposed setting is more challenging than previous works due to the high unlabeled to labeled data ratio, introducing a large distribution gap in between, and an absence of prior knowledge over novel classes. Additionally, since we test on a class-disjoint set, the representation needs to be highly generalized. We test existing semi-supervised learning and novel class discovery methods in our proposed setting and found they fail to generalize.

One observation we make is that addressing such a challenging setting with one-step training is difficult. Thus, we propose a novel *Progressive Sample Selection* (PSS) approach as illustrated by Fig. 1. Our method, partially inspired by [6], recurrently clusters a *selected* set of unlabeled data with representation learnt at the current iteration and adopts the cluster assignments as pseudo-labels to refine subsequent representations. However, PSS differs in that, within each iteration, we propose a novel sample selection method to gather samples which are closely clustered together via a density criterion.

Our key insight is that under such a selection criterion over the clustering density in the feature space, we choose samples signaling compact intra-class distance distributions and thus a higher homogeneity to reduce noise in the pseudo-labels. In traditional SSL methods, samples with high pseudo-label quality are often those represented confidently by known classes, or "close" to known classes semantically. However, we find that our selection method is also able to sample, with high quality, from dis-similar novel classes whose class centroids are far-apart in the feature space. These samples from distant novel classes help improve the model generalization to disjoint unseen classes at test-time. Compared to adding all unlabeled samples at once, our progressively selected samples improve generalization more effectively, as shown in Fig. 4.

We test our method on two open-world metric learning tasks: image retrieval for natural species, where the task is given a query image, to find nearest neighbor images across animal species, and 1:1 face verification, which classifies a pair of faces as being from the same person or different. The proposed progressive sample selection and representation learning method outperforms state-of-the-art semi-supervised learning and open-world representation learning methods. Specifically, it improves the Recall@1 performance from 55% to 57% over the image retrieval benchmark for nature species, and reduces the False Non Match Rate (FNMR) @ 1e–4 False Match Rate (FMR), from 22% to 21%, for face verification, relative to SOTA methods, as shown in Table 3 and 4.

To summarize, the key contributions of our method are as follows: 1) we formalize a practical open-world representation learning setting that reduces the gap between existing settings in the literature to the real-world application; 2) we propose a novel iterative method that progressively selects, at each iteration, samples that are most effective in improving representation generalization over test-time unseen classes; 3) we outperform state-of-the-art semi-supervised and novel class discovery methods using labeled and unlabeled data under our practical setting for open-world representation learning, over the nature species image retrieval and 1:1 face verification tasks.

2   Related Work

Our work is closely related to semi-supervised learning and novel class discovery, we review literature in these two fields in the following discussion. We also discuss different sample selections methods and literature that iterate between feature learning and pseudo labeling as we do in this work.

Semi-supervised Learning. Traditional SSL follows a closed-set setting which assumes the same set of classes in labeled and unlabeled data. The goal is to improve in-distribution classification performance with the help of an unlabeled dataset. The core challenge is in on how to leverage unlabeled data, which is roughly categorized into the following spectrums: consistency regularization [28,32,35,42], pseudo-labeling [20,29,44], generative methods [8,25,27] and graph based methods [2,23]. However, when the unlabeled set contains out-of-distribution (OOD) samples, termed as open-set SSL [26], traditional approaches inevitably suffer performance degradation [22,26,34]. To mitigate this adverse impact, recent works [11,16,31,49] proposed to detect and down play OOD samples for classification performance of in-distribution data. We encourage readers to refer [22,36,48] for more comprehensive review of SSL literature.

Novel Class Discovery. A related line of work is novel class discovery (NCD) [13]. Different from closed-set or open-set SSL which leverages an unlabeled image set to improve learning performance on seen classes, NCD aims at discovering new classes in an unlabeled image set, assuming disjoint classes for labeled and unlabeled images. In order to transfer the representation from the labeled set to the unlabeled one, prevailing works [12,18,50] opt to learn transformation invariant features from labeled set first then pairwise relationship among unlabeled samples. These two-step approaches are unified into one single objective in [10] with multi-view self-labeling strategy. NCD [13] makes the assumption that all unlabeled data comes from novel classes and the number of classes is known. To be less constrained, [37] introduced Generalized Category Discovery (GCD) and proposed contrastive training with semi-supervised k-means to cluster unlabelled data into seen and unseen classes. In contrast to novel class discovery, [5] considers an open-world setting, in which testing set contains both seen and unseen classes. It proposed to train a classifier with both supervised and pairwise unsupervised loss in a unified fashion. Different from [5], which use all the unlabeled data in training, we progressively select samples which are most informative, avoiding bring too many noisy labels into feature training.

Sample Selection. A good sample selection method [19] will make the curated dataset to contain less noise, class imbalance and redundancy. Such resultant datasets will allow models trained over them to maximize the information gain from unlabeled data. When the labeling algorithm is not robust enough, it is beneficial to add those high confidence unlabeled samples to the labeled set. Confidence score [33] is one of the leading metrics to measure the quality of assigned labels. [30] applied confidence threshold to select a disjoint face identity set and assigned pseudo labels. Similarly, [44] proposed to use classification score on all unlabeled samples and selected top-K examples of each target class. However, samples with such high scores do not help close the distribution gap between labeled and unlabeled data in our open world setting. Therefore, adding them to the training set makes no guarantee of improved recognition rates on unseen classes. [45] proposed a progressive labeling algorithm similar to ours. It selected the most representative samples by ranking the in-degree of nodes on a directed k-nearest neighbor (kNN) graph. Different from this handcrafted node similarity metric, our approach adopts a density criterion that exploits rich semantics between graph nodes and we employ a GNN clustering model [43] which learns such a criterion with supervision from class labels.

Iteration Between Clustering and Feature Learning. Some existing research studies model the clustering (pseudo labeling) and feature learning into a unified framework [6,7,21,41,46]. These two tasks are usually solved in an alternative fashion under the same objective, leading to iterative methods similar to ours. [7,21,41,46] assign pseudo labels to all unlabeled samples and apply them for feature learning in the next step. However, due to the imperfect performance of clustering, this can easily bring noisy labels into feature learning. Deep clustering [6], on the other hand, proposed to sample data from a uniform distribution over the classes to circumvent the issue caused by class imbalance. Different from these methods, we proposed to sample unlabeled samples progressively based on their clustering density to avoid noisy labels being used in feature learning.

3   Methods

3.1   Problem Formalization

We formalize a practical setting for open-world representation learning. Given a partially labeled dataset $\mathcal{D}$, we define the seen-class set $\mathcal{C}_{in}$, the unseen-classes set $\mathcal{C}_{out}$, and test class set $\mathcal{C}_{test}$. These three sets do not intersect with each other, and $|\mathcal{C}_{in}| \ll |\mathcal{C}_{out}|$. The training set consists of a labeled set $\mathcal{L}_{in}$ with $\mathcal{C}_{in}$ labels, and an unlabeled set $\mathcal{U} = \mathcal{U}_{in} \cup \mathcal{U}_{out}$, where $\mathcal{U}_{in}$ has $\mathcal{C}_{in}$ labels and $\mathcal{U}_{out}$ has $\mathcal{C}_{out}$ labels. The split of $\mathcal{U}_{in}$ and $\mathcal{U}_{out}$ is not known. We have $|\mathcal{L}_{in}| \ll |\mathcal{U}|$, and $|\mathcal{L}_{in}| : |\mathcal{U}| \approx 1 : 10$ in our setting. Figure 2 illustrates the dataset split. We aim to train a feature extractor f to obtain generalized representations.

Compared with existing open-world semi-supervised learning and novel class discovery settings [10,13], ours differs in the aspects: (1) the unlabeled data is

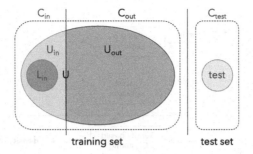

Fig. 2. Illustration of our practical open-world representation learning setting. We have a labeled training set L_{in} with seen classes $\mathcal{C}_{\text{in}}$, and an unlabeled training set $\mathcal{U} = \mathcal{U}_{\text{in}} \cup \mathcal{U}_{\text{out}}$ with both seen classes $\mathcal{C}_{\text{in}}$ and unseen classes $\mathcal{C}_{\text{out}}$, only the images are accessible and the discrimination of $\mathcal{U}_{\text{in}}$ and $\mathcal{U}_{\text{out}}$ is unknown. The test set is from disjoint test classes $\mathcal{C}_{\text{test}}$. We train on the labeled data $\mathcal{L}_{\text{in}}$ with ground truth labels; and the unlabeled data $\mathcal{U}$ with generated pseudo labels. The unlabeled data are selectively added during iterations

from both seen and unseen classes, instead of from only seen classes; (2) the unseen class number is not provided. Compared with the most similar existing setting in [37]: (1) We have much larger $|\mathcal{U}| : |\mathcal{L}_{\text{in}}|$ and $|\mathcal{C}_{\text{out}}| : |\mathcal{C}_{\text{in}}|$ ratios; and (2) test on a hold out test set. The test images and classes are not accessible during training. In terms of the above differences, our setting is more challenging and of practical significance. Specifically, the high unlabeled to labeled data ratio leads to large distribution gap between the unlabeled and labeled data. Testing on a class-disjoint set requires a highly generalized model. The setting is also closer to the real world use scenarios, such as face verification and image retrieval.

3.2 Progressive Sample Selection (PSS) Pipeline

We propose a novel *Progressive Sample Selection* (PSS) approach to tackle the challenges in our practical open-world representation learning setting. We design a progressive pipeline to gradually expand the set of images used to train our model with the goals of being more robust to out-of-distribution unseen-class data. We select samples based on their cluster density, selecting samples in clusters with high local homogeneity. This selects points with less noise at both small and large distances from seen classes. We show that by continuing to add samples at each training iteration with our selection method, we expand the feature space and improve the model's generalization ability.

PSS Pipeline. The overall PSS pipeline for open-set representation learning is shown in Fig. 3. The training set $\mathcal{T}_0$ is initialized as the labeled set $\mathcal{L}_{\text{in}}$ and expands during iterations. Each iteration contains three steps, in iteration i:

1. **Representation Learning.** Train a feature extractor f_i to learn representations on the training set $\mathcal{T}_i$. Note f_i is retrained in each iteration instead of finetuning on top of f_{i-1} to alleviate overfitting and avoid local optima.

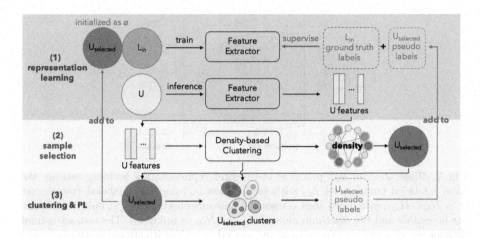

Fig. 3. The overall pipeline of Progressive Sample Selection (PSS). We progressively repeat three steps to train a generalized feature extractor with samples increasingly added to the training set in iterations. The feature extractor and density-based clustering model are shared in different steps. Best viewed in color (Color figure online)

2. **Sample selection.** Estimate the density of the feature space defined by f_i for each sample in the unlabeled training set $\mathcal{U}_i$. Select samples for inclusion in training the next iteration feature representation f_{i+1} that have a density estimate above a threshold τ and pass the selection together with $\mathcal{U}_i$ to the clustering step for pseudo labeling as $\mathcal{U}_{\text{selected}}$. The details are in Sect. 3.3.

3. **Clustering and pseudo labeling.** Cluster samples in $\mathcal{U}$ and assign pseudo labels to points in $\mathcal{U}_{\text{selected}}$ corresponding to their cluster assignment. Then update the training set $\mathcal{T}_{i+1} = \mathcal{T}_i \cup \mathcal{U}_{\text{selected}}$ and the unlabeled set $\mathcal{U}_{i+1} = \mathcal{U}_i \setminus \mathcal{U}_{\text{selected}}$, preparing for iteration $i + 1$ training. The details of clustering and pseudo labeling are in Sect. 3.4.

The above three steps are looped until the number of selected samples which are far away from the training set on the feature space is small. Finally, we re-train the feature extractor to learn better representations for retrieval or recognition.

3.3   Sample Selection

Due to the large unlabeled to labeled data ratio in our setting, a large class distribution gap exists between the unlabeled and labeled data. Thus, it is hard to get reasonable representations and clustering results for the subset of out-of-distribution data. In order to get high-quality training data and pseudo labels, we propose a novel sample selection method outlined above. We leverage Hi-LANDER [43] to both estimate the sample density and perform clustering but in principle these two systems could be independent estimators.

Hi-LANDER [43] is a hierarchical graph neural network model for image clustering which learns the grouping and model selection criteria in traditional clustering methods. It recurrently builds k-nearest-neighbor graphs over nodes which are grouped from connected components at different level of the hierarchy. It defines *Density* as the proportion of same-class neighbors weighted by similarity. Specifically, the estimated density $\hat{d}_i$ for the i-th sample is:

$$\hat{d}_i = \frac{1}{k} \sum_{j \in \mathcal{N}(i)} \hat{e}_{ij} \cdot a_{ij}, \quad \hat{e}_{ij} = P(y_i = y_j) - P(y_i \neq y_j) \tag{1}$$

where $\mathcal{N}(i)$ refers to the neighbors of sample i, $\hat{e}_{ij}$ is the edge linkage probability of sample i sharing the same class as its neighbour j, and a_{ij} is the feature similarity between the two. Further details can be found in Equation (4) in [43]. A sample with high density therefore has a neighborhood that contains more consistent labels as itself, exhibiting a higher homogeneity and less noisy labels in the clustering pseudo-labels.

In each iteration, samples are selected through the above defined density metric with a threshold τ. It is observed that using such as density selection criterion enforcing high homogeneity (thus high pseudo-label quality), we not only select samples that are close to known classes but also those that are far-apart from the centroids of existing classes in the feature space to close the distribution gap between labeled and unlabeled data, allowing improved generalization to unseen disjoint test-time classes (Fig. 5).

3.4 Clustering and Pseudo Labeling

After obtaining the $\mathcal{U}_{\text{selected}}$ from $\mathcal{U}_i$ with the density metric, we then generate pseudo labels for them using the clustering results of Hi-LANDER. Given the clusters, we assign one new class label to all selected unlabeled samples in each cluster. Assume the current training set $\mathcal{T}_i$ has m existing classes, samples in $\mathcal{U}_{\text{selected}}$ will then have their pseudo labels indexed from $m+1$. Note that for two same-class samples, this process might assign different pseudo labels to them. However, according to [10,17], over-clustering does not harm the downstream task performance, thus the class-split is acceptable.

With the selected samples and pseudo labels, the training set $\mathcal{T}_i$ is expanded to $\mathcal{T}_{i+1} = \mathcal{T}_i \cup \mathcal{U}_{\text{selected}}$. Finally, we re-train the feature extractor on $\mathcal{T}_{i+1}$ to learn more generalized representations.

4 Experiments

We evaluate PSS on fine-grained natural image retrieval and face verification benchmarks. First, we show ablation experiments over the design choices of PSS and demonstrate their significance in improving feature generalization. We then illustrate the performance comparison of PSS to state-of-the-art SSL and novel class discovery methods over the fine-grained nature species image-retrieval benchmark. Finally, we demonstrate the performance improvement of PSS in open-set face verification benchmarks.

4.1   Evaluation Protocols

Datasets. For fine-grained natural image retrieval, we use iNaturalist [15] dataset, which contains a training set of 325,846 images across 5,690 classes and a disjoint test set of 136,093 images across 2,452 test classes. We randomly sample about 16% of the training classes as the seen classes C_{in}, and take 60% of the images from each class in C_{in} as the labeled training set $\mathcal{L}_{in}$. The rest of the samples in the training set are used as the unlabeled training set $\mathcal{U}$. The test set has disjoint samples and classes to the training set. The attributes of three sets are shown in Table 1. The labeled training set $\mathcal{L}_{in}$ has about 9% samples over all the training samples. The ratios of both the labeled classes and the labeled samples are much smaller than previous open-set semi-supervised learning and novel class discovery settings.

For face verification training, we used the combined IMDB [39] and Deep-Glint [1] datasets. The IMDB consists of 1.3 Million images with 49,990 identities and the DeepGlint dataset contains around 6.2 Million images with 180k identities. We randomly sampled 90% of the IMDB data as $\mathcal{L}_{in}$ and the rest are treated as $\mathcal{U}$. Similar to iNatualist experiments, we divide the dataset into $\mathcal{L}_{in}$ and $\mathcal{U}$ sets and the statistics of these sets can be found in Table 1. There is roughly a 1:6 ratio between the labeled and unlabeled data. We evaluate our method using the IJB-C [24] face verification benchmarks on the 1:1 face verification task, which contains about 3,531 identities and 140k images. The IJB-C benchmark is disjoint from the IMDB and the DeepGlint data that we use for training.

Metrics. For image retrieval and face verification, we respectively use *Recall@k* (higher the better) and False Non-Match Rate (FNMR) at False Match Rate (FMR) equaling 1e-4 (lower the better) as the metric to evaluate our method.

4.2   Implementation Details

For image retrieval, we use Smooth-AP loss [4] to finetune a ResNet-50 [14] backbone. The embedded dimension is 128. The learning rate is 1e-5. We train the feature extractor on a single machine with 8 NVIDIA T4 GPUs. The hidden dimension of Hi-LANDER is 512, and use GAT [38] as the base graph neural network model. The k expansions in k-NN are 10,5,3.

For face verification, we use CosFace [40] for training our face embedding model. The embedding dimension is 128 and learning rate starts at 0.1 and decreases according to a cosine learning rate schedule. We train the embedding for 32 epochs on a distributed training system with 8 nodes, each with 8 NVIDIA Tesla V100 GPUs. We use the same Hi-LANDER setting as in image retrieval.

Section 4.3 describes the sample selection threshold and stopping criterion.

4.3   Ablation Experiments

We examine the effectiveness of our progressive system design by ablating our sample selection and progressive refinement. From Table 2, notice removing either our sample selection or progressive refinement results in a regression in performance. Note that for progressive methods, the training time expands linearly with the number of iterations and thus the accuracy improvements do come at the cost of training time. The sample selection, however, not only brings performance gains but also reduces the number of samples being trained, in-turn reducing training time. We illustrate these components in more detail on the nature species image retrieval benchmark below.

Table 1. The labeled, unlabeled and class-disjoint test dataset attributes

Split	iNarturalist		Face	
	#images	#classes	#images	#classes
$\mathcal{L}_{in}$	29,011	948	1,124,874	49990
$\mathcal{U}$	296,835	5,690	6,323,702	209,551
test	136,093	2,452	141,139	3,531

Table 2. Ablation of sample selection and iteration in our method. Both improve the performance. Sample selection also improves training efficiency

Sample selection	Iterate	#training data	#iterations	Recall@1	Recall@4	Recall@16	Recall@32
✗	✗	325,846	0	0.5421	0.7128	0.8318	0.8755
✓	✗	69,140	0	0.5522	0.7224	0.8413	0.8848
✗	✓	325,846	4	0.5548	0.7242	0.8407	0.8839
✓	✓	87,349	4	**0.5714**	**0.7357**	**0.8501**	**0.8914**

Progressive Pipeline. The proposed open-world representation learning setting is challenging considering the large ratio between unlabeled data and labeled data. The base feature learned from the labeled data has limited representation ability on the unlabeled data and thus the pseudo-labels suffer more noise. Our progressive pipeline continually updates the feature and improves the pseudo-label quality at each iteration. This assumption is verified in Table 2 and Table 3, where our iterative method outperforms the one-step baselines. Figure 4 shows the retrieval performance at each iteration of PSS compared with the DeepClustering [6] iterative method. We notice DeepClustering stops improving after 2 iterations, while for PSS performance does not plateau until iteration 4.

Sample Selection. The difference between our method and DeepClustering's [6] ability to continue to improve over iterations, lies in the process of sample selection. As mentioned in the progressive analysis, a large portion of the unlabeled data will be tagged with noisy pseudo-label since the generalization ability of the base feature is limited. Noisy pseudo-labels hurt model performance and diminishes the gain from correctly pseudo-labeled samples.

Usually, samples close to the existing labeled classes are easier to get high-quality pseudo-labels, since the learned feature are easier to generalize to those similar samples. Several existing sample selection works are adopting this intuition or its variants to keep pseudo-label quality, such as FixMatch [3], which only keeps samples assigned a high probability to a known class. In PSS, we use density defined in Hi-LANDER [43] as the selection metric. Intuitively, high density for a sample is an indicator of high-quality pseudo-label since the local intra-class homogeneity is kept. We can consider current feature "works" for that high-density sample by collecting same-class samples into its closest neighborhood. High density does not necessarily mean close distance to labeled classes. In Fig. 5, we indeed found the density and the distance-to-closest-labeled-class are

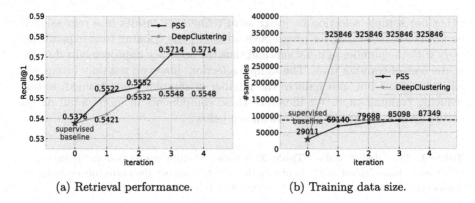

(a) Retrieval performance.   (b) Training data size.

Fig. 4. The retrieval performance (Recall@1) and training data size on iNaturalist in different iterations. The performance improves during iterations with more training data. DeepClustering is almost converged after iteration 2 while PSS still witnesses a performance boost at iteration 3. Meanwhile, PSS uses fewer samples to train the feature representation benefiting from sample selection

not negatively correlated, making it possible to select some high-quality pseudo-labeled samples which differ from the labeled classes. This is vital to generalize to unseen data for the challenging open-world representation learning setting and a major differentiator with existing sample selection methods. To verify this statement, we split the selected samples to equal-sized two parts based on the distance-to-closest-labeled-class. Samples with distance higher than 0.15 (mean distance for all the selected samples) are collected in the"far" part, vice versa. After feature learning with these two parts separately, we found that the samples far-away from existing labeled classes bring more gain on the test set. The *Recall@1* on the feature learnt with "far" part is 0.5524, while the one from "close" part is 0.5490 in iteration 1.

Density Thresholding Criterion. The density threshold is one of the hyper-parameters of PSS. The threshold we use is the density inflection point of the approximated upper-bound density-distance curve, as illustrated in Fig. 5 over the nature species image retrieval benchmark (the first iteration). It shows that the density of the inflection point is around 0.8 and thus we pick it as the sample selection threshold and keep it for subsequent iterations til convergence. For face verification, the same rule is applied and we select threshold of 0.9.

Stopping Criterion. The stopping criterion is usually empirical. We define our stopping criterion as the portion of samples who's distance to the nearest training class centroid is large (greater than 0.15). This portion drops iteration by iteration. When it drops to a certain level, the benefit effect from the informative large distance samples will be negated by the negative effect from noisy pseudo-labels and thus we stop the first iteration we see this indicator rise. Figure 6

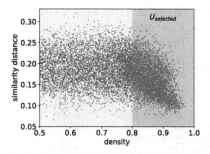
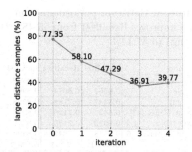

Fig. 5. The non-negative correlation between density and the cosine distance to the nearest training class centroid after iteration 1. Threshold 0.8 is selected for species retrieval

Fig. 6. The percentage of distances to the nearest training class centroid considered to be large (greater than 0.15) in $\mathcal{U}$ over different iterations

shows such stopping indicator value over the nature species retrieval task, which leads to stopping after the 4th iteration. For face verification, the same stopping criteria is applied and we stop at iteration 4.

4.4 Image Retrieval Results

We validate the effectiveness of PSS on natural images using fine-grained image retrieval as the downstream task.

We compare PSS with the supervised baseline trained with only labeled data $\mathcal{L}_{in}$, oracle trained with all training data $\mathcal{L}_{in} \cup \mathcal{U}$ with ground truth labels, traditional semi-supervised learning method Pseudo Labeling (PL) [20], open-set semi-supervised learning method UNO [10], one-step clustering method Hi-LANDER [43], and iterative clustering method DeepClustering [6]. UNO has classification heads for the training set but not for the disjoint-class test set, so we train a UNO model to generate pseudo labels for the unlabeled data $\mathcal{U}$, and finetune a pretrained feature extractor with Smooth-AP [4] loss. For Hi-LANDER, we apply a trained Hi-LANDER clustering model on $\mathcal{U}$ to generate pseudo labels and re-train the feature extractor with both $\mathcal{L}_{in}$ and $\mathcal{U}$. Here we do not compare with some other semi-supervised learning methods such as self-training [34] because they rely on the design of classification heads, which have difficulty expanding to the open-world retrieval task with unseen classes.

Table 3 shows the retrieval performance of PSS and the state-of-the-art SSL and novel class discovery methods on the hold out iNaturalist test set. All the previous methods, except UNO, boost the supervised baseline by training with more data. Though UNO performs excellently in terms of classification accuracy on the unlabeled training set, it does not work well in our setting since the large unlabeled to labeled distribution gap and it over-fits on the labeled data. The one-step methods PL, Hi-LANDER, and UNO add all the unlabeled data at once thus introduce more noises to the pseudo labels. Training with the noisy pseudo labels regress the performance boost. DeepClustering iteratively train with all

Table 3. Retrieval performance on iNaturalist. PSS improves Recall@1 from 55.48% (DeepClustering) to 57.14%

Method	Recall@1	Recall@4	Recall@16	Recall@32
Sup. baseline	0.5376	0.7135	0.8359	0.8817
Oracle	0.6554	0.8074	0.8966	0.9261
PL [20]	0.5447	0.7188	0.8398	0.8832
Hi-LANDER [43]	0.5421	0.7128	0.8318	0.8755
UNO [10]	0.5372	0.7138	0.8367	0.8808
DeepClustering [6]	0.5548	0.7242	0.8407	0.8839
PSS	**0.5714**	**0.7357**	**0.8501**	**0.8914**

Table 4. IJBC Face Verification. PSS reduces FNMR@FMR 1e-4 from best prior (DeepClustering)

Method	FNMR@FMR1e-4
Sup. baseline	0.3007
Oracle	0.0672
DB-SCAN [9]	0.4203
GCN-V [47]	0.2508
Hi-LANDER [43]	0.2472
RoyChowdhury et al. [30]	0.2706
DeepClustering [6]	0.2234
PSS	**0.2165**

the unlabeled data in each iteration. Though the progressive refinement brings performance boost by increasing quality of both features and pseudo labels, the pseudo labels are still noisy thus the gain is limited and stops increasing after two iterations (see Fig. 4). Benefiting from our progressive sample selection pipeline, PSS is able to steadily improve feature generalization to test-time disjoint novel classes over iterations due to its capability to choose distant samples which also exhibit high homogeneity and high pseudo-label quality. Although DeepClustering also achieves relatively high Recall@1 performance, it's much more costly than PSS in the feature training step. Even if we consider DeepClustering to have converged at iteration 2 while PSS stops at iteration 4, PSS improves training efficiency by 60% via training on less than 40% of the samples summed-up across all iterations compared to DeepClustering.

4.5   Face Verification Results

Figure 7 shows the performance gain of PSS over iterations and Fig. 8 shows the progressive number of samples selected. From iteration 1 to 3, the face verification performance steadily improves, with convergence at iteration 4.

We compare PSS with state-of-the-art semi-supervised and open-world representation learning methods [6,9,30,43,47] in Table 4. For DB-SCAN [9], GCN-V [47], Hi-LANDER [43], and RoyChowdhury et al. [30] which use clustering and pseudo-labeling, we perform a one-step feature training, where all unlabeled samples are gathered to generate pseudo-labels and used for training at once. For DeepClustering [6], we recurrently run the feature training with the same backbone architecture as PSS and pseudo-labeling via Hi-LANDER clustering in an alternating manner, however, it lacks the progressive sample selection. Due to its high training cost with full unlabeled and labeled data within each iteration (>7 million samples), we stop DeepClustering after iteration 2. PSS, on the other hand, uses a much more efficient number of samples across all iterations (<7 million in total). PSS significantly improves feature generalization over methods that directly use all samples. In addition, PSS achieves a training efficiency boost over DeepClustering, where it reduces FNMR@FMR=1e-4 from 22.34% to 21.66% with training over only < 50% of the samples summed-up across iterations.

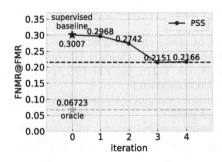 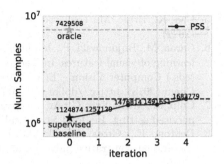

Fig. 7. IJBC Face Verification FNMR @ FMR 1e-4 (the lower, the better)

Fig. 8. Number of sampled selected by PSS for face verification

5 Conclusion

We propose a practical open-world representation learning setting to learn unseen category representations with partially labeled data. Our setting has large unlabeled to labeled data ratio, no prior knowledge over the number of unseen classes during training, and no access to the images that have the same labels as the test set. Existing open-world representation learning methods fail to generalize to the proposed setting because of the large distribution gap between the unlabeled and labeled data. To tackle this challenging setting, we propose a novel *Progressive Sample Selection* (PSS) approach to improve representation generalization by iteratively training with increasingly effective samples selected during iterations. We use estimated density in Hi-LANDER clustering model to select samples that are densely clustered together with high local intra-class homogeneity. These samples can be from novel classes that are far from the existing categories, thus help improve the model generalization to test-time disjoint unseen classes. Experiments indicate that our method outperforms the state-of-the-art semi-supervised learning methods and novel class discovery methods in natural image retrieval and face verification.

References

1. http://trillionpairs.deepglint.com/overview
2. Bengio, Y., Delalleau, O., Le Roux, N.: 11 label propagation and quadratic criterion (2006)
3. Berthelot, D., Carlini, N., Goodfellow, I., Papernot, N., Oliver, A., Raffel, C.A.: Mixmatch: a holistic approach to semi-supervised learning. Adv. Neural Inf. Process. Syst. **32**, 1–11 (2019)
4. Brown, A., Xie, W., Kalogeiton, V., Zisserman, A.: Smooth-AP: smoothing the path towards large-scale image retrieval. In: Vedaldi, A., Bischof, H., Brox, T., Frahm, J.-M. (eds.) ECCV 2020. LNCS, vol. 12354, pp. 677–694. Springer, Cham (2020). https://doi.org/10.1007/978-3-030-58545-7_39

5. Cao, K., Brbić, M., Leskovec, J.: Open-world semi-supervised learning. In: ICLR (2022)
6. Caron, M., Bojanowski, P., Joulin, A., Douze, M.: Deep clustering for unsupervised learning of visual features. In: Ferrari, V., Hebert, M., Sminchisescu, C., Weiss, Y. (eds.) Computer Vision – ECCV 2018. LNCS, vol. 11218, pp. 139–156. Springer, Cham (2018). https://doi.org/10.1007/978-3-030-01264-9_9
7. Culp, M., Michailidis, G.: An iterative algorithm for extending learners to a semisupervised setting. In: Joint Statistical Meetings (2007)
8. Denton, E., Gross, S., Fergus, R.: Semi-supervised learning with context-conditional generative adversarial networks. arXiv preprint arXiv:1611.06430 (2016)
9. Ester, M., Kriegel, H.P., Sander, J., Xu, X.: A density-based algorithm for discovering clusters in large spatial databases with noise. In: Proceedings of the Second International Conference on Knowledge Discovery and Data Mining, KDD 1996, pp. 226–231. AAAI Press (1996)
10. Fini, E., Sangineto, E., Lathuilière, S., Zhong, Z., Nabi, M., Ricci, E.: A unified objective for novel class discovery. In: Proceedings of the IEEE/CVF International Conference on Computer Vision (ICCV), pp. 9284–9292 (2021)
11. Guo, L.Z., Zhang, Z.Y., Jiang, Y., Li, Y.F., Zhou, Z.H.: Safe deep semi-supervised learning for unseen-class unlabeled data. In: International Conference on Machine Learning, pp. 3897–3906. PMLR (2020)
12. Han, K., Rebuffi, S.A., Ehrhardt, S., Vedaldi, A., Zisserman, A.: Automatically discovering and learning new visual categories with ranking statistics. arXiv preprint arXiv:2002.05714 (2020)
13. Han, K., Vedaldi, A., Zisserman, A.: Learning to discover novel visual categories via deep transfer clustering. In: Proceedings of the IEEE/CVF International Conference on Computer Vision, pp. 8401–8409 (2019)
14. He, K., Zhang, X., Ren, S., Sun, J.: Deep residual learning for image recognition. In: CVPR, pp. 770–778. IEEE Computer Society (2016)
15. Horn, G.V., et al.: The iNaturalist species classification and detection dataset. In: CVPR, pp. 8769–8778. Computer Vision Foundation/IEEE Computer Society (2018)
16. Huang, J., et al.: Trash to treasure: harvesting OOD data with cross-modal matching for open-set semi-supervised learning. In: Proceedings of the IEEE/CVF International Conference on Computer Vision, pp. 8310–8319 (2021)
17. Ji, X., Henriques, J.F., Vedaldi, A.: Invariant information clustering for unsupervised image classification and segmentation. In: Proceedings of the IEEE/CVF International Conference on Computer Vision (ICCV) (2019)
18. Jia, X., Han, K., Zhu, Y., Green, B.: Joint representation learning and novel category discovery on single-and multi-modal data. In: Proceedings of the IEEE/CVF International Conference on Computer Vision, pp. 610–619 (2021)
19. Killamsetty, K., Zhao, X., Chen, F., Iyer, R.: Retrieve: coreset selection for efficient and robust semi-supervised learning. Adv. Neural Inf. Process. Syst. **34**, 14488–14501 (2021)
20. Lee, D.H., et al.: Pseudo-label: the simple and efficient semi-supervised learning method for deep neural networks. In: Workshop on Challenges in Representation Learning, ICML, vol. 3, pp. 896 (2013)
21. Liao, R., Schwing, A., Zemel, R., Urtasun, R.: Learning deep parsimonious representations. In: NeurIPS (2016)
22. Luo, H., et al.: An empirical study and analysis on open-set semi-supervised learning. arXiv preprint arXiv:2101.08237 (2021)

23. Luo, Y., Zhu, J., Li, M., Ren, Y., Zhang, B.: Smooth neighbors on teacher graphs for semi-supervised learning. In: Proceedings of the IEEE Conference on Computer Vision and Pattern Recognition, pp. 8896–8905 (2018)
24. Maze, B., et al.: IARPA Janus benchmark - c: face dataset and protocol. In: 2018 International Conference on Biometrics (ICB), pp. 158–165 (2018). https://doi. org/10.1109/ICB2018.2018.00033
25. Odena, A.: Semi-supervised learning with generative adversarial networks. arXiv preprint arXiv:1606.01583 (2016)
26. Oliver, A., Odena, A., Raffel, C.A., Cubuk, E.D., Goodfellow, I.: Realistic evaluation of deep semi-supervised learning algorithms. Adv. Neural Inf. Process. Syst. **31**, 1–12 (2018)
27. Radford, A., Metz, L., Chintala, S.: Unsupervised representation learning with deep convolutional generative adversarial networks. arXiv preprint arXiv:1511.06434 (2015)
28. Rasmus, A., Berglund, M., Honkala, M., Valpola, H., Raiko, T.: Semi-supervised learning with ladder networks. Adv. Neural Inf. Process. Syst. **28**, 1–9 (2015)
29. Rosenberg, C., Hebert, M., Schneiderman, H.: Semi-supervised self-training of object detection models (2005)
30. RoyChowdhury, A., Yu, X., Sohn, K., Learned-Miller, E., Chandraker, M.: Improving face recognition by clustering unlabeled faces in the wild. In: Vedaldi, A., Bischof, H., Brox, T., Frahm, J.-M. (eds.) ECCV 2020. LNCS, vol. 12369, pp. 119–136. Springer, Cham (2020). https://doi.org/10.1007/978-3-030-58586-0_8
31. Saito, K., Kim, D., Saenko, K.: OpenMatch: open-set semi-supervised learning with open-set consistency regularization. Adv. Neural Inf. Process. Syst. **34**, 25956–25967 (2021)
32. Sajjadi, M., Javanmardi, M., Tasdizen, T.: Regularization with stochastic transformations and perturbations for deep semi-supervised learning. Adv. Neural Inf. Process. Syst. **29**, 1–9 (2016)
33. Sohn, K.: FixMatch: simplifying semi-supervised learning with consistency and confidence. Adv. Neural. Inf. Process. Syst. **33**, 596–608 (2020)
34. Su, J.C., Cheng, Z., Maji, S.: A realistic evaluation of semi-supervised learning for fine-grained classification. In: Proceedings of the IEEE/CVF Conference on Computer Vision and Pattern Recognition, pp. 12966–12975 (2021)
35. Tarvainen, A., Valpola, H.: Mean teachers are better role models: weight-averaged consistency targets improve semi-supervised deep learning results. Adv. Neural Inf. Process. Syst. **30**, 1–10 (2017)
36. van Engelen, J.E., Hoos, H.H.: A survey on semi-supervised learning. Mach. Learn. **109**(2), 373–440 (2019). https://doi.org/10.1007/s10994-019-05855-6
37. Vaze, S., Han, K., Vedaldi, A., Zisserman, A.: Generalized category discovery. arXiv preprint arXiv:2201.02609 (2022)
38. Veličković, P., Cucurull, G., Casanova, A., Romero, A., Liò, P., Bengio, Y.: Graph attention networks. In: International Conference on Learning Representations (2018). https://openreview.net/forum?id=rJXMpikCZ
39. Wang, F., et al.: The devil of face recognition is in the noise. arXiv preprint arXiv:1807.11649 (2018)
40. Wang, H., et al.: CosFace: large margin cosine loss for deep face recognition. In: Proceedings of the IEEE Conference on Computer Vision and Pattern Recognition (CVPR) (2018)
41. Xie, J., Girshick, R., Farhadi, A.: Unsupervised deep embedding for clustering analysis. In: ICML (2016)

42. Xie, Q., Dai, Z., Hovy, E., Luong, T., Le, Q.: Unsupervised data augmentation for consistency training. Adv. Neural. Inf. Process. Syst. **33**, 6256–6268 (2020)
43. Xing, Y., et al.: Learning hierarchical graph neural networks for image clustering. In: Proceedings of the IEEE/CVF International Conference on Computer Vision (ICCV), pp. 3467–3477 (2021)
44. Yalniz, I.Z., Jégou, H., Chen, K., Paluri, M., Mahajan, D.: Billion-scale semi-supervised learning for image classification. arXiv preprint arXiv:1905.00546 (2019)
45. Yan, X., Chen, R., Feng, L., Yang, J., Zheng, H., Zhang, W.: Progressive representative labeling for deep semi-supervised learning. arXiv preprint arXiv:2108.06070 (2021)
46. Yang, J., Parikh, D., Batra, D.: Joint unsupervised learning of deep representations and image clusters. In: CVPR (2016)
47. Yang, L., Chen, D., Zhan, X., Zhao, R., Loy, C.C., Lin, D.: Learning to cluster faces via confidence and connectivity estimation. In: Proceedings of the IEEE Conference on Computer Vision and Pattern Recognition (2020)
48. Yang, X., Song, Z., King, I., Xu, Z.: A survey on deep semi-supervised learning. arXiv preprint arXiv:2103.00550 (2021)
49. Yu, Q., Ikami, D., Irie, G., Aizawa, K.: Multi-task curriculum framework for open-set semi-supervised learning. In: Vedaldi, A., Bischof, H., Brox, T., Frahm, J.-M. (eds.) ECCV 2020. LNCS, vol. 12357, pp. 438–454. Springer, Cham (2020). https://doi.org/10.1007/978-3-030-58610-2_26
50. Zhong, Z., Fini, E., Roy, S., Luo, Z., Ricci, E., Sebe, N.: Neighborhood contrastive learning for novel class discovery. In: Proceedings of the IEEE/CVF Conference on Computer Vision and Pattern Recognition, pp. 10867–10875 (2021)

Improving Self-supervised Lightweight Model Learning via Hard-Aware Metric Distillation

Hao Liu[2] and Mang Ye[1,3(✉)]

[1] School of Computer Science, Wuhan University, Wuhan, China
mangye16@gmail.com
[2] School of Computer Science, Beijing Institute of Technology, Beijing, China
[3] Hubei Luojia Laboratory, Wuhan, China
https://github.com/liuhao-lh/SMD

Abstract. The performance of self-supervised learning (SSL) models is hindered by the scale of the network. Existing SSL methods suffer a precipitous drop in lightweight models, which is important for many mobile devices. To address this problem, we propose a method to improve the lightweight network (as student) via distilling the metric knowledge in a larger SSL model (as teacher). We exploit the relation between teacher and student to mine the positive and negative supervision from the unlabeled data, which captures more accurate supervision signals. To adaptively handle the uncertainty in positive and negative sample pairs, we incorporate a dynamic weighting strategy to the metric relation between embeddings. Different from previous self-supervised distillers, our solution directly optimizes the network from a metric transfer perspective by utilizing the relationships between samples and networks, without additional SSL constraints. Our method significantly boosts the performance of lightweight networks and outperforms existing distillers with fewer training epochs on the large-scale ImageNet. Interestingly, the SSL performance even beats the teacher network in several settings.

1 Introduction

As an effective way to explore the information in the data itself, self-supervised learning (SSL) can obtain discriminative task-agnostic representations, while allowing the training without prohibitively expensive data annotation. Recently, there has been impressive progress in SSL [4,6,7,11,15,35]. Some SSL models trained on the large-scale ImageNet without labels have achieved comparable or even better accuracy than the supervised models when transferred to downstream tasks, such as semi-supervised image classification and object detection.

Generally, the gap between supervised and self-supervised is much smaller when increasing the capacity of the network architecture [1]. Therefore, the top-performing SSL algorithms usually require large networks as their backbone. This greatly limits the applicability of SSL for many mobile devices with limited

S. Avidan et al. (Eds.): ECCV 2022, LNCS 13691, pp. 295–311, 2022.
https://doi.org/10.1007/978-3-031-19821-2_17

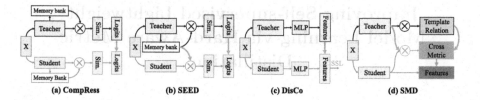

Fig. 1. Comparison with existing self-supervised distillers. X is the input images. The red arrow indicates the knowledge transfer direction. Both (a) CompRess [1] and (b) SEED [9] transfer the knowledge of the similarity between a sample and a negative memory bank. (c) DisCo [10] constrains the last embedding of the student to be consistent with that of the teacher. (d) Our SMD mines and optimizes the metric relationship between samples in a batch, which does not need to maintain a memory bank. It also utilizes embedding relations between the teacher and student models.

capacity, *i.e.*, the lightweight model is preferred in edge computing applications. However, existing SSL methods do not work well on the lightweight network. For example, the linear evaluation of MobileNet-V3-Large [19], its Top-1 accuracy on ImageNet using MoCo-V2 is only 36.2%, which is far from satisfying compared to its fully supervised counterparts 75.2% [10]. This motivates us to investigate a feasible solution to design powerful lightweight SSL models.

To learn better representations for lightweight self-supervised models, many researchers set out to solve this problem from the perspective of knowledge distillation. Most supervised distillers [18,29] cannot be extended to self-supervised distillation since the self-supervision paradigm does not contain any training labels. We illustrate some recently proposed self-supervised distillers in Fig. 1. CompRess [1] and SEED [9] utilize the memory bank in MoCo [15] for knowledge transfer. DisCo [10] and SimDis [12] extract extra supervision from the representation and optimize the student model by aligning the features between the same samples. However, they are constrained by the self-supervised learning framework that simply assumes non-target images as negative samples. None of them has explored the relationships between samples under the self-supervised knowledge distillation task.

In the well-trained larger SSL teacher space, we assume that the distance between positive sample pairs is small, and the distance between negative sample pairs is large. During the distillation, the lightweight student optimizes toward the teacher, *i.e.*, for the same sample, the distance between the teacher features and student features should not be large, where we name this distance as *teacher-to-student metric difference*. In the teacher space, if the distance between two samples is smaller than the above *teacher-to-student metric difference*, we can consider that the distance is small enough so that these two samples are treated as positive sample pairs. Otherwise, these two samples are negative pairs. Based on this idea, we divide unlabeled data into positive and negative sample pairs and thus perform effective knowledge distillation from the perspective of the metric relation under the self-supervised learning setting, *i.e.*, making positive pairs concentrated and negative pairs separated. We utilize the metric differences between the well-trained teacher and to-be-optimized student model, acting as a dynamic decision boundary to divide positive and negative sets without category label supervision.

In this work, we propose a novel Self-supervised Metric Distillation (SMD) for lightweight model learning. Specifically, we optimize the metric relation between teacher and student embeddings. Unlike previous self-supervised training and distillation methods, we focus on optimizing difficult pairs rather than all sample pairs. Therefore, we introduce a hard mining strategy to improve the widely adopted *Info-NCE* [23]. Inevitably, there will be some incorrectly divided positive and negative sample pairs. To reduce their influence, we generate weight coefficients based on the metric relation between teacher and student embeddings. This prevents incorrectly divided samples from affecting the optimization and also gives different sample pairs different optimization strengths, thereby effectively improving the performance of the student model. With the help of the above strategies, our SMD has achieved compelling results without any complex projectors [10,12] or a huge negative sample queue [1,9].

Our method performs more accurate optimization based on the positive and negative sample pairs mined by the teacher-guided metric difference. We present comprehensive experiments on CIFAR100 and ImageNet to evaluate our distillation method in the self-supervised manner. Furthermore, our method can also be deployed in a supervised distillation framework, which not only surpasses many supervised distillation methods but also obtains state-of-the-art results. Overall, our contributions can be summarized as follows:

- In the self-supervised distillation framework, we are the first to attempt to explore the explicit relationship between samples and find an effective strategy to divide positive and negative pairs from unlabeled data through the *teacher-to-student metric difference.*
- We design a self-supervised hard-aware metric distillation approach that optimizes the student embeddings by adaptively utilizing the teacher relation supervision, which can weaken the impact of incorrectly divided samples.
- Our method significantly improves the performance of lightweight models in the self-supervised knowledge distillation task and achieves a much higher accuracy than other methods in self-supervised knowledge distillation.
- Our method can also be seamlessly applied in the supervised distillation framework without network modification and achieves much a higher accuracy than existing supervised distillers. The learned student network even outperforms the teacher in some settings.

2   Related Work

Supervised Knowledge Distillation is commonly used in the supervised paradigm to improve the performance of lightweight models under extra supervision from powerful but large models, which is also called model compression [3]. Early work achieved this by aligning the network logits [18] or the intermediate representations [26]. Recently, many works have proposed to transfer carefully designed statistics from teacher to student networks, which includes attention maps [38], mutual information [2,29], probability distributions [25], maximum mean discrepancies [20] and activation boundaries of the hidden neurons [17].

Self-supervised Knowledge Distillation. Most effective distillation have a supervised loss term [5,18,29]. Thus, they cannot be directly applied to self-supervised models since the self-supervision paradigm does not contain any training labels. Some recent works have made some attempts to solve this problem. Both CompR [1] and SEED [9] are inherited from the idea of the negative sample queue in MoCo [15]. They use KL-divergence to align two probability distributions, which is obtained by computing the similarity between the sample features and the features stored in the queue. For DisCo [10] and SimDis [12], their core idea is to optimize the output of the teacher model and the student model for the same sample via L_2 loss. All these methods are constrained by the idea of the self-supervision training framework, where all samples except the target are considered as negative samples. Our SMD attempts to dig deeper into the relationship between samples from unlabeled data in the knowledge distillation framework and optimize specific sample pairs directly from a metric learning perspective, which as far as we know has not yet been investigated.

3   Proposed Method

Our SMD aims at optimizing the student features by distilling the feature embeddings learned from the teacher. The main idea is to find the set of positive and negative sample pairs from the unlabeled data, then optimize the relative distances between the fixed teacher features and optimizable student features, reinforcing the student features' discriminability under the teacher's supervision.

3.1   Difference-Guided Positive and Negative Mining

Given a well-trained self-supervised teacher model $f^t(\cdot)$ and a randomly initialized student model $f^s(\cdot)$, the student/teacher feature of an unlabeled input image x_i is represented as $f^s(x_i)/f^t(x_i)$. The core idea of the previous approaches [10,12] is to directly optimize the features between $f^s(x_i)$ and $f^t(x_i)$. This obviously ignores the influence of the critical negative samples [14,32]. However, it is not feasible to randomly choose one of the unlabeled data as the negative sample because the network performance will be affected if the selected one is a positive sample. Since there is a huge gap between a well pre-trained teacher model and a randomly initialized student model. This leads us to the following intuition: *Could we find the positive and negative samples in the unlabeled data based on the differences between teacher and student models?*

Take x_i as the anchor. For another image x_a in the batch, we calculate its teacher embedding $f^t(x_a)$. Let $D(\cdot)$ be a metric function measuring the distance between two images in the embedding space. A larger D indicates a

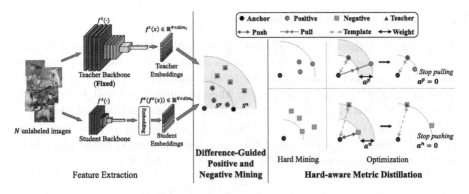

Fig. 2. Schematization of SMD: 1) *Feature Extraction:* Teacher and student extract embeddings for unlabeled images. 2) *Difference-Guided Positive and Negative Mining* Sect. 3.1: The positive and negative samples are divided according to the embeddings of teacher and student networks. The embeddings with red triangles (▲) are from the teacher network and those without red triangles are from the student network. 3) *Hard-aware Metric Distillation* Sect. 3.2: Find the hardest samples from the positive and negative set respectively, and then optimize the cross metric between student and teacher embeddings based on template relations. Best viewed in color. Zoom in for details. (Color figure online)

lower similarity between two embeddings. Here, we adopt the Euclidean distance $D(\boldsymbol{f}(x_i), \boldsymbol{f}(x_j)) = \|\bar{\boldsymbol{f}}(x_i) - \bar{\boldsymbol{f}}(x_j)\|_2$, in which $\bar{\boldsymbol{f}}(x_i)$ and $\bar{\boldsymbol{f}}(x_j)$ are normalized embedding features. Since the teacher is well trained, $D(\boldsymbol{f}^t(x_i), \boldsymbol{f}^t(x_a))$ is generally small if x_i and x_a belong to the same category. We identify x_i and x_a as a positive pair when $D(\boldsymbol{f}^t(x_i), \boldsymbol{f}^t(x_a))$ is smaller than a decision boundary, and vice versa [34]. Here, the decision boundary about D is critical. Setting it as a hyper-parameter is a spontaneous idea for tackling this problem, but it is impossible to separate all positive and negative sample pairs with only one hyper-parameter. During the distillation, the lightweight student optimizes toward the teacher, but the cumbersome teacher network and the lightweight student models are usually very different in structure, which will make it impossible for $\boldsymbol{f}^t(x_i)$ and $\boldsymbol{f}^s(x_i)$ to match perfectly. We name this little gap *teacher-to-student metric difference*, and tentatively believe that it can provide some useful information:

$$(x_i, x_a) \in \begin{cases} S_i^p, & D(\boldsymbol{f}^t(x_i), \boldsymbol{f}^t(x_a)) < D(\boldsymbol{f}^t(x_i), \boldsymbol{f}^s(x_i)), \\ S_i^n, & D(\boldsymbol{f}^t(x_i), \boldsymbol{f}^t(x_a)) \geq D(\boldsymbol{f}^t(x_i), \boldsymbol{f}^s(x_i)). \end{cases} \tag{1}$$

For x_i, other samples in the batch are divided into the positive set S_i^p and negative set S_i^n. Moreover, different samples have different *teacher-to-student metric differences* $D(\boldsymbol{f}^t(x_i), \boldsymbol{f}^s(x_i))$, which serve as the dynamical decision boundaries (Fig. 2).

3.2 Hard-Aware Metric Distillation

We assume that the obtained S_i^p and S_i^n are both reliable. The primary goal of our hard-aware metric distillation is to optimize the cross metric relation between teacher and student features in the embedding space, *i.e.*, for every sample x_i, pull $\boldsymbol{f}^t(x_i)$ and $\boldsymbol{f}^s(x_j)$ closer while pushing $\boldsymbol{f}^t(x_i)$ and $\boldsymbol{f}^s(x_k)$ apart, where $x_j \in S_i^p$, and $x_k \in S_i^n$. For simplicity, we use the shorthand notation $d_{ij}^p = D(\boldsymbol{f}^t(x_i), \boldsymbol{f}^s(x_j))$, $d_{ik}^n = D(\boldsymbol{f}^t(x_i), \boldsymbol{f}^s(x_k))$. The learning target is to increase all d_{ik}^n and decrease all d_{ij}^p. To achieve this, we adopt an *Info-NCE*-like loss [23] to distill the metric knowledge learned in the teacher network:

$$\mathcal{L}_i = -\log \frac{\sum_{k=1}^{K} \exp(d_{ik}^n / \tau)}{\sum_{k=1}^{K} \exp(d_{ik}^n / \tau) + \sum_{j=1}^{J} \exp(d_{ij}^p / \tau)}, \tag{2}$$

where τ is a temperature hyper-parameter. K and J represent the number of samples in S_i^n and S_i^p, respectively. For every x_i, the student network pulls all positive embeddings $\boldsymbol{f}^s(x_j)$ towards $\boldsymbol{f}^t(x_i)$, and pushes all negative embeddings $\boldsymbol{f}^s(x_k)$ away from $\boldsymbol{f}^t(x_i)$.

However, it is cost-prohibitive to perform the above optimization for all sample pairs even in a batch. To improve this, we revisit Eq. (2), in which τ is always set to quite small [9,15,33]. This will sharpen the probability distribution [18], which makes a few key samples dominate the entire loss. From this, we speculate that the hardest case should play a key role. We utilize an online batch hard mining strategy based on the S_i^p and S_i^n. Specifically, we select the positive and negative cross-model pairs within each sampled batch online. First, we calculate the cross-relation embedding distance of each image pair for the student and teacher networks in a batch. For each anchor's teacher embedding $\boldsymbol{f}^t(x_i)$, we select its hardest positive and hardest negative samples from the student embeddings. The online mining process is formulated as:

$$d_i^p = \max_{j \in S_i^p} d_{ij}^p, \quad d_i^n = \min_{k \in S_i^n} d_{ik}^n, \tag{3}$$

where d_i^p and d_i^n represent the hardest positive and negative pair mined from the student features for anchor x_i. With the selected hard positives and negatives, our learning target evolves from Eq. (2) to:

$$\mathcal{L}_i = -\log \frac{\exp(d_i^n / \tau)}{\exp(d_i^n / \tau) + \exp(d_i^p / \tau)}. \tag{4}$$

The denominator only contains one hardest positive pair and one hardest negative pair. By minimizing Eq. (4), we pull the hardest positive pair closer and push the hardest negative pair farther.

There will inevitably be some incorrectly divided sample pairs in S_i^p and S_i^n. Though Eq. (4) allows the optimization process to focus on a few key samples, it also amplifies the impact of these incorrectly divided pairs. We can prevent these wrong samples from hindering the optimization process if they can be ruled out, *i.e.*, assign zero weight to these samples. Here, we improve Eq. (4) by a teacher-guided self-supervised weighting mechanism, which re-assigns the contribution of different d_i^p and d_i^n in the overall optimization process:

$$\mathcal{L}_i^{md} = -\log \frac{\exp(a_i^n d_i^n / \tau)}{\exp(a_i^n d_i^n / \tau) + \exp(a_i^p d_i^p / \tau)}, \qquad (5)$$

where a_i^p and a_i^n are non-negative weighting factors.

Given an anchor sample x_i with teacher features $\boldsymbol{f}^t(x_i)$, we first get its hardest positive x_{j^h} and the hardest negative samples x_{k^h} from S_i^p and S_i^n. After identifying the hardest sample index from all the student features, we calculate the distances $D(\boldsymbol{f}^t(x_i), \boldsymbol{f}^t(x_{j^h}))$ and $D(\boldsymbol{f}^t(x_i), \boldsymbol{f}^t(x_{k^h}))$ within the teacher embedding space. These two distances are encoded as the main guidance for optimizing d_i^p and d_i^n, so a_i^p and a_i^n in Eq. (5) are defined in a teacher-guided self-supervised manner as:

$$\begin{cases} a_i^p = [d_i^p - D(\boldsymbol{f}^t(x_i), \boldsymbol{f}^t(x_{j^h}))]_+, \\ a_i^n = [D(\boldsymbol{f}^t(x_i), \boldsymbol{f}^t(x_{k^h})) - d_i^n]_+. \end{cases} \qquad (6)$$

where $D(\boldsymbol{f}^t(x_i), \boldsymbol{f}^t(x_{j^h}))$ and $D(\boldsymbol{f}^t(x_i), \boldsymbol{f}^t(x_{k^h}))$ are template relations; $[]_+$ is the "cut-off at zero" operation to ensure a_i^p and a_i^n are non-negative, and also stops the optimization process when the student network outperforms the teacher network. When the sample pair is incorrectly divided, optimizing Eq. (5) will go against our goal if all weighting factors are 1. With Eq. (6), the optimization will be stopped when the false-negative samples are pushed far beyond the template relation or false-positive samples are pulled close within the template relation. a_i^p and a_i^n will set the optimization of the incorrect pair right. Here the template relation is the lower bound of the worst case. When the sample pair is correctly divided, the ideal convergence status is that d_i^p and d_i^n are better than the template relation instead of pulling positive samples as close as possible and pushing negative samples as far as possible. This moderate training goal can also improve the generalization ability.

3.3 Learning Constraint

Embedding Alignment. Since student and teacher networks have different structures, their embedding spaces are often different. It is difficult for the student network to find the correct embedding space where the teacher network features are located since our method is to optimize the metric relationship between the features. To solve this, we added $\mathcal{L}_2$ constraint in the first few training epochs to directly align the embedding space of the teacher and student networks:

$$\mathcal{L}_i^{align} = ||\bar{\boldsymbol{f}}^t(x_i) - \bar{\boldsymbol{f}}^s(x_i)||^2.$$

Feature Embedding Transformation. To calculate d_i^p and d_i^n in Eq.(5), a straightforward solution is to directly adopt the backbone features of the student and teacher networks as $f^s(x)$ and $f^t(x)$. However, the student and teacher usually have different backbone structures, thus $f^s(x)$ and $f^t(x)$ are not directly comparable due to different dimensions dim_s and dim_t. Therefore, we introduce an embedding layer $e(\cdot)$ to encode the student backbone features $f^s(x)$. The embedding layer is composed of a FC layer. The output of embedding layer $f^e(f^s(x))$ with dimension dim_t takes the place of student backbone features $f^s(x)$ for hard-aware metric distillation. Compared with the backbone features, the feature dimension of $f^e(f^s(x))$ is easier to adjust when the teacher and student networks have different structures.

The overall training loss for our proposed SMD is:

$$\mathcal{L}_{SMD} = \frac{1}{N} \sum_{i=1}^{N} (\mathcal{L}_i^{md} + \mathcal{L}_i^{align}), \tag{7}$$

where N is the batch size. Experimentally, it is sufficient to add the $\mathcal{L}_2$ constraint only in the first one or two epochs, which only accounts for 0.2% to 1% of the whole training process. Without this constraint, the training would not converge in most scenarios from experiments in Sect. 4.4.

4   Experiments

4.1   Self-supervised Distillation on CIFAR100

Dataset. In this section, all the experiments are conducted on CIFAR-100 [21], which contains 50K training images and 10K test images from a total of 100 classes. The image size is 32×32.

Self-Supervised Pre-training of Vanilla Network. We use SimSiam [7] to pre-train the vanilla teacher and student network. ResNet [16] and Wide-ResNet [37] are selected as the teacher network. A projector (a two-layer multi-layer-perceptron (MLP) with batch normalization (BN)) and a predictor (a two-layer MLP and the output linear layer has no BN and ReLU) are appended at the end of the encoder (backbone) after average pooling. All networks are pre-trained for 800 epochs by a standard SGD optimizer with a momentum of 0.9 and a weight decay parameter of 5e-4. The initial learning rate is set as 0.06 and updated by a cosine decay scheduler with 10 warm-up epochs. The batch size is 512. For MobileNet and ShuffleNet, the initial learning rate is 0.012.

Self-Supervised Distillation on Student Network. We choose multiple lightweight networks as the student network: ResNet and Wide-ResNet with fewer layers, MobileNet [27] and ShuffleNet [22]. The hyper-parameter τ is set to 0.02. All training strategies are consistent with the vanilla network.

Linear and kNN Evaluation. In order to validate the effectiveness of our SMD, we treat the network as a frozen feature extractor after self-supervised pre-training/distillation and train a linear classifier on the labeled training set. The initial learning rate is set as 30 and updated by a cosine decay scheduler. The batch size is 256. SGD optimizer with momentum 0.9 is used for 100 epochs training and the weight decay is 0. We also perform classification using K-Nearest Neighbors (kNN) based on the backbone feature by taking the most frequent label of its K (K = 200) nearest neighbors.

Table 1. Results on the CIFAR-100 under self-supervised distillation framework. The kNN accuracy (%) and Top-1 classification accuracy (%) for transferring across some teacher and student architectures.

Methods	T:resnet 32×4 S:resnet 32		T:WRN-40-2 S:WRN-16-2		T:resnet 32×4 S:MobileNetV2		T:ResNet-50 S:ShuffleNetV2		T:WRN-40-2 S:ShuffleNetV2	
	kNN	Top-1	kNN	Top-1	kNN	Top-1	kNN	Top-1	kNN	Top-1
Teacher	60.63	67.27	56.16	63.16	61.89	69.96	60.63	67.27	56.16	63.16
Student	46.35	52.54	48.45	58.58	26.88	35.87	31.78	48.90	31.78	48.90
L_2	49.68	55.48	52.60	60.16	54.34	58.43	58.52	66.25	55.37	63.73
SSL+SMD	52.52	57.97	53.42	60.92	56.89	61.32	60.12	67.43	**57.32**	67.11
SMD	**52.54**	**58.15**	**53.53**	**60.98**	**57.12**	**61.89**	**60.21**	**67.70**	57.16	**67.88**

Table 1 compares Top-1 accuracy using kNN and using linear evaluation (Top-1) with different teacher-student combinations. We list the baseline results of self-supervised pre-training using SimSiam in the first and second rows for each teacher-student combination. We observe that our SMD consistently outperforms the student baseline. Moreover, the performance of the student network will be improved with a better teacher network. In addition, we explore several alternative distillation strategies. L_2: the core idea of [10] and [12]. The embeddings of the same image are pulled closer. _SMD+SSL_: add the self-supervised loss to our method. Our SMD has a considerable improvement compared to L_2 when the structure of the teacher and student network is quite different (the last three columns). We conjecture that optimizing more abstract metric knowledge is easier to generalize than directly pulling two embeddings that are not in the same space closer. Moreover, we study the effect of the original SSL supervision as supplementary loss (SSL+SMD) and find it is not necessary for distillation. Perhaps the goals of distillation and self-supervised learning are different. Distillation forces the student network to mimic the predictions of the teacher network while self-supervised learning attempts to discover and learn latent patterns from the data itself, where the former contains more fruitful information.

4.2   Self-supervised Distillation on ImageNet

Dataset. In this section, all the experiments are conducted on the large-scale ImageNet 2012 dataset [8], which provides 1,281,167 images from 1,000 classes for training and 50,000 for validation.

Self-Supervised Pre-training of Vanilla Network. We use the official model ResNet-50 (100 epochs) released by SimSiam [7] as the teacher network. The SimSiam baseline of the student models is trained with the official Sim-Siam strategy, where all networks are pre-trained for 100 epochs by an SGD optimizer with a momentum of 0.9 and a weight decay parameter of 1e-4. The initial learning rate is 0.1 with a 512 batch size and updated by a cosine decay scheduler.

Self-Supervised Distillation on Student Network. We choose multiple lightweight networks as the student network: ResNet with 18 and 34 layers, MobileNet-V3-Large [19], EfficientNet-B0 and EfficientNet-B1 [28]. τ is set to 0.04. All training strategies are consistent with the vanilla network.

Linear Evaluation. We train a linear classifier on top of the frozen network encoder after self-supervised pre-training/distillation. Use the LARS optimizer [36] for 90 epochs training with a cosine decay learning rate schedule. The base learning rate is 0.1, scaled linearly with the batch size (LearningRate = $0.1 \times$ BatchSize/256). The results are reported in terms of Top-1 and Top-5 accuracy.

Table 2. Comparison of distillation methods on full ImageNet. Top-1 and Top-5 linear evaluation accuracy (%) for multiple students on full ImageNet validation set. The teacher network for all methods is ResNet-50. MoCo-V2 and SimSiam denote self-supervised learning baselines before distillation. We denote by * methods where we use our re-implementation based on the paper; for all other methods we use the results reported by their original papers. The first row shows the supervised performances of student networks. "–" means the student network collapses or has poor results.

	Epoch	ResNet-18		ResNet-34		Efficient-B0		Efficient-B1		Mobile-V3	
		Top-1	Top-5	Top-1	Top-5	Top-1	Top-5	Top-1	Top-5	Top-1	Top-5
Supervised		69.5	89.1	73.3	91.4	77.3	95.3	79.2	94.5	75.2	92.2
MoCo-V2	200	52.5	77.0	57.4	81.6	42.2	68.5	50.7	74.6	36.3	62.2
SEED	200	57.9	82.0	58.5	82.6	61.3	82.7	61.4	83.1	55.2	80.3
DisCo	200	60.6	83.7	62.5	85.4	66.5	87.6	66.6	87.5	64.4	86.2
SimSiam	100	30.5	57.2	33.4	59.7	–	–	–	–	–	–
CompR-1q*	100	60.5	83.0	62.1	84.2	65.2	86.3	65.8	86.5	62.7	85.1
SMD	100	**61.8**	**84.3**	**64.1**	**86.0**	**66.5**	87.4	**66.8**	87.3	**64.5**	**86.7**

Table 2 compares the results of different distillation objectives on multiple teacher-student pairs. The SimSiam(baseline) even collapses in some cases, and related studies [9] conjecture that smaller models with fewer parameters cannot effectively learn instance-level discriminative representation with a large amount of unlabeled data. The student models distilled by SMD outperform the counterparts pre-trained by SimSiam by a large margin. Besides, we observe that our SMD consistently outperforms all other distillation objectives. Note that SEED [9] and DisCo [10] use the MoCo-V2 [15] training strategy that performs better on lightweight models and needs more training epochs. Due to the computational limitation, unlike SEED and DisCo, we use the SimSiam baseline that only needs to train 100 epochs. Almost all papers about self-supervised learning and distillation have verified that the final results benefit from more training epochs [6,10]. In addition, DisCo needs an MLP with a large dimension of the hidden layer to deal with the *distilling bottleneck* phenomenon. SEED needs to maintain a large negative sample queue with a length of 65,536. The additional parameters required by our SMD are only a fully connected layer used to align the feature dimensions of the teacher and student models. Our method achieves better results than other methods on a weaker baseline and fewer additional parameters, verifying that SMD can learn effective metric relationships from unlabeled data.

The self-supervised distillation performance is greatly influenced by the training strategy, so we re-implement CompR [1] by the training strategy of SMD. Under the same training strategy, our SMD also surpasses CompR-1q by a large margin. CompR relies heavily on a huge negative sample queue with a length of 128,000. When the size of the negative sample queue decreases, their performance drops rapidly [1]. It is worth noting that our method can outperform CompR by directly optimizing real-time instance features with online hard mining in a 256-size batch. Both SEED and CompR are derived from the idea of latent negative sampling [33]. They treat all non-target unlabeled samples as negative, which misclassifies some positive samples. Our SMD mines positive and negative pairs from unlabeled samples, which is a good solution to this problem.

Table 3. CIFAR-100 Top-1 *accuracy* (%) under supervised distillation framework, when the student and teacher share similar network architecture.

	WRN-40-2	WRN-40-2	resnet56	resnet110	resnet110	vgg13
	WRN-16-2	WRN-40-1	resnet20	resnet20	resnet32	vgg8
Teacher	75.61	75.61	72.34	74.31	74.31	74.64
Student	73.26	71.98	69.06	69.06	71.14	70.36
KD [18]	74.92	73.54	70.66	70.67	73.08	72.98
FitNet [26]	73.58	72.24	69.21	68.99	71.06	71.02
SP [30]	73.83	72.43	69.67	70.04	72.69	72.68
RKD [24]	73.35	72.22	69.61	69.25	71.82	71.48
KDCL [13]	73.93	73.12	70.58	70.36	72.67	72.94
CRD [29]	75.48	74.14	71.16	71.46	73.48	73.94
WCoRD [5]	75.88	74.73	71.56	71.57	73.81	74.55
SMD	**76.39**	**74.76**	**71.59**	**71.62**	**73.94**	**74.84**

4.3 Applicability on Supervised Distillation Framework

To further highlight the superiority of SMD, we deploy our method in a supervised distillation framework, the baseline of which is usually a supervised classification problem. In the distillation part, the state-of-the-art supervised distillation methods usually use label information for knowledge transfer. We apply

SMD to the supervised distillation framework without any modification. The only difference between the supervised distillation and the unsupervised distillation framework is that we must add a fully connected layer after the backbone of the student network and a classification loss will be trained together with our Eq.(7). Note that the distillation part of our SMD does not use any label information.

We evaluate our SMD on CIFAR-100 following the training procedure of CRD [29] in all the experiments for fair comparisons. All the models are trained for 240 epochs by SGD, and the learning rate drops by 0.1 after 150, 180, and 210 epochs. We set the weight decay to 5e-4, the batch size N to 64, and the momentum to 0.9. The initial learning rate is 0.05 for all models except MobileNet and ShuffleNet, where it is 0.01. τ is set to 0.04.

Table 3 and Table 4 list different teacher-student pairs to verify that our method is robust. We also listed some classic methods (KD [18] and FitNet [26]) and recently proposed methods with better performance [5,13,24,29,30]. For WCoRD and KDCL, we use the results that are reported in their original paper. For all other methods, we use author-provided or author-verified code from the CRD repository. We can observe that our SMD can consistently outperform all other distillation methods with a large margin, including the recent state-of-the-art CRD and WCoRD. Note that most of these methods require the label information in the distillation process to mine the relationships between samples. For example, CRD heavily relies on accurate negative samples provided by annotated labels. Our SMD does not require any label information in the distillation process and effectively completes knowledge transfer in a self-supervised manner. In particular, our students outperform the teachers in some cases (WRN-40-2 to WRN-16-2, vgg13 to vgg8, and WRN-40-2 to ShuffleNetV1). This benefits from "cut-off at zero" strategy in Eq.(6). The knowledge learned in the teacher model may be redundant, so the teacher is not the optimal solution. In the distillation task, the student uses the optimization directions provided by the teacher, combined with the directions of the student's gradients, jointly find-

Table 4. CIFAR-100 Top-1 *accuracy* (%) under supervised distillation framework, for transfer across very different teacher and student architectures.

	ResNet-50	ResNet-50	resnet32x4	resnet32x4	WRN-40-2
	MobileNetV2	vgg8	ShuffleNetV1	ShuffleNetV2	ShuffleNetV1
Teacher	79.34	79.34	79.42	79.42	75.61
Student	64.60	70.36	70.50	71.82	70.50
KD [18]	67.35	73.81	74.07	74.45	74.83
FitNet [26]	63.16	70.69	73.59	73.54	73.73
SP [30]	68.08	73.34	73.48	74.56	74.52
RKD [24]	64.43	71.50	72.28	73.21	72.21
KDCL [13]	67.64	73.03	74.32	75.35	74.79
CRD [29]	69.11	74.30	75.11	75.65	76.05
WCoRD [5]	70.45	74.86	75.40	75.96	76.32
SMD	**70.76**	**74.95**	**76.21**	**76.82**	**76.89**

ing an optimal solution. "cut-off at zero" retains this optimization state, rather than letting students continue optimizing towards the teacher.

4.4   Analysis

In this section, all experiments are conducted on two teacher-student combinations under the supervised distillation framework, MobileNetV2 supervised by ResNet-50 and resnet20 supervised by resnet56. We first comprehensively verify the correctness of the positive and negative sets obtained by Eq.(1). Following that, we show the necessity of the weighting factors, hard mining and L_2 loss.

Table 5. Statistical information for positive and negative mining. Total Accuracy (%), TP, TN, FP, and FN for MobileNetV2 with batch=64.

Epoch	Accuracy(%)	TP	TN	FP	FN
1 (10 iter)	2.25	92	0	4004	0
1 (30 iter)	76.73	102	3041	953	0
1 (100 iter)	99.37	104	3966	26	0
2	99.53	108	3969	17	2
150	99.17	81	3981	1	33
240	99.12	74	3986	0	36

Table 6. Statistical information in the mined hardest negatives/positives with and without weighting factors. TP, TN, FP, and FN for MobileNetV2 with batch=64.

Epoch	SMD				SMD *without* weighting factors			
	TP	TN	FP	FN	TP	TN	FP	FN
1 (30 iter)	5	63	59	1	0	6	6	0
1 (100 iter)	49	64	15	0	9	64	55	0
2	59	64	5	0	36	64	28	0
150	62	64	2	0	14	64	50	0
240	64	64	0	0	11	64	53	0

Difference-Guided Positive and Negative Mining. To verify the accuracy of the difference-guided positive and negative mining, we list the changes of the total accuracy with the number of iterations in Table 5. The overall accuracy increases rapidly as the number of iterations increases, and soon reaches 99%. This verifies that our method can make a preliminary division. The accuracy seems to be satisfactory, but the number of positive and negative sample pairs is unbalanced since every batch is obtained by random sampling. To comprehensively evaluate the results, we count the True Positive (TP), True Negative

(TN), False Positive (FP), and False Negative (FN) in a batch during the training. In the first few iterations, most of the samples are classified as positive pairs because the embedding spaces of teachers and students are not aligned and the *teacher-to-student metric difference* is large. After the two spaces are aligned, our method of obtaining positive and negative sets yields almost accurate results in the early epoch. This verifies that the *teacher-to-student metric difference* can indeed serve as a decision boundary that can be used to divide positive and negative samples. In the later stage, this difference will become very small because the student embedding has been trained toward the teacher embedding and our supervision mining method tends to divide more pairs as negative. Fortunately, these incorrectly divided pairs will not affect our performance due to the hard mining strategy and the weighting factors in Eq.(6). From another perspective, knowledge distillation aims to lower the gap between student and teacher spaces. The gradual shrinking of the decision boundary and positive examples will ensure that the embedding space learned by the student is similar to that of the teacher. In the limit, the two spaces will be perfectly aligned when the decision boundary is zero. This gradual way of adjusting the positive and negative pairs is conducive to SSL distillation.

Importance of Hard Mining. Hard mining is introduced based on the assumption that the hardest case plays a key role in optimization [31], and it also prevents all pairs from performing cost-prohibitive optimization. In addition to these, we find that hard mining can weaken the impact of incorrectly divided pairs. Table 6 lists the statistical results of our SMD in the mined hardest negatives/positives. In the later training stage, almost all the hardest samples are correct. Combined with the data in Table 5, we reasonably infer that although some FNs are positive, for the well-trained teacher, these FNs are further away from the anchor compared to the hardest negative samples. Therefore, these FNs do not affect our optimization after hard mining, nor do FPs.

Weighting Factors. We conducted a comparison using our SMD and SMD without a_i^p and a_i^n. The Top-1 result for MobileNetV2 decreases from 70.76 to 63.48. For resnet20, from 71.56 to 69.05. Adding such a weighting factor brings a substantial improvement. Table 6 also lists the statistical results in the mined hardest negatives/positives of SMD without weighting factors. At the 30th iteration, only 6 out of 64 samples find the corresponding positive and negative sample pairs. Since the student network has not converged, the remaining 58 samples cannot find the corresponding negative samples and fail to join the distillation (all other samples are classified as positive). From 150 to 240 epoch, the TP even gradually decreases. Hard mining allows distillation to focus on optimizing difficult samples, but it also can exacerbate errors due to samples with inevitable wrong division, resulting in even worse performance than baseline. By introducing these two dynamic weighting factors, the impact of incorrectly divided pairs is greatly mitigated. This brilliant design can also provide a moderate optimization target for the correct sample pairs, thereby significantly improving the distillation results.

Necessity of L_2 loss. When the L_2 loss was completely removed, the Top-1 accuracy for MobileNetV2 decreases to 65.65, but only a slight change for resnet20, to 71.64. We can infer that L_2 loss plays a key role although it only acts on the first two epochs. When the structural differences between the student and the teacher are too large and the embeddings of the student network fail to find the embedding space of the teacher network, SMD cannot converge without L_2 loss. Note that the absence of L_2 loss does not degrade the performance when the student network can easily find the embedding space of the teacher network. These observations suggest that L_2 loss can help align the embedding space, but the final performance of SMD will not benefit from it.

5   Conclusion

In this work, we propose SMD to effectively improve the lightweight SSL model via distilling the metric information. Our solution utilizes the relationship between samples from unlabeled data in the knowledge distillation framework, which has not yet been investigated. Moreover, we also incorporate a dynamic weighting strategy to handle pairwise uncertainty adaptively. Extensive experiments demonstrate that our proposed SMD achieves state-of-the-art performance on various benchmarks of lightweight models.

Acknowledgment. This work is supported by National Natural Science Foundation of China (62176188), Key Research and Development Program of Hubei Province (2021BAA187), Special Fund of Hubei Luojia Laboratory (220100015).

References

1. Abbasi Koohpayegani, S., Tejankar, A., Pirsiavash, H.: Compress: self-supervised learning by compressing representations. NeurIPS **33**, 12980–12992 (2020)
2. Ahn, S., Hu, S.X., Damianou, A., Lawrence, N.D., Dai, Z.: Variational information distillation for knowledge transfer. In: CVPR, pp. 9163–9171 (2019)
3. Buciluă, C., Caruana, R., Niculescu-Mizil, A.: Model compression. In: ACM SIGKDD, pp. 535–541 (2006)
4. Caron, M., Misra, I., Mairal, J., Goyal, P., Bojanowski, P., Joulin, A.: Unsupervised learning of visual features by contrasting cluster assignments. arXiv preprint arXiv:2006.09882 (2020)
5. Chen, L., Wang, D., Gan, Z., Liu, J., Henao, R., Carin, L.: Wasserstein contrastive representation distillation. In: CVPR, pp. 16296–16305 (2021)
6. Chen, T., Kornblith, S., Norouzi, M., Hinton, G.: A simple framework for contrastive learning of visual representations. In: ICML, pp. 1597–1607. PMLR (2020)
7. Chen, X., He, K.: Exploring simple siamese representation learning. In: CVPR, pp. 15750–15758 (2021)
8. Deng, J., Dong, W., Socher, R., Li, L.J., Li, K., Fei-Fei, L.: Imagenet: a large-scale hierarchical image database. In: CVPR, pp. 248–255. IEEE (2009)

9. Fang, Z., Wang, J., Wang, L., Zhang, L., Yang, Y., Liu, Z.: Seed: self-supervised distillation for visual representation. arXiv preprint arXiv:2101.04731 (2021)

10. Gao, Y., et al.: Disco: Remedy self-supervised learning on lightweight models with distilled contrastive learning. arXiv preprint arXiv:2104.09124 (2021)

11. Grill, J.B., et al.: Bootstrap your own latent: a new approach to self-supervised learning. arXiv preprint arXiv:2006.07733 (2020)

12. Gu, J., Liu, W., Tian, Y.: Simple distillation baselines for improving small self-supervised models. arXiv preprint arXiv:2106.11304 (2021)

13. Guo, Q., et al.: Online knowledge distillation via collaborative learning. In: CVPR, pp. 11020–11029 (2020)

14. Hadsell, R., Chopra, S., LeCun, Y.: Dimensionality reduction by learning an invariant mapping. In: 2006 IEEE Computer Society Conference on Computer Vision and Pattern Recognition (CVPR 2006), vol. 2, pp. 1735–1742. IEEE (2006)

15. He, K., Fan, H., Wu, Y., Xie, S., Girshick, R.: Momentum contrast for unsupervised visual representation learning. In: CVPR, pp. 9729–9738 (2020)

16. He, K., Zhang, X., Ren, S., Sun, J.: Deep residual learning for image recognition. In: CVPR, pp. 770–778 (2016)

17. Heo, B., Lee, M., Yun, S., Choi, J.Y.: Knowledge transfer via distillation of activation boundaries formed by hidden neurons. In: AAAI, vol. 33, pp. 3779–3787 (2019)

18. Hinton, G., Vinyals, O., Dean, J.: Distilling the knowledge in a neural network. arXiv preprint arXiv:1503.02531 (2015)

19. Howard, A., et al.: Searching for mobilenetv3. In: ICCV, pp. 1314–1324 (2019)

20. Huang, Z., Wang, N.: Like what you like: knowledge distill via neuron selectivity transfer. arXiv preprint arXiv:1707.01219 (2017)

21. Krizhevsky, A., Hinton, G., et al.: Learning multiple layers of features from tiny images (2009)

22. Ma, N., Zhang, X., Zheng, H.-T., Sun, J.: ShuffleNet V2: practical guidelines for efficient CNN architecture design. In: Ferrari, V., Hebert, M., Sminchisescu, C., Weiss, Y. (eds.) Computer Vision – ECCV 2018. LNCS, vol. 11218, pp. 122–138. Springer, Cham (2018). https://doi.org/10.1007/978-3-030-01264-9_8

23. Oord, A.v.d., Li, Y., Vinyals, O.: Representation learning with contrastive predictive coding. arXiv preprint arXiv:1807.03748 (2018)

24. Park, W., Kim, D., Lu, Y., Cho, M.: Relational knowledge distillation. In: CVPR, pp. 3967–3976 (2019)

25. Passalis, N., Tefas, A.: Learning deep representations with probabilistic knowledge transfer. In: Ferrari, V., Hebert, M., Sminchisescu, C., Weiss, Y. (eds.) ECCV 2018. LNCS, vol. 11215, pp. 283–299. Springer, Cham (2018). https://doi.org/10.1007/978-3-030-01252-6_17

26. Romero, A., Ballas, N., Kahou, S.E., Chassang, A., Gatta, C., Bengio, Y.: Fitnets: hints for thin deep nets. arXiv preprint arXiv:1412.6550 (2014)

27. Sandler, M., Howard, A., Zhu, M., Zhmoginov, A., Chen, L.C.: Mobilenetv 2: inverted residuals and linear bottlenecks. In: CVPR, pp. 4510–4520 (2018)

28. Tan, M., Le, Q.: Efficientnet: rethinking model scaling for convolutional neural networks. In: ICML, pp. 6105–6114. PMLR (2019)

29. Tian, Y., Krishnan, D., Isola, P.: Contrastive representation distillation. In: ICLR (2019)

30. Tung, F., Mori, G.: Similarity-preserving knowledge distillation. In: ICCV, pp. 1365–1374 (2019)

31. Wang, F., Liu, H.: Understanding the behaviour of contrastive loss. In: CVPR, pp. 2495–2504 (2021)

32. Weinberger, K.Q., Saul, L.K.: Distance metric learning for large margin nearest neighbor classification. J. Mach. Learn. Res. **10**(2) (2009)
33. Wu, Z., Xiong, Y., Yu, S.X., Lin, D.: Unsupervised feature learning via non-parametric instance discrimination. In: CVPR, pp. 3733–3742 (2018)
34. Ye, M., Li, H., Du, B., Shen, J., Shao, L., Hoi, S.C.: Collaborative refining for person re-identification with label noise. IEEE TIP **31**, 379–391 (2021)
35. Ye, M., Shen, J., Zhang, X., Yuen, P.C., Chang, S.F.: Augmentation invariant and instance spreading feature for softmax embedding. IEEE TPAMI **44**(02), 924–939 (2022)
36. You, Y., Gitman, I., Ginsburg, B.: Scaling sgd batch size to 32k for imagenet training, vol. 6, p. 12. arXiv preprint arXiv:1708.03888 (2017)
37. Zagoruyko, S., Komodakis, N.: Wide residual networks. arXiv preprint arXiv:1605.07146 (2016)
38. Zagoruyko, S., Komodakis, N.: Paying more attention to attention: improving the performance of convolutional neural networks via attention transfer. In: ICLR (2017). https://arxiv.org/abs/1612.03928

Object Discovery via Contrastive Learning for Weakly Supervised Object Detection

Jinhwan Seo[1] , Wonho Bae[2] , Danica J. Sutherland[2,3] ,
Junhyug Noh[4(✉)] , and Daijin Kim[1(✉)]

[1] Pohang University of Science and Technology, Pohang, South Korea
dkim@postech.ac.kr
[2] University of British Columbia, Endowment Lands, Canada
{whbae,dsuth}@cs.ubc.ca
[3] Alberta Machine Intelligence Institute, Edmonton, Canada
[4] Lawrence Livermore National Laboratory, Livermore, USA
noh1@llnl.gov

Abstract. Weakly Supervised Object Detection (WSOD) is a task that detects objects in an image using a model trained only on image-level annotations. Current state-of-the-art models benefit from self-supervised instance-level supervision, but since weak supervision does not include count or location information, the most common "argmax" labeling method often ignores many instances of objects. To alleviate this issue, we propose a novel multiple instance labeling method called *object discovery*. We further introduce a new contrastive loss under weak supervision where no instance-level information is available for sampling, called *weakly supervised contrastive loss* (WSCL). WSCL aims to construct a credible similarity threshold for object discovery by leveraging consistent features for embedding vectors in the same class. As a result, we achieve new state-of-the-art results on MS-COCO 2014 and 2017 as well as PASCAL VOC 2012, and competitive results on PASCAL VOC 2007. The code is available at https://github.com/jinhseo/OD-WSCL.

Keyword: Weakly Supervised Object Detection (WSOD)

1 Introduction

Object detection [18–21] has seen huge improvements since the introduction of deep neural networks and large-scale datasets [5,7,17]. It is, however, very expensive and time-consuming to annotate large datasets with fine-grained object bounding boxes. Recent work has thus attempted to use more cost-efficient annotations in an approach called Weakly Supervised Object Detection (WSOD), such as image, point, or "scribble" labels.

Supplementary Information The online version contains supplementary material available at https://doi.org/10.1007/978-3-031-19821-2_18.

S. Avidan et al. (Eds.): ECCV 2022, LNCS 13691, pp. 312–329, 2022.
https://doi.org/10.1007/978-3-031-19821-2_18

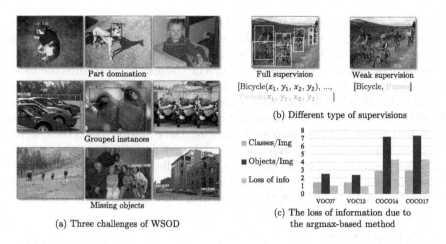

(a) Three challenges of WSOD

(b) Different type of supervisions

(c) The loss of information due to the argmax-based method

Fig. 1. (a) Three challenges of WSOD: part domination, grouped instances, and missing objects. (b) Unlike full supervision, there is no location and count information in weak supervision. (c) A large number of target objects are ignored in PASCAL VOC [7] and MS-COCO [17] due to the argmax-based method.

Although WSOD methods can be trained with much less annotation effort, however, the resulting models still perform far below their fully-supervised counterparts. We identify three categories of reasons for this deterioration, summarized in Fig. 1(a). First, *part domination* is when WSOD models focus only on the discriminative part of an object, perhaps caused by the fundamentally ill-posed nature of framing WSOD as a Multiple Instance Learning (MIL) problem [6] prone to local minima, as done by much previous work [2,29,32]. The second major issue of WSOD is *grouped instances*, where neighbouring instances of objects in the same category are grouped into one large proposal, rather than proposed separately. As image-level annotations reveal only the presence of each object class, without any information about object location or counts (see Fig. 1(b)), it has become conventional to take only the single highest-score proposal as a "pseudo groundtruth" [2,12,29]. This can help avoid false positives, but often causes *missing objects*, where less-obvious instances are ignored.

Current argmax-based algorithms for finding pseudo groundtruths turn out to be problematic even on extremely popular benchmark datasets. Labeling only one proposal per category misses 40% of labels on PASCAL VOC [7] (selecting 7,306 of 12,608 target objects on VOC07), and 60% on MS-COCO [17] (533,396 of 894,204 objects on COCO14). Similar patterns hold for VOC12 and COCO17 (see Fig. 1(c)). Object detection models trained with this limited and, indeed, potentially confusing supervision are substantially hindered, and mining more pseudo-labels is problematic since they are likely to be false positives.

We introduce a novel multiple instance labeling method which addresses the limitations of current labeling methods in WSOD. Our proposed object discovery module explores all proposed candidates using a similarity measure to the highest-scoring representation. We further suggest a weakly supervised contrastive loss (WSCL) to set a reliable similarity threshold. WSCL encourages a model to learn similar features for objects in the same class, and to learn discriminative features for objects in different classes. To make sure the model learn appropriate features, we provide a large number of positive and negative instances for WSCL through three feature augmentation methods suitable for WSOD. This well-behaved embedding space allows the object discovery module to find more reliable pseudo groundtruths. The resulting model then detects less-discriminative parts of target objects, misses fewer objects, and better distinguishes neighbouring object instances, as we will demonstrate experimentally in Sect. 5.1. As a result, the proposed approach beats state-of-the-art WSOD performance on both MS-COCO and PASCAL VOC by significant margins.

2   Related Work

2.1   Weakly Supervised Object Detection

Bilen *et al.* [2] introduced the first MIL-based end-to-end WSOD approach, known as WSDDN, which includes both classification and detection streams. Based on the MIL-based method, later works in WSOD have attempted to generate instance-level pseudo groundtruths in various ways.

Self-Supervised Pseudo Labeling Approach. To use instance-level supervision, Tang *et al.* [29] suggest Online Instance Classifier Refinement (OICR), which alternates between training instance classifier and selecting the most representative candidates. The online classifier rectifies initially detected instances through multiple stages and updates instance-level supervision determined by spatial relations. Tang *et al.* [28] expand clusters from OICR to include adjacent proposals that belong to the same cluster. Kosugi *et al.* [15] devise an instance labeling method to find positive instances based on a context classification loss, and to avoid negative instances using spatial constraints. Zeng *et al.* [36] show that the bottom-up evidence, unlike top-down class confidence, helps to recognize class-agnostic object boundaries. Chen *et al.* [4] propose a spatial likelihood voting (SLV) system to vote the bounding boxes with the highest likelihood in spatial dimension. Huang *et al.* [12] propose Comprehensive Attention Self-Distillation (CASD) that learns a balanced representation via input-wise and layer-wise feature learning. CASD aggregate attention maps, generated by multiple transformations and extracted from different levels of feature maps.

Multiple Instance Approach. Previous works focus on selecting valid pseudo groundtruths based on location information, but most still rely on the argmax labeling method which considers only one instance. Some attempts have been made, however, to provide multiple pseudo groundtruths. C-WSL [8] uses per-class object count annotations, which can help effectively separate grouped instances. OIM [16] exploits an object mining method to find undiscovered objects by calculating Euclidean distance between the core instance and its surrounding boxes. Ren *et al.* [22] propose not only Multiple Instance Self-Training (MIST) to generate top-k scored proposals as pseudo groundtruths, but also parametric dropblock to adversarially drop out discriminative parts. Yin *et al.* [35] introduce feature bank to provide one more pseudo groundtruth using the top-similarity scored instance. These algorithms [16,22,35] effectively find multiple instances per class, but their methods largely depend on heuristics, rather than learning. Our proposed method instead explores all possible pseudo groundtruths in a more reliable way, with learning guided by a contrastive loss.

2.2 Contrastive Learning

Contrastive losses have been successful in unsupervised and self-supervised learning for image classification tasks [3,14]. For object detection tasks, Xie *et al.* [33] and Sun *et al.* [27] demonstrate learning good embedding features via contrastive learning successfully improves the generalization ability of an object detector. One important factor of this success is to use effective mining strategies for positive and negative samples, which accelerates convergence and enhances the generalization ability of a model. In image classification tasks, these sample pairs are usually identified either by class labels [14] if available, or pairing images with versions that have been randomly altered with methods such as cropping, color distortion, or Gaussian blur [3]. Schroff *et al.* [24] introduce a hard positive and negative mining strategy based on the distance between anchor and positive samples, with full supervision. However, it is difficult to mine positive and negative samples in WSOD setting, which assumes no instance-level labels are available. Therefore, we propose feature augmentations to sample positives and negatives for contrastive learning in the WSOD setting. To the best of our knowledge, our method is the first approach to incorporate contrastive learning into WSOD tasks. Our proposed weakly supervised contrastive loss guides a model to learn consistent feature representations for objects in the same class and discriminative representations for ones in different classes, through mining positive and negative samples and augmenting intermediate features.

3 Background

As with most state-of-the-art WSOD models, our approach is also based on the MIL head of WSDDN [2], followed by the refinement head suggested by OICR [29]. In this section, we describe how MIL and refinement heads work.

3.1 Feature Extractor

Let a batch $B = \{I^n, R^n, Y^n\}_{n=1}^N$ contain an image I^n, proposals $R^n = \{r_1, ..., r_{M^n}\}$ with M^n proposals for the image I^n, and image-level labels $Y^n = [y_1^n, ..., y_C^n] \in \{0,1\}^C$ where C is the number of classes. Given an image I^n, a feature extractor generates features for downstream tasks as follows. A backbone network takes a given image as input and outputs a feature map, from which a Region of Interest (RoI) feature map $f^n \in \mathbb{R}^{D \times H \times W \times M^n}$ is generated through an RoI pooling layer. Two fully-connected (FC) layers, which we denote $\eta(\cdot)$, map f^n to RoI feature vectors $v^n \in \mathbb{R}^{D' \times M^n}$. To alleviate part domination, we also randomly mask out some blocks of the RoI map with Dropblock [22], generating $\tilde{f}^n$; we then generate regularized feature vectors $\tilde{v}^n = \eta(\tilde{f}^n)$. The MIL and refinement heads operate on $\tilde{v}^n$.

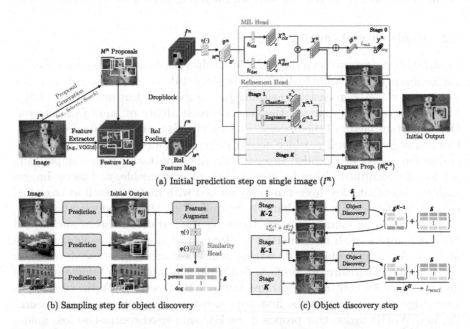

(a) Initial prediction step on single image (I^n)

(b) Sampling step for object discovery

(c) Object discovery step

Fig. 2. Overall architecture of the proposed method. Initial prediction in (a) collects top-scoring instances over all stages. Sampling step for Object Discovery in (b) iterates step (a) for all images in a batch, and applies feature augmentations described in Sect. 4.2. Object discovery in (c) mines additional pseudo groundtruths that are not recognized by the argmax method.

3.2   Multiple Instance Learning Head

As illustrated in Fig. 2(a), Multiple Instance Learning (MIL) head consists of classification and detection networks which take RoI feature vectors $\tilde{v}^n$ as input, and return classification scores $X_{cls}^n \in \mathbb{R}^{C \times M^n}$ and detection scores $X_{det}^n \in \mathbb{R}^{C \times M^n}$. Here, the X_{cls}^n are computed by a softmax operation along the classes (rows), whereas X_{det}^n are computed along the regions (columns). Proposal scores $X^n \in \mathbb{R}^{C \times M^n}$ are the element-wise product of classification and detection scores: $X^n = X_{cls}^n \odot X_{det}^n$. The image score of the c-th class, ϕ_c^n, is obtained by the sum of proposal scores over all regions: $\phi_c^n = \sum_{m=1}^{M^n} X_{c,m}^n$. Given an image-level label Y^n and image score ϕ_c^n, the multi-label classification loss L_{mil} is

$$L_{mil} = -\frac{1}{N} \sum_{n=1}^{N} \sum_{c=1}^{C} y_c^n \log \phi_c^n + (1 - y_c^n) \log(1 - \phi_c^n). \qquad (1)$$

3.3 Refinement Head

The goal of the refinement head is to integrate self-supervised training strategy into WSOD via instance-level supervision. At the k-th stage ($k \in \{1, ..., K\}$), an instance classifier generates proposal scores $X^{n,k} \in \mathbb{R}^{(C+1) \times M^n}$ where M^n is the number of proposals and $C + 1$ adds a background class to the C classes. Instance-level supervision at the k-th stage is determined by previous stage; in particular, the first instance classifier takes supervision from the output of MIL head. Instance-level pseudo labels for the n-th image $Y^{n,k} \in \mathbb{R}^{(C+1) \times M^n}$ are then set to 1 if the corresponding proposal sufficiently overlaps the highest scored proposal, otherwise 0 as defined in (2).

$$\bar{m}_c^{n,k} = \underset{m}{\operatorname{argmax}}\, x_{c,m}^{n,(k-1)}; \qquad y_{c,m}^{n,k} = \begin{cases} 1 & \text{if } IoU(r_m, r_{\bar{m}_c^{n,k}}) > 0.5 \\ 0 & \text{otherwise.} \end{cases} \qquad (2)$$

Finally, the instance classification loss L_{cls} is defined as

$$L_{cls} = -\frac{1}{N} \sum_{n=1}^{N} \frac{1}{K} \sum_{k=1}^{K} \frac{1}{M^n} \sum_{m=1}^{M^n} \sum_{c=1}^{C+1} w_m^{n,k} y_{c,m}^{n,k} \log x_{c,m}^{n,k} \qquad (3)$$

where $x_{c,m}^{n,k}$ denotes m-th proposal score of a class c at k-th stage, $w_m^{n,k}$ denotes a loss weight defined as $w_m^{n,k} = x_{c,\bar{m}_c^{n,k}}^{n,(k-1)}$ following OICR [29], and K is the total number of refinement stages.

In addition to instance classification, some work [34,36] has improved localization performance by adding a bounding box regression loss. Given $\hat{M}^n$ pseudo groundtruth bounding boxes $\hat{g}_m^{n,k}$, nearby predicted bounding boxes $g_m^{n,k}$, matched as in (2), are encouraged to align using a $smooth_{L1}$ regression loss:

$$L_{reg} = -\frac{1}{N} \sum_{n=1}^{N} \frac{1}{K} \sum_{k=1}^{K} \frac{1}{\hat{M}^n} \sum_{m=1}^{\hat{M}^n} w_m^{n,k} smooth_{L1}(g_m^{n,k}, \hat{g}_m^{n,k}). \qquad (4)$$

4 Our Approach

Most prior WSOD works [12,29] consider only top-scoring proposals, as described in (2). This strategy, however, has significant challenges in achieving our goal of detecting *all* objects present. To alleviate this issue, we propose a novel approach called *object discovery* which secures reliable pseudo groundtruths, by transferring instance-level supervision from previous to the next stage as illustrated in Sect. 3.3 and Fig. 2(c). To further enhance the object discovery module, we also introduce a new *similarity head* which maps RoI feature vectors to an embedding space, guided by a novel weakly supervised contrastive loss (WSCL).

4.1   Similarity Head

Parallel to the MIL and refinement heads, we construct a similarity head $\varphi(\cdot)$ that takes augmented RoI feature vectors as input described in Fig. 2. We will explain how RoI features are augmented in Sect. 4.2. The similarity head consists of two FC layers which map the inputs to a 128-dimensional space, followed by a normalization step. Thus, the outputs of the similarity head are expressed as $z^n = \varphi(v^n) \in \mathbb{R}^{128 \times M^n}$ where $||z_m^n||_2 = 1$. Note that the similarity head uses v^n, whereas MIL and refinement head use the region-dropped $\tilde{v}^n$.

4.2   Sampling Strategy for Object Discovery

Contrastive learning [3,14], in general, focuses on making "positive" and "negative" pairs have similar and different feature embeddings, respectively. Although it is possible to augment images and pass each to the backbone to obtain pair of samples from RoI features in WSOD setting where no instance-level supervisions are available, it is computationally inefficient: most of the features from the backbone are not used as RoI features. Instead of augmenting images, we propose three feature augmentation methods to generate views of samples, as shown in Fig. 3(a): *IoU sampling*, *random masking*, and *adding gaussian noise*.

IoU Sampling. The purpose of IoU sampling is to increase the number of samples by treating the proposals adjacent to the top-scoring proposal $\bar{m}_c^n$ in (2) as positives. The proposals that overlap more than a threshold τ_{IoU} with the top-scoring proposal at each stage k are considered positive samples, and the corresponding embedding vectors are formulated as

$$\mathcal{M}_c^{n,k} = \{m \mid IoU(r_m, r_{\bar{m}_c^{n,k}}) > \tau_{IoU}, m = 1, 2, ..., M^n\}$$

$$\mathcal{Z}_{IoU}^{n,c} = \{\varphi(\eta(f_m^n)) \mid m \in \bigcup_{k=0}^{K-1} \mathcal{M}_c^{n,k}\} \tag{5}$$

where M^n denotes the total number of proposals in n-th image, $\eta(\cdot)$ is the extractor of RoI feature vectors, and $\varphi(\cdot)$ denotes the similarity head.

Random Masking. Random masking randomly drops some regions across all channels of a RoI feature map. We first generate a random map $D : D_{i,j} \sim U(0,1) \in \mathbb{R}^{H \times W}$. Then the binary mask D_{drop} is determined by drop threshold

τ_{drop}, so if $D < \tau_{drop}$, D_{drop} is set to be 0, otherwise 1. Finally, a randomly-masked feature is obtained by taking spatial-wise multiplication of a RoI feature map f_m^n with D_{drop} followed by the similarity head,

$$\mathcal{Z}_{mask}^{n,c} = \{\varphi(\eta(f_m^n \odot D_{drop})) \mid m \in \bigcup_{k=0}^{K-1} \mathcal{M}_c^{n,k}\}. \tag{6}$$

Here, random masking is applied to the all proposals from IoU sampling at all stages, $\bigcup_{k=1}^{K} \mathcal{M}_c^{n,k}$, to obtain more positive samples.

Adding Gaussian Noise. To add Gaussian random noise to RoI feature maps, we create a random noise map $D_{noise} : D_{i,j} \sim N(0,1) \in \mathbb{R}^{H \times W}$. We add this to the RoI feature maps f_m^n by

$$\mathcal{Z}_{noise}^{n,c} = \{\varphi(\eta(f_m^n + f_m^n \odot D_{noise})) \mid m \in \bigcup_{k=0}^{K-1} \mathcal{M}_c^{n,k}\}. \tag{7}$$

Cross-Image Representations. Finally, we gather the augmented embedding vectors corresponding to the same object category from different images, as described in Fig. 3(b). We treat cross-batch representations from the same categories as positive examples in the mini-batch,

$$\mathcal{S}_c = \bigcup_{n=1}^{N} (\mathcal{Z}_{IoU}^{n,c} \cup \mathcal{Z}_{mask}^{n,c} \cup \mathcal{Z}_{noise}^{n,c}). \tag{8}$$

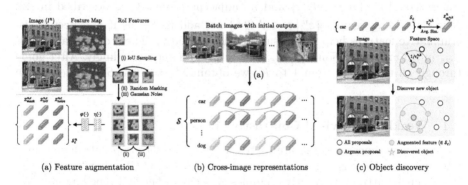

(a) Feature augmentation   (b) Cross-image representations   (c) Object discovery

Fig. 3. Three steps for object discovery module. (a) applies feature augmentation methods to embedding vectors of top-scoring proposals. (b) collects all augmented embedding vectors through all images in a batch. (c) determines new pseudo groundtruths based on the similarity with the embedding vector of the top-scoring instance $z_{\bar{m}_c^{n,k}}^n$ and similarity threshold $\tau_c^{n,k}$.

4.3   Object Discovery

Using the augmented RoI features introduced in the previous section, we discover many reliable instance-level pseudo groundtruths missed by previous methods that take only the top-scoring proposals. Intuitively, even though the classification score of a proposal may be low, if its embedding vector is close to that of the top-scoring proposal, it is likely that the proposal shares the same class as the top-scoring proposal. Therefore, instead of solely relying on classification scores, we exploit similarity scores between the embedding vectors of all proposals and the top-scoring (argmax) proposal at each stage k, to discover additional pseudo grountruths as shown in Fig. 3(c). To mine new pseudo groundtruths, we first compute a threshold $\tau_c^{n,k}$ that determines whether to label a proposal as a pseudo groundtruth for a class c at stage k:

$$\tau_c^{n,k} = \frac{1}{|\mathcal{S}_c|} \sum_{i=1}^{|\mathcal{S}_c|} sim(z_{\bar{m}_c^{n,k}}^n, \mathcal{S}_{c,i}), \tag{9}$$

where $z_{\bar{m}_c^{n,k}}^n$ denotes embedding vectors of top-scoring proposals at stage k, $\mathcal{S}_{c,i}$ denotes i-th element of $\mathcal{S}_c$, and $sim(\cdot, \cdot)$ is a dot product between inputs. Then, new pseudo groundtruth candidates $\acute{\mathcal{M}}_c^{n,k}$ are determined as the ones having higher similarity to the top-scoring proposal than similarity threshold $\tau_c^{n,k}$,

$$\acute{\mathcal{M}}_c^{n,k} = \{m \mid sim(z_m^n, z_{\bar{m}_c^{n,k}}^n) > \tau_c^{n,k}, m = 1, 2, ..., M^n\}. \tag{10}$$

Finally, we add new pseudo groundtruths denoted as $\tilde{\mathcal{M}}_c^{n,k}$ at stage k after applying Non-Maximum Suppression (NMS) [23] to $\acute{\mathcal{M}}_c^{n,k}$.

Consequently, we update instance-level supervision and embedding vectors for newly discovered pseudo groundtruths $\tilde{\mathcal{M}}_c^{n,k}$. We re-label instance-level supervision $\{y_{c,m}^{n,k} | m \in \tilde{\mathcal{M}}_c^{n,k}\}$ and its adjacent proposals as described in (2). New embedding vectors $\{z_m^n | m \in \tilde{\mathcal{M}}_c^{n,k}\}$ are add to S_c^k, as it is expected discriminative features help to measure precise similarity. Then, classification loss L_{cls} in (3) and regression loss L_{reg} in (4) are updated accordingly. After going through all the stages from 1 to K, we obtain $S^U = S^K \cup S$ as described in Fig. 2(c).

4.4   Weakly Supervised Contrastive Loss

To learn more consistent feature representations for the proposals in the same class, we propose weakly supervised contrastive loss (WSCL) that learns representations by attracting positive samples closer together and repelling negative samples away from positives samples in the embedding space. From a collection $S^U = \{s_i, t_i\}_{i=1}^{|S^U|}$ where s_i denotes i-th embedding vectors, t_i denotes the pseudo label of s_i, WSCL for i-th embedding vector denoted as L_{wscl}^i, is formulated as

$$L_{wscl}^i = -\frac{1}{N_{t_i} - 1} \sum_{j=1, j \neq i}^{|S^U|} \mathbb{1}\{t_i = t_j\} \cdot \log \frac{\exp(s_i \cdot s_j / \epsilon)}{\sum_{l=1, l \neq i}^{|S^U|} \exp(s_i \cdot s_l / \epsilon)} \tag{11}$$

where $N_{t_i} := \sum_{j=1}^{|\mathcal{S}^U|} \mathbb{1}\{t_i = t_j\}$, and ϵ is a temperature parameter introduced in [14]. Note that $\mathcal{S}^U = \bigcup_{c=1}^{C} \mathcal{S}_c^U$.

Instance Difficulty. Since confidence score of instance is noisy at early stages of training, we introduce instance difficulty ω to make training for WSCL easier. ω is the set of scores for all images in a batch where each score is the instance score from the MIL head over the sum of them at each image. Here, the size of ω is the same as $\mathcal{S}$. Then, the re-weighted contrastive loss is formulated as,

$$L_{wscl} = \frac{1}{|\mathcal{S}^U|} \sum_{i=1}^{|\mathcal{S}^U|} \omega_i \cdot L_{wscl}^i, \ \omega = \bigcup_{n=1}^{N} \left\{ X_{c,m}^n / \sum_{j=1}^{M^n} X_{c,j}^n \mid m \in \bigcup_{k=0}^{K-1} \mathcal{M}_c^{n,k} \right\} \quad (12)$$

Total Loss. Finally, the total loss of training the proposed model is defined as

$$L_{total} = L_{mil} + L_{cls} + L_{reg} + \lambda L_{wscl} \quad (13)$$

where λ is a loss weight to balance scale with the other losses.

5 Experiments

5.1 Experiment Setting

Datasets. To verify the robustness of our method, we evaluate it on four object detection datasets; VOC07 and VOC12 in PASCAL VOC [7], and COCO14 and COCO17 in MS-COCO [17], following the convention in WSOD tasks. We use trainval sets containing 5,011 and 11,540 images for VOC07 and VOC12, respectively, and test sets that contain 4,951 and 10,991 images, for evaluation. We further investigate the robustness of our method on MS-COCO datasets. For COCO14, we train our model on the train set of 82,783 images and test it with the validation set of 40,504 images. For COCO17, we split the dataset into the train set of 118,287 images and validation set of 5,000 images. We use only image-level annotations to train our model on all datasets.

Evaluation Metrics. On VOC07 and 12 datasets, we evaluate our model on the test set using mean Average Precision (mAP) metric with standard IoU criterion (0.5). MS-COCO is more challenging than PASCAL VOC as it has significantly more instances per image (about 2 *vs.* 7) and more classes (20 *vs.* 80). For this reason, MS-COCO is often not considered in the WSOD literature. We report the performance on MS-COCO datasets following the standard COCO metric which includes several metrics, such as, average precision (AP) and average recall (AR) with varying IoU thresholds *e.g.*, 0.5 and 0.75, and object sizes *e.g.*, small (s), medium (m), and large (l), but the most representative metric is the AP averaged over 10 IoU thresholds (from 0.5 to 0.95 for every 0.05 step).

Implementation Details. All the implementation is developed in PyTorch. For both VGG16 [26] and ResNet [11] models, we initialize parameters using ImageNet [5] pre-trained networks. For VGG16, following the previous methods [12,22], we replace a global average pooling layer with a RoI pooling layer, and remove the last FC layer leaving two FC layers, which all the heads including the similarity head are attached to. For ResNet, we modify the structure for WSOD as suggested in Sect. 4 of Shen *et al.* [25]. We use around 2,000 proposals per image for both proposal generation methods, SS [31] and MCG [1].

Hyperparameters. The batch size is set to 8 for PASCAL VOC and MS-COCO datasets. We train models for 30K, 60K and 130K iterations on VOC07, VOC12 and MS-COCO, respectively, using a SGD optimizer with the learning rate of 0.01 and weight decay of 0.0001 except for R50-WS and R101-WS [25] where the learning rate is set to 0.02 on both datasets. At inference time, the prediction scores are computed as the average of proposal scores for all k-stages, and the offsets from regression branch are incorporated to adjust the coordinates of bounding boxes. The final predictions are made after applying NMS of which threshold is set to 0.4 for both datasets. Following the previous methods [12, 22,29], the inputs are multi-scaled to $\{480, 576, 688, 864, 1000, 1200\}$ for both training and inference time. In the experiments, we set $\tau_{IoU} = 0.5$, $\tau_{drop} = 0.3$, $\tau_{nms} = 0.1$, $\lambda = 0.03$ ($\lambda = 0.01$ on COCO datasets) and $\epsilon = 0.2$ for WSCL and K=3 for the number of refinement stages. But, as we will show in an ablation study, the performance is not sensitive to the choice of hyperparameters.

Table 1. Comparison of the state-of-the-art algorithms on MS-COCO

Dataset	Backbone	Method	AP	AP^{50}	AP^{75}	AP^s	AP^m	AP^l	AR^1	AR^{10}	AR^{100}	AR^s	AR^m	AR^l
COCO14	VGG16	PCL [28]	8.5	19.4	–	–	–	–	–	–	–	–	–	–
		C-MIDN [9]	9.6	21.4	–	–	–	–	–	–	–	–	–	–
		WSOD2 [36]	10.8	22.7	–	–	–	–	–	–	-	-	-	–
		MIST [22]	11.4	24.3	9.4	3.6	12.2	17.6	13.5	22.6	23.9	8.5	25.4	38.3
		CASD [12]	12.8	26.4	–	–	–	–	–	–	–	–	–	–
		Ours	**13.7**	**27.7**	**11.9**	**4.4**	**14.5**	**21.2**	**14.7**	**24.8**	**26.9**	**8.8**	**27.8**	**44.0**
	ResNet50	MIST [22]	12.6	26.1	10.8	3.7	13.3	19.9	14.8	23.7	24.7	8.4	25.1	41.8
		CASD [12]	**13.9**	27.8	–	–	–	–	–	–	–	–	–	–
		Ours	**13.9**	**29.1**	**11.8**	**4.9**	**16.8**	**22.3**	**15.5**	**26.1**	**28.0**	**9.0**	**31.8**	**46.6**
	ResNet101	MIST [22]	13.0	26.1	10.8	3.7	13.3	19.9	14.8	23.7	24.7	8.4	25.1	41.8
		Ours	**14.4**	**29.0**	**12.4**	**4.8**	**17.3**	**23.8**	**15.8**	**27.0**	**30.0**	**9.2**	**33.6**	**51.0**
COCO17	VGG16	MIST [22]	12.4	25.8	10.5	3.9	13.8	19.9	14.3	23.3	24.6	**9.7**	26.6	39.6
		Ours	**13.6**	**27.4**	**12.2**	**4.9**	**15.5**	**21.6**	**14.6**	**24.8**	**26.8**	9.2	**28.7**	**43.8**
	ResNet50	Ours	13.8	27.8	12.1	5.7	17.7	23.8	15.1	26.6	29.7	10.1	33.7	50.7
	ResNet101	Ours	14.4	28.7	12.6	5.4	17.9	25.5	15.4	26.8	29.6	10.0	33.3	50.6

5.2   Quantitative Results

Comparison with State-of-the-Arts. In Table 1, we compare the proposed method with other state-of-the-art algorithms on COCO14 and 17. Regardless of backbone structure and dataset, our method achieves the new state-of-the-art performance for all the evaluation metrics. The fact that the performance of Ours in AR measurements are higher than the other methods implies that the proposed method successfully detects missing instances compared to the previous methods on MS-COCO, which contain many instances and categories per image. For instance, our method outperforms MIST [22] by a large margin in AR measurements; on average of 2.13% for $(AR^1, AR^{10}, AR^{100})$ and on average of 3.46% for (AR^s, AR^m, AR^l) with VGG16 on COCO14. Despite the significant improvement in AR, AP also improves by a large margin regardless of different subcategory of AP and backbone structure. Our method gains on average of 2.95% for (AP^{50}, AP^{75}) and on average of 2.23% for (AP^s, AP^m, AP^l) with VGG16 on COCO14. We observe similar tendency on COCO17 for all the backbones. As a result, our proposed method achieves the new state-of-the-art performance on both COCO14 and COCO17 (14.4%).

In Table 2, we compare the performance of the state-of-the-art methods on PASCAL VOC with both SS and MCG proposal methods. Since PASCAL VOC datasets contain less number of instances and categores per image, the gain achieved by our method is relatively lower than MS-COCO. It, however, outperforms other multiple instance labeling methods [8,16, 22] with clear margins. For example, Ours outperforms MIST [22] (the best performance multiple instance labeling method) by 1.2% and 2.5% on VOC07 and VOC12, respectively, with SS proposal method, and 2.2% and 2.3% with MCG proposal method. It also achieves the new state-of-the-art performance on VOC12 (54.6%) and compatible results on VOC07 (Ours: 56.1% *vs.* CASD: 56.8%). We use MCG for the rest of the experiments as it outperforms SS.

Table 2. Comparison of the state-of-the-art methods on PASCAL VOC.

Proposal	Method	VOC07	VOC12
SS [31]	WSDDN [2]	34.8	–
	OICR [29]	41.2	37.9
	PCL [28]	43.5	40.6
	C-WSL [8]	46.8	43.0
	WSRPN [30]	47.9	43.4
	C-MIL [32]	50.5	46.7
	C-MIDN [9]	52.6	50.2
	WSOD2 [36]	53.6	47.2
	OIM [16]	50.1	45.3
	SLV [4]	53.5	49.2
	MIST [22]	54.9	52.1
	CASD [13]	**56.8**	53.6
	Ours	56.1	**54.6**
MCG [1]	MIST [22]	56.5	53.9
	CASD [13]	57.4	–
	Ours	**58.7**	**56.2**

The Effectiveness of Each Component. To validate the effectiveness of each component of Object Discovery (OD) and WSCL modules, we provide experiment results on VOC07 with SS in Table 3(a). Note that we find the performance of OICR [29] can be further increased by adding the bounding box regression and dropblock [10] layers (45.0% → 52.3% on VOC07), thus, we call

Table 3. Experiment results with various settings on VOC07. (a) Different components of the proposed method. (b) Performance with ResNet backbones [25]. (c) Comparison of different combination of feature augmentation methods.

(a) Diff. components

OD	WSCL	mAP
		52.3
✓		56.1
	✓	54.5
✓	✓	**58.7**

(b) ResNet backbones

Method	R50-WS	R101-WS
OICR[29]	50.9	51.4
PCL[28]	50.8	53.3
C-MIL[32]	53.4	53.9
Ours	**56.6**	**56.5**

(c) Feature augmentation

Method	IoU	Mask	Noise	mAP
OICR$^+$				52.3
+Ours	✓			56.8
		✓		55.1
			✓	54.8
	✓	✓		57.4
	✓		✓	57.4
		✓	✓	55.2
	✓	✓	✓	**58.7**

OICR + Regression + Dropblock as OICR$^+$, and use it as the baseline throughout the experiments unless specified otherwise. In Table 3(a), each of OD and WSCL modules significantly improves OICR$^+$ baseline (+3.8 and +2.2) but the improvement is the highest when both OD and WSCL are applied simultaneously, which partially demonstrate that each module helps the other one as described in Sect. 4.

Robust Regardless of Backbone. In Table 1, we have shown that the proposed method performs well both in AP and AR metrics on MS-COCO datasets regardless of backbone structure. Although it is not a common practice to provide the performance with ResNet backbones on PASCAL VOC, we provide the performance of our method on ResNet in Table 3(b). It shows that Ours with ResNet backbones significantly outperforms the previous state-of-the-art methods as with the case with VGG backbone shown in Table 2. The performance of the previous methods are reported in [25].

5.3   Ablation Studies

Feature Augmentation Methods. To further verify the effectiveness of the proposed feature augmentation methods, we experiment with different combination of augmentation methods for the object discovery and WSCL modules in Table 3(c). The performance significantly improves from 52.3% to 55.1% and 54.8% with random masking and Gaussian noise, respectively, even without IoU sampling. With IoU sampling prior to random masking and Gaussian noise, the performance consistently improves further by 2.3% and 2.6% for random masking and Gaussian noise. Using all the proposed feature augmentations, the performance reaches 58.7% that is 6.4% higher than the baseline.

Sensitivity to Hyperparameters. In Fig. 4, we provide the experiment results with different values of the hyperparameters we introduce. Regardless of hyperparameter, the performance is not sensitive to the choice of values around the

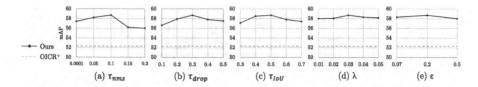

Fig. 4. Performance with different values of τ_{nms}, τ_{drop}, τ_{IoU}, λ and ϵ.

(a) Part domination   (b) Group instances   (c) Missing objects

Fig. 5. Qualitative results of OICR [29] and ours about the three challenges of WSOD: (a) part domination, (b) grouped instances and (c) missing objects. The images on the left and right indicate OICR and Ours, respectively.

optimal values we choose ($\tau_{nms} = 0.1, \tau_{drop} = 0.3, \tau_{IoU} = 0.5, \lambda = 0.03$ and $\epsilon = 0.2$). For instance, the gap between the highest and lowest performance for each hyperparameter is no more than 2.6% in mAP (highest with τ_{nms}), which demonstrates that our proposed method does not greatly depend on hyperparameter tuning. In (e), we use the same values of ϵ following the experiments conducted in other contrastive learning methods [3,14].

5.4   Qualitative Results

Three Challenges of WSOD. In Fig. 5, we provide the qualitative results that show how our method addresses three main challenges of WSOD – part domination, grouped instances and missing objects (described in Sect. 1), compared to OICR [29]. The left columns show the results from OICR [29] whereas the right columns show the results from our method. The part domination shown in (a) is largely alleviated, especially for the categories with various poses such as *dog, cat* and *person*. We also observe that grouped instances are separated into multiple bounding boxes in (b). Lastly, our method successfully detects many of instances that are ignored with the argmax labeling method as shown in (c).

Fig. 6. Comparison of pseudo groundtruths generated by (a) OICR [29], (b) MIST [22] and (c) Ours which shows pseudo groundtruths at different training steps. "Difficult" objects are often captured by Ours as shown in (d).

Selection of Pseudo Groundtruths. We visualize the pseudo groundtruths captured by OICR [29], MIST [22] and Ours in Fig. 6. OICR [29] selects only the top-scoring proposal per category ignoring all the other instances as shown in (a). Although multiple objects are captured by MIST [22] in (b), it also selects many false positives *e.g.*, object-like background. Ours also captures many false positives in early stages of training (Iter: 0 – 10K) but later in training, it mostly selects true positives (Iter: 20K – 30K). Our method can even detect some objects categorized as "difficult" (red boxes in (e)), which are not considered for detection performance as they are too hard even for humans to detect.

6 Conclusion

We propose a novel multiple instance labeling method to replace the conventional argmax-based pseudo groundtruth labeling method for weakly supervised object detection (WSOD). To this end, we introduce a contrastive loss for the WSOD setting that learns consistent embedding features for proposals in the same class, and discriminative features for ones in different classes. With these features, it is possible to mine a large number of reliable pseudo groundtruths, which provide richer supervision for WSOD tasks. As a result, we achieve the new state-of-the-art results on both PASCAL VOC and MS-COCO benchmarks.

Acknowledgements. This work was supported by Institute of Information & communications Technology Planning & Evaluation (IITP) grants funded by the Korea government (MSIT) (No.2017-0-00897, Development of Object Detection and Recognition for Intelligent Vehicles) and (No.B0101-15-0266, Development of High Performance Visual BigData Discovery Platform for Large-Scale Realtime Data Analysis), as well as by support provided by the Natural Sciences and Engineering Research Council of Canada and the Canada CIFAR AI Chairs program. Junhyug Noh was supported by LLNL under Contract DE-AC52-07NA27344.

References

1. Arbeláez, P., Pont-Tuset, J., Barron, J.T., Marques, F., Malik, J.: Multiscale combinatorial grouping. In: Proceedings of the IEEE Conference on Computer Vision and Pattern Recognition, pp. 328–335 (2014)
2. Bilen, H., Vedaldi, A.: Weakly supervised deep detection networks. In: The IEEE Conference on Computer Vision and Pattern Recognition (CVPR) (2016)
3. Chen, T., Kornblith, S., Norouzi, M., Hinton, G.: A simple framework for contrastive learning of visual representations. In: International Conference on Machine Learning, pp. 1597–1607. PMLR (2020)
4. Chen, Z., Fu, Z., Jiang, R., Chen, Y., Hua, X.S.: SLV: spatial likelihood voting for weakly supervised object detection. In: Proceedings of the IEEE/CVF Conference on Computer Vision and Pattern Recognition, pp. 12995–13004 (2020)
5. Deng, J., Dong, W., Socher, R., Li, L.J., Li, K., Fei-Fei, L.: Imagenet: a large-scale hierarchical image database. In: 2009 IEEE Conference on Computer Vision and Pattern Recognition, pp. 248–255. Ieee (2009)
6. Dietterich, T.G., Lathrop, R.H., Lozano-Pérez, T.: Solving the multiple instance problem with axis-parallel rectangles. Artif. Intell. **89**(1–2), 31–71 (1997)
7. Everingham, M., Eslami, S.M.A., Van Gool, L., Williams, C.K.I., Winn, J., Zisserman, A.: The pascal visual object classes challenge: a retrospective. Int. J. Comput. Vision **111**(1), 98–136 (2015)
8. Gao, M., Li, A., Yu, R., Morariu, V.I., Davis, L.S.: C-WSL: count-guided weakly supervised localization. In: Ferrari, V., Hebert, M., Sminchisescu, C., Weiss, Y. (eds.) ECCV 2018. LNCS, vol. 11205, pp. 155–171. Springer, Cham (2018). https://doi.org/10.1007/978-3-030-01246-5_10
9. Gao, Y., et al.: C-midn: Coupled multiple instance detection network with segmentation guidance for weakly supervised object detection. In: Proceedings of the IEEE/CVF International Conference on Computer Vision, pp. 9834–9843 (2019)
10. Ghiasi, G., Lin, T.Y., Le, Q.V.: Dropblock: a regularization method for convolutional networks. arXiv preprint arXiv:1810.12890 (2018)
11. He, K., Zhang, X., Ren, S., Sun, J.: Deep residual learning for image recognition. In: Proceedings of the IEEE Conference on Computer Vision and Pattern Recognition, pp. 770–778 (2016)
12. Huang, Z., Zou, Y., Bhagavatula, V., Huang, D.: Comprehensive attention self-distillation for weakly-supervised object detection. arXiv preprint arXiv:2010.12023 (2020)
13. Hwang, J., Kim, S., Son, J., Han, B.: Weakly supervised instance segmentation by deep community learning. In: Proceedings of the IEEE/CVF Winter Conference on Applications of Computer Vision, pp. 1020–1029 (2021)
14. Khosla, P., et al.: Supervised contrastive learning. arXiv preprint arXiv:2004.11362 (2020)
15. Kosugi, S., Yamasaki, T., Aizawa, K.: Object-aware instance labeling for weakly supervised object detection. In: The IEEE International Conference on Computer Vision (ICCV) (2019)
16. Lin, C., Wang, S., Xu, D., Lu, Y., Zhang, W.: Object instance mining for weakly supervised object detection. In: AAAI, pp. 11482–11489 (2020)
17. Lin, T.-Y., et al.: Microsoft COCO: common objects in context. In: Fleet, D., Pajdla, T., Schiele, B., Tuytelaars, T. (eds.) ECCV 2014. LNCS, vol. 8693, pp. 740–755. Springer, Cham (2014). https://doi.org/10.1007/978-3-319-10602-1_48

18. Liu, W., et al.: SSD: single shot multibox detector. In: Leibe, B., Matas, J., Sebe, N., Welling, M. (eds.) ECCV 2016. LNCS, vol. 9905, pp. 21–37. Springer, Cham (2016). https://doi.org/10.1007/978-3-319-46448-0_2

19. Long, J., Shelhamer, E., Darrell, T.: Fully convolutional networks for semantic segmentation. In: Proceedings of the IEEE Conference on Computer Vision and Pattern Recognition, pp. 3431–3440 (2015)

20. Redmon, J., Divvala, S., Girshick, R., Farhadi, A.: You only look once: unified, real-time object detection. In: Proceedings of the IEEE Conference on Computer Vision and Pattern Recognition, pp. 779–788 (2016)

21. Ren, S., He, K., Girshick, R., Sun, J.: Faster r-cnn: towards real-time object detection with region proposal networks. In: Advances in Neural Information Processing Systems, pp. 91–99 (2015)

22. Ren, Z., et al.: Instance-aware, context-focused, and memory-efficient weakly supervised object detection. In: Proceedings of the IEEE/CVF Conference on Computer Vision and Pattern Recognition, pp. 10598–10607 (2020)

23. Rosenfeld, A., Thurston, M.: Edge and curve detection for visual scene analysis. IEEE Trans. Comput. **100**(5), 562–569 (1971)

24. Schroff, F., Kalenichenko, D., Philbin, J.: Facenet: a unified embedding for face recognition and clustering. In: Proceedings of the IEEE Conference on Computer Vision and Pattern Recognition, pp. 815–823 (2015)

25. Shen, Y., et al.: Enabling deep residual networks for weakly supervised object detection. In: Vedaldi, A., Bischof, H., Brox, T., Frahm, J.-M. (eds.) ECCV 2020. LNCS, vol. 12353, pp. 118–136. Springer, Cham (2020). https://doi.org/10.1007/978-3-030-58598-3_8

26. Simonyan, K., Zisserman, A.: Very deep convolutional networks for large-scale image recognition. In: ICLR (2015)

27. Sun, B., Li, B., Cai, S., Yuan, Y., Zhang, C.: Fsce: few-shot object detection via contrastive proposal encoding. In: Proceedings of the IEEE/CVF Conference on Computer Vision and Pattern Recognition, pp. 7352–7362 (2021)

28. Tang, P.: Pcl: proposal cluster learning for weakly supervised object detection. IEEE Trans. Pattern Anal. Mach. Intell. **42**(1), 176–191 (2018)

29. Tang, P., Wang, X., Bai, X., Liu, W.: Multiple instance detection network with online instance classifier refinement. In: The IEEE Conference on Computer Vision and Pattern Recognition (CVPR) (2017)

30. Tang, P., et al.: Weakly supervised region proposal network and object detection. In: Ferrari, V., Hebert, M., Sminchisescu, C., Weiss, Y. (eds.) ECCV 2018. LNCS, vol. 11215, pp. 370–386. Springer, Cham (2018). https://doi.org/10.1007/978-3-030-01252-6_22

31. Uijlings, J.R., Van De Sande, K.E., Gevers, T., Smeulders, A.W.: Selective search for object recognition. Int. J. Comput. Vision **104**(2), 154–171 (2013)

32. Wan, F., Liu, C., Ke, W., Ji, X., Jiao, J., Ye, Q.: C-mil: continuation multiple instance learning for weakly supervised object detection. In: The IEEE Conference on Computer Vision and Pattern Recognition (CVPR) (2019)

33. Xie, E., et al.: Detco: unsupervised contrastive learning for object detection. In: Proceedings of the IEEE/CVF International Conference on Computer Vision, pp. 8392–8401 (2021)

34. Yang, K., Li, D., Dou, Y.: Towards precise end-to-end weakly supervised object detection network. In: Proceedings of the IEEE/CVF International Conference on Computer Vision (ICCV) (2019)

35. Yin, Y., Deng, J., Zhou, W., Li, H.: Instance mining with class feature banks for weakly supervised object detection. In: Proceedings of the AAAI Conference on Artificial Intelligence, pp. 3190–3198 (2021)
36. Zeng, Z., Liu, B., Fu, J., Chao, H., Zhang, L.: Wsod2: learning bottom-up and top-down objectness distillation for weakly-supervised object detection. In: Proceedings of the IEEE/CVF International Conference on Computer Vision, pp. 8292–8300 (2019)

Stochastic Consensus: Enhancing Semi-Supervised Learning with Consistency of Stochastic Classifiers

Hui Tang[1]📷, Lin Sun[2], and Kui Jia[1](✉)

[1] South China University of Technology, Guangzhou, China
eehuitang@mail.scut.edu.cn, kuijia@scut.edu.cn
[2] Magic Leap, Sunnyvale, CA, USA
lsun@magicleap.com

Abstract. Semi-supervised learning (SSL) has achieved new progress recently with the emerging framework of self-training deep networks, where the criteria for selection of unlabeled samples with pseudo labels play a key role in the empirical success. In this work, we propose such a new criterion based on consistency among multiple, stochastic classifiers, termed Stochastic Consensus (STOCO). Specifically, we model parameters of the classifiers as a Gaussian distribution whose mean and standard deviation are jointly optimized during training. Due to the scarcity of labels in SSL, modeling classifiers as a distribution itself provides additional regularization that mitigates overfitting to the labeled samples. We technically generate pseudo labels using a simple but flexible framework of deep discriminative clustering, which benefits from the overall structure of data distribution. We also provide theoretical analysis of our criterion by connecting with the theory of learning from noisy data. Our proposed criterion can be readily applied to self-training based SSL frameworks. By choosing the representative FixMatch as the baseline, our method with multiple stochastic classifiers achieves the state of the art on popular SSL benchmarks, especially in label-scarce cases.

Keywords: Semi-supervised learning · Stochastic classifiers · Consistency criterion · Deep discriminative clustering

1 Introduction

The practical success of deep learning across a range of application problems assumes the access to massive amounts of annotated training data. However, data annotations are usually costly, and in some cases they could be difficult to be acquired due to, e.g., the lack of domain expertise. The situation motivates topics of data-efficient learning, such as semi-supervised learning (SSL) [25], few-shot learning [15], and domain adaptation [57], etc. Among them, SSL is a more

---

Supplementary Information The online version contains supplementary material available at https://doi.org/10.1007/978-3-031-19821-2_19.

classical one that aims for model learning with a few number of labeled samples and a large number of unlabeled ones from the same data distribution.

Deep SSL achieves good progress recently, and the methods generally fall in three categories. Those in the first category are based on self-training with pseudo labels [18,25] ; they work better by selecting unlabeled samples with pseudo labels assigned by the previously learned model, and then updating the model in a supervised manner using both the labeled and pseudo-labeled data; the selection criteria are usually based on confidence filtering of pseudo labels [16,26,44,53], where the unlabeled samples with high confidence remain and others are discarded. Methods in the second category are based on consistency regularization that enforces the consistency of model predictions between a sample and its perturbed counterpart, including randomly augmented duplicates [42], virtual adversarial examples [33], similar/smooth neighbors [30], to name a few; the smoothness assumption is also considered in these methods, i.e., close input samples should have close labels. The last category of FixMatch [44] and CoMatch [26] has shown remarkable performance by integrating self-training and consistency regularization. In spite of these advances, we show in this paper that the selection criteria in existing methods can be further improved for better SSL.

Specifically, we propose a novel consistency criterion among multiple stochastic classifiers under the self-training framework of SSL, termed Stochastic Consensus (STOCO); Fig. 1 gives the illustration. The proposed criterion is partially inspired by co-training [3,6,8] and tri-training [41,55]; they leverage category predictions of one or two classifiers on unlabeled samples to enlarge the training set, wherein a design principle is based on majority voting that shares a similar insight with the popular techniques of ensemble learning [7,12]. In classical ensemble learning, the number of model parameters grows linearly with that of model classifiers. To improve the efficiency, we propose the use of stochastic classifiers [29] for consistency criterion, where parameters of multiple stochastic classifiers are sampled from a same Gaussian distribution whose mean and standard deviation are simultaneously optimized during training. In the extreme case, one can sample an infinite number of classifiers while keeping the model size unchanged. Due to the scarcity of labels in SSL, modeling classifiers as a distribution itself can provide regularization that mitigates overfitting to the labeled samples. We note that a recent work UPS [39] uses MC-dropout [17] to model randomness, which is model-dependent and data-independent, and yields diverse network structures; differently, STOCO uses stochastic classifiers, whose parameters are modeled as a learnable, model-agnostic Gaussian distribution that can *dynamically capture the pattern of sensible decision boundaries*, directly benefiting model generalization, as demonstrated in Sec. 4.

To implement our proposed consistency criterion, for any unlabeled sample, we compute the element-wise product of category predictions from multiple stochastic classifiers, and select samples with the maximum value in the product higher than a pre-defined threshold; we then take an average of the predictions from multiple classifiers, and generate pseudo labels from the thus obtained averages using a simple but flexible deep learning based discriminative clustering framework [13]. Intuitively, the pseudo labels are generated to both encourage the cluster size balance and respect the underlying data distribution. In this work, we provide theoretical analysis of our proposed criterion by connecting with the theory of learning from noisy data [1]. Our method can be readily applied to self-training based SSL frameworks. Choosing the representative Fix-Match as the baseline, our method with multiple stochastic classifiers achieves the state of the art on four popular benchmarks, especially in label-scarce cases.

2   Related Works

Over the past two decades, a huge literature has emerged on semi-supervised learning (SSL), including a broad variety of algorithms [14]. We focus on deep learning based ones, which can be mainly divided into three categories except for those meta-learning based SSL approaches [19,27,36,47].

Methods in the first category leverage the idea from the earlier works [32,43] that pseudo labels for unlabeled data are produced by the trained model itself and then used to refine the current model, termed as self-training. Such a simple strategy is widely adopted or developed in various fields [16,18,25,39,40,51,56, 57]. Lee [25] assigns the highest-score category to an unlabeled sample. Entropy minimization [18] directly uses predicted class probability distributions as pseudo labels. To improve, confidence thresholding [16] is often used to select reliable pseudo labels. Recently, UPS [39] utilizes both uncertainty and confidence of a network prediction to select a more accurate subset of pseudo labels.

The second category is consistency regularization, which enforces the consistent prediction between a sample and its counterpart perturbed by modifying the model [24,38,46,54] or input [2,30,33,42]. For example, Rasmus et al. [38] minimize the difference between the activations of the unperturbed parent model and those of the perturbed models after denoising ; Mean Teacher [46] is the moving average over weights of model parameters, whose predictions are used as targets; WCP [54] derives the worst-case perturbations on network weights and structures via optimizing with spectral methods and then stabilizes model predictions in presence of such perturbations; Sajjadi et al. [42] make the model prediction consistent for an individual unlabeled sample when it goes through multiple passes of random transformation ; VAT [33] reduces the divergence between model predictions of the vanilla unlabeled sample and its virtual adversarial counterpart; SNTG [30] constructs a graph based on mean teacher predictions to guide the student model so that the neighbors have similar features; PAWS [2] enforces the consistency of distance-based, non-parametrically predictions between the anchor and positive views of a same unlabeled image.

The last category includes methods combining self-training with consistency regularization [4,5,26,44,50,53]. Apart from mixup, ReMixMatch [4] encourages alignment between marginal class distributions of labeled and unlabeled data, and makes consistent predictions between a weakly-augmented image and multiple strongly-augmented images of the same sample. FixMatch [44] trains the model on the strongly-augmented version of a sample with the prediction on its weakly-augmented version as the pseudo label; pseudo labels are selected

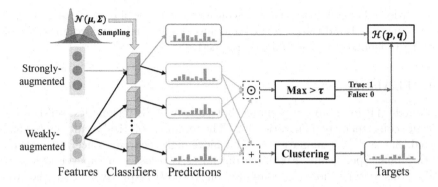

Features   Classifiers   Predictions   Targets

Fig. 1. Diagram for our method of stochastic consensus (STOCO). We sample multiple classifiers from a learned Gaussian distribution $\mathcal{N}(\boldsymbol{\mu}, \boldsymbol{\Sigma})$; for the weakly-augmented version of any unlabeled sample, we calculate the element-wise product of category predictions from these stochastic classifiers and select samples with the maximum value in the product higher than a pre-defined threshold τ; we take an average over the predictions from multiple classifiers, and generate pseudo labels from the thus obtained averages via deep discriminative clustering; then, with these derived targets, the model is trained using the strongly-augmented version of selected samples via a cross-entropy loss $\mathcal{H}(\boldsymbol{p}, \boldsymbol{q})$.

above a pre-defined confidence threshold. Flexibly adjusting class-wise confidence thresholds is introduced in [53], where the principle is to scale down the fixed threshold if one class has less highly confident samples. CoMatch [26] utilizes the similarities between embeddings of unlabeled samples to weight and sum their class probabilities as the pseudo label; a pseudo label graph is then constructed to regularize the embedding graph. Our method shares a similar motivation with these ones, but differs in the aim to progressively improve the noise rate of selected samples by applying the proposed consistency criterion among multiple stochastic classifiers, in a distinctive perspective of designing a more strict criterion, which is under-explored.

3   The Proposed Method

Consider a labeled batch with n_x pairs of samples and one-hot labels $\mathcal{X} = \{(\boldsymbol{x}_i, \boldsymbol{y}_i)\}_{i=1}^{n_x}$, and an unlabeled batch with n_u samples $\mathcal{U} = \{\boldsymbol{u}_i\}_{i=1}^{n_u}$, where $n_u = \gamma n_x$. Here, γ controls the relative size of $\mathcal{X}$ and $\mathcal{U}$. Let the number of classes be K. The objective of semi-supervised learning (SSL) is to predict class labels for unseen samples by learning a feature extractor $g(\cdot; \boldsymbol{\theta}_g)$ that lifts any input sample to the feature space $\mathcal{Z}$, and a classifier $f(\cdot; \boldsymbol{\theta}_f)$ that outputs class probabilities from the feature $\boldsymbol{z} \in \mathcal{Z}$, where $\boldsymbol{\theta}_g$ and $\boldsymbol{\theta}_f$ collect the network parameters of feature extractor and classifier respectively. Let $p(\mathbf{x}; \boldsymbol{\theta}_m)$ be the label distribution predicted by the classification model $f(g(\cdot))$, where $\boldsymbol{\theta}_m = \{\boldsymbol{\theta}_g, \boldsymbol{\theta}_f\}$ collects all parameters of the model. Let $\mathcal{H}(\cdot, \cdot)$ be the cross entropy between two probability distributions. For unlabeled data, we consider two types of data augmentation: a strong one (i.e., RandAugment [11]) and a weak one (i.e., standard flip-and-shift strategy), denoted by $\mathcal{A}(\cdot)$ and $\alpha(\cdot)$ respectively.

3.1 FixMatch

FixMatch [44] integrates two simple but effective SSL techniques, self-training [25] and consistency regularization [42]. The recent theoretical result [48] has suggested that such a combination could achieve high accuracy concerning ground-truth labels. Specifically, FixMatch optimizes two losses: a supervised loss $\mathcal{L}_s$ and an unsupervised loss $\mathcal{L}_u$, computed on $\mathcal{X}$ and $\mathcal{U}$ respectively. $\mathcal{L}_s$ is the cross entropy between predicted label distribution and ground-truth one, computed on the weakly-augmented labeled images:

$$\mathcal{L}_s = \frac{1}{n_x} \sum_{i=1}^{n_x} \mathcal{H}(p(\alpha(\boldsymbol{x}_i); \boldsymbol{\theta}_m), \boldsymbol{y}_i). \tag{1}$$

The computation of $\mathcal{L}_u$ is as follows. For the weakly-augmented unlabeled images $\{\alpha(\boldsymbol{u}_i)\}_{i=1}^{n_u}$, FixMatch first produces category predictions $\{p(\alpha(\boldsymbol{u}_i); \boldsymbol{\theta}_m)\}_{i=1}^{n_u}$; the images with $\max p(\alpha(\boldsymbol{u}_i); \boldsymbol{\theta}_m) > \tau$ are selected and their pseudo labels are generated by $\hat{y}_i = \arg\max p(\alpha(\boldsymbol{u}_i); \boldsymbol{\theta}_m)$, where the hyperparameter τ determines the threshold of traditional confidence filtering [16,40,44,50,57]; then, the model is trained on the strongly-augmented version of the selected samples to predict the generated pseudo labels. For any selected sample $\boldsymbol{u}_i$, we denote the one-hot pseudo label of $\alpha(\boldsymbol{u}_i)$ as $\hat{\boldsymbol{y}}_i$ and write $\mathcal{L}_u$ as the cross entropy between predicted label distribution of $\mathcal{A}(\boldsymbol{u}_i)$ and $\hat{\boldsymbol{y}}_i$:

$$\mathcal{L}_u = \frac{1}{n_u} \sum_{i=1}^{n_u} \mathbb{I}[\max p(\alpha(\boldsymbol{u}_i); \boldsymbol{\theta}_m) > \tau] \mathcal{H}(p(\mathcal{A}(\boldsymbol{u}_i); \boldsymbol{\theta}_m), \hat{\boldsymbol{y}}_i), \tag{2}$$

where $\mathbb{I}[\cdot]$ is an indicator. Combining $\mathcal{L}_s$ and $\mathcal{L}_u$ gives the overall loss of FixMatch:

$$\mathcal{L}_{overall} = \mathcal{L}_s + \lambda_u \mathcal{L}_u, \tag{3}$$

where λ_u is to make a trade-off in the joint optimization problem. Optimizing Eq. (3) implements self-training and consistency regularization simultaneously.

3.2 Our Method: Stochastic Consensus

FixMatch achieves the state-of-the-art performance by setting a high τ, which improves the quality of pseudo labels. However, its use of the traditional confidence criterion is sub-optimal since it only leverages the prediction information from one classifier. The earlier works of co-training [8] and tri-training [55] have suggested that the prediction information from other classifiers can be helpful. To this end, we propose for SSL a novel sample selection scheme, the consistency criterion among multiple classifiers, which can further improve the quality of pseudo labels. Generally, the model size will linearly increase as the number of classifiers grows. To enhance efficiency, we propose to use stochastic classifiers [29], which are modeled by a Gaussian distribution whose parameters are jointly learned in training. One can sample an arbitrary number of classifiers from the learned distribution while keeping the model size consistent. We thus term our proposed method as Stochastic Consensus (STOCO). Moreover, we use a simple but flexible deep learning based discriminative clustering framework [13] to generate a soft version of pseudo labels, which encourages cluster size balance while avoiding the introduction of additional hyperparameter: temperature T [4,5].

Consistency Criterion among Stochastic Classifiers. A Gaussian distribution $\mathcal{N}(\mu, \Sigma)$ is used to model the classifier $f(\cdot; \theta_f)$, i.e., $\theta_f \sim \mathcal{N}(\mu, \Sigma)$, where μ and Σ are the mean vector (by flattening the weight matrix) and diagonal covariance matrix respectively. With the reparametrisation trick [22], the overall loss will be back-propagated to the learnable parameters of μ and Σ. With diagonal Σ, we can always keep the model size as having two classifiers. To be specific, we first draw m vectors $\{\epsilon_j\}_{j=1}^m$ of the same size as μ from a standard Gaussian distribution. Then, m stochastic classifiers $\{\theta_f^j\}_{j=1}^m$ are derived by:

$$\theta_f^j = \mu + \sigma \odot \epsilon_j, \tag{4}$$

where σ is the diagonal of Σ and $\odot$ indicates element-wise product. Due to the nature of randomness in the independent sampling, classifiers in $\{\theta_f^j\}_{j=1}^m$ are different; meanwhile, they do not deviate too much from each other since they come from the same source, thus stabilizing training and avoiding degeneration. On the other hand, since SSL only has access to a few labeled samples, a set of sensible solutions might exist and thus it is natural to model the classifier as a distribution, which also acts as an implicit regularization to mitigate overfitting. These characteristics provide sufficient conditions for our consistency criterion. For a weakly-augmented version of a given unlabeled sample u_i, we extract the feature by $z_i^\alpha = g(\alpha(u_i); \theta_g)$. Each classifier in $\{\theta_f^j\}_{j=1}^m$ takes z_i^α as input and outputs the class probability distribution $p(z_i^\alpha; \theta_f^j)$. We take an ensemble of the predicted label distributions by computing the element-wise product:

$$\dot{p}(z_i^\alpha) = p(z_i^\alpha; \theta_f^1) \odot p(z_i^\alpha; \theta_f^2) \odot \cdots p(z_i^\alpha; \theta_f^m). \tag{5}$$

The sample will be selected if $\max \dot{p}(z_i^\alpha) > \tau$. The proposed criterion is in fact an evolved version of self-training, which selects unlabeled samples for one classifier if all classifiers are confident of the same class. Such a selection strategy is essentially majority voting, leading to more reliable results [7,12,37]. Without loss of generality, the cross entropy in $\mathcal{L}_u$ is computed between $p(z_i^A; \theta_f^1)$ and the one-hot form of $\hat{y}_i = \arg\max \dot{p}(z_i^\alpha)$, where $z_i^A = g(\mathcal{A}(u_i); \theta_g)$.

Pseudo Label Generation via Deep Discriminative Clustering. The core idea is to introduce an auxiliary distribution [13,20,49] by considering the overall data structure in the feature space, which enforces *structural regularization*. Specifically, given m predicted label distributions $\{p(z_i^\alpha; \theta_f^j)\}_{j=1}^m$ for the weakly-augmented version of an unlabeled sample u_i, we take the average as:

$$\bar{p}(z_i^\alpha) = \frac{1}{m} \sum_{j=1}^m p(z_i^\alpha; \theta_f^j), \tag{6}$$

which integrates the prediction information from all m stochastic classifiers and is still a probability distribution (i.e., $\sum \bar{p}(z_i^\alpha) = 1$). For unlabeled data $\{u_i\}_{i=1}^{n_u}$, we collectively write the predicted probability vectors $\{\bar{p}_i^\alpha\}_{i=1}^{n_u}$ as P, where $\bar{p}_i^\alpha = \bar{p}(z_i^\alpha)$. We also write $\bar{p}_{ik}^\alpha$ as the k-th element of $\bar{p}_i^\alpha$. To refine the model predictions iteratively, we then introduce a target counterpart $Q = \{\bar{q}_i^\alpha\}_{i=1}^{n_u}$, which is obtained by optimizing the following objective [13]:

$$\min_{Q} \text{KL}(P|Q) + \text{KL}(\varrho|\pi), \tag{7}$$

where $\varrho = 1/n_u \sum_{i=1}^{n_u} \bar{q}_i^\alpha$ is the empirical label distribution, π is the uniform distribution, and $\text{KL}(\cdot|\cdot)$ denotes the KL divergence between two distributions. The first term in Eq. (7) minimizes the divergence between P and Q, which avoids the targets deviating too much from the predictions and thus shows respect to the underlying data distribution; the second term minimizes the divergence between ϱ and π, which avoids degenerate solutions (i.e., cluster merging) and encourages cluster size balance. The closed-form solution of Q is derived by [13]:

$$\bar{q}_{ik}^\alpha = \frac{\bar{p}_{ik}^\alpha / (\sum_{i'} \bar{p}_{i'k}^\alpha)^{0.5}}{\sum_{k'} \bar{p}_{ik'}^\alpha / (\sum_{i'} \bar{p}_{i'k'}^\alpha)^{0.5}}, \tag{8}$$

which generates the pseudo labels to supervise the model learning, whose effectiveness has been demonstrated in various applications [9,21,28,34,45].

Given $\dot{p}(z_i^\alpha)$ and $\bar{q}_i^\alpha$ for any unlabeled sample, we have an improved version of the unsupervised loss $\mathcal{L}_u$ as:

$$\mathcal{L}_u = \frac{1}{n_u} \sum_{i=1}^{n_u} \mathbb{I}[\max \dot{p}(z_i^\alpha) > \tau] \mathcal{H}(p(z_i^\mathcal{A}; \theta_f^1), \bar{q}_i^\alpha). \tag{9}$$

3.3 Theoretical Analysis

We provide theoretical analysis for our method to show its progressively improved classification error by connecting with the theory in [1]. The work [1] adapts the probably approximately correct (PAC) learning theory from reliable data to noisy data, giving a learning algorithm guidance on how to handle incorrect training samples . The theory is explained below.

Theorem 1 ([1], Theorem 2). *If we draw a sequence ς of*

$$\zeta \geq \frac{2}{\epsilon^2(1 - 2\eta)^2} \ln(\frac{2N}{\delta}) \tag{10}$$

samples, then a hypothesis h that minimizes the disagreement with ς will have the PAC property:

$$\Pr[d(h, h^*) \geq \epsilon] \leq \delta, \tag{11}$$

where ϵ is the classification error rate of the worst-case hypothesis, η (< 0.5) is an upper bound on the classification noise rate, N is the number of hypotheses, δ is a confidence parameter, and $d(\cdot, \cdot)$ is the sum over the probability of elements from the symmetric difference between hypotheses h and h^* (the ground truth).

Theorem 1 tells that if the condition (10) is satisfied, then the difference between the conjectured rule h and the correct rule h^* will be small (less than ϵ) with a high probability (greater than $1 - \delta$). Following [55], we have:

$$v = \frac{c}{\epsilon^2} = \zeta(1 - 2\eta)^2, \tag{12}$$

where $c = 2\nu \ln(\frac{2N}{\delta})$, v is an intermediate variable, and ν is a positive number to make the condition (10) hold equality. During the model training of our method, the classification noise rate at the t-th iteration is estimated by:

$$\eta^t = \frac{\eta_x^t |\mathcal{X}| + \breve{\eta}_u^t |\mathcal{U}_l^t|}{|\mathcal{X} \cup \mathcal{U}_l^t|}, \tag{13}$$

where η_x^t denotes the classification noise rate on the labeled set $\mathcal{X}$, $\eta_x^t |\mathcal{X}|$ is accordingly the number of labeled samples mislabeled by the model, $\mathcal{U}_l^t$ indicates the set of unlabeled samples selected by our method, $\breve{\eta}_u^t$ denotes the estimation of the upper-bound classification noise rate on $\mathcal{U}_l^t$, and $\breve{\eta}_u^t |\mathcal{U}_l^t|$ is accordingly the number of mislabeled samples in $\mathcal{U}_l^t$. According to Eq. (12), v^t is computed by:

$$v^t = \zeta^t (1 - 2\eta^t)^2 = |\mathcal{X} \cup \mathcal{U}_l^t| \left(1 - 2\frac{\eta_x^t |\mathcal{X}| + \breve{\eta}_u^t |\mathcal{U}_l^t|}{|\mathcal{X} \cup \mathcal{U}_l^t|}\right)^2. \tag{14}$$

Eq. (12) shows that v is proportional to $1/\epsilon^2$, i.e., $\epsilon^t < \epsilon^{t-1}$ if $v^t > v^{t-1}$, suggesting that the classification model can be progressively improved via the use of $\mathcal{U}_l^t$ in training. The condition $v^t > v^{t-1}$ can be also written as:

$$|\mathcal{X} \cup \mathcal{U}_l^t| \left(1 - 2\frac{\eta_x^t |\mathcal{X}| + \breve{\eta}_u^t |\mathcal{U}_l^t|}{|\mathcal{X} \cup \mathcal{U}_l^t|}\right)^2 > |\mathcal{X} \cup \mathcal{U}_l^{t-1}| \left(1 - 2\frac{\eta_x^{t-1} |\mathcal{X}| + \breve{\eta}_u^{t-1} |\mathcal{U}_l^{t-1}|}{|\mathcal{X} \cup \mathcal{U}_l^{t-1}|}\right)^2. \tag{15}$$

Considering that η_x^t and η_x^{t-1} can be very small and assuming that $0 < \breve{\eta}_u^t, \breve{\eta}_u^{t-1} < 0.5$, we can simplify the condition (15) as:

$$0 < \frac{\breve{\eta}_u^t}{\breve{\eta}_u^{t-1}} < \frac{|\mathcal{U}_l^{t-1}|}{|\mathcal{U}_l^t|} < 1. \tag{16}$$

Our consistency criterion among multiple stochastic classifiers conducts a strict selection process, where one unlabeled sample will be selected if all classifiers have consistent and confident predictions, leading to a lower classification noise rate than the traditional confidence filter used in FixMatch. It implies that the assumption of $0 < \breve{\eta}_u^t, \breve{\eta}_u^{t-1} < 0.5$ would be implemented and thus the condition of $\breve{\eta}_u^t < \breve{\eta}_u^{t-1}$ would be met. On the other hand, the number of unlabeled samples selected by our method would increase in a gradual manner with the training due to the strict selection; consequently, the conditions of $|\mathcal{U}_l^t| > |\mathcal{U}_l^{t-1}|$ and $\breve{\eta}_u^t|\mathcal{U}_l^t| < \breve{\eta}_u^{t-1}|\mathcal{U}_l^{t-1}|$ would be satisfied. These analyses suggest that our method would iteratively improve the model performance, as demonstrated in Sec. 4.2.

4 Experiments

In this section, we follow FixMatch [44] in terms of hyperparameter setting and model architecture, and evaluate our method using FixMatch as the backbone on typical semi-supervised learning (SSL) benchmark datasets.

4.1 Setup

Datasets. We use the following four SSL benchmark datasets for our experiments with various number of labeled samples. *CIFAR-10* [23] contains $60,000$ colour images in 10 classes, with $6,000$ images per class. There are $50,000$ training images and $10,000$ test images. The 10 classes are completely mutually exclusive. We follow FixMatch and examine on the three settings of 40, 250, and $4,000$ labels. *CIFAR-100* [23] also has $60,000$ images in total but consists of 100 classes, resulting in a more chanllenging classification scenario. Each class has 600 images, where 500 images are for training and the remaining 100 are for testing. We experiment on 400-, $2,500$-, and $10,000$-label settings. *SVHN* [35] includes $73,257$ images for training and $26,032$ images for testing. There are 10 classes in SVHN, corresponding to 10 digits of $\{0, 1, \ldots, 9\}$. Images in SVHN have a colored background and multiple extremely blurred digits, which are taken from the real-world streets. We evaluate on the three settings of 40, 250, and $1,000$ labels. *STL-10* [10] is a dataset tailored for SSL, which comprises $5,000$ labeled color images of size 96×96 and $100,000$ unlabeled images. The unlabeled samples are drawn from a distribution slightly shifted from the one of labeled data, leading to a more realistic test. The labeled set is split into ten pre-defined folds of $1,000$ images each. We evaluate on five of these ten folds.

Implementation Details. For all experiments, we follow FixMatch's training protocol, including optimizer, learning rate schedule, and data preprocessing, and consistently apply the same hyperparameter setting, e.g., $\gamma = 7$, $\tau = 0.95$, and $\lambda_u = 1$. Besides, we empirically set the classifier number m as 5. For CIFAR-10 and SVHN, we use a Wide ResNet-28-2 [52] as the base network; for CIFAR-100, we use a Wide ResNet-28-8 that leverages more convolution filters to cope with larger label space; for STL-10, we use a Wide ResNet-37-2 that utilizes more convolution layers to handle higher input resolution. For inference, we use a fixed classifier determined by the learned mean μ and report the classification result of mean±std over five trials with different folds of labeled data.

Table 1. Ablation studies. We follow [4,26,44] to report error rates on a single 40-label split from CIFAR-10. STOCO (w/o CC and DDC) removes both consistency criterion among stochastic classifiers and pseudo label generation via deep discriminative clustering, namely FixMatch. STOCO (w/o CC) removes the consistency criterion only. STOCO ($m = 5$) is with 5 stochastic classifiers, i.e., our method.

Method	STOCO (w/o CC and DDC)	STOCO (w/o CC)	STOCO (m=1)	STOCO (m=2)	STOCO (m=5)	STOCO (m=10)	STOCO (m=15)	STOCO (m=20)
Error rate	11.27	9.25	8.46	6.68	4.74	4.86	6.79	7.19

4.2 Ablation Studies and Learning Analyses

Ablation Studies. To examine the effects of two key components in our method, we conduct careful ablation studies on CIFAR-10 with 40 labels by evaluating several variants of our method: **(1)** STOCO (w/o CC and DDC), which removes both consistency criterion among stochastic classifiers and pseudo label generation via deep discriminative clustering, namely FixMatch; **(2)** STOCO (w/o CC), which removes the consistency criterion only; **(3)** STOCO with varied number of stochastic classifiers, i.e., $m \in \{1, 2, 5, 10, 15, 20\}$. Results are shown in Table 1. We observe that our method ($m = 5$) degrades by 4.51% after removing the consistency criterion, and then by 2.02% after successively removing the deep discriminative clustering. This verifies that both components are indispensable and thus our method has a reasonable design. Given that the only difference between STOCO ($m = 1$) and STOCO (w/o CC) is whether they use a stochastic classifier, the former slightly outperforms the latter, showing the superiority of the stochastic classifier. The error rate decreases with the growth of m when $m \leq 5$, indicating that more classifiers can enhance the generalization ability via more strict sample selection; a reverse phenomenon is observed when $m > 5$, suggesting that the selection process is too strict to involve enough unlabeled samples in training so that the model cannot converge fast and well. Notably, our STOCO yields fairly stable performance when m varies in a wide range, suggesting the excellent robustness of our method.

Learning Analyses. As analyzed in Sect. 3.3, the proposed consistency criterion among multiple stochastic classifiers conducts a strict selection process, which would meet the three conditions of progressively improving model's generalization ability: **(1)** $|\mathcal{U}_l^t| > |\mathcal{U}_l^{t-1}|$, which states that the number of selected unlabeled samples should increase as the training proceeds; **(2)** $\breve{\eta}_u^t < \breve{\eta}_u^{t-1}$, which tells that the classification noise rate of the selected pseudo-labeled set should decrease iteratively; **(3)** $\breve{\eta}_u^t |\mathcal{U}_l^t| < \breve{\eta}_u^{t-1} |\mathcal{U}_l^{t-1}|$, which describes that the number of mislabeled samples in the selected pseudo-labeled set should reduce with the training. To verify these empirically, we conduct experiments on CIFAR-10 with 40, 250, and 4,000 labels, and examine how the following five quantities evolve during training; they are the training loss measured on the training set, test loss measured on the test set, mask rate that is the ratio of selected samples in an unlabeled batch, noise rate and mislabeled number that are respectively the ratio and number of incorrectly labeled samples in the selected pseudo-labeled

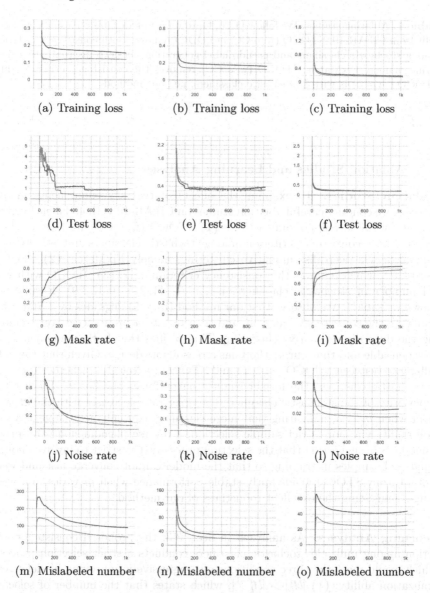

Fig. 2. Learning analyses on our STOCO. For all subfigures, the horizontal axis represents the training epoch; the colors of blue and orange correspond to the results of FixMatch and our method respectively. The results are obtained on CIFAR-10 with 40 (column 1), 250 (column 2), and 4,000 (column 3) labels. Refer to the main text for how these quantities are defined and computed. (Color figure online)

set, which are measured using the ground truth labels, just for visualization. In Fig. 2, we plot the evolving curves of these quantities during training, by comparing our method with the baseline FixMatch [44]. We highlight several

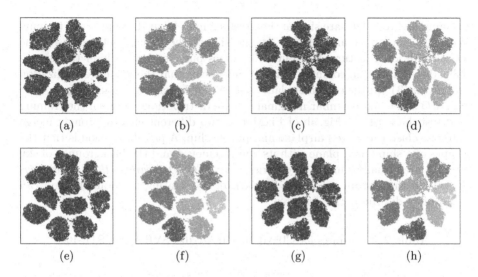

(a)   (b)   (c)   (d)

(e)   (f)   (g)   (h)

Fig. 3. The t-SNE visualization of features learned by FixMatch (left two columns) and our STOCO (right two columns). In columns 1 and 3, the colors of red and blue denote the training and test samples respectively; their counterparts whose classes are color-coded are in columns 2 and 4 respectively. Results in these plots are obtained on CIFAR-10 with 40 (a-d) and 250 (e-h) labels. (Color figure online)

observations below. **(1)** The training loss of our STOCO is lower than that of FixMatch since our proposed consistency criterion selects fewer unlabeled samples, which are the most confident ones with the largest easiness. **(2)** The test loss of our STOCO decreases and then stabilizes at a low level, showing the *progressively improved generalization performance*; particularly, in the extreme case where only 4 labels are available per class (cf. Fig. 2d), our STOCO exhibits a clear loss drop with the training when compared to FixMatch, verifying the better convergence performance of our method. **(3)** In the row of test loss, we find that FixMatch suffers a slight rise at the late stage of training whereas our STOCO does not, suggesting that *our method indeed has the effect of alleviating overfitting.* **(4)** As the training process proceeds, our STOCO has an increasing mask rate, and its noise rate and mislabeled number decrease, indicating that the three conditions are satisfied; notably, *our method achieves a much lower mislabeled number than FixMatch on all label settings*, demonstrating the superiority of our method. These observations corroborate our analyses in Sec. 3.3.

Feature Visualization. To get an intuitive sense of the effect of our method, we expose qualitative differences between the strong baseline FixMatch [44] and our method. We use t-SNE [31] to visualize features of both training and test data, which are extracted by the learned feature extractor of each method. The results on CIFAR-10 with 40 and 250 labels are plotted in Fig. 3. We emphasize several interesting observations below. **(1)** The marginal feature distributions of training and test data are similar, i.e., test samples lie in the support of training data (cf. columns 1 and 3). (2) As the size of the labeled set increases, the class-conditional feature distribution becomes purer and gets closer to the true label distribution (cf. columns 2 and 4), suggesting that the model generalization improves. (3) On the extremely label-scarce setting (cf. Fig. 3a and Fig. 3c), our STOCO yields more similar marginal feature distributions between the training and test data. (4) In Fig. 3b of FixMatch, two different classes wrongly merge into one cluster, e.g., red airplane and purple ship. A possible reason is that the shapes of a ship and a plane with its wings removed and the backgrounds of sky and sea are visually similar. In contrast, *our STOCO separates these ambiguous classes* in the feature space (cf. Fig. 3d), demonstrating that our method can learn more discriminative features.

Table 2. Error rates for CIFAR-10, CIFAR-100, SVHN, and STL-10.

Method	CIFAR-10			CIFAR-100			SVHN			STL-10
	40 labels	250 labels	4000 labels	400 labels	2500 labels	10000 labels	40 labels	250 labels	1000 labels	1000 labels
Π-Model [38]	–	54.26±3.97	14.016±0.38	–	57.256±0.48	37.886±0.11	–	18.966±1.92	7.546±0.36	26.236±0.82
Pseudo-Labeling [25]	–	49.786±0.43	16.096±0.28	–	57.386±0.46	36.216±0.19	–	20.216±1.09	9.946±0.61	27.996±0.83
Mean Teacher [46]	–	32.326±2.30	9.196±0.19	–	53.916±0.57	35.836±0.24	–	3.576±0.11	3.426±0.07	21.436±2.39
MixMatch [5]	47.546±11.50	11.056±0.86	6.426±0.10	67.616±1.32	39.946±0.37	28.316±0.33	42.556±14.53	3.986±0.23	3.506±0.28	10.416±0.61
UPS [39]	–	–	6.42	–	–	–	–	–	–	–
Meta-Semi [47]	–	–	6.106±0.10	–	–	29.696±0.18	–	–	–	8.036±0.24
UDA [50]	29.056±5.93	8.826±1.08	4.886±0.18	59.286±0.88	33.136±0.22	24.506±0.25	52.636±20.51	5.696±2.76	2.466±0.24	7.666±0.56
ReMixMatch [4]	19.106±9.64	5.446±0.05	4.726±0.13	44.286±2.06	27.436±0.31	23.036±0.56	*3.346±0.20*	2.926±0.48	2.656±0.08	**5.236±0.45**
FixMatch [44]	13.816±3.37	5.076±0.65	4.266±0.05	48.856±1.75	28.296±0.11	22.606±0.12	3.966±2.17	*2.486±0.38*	**2.286±0.11**	7.986±1.50
CoMatch [26]	6.916±1.39	4.916±0.33	–	–	–	–	–	–	–	–
FlexMatch [53]	**4.996±0.16**	*4.806±0.06*	*3.956±0.03*	**32.446±1.99**	**23.856±0.23**	**19.926±0.06**	5.366±2.38	–	2.866±0.91	*5.566±0.22*
STOCO	7.176±1.95	**4.776±0.30**	**3.866±0.05**	*41.456±1.21*	*27.416±0.35*	*21.826±0.20*	**2.856±0.16**	**2.476±0.14**	*2.386±0.06*	7.796±0.52

4.3 Comparison with the State-of-the-Art

We compare the proposed STOCO with the state-of-the-art methods on CIFAR-10 in Table 2, where results of existing methods are quoted from their respective papers or [44]. With 400 labels per class, all compared methods show small differences in performance; nevertheless, by combining SSL techniques, FixMatch greatly improves over Π-Model, Pseudo-Labeling, and Mean Teacher that are on their own; notably, our STOCO achieves the best result of 3.86%. With 25 labels per class, the methods based on technique combination are far ahead of those on their own by a margin larger than 20%, showing the huge advantages of technique combination; again, our method outperforms all the compared ones. With only 4 labels per class, the simpler FixMatch that combines self-training and consistency regularization is superior to the excellent ReMixMatch, which additionally integrates self-supervised learning and mixup; notably, with multiple stochastic classifiers, our STOCO produces a much better result than FixMatch and is on par with CoMatch, showing that our method is suitable for application scenarios with extremely scarce labels. Furthermore, we find that our method achieves a high classification accuracy of 7.17% on the challenging 40-label setting, which is only 2.40% and 3.31% lower than that on the 250- and 4000-label settings respectively, indicating that the benefit from increasing the number of labeled samples is limited on CIFAR-10 due to its simplicity.

The comparisons between different methods on the difficult CIFAR-100 are shown in Table 2, where most of the phenomena are similar to those on CIFAR-10. Besides, we emphasize the following several observations. **(1)** Compared to the results on CIFAR-10, these on CIFAR-100 still have a large room of improvement since the 100 classes in CIFAR-100 come from a fine-grained classification of 20 superclasses and thus are difficult to distinguish. **(2)** ReMixMatch performs better than FixMatch, especially on the hardest 400-label setting, which is due to its use of distribution alignment (empirically found by [44]). **(3)** Our STOCO improves over FixMatch by a large margin, e.g., 7.40% on the 400-label setting, demonstrating the effectiveness of our method in tackling different learning scenarios with varying label conditions. Note that recent methods achieve the SSL goal of performing better with less supervision by technique combination; differently, our method gets closer to the goal via the use of a sample selection criterion based on stochastic consensus.

The results on SVHN are reported in Table 2, from which we take similar observations to those above. It is noteworthy that with only 4 labels per class, our STOCO outperforms the state-of-the-art FlexMatch by 2.51%, confirming the superiority of our method. When increasing the number of labels in each class from 4 to 100, we find that the performance gain is small (0.47%). This suggests that for a simple task like SVHN, a few labels are enough to get a good classification model. Although the same number of labels are available for each class, the results on CIFAR-100 are much worse than those on SVHN, implying that the required number of labeled samples to achieve good performance is task-dependent. Establishing a principled metric is expected to estimate this number in practical applications, such that the manual labeling efforts can be reduced.

We also organize the results on STL-10 in Table 2. With 100 labeled samples per class involved in training, the SSL methods based on technique combination exhibit clear advantages over others in such a challenging test; in particular, our STOCO is comparable to the state-of-the-art ones.

5   Conclusion

Semi-supervised learning (SSL) is a popular field, which aims to reduce the labeling cost in cases requiring domain expertise, e.g., medical diagnosis and cultural relic identification. Recent SSL methods focus on integrating various SSL techniques including self-training, where the criterion for selecting unlabeled samples with pseudo labels plays an important role in the empirical success. However, we note that the research direction of sample selection criterion is under-explored in SSL. To this end, we propose a novel criterion based on consistency among multiple stochastic classifiers, termed Stochastic Consensus (STOCO), which can be readily applied to any self-training based SSL framework. We choose the representative FixMatch as the baseline and achieve the state of the art on typical SSL benchmarks, especially in label-scarce cases. STOCO improves the model's generalization ability without losing simplicity, which helps audience expansion in the academic community and industrial deployment in recognition systems.

Acknowledgments. This work is supported in part by Program for Guangdong Introducing Innovative and Enterpreneurial Teams (No.: 2017ZT07X183), National Natural Science Foundation of China (No.: 61771201), and Guangdong R&D key project of China (No.: 2019B010155001). Correspondence to Kui Jia (email: kuijia@scut.edu.cn).

References

1. Angluin, D., Laird, P.: Learning from noisy examples. Mach. Learn. **2**, 343–370 (1988)
2. Assran, M., et al.: Semi-supervised learning of visual features by non-parametrically predicting view assignments with support samples. In: ICCV, pp. 8443–8452 (2021)
3. Balcan, M.F., Blum, A., Yang, K.: Co-training and expansion: towards bridging theory and practice. In: NeurIPS, pp. 89–96 (2004)
4. Berthelot, D., et al.: Remixmatch: semi-supervised learning with distribution matching and augmentation anchoring. In: ICLR (2020)
5. Berthelot, D., Carlini, N., Goodfellow, I., Papernot, N., Oliver, A., Raffel, C.A.: Mixmatch: a holistic approach to semi-supervised learning. In: NeurIPS, vol. 32 (2019)
6. Blum, A., Mitchell, T.: Combining labeled and unlabeled data with co-training. In: COLT, pp. 92–100 (1998)
7. d'Alché Buc, F., Grandvalet, Y., Ambroise, C.: Semi-supervised marginboost. In: NeurIPS, pp. 553–560 (2001)
8. Chen, M., Weinberger, K.Q., Blitzer, J.: Co-training for domain adaptation. In: NeurIPS, vol. 24 (2011)
9. Chen, Z., Zhuang, J., Liang, X., Lin, L.: Blending-target domain adaptation by adversarial meta-adaptation networks. In: CVPR, pp. 2243–2252 (2019)
10. Coates, A., Ng, A., Lee, H.: An analysis of single-layer networks in unsupervised feature learning. In: Proceedings of the Fourteenth International Conference on Artificial Intelligence and Statistics, pp. 215–223 (2011)
11. Cubuk, E.D., Zoph, B., Shlens, J., Le, Q.: Randaugment: practical automated data augmentation with a reduced search space. In: NeurIPS, vol. 33, pp. 18613–18624 (2020)
12. Dietterich, T.G.: Ensemble methods in machine learning. In: MCS, pp. 1–15 (2000)
13. Dizaji, K.G., Herandi, A., Deng, C., Cai, W., Huang, H.: Deep clustering via joint convolutional autoencoder embedding and relative entropy minimization. In: ICCV, pp. 5747–5756 (2017)
14. van Engelen, J.E., Hoos, H.H.: A survey on semi-supervised learning. Mach. Learn. **109**(2), 373–440 (2019). https://doi.org/10.1007/s10994-019-05855-6
15. Fei-Fei, L., Fergus, R., Perona, P.: One-shot learning of object categories. IEEE TPAMI **28**, 594–611 (2006)
16. French, G., Mackiewicz, M., Fisher, M.: Self-ensembling for visual domain adaptation. In: International Conference on Learning Representations (2018). https://openreview.net/forum?id=rkpoTaxA-
17. Gal, Y., Ghahramani, Z.: Dropout as a bayesian approximation: Representing model uncertainty in deep learning. In: Balcan, M.F., Weinberger, K.Q. (eds.) Proceedings of International Conference Machine Learning. Proceedings of Machine Learning Research, 20–22 June 2016, vol. 48, pp. 1050–1059. PMLR, New York (2016). https://proceedings.mlr.press/v48/gal16.html

18. Grandvalet, Y., Bengio, Y.: Semi-supervised learning by entropy minimization. In: NeurIPS, pp. 529–536 (2004)

19. Guo, L.Z., Zhang, Z.Y., Jiang, Y., Li, Y.F., Zhou, Z.H.: Safe deep semi-supervised learning for unseen-class unlabeled data. In: III, H.D., Singh, A. (eds.) Proceedings of International Conference on Machine Learning. Proceedings of Machine Learning Research, 13–18 July 2020, vol. 119, pp. 3897–3906. PMLR (2020)

20. Jabi, M., Pedersoli, M., Mitiche, A., Ayed, I.B.: Deep clustering: on the link between discriminative models and k-means. IEEE TPAMI **43**, 1887–1896 (2021)

21. Karim, M.R., et al.: Deep learning-based clustering approaches for bioinformatics. Brief. Bioinf. **22**, 393–415 (2020)

22. Kingma, D., Welling, M.: Auto-encoding variational bayes. In: ICLR (2014)

23. Krizhevsky, A.: Learning multiple layers of features from tiny images. In: Technical report (2009)

24. Laine, S., Aila, T.: Temporal ensembling for semi-supervised learning. In: ICLR (2016)

25. Lee, D.H.: Pseudo-label : The simple and efficient semi-supervised learning method for deep neural networks. In: Proceedings of International Conference on Machine Learning Workshop (2013)

26. Li, J., Xiong, C., Hoi, S.C.: Comatch: semi-supervised learning with contrastive graph regularization. In: ICCV, pp. 9475–9484 (2021)

27. Li, W., Foo, C., Bilen, H.: Learning to impute: a general framework for semi-supervised learning. CoRR abs/1912.10364 (2019). http://arxiv.org/abs/1912.10364

28. Liang, J., Yang, J., Lee, H.-Y., Wang, K., Yang, M.-H.: Sub-GAN: an unsupervised generative model via subspaces. In: Ferrari, V., Hebert, M., Sminchisescu, C., Weiss, Y. (eds.) ECCV 2018. LNCS, vol. 11215, pp. 726–743. Springer, Cham (2018). https://doi.org/10.1007/978-3-030-01252-6_43

29. Lu, Z., Yang, Y., Zhu, X., Liu, C., Song, Y.Z., Xiang, T.: Stochastic classifiers for unsupervised domain adaptation. In: CVPR, pp. 9108–9117 (2020)

30. Luo, Y., Zhu, J., Li, M., Ren, Y., Zhang, B.: Smooth neighbors on teacher graphs for semi-supervised learning. In: CVPR, pp. 8896–8905 (2018)

31. van der Maaten, L., Hinton, G.: Visualizing data using t-sne. J. Mach. Learn. Res. **9**, 2579–2605 (2008)

32. McLachlan, G.J.: Iterative reclassification procedure for constructing an asymptotically optimal rule of allocation in discriminant analysis. J. Am. Stat. Assoc. **70**, 365–369 (1975)

33. Miyato, T., Maeda, S.I., Koyama, M., Ishii, S.: Virtual adversarial training: a regularization method for supervised and semi-supervised learning. IEEE TPAMI **41**, 1979–1993 (2019)

34. Mousavi, S.M., Zhu, W., Ellsworth, W., Beroza, G.: Unsupervised clustering of seismic signals using deep convolutional autoencoders. IEEE Geosci. Remote Sens. Lett. **16**, 1693–1697 (2019)

35. Netzer, Y., Wang, T., Coates, A., Bissacco, A., Wu, B., Ng, A.Y.: Reading digits in natural images with unsupervised feature learning. In: Workshop of Proceedings of Neural Information Processing System (2011)

36. Pham, H., Dai, Z., Xie, Q., Le, Q.V.: Meta pseudo labels. In: CVPR, pp. 11557–11568 (2021)

37. Quinlan, J.R.: Miniboosting decision trees (1999)

38. Rasmus, A., Valpola, H., Honkala, M., Berglund, M., Raiko, T.: Semi-supervised learning with ladder networks. In: NeurIPS, pp. 3546–3554 (2015)

39. Rizve, M.N., Duarte, K., Rawat, Y.S., Shah, M.: In defense of pseudo-labeling: an uncertainty-aware pseudo-label selection framework for semi-supervised learning. In: ICLR (2021). https://openreview.net/forum?id=-ODN6SbiUU

40. Rosenberg, C., Hebert, M., Schneiderman, H.: Semi-supervised self-training of object detection models. In: Seventh IEEE Workshops on Applications of Computer Vision, vol. 1, pp. 29–36 (2005)

41. Saito, K., Ushiku, Y., Harada, T.: Asymmetric tri-training for unsupervised domain adaptation. In: Proceedings of International Conference Machine Learning, pp. 2988–2997 (2017)

42. Sajjadi, M., Javanmardi, M., Tasdizen, T.: Regularization with stochastic transformations and perturbations for deep semi-supervised learning. In: NeurIPS, vol. 29 (2016)

43. Scudder, H.: Probability of error of some adaptive pattern-recognition machines. IEEE Trans. Inf. Theory **11**, 363–371 (1965)

44. Sohn, K., et al.: Fixmatch: simplifying semi-supervised learning with consistency and confidence. In: NeurIPS, vol. 33, pp. 596–608 (2020)

45. Tang, H., Chen, K., Jia, K.: Unsupervised domain adaptation via structurally regularized deep clustering. In: CVPR, pp. 8725–8735 (2020)

46. Tarvainen, A., Valpola, H.: Mean teachers are better role models: weight-averaged consistency targets improve semi-supervised deep learning results. In: NeurIPS, vol. 30 (2017)

47. Wang, Y., Guo, J., Song, S., Huang, G.: Meta-semi: a meta-learning approach for semi-supervised learning. CoRR abs/2007.02394 (2020). https://arxiv.org/abs/2007.02394

48. Wei, C., Shen, K., Chen, Y., Ma, T.: Theoretical analysis of self-training with deep networks on unlabeled data. In: ICLR (2021)

49. Xie, J., Girshick, R., Farhadi, A.: Unsupervised deep embedding for clustering analysis. In: Proceedings of International Conference on Machine Learning, pp. 478–487 (2016)

50. Xie, Q., Dai, Z., Hovy, E., Luong, T., Le, Q.: Unsupervised data augmentation for consistency training. In: NeurIPS, vol. 33, pp. 6256–6268 (2020)

51. Xie, Q., Luong, M.T., Hovy, E., Le, Q.V.: Self-training with noisy student improves imagenet classification. In: CVPR, pp. 10687–10698 (2020)

52. Zagoruyko, S., Komodakis, N.: Wide residual networks. In: BMVC (2016)

53. Zhang, B., et al.: Flexmatch: Boosting semi-supervised learning with curriculum pseudo labeling. In: Beygelzimer, A., Dauphin, Y., Liang, P., Vaughan, J.W. (eds.) NeurIPS (2021). https://openreview.net/forum?id=3qMwV98zLIk

54. Zhang, L., Qi, G.J.: Wcp: worst-case perturbations for semi-supervised deep learning. In: CVPR, pp. 3911–3920 (2020)

55. Zhou, Z.H., Li, M.: Tri-training: exploiting unlabeled data using three classifiers. IEEE Trans. Knowl. Data Eng. **17**, 1529–1541 (2005)

56. Zou, Y., Yu, Z., Liu, X., Kumar, B.V.K.V., Wang, J.: Confidence regularized self-training. In: ICCV, pp. 5981–5990 (2019)

57. Zou, Y., Yu, Z., Vijaya Kumar, B.V.K., Wang, J.: Unsupervised domain adaptation for semantic segmentation via class-balanced self-training. In: Ferrari, V., Hebert, M., Sminchisescu, C., Weiss, Y. (eds.) ECCV 2018. LNCS, vol. 11207, pp. 297–313. Springer, Cham (2018). https://doi.org/10.1007/978-3-030-01219-9_18

DiffuseMorph: Unsupervised Deformable Image Registration Using Diffusion Model

Boah Kim⬤, Inhwa Han⬤, and Jong Chul Ye$^{(\boxtimes)}$⬤

Korea Advanced Institute of Science and Technology (KAIST), Daejeon, South Korea
{boahkim,inhwahan,jong.ye}@kaist.ac.kr

Abstract. Deformable image registration is one of the fundamental tasks in medical imaging. Classical registration algorithms usually require a high computational cost for iterative optimizations. Although deep-learning-based methods have been developed for fast image registration, it is still challenging to obtain realistic continuous deformations from a moving image to a fixed image with less topological folding problem. To address this, here we present a novel diffusion-model-based image registration method, called DiffuseMorph. DiffuseMorph not only generates synthetic deformed images through reverse diffusion but also allows image registration by deformation fields. Specifically, the deformation fields are generated by the conditional score function of the deformation between the moving and fixed images, so that the registration can be performed from continuous deformation by simply scaling the latent feature of the score. Experimental results on 2D facial and 3D medical image registration tasks demonstrate that our method provides flexible deformations with topology preservation capability.

Keywords: Image registration · Diffusion model · Image deformation · Unsupervised learning

1 Introduction

Deformable image registration is to estimate non-rigid voxel correspondences between moving and fixed image pairs. This is especially important for medical image analysis such as disease diagnosis and treatment monitoring, since the anatomical structures or shapes of medical images are different according to subjects, scanning time, imaging modality, etc. Accordingly, various image registration methods have been studied over the past decades.

Part of this paper is presented at the 25th International Conference on Medical Image Computing and Computer Assisted Intervention, MICCAI 2022 [20].

Supplementary Information The online version contains supplementary material available at https://doi.org/10.1007/978-3-031-19821-2_20.

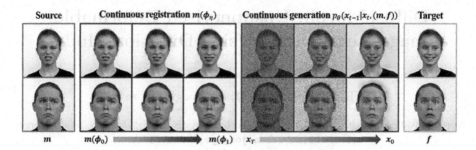

Fig. 1. DiffuseMorph provides not only deformable image registration along the continuous trajectory by simply scaling the latent features in generating deformation fields but also synthetic deformed images through continuous generation by the reverse diffusion process.

Classical image registration approaches usually attempt to align images by solving a computationally expensive optimization problem [1, 2, 22]. To address this computational issue, deep-learning-based image registration methods have been extensively studied [3, 6, 19, 26, 30], which train neural networks to estimate the registration field by taking the moving and fixed images as network inputs. These approaches provide fast deformation while maintaining registration accuracy. However, the supervised methods usually require the ground-truth registration fields [30, 31], and some of the existing unsupervised approaches need additional diffeomorphic constraints [10, 23] or the cycle-consistency [19] for topology preservation.

Recently, score-based diffusion models have shown high-quality performance in image generation [37, 38]. In particular, the denoising diffusion probabilistic model (DDPM) [14, 34] learns the Markov transformation from Gaussian noise to data distribution and provides diverse samples through the stochastic diffusion process by estimating the latent feature of score function, which has been applied to many areas of computer vision [8, 12, 18, 33, 35]. To generate images with desired semantics, conditional denoising diffusion models have been also presented [9, 32]. However, it is challenging to apply DDPM to the image registration task, since the proper registration should be performed through the deformation field for the moving image rather than image generation.

In this paper, by leveraging the property of the diffusion model where the estimated latent feature provides spatial information to generate images, we present a novel unsupervised deformable image registration approach, dubbed DiffuseMorph, by adapting the DDPM to generate deformation fields. Specifically, our proposed model is composed of a diffusion network and a deformation network: the former network learns a conditional score function of the deformation between moving and fixed images, and the latter network estimates the deformation field using the latent feature from the score function and provides deformed images. These two networks are jointly trained in an end-to-end learning manner so that DiffuseMorph not only estimates Markov transformation in the direction in which the moving image is deformed into the fixed image, but also produces the registration field for the moving image to be warped into the fixed image. Since the latent feature from the conditional score function of the diffusion model has spatial information of the condition, the linear scaling of the latent feature may provide deformation fields along the continuous trajectory from the moving to the fixed images.

Accordingly, as shown in Fig. 1, the proposed DiffuseMorph allows both image registration along the continuous trajectory and synthetic deformed image generation. Specifically, our trained model provide the continuous deformations from the moving image to the fixed image by simply interpolating the latent feature that is used as an input for the deformation network. In addition, the proposed model can quickly generate synthetic deformed images similar to the fixed images. Here, to further accelerate the diffusion procedure, instead of starting from random Gaussian noise, we present a generative process in which the moving image is propagated one step via forward diffusion and then iteratively refined through the reverse diffusion process of the DDPM. This reduces the number of diffusion steps significantly and makes the sample retain the original moving image content.

We demonstrate the performance of the proposed method on 2D facial expression registration and 3D medical image registration tasks. The experimental results verify that our model achieves high performance in registration accuracy. Also, thanks to the latent feature estimated from the diffusion model, our method enables real-time image registration along the continuous trajectory between the moving and fixed images, which is more realistic than the comparative learning-based registration methods. Our main contributions are summarized as:

- We propose DiffuseMorph, the first image registration method employing the denoising diffusion model conditioned on a pair of moving and fixed images.
- When the proposed model is trained, our model not only performs image registration along the continuous trajectory from the moving to fixed images by scaling the latent feature but also generates synthetic deformed images through the fast reverse diffusion process.
- We demonstrate that the proposed method can be applied to 2D and 3D image registration tasks and provide accurate deformation with comparable topology preservation over the existing methods.

2 Backgrounds and Related Works

2.1 Deformable Image Registration

Given a moving image m and a fixed image f, classical deformable image registration methods are performed by solving the following optimization problem:

$$\phi^* = \underset{\phi}{\operatorname{argmin}} \quad L_{sim}(m(\phi), f) + L_{reg}(\phi), \tag{1}$$

where ϕ^* is the optimal registration field to deform the moving image into the fixed image. L_{sim} is the dissimilarity function to compute the similarity between the deformed and fixed images, and L_{reg} is the regularization penalty of the registration field. By minimizing the energy function, the deformed image $m(\phi)$ is estimated by warping the moving image. In particular, diffeomorphic registration can be achieved when one imposes additional constraints on the field ϕ such that the deformation mapping is differentiable and invertible, thereby preserving the topology [2,4,39].

Learning-based Registration Methods. As the traditional registration approaches usually require large computation and long runtime, deep learning methods have been extensively studied lately, which estimates the deformation field in real time once a neural network is trained. However, supervised learning methods train the networks using the ground-truth registration fields [6,7,31,42], which needs high-quality labels for training. To alleviate this, weakly-supervised registration models that use pseudo-labels such as segmentation maps have been developed [16,41]. On the other hand, unsupervised learning approaches train the networks by computing similarity between the deformed image and the fixed reference [3,19,26,27,40]. To guarantee topology preservation, learning-based diffeomorphic registration methods are also presented [10,11,23], which have the layer of scaling and squaring integration for the diffeormorphic constraint.

These existing methods may provide intermediate deformations between the moving and fixed images by scaling the registration field or integrating the velocity field in shorter timescales. However, our method produces more realistic continuous deformation by scaling the latent feature that has spatial information of the moving and fixed images, improving the performance of image registration.

2.2   Denoising Diffusion Probabilistic Model

Recently, the denoising diffusion probabilistic model (DDPM) [14,34], one of the generative models, is presented to learn the Markov transformation from the simple Gaussian distribution to the data distribution. In the forward diffusion process, noises are gradually added to the data x_0 using a Markov chain, in which each step of sampling latent variables x_t for $t \in [0, T]$ is defined as a Gaussian transition:

$$q(x_t|x_{t-1}) = \mathcal{N}(x_t; \sqrt{1 - \beta_t}x_{t-1}, \beta_t I), \tag{2}$$

where $0 < \beta_t < 1$ is a variance of the noise. The resulting distribution of x_t given x_0 is then expressed as:

$$q(x_t|x_0) = \mathcal{N}(x_t; \sqrt{\alpha_t}x_0, (1 - \alpha_t)I), \tag{3}$$

where $\alpha_t = \Pi_{s=1}^t (1 - \beta_s)$. Accordingly, given $\epsilon \sim \mathcal{N}(0, I)$, x_t can be sampled by:

$$x_t = \sqrt{\alpha_t}x_0 + \sqrt{1 - \alpha_t}\epsilon. \tag{4}$$

For the generative process to perform the reverse diffusion, DDPM learns the parameterized Gaussian process $p_\theta(x_{t-1}|x_t)$, which is represented as:

$$p_\theta(x_{t-1}|x_t) = \mathcal{N}(x_{t-1}; \mu_\theta(x_t, t), \sigma_t^2 I), \tag{5}$$

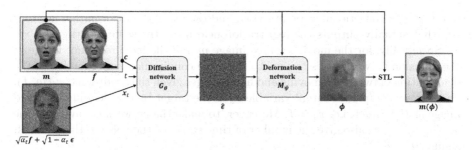

Fig. 2. The training framework of DiffuseMorph. Given a condition with a pair of a moving image m and a fixed image f, the diffusion network G_θ estimates the conditional score function of the deformation, and the deformation network M_ψ outputs the registration field ϕ. Then, using the spatial transformation layer (STL), the moving image is warped into the fixed image.

where σ_t is a fixed variance, and $\mu_\theta(x_t, t)$ is a learned mean defined as:

$$\mu_\theta(x_t, t) = \frac{1}{\sqrt{1-\beta_t}} \left(x_t - \frac{\beta_t}{\sqrt{1-\alpha_t}} \epsilon_\theta(x_t, t) \right), \tag{6}$$

where ϵ_θ is a parameterized model. In fact, the model $\epsilon_\theta(x_t, t)$ is just a scaled version of the score function $s_\theta(x_t, t)$ [36], which is the gradient of the $\log p_\theta(x_t)$. Once the model ϵ_θ is trained, the data is sampled by the following stochastic generation step: $x_{t-1} = \mu_\theta(x_t, t) + \sigma_t z$, where $\sigma_t^2 = \frac{1-\alpha_{t-1}}{1-\alpha_t} \beta_t$ and $z \sim \mathcal{N}(0, I)$.

Conditional Diffusion Models. In order to generate images with desired semantics, conditional diffusion models have been proposed recently [9,15,29, 32,35,37], which gives the conditional reference image to the network or the generative process. DDIM [35] proposes a deterministic non-Markovian generative process starting from an initial condition to control the image generation of the reverse diffusion process. SR3 [32] presents a method to train the DDPM with a conditioned image for the super-resolution task. ILVR [9] proposes a conditioning iterative generative process using an unconditional model. However, these diffusion model-based generative methods are concerned about image generation, and cannot be used for image registration as they do not produce any deformation field for the registration.

3   Proposed Method

3.1   Framework of DiffuseMorph

By leveraging the capability of DDPM, we aim to develop a novel diffusion model-based unsupervised image registration approach. Since the image registration is to warp the moving image using the deformation field, we design our model with two networks as illustrated in Fig. 2: one is a diffusion network G_θ

to estimate a conditional score function, and the other is a deformation network M_ψ that actually outputs the registration field using the score function.

Specifically, for the moving source image m and the fixed reference image f, the diffusion network G_θ is trained to learn the conditional score function of the deformation between the moving and fixed images given the condition $c = (m, f)$. For this, we sample the latent variable x_t of the target by (4), defining the fixed image as the target, i.e. $x_0 = f$. Moreover, to make the network G_θ aware of the level of noise, we also give the number of time steps for the noise to the network, similar to [14].

On the other hand, the deformation network M_ψ takes the latent feature of the conditional score function $\hat{\epsilon}$ that is an output of the diffusion network, as well as the moving source image m. Then the network outputs the registration field ϕ, providing the deformed image $m(\phi)$ by warping the moving image m using the spatial transformation layer (STL) [17]. To deform 2D/3D images in our experiments, we adopt the transformation function using bi-/tri-linear interpolation.

3.2   Loss Function

Recall that the diffusion network G_θ and the deformation network M_ψ are jointly trained in an end-to-end learning manner. Thus, for the training of our model, we design the objective function as follows:

$$\min_{G_\theta, M_\psi} L_{diffusion}(c, x_t, t) + \lambda L_{regist}(m, f), \qquad (7)$$

where $L_{diffusion}$ and L_{regist} are the diffusion loss and the registration loss, respectively, and λ is a hyper-parameter. The detailed description of each loss function is as follows.

Given the condition c and the perturbed data x_t at the time step $t \in [0, T_{train}]$, the diffusion loss is to learn the conditional score function:

$$L_{diffusion}(c, x_t, t) = \mathbb{E}_{\epsilon, x_t, t} ||G_\theta(c, x_t, t) - \epsilon||_2^2, \qquad (8)$$

where $\epsilon \sim \mathcal{N}(0, I)$. Also, the registration loss is to estimate the deformation field so that the deformed source image has similar shape of the fixed image, which is designed as the traditional energy function in (1):

$$L_{regist}(m, f) = -(m(\phi) \otimes f) + \lambda_\phi \sum ||\nabla \phi||^2, \qquad (9)$$

where $\phi = M_\psi(m, \hat{\epsilon})$ with $\hat{\epsilon}$ referring to the diffusion network output, and λ_ϕ is a hyper-parameter. The first term of (9) is the local normalized cross-correlation [3] between the deformed image and fixed image, and the second term is the smoothness penalty on the registration field. We set $\lambda_\phi = 1$.

It is remarkable that the net effect of the two loss functions is that G_θ is trained to estimate the latent feature for the conditional score function of the deformation, which has the spatial information of the moving and fixed images.

Fig. 3. In the inference phase, our model provides not only the image registration $m(\phi)$ that warps the moving image, but also generates synethetic images $\tilde{m}$.

Accordingly, the latent feature helps the proposed model to perform image registration along the continuous trajectory, which can provide topology preservation. Furthermore, when combined with the reverse diffusion process, the latent feature guides the reverse diffusion to generate the synthetic deformed image from the moving image initialization.

3.3 Image Registration Using DiffuseMorph

When the networks of the proposed model are trained, in the inference phase, they provide image registration by estimating the deformation field for the moving image to be aligned with the fixed image. Thanks to the end-to-end training of our model, the diffusion network allows the deformation network to generate the regular registration field. Specifically, using the learned parameters of $G_{\theta*}$ and $M_{\psi*}$, the registration field ϕ at $t = 0$ is estimated by:

$$\phi = M_{\psi*}(m, G_{\theta*}(c, x_0, t)), \tag{10}$$

where x_0 is set to the fixed target image f. Then, the deformed image $m(\phi)$ is computed using the estimated field ϕ through the spatial transformation layer. Therefore, our model performs image registration at a single step with the smooth registration field.

Image Registration Along Continuous Trajectory. In the image registration that warps the moving image into the fixed image, our model provides the continuous deformation of the moving image along the trajectory toward the fixed image. This is possible since the deformation network estimates the registration field according to the latent feature. Specifically, if the latent feature from the conditional score is set to zero, the deformation network outputs the registration field that hardly warps the moving image, whereas when the latent feature is given as in (10), the deformation network estimates the registration field that deforms the moving image into the fixed image.

Accordingly, as described in Algorithm 1, for the latent feature $\hat{\epsilon}^f = G_{\theta^*}(c, f, 0)$, the registration field ϕ_η for the continuous image deformation can be generated by simply interpolating the latent feature:

$$\phi_\eta = M_{\psi^*}(m, \hat{\epsilon}_\eta^f), \qquad (11)$$

where $\hat{\epsilon}_\eta^f = \eta \cdot \hat{\epsilon}^f$ for $0 \leq \eta \leq 1$.
We believe that this interesting phenomenon occurs from learning the conditional score function of deformation, as will be observed later in our experiments.

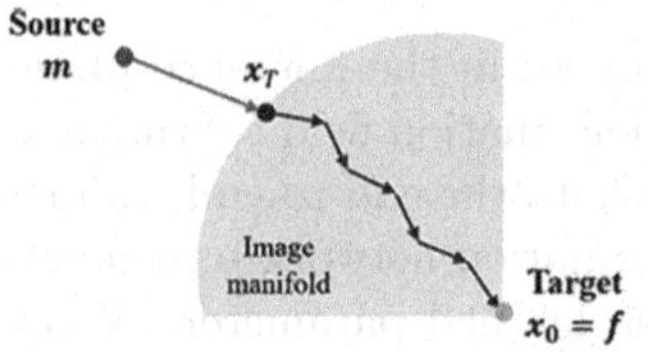

Algorithm 1. Continuous image registration

1: **Input:** Conditional images, $c = (m, f)$
2: **Output:** Deformed moving image, $m(\phi_\eta)$
3: Set the latent feature $\hat{\epsilon}^f = G_{\theta^*}(c, f, 0)$
4: **for** $\eta \in [0, 1]$ **do**
5: $\quad \hat{\epsilon}_\eta^f \leftarrow \eta \cdot \hat{\epsilon}^f$
6: $\quad \phi_\eta \leftarrow M_{\psi^*}(m, \hat{\epsilon}_\eta^f)$
7: **end for=**
8: **return** $m(\phi_\eta)$

Fig. 4. Generative process toward fixed target data distribution.

Algorithm 2. Synthetic image generation process

1: **Input:** Conditional images, $c = (m, f)$
2: **Output:** Synthetic deformed image, x
3: Set $T \in (0, T_{train})$
4: Sample $x_T = \sqrt{\alpha_T} m + \sqrt{1 - \alpha_T} \epsilon$, where $\epsilon \sim \mathcal{N}(0, I)$
5: **for** $t = T, T-1, ..., 1$ **do**
6: $\quad z \sim \mathcal{N}(0, I)$
7: $\quad x_{t-1} \leftarrow \frac{1}{\sqrt{1-\beta_t}}(x_t - \frac{\beta_t}{\sqrt{1-\alpha_t}} G_{\theta^*}(c, x_t, t)) + \sigma_t z$
8: **end for**
9: **return** x_0

Synthetic Image Generation via Reverse Diffusion. In our method, the latent feature generated by the diffusion network itself also guides the generation of synthetic deformed images through the reverse diffusion process. Here, as the diffusion network learns the conditional score function for the deformation between the moving image and the fixed image, our image generation starts from the moving image, in contrast to the existing conditional generative process of DDPM [9,32] that starts from the pure Gaussian noise $x_T \sim \mathcal{N}(0, I)$. When we set the initial state with the original moving image m, the one-step forward diffusion is performed by:

$$x_T = \sqrt{\alpha_T} m + \sqrt{1 - \alpha_T} \epsilon, \qquad (12)$$

where $\epsilon \sim \mathcal{N}(0, I)$, and α_T is the noise level at the time step $T \leq T_{train}$. Here, the time step T is set to a value not to lose the identity of the image. This forward sampling allows the moving image distribution to be close to the fixed image distribution, as illustrated in Fig. 4, which reduces the number of reverse diffusion steps and generation time.

Then, by starting from x_T, the generation of the synthetic image x_0 that fits into the fixed image f is performed by the following reverse diffusion process from $t = T$ to $t = 1$:

$$x_{t-1} = \frac{1}{\sqrt{1-\beta_t}} \left(x_t - \frac{\beta_t}{\sqrt{1-\alpha_t}} G_{\theta^*}(c, x_t, t) \right) + \sigma_t z, \tag{13}$$

where $z \sim \mathcal{N}(0, I)$. Here, in choosing the total steps of reverse diffusion, we employ [8] that presents an efficient inference method. Thus, one can flexibly set the number of sampling steps, and in our experiments, we set the reverse steps as 200 in maximum. The pseudocode of this generative process of DiffuseMorph is described in Algorithm 2.

4   Experimental Results

To demonstrate that DiffuseMorph generates high-quality deformed images from the moving to the fixed images, we apply our method to the various image registration tasks. We conduct the experiments on the intra-subject image registration using 2D facial expression images and 3D cardiac MR scans. Also, we apply our model to 3D brain MR registration, in which individual brain images are deformed to a common atlas. The datasets and training details are as follows, and more details are described in Supplementary Material.

Datasets. For 2D face images, Radboud Faces Database (RaFD) [25] was used. It contains 8 facial expressions collected from 67 subjects: neutral, angry, contemptuous, disgusted, fearful, happy, sad, and surprised. For each expression, 3 different gaze directions are provided. We cropped the data to 640×640, resized them into 128×128, and converted the RGB images to gray scale. We divided the data by 53, 7, and 7 subjects for training, validation, and test, respectively.

For 3D cardiac MR scans, we used ACDC dataset [5] that provides 100 4D temporal cardiac MRI data from the diastolic to systolic phases and segmentation maps at both ends of the phases. We resampled all scans with a voxel spacing of $1.5 \times 1.5 \times 3.15mm$, cropped them to $128 \times 128 \times 32$, and normalized the intensity into [-1, 1]. We used 90 and 10 scans for training and test.

Also, we used OASIS-3 dataset [24] for 3D brain MR registration. It provides brain MR images and corresponding volumetric segmentation maps from FreeSurfer [13]. We used 1156 T1-weighted scans that preprocessed by image resampling to $256 \times 256 \times 256$ grid with $1mm^3$ isotropic voxels, affine spatial normalization, and brain extraction. The images were cropped by $160 \times 192 \times 224$. We used 1027, 93, and 129 scans for training, validation, and test, respectively.

Implementation Details. Our model was implemented using PyTorch library in Python. We used the network architecture designed in DDPM [14] for the diffusion network, and set the noise level from 10^{-6} to 10^{-2} by linearly scheduling with $T_{train} = 2000$. Also, we used the backbone of VoxelMorph-1 [3] for the deformation network. Here, we configured layers of the networks according to the dimension of the image, e.g. 2D convolution layer for 2D image registration. For the face dataset, we set the hyper-parameter as $\lambda = 2$, and trained the model with the learning rate 5×10^{-6} for 40 epochs. For the cardiac MR data, we trained the model with $\lambda = 20$ and the learning rate 2×10^{-4} for 800 epochs. Also, we trained the model using the brain MR data for 60 epochs with $\lambda = 10$ and the learning rate 1×10^{-4}. Using a single Nvidia Quadro RTX 6000 GPU, we trained our model by Adam optimization algorithm [21].

Evaluation. To evaluate the registration performance, we computed the percentage of non-positive values of Jacobian determinant on the registration field ($|J_\phi| \leq 0$), which indicates that one-to-one mapping of the registration has been lost. Here, for the facial images, we measured NMSE and SSIM between deformed and fixed images. For the MR images, we computed Dice score between the deformed segmentation maps and the ground-truth labels for several anatomical structures. On the other hand, to evaluate the continuous deformation quality of cardiac scans, we computed PSNR and NMSE between the deformed images and the real data. For the comparative learning-based models, we used the same deformation network architecture and parameters for a fair comparison.

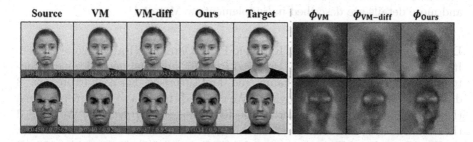

Fig. 5. Visual comparison results of image registration on the facial images (left) using the estimated registration fields (right). Results are deformed from the right-gazed sad to the front-gazed contemptuous images (top), and from the left-gazed disgusted to the front-gazed fearful images (bottom). The average values of NMSE/SSIM are displayed on each registration result.

Table 1. Quantitative evaluation results of the facial expression image registration. Standard deviations are shown in parentheses.

Method	NMSE $\times 10^{-1}$	SSIM	$|J_\phi| \leq 0$ (%)
Initial	0.363 (0.268)	0.823 (0.066)	0
VM [3]	0.047 (0.057)	0.936 (0.024)	0.050 (0.106)
VM-diff [10]	0.034 (0.015)	0.957 (0.013)	**0.014 (0.065)**
Ours	**0.032 (0.017)**	**0.964 (0.011)**	0.017 (0.056)

4.1   Results of Intra-subject 2D Face Image Registration

We compared DiffuseMorph against VM [3] and VM-diff [10]. We tested the image registration performance on the deformed images in RGB scale by applying the registration field to each RGB channel. Figure 5 shows visual comparisons of the registration results. Compared to VM and VM-diff, our model deforms the source image to be more accurately aligned with the target image. Also, as reported in Table 1, our model achieves lower NMSE and higher SSIM. Moreover, the metric of Jacobian determinant on registration fields of ours shows comparable values to VM-diff with the diffeomorphic constraint. These results indicate that the proposed DiffuseMorph provides high-quality image registration. More results of facial expression images can be found in Supplementary Material.

Continuous Image Deformation. We also performed continuous deformations of the facial expression from the moving source to the fixed target. Figure 6 shows the intermediate images of our model and the comparative methods. We obtained the results of VM by scaling the registration field, i.e. $\zeta \cdot \phi$ with $0 \leq \zeta \leq 1$, and those of VM-diff by integrating the velocity field along timescales, i.e. $\phi^{1/2^v}$ where v is the number of time steps. We can see that the estimated registration fields of VM only vary in their scale, but the relative spatial distribution does not change. Also, VM-diff does not provide regularly continuous deformation. On the other hand, in the proposed method, the registration field changes non-uniformly according to η, depending on the importance of variations at the intermediate deformation level. The improved performance of our method also can be also quantitatively verified using the facial landmarks extracted by *dlib* library in Python. Specifically, the visual results and MSE values in Fig. 6 show that our model provides superior performance for the continuous deformation, which indicates the importance of the conditional score for deformation.

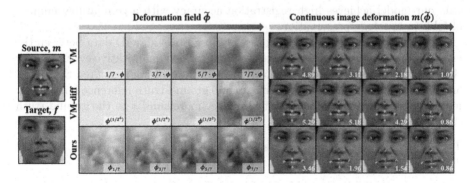

Fig. 6. Results of continuous image deformation of the facial images with facial landmarks. The deformation is performed from the right-gazed disgusted to the left-gazed contemptuous images. The average of MSE between the deformed and target landmarks is displayed on each result.

358   B. Kim et al.

Synthetic Deformed Image Generation.
To verify the capability of image generation from our DiffuseMorph, we evaluated
the generation using the facial images.
Here, the generative process was performed using the unseen images in the
training phase. Figure 7 shows the generated samples $\tilde{m}$ given the moving source
and fixed target images. The samples are
obtained from the noisy moving image
with the noise level α_{200} for the forward
diffusion. We set the number of reverse
diffusion steps to 80. As shown in the
results, our model provides the synthetic
deformed images similar to the target
images for various pairs of facial expressions. Also, when compared to the warped
image $m(\phi)$ using the registration field, we

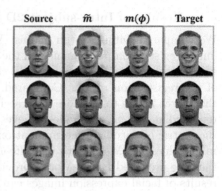

Fig. 7. Results of the synthetic
deformed image generation via our
generative process. The process of the
samples is included in Supplementary
Material.

can observe that the proposed generative process is effective to provide image
deformation if the moving image does not have teeth shown in the fixed image.

4.2 Results of Intra-subject 3D Cardiac MR Image Registration

We tested the image registration of the end-diastolic images aligned with the
end-systolic images. Table 2 reports the registration results with the average Dice
score for the segmentation maps of left blood pool (BP), myocardium (Myo),
left ventricle (LV), right ventricle (RV), and these total region, as well as the
Jacobian metrics. Compared to the baseline methods of VM [3] and VM-diff
[10], our model achieves high registration accuracy with a comparable number
of folds in topology preservation.

In addition, since the cardiac dataset we used provides 4D data between the
end-diastolic to the end-systolic phases, we performed quantitative evaluation for
the continuous deformation. As shown in Table 2, when we measured the PSNR
and NMSE between the deformed images and ground-truth reference images, our
method provides continuous deformed images more similar to the ground-truth

Table 2. Quantitative comparison results of the cardiac image registration. Standard
deviations are shown in parentheses.

Method	Image registration		Continuous deformation		
	Dice	$|J_\phi| \leq 0$ (%)	PSNR (dB)	NMSE $\times 10^{-8}$	Time (sec)
Initial	0.642 (0.188)	–	28.058 (2.205)	0.790 (0.516)	–
VM [3]	0.787 (0.113)	0.169 (0.109)	30.678 (2.652)	0.477 (0.453)	0.219
VM-diff [10]	0.794 (0.104)	0.291 (0.188)	29.481 (2.473)	0.602 (0.477)	2.902
Ours	**0.802 (0.109)**	**0.161 (0.082)**	**30.725 (2.579)**	**0.466 (0.432)**	0.456

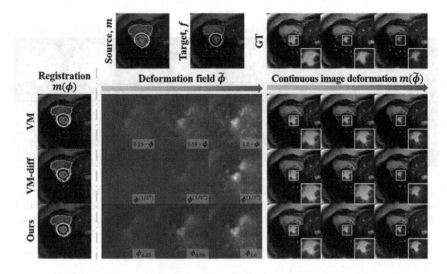

Fig. 8. Results of the image registration and continuous deformation on the cardiac MR images. The registration results show the overlaid contours of segmentation maps (green: RV, red: Myo, blue: BP). GT is the ground-truth data. (Color figure online)

images than the comparative methods. The visual comparison results in Fig. 8 also shows the superiority of our method. More visual results can be found in Supplementary Material.

4.3   Results of Atlas-based 3D Brain MR Image Registration

For the brain MR image registration, we compared our DiffuseMorph to the following comparative methods: SyN [2], VM [3], VM-diff [10], SYMNet [28], MSDIRNet [26], and CM [19]. As shown in the visual comparison results of Fig. 9, our model estimates smooth registration fields and yields deformed moving images that are more accurately aligned to the fixed images, compared to the baseline models. This also can be observed through the contours of the segmentation maps of several brain anatomical structures. We provided more visual results in Supplementary Material. Figure 10 and Table 3 report the results of quantitative evaluation. These show that the proposed method achieves higher Dice scores with less non-positive values of the Jacobian determinant over the existing learning-based methods, which empirically suggests that the proposed method can provide accurate image registration with improved topology preservation.

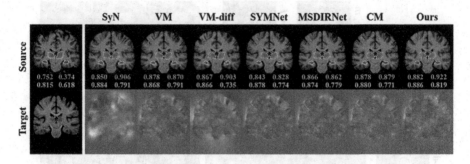

Fig. 9. Results of the image registration on the brain MR images (top) and the estimated registration fields (bottom). Segmentation maps of several anatomical structures are overlaid with the contours (blue: ventricles, green: thalami, orange: third ventricle, pink: hippocampi). The Dice scores for each structure are displayed with the corresponding colors on each result. (Color figure online)

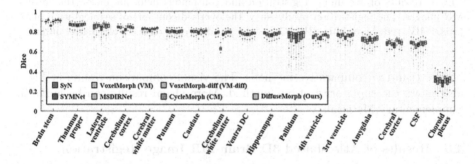

Fig. 10. Quantitative evaluation results of Dice scores on brain anatomical structures in the brain MR image registration experiment.

Table 3. Quantitative evaluation results of the brain MR image registration. Standard deviations are shown in parentheses.

Method	Dice	$|J_\phi| \leq 0$ (%)	Time (min)
Initial	0.616 (0.171)	0	0
SyN [2]	0.752 (0.140)	0.400 (0.100)	122, CPU
VM [3]	0.749 (0.145)	0.553 (0.075)	0.01, GPU
VM-diff [10]	0.731 (0.139)	0.631 (0.073)	0.01, GPU
SYMNet [28]	0.733 (0.148)	0.547 (0.049)	0.43, GPU
MSDIRNet [26]	0.751 (0.142)	0.804 (0.089)	2.06, GPU
CM [19]	0.750 (0.144)	0.510 (0.087)	0.01, GPU
Ours	**0.756 (0.139)**	**0.505 (0.058)**	0.01, GPU

Study on the Effect of Registration Loss. To explore the effect of the registration loss on the performance of our model, we performed a comparison study by varying the value of λ in (7) using brain MR data. As reported in Table 4, when λ is lower, the Dice score decreased but produced better regularity of registration fields. This indicates that the registration loss forces our model to provide more accurate image registration, but the trade-off needs to be balanced.

Table 4. Result of the study on the effect of registration loss. Standard deviations are shown in parentheses.

Method	Dice	$|J_\phi| \leq 0$ (%)
$\lambda = 2$	0.736 (0.152)	0.498 (0.098)
$\lambda = 5$	0.746 (0.143)	0.499 (0.070)
$\lambda = 10$	0.756 (0.139)	0.505 (0.058)

5   Conclusion

We presented a novel DiffuseMorph model for unsupervised image registration by employing the diffusion probabilistic model that is jointly trained with the deformation network. Thanks to the capability of learning the conditional score function of deformation, the proposed method not only generates synthetic deformed images but also provides high-quality image registration from the continuous deformation by estimating registration fields along the trajectory for the moving image toward the fixed image. We expect that DiffuseMorph can be a promising algorithm to generate temporal data using moving and fixed images.

Acknowledgments. This work was supported in part by the National Research Foundation (NRF) of Korea under Grant NRF-2020R1A2B5B03001980, in part by Field-oriented Technology Development Project for Customs Administration through NRF of Korea funded by the Ministry of Science & ICT and Korea Customs Service(NRF-2021M3I1A1097938), and in part by the KAIST Key Research Institute (Interdisciplinary Research Group) Project.

References

1. Ashburner, J.: A fast diffeomorphic image registration algorithm. Neuroimage **38**(1), 95–113 (2007)
2. Avants, B.B., Epstein, C.L., Grossman, M., Gee, J.C.: Symmetric diffeomorphic image registration with cross-correlation: evaluating automated labeling of elderly and neurodegenerative brain. Med. Image Anal. **12**(1), 26–41 (2008)
3. Balakrishnan, G., Zhao, A., Sabuncu, M.R., Guttag, J., Dalca, A.V.: An unsupervised learning model for deformable medical image registration. In: Proceedings of the IEEE Conference on Computer Vision and Pattern Recognition, pp. 9252–9260 (2018)
4. Beg, M.F., Miller, M.I., Trouvé, A., Younes, L.: Computing large deformation metric mappings via geodesic flows of diffeomorphisms. Int. J. Comput. Vision **61**(2), 139–157 (2005). https://doi.org/10.1023/B:VISI.0000043755.93987.aa

5. Bernard, O., et al.: Deep learning techniques for automatic MRI cardiac multi-structures segmentation and diagnosis: is the problem solved? IEEE Trans. Med. Imaging **37**(11), 2514–2525 (2018)

6. Cao, X., et al.: Deformable image registration based on similarity-steered CNN regression. In: Descoteaux, M., Maier-Hein, L., Franz, A., Jannin, P., Collins, D.L., Duchesne, S. (eds.) MICCAI 2017. LNCS, vol. 10433, pp. 300–308. Springer, Cham (2017). https://doi.org/10.1007/978-3-319-66182-7_35

7. Cao, X., Yang, J., Wang, L., Xue, Z., Wang, Q., Shen, D.: Deep learning based inter-modality image registration supervised by intra-modality similarity. In: Shi, Y., Suk, H.-I., Liu, M. (eds.) MLMI 2018. LNCS, vol. 11046, pp. 55–63. Springer, Cham (2018). https://doi.org/10.1007/978-3-030-00919-9_7

8. Chen, N., Zhang, Y., Zen, H., Weiss, R.J., Norouzi, M., Chan, W.: WaveGrad: estimating gradients for waveform generation. In: International Conference on Learning Representations (2020)

9. Choi, J., Kim, S., Jeong, Y., Gwon, Y., Yoon, S.: ILVR: conditioning method for denoising diffusion probabilistic models. In: Proceedings of the IEEE/CVF International Conference on Computer Vision, pp. 14367–14376 (2021)

10. Dalca, A.V., Balakrishnan, G., Guttag, J., Sabuncu, M.R.: Unsupervised learning for fast probabilistic diffeomorphic registration. In: Frangi, A.F., Schnabel, J.A., Davatzikos, C., Alberola-López, C., Fichtinger, G. (eds.) MICCAI 2018. LNCS, vol. 11070, pp. 729–738. Springer, Cham (2018). https://doi.org/10.1007/978-3-030-00928-1_82

11. Dalca, A.V., Balakrishnan, G., Guttag, J., Sabuncu, M.R.: Unsupervised learning of probabilistic diffeomorphic registration for images and surfaces. Med. Image Anal. **57**, 226–236 (2019)

12. Fadnavis, S., Batson, J., Garyfallidis, E.: Patch2self: denoising diffusion MRI with self-supervised learning. Adv. Neural. Inf. Process. Syst. **33**, 16293–16303 (2020)

13. Fischl, B.: FreeSurfer. Neuroimage **62**(2), 774–781 (2012)

14. Ho, J., Jain, A., Abbeel, P.: Denoising diffusion probabilistic models. Adv. Neural. Inf. Process. Syst. **33**, 6840–6851 (2020)

15. Ho, J., Saharia, C., Chan, W., Fleet, D.J., Norouzi, M., Salimans, T.: Cascaded diffusion models for high fidelity image generation. J. Mach. Learn. Res. **23**(47), 1–33 (2022)

16. Hu, Y., et al.: Weakly-supervised convolutional neural networks for multimodal image registration. Med. Image Anal. **49**, 1–13 (2018)

17. Jaderberg, M., Simonyan, K., Zisserman, A., et al.: Spatial transformer networks. Adv. Neural. Inf. Process. Syst. **28**, 2017–2025 (2015)

18. Jeong, M., Kim, H., Cheon, S.J., Choi, B.J., Kim, N.S.: Diff-TTS: a denoising diffusion model for text-to-speech. arXiv preprint arXiv:2104.01409 (2021)

19. Kim, B., Kim, D.H., Park, S.H., Kim, J., Lee, J.G., Ye, J.C.: CycleMorph: cycle consistent unsupervised deformable image registration. Med. Image Anal. **71**, 102036 (2021)

20. Kim, B., Ye, J.C.: Diffusion deformable model for 4D temporal medical image generation. In: Wang, L., Dou, Q., Fletcher, P.T., Speidel, S., Li, S. (eds) Medical Image Computing and Computer Assisted Intervention–MICCAI 2022. MICCAI 2022. Lecture Notes in Computer Science, vol 13431. Springer, Cham.(2022). https://doi.org/10.1007/978-3-031-16431-6_51

21. Kingma, D.P., Ba, J.: Adam: a method for stochastic optimization. In: ICLR (Poster) (2015)

22. Klein, S., Staring, M., Murphy, K., Viergever, M.A., Pluim, J.P.: Elastix: a toolbox for intensity-based medical image registration. IEEE Trans. Med. Imaging **29**(1), 196–205 (2009)
23. Krebs, J., Mansi, T., Mailhé, B., Ayache, N., Delingette, H.: Unsupervised probabilistic deformation modeling for robust diffeomorphic registration. In: Stoyanov, D., et al. (eds.) DLMIA/ML-CDS -2018. LNCS, vol. 11045, pp. 101–109. Springer, Cham (2018). https://doi.org/10.1007/978-3-030-00889-5_12
24. LaMontagne, P.J., et al.: Oasis-3: longitudinal neuroimaging, clinical, and cognitive dataset for normal aging and Alzheimer disease. MedRxiv (2019)
25. Langner, O., Dotsch, R., Bijlstra, G., Wigboldus, D.H., Hawk, S.T., Van Knippenberg, A.: Presentation and validation of the Radboud faces database. Cogn. Emot. **24**(8), 1377–1388 (2010)
26. Lei, Y., et al.: 4d-CT deformable image registration using multiscale unsupervised deep learning. Phys. Med. Biol. **65**(8), 085003 (2020)
27. Mahapatra, D., Antony, B., Sedai, S., Garnavi, R.: Deformable medical image registration using generative adversarial networks. In: 2018 IEEE 15th International Symposium on Biomedical Imaging (ISBI 2018), pp. 1449–1453. IEEE (2018)
28. Mok, T.C., Chung, A.: Fast symmetric diffeomorphic image registration with convolutional neural networks. In: Proceedings of the IEEE/CVF Conference on Computer Vision and Pattern Recognition, pp. 4644–4653 (2020)
29. Nichol, A.Q., Dhariwal, P.: Improved denoising diffusion probabilistic models. In: International Conference on Machine Learning, pp. 8162–8171. PMLR (2021)
30. Onofrey, J.A., Staib, L.H., Papademetris, X.: Semi-supervised learning of nonrigid deformations for image registration. In: Menze, B., Langs, G., Montillo, A., Kelm, M., Müller, H., Tu, Z. (eds.) MCV 2013. LNCS, vol. 8331, pp. 13–23. Springer, Cham (2014). https://doi.org/10.1007/978-3-319-05530-5_2
31. Rohé, M.-M., Datar, M., Heimann, T., Sermesant, M., Pennec, X.: SVF-Net: learning deformable image registration using shape matching. In: Descoteaux, M., Maier-Hein, L., Franz, A., Jannin, P., Collins, D.L., Duchesne, S. (eds.) MICCAI 2017. LNCS, vol. 10433, pp. 266–274. Springer, Cham (2017). https://doi.org/10.1007/978-3-319-66182-7_31
32. Saharia, C., Ho, J., Chan, W., Salimans, T., Fleet, D.J., Norouzi, M.: Image super-resolution via iterative refinement. arXiv preprint arXiv:2104.07636 (2021)
33. Sasaki, H., Willcocks, C.G., Breckon, T.P.: Unit-ddpm: unpaired image translation with denoising diffusion probabilistic models. arXiv preprint arXiv:2104.05358 (2021)
34. Sohl-Dickstein, J., Weiss, E., Maheswaranathan, N., Ganguli, S.: Deep unsupervised learning using nonequilibrium thermodynamics. In: International Conference on Machine Learning, pp. 2256–2265. PMLR (2015)
35. Song, J., Meng, C., Ermon, S.: Denoising diffusion implicit models. In: International Conference on Learning Representations (2020)
36. Song, Y., Ermon, S.: Generative modeling by estimating gradients of the data distribution. Adv. Neural Inf. Processi. Syst. **32**, 1–13 (2019)
37. Song, Y., Sohl-Dickstein, J., Kingma, D.P., Kumar, A., Ermon, S., Poole, B.: Score-based generative modeling through stochastic differential equations. In: International Conference on Learning Representations (2020)
38. Vahdat, A., Kreis, K., Kautz, J.: Score-based generative modeling in latent space. Adv. Neural. Inf. Process. Syst. **34**, 11287–11302 (2021)
39. Vercauteren, T., Pennec, X., Perchant, A., Ayache, N.: Diffeomorphic demons: efficient non-parametric image registration. Neuroimage **45**(1), S61–S72 (2009)

40. de Vos, B.D., Berendsen, F.F., Viergever, M.A., Sokooti, H., Staring, M., Išgum, I.: A deep learning framework for unsupervised affine and deformable image registration. Med. Image Anal. **52**, 128–143 (2019)
41. Xu, Z., Niethammer, M.: DeepAtlas: joint semi-supervised learning of image registration and segmentation. In: Shen, D., et al. (eds.) MICCAI 2019. LNCS, vol. 11765, pp. 420–429. Springer, Cham (2019). https://doi.org/10.1007/978-3-030-32245-8_47
42. Yang, X., Kwitt, R., Styner, M., Niethammer, M.: Quicksilver: fast predictive image registration-a deep learning approach. Neuroimage **158**, 378–396 (2017)

Semi-Leak: Membership Inference Attacks Against Semi-supervised Learning

Xinlei He[1]([✉]), Hongbin Liu[2], Neil Zhenqiang Gong[2], and Yang Zhang[1]

[1] CISPA Helmholz Center for Information Security, Saarbrücken, Germany
xinlei.he@cispa.de
[2] Duke University, Durham, USA

Abstract. Semi-supervised learning (SSL) leverages both labeled and unlabeled data to train machine learning (ML) models. State-of-the-art SSL methods can achieve comparable performance to supervised learning by leveraging much fewer labeled data. However, most existing works focus on improving the performance of SSL. In this work, we take a different angle by studying the training data privacy of SSL. Specifically, we propose the first data augmentation-based membership inference attacks against ML models trained by SSL. Given a data sample and the black-box access to a model, the goal of membership inference attack is to determine whether the data sample belongs to the training dataset of the model. Our evaluation shows that the proposed attack can consistently outperform existing membership inference attacks and achieves the best performance against the model trained by SSL. Moreover, we uncover that the reason for membership leakage in SSL is different from the commonly believed one in supervised learning, i.e., overfitting (the gap between training and testing accuracy). We observe that the SSL model is well generalized to the testing data (with almost 0 overfitting) but "memorizes" the training data by giving a more confident prediction regardless of its correctness. We also explore early stopping as a countermeasure to prevent membership inference attacks against SSL. The results show that early stopping can mitigate the membership inference attack, but with the cost of model's utility degradation. (Our code is available at https://github.com/xinleihe/Semi-Leak.)

Keywords: Membership inference attack · Semi-supervised learning

1 Introduction

Machine learning (ML) has made tremendous progress in the past decade. One of the key reasons for the great success of ML models can be credited to the large-scale labeled data. However, such labeled datasets are often hard to collect as

Supplementary Information The online version contains supplementary material available at https://doi.org/10.1007/978-3-031-19821-2_21.

S. Avidan et al. (Eds.): ECCV 2022, LNCS 13691, pp. 365–381, 2022.
https://doi.org/10.1007/978-3-031-19821-2_21

they rely on human annotations and expertise in the specific domain. Meanwhile, unlabeled datasets are easy to obtain. To better leverage the unlabeled data, semi-supervised learning (SSL) has been proposed. Concretely, SSL uses a small set of labeled data and a large set of unlabeled data to jointly train the ML model. In recent years, SSL shows its effectiveness on different tasks by leveraging much fewer labeled data [25,32,35]. For instance, by only using 250 labeled samples, FlexMatch [35] can achieve about 95% accuracy on CIFAR10.

Different from supervised learning where every data sample is treated equally in the training procedure, SSL takes different ways to handle the labeled and unlabeled data samples during the training. Concretely, the state-of-the-art SSL methods [25,32,35] leverage weak augmentation to the labeled samples and trains them in a supervised manner. For each unlabeled sample, it would generate a weakly-augmented view and a strongly-augmented view (by weak and strong augmentations), and the goal is to leverage the model's prediction probability (referred to as prediction or posteriors) of the weakly-augmented view to guide the training of the strongly-augmented view of the sample. Instead of directly using the posteriors as a "soft" label, those SSL methods switch the posteriors into a "sharpen" [32] or "hard" label [25,35]. Note that the sample is not used to train the model until the highest probability of the prediction on the weakly-augmented view exceeds a pre-defined threshold τ. In this way, the model trained by SSL can gradually learn more accurate predictions.

Despite being powerful, ML models are shown to be vulnerable to various privacy attacks [7,24,26], represented by membership inference attacks [18,23, 24,27]. The goal of membership inference attack is to determine whether a data sample is used to train a target ML model. Successful membership inference attacks can raise privacy concerns as they may reveal sensitive information of people. For instance, if an ML model is trained on the data for people with a certain sensitive attribute (e.g., diseases), identifying the person in the training dataset directly reveals this individual's sensitive attribute. So far, most of the efforts on membership inference attacks concentrate on models trained by supervised learning. Also, there are some exploratory researches investigating the privacy risks in self-supervised learning [9,16]. However, in SSL, the labeled and unlabeled samples are treated differently during the training. It is important to quantify whether this unique training paradigm would lead to different privacy risks for labeled and unlabeled samples. Also, as the different augmented views instead of the original samples are used to train the model, we are curious whether a more effective membership inference attack mechanism can be proposed against SSL. To be best of our knowledge, this is largely unexplored.

In this work, we fill the gap by proposing the first data augmentation-based membership inference attack method against SSL. A key advantage for SSL is that it only needs a small amount of labeled data and leverages the unlabeled data itself to guide the training. Concretely, for the labeled data, the model is trained in a supervised manner. For the unlabeled data, SSL leverage the data itself as the supervision. In particular, for each unlabeled training sample, a weakly augmented and a strongly augmented views will be fed into the target model and the training objective is to minimize the distance of the model's prediction on these two views. Our proposed data augmentation-based attack is based on the intuition that the model's prediction of these two views should be more similar if the sample belongs to the model's training set.

We conduct our evaluation on three SSL methods (FixMatch, FlexMatch, and UDA) and three commonly used SSL datasets (SVHN, CIFAR10, and CIFAR100). Our empirical results show that our proposed attack can consistently outperform baseline attacks and reaches the best performance. For instance, for FixMatch trained on CIFAR10 with 500 labeled samples, our attack achieves 0.780 AUC while the best baseline attack only has 0.722 AUC. This indicates that our attack can better unleash the membership information in SSL.

Moreover, we find that, unlike supervised learning where the membership leakage can be credited to the overfitting nature of the model [23,24] (i.e., the model predicts the training data more accurately than the testing data), models trained by SSL methods are well generalized and have almost no overfitting but still suffer high membership inference risk. Our analysis reveals that the model indeed "memorizes" the training data, but such memorization does not present as a more accurate prediction, but a more confident prediction. We show that the prediction entropy distribution of members and non-members has a large gap in models trained by SSL (measured by Jason-Shannon (JS) Distance).

Contributions. (1) We are the first to study the privacy risk of SSL through the lens of membership inference attacks and we propose a data augmentation-based attack that is tailored to SSL methods. (2) We conduct extensive experiments on SVHN, CIFAR10, and CIFAR100 datasets. Our results show that our proposed attack outperforms baseline attacks that are extended from existing works to SSL settings. (3) We show that the effectiveness of membership inference attacks against SSL is not credited to the model's overfitting level but credited to the model prediction's distinguishable entropy distributions for members and non-members (measured by Jason-Shannon Distance). (4) We study an early-stopping-based defense against our proposed attack. We show that this defense can decrease the attack AUC of our attack but sacrifice the testing accuracy of the trained models.

2 Preliminary and Related Work

2.1 Semi-supervised Learning

Semi-supervised learning (SSL) [2,13,17,25,32,35] aims to train accurate models via exploiting a large amount of unlabeled data when the labeled data is scarce. In this paper, we focus on the vision domain since most advanced SSL methods are designed for it. Generally speaking, state-of-the-art SSL techniques [25,32,35] produce "pseudo labels" for the unlabeled samples when the model's predictions are confident enough based on pre-defined threshold strategies. For example, Lee [13] first proposed to produce the class label that has the highest confidence score output by the classifier for unlabeled samples during training. After assigning pseudo labels to unlabeled samples, they can train classifiers in a supervised fashion with labeled and unlabeled samples. Recently, FixMatch [25] achieves state-of-the-art classification accuracy via assigning the strongly augmented unlabeled samples with the pseudo labels produced from the corresponding weakly augmented samples when the highest confidence score exceeds a certain threshold. While UDA [32] was proposed to treat the classifier's "sharpen" output confidence scores as the 'pseudo labels' rather than one class label. Similar to FixMatch, UDA trains strongly augmented unlabeled samples with the pseudo labels produced from the corresponding weakly augmented samples. FlexMatch [35] updates FixMatch by introducing the curriculum learning-based method to flexibly adjust the threshold for different classes during the training. Existing studies on SSL mainly focus on how to improve the performance, however, we are the first to show that state-of-the-art SSL methods are vulnerable to our tailored membership inference attacks, which exploit the strong/weak data augmentations used by state-of-the-art SSL methods.

2.2 Membership Inference Attacks

The goal of membership inference attack [3,4,8–11,15,16,18,21–24,27,30] is to determine whether a given data sample is used to train a target model. Multiple works studied the membership inference attacks against the supervised learning [5,8,15,19,23,24]. Shokri et al. [24] proposed the first black-box membership inference attack against machine learning models by leveraging multiple shadow models and attack models. The attack model takes a sample's posteriors generated from the target model as the input and predicts whether it is a member or not. Salem et al. [23] relaxed the assumption from Shokri et al. [24] and proposed novel model-independent and dataset-independent membership inference attacks. Nasr et al. [19] studied the white-box membership inference attacks in both centralized and federated learning settings. Li and Zhang [15] and Choo et al. [5] concentrated on a more restricted attack scenario (called label-only attack) where the target model only returns the predicted labels instead of posteriors when the adversary queries the target model with given samples. Roughly speaking, their proposed label-only attacks aim to infer a given sample's membership status via comparing a pre-defined threshold with the scale of adversarial perturbation that needs to be added to the given sample to change the target model's predicted label. However, these membership inference attacks are tailored to supervised learning and we show that semi-supervised learning is more vulnerable to our proposed data augmentation-based membership inference attack compared with existing membership inference attacks.

3   Conventional Membership Inference Attacks

In membership inference attack, the adversary aims to determine whether a given data sample x belongs to the target model T's training dataset or not given the adversary's background knowledge $\mathcal{K}$. A data sample x is called *member* (or *non-member*) if it belongs to (or does not belong to) the training dataset of the target model $\mathcal{T}$. Formally, we define the membership inference attack as $\mathcal{A} : x, \mathcal{T}, \mathcal{K} \rightarrow \{0, 1\}$, where the attack $\mathcal{A}$ is essentially a mapping function and 1 (or 0) means the data sample x is a member (or non-member).

3.1 Threat Model

Given a target model $\mathcal{T}$, we first assume that the adversary only has black-box access to it, which means that the adversary can only query the target model with a data sample x and obtain the target model's prediction on it (denoted as posteriors). Note that in this paper we consider the black-box attack since it is the most difficult and practical real-world scenario.

Following previous work [9,24,27], we assume that the adversary has a *shadow dataset* $\mathcal{D}_{shadow}$ that has the same distribution as the target model $\mathcal{T}$'s training dataset $\mathcal{D}_{target}^{train}$. The adversary can use the shadow dataset $\mathcal{D}_{shadow}$ to train a *shadow model* $\mathcal{S}$, which mimics the behavior of the target model $\mathcal{T}$ to better conduct the attacks. Also, we assume that the shadow model $\mathcal{S}$ has the same architecture as the target model. Such assumption is realistic as: (1) The adversary can leverage the same machine learning service to train the shadow model and (2) The adversary can perform hyperparameter stealing attacks [20,29] to obtain the target model's architecture.

3.2 Methodology

Generally speaking, the membership inference attack pipeline usually consists of three major components, i.e., shadow training, constructing attack training dataset, and attack model training or performing the attack.

Shadow Training. Shadow training [18,23,24] aims to train shadow models to mimic the behavior of the target model based on the adversary's background knowledge. Specifically, the adversary first evenly splits the shadow dataset $\mathcal{D}_{shadow}$ into two disjoint parts, i.e., shadow training data $\mathcal{D}_{shadow}^{train}$ and shadow testing data $\mathcal{D}_{shadow}^{test}$. The adversary then uses the $\mathcal{D}_{shadow}^{train}$ to train a shadow model $\mathcal{S}$ that mimics the behavior of the target model $\mathcal{T}$.

Constructing Attack Training Dataset. To construct the training dataset for the attack model, the adversary first uses $\mathcal{D}_{shadow}^{train}$ (contains members) and $\mathcal{D}_{shadow}^{test}$ (contains non-members) to query the shadow model $\mathcal{S}$ and obtain the corresponding posteriors. Following Salem et al. [23], we leverage the descendingly sorted posteriors as the inputting features for the attack model. Finally, we assign the membership status 1/0 for members/non-members as labels.

Training Neural Network-Based Attack Model. For neural network-based attacks [23,24] (denoted as $\mathcal{A}_{NN}$), the adversary aims to train a neural network-based attack model to distinguish members and non-members given the posteriors generated by the target model $\mathcal{T}$. After constructing the attack training dataset, the adversary trains an NN-based attack model on the constructed training dataset. Following previous works [9,16,23,24], we consider a multi-layer perceptron (MLP) as the neural network architecture for the attack model. Once the attack model is trained, it can be used by the adversary to predict whether a given data sample x is a member or non-member.

Metric-Based Attacks. Metric-based attacks [14,27,28,33] also require the adversary to train a shadow model $\mathcal{S}$. Unlike NN-based attacks that require training an attack model, metric-based attacks design a specific metric and calculate a threshold over the metrics by querying the shadow model $\mathcal{S}$ with $\mathcal{D}_{shadow}^{train}$ and $\mathcal{D}_{shadow}^{test}$. We adopt four state-of-the-art metric-based attacks following Song and Mittal. [27]: (1) Prediction correctness ($\mathcal{A}_{Corr}$) which considers a sample as a member if the label is correctly predicted by the target model; (2) Prediction confidence ($\mathcal{A}_{Conf}$) which judges a sample as a member if the prediction probability at the ground truth class is larger than a pre-defined threshold (learned from the shadow model); (3) prediction entropy ($\mathcal{A}_{Ent}$) which considers a sample as a member if the entropy of the prediction is smaller than a pre-defined threshold (learned from the shadow model); and (4) Modified prediction entropy ($\mathcal{A}_{Ment}$) which is similar to (3) but modifies the entropy function and combines the ground truth label as a new metric.

4 Our Method

The main difference between SSL methods and supervised learning methods is that SSL methods leverage a large amount of unlabeled samples together with a small amount of labeled samples to train the model. Recall that state-of-the-art SSL methods [25,31,35] leverage both weak and strong data augmentations to the unlabeled samples during the training. The key idea of these SSL methods is to train the model that maximizes the model's prediction agreement on weakly and strongly augmented views that come from the same unlabeled sample. In other words, for an unlabeled training sample, the trained model may tend to output more similar posteriors for its weakly and strongly augmented views. While for labeled training samples, the trained model may output similar posteriors for different weakly augmented views from the same sample since those posteriors result in the same predicted label. This observation may also hold for unlabeled samples since the posteriors of the same training unlabeled sample tend to produce the same "pseudo label". Intuitively speaking, the target model $\mathcal{T}$ may output similar (or dissimilar) posteriors for different weakly and/or strongly augmented views of member (or non-member).

Based on the above intuition, we propose a data augmentation-based membership inference attack (denoted as $\mathcal{A}_{DA}$) tailored to state-of-the-art SSL methods. $\mathcal{A}_{DA}$ follows the similar pipeline as NN-based attack $\mathcal{A}_{NN}$, i.e., shadow training and training an NN-based attack model.

However, our attack $\mathcal{A}_{DA}$ extracts membership features (i.e. the input for the attack model) in a different way from the attack $\mathcal{A}_{NN}$. Specifically, given a data sample x, we first generate K weakly augmented and K strongly augmented views of it, respectively. Then we use the augmented views to query the shadow model to obtain output posteriors. After that, we calculate three similarity matrices among: (1) K posteriors of weakly augmented views themselves, (2) K posteriors of strongly augmented views themselves, and (3) K posteriors of weakly augmented views and K posteriors of strongly augmented views, based on a predefined similarity metrics (e.g., JS Distance, Cosine Distance, etc.). Then we obtain three similarity matrices where each of them contains K^2 similarity values. We expand each similarity matrix into a vector and sort the values in each vector in descending order, respectively. Then we concatenate them together, and finally obtain a vector with $3K^2$ values. The obtained vectors are then assigned with the membership status as the labels. Once the attack model is trained, to determine whether a sample belongs to the target model's training dataset, we again generate K weakly and K strongly augmented views of it to query the target model, generate the attack input to query the attack model, and obtain its membership prediction. Figure 1 shows the overview of $\mathcal{A}_{DA}$ and the detailed algorithm is shown in Algorithm 1 in the supplemental material.

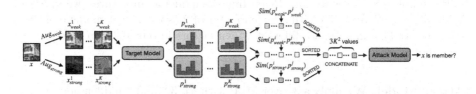

Fig. 1. Overview of our data augmentation based attack $\mathcal{A}_{DA}$.

5   Evaluation

5.1   Experimental Setup

Dataset Configuration. We evaluate the performance of target models and membership inference attacks on three commonly used SSL datasets, i.e., SVHN, CIFAR10, and CIFAR100. For each dataset, we first randomly split it into four equal parts, i.e., $\mathcal{D}_{target}^{train}$, $\mathcal{D}_{target}^{test}$, $\mathcal{D}_{shadow}^{train}$, and $\mathcal{D}_{shadow}^{test}$. We leverage $\mathcal{D}_{target}^{train}$ to train the target model and consider the samples from $\mathcal{D}_{target}^{train}$ as the members of the target model. Samples in $\mathcal{D}_{target}^{test}$ are considered as the non-members of the target model. $\mathcal{D}_{shadow}^{train}$ is used to build up the shadow model. Both $\mathcal{D}_{shadow}^{train}$ and

$\mathcal{D}_{shadow}^{test}$ are used to train the attack model. Note that the $\mathcal{D}_{target}^{train}$ is smaller than the original training dataset (e.g., for CIFAR10, $\mathcal{D}_{target}^{train}$ contains 15,000 samples while the original training dataset contains 50,000 samples), which may lead to lower target model performance.

Metric. We follow previous work [9,24,25,32,35] and adopt testing accuracy as the evaluation metric for target model performance. Regarding the attack, we leverage AUC as the evaluation metric [15,30] as we aim to quantify both the general membership privacy risk for members vs. non-members and the separate privacy risks for labeled/unlabeled members vs. non-members (unbalanced).

Target Model. For a fair comparison, we apply the same hyperparameters for FixMatch, UDA, and FlexMatch. Specifically, we apply SGD optimizer. The initial learning rate is set to 0.03 with a cosine learning rate decay which sets the learning rate to $\eta \ cos(\frac{\pi k}{2N})$, where η is the initial learning rate, k is the current training step, and N is the total number of training steps. We set $N = 100 \times 2^{10}$. We leverage an exponential moving average of model parameters with the momentum of 0.999. The labeled batch size (i.e., the batch size of the labeled data) is set to 64 and the ratio of unlabeled batch size to the labeled batch size is set to 7. Note that the threshold τ is set to 0.8 for UDA and 0.95 for FixMatch and FlexMatch following the original papers. We apply RandAugment [6] as the strong augmentation method in our experiments (see Section 8.1 in the supplementary material). Regarding the model architectures, we leverage Wide ResNet (WRN) [34] with a widen factor of 2 as the target model architecture and we also investigate different widen factors in our ablation studies (see Sect. 5.6).

Attack Model. We apply a 3-layer MLP with 64, 32, and 2 hidden neurons for each layer as the attack model's architecture. We train the attack model for 100 epochs using Adam optimizer with the learning rate of 0.001 and the batch size of 256. For our proposed attack, we set the number of augmented views used to query the target model to 10 and leverage JS Distance as the similarity function. Note that we also evaluate different numbers of augmented views and different similarity functions in our ablation studies (see Sect. 5.5).

5.2   Target Model Performance

We first evaluate the performance of the supervised models and the SSL models on the original classification tasks using $\mathcal{D}_{target}^{test}$. We use the full $\mathcal{D}_{target}^{train}$ to train the supervised models, while we use a small portion of labeled samples and treat the remaining samples as unlabeled ones in $\mathcal{D}_{target}^{train}$ when training the SSL models. We observe that SSL with more labeled samples can achieve better performance on the original classification tasks. For instance, on Fig. 2b, when the target model is FixMatch trained on CIFAR10, the classification accuracy is

0.866, 0.896, 0.903, and 0.904 with 500, 1,000, 2,000, and 4,000 labeled samples, respectively. This is expected as more labeled samples help the target model to better learn the decision boundary at the early stage. Another observation is that for a more complicated task, it may require more labeled samples to achieve comparable performance as the supervised models. We consider SVHN, CIFAR10, and CIFAR100 have increasing difficulty levels. Take models trained by UDA as a case study (green bar in Fig. 2), on SVHN, with only 500 labeled samples, the testing accuracy is 0.953, which is even better than the supervised model (0.951). We suspect the reason is that 500 labeled samples is enough to learn a relatively accurate decision boundary and the strong data augmentation used in SSL methods can better help the model to generalize to the unseen data. On the other hand, on CIFAR10 and CIFAR100, it may require 1,000 and 4,000 labeled samples to catch up with the performance of the supervised model. Such observation indicates that a larger portion of labeled data is still helpful for a more complicated task.

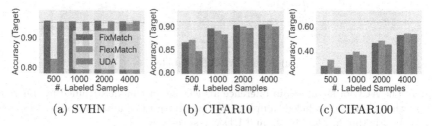

(a) SVHN   (b) CIFAR10   (c) CIFAR100

Fig. 2. Testing accuracy on the original classification tasks. Note that the red dash line denotes the performance of supervised models. (Color figure online)

5.3   Membership Inference Attack Performance

We then evaluate the performance of different membership inference attacks on SSL models. The results are summarized in Fig. 3. Note that we leverage AUC as the attack evaluation metric to better quantify the privacy leakage of all training data (first row) as well as the separate privacy leakage of labeled (second row) and unlabeled (third row) training data. We find that for the baseline attacks (i.e., except our $\mathcal{A}_{DA}$), $\mathcal{A}_{NN}$ and $\mathcal{A}_{Ent}$ perform the best, while other attacks like $\mathcal{A}_{Corr}$, $\mathcal{A}_{Conf}$, and $\mathcal{A}_{Ment}$ are less effective. For instance, on FlexMatch trained on CIFAR10 with 500 labeled samples (the middle one of Fig. 3a), the attack AUC is 0.726 for both $\mathcal{A}_{NN}$ and $\mathcal{A}_{Ent}$, while only 0.497, 0.643, and 0.642 for $\mathcal{A}_{Corr}$, $\mathcal{A}_{Conf}$, and $\mathcal{A}_{Ment}$. To better investigate the reason behind this, we further measure the attack AUC for labeled data and unlabeled data, respectively. We find that $\mathcal{A}_{Conf}$ and $\mathcal{A}_{Ment}$ achieve even better performance on labeled training samples than $\mathcal{A}_{NN}$ and $\mathcal{A}_{Ent}$. For instance, for FlexMatch trained on CIFAR100, the AUC (labeled) for $\mathcal{A}_{Conf}$ and $\mathcal{A}_{Ment}$ are both 0.955, while only

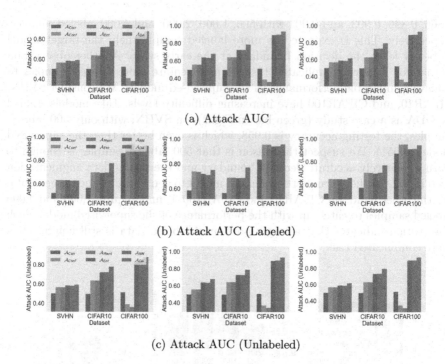

(a) Attack AUC

(b) Attack AUC (Labeled)

(c) Attack AUC (Unlabeled)

Fig. 3. The AUC of membership inference attacks against models trained by different SSL methods with 500 labeled samples. The first to third columns denote the models trained by FixMatch, FlexMatch, and UDA, respectively.

0.944 and 0.941 for $\mathcal{A}_{NN}$ and $\mathcal{A}_{Ent}$. This is expected as the labeled sample has a higher confidence score on its ground-truth label, which facilitates the attacks that leverage such information. However, this is not the case for the unlabeled samples. As we can observe that, for FlexMatch trained on CIFAR100, the AUC (unlabeled) is only 0.370 and 0.341 for $\mathcal{A}_{Conf}$ and $\mathcal{A}_{Ment}$, but 0.899 and 0.894 for $\mathcal{A}_{NN}$ and $\mathcal{A}_{Ent}$. This indicates that, for the unlabeled samples, the model may give similar correctness predictions on both unlabeled training samples and testing samples, which makes it harder to differentiate them. However, the model will give more confident predictions on unlabeled training samples than on testing samples, which results in better performance for $\mathcal{A}_{NN}$ and $\mathcal{A}_{Ent}$.

On the other hand, we also observe that our proposed data augmentation-based attack $\mathcal{A}_{DA}$ achieves consistently better overall performance on all datasets and SSL methods than those baseline attacks. Moreover, $\mathcal{A}_{DA}$ works better in determining the membership of unlabeled training samples. For instance, on FixMatch trained on CIFAR10, the unlabeled AUC is 0.780 for $\mathcal{A}_{DA}$ while only 0.722 for the best baseline attack ($\mathcal{A}_{NN}$). This is because $\mathcal{A}_{DA}$ unveils the pattern that the predictions of a sample's weak and strong augmented views should be closer if the sample is an unlabeled sample used during the training.

5.4 What Determines Membership Inference Attack in SSL

The effectiveness of membership inference attacks has been largely credited to the intrinsic overfitting phenomenon of the ML model [23,24]. Here overfitting denotes the model's training accuracy minus its testing accuracy. Such assumption has been verified on various ML models [9,18,23,24]. However, it is unclear whether such assumption still holds for SSL. If not, what is the reason for models trained by SSL to be vulnerable to membership inference attacks?

From Fig. 3, we find that $\mathcal{A}_{Ent}$ achieves good performance in predicting the membership status of a sample, which gives us the hint that the members' and non-members' predictions may have different entropy distributions. Here we leverage the JS Distance to quantify the difference between the entropy distribution of members' and non-members' predictions (we denote this measure as JS Distance (Entropy)).

To better quantify the correlation between different factors (e.g., overfitting, JS Distance (Entropy)) and the attack performance, we measure them under different training steps of the target models. Note that here we consider the $\mathcal{A}_{DA}$ as it performs the best in membership inference. Figure 4 shows the results of models trained by different SSL methods on the CIFAR100 with 500 labeled samples. The results for models trained on different datasets and with different numbers of labeled samples are shown in Section 8.3 in supplementary materials.

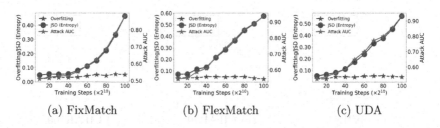

(a) FixMatch   (b) FlexMatch   (c) UDA

Fig. 4. The overfitting/JS Distance (Entropy) and attack AUC with respect to different training steps. The target model is trained on CIFAR100 with 500 labeled samples. Note that we consider the attack AUC of $\mathcal{A}_{DA}$, which is the strongest attack.

In Fig. 4, we observe that during the whole training procedure, the models trained by SSL have nearly 0 overfitting, which means that the models can always generalize well to the unseen data. However, we find that the attack AUC keeps increasing during the training. This indicates that the success of membership inference attacks is not necessarily related to the high overfitting level, which is overlooked by previous research. On the other hand, we observe that the JS Distance (Entropy) does increase during the training, which means that although the model does not predict more accurately to the member samples (mainly unlabeled samples) than the non-member samples, the model indeed makes a more confident prediction on member samples (i.e., with lower entropy of prediction). Our observation reveals that the models trained by SSL indeed "memorize" the training data. However, such memorization does not reflect in the overfitting, i.e., the gap between training and testing accuracy. Instead, it reflects in the more confident prediction of the members than the non-members.

5.5   Ablation Study (Attack Model)

Number of Views. We first investigate how the attack performance would be affected by different numbers of views generated by the weak and strong augmentations to query the target model. To this end, for the SSL methods trained on different datasets with only 500 labeled samples, we range the number of views from 1 to 100 and the attack performance is shown in Fig. 5. Note that we also show the results with 1,000, 2,000, and 4,000 labeled samples in Section 8.4 in the supplementary material. A clear trend is that more views lead to better attack performance. For instance, for FixMatch trained on CIFAR10 with 500 labeled samples (Fig. 5b), the attack AUC is 0.780 with 10 augmented views, while 0.806 for 100 augmented views. However, we find that the attack performance increases rapidly when the number of augmented views increases from 1 to 10, but plateaus from 10 to 100. Moreover, more views lead to more queries to the target model and higher computational cost. We consider 10 as a suitable number of views since it achieves comparable performance to 100 while spending less query budget.

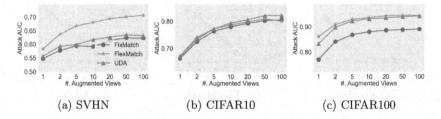

(a) SVHN   (b) CIFAR10   (c) CIFAR100

Fig. 5. The attack AUC of $\mathcal{A}_{DA}$ with different numbers of augmented views to query the target model. The target model is trained with 500 labeled samples.

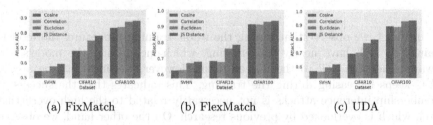

(a) FixMatch   (b) FlexMatch   (c) UDA

Fig. 6. The attack AUC of $\mathcal{A}_{DA}$ with different similarity functions. The target model is trained with 500 labeled samples.

Table 1. The target model performance and attack performance ($\mathcal{A}_{DA}$) when the target model has different capacities. The target model is trained by FixMatch on CIFAR100 with 500 labeled samples. ($\star$) denotes the default setting.

Architecture	Test ACC	Attack AUC	Attack AUC (Labeled)	Attack AUC (Unlabeled)
WRN28-1	0.217	0.726	0.954	0.718
WRN28-2 ($\star$)	0.276	0.874	0.896	0.873
WRN28-4	0.299	0.917	0.910	0.917
WRN28-8	0.305	0.927	0.918	0.927

Table 2. The target model performance and attack performance ($\mathcal{A}_{DA}$) when the target model leverages different unlabeled ratios during each training step. The target model is trained by FixMatch on CIFAR100 with 500 labeled samples. ($\star$) denotes the default setting.

Ratio	Test Acc	Attack AUC	Attack AUC (Labeled)	Attack AUC (Unlabeled)
1	0.210	0.578	0.965	0.565
2	0.263	0.646	0.942	0.636
4	0.273	0.785	0.946	0.779
7 ($\star$)	0.276	0.874	0.896	0.873
8	0.269	0.886	0.924	0.884
16	0.247	0.909	0.913	0.909

Similarity Function. Note that in our attack $\mathcal{A}_{DA}$, we can apply different similarity functions to measure the distance between the posteriors generated from different augmented views. Here we evaluate 4 distance metrics, i.e., Cosine Distance, Correlation Distance, Euclidean Distance, and JS Distance. The result for FixMatch, FlexMatch, and UDA trained on three different datasets with 500 labeled samples are summarized in Fig. 6. Note that we also show the results with 1,000, 2,000, and 4,000 labeled samples in Section 8.5 in the supplementary material. We find that JS Distance consistently outperforms the other three distance metrics and achieves the best performance. For instance, FixMatch trained on CIFAR10, the attack AUC is 0.679, 0.682, 0.749, and 0.780 for Cosine Distance, Correlation Distance, Euclidean Distance, and JS Distance. We suspect the reason is that JS Distance is designed to calculate the difference between two probabilities' distributions, which may better fit our scenario as the prediction posteriors are probability as well.

Moreover, we also find that the magnitude of data augmentation and the shadow model architecture only have limited impact on the attack performance (see Section 8.6 in the supplementary material for more details).

5.6   Ablation Study (Target Model)

We also investigate whether the target model's capacity and the unlabeled ratio (i.e., $\frac{batchsize(unlabeled)}{batchsize(labeled)}$ during each training step) would affect the performance. Note that here we select FixMatch trained on CIFAR100 with 500 labeled data as a case study, since the target model's capacity and the unlabeled ratio are general to different SSL methods, and CIFAR100 with 500 labeled data is the most challenging setting to train the target model (see Fig. 2). We consider an adaptive adversary [12] who is aware of the training details of the target model and can train the shadow model in the same way.

Model Capacity. The target model architecture we leverage in our paper is WRN28-2. To better quantify the impact of model capacity on the target and attack performance, we vary the width of WRN28 from 1 to 8 and the results are shown in Table 1. We can observe that a larger model capacity, in general, leads to a better target model's performance on the original classification task, but also increases the membership risk (especially for unlabeled samples). For instance, when the model capacity increase from WRN28-1 to WRN-28-8, the target testing accuracy increases from 0.217 to 0.305, while the attack AUC increases from 0.726 to 0.927. One reason is that, with larger model capacity, the model can "memorize" more different views of data samples, which not only facilitate target tasks, but also raise the membership risk.

Ratio of Unlabeled Samples in Each Training Step. We then investigate whether the unlabeled ratio (URatio) during each training step affects the attack performance. Concretely, we vary the unlabeled ratio from 1 to 16 while training the target model and Table 2 summarizes the results. We have two findings. First, the best target model performance reaches with the default setting (7). Second, the membership inference risk, in particular for the unlabeled data, keeps increasing when the ratio increases. On the other hand, the membership inference risk for labeled data slightly decreases (but still in a high level) while increasing the ratio. Therefore, a better choice may be leveraging a relatively small unlabeled ratio to achieve good target performance while reducing the membership risk for unlabeled samples.

6   Discussion on Defenses

We observe that the attack performance increases sharply at the late training steps (see Fig. 4), which indicates that early stopping may be a good strategy to mitigate membership inference attacks. We take CIFAR100 with 4,000 labeled samples as a case study and show the target/attack model performance with respect to different training steps in Figure 7 (in the supplementary material). We find that there is a trade-off between model utility and membership inference performance, i.e., it may reduce both the attack performance and the target model's utility. We note that previous work [16,27] also observe such a trade-off. Besides early stopping, we also evaluate three other defenses, i.e., top-k posteriors [24], model stacking [23], and DP-SGD [1]. Our case study (see Section 8.7 in the supplementary material) shows that early stopping achieves the best trade-off between model utility and membership inference performance.

7   Conclusion

In this paper, we perform the first training data privacy quantification against models trained by SSL through the lens of membership inference attack. Empirical evaluation shows that our proposed data augmentation-based attacks consistently outperform the baseline attacks, in particular for unlabeled training data. Moreover, we have an interesting finding that the reason leading to membership leakage in SSL is different from the commonly believed overfitting nature of ML models trained in supervised manners. The models trained by SSL are well generalized to the testing data (i.e., with almost 0 overfitting level). However, our attack can still successfully break the membership privacy. The reason is that the models trained by SSL "memorize" the training data by giving more confident predictions on them, regardless of the ground truth labels. We also find that early stopping can serve as a countermeasure against the attacks, but there is a trade-off between membership privacy and model utility.

Acknowledgments. This work is partially funded by the Helmholtz Association within the project "Trustworthy Federated Data Analytics" (TFDA) (funding number ZT-I-OO1 4) and National Science Foundation grant No. 1937786.

References

1. Abadi, M., et al.: Deep Learning with differential privacy. In: ACM SIGSAC Conference on Computer and Communications Security (CCS), pp. 308–318. ACM (2016)
2. Berthelot, D., Carlini, N., Goodfellow, I.J., Papernot, N., Oliver, A., Raffel, C.: MixMatch: a holistic approach to semi-supervised learning. In: Annual Conference on Neural Information Processing Systems (NeurIPS). NeurIPS (2019)
3. Carlini, N., Chien, S., Nasr, M., Song, S., Terzis, A., Tramèr, F.: Membership inference attacks from first principles. CoRR abs/2112.03570 (2021)
4. Chen, D., Yu, N., Zhang, Y., Fritz, M.: GAN-Leaks: A taxonomy of membership inference attacks against generative models. In: ACM SIGSAC Conference on Computer and Communications Security (CCS), pp. 343–362. ACM (2020)
5. Choo, C.A.C., Tramèr, F., Carlini, N., Papernot, N.: Label-only membership inference attacks. In: International Conference on Machine Learning (ICML), pp. 1964–1974. PMLR (2021)
6. Cubuk, E.D., Zoph, B., Shlens, J., Le, Q.: RandAugment: practical automated data augmentation with a reduced search space. In: Annual Conference on Neural Information Processing Systems (NeurIPS), pp. 18613–18624. NeurIPS (2020)

7. Fredrikson, M., Jha, S., Ristenpart, T.: Model inversion attacks that exploit confidence information and basic countermeasures. In: ACM SIGSAC Conference on Computer and Communications Security (CCS), pp. 1322–1333. ACM (2015)

8. He, X., Wen, R., Wu, Y., Backes, M., Shen, Y., Zhang, Y.: Node-level membership inference attacks against graph neural networks. CoRR abs/2102.05429 (2021)

9. He, X., Zhang, Y.: Quantifying and mitigating privacy risks of contrastive learning. In: ACM SIGSAC Conference on Computer and Communications Security (CCS), pp. 845–863. ACM (2021)

10. He, Y., Rahimian, S., Schiele, B., Fritz, M.: Segmentations-Leak: membership inference attacks and defenses in semantic image segmentation. In: Vedaldi, A., Bischof, H., Brox, T., Frahm, J.-M. (eds.) ECCV 2020. LNCS, vol. 12368, pp. 519–535. Springer, Cham (2020). https://doi.org/10.1007/978-3-030-58592-1_31

11. Hui, B., Yang, Y., Yuan, H., Burlina, P., Gong, N.Z., Cao, Y.: Practical blind membership inference attack via differential comparisons. In: Network and Distributed System Security Symposium (NDSS). Internet Society (2021)

12. Jia, J., Salem, A., Backes, M., Zhang, Y., Gong, N.Z.: MemGuard: defending against black-box membership inference attacks via adversarial examples. In: ACM SIGSAC Conference on Computer and Communications Security (CCS), pp. 259–274. ACM (2019)

13. Lee, D.H.: Pseudo-label: the simple and efficient semi-supervised learning method for deep neural networks. In: ICML Workshop on Challenges in Representation Learning (WREPL). ICML (2013)

14. Leino, K., Fredrikson, M.: Stolen memories: leveraging model memorization for calibrated white-box membership inference. In: USENIX Security Symposium (USENIX Security), pp. 1605–1622. USENIX (2020)

15. Li, Z., Zhang, Y.: Membership leakage in label-only exposures. In: ACM SIGSAC Conference on Computer and Communications Security (CCS), pp. 880–895. ACM (2021)

16. Liu, H., Jia, J., Qu, W., Gong, N.Z.: EncoderMI: membership inference against pretrained encoders in contrastive learning. In: ACM SIGSAC Conference on Computer and Communications Security (CCS). ACM (2021)

17. Miyato, T., Maeda, S., Koyama, M., Ishii, S.: Virtual adversarial training: a regularization method for supervised and semi-supervised learning. IEEE Trans. Pattern Anal. Mach. Intell. 41(8), 1979–1993 (2019)

18. Nasr, M., Shokri, R., Houmansadr, A.: Machine learning with membership privacy using adversarial regularization. In: ACM SIGSAC Conference on Computer and Communications Security (CCS), pp. 634–646. ACM (2018)

19. Nasr, M., Shokri, R., Houmansadr, A.: Comprehensive privacy analysis of deep learning: passive and active white-box inference attacks against centralized and federated learning. In: IEEE Symposium on Security and Privacy (S&P), pp. 1021–1035. IEEE (2019)

20. Oh, S.J., Augustin, M., Schiele, B., Fritz, M.: Towards reverse-engineering black-box neural networks. In: International Conference on Learning Representations (ICLR) (2018)

21. Pyrgelis, A., Troncoso, C., Cristofaro, E.D.: Knock Knock, Who's there? Membership inference on aggregate location data. In: Network and Distributed System Security Symposium (NDSS). Internet Society (2018)

22. Rahimian, S., Orekondy, T., Fritz, M.: Differential privacy defenses and sampling attacks for membership inference. In: PriML Workshop (PriML). NeurIPS (2020)

23. Salem, A., Zhang, Y., Humbert, M., Berrang, P., Fritz, M., Backes, M.: ML-Leaks: model and data independent membership inference attacks and defenses on machine learning models. In: Network and Distributed System Security Symposium (NDSS). Internet Society (2019)

24. Shokri, R., Stronati, M., Song, C., Shmatikov, V.: Membership inference attacks against machine learning models. In: IEEE Symposium on Security and Privacy (S&P), pp. 3–18. IEEE (2017)

25. Sohn, K., et al.: FixMatch: simplifying semi-supervised learning with consistency and confidence. In: Annual Conference on Neural Information Processing Systems (NeurIPS). NeurIPS (2020)

26. Song, C., Shmatikov, V.: Overlearning reveals sensitive attributes. In: International Conference on Learning Representations (ICLR) (2020)

27. Song, L., Mittal, P.: Systematic evaluation of privacy risks of machine learning models. In: USENIX Security Symposium (USENIX Security). USENIX (2021)

28. Song, L., Shokri, R., Mittal, P.: Privacy risks of securing machine learning models against adversarial examples. In: ACM SIGSAC Conference on Computer and Communications Security (CCS), pp. 241–257. ACM (2019)

29. Wang, B., Gong, N.Z.: Stealing hyperparameters in machine learning. In: IEEE Symposium on Security and Privacy (S&P), pp. 36–52. IEEE (2018)

30. Watson, L., Guo, C., Cormode, G., Sablayrolles, A.: On the importance of difficulty calibration in membership inference attacks. CoRR abs/2111.08440 (2021)

31. Xie, Q., Dai, Z., Du, Y., Hovy, E.H., Neubig, G.: Controllable invariance through adversarial feature learning. In: Annual Conference on Neural Information Processing Systems (NIPS), pp. 585–596. NIPS (2017)

32. Xie, Q., Dai, Z., Hovy, E.H., Luong, T., Le, Q.: Unsupervised data augmentation for consistency training. In: Annual Conference on Neural Information Processing Systems (NeurIPS). NeurIPS (2020)

33. Yeom, S., Giacomelli, I., Fredrikson, M., Jha, S.: Privacy risk in machine learning: analyzing the connection to overfitting. In: IEEE Computer Security Foundations Symposium (CSF), pp. 268–282. IEEE (2018)

34. Zagoruyko, S., Komodakis, N.: Wide residual networks. In: Proceedings of the British Machine Vision Conference (BMVC). BMVA Press (2016)

35. Zhang, B., et al.: FlexMatch: boosting semi-supervised learning with curriculum pseudo labeling. In: Annual Conference on Neural Information Processing Systems (NeurIPS). NeurIPS (2021)

OpenLDN: Learning to Discover Novel Classes for Open-World Semi-Supervised Learning

Mamshad Nayeem Rizve[1]([✉]), Navid Kardan[1], Salman Khan[2],
Fahad Shahbaz Khan[2], and Mubarak Shah[1]

[1] Center for Research in Computer Vision, UCF, Orlando, USA
{nayeemrizve,kardan}@knights.ucf.edu, shah@crcv.ucf.edu
[2] Mohamed bin Zayed University of AI, Abu Dhabi, UAE
{salman.khan,fahad.khan}@mbzuai.ac.ae

Abstract. Semi-supervised learning (SSL) is one of the dominant approaches to address the annotation bottleneck of supervised learning. Recent SSL methods can effectively leverage a large repository of unlabeled data to improve performance while relying on a small set of labeled data. One common assumption in most SSL methods is that the labeled and unlabeled data are from the same data distribution. However, this is hardly the case in many real-world scenarios, which limits their applicability. In this work, instead, we attempt to solve the challenging open-world SSL problem that does not make such an assumption. In the open-world SSL problem, the objective is to recognize samples of known classes, and simultaneously detect and cluster samples belonging to novel classes present in unlabeled data. This work introduces OpenLDN that utilizes a pairwise similarity loss to discover novel classes. Using a bi-level optimization rule this pairwise similarity loss exploits the information available in the labeled set to implicitly cluster novel class samples, while simultaneously recognizing samples from known classes. After discovering novel classes, OpenLDN transforms the open-world SSL problem into a standard SSL problem to achieve additional performance gains using existing SSL methods. Our extensive experiments demonstrate that OpenLDN outperforms the current state-of-the-art methods on multiple popular classification benchmarks while providing a better accuracy/training time trade-off. Code: https://github.com/nayeemrizve/OpenLDN.

Keywords: Open-world · Semi-supervised learning · Novel classes

1 Introduction

Deep learning methods have made significant progress on challenging supervised learning tasks [10, 13, 27, 28, 61]. However, the supervised learning paradigm

Supplementary Information The online version contains supplementary material available at https://doi.org/10.1007/978-3-031-19821-2_22.

assumes access to large amounts of manually labeled data which is time-consuming and expensive to acquire. Several approaches have been proposed to address this problem, including semi-supervised learning [6,46,62], active learning [21,36,55], self-supervised learning [14,18,26], transfer learning [37,56,73], and few-shot learning [20,53,58,66]. Among them, semi-supervised learning (SSL) is one of the dominant approaches which reduces the amount of annotation required by taking advantage of a large collection of unlabeled data.

Even though recent SSL methods [5,6,59,69] have achieved promising results, one of their primary assumptions is that both labeled and unlabeled data come from the same distribution. However, this assumption is difficult to satisfy in many real-world scenarios (open-world problems e.g. [4,33]). For instance, unlabeled data is commonly mined from the web sources which can include examples from unknown classes. It has been established that training with such examples generally deteriorates the performance of the standard SSL methods [16,47]. To mitigate the negative impact of unlabeled samples from unknown (novel) classes, different solutions have been proposed [16,23,75]. However, their main motivation is to merely ignore novel class samples to prevent performance degradation on known classes. In contrast, recently ORCA [7] generalizes the SSL problem with novel classes, where the objective is not only to retain the performance on known classes but also to recognize samples of novel classes. This realistic SSL setup is called open-world SSL problem and is the focus of this work.

This work proposes OpenLDN which employs a pairwise similarity loss to discover novel classes. This loss solves a pairwise similarity prediction task that determines whether an image pair belongs to the same class or not. Essentially, this task is akin to unsupervised clustering problem [11,67], thereby promoting novel class discovery by identifying coherent clusters. The fundamental challenge for solving pairwise similarity is to determine similarity relationship between a pair of images without accessing their class labels. One common way to overcome this challenge is to estimate the pairwise similarity relationship based on pretrained unsupervised/self-supervised features [7,24]. However, this process is computationally expensive. To avoid dependency on unsupervised/self-supervised pretraining, instead, we exploit the information available in the labeled examples from known classes for solving the pairwise similarity prediction task, and introduce a pairwise similarity prediction network to generate the similarity scores between a pair of images. To update the parameters of this network, we resort to a bi-level optimization rule [3,23], which transfers the information available in the labeled examples of known classes to utilize them in learning unknown classes. In particular, we *implicitly* optimize the parameters of the similarity prediction network based on the cross-entropy loss on labeled examples. This way, we solve the pairwise similarity prediction task without relying on unsupervised/self-supervised pretraining, which makes the overall training more efficient while providing substantial performance gains.

Learning pairwise similarity relationship based on output probabilities leads to implicitly discovering clusters according to the most probable class, hence, the discovery of novel classes. Once we learn to recognize novel classes, we can generate pseudo-labels for novel class samples. This subsequently allows us to transform the open-world SSL problem into a closed-world SSL problem by utilizing the generated pseudo-labels of unlabeled samples to incorporate novel class samples into the labeled set. This unique perspective of transforming the open-world problem into a closed-world one is particularly powerful since it allows us to leverage any off-the-shelf closed-world SSL method to achieve further improvements. However, one shortcoming of this strategy is that the generated pseudo-labels for novel classes tend to be noisy, which can in turn impede the subsequent training. To address this issue, we introduce *iterative pseudo-labeling*, a simple and efficient way to handle the noisy estimation of pseudo-labels.

In summary, our key contributions are: (1) we propose a novel algorithm, OpenLDN, to solve open-world SSL. OpenLDN applies a bi-level optimization rule to determine pairwise similarity relationship without relying on pretrained features, (2) we propose to transform the open-world SSL into a closed-world SSL problem by discovering novel classes; this allows us to leverage any off-the-shelf closed-world SSL method to further improve performance, and (3) we introduce *iterative pseudo-labeling*, a simple and efficient method to handle noisy pseudo-labels of novel classes, (4) our experiments show that OpenLDN outperforms the existing state-of-the-art methods by a significant margin.

2   Related Works

Semi-Supervised Learning: SSL is a popular approach to handle label annotation bottleneck in supervised learning [9,15,22,32,35,44,50]. Generally, these methods are developed for a closed-world setup, where unlabeled set only contains samples from the known classes. The two most dominant approaches for closed-world SSL are consistency regularization [41,45,54,63] and pseudo-labeling [2,43,51,57]. The consistency regularization based methods minimize a consistency loss between differently augmented versions of an image to extract salient features from the unlabeled samples. Pseudo-labeling based methods generate pseudo-labels for the unlabeled samples by a network trained on labeled data, and subsequently training on them in a supervised manner. Finally, the hybrid approaches [5,6,59] combine both consistency regularization and pseudo-labeling.

Recent works [16,47] demonstrate that the presence of novel class samples in the unlabeled set negatively impacts the performance on known classes. Different solutions have been proposed to address this issue [16,23,75]. A weight function is trained in [23] to down-weight the novel class samples. Novel class samples are filtered out in [16] based on confidence scores. Weighted batch normalization is introduced in [75] to achieve robustness against novel class samples. However, none of these methods attempt to solve the challenging open-world SSL problem, where the objective is to detect samples of novel classes and classify them. To the best of our knowledge, ORCA [7] is the only method that addresses this issue by introducing an uncertainty-aware adaptive margin based cross-entropy loss to mitigate excessive influence of known classes at early stages of training. However, to discover novel classes, ORCA relies on self-supervised pretraining, which is computationally costly. To overcome the reliance on self-supervised pretraining, the pairwise similarity loss in OpenLDN exploits the information available in labeled examples from known classes using a bi-level optimization rule.

Novel Class Discovery: Novel class discovery problem [19,24,25,29–31,74, 76,77] is closely related to unsupervised clustering [64,68,70,71]. The key difference between the novel class discovery and unsupervised clustering is that the former relies on an extra labeled set to learn the novel classes. To discover novel classes, [24] performs self-supervised pretraining followed by solving a pairwise similarity prediction task based on the rank statistics of the self-supervised features. [25] extends the deep clustering framework to discover novel classes. Pairwise similarity prediction task is also applied in [29,30] to categorize novel classes by transferring knowledge from the known classes. While novel class discovery methods generally use multiple objective functions, [19] simplifies this using multi-view pseudo-labeling and training with cross-entropy loss. The key difference between open-world SSL and novel class discovery is that the former does not assume that unlabeled data only contains novel class samples. Hence, novel class discovery methods are not readily applicable to open-world SSL problem. Additionally, our experimentation shows that OpenLDN outperforms the appropriately modified novel class discovery methods for open-world SSL by a considerable margin.

3   Method

To identify unlabeled samples from both known and novel classes, we introduce a pairwise similarity loss to implicitly cluster the unlabeled data into known and novel classes. This implicit clustering induces discovery of novel classes which is complemented by a cross-entropy loss and an entropy regularization term. Next, we generate pseudo-labels for novel class samples to transform the original open-world SSL problem into a closed-world SSL problem. This transformation allows us to take benefit of existing off-the-shelf closed-world SSL methods to learn on both known and novel classes, delivering further gains. An overview of our approach is provided in Fig. 1. In the following, we present the problem formulation and provide the details of our approach.

3.1   Problem Formulation

We denote scalars as a, vectors as $\mathbf{a}$, matrices as $\mathbf{A}$, and sets as $\mathbb{A}$. In a matrix, the first index always represents rows and the second index represents columns. Further, $\mathbf{A}_{i,:}$ and $\mathbf{A}_{:,k}$ refer to the ith row and k^{th} column in $\mathbf{A}$, respectively.

In open-world SSL problem we assume that there is a labeled set, $\mathbb{S}_L$, and an unlabeled set, $\mathbb{S}_U$. Let, $\mathbb{S}_L = \{\mathbf{x}_i^l, \mathbf{y}_i^l\}_{i=1}^{n_l}$ represent the labeled dataset with n_l samples, where $\mathbf{x}_i^l$ is a labeled sample and $\mathbf{y}_i^l$ is its corresponding label, which belongs to one of the c_l known classes. Similarly, $\mathbb{S}_U = \{\mathbf{x}_i^u\}_{i=1}^{n_u}$, consists of n_u unlabeled samples, where $\mathbf{x}_i^u$ belongs to one of the c_u classes, where c_u is the total number of classes in $\mathbb{S}_U$. In conventional closed-world SSL setting, it is assumed that the class categories for both labeled and unlabeled data are the same. However, in open-world SSL framework, $\mathbb{S}_U$ contains some samples that do not belong to any of the known classes. The samples belonging to unknown classes are called novel class samples where each sample belongs to one of the c_n novel classes, i.e., in open-world setting $c_u = c_l + c_n$.

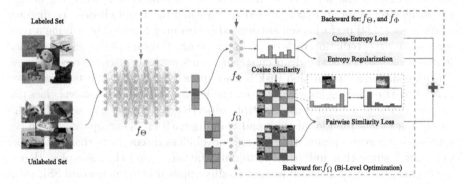

Fig. 1. *OpenLDN Overview - Learning to Discover Novel classes:* A set of labeled and unlabeled images are provided to the feature extractor, f_Θ, to obtain feature embeddings. The embeddings are passed to the classifier, f_Φ, to obtain output probabilities. We compute pairwise cosine similarity scores from the output probabilities for every possible pair in a batch. In parallel, the pairwise similarity prediction network, f_Ω, also outputs similarity scores based on pairs of feature embeddings. Afterwards, we calculate pairwise similarity loss (Eq. 2) to promote the discovery of novel classes. We also compute cross-entropy (CE) loss (Eq. 6) and entropy regularization loss (Eq. 7) to complement the pairwise similarity loss by learning from labeled and pseudo-labeled samples and avoiding trivial solutions, respectively. Next, we update the parameters of f_Θ and f_Φ to minimize the overall loss. Then we compute CE loss using only the labeled samples with updated f_Θ and f_Φ. Finally, we utilize a bi-level optimization rule to update f_Ω based on this CE loss (Eq. 4). The bi-level optimization rule helps to optimize f_Ω by transferring feature similarities from known to unknown classes.

3.2   Learning to Discover Novel Classes

To discover novel classes OpenLDN leverages a neural network, f_Θ, parameterized with Θ, as feature extractor. The feature extractor generates a feature embedding by projecting an input image $\mathbf{x}$ into the embedding space, $\mathbf{z} \in \mathbb{R}^d$, i.e., $f_\Theta : \mathbb{X} \mapsto \mathbb{Z}$. Here, $\mathbb{X}$, and $\mathbb{Z}$ are sets of input images and feature embeddings, respectively. Next, to recognise samples from novel classes, as well as to classify the samples from known classes, we apply a classifier, f_Φ, parameterized with Φ. This classifier projects the embedding vector $\mathbf{z}$ into an output classification space, $f_\Phi : \mathbb{Z} \mapsto \mathbb{R}^{c_l+c_n}$. In this output space, the first c_l logits correspond to the known classes, and the remaining c_n logits belong to novel classes.

The softmax probability scores, $\hat{\mathbf{y}} \in \mathbb{R}^{c_l+c_n}$, are obtained from these output scores using softmax activation function, i.e., $\hat{\mathbf{y}} = \text{Softmax}(f_\Phi \circ f_\Theta(\mathbf{x}))$.

Our overall objective to discover novel classes while recognizing known classes consists of three losses: a) a pairwise similarity loss $\mathcal{L}_{pair}$, b) a cross-entropy (CE) loss $\mathcal{L}_{ce}$, and c) an entropy regularization term $\mathcal{L}_{reg}$. The pairwise similarity loss helps the network to discover novel classes, whereas the CE loss helps classify known classes and novel classes by utilizing the groundtruth labels and generated pseudo-labels, while the entropy regularization helps in avoiding tirvial solutions. The overall objective function to discover novel classes is as follows:

$$\mathcal{L}_{nov} = \mathcal{L}_{pair} + \mathcal{L}_{ce} + \mathcal{L}_{reg}. \tag{1}$$

After training with $\mathcal{L}_{nov}$, samples that are assigned to any of the last c_n logits are considered novel class samples.

Pairwise Similarity Loss: Discovering novel classes is a core component of our proposed method, which is an unsupervised clustering problem, that can be expressed as a pairwise similarity prediction task [11,67]. In particular, there can only be two possible relationships between a pair of images with respect to clusters, either they belong to the same cluster or not. However, to solve a pairwise similarity prediction task supervision is needed. Previous methods [7,24] try to overcome this problem by generating pairwise pseudo-labels for all pairs of images by finding the nearest neighbors (labeled as members of the same cluster) based on pretrained features. However, such an approach is computationally expensive and suffers from noisy estimation of nearest neighbors.

In sharp contrast to this approach, instead of relying on unsupervised/self-supervised pretraining to obtain labels for the pairwise similarity prediction task, we learn to estimate the pairwise similarity scores based on the available groundtruth annotations which are more reliable. To this end, we introduce a pairwise similarity prediction network, f_Ω, parameterized by Ω. Given a pair of embedding vectors, f_Ω outputs a pairwise similarity score, i.e., $f_\Omega : \mathbb{Z} \times \mathbb{Z} \mapsto [0,1]$. The pairwise similarity score from f_Ω can be used as the supervisory signal for minimizing the pairwise similarity loss. To this end, given a batch of images, we compute the cosine similarity of output probabilities between all pairs of images. After that, for our pairwise similarity loss, we minimize l_2 loss between the computed cosine similarity scores of output probabilities and the estimated pairwise similarity scores from f_Ω. Note that minimizing pairwise similarity loss for cosine similarities of output probabilities is crucial since this will implicitly lead to formation of clusters based on maximum probability scores, consequently, the recognition of novel classes. The pairwise similarity loss is as follows:

$$\mathcal{L}_{pair} = \sum_{i \neq j} \left(\text{Sim}(\hat{\mathbf{Y}}_{i,:}, \hat{\mathbf{Y}}_{j,:}) - f_\Omega(\mathbf{Z}_{i,:}, \mathbf{Z}_{j,:}) \right)^2, \tag{2}$$

where, $\hat{\mathbf{Y}}$ is the output probability matrix, $\mathbf{Z}$ is the matrix of feature embeddings, $\text{Sim}(.,.)$ denotes the cosine similarity function.

To optimize the parameters of f_Ω, we devise a bi-level optimization procedure [3]. Since we do not have access to the labels of any unlabeled sample, especially the samples from the novel classes, we utilize the groundtruth labels of the labeled examples belonging to known classes. The main motivation behind this bi-level optimization is to acquire a set of parameters Ω that do not deteriorate the performance of $f_\Phi \circ f_\Theta$ on known classes. Thereby, we optimize f_Ω based on the cross-entropy loss computed on labeled examples. The optimization procedure is as follows:

First, we update the parameters of feature extractor and classifier with the combined loss introduced in Eq. 1 to discover novel classes.

$$(\Theta^*, \Phi^*) = (\Theta, \Phi) - \alpha_{(\Theta,\Phi)} \nabla_{(\Theta,\Phi)} \mathcal{L}_{nov}(\Theta, \Phi, \Omega). \tag{3}$$

where, $\alpha_{(\Theta,\Phi)}$ refers to the learning rate for optimizing the parameters Θ and Φ.

Next, we use the supervised cross-entropy loss, $\mathcal{L}_{ce}^l = -\sum_i \sum_k \mathbf{Y}_{i,k} \log \hat{\mathbf{Y}}_{i,k}$, computed over the labeled examples to update the parameters of f_Ω. Here, $\mathbf{Y}$ is the matrix of groundtruth labels. The update rule is according to,

$$\Omega^* = \Omega - \alpha_\Omega \nabla_\Omega \mathcal{L}_{ce}^l(\Theta^*, \Phi^*), \tag{4}$$

where, α_Ω is the learning rate for optimizing the parameters Ω. Since Ω is not explicit in the objective $\mathcal{L}_{ce}^l(\Theta^*, \Phi^*)$ in Eq. 4, we perform a bi-level optimization to calculate $\nabla_\Omega \mathcal{L}_{ce}^l(\Theta^*, \Phi^*)$. This nested optimization is available in most modern deep learning packages that support automatic differentiation [1,49].

This bi-level optimization procedure ensures that the parameters of f_Ω are updated in such a way that the classification performance on known classes does not deteriorate since this is one of the primary objectives in open-world SSL.

Learning with Labeled and Pseudo-labeled Data: In the above, we introduced the pairwise similarity loss to recognise novel classes by solving a pairwise similarity prediction task. Recall that our aim is to recognise novel classes in the unlabeled set and to classify the known classes, at the same time. This problem only allows access to a limited amount of annotations for known classes. The straightforward way to utilize these available annotations would be to minimize a cross-entropy loss on the labeled samples. However, this approach can create a strong bias towards known classes because of their strong training signal [7]. To mitigate this bias and to utilize the unlabeled samples more efficiently, we generate pseudo-labels for all the unlabeled data. The generated pseudo-labels can be used with groundtruth labels for minimizing cross-entropy loss.

Following the common practice [2,43,51], we generate pseudo-labels based on the network output probabilities. To reduce the possibility of erroneous training with unreliable pseudo-labels, we generate pseudo-labels only for sufficiently confident predictions. In addition, our pseudo-label based cross-entropy learning satisfies another commonly used objective in SSL works i.e., consistency regularization. This objective encourages perturbation invariant output distribution so that the decision boundaries lie in low density regions [12,65]. One way to satisfy this objective is to minimize the divergence between output probabilities of two randomly transformed versions of an image. However, it adds another term to the loss, and consequently a new hyperparameter. A more elegant way is to use the generated pseudo-label from one transformed version of an image as the target for the other version. We utilize the pseudo-labels generated from a weakly transformed version of an image $\mathbf{x}^w$ as the target for its strongly augmented version, $\mathbf{x}^s$. We state our pseudo-label generation process below:

$$\mathbb{S}_{PL} = \{(\mathbf{x}_i^s, \mathbb{1}_{\max(\hat{\mathbf{Y}}_{i,:}^w)}(\hat{\mathbf{Y}}_{i,:}^w)|\max(\hat{\mathbf{Y}}_{i,:}^w) > \tau\}, \tag{5}$$

where, $\tau = 0.5$ (midpoint in binary classification) to avoid per-dataset finetuning.

Once the pseudo-labels are generated we combine them with the groundtruth labels, $\mathbb{S} = \mathbb{S}_{PL} \cup \mathbb{S}_L$, and train the model using cross-entropy loss. In practice, we combine these two sets within a batch. Let $\mathbb{S}_B$ denote a batch, the cross-entropy loss on this set is defined as:

$$\mathcal{L}_{ce} = -\sum_{i \in \mathbb{S}_B} \sum_{k=1}^{c_u} \tilde{\mathbf{Y}}_{i,k} \log \hat{\mathbf{Y}}_{i,k}, \tag{6}$$

where, $\tilde{\mathbf{Y}}$ is the matrix of one-hot encoded ground-truth labels and the generated pseudo-labels.

Entropy Regularization: One of the well-known drawbacks of assigning unlabeled data to distinct categories based on a discriminative (such as cross-entropy) loss is that it can lead to a trivial solution where all the unlabeled samples are assigned to the same class [7,8,19,72]. Our pairwise similarity loss suffers from the same problem since such a solution will also minimize our pairwise similarity loss in Eq. 2. To address this, we incorporate an entropy regularization term in our training objective. One way to achieve this would be to apply entropy regularization to the output of each sample independently. However, this way of entropy minimization leads to substantial changes in the individual output probabilities which results in arbitrary class assignments for novel class samples. To avoid this problem, we apply entropy regularization over an aggregated statistic, in our case, the mean of the sample probabilities of an entire batch. This entropy regularization term prevents a single class from dominating the entire batch, where most of unlabeled samples are only assigned to one class. This term does not interfere with the balanced class assignments. The entropy regularization is defined as,

$$\mathcal{L}_{reg} = \sum_{k=1}^{c_u} \bar{\mathbf{y}}_k \log \bar{\mathbf{y}}_k, \tag{7}$$

where, $\bar{\mathbf{y}} = \frac{1}{b}\sum_{i=1}^{b} \hat{\mathbf{Y}}_{i,:}$ is the average probability of the batch, and b denotes the number of examples in a batch.

3.3   Closed-World Training with Iterative Pseudo-labeling

Once we discover novel classes in the unlabeled data we can reformulate the open-world SSL problem as a closed-world one to improve performance. To this end, we generate the pseudo-labels for all novel class samples using Eq. 8:

$$\check{\mathbf{Y}} = \mathbb{1}_{\max(\hat{\mathbf{Y}}_{i,:})}(\hat{\mathbf{Y}}_{i,:}). \tag{8}$$

Next, using generated pseudo-labels, we add novel class samples to the labeled set. At this point, we are able to apply any standard closed-world SSL method [6,59,63,69]. Unfortunately, pseudo-labels tend to contain noise that can hamper the performance. To mitigate the negative impact of noise, we propose to perform pseudo-labeling during the closed-world SSL training in an iterative manner. This new iterative pseudo-labeling approach can be related to EM algorithm. From this perspective, we iteratively attempt to update the pseudo-labels (expectation step), and train the network by minimizing the loss on those updated pseudo-labels (maximization step). It is important to note that OpenLDN, including the final closed-world SSL retraining, is computationally lighter or comparable to the unsupervised/self-supervised pretraining based approaches (Sect. 4.2). Besides, the transformation from the open-world SSL problem to a closed-world problem is a general solution which can be applied to other methods as well. We provide our overall training algorithm in supplementary materials.

4   Experimental Evaluation

Datasets: To demonstrate the effectiveness of OpenLDN, we conduct experiments on five common benchmark datasets: CIFAR-10 [38], CIFAR-100 [39], ImageNet-100 [17], Tiny ImageNet [42], and Oxford-IIIT Pet dataset [48]. Both CIFAR-10 and CIFAR-100 datasets contain 60K images (split into 50K/10k train/test set), and they have 10 and 100 categories, respectively. ImagNet1-100 dataset contains 100 image categories from ImageNet. Tiny ImageNet contains 100K/10K training/validation images from 200 classes. Finally, Oxford-IIIT Pet contains images from 37 categories split into 3680/3669 train/test set. In our experiments, we divide each of these datasets based on the percentage of known and novel classes. We consider the first c_l classes as known and the rest as novel. For known classes, we randomly select a portion of data to construct the labeled set and add the rest to the unlabeled set along with all novel class samples.

Implementation Details: We use ResNet-18 [28] as the feature extractor in all of our experiments except the experiments on ImageNet-100 dataset where we use ResNet-50. We instantiate our pairwise similarity prediction network, f_Ω, with an MLP consisting of a single hidden layer of dimension 100. The classifier, f_Φ, is a single linear layer. To discover novel classes, we train for 50 epochs with a batch size of 200 (480 for ImageNet-100) in all the experiments.

We always use Adam optimizer [34]. For training the feature extractor and the classifier, we set the learning rate to $5e^{-4}$ ($1e^{-2}$ for ImageNet-100). For the pairwise similarity prediction network, we use a learning rate of $1e^{-4}$. We use two popular closed-world SSL methods, Mixmatch [6] and UDA [69], for second stage closed-world SSL training. For this closed-world training, to preserve data balance, we select an equal number of pseudo-labels for each novel class. For iterative pseudo-labeling, we generate pseudo-labels every 10 epochs. Additional implementation details are available in the supplementary materials.

Evaluation Metrics: We report standard accuracy for known classes. In addition, following [7,19,24,25], we report clustering accuracy on novel classes. We leverage the Hungarian algorithm [40] to align the predictions and groundtruth labels before measuring the classification accuracy. Finally, we also report the joint accuracy on the novel and known classes by using the Hungarian algorithm.

Table 1. Accuracy on **CIFAR-10**, **CIFAR-100**, and **ImageNet-100** datasets with 50% classes as known and 50% classes as novel.

Method	CIFAR10			CIFAR100			ImageNet100		
	Known	Novel	All	Known	Novel	All	Known	Novel	All
FixMatch[59]	71.5	50.4	49.5	39.6	23.5	20.3	65.8	36.7	34.9
DS³L[23]	77.6	45.3	40.2	55.1	23.7	24.0	71.2	32.5	30.8
CGDL[60]	72.3	44.6	39.7	49.3	22.5	23.5	67.3	33.8	31.9
DTC [25]	53.9	39.5	38.3	31.3	22.9	18.3	25.6	20.8	21.3
RankStats[24]	86.6	81.0	82.9	36.4	28.4	23.1	47.3	28.7	40.3
UNO[19]	91.6	69.3	80.5	68.3	36.5	51.5	–	–	–
ORCA[7]	88.2	90.4	89.7	66.9	43.0	48.1	89.1	**72.1**	77.8
OpenLDN-MixMatch	95.2	92.7	94.0	73.5	46.8₊₃.₈	60.1₊₈.₆	–	–	–
OpenLDN-UDA	**95.7**₊₄.₁	**95.1**₊₄.₇	**95.4**₊₅.₇	**74.1**₊₅.₈	44.5	59.3	**89.6**₊₀.₅	68.6₋₃.₅	**79.1**₊₁.₃

4.1 Results

CIFAR-10, CIFAR-100, and ImageNet-100 Experiments: We present our experimental results on CIFAR-10, CIFAR-100, and ImageNet-100 datasets in Table 1. We conduct experiments with 50% novel classes on all three datasets, where we include 50% labeled data from known classes. We report additional results with less labeled data in supplementary material. For comparison, we primarily use the scores reported in [7]. Furthermore, as another competitive baseline, we modify a recent novel class discovery method, UNO [19], and include its performance for comparison. Table 1 shows that both OpenLDN-MixMatch and OpenLDN-UDA significantly outperform novel class discovery methods (DTC [25], RankStats [24], and UNO [19]) that have been modified for open-world SSL task. OpenLDN also outperforms other baseline methods: FixMatch [59], DS³L [23], and CGDL [60]. These results showcase the efficacy of

OpenLDN, where it outperforms previous state-of-the-art (ORCA [7]) by about 4.7–7.5% absolute improvement on different evaluation metrics on CIFAR-10 dataset. We observe a similar pattern on CIFAR-100 dataset, where OpenLDN outperforms ORCA and UNO by 12% and 8.6% respectively on the joint task of classifying known and novel classes. We also notice a similar trend on ImageNet-100 dataset. In parallel to outperforming all the baselines methods, OpenLDN achieves a modest 1.3% improvement over ORCA. These results validate the effectiveness of OpenLDN in solving open-world SSL problem.

Table 2. Accuracy on **Tiny ImageNet** and **Oxford-IIIT Pet** datasets with 50% classes as known and 50% classes as novel.

Method	Tiny ImageNet			Oxford-IIIT Pet		
	Known	**Novel**	**All**	**Known**	**Novel**	**All**
DTC [25]	28.8	16.3	19.9	20.7	16.0	13.5
RankStats [24]	5.7	5.4	3.4	12.6	11.9	11.1
UNO [19]	46.5	15.7	30.3	49.8	22.7	34.9
OpenLDN-MixMatch	52.3	19.5	36.0	**67.1**$_{\uparrow 17.3}$	27.3	47.7
OpenLDN-UDA	**58.3**$_{\uparrow 11.8}$	**25.5**$_{\uparrow 9.8}$	**41.9**$_{\uparrow 11.6}$	66.8	**33.1**$_{\uparrow 10.4}$	**50.4**$_{\uparrow 15.5}$

Tiny ImageNet and Oxford-IIIT Pet Experiments: We also conduct additional experiments on the challenging Tiny ImageNet dataset, where the total number of classes is significantly larger than CIFAR-10, CIFAR-100, and ImageNet-100 datasets. Moreover, to further demonstrate the effectiveness of OpenLDN, we also conduct experiments on a fine-grained dataset, i.e., Oxford-IIIT Pet. The results of these experiments are presented in Table 2. On Tiny ImageNet dataset we observe that OpenLDN significantly outperforms DTC and RankStat. Furthermore, OpenLDN-UDA achieves ∼60% relative improvement on novel classes over UNO. OpenLDN-MixMatch also achieves a significant improvement over UNO on novel and all classes. Furthermore, on fine-grained Oxford-IIIT Pet dataset, we make a similar comparison and observe that OpenLDN significantly outperforms all three novel class discovery methods by a large margin. To be precise, OpenLDN-Mixmatch achieves 12.8% absolute improvement over UNO on the joint classification task and similarly, OpenLDN-UDA achieves 15.5% absolute improvement. Experiments on both of these datasets demonstrate that OpenLDN can scale up to a large number of classes and is also effective for challenging fine-grained classification task.

4.2 Ablation and Analysis

We conduct extensive ablation studies on the CIFAR-100 dataset, with 50% labels, to study the contribution of different components of OpenLDN. The

Table 3. Ablation study on **CIFAR-100** with 50% classes as known and 50% classes as novel. Here, **EntReg** refers to entropy regularization, **SimLoss** means pairwise similarity loss, **CWT** refers to closed-world SSL training, and **ItrPL** denotes iterative pseudo-labeling. Each component of OpenLDN contributes towards final performance.

EntReg	SimLoss	CWT	ItrPL	Known	Novel	All
✗	✓	✗	✗	66.7	–	33.4
✓	✗	✗	✗	66.2	26.6	46.2
✓	✓	✗	✗	66.2	40.3	53.3
✓	✓	✓	✗	73.9	44.9	59.1
✓	✓	✓	✓	73.5	46.8	60.1

results are presented in Table 3. In this table, the first row demonstrates that without entropy regularization OpenLDN is unable to detect novel classes. We contribute this to overpowering of a single class (Sect. 3.2). Next, we evaluate the impact of our pairwise similarity loss with bi-level optimization rule. We observe that without pairwise similarity loss the performance of OpenLDN degrades by 13.7% on novel classes which makes it the most critical component of our proposed solution. We also observe that our pairwise similarity loss does not sacrifice known class performance to improve the performance on novel classes. This outcome is expected since one of the objectives of our bi-level optimization rule is to retain performance on known classes (Sect. 3.2). The fourth row demonstrates the effectiveness of transforming the open-world SSL problem into a closed-world one. Here, we observe that with this component we obtain a significant improvement in known class performance. In addition, we also notice a significant improvement in novel class performance. Interestingly, on this dataset, OpenLDN outperforms ORCA [7] (on joint classification task) even without the subsequent closed-world SSL training. Finally, Table 3 shows that including iterative pseudo-labeling proves to be effective, where we observe ∼2% performance boost on novel classes. In conclusion, this extensive ablation study empirically validates the effectiveness of different components of our solution.

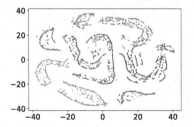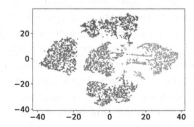

Fig. 2. Impact of closed-world training. t-SNE visualization of novel class probabilities on **CIFAR-10**: (left to right) before and after closed-world training.

Impact of Closed-World Training: In an attempt to further investigate the impact of closed-world SSL training, we perform a t-SNE visualization of probability outputs of the novel class samples on CIFAR-10 dataset in Fig. 2. Following our general setup, in this experiment, we consider 50% classes as novel. The results in Fig. 2 show that after novel class discovery training the novel classes form very distinct clusters. However, since novel classes are learned through auxiliary losses, without any direct supervision, there is some overlap between different classes. After training with a closed-world SSL method (MixMatch) we observe that these overlaps fade away and novel classes become well-separated and form compact clusters. This analysis further validates the complimentary effect of incorporating a closed-world SSL method after discovering novel classes.

Effect of Changing Pairwise Similarity Estimation: In another set of experiments, to analyze the effectiveness of our pairwise similarity estimation with bi-level optimization rule we conduct experiments with alternate pairwise similarity estimation methods on CIFAR-100 dataset. The results are reported in Table 4. In this table, to provide a baseline to compare other pairwise similarity estimation techniques, we include the perfor-

Table 4. Results with alternate pairwise similarity estimation methods on **CIFAR-100** dataset with 50% classes as known and 50% classes as novel.

Pairwise Sim. Est.	Known	Novel	All
No similarity	66.2	26.6	46.2
Soft Cosine	64.5	10.3	37.4
Hard Cosine (0.50)	53.7	2.1	27.9
Hard Cosine (0.95)	54.2	17.3	35.8
Nearest Neighbor	**66.4**	31.7	49.1
OpenLDN	66.2	**40.3**	**53.3**

mance of OpenLDN without any pairwise similarity loss in the first row. The next row in the table demonstrates the performance of OpenLDN when the pairwise similarity is directly estimated from the cosine similarity of features. Surprisingly this method of estimating pairwise similarity performs worse than our baseline without any pairwise similarity loss (first row). We hypothesize this phenomenon to instability of cosine similarity of features without any feature pretraining. In the next set of experiments (third and fourth rows), we utilize a hard version of this pairwise similarity estimation method, where we threshold the pairwise feature similarities using two different thresholds (0.50 and 0.95). After that, we minimize a binary cross-entropy loss as the pairwise similarity loss. The results of these two experiments are reported in third and fourth row, where a further drop in performance is observed. One possible explanation is that without any feature pretraining this kind of pairwise similarity estimation leads to a lot of false positives (from novel classes) which in turn reduces the score of known classes. Finally, in the next row of the table, we use a nearest neighbor based pairwise similarity estimation technique similar to ORCA [7]. As indicated in the table, this nearest neighbor based similarity estimation improves over the baseline without any pairwise similarity loss. However, our pairwise similarity estimation based on the bi-level optimization rule outperforms this nearest neighbor based estimation technique by a significant margin; we obtain

~9% absolute improvement on novel classes. These set of experiments further validate our claim that common pairwise similarity estimation techniques are not potent without feature pretraining, whereas, the proposed pairwise similarity estimation in OpenLDN is able to learn these pairwise similarities effectively.

Computational Cost Analysis: One of the primary advantages of OpenLDN is that unlike ORCA it does not require any feature initialization technique. This enables OpenLDN to be computationally efficient in comparison to ORCA. To demonstrate the efficiency of OpenLDN we report the performance on CIFAR-100 dataset across different training budgets in Fig. 3. We notice that, ORCA with SimCLR pretraining takes ~ 28 h with our computing

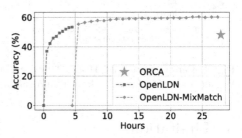

Fig. 3. Accuracy with respect to wall-clock time on **CIFAR-100** dataset. OpenLDN outperforms ORCA in less than 3 h.

resources. We also observe that OpenLDN outperforms ORCA under 3 h on this dataset even without the closed-world SSL training. On the other hand, the closed-world SSL training reaches a reasonable performance very fast and improves relatively slowly over time. Therefore, if computational budget is of concern we can stop training at an earlier stage without making a noticeable trade-off in performance.

Unknown Number of Novel Classes: In our experiments, we assume that the number of novel classes is known in advance. This follows novel class discovery methods [19,24,25], and exiting work on open-world SSL [7]. However, this is a limiting assumption since in real-world applications the number of novel classes is rarely known a priori. Therefore, estimating the number of novel classes is crucial for wider adoption. To the best of our knowledge, DTC [25] is the only method that proposes a solution for estimating the number of novel classes. However, in our experiments we find that DTC only works for small number of unknown classes and fails to estimate the number of novel classes for CIFAR-100 dataset, where 50% of classes are novel. Therefore, instead of estimating the number of novel classes by DTC, we analyze the performance of OpenLDN with the assumption that a reasonable method for estimating the number of novel classes is provided. We further assume that the hypothetical method will either overestimate or underestimate the number of novel classes. We conduct two sets of experiments to investigate both these cases. The results are demonstrated in Fig. 4. We observe that performance of OpenLDN is stable over a wide range of estimation errors. We also notice that even with 50% estimation error OpenLDN outperforms ORCA on CIFAR-100 dataset. In summary, these experiments demonstrate that OpenLDN can be applied in a more realistic setup if a reasonable method for estimating the number of novel classes is available.

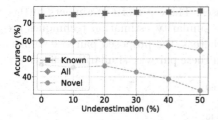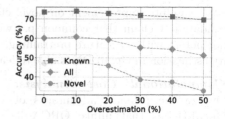

Fig. 4. Performance on **CIFAR-100** dataset with unknown number of novel classes. We set first 50% classes as known and remaining 50% classes as novel.

5   Limitations

In this work, we focus on the more general open-world SSL problem, where the unlabeled set can include unknown class samples. However, our proposed solution is based on a few assumptions. Most notably, following prior works, we assume that the known classes are similar to novel classes, thus they will share some relevant information that can be exploited for discovering novel classes. However, in some extreme cases, this assumption might be violated. Besides, in our entropy regularization term, we encourage the outputs to be uniform. For imbalanced data, this can lead to suboptimal results. One solution is to apply the prior target distribution [52] instead of uniform distribution in the entropy regularization loss. This prompts a new avenue of research that investigate novel methods to estimate prior target distribution in open-world environments.

6   Conclusion

In this work, we propose OpenLDN to solve open-world SSL problem. OpenLDN utilizes a pairwise similarity loss to discover and cluster novel classes by solving a pairwise similarity prediction task. One advantage of our solution is that the proposed pairwise similarity objective does not rely on any additional self-supervised pretraining, but instead, it exploits the information readily available in the labeled set using a bi-level optimization rule. Moreover, our solution brings in a unique perspective towards solving open-world SSL problems by transforming it into a closed-world SSL problem. This insight provides the opportunity to leverage all recent advancements in closed-world SSL methods readily in the context of open-world SSL. Finally, we introduce iterative pseudo-labeling as a simple and effective tool to address the noise present in generated pseudo-labels for novel classes without adding any significant computational overhead. OpenLDN is able to outperform the state-of-the-art open-world SSL methods while incurring a lower computational cost. We demonstrate the superior performance of OpenLDN over a wide range of vision datasets.

References

1. Abadi, M., et al.: TensorFlow: large-scale machine learning on heterogeneous systems (2015). Software available from tensorflow.org. https://www.tensorflow.org/
2. Arazo, E., Ortego, D., Albert, P., O'Connor, N.E., McGuinness, K.: Pseudo-labeling and confirmation bias in deep semi-supervised learning. In: 2020 International Joint Conference on Neural Networks (IJCNN), pp. 1–8. IEEE (2020)
3. Bard, J.F.: Practical Bilevel Optimization: Algorithms and Applications, vol. 30. Springer, New York (2013). https://doi.org/10.1007/978-1-4757-2836-1
4. Bendale, A., Boult, T.: Towards open world recognition. In: Proceedings of the IEEE Conference on Computer Vision and Pattern Recognition, pp. 1893–1902 (2015)
5. Berthelot, D., et al.: RemixMatch: semi-supervised learning with distribution matching and augmentation anchoring. In: International Conference on Learning Representations (2020)
6. Berthelot, D., Carlini, N., Goodfellow, I., Papernot, N., Oliver, A., Raffel, C.A.: MixMatch: a holistic approach to semi-supervised learning. In: Advances in Neural Information Processing Systems 32, pp. 5049–5059. Curran Associates, Inc. (2019)
7. Cao, K., Brbic, M., Leskovec, J.: Open-world semi-supervised learning. In: International Conference on Learning Representations (2022). https://openreview.net/forum?id=O-r8LOR-CCA
8. Caron, M., Bojanowski, P., Joulin, A., Douze, M.: Deep clustering for unsupervised learning of visual features. In: Ferrari, V., Hebert, M., Sminchisescu, C., Weiss, Y. (eds.) Computer Vision – ECCV 2018. LNCS, vol. 11218, pp. 139–156. Springer, Cham (2018). https://doi.org/10.1007/978-3-030-01264-9_9
9. Caron, M., Misra, I., Mairal, J., Goyal, P., Bojanowski, P., Joulin, A.: Unsupervised learning of visual features by contrasting cluster assignments. In: Advances in Neural Information Processing Systems 33 (2020)
10. Carreira, J., Zisserman, A.: Quo vadis, action recognition? A new model and the kinetics dataset. In: Proceedings of the IEEE Conference on Computer Vision and Pattern Recognition, pp. 6299–6308 (2017)
11. Chang, J., Wang, L., Meng, G., Xiang, S., Pan, C.: Deep adaptive image clustering. In: Proceedings of the IEEE international Conference on Computer Vision, pp. 5879–5887 (2017)
12. Chapelle, O., Zien, A.: Semi-supervised classification by low density separation. In: AISTATS, vol. 2005, pp. 57–64. Citeseer (2005)
13. Chen, L.-C., Zhu, Y., Papandreou, G., Schroff, F., Adam, H.: Encoder-decoder with atrous separable convolution for semantic image segmentation. In: Ferrari, V., Hebert, M., Sminchisescu, C., Weiss, Y. (eds.) ECCV 2018. LNCS, vol. 11211, pp. 833–851. Springer, Cham (2018). https://doi.org/10.1007/978-3-030-01234-2_49
14. Chen, T., Kornblith, S., Norouzi, M., Hinton, G.: A simple framework for contrastive learning of visual representations. arXiv preprint arXiv:2002.05709 (2020)
15. Chen, T., Kornblith, S., Swersky, K., Norouzi, M., Hinton, G.E.: Big self-supervised models are strong semi-supervised learners. In: Advances in Neural Information Processing Systems 33 (2020)
16. Chen, Y., Zhu, X., Li, W., Gong, S.: Semi-supervised learning under class distribution mismatch. In: Proceedings of the AAAI Conference on Artificial Intelligence, vol. 34, pp. 3569–3576 (2020)
17. Deng, J., Dong, W., Socher, R., Li, L.J., Li, K., Fei-Fei, L.: ImageNet: a large-scale hierarchical image database. In: 2009 IEEE Conference on Computer Vision and Pattern Recognition, pp. 248–255. IEEE (2009)

18. Doersch, C., Gupta, A., Efros, A.A.: Unsupervised visual representation learning by context prediction. In: Proceedings of the IEEE International Conference on Computer Vision, pp. 1422–1430 (2015)
19. Fini, E., Sangineto, E., Lathuilière, S., Zhong, Z., Nabi, M., Ricci, E.: A unified objective for novel class discovery. In: Proceedings of the IEEE/CVF International Conference on Computer Vision, pp. 9284–9292 (2021)
20. Finn, C., Abbeel, P., Levine, S.: Model-agnostic meta-learning for fast adaptation of deep networks. Proceedings of Machine Learning Research, International Convention Centre, Sydney, Australia, 06–11 August 2017, vol. 70, pp. 1126–1135. PMLR (2017). http://proceedings.mlr.press/v70/finn17a.html
21. Gal, Y., Islam, R., Ghahramani, Z.: Deep Bayesian active learning with image data. In: International Conference on Machine Learning, pp. 1183–1192. PMLR (2017)
22. Gammerman, A., Vovk, V., Vapnik, V.: Learning by transduction. In: Proceedings of the Fourteenth Conference on Uncertainty in Artificial Intelligence, UAI 1998, pp. 148–155. Morgan Kaufmann Publishers Inc., San Francisco (1998)
23. Guo, L.Z., Zhang, Z.Y., Jiang, Y., Li, Y.F., Zhou, Z.H.: Safe deep semi-supervised learning for unseen-class unlabeled data. In: International Conference on Machine Learning, pp. 3897–3906. PMLR (2020)
24. Han, K., Rebuffi, S.A., Ehrhardt, S., Vedaldi, A., Zisserman, A.: Automatically discovering and learning new visual categories with ranking statistics. In: International Conference on Learning Representations (2020)
25. Han, K., Vedaldi, A., Zisserman, A.: Learning to discover novel visual categories via deep transfer clustering. In: Proceedings of the IEEE/CVF International Conference on Computer Vision, pp. 8401–8409 (2019)
26. He, K., Fan, H., Wu, Y., Xie, S., Girshick, R.: Momentum contrast for unsupervised visual representation learning. In: Proceedings of the IEEE/CVF Conference on Computer Vision and Pattern Recognition, pp. 9729–9738 (2020)
27. He, K., Gkioxari, G., Dollár, P., Girshick, R.: Mask R-CNN. In: Proceedings of the IEEE International Conference on Computer Vision, pp. 2961–2969 (2017)
28. He, K., Zhang, X., Ren, S., Sun, J.: Deep residual learning for image recognition. In: Proceedings of the IEEE Conference on Computer Vision and Pattern Recognition, pp. 770–778 (2016)
29. Hsu, Y.C., Lv, Z., Kira, Z.: Learning to cluster in order to transfer across domains and tasks. In: International Conference on Learning Representations (2018). https://openreview.net/forum?id=ByRWCqvT-
30. Hsu, Y.C., Lv, Z., Schlosser, J., Odom, P., Kira, Z.: Multi-class classification without multi-class labels. In: International Conference on Learning Representations (2019). https://openreview.net/forum?id=SJzR2iRcK7
31. Jia, X., Han, K., Zhu, Y., Green, B.: Joint representation learning and novel category discovery on single-and multi-modal data. In: Proceedings of the IEEE/CVF International Conference on Computer Vision, pp. 610–619 (2021)
32. Joachims, T.: Transductive inference for text classification using support vector machines. In: ICML, vol. 99, pp. 200–209 (1999)
33. Kardan, N., Stanley, K.O.: Mitigating fooling with competitive overcomplete output layer neural networks. In: 2017 International Joint Conference on Neural Networks (IJCNN), pp. 518–525. IEEE (2017)
34. Kingma, D.P., Ba, J.: Adam: a method for stochastic optimization. arXiv preprint arXiv:1412.6980 (2014)

35. Kingma, D.P., Mohamed, S., Rezende, D.J., Welling, M.: Semi-supervised learning with deep generative models. In: Advances in Neural Information Processing Systems, pp. 3581–3589 (2014)
36. Konyushkova, K., Sznitman, R., Fua, P.: Learning active learning from data. In: Guyon, I., et al. (eds.) Advances in Neural Information Processing Systems, vol. 30. Curran Associates, Inc. (2017). https://proceedings.neurips.cc/paper/2017/file/8ca8da41fe1ebc8d3ca31dc14f5fc56c-Paper.pdf
37. Kornblith, S., Shlens, J., Le, Q.V.: Do better ImageNet models transfer better? In: Proceedings of the IEEE Conference on Computer Vision and Pattern Recognition, pp. 2661–2671 (2019)
38. Krizhevsky, A., Nair, V., Hinton, G.: CIFAR-10 (Canadian Institute for Advanced Research)
39. Krizhevsky, A., Nair, V., Hinton, G.: CIFAR-100 (Canadian Institute for Advanced Research)
40. Kuhn, H.W.: The Hungarian method for the assignment problem. Naval Res. Logist. Q. **2**(1–2), 83–97 (1955)
41. Laine, S., Aila, T.: Temporal ensembling for semi-supervised learning. In: ICLR (Poster). OpenReview.net (2017)
42. Le, Y., Yang, X.: Tiny ImageNet visual recognition challenge. CS 231N **7**(7), 3 (2015)
43. Lee, D.H.: Pseudo-label: the simple and efficient semi-supervised learning method for deep neural networks (2013)
44. Liu, B., Wu, Z., Hu, H., Lin, S.: Deep metric transfer for label propagation with limited annotated data. In: Proceedings of the IEEE International Conference on Computer Vision Workshops (2019)
45. Miyato, T., Maeda, S., Koyama, M., Ishii, S.: Virtual adversarial training: a regularization method for supervised and semi-supervised learning. IEEE Trans. Pattern Anal. Mach. Intell. **41**, 1979–1993 (2018)
46. Miyato, T., Maeda, S., Koyama, M., Ishii, S.: Virtual adversarial training: a regularization method for supervised and semi-supervised learning. IEEE Trans. Pattern Anal. Mach. Intell. **41**(8), 1979–1993 (2018)
47. Oliver, A., Odena, A., Raffel, C., Cubuk, E.D., Goodfellow, I.J.: Realistic evaluation of deep semi-supervised learning algorithms. arXiv preprint arXiv:1804.09170 (2018)
48. Parkhi, O.M., Vedaldi, A., Zisserman, A., Jawahar, C.V.: Cats and dogs. In: IEEE Conference on Computer Vision and Pattern Recognition (2012)
49. Paszke, A., et al.: Automatic differentiation in PyTorch (2017)
50. Pu, Y., et al.: Variational autoencoder for deep learning of images, labels and captions. In: Advances in Neural Information Processing Systems, pp. 2352–2360 (2016)
51. Rizve, M.N., Duarte, K., Rawat, Y.S., Shah, M.: In defense of pseudo-labeling: an uncertainty-aware pseudo-label selection framework for semi-supervised learning. In: International Conference on Learning Representations (2021). https://openreview.net/forum?id=-ODN6SbiUU
52. Rizve, M.N., Kardan, N., Shah, M.: Towards realistic semi-supervised learning. In: Farinella, T. (ed.) ECCV 2022. LNCS, vol. 13691, pp. xx–yy. Springer, Cham (2022)
53. Rizve, M.N., Khan, S., Khan, F.S., Shah, M.: Exploring complementary strengths of invariant and equivariant representations for few-shot learning. In: Proceedings of the IEEE/CVF Conference on Computer Vision and Pattern Recognition, pp. 10836–10846 (2021)

54. Sajjadi, M., Javanmardi, M., Tasdizen, T.: Regularization with stochastic trans-formations and perturbations for deep semi-supervised learning. In: Lee, D.D., Sugiyama, M., Luxburg, U.V., Guyon, I., Garnett, R. (eds.) Advances in Neural Information Processing Systems 29, pp. 1163–1171. Curran Associates, Inc. (2016)
55. Sener, O., Savarese, S.: Active learning for convolutional neural networks: a core-set approach. In: International Conference on Learning Representations (2018). https://openreview.net/forum?id=H1aIuk-RW
56. Sharif Razavian, A., Azizpour, H., Sullivan, J., Carlsson, S.: CNN features off-the-shelf: an astounding baseline for recognition. In: Proceedings of the IEEE Confer-ence on Computer Vision and Pattern Recognition Workshops, pp. 806–813 (2014)
57. Shi, W., Gong, Y., Ding, C., Ma, Z., Tao, X., Zheng, N.: Transductive semi-supervised deep learning using min-max features. In: Ferrari, V., Hebert, M., Smin-chisescu, C., Weiss, Y. (eds.) ECCV 2018. LNCS, vol. 11209, pp. 311–327. Springer, Cham (2018). https://doi.org/10.1007/978-3-030-01228-1_19
58. Snell, J., Swersky, K., Zemel, R.: Prototypical networks for few-shot learning. In: Advances in Neural Information Processing Systems, pp. 4077–4087 (2017)
59. Sohn, K., et al.: FixMatch: simplifying semi-supervised learning with consistency and confidence. In: Larochelle, H., Ranzato, M., Hadsell, R., Balcan, M.F., Lin, H. (eds.) Advances in Neural Information Processing Systems, vol. 33, pp. 596–608. Curran Associates, Inc. (2020). https://proceedings.neurips.cc/paper/2020/file/06964dce9addb1c5cb5d6e3d9838f733-Paper.pdf
60. Sun, X., Yang, Z., Zhang, C., Ling, K.V., Peng, G.: Conditional Gaussian distri-bution learning for open set recognition. In: Proceedings of the IEEE/CVF Con-ference on Computer Vision and Pattern Recognition, pp. 13480–13489 (2020)
61. Szegedy, C., Vanhoucke, V., Ioffe, S., Shlens, J., Wojna, Z.: Rethinking the incep-tion architecture for computer vision. In: Proceedings of the IEEE Conference on Computer Vision and Pattern Recognition, pp. 2818–2826 (2016)
62. Tarvainen, A., Valpola, H.: Mean teachers are better role models: weight-averaged consistency targets improve semi-supervised deep learning results. arXiv preprint arXiv:1703.01780 (2017)
63. Tarvainen, A., Valpola, H.: Mean teachers are better role models: weight-averaged consistency targets improve semi-supervised deep learning results. In: Guyon, I., et al. (eds.) Advances in Neural Information Processing Systems 30, pp. 1195–1204. Curran Associates, Inc. (2017)
64. Van Gansbeke, W., Vandenhende, S., Georgoulis, S., Proesmans, M., Van Gool, L.: SCAN: learning to classify images without labels. In: Vedaldi, A., Bischof, H., Brox, T., Frahm, J.-M. (eds.) ECCV 2020. LNCS, vol. 12355, pp. 268–285. Springer, Cham (2020). https://doi.org/10.1007/978-3-030-58607-2_16
65. Verma, V., Kawaguchi, K., Lamb, A., Kannala, J., Bengio, Y., Lopez-Paz, D.: Interpolation consistency training for semi-supervised learning. arXiv preprint arXiv:1903.03825 (2019)
66. Vinyals, O., Blundell, C., Lillicrap, T., kavukcuoglu, k., Wierstra, D.: Matching networks for one shot learning. In: Lee, D.D., Sugiyama, M., Luxburg, U.V., Guyon, I., Garnett, R. (eds.) Advances in Neural Information Processing Systems 29, pp. 3630–3638. Curran Associates, Inc. (2016). http://papers.nips.cc/paper/6385-matching-networks-for-one-shot-learning.pdf
67. Wu, J., et al.: Deep comprehensive correlation mining for image clustering. In: Proceedings of the IEEE/CVF International Conference on Computer Vision, pp. 8150–8159 (2019)

68. Xie, J., Girshick, R., Farhadi, A.: Unsupervised deep embedding for clustering analysis. In: International Conference on Machine Learning, pp. 478–487. PMLR (2016)
69. Xie, Q., Dai, Z., Hovy, E., Luong, M.T., Le, Q.V.: Unsupervised data augmentation for consistency training. arXiv preprint arXiv:1904.12848 (2019)
70. Yang, B., Fu, X., Sidiropoulos, N.D., Hong, M.: Towards k-means-friendly spaces: simultaneous deep learning and clustering. In: International Conference on Machine Learning, pp. 3861–3870. PMLR (2017)
71. Yang, J., Parikh, D., Batra, D.: Joint unsupervised learning of deep representations and image clusters. In: Proceedings of the IEEE Conference on Computer Vision and Pattern Recognition, pp. 5147–5156 (2016)
72. Asano, Y.M., Rupprecht, C., Vedaldi, A.: Self-labelling via simultaneous clustering and representation learning. In: International Conference on Learning Representations (2020). https://openreview.net/forum?id=Hyx-jyBFPr
73. Zamir, A.R., Sax, A., Shen, W., Guibas, L.J., Malik, J., Savarese, S.: Taskonomy: Disentangling task transfer learning. In: Proceedings of the IEEE Conference on Computer Vision and Pattern Recognition, pp. 3712–3722 (2018)
74. Zhao, B., Han, K.: Novel visual category discovery with dual ranking statistics and mutual knowledge distillation. In: Advances in Neural Information Processing Systems 34, pp. 22982–22994 (2021)
75. Zhao, X., Krishnateja, K., Iyer, R., Chen, F.: Robust semi-supervised learning with out of distribution data. arXiv preprint arXiv:2010.03658 (2020)
76. Zhong, Z., Fini, E., Roy, S., Luo, Z., Ricci, E., Sebe, N.: Neighborhood contrastive learning for novel class discovery. In: Proceedings of the IEEE/CVF Conference on Computer Vision and Pattern Recognition, pp. 10867–10875 (2021)
77. Zhong, Z., Zhu, L., Luo, Z., Li, S., Yang, Y., Sebe, N.: OpenMix: reviving known knowledge for discovering novel visual categories in an open world. In: Proceedings of the IEEE/CVF Conference on Computer Vision and Pattern Recognition, pp. 9462–9470 (2021)

Embedding Contrastive Unsupervised Features to Cluster In- And Out-of-Distribution Noise in Corrupted Image Datasets

Paul Albert[(✉)], Eric Arazo, Noel E. O'Connor, and Kevin McGuinness

School of Electronic Engineering, Insight SFI Centre for Data Analytics, Dublin City University (DCU), Dublin, Ireland
`paul.albert@insight-centre.org`

Abstract. Using search engines for web image retrieval is a tempting alternative to manual curation when creating an image dataset, but their main drawback remains the proportion of incorrect (noisy) samples retrieved. These noisy samples have been evidenced by previous works to be a mixture of in-distribution (ID) samples, assigned to the incorrect category but presenting similar visual semantics to other classes in the dataset, and out-of-distribution (OOD) images, which share no semantic correlation with any category from the dataset. The latter are, in practice, the dominant type of noisy images retrieved. To tackle this noise duality, we propose a two stage algorithm starting with a detection step where we use unsupervised contrastive feature learning to represent images in a feature space. We find that the alignment and uniformity principles of contrastive learning allow OOD samples to be linearly separated from ID samples on the unit hypersphere. We then spectrally embed the unsupervised representations using a fixed neighborhood size and apply an outlier sensitive clustering at the class level to detect the clean and OOD clusters as well as ID noisy outliers. We finally train a noise robust neural network that corrects ID noise to the correct category and utilizes OOD samples in a guided contrastive objective, clustering them to improve low-level features. Our algorithm improves the state-of-the-art results on synthetic noise image datasets as well as real-world web-crawled data. Our work is fully reproducible github.com/PaulAlbert31/SNCF.

Keywords: Computer vision · Image classification · Label noise · Out-of-distribution noise

1 Introduction

Convolutional neural networks (CNN) show remarkable classification accuracies on large image datasets carefully curated by large numbers of annotators [18, 26],

---

Supplementary Information The online version contains supplementary material available at https://doi.org/10.1007/978-3-031-19821-2_23.

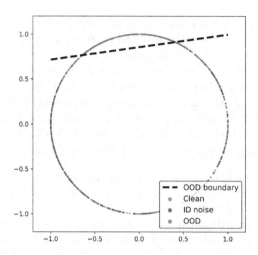

Fig. 1. Visualization of the linear separation between ID unsupervised contrastive representations on the 2D hypersphere. CIFAR-10 corrupted with $r_{in} = r_{out} = 0.2$, OOD from ImageNet32. Linear separability in 2D at the dataset level is 92.49% but increases to 98%+ for 128D

which entails that the data gathering and labeling process has become a significant part of the effort required when designing a deep learning image classification algorithm. Recent research proposes to reduce the cost of the data gathering effort in multiple ways, including semi-supervised learning [9] where only a small part of the images have been labeled by humans, which is often the most time consuming part of the dataset building process; unsupervised learning [5], where visual features are learned without the need for labels; and web-crawled datasets [24] constructed from search engine queries, although this results in the inclusion of incorrect samples assigned to the incorrect class or not belonging to the distribution and corrupting the CNN's convergence. This paper tackles this latter challenge. Designing algorithms capable of training highly accurate CNNs even when trained on imperfect web-crawled data is an important step towards the widespread deployment and take up of computer vision algorithms in practice. CNNs have been shown to completely overfit noisy samples in a dataset without proper regularization [48], which degrades performance. More specifically, the noise observed in web-crawled datasets has been categorized as both in-distribution and out-of-distribution, the latter being the dominant type [1]. While in-distribution (ID) noisy images can be directly used to train the network after correcting their assigned label, out-of-distribution (OOD) images cannot be assigned to any category. Since a trusted in-distribution dataset is unavailable and the identity of clean and noisy samples is unknown, out-of-distribution detection algorithms [11,13,47], which use a classifier trained on clean data to be able to detect OOD samples post training, cannot be used. This further complicates the noise detection process. Once noisy images have been identified, simply ignoring out-of-distribution images has been shown to be sub-optimal as these samples still contain meaningful information for learning low-level features that can be leveraged to improve the representations learned [14,46]. This paper proposes to tackle the in-distribution and out-of-distribution duality of the noise present in web-crawled datasets specifically to improve the final classification accuracy. To detect the noise, we observe that unsupervised contrastive representations for OOD samples are linearly separated from ID ones on the hypersphere (see Fig. 1) and train a robust network that will use current representations to correct ID noisy samples and use OOD data to improve low-level representations using contrastive learning. Our contributions are:

- A dual noise detection approach utilizing the alignment and uniformity principles of contrastive learning to detect noisy samples in a spectral embedding of unsupervised representations.
- A noise robust algorithm capable of training a CNN on a dataset corrupted with in-distribution and out-of-distribution noise, correcting the label of in-distribution whilst using out-of-distribution noise to improve low-level features.
- Experiments on controlled and real world noisy datasets demonstrating the state-of-the-art performance of our algorithm.

2   Related Work

2.1   Web-Crawled Datasets

Web-crawled datasets are a low supervision alternative to dataset building that helps to democratize deep learning approaches. Here we will give some examples. Webvision [24] is a dataset constituted of 2.4 million images gathered using search queries on the same 1k classes as the ILSVRC12 [20] challenge. Albert *et al.* [1] have shown that the noise present in Webvision is predominantly out-of-distribution. Clothing1M [44] is a 1M images clothes classification dataset, popular dataset in the label noise community which, as shown by the authors, only contains ID noise. More recently, Sun *et al.* [37] released additional web datasets for fine grained classification tasks.

2.2   Tackling ID and OOD Noise

Most of the noise robust algorithms that showed improvements on web-noise assume that all the noise is ID. The strategies used to combat ID noise include: robust loss functions [30,31], meta-learning [41,45], sample weighing using a mentor network [16,17], network regularization [25,49], semi-supervised learning [22,28,51], contrastive learning to detect the noise in MOIT [29] or improve the label correction using nearest neighbor clustering together with a semi-supervised correction in ScanMix [33]. Another class of noise robust algorithms have emerged recently to tackle noisy datasets presenting both in- and out-of-distribution noise. EvidentialMix [32] and DSOS [1] differentiates between ID noisy and OOD data using a custom noise landscape and JoSRC [46] evidences

OOD samples as having a low agreement between two consistent views of the same image. The methods we compare against are described in more details in Sect. 4.1 and we direct the interested reader to a recent label noise survey by Song et al. [15] for an in-depth overview of state-of-the-art label noise robust algorithms.

3 Algorithm Description

This paper studies image classification in the presence of label noise, where part of the available image dataset $\mathcal{X} = \{x_i\}_{i=1}^{N}$ and its associated classification labels $\mathcal{Y} = \{y_i\}_{i=1}^{N}$, with the class distribution $\{c\}_{c=1}^{C}$, is corrupted by N_o out-of-distribution samples and N_n in-distribution noisy samples, where $N_c = N - N_o - N_n$ is the number of in-distribution clean examples. N_o, N_n as well as the identity of the ID noisy and OOD samples are unknown. Examples of such datasets are web-crawled datasets: Webvision [24], Clothing1M [44], and the Webly Supervised Fine-Grained Recognition datasets [37]. We propose here an algorithm capable of training a convolutional neural network (CNN) Ψ on the corrupted dataset $\mathcal{X}$ without over-fitting to the noise and capable to accurately classify examples belonging to the class distribution.

3.1 Unsupervised Feature Learning

First, our algorithm learns unsupervised representations from the images themselves, independently of their label. We aim here to relate images to each other in order to capture clusters of similar images. To do so, we train the N-pairs unsupervised contrastive learning algorithm which has been successfully used in metric learning [36] and unsupervised learning on images and text [21]. Given two mini-batches of size B formed from two strongly data augmented views x_i' and x_i'' of $x_i \in \mathcal{X}$, we enforce u_i' and u_i'', their associated contrastive representations through Ψ, to be similar to each other and dissimilar to every other image in the batch. We compute the unsupervised contrastive loss

$$l_{unsup} = -\frac{1}{B} \sum_{i=1}^{B} \log \left(\frac{\exp\left(ip(u_i'', u_i')/\tau_2\right)}{\sum_{k=1}^{B} \exp\left(ip(u_k'', u_i')/\tau_2\right)} \right), \tag{1}$$

where $ip(u_1, u_2) = \frac{u_1^T . u_2}{\|u_1\|_2 \|u_2\|_2}$ is the inner product operation, measuring the similarity between contrastive representations, and τ_2 a temperature hyper-parameter, fixed to 0.2 for every experiment. Mixup [49] can be optionally used to further augment x_i' by linearly interpolating it with other augmented samples from the mini-batch with a parameter μ drawn from a beta distribution with parameter 1 to produce $x_{mix}' = \mu x_i' + (1 - \mu)x_j'$ with x_j' a random sample from the mini-batch (different for every x_i) and u_{mix}' the associated representation of x_{mix}'. We then use

$$l_{mix} = -\frac{1}{B}\sum_{i=1}^{B}\log\left(\mu\frac{\exp\left(ip(u_i'', u_{mix}')/\tau_2\right)}{\sum_{k=1}^{B}\exp\left(ip(u_k'', u_{mix}')/\tau_2\right)}\right.$$
$$\left. + (1-\mu)\frac{\exp\left(ip(u_j'', u_{mix}')/\tau_2\right)}{\sum_{k=1}^{B}\exp\left(ip(u_k'', u_{mix}')/\tau_2\right)}\right), \tag{2}$$

the N-pairs loss paired with mixup as a data augmentation. This unsupervised contrastive objective has been proposed as part of the iMix [21] algorithm.

3.2   Embedding of Unsupervised Features

We propose not to use the learned unsupervised features directly but instead to perform a non-linear spectral dimensionality reduction on an affinity matrix (embedding). The aim of the embedding is to capture the affinities between samples and their neighbors where ID clean samples will be very similar to other samples from the same class, ID noisy samples will be similar to other ID samples from a different class and OOD samples dissimilar to any ID sample. This motivates computing the embedding at the dataset level to ensure that the similarity of ID noise to other classes is captured. We first compute the sparse similarity matrix S of size $N \times N$ where for each sample in the dataset, we compute the affinity to a fixed neighborhood size of 50 neighbors.

$$S_{ij} = \left(u_i^T u_j / \|u_i\|_2 \|u_j\|_2\right)^\gamma, \tag{3}$$

with u_i the unsupervised representation for sample x_i (not augmented) and $\gamma = 3$ a hyper-parameter regulating the importance of distant neighbors. With I_N the identity matrix of size N and D the diagonal normalization matrix where $D_{ii} = \sum_{j=1}^{N} S_{ij}$, we compute the normalized Laplacian

$$L = I_N - D^{-1/2}SD^{-1/2}. \tag{4}$$

We finally compute the first k eigenvectors of the normalized Laplacian L by solving

$$(L - \lambda)V = 0 \tag{5}$$

and concatenating the first k eigenvectors V of L (by increasing order of the eigenvalues λ, omitting the smallest), providing us with k features per sample to form the embedding E. In practice we use $k = 20$ for every dataset. This embedding process is commonly referred to as spectral embedding [27,35].

3.3   Unsupervised Clustering of Noise

Using the embedding E, we cluster embedded unsupervised features to identify three kinds of samples: clean ID, noisy ID, and OOD. In the generic case where the three types of noise are expected in the dataset, we apply the clustering at the class level and aim to discover three clusters for each class: a high density cluster of ID clean samples, a low density cluster of OOD samples and ID noisy outliers.

In the case where no ID noise is present, we observe the cluster separation at the dataset level and use a two mode Gaussian mixture to retrieve each cluster.

Why Does OOD Noise Cluster? Contrary to previous research where OOD noise is considered an outlier to the distribution [43], we observe in this paper that unsupervised contrastive learning can be effectively used to cluster noise in the feature space. We expand here on our intuition as to why this works using the alignment and uniformity principles for contrastive learning formalized by Wang *et al.* [42]. Unsupervised contrastive learning pulls together augmented representations of a same image while pushing apart representations of any other sample in the mini-batch. Since images from a same class will be similar to each other's augmentations, they will cluster together in the feature space to create one (or more) mode for the class (alignment principle). On the other hand, by considering OOD samples as being uniformly sampled from the set of all images, meaning much more varied in appearance than the ID set, we would expect that no compact mode would appear and that these samples would remain uniformly distributed in the feature space yet separated from the ID examples, pulled together into their respective class modes (uniformity principle). Since the features are L^2 normalized during training they exist on the surface of a unit hypersphere and one side of the sphere will contain well represented ID classes, clustered into their respective modes, while OOD noise will remain uniformly distributed be on the other side of the hypersphere and linearly separable from ID samples. Section 4.2 proposes experiments to evidence the linear separability of ID and OOD samples in the unsupervised contrastive feature space. The spectral embedding we propose has a key role to play in the clustering of the OOD noise which, although separable from the ID samples, is much more spread-out that the compact class modes of ID images. We remedy this problem by computing the affinities in S not over a fixed distance threshold but using a fixed number of neighbors.

OPTICS [2] is an algorithm which allows us to detect clusters as well as outliers: each feature point is ordered to create a chain where neighboring points are ordered next to each other. Each feature point is then labeled with a reachability cost to neighbors in a neighborhood of size V. The higher the cost, the more likely a sample is to be an outlier. Finally, clusters are identified in the ordering where "valleys" of low reachability cost evidence a cluster, themselves separated with high cost outliers.

Discovering Clean and Noisy Clusters. Because the difficulty of learning similar unsupervised features varies from class to class in an image dataset, we propose to modify the OPTICS algorithm to become more flexible to our problem. We aim here to be able to detect varying valley sizes in the ordered reachability plot where different classes in the image dataset will have more compact classes (fine grained classes) than others (classes with highly diverse examples). In practice, we compute three different reachability orderings for three different neighborhood sizes V (75, 50, 25 neighbors), which allows us to account for cluster compactness variations across classes and noise levels. The algorithm chooses the optimal cluster assignment at the class level as being the cluster with the lower amount of outliers given at least two clusters are identified (clean and OOD). This allows us to reduce the amount of hyper-parameters to tune for the clustering to the ξ parameter of OPTICS which controls the decision boundary between clusters and outliers. Higher values for ξ imply a higher tolerance threshold meaning a lower amount of outliers.

No ID Noise. In the case where we expect no ID noisy samples in the dataset, we only aim to discover a clean and an OOD cluster without outliers. In this case, the OOD cluster can be retrieved at the dataset level and we choose instead to fit a 2 component Gaussian mixture on the embedded features to retrieve the clusters.

Clean or OOD. Once the clusters are evidenced in the ordering, the final step for the detection is to classify the clusters into clean or OOD. Although the average reachability score within the cluster could at first glance be considered a good indication of the OOD nature of a cluster, by computing the affinity matrix over a fixed neighborhood size, distances are not accurately preserved. We propose instead to compute the density of the cluster in the original unsupervised feature space, where for each sample in the dataset we compute the average distance to all other points in the cluster. We then select the cluster with the lowest density as the OOD cluster.

3.4 Spectral Noise Clustering from Contrastive Features (SNCF)

Clustering the embedded unsupervised feature space provides three subsets of $\mathcal{X}$: $\mathcal{X}_c, \mathcal{X}_n$ and $\mathcal{X}_o$, respectively the clean, ID noisy and OOD subsets. We aim to use all the available samples to train our CNN and do so by correcting ID noisy samples to their true label and using OOD samples to learn more robust low-level features. We train from scratch on each type of noise separately without using the unsupervised features to initialize the classification network.

Correcting In-Distribution Noise. Although the unsupervised features allow the detection of incorrectly assigned samples, we find that this is not sufficient to accurately assign ID noise to the right class, especially since they might be close to other ID noisy samples themselves assigned to another incorrect class. We propose instead to correct the ID noise during the supervised training phase, using knowledge learned on clean ID samples during a warm-up pre-training. We then estimate the true labels of the detected ID noise using a consistency regularization approach. For every ID noisy sample in $\mathcal{X}_n$ two weakly augmented versions are produced. The network then predicts on both samples ($p_{i,1}$ and $p_{i,2}$) and returns an average prediction, which, after temperature sharpening τ_1 and normalization, is used as the corrected class assignment: $y_i = \left(\frac{p_{i,1}+p_{i,2}}{2} \right)^{\tau_1}$ with $\tau_1 = 2$ in every experiment. We find temperature sharpening to be necessary to reduce the entropy of the guessed label and to encourage the network to produce more confident predictions.

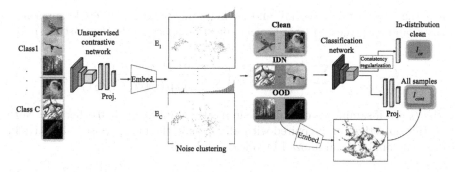

Fig. 2. Visualization of the algorithm. The unsupervised features are embedded to create E and evaluated at the class level ($E_1, \ldots E_C$) to cluster clean and OOD samples. The detected OOD samples are re-embedded from their unsupervised features to detect clusters of similar images. We correct the ID noise using consistency regularization and the OOD sample's cluster assignments are used together with the classes of all in-distribution samples in a guided contrastive objective

Out-of-Distribution Samples. OOD samples cannot be corrected to any label in the distribution but we propose to include them in an additional guided contrastive loss minimization objective to learn low level features. Once the noise detection algorithm has run, we re-embed the unsupervised features of detected OOD noise and use OPTICS to discover clusters of the most similar samples in the OOD data. At training time, we augment each sample in the dataset into one weakly and one strongly augmented view, producing two mini-batches of the same images augmented differently. We then enforce ID samples belonging to the same class (corrected for the ID noise) as well as OOD samples from the same unsupervised cluster to be similar while being dissimilar to every other example in the mini-batch. OOD samples not assigned to any unsupervised cluster are considered similar to their augmented view only. This guided contrastive objective is described in Eq. 7. Note here that the similarities are enforced between the two mini-batches of augmented views alone. We attempted to enforce similarities inside the same augmented batch but noticed no accuracy improvements.

3.5 Loss Objectives

We consider here that p_i is the current softmax prediction of Ψ on sample $x_i \in \mathcal{X}$. Our algorithm aims to optimize over two objectives during training. The first is the classification objective on the detected clean samples $\mathcal{X}_c$ and the ID samples from $\mathcal{X}_n$ whose label has been corrected. We use the cross entropy loss:

$$l_{ce} = \sum_{i=1}^{N_c+N_n} y_i^T \log(p_i). \tag{6}$$

Secondly, we minimize the guided contrastive learning objective, grouping samples of the same class and OOD samples from the same OOD cluster together using their respectively weakly and strongly augmented projected representations r_i and r_i', projected from the classification space to the contrastive space

$$l_{cont} = -\frac{1}{N}\sum_{i=1}^{N}\frac{1}{B}\sum_{b=1}^{B}e_{i,b}\log\left(\frac{\exp\left(ip(r_b, r_i')/\tau_2\right)}{\sum_{k=1}^{B}\exp\left(ip(r_k, r_i')/\tau_2\right)}\right), \tag{7}$$

with $e_{i,b} = 1$ if sample i is considered similar to sample b, $e_{i,b} = 0$ otherwise. Note that this objective can be paired with mixup as in the unsupervised objective in Eq. 2. The final loss minimized by our algorithm is:

$$l = l_{ce} + \beta l_{cont}, \tag{8}$$

where β is an hyper-parameter (typically 1). Figure 2 illustrates the algorithm.

4   Experiments

4.1   Implementation Details

We form each mini-batch be aggregating an equal number of clean ID, noisy ID and OOD samples. Since the OOD is ignored in the ID objective (Eq. 6) and in order to have the same batch size for the ID and the contrastive forward pass, we form the ID mini-batch by aggregating two weakly augmented views of the clean data with one weakly augmented view for the ID noisy data (ID clean, ID noisy, OOD for the contrastive mini-batch). For the weak data augmentations we use cropping with padding and random horizontal flip and the strong SimCLR augmentations [6]. We warm-up the network on the detected clean data from scratch for 15 epochs in every experiment (except 5 for WebVision) and start both the ID noise correction and the guided contrastive objective after this. For a fair comparison with other approaches, the unsupervised features are not used to initialize the network in the robust classification phase. More experiments are proposed in the supplementary material. Since our algorithm minimizes a contrastive loss, we find that adding a non-linear projection head [6,7] to project features from the classification space to the contrastive space is beneficial in reconciling the training objectives. The final number of projected contrastive features is 128 and the projection head is not used at test time. We use stochastic gradient descent (SGD) with a weight decay of 5×10^{-4} and mixup [49] augmentation with $\alpha = 1$ for all experiments.

Training the Unsupervised Algorithm. We train the unsupervised algorithm using the same network as the robust classification phase. In cases where the resolution is 227×227 or above, we train and evaluate the unsupervised features at resolution 84×84 as this helps to keep training time and memory consumption reasonable yet still separates the OOD and ID clusters. The algorithm is trained for 2000 epochs, with a batch size of 256, starting with a learning rate of 0.01 and reducing it by a factor of 10 at epochs 1000, 1500. We use the mixup version on the unsupervised objective (iMix [21]).

Synthetically Corrupted Datasets. We conduct a first series of experiments on synthetically corrupted versions of CIFAR-100 [19] where we control the ID noise and OOD noise. We use the same configuration as in Albert *et al.* [1] and note r_{in} and r_{out} the corruption ratios for ID noisy and OOD noise respectively with $r_{in} + r_{out}$ the total noise level. Our focus here is on the OOD noise rate more than ID noise, which is less present in web-crawled datasets [1]. We introduce OOD noise by replacing original images with images from another dataset, either ImageNet32 [8] or Places365 [50]. For the ID noise, we randomly flip the labels of a portion of the dataset to a random label (uniform noise). The dataset size remains 50K images after noise injection. We train on CIFAR-100 using a PreActResNet18 [18] trained with a batch size of 256 for 100 epochs with a learning rate of 0.1, reducing it by a factor of 10 at epochs 50 and 80.

Web Noise Corruption. We conduct experiments on miniImageNet [40] corrupted by web noise from Jiang *et al.* [17] (Controlled Noisy Web Labels, CNWL) where the severity of the web noise corruption is controlled. This dataset is an example where ID noise is very limited and where we find that using the 2 components GMM is sufficient to detect the noise at the dataset level (see Sect. 3.3). We train on this dataset at two different resolutions, first 299×299, which is the original configuration proposed by Jiang *et al.* [17] and second the 32×32 resolution adopted in recent works [10,33,45]. For the 299×299 configuration, we train an InceptionResNetV2 [38] with a batch size of 64 for 200 epochs with a learning rate of 0.01, reducing it by a factor of 10 at epochs 100, 160. For the 32×32 configuration, we use the same configuration as CIFAR-100.

Real-World Dataset. We evaluate our model on the (mini)Webvision [24] dataset reduced to the first 50 classes (65k images). We train an InceptionResNetV2 [38] at a 227×227 resolution with a batch size of 64 for 100 epochs with a learning rate of 0.01, reducing it by 10 at epochs 50, 80.

Baselines. We introduce here the state-of-the-art approaches we compared with as well as the abbreviations used in the tables. Cross-entropy (CE), dropout (D), and mixup (M) are simple baselines obtained by training with no noise correction and dropout [4] or mixup [49] as regularization. MentorNet [16] (MN) and MentorMix [17] (MM) use teacher networks to weight noisy samples. FaMUS [45] (FaMUS) uses meta learning to learn to correct noisy samples. Bootstrapping [31] (B) corrects noisy samples using a fixed interpolation with pseudo-labels; Dynamic Bootstrapping [3] (DB) expands the idea by correcting only high loss noisy samples retrieved using a beta mixture. The S-model [12] (SM) corrects noisy samples using a noise adaptation layer optimized using an expectation maximization algorithm. DivideMix [22] (DM) uses a Gaussian mixture to detect high loss samples and correct them using a semi-supervised consistency regularization algorithm; the idea is expanded upon in PropMix [10] (PM) where self-supervised initialization is used and only the simplest of the noisy samples are corrected while the hardest are discarded. ScanMix [33] (SM) also improves on DM by correcting the label using a semi-supervised contrastive algorithm together with a semantic clustering in an self-supervised feature space, optimized using an EM algorithm. EvidentialMix [32] (EDM) refines the noisy sample detection of DM to account for OOD samples and uses the evidential loss [34] to evidence separate OOD and ID noisy modes. JoSRC [46] (JoSRC) proposes to use the Jensen-Shannon divergence between a consistency regularization guessed label and the original label to detect noisy samples and further select samples with low agreement between views as OOD. Robust Representation Learning [23] (RRL) trains a weakly supervised prototype objective to promote clean samples to be close to their class prototypes. Finally, Dynamic Softening for Out-of-distribution Samples [1] (DSOS) computes the collision entropy of the interpolation between the original label and network prediction to separate ID noisy and OOD samples.

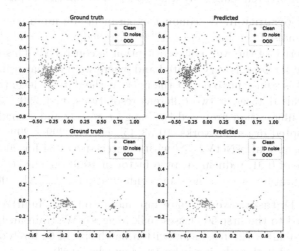

Fig. 3. Feature embedding for class 1 of CIFAR-100 corrupted with $r_i = r_o = 0.2$ (ImageNet32 OOD). The top row presents a 2D visualization obtained using Isomap [39] of the raw contrastive features and the second row presents a Isomap visualization of the embedding E. Embedding the features allows to evidence the OOD cluster

4.2   Clustering the Unsupervised Features

This section presents the experiments on the linear separability of ID and OOD data in an unsupervised feature space, the importance of embedding the unsupervised features when clustering the noise and the accuracy our noise retrieval algorithm. First, to validate our hypothesis over the separability of ID and OOD samples in the unsupervised feature space, we propose to train a linear classifier on the unsupervised features and evaluate its capacity to linearly separate the two distributions. We observe that the classifier can linearly separate the two distribution with error rates below 3% for synthetically corrupted CIFAR-100 with $r_{in} = r_{out} = 0.2$ and below 1% for miniImagenet corrupted with web noise (CNWL). The linear separability is less accurate when using Places365 as the OOD corruption dataset; we argue that this is because of lower image variability in the dataset, justified by the lower number of classes and the fine-grained nature of the classification task. A table and more visualizations of the separation on the 2D-hypersphere are available in the supplementary material. Second, Fig. 3 provides a visualization of the importance of embedding the unsupervised features to perform the noise clustering for a class of CIFAR-100 where we compare applying the clustering algorithm on the raw unsupervised contrastive features against the spectral embedding E. The left column is the ground-truth and the right represent the detection made by the clustering algorithm. We use Isomap [39] to reduce the dimentionality to 2 to be able to visualize the features. The spectral embedding E is essential to evidence the OOD cluster, not originally present in the raw features.

Table 1. Mitigating ID noise and OOD noise on CIFAR-100 corrupted with ImageNet32 or Places365 images. We run all the algorithms using publicly available implementations by authors. We report best and last accuracy. We bold (underline) the highest best (final) accuracy

Corruption	r_{out}	r_{in}	CE	M	DB	JoSRC	ELR	EDM	DSOS	RRL	Ours
INet32	0.2	0.2	63.68/55.52	66.71/62.52	65.61/65.61	67.37/64.17	68.71/68.51	71.03/70.42	70.54/70.54	72.64/72.33	**72.95**/<u>72.70</u>
	0.4	0.2	58.94/44.31	59.54/53.16	54.79/54.42	61.70/61.37	63.21/63.07	61.89/61.83	62.49/62.05	66.04/65.44	**67.62**/<u>67.14</u>
	0.6	0.2	46.02/26.03	42.87/40.39	42.50/42.50	37.95/37.11	44.79/44.60	21.88/14.59	49.98/49.14	26.76/24.51	**53.26**/<u>51.26</u>
	0.4	0.4	41.39/18.45	38.37/33.85	35.90/35.90	41.53/41.44	34.82/34.21	24.15/01.62	43.69/42.88	31.29/30.64	**54.04**/<u>52.66</u>
Places365	0.2	0.2	59.88/53.61	66.31/59.69	65.86/65.83	67.06/66.73	68.58/68.45	70.46/70.25	69.72/69.12	**72.62**/<u>72.49</u>	71.25/71.14
	0.4	0.2	53.46/42.46	59.75/48.55	55.81/55.61	60.83/60.64	62.66/62.34	61.80/61.55	59.47/59.47	**65.82**/<u>65.79</u>	64.03/63.48
	0.6	0.2	39.55/21.42	39.17/33.69	40.75/40.61	39.83/39.63	37.10/36.51	23.67/14.66	35.48/35.41	49.27/49.27	**49.83**/<u>49.83</u>
	0.4	0.4	32.06/13.85	34.36/27.63	35.05/34.86	33.23/32.58	34.71/33.86	20.33/11.88	29.54/29.48	26.67/24.34	**50.95**/<u>47.61</u>

Table 2. Ablation study on CIFAR-100 corrupted with ImageNet32 with $r_{out} = 0.4$ and $r_{in} = 0.2$. corr = correction and rm = remove

		Embed	Contrastive	Best	Last
No noise corr	CE	✗	✗	58.94	44.31
	+ mixup	✗	✗	59.54	53.16
	+ guided contrastive	✗	✓	62.83	56.29
Noise corr	ID corr only	✗	✗	57.02	55.43
	rm OOD only	✗	✗	60.73	53.88
	ID corr and rm OOD	✗	✗	54.81	54.20
	ID corr only	✓	✗	61.40	58.90
	rm OOD only	✓	✗	60.87	54.08
	ID corr and rm OOD	✓	✗	61.83	61.45
	ID corr only	✓	✓	63.91	62.94
	ID corr and rm OOD	✓	✓	64.51	64.04
	OOD corr only	✓	✓	63.41	58.39
	ID + OOD corr	✓	✓	65.22	64.42
Other	+ equal sampling	✓	✓	67.62	67.14
	- mixup	✓	✓	61.66	59.40

4.3   Synthetic Noise Corruption

We study the capacity of our algorithm to mitigate ID noise and OOD noise on synthetically corrupted version of the CIFAR-100 dataset. Table 1 reports results when using ImageNet32 or Places365 as a OOD corruption. We notice that the OOD corruption using the Places365 dataset is more harmful than corrupting with ImageNet32, especially for high noise levels.

4.4   Ablation Study

Table 2 illustrates the importance of each element of the proposed method on CIFAR-100 corrupted with OOD noise from ImageNet32. We study multiple cases including retrieving OOD and ID clusters on the un-embedded raw unsupervised contrastive features (Noise corr without embedding); correcting only the OOD or ID examples while considering the rest clean (ID/OOD corr only); joint effect of the ID and OOD correction (ID + OOD corr); studying the effect of removing the OOD samples from the training set instead of using them in the guided contrastive objective in Eq. 7 (ID corr and rm OOD); running the algorithm without mixup (- mixup). We point out how important mixup is (especially in the classification loss) to avoid overfitting to the noise. Figure 4 reports the quality of our robust classification algorithm on ID and OOD clustering for

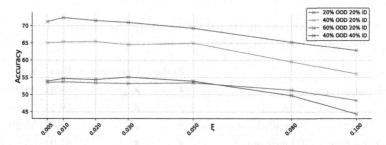

Fig. 4. Hyper-parameter tuning for OPTICS. We report accuracy results obtained for ID/OOD clustering setting different ξ values in OPTICS

Table 3. Web-corrupted miniImageNet from the CNWL [17] (32 × 32). We run our algorithm; other results are from [10]. We denote with ⋆ algorithms using an ensemble of networks to predict and with † algorithms using unsupervised initialization. We report best accuracy

Noise level	CE	M	⋆DM	MM	FaMUS	⋆†SM	⋆†PM	Ours
20	47.36	49.10	50.96	51.02	51.42	59.06	61.24	61.56
40	42.70	46.40	46.72	47.14	48.03	54.54	56.22	59.94
60	37.30	40.58	43.14	43.80	45.10	52.36	52.84	54.92
80	29.76	33.58	34.50	33.46	35.50	40.00	43.42	45.62

different values of ξ in OPTICS where values inferior to 0.03 lead to the best results. We choose $\xi = 0.01$ for all datasets.

4.5   Results on Web-Noise

We consider here the controlled noisy web labels (CNWL) dataset, where mini-ImageNet is corrupted with OOD images from web queries. Table 3 reports results when training at resolution 32×32 and Table 4 at resolution 299×299. Finally, in Table 5 we train on the first 50 classes of the Webvision dataset (mini-Webvision) a real world web-crawled dataset and report top-1 and top-5 accuracy results on the validation set on Webvision and on the test set on the ImageNet1k (ILSVRC12) dataset. Since our algorithm uses only one network and to compare against ensemble methods, we report an additional result where we ensemble two networks trained from different random initializations. We also report results when training for 150 epochs to compare fairly against FaMUS. Our algorithm slightly outperforms the state-of-the-art for top-1 accuracy but more convincingly so for top-5 accuracy on Webvision. Because of the guided contrastive loss, the network learns more generalizable features which reduce the risk of catastrophic classification errors (when the predicted class is completely semantically different from the correct predictions). mini-Webvision in particular proposes fine grained classification on species of birds, amphibians and marine animals which reward generalizable features for top-5 evaluation.

Table 4. Web noise on web corrupted miniImageNet (Red MiniImageNet [17]) trained at a high resolution (299×299). We run our algorithm, other results are from [1]. We report best accuracy

Noise level	CE	D	SM	B	M	MN	MM	DSOS	Ours
0	70.9/68.5	71.8/65.7	71.4/68.4	71.8/68.4	72.8/72.3	71.2/68.9	74.3/73.7	74.52/74.10	**74.80**/<u>74.60</u>
30	66.1/56.5	66.6/55.0	65.2/56.3	66.6/56.7	66.8/61.8	66.2/64.0	68.3/67.2	69.84/67.86	**69.96**/<u>69.64</u>
50	60.9/51.7	62.1/50.01	61.3/51.3	62.6/52..5	63.2/58.4	61.7/58.0	63.3/61.8	66.14/65.18	**66.48**/<u>66.38</u>
80	48.8/39.8	49.5/37.6	49.0/40.6	50.1/40.1	50.7/45.5	49.3/43.4	50.2/48.4	55.26/52.24	**55.54**/<u>54.96</u>

Table 5. Classification accuracy for the proposed and other state-of-the-art methods. We denote with $\star$ algorithms using an ensemble of networks to predict and with $\dagger$ algorithms using unsupervised initialization. We train the network on the mini-Webvision dataset and test on the ImageNet 1k test set (ILSVRC12). We bold the best results

		100 epochs										150 epochs	
		M	MM	$\star$DM	$\star$ELR+	RRL	$\star$DSOS	$\star\dagger$PM	$\star\dagger$SM	Ours	$\star$Ours	FaMUS	$\star$Ours
mini-WebVision	top-1	75.44	76.0	77.32	77.78	77.80	78.76	78.84	**80.04**	78.16	79.84	79.40	**80.24**
	top-5	90.12	90.2	91.64	91.68	91.30	92.32	90.56	93.04	92.60	**93.64**	92.80	93.44
ILSVRC12	top-1	71.44	72.9	75.20	70.29	74.40	75.88	--	75.76	74.20	**76.64**	77.00	77.12
	top-5	89.40	91.10	90.84	89.76	90.90	92.36	--	92.60	93.32	**94.20**	92.76	94.32

5   Conclusion

This paper proposes to use the alignment and uniformity principles of unsupervised contrastive learning to detect clean and OOD label noise clusters in an embedded feature space. We show that the unsupervised contrastive features for OOD and ID samples are, to a large extent, linearly separated on the unit hypersphere and compute a fixed neighborhood spectral embedding to reduce differences in cluster densities. We adapt the OPTICS algorithm, ordering samples in a neighbor chain and computing the reachability cost to neighbors. Clusters are evidenced by valleys in the reachability plot and a voting system automatically selects the best cluster assignement at the class level given multiple neighborhood sizes. Once the noise has been identified, we train a robust classifier that corrects the labels of known ID noisy samples using a consistency regularization estimation and uses ID and OOD samples together in an auxiliary guided contrastive objective. We report state-of-the-art results on a variety of noisy datasets including synthetically corrupted versions of CIFAR-100, controlled web noise in miniImageNet, and mini-Webvision as a real-world web-crawled dataset.

Acknowledgments. This publication has emanated from research conducted with the financial support of Science Foundation Ireland (SFI) under grant number 16/RC/3835 - Vistamilk and 12/RC/2289_P2 - Insight as well as the support of the Irish Centre for High End Computing (ICHEC).

References

1. Albert, P., Ortego, D., Arazo, E., O'Connor, N., McGuinness, K.: Addressing out-of-distribution label noise in webly-labelled data. In: Winter Conference on Applications of Computer Vision (WACV) (2022)
2. Ankerst, M., Breunig, M.M., Kriegel, H.P., Sander, J.: Optics: ordering points to identify the clustering structure. ACM SIGMOD Rec. **28**(2), 49–60 (1999)
3. Arazo, E., Ortego, D., Albert, P., O'Connor, N., McGuinness, K.: Unsupervised label noise modeling and loss correction. In: International Conference on Machine Learning (ICML) (2019)
4. Arpit, D., et al.: A closer look at memorization in deep networks. In: International Conference on Machine Learning (ICML) (2017)
5. Borgli, H., et al.: HyperKvasir, a comprehensive multi-class image and video dataset for gastrointestinal endoscopy. Sci. Data **7**, 1–14 (2020)
6. Chen, T., Kornblith, S., Norouzi, M., Hinton, G.: A simple framework for contrastive learning of visual representations. In: International Conference on Machine Learning (ICML) (2020)
7. Chen, T., Kornblith, S., Swersky, K., Norouzi, M., Hinton, G.: Big self-supervised models are strong semi-supervised learners. arXiv:2006.10029 (2020)
8. Chrabaszcz, P., Loshchilov, I., Hutter, F.: A downsampled variant of ImageNet as an alternative to the CIFAR datasets. arXiv:1707.08819 (2017)
9. Coates, A., Ng, A., Lee, H.: An analysis of single-layer networks in unsupervised feature learning. In: International Conference on Artificial Intelligence and Statistics (AISTATS) (2011)

10. Cordeiro, F.R., Belagiannis, V., Reid, I., Carneiro, G.: PropMix: hard sample filtering and proportional MixUp for learning with noisy labels. arXiv:2110.11809 (2021)
11. Fort, S., Ren, J., Lakshminarayanan, B.: Exploring the limits of out-of-distribution detection. In: Advances in Neural Information Processing Systems (NeurIPS) (2021)
12. Goldberger, J., Ben-Reuven, E.: Training deep neural-networks using a noise adaptation layer. In: International Conference on Learning Representations (ICLR) (2017)
13. Hendrycks, D., Mazeika, M., Dietterich, T.: Deep anomaly detection with outlier exposure. In: International Conference on Learning Representations (ICLR) (2019)
14. Huang, J., et al.: Trash to treasure: harvesting OOD data with cross-modal matching for open-set semi-supervised learning. In: IEEE/CVF International Conference on Computer Vision (ICCV) (2021)
15. Hwanjun, S., Minseok, K., Dongmin, P., Jae-Gil, L.: Learning from noisy labels with deep neural networks: a survey. arXiv:2007.08199 (2020)
16. Jiang, L., Zhou, Z., Leung, T., Li, L., Fei-Fei, L.: MentorNet: learning data-driven curriculum for very deep neural networks on corrupted labels. In: International Conference on Machine Learning (ICML) (2018)
17. Jiang, L., Huang, D., Liu, M., Yang, W.: Beyond synthetic noise: deep learning on controlled noisy labels. In: International Conference on Machine Learning (ICML) (2020)
18. Kaiming, H., Xiangyu, Z., Shaoqing, R., Jian, S.: Deep residual learning for image recognition. In: IEEE Conference on Computer Vision and Pattern Recognition (CVPR) (2016)
19. Krizhevsky, A., Hinton, G.: Learning multiple layers of features from tiny images. University of Toronto, Technical report (2009)
20. Krizhevsky, A., Sutskever, I., Hinton, G.: ImageNet classification with deep convolutional neural networks. In: Advances in Neural Information Processing Systems (NeurIPS) (2012)
21. Lee, K., Zhu, Y., Sohn, K., Li, C.L., Shin, J., Lee, H.: i-Mix: a strategy for regularizing contrastive representation learning. In: International Conference on Learning Representations (ICLR) (2021)
22. Li, J., Socher, R., Hoi, S.: DivideMix: learning with noisy labels as semi-supervised learning. In: International Conference on Learning Representations (ICLR) (2020)
23. Li, J., Xiong, C., Hoi, S.C.: Learning from noisy data with robust representation learning. In: IEEE/CVF International Conference on Computer Vision (ICCV) (2021)
24. Li, W., Wang, L., Li, W., Agustsson, E., Van Gool, L.: WebVision database: visual learning and understanding from web data. arXiv:1708.02862 (2017)
25. Liu, S., Niles-Weed, J., Razavian, N., Fernandez-Granda, C.: Early-learning regularization prevents memorization of noisy labels. In: Advances in Neural Information Processing Systems (NeurIPS) (2020)
26. Mingxing, T., Quoc, L.: EfficientNet: rethinking model scaling for convolutional neural networks. In: International Conference on Machine Learning (ICML) (2019)
27. Ng, A.Y., Jordan, M.I., Weiss, Y.: On spectral clustering: analysis and an algorithm. In: Advances in Neural Information Processing Systems (NeurIPS) (2002)
28. Ortego, D., Arazo, E., Albert, P., O'Connor, N., McGuinness, K.: Towards robust learning with different label noise distributions. In: International Conference on Pattern Recognition (ICPR) (2020)

29. Ortego, D., Arazo, E., Albert, P., O'Connor, N.E., McGuinness, K.: Multi-objective interpolation training for robustness to label noise. In: IEEE/CVF Conference on Computer Vision and Pattern Recognition (CVPR) (2021)

30. Patrini, G., Rozza, A., Krishna Menon, A., Nock, R., Qu, L.: Making deep neural networks robust to label noise: a loss correction approach. In: IEEE Conference on Computer Vision and Pattern Recognition (CVPR) (2017)

31. Reed, S., Lee, H., Anguelov, D., Szegedy, C., Erhan, D., Rabinovich, A.: Training deep neural networks on noisy labels with bootstrapping. In: International Conference on Learning Representations (ICLR) (2015)

32. Sachdeva, R., Cordeiro, F.R., Belagiannis, V., Reid, I., Carneiro, G.: EvidentialMix: learning with combined open-set and closed-set noisy labels. In: IEEE/CVF Winter Conference on Applications of Computer Vision (WACV) (2020)

33. Sachdeva, R., Cordeiro, F.R., Belagiannis, V., Reid, I., Carneiro, G.: ScanMix: learning from severe label noise via semantic clustering and semi-supervised learning. arXiv:2103.11395 (2021)

34. Sensoy, M., Kaplan, L., Kandemir, M.: Evidential deep learning to quantify classification uncertainty. In: Advances in Neural Information Processing Systems (NeurIPS) (2018)

35. Shi, J., Malik, J.: Normalized cuts and image segmentation. IEEE Trans. Pattern Anal. Mach. Intell. (TPAMI) 22(8), 888–905 (2000)

36. Sohn, K.: Improved deep metric learning with multi-class n-pair loss objective. In: Advances in Neural Information Processing Systems (NeurIPS) (2016)

37. Sun, Z., et al.: Webly supervised fine-grained recognition: benchmark datasets and an approach. In: IEEE/CVF International Conference on Computer Vision (ICCV) (2021)

38. Szegedy, C., Ioffe, S., Vanhoucke, V., Alemi, A.: Inception-v4, inception-resnet and the impact of residual connections on learning. In: Association for the Advancement of Artificial Intelligence (AAAI) (2016)

39. Tenenbaum, J.B., de Silva, V., Langford, J.C.: A global geometric framework for nonlinear dimensionality reduction. Science 290(5500), 2319–2323 (2000)

40. Vinyals, O., Blundell, C., Lillicrap, T., Kavukcuoglu, K., Wierstra, D.: Matching networks for one shot learning. In: Advances in Neural Information Processing Systems (NeuRIPS) (2016)

41. Vyas, N., Saxena, S., Voice, T.: Learning soft labels via meta learning. arXiv:2009.09496 (2020)

42. Wang, T., Isola, P.: Understanding contrastive representation learning through alignment and uniformity on the hypersphere. In: International Conference on Machine Learning (ICLR) (2020)

43. Wang, Y., et al.: Iterative learning with open-set noisy labels. In: IEEE Conference on Computer Vision and Pattern Recognition (CVPR) (2018)

44. Xiao, T., Xia, T., Yang, Y., Huang, C., Wang, X.: Learning from massive noisy labeled data for image classification. In: IEEE Conference on Computer Vision and Pattern Recognition (CVPR) (2015)

45. Xu, Y., Zhu, L., Jiang, L., Yang, Y.: Faster meta update strategy for noise-robust deep learning. In: IEEE/CVF Conference on Computer Vision and Pattern Recognition (CVPR) (2021)

46. Yao, Y., et al.: Jo-SRC: a contrastive approach for combating noisy labels. In: IEEE/CVF Conference on Computer Vision and Pattern Recognition (CVPR) (2021)

47. Yu, Q., Aizawa, K.: Unsupervised out-of-distribution detection by maximum classifier discrepancy. In: IEEE International Conference on Computer Vision (ICCV) (2019)
48. Zhang, C., Bengio, S., Hardt, M., Recht, B., Vinyals, O.: Understanding deep learning requires re-thinking generalization. In: International Conference on Learning Representations (ICLR) (2017)
49. Zhang, H., Cisse, M., Dauphin, Y., Lopez-Paz, D.: mixup: Beyond empirical risk minimization. In: International Conference on Learning Representations (ICLR) (2018)
50. Zhou, B., Lapedriza, A., Khosla, A., Oliva, A., Torralba, A.: Places: a 10 million image database for scene recognition. IEEE Trans. Pattern Anal. Mach. Intell. **40**(6), 1452–1464 (2017)
51. Zhou, T., Wang, S., Bilmes, J.: Robust curriculum learning: from clean label detection to noisy label self-correction. In: International Conference on Learning Representations (ICLR) (2020)

Unsupervised Few-Shot Image Classification by Learning Features into Clustering Space

Shuo Li[1,2,3,4] ⓘ, Fang Liu[1,2,3,4](✉) ⓘ, Zehua Hao[1,2,3,4], Kaibo Zhao[1,2,3,4], and Licheng Jiao[1,2,3,4] ⓘ

[1] Key Laboratory of Intelligent Perception and Image Understanding of Ministry of Education, Xi'an, China
[2] International Research Center for Intelligent Perception and Computation, Xi'an, China
[3] Joint International Research Laboratory of Intelligent Perception and Computation, Xi'an, China
[4] School of Artificial Intelligent, Xidian University, Xi'an 710071, P.R. China
{alisure,zhhao_1995}@stu.xidian.edu.cn, f63liu@163.com, lchjiao@mail.xidian.edu.cn

Abstract. Most few-shot image classification methods are trained based on tasks. Usually, tasks are built on base classes with a large number of labeled images, which consumes large effort. Unsupervised few-shot image classification methods do not need labeled images, because they require tasks to be built on unlabeled images. In order to efficiently build tasks with unlabeled images, we propose a novel single-stage clustering method: Learning Features into Clustering Space (LF2CS), which first set a separable clustering space by fixing the clustering centers and then use a learnable model to learn features into the clustering space. Based on our LF2CS, we put forward an image sampling and c-way k-shot task building method. With this, we propose a novel unsupervised few-shot image classification method, which jointly learns the learnable model, clustering and few-shot image classification. Experiments and visualization show that our LF2CS has a strong ability to generalize to the novel categories. From the perspective of image sampling, we implement four baselines according to how to build tasks. We conduct experiments on the Omniglot, miniImageNet, tieredImageNet and CIFARFS datasets based on the Conv-4 and ResNet-12 backbones. Experimental results show that ours outperform the state-of-the-art methods.

Keywords: Few-shot learning · Unsupervised few-shot image classification · Single-stage clustering · Learning features into clustering space

1 Introduction

Few-Shot Learning (FSL) aims to learn the novel categories by a small number of images, and usually includes an auxiliary dataset for training [41–43]. The

S. Avidan et al. (Eds.): ECCV 2022, LNCS 13691, pp. 420–436, 2022.
https://doi.org/10.1007/978-3-031-19821-2_24

purpose of image classification is to predict the category of image x, while few-shot image classification predicts which of $c \times k$ images (c categories and each category has k images) are of the same category as image x. Few-shot image classification usually organizes images into a c-way k-shot form, which is called a task. FSL learns meta-knowledge related to tasks, rather than knowledge related to specific categories, thereby generalizing the meta-knowledge to the novel categories. The auxiliary dataset usually contains a large number of annotated images. For example, the training set of tieredImageNet [38] contains 448,695 images. When FSL methods are directly applied to a new field, we need to label the auxiliary dataset, which will consume large effort. To alleviate the burden caused by the auxiliary dataset, Unsupervised FSL (UFSL) has attracted attention [2,6,16,17,20,21,25,36]. Under the setting of supervised FSL, the labels of the auxiliary dataset are used to build tasks (as shown in Fig. 1 (a)), while under the setting of UFSL, the auxiliary dataset has no available labels. Our work will explore how to build tasks through unlabeled auxiliary dataset.

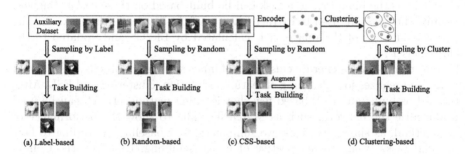

Fig. 1. The four baselines from the view of sampling. (a) Label-based baseline, which is a supervised baseline. Since the images have category labels, two of the four sampled images belong to the same category. (b) Random-based baseline, in which four images are randomly sampled, and the label of task is randomly determined. (c) CSS-based baseline, in which three images are randomly sampled, and then one of the images is selected to obtain another view through data augmentation. (d) Clustering-based baseline, in which first all images are divided into multiple clusters by a clustering algorithm, and then four images are selected with cluster ids as labels.

There are two common unsupervised ways to build tasks from the auxiliary dataset: 1) CSS-based methods (Comparative Self-Supervised, as shown in Fig. 1(c)) use data augmentations to obtain another view of the images to construct the image pairs, and then use the image pairs to build tasks [17,20]; 2) Clustering-based methods (as shown in Fig. 1(d)), by a clustering algorithm, divide the images into clusters to obtain the pseudo-labels, and then use the pseudo-labels to build tasks [5,16]. Since CSS-based methods build tasks based on the different views, these methods are concise and effective, but the diversity of tasks may be poor. Also, since Clustering-based methods build tasks based on the clusters, the diversity of tasks may be good, but these methods usually contain multiple steps. For example, CACTUs [16] use the existing unsupervised model [7] to extract features, and then cluster these features to obtain the cluster ids (cluster assignments). This method takes features learning and clustering as two independent steps and requires additional unsupervised models.

To combine the advantages of both methods, we propose a Learn Features into Clustering Space (LF2CS) method, which is a single-stage clustering method. By fixing the clustering center matrix to the identity matrix, LF2CS sets a separable clustering space, and then uses a learnable model to learn features into the clustering space. By this way, LF2CS does not require any other images when determining the cluster id of each image. Based on LF2CS, we put forward an image sampling and task building method, and thus propose a clustering-based unsupervised few-shot image classification method, as shown in Fig. 2. First, each image x_i is fed into a random initialized network to obtain the feature z_i, and LF2CS is used to obtain the initial cluster id $\hat{y}_i$, so that the cluster ids $\hat{Y}$ of all images can be initialized. Then, for each image x_i, $c \times k$ images are sampled based on the cluster ids $\hat{Y}$, in which k images have the same cluster id as the image x_i, so a task can be built based on these $c \times k + 1$ images. Finally, encoders are used to extract features of the images in the task, and the new cluster id $\hat{y}_i$ of the image x_i is calculated by LF2CS and updated to the cluster ids $\hat{Y}$.

Our method first generate cluster ids of images, then samples images to build tasks, and realizes joint learning of feature extraction, clustering and FSL. After the task is built, any task-based few-shot learning method [41–43] can be used to optimize the network, such as MatchNet [43]. To show the performance of our method, as shown in Fig. 1, we summarize four baselines according to how to build tasks from the perspective of image sampling. Based on the Conv-4 [43] and ResNet-12 backbones, we conduct experiments on the Omniglot [23], miniImageNet [43], tieredImageNet [38], and CIFARFS [3] datasets. In summary, our main contributions are as follows:

1) By fixing the clustering center matrix to the identity matrix, we first set a separable clustering space and then use a learnable model to learn features into the clustering space;
2) A clustering-based unsupervised few-shot image classification method is proposed through image sampling and task building, which jointly learns feature learning, clustering, and few-shot image classification;
3) From the view of sampling, we implement four baselines according to how to build tasks: Label-based, Random-based, CSS-based, and Clustering-based;
4) We conduct experiments on a series of benchmarks based on Conv-4 and ResNet-12, and experimentals show that our method has a strong ability to generalize to the novel categories and achieves the state-of-the-art results.

2   Related Work

2.1   Few-Shot Learning

FSL aims to learn the novel categories through few labeled images, and it usually contains a labeled auxiliary dataset [12,26,30,32]. There are many methods: Metric-based, Finetune-based, and Parameterize-based, etc. Metric-based methods are to learn the ability of similarity measure [28,41–43]. Finetune-based methods are to finetune a base-learner for new tasks by its few samples and make the base-learner converge fast within fewer parameter update steps [11,37,40]. Parameterize-based methods are to parameterize the base-learner or its subcomponents, thereby generalizing the meta-learner to new tasks [4,8,44].

2.2   Unsupervised Feature Learning

Unsupervised feature learning includes many methods, and we mainly introduce clustering and self-supervised learning. Clustering aims to divide the data into different clusters based on the inherent information of data, such as Gaussian Mixture model [1], K-means [18], spectral clustering [48], hierarchical clustering [19], etc. Recently, deep-based clustering methods [7,27,45,47] have shown superior performance. Self-supervised learning uses the data itself to construct some supervised signals to replace the label, such as colorization [46], solving jigsaw puzzle [34], rotation [13], etc. Recently, comparative self-supervised learning methods [9,10,14,15,31] have made great progress, which learn from multiple views of the images. These methods obtain multiple different views, thereby constructing positive and negative image pairs, so that the positive image pair are similar in the feature space, and the negative image pair are not similar [15].

2.3   Unsupervised Few-Shot Learning

Different from FSL, UFSL usually contains an unlabeled auxiliary dataset. There are two common methods: CSS-based and Clustering-based. CSS-based methods use data augmentations to obtain mutiply views of image to construct image pairs which are used to build tasks. Generally, the data augmentations contain common image transforms [2,6,17,20,25,36], such as random resized crop and color jitter, and (or) generative models [21,36], such as autoencoders and generative adversarial networks. Clustering-based methods [5,16] divide the images in the auxiliary dataset into multiple clusters to obtain the pseudo-labels of the images, and then use the pseudo-labels to build tasks.

3   Our Approach

3.1   Unsupervised Few-Shot Learning

In FSL, an auxiliary dataset $D_{aux} = \{(x_i, y_i)\}_{i=1}^{N_{aux}}$ (N_{aux} is the number of images) is used to train a learnable model, and then applies the model to a

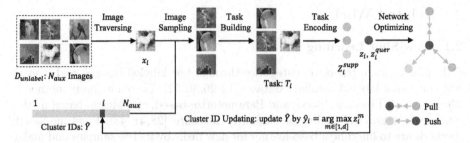

Fig. 2. The overall pipeline of our approach. The 3-way 1-shot task is used as an example to show our method. Clusters IDs $\hat{Y}$ stores the cluster ids of all images in $D_{unlabel}$, and $|\hat{Y}| = N_{aux}$. First, for the image x_i, its cluster id $\hat{y}_i$ is obtained from $\hat{Y}$ (Image Traversing). Then, according to $\hat{y}_i$ and $\hat{Y}$, three images are sampled from $D_{unlabel}$: the cluster id of one image is $\hat{y}_i$, and the cluster id of the other two images is not $\hat{y}_i$ (Image Sampling), so the 3-way 1-shot task can be built (Task Building). Then, the feature of task is obtained by encoders (Task Encoding), and encoders are optimized by reducing the distance of features with the same cluster id as the image x_i (Pull) and increasing the distance of features with different cluster ids to the image x_i (Push) (Network Optimizing). Finally, the cluster id $\hat{y}_i$ is updated (Cluster ID Updating).

target dataset $D_{target} = \{\{(x_i, y_i)\}_{i=1}^{N_{label}}, \{x_j\}_{j=1}^{N_{unlabel}}\}$ (where $N_{label} \ll N_{unlabel}$, N_{label} and $N_{unlabel}$ are the number of labeled and unlabeled images), so that the target dataset with few labeled images can be classified. D_{aux} and D_{target} are also known as the base classes and the novel classes, respectively. D_{aux} contains a large number of labeled images. UFSL aims to train a model using an unlabeled auxiliary dataset $D_{unlabel} = \{x_i\}_{i=1}^{N_{aux}}$ which contains a large number of unlabeled images, and then also applies the model to D_{target}.

Task-based FSL organizes images into tasks in the form of c-way k-shot. Task T_i is composed of the support set T_i^{supp}, the query set T_i^{quer} and the label y_i^{task}:

$$T_i = \{T_i^{supp}, T_i^{quer}, y_i^{task}\} = \{\{(x_j, y_j)\}_{j=1}^{c \times k}, \{x_i\}, y_i^{task}\}, \tag{1}$$

where $y_i^{task} \in \{0,1\}^{c \times k}$, T_i^{supp} contains c classes and each class has k labeled images. Note that in our work, T_i^{quer} contains only one image x_i. Under the setting of supervised FSL, since the image label is available on the base classes, the task T_i is built in an supervised way. Under the setting of UFSL, the task T_i needs to be built in an unsupervised way. The difference between most UFSL methods is how to build tasks in the base classes. There are two common unsupervised ways to build tasks: Clustering-based and CSS-based. Clustering-based methods divide the images of $D_{unlabel}$ into multiple clusters, and then uses the cluster ids as the pseudo-labels to build tasks. CSS-based methods build tasks based on different views of the same image.

3.2 Learn Features into Clustering Space

In DeepCluster [7], Caron *et. al* alternates between clustering the image features to generate pseudo-labels (Eq. 2) and updating the parameters of the learnable model f_θ by predicting pseudo-labels (Eq. 3):

$$\min_{C \in \mathbb{R}^{d \times K}} \frac{1}{N} \sum_{i=1}^{N} \min_{\hat{y}_i \in \{0,1\}^K} ||f_\theta(x_i) - C\hat{y}_i||_2^2, \tag{2}$$

$$\min_{\theta} \frac{1}{N} \sum_{i=1}^{N} \mathcal{L}(f_\theta(x_i), \hat{y}_i), \tag{3}$$

where θ is the parameter of the network $f_\theta(\cdot)$, C is the cluster center matrix, K is the number of clusters, d is the output feature dimension of $f_\theta(\cdot)$, and $\hat{y}_i$ is the cluster id of the image x_i and $\hat{y}_i^T 1_K = 1$. This method has some limitations: all features need to be extracted before clustering, feature learning and clustering are two independent step, and clustering result usually depends on the initialization of the cluster centers.

Different from [7], we preset a separable d-dimensional clustering space by setting $K = d$ and fixing the matrix C to the identity matrix $E \in \mathbb{R}^{d \times d}$. Since it is located on the coordinate axis of this space, all cluster centers are orthogonal, this clustering space has strong separability. Therefore, Eq. 2 is simplified to:

$$\frac{1}{N} \sum_{i=1}^{N} \min_{\hat{y}_i \in \{0,1\}^d} ||f_\theta(x_i) - E\hat{y}_i||_2^2. \tag{4}$$

In order to make Eq. 4 feasible, the network $f_\theta(\cdot)$ need to be used to learn features of all images into the d-dimensional clustering space. We call this Learn Features into Clustering Space (LF2CS). Specifically, given an image x_i, the feature $z_i = f_\theta(x_i)$ and the cluster to which x_i belongs can be quickly calculated by:

$$\hat{y}_i = \arg\min_{m \in [1,d]} ||z_i - E_m||_2^2 = \arg\max_{m \in [1,d]} z_i^m, \tag{5}$$

where $z_i \in \mathbb{R}^d$, $E_m \in \mathbb{R}^d$, E_m is the cluster center of cluster m, z_i^m is the m-th value of z_i, and $\hat{y}_i$ is the cluster id of x_i. By treating $\hat{y}_i$ as the pseudo-label of x_i, the parameter of $f_\theta(x_i)$ can be updated by Eq. 3.

From Eq. 5, it can be seen that given a feature z_i, cluster center, which is closest to z_i, can be quickly calculated. The advantage of this is that the cluster id $\hat{y}_i$ of the image x_i can be calculated in a simple way, without the need of other image features. Our LF2CS eliminates the process of solving cluster centers in Eq. 2 by iterative algorithms, such as K-means. Therefore, our LF2CS is a single-stage clustering algorithm, instead of alternating between Eq. 3 and Eq. 2.

Avoiding Trivial Solution. Most clustering-based methods have trivial solutions [7,27]. In order to avoid invalid solutions, our LF2CS forces all images to be scattered into the clustering space by limiting the maximum number of images in each cluster. When the number of images in the m-th cluster exceeds $n_{max} = N_{aux}/d$, we will no longer assign any images to the m-th cluster, but look for the next cluster that satisfies the constraint. The maximum number of images n_{max} per cluster means that each cluster is almost the same size. In this way, our method avoids both over-clustering (many clusters are relatively small) and under-clustering (some clusters are relatively large).

3.3 Image Sampling and Task Building

Given an unlabeled auxiliary dataset $D_{unlabel} = \{x_i\}_{i=1}^{N_{aux}}$, our goal is to build tasks from unlabeled images. In order to record the cluster to which each image belongs, $\hat{Y} = \{\hat{y}_i\}_{i=1}^{N_{aux}}$ is used to store the cluster ids of all images, that is, $\hat{y}_i$ is the cluster id of the image x_i, where $\hat{y}_i \in [1, d]$. To facilitate joint training, we use mini-batch of tasks in training for each optimization step, instead of episode

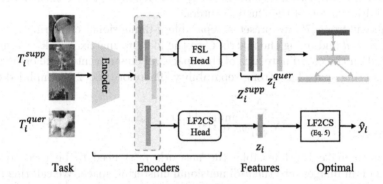

Fig. 3. Task Encoding and Network Optimizing. Both FSL Head and LF2CS Head are a fully connected layer. We call Encoder, FSL Head, and LF2CS Head as Encoders. We treat the optimization as a multi-task learning problem: LF2CS and few-shot image classification. Note that $z_i^{quer} \in \mathbb{R}^q$ and $z_i \in \mathbb{R}^d$.

[43]. When evaluating, like other methods [41–43], we use episode as input. To build c-way k-shot task, the image x_i is used as the query set T_i^{quer}, $c \times k$ images are selected as the support set T_i^{supp} through the cluster id $\hat{y}_i$. Specifically, we get c clusters by $\hat{y}_i$ and randomly selecting other $c - 1$ clusters:

$$\hat{Y}_c = \{\hat{y}_i\} \cup \{c_j\}_{j=1}^{c-1}, \quad s.t. \ c_j \neq \hat{y}_i, \tag{6}$$

where c_j is a cluster id and $\hat{Y}_c$ is the set of c cluster ids. According to $\hat{Y}$, by randomly selecting k images from $D_{unlabel}$ for each cluster id in $\hat{Y}_c$, we can get $c \times k$ images which are treated as the support set T_i^{supp}. Since the images with the same cluster id are usually treated as the same category, the task $T_i = \{T_i^{supp}, T_i^{quer}, y_i^{task}\}$ is built successfully, where y_i^{task} can be obtained by whether the cluster ids of the images in the query set T_i^{quer} and the support set T_i^{supp} are the same. The new cluster id $\hat{y}_i$ of the image x_i can be calculated by Eq. 5, and then $\hat{Y}$ is updated by replacing the old cluster id with the new one.

3.4   Task Encoding and Network Optimizing

As shown in Fig. 3, we use the Encoder to embed images of the task T_i. In our method, the Encoder is Conv-4 or ResNet-12. FSL Head is used to learn features for few-shot image classification, and LF2CS Head is used to learn features into the clustering space. Both FSL Head and LF2CS Head are a fully connected layer, which are used to embed features for clustering and few-shot image classification. The output dimension of FSL Head is q and the output dimension of LF2CS Head is d. The feature $z_i \in \mathbb{R}^d$ is extracted by feeding the image x_i in the query set T_i^{quer} to Encoder and LF2CS Head, and the feature $z_i^{quer} \in \mathbb{R}^q$ also is extracted by feeding the image x_i in the query set T_i^{quer} to Encoder and FSL Head. In addition, the features $Z_i^{supp} = \{z_{i,j}^{supp}\}_{j=1}^{c \times k}$ are extracted by feeding images in the support set T_i^{supp} to Encoder and FSL Head, where $z_{i,j}^{supp} \in \mathbb{R}^q$ is the feature of the j-th image in the support set T_i^{supp}.

Algorithm 1 The overall pipeline of our method.

Input: the dataset $D_{unlabel} = \{x_i\}_{i=1}^{N_{aux}}$, max iteration T_{max};
Output: Encoders.

1: Initialize the parameters of Encoders;
2: **for** $i = \{1, 2, ..., N_{aux}\}$ **do**
3:    Extract z_i and compute $\hat{y}_i$; // Initialize $\hat{Y}$;
4: **end for**
5: **for** $t = \{1, 2, ..., T_{max}\}$ **do**
6:    // Image Traversing
7:    **for** $i = \{1, 2, ..., N_{aux}\}$ **do**
8:        Get $\hat{Y}_c$ by $\hat{y}_i$ and Select $c \times k$ images as T_i^{supp}; // Image Sampling
9:        Build task $T_i = \{T_i^{supp}, T_i^{quer}, y_i^{task}\}$; // Task Building
10:       Get features $z_i, z_i^{quer}, Z_i^{supp}$ by Encoders; // Task Encoding
11:       Compute loss $\mathcal{L}$ by Eq.8 and Update the parameters; // Network Optimizing
12:       Calculate the cluster id $\hat{y}_i$ and Update $\hat{Y}$ by $\hat{y}_i$; // Cluster ID Updating
13:    **end for**
14: **end for**
15: **return** Encoders;

After the task is built, any task-based few-shot learning method [41–43] can be used to optimize the network. We optimize the network based on MatchNet [43] and use the softmax over cosine to measure similarity between features:

$$p_i^{task} = \{p_{i,j}^{task}\}_{j=1}^{c \times k} = \left\{ \frac{exp(cos(z_{i,j}^{supp}, z_i^{quer}))}{\sum\limits_{z_{i,l}^{supp} \in Z_i^{supp}} exp(cos(z_{i,l}^{supp}, z_i^{quer}))} \right\}_{j=1}^{c \times k}, \quad (7)$$

where $cos(\cdot, \cdot)$ is the cosine similarity. FSL can be optimized by MSE (Mean Squared Error) loss between p_i^{task} and the task label y_i^{task}, and LF2CS can be optimized by CE (Cross Entropy) loss between the feature z_i and the cluster id $\hat{y}_i$. The optimization of our method can be treated as a multi-task learning problem. Therefore, we jointly learn LF2CS and FSL, and the total loss is:

$$\mathcal{L} = MSE(p_i^{task}, y_i^{task}) + CE(z_i, \hat{y}_i), \quad (8)$$

where $y_i^{task} \in \{0,1\}^{c \times k}$, $p_i^{task} \in \mathbb{R}^{c \times k}$, $z_i \in \mathbb{R}^d$, and $\hat{y}_i \in [1,d]$. In the CE loss, $\hat{y}_i$ is converted to a one-hot vector. Taking Eq. 8 as our total loss, our method increases the similarity of features with the same cluster id and reduces the similarity of features with different cluster ids.

For easy understanding, we show the overall pipeline of our method in Algorithm 1. Please refer to https://github.com/xidianai/LF2CS for the code.

4   Experimental Results

4.1   Setup

Our method includes an Encoder and two linear head (FSL Head and LF2CS Head). For Encoder, we use two widely used networks (Conv-4 [43] and ResNet-12). For each Head, we use a fully connected layer. The output dimension q of FSL Head is 1024, and the output dimension d of LF2CS Head is 1024. All our models are trained from scratch without any pre-trained weights. We use the SGD optimizer with learning rate of 0.01, weight decay of 5e-4 and batch size of 64. We use the learning rate strategy shown in Fig. 5 and train the model for 1,500 epochs. All our experiments are implemented based on PyTorch [35]. We use the evaluate strategies used in [42]. Following [42], each class uses 15 query samples in each episode: for c-way k-shot, each episode contains $15 \times c$ query images and $c \times k$ support images. All accuracies are averaged over 1,000

Table 1. Few-shot image classification accuracies of 5-way and 20-way on Omniglot. All accuracies are averaged over 1000 test episodes and are reported with 95% confidence intervals. The backbone of all methods is Conv-4. Bold represent the best values.

	Method	5-Way Acc.		20-Way Acc.	
		1-Shot	5-Shot	1-Shot	5-Shot
FSL	MatchNet [43]	98.10±-%	98.90±-%	93.80±-%	98.50±-%
	MAML [11]	98.70±0.40%	99.90±0.10%	95.80±0.30%	98.90±0.20%
	ProtoNet [41]	98.80±-%	99.70±-%	96.00±-%	98.90±-%
	Meta-SGD [29]	99.50±-%	99.90±-%	95.90±-%	99.00±-%
	RelationNet [42]	99.60±0.20%	99.80±0.10%	97.60±0.20%	99.10±0.10%
	Baselines: Label	97.92±0.22%	99.47±0.08%	92.84±0.21%	97.68±0.10%
UFSL	CACTUs [16]	68.84±-%	87.78±-%	48.09±-%	73.36±-%
	UMTRA [20]	83.80±-%	95.43±-%	74.25±-%	92.12±-%
	LASIUM [21]	83.26±0.55%	95.29±0.22%	-	-
	ProtoTransfer [33]	88.00±-%	96.48±-%	72.27±-%	89.08±-%
	AAL [2]	88.40±0.75%	98.00±0.32%	70.20±0.86%	88.30±1.22%
	ULDA [36]	91.00±0.42%	98.14±0.15%	78.05±0.31%	94.08±0.13%
	UFLST [17]	97.03±-%	99.19±-%	91.28±-%	97.37±-%
	Baselines: Random	58.50±0.70%	71.73±0.59%	33.94±0.31%	47.14±0.32%
	Baselines: CSS	83.97±0.56%	94.65±0.26%	65.25±0.34%	84.74±0.22%
	Baselines: Clustering	83.14±0.62%	91.67±0.36%	61.52±0.36%	77.05±0.28%
	Ours: LF2CS	**97.31±0.25%**	**99.32±0.10%**	**91.72±0.22%**	**97.65±0.09%**

test episodes and are reported with 95% confidence intervals. We also use KNN to evaluate our LF2CS, and set the number of nearest neighbor samples to 100. The top-1 and top-5 accuracy of KNN are used to report the results.

4.2   Unsupervised Few-Shot Image Classification Results

Results on Omniglot. The Omniglot [23] dataset consists of 1,623 characters from 50 different alphabets and each character contains 20 samples drawn by different people. Following [41,43], we resize the sample to 28×28. We use 1,028 characters for training, 172 characters for validation, and the remaining 423 characters for testing. On the Omniglot dataset, we only use Conv-4 as the backbone of Encoder. Table 1 shows the few-shot image classification accuracies on Omniglot. Compared with other unsupervised baselines, the method of building tasks by randomly selecting images (Random-based) has the worst accuracies and our LF2CS has the best accuracies in all cases. Compared with other unsupervised methods, ours do 97.31% for 5-way 1-shot with Conv-4 as the backbone, which has also reached the level of supervised methods.

Table 2. 5-way 1-shot and 5-way 5-shot few-shot image classification accuracies on the miniImageNet dataset. All accuracies are averaged over 1000 test episodes and reported with 95% confidence intervals. Bold represent the best values.

	Method	Backbone	5-Way 1-Shot	5-Way 5-Shot
FSL	MatchNet [43]	Conv-4	46.60±-%	60.00±-%
	ProtoNet [41]	Conv-4	49.42±0.78%	68.20±0.66%
	RelationNet [42]	Conv-4	50.44±0.82%	65.32±0.70%
	MAML [11]	Conv-4	48.70±1.84%	63.11±0.92%
	MetaOptnet [24]	ResNet-12	62.64±0.61%	78.63±0.46%
	Baselines: Label	Conv-4	52.53±0.62%	65.98±0.53%
	Baselines: Label	ResNet-12	60.06±0.69%	71.76±0.58%
UFSL	UFLST [17]	Conv-4	33.77±0.70%	45.03±0.73%
	AAL [2]	Conv-4	37.67±0.39%	40.29±0.68%
	CACTUs [16]	Conv-4	39.90±0.74%	53.97±0.70%
	UMTRA [20]	Conv-4	39.93±-%	50.73±-%
	LASIUM [21]	Conv-4	40.19±0.58%	54.56±0.55%
	ULDA [36]	Conv-4	40.63±0.61%	56.18±0.59%
	CSSL-FSL [25]	ResNet-50	48.53±1.26%	63.13±0.87%
	No-Labels [6]	ResNet-50	50.10±0.20%	60.10±0.20%
	Baselines: Random	Conv-4	25.29±0.39%	28.86±0.39%
	Baselines: CSS	Conv-4	41.00±0.56%	52.17±0.54%
	Baselines: Clustering	Conv-4	41.01±0.59%	51.52±0.55%
	Ours: LF2CS	Conv-4	**48.32±0.64%**	**61.52±0.52%**
	Baselines: Random	ResNet-12	29.92±0.46%	36.82±0.48%
	Baselines: CSS	ResNet-12	45.42±0.60%	58.37±0.54%
	Baselines: Clustering	ResNet-12	48.48±0.63%	61.10±0.58%
	Ours: LF2CS	ResNet-12	**53.14±0.62%**	**67.36±0.50%**

Results on MiniImageNet. The miniImageNet [43] dataset consists of 100 categories sampled from ImageNet [39], all images are 84×84 in size, and each category has 600 images. Following [43], we divide all categories into 64 (training), 16 (validation), and 20 (test) categories. Table 2 shows the few-shot image classification accuracies on miniImageNet. We compare with 5 supervised methods and 8 unsupervised methods. Compared with other unsupervised baselines, the method of building tasks by randomly selecting images has the worst accuracies, while our methods have the best accuracies. Especially, our ResNet-12 reaches 53.14% for 5-way 1-shot, which has better results than all unsupervised methods. Compared with other unsupervised methods, our methods have a smaller gap with the supervised few-shot image classification methods.

Table 3. 5-way 1-shot and 5-way 5-shot few-shot image classification accuracies on the tieredImageNet dataset. All accuracies are averaged over 1000 test episodes and reported with 95% confidence intervals. Bold represent the best values.

	Method	Backbone	5-Way 1-Shot	5-Way 5-Shot
FSL	ProtoNet [41]	Conv-4	53.31±0.89%	72.69±0.74%
	RelationNet [42]	Conv-4	54.48±0.93%	71.32±0.78%
	MAML [11]	Conv-4	51.67±1.81%	70.30±1.75%
	MetaOptnet [24]	ResNet-12	65.99±0.72%	81.56±0.53%
	Baselines: Label	Conv-4	56.09±0.72%	68.86±0.60%
	Baselines: Label	ResNet-12	64.67±0.76%	76.71±0.57%
UFSL	ULDA [36]	Conv-4	41.77±0.65%	56.78±0.63%
	Baselines: Random	Conv-4	24.81±0.36%	28.80±0.40%
	Baselines: CSS	Conv-4	40.74±0.59%	52.72±0.58%
	Baselines: Clustering	Conv-4	42.60±0.62%	55.11±0.57%
	Ours: LF2CS	Conv-4	**49.15±0.65%**	**62.54±0.58%**
	Baselines: Random	ResNet-12	31.58±0.50%	38.82±0.53%
	Baselines: CSS	ResNet-12	43.13±0.62%	56.36±0.56%
	Baselines: Clustering	ResNet-12	44.93±0.64%	57.53±0.59%
	Ours: LF2CS	ResNet-12	**53.16±0.66%**	**66.59±0.57%**

Results on TieredImageNet. The tieredImageNet [38] dataset consists of 608 classes with a total of 779,165 images of size 84×84. These classes are selected from 34 higher-level nodes in the ImageNet hierarchy. Following [38], 351 classes from 20 high level nodes are used for training, 97 classes from 6 nodes for validation and 160 classes from 8 nodes for testing. Table 3 shows the few-shot image classification accuracies on tieredImageNet. Compared with other unsupervised methods, our methods have the best accuracies. Among them, our ResNet-12 has an accuracy of 53.16% for 5-way 1-shot and 66.59% for 5-way 5-shot. Compared with other unsupervised baselines, our methods have a smaller gap with the supervised few-shot image classification methods.

Results on CIFARFS. The CIFARFS [3] dataset consists of 100 classes sampled from CIFAR100 [22]. All the images are 32×32 in size. Following [3], we divide all classes into 64, 16, and 20 classes for training, validation, and testing, respectively. We compare with four supervised methods and one unsupervised method. Table 4 shows the few-shot accuracies on CIFARFS. Compared with other unsupervised methods, our methods have the best accuracies. For 5-way 1-shot, our method based on the Conv-4 backbone achieves an accuracy of 51.52%.

4.3   Ablation Experiments and Visualization

The Performance of LF2CS. The number of clusters is the same as the dimension d, which usually affects the clustering results. We conduct experiments to observe the effect of the dimension d. Encoder also plays an important role on the clustering results, and we evaluate our LF2CS on two architectures: Conv-4 [43] and ResNet-12. Figure 4 shows the top-1 KNN accuracies and training time per epoch on miniImageNet. Table 5 shows the accuracies of LF2CS with different Encoder on miniImageNet. We report the results with top-1 and top-5 KNN accuracies, and 5-way 1-shot and 5-way 5-shot few-shot accuracies. Note that the categories in training, validation and test sets do not intersect. From Fig. 4, we can find that as the dimension d increases, the KNN accuracy and training time also increase. To balance the time and accuracy, the dimension d

Table 4. Few-shot image classification accuracies on the CIFARFS dataset. All accuracies are averaged over 1000 test episodes and reported with 95% confidence intervals. Bold represent the best values.

	Method	Backbone	5-way 1-shot	5-way 5-shot
FSL	ProtoNet	Conv-4	55.50±0.70%	72.60±0.60%
	RelationNet	Conv-4	55.00±1.00%	69.30±0.80%
	MAML	Conv-4	58.90±1.90%	71.50±1.00%
	MetaOptnet	ResNet-12	72.08±0.70%	85.00±0.50%
	Baselines: Label-based	Conv-4	65.65±0.74%	76.75±0.57%
	Baselines: Label-based	ResNet-12	67.14±0.76%	77.46±0.54%
UFSL	No-Labels	ResNet-50	53.00±0.20%	62.50±0.20%
	Baselines: Random-based	Conv-4	30.87±0.47%	38.03±0.49%
	Baselines: CSS-based	Conv-4	42.59±0.65%	55.64±0.59%
	Baselines: Clustering-based	Conv-4	44.72±0.66%	58.21±0.57%
	Ours: LF2CS	Conv-4	**51.52±0.72%**	**66.82±0.57%**
	Baselines: Random-based	ResNet-12	34.25±0.55%	44.48±0.55%
	Baselines: CSS-based	ResNet-12	46.46±0.67%	61.39±0.59%
	Baselines: Clustering-based	ResNet-12	44.88±0.67%	58.50±0.59%
	Ours: LF2CS	ResNet-12	**55.04±0.72%**	**70.62±0.57%**

is set to 1024. From the few-shot accuracies in Table 5, it can be seen that LF2CS has a strong generalization ability to the novel categories, such as 48.41% in the training set v.s. 48.32% in the test set with Conv-4 as the backbone and 53.59% in the training set v.s. 53.14% in the test set with ResNet-12 as the backbone.

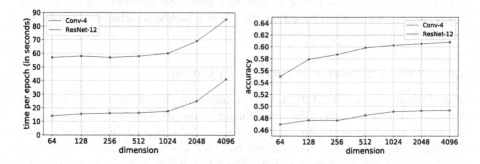

Fig. 4. Left: The Top-1 KNN accuracies in test set on miniImageNet; Right: The training time per epoch of different dimension of LF2CS Head on miniImageNet.

Table 5. Top-1 and Top-5 KNN accuracies, and 5-way 1-shot and 5-way 5-shot few-shot accuracies of LF2CS Head with different Encoder on the training, validation and test sets of miniImageNet. All few-shot accuracies are averaged over 1000 test episodes and reported with 95% confidence intervals. The dimension d is 1024.

SubSet	Encoder	Top-1	Top-5	5-Way 1-Shot	5-Way 5-Shot
Training	Conv-4	36.85%	69.36%	48.41±0.62%	62.28±0.50%
	ResNet-12	53.42%	81.61%	53.59±0.65%	68.06±0.51%
Validation	Conv-4	50.49%	88.86%	46.71±0.65%	59.32±0.53%
	ResNet-12	62.17%	92.34%	51.69±0.67%	65.41±0.53%
Test	Conv-4	49.10%	88.00%	48.32±0.64%	61.52±0.52%
	ResNet-12	60.25%	91.38%	53.14±0.62%	67.36±0.50%

The Change of the Cluster Assignments. Now, we show the gradual change of the cluster ids over time. During the training process, we have counted the change of the cluster ids. The change of learning rate is shown in the left of Fig. 5. There are two curves in the right of Fig. 5. The first represents the change ratio of cluster ids and the second represents the ratio of cluster ids that do not meet the limit on the number of clusters. At the beginning of training, the change ratio of cluster ids and the ratio of cluster ids that do not meet the limit on the number of clusters are almost 98% or more. It is almost completely random. But as the training progresses, the ratio of cluster ids that do not meet the limit on the number of clusters dropped sharply. That is to say, the number of images that do not meet the limit is rapidly decreasing. As the training progresses, the change ratio of cluster assignments is also reduced. At the end of training, only 20% of the cluster assignments changed.

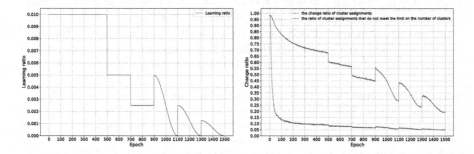

Fig. 5. The gradual change of the cluster ids over time. Left: The learning rate decay using cosine strategy; Right: The change ratio of the cluster ids (assignments).

Fig. 6. Visualize images in some clusters on the miniImageNet dataset. Each row of images represents the same clusters. The images of left, middle, and right come from the training, validation and test sets, respectively.

The Visualization of Images in Some Clusters. Since task is built by selecting images from clusters, the clustering results affect the quality of tasks. When there are more images belonging to the same category in the same cluster, the quality of the task will be higher. Therefore, visualizing the images of the same cluster will help to understand our method. Figure 6 shows some images in some clusters, which are divided into three parts. The left, middle, and right show the images in the training, validation, and test sets of miniImageNet, respectively. Obviously, we can see that each cluster represents a certain vision semantics of images. For example, the first row has a similar texture, and the last row has a similar shape.

5   Conclusion

In our work, we propose a novel single-stage clustering method: Learning Features into Clustering Space (LF2CS), which fixes the cluster center matrix to the identity matrix, thereby setting a strongly separable clustering space, and then learns features into the clustering space. Based on this, we put forward an image sampling and task building method, and with this, we propose an unsupervised few-shot image classification method. Experimental results and visualization show that our LF2CS has a strong ability to generalize to the novel categories. Based on Conv-4 and ResNet-12, we conduct experiments on four FSL datasets, and our method achieves the state-of-the-art results.

Acknowledgements. This work was supported in part by the National Natural Science Foundation of China (No.62076192), Key Research and Development Program in Shaanxi Province of China (No.2019ZDLGY03-06), the State Key Program of National Natural Science of China (No.61836009), in part by the Program for Cheung Kong Scholars and Innovative Research Team in University (No. IRT_15R53), in part by The Fund for Foreign Scholars in University Research and Teaching Programs (the 111 Project) (No. B07048), in part by the Key Scientific Technological Innovation Research Project by Ministry of Education, the National Key Research and Development Program of China.

References

1. Abramson, N., Braverman, D.J., Sebestyen, G.S.: Pattern recognition and machine learning. JASA **103**(482), 886–887 (2006)
2. Antoniou, A., Storkey, A.J.: Assume, augment and learn: Unsupervised few-shot meta-learning via random labels and data augmentation. CoRR abs/1902.09884 (2019)
3. Bertinetto, L., Henriques, J.F., Torr, P.H.S., Vedaldi, A.: Meta-learning with differentiable closed-form solvers. In: ICLR (2019)
4. Bertinetto, L., Henriques, J.F., Valmadre, J., Torr, P.H.S., Vedaldi, A.: Learning feed-forward one-shot learners. In: NIPS, pp. 523–531 (2016)
5. Bertugli, A., Vincenzi, S., Calderara, S., Passerini, A.: Few-shot unsupervised continual learning through meta-examples. CoRR abs/2009.08107 (2020)
6. Bharti, A., Balasubramanian, V.N., Jawahar, C.V.: Few shot learning with no labels. CoRR abs/2012.13751 (2020)
7. Caron, M., Bojanowski, P., Joulin, A., Douze, M.: Deep clustering for unsupervised learning of visual features. In: ECCV. vol. 11218, pp. 139–156 (2018)
8. Chen, M., et al.: Diversity transfer network for few-shot learning. In: AAAI, pp. 10559–10566 (2020)
9. Chen, T., Kornblith, S., Norouzi, M., Hinton, G.E.: A simple framework for contrastive learning of visual representations. In: ICML, vol. 119, pp. 1597–1607 (2020)
10. Cui, Y., Liu, F., Liu, X., Li, L., Qian, X.: TCSPANET: two-staged contrastive learning and sub-patch attention based network for polsar image classification. Remote Sens. **14**(10), 2451 (2022)
11. Finn, C., Abbeel, P., Levine, S.: Model-agnostic meta-learning for fast adaptation of deep networks. In: ICML, vol. 70, pp. 1126–1135 (2017)

12. Frikha, A., Krompaß, D., Köpken, H., Tresp, V.: Few-shot one-class classification via meta-learning. In: AAAI, pp. 7448–7456 (2021)
13. Gidaris, S., Singh, P., Komodakis, N.: Unsupervised representation learning by predicting image rotations. In: ICLR (2018)
14. Grill, J., et al.: Bootstrap your own latent - a new approach to self-supervised learning. In: NeurIPS (2020)
15. He, K., Fan, H., Wu, Y., Xie, S., Girshick, R.B.: Momentum contrast for unsupervised visual representation learning. In: CVPR, pp. 9726–9735 (2020)
16. Hsu, K., Levine, S., Finn, C.: Unsupervised learning via meta-learning. In: ICLR (2019)
17. Ji, Z., Zou, X., Huang, T., Wu, S.: Unsupervised few-shot feature learning via self-supervised training. Front. Comput. Neurosci. **14**, 83 (2020)
18. Jiao, L., Ronghua, S., Fang, L., Weitong, Z.: Brain and Nature-Inspired Learning, Computation and Recognition. Elsevier, Amsterdam (2020)
19. Karypis, G., Han, E., Kumar, V.: Chameleon: Hierarchical clustering using dynamic modeling. Computer **32**(8), 68–75 (1999)
20. Khodadadeh, S., Bölöni, L., Shah, M.: Unsupervised meta-learning for few-shot image classification. In: NeurIPS, pp. 10132–10142 (2019)
21. Khodadadeh, S., Zehtabian, S., Vahidian, S., Wang, W., Lin, B., Bölöni, L.: Unsupervised meta-learning through latent-space interpolation in generative models. CoRR abs/2006.10236 (2020)
22. Krizhevsky, A.: Learning Multiple Layers of Features from Tiny Images, pp. 32–33 (2009)
23. Lake, B.M., Salakhutdinov, R., Tenenbaum, J.B.: Human-level concept learning through probabilistic program induction. Science **350**(6266), 1332–1338 (2015)
24. Lee, K., Maji, S., Ravichandran, A., Soatto, S.: Meta-learning with differentiable convex optimization. In: CVPR, pp. 10657–10665 (2019)
25. Li, J., Liu, G.: Few-shot image classification via contrastive self-supervised learning. arXiv abs/2008.09942 (2020)
26. Li, J., Wang, Z., Hu, X.: Learning intact features by erasing-inpainting for few-shot classification. In: AAAI, pp. 8401–8409 (2021)
27. Li, S., Liu, F., Jiao, L., Chen, P., Li, L.: Self-supervised self-organizing clustering network: a novel unsupervised representation learning method. IEEE Trans. Neural Netw. Learn. Syst. pp. 1–15 (2022)
28. Li, W., Xu, J., Huo, J., Wang, L., Gao, Y., Luo, J.: Distribution consistency based covariance metric networks for few-shot learning. In: AAAI, pp. 8642–8649 (2019)
29. Li, Z., Zhou, F., Chen, F., Li, H.: Meta-sgd: learning to learn quickly for few shot learning. CoRR abs/1707.09835 (2017)
30. Liu, C., Fu, Y., Xu, C., Yang, S., Li, J., Wang, C., Zhang, L.: Learning a few-shot embedding model with contrastive learning. In: AAAI, pp. 8635–8643 (2021)
31. Liu, F., Qian, X., Jiao, L., Zhang, X., Li, L., Cui, Y.: Contrastive learning-based dual dynamic GCN for SAR image scene classification. IEEE Trans. Neural Netw. Learn. Syst. pp. 1–15 (2022)
32. Lu, J., Gong, P., Ye, J., Zhang, C.: Learning from very few samples: a survey. CoRR abs/2009.02653 (2020)
33. Medina, C., Devos, A., Grossglauser, M.: Self-supervised prototypical transfer learning for few-shot classification. CoRR abs/2006.11325 (2020)
34. Noroozi, M., Favaro, P.: Unsupervised learning of visual representations by solving jigsaw puzzles. In: Leibe, B., Matas, J., Sebe, N., Welling, M. (eds.) ECCV 2016. LNCS, vol. 9910, pp. 69–84. Springer, Cham (2016). https://doi.org/10.1007/978-3-319-46466-4_5

35. Paszke, A., et al.: Pytorch: an imperative style, high-performance deep learning library. In: NeurIPS, pp. 8024–8035 (2019)
36. Qin, T., Li, W., Shi, Y., Gao, Y.: Unsupervised few-shot learning via distribution shift-based augmentation. CoRR abs/2004.05805 (2020)
37. Ravi, S., Larochelle, H.: Optimization as a model for few-shot learning. In: ICLR (2017)
38. Ren, M., et al.: Meta-learning for semi-supervised few-shot classification. In: ICLR (2018)
39. Russakovsky, O., et al.: ImageNet large scale visual recognition challenge. Int. J. Comput. Vis. **115**(3), 211–252 (2015). https://doi.org/10.1007/s11263-015-0816-y
40. Shen, Z., Liu, Z., Qin, J., Savvides, M., Cheng, K.: Partial is better than all: revisiting fine-tuning strategy for few-shot learning. In: AAAI, pp. 9594–9602 (2021)
41. Snell, J., Swersky, K., Zemel, R.S.: Prototypical networks for few-shot learning. In: NIPS, pp. 4077–4087 (2017)
42. Sung, F., Yang, Y., Zhang, L., Xiang, T., Torr, P.H.S., Hospedales, T.M.: Learning to compare: Relation network for few-shot learning. In: CVPR, pp. 1199–1208 (2018)
43. Vinyals, O., Blundell, C., Lillicrap, T., Kavukcuoglu, K., Wierstra, D.: Matching networks for one shot learning. In: NIPS, pp. 3630–3638 (2016)
44. Wang, Y.-X., Hebert, M.: Learning to learn: model regression networks for easy small sample learning. In: Leibe, B., Matas, J., Sebe, N., Welling, M. (eds.) ECCV 2016. LNCS, vol. 9910, pp. 616–634. Springer, Cham (2016). https://doi.org/10.1007/978-3-319-46466-4_37
45. Xie, J., Girshick, R.B., Farhadi, A.: Unsupervised deep embedding for clustering analysis. In: ICML, vol. 48, pp. 478–487 (2016)
46. Zhang, R., Isola, P., Efros, A.A.: Colorful image colorization. In: Leibe, B., Matas, J., Sebe, N., Welling, M. (eds.) ECCV 2016. LNCS, vol. 9907, pp. 649–666. Springer, Cham (2016). https://doi.org/10.1007/978-3-319-46487-9_40
47. Zhang, W., Jiao, L., Liu, F., Yang, S., Song, W., Liu, J.: Sparse feature clustering network for unsupervised SAR image change detection. IEEE Trans. Geosci. Remote Sens. **60**, 1–13 (2022)
48. Zhang, X., Jiao, L., Liu, F., Bo, L., Gong, M.: Spectral clustering ensemble applied to SAR image segmentation. IEEE Trans. Geosci. Remote Sens. **46**(7), 2126–2136 (2008)

Towards Realistic Semi-supervised Learning

Mamshad Nayeem Rizve[(✉)], Navid Kardan, and Mubarak Shah

Center for Research in Computer Vision, UCF, Orlando, USA
{nayeemrizve,kardan}@knights.ucf.edu, shah@crcv.ucf.edu

Abstract. Deep learning is pushing the state-of-the-art in many computer vision applications. However, it relies on large annotated data repositories, and capturing the unconstrained nature of the real-world data is yet to be solved. Semi-supervised learning (SSL) complements the annotated training data with a large corpus of unlabeled data to reduce annotation cost. The standard SSL approach assumes unlabeled data are from the same distribution as annotated data. Recently, a more realistic SSL problem, called open-world SSL, is introduced, where the unannotated data might contain samples from unknown classes. In this paper, we propose a novel pseudo-label based approach to tackle SSL in open-world setting. At the core of our method, we utilize sample uncertainty and incorporate prior knowledge about class distribution to generate reliable class-distribution-aware pseudo-labels for unlabeled data belonging to both known and unknown classes. Our extensive experimentation showcases the effectiveness of our approach on several benchmark datasets, where it substantially outperforms the existing state-of-the-art on seven diverse datasets including CIFAR-100 ($\sim$17%), ImageNet-100 ($\sim$5%), and Tiny ImageNet ($\sim$9%). We also highlight the flexibility of our approach in solving novel class discovery task, demonstrate its stability in dealing with imbalanced data, and complement our approach with a technique to estimate the number of novel classes. Code: https://github.com/nayeemrizve/TRSSL

Keywords: Semi-supervised learning · Open-world · Uncertainty

1 Introduction

Deep learning systems have made tremendous progress in solving many challenging vision problems [1,11,20,24,25,53]. However, most of this progress has been made in controlled environments, which limits their application in real-world scenarios. For instance, in classification, we should know all the classes in advance. However, many real-world problems cannot be expressed with this constraint,

---

Supplementary Information The online version contains supplementary material available at https://doi.org/10.1007/978-3-031-19821-2_25.

where we constantly encounter new concepts while exploring an unconstrained environment. A practical learning model should be able to properly detect and handle new situations. Open-world problems [4,9,23,29,33,34,58] try to model this unconstrained nature of real-world data.

Despite abundance of real-world data, it is often required to annotate raw data before passing it to supervised models, which is quiet costly. One of the dominant approaches to reduce the cost of annotation is semi-supervised learning (SSL) [6,43,48,61,62], where the objective is to leverage a set of unlabeled data in conjunction with a limited labeled set to improve performance. Following [9], in this work, we consider the unlabeled set to possibly contain samples from unknown (novel) classes that are not present in the labeled set. This problem is called open-world SSL [9]. Here, the goal is to identify novel-class samples and classify them, as well as to improve known-class performance by utilizing unlabeled known-class samples.

At first sight, the major difficulty with open-world SSL might be related to breaking the closed-world assumption. In fact, it is common knowledge that presence of samples from novel classes deteriorates the performance of standard SSL methods drastically [14,50]. This leads to introduction of new approaches that mitigate this issue based on identifying, and subsequently reducing the effect of novel class samples to generalize SSL to more practical settings [14,21,68]. However, open-world SSL requires *identifying and assigning samples to novel classes*, which contrasts with this simpler objective of ignoring them. To the best of our knowledge ORCA [9] is the only prior work that proposes a solution for this challenging problem, where the authors also demonstrate that open-world SSL problem cannot be solved by simple extensions of existing SSL approaches.

Improving upon ORCA, this paper introduces a streamlined approach for open-world SSL problem, which does not require careful design choices for multiple objectives, and does not rely on feature initialization. Our approach substantially improves state-of-the-art performance on multiple datasets (Fig. 1). Furthermore, distinctly from previous work, our algorithm can naturally handle arbitrary class distributions such as imbalanced data. Finally, we propose a method to estimate the number of unknown classes for more practical applications.

For solving the open-world SSL problem, we employ an intuitive pseudo-labeling approach. Our pseudo-label generation process takes different

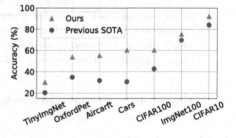

Fig. 1. Performance of our proposed method with respect to previous SOTA method on Tiny ImageNet, Oxford-IIIT Pet, FGVC-Aircraft, Stanford-Cars, CIFAR-100, ImageNet-100, and CIFAR-10 datasets respectively.

challenges associated with the open-world SSL problem—simultaneously classifying samples from both known and unknown classes, and handling arbitrary class distribution—into account. Furthermore, we incorporate sample uncertainty into pseudo-label learning to address the unreliable nature of generated pseudo-labels. We make two major technical contributions in this work: (1) we propose a novel pseudo-label generation method, which takes advantage of the prior knowledge about class distribution and generate pseudo-labels accordingly using Sinkhorn-Knopp algorithm [2,10,60,66]. Our proposed solution can take advantage of any arbitrary data distribution which includes imbalanced distributions. (2) we introduce a novel uncertainty-guided temperature scaling technique to address the unreliable nature of the generated pseudo-labels. Additionally, we propose a simple yet effective method for estimating the number of novel classes, allowing for a more realistic application of our method. Our extensive experimentation on four standard benchmark datasets and also three additional fine-grained datasets demonstrate that the proposed method significantly outperforms the existing works (Fig. 1). Finally, our experimentation with data imbalance (Sect. 4.3) signifies that the proposed method can work satisfactorily even when no prior knowledge is available about the underlying class distribution.

2   Related Works

Open-World Learning. To address the unconstrained nature of real-world data, multiple research directions have been explored. In this work, we refer to all these different approaches as open-world learning method. Open-set recognition (OSR) [27,45,58], open-world recognition (OWR) [4,7,29,65], out-of-distribution detection [31,32,44,45,67], and novel class discovery (NCD) [17,22,23,26,69] are some of the notable open-world learning approaches.

Open-set recognition methods aim to identify novel class samples during inference to avoid assigning them to one of the known/seen classes. One of the early works on OSR was proposed in [58], where a one-vs-all strategy was applied to prevent assigning novel class samples to known classes. [27] extends OSR to multi-class setup by using probabilistic modeling to adjust the classification boundary. Instead of designing robust models for OSR, ODIN [45] detects novel class samples (out-of-distribution) based on difference in output probabilities caused by changing the softmax temperature and adding small controlled perturbations to the inputs. Even though OSR is a related problem, the focus of this work is more general where our goal is to not only detect novel class samples but also to cluster them.

OWR methods such as [4] work in an incremental manner, where once the model determines instances from novel classes an oracle can provide class labels for unknown samples to incorporate them into the seen set. To incorporate new classes, [65] maintains a dynamic list of exemplar samples for each class, and unknown examples are detected by finding the similarity with these exemplars. Finally, authors in [29] propose contrastive clustering and energy based unknown sample detection for open-world object detection. The key difference between these methods and ours is that we do not rely on an oracle to learn novel classes.

NCD methods are most closely related to our task. The main objective of NCD methods is to cluster novel class samples in the unlabeled set. To this end, authors in [26] leverage the information available in the seen classes by training a pairwise similarity prediction network that they later apply to cluster novel class samples. Similar to their approach, a pairwise similarity task is solved to discover novel classes based on a novel rank statistics in [22]. Most NCD methods rely on multiple objective functions and require some sort of feature pretraining approach. This is addressed in [17] by utilizing multi-view pseudo-labeling and overclustering while only relying on cross-entropy loss. The main difference between NCD problem and our task is that we do not assume unlabeled data only includes novel class samples. Besides, in contrast to most of these methods, our proposed solution requires only one loss function and does not make architectural changes to treat seen and novel classes differently. Additionally, our extensive experimentation demonstrates that extension of these methods is not very effective for open-world SSL problem.

Semi-supervised Learning. Extensive research has been conducted on closed-world SSL [5,6,10,13,19,28,36,41,43,46,48,52,57,59,61,62]. The closed-world SSL methods achieve impressive performance on standard benchmark datasets. However, these methods assume that the unlabeled data only contains samples from seen classes, which is very restrictive. Moreover, recent works [14,50] suggest that presence of novel class samples deteriorates performance of SSL methods. Robust SSL methods [14,21,68] address this issue by filtering out or reweighting novel class samples. The realistic open-world SSL problem as proposed in [9] requires clustering the novel class samples which is not addressed by robust SSL methods. To the best of our knowledge, ORCA [9] is the only prior work that solves this challenging problem. ORCA achieves very promising performance in comparison to other novel class discovery or robust SSL based baselines. However, to solve this problem ORCA leverages self-supervised pretraining and multiple objective functions. In a concurrent work, [55] proposes a solution to open-world SSL that does not rely on feature pretraining. However, similar to ORCA, their approach relies on multiple objectives. In contrast, our proposed solution outperforms ORCA by a large margin without relying on either of them.

3   Method

Similar to standard closed-world SSL, the training data for open-world SSL problem consists of a labeled set, $\mathbb{D}_L$, and an unlabeled set, $\mathbb{D}_U$. The labeled set, $\mathbb{D}_L$ encompasses N_L labeled samples s.t. $\mathbb{D}_L = \left\{ \mathbf{x}_l^{(i)}, \mathbf{y}_l^{(i)} \right\}_{i=1}^{N_L}$, where $\mathbf{x}_l^{(i)}$ is an input and $\mathbf{y}_l^{(i)}$ is its corresponding label (in one-hot encoding) belonging to one of the $\mathbb{C}_L$ classes. On the other hand, the unlabeled set, $\mathbb{D}_U$, consists of N_U (in practice, $N_U \gg N_L$) unlabeled samples s.t. $\mathbb{D}_U = \left\{ \mathbf{x}_u^{(i)} \right\}_{i=1}^{N_U}$, where $\mathbf{x}_u^{(i)}$ is a sample without any label that belongs to one of the $\mathbb{C}_U$ classes. The primary distinction between the closed-world and open-world SSL formulation is that the closed-world SSL assumes $\mathbb{C}_L = \mathbb{C}_U$, whereas in open-world SSL $\mathbb{C}_L \subset \mathbb{C}_U$. We refer to $\mathbb{C}_U \setminus \mathbb{C}_L$, as novel classes, $\mathbb{C}_N$. Note that unlike previous works on novel class discovery problem [17,22,69], we do not need to know the number of novel classes, $|\mathbb{C}_N|$, in advance. During test time, the objective is to assign samples from novel classes to their corresponding novel class in $\mathbb{C}_N$, and to classify the samples from seen classes into one of the $|\mathbb{C}_L|$ classes.

In the following subsections, we first introduce our class-distribution-aware pseudo-label based training objective to classify the samples from seen classes, while attributing the samples from novel classes to their respective categories (Sect. 3.1). After that, we introduce uncertainty-guided temperature scaling to incorporate reliability of pseudo-labels into the learning process (Sect. 3.2) (Fig. 2).

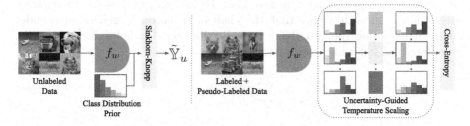

Fig. 2. *Training Overview:* **Left:** generating pseudo-labels. Our model generates pseudo-labels for the unlabeled samples using Sinkhorn-Knopp while taking class distribution prior into account. **Right:** reliable training with both labeled and unlabeled samples. We use the ground-truth labels and generated pseudo-labels to train in a supervised manner. To address the unreliable nature of pseudo-labels in open-world SSL, we apply uncertainty-guided temperature scaling (darker color refers to higher uncertainty). (Color figure online)

3.1 Class-Distribution-Aware Pseudo-labeling

To achieve the dual objective of open-world SSL problem, i.e., identifying samples from the seen classes and clustering the samples from novel classes, we design a single classification objective. To this end, we utilize a neural network, f_w, to map the input data $\mathbf{x}$ into the output space of class scores (logits), $\mathbf{z} \in \mathbb{R}^{|\mathbb{C}_L|+|\mathbb{C}_N|}$, s.t. $f_w : \mathbb{X} \to \mathbb{Z}$; here, $\mathbb{X}$ is the set of input data and $\mathbb{Z}$ is the set of output logits. In our setup, the first $|\mathbb{C}_L|$ entries of the class score vector (logits), $\mathbf{z}$, correspond to seen classes and the remaining $|\mathbb{C}_N|$ elements correspond to novel classes. Finally, we transform these logits to probability distribution, $\hat{\mathbf{y}}$, using softmax activation function: $\hat{\mathbf{y}}_j = \exp(\mathbf{z_j})/\sum_k \exp(\mathbf{z_k})$.

The neural network, f_w, can be trained using cross-entropy loss if the labels for all the input samples are available. However, in open-world SSL problem the samples in $\mathbb{D}_U$ lack label. To address this issue, pseudo-labels, $\tilde{\mathbf{y}}_u \in \hat{\mathbb{Y}}_u$, are generated for all unlabeled samples. After that, cross entropy loss is applied to train the model using the available ground-truth labels, $\mathbf{y}_l \in \mathbb{Y}_l$, and generated pseudo-labels. Here, we assume one-hot encoding for $\mathbf{y}_l$ and $\mathbb{Y}$ denotes the set of all labels, where $\mathbb{Y} = \mathbb{Y}_l \cup \tilde{\mathbb{Y}}_u$. Now, the cross-entropy loss is defined using,

$$\mathcal{L}_{ce} = -\frac{1}{N} \sum_{i=1}^{N} \sum_{j=1}^{C} \mathbf{y}_j^{(i)} \log \hat{\mathbf{y}}_j^{(i)}, \tag{1}$$

where, $C = |\mathbb{C}_L| + |\mathbb{C}_N|$ is total number of classes, $N = N_L + N_U$ is the total number of samples, $\mathbf{y} \in \mathbb{Y}$, and $\mathbf{y}_j^{(i)}$ is the jth element of the class label vector, $\mathbf{y}^{(i)}$, for training instance i.

Next, we discuss the class-distribution-aware pseudo-label generation process. Since pseudo-label generation process is inherently ill-posed, we can guide this process by injecting an inductive bias. To this end, we propose to generate pseudo-labels in such a way that the class distribution of generated pseudo-labels should follow the underlying class distribution of samples. More formally, we enforce the following constraint:

$$\forall j \sum_{i}^{N_U} \tilde{\mathbf{y}}_j^{(i)} = N_U^{C_j}, \tag{2}$$

where, $N_U^{C_j}$ is the number of samples in jth class.

One common strategy to satisfy this objective is to apply an entropy maximization term coupled with optimizing a pairwise similarity score objective [9,63]. However, this approach implicitly assumes that the classes are balanced and optimizing the pairwise objective requires a good set of initial features; besides, coordinating these two objectives requires careful design. This paper pursues a more streamlined approach by generating pseudo-labels such that they directly satisfy the constraints in Eq. 2. Fortunately, this constrained pseudo-label generation problem is inherently a transportation problem [8,30], where we want to assign unlabeled samples to one of the seen/novel classes based on output probabilities. Such an assignment can be captured with an assignment matrix, $\mathbf{A}$, which can be interpreted as (normalized) pseudo-labels. Following Cuturi's notation [15], every such assignment $\mathbf{A}$, called a transport matrix, that satisfies the constraint in Eq. 2 is a member of a transportation polytope, $\mathcal{A}$.

$$\mathcal{A} := \left\{ \mathbf{A} \in \mathbb{R}^{N_U \times C} | \forall j \sum \mathbf{A}_{:,j} = \frac{N_U^{C_j}}{N_U}, \forall i \sum \mathbf{A}_{i,:} = \frac{1}{N_U} \right\}. \tag{3}$$

Note that every transport matrix $\mathbf{A}$ is a joint probability, therefore, it is a normalized matrix. By considering the cross-entropy cost of assigning unlabeled samples based on model predictions to different classes, an optimal solution can be found within the transportation polytope $\mathcal{A}$. More formally, we solve $\min_{\mathbf{A} \in \mathcal{A}} -Tr(\mathbf{A}^T \log(\hat{\mathbf{Y}}_U / N_U))$ optimization problem, where $\hat{\mathbf{Y}}_U$ is the matrix of output probabilities generated by the model for the unlabeled samples. Unfortunately, enforcing the constraint described in Eq. 2 is non-trivial for novel classes since we do not know the specific order of novel classes. To address this issue, we need to solve a permutation problem while obtaining the optimal assignment matrix, $\mathbf{A}$. To this end, we introduce a permutation matrix $\mathbf{P}_\pi$ and reformulate the optimization problem as $\min_{\mathbf{A} \in \mathcal{A}} -Tr((\mathbf{A}\mathbf{P}_\pi)^T \log(\hat{\mathbf{Y}}_U/N_U))$. Here, the permutation matrix $\mathbf{P}_\pi$ reorders the columns of the assignment matrix. We estimate the permutation matrix $\mathbf{P}_\pi$ from the order of the marginal of output probabilities $\hat{\mathbf{Y}}_U$. This simple reordering ensures that per class constraint is aligned with the output probabilities. After determining the permutation, finding the optimal solution for $\mathbf{A}$ becomes an instance of the optimal transport problem. Hence, can be solved using Sinkhorn-Knopp algorithm. Cuturi [15] proposes a fast version of Sinkhorn-Knopp algorithm. In particular, [15] shows that a fast estimation of the optimal assignment can be obtained by:

$$\mathbf{A} = \mathrm{diag}(\mathbf{m})(\hat{\mathbf{Y}}_U/N_U)^\lambda \mathrm{diag}(\mathbf{n}), \tag{4}$$

where λ is a regularization term that controls the speed of convergence versus precision of the solution, vectors $\mathbf{m}$ and $\mathbf{n}$ are used for scaling $\hat{\mathbf{Y}}_U/N_U$ so that the transportation matrix $\mathbf{A}$ is also a probability matrix. This is an itereative procedure where $\mathbf{m}$ and $\mathbf{n}$ are updated according to the following rules:

$$\mathbf{m} \leftarrow [(\hat{\mathbf{Y}}_U/N_U)^\lambda \mathbf{n}]^{-1}, \mathbf{n} \leftarrow [\mathbf{m}^T(\hat{\mathbf{Y}}_U/N_U)^\lambda]^{-1}. \tag{5}$$

Another aspect of our pseudo-label generation is inducing perturbation invariant features. Generally learning invariant features is achieved by minimizing a consistency loss that minimizes the distance between the output representation of two transformed versions of the same image [6,57,64]. To achieve this, for the unlabeled data, given image $\mathbf{x}$, we generate two augmented versions of this image, $\mathbf{x}_{\tau_1} = \tau_1(\mathbf{x})$, and $\mathbf{x}_{\tau_2} = \tau_2(\mathbf{x})$, where $\tau_1(.)$, and $\tau_2(.)$ are two stochastic transformations. The generated pseudo-labels for these two augmented images are $\tilde{\mathbf{y}}_{\tau_1}$, and $\tilde{\mathbf{y}}_{\tau_2}$, respectively. To learn transformation invariant representation using cross-entropy loss, we treat $\tilde{\mathbf{y}}_{\tau_2}$ as the corresponding pseudo-label of $\mathbf{x}_{\tau_1}$ and vice versa. This cross pseudo-labeling encourages learning of perturbation invariant features without introducing a new loss function.

Finally, in its original formulation Sinkhorn-Knopp algorithm generates hard pseudo-labels [15]. However, recent literature [10] reports better performance by applying soft pseudo-labels. In our work we utilize a mixture of soft and hard pseudo-labels (mixed pseudo-labels), which we found to be beneficial (Sect. 4.3). To be specific, to encourage confident learning for novel classes, we generate hard pseudo-labels for unlabeled samples which are strongly assigned to novel classes. For the rest of the unlabeled samples, we use soft pseudo-labels.

3.2 Uncertainty-Guided Temperature Scaling

Since we generate pseudo-labels by relying on the confidence scores of the network, final performance is affected by their reliability. We can capture the reliability of prediction confidences by measuring their uncertainty. One simple way to do that in the standard neural networks is to perform Monte Carlo sampling in the network parameter space [18] or in the input space [3,54]. Since we do not want to modify the network parameters, we decide to perform stochastic sampling in input space. To this end, we apply stochastic transformations on input data and estimate the sample uncertainty, u(.), by calculating the variance over the applied stochastic transformations [16,49,54]:

$$u(\mathbf{x}) = \text{Var}(\hat{\mathbf{y}}) = \frac{1}{T} \sum_{i=1}^{T} (\hat{\mathbf{y}}_{\tau_i} - \text{E}(\hat{\mathbf{y}}))^2, \tag{6}$$

where, $\hat{\mathbf{y}}_{\tau_i} = \text{Softmax}(f_w(\tau_i(\mathbf{x})))$, $\tau_i(.)$ represents a stochastic transformation applied to the input $\mathbf{x}$, and $\text{E}(\hat{\mathbf{y}}) = \frac{1}{T} \sum_{i=1}^{T} \hat{\mathbf{y}}_{\tau_i}$.

Next, we want to incorporate this uncertainty information into our training process. One strategy to achieve this is to select more reliable pseudo-labels by filtering out unreliable samples based on their uncertainty score [54]. However, two potential drawbacks of this approach are introducing a new hyperparameter and discarding a portion of available data. Therefore, to tackle both of these drawbacks, we introduce uncertainty-guided temperature scaling.

Recall that in our training we use softmax probabilities for cross-entropy loss. Temperature scaling is a strategy to modify the softness of the output probability distribution. In standard softmax probability computation, the temperature value is set to 1. A higher value of temperature increases the entropy or uncertainty of the softmax probability, whereas a lower value makes it more certain. Existing works [9,12,17,35] apply a fixed temperature value (whether high or low) as a hyperparameter. In contrast, we propose to use a different temperature for each sample during the course of training which is influenced by the certainty of its pseudo-label. The main idea is that if the network is certain about its prediction on a particular sample we make this prediction more confident and vice versa. Based on this idea we modify the softmax probability computation in the following way:

$$\hat{\mathbf{y}}_j^{(i)} = \frac{\exp(\mathbf{z}_j^{(i)}/u(\mathbf{x}^{(i)}))}{\sum_k \exp(\mathbf{z}_k^{(i)}/u(\mathbf{x}^{(i)}))}, \tag{7}$$

where $u(\mathbf{x}^{(i)})$ is the uncertainty of sample $\mathbf{x}^{(i)}$ that is obtained from Eq. 6.

In practice, the sample uncertainties calculated by Eq. 6 have low magnitudes. Therefore, we normalize these uncertainty values across the entire dataset before plugging them into Eq. 7.

Our training algorithm is provided in supplementary materials.

4   Experiments and Results

4.1   Experimental Setup

In the following, we describe our experimental setup including dataset descriptions, implementation details, evaluation details, and specifics of our baselines.

Datasets. We conduct experiments on four commonly used computer vision benchmark datasets: CIFAR-10 [38], CIFAR-100 [39], ImageNet-100 [56] and Tiny ImageNet [42]. The datasets are selected in increasing order of difficulty based on the number of classes. We also evaluate our method on three drastically different fine-grained classification datasets: Oxford-IIIT Pet [51], FGVC-Aircraft [47], and Stanford-Cars [37]. A detailed description of these datasets is provided in supplementary materials. For all the datasets, we use the first 50% classes as seen and the remaining 50% classes as novel. We use 10% data from the seen classes as the labeled set and use the remaining 90% data, along with the samples from novel classes, as unlabeled set for our experiments on standard benchmark datasets. For fine-grained datasets, we use 50% data from seen classes as labeled. Additional results with other data percentage are provided in the supplementary materials.

Implementation Details. Following ORCA [9], for a fair comparison, we use ResNet-50 [25] for ImageNet-100 experiments and ResNet-18 [25] for all the other experiments. We apply l_2 normalization to the weights of the last linear layer. For CIFAR-10, CIFAR-100, and Tiny ImageNet experiments, we train our model for 200 epochs. For the other datasets, we train these model for 100 epochs. We use a batchsize of 256 for all of our experiments except ImageNet-100 where similar to [9] we use a batchsize of 512. For optimizing the network parameters, we use SGD optimizer with momentum. We use a cosine annealing based learning rate scheduler accompanied by a linear warmup, where we set the base learning rate to 0.1 and set the warmup length to 10 epochs. For network parameters, we set the weight decay to 1e-4. Following [10], we set the value of λ to 0.05 and perform 3 iterations for pseudo-label generation using the Sinkhorn-Knopp algorithm. Additional implementation details are provided in supplementary materials.

Evaluation Details. For evaluation, we report standard classification accuracy on seen classes. On novel classes, we report clustering accuracy following [9,17, 22,23]. To this end, we consider the class prediction as cluster ID. Next, we use the Hungarian algorithm [40] to match cluster IDs with ground-truth classes. Once the matches are obtained, we calculate classification accuracy with the corresponding cluster IDs. Besides, if a novel class sample gets assigned to one of the seen classes, we consider that as a misclassified prediction and remove that sample before matching the cluster IDs with ground-truth class labels. We also report clustering accuracy for all the classes.

Comparison Details. We compare the performance of our method on CIFAR-10, CIFAR-100, and ImageNet-100 datasets with the results reported in [9]. The remaining four datasets do not have any publicly available evaluation for open-world SSL problem. Therefore, we extend three recent novel class discovery methods [17,22,23] to open-world SSL setting using publicly available codebase. For [22,23], we extend the unlabeled head to include logits for seen classes by following [9]. However, neither of these methods has any explicit classification loss for seen classes in the unlabeled head. Therefore, there is no straightforward way to map the seen class samples into their corresponding class logits. For reporting scores on seen classes, we use the Hungarian algorithm for these two methods. In [17], pseudo-labels are generated for the novel class samples on the unlabeled head. To make it compatible with open-world SSL setting, we generate pseudo-labels from the concatenated prediction of the labeled and unlabeled heads during training. Since this method has explicit classification loss, we report standard classification accuracy on seen classes.

4.2   Main Results

Standard Benchmark Datasets. We compare our method with existing literature on open-world SSL problem [9] and other related approaches that have been modified for this problem in Table 1 and 2. On CIFAR-10 we observe that our proposed method outperforms ORCA [9] on both seen and novel classes by 12.1% and 4.1%, respectively. Our proposed method also outperforms other novel class discovery methods [17,22,23] by a large margin. The same trend is observed for FixMatch [61] (a state-of-the-art closed-world SSL method). Finally, our proposed method outperforms DS^{3}L [21], a popular robust SSL method. Interestingly, improvement of our proposed method is more prominent on CIFAR-100 dataset, which is more challenging because of the higher number of classes. On CIFAR-100 dataset, our proposed method outperforms ORCA by around 20% on novel classes and 16% on seen classes. Noticeably, we observe that UNO [17] marginally outperforms ORCA on this dataset. However, our proposed method outperforms UNO by a significant margin. Next, we evaluate on two variants of ImageNet: ImageNet-100, and Tiny ImageNet. We observe a similar trend on ImageNet-100 dataset, where we observe an overall improvement of 5.7% over ORCA. After that, we conduct experiments on challenging Tiny ImageNet dataset. This dataset is more challenging than CIFAR-100 and ImageNet-100 dataset since it has 200 classes. Besides, without transfer learning, even the performance of supervised methods is relatively low on this dataset. Overall, our proposed method outperforms the second best method, UNO, by 9.9%, which is almost 50% relative improvement on this challenging dataset. The results on

Table 1. Average accuracy on the **CIFAR-10**, **CIFAR-100**, and **ImageNet-100** datasets with 50% classes as seen and 50% classes as novel. The results are averaged over three independent runs.

Method	CIFAR-10			CIFAR-100			ImageNet-100		
	Seen	Novel	All	Seen	Novel	All	Seen	Novel	All
FixMatch [61]	64.3	49.4	47.3	30.9	18.5	15.3	60.9	33.7	30.2
DS^{3}L [21]	70.5	46.6	43.5	33.7	15.8	15.1	64.3	28.1	25.9
DTC [23]	42.7	31.8	32.4	22.1	10.5	13.7	24.5	17.8	19.3
RankStats [22]	71.4	63.9	66.7	20.4	16.7	17.8	41.2	26.8	37.4
UNO [17]	86.5	71.2	78.9	53.7	33.6	42.7	66.0	42.2	53.3
ORCA [9]	82.8	85.5	84.1	52.5	31.8	38.6	83.9	60.5	69.7
Ours	94.9	89.6	92.2	68.5	52.1	60.3	82.6	67.8	75.4

Table 2. Average accuracy on the **Tiny ImageNet**, **Oxford-IIIT Pet**, **FGVC-Aircraft**, and **Stanford-Cars** datasets with 50% classes as seen and 50% classes as novel. The results are averaged over three independent runs.

Method	Tiny ImageNet			Oxford-IIIT Pet			FGVC-Aircraft			Stanford-Cars		
	Seen	Novel	All	Seen	Novel	All	Seen	Novel	All	Seen	Novel	All
DTC [23]	13.5	12.7	11.5	20.7	16.0	13.5	16.3	16.5	11.8	12.3	10.0	7.7
RankStats [22]	9.6	8.9	6.4	12.6	11.9	11.1	13.4	13.6	11.1	10.4	9.1	6.6
UNO [17]	28.4	14.4	20.4	49.8	22.7	34.9	44.4	24.7	31.8	49.0	15.7	30.7
Ours	39.5	20.5	30.3	70.9	36.1	53.9	69.5	41.2	55.4	83.5	37.1	60.4

these four datasets demonstrate that *the proposed method not only outperforms previous methods but also excels in scenarios where the number of classes is significantly higher which is always a challenge for clustering methods.*

Fine-Grained Datasets. Finally, we evaluate our method on three fine-grained classification datasets with different number of classes. This evaluation is particularly important since fine-grained classification captures challenges associated with many real-world applications. We hypothesize that, fine-grained classification is a harder problem for open-world semi-supervised learning since the novel classes are visually similar to seen classes. In these experiments we compare the performance of the proposed method with three novel class discovery methods, DTC [23], RankStat [22], and UNO [17]. We report our results in Table 2. Once again our method outperforms all three methods on these fine-grained classification datasets by a significant margin. To be specific, in overall, the proposed method achieves 50–100% relative improvement compared to the second best method UNO. Together, our previous results combined with these fine-grained results, showcase the efficacy of our proposed method and indicate a wider application for more practical settings.

Table 3. Ablataion study on **CIFAR-10**, **CIFAR-100**, and **Tiny ImageNet** datasets with 50% classes as seen and 50% classes as novel. Here, **UTS** refers to uncertainty-guided temperature scaling, **MPL** refers to mixed pseudo-labeling, and **Oracle** refers to having prior knowledge about the number of novel classes.

UTS	MPL	Oracle	CIFAR-10			CIFAR-100			Tiny ImageNet		
			Seen	Novel	All	Seen	Novel	All	Seen	Novel	All
✗	✗	✓	96.0	84.4	90.2	69.2	46.5	57.9	38.1	17.5	28.1
✓	✗	✓	95.0	86.6	90.8	69.4	46.6	57.9	41.3	16.0	29.2
✗	✓	✓	95.8	87.9	91.9	66.9	48.1	57.5	34.9	21.0	28.2
✓	✓	✗	94.9	89.6	92.2	65.5	44.2	54.8	40.3	19.3	30.2
✓	✓	✓	94.9	89.6	92.2	68.5	52.1	60.3	39.5	20.5	30.3

4.3   Ablation and Analysis

To investigate the impact of different components, we conduct extensive ablation study on CIFAR-10, CIFAR-100, and Tiny ImageNet datasets. We report the results in Table 3. The first row depicts the performance of our proposed method without uncertainty-guided temperature scaling, and mixed pseudo-labeling. Here, we can see that our proposed method is able to achieve reasonable performance solely based on distribution-aware pseudo-labels. Next, we investigate the impact of removing mixed pseudo-labeling. We observe that the performance on novel classes drops considerably; 3% on CIFAR-10, 5.5% on CIFAR-100, and 4.5% on the Tiny ImageNet dataset. This shows that mixed pseudo-labeling encourages confident learning for novel classes and is a crucial component of our method. After that, we investigate the effect of uncertainty-guided temperature scaling. We observe that the overall performance on all three datasets drops from 0.3%-2.8%. We also observe that the performance degradation is more severe on harder datasets (6.9% relative degradation on Tiny ImageNet compared to 4.6% on CIFAR-100). Next, we report scores with the estimated number of novel classes (Sect. 4.3) for completeness (without Oracle in Table 3). We observe that even with the estimated number of novel classes, our method greatly outperforms ORCA and UNO. Our ablation study as a whole demonstrates that every component of our proposed method is crucial and makes a noticeable contribution to the final performance while achieving their designated goal.

Table 4. Estimation of the number of novel classes. The table shows the estimated number of classes vs the actual number of classes in different datasets.

Dataset	GT	Estimated	Error
CIFAR-10	10	10	0%
CIFAR-100	100	117	17%
ImageNet-100	100	139	39%
Tiny ImageNet	200	192	−4%

Estimating Number of Novel Classes. A realistic semi-supervised learning system should make minimal assumption about the nature of the problem. For open-world SSL problem, determining the number of novel classes is a crucial step since without explicit determination of the number of classes either a method will have to assume that the number of novel classes is known in advance or set an upper limit for the number of novel classes. A more practical approach is to estimate the number of unkown classes. Therefore, this work proposes a solution to explicitly estimate the number of novel classes. To this end, we leverage self-supervised features from SimCLR [12].

To estimate the number of novel classes, we perform k-means clustering on SimCLR features with different values of k. We determine the optimal k by evaluating the performance of generated clusters on the labeled samples. We empirically find that this approach generally underestimates the number of novel classes. This is to be expected since clustering

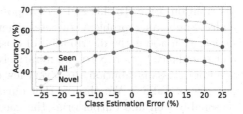

Fig. 3. Accuracy as a function of class estimation error on **CIFAR-100** dataset.

accuracy usually decreases with increasing number of clusters due to assignment of labeled samples to unknown clusters. To mitigate this issue, we perform a sample reassignment technique, where we reallocate the labeled samples assigned to unknown clusters (misclassified samples) to their nearest labeled clusters based on their distance from the cluster centers. Additional details are provided in the supplementary materials.

We report the performance of our estimation method in Table 4. We observe that on all four datasets our proposed estimation method leads to reasonable performance. In addition to this, we conduct a series of experiments on CIFAR-100 dataset to determine the sensitivity of the proposed method to the novel class estimation error. The results are reported in Fig. 3 where we observe that our proposed method performs reasonably well over a wide range of estimation error. Please note that even with 25% overestimation and underestimation errors, our proposed method outperforms ORCA and UNO (Table 1). These results reaffirms the practicality of the proposed solution.

Data Imbalance. Even though most standard benchmark vision datasets are class balanced, in real-world this is hardly the case. Instead, real-world data often demonstrates long-tailed distribution. Since our proposed method can take any arbitrary distribution into account for generating pseudo-labels, it can naturally take imbalance into account. To demonstrate the effectiveness of our proposed method on imbalanced data, we conduct experiments on CIFAR-100 dataset and report the results in Table 5. We observe that for both imbalance factors (exponential) of 10 and 20, our proposed method with imbalance class distribution prior improves over the balanced prior baseline by 1.1% and 3.1%, respectively. We also conduct another set of experiments where we assume no access to class

Table 5. Performance on **CIFAR-100** dataset with different imabalance factors (**IF**) with 50% classes as seen and 50% classes as novel.

Method	IF = 10			IF = 20		
	Seen	Novel	All	Seen	Novel	All
Balanced class distribution Prior	48.4	28.6	38.9	44.4	22.9	33.8
Imbalanced class distribution Prior	50.5	30.8	41.0	48.8	24.6	36.9
Estimated class distribution Prior	50.2	31.3	41.3	44.2	24.0	35.3

distribution prior. To this end, we propose a simple extension of our method to address imbalance problem. In cases where we do not have access to the prior information about the distribution of classes, to train our model, we start with a class-balanced prior. Next, we iteratively update our prior based on the latest posterior class distribution after every few epochs. The results are reported in the last row of Table 5. We observe that our simple estimation technique performs reasonably well and outperforms the class-balanced baseline with a noticeable margin. In summary, these experiments validate that our proposed method can effectively take advantage of underlying data distribution and work reasonably well even when we do not have access to the class distribution prior.

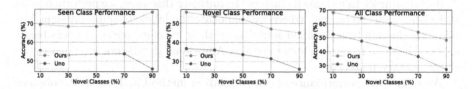

Fig. 4. Accuracy on seen (left), novel (middle), and all classes (right), as a function of different percentage of novel classes on the **CIFAR-100** dataset.

Different Percentage of Novel Classes. In all of our experiments, we consider 50% classes as seen and the remaining 50% as novel. To further investigate how our method performs under different conditions, we vary percentages of novel classes. We conduct this experiment on CIFAR-100 dataset. The results are presented in Fig. 4, where we vary the number of novel classes from 10% to 90%. For this analysis, we compare the performance with UNO. The left figure in Fig. 4 shows that our performance on seen classes remains relatively the same as we increase the percentage of novel classes. Furthermore, we observe that our seen class accuracy increases considerably when the percentage of novel classes is very high (90%) which is to be expected since this is an easier classification task for seen classes. However, for UNO, we notice a significant performance drop as the number of novel classes increases which shows that UNO is not sufficiently stable for this challenging setup. On novel classes (Fig. 4-middle), as we expect, we observe a steady drops in performance as the number of novel classes increase. However, as depicted in this graph, even at a very high novel class ratio, our proposed method can successfully provide a very good performance. Note that, we do not include ORCA in this experiment since their code is not publicly available. However, a similar analysis for ORCA is available in their supplementary materials with 50% labeled data. We observe that our novel class performance is noticeably higher than ORCA even though we only employ 10% labeled data. Finally, in Fig. 4-right we observe that the overall performance degrades predictably as we increase the percentage of novel classes.

Novel Class Discovery. In this work, we propose a general solution for open-world SSL problem which can be easily modified for the novel class discovery

Table 6. Performance on novel class discovery task on **CIFAR-100** dataset with 50% classes as seen and 50% classes as novel.

Method	Novel
k-means	28.3
DTC [23]	35.9
RankStats [22]	39.2
RankStats+ [22]	44.1
UNO [17]	52.9
Ours	57.5

problem, where the principal assumption is that the unlabeled data contains only novel class samples. In this set of experiments we apply our proposed method on the novel class discovery task by generating pseudo-labels only for novel classes. We do not make any other modification to the original method for this task. The findings from these experiments are reported in Table 6. We conduct experiments on CIFAR-100-50, i.e., 50 classes are set as novel. For comparison, we use the results reported in UNO [17]. To the best of our knowledge, UNO reports the best scores for this particular experimental setup. Table 6 demonstrates that the porposed method outperforms k-means, DTC [23], RankStats [22], and RankStats+ by a significant margin. Importantly, our method also outperforms the current state-of-the-art method for novel class discovery, UNO, by 4.6%. Interestingly, this experiment demonstrates that *our proposed method is a versatile solution which can be readily applied to novel class discovery problem.*

5   Conclusion

In this work, we propose a practical method for open-world SSL problem. Our proposed method generates pseudo-labels according to class distribution prior to solve open-world SSL problem in realistic settings with arbitrary class distributions. We extend our method to handle practical scenarios where neither the number of unkown classes nor the class distribution prior is available. Furthermore, we introduce uncertainty-guided temperature scaling to improve the reliability of pseudo-label learning. Our extensive experiments on seven diverse datasets demonstrate the effectiveness of our approach, where it significantly improves the state-of-the-art. Finally, we show that our method can be readily applied to novel class discovery problem to outperform the existing solutions.

References

1. Anderson, P., et al.: Bottom-up and top-down attention for image captioning and visual question answering. In: Proceedings of the IEEE Conference on Computer Vision and Pattern Recognition (CVPR), June 2018
2. Asano, Y., Patrick, M., Rupprecht, C., Vedaldi, A.: Labelling unlabelled videos from scratch with multi-modal self-supervision. In: Advances in Neural Information Processing Systems, vol. 33, pp. 4660–4671 (2020)
3. Ayhan, M.S., Berens, P.: Test-time data augmentation for estimation of heteroscedastic aleatoric uncertainty in deep neural networks. In: International Conference on Medical Imaging with Deep Learning (2018)
4. Bendale, A., Boult, T.: Towards open world recognition. In: Proceedings of the IEEE Conference on Computer Vision and Pattern Recognition, pp. 1893–1902 (2015)
5. Berthelot, D., et al.: ReMixMatch: semi-supervised learning with distribution matching and augmentation anchoring. In: International Conference on Learning Representations (2020)
6. Berthelot, D., Carlini, N., Goodfellow, I., Papernot, N., Oliver, A., Raffel, C.A.: MixMatch: a holistic approach to semi-supervised learning. In: Advances in Neural Information Processing Systems, vol. 32, pp. 5049–5059. Curran Associates, Inc. (2019)
7. Boult, T.E., Cruz, S., Dhamija, A.R., Gunther, M., Henrydoss, J., Scheirer, W.J.: Learning and the unknown: surveying steps toward open world recognition. In: Proceedings of the AAAI Conference on Artificial Intelligence, vol. 33, pp. 9801–9807 (2019)
8. Brenier, Y.: D'ecomposition polaire et r'earrangement monotone des champs de vecteurs. CR Acad. Sci. Paris Sér. I Math. **305**, 805–808 (1987)
9. Cao, K., Brbic, M., Leskovec, J.: Open-world semi-supervised learning. In: International Conference on Learning Representations (2022). https://openreview.net/forum?id=O-r8LOR-CCA
10. Caron, M., Misra, I., Mairal, J., Goyal, P., Bojanowski, P., Joulin, A.: Unsupervised learning of visual features by contrasting cluster assignments. arXiv preprint arXiv:2006.09882 (2020)
11. Chen, L.-C., Zhu, Y., Papandreou, G., Schroff, F., Adam, H.: Encoder-decoder with atrous separable convolution for semantic image segmentation. In: Ferrari, V., Hebert, M., Sminchisescu, C., Weiss, Y. (eds.) ECCV 2018. LNCS, vol. 11211, pp. 833–851. Springer, Cham (2018). https://doi.org/10.1007/978-3-030-01234-2_49
12. Chen, T., Kornblith, S., Norouzi, M., Hinton, G.: A simple framework for contrastive learning of visual representations. arXiv preprint arXiv:2002.05709 (2020)
13. Chen, T., Kornblith, S., Swersky, K., Norouzi, M., Hinton, G.E.: Big self-supervised models are strong semi-supervised learners. In: Advances in Neural Information Processing Systems, vol. 33 (2020)
14. Chen, Y., Zhu, X., Li, W., Gong, S.: Semi-supervised learning under class distribution mismatch. In: Proceedings of the AAAI Conference on Artificial Intelligence, vol. 34, pp. 3569–3576 (2020)
15. Cuturi, M.: Sinkhorn distances: lightspeed computation of optimal transport. In: Advances in Neural Information Processing Systems, vol. 26, pp. 2292–2300 (2013)
16. Feinman, R., Curtin, R.R., Shintre, S., Gardner, A.B.: Detecting adversarial samples from artifacts. arXiv preprint arXiv:1703.00410 (2017)

17. Fini, E., Sangineto, E., Lathuilière, S., Zhong, Z., Nabi, M., Ricci, E.: A unified objective for novel class discovery. In: Proceedings of the IEEE/CVF International Conference on Computer Vision, pp. 9284–9292 (2021)
18. Gal, Y., Ghahramani, Z.: Dropout as a Bayesian approximation: representing model uncertainty in deep learning. In: International Conference on Machine Learning, pp. 1050–1059. PMLR (2016)
19. Gammerman, A., Vovk, V., Vapnik, V.: Learning by transduction. In: Proceedings of the Fourteenth Conference on Uncertainty in Artificial Intelligence, UAI 1998, pp. 148–155. Morgan Kaufmann Publishers Inc., San Francisco (1998)
20. Girshick, R.: Fast R-CNN. In: Proceedings of the IEEE International Conference on Computer Vision, pp. 1440–1448 (2015)
21. Guo, L.Z., Zhang, Z.Y., Jiang, Y., Li, Y.F., Zhou, Z.H.: Safe deep semi-supervised learning for unseen-class unlabeled data. In: International Conference on Machine Learning, pp. 3897–3906. PMLR (2020)
22. Han, K., Rebuffi, S.A., Ehrhardt, S., Vedaldi, A., Zisserman, A.: Automatically discovering and learning new visual categories with ranking statistics. In: International Conference on Learning Representations (2020)
23. Han, K., Vedaldi, A., Zisserman, A.: Learning to discover novel visual categories via deep transfer clustering. In: Proceedings of the IEEE/CVF International Conference on Computer Vision, pp. 8401–8409 (2019)
24. He, K., Gkioxari, G., Dollár, P., Girshick, R.: Mask R-CNN. In: Proceedings of the IEEE International Conference on Computer Vision, pp. 2961–2969 (2017)
25. He, K., Zhang, X., Ren, S., Sun, J.: Deep residual learning for image recognition. In: Proceedings of the IEEE Conference on Computer Vision and Pattern Recognition, pp. 770–778 (2016)
26. Hsu, Y.C., Lv, Z., Kira, Z.: Learning to cluster in order to transfer across domains and tasks. In: International Conference on Learning Representations (2018). https://openreview.net/forum?id=ByRWCqvT-
27. Jain, L.P., Scheirer, W.J., Boult, T.E.: Multi-class Open set recognition using probability of inclusion. In: Fleet, D., Pajdla, T., Schiele, B., Tuytelaars, T. (eds.) ECCV 2014. LNCS, vol. 8691, pp. 393–409. Springer, Cham (2014). https://doi.org/10.1007/978-3-319-10578-9_26
28. Joachims, T.: Transductive inference for text classification using support vector machines. In: ICML, vol. 99, pp. 200–209 (1999)
29. Joseph, K., Khan, S., Khan, F.S., Balasubramanian, V.N.: Towards open world object detection. In: Proceedings of the IEEE/CVF Conference on Computer Vision and Pattern Recognition, pp. 5830–5840 (2021)
30. Kantorovich, L.: On translation of mass. In: Dokl. AN SSSR, vol. 37, p. 20 (1942)
31. Kardan, N., Shah, M., Hill, M.: Self-joint supervised learning. In: International Conference on Learning Representations (2021)
32. Kardan, N., Sharma, A., Stanley, K.O.: Towards consistent predictive confidence through fitted ensembles. In: 2021 International Joint Conference on Neural Networks (IJCNN), pp. 1–9. IEEE (2021)
33. Kardan, N., Stanley, K.O.: Fitted learning: models with awareness of their limits. arXiv preprint arXiv:1609.02226 (2016)
34. Kardan, N., Stanley, K.O.: Mitigating fooling with competitive overcomplete output layer neural networks. In: 2017 International Joint Conference on Neural Networks (IJCNN), pp. 518–525. IEEE (2017)
35. Khosla, P., et al.: Supervised contrastive learning. arXiv preprint arXiv:2004.11362 (2020)

36. Kingma, D.P., Mohamed, S., Rezende, D.J., Welling, M.: Semi-supervised learning with deep generative models. In: Advances in Neural Information Processing Systems, pp. 3581–3589 (2014)
37. Krause, J., Stark, M., Deng, J., Fei-Fei, L.: 3D object representations for fine-grained categorization. In: 4th International IEEE Workshop on 3D Representation and Recognition (3DRR 2013), Sydney, Australia (2013)
38. Krizhevsky, A., Nair, V., Hinton, G.: CIFAR-10 (Canadian Institute for Advanced Research)
39. Krizhevsky, A., Nair, V., Hinton, G.: CIFAR-100 (Canadian Institute for Advanced Research)
40. Kuhn, H.W.: The Hungarian method for the assignment problem. Naval Res. Logistics Q. **2**(1–2), 83–97 (1955)
41. Laine, S., Aila, T.: Temporal ensembling for semi-supervised learning. In: ICLR (Poster) (2017). OpenReview.net
42. Le, Y., Yang, X.: Tiny ImageNet visual recognition challenge. CS 231N **7**(7), 3 (2015)
43. Lee, D.H.: Pseudo-label: the simple and efficient semi-supervised learning method for deep neural networks (2013)
44. Lee, K., Lee, K., Lee, H., Shin, J.: A simple unified framework for detecting out-of-distribution samples and adversarial attacks. In: Advances in Neural Information Processing Systems, vol. 31 (2018)
45. Liang, S., Li, Y., Srikant, R.: Enhancing the reliability of out-of-distribution image detection in neural networks. arXiv preprint arXiv:1706.02690 (2017)
46. Liu, B., Wu, Z., Hu, H., Lin, S.: Deep metric transfer for label propagation with limited annotated data. In: Proceedings of the IEEE International Conference on Computer Vision Workshops (2019)
47. Maji, S., Kannala, J., Rahtu, E., Blaschko, M., Vedaldi, A.: Fine-grained visual classification of aircraft. Technical report (2013)
48. Miyato, T., Maeda, S.-I., Koyama, M., Ishii, S.: Virtual adversarial training: a regularization method for supervised and semi-supervised learning. IEEE Trans. Pattern Anal. Mach. Intell. **41**, 1979–1993 (2018)
49. Mukherjee, S., Awadallah, A.: Uncertainty-aware self-training for few-shot text classification. In: Larochelle, H., Ranzato, M., Hadsell, R., Balcan, M.F., Lin, H. (eds.) Advances in Neural Information Processing Systems, vol. 33, pp. 21199–21212. Curran Associates, Inc. (2020). https://proceedings.neurips.cc/paper/2020/file/f23d125da1e29e34c552f448610ff25f-Paper.pdf
50. Oliver, A., Odena, A., Raffel, C., Cubuk, E.D., Goodfellow, I.J.: Realistic evaluation of deep semi-supervised learning algorithms. arXiv preprint arXiv:1804.09170 (2018)
51. Parkhi, O.M., Vedaldi, A., Zisserman, A., Jawahar, C.V.: Cats and dogs. In: IEEE Conference on Computer Vision and Pattern Recognition (2012)
52. Pu, Y., et al.: Variational autoencoder for deep learning of images, labels and captions. In: Advances in Neural Information Processing Systems, pp. 2352–2360 (2016)
53. Qi, C.R., Su, H., Mo, K., Guibas, L.J.: PointNet: deep learning on point sets for 3D classification and segmentation. In: Proceedings of the IEEE Conference on Computer Vision and Pattern Recognition (CVPR), July 2017
54. Rizve, M.N., Duarte, K., Rawat, Y.S., Shah, M.: In defense of pseudo-labeling: an uncertainty-aware pseudo-label selection framework for semi-supervised learning. In: International Conference on Learning Representations (2021). https://openreview.net/forum?id=-ODN6SbiUU

55. Rizve, M.N., Kardan, N., Khan, S., Khan, F.S., Shah, M.: Openldn: Learning to discover novel classes for open-world semi-supervised learning. In: Farinella, T. (ed.) ECCV 2022, LNCS 13691, pp. 382–401. Springer, Heidelberg (2022)

56. Russakovsky, O., et al.: ImageNet large scale visual recognition challenge. Int. J. Comput. Vis. **115**(3), 211–252 (2015)

57. Sajjadi, M., Javanmardi, M., Tasdizen, T.: Regularization with stochastic transformations and perturbations for deep semi-supervised learning. In: Lee, D.D., Sugiyama, M., Luxburg, U.V., Guyon, I., Garnett, R. (eds.) Advances in Neural Information Processing Systems, vol. 29, pp. 1163–1171. Curran Associates, Inc. (2016)

58. Scheirer, W.J., de Rezende Rocha, A., Sapkota, A., Boult, T.E.: Toward open set recognition. IEEE Trans. Pattern Anal. Mach. Intell. **35**(7), 1757–1772 (2012)

59. Shi, W., Gong, Y., Ding, C., Ma, Z., Tao, X., Zheng, N.: Transductive semi-supervised deep learning using min-max features. In: Ferrari, V., Hebert, M., Sminchisescu, C., Weiss, Y. (eds.) ECCV 2018. LNCS, vol. 11209, pp. 311–327. Springer, Cham (2018). https://doi.org/10.1007/978-3-030-01228-1_19

60. Sinkhorn, R., Knopp, P.: Concerning nonnegative matrices and doubly stochastic matrices. Pac. J. Math. **21**(2), 343–348 (1967)

61. Sohn, K., et al.: FixMatch: simplifying semi-supervised learning with consistency and confidence. arXiv preprint arXiv:2001.07685 (2020)

62. Tarvainen, A., Valpola, H.: Mean teachers are better role models: weight-averaged consistency targets improve semi-supervised deep learning results. In: Guyon, I., et al. (eds.) Advances in Neural Information Processing Systems, vol. 30, pp. 1195–1204. Curran Associates, Inc. (2017)

63. Van Gansbeke, W., Vandenhende, S., Georgoulis, S., Proesmans, M., Van Gool, L.: SCAN: Learning to classify images without labels. In: Vedaldi, A., Bischof, H., Brox, T., Frahm, J.-M. (eds.) ECCV 2020. LNCS, vol. 12355, pp. 268–285. Springer, Cham (2020). https://doi.org/10.1007/978-3-030-58607-2_16

64. Verma, V., Lamb, A., Kannala, J., Bengio, Y., Lopez-Paz, D.: Interpolation consistency training for semi-supervised learning. In: IJCAI (2019)

65. Xu, H., Liu, B., Shu, L., Yu, P.: Open-world learning and application to product classification. In: The World Wide Web Conference, pp. 3413–3419 (2019)

66. Asano, Y.M., Rupprecht, C., Vedaldi, A.: Self-labelling via simultaneous clustering and representation learning. In: International Conference on Learning Representations (2020). https://openreview.net/forum?id=Hyx-jyBFPr

67. Zaeemzadeh, A., Bisagno, N., Sambugaro, Z., Conci, N., Rahnavard, N., Shah, M.: Out-of-distribution detection using union of 1-dimensional subspaces. In: Proceedings of the IEEE/CVF Conference on Computer Vision and Pattern Recognition, pp. 9452–9461 (2021)

68. Zhao, X., Krishnateja, K., Iyer, R., Chen, F.: Robust semi-supervised learning with out of distribution data. arXiv preprint arXiv:2010.03658 (2020)

69. Zhong, Z., Zhu, L., Luo, Z., Li, S., Yang, Y., Sebe, N.: OpenMix: reviving known knowledge for discovering novel visual categories in an open world. In: Proceedings of the IEEE/CVF Conference on Computer Vision and Pattern Recognition (CVPR), pp. 9462–9470, June 2021

Masked Siamese Networks
for Label-Efficient Learning

Mahmoud Assran[✉], Mathilde Caron, Ishan Misra, Piotr Bojanowski,
Florian Bordes, Pascal Vincent, Armand Joulin, Mike Rabbat,
and Nicolas Ballas

Meta AI (FAIR), New York, USA
massran@fb.com

Abstract. We propose Masked Siamese Networks (MSN), a self-supervised learning framework for learning image representations. Our approach matches the representation of an image view containing randomly masked patches to the representation of the original unmasked image. This self-supervised pre-training strategy is particularly scalable when applied to Vision Transformers since only the unmasked patches are processed by the network. As a result, MSNs improve the scalability of joint-embedding architectures, while producing representations of a high semantic level that perform competitively on low-shot image classification. For instance, on ImageNet-1K, with only 5,000 annotated images, our base MSN model achieves 72.4% top-1 accuracy, and with 1% of ImageNet-1K labels, we achieve 75.7% top-1 accuracy, setting a new state-of-the-art for self-supervised learning on this benchmark. Our code is publicly available at https://github.com/facebookresearch/msn.

Keywords: Self-supervised representation learning · Low-shot classification · Vision transformers · Siamese networks

1 Introduction

Self-Supervised Learning (SSL) has emerged as an effective strategy for unsupervised learning of image representations, eliminating the need to manually annotate vast quantities of data. By training large models on unlabeled data, SSL aims to learn representations that can be effectively applied to a downstream prediction task with few labels [15].

One of the core ideas of SSL is to remove a portion of the input and learn to predict the removed content [43]. Auto-regressive models and denoising auto-encoders instantiate this principle in vision by predicting the missing parts at the pixel or token level [3,5,12,27,50]. Masked auto-encoders in particular, which learn representations by reconstructing randomly masked patches from

Supplementary Information The online version contains supplementary material available at https://doi.org/10.1007/978-3-031-19821-2_26.

an input, have been successfully applied in vision [5,27,52,55]. However, optimizing a reconstruction loss requires modelling low-level image details that are not necessary for classification tasks involving semantic abstraction. Thus, the resulting representations often need to be fine-tuned for semantic recognition tasks which can lead to overfitting in low-shot settings. Nevertheless, masked auto-encoders have enabled the training of large-scale models and demonstrated state-of-the-art performance when fine-tuning on large labeled datasets, with millions of labels [3,5,27,55].

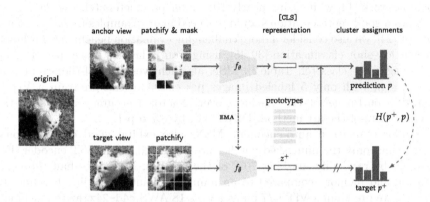

Fig. 1. Masked Siamese Networks. First use random data augmentations to generate two views of an image, referred to as the anchor view and the target view. Subsequently, a random mask is applied to the anchor view, while the target view is left unchanged. The objective is then to assign the representation of the masked anchor view to the same clusters as the representation of the unmasked target view. A standard cross-entropy loss is used as the criterion to optimize.

Joint-embedding architectures, on the other hand, avoid reconstruction. Approaches such as Siamese Networks [6,10,11,15,25,28,57] learn a representation by training an encoder network to produce similar embeddings for two different views of the same image [9,22]. Here the views are typically constructed by applying different image transforms—such as random scaling, cropping, and color jitter—to the input [41,53]. The inductive bias introduced by this invariance-based pre-training typically produces strong off-the-shelf representations of a high semantic level [11] but often disregards rich local structure that can be helpful to model.

In this work, we propose Masked Siamese Networks (MSNs), a self-supervised learning framework that leverages the idea of mask-denoising while avoiding pixel and token-level reconstruction. Given two views of an image, MSN randomly masks patches from one view while leaving the other view unchanged. The objective is to train a neural network encoder, parametrized with a vision transformer (ViT) [21], to output similar embeddings for the two views. In this procedure, MSN does not predict the masked patches at the input level, but rather performs the denoising step implicitly at the representation level by ensuring that the representation of the masked input matches the representation of the unmasked one. Figure 1 shows a schematic of the method.

Empirically, we demonstrate that MSNs learn strong off-the-shelf representations that excel at low-shot prediction (cf. Fig. 2). In particular, MSN achieves good classification performance using 100× fewer labels than current mask-based auto-encoders [27,54]. In the standard 1% ImageNet low-shot classification task, an MSN-trained ViT-B/4 (using a patch size of 4x4 pixels) achieves 75.7% top-1 accuracy, outperforming the previous 800M parameter state-of-the-art convolutional network [14] while using nearly 10× fewer parameters (cf. Fig. 2a).

Since a good representation should not need many examples to learn about a concept [24], we also consider a more challenging evaluation benchmark for label-efficient low-shot classification [39,45], using from 1 labeled image per class up to 5 images per class (cf. Table 2). MSN also achieves state-of-the-art in that regime; e.g., with only 5 labeled images per class, we can pre-train a ViT-B with MSN on ImageNet-1K to achieve over 72% top-1 accuracy, surpassing the previous state-of-the-art method, DINO [11], by 8% top-1.

Similar to masked auto-encoders, MSNs also exhibit good computational scaling since only the unmasked patches are processed by the ViT encoder. For example, by randomly masking 70% of the patches, MSN uses half the computation and memory compared to an unmasked joint-embedding baseline. In practice, we pre-train a ViT-L/7 on as few as 18 AWS p4d-24xlarge machines. Without masking, the same job requires over 42 machines.

Finally, we also show that MSNs are competitive with prior works on other self-supervised benchmarks that use many labels for evaluation (e.g., fine-tuning, linear-evaluation, transfer learning).

2 Prerequisites

Problem Formulation. Consider a large collection of unlabeled images, $\mathcal{D} = (\mathbf{x}_i)_{i=1}^{U}$, and a small dataset of annotated images, $\mathcal{S} = (\mathbf{x}_{si}, y_i)_{i=1}^{L}$, with $L \ll U$. Here, the images in $\mathcal{S}$ may overlap with the images in the dataset $\mathcal{D}$. Our goal is to learn image representations by first pre-training on $\mathcal{D}$ and then adapting the representation to the supervised task using $\mathcal{S}$.

Siamese Networks. The goal of siamese networks [7,9], as they are used in self-supervised learning, is to learn an encoder that produces similar image embeddings for two views of an image. Specifically, given an encoder $f_\theta(\cdot)$ and two views $\mathbf{x_i}$ and $\mathbf{x_i^+}$ of an image, the encoder independently processes each view and outputs representations z_i and z_i^+ respectively, referred to as the anchor representation and the target representation. The objective of siamese networks is to learn an encoder that is not sensitive to differences between views, so the representations z_i and z_i^+ should match. In practice, the encoder $f_\theta(\cdot)$ is usually parameterized as a deep neural network with learnable parameters θ.

The main challenge with siamese architectures is to prevent representation collapse in which the encoder produces a constant image embedding regardless of the input. Several approaches have been investigated in the literature. Contrastive losses explicitly push away embeddings of different images [9,15,28]. Information maximization approaches try to maximize the entropy of the average prediction [1,11] or spread out the embeddings uniformly on the surface of a sphere [10]. Asymmetric approaches rely on an asymmetric architectural choice such as stop-gradient operations and a momentum encoder [15,25] to prevent collapse. Other approaches try to decorrelate the vector components of the embeddings to minimize redundancy across samples [6,57].

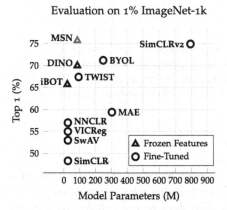
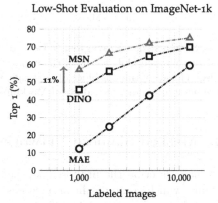

(a) Evaluation using 1% of ImageNet-1K labels (~13 imgs/class). Evaluation with *Frozen Features* corresponds to freezing the weights and training a logistic regression classifier with the available labeled samples. Evaluation with *Fine-Tuning* corresponds to adding a linear head and fine-tuning the model+head, end-to-end.

(b) Low-shot evaluation comparing MSN (ViT-L/7) to the best publicly available models in low-shot classification for DINO (ViT-B/8) and MAE (ViT-L/16). MSN and DINO use a linear probe, whereas MAE uses partial fine-tuning, where the last block of the pre-trained model along with a linear head are adapted.

Fig. 2. Low-shot Evaluation of self-supervised models, pre-trained on ImageNet-1K. (Left) MSN matches the previous 800M parameter state-of-the-art, while using a model that is 10× smaller, and no fine-tuning. (Right) MSN achieves good classification performance using less labels than current mask-based auto-encoders.

Vision Transformer. We use a standard Vision Transformer (ViT) architecture [21] as the encoder. Vision Transformers first extract a sequence of non-overlapping patches of resolution $N \times N$ from an image. Next, they apply a linear layer to extract patch tokens, and subsequently add learnable positional embeddings to them. An extra learnable [CLS] token is added to the sequence. This token aims to aggregate information from the full sequence of patches [11,21].

The sequence of tokens is then fed to a stack of Transformer layers [49]. A Transformer layer is composed of a self-attention [49] and a fully-connected layer with skip connections [29]. Self-attention uses an attention mechanism [4] applied to the entire sequence of elements to update the representation. The output representation associated to the [CLS] token is used as the output of the encoder.

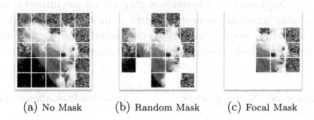

(a) No Mask   (b) Random Mask   (c) Focal Mask

Fig. 3. Masking strategies. When applying a Random Mask, we randomly drop patches across a global view of the image. When applying a Focal Mask, we randomly select a local continuous block of an image, and mask everything around it. We typically leverage both Random and Focal Masking strategies when pre-training with MSNs.

3   Masked Siamese Networks

We now describe the proposed Masked Siamese Network (MSN) training procedure, which combines invariance-based pre-training with mask denoising; see Fig. 1 for a schematic. MSNs first use random data augmentations to generate two views of an image, referred to as the anchor view and the target view. Subsequently, a random mask is applied to the anchor view, while the target view is left unchanged. Similar to clustering-based SSL approaches [1,10,11], learning occurs by computing a soft-distribution over a set of prototypes for both the anchor and target views. The objective is then to assign the representation of the masked anchor view to the same prototypes as the representation of the unmasked target view. We use a standard cross-entropy loss to optimize this criterion.

In contrast to previous work on masked image modelling, the mask-denoising process in MSN is discriminative, rather than generative [5,27,52,55,61]. MSN architectures do not directly predict pixel values (or tokens) for the masked patches. Instead, the loss is applied directly to the output corresponding to the [CLS] token of the encoder.

Input Views. In each iteration of pre-training, we sample a mini-batch of $B \geq 1$ images. For an index $i \in [B]$, let $\mathbf{x}_i$ denote the ith image in the mini-batch. For each image $\mathbf{x}_i$, we first apply a random set of data augmentations to generate a target view, denoted $\mathbf{x}_i^+$, and $M \geq 1$ anchor views, denoted $\mathbf{x}_{i,1}, \mathbf{x}_{i,2}, \ldots, \mathbf{x}_{i,M}$.

Patchify and Mask. Next, we "patchify" each view by converting it into a sequence of non-overlapping $N \times N$ patches. After patchifying the anchor view $\mathbf{x}_{i,m}$, we also apply the additional step of masking by randomly dropping some of the patches. We denote by $\hat{\mathbf{x}}_{i,m}$ the sequence of masked anchor patches, and by $\hat{\mathbf{x}}_i^+$ the sequence of unmasked target patches. Because of masking, the anchor sequence $\hat{\mathbf{x}}_{i,m}$ can have a different length than the patchified target sequence $\hat{\mathbf{x}}_i^+$, even if both image views originally have the same resolution.

We investigate two strategies for masking the anchor views, Random Masking and Focal Masking, which are depicted in Fig. 3. When applying Random Masking, we randomly drop potentially non-contiguous patches across the sequence. Conversely, when applying Focal Masking, we randomly select a local continuous block of the anchor view and drop all the patches around it.

Encoder. Given a parameterized anchor encoder, denoted $f_\theta(\cdot)$, let $z_{i,m} \in \mathbb{R}^d$ denote the representation computed from the patchified (and masked) anchor view $\hat{\mathbf{x}}_{i,m}$. Similarly, given a parameterized target encoder $f_{\bar\theta}(\cdot)$, with a potentially different set of parameters $\bar\theta$, let $z_i^+ \in \mathbb{R}^d$ denote the representation computed from the patchified target view $\hat{\mathbf{x}}_i^+$. In MSNs, the parameters $\bar\theta$ of the target encoder are updated via an exponential moving average of the anchor encoder parameters [25]. Both encoders correspond to the trunk of a ViT [21]. We take the output of the network to be the representation corresponding to the [CLS] token.

Similarity Metric and Predictions. Let $\mathbf{q} \in \mathbb{R}^{K \times d}$ denote $K > 1$ learnable prototypes, each of dimension d. To train the encoder, we compute a distribution based on the similarity between these prototypes and each anchor and target view pair, and we penalize the encoder for differences between these distributions. More precisely, for an anchor representation $z_{i,m}$, we compute a "prediction" $p_{i,m} \in \Delta_K$ in the K-dimensional simplex by measuring the cosine similarity to the prototypes matrix $\mathbf{q}$. For L_2-normalized representations and prototypes, the predictions $p_{i,m}$ can be concisely written as

$$p_{i,m} := \text{softmax}\left(\frac{z_{i,m} \cdot \mathbf{q}}{\tau}\right),$$

where $\tau \in (0,1)$ is a temperature. Similarly, for each target representation z_i^+, we generate a prediction $p_i^+ \in \Delta_K$ by measuring the cosine similarity to the same prototypes matrix $\mathbf{q}$. When computing the target predictions, we also use a temperature parameter $\tau^+ \in (0,1)$. Note, we always choose $\tau^+ < \tau$ to encourage sharper target predictions, which implicitly guides the model to produce confident low entropy anchor predictions. As we show in Appendix D, target sharpening coupled with mean-entropy maximization is provably sufficient to eliminate collapsing solutions in the MSN framework.

Training Objective. As previously mentioned, to train the encoder, we penalize when the anchor prediction $p_{i,m}$ is different from the target prediction p_i^+. We enforce this criterion using a standard cross-entropy loss $H(p_{i,m}, p_i^+)$.

We also incorporate the mean entropy maximization (ME-MAX) regularizer, also used in [1,33], to encourage the model to utilize the full set of prototypes. Denote the average prediction across all the anchor views by

$$\bar{p} := \frac{1}{MB} \sum_{i=1}^{B} \sum_{m=1}^{M} p_{i,m}.$$

The ME-MAX regularizer simply seeks to maximize the entropy of $\bar{p}$, denoted $H(\bar{p})$, or equivalently, minimize the negative entropy of $\bar{p}$. Thus, the overall objective to be minimized when training the encoder parameters θ and prototypes $\mathbf{q}$ is

$$\frac{1}{MB} \sum_{i=1}^{B} \sum_{m=1}^{M} H(p_{i,m}, p_i^+) - \lambda H(\bar{p}), \tag{1}$$

where $\lambda > 0$ controls the weight of the ME-MAX regularization. Note that when training, we only compute gradients with respect to the anchor predictions $p_{i,m}$, not the target predictions p_i^+.

4   Related Work

Unsupervised pre-training for vision has seen rapid progress with the development of view-invariant representation learning and joint embedding architectures [6,11,15,25,28,53]. Most similar to our approach is DINO [11] which leverages a Siamese Network with a cross-entropy loss and a momentum encoder. DINO also uses multi-crop training, which is a form of focal masking, but it requires an unmasked anchor view during training. MSN can be seen as a generalization of DINO, leveraging both random and focal masking without requiring any unmasked anchor views. Since the cross-entropy loss in Eq. (1) is only differentiated with respect to the anchor predictions, not the target, MSN only backpropagates through the anchor network and only needs to store the activation associated with the masked view. MSN therefore reduces the computational and memory requirements. MSN also differs from DINO in its mechanism for preventing representation collapse (entropy maximization as opposed to centering and sharpening). Our empirical results show that MSN compares favourably to DINO across various degrees of supervision for the downstream task.

A prominent line of work in SSL is to remove a portion of the input and learn to reconstruct the removed content [18]. For example, in the field of image recognition, some works have proposed to predict augmented image channels [60], which can be regarded as a form of image colorization [34,35,59]. Other approaches propose to remove and learn to regress entire image regions: the seminal Context Encoders of Pathak et al. [43] train a network to generate missing image patches based on their surroundings. Recent works revisit this idea and investigate the pre-training of ViTs with masked auto-encoders [5,12,27,52,55]. These approaches corrupt images with mask-noise and predict missing input values at the pixel level [21,27,54] or using a tokenizer [5,52]. Our approach does not predict the missing value at the input level, but instead performs the denoising step implicitly by ensuring that the global representation of the noisy input matches that of the uncorrupted input.

Some recent approaches have started to explore the combination of joint-embedding architectures and denoising pre-training tasks [3,23,61]. Those approaches mask an image by replacing the masked patches with a learnable mask token, and output a single vector for each masked patch. The objective is then to directly match each computed patch vector to the equivalent patch token extracted from a target encoder. Different from these approaches, we only match the view representations globally and do not consider a patch level loss. Consequently, we can completely ignore the masked patches, significantly reducing the computational and memory requirements. For example, when training our largest model, a ViT-L/7, we mask over 70% of the input patches, and reduce memory and computational overhead by half.

Table 1. Extreme low-shot. We evaluate the label-efficiency of self-supervised models pretrained on the ImageNet-1K dataset. For evaluation, we use an extremely small number of the ImageNet-1K labels and report the mean top-1 accuracy and standard deviation across 3 random splits of the data.

			Images per Class		
Method	Architecture	Epochs	1	2	5
iBOT [61]	ViT-S/16	800	40.4 ± 0.5	50.8 ± 0.8	59.9 ± 0.2
	ViT-B/16	400	46.1 ± 0.3	56.2 ± 0.7	64.7 ± 0.3
DINO [11]	ViT-S/16	800	38.9 ± 0.4	48.9 ± 0.3	58.5 ± 0.1
	ViT-B/16	400	41.8 ± 0.3	51.9 ± 0.6	61.4 ± 0.2
	ViT-S/8	800	45.5 ± 0.4	56.0 ± 0.7	64.7 ± 0.4
	ViT-B/8	300	45.8 ± 0.5	55.9 ± 0.6	64.6 ± 0.2
MAE [27]	ViT-B/16	1600	8.2 ± 0.3	25.0 ± 0.3	40.5 ± 0.2
	ViT-L/16	1600	12.3 ± 0.2	19.3 ± 1.8	42.3 ± 0.3
	ViT-H/14	1600	11.6 ± 0.4	18.6 ± 0.2	32.8 ± 0.2
MSN (Ours)	ViT-S/16	800	47.1 ± 0.1	55.8 ± 0.6	62.8 ± 0.3
	ViT-B/16	600	49.8 ± 0.2	58.9 ± 0.4	65.5 ± 0.3
	ViT-B/8	600	55.1 ± 0.1	64.9 ± 0.7	71.6 ± 0.3
	ViT-L/7	200	$\mathbf{57.1 \pm 0.6}$	$\mathbf{66.4 \pm 0.6}$	$\mathbf{72.1 \pm 0.2}$

5 Results

We evaluate MSN representations learned on the ImageNet-1K dataset [44]. We first consider low-shot evaluation on ImageNet-1K using as few as 1–5 images per class. We also compare with the state-of-the-art in settings where more supervision is available and investigate transfer-learning performance. Finally, we conduct ablation experiments with MSN. By default, we pre-train with a batch-size of 1024 images, generating several anchor views from each image: 1 view with a random mask, and 10 views with focal masks. We find that the optimal masking ratio is model-dependent, with larger models benefiting from more aggressive patch dropping. We describe MSN implementation details in Appendix C.

5.1   Label-Efficient Learning

The premise of SSL is to learn representations on unlabeled data that can be effectively applied to prediction tasks with few labels [14]. In this section we explore the performance of self-supervised approaches when very few labeled examples are available.

Table 2. Low-shot evaluation on ImageNet-1K using 1% of the labels (approximately 13 images per class). [†]Indicates evaluations we computed using publicly available models.

Method	Architecture	Params.	Top 1
Comparing similar architectures			
Barlow-Tw. [57]	RN50	24M	55.0
SimCLRv2 [14]	RN50	24M	57.9
PAWS [1]	RN50	24M	66.5
DINO [11]	ViT-S/16	22M	64.5
iBOT [61]	ViT-S/16	22M	65.9
MSN	ViT-S/16	22M	**67.2**
Comparing larger architectures			
BYOL [25]	RN200 (2×)	250M	71.2
SimCLRv2 [14]	RN151+SK (3×)	795M	74.9
iBOT [61][†]	ViT-B/16	86M	69.7
DINO [11][†]	ViT-B/8	86M	70.0
MSN	ViT-B/4	86M	**75.7**

Extreme Low-Shot. We first evaluate the classification performance of unsupervised models that have been pre-trained on ImageNet-1K, by using 1, 2, and 5 labeled images per class for supervised evaluation. We compare MSN to the joint-embedding approach, DINO [14], the auto-encoding approach, MAE [27],

and the hybrid approach, iBOT [61], which combines a joint-embedding architecture with a token-based patch-level loss. We download the official released
models of each related approach for evaluation.

To adapt the joint-embeddings models to the supervised task, we freeze the
weights of the pre-trained model and train a linear classifier on top using 1,
2 or 5 labeled samples (see Appendix C). For MAE, we rely on partial fine-
tuning [27], except for the 1 image per class setting, and all results with the ViT-
H/14 architecture, which use a linear classifier. Partial fine-tuning corresponds
to fine-tuning the last block of the pre-trained model along with a linear head.
MAE benefits from partial fine-tuning, but for sufficiently large models, such as
the ViT-H/14, this leads to significant overfitting in the low-shot regime. We
compare both protocols in more detail in Appendix E.

Table 1 reports the extreme low-shot evaluation results. MSN outperforms the
other representation learning approaches across all levels of supervision. Moreover, the improvement offered by MSN increases as the amount of available
labeled data is decreased. The performance of MSN also benefits from increased
model size—settings with less labeled data appear to benefit more from increased
model depth and smaller patch sizes.

Table 3. Linear evaluation on ImageNet-1K using 100% of the labels.

Method	Architecture	Params.	Epochs	Top 1
Comparing similar architectures				
SimCLRv2 [14]	RN50	24M	800	71.7
BYOL [25]	RN50	24M	1000	74.4
DINO [11]	ViT-S/16	22M	800	77.0
iBOT [61]	ViT-S/16	22M	800	**77.9**
MSN	ViT-S/16	22M	600	76.9
Comparing larger architectures				
MAE [27]	ViT-H/14	632M	1600	76.6
BYOL [25]	RN200 (2×)	250M	800	79.6
SimCLRv2 [14]	RN151+SK (3×)	795M	800	79.8
iBOT [61]	ViT-B/16	86M	400	79.4
DINO [11]	ViT-B/8	86M	300	80.1
MoCov3 [16]	ViT-BN-L/7	304M	300	**81.0**
MSN	ViT-L/7	304M	200	**80.7**

We also observe that joint-embedding approaches appear to be more robust
to the limited availability of downstream supervision than reconstruction-based
auto-encoding approaches. To explain this observation, we refer to the Masked

Auto-Encoders paper [27] which conjectures that using a pixel reconstruction loss results in encoder representations of a lower semantic level than other methods. Conversely, the inductive bias introduced by invariance-based pre-training appears to be helpful in the low-shot regime.

1% ImageNet-1K. Table 2 reports a comparison on the 1% ImageNet-1K task, which is a standard benchmark for low-shot evaluation of self-supervised models [13]. For reference, the best reported result in the literature on 1% labeled data is 76.6%, achieved with a multi-stage semi-supervised pipeline, i.e., self-distilling from a fine-tuned ResNet-152 with 3× wider channels and selective kernels [14]. Here we focus on comparing to other models trained in a self-supervised setting. Our best MSN model using a ViT-L/7 achieves 75.1% top 1 accuracy, surpassing the previous 800M parameter state-of-the-art convolutional network [14] while using significantly fewer parameters and no fine-tuning. When focusing the comparison on similar architectures (models with similar FLOP counts), MSN also consistently improves upon previous approaches.

5.2   Linear Evaluation and Fine-Tuning

In this section we compare with the state-of-the-art on standard evaluation benchmarks where more supervised samples are available to adapt the representation. We use the full ImageNet-1K training images with 1.28M labels.

Table 4. End-to-end fine-tuning of a ViT-B/16 encoder on ImageNet-1K using 100% of the labels. MSN obtains competitive performance with both joint-embedding approaches and auto-encoding approaches.

Initialization	Pretrain Epochs	Top 1
DINO [11]	800	83.6
BEiT [5]	800	83.2
iBOT [27]	800	83.8
MAE [27]	1600	83.6
SimMIM [55]	-	83.8
MaskFeat [52]	-	84.0
Data2Vec [3]	800	**84.2**
MSN	600	83.4

Linear Evaluation. We evaluate self-supervised pretrained models by freezing their weights and training a linear classifier. Table 3 reports the linear evaluation results on ImageNet-1K. We observe that MSN performs competitively with the state-of-the-art. The best MSN model achieves 80.7% top-1 accuracy.

Fine-Tuning. In this evaluation setting, we finetune all the weights of the self-supervised model using all the labels from the ImageNet-1K training set. We focus on the ViT-B/16 architecture. We adopt the same fine-tuning protocol as [5], and provide the details in Appendix C. Table 4 reports the comparison with fine-tuning evaluation using 100% labels on ImageNet-1K. MSN is competitive with joint-embedding approaches, such as DINO, and generative auto-encoding approaches, such as MAE.

5.3   Transfer Learning

We also report transfer learning experiments on the CIFAR10, CIFAR100 and iNaturalist datasets in Table 5 when using a self-supervised ViT-B/16 pre-trained on ImageNet-1K. Across all tasks, various levels of supervision, and evaluation methods, MSN either outperforms or achieves similar results to DINO pre-training. Recall that MSN pre-training is also less computationally expensive than DINO pre-training due to the anchor masking.

Table 5. Transfer Learning with a ViT-Base/16 pre-trained on ImageNet-1K. Across all tasks, various levels of supervision, and evaluation methods, MSN either outperforms or achieves similar results to DINO pre-training. The MSN model is trained with a masking ratio of 0.3; i.e., dropping 30% of patches, and thus reduces the computational cost of pre-training relative to DINO.

Evaluation	Method	Top 1				
		CIFAR10		CIFAR100	iNat18	iNat19
		4000 labels	50000 labels			
Fine-Tuning	DINO	–	99.0	90.5	72.0	78.2
	MSN	–	99.0	90.5	72.1	78.1
Linear Eval.	DINO	93.2	95.3	82.9	–	–
	MSN	93.8	95.7	82.8	–	–

5.4   Ablations

We now conduct a series of experiments to gain insights into the important design decisions used in MSN such as the masking strategy and the data augmentation strategy. We measure the accuracy of the models by training a logistic regression classifier on the frozen trunk using 1% of ImageNet-1K labels (∼13 imgs/class).

Combining Random and Focal Masking. In MSN we apply both random and focal masking to the anchor views. Focal masking corresponds to selecting a small crop from the anchor view. Random masking corresponds to randomly dropping potentially non-contiguous patches from the anchor view.

Table 6. Masking strategy. Impact of masking strategy on low-shot accuracy (1% of ImageNet-1K labels) of a ViT-B/16. We only generate one anchor view of each image, except in the last row, where we generate two views, one with a Random Mask and one with a Focal Mask. A random masking ratio of 0.5 is used. Applying a random mask to the anchor view is better than applying no mask. By combining both random and focal masking strategies, we obtain the strongest performance.

Anchor View	Top 1
No Mask	49.3
Focal Mask	39.3
Random Mask	52.3
Random Mask + Focal Mask	**59.8**

Table 6 reports the effect on low-shot evaluation when using a) No Masking, b) Focal Masking, c) Random Masking, or d) Random and Focal Masking. Applying a random mask to the anchor view is always better than applying no mask. By contrast, applying only a focal mask degrades the performance, which highlights the importance of maintaining a global view during pre-training. By combining both random and focal masking strategies, we obtain the strongest performance.

Random Masking Ratio. Here we explore the relationship between the optimal masking ratio and the model size. Table 7 reports the low-shot learning performance for various random masking ratios as we increase the model size.[1]

Table 7. Masking ratio. Impact of pre-training random masking ratio (fraction of randomly dropped patches in each random mask) on ImageNet 1% accuracy. Accuracy of larger models improves when leveraging aggressive masking during pre-training.

	Top 1			
	Random Masking Ratio			
Architecture	0.15	0.3	0.5	0.7
ViT-S/16	**66.3**	66.0	64.8	–
ViT-B/16	68.8	**69.6**	–	–
ViT-L/16	NaN	NaN	**70.1**	69.4

When increasing the model size, we find that increasing the masking ratio (dropping more patches) is helpful for improving low-shot performance. We also

---

[1] Note that the performance of the ViT-S/16 can be improved by removing the Sinkhorn normalization, as we do in Table 2, however for consistency of evaluation with other models, we keep it in for this ablation.

find that the ViT-L/16 runs with weak masking are unstable, while the runs with more aggressive masking are quite stable. However, we do not have sufficient evidence to claim that increasing the masking ratio always improves the stability of large ViT pre-training.

Augmentation Invariance and Low-Shot Learning. We explore the importance of data-augmentation invariance for low-shot learning. We pretrain a ViT-B/16 with MSN, where the teacher and anchor networks either share the input image view or use different input views; in both cases, the anchor view is always masked. The views are constructed by applying random ColorJitter, Crop, Horizontal Flips, and GaussianBlur to the input image.

Table 8 reports top-1 accuracy when evaluating with 1% of ImageNet-1K labels. Sharing the view leads to a top-1 accuracy of 7%; MSN finds a shortcut solution relying on color statistics. Using different colors in the input views resolves this pathological behaviour and achieves a top-1 of 48.3%. Further applying the geometric data-augmentations independently to the two views (as opposed to sharing views) further improves the performance to 52.3%, showing the importance of learning view-invariant representations in the low-shot setting.

Random Masking Compute and Memory. We look at the effect of the random masking ratio, i.e., the fraction of dropped patches from the global anchor view, on the computational requirements of large model pre-training. In each iteration we also generate 10 focal views (small crops) of each input image; the random masking ratio has no impact on these views.

Table 8. Impact of view-sharing during pre-training when evaluating on ImageNet 1%. The target view is constructed by applying random ColorJitter, Crop, Horizontal Flips, and GaussianBlur to the input image. When using the same image view, MSN finds a shortcut solution. Using color jitter prevents this pathological behaviour. Randomly applying additional geometric data transformations to the anchor further improves performance, demonstrating the importance of view invariance in the low-shot setting.

Anchor View Generation	Top 1
Target View	7.0
Target View + ColorJitter	48.7
Target View + ColorJitter + Crop + Flip + GaussianBlur	**52.3**

Table 9. Impact of random masking ratio on GPU memory usage and runtime when pre-training a ViT-L/7. Measurements are conducted on a single AWS `p4d-24xlarge` machine, containing 8 A100 GPUs, using a batch-size of 2 images per GPU. In each iteration we also generate 10 focal views (small crops) of each input image; the random masking ratio has no impact on these views. Using more aggressive masking of the global view progressively reduces device memory utilization and speeds up training.

Masking Ratio	Mem./GPU	Throughput
0.0	26G	415 imgs/s
0.3	21G	480 imgs/s
0.5	18G	525 imgs/s
0.7	17G	600 imgs/s

Table 9 reports the memory consumption and throughput (imgs/s) of a ViT-L/7 model on a single AWS `p4d-24xlarge` machine using a batch-size of 2 images per GPU. As expected, using more aggressive masking of the global view progressively reduces device memory utilization and speeds up training. For example, by randomly masking 70% of the patches, we can use MSN to pre-train a full-precision ViT-Large with a patch-size of 7×7 on as few as 18 AWS `p4d-24xlarge` machines. Without masking, the same job requires over 42 machines when using the default batch-size of 1024 images.

6   Conclusion

We propose Masked Siamese Networks (MSNs), a self-supervised learning framework that leverages the idea of mask-denoising while avoiding pixel and token-level reconstruction. We demonstrate empirically that MSNs learn strong off-the-shelf representations that excel at label-efficient learning, while simultaneously improving the scalability of joint-embedding architectures. By relying on view-invariant representation learning, MSN does require the specification of data transformations, and it may be that the optimal transformations and invariances are dataset and task dependant. In future work, we plan to explore more flexible mechanisms to learn those transformations and also explore the use of equivariant representations.

References

1. Assran, M., et al.: Semi-supervised learning of visual features by non-parametrically predicting view assignments with support samples. In: ICCV (2021)
2. Atito, S., Awais, M., Kittler, J.: SiT: self-supervised vision transformer. arXiv preprint arXiv:2104.03602 (2021)
3. Baevski, A., Hsu, W.N., Xu, Q., Babu, A., Gu, J., Auli, M.: Data2vec: a general framework for self-supervised learning in speech, vision and language. arXiv preprint arXiv:2202.03555 (2022)

4. Bahdanau, D., Cho, K., Bengio, Y.: Neural machine translation by jointly learning to align and translate. arXiv preprint arXiv:1409.0473 (2014)

5. Bao, H., Dong, L., Wei, F.: BEiT: BERT pre-training of image transformers. arXiv preprint arXiv:2106.08254 (2021)

6. Bardes, A., Ponce, J., LeCun, Y.: VICReg: variance-invariance-covariance regularization for self-supervised learning. arXiv preprint arXiv:2105.04906 (2021)

7. Becker, S., Hinton, G.E.: Self-organizing neural network that discovers surfaces in random-dot stereograms. Nature **355**(6356), 161–163 (1992)

8. Bordes, F., Balestriero, R., Vincent, P.: High fidelity visualization of what your self-supervised representation knows about. arXiv preprint arXiv:2112.09164 (2021)

9. Bromley, J., et al.: Signature verification using a "Siamese" time delay neural network. Int. J. Pattern Recognit Artif Intell. **7**(04), 669–688 (1993)

10. Caron, M., Misra, I., Mairal, J., Goyal, P., Bojanowski, P., Joulin, A.: Unsupervised learning of visual features by contrasting cluster assignments. In: NeurIPS (2020)

11. Caron, M., et al.: Emerging properties in self-supervised vision transformers. In: ICCV (2021)

12. Chen, M., et al.: Generative pretraining from pixels. In: International Conference on Machine Learning, pp. 1691–1703. PMLR (2020)

13. Chen, T., Kornblith, S., Norouzi, M., Hinton, G.: A simple framework for contrastive learning of visual representations. preprint arXiv:2002.05709 (2020)

14. Chen, T., Kornblith, S., Swersky, K., Norouzi, M., Hinton, G.: Big self-supervised models are strong semi-supervised learners. arXiv preprint arXiv:2006.10029 (2020)

15. Chen, X., He, K.: Exploring simple Siamese representation learning. arXiv preprint arXiv:2011.10566 (2020)

16. Chen, X., Xie, S., He, K.: An empirical study of training self-supervised vision transformers. arXiv preprint arXiv:2104.02057 (2021)

17. Cubuk, E.D., Zoph, B., Mane, D., Vasudevan, V., Le, Q.V.: AutoAugment: learning augmentation strategies from data. In: CVPR (2019)

18. Devlin, J., Chang, M.W., Lee, K., Toutanova, K.: BERT: pre-training of deep bidirectional transformers for language understanding. arXiv preprint arXiv:1810.04805 (2018)

19. Doersch, C., Gupta, A., Efros, A.A.: Unsupervised visual representation learning by context prediction. In: Proceedings of the IEEE International Conference on Computer Vision, pp. 1422–1430 (2015)

20. Donahue, J., Simonyan, K.: Large scale adversarial representation learning. In: Advances in Neural Information Processing Systems, vol. 32 (2019)

21. Dosovitskiy, A., et al.: An image is worth 16×16 words: transformers for image recognition at scale. arXiv preprint arXiv:2010.11929 (2020)

22. Dosovitskiy, A., Springenberg, J.T., Riedmiller, M.A., Brox, T.: Discriminative unsupervised feature learning with convolutional neural networks. CoRR (2014)

23. El-Nouby, A., Izacard, G., Touvron, H., Laptev, I., Jegou, H., Grave, E.: Are large-scale datasets necessary for self-supervised pre-training? arXiv preprint arXiv:2112.10740 (2021)

24. Goyal, P., Mahajan, D., Gupta, A., Misra, I.: Scaling and benchmarking self-supervised visual representation learning. In: ICCV (2019)

25. Grill, J.B., et al.: Bootstrap your own latent: a new approach to self-supervised learning. In: NeurIPS (2020)

26. Gupta, K., Somepalli, G., Anubhav, A., Magalle Hewa, V.Y.J., Zwicker, M., Shrivastava, A.: PatchGame: learning to signal mid-level patches in referential games. In: Advances in Neural Information Processing Systems, vol. 34, pp. 26015–26027 (2021)

27. He, K., Chen, X., Xie, S., Li, Y., Dollár, P., Girshick, R.: Masked autoencoders are scalable vision learners. arXiv preprint arXiv:2111.06377 (2021)
28. He, K., Fan, H., Wu, Y., Xie, S., Girshick, R.: Momentum contrast for unsupervised visual representation learning. arXiv preprint arXiv:1911.05722 (2019)
29. He, K., Zhang, X., Ren, S., Sun, J.: Deep residual learning for image recognition. In: CVPR (2016)
30. Hendrycks, D., et al.: The many faces of robustness: a critical analysis of out-of-distribution generalization. In: ICCV (2021)
31. Hendrycks, D., Dietterich, T.: Benchmarking neural network robustness to common corruptions and perturbations. In: Proceedings of the International Conference on Learning Representations (2019)
32. Hendrycks, D., Zhao, K., Basart, S., Steinhardt, J., Song, D.: Natural adversarial examples. In: CVPR (2021)
33. Joulin, A., Bach, F.: A convex relaxation for weakly supervised classifiers. arXiv preprint arXiv:1206.6413 (2012)
34. Larsson, G., Maire, M., Shakhnarovich, G.: Learning representations for automatic colorization. In: ECCV (2016)
35. Larsson, G., Maire, M., Shakhnarovich, G.: Colorization as a proxy task for visual understanding. In: CVPR (2017)
36. Li, C., et al.: Efficient self-supervised vision transformers for representation learning. arXiv preprint arXiv:2106.09785 (2021)
37. Li, Z., et al.: MST: masked self-supervised transformer for visual representation. Adv. Neural. Inf. Process. Syst. **34**, 13165–13176 (2021)
38. Loshchilov, I., Hutter, F.: Decoupled weight decay regularization. arXiv preprint arXiv:1711.05101 (2017)
39. Lucas, T., Weinzaepfel, P., Rogez, G.: Barely-supervised learning: semi-supervised learning with very few labeled images. preprint arXiv:2112.12004 (2021)
40. Mairal, J.: Cyanure: an open-source toolbox for empirical risk minimization for Python, C++, and soon more. arXiv preprint arXiv:1912.08165 (2019)
41. Misra, I., van der Maaten, L.: Self-supervised learning of pretext-invariant representations. In: CVPR (2020)
42. Noroozi, M., Favaro, P.: Unsupervised learning of visual representations by Solving Jigsaw Puzzles. In: Leibe, B., Matas, J., Sebe, N., Welling, M. (eds.) ECCV 2016. LNCS, vol. 9910, pp. 69–84. Springer, Cham (2016). https://doi.org/10.1007/978-3-319-46466-4_5
43. Pathak, D., Krahenbuhl, P., Donahue, J., Darrell, T., Efros, A.A.: Context encoders: feature learning by inpainting. In: CVPR (2016)
44. Russakovsky, O., et al.: ImageNet large scale visual recognition challenge. Int. J. Comput. Vision **115**(3), 211–252 (2015)
45. Sohn, K., et al.: FixMatch: simplifying semi-supervised learning with consistency and confidence. arXiv preprint arXiv:2001.07685 (2020)
46. Tian, Y., Krishnan, D., Isola, P.: Contrastive multiview coding. In: Vedaldi, A., Bischof, H., Brox, T., Frahm, J.-M. (eds.) ECCV 2020. LNCS, vol. 12356, pp. 776–794. Springer, Cham (2020). https://doi.org/10.1007/978-3-030-58621-8_45
47. Touvron, H., Cord, M., Douze, M., Massa, F., Sablayrolles, A., Jégou, H.: Training data-efficient image transformers & distillation through attention. In: International Conference on Machine Learning, pp. 10347–10357. PMLR (2021)
48. Trinh, T.H., Luong, M.T., Le, Q.V.: Selfie: self-supervised pretraining for image embedding. arXiv preprint arXiv:1906.02940 (2019)
49. Vaswani, A., et al.: Attention is all you need. In: NeurIPS (2017)

50. Vincent, P., Larochelle, H., Lajoie, I., Bengio, Y., Manzagol, P.A., Bottou, L.: Stacked denoising autoencoders: Learning useful representations in a deep network with a local denoising criterion. J. Mach. Learn. Res. **11**(12) (2010)

51. Wang, H., Ge, S., Lipton, Z., Xing, E.P.: Learning robust global representations by penalizing local predictive power. In: Advances in Neural Information Processing Systems, pp. 10506–10518 (2019)

52. Wei, C., Fan, H., Xie, S., Wu, C.Y., Yuille, A., Feichtenhofer, C.: Masked feature prediction for self-supervised visual pre-training. arXiv preprint arXiv:2112.09133 (2021)

53. Wu, Z., Xiong, Y., Yu, S.X., Lin, D.: Unsupervised feature learning via non-parametric instance discrimination. In: CVPR (2018)

54. Xie, Q., Dai, Z., Hovy, E., Luong, M.T., Le, Q.V.: Unsupervised data augmentation. arXiv preprint arXiv:1904.12848 (2019)

55. Xie, Z., et al.: SimMIM: a simple framework for masked image modeling. arXiv preprint arXiv:2111.09886 (2021)

56. Yun, S., Han, D., Oh, S.J., Chun, S., Choe, J., Yoo, Y.: CutMix: regularization strategy to train strong classifiers with localizable features. In: ICCV (2019)

57. Zbontar, J., Jing, L., Misra, I., LeCun, Y., Deny, S.: Barlow twins: self-supervised learning via redundancy reduction. arXiv preprint arXiv:2103.03230 (2021)

58. Zhang, H., Cisse, M., Dauphin, Y.N., Lopez-Paz, D.: mixup: beyond empirical risk minimization. arXiv preprint arXiv:1710.09412 (2017)

59. Zhang, R., Isola, P., Efros, A.A.: Colorful image colorization. In: Leibe, B., Matas, J., Sebe, N., Welling, M. (eds.) ECCV 2016. LNCS, vol. 9907, pp. 649–666. Springer, Cham (2016). https://doi.org/10.1007/978-3-319-46487-9_40

60. Zhang, R., Isola, P., Efros, A.A.: Split-brain autoencoders: unsupervised learning by cross-channel prediction. In: CVPR (2017)

61. Zhou, J., et al.: iBOT: image BERT pre-training with online tokenizer. arXiv preprint arXiv:2111.07832 (2021)

62. Zhu, R., Zhao, B., Liu, J., Sun, Z., Chen, C.W.: Improving contrastive learning by visualizing feature transformation. In: Proceedings of the IEEE/CVF International Conference on Computer Vision, pp. 10306–10315 (2021)

Natural Synthetic Anomalies for Self-supervised Anomaly Detection and Localization

Hannah M. Schlüter[1]([✉]) [ID], Jeremy Tan[1] [ID], Benjamin Hou[1] [ID],
and Bernhard Kainz[1,2] [ID]

[1] Imperial College London, London, UK
hmschlue@mit.edu, {j.tan17,benjamin.hou11,b.kainz}@imperial.ac.uk
[2] Friedrich-Alexander-Universität Erlangen-Nürnberg, Erlangen, Germany

Abstract. We introduce a simple and intuitive self-supervision task, Natural Synthetic Anomalies (NSA), for training an end-to-end model for anomaly detection and localization using only normal training data. NSA integrates Poisson image editing to seamlessly blend scaled patches of various sizes from separate images. This creates a wide range of synthetic anomalies which are more similar to natural sub-image irregularities than previous data-augmentation strategies for self-supervised anomaly detection. We evaluate the proposed method using natural and medical images. Our experiments with the MVTec AD dataset show that a model trained to localize NSA anomalies generalizes well to detecting real-world a priori unknown types of manufacturing defects. Our method achieves an overall detection AUROC of **97.2** outperforming all previous methods that learn without the use of additional datasets. Code available at https://github.com/hmsch/natural-synthetic-anomalies.

Keywords: Image anomaly localization, self-supervised learning

1 Introduction

Anomaly detection is a binary classification task where the aim is to separate normal data from anomalous examples. There are different types of anomaly detection depending on what training data and labels are available. A difficult yet realistic setting is to detect and localize unknown types of anomalies while only having access to normal data during training. To be useful in real applications, an automated system must be able to detect subtle and rare anomalies; irregularities that are either impossible to spot for humans because of contextual uniformity or get lost due to task-remote stimuli that lead to inattentional blindness [16].

Attempting to detect rare anomalies often means that it is impossible to acquire sufficient amounts of human-annotated training data for a supervised method. Obtaining precise ground-truth annotations is time-consuming

---

Supplementary Information The online version contains supplementary material available at https://doi.org/10.1007/978-3-031-19821-2_27.

S. Avidan et al. (Eds.): ECCV 2022, LNCS 13691, pp. 474–489, 2022.
https://doi.org/10.1007/978-3-031-19821-2_27

and requires expert knowledge depending on the application domain. Anomaly detection based on only normal data has applications in many areas including defect detection in industrial production pipelines [2,5,6,14,23,32], unsupervised lesion detection in medical images [17,20,27–29,38], or finding unusual events in surveillance videos [1,5,6].

The main challenge of unsupervised approaches is designing a training setup that will encourage the model to learn features relevant to anomaly detection without having any prior knowledge of the types of anomalies to expect. A common theme among top-performing approaches [6,11,23,24] for anomaly detection in natural images, specifically on the MVTec AD benchmark, is to sidestep this challenge by relying on deep features from pre-trained ImageNet models.

We find approaches that learn from scratch more interesting. They are more widely applicable to other domains where the usefulness of ImageNet pre-training is limited, such as medical imaging [22]. Many rely on learning a compressed representation of normal data and use these embeddings or reconstructions derived from them to define an anomaly score. Self-supervised learning is thus becoming a prominent strategy in anomaly detection. By designing an appropriate task, self-supervision can be an effective proxy for supervised learning, bypassing the need for labeled data. While various self-supervised tasks, such as context prediction [7] or estimating geometric transformations [8,9], can be used to learn a compressed representation of the data, recent works [14,28,29,36] show that data-augmentation strategies mimicking real defects are particularly effective for sub-image anomaly detection. These methods create synthetic anomalies by replacing or blending image patches with content from other images or image locations. However, recently proposed synthesis strategies [14,36] feature obvious discontinuities. This is raising concerns that the model may overfit to prior assumptions that are inherently encoded in synthetic manipulations. To prevent this, one can either resort to simpler encoders [14], which impedes end-to-end localization, or add additional networks for reconstruction [36], which greatly increases model size, computational costs, and training time. Even methods that linearly interpolate similar patches to create more subtle irregularities can suffer from the same problem [28]. [29] solves this problem by using Poisson image editing [21], but the resulting anomalies are so subtle that they may represent variations of the normal class rather than true anomalies.

Contribution. We introduce a simple and intuitive self-supervised method for sub-image anomaly detection and localization. Our Natural Synthetic Anomalies (NSA), are a) more natural than the current state-of-the-art CutPaste [14], FPI [28], or DRAEM [36] due to the use of Poisson image editing, b) more diverse than CutPaste, FPI, or PII anomalies due to rescaling, shifting and a new Gamma-distribution-based patch shape sampling strategy, and c) more relevant to the task by imposing background constraints and using pixel-level labels derived from the resulting difference to the normal image rather than interpolation factors as used in FPI and PII. Like FPI and PII, NSA can be used to train an end-to-end model for anomaly detection and localization rather than generating compressed representations for a multi-stage pipeline.

We evaluate the proposed method on the MVTec AD dataset [2] which contains normal training data and both normal and anomalous test data for a wide range of natural and manufacturing defects for 10 object and 5 texture classes. NSA achieves the new state-of-the-art localization (96.3 AUROC) and detection (97.2 AUROC) performance among methods that do not use additional datasets. It also performs comparably to the best methods that use additional data and much bigger models [6,36]. [6] uses a model pre-trained on ImageNet. Compared to the large amount of data in ImageNet, our method only uses MVTec AD data, which contains between 60 and 391 training images per class.

NSA is a very general method for creating diverse and realistic synthetic anomalies in images. Since it does not rely on pre-training with ImageNet or any other dataset, it can easily be adapted to domains beyond natural images. Thus, we also evaluate NSA using a curated subset of a public chest X-ray dataset [33] where it outperforms other state-of-the-art self-supervised methods for disease detection.

2   Related Work

Reconstruction-based anomaly detection establishes pixel-level and image-level anomaly scores from the pixel-wise reconstruction error using variational autoencoders (VAE) [38], Bayesian autoencoders [20], generative adversarial networks (GAN) [27], or the restoration distance using a vector-quantized VAE (VQ-VAE) [17,32] trained with normal data. Anomaly scores can be improved by leveraging additional information derived from the model, such as the discriminator output when using a GAN [27], the KL-divergence of the latent representation of a VAE for image-level scores or its gradient for pixel-level scores [38], or the likelihood of the latent representation under a learnt prior using a VQ-VAE [17,32] or latent space autoregression [1]. A downside of these approaches is that it is difficult to control the capacity of the model. Depending on regularization, the model cannot reconstruct all details of normal examples well or may be able to reconstruct anomalous regions too.

Embedding-based anomaly detection derives an anomaly score from the distance between embedding vectors of normal training images and test examples. An embedding-similarity metric can be defined using any method for one-class classification such as support vector data description (SVDD) used in [34], Gaussian distributions used in [6,14,23], or nearest neighbour search used in [5,24]. Features for the embedding vectors are often extracted from pre-trained deep neural networks [5,6,23,24], but can also be learned from scratch using a self-supervised task [14] or together with the one-class classification objective in Deep-SVDD [26] and Deep One-Class Classification (DOCC) [25] or a combination thereof [34]. When using embeddings of the entire image, embedding-based approaches can perform detection but not localization and are hence less interpretable. To circumvent this issue, [6,14,24,34] work with patch-level embeddings to create an anomaly map while [5] compares test images to their nearest neighbors from the training set at the pixel-level. In a similar vein, flow-based methods can perform density estimation [10]. However, these methods can sometimes assign higher likelihood to outlier samples [18] and typically need pre-trained feature extractors to achieve better performance [35].

Self-supervised Learning. A supervisory signal from a proxy task defined based on unlabeled data, such as predicting the relative position of patches [7] or estimating geometric transformations [8,9], can help the model learn useful features for a downstream task. While [7–9] use features learned from the proxy task to discover different object classes, self-supervised learning has also been successfully applied to sub-image anomaly detection [14,28,29,34,36]. In [28,29], the output for the self-supervised task is a prediction of the interpolation factor where a foreign patch from another observation in the training distribution has been blended into the current image. This output is used directly as an anomaly score without any further training step. We also employ this general setup for our method. In [36], the foreign patches are first removed by a reconstructive sub-network and then a discriminative sub-network produces an anomaly map by comparing the input image with foreign patches to the reconstruction.

Poisson Image Editing. Pasting part of one image into another causes obvious discontinuities. [21] developed a method to seamlessly clone an object from one image into another image. For a source image given by g and a destination image given by f^*, we seek an interpolant f over the interior of a region Ω with boundary $\partial\Omega$ that solves the minimization problem given by (1). According to [21], this has the unique solution of the Poisson partial differential equations (2) with Dirichlet boundary conditions given by the destination image.

$$f = \arg\min_f \iint_\Omega |\nabla f - \mathbf{v}|^2 \text{ with } f|_{\partial\Omega} = f^*|_{\partial\Omega} \tag{1}$$

$$\Delta f = \operatorname{div}\mathbf{v} \text{ over } \Omega, \text{ with } f|_{\partial\Omega} = f^*|_{\partial\Omega} \tag{2}$$

[21] gives two options for defining the guidance field $\mathbf{v}$: a) use the source image gradient (3) or b) a mix of source and destination gradients (4).

$$\mathbf{v} = \nabla g \tag{3}$$

$$\forall \mathbf{x} \in \Omega, \mathbf{v}(\mathbf{x}) = \begin{cases} \nabla f^*(\mathbf{x}), & \text{if } |\nabla f^*(\mathbf{x})| > |\nabla g(\mathbf{x})|, \\ \nabla g(\mathbf{x}), & \text{otherwise} \end{cases} \tag{4}$$

In practice, a finite difference discretization of (2) is solved numerically. Seamless cloning is implemented in the OpenCV library [3] which we use in our self-supervised task. A Poisson image editing approach has also recently been used for anomaly detection in medical images [29].

3   NSA Self-supervised Task

As only normal data is available at training time, the model needs to be trained using a proxy task. In our case, the task is to localize synthetic anomalies created from normal data by blending a patch from a source image into the destination image as follows:

1. Select a random rectangular patch in the source image.
2. Randomly resize the patch and select a different destination location.
3. Seamlessly blend the patch into the destination image.
4. Optionally, repeat steps 1–3 to add multiple patches to the same image.
5. Create a pixel-wise label mask.

Patch Sampling and Constraints: Given two normal $W \times H$ training images x_s and x_d, we select a random rectangular patch p_s with width w and height h sampled from a truncated Gamma distribution, and center (c_x, c_y) in the source image x_s sampled from a uniform distribution:

$$w = W \min\left(\max\left(w_{\min}, 0.06 + r_w\right), w_{\max}\right), \quad \text{with} \quad r_w \sim \text{Gamma}(2, 0.1) \quad (5)$$

$$h = H \min\left(\max\left(h_{\min}, 0.06 + r_h\right), h_{\max}\right), \quad \text{with} \quad r_h \sim \text{Gamma}(2, 0.1) \quad (6)$$

$$c_x \sim U\left(W\frac{w_{\min}}{2}, W - W\frac{w_{\min}}{2}\right), \quad c_y \sim U\left(H\frac{h_{\min}}{2}, H - H\frac{h_{\min}}{2}\right) \quad (7)$$

Sampling the width and height from a truncated Gamma distribution means we assume anomalies are local (small) but want the model to be able to recognize larger irregularities too. Hence, some long slim rectangles and occasionally large patches are generated. The width and height bounds are selected based on the dimensions of the object. For images containing an object and a plain background, we calculate object masks m_s and m_d by thresholding the pixel-wise absolute difference to the background brightness b. For each pixel i the masks are given by:

$$m_s^{(i)} = |x_s^{(i)} - b| < t_{\text{brightness}}, \quad m_d^{(i)} = |x_d^{(i)} - b| < t_{\text{brightness}} \quad (8)$$

We apply (7) repeatedly until $(p_s \cap m_s)/(wh) > t_{\text{object}}$ to ensure the patch contains part of the object. Then we resize the patch to obtain p_s' with width $w' = sw$ and height $h' = sh$. We select a destination patch p_d in the destination image x_d with the same dimensions and center (c_x', c_y') where:

$$s = \max\left(\frac{w_{\min}}{w}, \frac{h_{\min}}{h}, \min\left(r_s, \frac{w_{\max}}{w}, \frac{h_{\max}}{h}\right)\right) \quad \text{with} \quad r_s \sim N(1, 1/4) \quad (9)$$

$$c_x' \sim U\left(W\frac{w'}{2}, W - W\frac{w'}{2}\right), \quad c_y' \sim U\left(H\frac{h'}{2}, H - H\frac{h'}{2}\right) \quad (10)$$

To prevent creating many examples of patches floating in the background, we apply (10) repeatedly until

$$(p_d \cap m_d)/(w'h') > t_{\text{object}} \qquad \text{(contains part of the object)}, \quad (11)$$

$$(m_{p_d} \cap m_{p_s'})/|m_{p_s'}| > t_{\text{overlap}} \qquad \begin{array}{l}\text{(object portions of patch and} \\ \text{destination image overlap)}\end{array} \quad (12)$$

where m_{p_d} and $m_{p_s'}$ are the object masks of the source and destination patches. We seamlessly blend p_s' into x_d at location (c_x', c_y') to obtain the training sample $\tilde{x}$. After blending the first patch, we add up to $n - 1$ further patches by flipping

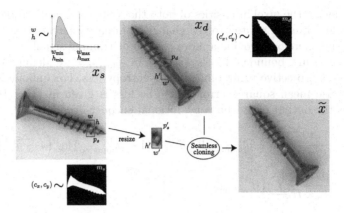

Fig. 1. NSA anomalies are created by seamlessly cloning a patch from a normal training image into another normal training image.

$n - 1$ coins whether to add another patch or not. Figure 1 shows a simplified outline of how the synthetic anomalies are created.

Hyperparameters as Assumptions: The patch selection procedure has a number of hyperparameters which characterize our synthetic out-distribution. Ideally, we would want this synthetic out-distribution to match the real out-distribution as closely as possible but since the real distribution is unknown at training time, we cannot use it to select the hyperparameters and sampling distributions. As [37] proved for generative models, no test statistic is useful for all possible out-distributions and some assumptions must be made to increase the likelihood that the test is useful for relevant or probable out-distributions. For our method, we try to keep these assumptions as broad as possible by generating many different sizes, locations, quantities, and shapes of anomalies and only disregarding those which are obviously irrelevant due to extreme sizes compared to the object or little overlap with the object.

Labels: We use the local intensity differences where a foreign patch has been introduced to create a pixel-wise label $\widetilde{y}$ which is either a) binary: whether there is a difference or not, b) continuous based on the mean absolute intensity difference across C color channels, or c) a logistic function of the previous. All labels are median filtered to be more coherent. Before filtering, the label values at each pixel i are calculated as follows:

$$\widetilde{y}^{(i)}_{\text{binary}} = \begin{cases} 1, & \text{if } \widetilde{x}^{(i)} \neq x^{(i)}_d \\ 0, & \text{otherwise} \end{cases}, \qquad \widetilde{y}^{(i)}_{\text{continuous}} = \frac{1}{C} \sum_{c=1}^{C} |\widetilde{x}^{(i,c)} - x^{(i,c)}_d| \qquad (13)$$

$$\widetilde{y}^{(i)}_{\text{logistic}} = \frac{\widetilde{y}^{(i)}_{\text{binary}}}{1 + \exp\left(-k\left(\widetilde{y}^{(i)}_{\text{continuous}} - y_0\right)\right)} \qquad (14)$$

In contrast, FPI [28] and PII [29] use the patch interpolation factor as a label. This is somewhat ill-posed because the interpolation factor cannot be determined without knowing the pixel intensities of both the source and destination patches. Our labels are directly related to the change in intensity (created by the patch blending) and therefore provide a more consistent training signal.

Loss: When using bounded labels ($\widetilde{y}_{\text{binary}}$ or $\widetilde{y}_{\text{logistic}}$) we define our pixel-wise regression objective using binary cross-entropy loss. For unbounded labels ($\widetilde{y}_{\text{cont.}}$) we use mean squared error loss. The loss is given in (15)–(16) where $\widehat{y} = f(\widetilde{x})$ is the output of a deep convolutional encoder-decoder.

$$\mathcal{L}_{\text{bce}} = \frac{1}{W \times H} \sum_i - \widetilde{y}_{\text{bounded}}^{(i)} \log \widehat{y}^{(i)} - (1 - \widetilde{y}_{\text{bounded}}^{(i)}) \log \left(1 - \widehat{y}^{(i)}\right) \quad (15)$$

$$\mathcal{L}_{\text{mse}} = \frac{1}{W \times H} \sum_i \left(\widetilde{y}_{\text{continuous}}^{(i)} - \widehat{y}^{(i)}\right)^2 \quad (16)$$

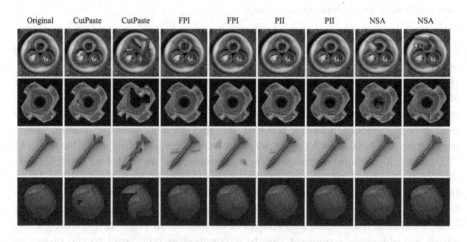

Fig. 2. Synthetic anomalies created with CutPaste, FPI, PII, and NSA.

By varying size, aspect ratio, source and destination location, and resizing the scale of the patches, this method dynamically creates a wide range of synthetic anomalies during training. The examples feature changes in size, shape, texture, location, and color of local image components as well as missing components by blending in a patch containing some background, while staying true to the overall distribution of the images and avoiding obvious discontinuities. Hence, these examples are a more realistic approximation of natural sub-image anomalies than CutPaste augmentations constructed by simply pasting patches at different locations [14] and more diverse than interpolating patches from two separate images at corresponding locations as in FPI [28] and PII [29] although still noticeably artificial to a human observer (Fig. 2).

4   Experiments

We compare end-to-end detection and localization models trained using our self-supervised task to end-to-end models trained using our implementations of FPI [28], PII [29], and CutPaste augmentation [14] on the MVTec AD dataset [2] and a curated subset of a public chest X-ray dataset [33]. We assess performance using the area under the receiver operating characteristic curve (AUROC).

Datasets: MVTec AD [2] contains normal training data and normal and anomalous test data featuring various types of natural and manufacturing defects for 10 object and 5 texture classes.

The NIH chest X-ray dataset [33] contains normal images as well as 14 different types of pathological patterns. There is a lot of natural variation in the normal class which is challenging for unsupervised methods. However, the most obvious differences are easily explained by the different views and the gender of the patients. We reduce this variation by reducing the curated subset defined in [31] further to only posteroanterior (back-to-front) view images of patients aged over 18 and separating them by gender. This leaves us with 1973 normal training images, 299 normal and 139 abnormal test images of male patients. For female patients, we have 1641 normal training, 244 normal and 123 abnormal test images. We call this dataset re-curated chest X-ray (rCXR) in the following. Note that the authors of PII [29] used the full NIH chest X-ray rather than the curated subset defined in [31].

4.1   Network Architecture and Training Setup

We use an encoder-decoder architecture with ResNet-18 [12] without the classification layers as the encoder, two 1×1 convolutions in the bottleneck to reduce the number of channels and a simpler ResNet-based decoder. The final activation is sigmoid and we use binary-crossentropy loss for all models besides NSA (continuous) for which we use ReLU activation and mean squared error loss as the labels are unbounded. The models are trained on batches of size 64 using Adam [13] with a cosine-annealing learning rate [15] that decays from 10^{-3} to 10^{-6} over 320 epochs. For non-aligned objects, the loss takes longer to converge, so we use 560 epochs for the hazelnut, metal nut, and screw classes in the MVTec AD dataset. For rCXR, we use 240 epochs. The same training hyperparameters are used for all variants of the self-supervised task. Hyperparameters for the self-supervised task are given in the supplementary material. Note that in our implementation of FPI, PII, and CutPaste we use object masks and the patch sizes are sampled from a truncated Gamma distribution rather than a uniform distribution [14,28,29] to allow for a more fair comparison with NSA. We call our CutPaste baseline CutPaste (end-to-end) to distinguish it from the multi-stage framework used in [14].

The MVTec AD images have high resolutions of up to 1024×1024 pixels and use the RGB color scheme. We resize object images to 256×256 pixels, apply a random rotation of up to 5 degrees for non-aligned and rotation invariant objects (bottle, hazelnut, metal nut, screw), center-crop to 230×230 pixels and crop a random 224×224 part of the image before creating self-supervised training examples to achieve slight rotation and translation invariance. When testing we use 224×224 center-crops of 256×256 object images. For texture classes, we use random 256×256 crops of 264×264 images for training and 256×256 images for testing. Intensities are normalized using the mean and standard deviation of ImageNet as commonly used before feeding them into the model.

The rCXR images have a resolution of 1024×1024 pixels in grayscale. We resize them to 256×256 pixels for training and apply a random rotation of up to 3 degrees, center-crop to 230×230 pixels and take a random crop of 224×224 pixels. For testing we use 224×224 center-crops of 256×256 resampled images. *Implementation:* We use PyTorch [19] V1.8.1 and train each model on an Nvidia GeForce GTX 1080 GPU while the self-supervised examples are created in parallel using 8 processes on an Intel Core i7-7700K CPU. The code is available at https://github.com/hmsch/natural-synthetic-anomalies.

4.2   Results and Evaluation

Defect Detection. In Table 1 we compare the detection performance of our models trained using variations of NSA, FPI [28], PII [29], and CutPaste [14] to CutPaste (3-way) from [14] which was previously the top-performing approach for defection detection in the MVTec AD dataset [2] without using additional datasets. For NSA, we report the mean and standard error of the detection AUROC for each class as well as the object, texture, and overall averages across five different random seeds. Our best method, NSA (logistic), achieves an overall image-level AUROC of **97.2** outperforming CutPaste (3-way) [14] by 2.0 which is well outside of the standard error range. A single NSA (logistic) model is also better than an ensemble of 5 CutPaste (3-way) models [14] (96.1 AUROC) and comparable to EfficientNet [30] pre-trained with ImageNet and finetuned with CutPaste (3-way) [14] (97.1 AUROC).

Methods using pre-trained ImageNet models, such as PaDiM [6] (97.9 AUROC), do not provide a fair comparison to our from-scratch approach. DRAEM [36] is a more relevant competitor. It uses the describable textures dataset (DTD) [4] not for pre-training but for creating its synthetic anomalies. DRAEM's training objective consists of localizing and correcting the synthetic anomalies, while our model performs anomaly localization. DRAEM (98.0 AUROC) outperforms our approach slightly overall, however both approaches give comparable results for many classes despite the fact that our models only have around 11 million parameters while DRAEM's two components add up to over 97 million parameters. We note that no standard errors were reported for DRAEM's results. The authors of DRAEM claim that realism of the synthetic anomalies is not important for their method. However, their own ablation study indicates that using plain solid colors instead of real textures from DTD, causes localization AUROC and AP to drop from 97.1 and 68.4 down to 92.6 and 56.5, respectively [36]. As such, external data from DTD, which is designed to span a range of textures found in the wild [4], may help to produce synthetic anomalies that overlap more with real anomalies. Furthermore, when using a similar training setup as ours, *i.e.*, without its reconstructive sub-network, DRAEM performs worse (93.9 AUROC) than NSA which uses more realistic synthetic anomalies.

Table 1. Image-level AUROC % for MVTec AD and standard error across five different random seeds. For our models, the image-level is the average pixel score across the image. Best scores between DRAEM [36], CutPaste (3-way) [14], and NSA within standard error are bold-faced. Note that DRAEM uses additional data.

		SOTA		Our experiments					
		DRAEM [36]	CutPaste (3-way) [14]	CutPaste (end-to-end)	FPI	PII	NSA (binary)	NSA (continuous)	NSA (logistic)
Object	Bottle	**99.2**	98.3 ±0.5	100.0	90.2	97.6	97.6 ±0.2	97.5 ±0.2	97.7 ±0.3
	Cable	91.8	80.6 ±0.5	75.4	68.0	68.9	92.1 ±2.4	90.2 ±3.0	**94.5** ±1.0
	Capsule	**98.5**	96.2 ±0.5	89.2	87.5	84.9	93.2 ±0.8	92.8 ±2.2	95.2 ±1.7
	Hazelnut	**100.0**	97.3 ±0.3	81.4	86.0	82.7	93.5 ±1.9	89.3 ±4.9	94.7 ±1.1
	Metal nut	98.7	**99.3** ±0.2	70.6	88.4	98.9	**99.4** ±0.3	94.6 ±2.1	98.7 ±0.7
	Pill	98.9	92.4 ±1.3	90.3	71.8	86.3	97.0 ±0.9	94.3 ±1.1	**99.2** ±0.6
	Screw	**93.9**	86.3 ±1.0	65.5	61.2	74.7	90.3 ±1.2	90.1 ±0.9	90.2 ±1.4
	Toothbrush	**100.0**	98.3 ±0.9	96.7	85.8	93.1	**100.0** ±0.0	99.6 ±0.5	**100.0** ±0.0
	Transistor	93.1	**95.5** ±0.5	88.2	79.6	90.1	93.5 ±0.9	92.8 ±2.2	**95.1** ±0.2
	Zipper	**100.0**	99.4 ±0.2	98.7	97.7	99.8	99.8 ±0.1	99.5 ±0.7	99.8 ±0.1
	Average	**97.4**	94.3 ±0.6	85.6	81.6	87.7	95.6 ±0.5	94.1 ±1.0	96.5 ±0.3
Texture	carpet	**97.0**	93.1 ±1.1	53.1	56.0	65.6	85.6 ±7.6	90.9 ±2.2	95.6 ±0.6
	Grid	**99.9**	**99.9** ±0.1	99.7	99.5	100.0	**99.9** ±0.1	98.5 ±3.3	**99.9** ±0.1
	Leather	**100.0**	**100.0** ±0.0	86.6	91.7	100.0	99.9 ±0.1	**100.0** ±0.0	99.9 ±0.1
	Tile	99.6	93.4 ±1.0	87.8	90.2	98.4	99.7 ±0.2	**100.0** ±0.0	**100.0** ±0.0
	Wood	**99.1**	98.6 ±0.5	84.6	74.4	91.9	96.7 ±1.2	97.8 ±0.8	97.5 ±1.5
	Average	**99.1**	97.0 ±0.5	82.4	82.4	91.2	96.4 ±1.4	97.5 ±0.9	98.6 ±0.3
Overall average		**98.0**	95.2 ±0.6	84.5	81.9	88.9	95.9 ±0.7	95.2 ±0.5	97.2 ±0.3

Synthetic Anomalies Should be as Diverse and Realistic as Possible. In our experiments, models trained with self-supervised examples created using Poisson blending clearly outperform models trained with simpler data-augmentation strategies like CutPaste [14] and FPI [28]. Examples created with Poisson blending are more visually similar to real-world defects as they do not have artificial discontinuities (Fig. 2) and according to Table 1, the corresponding models generalize better to real defects. Although PII [29] performs well for most texture classes, NSA, which also shifts and resizes the patches, performs much better for objects. Since PII and FPI use the same source and destination location for the patches, their synthetic anomalies are very subtle for aligned object classes and much subtler than the real defects in the MVTec AD dataset. In classes with lower AUROC, the synthetic training anomalies may have less similarity to the real test anomalies. These classes also tend to have higher standard error. In contrast, classes with high AUROC have low standard error. This could indicate that for these classes the self-supervised task can sensitize the network to the distribution of real anomalies reliably. It may also be possible to use the variance between random seeds to gauge the reliability of predictions.

Labels Should Approximate the Degree of Abnormality. Aside from abnormal irregularities there can also be natural variation between and within the images of each class. When training a model with binary labels, the final activations tend to saturate and the predictions do not give any measure of how anomalous the regions with high scores are. Training a model with continuous labels teaches the model to differentiate between different degrees of anomalies. When using unbounded continuous labels, training is less stable and the AUROC scores have a high standard error. Models trained with bounded continuous labels outperform the binary ones most in classes with high inherent variation such as cable, hazelnut, transistor, carpet, and wood (Table 1) when using a threshold independent metric such as AUROC. PII [29] also uses continuous labels; pixels corresponding to the foreign patch are assigned to a uniform value equivalent to the interpolation factor. However, NSA (logistic) outperforms PII for some textures and most objects, including unaligned objects. For aligned objects, NSA creates more diverse anomalies than PII because the location of the source and destination patches can be different. But for unaligned objects, this advantage is negligible. Despite the similarity in generated anomalies, NSA still yields higher performance in these classes. A possible explanation is that the labels for NSA (logistic) are inhomogeneous and based on the outcome of the blending rather than its setup and hence more accurately represent the degree of abnormality.

Defect Localization. In Table 2 we report the pixel-level performance of the models from Table 1. Although NSA performs well for objects on the image-level when trained with unbounded continuous labels, pixel-wise performance is much better for NSA with bounded binary or continuous labels. NSA (logistic) achieves a **96.3** average pixel-level AUROC performing similarly to CutPaste (3-way) [14] (96.0 AUROC). It also reaches similar performance to DRAEM [36] for many classes although DRAEM achieves a higher overall score (97.3 AUROC). Figure 3 shows that NSA (logistic) can localize a wide range of real-world defects accurately including anomalies that are very different from the synthetic anomalies seen during training (*e.g.*, white writing on hazelnuts, misplaced transistors, stained tiles and carpet).

Medical Imaging. In Table 3, we compare the performance of NSA and end-to-end models trained using other self-supervised tasks for the task of binary classification of rCXR images into healthy (normal) and pathological (abnormal) categories. Models trained using NSA clearly outperform end-to-end models trained with FPI [28] or CutPaste [14]. NSA also outperforms PII [29]. However, the type of label used for NSA is less important for this dataset. Since there is high inter-sample variability in the normal data, it is possible that all synthetic anomalies created by NSA would be considered abnormal. So, approximating the degree of abnormality with a continuous label does not improve over the binary labels when evaluating the model with real anomalies.

We do not report pixel-level metrics, as we only have very rough bounding boxes for less than 10% of the test set. Figure 4 shows example predictions for several healthy and pathological cases. The localization predictions are good for examples 1–5, 7, and 8, but the model fails to detect any abnormal findings in the 6th example and disagrees with the bounding box annotation for bottom examples 9 and 10. We did not compare to CutPaste (3-way) [14] here as there is no reference implementation available.

Limitations. The 9th example in Fig. 4 shows cardiomegaly, *i.e.*, an enlarged heart, for which the bounding box contains the entire heart. But the model

Table 2. Pixel-level AUROC % with standard error for the MVTec AD models from Table 1. Note that DRAEM uses additional data.

		SOTA		Our experiments					
		DRAEM [36]	CutPaste (3-way) [14]	CutPaste (end-to-end)	FPI	PII	NSA (binary)	NSA (continuous)	NSA (logistic)
Object	Bottle	**99.1**	97.6 ±0.1	97.7	91.8	93.1	98.4 ±0.2	97.3 ±0.5	98.3 ±0.1
	Cable	**94.7**	90.0 ±0.2	81.0	66.5	70.2	93.3 ±3.4	91.0 ±2.8	96.0 ±1.4
	Capsule	94.3	97.4 ±0.1	97.5	95.9	90.2	**98.1** ±0.2	91.6 ±5.6	97.6 ±0.9
	Hazelnut	**99.7**	97.3 ±0.1	94.8	89.8	97.0	97.2 ±0.6	97.7 ±0.6	97.6 ±0.6
	Metal nut	**99.5**	93.1 ±0.4	68.1	96.2	95.4	98.2 ±0.2	97.3 ±0.3	98.4 ±0.2
	Pill	97.6	95.7 ±0.1	98.1	62.3	95.3	98.5 ±0.2	**97.1** ±2.7	98.5 ±0.3
	Screw	**97.6**	96.7 ±0.1	90.7	90.4	92.8	96.7 ±0.4	92.3 ±5.3	96.5 ±0.1
	Toothbrush	**98.1**	**98.1** ±0.0	95.7	81.8	81.3	95.6 ±0.6	94.5 ±0.7	94.9 ±0.7
	Transistor	**90.9**	93.0 ±0.2	85.9	78.5	86.9	87.8 ±1.9	80.2 ±3.3	88.0 ±1.8
	Zipper	98.8	99.3 ±0.0	92.9	91.8	93.8	94.2 ±0.2	90.7 ±1.5	94.2 ±0.3
	Average	**97.0**	95.8 ±0.1	90.2	84.5	89.6	95.8 ±0.4	93.0 ±1.7	96.0 ±0.4
Texture	Carpet	95.5	**98.3** ±0.0	83.3	70.8	97.2	94.5 ±4.1	81.8 ±6.8	95.5 ±2.3
	Grid	**99.7**	97.5 ±0.1	97.6	94.2	98.9	99.1 ±0.0	98.0 ±0.3	99.2 ±0.1
	Leather	98.6	99.5 ±0.0	96.4	88.3	99.2	**99.6** ±0.0	99.5 ±0.2	99.5 ±0.1
	Tile	99.2	90.5 ±0.2	72.7	65.0	98.0	99.0 ±0.2	97.4 ±0.7	**99.3** ±0.0
	Wood	**96.4**	95.5 ±0.1	84.0	71.1	91.1	94.0 ±0.8	90.6 ±3.7	90.7 ±1.9
	Average	**97.9**	96.3 ±0.1	86.8	77.9	96.9	97.3 ±0.7	93.5 ±0.9	96.8 ±0.7
Overall average		**97.3**	96.0 ±0.1	89.1	82.3	92.0	96.3 ±0.2	93.1 ±1.1	96.3 ±0.4

Table 3. Image-level AUROC % for rCXR and standard error across five different random seeds. Best scores per row within standard error are bold-faced.

	CutPaste (end-to-end)	FPI	PII	NSA(binary)	NSA(continuous)	NSA(logistic)
Male	59.8	73.7	91.7 ±0.6	**94.0** ±0.5	93.4 ±0.3	**94.0** ±0.6
Female	56.2	67.4	92.8 ±0.4	**94.3** ±0.6	93.0 ±0.4	**94.0** ±0.5

only activates for portions of the heart that exceed the normal size found in healthy patients. In these cases, the model lacks the semantic understanding that radiologists use to categorize diseases. In the 10th example, the model activates more for the tubes on the patient's right side than for the finding inside of the bounding box. Unlike a human radiologist, an anomaly detection model cannot be expected to automatically classify clinically correctly placed lines, tubes, or cardiac devices as normal if they are not expected in the healthy training distribution.

Our method sometimes fails to detect very small defects (see capsule, hazelnut, screw, and wood examples in Fig. 5), predicts too large regions or has false positives (see bottle, cable, zipper, carpet, leather in Fig. 5). The transistor class has several examples of misplaced or missing transistors. These are detected but the predicted localization does not match the large human annotation (Fig. 5) resulting in a low localization AUROC (Table 2). Patch-wise localization, as used for CutPaste [14] and PaDiM [6] among others, can detect the missing transistor for each patch and hence produce a segmentation map closer to the human annotation. However, for these large anomalies the type of defect is immediately obvious to a human inspector once detected so we argue that precise localization would not be necessary for most applications.

Since the model does not see any real anomalies during training, it may predict statistically unlikely normal variations as abnormal and fails to recognize subtle anomalies that are very different from the synthetic anomalies seen during training. Hence, predictions from a self-supervised anomaly detection model

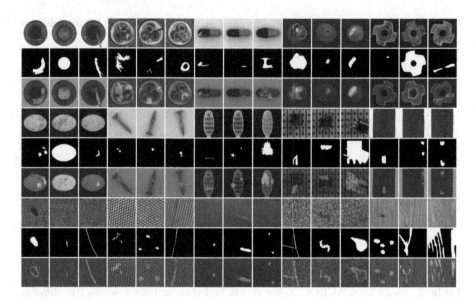

Fig. 3. Examples of defect localization in the MVTec AD dataset using models trained with NSA (logistic). From top to bottom: input images, human annotation, heatmap of pixel-level predictions. Best viewed in a digital version.

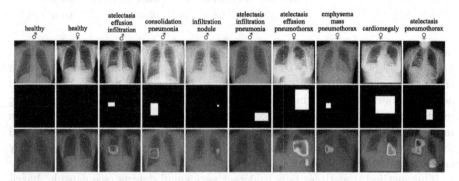

Fig. 4. Example localization predictions for chest X-ray disease detection using models trained with NSA (binary). From top to bottom: input images, rough bounding box from a radiologist, heatmap of pixel-level predictions. Each case is labeled with pathology keywords that [33] mined from radiologist reports.

should not be used on their own for decision making. Such models can however be useful as an instant second observer and for quality control. As far as we are aware, there are no further potential negative societal impacts of this work.

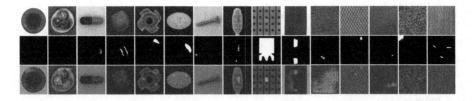

Fig. 5. Failure cases for MVTec AD defect localization using models trained with NSA (logistic). Examples include false pos./negatives and incorrect localization. From left to right: input, human annotation, heatmap of pixel-level predictions.

5   Conclusion

We propose a self-supervised task that creates diverse and realistic synthetic anomalies. These training examples are generated under controlled conditions that help to produce relevant and subtle anomalies. This provides a more consistent training signal and results in better detection of real anomalies. The formulation of the loss and synthetic labels yields an effective and computationally efficient training task. This helps NSA outperform state-of-the-art methods on both natural and medical imaging datasets, demonstrating its generalizability. In the future, additions such as quantifying uncertainty or exploiting classes of known anomalies could help facilitate the use of NSA in critical applications.

Acknowledgments. This work was supported by the UK Research and Innovation London Medical Imaging and Artificial Intelligence Centre for Value Based Healthcare and the iFind project, Wellcome Trust IEH Award [102431].

References

1. Abati, D., Porrello, A., Calderara, S., Cucchiara, R.: Latent space autoregression for novelty detection. In: IEEE Conference on Computer Vision and Pattern Recognition, CVPR 2019, Long Beach, CA, USA, 16–20 June 2019, pp. 481–490. Computer Vision Foundation/IEEE (2019)
2. Bergmann, P., Batzner, K., Fauser, M., Sattlegger, D., Steger, C.: The MVTec anomaly detection dataset: a comprehensive real-world dataset for unsupervised anomaly detection. Int. J. Comput. Vision **129**(4), 1038–1059 (2021). https://doi. org/10.1007/s11263-020-01400-4
3. Bradski, G.: The OpenCV library. Dr. Dobb's J. Softw. Tools (2000)
4. Cimpoi, M., Maji, S., Kokkinos, I., Mohamed, S., Vedaldi, A.: Describing textures in the wild. In: 2014 IEEE Conference on Computer Vision and Pattern Recognition, pp. 3606–3613 (2014)
5. Cohen, N., Hoshen, Y.: Sub-image anomaly detection with deep pyramid correspondences (2021)
6. Defard, T., Setkov, A., Loesch, A., Audigier, R.: PaDiM: a patch distribution modeling framework for anomaly detection and localization. In: Del Bimbo, A., et al. (eds.) ICPR 2021. LNCS, vol. 12664, pp. 475–489. Springer, Cham (2021). https://doi.org/10.1007/978-3-030-68799-1_35
7. Doersch, C., Gupta, A., Efros, A.A.: Unsupervised visual representation learning by context prediction. In: 2015 IEEE International Conference on Computer Vision (ICCV), pp. 1422–1430 (2015)

8. Gidaris, S., Singh, P., Komodakis, N.: Unsupervised representation learning by predicting image rotations. In: International Conference on Learning Representations (2018)
9. Golan, I., El-Yaniv, R.: Deep anomaly detection using geometric transformations. In: Proceedings of the 32nd International Conference on Neural Information Processing Systems, NIPS 2018, pp. 9781–9791. Curran Associates Inc., Red Hook (2018)
10. Grathwohl, W., Chen, R.T.Q., Bettencourt, J., Sutskever, I., Duvenaud, D.: FFJORD: free-form continuous dynamics for scalable reversible generative models. In: 7th International Conference on Learning Representations, ICLR 2019, 6–9 May 2019, New Orleans, LA, USA (2019). OpenReview.net
11. Gudovskiy, D.A., Ishizaka, S., Kozuka, K.: CFLOW-AD: real-time unsupervised anomaly detection with localization via conditional normalizing flows. In: 2022 IEEE/CVF Winter Conference on Applications of Computer Vision (WACV), pp. 1819–1828 (2022)
12. He, K., Zhang, X., Ren, S., Sun, J.: Deep residual learning for image recognition. In: 2016 IEEE Conference on Computer Vision and Pattern Recognition (CVPR), pp. 770–778 (2016)
13. Kingma, D.P., Ba, J.: Adam: a method for stochastic optimization. In: 3rd International Conference on Learning Representations, ICLR 2015, San Diego, CA, USA, 7–9 May 2015, Conference Track Proceedings (2015)
14. Li, C.L., Sohn, K., Yoon, J., Pfister, T.: CutPaste: self-supervised learning for anomaly detection and localization. In: Proceedings of the IEEE/CVF Conference on Computer Vision and Pattern Recognition (CVPR), pp. 9664–9674, June 2021. https://doi.org/10.1109/CVPR46437.2021.00954
15. Loshchilov, I., Hutter, F.: SGDR: stochastic gradient descent with warm restarts. In: 5th International Conference on Learning Representations, ICLR 2017, Toulon, France, 24–26 April 2017, Conference Track Proceedings (2017). OpenReview.net
16. Mack, A., Rock, I., et al.: Inattentional Blindness. MIT Press (1998)
17. Marimont, S.N., Tarroni, G.: Anomaly detection through latent space restoration using vector quantized variational autoencoders. In: 2021 IEEE 18th International Symposium on Biomedical Imaging (ISBI), pp. 1764–1767 (2021)
18. Nalisnick, E.T., Matsukawa, A., Teh, Y.W., Görür, D., Lakshminarayanan, B.: Do deep generative models know what they don't know? In: 7th International Conference on Learning Representations, ICLR 2019, New Orleans, LA, USA, 6–9 May 2019 (2019). OpenReview.net
19. Paszke, A., et al.: PyTorch: an imperative style, high-performance deep learning library. In: Advances in Neural Information Processing Systems, vol. 32, pp. 8024–8035. Curran Associates, Inc. (2019)
20. Pawlowski, N., et al.: Unsupervised lesion detection in brain CT using Bayesian convolutional autoencoders. In: OpenReview (2018)
21. Pérez, P., Gangnet, M., Blake, A.: Poisson image editing. In: ACM SIGGRAPH 2003 Papers, SIGGRAPH 2003, pp. 313–318. Association for Computing Machinery, New York (2003)
22. Raghu, M., Zhang, C., Kleinberg, J., Bengio, S.: Transfusion: understanding transfer learning for medical imaging. In: Wallach, H., Larochelle, H., Beygelzimer, A., d' Alché-Buc, F., Fox, E., Garnett, R. (eds.) Advances in Neural Information Processing Systems, vol. 32. Curran Associates, Inc. (2019)

23. Rippel, O., Mertens, P., Merhof, D.: Modeling the distribution of normal data in pre-trained deep features for anomaly detection. In: 25th International Conference on Pattern Recognition, ICPR 2020, Virtual Event/Milan, Italy, 10–15 January 2021, pp. 6726–6733. IEEE (2020)

24. Roth, K., Pemula, L., Zepeda, J., Schölkopf, B., Brox, T., Gehler, P.: Towards total recall in industrial anomaly detection. In: Proceedings of the IEEE/CVF Conference on Computer Vision and Pattern Recognition (CVPR), pp. 14318–14328, June 2022

25. Ruff, L., et al.: A unifying review of deep and shallow anomaly detection. Proc. IEEE **109**, 756–795 (2021)

26. Ruff, L., et al.: Deep one-class classification. In: Proceedings of the 35th International Conference on Machine Learning. Proceedings of Machine Learning Research, vol. 80, pp. 4393–4402. PMLR (2018)

27. Schlegl, T., Seeböck, P., Waldstein, S.M., Langs, G., Schmidt-Erfurth, U.: f-AnoGAN: fast unsupervised anomaly detection with generative adversarial networks. Med. Image Anal. **54**, 30–44 (2019)

28. Tan, J., Hou, B., Batten, J., Qiu, H., Kainz, B.: Detecting outliers with foreign patch interpolation. Mach. Learn. Biomed. Imaging **2022**, 1–27 (2022). https://melba-journal.org/papers/2022:013.html

29. Tan, J., Hou, B., Day, T., Simpson, J., Rueckert, D., Kainz, B.: Detecting outliers with poisson image interpolation. In: de Bruijne, M., et al. (eds.) MICCAI 2021. LNCS, vol. 12905, pp. 581–591. Springer, Cham (2021). https://doi.org/10.1007/978-3-030-87240-3_56

30. Tan, M., Le, Q.: EfficientNet: Rethinking model scaling for convolutional neural networks. In: Proceedings of the 36th International Conference on Machine Learning. Proceedings of Machine Learning Research, vol. 97, pp. 6105–6114. PMLR (06 2019)

31. Tang, Y.X., et al.: Automated abnormality classification of chest radiographs using deep convolutional neural networks. NPJ Digit. Med. **3**(1), 1–8 (2020)

32. Wang, L., Zhang, D., Guo, J., Han, Y.: Image anomaly detection using normal data only by latent space resampling. Appl. Sci. **10**(23) (2020)

33. Wang, X., Peng, Y., Lu, L., Lu, Z., Bagheri, M., Summers, R.M.: ChestX-ray8: hospital-scale chest X-ray database and benchmarks on weakly-supervised classification and localization of common thorax diseases. In: Proceedings of the IEEE Conference on Computer Vision and Pattern Recognition, pp. 2097–2106 (2017). https://doi.org/10.1109/CVPR.2017.369

34. Yi, J., Yoon, S.: Patch SVDD: patch-level SVDD for anomaly detection and segmentation. In: Proceedings of the Asian Conference on Computer Vision (ACCV) (2020)

35. Yu, J., et al.: FastFlow: unsupervised anomaly detection and localization via 2d normalizing flows. CoRR abs/2111.07677 (2021)

36. Zavrtanik, V., Kristan, M., Skocaj, D.: DRAEM-a discriminatively trained reconstruction embedding for surface anomaly detection. In: Proceedings of the IEEE/CVF International Conference on Computer Vision, pp. 8330–8339 (2021). https://doi.org/10.1109/ICCV48922.2021.00822

37. Zhang, L., Goldstein, M., Ranganath, R.: Understanding failures in out-of-distribution detection with deep generative models. In: Meila, M., Zhang, T. (eds.) Proceedings of the 38th International Conference on Machine Learning. Proceedings of Machine Learning Research, vol. 139, pp. 12427–12436. PMLR, 18–24 July 2021

38. Zimmerer, D., Isensee, F., Petersen, J., Kohl, S., Maier-Hein, K.: Unsupervised anomaly localization using variational auto-encoders. In: Shen, D., et al. (eds.) MICCAI 2019. LNCS, vol. 11767, pp. 289–297. Springer, Cham (2019). https://doi.org/10.1007/978-3-030-32251-9_32

Understanding Collapse in Non-contrastive Siamese Representation Learning

Alexander C. Li[1]([✉])(iD), Alexei A. Efros[2](iD), and Deepak Pathak[1](iD)

[1] Carnegie Mellon University, Pittsburgh, USA
alexanderli@cmu.edu
[2] University of California, Berkeley, USA

Abstract. Contrastive methods have led a recent surge in the performance of self-supervised representation learning (SSL). Recent methods like BYOL or SimSiam purportedly distill these contrastive methods down to their essence, removing bells and whistles, including the negative examples, that do not contribute to downstream performance. These "non-contrastive" methods surprisingly work well without using negatives even though the global minimum lies at trivial collapse. We empirically analyze these non-contrastive methods and find that SimSiam is extraordinarily sensitive to model size. In particular, SimSiam representations undergo partial dimensional collapse if the model is too small relative to the dataset size. We propose a metric to measure the degree of this collapse and show that it can be used to forecast the downstream task performance without any fine-tuning or labels. We further analyze architectural design choices and their effect on the downstream performance. Finally, we demonstrate that shifting to a continual learning setting acts as a regularizer and prevents collapse, and a hybrid between continual and multi-epoch training can improve linear probe accuracy by as many as 18% points using ResNet-18 on ImageNet.

Keywords: Self-supervised learning · Continual learning

1 Introduction

Self-supervised representation learning (SSL) has seen steady progress in the last several years. Recent success has been obtained via Siamese representation learning. Given an input image, the neural network encoder is trained such that the feature encoding of different augmentations, aka "views", of the image are close to each other. However, trivially training such an image encoder leads to collapse, where the encoder outputs a constant representation irrespective of

Supplementary Information The online version contains supplementary material available at https://doi.org/10.1007/978-3-031-19821-2_28.

S. Avidan et al. (Eds.): ECCV 2022, LNCS 13691, pp. 490–505, 2022.
https://doi.org/10.1007/978-3-031-19821-2_28

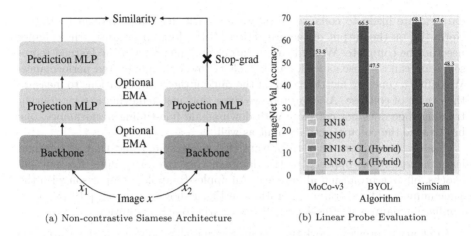

(a) Non-contrastive Siamese Architecture   (b) Linear Probe Evaluation

Fig. 1. Non-contrastive methods and sensitivity to model size. Left: given augmentations x_1 and x_2 of the same starting image, non-contrastive Siamese methods learn to use x_1 to predict the representation of x_2. SimSiam uses only the stop-grad, whereas BYOL additionally uses an exponential moving average for the second branch. Right: in contrast to methods like MoCo-v3 [7] or BYOL [12], SimSiam linear probe accuracy drops dramatically when the model is too small relative to the dataset complexity. We can close the performance gap and outperform BYOL on ResNet-18 by applying a hybrid of continual and multi-epoch training as discussed in Sect. 4.

input. Contrastive methods avoid this collapse by encouraging the learned representations to be far apart for views coming from very different images. There are many ways to implement this contrastive objective, either via instance discrimination, where augmentations from the same image are treated as positives and from different images as negatives [1,4,13,16,22], or by contrasting different clusters of positives [2,3]. These approaches work well but are bottlenecked by their reliance on negatives, as it is tricky to ensure that the negative samples are not too easy to distinguish [30].

Recent methods have found an alternative by removing the negatives altogether and adding architectural constraints, e.g. the momentum encoder in BYOL [27] or the stop gradient in SimSiam [5]. These "non-contrastive" models achieve strong results in the typical ImageNet pre-training setting, which is surprising because there is no strict constraint to prevent the aforementioned collapse. Some prior work has analyzed learning non-contrastive learning dynamics in a simple linear model [29], but analysis of when collapse happens is still ad hoc and largely anecdotal.

In this work, we seek to empirically understand the scenarios under which collapse occurs in these non-contrastive Siamese networks and suggest potential ways to avoid it. Contrary to previous methods that claim that the stop-gradient, prediction head, and high predictor learning rate are enough to prevent the collapse [5,29], we show that collapse additionally depends on the model capacity relative to the data complexity. For instance, small networks trained on large datasets are likely to collapse despite using tricks like stop-gradient or Batch-Norm [17] on the output of the projection MLP. More importantly, the collapse need not be complete. We find that a subset of dimensions in the learned representation can collapse as well, which leads to lower than expected performance. We define a concrete metric based on the rank of the representations to measure the degree of collapse. As expected, we show that just achieving low loss during training time does not correlate with downstream fine-tuning performance; one has to take the collapse into account as well.

Finally, we explore ways to prevent this collapse and find that a continual learning regime, as opposed to the dominant practice of training for multiple epochs, offers a promising alternative. An apples-to-apples comparison with the same number of total training iterations in Fig. 1 shows a gain of up to 18% over vanilla SimSiam using ResNet18. We summarize our contributions below:

- Contrary to previous work that claims SimSiam has no issues with collapse, we show that SimSiam performance drops significantly when the model capacity is too small relative to the data complexity.
- We define a rank-based metric to measure the degree of *partial dimensional collapse*, i.e., the representations contain redundant information which leads to the decline in downstream performance.
- Linear regression, using our collapse metric and the SimSiam loss, can accurately predict the linear probing accuracy. This can be used to compare models without using labels or additional training time.
- We show that model width is more important for downstream performance than depth, even when the total number of parameters is accounted for.
- We show that switching to a continual learning setting eliminates collapse and restores SimSiam accuracy by as much as 18% points.

2   Related Work

Self-supervised Learning. Contrastive learning approaches learn a representation space where positive sample pairs are closer and negative sample pairs are driven further apart [4,13,15,16,22,24]. Often, for a given image from the dataset, a positive sample pair is constructed using an image augmentation. Negative sample pairs are generated by randomly sampling different images from the dataset. One of the drawbacks of these approaches is that training with explicit negative pairs might cause representations of very similar images to be pushed too far apart, depending on how the negatives are mined. More recent non-contrastive approaches are able to learn representations without the need for negative samples at all [5,12], using only image augmentations and stop gradient.

Understanding Self-supervised Learning. [29] analyzes a surprisingly predictive linear model that represents the BYOL and SimSiam settings. However, their linear model makes no predictions about the effect of model capacity or dataset complexity. Most prior work has focused on understanding contrastive learning [18,25,28], but understanding of non-contrastive Siamese learning remains limited.

Continual Learning. Continual learning focuses on how to train models when presented with a stream of (potentially correlated) data. Typically, sticking to the multi-epoch procedure and just taking gradient steps on the data as it arrives, without any modification to the training algorithm, leads to catastrophic forgetting [11,19], where model performance deteriorates on past data. A wide variety of continual learning methods have been proposed to address this problem. Regularization-based methods such as elastic weight consolidation [19] or sharpness-based regularization [8] seek to constrain the parameters that strongly affect the loss. Replay-based or coreset methods store summary information about previous data, such as class-based cluster centers [26]. However, these continual learning methods have always performed worse than a model that can train on all of the data at once, i.e. multi-epoch training is preferable to continual learning. In this paper, we surprisingly draw the opposite conclusion: continual learning, without applying any fancy tricks, yields much higher downstream performance than multi-epoch training.

3   Relative Underparameterization Causes Collapse

Smaller networks, such as ResNet-18 and ResNet-34 [14], are useful for a variety of reasons. They train faster and require less GPU memory, which is especially desirable for academics or practitioners with limited compute resources. Smaller networks also have lower latency, higher throughput, and better energy efficiency at inference time. Typically, we expect model accuracy or other metrics to fall gracefully as we reduce the size of the model. However, Fig. 1 shows that Sim-Siam performance drops significantly when using ResNet-18 instead of ResNet-50. This is unexpected, as these networks still have enough capacity to fit the SimSiam objective (see the performance with BYOL, which uses the same loss function). Furthermore, SimSiam with ResNet-18 has been shown [6] to match the performance of contrastive learning algorithms like SimCLR [4] on simple datasets like CIFAR-10 [20]. In this section, we seek to explain why smaller SimSiam models tend to have drastically lower performance on larger datasets.

3.1   Experimental Setup

Non-contrastive Siamese methods, e.g. BYOL and SimSiam, have the same general architecture, shown in Fig. 1(a). Two views x_1 and x_2 of the same image are generated with two different augmentations, and x_1 is passed into the online backbone network on the left, while x_2 is passed into the target backbone network on the right. The backbone is typically a ResNet variant [14]. The outputs of these two backbone networks are passed into the corresponding projection MLPs, and then a prediction MLP is used to predict the projected representation of x_2 from the projected representation of x_1. SimSiam uses the same network for the online and target backbone and projection networks and uses a stop-gradient to prevent gradient signal from propagating through the second branch. BYOL also uses a stop-grad, but additionally uses an exponential moving average (EMA) to update the target backbone and projection networks.

SimSiam Configuration. Unless otherwise stated, we use the same hyperparameters for each SimSiam model, from the original SimSiam ResNet-50 configuration [6]: we use batch size 256, which works well for ResNet-50 in the 100-epoch pre-training setting, and use SGD with learning rate 0.05, momentum 0.9, and cosine learning rate decay. Regardless of how much data we train on, or in what order the data is used, we train the model for 500 thousand gradient steps, which is equivalent to 100 epochs on 100% of ImageNet with a batch size of 256.

Linear Probe Configuration. Following the procedure in [6], we replace the projection and prediction heads with a fully connected layer and freeze the ResNet backbone. We perform 90 epochs of linear probing with the LARS optimizer, learning rate 0.1, and cosine learning rate decay. We use the standard augmentations: RandomResizedCrop, random horizontal flip, and normalization.

K-nearest Neighbors Configuration. We remove the projection and prediction heads, and just use the ResNet backbone to compute representations. For each image in the ImageNet-1k training and validation sets, we resize the image to 256×256, followed by a 224×224 center crop and normalization. We use cosine similarity to determine the nearest neighbors of each of the validation images, as this consistently yielded higher accuracies than the Euclidean distance. We select the value of k that maximizes the validation accuracy. The k-NN accuracy is fast to compute, requiring only about 10 min on an RTX 3090 GPU, compared to roughly 16 h for linear probing. k-NN is also consistent and does not vary across evaluations, unlike learned linear probing.

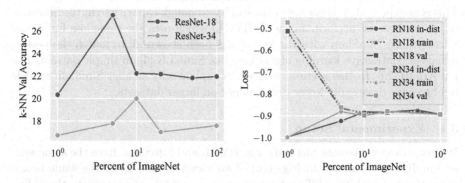

Fig. 2. SimSiam performance as a function of dataset size. For the ResNet-18 and ResNet-34 architectures, we train 6 SimSiam models from scratch, each on a different size subset of ImageNet (1%, 5%, 10%, 20%, 50%, and 100%). Left: as we increase the amount of training data, the linear probing accuracy and k-NN accuracy increase until a certain model size to dataset size ratio, after which accuracy begins to fall. Right: This increase and decrease in performance is not apparent if we only look at the SimSiam loss, whether it is on the training set, validation set, or in-distribution subset.

3.2   Performance Impact of Model Size Relative to Dataset Size

If ResNet-18 works well with SimSiam on CIFAR-10, but does poorly on ImageNet-1k, what causes this difference? The complexity of the dataset matters as ImageNet is much more difficult to fit than CIFAR-10 (i.e. it has a larger *intrinsic dimension* [21]). Model size also matters as SimSiam + ResNet-50 is capable of SOTA performance on certain SSL benchmarks. Hence, we hypothesize that it is actually the ratio of model capacity relative to the dataset complexity that determines the SimSiam performance. The larger and more complex the dataset, the bigger the model needs to be.

To test our hypothesis, we perform an experiment where we train ResNet-18 and ResNet-34 SimSiam models for the same number of gradient steps but on different amounts of data from ImageNet-1k [9], ranging in {1%, 5%, 10%, 20%, 50%, 100%}. By varying the size of the training set, we change how difficult it is to fit. Figure 2 (left) shows the k-NN validation accuracy of these models. Both architectures have a "sweet spot" in the size of the training set. ResNet-18 peaks at 5% of ImageNet-1k, whereas ResNet-34 peaks with more data at 10%. After the peak, k-NN accuracy falls and stays relatively flat. This supports our hypothesis since more data helps up to a certain threshold. However, this increase and decrease in accuracy is not visible in any of the loss metrics shown in Fig. 2 (right). The ResNet-18 accuracy peaks at 5% of ImageNet, and the ResNet-34 accuracy peaks at 10% of ImageNet, yet the in-distribution loss monotonically increases and the full training and validation losses monotonically decrease.

It is worth noting that the loss on the training subset and the loss on the validation set coincide almost perfectly for every subset of at least 10%. This indicates that the SimSiam model is not overfitting in the classical train/test sense, and theories such as "deep double descent" [23], which characterize the size of the effect of model size on the generalization gap between the train and test loss, do not explain the effect of varying model size or dataset size.

One thing we notice is that ResNet-34 consistently performs worse than ResNet-18, which we analyze below.

3.3   Performance Impact of Model Architecture

Table 1. Network width matters more than depth or number of parameters.

Block type	Layers	Width multiplier	Repr. dim.	Params	Lin. Acc.
Basic	18	1x	512	11.7M	30.0%
Basic	34	1x	512	21.8M	16.8%
Bottleneck	50	1x	2048	25.6M	68.1%
Bottleneck	26	1x	2048	16.0M	61.7%
Bottleneck	26	2x	2048	39.6M	62.6%
Basic	50	1x	512	31.9M	17.5%

We analyze what architectural components determine model capacity in the non-contrastive SSL. In Table 1, we show the performance of various ResNet variants trained with SimSiam. The top three rows are vanilla ResNet-18, -34, and -50 models, and the last 3 correspond to new variants that mix various components. First, we find that increasing depth does not always improve performance, especially if the model is not wide enough. Increasing the depth from ResNet-18 to ResNet-34 to a depth-50 network with Basic blocks actually decreases downstream performance. We hypothesize that increased depth may make it easier for SimSiam to lose information at every layer and compute collapsed representations, since the size of the vector passed between layers is limited.

In contrast, using Bottleneck residual blocks (1×1 conv to decrease the number of channels, then 3×3 conv, then 1×1 to increase the number of channels) to increase the width of the network is much more effective. This achieves 61.7% linear probing accuracy with fewer parameters than even a ResNet-34. Doubling the width of that network further increases accuracy by another 0.9%. Overall, model capacity corresponds more to width than depth. We also tried training Vision Transformers [10] with SimSiam, but found uniformly negative results. We discuss this in Appendix 4.1.

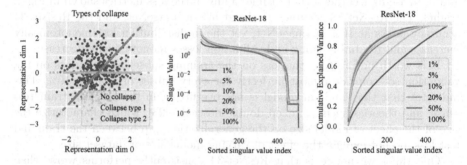

Fig. 3. Partial dimensional collapse for large subsets. Left: the obvious form of dimensional collapse is when a particular dimension collapses to a constant value. Less obvious is when two representation dimensions covary together, i.e. one can be predicted from the other. There appears to be variation in each dimension, but the second dimension conveys no additional information. The singular values from PCA capture both kinds of collapse. Middle: we plot the singular values of representations computed by SimSiam ResNet-18 models trained on different size subsets of ImageNet. Right: the cumulative explained variance corresponding to the cumulative sum of the singular values, divided by the total. The faster this rises, the more collapse has occurred.

3.4   Performance Drops Due to Partial Dimensional Collapse

We now discuss the drop in performance of ResNet18 and ResNet34 described in Sect. 3.2 and argue that it is caused by *partial dimensional collapse*, where some parts of the representations either are constant across the dataset or covary with other parts of the representation. Dimensional collapse reduces the amount of information contained in the learned representations and is possible because SimSiam lacks any repulsive term to push representations apart.

Figure 3 (left) shows a toy visualization of each kind of collapse. A key observation is that collapse can occur even if every representation dimension has high variance (see collapse type 2). This form of collapse is not captured by the collapse metric in [6], which for every dimension measures the standard deviation of that representation dimension across examples. In contrast, after using our model to obtain a d-dimensional representation for each image in the training set of N samples, we perform PCA on the resulting $N \times d$ representation matrix to obtain d singular values $\sigma_1 \geq \sigma_2 \geq \cdots \geq \sigma_d$. More collapse should show up as smaller singular values, and PCA finds orthogonal axes that maximize variance, so it is capable of capturing both kinds of collapse.

In Fig. 3 (middle), we examine the singular values of ResNet-18 models trained with varying amounts of data. At 5% of ImageNet and beyond, roughly the last 80 singular values collapse to 0, and the last 300 singular values noticeably decay more when the model is trained on more data. To visualize the *degree* of collapse, we look at the cumulative explained variance of the singular values:

$$(\text{Cumulative explained variance})_j = \frac{\sum_{i=1}^{j} \sigma_i}{\sum_{k=1}^{d} \sigma_k} \tag{1}$$

The cumulative explained variance measures the rank of the representations and rises monotonically from 0 to 1; the more quickly it does so, the more the model has collapsed. The $\{10\%, 20\%, 50\%, \text{and } 100\%\}$ ResNet-18 models have roughly the same explained variance curves, indicating the same high degree of collapse, which fits the fact that the k-NN accuracy flatlines for these models in Fig. 2. The 1% model exhibits no collapse at all, and the 5% model collapses to a small degree. Despite collapsing more than the 1% model, the 5% ResNet-18 model has the best k-NN accuracy. We hypothesize that this is because it has much lower SimSiam loss. We explore this tradeoff in Sect. 3.5.

In contrast to [6], which poses collapse as an "all-or-nothing" phenomenon that can occur when removing the stop-gradient or the prediction head, we find that collapse exists on a spectrum. Partial dimensional collapse is not unique to noncontrastive methods like SimSiam. Prior work found that contrastive methods like SimCLR can have partial dimensional collapse in the projected embedding space (output of the projection MLP) [18], which is different from the representation space as shown here (input to the projection MLP).

3.5   Predicting Performance from Collapse Metric and SimSiam Loss

There is a fundamental tradeoff between dimensional collapse and the SimSiam prediction loss. More collapse reduces the entropy in the representations and makes them more predictable, which decreases the loss, but this comes at the

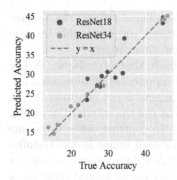

	AUC Only	Loss Only	Use Both
R^2	0.21	0.06	0.95
Pearson's r	0.46	0.24	0.98
Spearman's ρ	0.48	0.09	0.97
AUC coeff.	-34.7	-	-79.5
Train loss coeff.	-	-14.9	-106.0

Fig. 4. Accuracy is predictable from loss and collapse. We train a collection of ResNet-18 and ResNet-34 models using a variety of ImageNet subset sizes and training methods (see Sect. 4). We then fit a simple linear model to predict the validation linear probing accuracy from the loss on the full training set and the area under the explained variance curve. The simple linear model is highly predictive across both architectures, with $R^2 = 0.95$ indicating a very good linear fit. Note that either of these features alone is a poor predictor for downstream accuracy.

cost of lower representation quality. In this section, we quantify how these two properties can accurately predict model performance on a downstream task.

We form a collection of 22 trained ResNet-18 and ResNet-34 models, consisting of the models trained on different size ImageNet subsets (from Sect. 3.2) and models trained using different data orderings (from Sect. 4). For each model, we compute the SimSiam loss on the full 1.2M image training set, the validation accuracy of a linear probe trained on ImageNet, and a metric that measures the degree of dimensional collapse in the representations. Following the same PCA procedure as Sect. 3.4, we compute the d singular values $\sigma_1, \ldots, \sigma_d$ of the representations of the full training set. Our collapse metric corresponds to the area under the cumulative explained variance of the singular values:

$$\text{AUC} = \frac{\frac{1}{d} \sum_{i=1}^{d} \sum_{j=1}^{i} \sigma_j}{\sum_{k=1}^{d} \sigma_k} \tag{2}$$

The AUC can range from 0.5 to 1, and larger AUC values reflect more collapse. AUC = 0.5 means all of the singular values are identical, which indicates that no collapse is occurring. AUC = 1 means that the last $d - 1$ singular values are 0, which indicates severe dimensional collapse.

Using values computed from our collection of 22 SimSiam models, we fit a linear model to predict the validation accuracy from the loss and AUC. Figure 4 shows that this linear model is highly accurate, with $R^2 = 0.950$. Strongly negative coefficients on the loss and AUC make sense: lower loss and less collapse result in more useful features. Figure 4 (left) shows that this linear fit works for both ResNet-18 and ResNet-34, with accurate predictions for most models. Note that the loss and AUC are only jointly predictive; using only loss or only AUC poorly predicts the downstream accuracy.

This finding has two implications. First, it allows estimating models' relative performance without using any labels. We can simply compute the loss on the full training set (or the validation loss, which Fig. 2 indicates is very close to the full training loss), as well as the singular values of the representations on the training set. If one model dominates the other in both metrics, i.e. it has lower loss and less collapse, then it is obviously better. Otherwise, we weight the loss and collapse metric by this linear formula to choose which model to fine-tune for a desired downstream task. In addition to not requiring labels, this procedure also eliminates the need to fine-tune multiple models to see which is best. Second, this means that we can improve SimSiam performance either by driving the loss down or by reducing collapse. Section 4 presents methods that focus on the latter.

4 Continual Training Prevents Collapse

Section 3 showed that SimSiam models tend to collapse if the training set is too large relative to the size of the network. At first glance, it seems that the only solutions are to use a larger model, which requires more time and compute, or to switch to a different self-supervised learning algorithm, which may itself have its own disadvantages (e.g. SimCLR [4] requires big batch sizes, and BYOL requires twice as many forward passes per update). However, in this section, we find that SimSiam's dimensional collapse has a simple solution that requires no change to the architecture, loss function, or hyperparameters. Motivated by the observation in Fig. 3 that shows that collapse does not occur in models trained on small subsets of the data, we simply partition the training set into small subsets and train on them in sequence. We show that changing the data order by switching to a *continual learning setup* is surprisingly highly effective at preventing dimensional collapse in small models.

We change only the order in which data is presented to the model; we use the same architectures, loss function, and hyperparameters as before. We compare three possible data orderings:

1. Multiple pass: this is the standard multi-epoch training procedure. The model is trained for E epochs, and each training image is used once each epoch.
2. Single pass: this is the *data-incremental* setting from continual learning. The data is randomly shuffled and partitioned into C chunks, which "arrive" one after another. When a chunk arrives, we take N stochastic gradient steps, after which we *throw away the chunk and stop using its images*. By default, we set the number of chunks to $C = 100$.
3. Cumulative: this is akin to the incremental learning setting with a replay buffer that is large enough to hold the entire training set. When a chunk arrives, we add its images to the replay buffer and then take N stochastic gradient steps. As more chunks arrive, the total size of the replay buffer increases and approaches the "multiple pass" setting towards the end.

For each data ordering, we do the same total number of gradient steps. Figure 5 illustrates how data is presented and used in each training procedure.

Multiple pass:

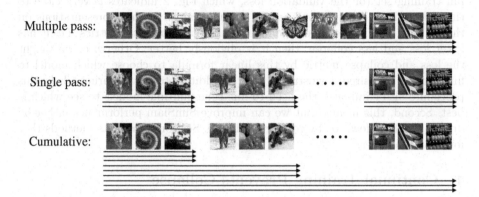

Single pass:

Cumulative:

Fig. 5. Illustration of each data ordering method. "Multiple pass" training consists of making E passes over the training set, so each data point is seen infrequently but uniformly across training. "Single pass" is a form of continual learning that splits the dataset into chunks. It trains intensely on a chunk, then throws it away and moves on to the next chunk. "Cumulative" also splits the dataset into chunks, but never throws away data. It accumulates data as it arrives, and begins to approximate "multiple pass" training towards the end of training.

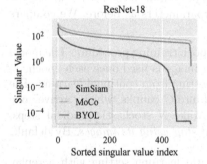

Training method	MoCo-v3	BYOL
Multiple pass	**53.8**	**47.6**
Single pass	48.9	44.2

Fig. 6. MoCo and BYOL do not collapse, even when trained with small models. Thus, as expected, single pass training does not improve linear probe accuracy on ImageNet over the multiple pass setting.

4.1 Results

Table 2 shows the result when using these 3 data orderings to train ResNet-18, ResNet-34, and ResNet-50 architectures. Continual training ("single pass") *improves validation accuracy by 14.5% points (ResNet-18) and 32.5% points (ResNet-34)* over the "multiple pass" baseline, but leads to a 12.2% drop for ResNet-50. Figure 7 shows that continual training helps ResNet-18 and ResNet-34 by preventing collapse, but ResNet-50 with "multiple pass" training does not collapse in the first place since ResNet-50 is sufficiently big. Thus, continual training for ResNet-50 just introduces catastrophic forgetting [11,19], making it more difficult to achieve low SimSiam loss.

Accumulating data seems like a more natural idea since it acts as a curriculum and slowly gives the model time to fit each new image, but it yields minor results. It results in a 2–6 percentage point improvement over multi-epoch training for ResNet-18 and ResNet-34 and is close to matching multi-epoch training for ResNet-50. However, this is still far behind "current," and Fig. 7 shows that "accumulate" does not significantly help prevent collapse.

Finally, continual training does not help with other SSL algorithms, such as MoCo-v3 [7] or BYOL [12], as shown in Fig. 6. This makes sense since the plot of their singular values shows that these methods do not collapse. This indicates that the exponential moving average (EMA) in BYOL prevents collapse and is actually crucial outside of the standard ImageNet-1k pre-training benchmark with ResNet-50. Note that using EMA introduces two additional costs at training time. First, the EMA itself requires maintaining two sets of weights that are constantly updated, which uses more GPU memory. Second, calculating the symmetrized loss of 2 sets of views requires twice as many forward passes, since the target network has different parameters than the online network.

In contrast, our proposed data ordering methods allow us to keep the efficiency of SimSiam with no additional overhead. Furthermore, switching to the continual setting offers its own advantages. Continual methods are faster to train, especially with limited resources, since fitting the entire chunk in system memory allows for much faster access than epoch-wise retrieval from disk or an NFS. Continual methods are also very well suited for real-life applications, where data often arrives in a stream. Algorithmic improvements for SSL in this continual training will likely transfer well to these practical settings.

Table 2. ImageNet top-1 linear probing validation accuracy for different SimSiam training methods. We show the mean and standard deviation over 3 random seeds.

Training method	ResNet-18	ResNet-34	ResNet-50
Mutiple pass	30.0 ± 1.8	16.8 ± 3.2	**68.1**
Cumulative	33.0 ± 1.9	22.2 ± 2.3	67.7
Single pass	44.5 ± 0.8	45.0 ± 1.1	55.9
Hybrid (switch at 40)	$\mathbf{48.3 \pm 0.7}$	$\mathbf{50.3 \pm 0.6}$	67.6

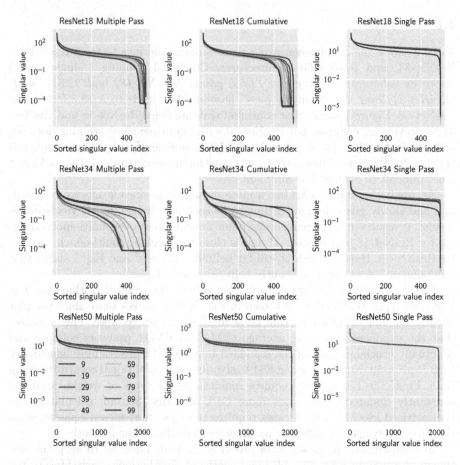

Fig. 7. Evolution of dimensional collapse across training. Each line shows the singular values corresponding to an intermediate training checkpoint. For "multiple passes" with both ResNet-18 and ResNet-34, more singular values collapse towards 0, indicating that dimensional collapse is happening. In contrast, the "single pass" strategy avoids collapse and in fact *increases* the singular values across training. ResNet-50 does not collapse even in the multi-epoch setting, so continual training does not help here.

4.2   Hybrid of Continual and Multi-epoch Training

Even though the pseudo-curriculum implemented in the "cumulative" data ordering did not improve performance, warming up the network with one method and then finishing training with another could be useful for simultaneously (a) preventing collapse while (b) driving the SimSiam loss lower. We experiment with doing continual training for the first part of training, then switching to multi-epoch training for the rest of training. Figure 8 shows how the k-NN accuracy and AUC collapse metric change over the course of training. Continual training for 40 chunks followed by multi-epoch training achieves the highest k-

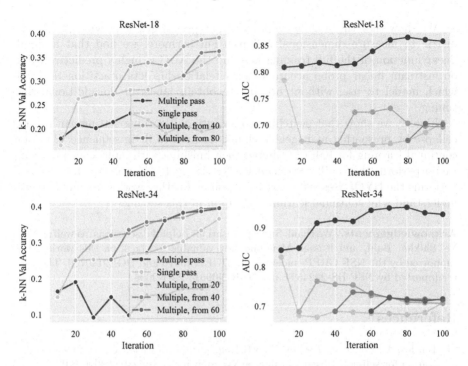

Fig. 8. Hybrid of Continual and Multi-epoch Training Improves Performance. We take an intermediate "single pass" checkpoint and fine-tune it with multi-epoch training. Our partial collapse metric (AUC) shows that multi-epoch fine-tuning tries to collapse immediately, but the initialization is good enough that it recovers.

NN validation accuracy, but only works because of the continual training in the beginning. Right after switching training methods, the model begins to collapse, but the initialization from continual training gives the model more room to recover. Table 2 shows that this hybrid method achieves 48.3% linear probing accuracy with ResNet-18, *18.3% points better than the multi-epoch baseline.* It is also within 0.5% of multi-epoch training on ResNet-50, indicating that hybrid training is a good default method to use for all architectures.

5   Conclusion

Our work provides a new understanding of non-contrastive SSL methods like SimSiam and BYOL. We find that tricks like EMA, while unnecessary on ImageNet when using large models like ResNet-50, are indeed important when using smaller models on complex datasets. We show that the ratio between model capacity and dataset complexity determines when collapse occurs, and that smaller models like ResNet-18 and ResNet-34 suffer from increasing amounts of collapse when trained on larger subsets of ImageNet. We also show that increasing model width is better at improving performance than increasing depth.

We show that the singular values of the representations provide an effective metric to measure dimensional collapse. Furthermore, we find that a simple linear function of the full training loss and the AUC is highly predictive of the downstream linear probe accuracy. This relationship lets practitioners decide which model to use, without needing to obtain labels or do additional fine-tuning.

Finally, we show that switching to a continual learning setting can prevent collapse by presenting manageable chunks of data to fit in sequence. By doing continual learning for half of training, then finishing with multi-epoch training, we outperform the vanilla SimSiam ResNet-18 by 18.3% points. This also outperforms the BYOL ResNet-18 by 1.1% points. Further work is required to fully understand why continual learning is helpful in this setting.

Acknowledgements. We thank Sudeep Dasari for helpful discussions, as well as Yufei Ye, Shikhar Bahl, and Russell Mendonca for valuable feedback on this work. AL is supported by the NSF GRFP under grants DGE1745016 and DGE2140739. The work is supported by NSF IIS-2024594 and ONR N00014-22-1-2096.

References

1. Bardes, A., Ponce, J., LeCun, Y.: VICReg: variance-invariance-covariance regularization for self-supervised learning. arXiv preprint arXiv:2105.04906 (2021)
2. Caron, M., Bojanowski, P., Joulin, A., Douze, M.: Deep clustering for unsupervised learning of visual features. In: Ferrari, V., Hebert, M., Sminchisescu, C., Weiss, Y. (eds.) Computer Vision – ECCV 2018. LNCS, vol. 11218, pp. 139–156. Springer, Cham (2018). https://doi.org/10.1007/978-3-030-01264-9_9
3. Caron, M., Misra, I., Mairal, J., Goyal, P., Bojanowski, P., Joulin, A.: Unsupervised learning of visual features by contrasting cluster assignments. In: NeurIPS (2020)
4. Chen, T., Kornblith, S., Norouzi, M., Hinton, G.: A simple framework for contrastive learning of visual representations. preprint arXiv:2002.05709 (2020)
5. Chen, X., He, K.: Exploring simple Siamese representation learning. preprint arXiv:2011.10566 (2020)
6. Chen, X., He, K.: Exploring simple Siamese representation learning. In: Proceedings of the IEEE/CVF Conference on Computer Vision and Pattern Recognition, pp. 15750–15758 (2021)
7. Chen, X., Xie, S., He, K.: An empirical study of training self-supervised vision transformers. In: Proceedings of the IEEE/CVF International Conference on Computer Vision, pp. 9640–9649 (2021)
8. Deng, D., Chen, G., Hao, J., Wang, Q., Heng, P.A.: Flattening sharpness for dynamic gradient projection memory benefits continual learning. In: Advances in Neural Information Processing Systems, vol. 34 (2021)
9. Deng, J., Dong, W., Socher, R., Li, L.J., Li, K., Fei-Fei, L.: ImageNet: a large-scale hierarchical image database. In: 2009 IEEE Conference on Computer Vision and Pattern Recognition, pp. 248–255. IEEE (2009)
10. Dosovitskiy, A., et al.: An image is worth 16×16 words: transformers for image recognition at scale. preprint arXiv:2010.11929 (2020)
11. French, R.M.: Catastrophic forgetting in connectionist networks. Trends Cogn. Sci. **3**(4), 128–135 (1999)

12. Grill, J.B., et al.: Bootstrap your own latent: a new approach to self-supervised learning. In: NeurIPS (2020)
13. He, K., Fan, H., Wu, Y., Xie, S., Girshick, R.: Momentum contrast for unsupervised visual representation learning. In: CVPR (2020)
14. He, K., Zhang, X., Ren, S., Sun, J.: Deep residual learning for image recognition. In: CVPR (2016)
15. Henaff, O.: Data-efficient image recognition with contrastive predictive coding. In: International Conference on Machine Learning, pp. 4182–4192. PMLR (2020)
16. Hénaff, O.J., et al.: Data-efficient image recognition with contrastive predictive coding. preprint arXiv:1905.09272 (2019)
17. Ioffe, S., Szegedy, C.: Batch normalization: accelerating deep network training by reducing internal covariate shift. In: International Conference on Machine Learning, pp. 448–456. PMLR (2015)
18. Jing, L., Vincent, P., LeCun, Y., Tian, Y.: Understanding dimensional collapse in contrastive self-supervised learning. arXiv preprint arXiv:2110.09348 (2021)
19. Kirkpatrick, J., et al.: Overcoming catastrophic forgetting in neural networks. Proc. Natl. Acad. Sci. **114**(13), 3521–3526 (2017)
20. Krizhevsky, A., Hinton, G., et al.: Learning multiple layers of features from tiny images (2009)
21. Li, C., Farkhoor, H., Liu, R., Yosinski, J.: Measuring the intrinsic dimension of objective landscapes. arXiv preprint arXiv:1804.08838 (2018)
22. Misra, I., Maaten, L.V.D.: Self-supervised learning of pretext-invariant representations. In: CVPR (2020)
23. Nakkiran, P., Kaplun, G., Bansal, Y., Yang, T., Barak, B., Sutskever, I.: Deep double descent: where bigger models and more data hurt (2019). arXiv preprint arXiv:1912.02292 (2019)
24. Oord, A.V.D., Li, Y., Vinyals, O.: Representation learning with contrastive predictive coding. preprint arXiv:1807.03748 (2018)
25. Purushwalkam, S., Gupta, A.: Demystifying contrastive self-supervised learning: invariances, augmentations and dataset biases. Adv. Neural. Inf. Process. Syst. **33**, 3407–3418 (2020)
26. Rebuffi, S.A., Kolesnikov, A., Sperl, G., Lampert, C.H.: iCaRl: incremental classifier and representation learning. In: Proceedings of the IEEE Conference on Computer Vision and Pattern Recognition, pp. 2001–2010 (2017)
27. Richemond, P.H., et al.: BYOL works even without batch statistics. preprint arXiv:2010.10241 (2020)
28. Tian, Y.: Deep contrastive learning is provably (almost) principal component analysis. arXiv preprint arXiv:2201.12680 (2022)
29. Tian, Y., Chen, X., Ganguli, S.: Understanding self-supervised learning dynamics without contrastive pairs. arXiv preprint arXiv:2102.06810 (2021)
30. Wu, Z., Xiong, Y., Yu, S.X., Lin, D.: Unsupervised feature learning via non-parametric instance discrimination. In: CVPR (2018)

Federated Self-supervised Learning for Video Understanding

Yasar Abbas Ur Rehman[1], Yan Gao[2]([✉]), Jiajun Shen[1],
Pedro Porto Buarque de Gusmão[2], and Nicholas Lane[2,3]

[1] TCL AI Lab, Hong Kong, Hong Kong
[2] University of Cambridge, Cambridge, UK
yg381@cam.ac.uk
[3] Samsung AI Cambridge, Cambridge, UK

Abstract. The ubiquity of camera-enabled mobile devices has lead to
large amounts of unlabelled video data being produced at the edge.
Although various self-supervised learning (SSL) methods have been proposed to harvest their latent spatio-temporal representations for task-
specific training, practical challenges including privacy concerns and
communication costs prevent SSL from being deployed at large scales.
To mitigate these issues, we propose the use of Federated Learning (FL)
to the task of video SSL. In this work, we evaluate the performance of
current state-of-the-art (SOTA) video-SSL techniques and identify their
shortcomings when integrated into the large-scale FL setting simulated
with kinetics-400 dataset. We follow by proposing a novel federated SSL
framework for video, dubbed FedVSSL, that integrates different aggregation strategies and partial weight updating. Extensive experiments
demonstrate the effectiveness and significance of FedVSSL as it outperforms the centralized SOTA for the downstream retrieval task by 6.66%
on UCF-101 and 5.13% on HMDB-51.

Keywords: Self-supervised learning · Federated learning · Video
understanding · Model aggregation

1 Introduction

A plethora of video content, often unlabelled and of private nature, is generated
everyday from cameras in cellphones, tablets, and other mobile devices [1,10,
21,31,38]. Being able to repurpose this data to solve various tasks in computer
vision has been of great interest to researchers since the last decade [4,7,10,
13,23,32,40,41]. Self-Supervised Learning (SSL) allows us to harvest these data
contents by learning *intermediate* visual representations from unlabelled data,
which can then be used as a starting point to solve specific downstream tasks
(e.g., human action recognition [36], temporal action detection [45]). In practice,
however, deploying SSL in its naïve form would require massive amounts of

---

Equal contribution—Y. A. U. Rehman and Y. Gao.

S. Avidan et al. (Eds.): ECCV 2022, LNCS 13691, pp. 506–522, 2022.
https://doi.org/10.1007/978-3-031-19821-2_29

data to be sent to a centralized server for processing, posing significant concerns around privacy, [15,17], communication, and storage costs, ultimately limiting the technology to small datasets.

A natural way to mitigate those issues is to combine SSL with the novel decentralized machine learning technique known as Federated Learning (FL) [29]. In FL, distributed population of edge devices collaboratively train a shared model while keeping their personal data private. Essentially, FL dilutes the burden of training across devices and avoids privacy and storage issues by not collecting users' data samples. The potential integration of video-SSL and FL into one coherent system offers lots of benefits in addition to data privacy. It enables large-scale decentralized feature learning from real-world data without requiring any costly and laborious data annotations. This can practically improve the performance and enables a vast majority of vision models for video applications [10], which have been under the shadow otherwise. Surprisingly, bearing such potential benefits there is no prior work that has so far studied video-SSL in FL.

In this paper, we conduct the first comprehensive study on video-SSL training in *cross-device* FL environment [20]. Our key findings from this study shows that: (1) The vanilla FL pretraining of video-SSL approaches are surprisingly not affected by the distribution of the data either being IID or non-IID. (2) Video-SSL with FL performs significantly better than the corresponding centralized SSL pretraining on video retrieval tasks and comparatively worse when the model is fined-tuned for action recognition. (3) We also show that the video SSL methods in FL settings are computationally efficient, regularized, and resilient to small-scale perturbation, compared to their centralized counterparts.

Based on the findings of our study of video-SSL with FL, we propose a novel federated learning framework, **FedVSSL**, designed specifically for video SSL. This framework allows to transceive only the backbone parameters of the video-SSL model during each communication round in FL. It then leverages a novel aggregation strategy, inspired by stochastic weighted averaging (SWA) [16], to aggregate and update the weights of the clients (performing video-SSL) at the server. FedVSSL obtains the state-of-the-art (SOTA) performance in video clip retrieval and competitive performance on action recognition against FedAvg and centralized video-SSL. The main contributions of this work are as follows:

1. We conduct the first systematic study of training video-SSL methods in FL *cross-device* settings with a large number of distributed clients. This establishes a baseline for naïvely implementing various video-SSL techniques using FL; shedding light on the basic problems of integrating video-SSL with FL into one coherent system.
2. Based on the above, we propose a general FL framework, FedVSSL, based on SWA [16] for pretraining video-SSL methods in FL. Our method obtains SOTA performance in video clip retrieval and competitive performance on action recognition against FedAvg and centralized video-SSL.
3. We release our code and models on GitHub[1] to allow for reproducibility and stimulate further research in the field.

---

[1] https://github.com/yasar-rehman/FEDVSSL.

2   Background and Related Work

2.1   Video Self-supervised Representation Learning

Video-SSL approaches often rely on solving a pretext task [8] in an unsupervised fashion to learn representations that can be reused in solving other downstream tasks. The pretext tasks in video-SSL are either based on contrastive methods, non-contrastive methods, or a combination of both. Contrastive methods exploit the similarity between the two augmented views of the input samples using contrastive learning to learn the spatio-temporal representation from the unlabeled data [8,11,12,28,34]. On the other hand, non-contrastive approaches utilize specialized pretext tasks to generate pseudo signals to learn the spatio-temporal representation in a supervised manner, usually requiring just a single input [2,18,19,26,30,39,40,42,43].

Regardless of the specific SSL method being deployed, a recent study has shown that SSL models become more robust on a wide range of vision-based tasks when pretrained on real-world and uncurated data [10]. Bearing such tremendous potential, video-SSL models can extend the horizons of the many vision-based applications. However, the utility of these video-SSL models is significantly limited by the scale of the datasets available on the training server due to issues such as data privacy, communication cost and large data storage requirements. In this paper, we extend the utility of video-SSL methods beyond the centralized servers. This would allow harvesting of information from an unprecedented amount of user data, offering new opportunities to advance the quality and robustness of video-SSL models.

2.2   Federated Visual Representation Learning

Federated Learning (FL) [29] has received a lot of attention in recent years. In this new paradigm, the server now needs to *aggregate* incoming weights from clients to progressively produce better networks. In its original form [29], aggregation was performed using FedAvg, an *aggregation strategy* that generates a model via a weighted sum of clients' parameters. However, this simple aggregation method can perform particularly poorly in realistic scenarios where clients have very different data distributions, i. e. the available datasets are essentially not Independent and Identically Distributed (IID).

In the past few years, a number of aggregation strategies have been proposed to improve upon the original FedAvg. Authors in [9] introduce local-model training loss as a weighting coefficient for aggregation. Adaptive federated optimization approaches, proposed in [33], incorporate knowledge of past iterations by applying a separate gradient-based optimization on the server-side. Specific to SSL, authors in [44] suggest using contrastive-learning on the server-side based on the logits sent by the clients, thus imposing some privacy issues.

Besides choosing a specific aggregation method when training using SSL in FL, we must also decide which parts of the networks need to be aggregated as some of the weights are associated with latent representations (backbone) while others are simply used for solving the pretext tasks (head). To this end, authors in [46] proposed FedU, that determines the update of the clients' model classification head based on the degree of backbone model divergence between the server and the clients.

It is important to note that the above-mentioned works were applied to small-scale *image-based* datasets [24,35] and that their proposed aggregation methods *rely on the usual class-label based definition of non-IID*. However, SSL should not depend on class-based labels, which prompts the question of whether such a definition of non-IID datasets bears any impact in video-SSL in FL. To the best of our knowledge, ours is the first FL SSL training framework tailored to *video* that is capable of producing SOTA models better than their centralized counterparts, regardless of the pretext class-label non-IID partitioning. We do this by correctly selecting only the backbone weights for aggregation.

3 Methodology

In this section, we provide the details of our systematic study on video-SSL using Federated Learning. Based on our findings, we follow by describing our proposed FedVSSL approach.

3.1 Federated Video-SSL System Design

We begin with a vanilla FL system that can be integrated with the video-SSL learning. The resulting FL video-SSL system is depicted in Fig. 1-Stage 1. We consider having n partitions $\{d_i\}_{i=1}^n$ of dataset D distributed among $\{c_i | c_i \in C\}_{i=1}^n$ decentralized clients in a Non-IID fashion. Each decentralized client learns intermediate features collaboratively by training the video-SSL approach on their respective local data partition for a few epochs before performing synchronization through the server. The synchronization includes receiving the clients' model parameters, performing model aggregation, and sending back the global model again to clients. More specifically, our training pipeline can be described as follows:

1. Each client c_i holds a set of local parameters $\{\theta_i^b, \theta_i^{p_t}\}$ for a backbone network $f(\theta^b)$ parameterized by the weights θ^b followed by a predictor head network $f(\theta^{p_t})$ parameterized by the weights θ^{p_t}. Note that all clients use the same model architecture but the parameter weights $\{\theta_i^b, \theta_i^{p_t}\}_{1 \leq i \leq n}$ can be non-consensus. During each FL round r, local video-SSL pretraining and synchronization will be conducted intersectively.

2. During the communication/synchronization step, each client would receive global values for the weights θ_g^b and $\theta_g^{p_t}$ aggregated on the server based on certain FL aggregation strategies.

3. During each round r, a random subset of clients, M, is selected to perform video-SSL training. Each participant $m \in M$ optimizes its local model's parameters $\{\theta_m^b, \theta_m^{p_t}\}$ for E number of local epochs.

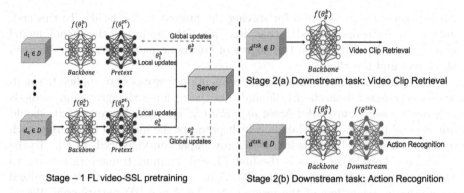

Fig. 1. System overview: Stage-1 (left) represents the FL video-SSL pretraining. For the downstream tasks; video clip retrieval is seen in Stage-2(a) and action recognition is depicted in Stage-2(b)

The local training steps in each client completely follows the setup of the video-SSL algorithms, including the pre-training task together with the task-specific loss function design. The optimization is performed with SGD by minimizing the objective $J_m^{p_t}(\theta^b, \theta^{pt})$:

$$J_m^{p_t}(\theta^b, \theta^{pt}) = \mathbb{E}_{\mathbf{x} \sim d_m} \mathcal{L}_m(\mathbf{x}, y_{pt}, \theta^b, \theta^{pt}), \tag{1}$$

where $(\mathbf{x}, y_{pt})$ is the data with its corresponding pseudo labels for the specific pretext task p_t. At the end of the R rounds, the final global model parameters θ_g^b for the backbone network can be used to extract spatio-temporal representations from videos for downstream tasks. We then follow the common practice of evaluating the performance of representation learning as done in traditional video-SSL work [41,42]. The representations learned by the global model parameters θ_g^b are evaluated by solving the downstream tasks tsk as is shown in Fig. 1 - Stage 2. In this work, we consider two downstream tasks:

Action Recognition: A classification head (fully connected layer) represented by $f(\theta^{tsk})$ is attached following the final layer of $f(\theta_g^b)$, resulting in the model F_{tsk} parameterized by $\{\theta_g^b, \theta^{tsk}\}$. The F_{tsk} is then fine-tuned in two ways: (1) fine-tuning the whole network $\{\theta_g^b, \theta^{tsk}\}$, and (2) fine-tuning only the linear classification layer $f(\theta^{tsk}$, i.e., linear probe.

Video Clip Retrieval: For the video clip retrieval, we determine the video label by majority voting of K-nearest neighbor (KNN) by directly using the parameters learned by $f(\theta_g^b)$ after the FL video-SSL pretraining and followed the protocol as described in [42].

The above generic video federated-SSL system allows us to perform a systematic analysis of the video-SSL approaches and its implications in FL environment against a number of key factors:

Video-SSL in Vanilla FL Settings. In this scenario, our main objective is to evaluate the performance gap between pretraining video-SSL algorithms in

FL and centralized environment. This evaluation will then quantify how different video-SSL methods behave in FL settings with IID and Non-IID data.

Aggregation Strategies. The aggregation method plays an important role towards superior performance of the final feature representations learned in FL video-SSL pretraining. We intend to study the effects of different aggregation strategies on the feature representations learned during FL pretraining of video-SSL approaches and hence the downstream tasks.

Loss-Surface and Model Stability of Video-SSL in FL. These analyses enable us to perform a side-by-side comparison of the key properties of pretraining video-SSL approaches in FL settings against their centralized counterpart. For example, recent work indicates that averaging the weights of the neural networks leads to wider minima [16,27] which subsequently provides better generalization. A natural question arises as to whether the aggregation strategies, based on weight averaging, by performing FL video-SSL pretraining could provide wider minima? Moreover, do such wider minima potentially lead to model stability against small-scale perturbations that naturally occur during the communication between edge devices and the server in FL?

Training Efficiency and Communication Cost. The total time for pretraining video-SSL in FL settings depends on the number of epochs during local training on each client and the number of communication rounds between the clients and the server. It is important to compute the number of communication rounds necessary to achieve a target performance with FL video-SSL training in order to find an optimal balance between the performance of video-SSL and FL system resources.

3.2   Proposed Method

Based on the observations of the systematic study of the video-SSL approaches in *cross-device* FL settings, we proposed a novel FL framework, *FedVSSL*, designed specifically for video-SSL in FL environment. The key characteristics of this framework are as follows: (1) Transceive only the backbone model parameters θ_g^b between the server and the clients. (2) FedVSSL aggregation strategy for pretraining video-SSL approaches in FL cross-device settings.

Transceive only Backbone Weights. Since each c_i client model contains two modules $(f(\theta_{c_i}^b)$ and $f(\theta_{c_i}^{p_t}))$, we analyse the characteristics of both modules and hypothesize that it is beneficial to only upload and aggregate the parameters θ^b of the backbone model at the server (see Table 4). The backbone module learns hierarchical deep features from the local data, representing the role of encoder. The classification head is more representative of local data distribution, which learns data-oriented features. We argue that only aggregating the backbone parts could increase generalization of the model, while retaining the classification head and updating it locally could capture more characteristics of non-IID data from clients. More evidence from Fig. 5 validates our hypothesis.

FedVSSL Aggregation. The motivation behind proposing FedVSSL aggregation is two folds: First, to integrate the FL aggregation strategies based on weighted averaging under a common framework. Second, to induce the knowledge from the past global models while performing model parameters aggregation.

After local pretraining at round r, the server collects the participating clients' locally updated weights θ_m^b, and the local gradients $g^{(m)}(r)$ from client m at round r is computed as: $g^{(m)}(r) = \theta_m^b(r) - \theta_g^b(r-1)$. The update rule for θ_g^b of the global model F_g for round r can then be stated as follows:

$$\theta_g^b(r) = \frac{(\sum_{i=1}^{\beta} \theta_g^b(r-i)) + \tilde{\theta}_g^b(r)}{\beta + 1}, \qquad (2)$$

where $\tilde{\theta}_g^b(r) = \theta_g^b(r-1) - \eta_s \Delta_r$ and η_s is the server learning rate. The averaging is performed over $\beta + 1$ global models. Equation 2 simply represents the stochastic weight averaging (SWA) [16] of the global models. As [16] reported, simple averaging of the multiple checkpoints of training models obtains better generalisation than conventional training. The Δ_r represents overall local gradients over m clients computed from a weighted combination of different aggregation strategies. Here we choose two aggregation strategies: FedAvg [29] and Loss [9], which aggregate the client models based on the number of samples or local training loss respectively. Then, Δ_r can be written as follows:

$$\Delta_r = \alpha \Delta_r^{Loss} + (1 - \alpha) \Delta_r^{FedAvg}. \qquad (3)$$

The α in Eq. 3 controls the amount of the contribution of each aggregation strategy. Equation 2 is the generalized representation of our FedVSSL aggregation rule. For example, setting $\beta = 0$ in Eq. 2 reduces the update rule to a weighted combination of FedAvg and Loss. On the other hand, setting $\alpha = 0$ or 1 reduces the update rule to running mean of FedAvg or Loss, respectively. The overall algorithm is summarised in Algorithm 1.

4 Experiments and Results

In this section, we first describe our experiment setup in Sect. 4.1 & Sect. 4.2). We conduct a systematic analysis of the behavior of video-SSL models in vanilla FL settings in Sect. 4.3, followed by a discussion for the results of our proposed FedVSSL in Sect. 4.4.

4.1 Datasets

For the pretraining stages of all video-SSL approaches, we utilize kinetics-400 (K400) dataset [21] with 219k training samples distributed among 400 action classes. For downstream task, we utilize the UCF-101 [36] (UCF) dataset containing 13,320 video samples for 101 action classes, and HMDB-51 [25] (HMDB) dataset with 7k video samples distributed among 51 action classes.

Algorithm 1. Federated Video Self-supervised Learning (FedVSSL)

Input: $R, M, N, n_m, \eta_s, \eta_l, \alpha, \beta$
Output: θ^b
Central server does:
1: **for** $r = 1, ..., R$ **do**
2:     Server randomly sample M clients.
3:     **for** each m in M **do**
4:         $\theta_m^b(r), n_m, \mathcal{L}_m^{pt} = \textbf{TrainLocally}(m, \theta_g^b(r))$
5:         $g^{(m)}(r) = \theta_m^b(r) - \theta_g^b(r-1)$
6:         $\Delta_r^{FedAvg} = \sum_{m=1}^{M} \frac{n_m}{\sum_{m=1}^{m} n_m} g^{(m)}(r)$
7:         $\Delta_r^{Loss} = \sum_{m=1}^{M} \frac{\exp(-\mathcal{L}_{(m)}^{Pt})}{\sum_{m=1}^{M} \exp(-\mathcal{L}_{(m)}^{Pt})} g^{(m)}(r)$
8:         $\Delta_r = \alpha \Delta_r^{Loss} + (1-\alpha) \Delta_r^{FedAvg}$
9:         Update global model weights $\tilde{\theta}_g^b(r) \leftarrow \theta_g^b(r-1) - \eta_s \Delta_r$.
10:       Compute $\theta_g^b(r) = \frac{(\sum_{i=1}^{\beta} \tilde{\theta}_g^b(r-i)) + \theta_g^b(r)}{\beta+1}$.

TrainLocally $(m, \theta_g^b(r))$:
1: **for** $k = 1, ..., E$ **do**
2:     $\{\theta_m^b, \theta_m^{pt}\}(k+1) \leftarrow \text{SSL}(\theta_g^b(k), \theta_m^{pt}(k), \eta_l)$ based on Eq. 1.
3: Upload $\theta_m^b, n_m, \mathcal{L}_m^{pt}$ to the server.

Kinectics-400 Non-IID. Each video sample in K400 comes from a different source, which conforms to the definition of non-IID based on video source-level. To make it more realistic, we generate the non-IID version of K400 based on actual class-labels [29]. We randomly partition the dataset into 100 shards to mimic the setting of having 100 disjoint clients participating in FL. Each client contains 8 classes resulting in each client having 2285 samples on average. Note that there is no overlap of samples between different clients.

4.2 Architecture and Implementation

Video-SSL Approaches. In this work, we consider three SOTA video-SSL algorithms, all of which propose to solve different pretext tasks for video representation learning. More specifically, VCOP [42] learns to determine the permutation order of shuffled clips, Speed [2,5,43] learns to predict the playback speed of videos, and CtP [39] predicts the positions and sizes of a synthetic image patch in a sequence of video frames. For all video-SSL approaches, we use R3D-18 [37] architecture as the backbone $f(\theta^b)$. The architecture choices of prediction heads for different pretext tasks and downstream tasks follow the settings in the original papers. It should be noted that our federated framework is agnostic to different architectures and video-SSL approaches. We develop the FL version of the video-SSL approaches considered in this work on top of Flower [3] federated learning platform by incorporating various video-SSL algorithms developed in MMCV framework [6,39]. Unless otherwise specified, we keep the settings of the video-SSL approaches as provided by [39] during the pretraining tasks and downstream tasks.

Table 1. Action recognition accuracy (Top-1%) and video clip retrieval accuracy (Top-1%, Top5%) on UCF and HMDB for three video-SSL methods. F-T represents fine-tune and L-P stands for linear probe. Δ represents the difference between centralized and corresponding FL performance. "+" and "−" show % improvement and degradation respectively. * means the results are reproduced using the implementation in [39]

SSL method	Action recognition				Video clip retrieval			
	UCF		HMDB		UCF		HMDB	
	F-T	L-P	F-T	L-P	R@1	R@5	R@1	R@5
VCOP*	71.29	24.93	38.56	13.53	15.52	28.26	8.11	22.22
VCOP(Fed)	69.26	20.00	33.27	12.22	13.72	24.85	6.41	19.94
Δ	(−2.03)	(−4.93)	(−5.29)	(−1.31)	(−1.8)	(−3.41)	(−1.7)	(−2.28)
Speed*	81.15	29.32	47.58	14.90	16.84	36.58	6.93	21.05
Speed (Fed)	73.16	35.63	38.43	21.57	21.97	41.61	10.98	28.30
Δ	(−7.99)	(+6.31)	(−9.05)	(+6.67)	(+4.05)	(+3.94)	(+3.92)	(+7.25)
CtP*	**86.20**	**48.14**	**57.00**	**30.65**	29.0	47.30	11.80	30.10
CtP (Fed)	81.95	46.13	49.15	28.63	**29.29**	**48.90**	**13.66**	**32.42**
Δ	(−4.25)	(−2.01)	(−7.85)	(−2.02)	(+0.29)	(+1.6)	(+1.86)	(+2.32)

FL Pretraining. We perform the FL pretraining of the video-SSL pretext-task p_t using Algorithm 1. The local pretraining on each client lasts for E epochs per FL round R, where we set $E = 1$ in our experiments. We set the total number of rounds R to 540 to ensure that each client acquires sufficient participation during FL pretraining. The selection of the number of E and R is based on our empirical observations. Each round, we randomly select $M = 5$ clients from the pool of 100 clients to participate in training and each client trains its local model using SGD optimizer without momentum. We set a constant learning rate of 0.01 for CtP and Speed and 0.001 for VCOP. Weight decay is set to 10^{-4} and training batch-size is set to 4. On the server side, in addition to our proposed method FedVSSL, we consider three existing aggregation strategies including FedAvg, Loss and FedU.

Downstream Tasks. For the fine-tuning stage of action recognition, we follow the configuration in CtP framework [39]. The $F_{d_{tsk}}$ is fine-tuned using the SGD optimizer with an initial learning rate of 0.01, momentum of 0.9, and weight decay of 5×10^{-4}. The learning rate is decayed by a factor of 0.1 after 60 and 120 epochs, respectively. The batch-size is set 32, and the fine-tuning stage lasts for 150 epochs. For linear probe, we keep the same settings as for the fine-tuning of the whole network, except that we train only $f(\theta^{d_{tsk}})$ layer of $F_{d_{tsk}}$ for 100 epochs. The learning rate is decayed by the factor of 0.1 after 60 and 80 epochs. For the video clip retrieval task, we follow the approach described in Sect. 3.1.

4.3   Video-SSL in Vanilla FL Settings

Here we investigate the performance of video-SSL in vanilla FL settings against the key factors listed in Sect. 3.1.

Table 2. Action recognition and video clip retrieval accuracies (%) on UCF and HMDB for the federated CtP models pretrained with one local epoch per round. C represents the number of clients, and Cpc stands for the number of classes per client

Method	C/Cpc	Data	Fine-tuning		Retrieval			
			UCF	HMDB	UCF		HMDB	
			Top-1	Top-1	R@1	R@5	R@1	R@5
CtP(Fed.)	100/-	IID	81.92	48.49	29.42	47.90	13.80	34.56
	100/8	Non-IID	81.95	49.15	29.29	48.90	13.66	32.42
	100/4	Non-IID	81.15	47.78	29.18	48.37	14.70	32.94
CtP(Cent.)	-	IID	86.2	57.00	29.00	47.30	11.80	30.10

Centralized vs. Federated Video-SSL. In this experiment, we draw a first investigation for the performance of video-SSL approaches using FedAvg in centralized and vanilla FL settings with Non-IID video data. We report this comparison in terms of three downstream tasks, i.e., fine-tuning, linear probe, video clip retrieval, on UCF and HMDB datasets (Table 1). First, CtP obtains the best performance for all tasks in both centralized and FL settings. Second, when the trained network is fine-tuned for the action recognition task, the centralized video-SSL approaches perform better compared to their corresponding FL counterparts. However, the degradation in the performance is not drastic. We conjecture that it is caused by the smoother and flatter manifold in the models in FL settings, which would be more challenging to fine-tune. Third, the linear-probe results for action recognition show mixed results due to the fact that only the classification head participates in the training. Finally, the video clip retrieval results are more competitive with the FL version of Speed and CtP, which achieve better performance than their centralized counterparts.

Given the fact that the video-SSL benefits from the large-scale datasets and the performance degradation of the FL version of the video-SSL is acceptable (even in the Non-IID case with FedAvg), it makes the FL a natural choice for video-SSL approaches.

Performance with IID vs. Non-IID Data. Conventional FL methods are designed to solve a supervised/semi-supervised learning task within an IID/Non-IID data distribution based on the actual class-labels. To understand the impact of data distribution on federated video-SSL training, we simulate IID and Non-IID settings based on class-labels and compare the performance of downstream task in Table 2. The Non-IID versions of K-400 are generated with two variations of the distribution of the samples among 100 clients, with 4 and 8 classes per client respectively. We report the fine-tuning and video clip retrieval accuracy on UCF and HMDB, by pretraining CtP video-SSL approach on all settings.

One can see from Table 2 that pretraining the CtP video-SSL approach using standard FedAvg with IID and different degrees of Non-IID levels achieve comparatively similar performance on the fine-tuning and video clip retrieval task.

Table 3. Video clip retrieval accuracies (%) and fine-tuning accuracies (%) on UCF and HMDB for CtP video-SSL approach using various aggregation strategies. The SSL pretraining is performed on K400 (Non-IID). Cent[†] represents the centralized training for 27 epochs which equals to 540 rounds in our FL setting

Method	Retrieval				Fine-tuning	
	UCF		HMDB		UCF	HMDB
	R@1	R@5	R@1	R@5	Top-1	Top-1
Centralized	29.00	47.3	11.80	30.1	86.20	57.00
Centralized[†]	27.65	47.67	12.81	31.05	83.64	53.73
FedAvg (Baseline)	32.62	50.41	**16.54**	35.29	79.91	52.88
Loss-based	32.54	50.01	14.44	34.97	79.43	50.63
FedU	**34.07**	**52.29**	14.90	**36.67**	**80.17**	**53.73**

This could be explained by the generation process of IID/Non-IID data based the actual class-labels. The video-SSL methods learn representations by generating pseudo labels based on the pretext task it solves, which is independent of actual class-labels. Hence, the IID/Non-IID data distribution has a slight impact to the SSL model training. In addition, we find that there exists a degradation in the fine-tuning performance of federated CtP video-SSL compared to its centralized counterpart. Interestingly, the FL version of CtP video-SSL approach gives better video clip retrieval performance when compared to its centralized counterpart with both IID and different degrees of Non-IID levels.

Performance of Aggregation Strategies. The aggregation method often plays an important role towards superior performance of models trained in FL environments. In this experiment, we investigate the impact of FL aggregation strategies on the pretraining by evaluating the final performance of video-SSL approaches in Non-IID FL settings. In Table 3, we show the performance of CtP video-SSL approach on UCF and HMDB against a range of aggregation strategies that include FedAvg [29], Loss [9], and FedU [46]. It can be observed that FedAvg performs better on HMDB and obtains similar performance with Loss method on UCF. Additionally, except for retrieval accuracy on HMDB, FedU outperforms others on both video clip retrieval and fine-tuning mainly due to its dynamic aggregation mechanism.

Loss Surface and Model Stability of Video-SSL in FL. To understand why the federated video-SSL models gain higher retrieval accuracy than centralized models, we further analyze the loss landscape around the pretrained model both in centralized and FL settings. To compute this, we utilize the filter normalization method as proposed in [27]. The results are shown in Fig. 2 for CtP video-SSL approach. We find that the loss landscape of model pretrained with FedAvg is flatter than the model pretrianed with the centralized video-SSL. The width of the optima is critically related to generalization, which enables the

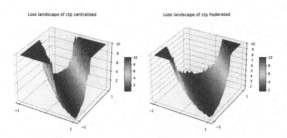

Fig. 2. Loss landscape of the final $f(\theta^b)$ pretrained in a centralized (left) and FL with FedAvg (right) settings

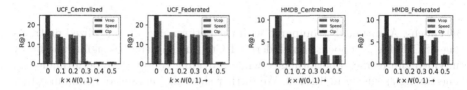

Fig. 3. Top1% action retrieval accuracy on UCF and HMDB by adding perturbation to all the weights of the pretrained $f(\theta^b)$ network. The perturbation is sampled from a normal distribution $N(0,1)$ and multiplied by a factor k

model to converge in a point centered in this region [14,16,22]. This often leads to slightly worse training loss but substantially better test accuracy.

We then explore whether such wider optima could increase model stability against small perturbations. To achieve this, we perturb the weights of the backbone pretrained with centralized and federated video-SSL approach. The perturbations are sampled from a uniform normal distribution with zero mean and unit variance, i.e., $\mathcal{N}(0,1)$. We start with the perturbation level of 0 and incrementally increase the level of perturbation by a factor of 0.1, i.e., $(\{\mathcal{N}(0,1) \times x | 0 \le x \le 0.5\})$. The results are shown in Fig. 3 for the top-1% video clip retrieval accuracy for the centralized video-SSL approach and its corresponding FL counterparts, on UCF and HMDB datasets. One can see from that as the level of perturbation is increased from 0 to 0.1 the top-1% accuracy drops significantly for both centralized CtP video-SSL and its FL counterparts. However, as the level for perturbation is further increased we find that the FL versions of the video-SSL approach show good stability compared to its centralized counterpart on both datasets. Overall, the federated training boosts generalization and stability of video-SSL models.

Training Efficiency and Communication Cost. In this experiment, we analyze the computational efficiency of pretraining CtP approach in both FL and centralized settings. We find that our FL pretraining of CtP for 540 rounds, with 100 clients and 5% client sampling rate (in ideal scenarios), is equivalent to 27 epochs (30%) of centralized pretraining. This results in 62.5% of GPU time saving compared to the centralized pretraining of the CtP that lasts for

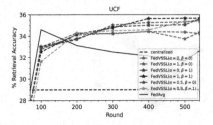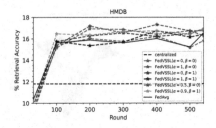

Fig. 4. Top 1% retrieval accuracy (%) w.r.t communication rounds for our proposed FL methods on UCF (left) and HMDB (right). Our proposed methods require less than 200 rounds to reach the centralized target accuracy on both datasets

90 epochs. Additionally, compared with the performance of centralized pretraining of CtP for 27 epochs, our federated CtP model achieves significant boost in video clip retrieval performance while providing competitive performance on fine-tuning as shown in Table 3. We further show the number of communication rounds required by federated video-SSL models to achieve the centralized target video clip retrieval accuracy. One can see from Fig. 4 that the FL model trained with FedAvg requires less than 100 rounds to reach the centralized target accuracy on UCF and HMDB datasets. Indeed, our proposed FedVSSL shows even better performance and convergence behaviour.

4.4   Results on FedVSSL

In this section, we investigate the performance of our proposed FVSSL method, conduct ablation studies by varying α and β in Eq. 2 and Eq. 3, and report the results on UCF and HMDB in Table 4. One can see that the performance of all proposed methods are competitive, which demonstrates that the learned representations are qualified for the downstream applications.

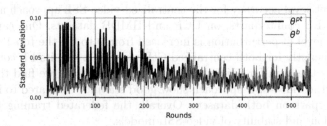

Fig. 5. Standard deviations of the L_2 difference between the global model weights and the locally trained model weights at each round of FL video-SSL pretraining with FedAvg. Both backbone θ^b and prediction head θ^{pt} are aggregated on the server

First, all models trained with FedVSSL provide superior retrieval performance. Concretely, (FedVSSL with $\alpha = 0.9, \beta = 0$) we improve the video

Table 4. Video clip retrieval accuracies (%) and fine-tuning accuracies (%) on UCF101 and HMDB51 for CtP video-SSL approach using our proposed FedVSSL methods. The SSL pretraining is performed on K400 (Non-IID)

Method	Retrieval				Fine-tuning		Linear-probe	
	UCF		HMDB		UCF	HMDB	UCF	HMDB
	R@1	R@5	R@1	R@5	Top-1	Top-1	Top-1	Top-1
Centralized	29.00	47.3	11.80	30.1	86.20	57.00	48.14	30.65
FedAvg (Baseline)	32.62	50.41	16.54	35.29	79.91	52.88	45.31	31.44
FedVSSL ($\alpha=0, \beta=0$)	34.34	51.71	15.82	36.01	79.91	52.94	47.95	31.12
FedVSSL ($\alpha=1, \beta=0$)	34.23	52.21	16.73	**38.30**	79.14	51.11	47.90	29.48
FedVSSL ($\alpha=0, \beta=1$)	35.61	52.18	**16.93**	37.78	79.43	51.90	47.66	30.00
FedVSSL ($\alpha=1, \beta=1$)	**35.66**	52.34	16.41	36.93	78.99	51.18	48.93	31.44
FedVSSL ($\alpha=0.9, \beta=0$)	35.50	**54.27**	16.27	37.25	**80.62**	**53.14**	**50.36**	**32.68**
FedVSSL ($\alpha=0.9, \beta=1$)	35.34	52.34	**16.93**	37.39	79.41	51.50	50.30	42.42

clip retrieval performance over FedAvg baseline by 2.88% (top1%) and 3.86% (top5%) on UCF, and 1.96% (top5%) on HMDB. We obtained 0.71% and 0.26% improvement (top1%) in the category of fine-tuning on UCF and HMDB, respectively compared to FedAvg baseline. In the category of Linear-probe, we obtained 5.05% and 1.24% improvement (top1%) on UCF and HMDB, respectively compared to the FedAvg baseline. Second, the component of SWA ($\beta=1$) in FedVSSL has a distinct benefit on the improvement of retrieval performance. Third, the top-1% retrieval accuracy of FedVSSL ($\alpha=0, \beta=0$) outperforms the FedAvg baseline by 1.72% on UCF dataset, which highlights the benefits of only updating backbone.

One can see from Fig. 5 that the standard deviation of the L_2 distance for the backbone model parameter is more consistent throughout the FL pretraining compared to that of prediction model parameters. This indicates that the backbone weights cause less divergence in FL pretraining of video-SSL which may provide significant efficiency and performance boost in the FL scenarios with stringent communication budget.

5   Conclusions

In this paper, we presented the first systematic study on video-SSL for FL. Our key findings include (1) the importance of aggregating just the backbone network and that (2) non-IID definition based on class-labels bears no impact on pretext training as they are not used by that task. Based on these findings, we proposed FedVSSL, an aggregation strategy tailored to video. FedVSSL was able to outperform the centralized SOTA for the downstream retrieval task by 6.66% on UCF-101 dataset and by 5.13% on HMDB-51 using non-contrastive methods. We hope this work will enable future research towards further combining FL and

SSL for video representation learning. These are complementary technologies that can together harvest rich visual information from edge devices while still preserving user privacy.

References

1. Aytar, Y., Vondrick, C., Torralba, A.: SoundNet: learning sound representations from unlabeled video. In: Advances in Neural Information Processing Systems, vol. 29 (2016)
2. Benaim, S., et al.: SpeedNet: learning the speediness in videos. In: Proceedings of the IEEE/CVF Conference on Computer Vision and Pattern Recognition, pp. 9922–9931 (2020)
3. Beutel, D.J., Topal, T., Mathur, A., Qiu, X., Parcollet, T., Lane, N.D.: Flower: a friendly federated learning research framework. arXiv preprint arXiv:2007.14390 (2020)
4. Chen, T., Kornblith, S., Norouzi, M., Hinton, G.: A simple framework for contrastive learning of visual representations. In: International Conference on Machine Learning, pp. 1597–1607. PMLR (2020)
5. Cho, H., Kim, T., Chang, H.J., Hwang, W.: Self-supervised visual learning by variable playback speeds prediction of a video. IEEE Access **9**, 79562–79571 (2021)
6. Contributors, M.: MMCV: OpenMMLab computer vision foundation (2018). https://github.com/open-mmlab/mmcv
7. Doersch, C., Gupta, A., Efros, A.A.: Unsupervised visual representation learning by context prediction. In: Proceedings of the IEEE International Conference on Computer Vision, pp. 1422–1430 (2015)
8. Feichtenhofer, C., Fan, H., Xiong, B., Girshick, R., He, K.: A large-scale study on unsupervised spatiotemporal representation learning. In: Proceedings of the IEEE/CVF Conference on Computer Vision and Pattern Recognition, pp. 3299–3309 (2021)
9. Gao, Y., et al.: End-to-end speech recognition from federated acoustic models. arXiv preprint. arXiv:2104.14297 (2021)
10. Goyal, P., et al.: Vision models are more robust and fair when pretrained on uncurated images without supervision. arXiv preprint arXiv:2202.08360 (2022)
11. Han, T., Xie, W., Zisserman, A.: Video representation learning by dense predictive coding. In: Proceedings of the IEEE/CVF International Conference on Computer Vision Workshops (2019)
12. Han, T., Xie, W., Zisserman, A.: Self-supervised co-training for video representation learning. In: Advances in Neural Information Processing Systems, vol. 33, pp. 5679–5690 (2020)
13. He, K., Fan, H., Wu, Y., Xie, S., Girshick, R.: Momentum contrast for unsupervised visual representation learning. In: Proceedings of the IEEE/CVF Conference on Computer Vision and Pattern Recognition, pp. 9729–9738 (2020)
14. Hochreiter, S., Schmidhuber, J.: Flat minima. Neural Comput. **9**(1), 1–42 (1997)
15. Hu, Z., Xie, H., Yu, L., Gao, X., Shang, Z., Zhang, Y.: Dynamic-aware federated learning for face forgery video detection. ACM Trans. Intell. Syst. Technol. (TIST) **13**, 1–25 (2022)
16. Izmailov, P., Podoprikhin, D., Garipov, T., Vetrov, D., Wilson, A.G.: Averaging weights leads to wider optima and better generalization. In: 34th Conference on Uncertainty in Artificial Intelligence 2018, UAI 2018, pp. 876–885. Association For Uncertainty in Artificial Intelligence (AUAI) (2018)

17. Jain, A.K., Deb, D., Engelsma, J.J.: Biometrics: trust, but verify. arXiv preprint arXiv:2105.06625 (2021)
18. Jenni, S., Meishvili, G., Favaro, P.: Video representation learning by recognizing temporal transformations. In: Vedaldi, A., Bischof, H., Brox, T., Frahm, J.-M. (eds.) ECCV 2020. LNCS, vol. 12373, pp. 425–442. Springer, Cham (2020). https://doi.org/10.1007/978-3-030-58604-1_26
19. Jing, L., Yang, X., Liu, J., Tian, Y.: Self-supervised spatiotemporal feature learning via video rotation prediction. arXiv preprint arXiv:1811.11387 (2018)
20. Kairouz, P., et al.: Advances and open problems in federated learning. arXiv preprint arXiv:1912.04977 (2019)
21. Kay, W., et al.: The kinetics human action video dataset. arXiv preprint arXiv:1705.06950 (2017)
22. Keskar, N.S., Mudigere, D., Nocedal, J., Smelyanskiy, M., Tang, P.T.P.: On large-batch training for deep learning: generalization gap and sharp minima. arXiv preprint arXiv:1609.04836 (2016)
23. Kolesnikov, A., Zhai, X., Beyer, L.: Revisiting self-supervised visual representation learning. In: Proceedings of the IEEE/CVF Conference on Computer Vision and Pattern Recognition, pp. 1920–1929 (2019)
24. Krizhevsky, A.: Learning multiple layers of features from tiny images (2009)
25. Kuehne, H., Jhuang, H., Garrote, E., Poggio, T., Serre, T.: HMDB: a large video database for human motion recognition. In: Proceedings of the International Conference on Computer Vision (ICCV) (2011)
26. Lee, H.Y., Huang, J.B., Singh, M., Yang, M.H.: Unsupervised representation learning by sorting sequences. In: Proceedings of the IEEE International Conference on Computer Vision, pp. 667–676 (2017)
27. Li, H., Xu, Z., Taylor, G., Studer, C., Goldstein, T.: Visualizing the loss landscape of neural nets. In: Proceedings of the 32nd International Conference on Neural Information Processing Systems, pp. 6391–6401 (2018)
28. Li, T., Wang, L.: Learning spatiotemporal features via video and text pair discrimination. arXiv preprint arXiv:2001.05691 (2020)
29. McMahan, B., Moore, E., Ramage, D., Hampson, S., Arcas, B.A.: Communication-efficient learning of deep networks from decentralized data. In: Artificial Intelligence and Statistics, pp. 1273–1282. PMLR (2017)
30. Misra, I., Zitnick, C.L., Hebert, M.: Shuffle and learn: unsupervised learning using temporal order verification. In: Leibe, B., Matas, J., Sebe, N., Welling, M. (eds.) ECCV 2016. LNCS, vol. 9905, pp. 527–544. Springer, Cham (2016). https://doi.org/10.1007/978-3-319-46448-0_32
31. Park, H., Sjosund, L., Yoo, Y., Monet, N., Bang, J., Kwak, N.: SINet: extreme lightweight portrait segmentation networks with spatial squeeze module and information blocking decoder. In: Proceedings of the IEEE/CVF Winter Conference on Applications of Computer Vision, pp. 2066–2074 (2020)
32. Piergiovanni, A., Angelova, A., Ryoo, M.S.: Evolving losses for unsupervised video representation learning. In: Proceedings of the IEEE/CVF Conference on Computer Vision and Pattern Recognition, pp. 133–142 (2020)
33. Reddi, S.J., et al.: Adaptive federated optimization. In: International Conference on Learning Representations (2020)
34. Romijnders, R., et al.: Representation learning from videos in-the-wild: an object-centric approach. In: Proceedings of the IEEE/CVF Winter Conference on Applications of Computer Vision, pp. 177–187 (2021)
35. Russakovsky, O., et al.: ImageNet large scale visual recognition challenge. Int. J. Comput. Vision 115(3), 211–252 (2015)

36. Soomro, K., Zamir, A.R., Shah, M.: UCF101: a dataset of 101 human actions classes from videos in the wild (2012)
37. Tran, D., Wang, H., Torresani, L., Ray, J., LeCun, Y., Paluri, M.: A closer look at spatiotemporal convolutions for action recognition. In: Proceedings of the IEEE Conference on Computer Vision and Pattern Recognition, pp. 6450–6459 (2018)
38. Vondrick, C., Pirsiavash, H., Torralba, A.: Anticipating visual representations from unlabeled video. In: Proceedings of the IEEE Conference on Computer Vision and Pattern Recognition, pp. 98–106 (2016)
39. Wang, G., Zhou, Y., Luo, C., Xie, W., Zeng, W., Xiong, Z.: Unsupervised visual representation learning by tracking patches in video. In: Proceedings of the IEEE/CVF Conference on Computer Vision and Pattern Recognition, pp. 2563–2572 (2021)
40. Wang, J., Jiao, J., Liu, Y.-H.: Self-supervised video representation learning by pace prediction. In: Vedaldi, A., Bischof, H., Brox, T., Frahm, J.-M. (eds.) ECCV 2020. LNCS, vol. 12362, pp. 504–521. Springer, Cham (2020). https://doi.org/10.1007/978-3-030-58520-4_30
41. Wang, X., Gupta, A.: Unsupervised learning of visual representations using videos. In: Proceedings of the IEEE International Conference on Computer Vision, pp. 2794–2802 (2015)
42. Xu, D., Xiao, J., Zhao, Z., Shao, J., Xie, D., Zhuang, Y.: Self-supervised spatiotemporal learning via video clip order prediction. In: Proceedings of the IEEE/CVF Conference on Computer Vision and Pattern Recognition, pp. 10334–10343 (2019)
43. Yao, Y., Liu, C., Luo, D., Zhou, Y., Ye, Q.: Video playback rate perception for self-supervised spatio-temporal representation learning. In: Proceedings of the IEEE/CVF Conference on Computer Vision and Pattern Recognition, pp. 6548–6557 (2020)
44. Zhang, F., et al.: Federated unsupervised representation learning. arXiv preprint arXiv:2010.08982 (2020)
45. Zhao, Y., Xiong, Y., Wang, L., Wu, Z., Tang, X., Lin, D.: Temporal action detection with structured segment networks. In: Proceedings of the IEEE International Conference on Computer Vision, pp. 2914–2923 (2017)
46. Zhuang, W., Gan, X., Wen, Y., Zhang, S., Yi, S.: Collaborative unsupervised visual representation learning from decentralized data. In: Proceedings of the IEEE/CVF International Conference on Computer Vision, pp. 4912–4921 (2021)

Towards Efficient and Effective Self-supervised Learning of Visual Representations

Sravanti Addepalli$^{(\boxtimes)}$ ⓘ, Kaushal Bhogale ⓘ, Priyam Dey ⓘ,
and R. Venkatesh Babu ⓘ

Video Analytics Lab, Department of Computational and Data Sciences,
Indian Institute of Science, Bangalore, India
sravantia@iisc.ac.in

Abstract. Self-supervision has emerged as a propitious method for visual representation learning after the recent paradigm shift from hand-crafted pretext tasks to instance-similarity based approaches. Most state-of-the-art methods enforce similarity between various augmentations of a given image, while some methods additionally use contrastive approaches to explicitly ensure diverse representations. While these approaches have indeed shown promising direction, they require a significantly larger number of training iterations when compared to the supervised counterparts. In this work, we explore reasons for the slow convergence of these methods, and further propose to strengthen them using well-posed auxiliary tasks that converge significantly faster, and are also useful for representation learning. The proposed method utilizes the task of rotation prediction to improve the efficiency of existing state-of-the-art methods. We demonstrate significant gains in performance using the proposed method on multiple datasets, specifically for lower training epochs.

1 Introduction

The unprecedented progress achieved using Deep Neural Networks over the past decade was fuelled by the availability of large-scale labelled datasets such as ImageNet [9], coupled with a massive increase in computational capabilities. While their initial success was contingent on the availability of annotations in a supervised learning framework [17,22,24,32], recent years have witnessed a surge in self-supervised learning methods, which could achieve comparable performance, albeit using a higher computational budget and larger model capacities [3,4,6,15]. Early self-supervised approaches [13,26,34] aimed at learning representations while solving specialized tasks that require a semantic understanding of the content to accomplish. While generative networks such as task-specific

---

S. Addepalli and K. Bhogale—Equal contribution.

Supplementary Information The online version contains supplementary material available at https://doi.org/10.1007/978-3-031-19821-2_30.

S. Avidan et al. (Eds.): ECCV 2022, LNCS 13691, pp. 523–538, 2022.
https://doi.org/10.1007/978-3-031-19821-2_30

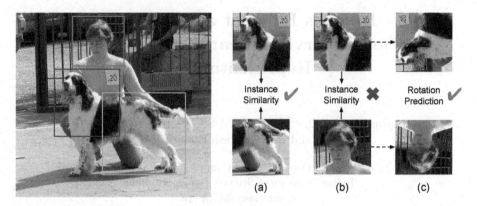

Fig. 1. We demonstrate noise in the training objective of instance-similarity based learning tasks. Consider the three random crops shown in the input image. The two crops in (a) are desirable, while the crops shown in (b) give an incorrect signal to the network. Since the task of rotation prediction shown in (c) aims to predict the rotation angle of each cropped image independently, there is no noise in the training objective.

encoder-decoder architectures [21,29,35] and Generative Adversarial Networks (GANs) [12,14] could learn useful representations, they were superseded by the use of discriminative tasks such as solving Jigsaw puzzles [26] and rotation prediction [13], as the latter could be achieved using lower model capacities and lesser compute. The surprisingly simple task of rotating every image by a random angle from the set $\{0°, 90°, 180°, 270°\}$, and training the network to predict this angle was seen to outperform other handcrafted task based methods with a similar convergence rate as supervised training [13]. Compared to these pretext task based methods, recent approaches have achieved a significant boost in performance by learning similar representations across various augmentations of a given image [3,4,6,15,16]. While these methods show improvements at a low training budget as well, they achieve a further boost when trained for a larger number of epochs [6], indicating that improving the convergence of such methods can lead to valuable gains at a low computational cost.

In this work, we empirically show that a key reason for the slow convergence of instance-similarity based approaches is the presence of noise in the training objective, owing to the nature of the learning task, as shown in Fig. 1. We further propose to strengthen the recent state-of-the-art instance-similarity based self-supervised learning algorithms such as BYOL [15] and SwAV [3] using a noise-free auxiliary training objective such as rotation prediction in a multi-task framework. As shown in Fig. 4, this leads to a similar convergence rate as RotNet [13], while also resulting in better representations from the instance-similarity based objective. We further study the invariance of the network to geometric transformations, and show that in natural images, rotation invariance hurts performance and learning covariant representations across multiple rotated views leads to improved results. We demonstrate significant gains in performance across multiple datasets - CIFAR-10, CIFAR-100 [23] and ImageNet-100 [9,33], and the scalability of the proposed approach to ImageNet-1k [9] as well.

Our code is available here: https://github.com/val-iisc/EffSSL.

2 Related Works

2.1 Handcrafted Pretext Task Based Methods

Discriminative pretext tasks use pseudo-labels that are generated automatically without the need for human annotations. This includes tasks based on spatial context of images such as context prediction [10], image jigsaw puzzle [26] and counting visual primitives [27].

RotNet: Rotation prediction, proposed by Gidaris et al. [13], has been one of the most successful pretext tasks for the learning of useful semantic representations. In this approach, every image is transformed using all four rotation transformations, and the network is trained to predict the corresponding rotation angle used for transforming the image. Due to its simplicity and effectiveness, the rotation task has been used to improve the training of GANs [5,14] as well.

Multi-task Learning: Doersch and Zisserman [11] investigated methods for combining several pretext tasks in a multi-task learning framework to learn better representations. Contrary to a general multi-task learning setting, in this work we aim to improve instance similarity based tasks such as BYOL [15] and SwAV [3] using handcrafted pretext tasks. We empirically show that the training objective of instance-similarity based tasks is noisy, and combining it with the well-defined objective of rotation prediction leads to improved performance.

2.2 Instance Discriminative Approaches

Recent approaches aim to learn similar representations for different augmentations of the same image, while generating diverse representations across different images. Several works achieve this using contrastive learning approaches [4,16,18,25,28], where multiple augmentations of a given image are considered as positives, and augmentations of other images are considered as negatives. PIRL [25] and MoCo [16] maintain a queue to sample more negatives.

SimCLR: The work by Chen et al. [4] presents a Simple Framework for Contrastive Learning of Visual Representations (SimCLR), that utilizes existing architectures such as ResNet [17], and avoids the need for memory banks. The authors proposed the use of multiple data augmentations and a learnable nonlinear transformation between representations to improve the effectiveness of contrastive learning. Two independent augmentations for every image are considered as positives in the contrastive learning task, while the augmentations of all other images are considered as negatives. The network is trained by minimizing the normalized temperature-scaled cross entropy loss (NT-Xent) loss.

BYOL, SimSiam: While prior approaches relied on the use of negatives for training, Grill et al. [15] proposed Bootstrap Your Own Latent (BYOL), which could achieve state-of-the-art performance without the use of negatives. The two augmentations of a given image are passed through two different networks - the base encoder and the momentum encoder. The base encoder is trained such that the representation at its output can be used to predict the representation at the output of the momentum encoder, using a predictor network. Chen and He [6] show that it is indeed possible to avoid a collapsed representation even without the momentum encoder using Simple Siamese (SimSiam) networks, and that the stop-gradient operation is crucial for achieving this.

Clustering Based Methods, SwAV: Clustering-based self-supervised approaches use pseudo-labels from the clustering algorithm to learn representations. DeepCluster [2] alternates between using k-means clustering for producing pseudo-labels, and training the network to predict the same. Asano *et al.* [1] show that degenerate solutions exist in the DeepCluster [2] algorithm. To address this, they cast the pseudo-label assignment problem as an instance of the optimal transport problem and solve it efficiently using a fast variant of the Sinkhorn-Knopp algorithm [7]. SwAV [3] also uses the Sinkhorn-Knoop algorithm for clustering the data while simultaneously enforcing consistency between cluster assignments by Swapping Assignments between Views (SwAV), and using them as targets for training.

2.3 Relation with Concurrent Works

There has been some recent interest towards improving instance-similarity based approaches by combining them with pretext tasks [8,20] . In particular, Kinakh et al. [20] show that the use of pretext auxiliary tasks in addition to the contrastive loss can boost the accuracy of models like ScatNet and ResNet-18 on small-scale datasets like STL-10 and CIFAR-100-20. Dangovski et al. [8] claim that learning equivariant representations is better than learning invariant representations, and hence the auxiliary rotation prediction task helps. Our work complements these efforts, and highlights a key issue in the instance-discriminative learning objective: the *impact of noise* in their slow convergence, and shows that combining them with a *noise-free* auxiliary pretext task can significantly improve their efficiency and effectiveness.

3 Motivation

The evolution of self-supervised learning algorithms from handcrafted pretext task-based methods [13,26,34] to instance discriminative approaches [3,4,6,15, 16] has indeed led to a significant boost in the performance of downstream tasks. However, as shown in Fig. 4, the latter require a larger number of training epochs for convergence. In this section, we show using controlled experiments that the slow convergence of instance-discriminative algorithms can be attributed to a noisy training objective, and eliminating this noise can lead to improved results.

3.1 Impact of False Negatives in SimCLR

The contrastive learning objective in SimCLR [4] considers two augmentations of a given image as positives and the augmentations of all other images in the

Table 1. Eliminating False Negatives in contrastive learning across varying levels of supervision (% Labels). Elimination of noise in the training objective leads to higher linear evaluation accuracy (%) within a fixed training budget.

% Labels	SimCLR [4]	Ours	Gain (%)
0	88.77	90.91	2.14
30	92.26 +3.49	93.94	1.68
50	92.93 +0.67	94.02	1.09
100	93.27 +0.34	94.15	0.88

Table 2. Eliminating False Positives in BYOL [15] across varying levels of supervision (% Good Crops). Elimination of noise in the training objective leads to higher linear evaluation accuracy (%) within a fixed training budget.

% Good Crops	BYOL [15]	Ours	Gain (%)
0	63.64	68.62	4.98
25	64.50+0.86	68.30	3.80
50	66.30+1.80	68.90	2.60
100	66.72+0.42	70.26	3.54

batch as negatives. These negatives could belong to the same class as the anchor image, and possibly be as similar to the anchor image as the corresponding positive, leading to a noisy training objective. While the probability of same class negatives is higher when batch size is higher than the number of classes, this issue can occur even otherwise, when there exist negative images that are more similar to the anchor when compared to the positive. Khosla et al. [19] use supervision from labels in a Supervised Contrastive (SupCon) framework to convert the same-class false negatives to additional positives, and show an improvement over supervised learning methods.

In order to specifically study the impact of eliminating false-negatives, we first perform experiments by using labels to avoid using the same class samples as negatives. We do not add these eliminated negatives as positives, in order to avoid excessive supervision. In Table 1 we present results of an experiment on the CIFAR-10 dataset, where the same-class negatives in SimCLR are eliminated using a varying fraction of labels. The fraction of labels serves as an upper bound to the amount of noise reduction in the training objective, considering that other sources of noise such as false-positives are still not eliminated. Using 30% labels, we achieve a 3.49% increase in accuracy when compared to the SimCLR baseline (0% labels case). It is also interesting to note that the boost in accuracy is highest for 30% supervision and reduces as the fraction of labels increase. This indicates that the network can possibly overcome the impact of noise more effectively when the amount of noise is lower. Overall, we obtain 4.5% boost in the case where all the labels are used. By jointly training SimCLR with the task of rotation prediction (Ours), we achieve highest gains in the case of 0% labels or the no supervision case, and significantly lower gains as the amount of labels increase. We discuss this in greater detail in Sect. 5.2.

3.2 Impact of False Positives in BYOL

Since BYOL does not use a contrastive learning objective, it is not directly impacted by noise due to false negatives. However, as shown in Fig. 1(b), the augmentations considered may not be similar to each other, leading to false positives. Selvaraju et al. [31] show that unsupervised saliency maps can be used for the selection of better crops, and also as a supervisory signal in the training objective. This leads to improved performance on scene datasets which contain multiple objects. Inspired by this, we use Grad-CAM [30] based saliency maps from a supervised ImageNet pre-trained network to select crops such that the ratio of mean saliency score of the cropped image and that of the full image is higher than a certain threshold (Details in Sect. 2 of the Supplementary). It is to be noted that the only difference with respect to BYOL is in the use of supervised saliency maps for the selection of crops. Alternatively, unsupervised saliency maps could also be used for the same. We demonstrate results of this experiment on the ImageNet-100 dataset in Table 2. We observe that by using saliency-maps for crop selection, the accuracy improves by 3.08% for a fixed training budget. While this experiment shows the impact of reducing the false positives in the BYOL objective, it does not completely eliminate noise in the training objective, since the saliency maps themselves are obtained from a Deep Neural Network, and hence may not be very accurate.

4   Proposed Method

In this section, we examine the advantages of instance-discriminative approaches and handcrafted pretext-task based methods, and further discuss our proposed approach which integrates both methods to overcome their limitations.

The key ingredients for the success of a self-supervised learning algorithm are (i) Well-posedness of the learning task; (ii) Extent of correlation between representations that help accomplish the pretext task, and ideal representations, whose quality is evaluated using downstream tasks.

The success of instance-similarity based approaches in achieving state-of-the-art performance on downstream tasks indeed shows that the representations learnt using such tasks are well correlated with ideal representations. However, these methods require to be trained on a significantly larger number of training epochs when compared to the supervised counterparts. As seen in the previous section, a possible reason for the slow convergence of these methods is the noise in training objective due to the presence of false positives and false negatives. While it is possible to overcome this noise using additional supervision from (unsupervised) pre-trained models, such as the use of saliency maps for crop selection, these methods are not very successful as this supervisory signal is also not perfect in practice. Moreover, this method assumes the availability of a network which is pre-trained on a relevant dataset, which may not always hold true, and hence adds to the training cost. We observe that the boost in performance is not good enough to justify the additional computational overhead. If the same computational budget is invested in the main self-supervised task, it leads to better performance (Details in Sect. 2 of the Supplementary).

On the other hand, task-based objectives such as rotation prediction score higher on the well-posedness of the learning task. In this task, a known random rotation transformation is applied to an image, and the task of the network is to predict the angle of rotation. Since the rotation angle is known a priori, there is

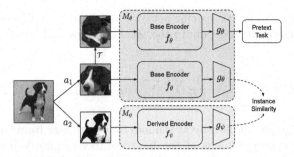

Fig. 2. Schematic diagram illustrating the proposed approach. A pretext task such as rotation prediction is combined with base methods like BYOL and SimCLR. For methods like BYOL and MoCo, the derived network M_ψ is a momentum-averaged version of M_θ, and for methods like SimCLR, M_θ and M_ψ share the same parameters.

very little scope for noise in labels or in the learning objective, leading to faster training convergence.

In this work, we propose to enhance the convergence of instance-similarity based approaches using pretext-task based objectives such as rotation prediction. The proposed approach can be used to enhance many existing instance-discrimination based algorithms (referred to as base algorithm) as shown in Sect. 5. A schematic diagram of our proposed approach is presented in Fig. 2.

We term the main feature extractor to be learned as the base encoder, and denote it as f_θ. Some of the self-supervised learning algorithms use an additional encoder, which is derived from the weights of the base encoder. We call this as a derived encoder and represent it using f_ψ. It is to be noted that the derived encoder may be also be identical to the base encoder, which represents an identity mapping between θ and ψ. As proposed by Chen et al. [4], many of the approaches use a learnable nonlinear transformation between the representations and the final instance-discriminative loss. We denote this projection network and its derived network using g_θ and g_ϕ respectively. We note that the base algorithm may have additional layers between the projection network and the final loss, such as the predictor in BYOL [15] and SimSiam [6], which are not explicitly shown in Fig. 2.

An input image x is first subject to two augmentations a_1 and a_2 to generate x^{a_1} and x^{a_2}. We use the augmentation pipeline from the respective base algorithm such as BYOL or SimCLR. These augmented images are passed through the base encoder f_θ and the derived encoder f_ϕ respectively, and the outputs of the projection networks g_θ and g_ϕ are used to compute the training objective of the respective base algorithm. The augmentation x^{a_1} is further transformed using a rotation transformation t which is randomly sampled from the set $\mathcal{T} = \{0°, 90°, 180°, 270°\}$. The rotated image $x^{a_1,t}$ is passed through the base encoder f_θ and projection network g_θ which are shared with the instance-based task. We represent the overall network formed by the composition of f_θ and g_θ by M_θ, and similarly the composition of f_ψ and g_ψ by M_ψ. The representation

$M_\theta(x^{a_1,t})$ is input to a task-specific network h_θ whose output is a 4-dimensional softmax vector over the outputs in the set $\mathcal{T}$. The overall training objective is as follows:

$$\mathcal{L} = \mathcal{L}_{\text{base}} + \lambda \cdot \frac{1}{2B} \sum_{i=0}^{B-1} \sum_{m=1}^{2} \ell_{CE}(h_\theta(M_\theta(x_i^{a_m,t_k}), t_k)) \tag{1}$$

Here t_k is sampled uniformly at random for each image from the set $\mathcal{T}$. $\mathcal{L}_{\text{base}}$ represents the symmetric loss of the base instance-similarity based algorithm used. We describe the base loss for BYOL [15] and SimCLR [4] in Sec. 1 of the Supplementary. λ is the weighting factor between rotation task and the instance-similarity objective. While the RotNet algorithm [13] uses all four rotations for every image, we consider only two in the overall symmetric loss. Therefore, when compared to the base algorithm, the computational overhead of the proposed method is limited to one additional forward propagation for every augmentation, which is very low when compared to the other components of training such as data loading and backpropagation. There is no additional overhead in backpropagation since the combined loss (Eq. 1) is used for training.

5   Experiments and Analysis

In this section, we first describe our experimental settings (Sect. 5.1), following which we present an empirical analysis to highlight the importance of the auxiliary task towards improving the efficiency and effectiveness of the base learning algorithm (Sect. 5.2). We further compare the properties of the learned representations using different training methods and show that learning representations that are covariant to rotation also aids in boosting performance (Sect. 5.3). We finally compare the results of the proposed method with the state-of-the-art approaches in Sect. 5.4.

5.1   Experimental Setup

We run our experiments either on a single 32 GB V100 GPU, or across two such GPUs unless specified otherwise. We train our models with ResNet-18 [17] architecture on CIFAR-10 and CIFAR-100 [23] dataset and with ResNet-50 [17] architecture on ImageNet-1k [9] dataset. Our primary evaluations are run for 200 epochs on CIFAR-10 and CIFAR-100, and 100 epochs on ImageNet-100 [9] dataset. We show additional evaluations across varying number of training epochs in Sect. 5.4. We describe the training hyperparameters in Sect. 4 of the Supplementary. We use the respective base algorithm or the proposed approach to learn the base encoder f_θ, and evaluate its effectiveness by training a linear classifier over this, as is common in prior works [3,4,6,15]. In this step, the weights of the base encoder are frozen. We additionally report results in a semi-supervised (Sect. 5.4) and transfer learning setting (Sect. 7 of the Supplementary) as well.

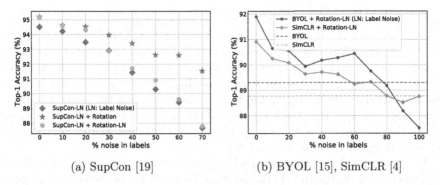

(a) SupCon [19]   (b) BYOL [15], SimCLR [4]

Fig. 3. The plots demonstrate the impact of label noise in different training objectives on CIFAR-10 dataset. The proposed method (+ Rotation) results in higher performance boost when the amount of label noise in the base method is larger. Addition of label noise to the rotation task reduces the gain in performance.

5.2   Robustness to Noise in the Training Objective

As discussed in Sect. 3, instance-similarity based tasks such as SimCLR [4] and BYOL [15] suffer from noise in the training objective, and eliminating this noise can lead to significant performance gains in a fixed training budget. We additionally report results of the proposed approach integrated with SimCLR and BYOL in Tables 1 and 2 respectively, and obtain gains over the base approach across varying settings of supervision levels. However, as can be seen from the column Gain (%), the gains using the proposed approach reduce with increasing levels of supervision. This is aligned with our hypothesis that the rotation task helps in overcoming the impact of noise in the base instance-similarity task, and therefore, when additional supervision already achieves this objective, gains using the proposed approach are lower.

Label Noise in a Supervised Learning Setting: We consider the task of supervised learning using the supervised contrastive (SupCon) learning objective proposed by Khosla et al. [19]. The training objective is similar to that of SimCLR [4] with the exception that same-class negatives are treated as positives. The authors demonstrate that this method outperforms standard supervised training as well. We choose this training objective as this is similar to the instance-similarity based tasks we consider in this paper, while also having significantly lesser noise due to the elimination of false negatives in training. As shown in Fig. 3a, even in this setting, the proposed method achieves 0.68% improvement, achieving a new state-of-the-art in supervised learning. In order to highlight the impact of noise in training, we run a controlled set of experiments by adding a fixed amount of label noise in each run. The plot in Fig. 3a shows the trend in accuracy of the SupCon algorithm with increasing label noise. The proposed method achieves a significant boost over the SupCon baseline consistently across different noise levels. Further, as the amount of noise in training increases, we achieve higher gains using the proposed approach, indicating that the rotation task is indeed helping overcome noise in the training objective.

We also consider a set of experiments where an equal amount of label noise is added to the SupCon training objective and to the rotation prediction task. We note that in majority of the runs (excluding the case of noise above 70%), the accuracy is very similar to the SupCon baseline with the same amount of noise. This indicates that the knowledge of true labels in handcrafted tasks such as rotation prediction is the key factor that contributes to the improvement achieved using the proposed approach.

We perform the experiments of adding label noise to the rotation prediction task when combined with BYOL and SimCLR as well. As shown in Fig. 3b we find that the gains with the rotation prediction task drops considerably over 0–20% label noise, indicating that a similar amount of noise ($\sim$20%) is present in the BYOL/SimCLR training objectives as well. Further, addition of rotation prediction task helps marginally (0.47–1.38%) even with higher amount of noise (30–60%) in rotation annotations. This indicates that, while the rotation prediction primarily helps by providing a noise-free training objective, it aids the main task in other ways too. We investigate this in the following section.

5.3   Learning Rotation-Covariant Representations

The task of enforcing similarity across various augmentations of a given image yields representations that are invariant to such transformations. In sharp contrast, the representations learned by humans are covariant with respect to factors such as rotation, color and scale, although we are able to still correlate multiple transformations of the same object very well. This hints at the fact that learning covariant representations could help the accuracy of downstream tasks such as object detection and classification.

In Table 3, we compare the rotation sensitivity and contrastive task accuracy of representations at the output of the base encoder f_θ, and the projection network g_θ. We follow the process described by Chen et al. [4] to obtain these results. We freeze the network till the respective layer (f_θ or g_θ) and train a rotation task classifier over this using a 2-layer MLP head. We measure the rotation task accuracy, which serves as an indication of the amount of rotation sensitivity in the base network. We further compute the contrastive task accuracy on the representations learned, by checking whether the two augmentations of a given image are more similar to each other when compared to augmentations of other images in the same batch.

Interestingly, a fully supervised network is more sensitive to rotation (80.54%) when compared to the representations learned using BYOL (73.4%). Chen et al. [4] also show that rotation augmentation hurts performance of SimCLR. These observations indicate that invariance to rotation hurts performance, and reducing this lead to better representations. While RotNet has higher accuracy on the rotation task, it does significantly worse on the instance discrimination task, leading to sub-optimal performance compared to BYOL. In the proposed method, we achieve better rotation task accuracy with a small drop in the con-

Table 3. Task Performance (%): Evaluation of representations learned using various algorithms on the task of rotation prediction and instance-discrimination.

Method	Linear	Rotation Acc		Contrastive Acc	
		f(.)	g(f(.))	f(.)	g(f(.))
Supervised	94.03	80.54	–	46.36	–
BYOL	89.30	73.40	58.32	78.53	78.82
Rotation	84.00	93.69	93.46	31.61	1.52
BYOL+Rotation	91.89	93.73	93.54	72.85	67.81

Table 4. BYOL + Rotation with **varying noise in the rotation labels**. Rotation prediction accuracy correlates with linear evaluation accuracy.

Rotation noise	Linear	Rotation Acc		Contrastive Acc	
		f(.)	g(f(.))	f(.)	g(f(.))
30%	89.93	91.88	91.78	73.42	64.25
50%	90.28	89.95	85.82	78.18	77.39
70%	89.75	80.49	67.26	78.55	77.31
80%	89.18	77.43	63.53	77.26	76.92

trastive task accuracy when compared to BYOL. This also results in an overall higher performance after Linear evaluation.

We also investigate rotation invariance for the experiments in Sect. 5.2 with BYOL as the base method, where noise is added to the rotation task. As shown in Table 4, we find that as the amount of noise increases in the rotation task, the amount of rotation invariance increases, leading to a drop in accuracy. Even with 50% noise in the rotation task, we achieve 16.55% boost in rotation performance, leading to 0.98% improvement in the accuracy after linear evaluation. Since the BYOL learning task possibly contains lesser noise compared to this, the gain in performance can be justified by the fact that rotation-covariant representations lead to improved performance on natural image datasets.

5.4   Comparison with the State-of-the-Art

We compare the performance of the proposed method with the respective baselines in the setting of linear evaluation on CIFAR-10, CIFAR-100 (Table 5), ImageNet-100 and ImageNet-1k (Table 6) datasets. We perform extensive hyperparameter search to obtain reliable results on the baseline methods for CIFAR-10 and CIFAR-100, since most existing works report the optimal settings for ImageNet-1k training alone. As shown in Table 5, although the performance of Rotation prediction [13] itself is significantly worse that other methods, we obtain gains of 2.14%, 2.59%, 3.6% and 2.14% on CIFAR-10 and 2.44%, 6.4%, 7.1% and 3.11% on CIFAR-100 by using the proposed method with SimCLR [4], BYOL [15], SwAV [3] and SimSiam [6] respectively.

We present results on CIFAR-10 dataset with varying number of training epochs in Fig. 4a using BYOL as the base approach. Across all settings, we obtain improved results over the BYOL baseline. The proposed method achieves the same accuracy as the baseline in one-third the training time (shown using blue dotted line) as shown in Fig. 4a. We show the difference in accuracy with respect to accuracy obtained with 50 epochs of training in Fig. 4a, to clearly visualize the convergence rate of different methods. It can be seen that the proposed method has a similar convergence trend as the Rotation task, while outperforming BYOL in terms of Top-1 Accuracy, highlighting that integrating these methods indeed combines the benefits of both methods.

We present results on ImageNet-100 dataset in Table 6. To limit the computational cost on our ImageNet-100 and ImageNet-1k runs, we either use the

Table 5. CIFAR-10, CIFAR-100: Accuracy (%) of the proposed method compared to baselines under two evaluation settings - K-Nearest Neighbor (KNN) classification with K = 200 and Linear classifier training. The proposed method achieves significant performance gains across all settings.

Method	CIFAR-10 (200 epochs)		CIFAR-100 (200 epochs)	
	KNN	Linear	KNN	Linear
Rotation Pred. [13]	78.01	84.00	36.25	50.87
SimCLR [4]	86.37	88.77	55.10	62.96
SimCLR + Ours	88.69	90.91	57.09	65.40
BYOL [15]	86.56	89.30	54.37	60.67
BYOL + Ours	89.80	91.89	58.41	67.03
SwAV [3]	80.65	83.60	40.35	51.50
SwAV + Ours	85.26	87.20	50.09	58.60
SimSiam [6]	87.05	89.77	56.90	64.27
SimSiam + Ours	**90.35**	**91.91**	**58.92**	**67.38**

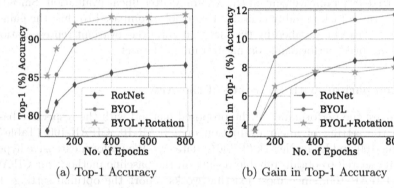

(a) Top-1 Accuracy   (b) Gain in Top-1 Accuracy

Fig. 4. (a) Accuracy (%) after Linear layer training for BYOL [15], RotNet [13] and the proposed method (BYOL+Rotation) on CIFAR-10. The proposed method achieves the same accuracy as the baseline in one-third the training time (shown using blue dotted line). (b) Gain in Top-1 Accuracy (%), or the difference between accuracy of the current epoch and epoch-50. Plot (a) shows the improvement in effectiveness of the proposed approach and plot (b) shows the improvement in efficiency or convergence rate. (Color figure online)

tuned hyperparameters from the official repository, or follow the settings from other popular repositories that report competent results. Due to the unavailability of tuned hyperparameters on this dataset for SimSiam, we skip reporting results of this method on ImageNet-100. We achieve gains of 2.58%, 1.22% and 2.2% on BYOL [15], SimCLR [4] and SwAV [3] respectively in Top-1 accuracy. We obtain the best results by integrating the proposed method with SwAV, and hence report ImageNet-1k results on the same method, in order to demonstrate the scalability of the proposed method to a large-scale dataset. We present the

Table 6. ImageNet-100 and ImageNet-1k: Performance (%) of the proposed method when compared to baselines under three evaluation settings - Linear classifier training and Semi-Supervised Learning with 1% and 10% labels. The proposed method achieves significant performance gains.

Method	Linear Acc	Semi-supervised 1% labels		Semi-supervised 10% labels	
	Top-1	Top-1	Top-5	Top-1	Top-5
ImageNet-100 (100 epochs, ResNet-18)					
Rotation Prediction [13]	53.86	34.72	65.70	51.18	81.38
BYOL [15]	71.02	46.60	75.50	68.00	89.80
BYOL + Ours	73.60	56.40	83.50	72.30	91.40
SimCLR [4]	72.02	57.28	83.69	71.44	91.72
SimCLR + Ours	73.24	**57.80**	**83.84**	**72.52**	**92.10**
SwAV [3]	72.20	49.38	78.41	67.56	90.78
SwAV + Ours	**74.40**	52.02	80.01	69.68	91.43
ImageNet-1k (30 epochs, ResNet-50)					
SwAV [3]	54.90	32.20	58.20	51.82	77.60
SwAV + Ours	**57.30**	**32.80**	**59.12**	**53.80**	**78.54**

result of 30-epochs of training on ImageNet-1k in Table 6. Using the proposed approach, we obtain a boost of 2.4% in Top-1 accuracy over the SwAV baseline. We present additional results on longer training epochs in Sec. 8 of the Supplementary.

Furthermore, we present results on ImageNet-100 dataset with varying number of training epochs in Fig. 5. Using the proposed method, we achieve gains across all settings with respect to the number of training epochs. We obtain improved results over the base methods in semi-supervised learning (Table 6) and transfer learning settings as well. We discuss the transfer learning results in Sect. 7 of the Supplementary.

5.5   Integration with Other Tasks

In this work, we empirically show that combining instance-discriminative tasks with well-posed handcrafted pretext tasks such as Rotation prediction [13] can indeed lead to more effective and efficient learning of visual representations. While we choose the Rotation prediction task due to its simplicity in implementation, and applicability to low resolution images (such as CIFAR-10), it is indeed possible to achieve gains by using other well-posed tasks as well. In Table 7, we report results on the ImageNet-100 [33] dataset by combining the base BYOL [15] algorithm individually with Rotation prediction [13], Jigsaw puzzle solving [26] and both. Although the Jigsaw puzzle solving task is sub-optimal when compared to the Rotation prediction task, we achieve similar gains in performance when these tasks are combined with BYOL. We obtain the best gains (3.7%) when we combine both tasks with BYOL. This shows that the analysis on well-defined tasks being able to aid the learning of instance-discriminative tasks that are noisy is indeed generic, and not specific to the Rotation prediction task alone.

Table 7. Combining BYOL with handcrafted pretext tasks: Accuracy in (%) after linear evaluation, of various algorithms on ImageNet-100 dataset.

	Top-1 (%)	Top-5 (%)
RotNet [13] (R)	53.86	81.26
Jigsaw [26] (J)	42.01	72.10
BYOL [15]	71.02	91.78
BYOL + R	73.60	**92.98**
BYOL + J	73.60	92.72
BYOL + J + R	**74.72**	92.94

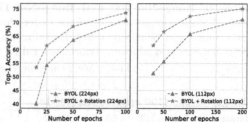

Fig. 5. Accuracy (%) after Linear layer training for BYOL and the proposed method (BYOL+Rotation) for ImageNet-100. The proposed method achieves significant gains over the baseline in all settings.

6   Conclusions

In this work, we investigate reasons for the slow convergence of recent instance-similarity based methods, and propose to improve the same by jointly training them with well-posed tasks such as rotation prediction. While instance-discriminative approaches learn better representations, handcrafted tasks have the advantage of faster convergence as the training objective is well defined and there is typically no (or very less) noise in the generated pseudo-labels. The complementary nature of the two kinds of tasks makes it suitable to achieve the gains associated with both by combining them. Using the proposed approach, we show significant gains in performance under a fixed training budget, along with improvements in training efficiency. We show similar gains in performance by combining the base algorithms with the task of Jigsaw puzzle solving as well. We hope that our work will revive research interest in designing specialized tasks, so that they can be help boost the effectiveness and efficiency of state-of-the-art methods.

Acknowledgments. This work was supported by the Qualcomm Innovation Fellowship. We are thankful for the support.

References

1. Asano, Y.M., Rupprecht, C., Vedaldi, A.: Self-labelling via simultaneous clustering and representation learning. In: International Conference on Learning Representations (ICLR) (2020)
2. Caron, M., Bojanowski, P., Joulin, A., Douze, M.: Deep clustering for unsupervised learning of visual features. In: Ferrari, V., Hebert, M., Sminchisescu, C., Weiss, Y. (eds.) Computer Vision – ECCV 2018. LNCS, vol. 11218, pp. 139–156. Springer, Cham (2018). https://doi.org/10.1007/978-3-030-01264-9_9
3. Caron, M., Misra, I., Mairal, J., Goyal, P., Bojanowski, P., Joulin, A.: Unsupervised learning of visual features by contrasting cluster assignments. In: Advances in Neural Information Processing Systems (NeurIPS) (2020)

4. Chen, T., Kornblith, S., Norouzi, M., Hinton, G.: A simple framework for contrastive learning of visual representations. In: Proceedings of the 37th International Conference on Machine Learning (ICML) (2020)
5. Chen, T., Zhai, X., Ritter, M., Lucic, M., Houlsby, N.: Self-supervised GANs via auxiliary rotation loss. In: Proceedings of the IEEE/CVF Conference on Computer Vision and Pattern Recognition (CVPR) (2019)
6. Chen, X., He, K.: Exploring simple siamese representation learning. In: Proceedings of the IEEE/CVF Conference on Computer Vision and Pattern Recognition (CVPR) (2021)
7. Cuturi, M.: Sinkhorn distances: lightspeed computation of optimal transport. In: Advances in Neural Information Processing Systems (NeurIPS) (2013)
8. Dangovski, R., et al.: Equivariant self-supervised learning: encouraging equivariance in representations. In: International Conference on Learning Representations (ICLR) (2022)
9. Deng, J., Dong, W., Socher, R., Li, L.J., Li, K., Fei-Fei, L.: ImageNet: a large-scale hierarchical image database. In: Proceedings of the IEEE Conference on Computer Vision and Pattern Recognition (CVPR) (2009)
10. Doersch, C., Gupta, A., Efros, A.A.: Unsupervised visual representation learning by context prediction. In: IEEE International Conference on Computer Vision (ICCV) (2015)
11. Doersch, C., Zisserman, A.: Multi-task self-supervised visual learning. In: IEEE International Conference on Computer Vision (ICCV) (2017)
12. Donahue, J., Krähenbühl, P., Darrell, T.: Adversarial feature learning. In: International Conference on Learning Representations (ICLR) (2017)
13. Gidaris, S., Singh, P., Komodakis, N.: Unsupervised representation learning by predicting image rotations. In: International Conference on Learning Representations (ICLR) (2018)
14. Goodfellow, I., et al.: Generative adversarial nets. In: Advances in Neural Information Processing Systems (NeurIPS) (2014)
15. Grill, J.B., et al.: Bootstrap your own latent - a new approach to self-supervised learning. In: Advances in Neural Information Processing Systems (NeurIPS) (2020)
16. He, K., Fan, H., Wu, Y., Xie, S., Girshick, R.: Momentum contrast for unsupervised visual representation learning. In: Proceedings of the IEEE/CVF Conference on Computer Vision and Pattern Recognition (CVPR) (2020)
17. He, K., Zhang, X., Ren, S., Sun, J.: Deep residual learning for image recognition. In: IEEE Conference on Computer Vision and Pattern Recognition (CVPR) (2016)
18. Hénaff, O.J., et al.: Data-efficient image recognition with contrastive predictive coding. In: Proceedings of the 37th International Conference on Machine Learning (ICML) (2020)
19. Khosla, P., et al.: Supervised contrastive learning. In: Advances in Neural Information Processing Systems (NeurIPS) (2020)
20. Kinakh, V., Voloshynovskiy, S., Taran, O.: ScatsimCLR: self-supervised contrastive learning with pretext task regularization for small-scale datasets. In: 2nd Visual Inductive Priors for Data-Efficient Deep Learning Workshop (2021)
21. Kingma, D.P., Welling, M.: Auto-encoding variational bayes. arXiv preprint arXiv:1312.6114 (2013)
22. Krizhevsky, A., Sutskever, I., Hinton, G.E.: ImageNet classification with deep convolutional neural networks. In: Advances in Neural Information Processing Systems (NeurIPS) (2012)
23. Krizhevsky, A., et al.: Learning multiple layers of features from tiny images (2009)

24. LeCun, Y., Bengio, Y., Hinton, G.: Deep learning. Nature **521**(7553), 436–444 (2015)
25. Misra, I., van der Maaten, L.: Self-supervised learning of pretext-invariant representations. In: Proceedings of the IEEE/CVF Conference on Computer Vision and Pattern Recognition (CVPR) (2020)
26. Noroozi, M., Favaro, P.: Unsupervised learning of visual representations by solving Jigsaw puzzles. In: Leibe, B., Matas, J., Sebe, N., Welling, M. (eds.) ECCV 2016. LNCS, vol. 9910, pp. 69–84. Springer, Cham (2016). https://doi.org/10.1007/978-3-319-46466-4_5
27. Noroozi, M., Pirsiavash, H., Favaro, P.: Representation learning by learning to count. In: Proceedings of the IEEE International Conference on Computer Vision (ICCV) (2017)
28. Oord, A.v.d., Li, Y., Vinyals, O.: Representation learning with contrastive predictive coding. arXiv preprint arXiv:1807.03748 (2018)
29. Pathak, D., Krahenbuhl, P., Donahue, J., Darrell, T., Efros, A.A.: Context encoders: feature learning by inpainting. In: Proceedings of the IEEE Conference on Computer Vision and Pattern Recognition (CVPR) (2016)
30. Selvaraju, R.R., Cogswell, M., Das, A., Vedantam, R., Parikh, D., Batra, D.: Grad-CAM: visual explanations from deep networks via gradient-based localization. In: Proceedings of the IEEE International Conference on Computer Vision (ICCV) (2017)
31. Selvaraju, R.R., Desai, K., Johnson, J., Naik, N.: Casting your model: learning to localize improves self-supervised representations. In: Proceedings of the IEEE/CVF Conference on Computer Vision and Pattern Recognition (CVPR) (2021)
32. Szegedy, C., et al.: Going deeper with convolutions. In: Proceedings of the IEEE Conference on Computer Vision and Pattern Recognition (CVPR) (2015)
33. Tian, Y., Krishnan, D., Isola, P.: Contrastive multiview coding. In: Vedaldi, A., Bischof, H., Brox, T., Frahm, J.-M. (eds.) ECCV 2020. LNCS, vol. 12356, pp. 776–794. Springer, Cham (2020). https://doi.org/10.1007/978-3-030-58621-8_45
34. Zhang, R., Isola, P., Efros, A.A.: Colorful image colorization. In: Leibe, B., Matas, J., Sebe, N., Welling, M. (eds.) ECCV 2016. LNCS, vol. 9907, pp. 649–666. Springer, Cham (2016). https://doi.org/10.1007/978-3-319-46487-9_40
35. Zhang, R., Isola, P., Efros, A.A.: Split-brain autoencoders: Unsupervised learning by cross-channel prediction. In: Proceedings of the IEEE Conference on Computer Vision and Pattern Recognition (CVPR) (2017)

DSR – A Dual Subspace Re-Projection Network for Surface Anomaly Detection

Vitjan Zavrtanik[✉], Matej Kristan, and Danijel Skočaj

University of Ljubljana, Faculty of Computer and Information Science,
Ljubljana, Slovenia
{vitjan.zavrtanik,matej.kristan,danijel.skocaj}@fri.uni-lj.si

Abstract. The state-of-the-art in discriminative unsupervised surface anomaly detection relies on external datasets for synthesizing anomaly-augmented training images. Such approaches are prone to failure on near-in-distribution anomalies since these are difficult to be synthesized realistically due to their similarity to anomaly-free regions. We propose an architecture based on quantized feature space representation with dual decoders, DSR, that avoids the image-level anomaly synthesis requirement. Without making any assumptions about the visual properties of anomalies, DSR generates the anomalies at the feature level by sampling the learned quantized feature space, which allows a controlled generation of near-in-distribution anomalies. DSR achieves state-of-the-art results on the KSDD2 and MVTec anomaly detection datasets. The experiments on the challenging real-world KSDD2 dataset show that DSR significantly outperforms other unsupervised surface anomaly detection methods, improving the previous top-performing methods by 10% AP in anomaly detection and 35% AP in anomaly localization. Code is available at: https://github.com/VitjanZ/DSR_anomaly_detection.

Keywords: Surface anomaly detection · Discrete feature space · Simulated anomaly generation

1 Introduction

Surface anomaly detection addresses localization of image regions that deviate from normal object appearance. This is a fundamental problem in industrial inspection, in which the anomalies are defects on production line objects. In the most challenging situations, the distribution of the normal appearance of the inspected objects is very close to the distribution of anomaly appearances, while anomalies often occupy only a small portion of the object. Furthermore, the anomalies are rare in practical production lines, making the acquisition of a suitable data set for training supervised methods infeasible. The methods thus

Supplementary Information The online version contains supplementary material available at https://doi.org/10.1007/978-3-031-19821-2_31.

focus on leveraging only anomaly-free images, since these can be abundantly obtained.

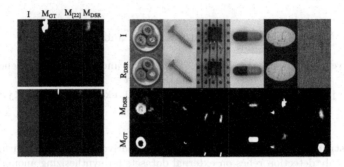

Fig. 1. The dual decoder architecture with discrete feature space allows DSR robust object-specific reconstruction (R_{DSR}) and accurate detection of near-in-distribution anomalies, which present a considerable challenge for the recent state-of-the-art ($M_{[22]}$).

Most anomaly detection approaches are based on computing the difference between the inspected image and its image-level or feature-level reconstruction [1–3,5,18,22], with their reconstruction method trained only on anomaly-free images. These approaches assume that anomalies will be poorly reconstructed since they have never been observed during training and that the reconstruction failure on anomalies can be well detected by L_2 or SSIM [20] difference with the input image.

However, L_2 and SSIM measures can only detect anomalies that differ substantially from normal appearance. Subsequent works have addressed this problem by either learning the distance measure with a discriminative network [21] or by classifying the anomalies directly on the input image [11]. These methods require annotated anomalies at training time, and resort to simulation of anomalies from auxiliary datasets and copy-pasting and blending them with the anomaly-free training images. While these methods by far outperform the reconstruction-only methods, they rely substantially on the quality of the auxiliary dataset and the simulation process quality; their performance still degrades on near-in-distribution anomalies (Fig. 1) since it is difficult to simulate these realistically.

In this paper we address two drawbacks of the surface anomaly detection state-of-the-art: the reliance on the auxiliary anomaly simulation datasets and poor near-in-distribution anomaly detection. We propose a dual subspace re-projection surface anomaly detection network (DSR). The network leverages the framework of discretized latent feature space image representation [16], and jointly learns a general and a normal-appearance-specific subspace re-projection to emphasize the anomaly detection capability. The proposed architecture avoids reliance on auxiliary anomaly datasets in training anomaly discrimination. We propose a new anomaly simulation technique that generates the anomalies directly from the network's discretized latent space of natural images, leading to significant performance improvements on near-in-distribution anomaly detection (Fig. 1).

Our contribution is thus twofold: (i) the dual image reconstruction branch architecture with discretized latent representation and (ii) the latent space anomaly generation method that leverages the learned representation of natural images. DSR substantially outperforms the state-of-the-art in near-in-distribution anomaly detection on the recent challenging KSDD2 [6] and delivers state-of-the-art performance on the standard MVTec anomaly detection dataset [3].

2 Related Work

Many recent surface anomaly detection methods are based on image reconstruction [1,2,5], where an encoder-decoder network is trained for image reconstruction on anomaly free images. The anomaly detection capability of these methods is based on the assumption that the trained networks will be unable to accurately reconstruct anomalous regions due to never seeing them during training, making anomalies detectable by comparing the input image to its reconstruction. The core assumption often does not hold, especially in more diverse datasets, as the reconstruction networks learn to generalize well which enables accurate anomaly reconstruction, hampering the downstream anomaly detection performance. Similarly, in [22] iterative inpainting is used for image reconstruction, however, the method is sensitive to random pattern regions that are difficult to inpaint and which cause false positive detections.

Several recent approaches utilize the ability of pretrained networks to extract informative features from an image. In [4] a network is trained on anomaly free images to reconstruct features extracted by the pretrained network. In [19] a feature map is generated as a concatenation of several layers of a pretrained network. An auto-encoder is then trained to reconstruct the resulting feature map. As with image reconstruction based anomaly detection methods, the networks in [4,19] are assumed to be unable to reconstruct the features extracted by the pretrained networks. In [17], a pretrained network is also used to extract informative features from anomaly free data, however instead of relying on reconstruction for anomaly detection, a multivariate gaussian is fit to the anomaly-free data. A Mahalanobis distance is then used as an anomaly score. A similar approach is used in [7], however, a Gaussian is fit at each location in the feature map.

Discriminative unsupervised anomaly detection methods [11,12,21] utilize synthetically generated anomalies to train a discriminative anomaly detection network. In order to alleviate overfitting on the synthetic anomaly appearance, in [21] a reconstruction network is used to restore the normal appearance of the synthetic anomalies. The discriminative network then learns a distance function between the original image and its reconstruction to perform anomaly detection. Due to a limited distribution of the generated synthetic anomalies, the reconstruction network may overfit to the synthetic appearance and fail to restore

normality in near-distribution anomalies, leading to a reduction in performance
in downstream anomaly detection.

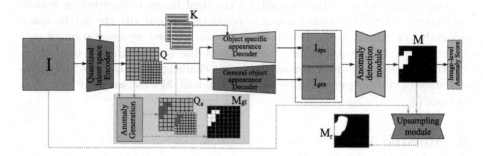

Fig. 2. The DSR architecture. During training, the non-anomalous image quantized feature maps (Q_{hi}, Q_{lo}) are replaced by the anomaly augmented feature maps $(Q_{a,hi}, Q_{a,lo})$ generated by the latent space sampling procedure (shaded block). The pathway marked with green arrows are used when training the Upsampling module with simulated smudges and at inference.

3   DSR

The DSR architecture is outlined in Fig. 2. The input image is projected into a
quantized latent space (Sect. 3.1) and then decoded in parallel by two decoders
specialized on different appearance subspaces. One decoder, the general object
appearance decoder (Sect. 3.2), is trained for high-fidelity reconstruction of arbitrary natural images, while the second, object-specific decoder (Sect. 3.3), is
restricted to reconstructing only normal local appearances of the selected object.
The two reconstructed images are then analyzed by the anomaly detection module (Sect. 3.4). The output localization map is at feature resolution and is upsampled to the input image resolution by the Upsampling module (Sect. 3.5). DSR
is trained by a novel technique of sampling the quantized latent feature space for
generating near-in-distribution anomalies (Sect. 3.6). The DSR training regime
is explained in Sect. 3.7.

3.1   Quantized Latent Space Encoder

DSR leverages quantized feature space representation, which has recently demonstrated strong modelling capabilities of complex natural image distributions ,e.g.,
[9,15]. The approach is based on quantizing the extracted features with features
from a codebook **K** which has been trained for optimal decoding of spatial configurations of quantized features into high-fidelity images.

In particular, the quantized latent space encoder module in Fig. 2 accepts
the input image **I** and projects it into a feature space **F** using a Resnet-based

encoder. A quantized feature representation $\mathbf{Q}$ of the input image is obtained by replacing each feature vector $\mathbf{F}_{ij}$ with its nearest neighbor $\mathbf{e}_l$ in $\mathbf{K}$, i.e.,

$$Q_{i,j} = q(F_{i,j}) = \underset{\mathbf{e}_l \in \mathbf{K}}{\operatorname{argmin}} \left(||\mathbf{F}_{i,j} - \mathbf{e}_l|| \right). \tag{1}$$

In the following, we refer to this operation as vector quantization (VQ). Note that the input image is encoded at two levels of detail using low- and high-resolution codebooks ($\mathbf{K}_{lo}$, $\mathbf{K}_{hi}$), producing $\mathbf{Q}_{lo}$ and $\mathbf{Q}_{hi}$. The two-level VQ has recently been reported to produce superior reconstructions [16]. The architecture of the quantized latent space encoder is shown in Fig. 3. The quantized feature maps Q_{hi} and Q_{low} produced by the quantized latent space encoder are 4× and 8× smaller than the original input image, respectively.

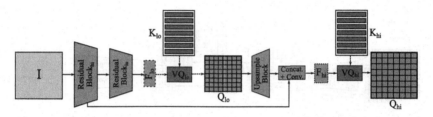

Fig. 3. The quantized latent space encoder architecture. Two residual blocks extract image features at different spatial resolutions. The low-resolution features F_{lo} are quantized by the codebook K_{lo} into a feature representation Q_{lo}. The high-resolution features are concatenated by upsampled Q_{lo}, followed by a convolutional block and quantized by the codebook K_{hi} into a high-resolution representation Q_{hi}.

3.2   General Object Appearance Decoder

The subspace of VQ encoded natural images is captured by specific *spatial configurations* of quantized feature vectors. We apply a *general object appearance decoder* to learn decoding of these configurations into image reconstructions. The decoder first upsamples the low resolution $\mathbf{Q}_{lo}$ and concatenates it with the $\mathbf{Q}_{hi}$, which is followed by two ResNet blocks and two transposed convolution upsampling blocks that map into the reconstructed image $\mathbf{I}_{gen}$.

3.3   Object-specific Appearance Decoder

The tasks of the second decoder, the *object-specific appearance decoder* (see Fig. 4) is to restore local visual anomalies into feasible normal appearances of the object instances observed during training. In particular, we would like to restrict the appearance subspace, i.e., the allowed spatial VQ feature configurations, into configurations that agree with normal appearances. This is achieved by a *subspace restriction module* (Fig. 4), which transforms both high- and low-resolution general input VQ representations ($\mathbf{Q}=\{\mathbf{Q}_{hi}, \mathbf{Q}_{lo}\}$) into non-quantized object-specific subspace configurations ($\tilde{\mathbf{F}}=\{\tilde{\mathbf{F}}_{lo}, \tilde{\mathbf{F}}_{hi}\}$). This is followed by a VQ projection (with codebooks $\mathbf{K}=\{K_{hi}, K_{lo}\}$) into object subspace-restricted quantized feature configurations ($\tilde{\mathbf{Q}}=\{\tilde{\mathbf{Q}}_{hi}, \tilde{\mathbf{Q}}_{lo}\}$). The quantized representations are concatenated (the low-resolution representation is upsampled first) and decoded into reconstructed anomaly-free image $\mathbf{I}_{spc}$ using a convolutional decoder. The subspace restriction modules (Fig. 4) are encoder-decoder convolutional networks with three downsampling and corresponding upsampling blocks. The image reconstruction network consists of two downsampling convolutional blocks, followed by four transposed convolution upsampling blocks. Examples of images with anomalies present and their anomaly-free reconstructions are shown in Fig. 5.

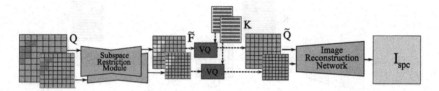

Fig. 4. The object-specific appearance decoder architecture. The features in the quantized features maps $\mathbf{Q}$ are reduced by a subspace restriction module into non-quantized features $\tilde{\mathbf{F}}$ that are then vector-quantized (VQ) by the codebooks $\mathbf{K}$ into $\tilde{\mathbf{Q}}$, which are then decoded into an anomaly-free image $\mathbf{I}_{spc}$.

Fig. 5. The object-specific decoder reconstructs the anomalous images (left) into anomaly-free images (right) with remarkable fidelity. In the second example, it even correctly reconstructs the anomalous green wire into blue. (Color figure online)

3.4   Anomaly Detection Module

The purpose of the anomaly detection module is to localize the anomaly by inspecting the input image reconstruction generated by the general object appearance decoder ($\mathbf{I}_{gen}$) and the object-specific appearance decoder ($\mathbf{I}_{spc}$). The reconstructed images are concatenated depth-wise and decoded into a segmentation mask $\mathbf{M}$ by a Unet-based architecture. $\mathbf{M}$ is the output anomaly map indicating the pixel-level location of the anomalies in the image. To compute also the image-level anomaly score, we apply a simple segmentation mask interpretation procedure as in [22] – the segmentation mask is smoothed by a 21×21 averaging filter and globally max-pooled into a single score.

3.5   Upsampling Module

The generated segmentation mask $\mathbf{M}$ is of the same resolution as the feature maps. A simple Unet-like upsampling module is thus used to resample the mask to full resolution. The input to the network is a depth-wise concatenation of the input image $\mathbf{I}$ and bilinearly upsampled mask $\mathbf{M}$. The output is the final full-resolution mask $\mathbf{M_r}$ (Fig. 2).

3.6   Feature-space Surface Anomaly Generation

The purpose of anomaly generator is to simulate near-in-distribution anomalies of various shapes and sizes with diverse visual appearances to (i) learn normal appearance subspace restriction in the object-specific appearance decoder (Sect. 3.3) and (ii) to specialize the anomaly detection module (Sect. 3.4) for detection of potentially gentle appearance deviations of anomalies from a diverse within-class normal appearance.

We propose a method that leverages the learned quantized subspace in DSR to generate such training anomalies as follows. An anomaly-free input image $\mathbf{I}$ is encoded into a VQ subspace representation $\mathbf{Q}$ and an anomaly mask $\mathbf{M_{gt}}$ is generated by sampling a Perlin noise [14], with values 1 indicating anomalous pixels. The features in $\mathbf{Q}$ corresponding to the anomaly indicators in $\mathbf{M_{gt}}$ are replaced by sampling from the set of codebook features $\mathbf{K}$.

Sampling without constraints will likely lead to significant appearance changes on anomalous pixels, resulting in trivial out-of-distribution reconstructed images. On the other hand, if the closest vectors are sampled that are too similar to the normal appearance, they will likely lead to false-positive detections.

We thus first define a similarity bound on all features for a given image $n \sim \mathcal{U}[\lambda_s N_K, N_K]$, where N_K is the number of codebook vectors and λ_s is the similarity bound parameter. Then we replace each feature in $\mathbf{Q}$, indicated by $\mathbf{M_{gt}}$, with one of its near neighbors from the codebook feature vectors, sampled uniformly, i.e., $k \sim \mathcal{U}[\lambda_s N_K, n]$. In all experiments λ_s is 0.05, therefore, excluding the 5% of most similar vectors to prevent false-positive generation, while prioritizing the selection of the features close to the vector to be replaced to encourage the generation of near-in-distribution anomalies.

3.7   DSR Training Procedure

The DSR is trained in three stages. In the **first stage**, the quantized latent space encoder (Sect. 3.1), along with the VQ codebook and the general object appearance decoder are trained on ImageNet [8] to learn the subspace of natural images, which allows a high-fidelity reconstruction of general images. We use the procedure from [13] that minimizes the image reconstruction loss as well as the difference between the feature space projection $\mathbf{F}$ computed in the quantized latent space encoder (Figs. 2 and 3) and its quantized version $\mathbf{Q}$, i.e.,

$$\mathcal{L}_{\text{st1}} = L_2(\mathbf{I}, \mathbf{I}_{\text{gen}}) + L_2(sg[\mathbf{F}], \mathbf{Q}) + \lambda_1 L_2(\mathbf{F}, sg[\mathbf{Q}]), \qquad (2)$$

where $L_2(\cdot)$ is the Euclidean distance and $sg[\cdot]$ is the stop gradient operator constraining the operand to be a non-updated constant [13]. After training, the discrete latent space encoder, the codebook and the general object appearance decoder (coloured in magenta in Fig. 2) are fixed.

In the second, **anomaly detection training stage**, the detection parts of DSR are trained on images of the selected object type. Anomaly-free training images are projected through the quantized latent space encoder into their quantized feature representation $\mathbf{Q}$. The surface anomaly generation method presented in Sect. 3.6 then generates the anomalies at the feature level, $\mathbf{Q}_{\text{a}}$, along with their ground truth masks $\mathbf{M}_{\text{gt}}$. The representation $\mathbf{Q}_{\text{a}}$ (that replaces $\mathbf{Q}$ in Fig. 2) is then forward passed and decoded into the anomaly mask $\mathbf{M}$.

The anomaly detection module and the object-specific appearance decoder are trained by minimizing the focal loss between the ground truth $\mathbf{M}_{\text{gt}}$ and predicted anomaly mask $\mathbf{M}$, the L_2 distance between the subspace-restricted configurations $\tilde{\mathbf{F}}$ computed in the object-specific appearance decoder (Fig. 4) and the non-anomalous input image quantized representation $\mathbf{Q}$, and the L_2 distance between the non-anomalous input image $\mathbf{I}$ and its object-specific reconstruction $\mathbf{I}_{\text{spc}}$, i.e.,

$$\mathcal{L}_{\text{st2}} = \mathcal{L}_{\text{foc}}(\mathbf{M}_{\text{gt}}, \mathbf{M}) + \lambda_2 L_2(\tilde{\mathbf{F}}, \mathbf{Q}) + \lambda_3 L_2(\mathbf{I}, \mathbf{I}_{\text{spc}}). \qquad (3)$$

Finally, the Upsampling module is trained. After the anomaly detection network has been trained, images with copy-pasted smudges are generated and the low-resolution anomaly masks are computed as detection network outputs. Since the full-resolution masks are known from the smudge pasting on the original image, the upsampling network can be trained with a focal loss.

4   Experiments

4.1   Implementation Details

In the first training stage (Sect. 3.7) quantized latent space encoder, general object appearance decoder and the latent vector codebook are trained for image reconstruction on ImageNet [8] for $200,000$ iterations with a batch size of 32 and a learning rate of 0.0002. The codebooks K_{hi} and K_{lo} each contain 4096 latent vectors of dimension 128. In the second training stage (Sect. 3.7) the object-specific appearance decoder and the anomaly detection model are trained for $100,000$ iterations with a batch size of 8 with a learning rate of 0.0002. The learning rate is decreased by a factor of 10 after $80,000$ iterations. The λ_2 and λ_3

values in Eq. 3 are set to 1 and 10, respectively. In the third stage the Upsampling module is then trained for 20,000 iterations with a learning rate of 0.0002 and a batch size of 8. The training hyperparameters and network architectures remain constant throughout our experiments.

4.2   Experimental Results on KSDD2

The recently proposed KSDD2 [6] surface anomaly detection dataset is currently the most challenging dataset with near-in-distribution surface anomalies (see Fig. 6). KSDD2 was acquired on real industrial production lines and contains a wide variety of anomalies, many of which are particularly challenging due to their similarity to the normal appearances in the training set.

Fig. 6. Normal (left) and anomalous (right) images from KSDD2. The anomalies (marked with white arrows) are very similar to the normal appearance in this dataset.

The dataset contains 2085 anomaly-free and 246 anomalous training images to test anomaly detection under unsupervised and supervised setups. For example, in the unsupervised setup, only anomaly-free training images may be used. The test set contains 894 anomaly-free and 110 anomalous images. We follow the evaluation procedure defined in [6], with the AP metric for image-level anomaly detection (AP_{det}), and present also anomaly localization results in terms of pixel-level AP (AP_{loc}).

Additional anomalous training samples available in KSDD2 [6] enable comparison of DSR with the supervised defect detection methods. Note that, although the acquisition of anomalous examples is difficult in practice, in many cases these are available, albeit in small quantities. Most of unsupervised anomaly detection methods, however, do not, or even can not, make use of this additional information, if available. The proposed DSR method can be easily adapted to take such annotations of anomalous images into account. In addition to the generated synthetic anomalies, the real-world anomalies with known ground truth can be utilised to train the anomaly detection module.

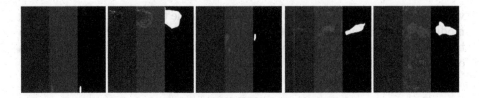

Fig. 7. Qualitative results of the unsupervised DSR on the KSDD2 dataset: the input image, the overlaid predicted mask and the ground truth.

Comparison with the State-of-the-art. The results of unsupervised surface anomaly detection methods are shown in Table 1. DSR significantly outperforms other state-of-the-art unsupervised methods such as MAD [17], PaDim [7] and DRAEM [21], achieving higher AP scores for anomaly detection and localization. It outperforms the previous best image-level AP score by 7.9 p.p. Qualitative examples of the unsupervised DSR are presented in Fig. 7 and show that despite a quite heterogeneous normal appearance, that can also be observed in Fig. 6, the visual defects are successfully detected and localized.

Extension to Supervised Learning In contrast to most of the unsupervised visual anomaly detection methods, DSR can also utilise pixel-level anotations, if they are available, making it applicable in low-shot anomaly detection scenarios. We evaluated the proposed approach in the supervised setting. Table 2 shows the comparison with the method from [6] that is specifically designed for supervised defect detection and can operate with various levels of supervision. In KSDD2, there are 246 anomalous samples available, and if image-level labels are available but none of them is segmented, the method [6] operates in the weakly supervised mode ($N = 0$).

Table 1. Anomaly detection (AP_{det}) and localization (AP_{loc}) on the KSDD2 dataset.

Method	US [4]	MAD [17]	DRÆM [21]	PaDim [7]	DSR
AP_{det}	65.3	79.3	77.8	55.6	**87.2**
AP_{loc}	-	-	42.4	45.3	**61.4**

The completely unsupervised DSR, without taking these additional positive training samples into account, outperforms the weakly supervised method [6] for 13.9 p.p. in AP_{det} and achieves a good localization result, whereas [6] is unable to produce meaningful segmentation maps. When a number of anomalous training images are also segmented ($N > 0$), the results improve even further, and significantly outperform the results of [6]. When using the full annotated training set of 246 segmented examples, DSR achieves anomaly detection performance near that of the fully supervised method [6] and outperforms the recent fully supervised method presented in [10]. Furthermore, DSR achieves the highest localization performance AP_{loc} under all training settings, significantly outperforming [6]. These results demonstrate that DSR can efficiently work in supervised settings as well, utilising all information available.

Table 2. Anomaly detection and localization on the KSDD2 dataset in a supervised settings w.r.t. number of used anomalous training images N with ground truth masks.

	Method N:	0	16	53	246
AP_{det}	[6]	73.3	83.2	89.1	**95.4**
	DSR	**87.2**	**91.4**	**94.6**	95.2
	[10]	-	-	-	93.3
AP_{loc}	[6]	1.0	45.1	52.2	67.6
	DSR	**61.4**	**71.2**	**81.6**	**85.5**

4.3 Experimental Results on MVTec

We also perform experiments on the MVTec anomaly detection dataset [3], which contains 15 different texture and object classes, and has been established as the standard surface anomaly evaluation benchmark [7,11,17,21]. The training set consists only of anomaly-free images, while the test set is comprised of anomalous as well as anomaly-free images. The widely used AUROC metric is applied for image-level anomaly detection. Because only a fraction of the pixels in the test set are anomalous, the pixel-wise average-precision metric AP [21] is used to evaluate the anomaly localization performance. It is more robust to class imbalance and better suited for anomaly localization evaluation than the commonly used pixel-wise AUROC.

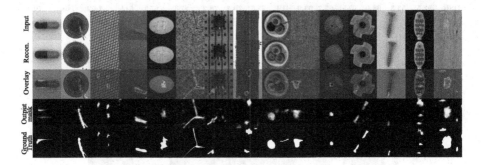

Fig. 8. Qualitative results on the MVTec dataset: the input images, outputs of the reconstruction network, input images with overlaid output masks, the output masks and the ground truth masks are shown in individual rows.

Table 3. Results of anomaly detection on MVTec dataset (AUROC) with the average score over all classes (*avg*) in the last column.

Method	bottle	capsule	grid	leather	pill	tile	trans.	zipper	cable	carpet	hazelnut	m. nut	screw	toothbrush	wood	average
[4]	99.0	86.1	81.0	88.2	87.9	99.1	81.8	91.9	86.2	91.6	93.1	82.0	54.9	95.3	97.7	87.7
[22]	99.9	88.4	99.6	100	83.8	98.7	90.9	98.1	81.9	84.2	83.3	88.5	84.5	100	93.0	91.7
[17]	100	92.3	92.9	100	83.3	97.4	95.9	97.9	94.0	95.5	98.7	93.1	81.2	95.8	97.6	94.4
[7]	99.8	91.5	95.7	100	94.4	97.4	97.8	90.9	92.2	99.9	93.3	99.2	84.4	97.2	98.8	95.5
[11]	98.2	98.2	100	100	94.9	94.6	96.1	99.9	81.2	93.9	98.3	99.9	88.7	99.4	99.1	96.1
[21]	99.2	98.5	99.9	100	98.9	99.6	93.1	100	91.8	97.0	100	98.7	93.9	100	99.1	98.0
DSR	100	98.1	100	100	97.5	100	97.8	100	93.8	100	95.6	98.5	96.2	99.7	96.3	98.2

Comparison with the State-of-the-art. We evaluate DSR against recent state-of-the-art surface anomaly detection methods. The experimental results are presented in Tables 3 and 4 for image-level anomaly detection and for pixel-level anomaly localization, respectively, and show that DSR outperforms the recent state-of-the-art approaches. It achieves an average AUROC of 98.2%, while maintaining a strong anomaly localization performance with an AP score of 70.2%. DSR outperforms the previous top performer in anomaly detection DRAEM [21] on the mean AUROC score by 0.2 percentage points (p.p.) and achieves superior performance on classes such as transistor, cable, carpet and screw, where near-distribution anomalies such as deformations are more prevalent. Qualitative results on the MVTec dataset are shown in Fig. 8 and demonstrate that the detected anomalous regions resemble the ground truth anomaly maps to a high degree.

Table 4. Results (AP) of anomaly localization on MVTec dataset.

Method	bottle	capsule	grid	leather	pill	tile	trans.	zipper	cable	carpet	hazelnut	m. nut	screw	toothbrush	wood	average
[4]	74.2	25.9	10.1	40.9	62.0	65.3	27.1	36.1	48.2	52.2	57.8	83.5	7.8	37.7	53.3	45.5
[22]	76.4	38.2	36.4	49.1	51.6	52.6	39.2	63.4	24.4	61.4	33.8	64.3	43.9	50.6	38.2	48.2
[7]	77.3	46.7	35.7	53.5	61.2	52.4	72.0	58.2	45.4	60.7	61.1	77.4	21.7	54.7	46.3	55.0
[21]	86.5	49.4	65.7	75.3	48.5	92.3	50.7	81.5	52.4	53.5	92.9	96.3	58.2	44.7	77.7	68.4
DSR	91.5	53.3	68.0	62.5	65.7	93.9	41.1	78.5	70.4	78.2	87.3	67.5	52.5	74.2	68.4	70.2

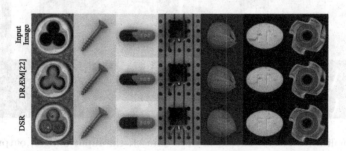

Fig. 9. Qualitative reconstruction results. DSR far better reconstructs the anomalies by their corresponding in-distribution appearance than the state-of-the-art DRÆM [21].

Further qualitative comparison is shown in Fig. 9. Both DSR and DRÆM [21] are trained to restore the normality of images corrupted by simulated anomalies. However, DRÆM [21] generates the anomalies in the image space from an out-of-distribution dataset, while DSR generates the anomalies within the quantized feature space, making it more difficult for the reconstruction network to overfit to the simulated anomaly appearance. This results in DSR having a more robust image normality restoration capability that is insensitive to near-in-distribution anomalies such as deformations. Figure 9 compares the reconstruction results of both methods. Note that DSR produces a more realistic reconstruction. Due to the reconstruction network not overfitting to the synthetic anomaly appearance, DSR can recognize deformations as deviations from normality and reconstruct them accordingly.

4.4   Ablation Study

Additional experiments on the MVTec dataset provide further insights into DSR.

Anomaly Source Evaluation. We evaluate the impact of training using our feature-based anomalies and compare it to the training with image-based anomalies generated from out-of-distribution datasets as proposed in [21]. The results are shown in Table 6(a), where DSR_{img} denotes the results when using image-based anomalies during training. We can see that feature-based anomaly generation (DSR) outperforms the image-based approach in anomaly localization and detection.

Anomaly Feature Sampling. To generate simulated anomalies, DSR samples vectors from the codebook K according to a designed process presented in Sect. 3.6. We compare this approach to one that samples the codebook with a uniform probability for each vector. The results (DSR_{random}) presented in Table 6(b) show a significant drop in performance. The sampling method, therefore, plays an important role. The proposed approach generates anomalous regions from vectors that are close to the extracted vectors generating simulated near-distribution anomalies that leads to superior results in terms of anomaly detection as well as localization. DSR is robust to the choice of the similarity bound parameter, retaining a good anomaly detection performance for a wide range of λ_s values (Table 5).

Table 5. Results on MVTec using various similarity bound λ_s values.

λ_s	0.01	0.02	0.05	0.1	0.2	0.5
$AUROC_{det}$	97.5	98.0	98.2	97.7	97.1	95.5

Reconstruction Loss Components. Table 6(c) shows the impact of individual reconstruction loss components of Eq. (3), where the reconstruction is conditioned both on the feature L_{feat} and image L_{img} reconstruction losses, which are the second and the third components in Eq. (3), respectively. During training

$\mathrm{DSR}_{L_{img}}$ uses only the image reconstruction loss and $\mathrm{DSR}_{L_{feat}}$ uses only the feature reconstruction loss. There is a significant loss in performance when using only individual loss components. Relying on both image and feature reconstruction losses during training results in a more robust normality reconstruction model leading to a 2 p.p. higher average image-level AUROC as well as significantly higher localization AP scores.

Upsampling module. Table 6(d) shows the effect of removing the Upsampling module of the network, leading to a drop in localization performance. The anomaly detection performance remains the same as the image-level score is extracted from the lower resolution output anomaly map M.

Table 6. Ablation study results on MVTec: (a) using out-of-distribution texture-based anomalies (DSR_{img}) in training; (b) unconstrained uniform anomaly sampling (DSR_{random}); (c) training with only image reconstruction loss ($\mathrm{DSR}_{L_{img}}$) and with only the feature reconstruction loss ($\mathrm{DSR}_{L_{feat}}$); (d) Performance without the Upsampling module (DSR_{U-}).

		(a)	(b)	(c)		(d)
Experiment	DSR	DSR_{img}	DSR_{random}	$\mathrm{DSR}_{L_{img}}$	$\mathrm{DSR}_{L_{feat}}$	DSR_{U-}
AUROC_{det}	98.2	97.8	95.6	96.3	95.2	98.2
AP_{loc}	70.2	67.5	62.5	67.0	61.8	65.2

5 Conclusion

We proposed DSR, a discriminative surface anomaly detection method based on dual image reconstruction branch architecture with discretized latent representation. Such representation allows controlled generation of synthetic anomalies in feature space, which, in contrast to the state-of-the-art methods that generate anomalies in image space, makes no assumption about the anomaly appearance and does not rely on image-level heuristics. Our anomaly generation approach produces near-in-distribution synthetic anomalies resulting in more robustly trained reconstruction capabilities and detection of anomalies whose appearance is close to the normal appearance.

On the recent challenging real-world KSDD2 dataset [6], it outperforms all other unsupervised surface anomaly detection methods by 10% AP in anomaly detection and 35% AP in anomaly localization tasks. DSR also significantly outperforms the weakly-supervised model presented in [6]. Moreover, we showed that the proposed approach can be extended to utilise also pixel-wise annotated anomalous training samples. When used in such supervised settings, it considerably improves the results of related supervised methods [6] when only a few annotated examples are available. This demonstrates the potential of DSR to be used in real-world settings where the number of available anomalous images is typically too low to train fully supervised methods. DSR also achieves state-of-the-art results on the standard MVTec anomaly detection dataset [3].

The ablation study shows that the sampling method used for anomaly generation impacts the final anomaly detection results significantly, which suggests that a more complex feature sampling method may improve results further, which we leave for our future research endeavours.

In addition to it's good performance across several tasks and it's ability to utilize anomalous training samples that are available in some practical scenarios, DSR is fast, running at 58 FPS, making it a good choice for real-world industrial applications with real-time requirements.

References

1. Akcay, S., Atapour-Abarghouei, A., Breckon, T.P.: GANomaly: semi-supervised anomaly detection via adversarial training. In: Jawahar, C.V., Li, H., Mori, G., Schindler, K. (eds.) ACCV 2018. LNCS, vol. 11363, pp. 622–637. Springer, Cham (2019). https://doi.org/10.1007/978-3-030-20893-6_39
2. Akçay, S., Atapour-Abarghouei, A., Breckon, T.P.: Skip-GANomaly: skip connected and adversarially trained encoder-decoder anomaly detection. In: 2019 International Joint Conference on Neural Networks (IJCNN), pp. 1–8. IEEE (2019)
3. Bergmann, P., Fauser, M., Sattlegger, D., Steger, C.: MVTec AD - a comprehensive real-world dataset for unsupervised anomaly detection. In: Proceedings of the IEEE Conference on Computer Vision and Pattern Recognition, pp. 9592–9600 (2019)
4. Bergmann, P., Fauser, M., Sattlegger, D., Steger, C.: Uninformed students: Student-teacher anomaly detection with discriminative latent embeddings. In: Proceedings of the IEEE/CVF Conference on Computer Vision and Pattern Recognition, pp. 4183–4192 (2020)
5. Bergmann, P., Löwe, S., Fauser, M., Sattlegger, D., Steger, C.: Improving unsupervised defect segmentation by applying structural similarity to autoencoders. In: 14th International Joint Conference on Computer Vision, Imaging and Computer Graphics theory and Applications, vol. 5, pp. 372–380 (2018)
6. Božič, J., Tabernik, D., Skočaj, D.: Mixed supervision for surface-defect detection: from weakly to fully supervised learning. Comput. Ind. **129**, 103459 (2021)
7. Defard, T., Setkov, A., Loesch, A., Audigier, R.: PaDiM: a patch distribution modeling framework for anomaly detection and localization. In: Del Bimbo, A., Cucchiara, R., Sclaroff, S., Farinella, G.M., Mei, T., Bertini, M., Escalante, H.J., Vezzani, R. (eds.) ICPR 2021. LNCS, vol. 12664, pp. 475–489. Springer, Cham (2021). https://doi.org/10.1007/978-3-030-68799-1_35
8. Deng, J., Dong, W., Socher, R., Li, L.J., Li, K., Fei-Fei, L.: ImageNet: a large-scale hierarchical image database. In: 2009 IEEE Conference on Computer Vision and Pattern Recognition, pp. 248–255. IEEE (2009)
9. Esser, P., Rombach, R., Ommer, B.: Taming transformers for high-resolution image synthesis. In: Proceedings of the IEEE/CVF Conference on Computer Vision and Pattern Recognition (CVPR), pp. 12873–12883, (2021)
10. Lei, L., Sun, S., Zhang, Y., Liu, H., Xu, W.: PSIC-Net: pixel-wise segmentation and image-wise classification network for surface defects. Machines **9**, 221 (2021). https://doi.org/10.3390/MACHINES9100221. https://www.mdpi.com/2075-1702/9/10/221/htm

11. Li, C.L., Sohn, K., Yoon, J., Pfister, T.: CutPaste: self-supervised learning for anomaly detection and localization. In: Proceedings of the IEEE/CVF Conference on Computer Vision and Pattern Recognition, pp. 9664–9674 (2021)

12. Lv, C., Shen, F., Zhang, Z., Xu, D., He, Y.: A novel pixel-wise defect inspection method based on stable background reconstruction. IEEE Trans. Instrum. Meas. **70**, 1–13 (2021). https://doi.org/10.1109/TIM.2020.3038413

13. van den Oord, A., Vinyals, O., Kavukcuoglu, K.: Neural discrete representation learning. In: Guyon, I., et al. (eds.) Advances in Neural Information Processing Systems, vol. 30, pp. 6306–6315. Curran Associates, Inc. (2017) https://proceedings.neurips.cc/paper/2017/file/7a98af17e63a0ac09ce2e96d03992fbc-Paper.pdf https://proceedings.neurips.cc/paper/2017/file/7a98af17e63a0ac09ce2e96d03992fbc-Paper.pdf

14. Perlin, K.: An image synthesizer. ACM Siggraph Comput. Graph. **19**(3), 287–296 (1985)

15. Ramesh, A., et al.: Zero-shot text-to-image generation. arXiv preprint arXiv:2102.12092 (2021)

16. Razavi, A., van den Oord, A., Vinyals, O.: Generating diverse high-fidelity images with VQ-VAE-2. In: Wallach, H., Larochelle, H., Beygelzimer, A., d' Alché-Buc, F., Fox, E., Garnett, R. (eds.) Adv. Neural Inf. Process. Sys. vol. 32, pp. 14866–14876. Curran Associates, Inc. (2019) https://proceedings.neurips.cc/paper/2019/file/5f8e2fa1718d1bbcadf1cd9c7a54fb8c-Paper.pdf https://proceedings.neurips.cc/paper/2019/file/5f8e2fa1718d1bbcadf1cd9c7a54fb8c-Paper.pdf

17. Rippel, O., Mertens, P., Merhof, D.: Modeling the distribution of normal data in pre-trained deep features for anomaly detection. In: ICPR (2020)

18. Schlegl, T., Seeböck, P., Waldstein, S.M., Langs, G., Schmidt-Erfurth, U.: f-AnoGAN: fast unsupervised anomaly detection with generative adversarial networks. Med. Image Anal. **54**, 30–44 (2019)

19. Shi, Y., Yang, J., Qi, Z.: Unsupervised anomaly segmentation via deep feature reconstruction. Neurocomputing **424**, 9–22 (2021)

20. Wang, Z., Bovik, A.C., Sheikh, H.R., Simoncelli, E.P.: Image quality assessment: from error visibility to structural similarity. IEEE Trans. Image Process. **13**(4), 600–612 (2004)

21. Zavrtanik, V., Kristan, M., Skočaj, D.: DRAEM - a discriminatively trained reconstruction embedding for surface anomaly detection. In: Proceedings of the IEEE/CVF International Conference on Computer Vision (ICCV), pp. 8330–8339, (2021)

22. Zavrtanik, V., Kristan, M., Skočaj, D.: Reconstruction by inpainting for visual anomaly detection. Pattern Recognit. **112**, 107706 (2021). https://doi.org/10.1016/j.patcog.2020.107706. https://www.sciencedirect.com/science/article/pii/S0031320320305094

PseudoAugment: Learning to Use Unlabeled Data for Data Augmentation in Point Clouds

Zhaoqi Leng[1]([✉]), Shuyang Cheng[1], Benjamin Caine[2], Weiyue Wang[1],
Xiao Zhang[1], Jonathon Shlens[2], Mingxing Tan[1], and Dragomir Anguelov[1]

[1] Waymo, Mountain View, USA
lengzhaoqi@waymo.com
[2] Google, Mountain View, USA

Abstract. Data augmentation is an important technique to improve data efficiency and to save labeling cost for 3D detection in point clouds. Yet, existing augmentation policies have so far been designed to only utilize labeled data, which limits the data diversity. In this paper, we recognize that pseudo labeling and data augmentation are complementary, thus propose to leverage unlabeled data for data augmentation to enrich the training data. In particular, we design three novel pseudo-label based data augmentation policies (PseudoAugments) to fuse both labeled and pseudo-labeled scenes, including frames (PseudoFrame), objects (PseudoBBox), and background (PseudoBackground). PseudoAugments outperforms pseudo labeling by mitigating pseudo labeling errors and generating diverse fused training scenes. We demonstrate PseudoAugments generalize across point-based and voxel-based architectures, different model capacity and both KITTI and Waymo Open Dataset. To alleviate the cost of hyperparameter tuning and iterative pseudo labeling, we develop a population-based data augmentation framework for 3D detection, named AutoPseudoAugment. Unlike previous works that perform pseudo-labeling offline, our framework performs PseudoAugments and hyperparameter tuning in one shot to reduce computational cost. Experimental results on the large-scale Waymo Open Dataset show our method outperforms state-of-the-art auto data augmentation method (PPBA) and self-training method (pseudo labeling). In particular, AutoPseudoAugment is about 3× and 2× data efficient on vehicle and pedestrian tasks compared to prior arts. Notably, AutoPseudoAugment nearly matches the full dataset training results, with just 10% of the labeled run segments on the vehicle detection task.

1 Introduction

3D object detection from LiDAR point cloud data is a core component of autonomous driving. Building accurate 3D object detection systems requires vast quantities of labeled scenes with accurate 3D bounding box annotations. While unlabeled LiDAR data is readily available, labeling itself is costly, e.g.,

© The Author(s), under exclusive license to Springer Nature Switzerland AG 2022
S. Avidan et al. (Eds.): ECCV 2022, LNCS 13691, pp. 555–572, 2022.
https://doi.org/10.1007/978-3-031-19821-2_32

6.4 h of LiDAR data contains more than 10 million human labeled 3D boxes [57]. Because of this, an effective way to increase the data efficiency for model training would be very appealing.

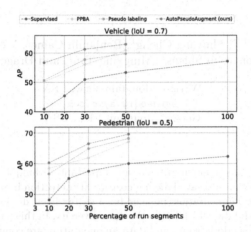

Fig. 1. AutoPseudoAugment is more data efficient than auto data augmentation and self-training methods. Data augmentation only (PPBA [8]), self-training (Pseudo labeling [4]) and our method (AutoPseudoAugment) are evaluated using 3D detection AP at Level 1 difficulty on the *validation* split of the Waymo Open Dataset [57]. Using 10% of labeled run segments, AutoPseudoAugment is about 3× data efficient as PPBA and Pseudo label method on the vehicle class and 2× on the pedestrian class. AutoPseudoAugment is nearly 10× and more than 5× data efficient compared to the supervised (no augmentation) vehicle and pedestrian baselines.

Data augmentation represents an effective way to increase data efficiency for labeled data. Data augmentations for 3D detection generally come in two forms: global augmentations like scene rotations, or local augmentations like ground truth augmentation, where crops of ground truth objects from the training set are inserted into the scene. Pasting ground truth objects into the scene has been shown to be extremely effective on various 3D detection datasets [8, 25, 30, 63–65, 69].

However, these augmentation techniques are typically limited to the labeled training data. A simple way to incorporate unlabeled data into training is pseudo labeling, but naively applying existing 3D data augmentation policies to pseudo labeled frames has an intrinsic limitation, i.e., pseudo labeled frames contain numerous false positive/negative bounding boxes and points. Several recent studies on 3D pseudo labeling [4, 44] have tried to use large-capacity teacher models to mitigate this issue, but the intrinsic pseudo-labeling errors persist. Here, we seek to an alternative approach: *mitigating the pseudo labeled errors by new data augmentation policies.*

Another challenge is how to effectively combine labeled and unlabeled data via data augmentation. Previous approaches treat pseudo-labeled frames as

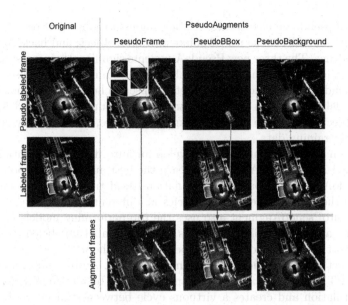

Fig. 2. Visualization of PseudoAugments. PseudoAugments contain three new data augmentation policies: PseudoFrame, PseudoBBox, and PseudoBackground. **PseudoFrame** replaces the labeled frame with a pseudo-labeled frame and drops points of low-confidence bounding boxes in the pseudo-labeled frames. **PseudoB-Box** pastes high-confidence bounding boxes and corresponding point clouds from a pseudo-labeled frame to a labeled frame. **PseudoBackground** removes all points within bounding boxes in a pseudo-labeled frame, and replaces the background point clouds in the labeled frame with the background point clouds of the pseudo-labeled frame. The augmented frames are used as labeled frames during training.

a whole and do not recognize the compositional nature of 3D point clouds scenes [4,44]. This limits the diversity of training data. A simple way to fuse labeled and pseudo-labeled frame is to generalize the existing copy-pasting object data augmentation to leverage unlabeled objects. Interestingly, we observe that only pasting objects between labeled and pseudo-labeled frames is not enough [8,25,30,63–65,69], because we miss out the diverse background scenes in the pseudo labeled dataset. Especially for 3D point clouds, more than 90% of the points are backgrounds, which provide critical ingredients for 3D detectors to learn to detect objects in new scenarios. Thus, it is necessary to develop a set of data augmentation policies that *take advantage of both foreground objects and background points in the pseudo labeled frames along with labeled frames to generate combinatorial number of point clouds.*

In this work, we propose a set of data augmentation policies tailored for pseudo labeled data, named *PseudoAugments*. As shown in Fig. 2, our PseudoAugments contain three new data augmentation policies: *PseudoFrame* removes low confidence points, *PseudoBBox* pastes pseudo objects onto labeled scenes, and *PseudoBackground* swaps the background point clouds between labeled and pseudo-labeled scenes. All our augmentations allow pseudo-labeling uncertainty, and only make use of points of frame, object, and background with high-confidence. The three new PseudoAugments significantly increase the diversity of training data by enabling a combinatorial number of new *fused* training scenes, including 1) ground truth objects on pseudo labeled background scenes, 2) pseudo labeled objects on ground truth background scenes, and 3) pseudo labeled objects on pseudo labeled background scenes, which greatly enrich the diversity of training data.

Based on PseudoAugments, we develop an auto data augmentation framework named AutoPseudoAugment to learn the best augmentation policies. Our AutoPseudoAugment is based on population-based training (PBT) and online search for the best augmentation policies at different training stages. On top of PBT, AutoPseudoAugment also uses the top-performing models in previous generations as an ensemble of teachers to pseudo label unlabeled data, which further boost the quality of pseudo labeled data without the need of training a separated set of high-capacity teacher models [4,44]. AutoPseudoAugment also extends PBT beyond simple hyperparameter tuning by introducing population-based distillation and creates a virtuous cycle between students and teachers, where good teachers in previous generations improves the quality of student models, which become better teachers to pseudo label for future generations.

Our main contribution can be summarized as follows:

1. **PseudoAugments: unifying data augmentation and pseudo labeling.** We identify data augmentation and pseudo labeling are complementary and introduce PseudoFrame, PseudoBBox, PseudoBackground data augmentation policies to take advantage of the composability of unlabeled 3D point clouds while mitigating errors.
2. **AutoPseudoAugment: efficient one-shot framework for PseudoAugment.** Our framework extends PBT by introducing population-based distillation. AutoPseudoAugment does auto hyperparameters search and self-training in one-shot, which reduces the training cost.
3. **Extensive experimental evaluations.** We demonstrate PseudoAugments generalize to different network architectures, model sizes, and datasets. In addition, AutoPseudoAugment outperforms both state-of-the-art auto data augmentation method (PPBA [8]) and pseudo labeling [4]. In particular, leveraging unlabeled data, AutoPseudoAugment requires 10% of labeled run segments to achieve similar performance as PPBA training on 30% of run segments and nearly matches the model performance trained on all labeled data without data augmentation, shown in Fig. 1.

2   Related Work

2.1   Data Augmentation

Data augmentation has been widely adopted to improve the performance of models trained with supervised learning, such as image classification [10,13,

29, 49, 54, 59, 66], 2D object detection [14, 23], image segmentation [15, 38, 46, 48], point cloud classification and detection [7–9, 18, 28, 30, 31, 34, 39, 50, 51, 63, 67, 69].

Due to the number of hyperparameters introduced by using a suite of data augmentations during training, designing a strong augmentation policy for a given task and dataset requires extensive experimentation. Automated data augmentation algorithms [11, 12, 24, 33, 35, 45] were proposed to search data augmentation policies. Recently, PointAugment [34] and PPBA [8] introduced automated data augmentation for point clouds, which showed strong empirical results.

Unlike existing data augmentation methods, which only operates on labeled data, our PseudoAugments are designed to improve the quality of pseudo labeled data and generate combinatorially diverse scenes by fusing labeled and pseudo labeled frames. Different from automated data augmentation frameworks, in particular population-based data augmentation [8, 24], our AutoPseudoAugment framework enables hyperparameters tuning and self-training in one-shot. It reduces the training cost especially for iterative self-training [62] and outperformed the state-of-the-art data augmentation framework for 3D point clouds, shown in Table 4.

2.2 Self-training

Self-training [4, 6, 36, 62], also referred to as pseudo-labeling [32], aims to learn from a combination of labeled and unlabeled data. In self-training, a trained teacher network is used to predict labels (pseudo labels) on unlabeled data, and a student model is later trained on the combination of the original labeled examples and the new pseudo-labeled examples. Self-training has been applied to a wide variety of tasks, including classification [1, 55, 62], semantic segmentation [6, 22, 40, 61], object detection [4, 47, 56, 70], speech recognition [27, 41].

Different from prior works on pseudo labeling for 3D point cloud [4, 44, 60], where unlabeled frames are used as a whole, our PseudoAugments enables combinatorial new training data by fusing labeled and unlabeled frames. In this work, we aim to demonstrate simple PseudoAugment policies are effective and general methods, while advanced techniques such as IoU-based filtering [60], part&shape-aware data augmentation [9, 67], and randering-based method [18] could further improve the quality of PseudoAugments.

2.3 Object Detection for Point Clouds

There exists a large collection of different architectures for performing 3D Object Detection. The majority of methods [7, 16, 19, 30, 63, 65, 69] discretize the space into either a 2D (Birds eye view) or 3D grid, and perform either 2D or 3D convolutions on this grid. Some methods alternatively opt to work with the range image view, performing convolutions on the spherical LiDAR image [2, 17, 37]. There also exists a third class of methods, that opt to learn features directly from the raw point cloud [39, 42, 43, 53], along with a handful of techniques that blend approaches [51,52,58,68]. Because our method is architecture-agnostic, we view these innovations as complimentary, as our method should benefit current and future architectures.

3   Methods

In this section, we first motivate PseudoAugment policies and explain their designs, then we detail the AutoPseudoAugment framework including our overall data augmentation search process and how this interacts with these PseudoAugment policies. A summary of the algorithm can be found in Algorithm 1.

Algorithm 1. AutoPseudoAugment contains two new elements: population-based distillation and PseudoAugments.

Input: data and label $(\mathcal{A}, \mathcal{B})$ and unlabeled data $\mathcal{C}$
Init: set training step $t = 0$, total training steps $\mathcal{N}$, generation step K, randomly initialize M models with random PseudoAugment hyperparameters θ.
while $t \neq \mathcal{N}$ **do**
  if $mod(t, K) == 0$ **then**
    # **Population based distillation**
    Select the top N models in the previous generation to pseudo label unlabeled data $\mathcal{C}$ and store into a pseudo database which contains unlabeled data and pseudo label $(\mathcal{C}, \mathcal{D})$
    # **Standard progressive PBT exploitation and exploration**
    Update hyperparameters θ and model parameters based on PBT [8, 26]
  else
    # **Model trained with PseudoAugment policies**
    Independently train M models in parallel while using the pseudo database $(\mathcal{C}, \mathcal{D})$ to augment the training data $(\mathcal{A}, \mathcal{B})$ through PseudoAugment policies.
  end if
end while

3.1   PseudoAugments

The primary goal of PseudoAugments is to generate more diverse training data by fusing pseudo-labeled and labeled frames, while reducing misclassified points and objects in pseudo-labeled frame. We proposed three new data augmentation polices which corresponds three different ways of utilizing pseudo-labeled data: PseudoFrame, PseudoBBox, PseudoBackground.

PseudoFrame. PseudoFrame extends the self-training approach, where a pseudo-labeled frame is used as if a labeled frame during training. Unlike [4], where pseudo bounding boxes with low prediction confidence are dropped to suppress false positive bounding boxes, PseudoFrame augments pseudo-labeled frames by truncating point clouds within those low confidence pseudo bounding boxes, shown in Fig. 2. In fact, pseudo labeling is suboptimal compared to PseudoFrame, regardless of what the confidence threshold is, e.g., setting a high threshold will introduce false negative points in the scenes while setting a low threshold will lead to additional false positive pseudo-labeled bounding boxes in the scenes. PseudoFrame resolves this challenge by simply dropping point clouds

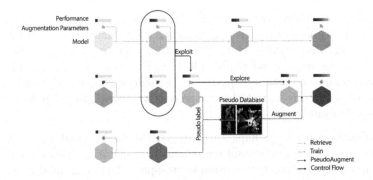

Fig. 3. Schematic diagram of AutoPseudoAugment. AutoPseudoAugment extends the idea of population-based data augmentation by introducing population-based distillation. Population-based distillation is done at the end of each generation, where we select top-performing models (green and grey hexagons) in previous generations as an ensemble of teachers to pseudo label unlabeled data. The pseudo-labeled frames are stored in a pseudo database, which are used to augment input point clouds in the next generation of training. In practice, we follow the recommendations of PPBA [8] and only explore up to three augmentation policy choices per generation, with exploration rate 0.8. More details on population based data augmentation can be found in [8,24].

in confusing (low confidence) pseudo boxes, which increases the effective quality of pseudo-labeled data, Fig. 4, and leads to higher quality student models, Table 1. The PseudoFrame policy is simple and contains only two hyperparameters: the probability of applying this policy (range $[0, 1]$), and the threshold of the classification confidence score for both dropping bounding boxes as well points (range $[0.5, 1]$).

Though PseudoFrame can leverage unlabeled data and increase the effective quality of pseudo-labeled data, the labeled frames and pseudo-labeled frames are still trained independently. To further increase the diversity of the training data, we introduce two more data augmentation policies, i.e., PseudoBBox and PseudoBackground, to fuse labeled frames and pseudo-labeled frames, which introduce combinartorial number of new training data.

PseudoBBox. Unlike pasting ground truth objects from the labeled frames [8,30,39,63], PseudoBBox is designed to introduce diverse pseudo objects into a training example while reducing the likelihood of pasting false positive points as objects, shown in Fig. 2. PseudoBBox fuses pseudo-labeled frames and labeled frames by pasting pseudo-labeled foreground objects onto labeled scenes. The PseudoBBox policy contains three parameters: the probability of applying this policy (range $[0, 1]$), the number of objects that will be added (range $[0, 20]$), and the threshold of the classification confidence score (range $[0.5, 1]$) required for an object to be inserted into a scene.

To align pasted objects to the new background scene, we adjust the Z value based on an estimate of the ground plane's Z coordinate[1]. We oversample $10\times$ pseudo objects and reject pseudo objects that overlap with any other pseudo objects and existing ground truth objects in the scene, then sample from the reminding pseudo objects and paste the predefined number of pseudo objects into the scene. If the pasted objects overlap with background points, we will remove background points.

PseudoBackground. Perhaps surprisingly, the background point clouds in unlabeled data contain important ingredients for generating diverse fused scenes, which are not recognized before. Simply swapping the background point clouds in labeled frames and unlabeled frames, we can generate diverse fused training scenes with ground truth objects on top of background point clouds from pseudo-labeled scenes. Different from PseudoFrame and PseudoBBox, we aggressively reject both true negative and false negative points in point clouds by removing all points within pseudo bounding boxes with object classification confidence scores above 0.1, and use reminding points as the background point clouds. Thus, the PseudoBackground is simple and contains only one hyperparameter, i.e., the probability of applying this operator (range $[0, 1]$). We align the ground plane of the new pseudo background point cloud with the existing point cloud and reject pseudo background point clouds when overlapping with bounding boxes, following the process described above for PseudoBoundingBox.

3.2 AutoPseudoAugment

AutoPseudoAugment is a data augmentation framework designed for efficient hyperparameter tuning while applying PseudoAugments in one shot, shown in Algorithm 1.

Population-Based Distillation. Motivated by the recent success of population-based augmentation [8,24], we apply PBT to find the optimal hypperparameters in PseudoAugments. However, traditionally, hyperparameter tuning and self-training are decoupled. Especially for iterative self-training [62], tuning the hyperarameters for the student model in each iteration will incur significant computation cost. To mitigate this challenge, we propose population-based distillation, where we take advantage of the models in previous generations as an ensemble of teachers to pseudo label unlabeled data, shown in Fig. 3.

Unlike PBT, where past generation model checkpoints are discarded when training the current generation, we recycle and use the top N model checkpoints in the previous generation as teachers. Because the previous generation checkpoints are trained with different schedules of data augmentation policies, they naturally form a diverse set of teachers. Thus, population-based distillation achieves both hyperparameter tuning and ensemble distillation at once.

---

[1] We estimate this with linear regression of the bottom center of the foreground ground truth or pseudo-labeled objects. If less than 3 bounding boxes are in the scene, we use the histogram of point clouds Z coordinate to estimate the ground plane.

In addition to our three new PseudoAugment policies PseudoFrame, PseudoBBox, and PseudoBackground, we adopt the full suite of data augmentations used by PPBA [8]. In order to further increase the diversity of our training data, we apply our three PseudoAugment policies *before* we apply other geometric-based data augmentations, allowing pseudo-label augmented scenes to be further augmented by other common data augmentations. Our final order of augmentations that could potentially be applied (given the choices of the policy) are: PseudoFrame, PseudoBoundingBox, PseudoBackground, RandomRotation, WorldScaling, GlobalTranslateNoise, FrustumDropout, FrustumNoise, RandomDropLaserPoints.

In this section, we extensively evaluate PseudoAugments policies and AutoPseudoAugment framework using voxel-based PointPillars model[2] [30] and point-based StarNet model [2] [39] on KITTI [20] and Waymo Open Dataset [57].

For the following experiments, we train two separate models to detect vehicles and pedestrians and adopt the same training setting as prior works [4,8,39]. To study the data efficiency, we create a smaller training set consisting of 10%, 30% and 50% of the run segments from the Waymo Open Dataset training set to use as our labeled dataset, while using the remaining run segments as an unlabeled dataset. We want to highlight that 10% of the Waymo Open Dataset contains a considerable amount of 3D labeled bounding boxes (more than 1 million) which is on par with other full training dataset such as KITTI, NuScenes, and Argoverse dataset [3,5,21]. For hyperparameter tuning on Waymo Open Dataset, we create a random subsampling of the validation set, using 10% of examples (4109 samples) as *mini-val* and use Level 1 difficulty average precision (AP) as our objective value.

4 Experiments

4.1 PseudoAugments Helps Quality and Diversity

In this section, we show PseudoAugments reduce the errors in pseudo labeled scenes via PseudoFrame and can generate diverse fused scenes when applying PseudoBBox and PseudoBackground, which outperform pseudo labeling method for both vehicle and pedestrian detection tasks. We follow the implementation in [4] and train teacher models on 10% of the training run segments using random Z rotation and random flip Y data augmentation for 150 epochs. We use the teacher models to pseudo label the reminding 90% of the training run segments and remove pseudo-labeled bounding boxes with classification score below 0.5. When training the student models, we use 1:1 ratio of labeled and pseudo labeled scene in each mini batch. Since the training data is increased 10×, we train the student model for 10× steps to take advantage of the additional pseudo labeled data, results shown in Table 1.

---

[2] Code for both models are available at https://github.com/tensorflow/lingvo/tree/master/lingvo/tasks/car under Apache License 2.0.

Table 1. PseudoAugments improve upon Pseudo labeling method. PseudoAugments reduce errors in the pseudo-labeled scenes by dropping low-confidence points, and improves data diversity by introducing fused pseudo-labeled scenes. Supervised PointPillars models are trained on 10% run segments and used as teachers. Pseudo labeling drops pseudo-labeled bounding boxes below confidence threshold 0.5, while PseudoFrame augments pseudo-labeled scenes by dropping both bouding boxes and point clouds within those bounding boxes below threshold 0.5. The improvements from PseudoAugments are additive. Introducing PseudoBBox and PseudoBackground further enrichs the training data, which leads to better student models. 3D detection Level 1 AP are evaluated on the Waymo Open Dataset *validation set*.

Setup	Effects	Vehicle L1 AP	Pedestrian L1 AP
Supervised (Teacher)		49.6	53.9
Pseudo labeling [4]		50.7 (+1.1)	56.7 (+2.8)
PseudoFrame only (Ours)	Reducing errors	51.1 (+1.5)	57.2 (+3.3)
PseudoBBox only (Ours)	Fusing scenes	53.4 (+3.8)	57.0 (+3.1)
PseudoBackground only (Ours)	Fusing scenes	51.9 (+2.3)	57.7 (+3.8)
All PseudoAugments (Ours)	Reducing errors + fusing scenes	**54.3 (+4.7)**	**58.4 (+4.5)**

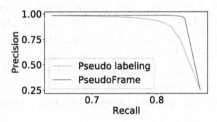

Fig. 4. PseudoFrame improves quality of pseudo labeled point clouds. Precision and recall are defined based on whether a point is inside labeled/pseudo labeled vehicle or pedestrian bounding boxes. Vanilla pseudo labeling approach only adds pseudo bounding boxes if the prediction confidence is higher than 0.5, but keeps all the false-negative points; In contrast, our PseudoFrame also drops points in low-confidence bounding boxes, thus reducing false negatives and improving precision-recall of pseudo labeled frames.

PseudoFrame Improves Data Quality. PseudoFrame augments the pseudo labeled scenes by removing point clouds in not so confident pseudo bounding boxes. Here, we remove bounding boxes and corresponding point clouds with classification confidence score below 0.5. As shown in Fig. 4, simply removing those point clouds is an effective data augmentation to increase the prevision-recall of pseudo labeled points. PseudoFrame improves the quality of student models (+0.4 on Vehicle AP and +0.5 on Pedestrian AP) compared to Pseudo labeling, shown in Table 1.

PseudoBBox and PseudoBackground Increase Diversity. PseudoBBox and PseudoBackground increase the diversity of the training scenes by fusing pseudo labeled and labeled scenes, as shown in Fig. 2. To find the optimal hyperparameters, we randomly sample 16 different combinations of hyperparameters from the search space detailed in Subsect. 3.1. Introducing fused scenes further improves the quality of student models (+3.2 on Vehicle AP and +1.2 on Pedestrian AP) compared to only applying PseudoFrame data augmentation, Table 1, which shows the benefit of PseudoBBox and PseudoBackground is additive.

4.2   Generalization of PseudoAugments

In the previous section, we demonstrate PseudoAugments improves upon pseudo labeling method on PointPillars models. In this section, we show PsueodAugments generalizes to different model sizes and architectures. In addition to Point-Pillars model, which is a voxel-based architecture [30], we evaluate PseudoAugment on larger PointPillars models and point-based StarNet [39] models. We use the same pseudo labeled data as in Subsect. 4.1, which is labeled by the supervised PointPillars models shown in Table 1. We show besides self-training using the same model size and architectures, PseudoAugments enables self-training from a smaller model to a larger model and across different architectures. Our results show PseudoAugments lead to higher improvements compared to pseudo labeling, Table 2. For the following experiments, we adopt the same training settings as in Subsect. 3.1.

Table 2. PseudoAugments generalize to larger capacity models and different architectures. PseudoAugments outperform pseudo labeling on 10% run segments using PointPillars [30], in Table 1, as teachers. (a) self-training from PointPillars teachers to larger PointPillars models (Pillars2X) and (b) self-training from PointPillars teachers to StarNet models [39]. Note that PseudoAugments improve the vehicle detection quality of Pillars2X whereas pseudo labeling is unable to. 3D detection Level 1 AP are evaluated on the Waymo Open Dataset *validation set*.

Setup	Vehicle AP	Pedestrian AP
Supervised	52.1	56.9
Pseudo labeling [4]	51.6 (-0.5)	57.8 (+0.9)
All PseudoAugments (Ours)	**55.7(+5.5)**	**59.7 (+2.8)**

(a) Pillars2X.

Setup	Vehicle AP	Pedestrian AP
Supervised	43.7	60.6
Pseudo labeling [4]	48.2 (+4.5)	63.5 (+2.9)
All PseudoAugments (Ours)	**51.2 (+7.5)**	**64.7 (+4.1)**

(b) StarNet models.

Generalize to Larger Models. We double the channel numbers of every convolution layers in the PointPillars model and denote it as Pillars2X. We train Pillars2X on the same supervised 10% run segments as the supervised training baseline, which has higher quality compared to the standard (1x) PointPillars, shown in Table 2a. Interestingly, the pseudo labeling method failed to improve the vehicle Pillars2X model when we use a weaker (1X) model as teacher (52.1 AP for supervised Pillars2X and 49.6 AP for supervised PointPillars on vehicle detection). This indicates errors in pseudo labeled frames diminishe the benefit of introducing unseen scenes to diversify the training data. Whereas, applying PseudoAugments overcomes this limitation and leads to significant improvement (+4.1 on Vehicle AP and +1.9 on Pedestrian AP) compared to pseudo labeling.

Generalize to Different Architectures. Unlike voxel-based PointPillars, StarNet is a point-based 3D detector and learns feature representations directly from raw point clouds. Our results show, using PointPillars model as teacher, PseudoAugments significantly improves quality of the StarNet student models (+3.0 on Vehicle AP and + 1.2 on Pedestrian AP) compared to pseudo labeling method Table 2b. This shows PseudoAugments are model agnostic and outperform pseudo labeling method when self-training between very different model architectures.

4.3   Generalize to KITTI Dataset

In this section, we show PseudoAugments is a general method that is effetive on significantly different datasets. Different from Waymo Open Dataset [57], KITTI [20] dataset was collected in different cities and has different point and object density per frame. Here, we follow the common practice and split the KITTI dataset in half, i.e., one used for training and the other half used for validation. We randomly select 10% of the training frames as a mini training split, while removing labels on the rest 90% of the training frames. We train PointPillars teacher models on the mini training split with random flip and random world scaling data augmentations. Our results, in Table 3, show using PseudoAugments consistently outperform pseudo labeling on detecting objects at all difficulties.

Table 3. PseudoAugments generalize to KITTI dataset. PseudoAugments outperform pseudo labeling on 10% KITTI training frames using PointPillars [30] as teachers. 3D detection APs for easy, moderate, and hard (E/M/H) objects are evaluated on the KITTI *validation set.*

Setup	Vehicle (E/M/H)	Ped&Cyc (E/M/H)
Supervised (Teacher)	55.6/49.2/46.1	46.3/33.4/30.2
Pseudo labeling [4]	64.3/51.4/49.0	49.3/35.9/32.6
All PseudoAugments (Ours)	**65.5/56.5/53.7**	**55.2/40.8/37.5**

4.4   AutoPseudoAugment Improves Data Efficiency

In previous sections, we demonstrate PseudoAugments are strong data augmentation methods that improves upon pseudo labeling. In this section, we show AutoPseudoAugment leverages PseudoAugments and further advances state-of-the-art auto data augmentation methods for 3D point clouds (PPBA) [8].

When the models are trained on 10% labeled run segments, we use generation step 1000 for both PPBA and AutoPseudoAugment. On 30% and 50% run segments, we increase the generation step to 2000. Even though AutoPseudoAugment introduces additional PseudoAugment policies compared to PPBA, we use the same number of tuners (population size 16) for AutoPseudoAugment and PPBA. We follow the other training settings in [8]. At the end of each generation, we select the top 10 models in previous generations with L1 AP above 0.35 as ensemble of teachers to pseudo label unlabeled data.

AutoPseudoAugment Outperforms Both Pseudo Labeling and PPBA Mmethods. Our AutoPseudoAugment framework subsumes both the auto data augmentation and pseudo labeling, which takes advantage of additional unlabeled data while tuning hyperparameters online. More importantly, PseudoAugments generate high-quality fused scenes, which greatly increases the diversity of the training data. As shown in Table 4, AutoPseudoAugment outperforms both PPBA and Pseudo labeling on 10%, 30%, and 50% labeled run segments.

To estimate the data efficiency, we train PointPillars models without data augmentation on 10%, 20%, 30%, 50% and 100% of training run segments, shown in Fig. 1. According to this metric, our AutoPseudoAugment at 10% run segments (56.7 AP) is almost 10× more data efficient on the vehicle class, which nearly matches the model trained with 100% labeled data (57.2 AP). On pedestrian class, AutoPseudoAugment at 10 % run segments (60.3 AP) shows 5× data efficient and suprasses no augmentation baseline model trained on 50 % of the run segments (60.0 AP), shown in Fig. 1.

Table 4. AutoPseudoAugment is more data efficient than SOTA auto data augmentation method (PPBA) and self-training method (Pseudo labeling). AuotoPseudoAugment outperforms both PPBA and Pseudo labeling when trained on 10%, 30%, and 50% of the labeled training data. For vehicles, with 10% labeled run segments, AutoPseudoAugment achieves about 6 better L1 AP than others, and matches the quality of 30% labeled run segments for PPBA and Pseudo labeling. 3D detection Level 1 and 2 detection AP and APH of PointPillars model are evaluated on the Waymo Open Dataset *validation* set.

Setup	Type of data	AutoML	Vehicle					
			10 %		30 %		50 %	
			AP (L1/L2)	APH (L1/L2)	AP (L1/L2)	APH (L1/L2)	AP (L1/L2)	APH (L1/L2)
PPBA [8]	Labeled only	✓	50.2/43.4	49.7/42.9	56.0/48.7	55.5/48.2	60.9/53.0	60.4/52.6
Pseudo labeling [4]	Labeled+Unlabeled		50.7/43.9	50.2/43.5	57.8/50.2	57.3/49.8	59.8/52.0	59.3/51.6
AutoPseudoAugment	Labeled+Unlabeled+Fused	✓	**56.7/49.2**	**56.3/48.8**	**61.3/53.5**	**60.9/53.1**	**63.0/55.1**	**62.5/54.6**
Setup	Type of data	AutoML	Pedestrian					
			10 %		30 %		50 %	
			AP (L1/L2)	APH (L1/L2)	AP (L1/L2)	APH (L1/L2)	AP (L1/L2)	APH (L1/L2)
PPBA [8]	Labeled only	✓	58.5/50.3	45.7/39.2	61.9/53.7	49.4/42.7	67.1/58.6	54.6/47.5
Pseudo labeling [4]	Labeled+Unlabeled		56.7/48.5	36.7/31.6	64.9/56.2	48.4/41.8	68.2/59.3	54.5/47.2
AutoPseudoAugment	Labeled+Unlabeled+Fused	✓	**60.3/52.1**	**48.3/41.7**	**66.5/57.8**	**55.1/47.7**	**69.6/60.8**	**58.9/51.4**

4.5   Each PseudoAugment Is Effective

Previous sections show the benefit of PseudoAugments are additive to Pseudo labeling and PPBA. In this section, we train PointPillars models on 10% run segments with only one data augmentation to tease apart the contribution of each PseudoAugment. As a reference, we also show the performance of common data augmentation policies such as random global Z rotation, random global

Y rotation, and ground truth bounding box data augmentations [8,30,39,63]. Compared to common data augmentation methods, standalone PseudoAugment achieves comparable improvements, shown in Table 5.

Table 5. Comparing PseudoAugments with common data augmentations. PointPillars models are trained with only one data augmentation method on 10% of the labeled run segments. 3D detection Level 1 AP on Waymo Open Dataset *validation set* are reported.

	No Aug	Common data augmentations			PseudoAugments (Ours)		
		RotateZ	FlipY	GTBBox	PseudoBBox	PseudoBackground	PseudoFrame
Vehicle	41.4	45.5 (+4.1)	44.4 (+3.0)	44.7 (+3.3)	46.4 (+5.0)	43.0 (+1.6)	45.6 (+4.2)
Pedestrian	49.1	52.7 (+3.6)	52.0 (+2.9)	50.4 (+1.3)	50.3 (+1.2)	52.2 (+3.1)	49.8 (+0.7)

PseudoBBox Introduces Diverse Foreground Objects. Unlike using ground truth bounding boxes, PseudoBBox leverages unseen objects in unlabeled data to enrich the training data. On vehicle detection tasks, PseudoBBox significantly outperforms ground truth bounding box (GTBBox) augmentation (+1.7 AP), which highlights the importance of using unseen objects in unlabeled data.

PseudoBackground is Important. Interestingly, we observe that utilizing the background point clouds in unlabeled data is important, especially for pedestrian detection. Taking advantage of the unseen backgrounds (PseudoBackground + 3.1 AP) is even more effective to improve model quality compared to using unseen object (PseudoBBox +1.6 AP) for detecting pedestrian.

5   Conclusion

Despite many prior works on data augmentation for 3D point clouds, data augmentation was mostly based on labeled data. In this paper, we propose to use unlabeled point clouds to augment training data and introduce PseudoAugments, which utilizes unlabeled point clouds to improve 3D detection. PseudoAugments mitigate intrinsic errors in pseudo labeled scenes while introducing diverse training data by fusing labeled and pseudo labeled scenes. We perform extensive studies and comparisons to show that PseudoAugments generalize to different architectures, model sizes, and datasets and demonstrate that AutoPseudoAugment framework outperforms existing state-of-the-art data augmentation method PPBA [8] and pseudo labeling [4] at various ratio of labeled and unlabeled data.

Acknowledgments. We would like to thank Yuning chai, Vijay Vasudevan, Jiquan Ngiam and the rest of Waymo and Google Brain teams for value feedback and infra supports.

References

1. Berthelot, D., Carlini, N., Goodfellow, I., Papernot, N., Oliver, A., Raffel, C.A.: MixMatch: a holistic approach to semi-supervised learning. In: Advances in Neural Information Processing Systems, pp. 5049–5059 (2019)
2. Bewley, A., Sun, P., Mensink, T., Anguelov, D., Sminchisescu, C.: Range conditioned dilated convolutions for scale invariant 3D object detection (2020)
3. Caesar, H., et al.: nuScenes: a multimodal dataset for autonomous driving. Corr abs/1903.11027 (2019) (1903)
4. Caine, B., et al.: Pseudo-labeling for scalable 3D object detection. arXiv preprint arXiv:2103.02093 (2021)
5. Chang, M.F., et al.: Argoverse: 3D tracking and forecasting with rich maps. In: Proceedings of the IEEE Conference on Computer Vision and Pattern Recognition, pp. 8748–8757 (2019)
6. Chen, L.C., et al.: Semi-supervised learning in video sequences for urban scene segmentation. arXiv preprint arXiv:2005.10266 (2020)
7. Chen, X., Ma, H., Wan, J., Li, B., Xia, T.: Multi-view 3D object detection network for autonomous driving. In: Proceedings of the IEEE Conference on Computer Vision and Pattern Recognition, pp. 1907–1915 (2017)
8. Cheng, S., et al.: Improving 3D object detection through progressive population based augmentation. arXiv preprint arXiv:2004.00831 (2020)
9. Choi, J., Song, Y., Kwak, N.: Part-aware data augmentation for 3D object detection in point cloud. In: 2021 IEEE/RSJ International Conference on Intelligent Robots and Systems (IROS), pp. 3391–3397. IEEE (2021)
10. Ciregan, D., Meier, U., Schmidhuber, J.: Multi-column deep neural networks for image classification. In: Proceedings of IEEE Conference on Computer Vision and Pattern Recognition, pp. 3642–3649. IEEE (2012)
11. Cubuk, E.D., Zoph, B., Mane, D., Vasudevan, V., Le, Q.V.: AutoAugment: learning augmentation policies from data. arXiv preprint arXiv:1805.09501 (2018)
12. Cubuk, E.D., Zoph, B., Shlens, J., Le, Q.V.: RandAugment: practical automated data augmentation with a reduced search space. In: Proceedings of the IEEE/CVF Conference on Computer Vision and Pattern Recognition Workshops, pp. 702–703 (2020)
13. DeVries, T., Taylor, G.W.: Improved regularization of convolutional neural networks with cutout. arXiv preprint arXiv:1708.04552 (2017)
14. Dwibedi, D., Misra, I., Hebert, M.: Cut, paste and learn: surprisingly easy synthesis for instance detection. In: Proceedings of the IEEE International Conference on Computer Vision, pp. 1301–1310 (2017)
15. Eaton-Rosen, Z., Bragman, F., Ourselin, S., Cardoso, M.J.: Improving data augmentation for medical image segmentation (2018)
16. Fan, L., et al.: Embracing single stride 3D object detector with sparse transformer. In: Proceedings of the IEEE/CVF Conference on Computer Vision and Pattern Recognition, pp. 8458–8468 (2022)
17. Fan, L., Xiong, X., Wang, F., Wang, N., Zhang, Z.: RangeDet: in defense of range view for lidar-based 3D object detection. In: Proceedings of the IEEE/CVF International Conference on Computer Vision, pp. 2918–2927 (2021)
18. Fang, J., Zuo, X., Zhou, D., Jin, S., Wang, S., Zhang, L.: LiDAR-AUG: a general rendering-based augmentation framework for 3D object detection. In: Proceedings of the IEEE/CVF Conference on Computer Vision and Pattern Recognition, pp. 4710–4720 (2021)

19. Ge, R., et al.: AFDet: anchor free one stage 3D object detection (2020)
20. Geiger, A., Lenz, P., Stiller, C., Urtasun, R.: Are we ready for autonomous driving? The KITTI vision benchmark suite. In: Conference on Computer Vision and Pattern Recognition(CVPR) (2012)
21. Geiger, A., Lenz, P., Stiller, C., Urtasun, R.: Vision meets robotics: the KITTI dataset. Int. J. Robot. Res. **32**(11), 1231–1237 (2013)
22. Ghiasi, G., et al.: Simple copy-paste is a strong data augmentation method for instance segmentation. In: Proceedings of the IEEE/CVF Conference on Computer Vision and Pattern Recognition, pp. 2918–2928 (2021)
23. Girshick, R., Radosavovic, I., Gkioxari, G., Dollár, P., He, K.: Detectron (2018)
24. Ho, D., Liang, E., Chen, X., Stoica, I., Abbeel, P.: Population based augmentation: Efficient learning of augmentation policy schedules. In: International Conference on Machine Learning, pp. 2731–2741. PMLR (2019)
25. Hu, P., Ziglar, J., Held, D., Ramanan, D.: What you see is what you get: exploiting visibility for 3D object detection. In: Proceedings of the IEEE/CVF Conference on Computer Vision and Pattern Recognition, pp. 11001–11009 (2020)
26. Jaderberg, M., et al.: Population based training of neural networks. arXiv preprint arXiv:1711.09846 (2017)
27. Kahn, J., Lee, A., Hannun, A.: Self-training for end-to-end speech recognition. In: ICASSP 2020–2020 IEEE International Conference on Acoustics, Speech and Signal Processing (ICASSP), pp. 7084–7088. IEEE (2020)
28. Kim, S., Lee, S., Hwang, D., Lee, J., Hwang, S.J., Kim, H.J.: Point cloud augmentation with weighted local transformations. In: Proceedings of the IEEE/CVF International Conference on Computer Vision, pp. 548–557 (2021)
29. Krizhevsky, A., Sutskever, I., Hinton, G.E.: ImageNet classification with deep convolutional neural networks. In: Advances in Neural Information Processing Systems (2012)
30. Lang, A.H., Vora, S., Caesar, H., Zhou, L., Yang, J., Beijbom, O.: PointPillars: fast encoders for object detection from point clouds. In: Proceedings of the IEEE Conference on Computer Vision and Pattern Recognition, pp. 12697–12705 (2019)
31. Lee, D., et al.: Regularization strategy for point cloud via rigidly mixed sample. In: Proceedings of the IEEE/CVF Conference on Computer Vision and Pattern Recognition, pp. 15900–15909 (2021)
32. Lee, D.H.: Pseudo-label: the simple and efficient semi-supervised learning method for deep neural networks. In: Workshop on Challenges in Representation Learning, ICML, vol. 3 (2013)
33. Lemley, J., Bazrafkan, S., Corcoran, P.: Smart augmentation learning an optimal data augmentation strategy. IEEE Access **5**, 5858–5869 (2017)
34. Li, R., Li, X., Heng, P.A., Fu, C.W.: PointAugment: an auto-augmentation framework for point cloud classification. arXiv preprint arXiv:2002.10876 (2020)
35. Lim, S., Kim, I., Kim, T., Kim, C., Kim, S.: Fast autoaugment. arXiv preprint arXiv:1905.00397 (2019)
36. McLachlan, G.J.: Iterative reclassification procedure for constructing an asymptotically optimal rule of allocation in discriminant analysis. J. Am. Stat. Assoc. **70**(350), 365–369 (1975)
37. Meyer, G.P., Laddha, A., Kee, E., Vallespi-Gonzalez, C., Wellington, C.K.: LaserNet: an efficient probabilistic 3D object detector for autonomous driving. In: Proceedings of the IEEE Conference on Computer Vision and Pattern Recognition, pp. 12677–12686 (2019)
38. Milletari, F., Navab, N., Ahmadi, S.A.: V-Net: fully convolutional neural networks for volumetric medical image segmentation, pp. 565–571 (2016)

39. Ngiam, J., et al.: StarNet: targeted computation for object detection in point clouds. arXiv preprint arXiv:1908.11069 (2019)

40. Papandreou, G., Chen, L.C., Murphy, K.P., Yuille, A.L.: Weakly-and semi-supervised learning of a deep convolutional network for semantic image segmentation. In: Proceedings of the IEEE International Conference on Computer Vision, pp. 1742–1750 (2015)

41. Park, D.S., et al.: Improved noisy student training for automatic speech recognition. arXiv preprint arXiv:2005.09629 (2020)

42. Qi, C.R., Liu, W., Wu, C., Su, H., Guibas, L.J.: Frustum PointNets for 3D object detection from RGB-D data. In: Proceedings of the IEEE Conference on Computer Vision and Pattern Recognition, pp. 918–927 (2018)

43. Qi, C.R., Su, H., Mo, K., Guibas, L.J.: PointNet: deep learning on point sets for 3D classification and segmentation. In: Proceedings of the IEEE Conference on Computer Vision and Pattern Recognition, pp. 652–660 (2017)

44. Qi, C.R., et al.: Offboard 3D object detection from point cloud sequences. In: Proceedings of the IEEE/CVF Conference on Computer Vision and Pattern Recognition, pp. 6134–6144 (2021)

45. Ratner, A.J., Ehrenberg, H., Hussain, Z., Dunnmon, J., Ré, C.: Learning to compose domain-specific transformations for data augmentation. In: Advances in Neural Information Processing Systems, pp. 3239–3249 (2017)

46. Ronneberger, O., Fischer, P., Brox, T.: U-Net: convolutional networks for biomedical image segmentation (2015)

47. Rosenberg, C., Hebert, M., Schneiderman, H.: Semi-supervised self-training of object detection models (2005)

48. Roth, H.R., et al.: Anatomy-specific classification of medical images using deep convolutional nets. arXiv preprint arXiv:1504.04003 (2015)

49. Sato, I., Nishimura, H., Yokoi, K.: APAC: augmented pattern classification with neural networks. arXiv preprint arXiv:1505.03229 (2015)

50. Sheshappanavar, S.V., Singh, V.V., Kambhamettu, C.: PatchAugment: local neighborhood augmentation in point cloud classification. In: Proceedings of the IEEE/CVF International Conference on Computer Vision, pp. 2118–2127 (2021)

51. Shi, S., et al.: PV-RCNN: point-voxel feature set abstraction for 3D object detection. arXiv preprint arXiv:1912.13192 (2019)

52. Shi, S., et al.: PV-RCNN++: point-voxel feature set abstraction with local vector representation for 3D object detection. arXiv preprint arXiv:2102.00463 (2021)

53. Shi, S., Wang, X., Li, H.: PointRCNN: 3D object proposal generation and detection from point cloud. In: Proceedings of the IEEE Conference on Computer Vision and Pattern Recognition, pp. 770–779 (2019)

54. Simard, P.Y., Steinkraus, D., Platt, J.C., et al.: Best practices for convolutional neural networks applied to visual document analysis. In: Proceedings of International Conference on Document Analysis and Recognition (2003)

55. Sohn, K., et al.: FixMatch: simplifying semi-supervised learning with consistency and confidence. arXiv preprint arXiv:2001.07685 (2020)

56. Sohn, K., et al.: A simple semi-supervised learning framework for object detection. arXiv preprint arXiv:2005.04757 (2020)

57. Sun, P., et al.: Scalability in perception for autonomous driving: Waymo open dataset. In: Proceedings of the IEEE/CVF Conference on Computer Vision and Pattern Recognition, pp. 2446–2454 (2020)

58. Sun, P., et al.: RSN: range sparse net for efficient, accurate LiDAR 3D object detection. In: Proceedings of the IEEE/CVF Conference on Computer Vision and Pattern Recognition, pp. 5725–5734 (2021)

59. Wan, L., Zeiler, M., Zhang, S., Le Cun, Y., Fergus, R.: Regularization of neural networks using DropConnect. In: International Conference on Machine Learning, pp. 1058–1066 (2013)
60. Wang, H., Cong, Y., Litany, O., Gao, Y., Guibas, L.J.: 3DIoUMatch: leveraging IoU prediction for semi-supervised 3D object detection. In: Proceedings of the IEEE/CVF Conference on Computer Vision and Pattern Recognition, pp. 14615–14624 (2021)
61. Wei, Y., et al.: STC: a simple to complex framework for weakly-supervised semantic segmentation. IEEE Trans. Pattern Anal. Mach. Intell. **39**(11), 2314–2320 (2016)
62. Xie, Q., Luong, M.T., Hovy, E., Le, Q.V.: Self-training with noisy student improves ImageNet classification. In: Conference on Computer Vision and Pattern Recognition (CVPR) (2020). https://arxiv.org/abs/1911.04252
63. Yan, Y., Mao, Y., Li, B.: Second: sparsely embedded convolutional detection. Sensors **18**(10), 3337 (2018)
64. Yang, B., Liang, M., Urtasun, R.: HDNET: exploiting HD maps for 3D object detection. In: Conference on Robot Learning, pp. 146–155. PMLR (2018)
65. Yang, B., Luo, W., Urtasun, R.: PIXOR: real-time 3D object detection from point clouds. In: Proceedings of the IEEE conference on Computer Vision and Pattern Recognition, pp. 7652–7660 (2018)
66. Zhang, H., Cisse, M., Dauphin, Y.N., Lopez-Paz, D.: mixup: Beyond empirical risk minimization. arXiv preprint arXiv:1710.09412 (2017)
67. Zheng, W., Tang, W., Jiang, L., Fu, C.W.: SE-SSD: self-ensembling single-stage object detector from point cloud. In: Proceedings of the IEEE/CVF Conference on Computer Vision and Pattern Recognition, pp. 14494–14503 (2021)
68. Zhou, Y., et al.: End-to-end multi-view fusion for 3D object detection in LiDAR point clouds. In: Conference on Robot Learning, pp. 923–932 (2020)
69. Zhou, Y., Tuzel, O.: VoxelNet: end-to-end learning for point cloud based 3D object detection. In: Proceedings of the IEEE Conference on Computer Vision and Pattern Recognition, pp. 4490–4499 (2018)
70. Zoph, B., et al.: Rethinking pre-training and self-training. In: Advances in Neural Information Processing Systems 33 (2020)

MVSTER: Epipolar Transformer for Efficient Multi-view Stereo

Xiaofeng Wang[1,2], Zheng Zhu[3], Guan Huang[3], Fangbo Qin[1], Yun Ye[3], Yijia He[4], Xu Chi[3], and Xingang Wang[1(✉)]

[1] Institute of Automation, Chinese Academy of Sciences, Beijing, China
{wangxiaofeng2020,qinfangbo2013,xingang.wang}@ia.ac.cn
[2] School of Artificial Intelligence, University of Chinese Academy of Science, Beijing, China
[3] PhiGent Robotics, Beijing, China
zhengzhu@ieee.org, {guang.huan,yun.ye,xu.chi}@phigent.ai
[4] Kwai Inc., Beijing, China

Abstract. Learning-based Multi-View Stereo (MVS) methods warp source images into the reference camera frustum to form 3D volumes, which are fused as a cost volume to be regularized by subsequent networks. The fusing step plays a vital role in bridging 2D semantics and 3D spatial associations. However, previous methods utilize extra networks to learn 2D information as fusing cues, underusing 3D spatial correlations and bringing additional computation costs. Therefore, we present MVSTER, which leverages the proposed epipolar Transformer to learn both 2D semantics and 3D spatial associations efficiently. Specifically, the epipolar Transformer utilizes a detachable monocular depth estimator to enhance 2D semantics and uses cross-attention to construct data-dependent 3D associations along epipolar line. Additionally, MVSTER is built in a cascade structure, where entropy-regularized optimal transport is leveraged to propagate finer depth estimations in each stage. Extensive experiments show MVSTER achieves state-of-the-art reconstruction performance with significantly higher efficiency: Compared with MVSNet and CasMVSNet, our MVSTER achieves 34% and 14% relative improvements on the DTU benchmark, with 80% and 51% relative reductions in running time. MVSTER also ranks first on Tanks&Temples-Advanced among all published works. Code is available at https://github.com/JeffWang987/MVSTER.

Keywords: Multi-view stereo · Transformer · Depth estimation · Optimal transport

1 Introduction

Given multiple 2D RGB observations and camera parameters, Multi-View Stereo (MVS) aims to reconstruct the dense geometry of the scene. MVS is a funda-

---

Supplementary Information The online version contains supplementary material available at https://doi.org/10.1007/978-3-031-19821-2_33.

mental task in 3D computer vision, with applications ranging from autonomous navigation to virtual/augmented reality. Despite being extensively studied by traditional geometric methods [19,43,50,58] for years, MVS is still challenged by unsatisfactory reconstructions under conditions of illumination changes, non-Lambertian surfaces and textureless areas [28,44].

Recent researches [65,66] have relieved the aforementioned problems via learning-based methods. Typically, they extract image features through 2D Convolutional Neural Networks (CNN). Then, source features are warped into reference camera frustum to form source volumes, which are fused as a cost volume to produce depth estimations. Fusing source volumes is an essential step in the whole pipeline and many MVS approaches [53,57,65,68,70] put efforts into it. The core of the fusing step is to explore correlations between multi-view images. MVSNet [65] follows the philosophy that various images contribute equally to the 3D cost volume, and utilizes variance operation to fuse different source volumes. However, such fusing method ignores various illumination and visibility conditions of different views. To alleviate this problem, [14,20,53] enrich 2D feature semnatics via Deformable Convolution Network (DCN) [12], and [68,70] leverage extra networks to learn per-pixel weights as a guidance for fusing multi-view features. However, these methods introduce onerous network parameters and restrict efficiency. Besides, they only concentrate on 2D local similarities as a criteria for correlating multiple views, neglecting depth-wise 3D associations, which could lead to inconsistency in 3D space [25].

Therefore, in this paper, we explore an efficient approach to model 3D spatial associations for fusing source volumes. Our intuition is to learn 3D relations from data itself, without introducing extra learning parameters. Recent success in attention mechanism prompts that Transformer [51] is appropriate for modeling 3D associations. The key advantage of Transformer is it leverages cross-attention to build data-dependent correlations, introducing minimal learnable parameters. Besides, compared with CNN, Transformer has expanded receptive field, which is more adept at constructing long-range 3D relations. Therefore, we propose the epipolar Transformer, which efficiently builds multi-view 3D correlations along the epipolar line. Specifically, we firstly leverage an auxiliary monocular depth estimator to enhance the 2D semantics of the *query* feature. The auxiliary branch guides our network to learn depth-discriminative features, and it can be detached after training, which brings no extra computation cost. Subsequently, cross-attention is utilized to model 3D associations explicitly from features on epipolar lines, without introducing sophisticated networks. Additionally, we formulate the depth estimation as a depth-aware classification problem and solve it with entropy-regularized optimal transport [38], which propagates finer depth maps in a cascade structure.

Owing to the epipolar Transformer, MVSTER obtains enhanced reconstruction results with fewer depth hypotheses. Compared with MVSNet [65] and CasMVSNet [23], our method reduces 88% and 73% relative depth hypotheses, making 80% and 51% relative reduction in running time, yet obtaining 34% and 14% relative improvements on the DTU benchmark, respectively. Besides, our method ranks first among all published works on Tanks&Temples-Advanced. The main technique contributions are four-fold as follows:

- We propose a novel end-to-end Transformer-based method for multi-view stereo, named MVSTER. It leverages the proposed epipolar Transformer to efficiently learn 3D associations along epipolar line.
- An auxiliary monocular depth estimator is utilized to guide the *query* feature to learn depth-discriminative information during training, which enhances feature semantics yet brings no efficiency compromises.
- We formulate depth estimation as a depth-aware classification problem and solve it with the entropy-regularized optimal transport, which produces finer depth estimations propagated in the cascade structure.
- Extensive experiments on DTU, Tanks&Temples, BlendedMVS, and ETH3D show our method achieves superior performance with significantly higher efficiency than existing methods.

2   Related Work

Learning-Based MVS. With the rapid progress of deep learning in 3D perception [16,26,33,35,39,40,46,75], the MVS community is gradually dominated by learning-based methods [23,34,53,57,61,65,66,68]. They achieve better reconstruction results than traditional methods [5,18,19,43,50]. Learning-based MVS approaches project source images into reference camera frustum to form multiple 3D volumes, which are fused through variance operation [8,23,61,63,65,66]. Such a fusing method follows the philosophy that the feature volumes from various source images contribute equally [65], neglecting heterogeneous illumination and scene content variability [68]. To remedy the aforementioned problem, PVA-MVSNet [68] proposes a self-adaptive view aggregation module to learn the different significance in source volumes. Vis-MVSNet [70] computes pixel-visibility to represent matching quality, which serves as a volume fusing weight. AA-RMVSNet [57] leverages expensive DCNs [12] to enhance intra-view semantics, and it aggregates inter-view with pixel-wise weight. However, these methods use CNN-based module aggregating local features as fusing guidance, which lacks long-range 3D associations and thus restricts their performance under challenging conditions. Besides, such aggregation modules bring extra computation cost burdening the network. In contrast, the proposed epipolar Transformer learns both 2D semantics and 3D spatial relations from data itself, without bringing onerous network parameters.

Transformers in 3D Vision. Transformers [2,13,42,49,51] find their initial applications in natural language processing and have drawn attention from computer vision community [6,7,15,32,54,62,74]. In tasks for 3D vision, BEVerse [72] and SurroundDepth [56] uses view Transformer to build correlations between images from different views. STTR [30] formulates stereo depth estimation as a sequence-to-sequence correspondence problem that is optimized by self-attention and cross-attention. Recently, Transformer extends its application to MVS. LANet [71], TransMVSNet [14] introduces an attention mechanism extracting dense features with global contexts, which expands the network receptive field. However, these methods densely correlate each pixel within 2D feature maps, which makes significant efficiency compromises. On the contrary, our epipolar Transformer leverages geometric knowledge, restricting attention associations within the epipolar line, which significantly reduces dispensable feature correlations and makes our pipeline more efficient. Besides, MVSTER only leverages the essential cross-attention of Transformer [51], without introducing sophisticated architecture (*i.e.*, position encoding, Feedforward Neural Network (FNN) and self-attention), which further boosts efficiency.

Auxiliary Task Learning. Auxiliary branch learning is demonstrated effective in multiple vision tasks [24,36,41,73]. In general, the auxiliary tasks are selected to be positively related to the main task, thus taking effect during training. In addition, the branch can be discarded after training, bringing no burden during inference. ManyDepth [55] is a self-supervised monocular depth estimator, utilizing MVS cost volume as an auxiliary branch, which enhances estimation reliability. This inspires us that MVS assists monocular depth estimation, and vice versa. Therefore, an auxiliary monocular depth estimation branch is leveraged in MVSTER to learn depth-discriminative features.

3   Method

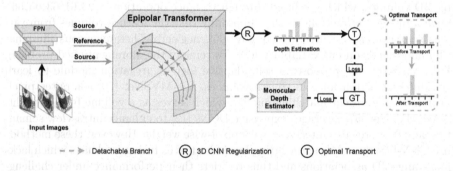

Fig. 1. MVSTER architecture. MVSTER firstly extracts features via FPN, then the multi-view features are aggregated by the epipolar Transformer, where the auxiliary branch makes monocular depth estimation to enhance context. Subsequently, the aggregated feature volume is regularized by 3D CNNs, producing depth estimations. Finally, optimal transport is utilized to optimize the predicted depth.

In this section, we give a detailed description of MVSTER. The network architecture is illustrated in Fig. 1. Given a reference image and its corresponding source images, we firstly extract 2D multi-scale features using Feature Pyramid Network (FPN) [31]. Source image features are then warped into reference camera frustum to construct source volumes via differentiable homography (Sect. 3.1). Subsequently, we leverage the epipolar Transformer to aggregate source volumes and produce the cost volume, which is regularized by lightweight 3D CNNs to make depth estimations (Sect. 3.2). Our pipeline is further built in a cascade structure, propagating depth map in a coarse to fine manner (Sect. 3.3). To reduce erroneous depth hypotheses during depth propagating, we formulate depth estimation as a depth-aware classification problem and optimize it with optimal transport. Finally, the network losses are given (Sect. 3.4).

3.1 2D Encoder and 3D Homography

Given a reference image $\mathbf{I}_{i=0} \in \mathbb{R}^{H \times W \times 3}$ and its neighboring source images $\mathbf{I}_{i=1,\ldots,N-1} \in \mathbb{R}^{H \times W \times 3}$, the first step is to extract the multi-scale 2D features of these inputs. A FPN-like network is applied, where the images are downscaled M times to build deep features $\mathbf{F}_{i=0,\ldots,N-1}^{k=0,\ldots,M-1} \in \mathbb{R}^{H_k \times W_k \times C_k}$. The scale $k = 0$ denotes the original size of images. The subsequent formulations can be generalized to a specific scale k, so k is omitted for simplicity.

Following previous learning-based methods [14,53,65,66], we utilize plane sweep stereo [10] that establishes multiple front-to-parallel planes in the reference view. Specifically, equipped with camera intrinsic parameters $\{\mathbf{K}_i\}_{i=0}^{N-1}$ and transformations parameters $\{[\mathbf{R}_{0,i} \mid \mathbf{t}_{0,i}]\}_{i=1}^{N-1}$ from source views to reference view, source features can be warped into the reference camera frustum:

$$\mathbf{p}_{s_i,j} = \mathbf{K}_i \cdot \left(\mathbf{R}_{0,i} \cdot \left(\mathbf{K}_0^{-1} \cdot \mathbf{p}_r \cdot d_j\right) + \mathbf{t}_{0,i}\right), \tag{1}$$

where d_j denotes j-th hypothesized depth of pixel $\mathbf{p}_r$ in the reference feature, and $\mathbf{p}_{s_i,j}$ is the corresponding pixel in the i-th source features. After the warping operation, $N-1$ source volumes $\{\mathbf{V}_i\}_{i=1}^{N-1} \in \mathbb{R}^{H \times W \times C \times D}$ are constructed, where D is the total number of hypothesized depths.

3.2 Epipolar Transformer

Next, we introduce the epipolar Transformer to aggregate source volumes from different views. The original attention function in Transformer [51] can be described as mapping a *query* and a set of *key-value* pairs to an output. Similarly, in the proposed epipolar Transformer, the reference feature is leveraged as the user *query* to match source features (*keys*) along the epipolar line, thus enhancing the corresponding depth *value*. Specifically, we enrich the reference *query* via an auxiliary task of monocular depth estimation. Subsequently, cross-attention computes associations between *query* and source volumes under epipolar constraint, generating attention guidance to aggregate the feature volumes from different views. The aggregated features are then regularized by lightweight 3D CNNs. In the following, we firstly give details about the *query* construction, then elaborate on the epipolar Transformer guided feature aggregation. Finally, the lightweight regularization strategy is given.

Query Construction. As aforementioned, we deem the reference feature as a *query* for the epipolar Transformer. However, features extracted by shallow 2D CNNs become less discriminative at non-Lambertian and low-texture regions. To remedy this problem, [14,20,53,57] utilize expensive DCNs [12] or ASPP [47] to enrich features. In contrast, we propose a more efficient way to enhance our *query*: building an auxiliary monocular depth estimation branch to regularize the *query* and learn depth-discriminative features.

A common decoder [22] used in the monocular depth estimation task is applied in our auxiliary branch. Given multi-scale reference features $\{\mathbf{F}_0^k\}_{k=0}^{M-1}$ that are extracted via FPN, we expand a low resolution feature map through interpolation, and concatenate it with the subsequent scale feature. The aggregated feature maps are fed into regression head [21,22] to make monocular depth estimations:

$$\mathbf{M}_k = \mathbf{\Phi}([\mathbf{I}(\mathbf{F}_0^k), \mathbf{F}_0^{k+1}]), \tag{2}$$

where $\mathbf{\Phi}(\cdot)$ is monocular depth decoder, $\mathbf{I}(\cdot)$ is the interpolation function and $[\cdot, \cdot]$ denotes concatenation operation. Subsequently, the monocular depth estimation is repeated for queries with different scales. Notably, such auxiliary branch is only used in the training phase, guiding our network to learn depth-aware features.

Epipolar Transformer Guided Aggregation. The aggregation pipeline is depicted in Fig. 2(a), which aims at building 3D associations of the *query* feature. However, depth-wise 3D spatial information is not explicitly delivered by the 2D query feature map, so we firstly restore the depth information via homography warping. According to the warping operation in Eq. (1), the hypothesized depth locations of *query* feature $\mathbf{p}_r$ are projected onto the source image epipolar line, resulting in the source volume features $\{\mathbf{p}_{s_i,j}\}_{j=0}^{D-1}$, which are regarded as the *keys* for the epipolar Transformer. Consequently, the *key* features along the epipolar line are leveraged to construct depth-wise 3D associations of the *query* feature, which is implemented with the cross-attention operation:

$$\mathbf{w}_i = \text{softmax}(\frac{\mathbf{v_i}^{\mathsf{T}}\mathbf{p}_r}{t_e\sqrt{C}}), \tag{3}$$

where $\mathbf{v_i} \in \mathbb{R}^{C \times D}$ is calculated by stacking $\{\mathbf{p}_{s_i,j}\}_{j=0}^{D-1}$ along depth dimension, t_e is the temperature parameter, and $\mathbf{w}_i$ is the attention correlating *query* and *keys*. We visualize an example of real images in Fig. 2(b), where the attention focuses on the most matched location on the epipolar line.

The calculated attention $\mathbf{w}_i$ between *query* and *keys* is utilized to aggregate *values*. As for the Transformer *value* design, we follow [53,59,70] to use group-wise correlation, which measures the visual similarity between reference feature and source volumes in an efficient manner:

$$\mathbf{s}_i^g = \frac{1}{G} \langle \mathbf{v}_i^g, \mathbf{p}_r^g \rangle, \tag{4}$$

where $g = 0, ..., G-1$, $\mathbf{v}_i^g \in \mathbb{R}^{\frac{C}{G} \times D}$ is the g-th group feature of $\mathbf{v}_i$, $\mathbf{p}_r^g \in \mathbb{R}^{\frac{C}{G} \times 1}$ is the g-th group feature of $\hat{\mathbf{p}}_r$, and $\langle \cdot, \cdot \rangle$ is the inner product. $\{\mathbf{s}_i^g\}_{g=0}^{G-1}$ are then

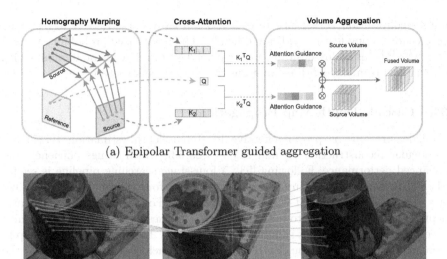

(a) Epipolar Transformer guided aggregation

(b) Visualization of attention on the DTU dataset

Fig. 2. (a) The epipolar Transformer aggregation. Homography warping is leveraged to restore depth-wise information of the reference feature, then cross-attention computes 3D associations between query and source volumes under epipolar constraint, generating attention guidance to aggregate the feature volumes from different views. (b) Visualization of the cross-attention score on scan 1 of the DTU dataset, where the opacity of dots on the epipolar line represents the attention score.

stacked along channel dimension to get $\mathbf{s}_i \in \mathbb{R}^{G \times D}$, which is the *value* for our Transformer. Finally, *values* are aggregated by epipolar attention score $\mathbf{w}_i$ to determine the final cost volume:

$$\mathbf{c} = \frac{\sum_{i=1}^{N-1} \mathbf{w}_i \mathbf{s}_i}{\sum_{i=1}^{N-1} \mathbf{w}_i}. \tag{5}$$

In summary, for the proposed epipolar Transformer, a detachable monocular depth estimation branch is firstly leveraged to enhance depth-discriminative 2D semantics, then the cross-attention between *query* and *keys* is utilized to construct depth-wise 3D associations. Finally, the combined 2D and 3D information serves as guidance for aggregating different views. As shown in Eq. (3)–(5), the epipolar Transformer is designed as an efficient aggregation module, where no learnable parameter is introduced, and the epipolar Transformer only learns data-dependent associations.

Lightweight Regularization. Due to non-Lambertian surfaces or object occlusions, the raw cost volume is noise-contaminated [65]. To smoothen the final depth map, 3D CNNs are utilized to regularize the cost volume. Considering we have embedded 3D associations into the cost volume, depth-wise feature encoding is omitted in our 3D CNNs, which makes it more efficient. Specifically, we reduce convolution kernel size from $3 \times 3 \times 3$ to $3 \times 3 \times 1$, only aggregating cost volume along feature width and height. The regularized probability volume $\mathbf{P} \in \mathbb{R}^{H \times W \times D}$ is highly desirable in per-pixel depth confidence prediction, which is leveraged to make depth estimations in the cascade structure.

3.3   Cascade Depth Map Propagation

Cascade structure is proven effective in stereo depth estimation [17,45,48], monocular reconstruction [4] and MVS [9,23,53], which brings efficiency and enhanced performance. Following [53], a four-stage searching pipeline is set for MVSTER, where the resolutions of inputs for the four stages are $H \times W \times 64$, $\frac{H}{2} \times \frac{W}{2} \times 32$, $\frac{H}{4} \times \frac{W}{4} \times 16$ and $\frac{H}{8} \times \frac{W}{8} \times 8$ respectively. Following [53,59], the inverse depth sampling is utilized to initialize depth hypotheses in the first stage, which is equivalent to equidistant sampling in pixel space. To propagate depth map in a coarse to fine manner, the depth hypotheses of each stage are centered at the previous stage's depth prediction, and D_k hypotheses are uniformly generated within the hypothesized depth range.

3.4   Loss

Although cascade structure benefits from coarse to fine pipeline, it has difficulty recovering from errors introduced at previous stages [23]. To alleviate this problem, a straightforward way is to generate a finer depth map at each stage, especially avoiding predicting depth far away from the ground truth. However, previous methods [14,57,66] simply regard depth estimation as a multi-class classification problem, which treats each hypothesized depth equally without considering the distance relationship between them. For example in Fig. 3, given a ground truth depth probability distribution, the cross-entropy losses of case 1 and case 2 are the same. However, the depth prediction of case 1 is out of the valid range and can not be properly propagated to the next stage.

In this paper, the depth prediction is formulated as a depth-aware classification problem, which emphasizes the penalty of the predicted depth that is distant from the ground truth. Specifically, we measure the distance between the predicted distribution $\mathbf{P}_i \in \mathbb{R}^D$ and the ground truth distribution $\mathbf{P}_{\theta,i} \in \mathbb{R}^D$ with the off-the-shelf Wasserstein distance [3]:

$$d_w(\mathbf{P}_i, \mathbf{P}_{\theta,i}) = \inf_{\gamma \in \Pi(\mathbf{P}_i, \mathbf{P}_{\theta,i})} \sum_{x,y} |x - y| \gamma(x, y), \qquad (6)$$

where inf stands for infimum, and $\Pi(\mathbf{P}_i, \mathbf{P}_{\theta,i})$ is the set of all possible distributions whose marginal distributions are $\mathbf{P}_i$ and $\mathbf{P}_{\theta,i}$, which satisfies $\sum_x \gamma(x, y) = \mathbf{P}_i(y)$ and $\sum_y \gamma(x, y) = \mathbf{P}_{\theta,i}(x)$. Such formulation is inspired by the optimal transport problem [38] that calculates the minimum work transporting $\mathbf{P}_i$ to $\mathbf{P}_{\theta,i}$, which can be differentially solved via the sinkhorn algorithm [11].

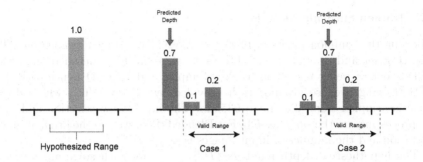

Fig. 3. Example illustrating that cross-entropy loss is not aware of the relative distance between each hypothesized depth. The left-most subfigure is the ground truth. Case 1, Case 2 are two predicted depth distributions.

In summary, the loss function consists of two parts: Wasserstein loss measuring the distance between predicted depth distribution and ground truth, and L_1 loss optimizing monocular depth estimation:

$$Loss = \sum_{k=0}^{M-1} \sum_{i \in \mathbf{p}_{valid}} d_w(\mathbf{P}_i^k, \mathbf{P}_{\theta,i}^k) + \lambda L_1(\mathbf{M}_i^k, \mathbf{P}_{\theta,i}^k), \tag{7}$$

where $\mathbf{p}_{valid}$ refers to the set of valid ground truth pixels, and λ is the loss weight. The total loss is calculated for M stages.

4   Experiments

4.1   Datasets

MVSTER is evaluated on DTU [1], Tanks&Temples [28], BlendedMVS [67] and ETH3D [44] to verify its effectiveness. Among the four datasets, DTU is an indoor dataset under laboratory conditions, which contains 124 scenes with 49 views and 7 illumination conditions. Following MVSNet [65], DTU is split into **training**, **validation** and **test** set. Tanks&Temples is a public benchmark providing realistic video sequences, which is divided into the intermediate set and a more challenging advanced set. BlendedMVS is a large-scale synthetic dataset that contains 106 **training** scans and 7 **validation** scans. ETH3D benchmark introduces high-resolution images with strong view-point variations, which is split into **training** and **test** sets. As for the evaluation metrics, DTU, Tanks&Temples, and ETH3D evaluate point cloud reconstructions using overall metrics [1] and F_1 score [28,44]. BlendedMVS evaluates depth map estimations using depth-wise metric [67]: EPE stands for L_1 distance between predicted depth map and ground truth, e_1 and e_3 represent the proportion of pixels with depth error larger than 1 and 3.

4.2   Implementation Details

Following the common practice [14,37,52], MVSTER is firstly trained on DTU training set and evaluated on DTU test set, then it is finetuned on Blend-edMVS before being tested on Tanks&Temples and ETH3D benchmark. For DTU training, we use ground truth provided by MVSNet [65], whose depth range is sampled from 425mm to 935mm. The input view selection and data pre-processing are the same as [53]. For BlendedMVS, we use the original image resolution and the number of input images is set as 7.

The hypothesized depth numbers $\{D_k\}_{k=0,...,3}$ for each stage are set as 8, 8, 4, 4. Following [37,57], the hypothesized number of the 1st stage is doubled when MVSTER is tested on Tanks&Temples and ETH3D. The group correlation $\{G_k\}_{k=0,...,3}$ are set as 8, 8, 4, 4. For inverse depth sampling, the inverse depth range R_k satisfies $\frac{1}{R_k} = \frac{1}{D_{k-1}-1} \frac{1}{R_{k-1}}$. For the epipolar Transformer, the temperature parameter t_e is set as 2. And the loss weight λ is set as 0.0003 in the experiments. We train MVSTER for 10 epochs and optimize it with Adam [27] ($\beta_1 = 0.9, \beta_2 = 0.999$). MVSTER is trained on four NVIDIA RTX 3090 GPUs with batch size 2 on each GPU. The learning rate is initially set as 0.001, which decays by a factor of 2 after 6, 8 and 9 epochs.

For point cloud reconstruction, we follow previous methods [23,65,66] to use both geometric and photometric constraints for depth filtering. We set the view consistency number and the photometric probability threshold as 4 and 0.5, respectively. The final depth fusion steps also follow previous methods [23,65,66].

4.3   Benchmark Performance

Evaluation on DTU We compare MVSTER with traditional methods [19,43, 50], published learning-based methods [9,23,53,57,65,66,68,69] and approaches from recent technical reports [14,37,52,76]. The input images are set as different resolutions (MVSTER*: 1600×1200 and MVSTER: 864×1152) to compare with previous methods, and the number of views is set as 5. The quantitative results are shown in Table 1, where MVSTER* achieves a state-of-the-art overall score and completeness score among all the competitors. Significantly, the inference time of MVSTER* is 0.17s, which is faster than the previous fastest method [53]. Additionally, MVSTER with lower resolution (864 × 1152) still outperforms all published works, and it runs at 0.09s per image with 2764 MB GPU memory consumption, which sets a new state of the art for efficient learning-based MVS. Qualitative results reconstructed by MVSTER are shown in the supplement.

Evaluation on Tanks&Temples. MVSTER is tested on Tanks&Temples to demonstrate the generalization ability. We use the original image resolution and set the number of views as 7. The depth range, camera parameters, and view selection strategies are aligned with PatchmatchNet [53]. And we follow the dynamic consistency checking method in depth filtering [61]. We compare MVSTER with traditional methods [43,58], published learning-based methods [23,34,53,57,66], and approaches from recent technique reports [14,37,52,64].

Table 1. Quantitative results of different methods on the DTU `evaluation` set. Methods with * denote their input resolution is 1600 × 1200. The last four methods with gray font come from technical reports.

Method	Acc.↓	Comp.↓	Overall↓	Runtime (s)↓
Gipuma [19]	**0.283**	0.873	0.578	–
COLMAP [43]	0.400	0.664	0.532	–
Tola [50]	0.342	1.190	0.766	–
MVSNet [65]	0.396	0.527	0.462	0.85
R-MVSNet [66]	0.383	0.452	0.417	0.89
CasMVSNet [23]	0.325	0.385	0.355	0.35
UCS-Net* [9]	0.338	0.349	0.344	0.32
PatchmatchNet* [53]	0.427	0.277	0.352	0.18
AA-RMVSNet [57]	0.376	0.339	0.357	–
MVSTER	0.350	0.276	0.313	**0.09**
MVSTER*	0.340	**0.266**	**0.303**	0.17
TransMVSNet [14]	0.321	0.289	0.305	0.99
MVS2D* [64]	0.394	0.290	0.342	0.13
UniMVSNet [37]	0.352	0.278	0.315	-
IterMVS* [52]	0.373	0.354	0.363	0.18

Advanced set quantitative results are shown in Table 2, where MVSTER achieves the highest mean F-score among all published works, and the inference time per image is 0.26s. Although our performance is 1.4% lower than the recent UniMVS-Net [37], the inference speed of MVSTER is 3× faster than UniMVSNet. For Tanks&Temples-Intermediate, MVSTER achieves a 60.92 mean F-score, which is 7.8% better than the previous most efficient method [53]. Overall, MVSTER shows strong generalization ability with great efficiency.

Evaluation on ETH3D. For evaluation on the ETD3D dataset, the input images are resized to 1920 × 1280 and the number of inputs is set as 7. The depth range, camera parameters, and view selection strategies are aligned with Patch-matchNet [53]. We compare MVSTER with traditional methods [18,43,43,58], published learning-based methods [29,53] and approaches from technique reports [52,60]. The running time per image is 0.30s and the quantitative results are shown in Table 3. On the `training` set, MVSTER achieves better F_1-score than the most competitive traditional method ACMH [58] and the recent IterMVS [52]. On the `test` set, our method obtains 8.9% improvement over the previous most efficient method [53], which is comparable to the recent IterMVS [52]. This demonstrates MVSTER can be well generalized to high-resolution images.

4.4   Ablation Study

The ablation study is conducted to analyze the effectiveness of each component, which is measured with DTU's point cloud reconstruction metric [1] and Blend-

Table 2. Quantitative results on Tanks&Temples-advanced. The evaluation metric is the mean F-score and the last four methods with gray font come from technical reports.

Method	Mean F-score	Aud.	Bal.	Cou.	Mus.	Pal.	Tem
COLMAP [43]	27.24	16.02	25.23	34.70	41.51	18.05	27.94
ACMH [58]	34.02	23.41	32.91	41.17	48.13	23.87	34.60
R-MVSNet [66]	29.55	19.49	31.45	29.99	42.31	22.94	31.10
CasMVSNet [23]	31.12	19.81	38.46	29.10	43.87	27.36	28.11
PatchmatchNet [53]	32.31	23.69	37.73	30.04	41.80	28.31	32.29
EPP-MVSNet [34]	35.72	21.28	39.74	35.34	49.21	30.00	38.75
AA R-MVSNet [57]	33.53	20.96	40.15	32.05	46.01	29.28	32.71
MVSTER	**37.53**	**26.68**	**42.14**	35.65	**49.37**	**32.16**	**39.19**
TransMVSNet [14]	37.00	24.84	44.69	34.77	46.49	34.69	36.62
MVSTR [76]	32.85	22.83	39.04	33.87	45.46	27.95	27.97
UniMVSNet [37]	38.96	28.33	44.36	39.74	52.89	33.80	34.63
IterMVS [52]	34.17	25.90	38.41	31.16	44.83	29.59	35.15

Table 3. Quantitative results on the ETH3D benchmark, which is split into a **training** set and a **test** set. The last two methods with gray font come from technical reports.

Methods	Training set			Test set		
	Acc.	Comp.	F_1-score	Acc.	Comp.	F_1-score
Gipuma [43]	84.44	34.91	36.38	86.47	24.91	45.18
PMVS [18]	90.23	32.08	46.06	90.08	31.84	44.16
COLMAP [43]	**91.85**	55.13	67.66	**91.97**	62.98	73.01
ACMH [58]	88.94	61.59	70.71	89.34	68.62	75.89
PatchmatchNet [53]	64.81	65.43	64.21	69.71	77.46	73.12
PatchMatch-RL [29]	76.05	62.22	67.78	74.48	72.89	72.38
MVSTER	76.92	**68.08**	**72.06**	77.09	**82.47**	**79.01**
PVSNet [60]	67.84	69.66	67.48	66.41	80.05	72.08
IterMVS [52]	79.79	66.08	71.69	84.73	76.49	80.06

edMVS's depth estimation metric [67]. Unless specified, the image resolutions for DTU and BlendedMVS are 864×1152 and 576×768.

Epipolar Transformer (ET). Existing methods for aggregating different views in learning-based MVS can be categorized as two types: (i) variance fusing [9,23,63,65,66], (ii) CNN-based fusing [53,57,68,70]. In this experiment, the aforementioned two methods are compared with the ET module under three conditions[1]. The quantitative results are concluded in Table 4. We observe that reducing hypothesized depth number can significantly decrease inference time. Compared with the hypothesized number used by MVSNet [65] and CasMVS-Net [23], our method relatively reduces 70% and 53% running time. However,

---

[1] Three hypothesized depth number: (i) $D : 192$ used by one-stage methods [57,65,66], (ii) $D : 48, 32, 8$ used by three-stage methods [14,23], and (iii) $D : 8, 8, 4, 4$ used by MVSTER. All of these conditions follow implementation details described in Sect. 4.2.

the variance fusing strategy shows restricted improvement in the third condition with fewest hypothesized number. CNN-based fusing alleviates the problem by enhancing local visual similarity, but it relatively brings 45%, 46%, 89% computation cost in three cases. In contrast, the ET module shows consistent performance improvement under different hypothesized cases, which demonstrates that 3D spatial associations are beneficial for aggregating multi-view features. Significantly, the ET module learns data-dependent fusing guidance, introducing minimal network parameters and bringing no extra computation cost.

Table 4. Quantitative results of different fusing methods under conditions with different hypothesized depth numbers.

Method	Hypo. Num	Overall↓	EPE ↓	e_1↓	e_3↓	Runtime (s)↓	Param (M)↓
Variance Fusion	192	0.460	1.62	19.34	9.84	0.40	0.34
CNN Fusion	192	0.442	1.58	**17.89**	9.47	0.58	0.35
ET (Ours)	192	**0.435**	**1.54**	17.93	**9.32**	**0.40**	**0.34**
Variance Fusion	48,32,8	0.335	1.28	14.82	7.55	0.28	0.93
CNN Fusion	48,32,8	0.327	**1.07**	14.33	7.03	0.41	0.94
ET (Ours)	48,32,8	**0.323**	1.09	**14.17**	**6.89**	**0.28**	**0.93**
Variance Fusion	8,8,4,4	0.334	1.39	15.32	7.92	0.09	0.98
CNN Fusion	8,8,4,4	0.320	1.33	**14.80**	7.32	0.17	1.01
ET (Ours)	8,8,4,4	**0.313**	**1.31**	14.98	**7.27**	**0.09**	**0.98**

Monocular Depth Estimator (MDE) In this experiment, the proposed MDE module is compared with DCN used by [14,53,57] and ASPP used by [20]. The results are shown in Table 5. We observe that the ASPP restricts the reconstruction performance, and DCN enhances reconstruction results with reduced depth error e_1. However, DCN brings high computation costs and introduces onerous learning parameters. In contrast, the MDE module shows comparable performance improvement with DCN but introduces no extra computation burden. We also provide an example in Fig. 4, where the MDE module enhances features details at object boundaries, which could reduce ambiguity for depth estimations within boundary areas.

Table 5. Comparison of our MDE module with DCN and ASPP.

Method	Overall↓	EPE ↓	e_1↓	e_3↓	Runtime (s)↓	Param (M)↓
Raw feature	0.317	1.35	15.00	7.37	0.09	0.98
DCN	**0.313**	1.33	**14.82**	7.55	0.23	1.51
ASPP	0.327	1.34	15.30	7.53	0.15	1.16
MDE (Ours)	**0.313**	**1.31**	14.98	**7.27**	**0.09**	**0.98**

Optimal Transport in Depth Propagation (OT). Learning-based MVS methods usually use L_1 loss to regress the depth map [23,65] or use cross-entropy loss to classify depth [14,66]. In this experiment, the two losses are compared

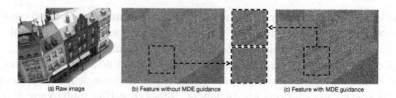

Fig. 4. An example shows that MDE guides the FPN feature to deliver more details at object boundaries. For better visualization, we leverage PCA to reduce the number of feature channels to 3 and color the channels with RGB.

with the Wasserstein loss computed by OT. Apart from the aforementioned evaluation metrics, we introduce S_3 EPE and S_4 EPE, which stand for EPE of stage 3 and stage 4 depth estimations on DTU. As shown in Table 6, OT improves point cloud reconstruction performance and reduces depth error. Especially, it greatly reduces depth error of the last two stages, which demonstrates OT is effective in propagating finer depth maps to later stages.

Table 6. Comparison of optimal transport with L_1 loss and cross-entropy loss.

Method	Overall↓	EPE ↓	e_1 ↓	e_3 ↓	S_3 EPE ↓	S_4 EPE↓
L_1 Loss	0.321	1.47	15.32	7.53	7.02	6.32
CE Loss	0.314	1.34	**14.96**	7.40	7.12	6.64
OT (Ours)	**0.313**	**1.31**	14.98	**7.27**	**6.41**	**5.90**

5   Conclusions

In this paper, we present the epipolar Transformer for efficient MVS, termed as MVSTER. The proposed epipolar Transformer leverages both 2D semantics and 3D spatial associations to efficiently aggregate multi-view features. Specifically, MVSTER enriches 2D depth-discriminative semantics via an auxiliary monocular depth estimator. And the cross-attention on the epipolar line constructs 3D associations without learnable parameters. The combined 2D and 3D information serves as guidance to aggregate different views. Moreover, we formulate depth estimation as a depth-aware classification problem, which produces finer depth estimations propagated in the cascade structure. Extensive experiments on DTU, Tanks&Temple, BlendedMVS, and ETH3D show our method achieves stage-of-the-art performance with significantly higher efficiency. We hope that MVSTER can serve as an efficient baseline for learning-based MVS, and further work may focus on simplifying 2D extractors and 3D CNNs.

Acknowledgments. This project was supported by the National Natural Science Foundation of China (No. 62073317).

References

1. Aanæs, H., Jensen, R.R., Vogiatzis, G., Tola, E., Dahl, A.B.: Large-scale data for multiple-view stereopsis. Int. J. Comput. Vis. **120**, 153–168 (2016)
2. Abnar, S., Zuidema, W.H.: Quantifying attention flow in transformers. In: Association for Computational Linguistics (2020)
3. Arjovsky, M., Chintala, S., Bottou, L.: Wasserstein GAN. arXiv preprint arXiv:1701.07875 (2017)
4. Bozic, A., Palafox, P., Thies, J., Dai, A., Nießner, M.: TransFormerfusion: monocular RGB scene reconstruction using transformers. In: Advances in Neural Information Processing Systems (2021)
5. Campbell, N.D.F., Vogiatzis, G., Hernández, C., Cipolla, R.: Using multiple hypotheses to improve depth-maps for multi-view stereo. In: Forsyth, D., Torr, P., Zisserman, A. (eds.) ECCV 2008. LNCS, vol. 5302, pp. 766–779. Springer, Heidelberg (2008). https://doi.org/10.1007/978-3-540-88682-2_58
6. Carion, N., Massa, F., Synnaeve, G., Usunier, N., Kirillov, A., Zagoruyko, S.: End-to-end object detection with transformers. In: Vedaldi, A., Bischof, H., Brox, T., Frahm, J.-M. (eds.) ECCV 2020. LNCS, vol. 12346, pp. 213–229. Springer, Cham (2020). https://doi.org/10.1007/978-3-030-58452-8_13
7. Chen, M., et al.: Generative pretraining from pixels. In: International Conference on Machine Learning (2020)
8. Chen, R., Han, S., Xu, J., Su, H.: Point-based multi-view stereo network. In: IEEE International Conference on Computer Vision (2019)
9. Cheng, S., et al.: Deep stereo using adaptive thin volume representation with uncertainty awareness. In: IEEE Conference on Computer Vision and Pattern Recognition (2020)
10. Collins, R.T.: A space-sweep approach to true multi-image matching. In: IEEE Conference on Computer Vision and Pattern Recognition (1996)
11. Cuturi, M.: Sinkhorn distances: lightspeed computation of optimal transport. In: Advances in Neural Information Processing Systems (2013)
12. Dai, J., et al.: Deformable convolutional networks. In: IEEE International Conference on Computer Vision (2017)
13. Devlin, J., Chang, M., Lee, K., Toutanova, K.: BERT: pre-training of deep bidirectional transformers for language understanding. In: Conference of the North American Chapter of the Association for Computational Linguistics: Human Language Technologies (2019)
14. Ding, Y., et al.: TransMVSNet: global context-aware multi-view stereo network with transformers. arXiv preprint arXiv:2111.14600 (2021)
15. Dosovitskiy, A., et al.: An image is worth 16x16 words: transformers for image recognition at scale. In: International Conference on Learning Representations (2021)
16. Dosovitskiy, A., et al.: FlowNet: learning optical flow with convolutional networks. In: IEEE International Conference on Computer Vision (2015)
17. Duggal, S., Wang, S., Ma, W., Hu, R., Urtasun, R.: DeepPruner: learning efficient stereo matching via differentiable PatchMatch. In: IEEE International Conference on Computer Vision (2019)
18. Furukawa, Y., Ponce, J.: Accurate, dense, and robust multiview stereopsis. IEEE Trans. Pattern Anal. Mach. Intell. (2010)
19. Galliani, S., Lasinger, K., Schindler, K.: Massively parallel multiview stereopsis by surface normal diffusion. In: IEEE International Conference on Computer Vision (2015)

20. Giang, K.T., Song, S., Jo, S.: Curvature-guided dynamic scale networks for multi-view stereo. arXiv preprint arXiv:2112.05999 (2021)
21. Godard, C., Aodha, O.M., Brostow, G.J.: Unsupervised monocular depth estimation with left-right consistency. In: IEEE Conference on Computer Vision and Pattern Recognition (2017)
22. Godard, C., Aodha, O.M., Firman, M., Brostow, G.J.: Digging into self-supervised monocular depth estimation. In: IEEE International Conference on Computer Vision (2019)
23. Gu, X., Fan, Z., Zhu, S., Dai, Z., Tan, F., Tan, P.: Cascade cost volume for high-resolution multi-view stereo and stereo matching. In: IEEE Conference on Computer Vision and Pattern Recognition (2020)
24. He, C., Zeng, H., Huang, J., Hua, X., Zhang, L.: Structure aware single-stage 3d object detection from point cloud. In: IEEE Conference on Computer Vision and Pattern Recognition (2020)
25. He, Y., Yan, R., Fragkiadaki, K., Yu, S.: Epipolar transformer for multi-view human pose estimation. In: IEEE Conference on Computer Vision and Pattern Recognition (2020)
26. Ke, Q., Bennamoun, M., An, S., Sohel, F.A., Boussaïd, F.: A new representation of skeleton sequences for 3d action recognition. In: IEEE Conference on Computer Vision and Pattern Recognition (2017)
27. Kingma, D.P., Ba, J.: Adam: a method for stochastic optimization. In: International Conference on Learning Representations (2015)
28. Knapitsch, A., Park, J., Zhou, Q., Koltun, V.: Tanks and temples: benchmarking large-scale scene reconstruction. ACM Trans. Graph. **36**, 1–13 (2017)
29. Lee, J.Y., DeGol, J., Zou, C., Hoiem, D.: PatchMatch-RL: Deep MVS with pixel-wise depth, normal, and visibility. In: IEEE International Conference on Computer Vision (2021)
30. Li, Z., et al.: Revisiting stereo depth estimation from a sequence-to-sequence perspective with transformers. In: IEEE International Conference on Computer Vision (2021)
31. Lin, T., Dollár, P., Girshick, R.B., He, K., Hariharan, B., Belongie, S.J.: Feature pyramid networks for object detection. In: IEEE Conference on Computer Vision and Pattern Recognition (2017)
32. Liu, Z., et al.: Swin transformer: hierarchical vision transformer using shifted windows. IEEE International Conference on Computer Vision (2021)
33. Luo, S., Hu, W.: Diffusion probabilistic models for 3D point cloud generation. In: IEEE Conference on Computer Vision and Pattern Recognition (2021)
34. Ma, X., Gong, Y., Wang, Q., Huang, J., Chen, L., Yu, F.: EPP-MVSNet: epipolar-assembling based depth prediction for multi-view stereo. In: IEEE International Conference on Computer Vision (2021)
35. Mildenhall, B., Srinivasan, P.P., Tancik, M., Barron, J.T., Ramamoorthi, R., Ng, R.: NeRF: representing scenes as neural radiance fields for view synthesis. In: Vedaldi, A., Bischof, H., Brox, T., Frahm, J.-M. (eds.) ECCV 2020. LNCS, vol. 12346, pp. 405–421. Springer, Cham (2020). https://doi.org/10.1007/978-3-030-58452-8_24
36. Mordan, T., Thome, N., Hénaff, G., Cord, M.: Revisiting multi-task learning with ROCK: a deep residual auxiliary block for visual detection. In: Advances in Neural Information Processing Systems (2018)
37. Peng, R., Wang, R., Wang, Z., Lai, Y., Wang, R.: Rethinking depth estimation for multi-view stereo: a unified representation and focal loss. arXiv preprint arXiv:2201.01501 (2022)

38. Peyré, G., Cuturi, M.: Computational optimal transport. Found. Trends Mach. Learn. (2019)
39. Qi, C.R., Su, H., Mo, K., Guibas, L.J.: PointNet: deep learning on point sets for 3D classification and segmentation. In: IEEE Conference on Computer Vision and Pattern Recognition (2017)
40. Qi, C.R., Yi, L., Su, H., Guibas, L.J.: PointNet++: deep hierarchical feature learning on point sets in a metric space. In: Advances in Neural Information Processing Systems (2017)
41. Qin, J., Wu, J., Xiao, X., Li, L., Wang, X.: Activation modulation and recalibration scheme for weakly supervised semantic segmentation. In: AAAI Conference on Artificial Intelligence (2021)
42. Radford, A., Narasimhan, K., Salimans, T., Sutskever, I.: Improving language understanding by generative pre-training. OpenAI Preprint (2018)
43. Schönberger, J.L., Frahm, J.: Structure-from-motion revisited. In: IEEE Conference on Computer Vision and Pattern Recognition (2016)
44. Schöps, T., et al.: A multi-view stereo benchmark with high-resolution images and multi-camera videos. In: IEEE Conference on Computer Vision and Pattern Recognition (2017)
45. Shen, Z., Dai, Y., Rao, Z.: CFNet: cascade and fused cost volume for robust stereo matching. In: IEEE Conference on Computer Vision and Pattern Recognition (2021)
46. Shi, S., et al.: PV-RCNN: point-voxel feature set abstraction for 3D object detection. In: IEEE Conference on Computer Vision and Pattern Recognition (2020)
47. Sinha, A., Murez, Z., Bartolozzi, J., Badrinarayanan, V., Rabinovich, A.: DELTAS: depth estimation by learning triangulation and densification of sparse points. In: Vedaldi, A., Bischof, H., Brox, T., Frahm, J.-M. (eds.) ECCV 2020. LNCS, vol. 12366, pp. 104–121. Springer, Cham (2020). https://doi.org/10.1007/978-3-030-58589-1_7
48. Tankovich, V., et al.: HitNet: hierarchical iterative tile refinement network for real-time stereo matching. In: IEEE Conference on Computer Vision and Pattern Recognition, pp. 14362–14372 (2021)
49. Tenney, I., Das, D., Pavlick, E.: BERT rediscovers the classical NLP pipeline. In: Association for Computational Linguistics (2019)
50. Tola, E., Strecha, C., Fua, P.: Efficient large-scale multi-view stereo for ultra high-resolution image sets. Mach. Vis. Appl. **23**, 903–920 (2012)
51. Vaswani, A., et al.: Attention is all you need. In: Advances in Neural Information Processing Systems (2017)
52. Wang, F., Galliani, S., Vogel, C., Pollefeys, M.: IterMVS: iterative probability estimation for efficient multi-view stereo. arXiv preprint arXiv:2112.05126 (2021)
53. Wang, F., Galliani, S., Vogel, C., Speciale, P., Pollefeys, M.: PatchmatchNet: learned multi-view PatchMatch stereo. In: IEEE Conference on Computer Vision and Pattern Recognition (2021)
54. Wang, H., Zhu, Y., Green, B., Adam, H., Yuille, A., Chen, L.-C.: Axial-DeepLab: stand-alone axial-attention for panoptic segmentation. In: Vedaldi, A., Bischof, H., Brox, T., Frahm, J.-M. (eds.) ECCV 2020. LNCS, vol. 12349, pp. 108–126. Springer, Cham (2020). https://doi.org/10.1007/978-3-030-58548-8_7

55. Watson, J., Aodha, O.M., Prisacariu, V., Brostow, G.J., Firman, M.: The temporal opportunist: self-supervised multi-frame monocular depth. In: IEEE Conference on Computer Vision and Pattern Recognition (2021)
56. Wei, Y., et al.: SurroundDepth: entangling surrounding views for self-supervised multi-camera depth estimation. arXiv preprint arXiv:2204.03636 (2022)
57. Wei, Z., Zhu, Q., Min, C., Chen, Y., Wang, G.: AA-RMVSNet: adaptive aggregation recurrent multi-view stereo network. In: IEEE International Conference on Computer Vision (2021)
58. Xu, Q., Tao, W.: Multi-scale geometric consistency guided multi-view stereo. In: IEEE Conference on Computer Vision and Pattern Recognition (2019)
59. Xu, Q., Tao, W.: Learning inverse depth regression for multi-view stereo with correlation cost volume. In: AAAI Conference on Artificial Intelligence (2020)
60. Xu, Q., Tao, W.: PVSNet: pixelwise visibility-aware multi-view stereo network. arXiv preprint arXiv:2007.07714 (2020)
61. Yan, J., et al.: Dense hybrid recurrent multi-view stereo net with dynamic consistency checking. In: European Conference on Computer Vision (2020)
62. Yang, F., Yang, H., Fu, J., Lu, H., Guo, B.: Learning texture transformer network for image super-resolution. In: IEEE Conference on Computer Vision and Pattern Recognition (2020)
63. Yang, J., Mao, W., Alvarez, J.M., Liu, M.: Cost volume pyramid based depth inference for multi-view stereo. In: IEEE Conference on Computer Vision and Pattern Recognition (2020)
64. Yang, Z., Ren, Z., Shan, Q., Huang, Q.: MVS2D: efficient multi-view stereo via attention-driven 2D convolutions. arXiv preprint arXiv:2104.13325 (2021)
65. Yao, Y., Luo, Z., Li, S., Fang, T., Quan, L.: MVSNet: depth inference for unstructured multi-view stereo. In: Ferrari, V., Hebert, M., Sminchisescu, C., Weiss, Y. (eds.) ECCV 2018. LNCS, vol. 11212, pp. 785–801. Springer, Cham (2018). https://doi.org/10.1007/978-3-030-01237-3_47
66. Yao, Y., Luo, Z., Li, S., Shen, T., Fang, T., Quan, L.: Recurrent MVSNet for high-resolution multi-view stereo depth inference. In: IEEE Conference on Computer Vision and Pattern Recognition (2019)
67. Yao, Y., et al.: BlendedMVS: a large-scale dataset for generalized multi-view stereo networks. In: IEEE Conference on Computer Vision and Pattern Recognition (2020)
68. Yi, H., et al.: Pyramid multi-view stereo net with self-adaptive view aggregation. In: Vedaldi, A., Bischof, H., Brox, T., Frahm, J.-M. (eds.) ECCV 2020. LNCS, vol. 12354, pp. 766–782. Springer, Cham (2020). https://doi.org/10.1007/978-3-030-58545-7_44
69. Yu, Z., Gao, S.: Fast-MVSNet: sparse-to-dense multi-view stereo with learned propagation and gauss-newton refinement. In: IEEE Conference on Computer Vision and Pattern Recognition (2020)
70. Zhang, J., Yao, Y., Li, S., Luo, Z., Fang, T.: Visibility-aware multi-view stereo network. In: British Machine Vision Conference (2020)
71. Zhang, X., Hu, Y., Wang, H., Cao, X., Zhang, B.: Long-range attention network for multi-view stereo. In: IEEE Winter Conference on Applications of Computer Vision (2021)
72. Zhang, Y., et al.: BEVerse: unified perception and prediction in birds-eye-view for vision-centric autonomous driving. arXiv preprint arXiv:2205.09743 (2022)
73. Zhao, M., Zhang, J., Zhang, C., Zhang, W.: Leveraging heterogeneous auxiliary tasks to assist crowd counting. In: IEEE Conference on Computer Vision and Pattern Recognition (2019)

74. Zhao, Z., Wu, Z., Zhuang, Y., Li, B., Jia, J.: Tracking objects as pixel-wise distributions. arXiv preprint arXiv:2207.05518 (2022)

75. Zhou, Y., Tuzel, O.: VoxelNet: end-to-end learning for point cloud based 3D object detection. In: IEEE Conference on Computer Vision and Pattern Recognition (2018)

76. Zhu, J., Peng, B., Li, W., Shen, H., Zhang, Z., Lei, J.: Multi-view stereo with transformer. arXiv preprint arXiv:2112.00336 (2021)

RelPose: Predicting Probabilistic Relative Rotation for Single Objects in the Wild

Jason Y. Zhang[✉], Deva Ramanan, and Shubham Tulsiani

Carnegie Mellon University, Pittsburgh, PA 15213, USA
jasonyzhang@cmu.edu

Abstract. We describe a data-driven method for inferring the camera viewpoints given multiple images of an arbitrary object. This task is a core component of classic geometric pipelines such as SfM and SLAM, and also serves as a vital pre-processing requirement for contemporary neural approaches (e.g. NeRF) to object reconstruction and view synthesis. In contrast to existing correspondence-driven methods that do not perform well given sparse views, we propose a top-down prediction based approach for estimating camera viewpoints. Our key technical insight is the use of an energy-based formulation for representing distributions over relative camera rotations, thus allowing us to explicitly represent multiple camera modes arising from object symmetries or views. Leveraging these relative predictions, we jointly estimate a consistent set of camera rotations from multiple images. We show that our approach outperforms state-of-the-art SfM and SLAM methods given sparse images on both seen and unseen categories. Further, our probabilistic approach significantly outperforms directly regressing relative poses, suggesting that modeling multimodality is important for coherent joint reconstruction. We demonstrate that our system can be a stepping stone toward in-the-wild reconstruction from multi-view datasets. The project page with code and videos can be found at jasonyzhang.com/relpose.

Keywords: Pose prediction · Sparse-view 3D

1 Introduction

Recovering 3D from 2D images of an object has been a central task in vision across decades. Given multiple views, structure-from-motion (SfM) based methods can infer a 3D representation of the underlying instance while also associating each image with a camera viewpoint. However, these correspondence-driven methods cannot robustly handle sparsely sampled images that minimally overlap, and typically require many (>20) images for a 360-degree 3D inference.

Supplementary Information The online version contains supplementary material available at https://doi.org/10.1007/978-3-031-19821-2_34.

S. Avidan et al. (Eds.): ECCV 2022, LNCS 13691, pp. 592–611, 2022.
https://doi.org/10.1007/978-3-031-19821-2_34

Unfortunately, this requirement of densely sampled views can be prohibitive-online marketplaces often have only a few images per instance, and a user casually reconstructing a novel object would also find capturing such views tedious. Although the recently emerging neural 3D reconstruction techniques also typically leverage similarly dense views, some works have shown promise that a far smaller number of images can suffice for high-quality 3D reconstruction. These successes have however still relied on precisely [60] or approximately [20,27,82] known camera viewpoints for inference. To apply these methods at scale, we must therefore answer a fundamental question-*given sparsely sampled images of a generic object, how can we obtain the associated camera viewpoints?*

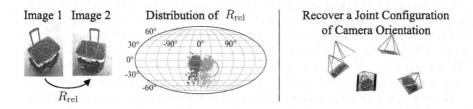

Fig. 1. Probabilistic Camera Rotation Estimation for Generic Objects. *Left*: Given two images of the same object, we predict a conditional distribution of relative camera viewpoint (rotation) that effectively handles symmetries and pose ambiguities. *Right*: Given a set of images, our approach outputs a configuration of camera rotations.

Existing methods do not provide a conclusive answer to this question. On the one hand, bottom-up correspondence-based techniques are not robustly applicable for sparse-view inference. On the other, recent neural multi-view methods can optimize already known approximate camera poses but provide no mechanism to obtain these to begin with. In this work, our goal is to fill this void and develop a method that, given a small number of unposed images of a generic object, can associate them with (approximate) camera viewpoints. Towards this goal, we focus on inferring the camera rotation matrices corresponding to each input image and propose a top-down approach to predict these. However, we note that the 'absolute' rotation is not well-defined given an image of a generic object-it assumes a 'canonical' pose which is not always known a-priori (e.g. what is an identity rotation for a pen? or a plant?). In contrast, the *relative* rotation between two views is well-defined even if a canonical pose for the instance is not. Thus, instead of adopting the common paradigm of single-image based pose prediction, we learn to estimate the relative pose given a pair of input images. We propose a system that leverages such pairwise predictions to then infer a consistent set of global rotations given multiple images of a generic object (Fig. 1).

A key technical question that we consider is regarding the formulation of such pairwise pose estimation. Given two informative views of a rotationally asymmetric object, a regression-based approach may be able to accurately predict their relative transformation. The general case however, can be more challenging - given two views of a cup but with the handle only visible in one, the relative pose is ambiguous given just the two images. To allow capturing this uncertainty, we formulate an energy-based relative pose prediction network that, given two images *and* a candidate relative rotation, outputs an energy corresponding to the (unnormalized) log-probability of the hypothesis. This probabilistic estimation of relative pose not only makes the learning more stable, but more importantly, provides a mechanism to estimate a *joint distribution* over viewpoints given multiple images. We show that optimizing rotations to improve this joint likelihood yields coherent poses given multiple images and leads to significant improvements over naive approaches that do not consider the joint likelihoods (Fig. 2).

We train our system using instances from over 40 commonplace object categories, and find that not only can it infer accurate (relative) poses for novel instances of these classes, it even generalizes to instances from unseen categories. Our approach can thus be viewed as a stepping stone toward sparse-view 3D reconstruction of generic objects; just as classical techniques provide precise camera poses that (neural) multi-view reconstruction methods can leverage, our work provides a similar, albeit coarser, output that can be used to initialize inference in current (and future) sparse-view reconstruction methods. While our system only outputs camera rotations, we note that a reasonable corresponding translation can be easily initialized assuming object-facing viewpoints, and we show that this suffices in practice for bootstrapping sparse-view reconstruction.

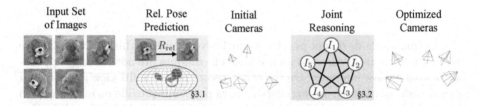

Fig. 2. Overview. From a set of images, we aim to recover corresponding camera poses (rotations). To do this, we train a pairwise pose predictor that takes in two images and a candidate relative rotation and predicts energy. By repeatedly querying this network, we recover a probability distribution over conditional relative rotations (see Sect. 3.1). We use these pairwise distributions to induce a joint likelihood over the camera transformations across multiple images, and iteratively improve an initial estimate by maximizing this likelihood (see Sect. 3.2).

2   Related Work

Structure-from-Motion (SfM). At a high level, structure-from-motion aims to recover 3D geometry and camera parameters from image sets. This is done classically by computing local image features [2,21,30,66], finding matches across images [31], and then estimating and verifying epipolar geometry using bundle adjustment [67]. Later works have scaled up the SfM pipeline using sequential algorithms, demonstrating results on hundreds or even thousands of images [18, 52,54,55,58].

The advent of deep learning has augmented various stages of the classical SfM pipeline. Better feature descriptors [14,15,46,49,57,72,79] and improved featured matching [9,16,29,53,68] have significantly outperformed their hand-crafted counterparts. BA-Net [63] and DeepSFM [75] have even replaced the bundle-adjustment process by optimizing over a cost volume. Most recently, Pixel-Perfect SfM [28] uses a featuremetric error to post-process camera poses to achieve sub-pixel accuracy.

While these methods can achieve excellent localization, all these approaches are bottom-up: beginning with local features that are matched across images. However, matching features requires sufficient overlap between images, which may not be possible given wide baseline views. While our work also aims to localize camera poses given image sets, our approach fundamentally differs because it is top-down and does not rely on low-level correspondences.

Simultaneous Localization and Mapping (SLAM). Related is the task of Monocular SLAM, which aims to localize and map the surroundings from a video stream. Indirect SLAM methods, similar to SfM, match local features across different images to localize the camera [5,37,38,51]. Direct SLAM methods, on the other hand, define a geometric objective function to directly optimize over a photometric error [11,17,56,87].

There have also been various attempts to introduce deep learning into SLAM pipelines. As with SfM, learned feature descriptors and matching have helped improve accuracy on SLAM subproblems and increased robustness. End-to-end deep SLAM methods [40,73,74,84] have improved the robustness of SLAM compared to classical methods, but have generally not closed the gap on performance. One notable exception is the recent DROID-SLAM [64], which combines the robustness of learning-based SLAM with the accuracy of classical SLAM.

These approaches all assume *sequential* streams and generally rely on matching or otherwise incorporating temporal locality between neighboring frames. We do not make any assumptions about the order of the image inputs nor the amount of overlap between nearby frames.

Single-view Pose Prediction. The task of predicting a (6-DoF) pose from a single image has a long and storied history, the surface of which can barely be scratched in this section. Unlike relative pose between multiple images, the (absolute) pose given a single image is only well-defined if there exists a canonical coordinate system. Most single-view pose prediction approaches therefore deal with a fixed set of categories, each of which has a canonical coordinate system defined *a priori* [4,7,23,24,26,39,42,43,59,65,71,77]. Other methods that are category-agnostic take in a 3D mesh or point cloud as input, which provides a local coordinate system [44,76,78,81].

Perhaps most relevant to us are approaches that not only predict pose but also model inherent uncertainty in the pose prediction [3,10,12,13,19,25,33,36, 39,45,47,61]. Like our approach, VpDR-Net [41] uses relative poses as supervision but still predicts absolute pose (with a unimodal Gaussian uncertainty model). Implicit-PDF [39] is the most similar approach to ours and served as an inspiration. Similar to our approach, Implicit-PDF uses a neural network to implicitly represent probability using an energy-based formulation which elegantly handles symmetries and multimodal distributions. Unlike our approach, Implicit-PDF (and all other single-view pose prediction methods) predict *absolute* pose, which does not exist in general for generic or novel categories. Instead, we model probability distributions over relative pose given pairs of images.

Learning-Based Relative Pose Prediction. When considering generic scenes, prior works have investigated the task of relative pose prediction given two images. However, these supervised [69] or self-supervised [32,70,80,85] methods typically consider prediction of motion between consecutive frames and are not easily adapted to wide-baseline prediction. While some approaches have investigated wide baseline prediction [1,34], regression-based inference does not effectively capture uncertainty unlike our energy-based model. Perhaps most similar to ours is DirectionNet [8] which also predicts a camera distribution for wide baseline views. While DirectionNet only uses the expected value of the distribution and thus ignores symmetry, we take advantage of multimodal distributions to improve our joint pose estimation.

3   Method

Given a set of N images $\{I_1, \ldots I_N\}$ depicting a *generic* object in-the-wild, we aim to recover a set of N rotation matrices $\{R_1, \ldots, R_N\}$ such that rotation matrix R_i corresponds to the viewpoint of the camera used to take image i. Note that while we do not model translation, it can be easily initialized using object-facing viewpoints for 3D object reconstruction [27,82] or a pose graph for SLAM [6]. We are primarily interested in settings with only sparse views and wide baselines. While bottom-up correspondence based techniques can reliably recover camera pose given dense views, they do not adapt well to sparse views with minimal overlap. We instead propose a prediction-based top-down approach that can learn and exploit the global structure directly.

The basic building block of our prediction system (visualized in Fig. 3) is a pairwise pose predictor that infers *relative* camera orientations given pairs of images. However, symmetries in objects and possibly uninformative viewpoints make this an inherently uncertain prediction task. To allow capturing this uncertainty, we propose an energy-based approach that models the *multi-modal distribution* over relative poses given two images.

Given the predicted distributions over pairwise relative rotations, we show that these can be leveraged to induce a *joint* distribution over the rotations. Starting with a greedy initialization, we present a coordinate-ascent approach that jointly reasons over and improves the set of inferred rotations. We describe

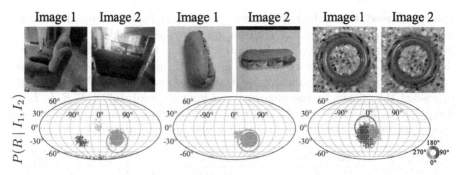

Fig. 3. Predicted conditional distribution of image pairs from unseen categories. Here, we visualize the predicted conditional distribution of image pairs. Inspired by [39], we visualize the rotation distribution (Algorithm 1) by plotting yaw as latitude, pitch as longitude, and roll as the color. The size of each circle is proportional to the probability of that rotation. We omit rotations with negligible probability. The center of the open circle represents the ground truth. We can see that network predicts 4 modes for the couch images, corresponding roughly to 90 °C increments, with the greatest probability assigned to the correct 90 °C rotation. The relative pose of the hot dog is unambiguous and thus only has one mode. While the relative pose for the frisbee has close to no pitch or yaw, the roll remains ambiguous, hence the variety in colors. See the supplement for a visualization of how to interpret the relative rotations.

our approach for modeling probability distributions over relative poses between two images in Sect. 3.1, and build on this in Sect. 3.2 to recover a joint set of poses across multiple images. Finally, we discuss implementation details in Sect. 3.3.

3.1 Estimating Pair-Wise Relative Rotations

Given a pair of images depicting an arbitrary object, we aim to predict a distribution over the relative rotation corresponding to the camera transformation between the two views. As there may be ambiguities when inferring the relative pose given two images, we introduce a formulation that can model uncertainty.

```
procedure PAIRWISEDISTRIBUTION(I₁, I₂)
    queries ← SAMPLEROTATIONSUNIF(50000)
    energies ← f(I₁, I₂, queries)
    probs ← SOFTMAX(energies)
    return queries, probs
end procedure
```

Algorithm 1: Pseudo-code for recovering a pairwise distribution. We describe how to recover the distribution of the relative pose given images.

Energy-Based Formulation. We wish to model the conditional distribution over a relative rotation matrix R given input images I_1 and I_2: $P(R \mid I_1, I_2)$. Inspired by recent work on *implicitly* representing the distribution over rotations using a neural network [39], we propose using an energy-based relative pose estimator. More specifically, we train a network $f(R, I_1, I_2)$ that learns to predict the energy, or the unnormalized joint log-probability, $P(R, I_1, I_2) = \alpha \exp f(R, I_1, I_2)$ where α is the constant of integration. From the product rule, we can recover the conditional probability as a function of f:

$$P(R \mid I_1, I_2) = \frac{P(R, I_1, I_2)}{P(I_1, I_2)} \approx \frac{\alpha \exp f(R, I_1, I_2)}{\sum_{R'} \alpha \exp f(R', I_1, I_2)} = \frac{\exp f(R, I_1, I_2)}{\sum_{R'} \exp f(R', I_1, I_2)}$$
(1)

We marginalize over rotations to avoid having to compute α (see Algorithm 1), but note that the number of sampled rotations should be large for the approximation to be accurate. It is therefore important to use a lightweight network f since it is queried once per sampled rotation in the denominator.

Training. We train our network by maximizing the log-likelihood of the conditional distribution, or equivalently minimizing the negative log-likelihood:

$$\mathcal{L} = -\log P(R_1^\top R_2 \mid I_1, I_2)$$
(2)

where R_1 and R_2 are the ground truth poses of I_1 and I_2 respectively. Note that while the 'absolute' poses (R_1, R_2) are in an arbitrary coordinate system (depending on e.g. SLAM system outputs), the relative pose $R_1^\top R_2$ between two views is agnostic to this incidental canonical frame. Following (1), we sample multiple candidate rotation matrices to compute the conditional probability.

Inference. Recovering the optimal transformation from the pose of I_1 to I_2 amounts to optimizing f over the space of rotations:

$$R^* = \arg\max_{R \in \mathbf{SO}(3)} P(R \mid I_1, I_2) = \arg\max_{R \in \mathbf{SO}(3)} f(R, I_1, I_2)$$
(3)

In practice, the loss landscape of f is often un-smooth, so we find that sampling and scoring rotations based on f to be more effective than gradient ascent.

We can also compute the conditional distribution of the relative rotation from I_1 to I_2 by sampling rotations over $\mathbf{SO}(3)$. The probability associated with each rotation can be computed using a softmax function, as described Algorithm 1 and derived in (1). Inspired by [39], we can visualize the distribution of rotations by projecting the rotation matrices on a 2-sphere using pitch and yaw and coloring the rotation based on roll. See Fig. 3 and the supplement for sample results.

3.2   Recovering Joint Poses

In the previous section, we describe an energy-based relative pose predictor conditioned on pairs of images. Using this network, we recover a coherent set of rotations when given a set of images.

Greedy Initialization. Given predictions for relative rotations between every pair of images, we aim to associate each image with an absolute rotation. However, as the relative poses are invariant up to a global rotation, we can treat the pose of the first image as the identity matrix: $R_1 = I$. We note that the rotations for the other images can be uniquely induced given any $N - 1$ relative rotations that span a tree.

---

procedure COORDASC(Images $\{I_i\}_N$)
  $\{R_i\}_N \leftarrow$ INITIALIZEROTATIONS($\{I_i\}_N$)
  for $t \in 1, \ldots,$ Num Iterations **do**
    $k \leftarrow$ RANDOMINTEGER(N)
    ▷ R'_k ($Q{\times}3{\times}3$): Q replacements for R_k
    $R'_k \leftarrow$ SAMPLEROTATIONSUNIF($Q{=}250000$)
    energs $\leftarrow$ ZEROS(Q)
    for $i \in 1, \ldots, N$ **and** $i \neq k$ **do**
      $R \leftarrow$ REPEAT(R_i, Q) ▷ $3{\times}3{\rightarrow}Q{\times}3{\times}3$
      energs $\leftarrow$ energs $+ f(I_i, I_k, R^{\top} R'_k)$
      energs $\leftarrow$ energs $+ f(I_k, I_i, R'^{\top}_k R)$
    end for
    $R_k \leftarrow R'_k[$ARGMAX(energs)$]$
  end for
end procedure

Algorithm 2: Pseudo-code for joint inference using relative pose predictor. We describe how to recover the joint poses given n images via coordinate ascent.

Sequential Chain. Perhaps the simplest way to construct such a tree is to treat the images as part of an ordered sequence. Given $R_1 = I$, all subsequent poses can be computed by using the best scoring relative pose from the previous image: $R_i = R_{i-1} R^*_{(i-1) \rightarrow i}$, denoting $R_{i \rightarrow j}$ as the relative rotation matrix $R_i^{\top} R_j$. However, this assumes that the images are captured sequentially (e.g. in a video) and may not be applicable for settings such as online marketplaces.

Maximum Spanning Tree. We improve over the naive linear chain by recognizing that some pairs of images may produce more confident predictions. Given N images, we construct a directed graph with $N \cdot (N - 1)$ edges, where the weight of edge $(i, j) = P(R^*_{i \rightarrow j} | I_i, I_j)$. We then construct a Maximum Spanning Tree (MST) that covers all images with the most confident set of relative rotations.

Reasoning over All Images Jointly. Both of the previous methods, which select a subset of edges, do not perform any joint reasoning and discard all but the highest scoring mode for each pair of images. Instead, we can take advantage of our energy-based formulation to enforce global consistency.

Given our pairwise conditional probabilities, we can define a joint distribution over the set of rotations:

$$P\left(\{R_i\}_{i=1}^N \mid \{I_i\}_{i=1}^N\right) = \alpha \exp\left(\sum_{(i,j) \in \mathcal{P}} f(R_{i \rightarrow j} \mid I_i, I_j) \right) \qquad (4)$$

where $\mathcal{P} = \{(i, j) \mid (i, j) \in [N] \times [N], i \neq j\}$ is the $N(N-1)$ set of pairwise permutations and α is the normalizing constant. Intuitively, this corresponds to the distribution modeled by a factor graph with a potential function corresponding to each pairwise edge.

We then aim to find the most likely set of rotations $\{R_1, \ldots, R_N\}$ under this conditional joint distribution (assuming $R_1 = I$). While it is not feasible to analytically obtain the global maxima, we adopt an optimization-based approach and iteratively improve the current estimate. More specifically, we initialize the set of poses with the greedy MST solution and at each iteration, we randomly select a rotation R_k to update. Assuming fixed values for $\{R_i\}_{i \neq k}$, we then search for the rotation R_k under the conditional distribution that maximizes the overall likelihood. We show in supplementary that this in fact corresponds to computing the most likely hypothesis under the distribution $P(R_k' \mid \{R_i\}_{i \neq k}, \{I_i\}_i)$:

$$\log P(R_k' \mid \{R_i\}_{i \neq k}, \{I_i\}_i) = \sum_{i \neq k} \left(f(R_{i \to k'}, I_i, I_k) + f(R_{k' \to i}, I_k, I_i) \right) + C \quad (5)$$

Analogous to our approach for finding the optimal solution for a single relative rotation, we sample multiple hypotheses for the rotation R_k, and select the hypothesis that maximizes (5). We find that this search-based block coordinate ascent helps us consistently improve over the initial solution while avoiding the local optima that a continuous optimization is susceptible to. We provide pseudo-code in Algorithm 2 and visualize one iteration of coordinate ascent in Fig. 4.

3.3 Implementation Details

Network Architecture. We use a ResNet-50 [22] with anti-aliasing [83] to extract image features. We use a lightweight 3-layer MLP that takes in a concatenation of 2 sets of image features and a rotation matrix to predict energy. We use positional encoding [35,62] directly on flattened 3×3 rotation matrix, similar to [39]. See the supplement for architecture diagrams.

Number of Rotation Samples. We use the equivolumetric sampling in [39] to compute query rotations (37k total rotations) during training. For each iteration of coordinate ascent, we randomly sample 250k rotation matrices. For visualizing distributions, we randomly sample 50k rotations.

Runtime. We train the pairwise estimator with a batch size of 64 images for approximately 2 days on 4 NVIDIA 2080TI GPUs. Inference for 20 images takes around 1–2 s to construct an MST and around 2 min for 200 iterations of coordinate ascent on a single 2080TI. Note that the runtime of the coordinate ascent scales linearly with the number of images.

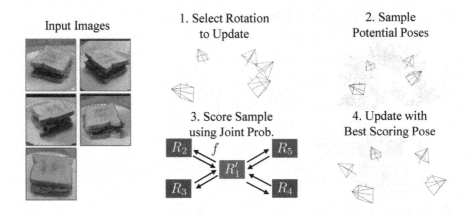

Fig. 4. Recovering Joint Poses with Coordinate Ascent. Given a set of images $\{I_1, \ldots, I_N\}$, we initialize a set of corresponding poses $\{R_1, \ldots, R_N\}$. During each iteration of coordinate ascent, we: 1) randomly select one pose R_k to update (the red camera in this case); 2) sample a large number (250k) of candidate poses; 3) score each pose according to the joint distribution conditioned on the other poses and images (5); and 4) update with the highest scoring pose. See Sect. 3.2 for more detail.

4 Evaluation

4.1 Experimental Setup

Dataset. We train and test on the Common Objects in 3D dataset (CO3D) [48], a large-scale dataset consisting of turntable-style videos of 51 common object categories. We train on the subset of the dataset that has camera poses, which were acquired by running COLMAP [54] over all frames of the video.

To train our network, we sample random frames and their associated camera poses from each video sequence. We train on 12,299 video sequences (from the **train-known** split) from 41 categories, holding out 10 categories to test generalization. We evaluate on 1,711 video sequences (from the **test-known** split) over all 41 trained categories (seen) as well as the 10 held out categories (unseen). The 10 held out categories are: **ball**, **book**, **couch**, **frisbee**, **hotdog**, **kite**, **remote**, **sandwich**, **skateboard**, and **suitcase**. We selected these categories randomly after excluding some of the categories with the most training images.

Task and Metrics. We consider the task of sparse-view camera pose estimation with $N = 3$, 5, 10, and 20 images, subsampled from a video sequence. This is highly challenging, especially when $N \leq 10$, because the ground truth camera poses have wide baselines.

We consider two possible ways to select N frames from a video sequence. First, we can randomly sample a set of N indices per video sequence (Random). Alternatively, we can use N uniformly-spaced frame indices (Uniform). We note

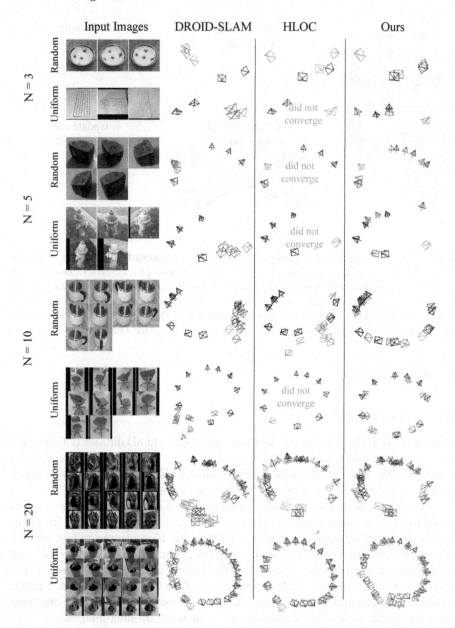

Fig. 5. Qualitative Comparison of Recovered Camera Poses with Baselines. We visualize the camera poses (rotations) predicted by DROID-SLAM, COLMAP with SuperPoint/SuperGlue, and our method given sparse image frames. The black cameras correspond to the ground truth. We only visualize the rotations predicted by each method, and set the translation such that the object center is a fixed distance away along the camera axis. As the poses are agnostic to a global rotation, we align the predicted cameras across all methods to the ground truth coordinate system by setting the recovered camera pose for the first image to the corresponding ground truth (visualized in green). Odd rows correspond to randomly sampled image frames, while even rows correspond to uniformly-spaced image frames. (Colot figure online)

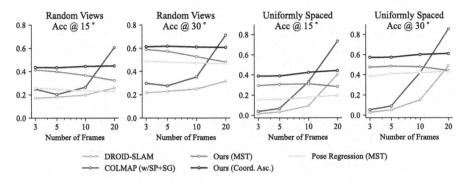

Fig. 6. Mean Accuracy on *Seen* Categories. We evaluate our approach against competitive SLAM (DROID-SLAM) and SfM (COLMAP with SuperPoint + Super-Glue) baselines in sparse-view settings. We also train a direct relative rotation predictor (Pose Regression) that is not probabilistic and uses the MST generated by our method to recover joint pose. We consider both randomly sampling and uniformly spacing frames from a video sequence. We report the proportion of pairwise relative poses that are within 15 and 30 °C of the ground truth, averaged over all seen categories. We find that our approach shines with fewer views because it does not rely on correspondences and thus can handle wide baseline views. Correspondence-based approach need about 20 images to begin to work.

that because CO3D video sequences are commonly taken in a turntable fashion, the uniformly spaced sampling strategy may be more representative of real world distributions of sparse view image sets. We report metrics on both task setups.

Because the global transformation of the camera poses is ambiguous, we evaluate each pair of relative rotations. For each of the $N(N-1)$ pairs, we compare the angular difference between the relative predicted rotation and the relative ground truth rotation using Rodrigues' formula [50]. We report the proportion of relative rotations that are within 15 and 30 °C of the ground truth. We note that rotation errors within this range are relatively easy to handle by downstream 3D reconstruction tasks (See Fig. 10 for an example).

Baselines. We compare against DROID-SLAM [64], a current state-of-the-art SLAM approach that incorporates learning in an optimization framework. Note that DROID-SLAM requires trajectories and camera intrinsics. Thus, we provide the DROID-SLAM baseline with sorted frame indices and intrinsics, but do not provide these to any other method.

We also compare with a state-of-the-art structure-from-motion pipeline that uses COLMAP [54] with SuperPoint feature extraction [14] and SuperGlue matching [53]. We used the implementation provided by [52]. For instances for which COLMAP does not converge or is unable to localize some cameras, we treat the missing poses as identity rotation for evaluation. We note that DROID-SLAM also outputs approximate identity rotations when the optimization fails.

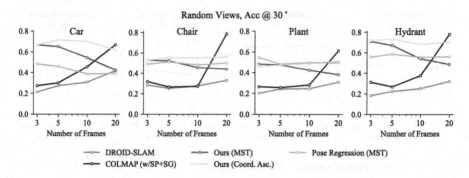

Fig. 7. Accuracy on Subset of *Seen* Categories. Here we compare all approaches on a representative subset of seen categories. We find that direct regression of relative poses (purple) struggles more on categories with symmetry (Car, Hydrant) than categories without symmetry (Chair, Plant), suggesting that multimodal prediction is important for resolving ambiguity. (Color figure online)

Ablations. In the spirit of learning-based solutions that directly regress pose, we train a network that predicts relative rotation directly given two images. Similar to our energy-based predictor, we pass the concatenated images features from a ResNet-50 into an MLP. We double the number of layers from 3 to 6 and add a skip connection to give this network increased capacity. Rotations are predicted using the 6D rotation representation [86]. See the supplement for additional architecture details. The relative pose regressor cannot directly predict poses for more than two images. To recover sets of poses from sets of images, we use the MST graph recovered by our method to link the pairs of relative rotations (we find that this performs better than linking the relative rotations sequentially).

To demonstrate the benefits of joint reasoning, we additionally report the performance of our method using the greedy Maximum Spanning Tree (MST) solution. The performance of the sequential solution is in the supplement.

4.2   Quantitative Evaluation

We evaluate all approaches on sparse-view camera pose estimation by averaging over all seen categories in Fig. 6. We find that our approach outperforms all baselines for $N \leq 10$ images. Correspondence-based approaches (DROID-SLAM and COLMAP) do not work until roughly 20 images, at which point image frames have sufficient overlap for local correspondences. However, real world multi-view data (e.g. marketplace images) typically have much fewer images. We find that coordinate ascent helps our approach scale with more image frames whereas the greedy maximum spanning tree accumulates errors with more frames.

Directly predicting relative poses does not perform well, possibly because pose regression cannot model multiple modes, which is important for symmetrical objects. We visualize the performance for four categories in Fig. 7. We find that the performance gap between our approach and direct regression is larger for

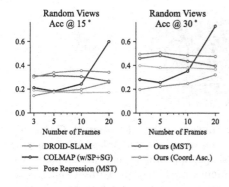

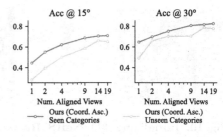

Fig. 8. Mean Accuracy on *Unseen* Categories. We evaluate our approach on held out categories from CO3D.

Fig. 9. Novel View Registration. Here, we evaluate the task of registering a new view given previously aligned cameras. We find that adding more views improves performance, suggesting that additional views reduce ambiguity.

objects with some symmetry (car, hydrant) than for objects without symmetry (chair, plant). Moreover, unlike our energy-based approach that models a joint distribution, a regression-based method does not allow similar joint reasoning.

We also test the generalization of our approach for *unseen* categories in Fig. 8. We still find that our method significantly outperforms all other approaches with sparse view ($N \leq 10$) even for never-before-seen object categories, indicating its ability to handle generic objects beyond training. The per-category evaluation for both seen and unseen categories are in the supplement.

Novel View Registration. In our standard SfM-inspired task setup, we aim to recover N camera poses given N images. Intuitively, adding images reduces ambiguity, but recovering additional cameras is also more challenging. To disambiguate between the two, we evaluate the task of registering new views given previously aligned images in Fig. 9. Given $N+1$ images, of which N have aligned cameras, we use our energy-based regressor to recover the remaining camera (equivalent to one iteration of coordinate ascent). We find that adding images improves accuracy, suggesting that additional views can reduce ambiguity.

4.3 Qualitative Results

We show qualitative results on the outputs of our pairwise predictor in Fig. 3. The visualized distributions suggest that our model is learning useful information about symmetry and can model multiple modes even for unseen categories.

We visualize predicted camera poses for DROID-SLAM, COLMAP, and our method with coordinate ascent in Fig. 5. Unable to bridge the domain gap from narrow baseline video frames, DROID-SLAM often gets stuck in the trajectory. Although COLMAP sometimes fails to converge, it performs well for $N = 20$. Our approach consistently outputs plausible interpretations but is unable to achieve *precise* localization. See supplementary for visualizations on randomly selected sequences and more category-specific discussion.

Fig. 10. Initializing 3D NeRS Reconstruction using Predicted Cameras. NeRS [82] is a representative 3D reconstruction approach that takes noisy cameras as initialization and jointly optimizes object shape, appearance, and camera poses. We run our method with coordinate ascent on 7 input images of a fire hydrant and 4 input images of a motorbike to obtain the camera initialization (green), which we provide to NeRS. NeRS then finetunes the cameras (red) and outputs a 3D reconstruction. (Color figure online)

We also validate that our camera pose estimations can be used for downstream 3D reconstruction. We use our camera poses to initialize NeRS [82], a representative sparse-view surface-based approach that requires a (noisy) camera initialization. Using our cameras, we successfully reconstruct a 3D model of a fire hydrant from 7 images and a motorbike from 4 images in Fig. 10. Note that the camera pose initialization in the original NeRS paper was manually selected.

5   Discussion

We presented a prediction-based approach for estimating camera rotations given (a sparse set of) images of a generic object. Our energy-based formulation allows capturing the underlying uncertainty in relative poses, while also enabling joint reasoning over multiple images. We believe our system's robustness under sparse views can allow it to serve as a stepping stone for initializing (neural) reconstruction methods in the wild, but also note that there are several open challenges. First, our work reasoned about the joint distribution using only pairwise potentials and developing efficient higher-order energy models may further improve performance. Moreover, while we outperform existing techniques given sparse-views, the correspondence-driven methods are more accurate given a large number of views, and we hope future efforts can unify the two approaches. Finally, our approach may not be directly applicable to reasoning about camera transformations for arbitrary scenes as modeling camera translation would be more important compared to object-centric images.

Acknowledgements. We would like to thank Gengshan Yang, Jonathon Luiten, Brian Okorn, and Elliot Wu for helpful feedback and discussion. This work was supported in part by the NSF GFRP (Grant No. DGE1745016), Singapore DSTA, and CMU Argo AI Center for Autonomous Vehicle Research.

References

1. Balntas, V., Li, S., Prisacariu, V.: RelocNet: continuous metric learning relocalisation using neural nets. In: Ferrari, V., Hebert, M., Sminchisescu, C., Weiss, Y. (eds.) Computer Vision – ECCV 2018. LNCS, vol. 11218, pp. 782–799. Springer, Cham (2018). https://doi.org/10.1007/978-3-030-01264-9_46
2. Bay, H., Tuytelaars, T., Van Gool, L.: SURF: speeded up robust features. In: Leonardis, A., Bischof, H., Pinz, A. (eds.) ECCV 2006. LNCS, vol. 3951, pp. 404–417. Springer, Heidelberg (2006). https://doi.org/10.1007/11744023_32
3. Brachmann, E., Michel, F., Krull, A., Yang, M.Y., Gumhold, S., et al.: Uncertainty-driven 6D pose estimation of objects and scenes from a single RGB image. In: CVPR (2016)
4. Bukschat, Y., Vetter, M.: EfficientPose: an efficient, accurate and scalable end-to-end 6D multi object pose estimation approach. arXiv:2011.04307 (2020)
5. Campos, C., Elvira, R., Gómez, J.J., Montiel, J.M.M., Tardós, J.D.: ORB-SLAM3: an accurate open-source library for visual visual-inertial and multi-map SLAM. T-RO 37(6), 1874–1890 (2021)
6. Carlone, L., Tron, R., Daniilidis, K., Dellaert, F.: Initialization techniques for 3D SLAM: a survey on rotation estimation and its use in pose graph optimization. ICRA (2015)
7. Chen, B., Chin, T.J., Klimavicius, M.: Occlusion-robust object pose estimation with holistic representation. In: WACV (2022)
8. Chen, K., Snavely, N., Makadia, A.: Wide-baseline relative camera pose estimation with directional learning. In: CVPR (2021)
9. Choy, C.B., Gwak, J., Savarese, S., Chandraker, M.: Universal correspondence network. In: NeurIPS (2016)
10. Corona, E., Kundu, K., Fidler, S.: Pose estimation for objects with rotational symmetry. In: IROS (2018)
11. Davison, A.J., Reid, I.D., Molton, N.D., Stasse, O.: MonoSLAM: real-time single camera SLAM. TPAMI 29(6), 1052–1067 (2007)
12. Deng, X., Mousavian, A., Xiang, Y., Xia, F., Bretl, T., Fox, D.: PoseRBPF: a rao-blackwellized particle filter for 6D object pose tracking. In: RSS (2019)
13. Deng, X., Xiang, Y., Mousavian, A., Eppner, C., Bretl, T., Fox, D.: Self-supervised 6D object pose estimation for robot manipulation. In: ICRA (2020)
14. DeTone, D., Malisiewicz, T., Rabinovich, A.: SuperPoint: self-supervised interest point detection and description. In: CVPR-W (2018)
15. Dusmanu, M., et al.: D2-Net: a trainable CNN for joint detection and description of local features. In: CVPR (2019)
16. Dusmanu, Mihai, Schönberger, Johannes L.., Pollefeys, Marc: Multi-view optimization of local feature geometry. In: Vedaldi, Andrea, Bischof, Horst, Brox, Thomas, Frahm, Jan-Michael. (eds.) ECCV 2020. LNCS, vol. 12346, pp. 670–686. Springer, Cham (2020). https://doi.org/10.1007/978-3-030-58452-8_39
17. Engel, J., Koltun, V., Cremers, D.: Direct sparse odometry. TPAMI (2018)
18. Furukawa, Y., Curless, B., Seitz, S.M., Szeliski, R.: Towards internet-scale multiview stereo. In: CVPR (2010)
19. Gilitschenski, I., Sahoo, R., Schwarting, W., Amini, A., Karaman, S., Rus, D.: Deep orientation uncertainty learning based on a Bingham loss. In: ICLR (2019)
20. Goel, S., Gkioxari, G., Malik, J.: Differentiable stereopsis: meshes from multiple views using differentiable rendering. In: CVPR (2022)

21. Harris, C., Stephens, M.: A Combined corner and edge detector. In: Alvey Vision Conference (1988)
22. He, K., Zhang, X., Ren, S., Sun, J.: Deep residual learning for image recognition. In: CVPR (2016)
23. Iwase, S., Liu, X., Khirodkar, R., Yokota, R., Kitani, K.M.: RePOSE: fast 6D object pose refinement via deep texture rendering. In: ICCV (2021)
24. Kehl, W., Manhardt, F., Tombari, F., Ilic, S., Navab, N.: SSD-6D: making RGB-based 3D detection and 6D pose estimation great again. In: ICCV (2017)
25. Kendall, A., Cipolla, R.: Modelling uncertainty in deep learning for camera relocalization. In: ICRA (2016)
26. Kendall, A., Grimes, M., Cipolla, R.: PoseNet: a convolutional network for real-time 6-DOF camera relocalization. In: ICCV (2015)
27. Lin, C.H., Ma, W.C., Torralba, A., Lucey, S.: BARF: bundle-adjusting neural radiance fields. In: ICCV (2021)
28. Lindenberger, P., Sarlin, P.E., Larsson, V., Pollefeys, M.: Pixel-perfect structure-from-motion with featuremetric refinement. In: ICCV (2021)
29. Liu, C., Yuen, J., Torralba, A.: SIFT flow: dense correspondence across scenes and its applications. TPAMI **33**(5), 978–994 (2010)
30. Lowe, D.G.: Distinctive image features from scale-invariant keypoints. IJCV **60**(2), 91–110 (2004)
31. Lucas, B.D., Kanade, T.: An iterative image registration technique with an application to stereo vision. In: IJCAI (1981)
32. Mahjourian, R., Wicke, M., Angelova, A.: Unsupervised learning of depth and ego-motion from monocular video using 3D geometric constraints. In: CVPR (2018)
33. Manhardt, F., et al.: Explaining the ambiguity of object detection and 6D pose from visual data. In: ICCV (2019)
34. Melekhov, I., Ylioinas, J., Kannala, J., Rahtu, E.: Relative camera pose estimation using convolutional neural networks. In: ACIVS (2017)
35. Mildenhall, B., Srinivasan, P.P., Tancik, M., Barron, J.T., Ramamoorthi, R., Ng, R.: NeRF: representing scenes as neural radiance fields for view synthesis. In: Vedaldi, A., Bischof, H., Brox, T., Frahm, J.-M. (eds.) ECCV 2020. LNCS, vol. 12346, pp. 405–421. Springer, Cham (2020). https://doi.org/10.1007/978-3-030-58452-8_24
36. Mohlin, D., Sullivan, J., Bianchi, G.: Probabilistic orientation estimation with matrix fisher distributions. In: NeurIPS (2020)
37. Mur-Artal, R., Montiel, J.M.M., Tardos, J.D.: ORB-SLAM: a versatile and accurate monocular SLAM system. T-RO **31**(5), 1147–1163 (2015)
38. Mur-Artal, R., Tardós, J.D.: ORB-SLAM2: an open-source SLAM system for monocular stereo and RGB-D cameras. T-RO **33**(5), 1255–1262 (2017)
39. Murphy, K.A., Esteves, C., Jampani, V., Ramalingam, S., Makadia, A.: Implicit-PDF: non-parametric representation of probability distributions on the rotation manifold. In: ICML (2021)
40. Newcombe, R.A., Lovegrove, S.J., Davison, A.J.: DTAM: dense tracking and mapping in real-time. In: ICCV (2011)
41. Novotny, D., Larlus, D., Vedaldi, A.: Learning 3D object categories by looking around them. In: ICCV (2017)
42. Novotny, D., Ravi, N., Graham, B., Neverova, N., Vedaldi, A.: C3DPO: canonical 3D pose networks for non-rigid structure from motion. In: ICCV (2019)
43. Oberweger, M., Rad, M., Lepetit, V.: Making deep heatmaps robust to partial occlusions for 3D object pose estimation. In: Ferrari, V., Hebert, M., Sminchisescu,

C., Weiss, Y. (eds.) ECCV 2018. LNCS, vol. 11219, pp. 125–141. Springer, Cham (2018). https://doi.org/10.1007/978-3-030-01267-0_8

44. Okorn, B., Gu, Q., Hebert, M., Held, D.: ZePHyR: zero-shot pose hypothesis scoring. In: ICRA (2021)
45. Okorn, B., Xu, M., Hebert, M., Held, D.: Learning orientation distributions for object pose estimation. In: IROS (2020)
46. Pautrat, R., Larsson, V., Oswald, M.R., Pollefeys, M.: Online invariance selection for local feature descriptors. In: Vedaldi, A., Bischof, H., Brox, T., Frahm, J.-M. (eds.) ECCV 2020. LNCS, vol. 12347, pp. 707–724. Springer, Cham (2020). https://doi.org/10.1007/978-3-030-58536-5_42
47. Prokudin, S., Gehler, P., Nowozin, S.: Deep directional statistics: pose estimation with uncertainty quantification. In: Ferrari, V., Hebert, M., Sminchisescu, C., Weiss, Y. (eds.) ECCV 2018. LNCS, vol. 11213, pp. 542–559. Springer, Cham (2018). https://doi.org/10.1007/978-3-030-01240-3_33
48. Reizenstein, J., Shapovalov, R., Henzler, P., Sbordone, L., Labatut, P., Novotny, D.: Common objects in 3D: large-scale learning and evaluation of real-life 3D category reconstruction. In: ICCV (2021)
49. Revaud, J., De Souza, C., Humenberger, M., Weinzaepfel, P.: R2D2: reliable and repeatable detector and descriptor. In: NeurIPS (2019)
50. Rodrigues, O.: Des lois géométriques qui régissent les déplacements d'un système solide dans l'espace, et de la variation des coordonnées provenant de ces déplacements considérés indépendamment des causes qui peuvent les produire. Journal de Mathématiques Pures et Appliquées **5** (1840)
51. Rosinol, A., Abate, M., Chang, Y., Carlone, L.: Kimera: an open-source library for real-time metric-semantic localization and mapping. In: ICRA (2020)
52. Sarlin, P.E., Cadena, C., Siegwart, R., Dymczyk, M.: From coarse to fine: robust hierarchical localization at large scale. In: CVPR (2019)
53. Sarlin, P.E., DeTone, D., Malisiewicz, T., Rabinovich, A.: SuperGlue: learning feature matching with graph neural networks. In: CVPR (2020)
54. Schönberger, J.L., Frahm, J.M.: Structure-from-motion revisited. In: CVPR (2016)
55. Schönberger, J.L., Zheng, E., Frahm, J.-M., Pollefeys, M.: Pixelwise view selection for unstructured multi-view stereo. In: Leibe, B., Matas, J., Sebe, N., Welling, M. (eds.) ECCV 2016. LNCS, vol. 9907, pp. 501–518. Springer, Cham (2016). https://doi.org/10.1007/978-3-319-46487-9_31
56. Schops, T., Sattler, T., Pollefeys, M.: BAD SLAM: bundle adjusted direct RGB-D SLAM. In: CVPR (2019)
57. Simonyan, K., Vedaldi, A., Zisserman, A.: Learning local feature descriptors using convex optimisation. TPAMI **36**(8), 1573–1585 (2014)
58. Snavely, N., Seitz, S.M., Szeliski, R.: Photo tourism: exploring photo collections in 3D. In: SIGGRAPH. ACM (2006)
59. Song, C., Song, J., Huang, Q.: HybridPose: 6D object pose estimation under hybrid representations. In: CVPR (2020)
60. Sun, X., et al.: Pix3D: dataset and methods for single-image 3D shape modeling. In: CVPR (2018)
61. Sundermeyer, M., Marton, Z.-C., Durner, M., Brucker, M., Triebel, R.: Implicit 3D orientation learning for 6D object detection from RGB images. In: Ferrari, V., Hebert, M., Sminchisescu, C., Weiss, Y. (eds.) ECCV 2018. LNCS, vol. 11210, pp. 712–729. Springer, Cham (2018). https://doi.org/10.1007/978-3-030-01231-1_43
62. Tancik, M., et al.: Fourier features let networks learn high frequency functions in low dimensional domains. In: NeurIPS (2020)

63. Tang, C., Tan, P.: BA-Net: dense bundle adjustment network. In: ICLR (2019)
64. Teed, Z., Deng, J.: DROID-SLAM: deep visual SLAM for monocular, stereo, and RGB-D cameras. In: NeurIPS (2021)
65. Tekin, B., Sinha, S.N., Fua, P.: Real-time seamless single shot 6D object pose prediction. In: CVPR (2018)
66. Tola, E., Lepetit, V., Fua, P.: Daisy: an efficient dense descriptor applied to wide-baseline stereo. TPAMI **32**(5), 815–830 (2009)
67. Triggs, B., McLauchlan, P.F., Hartley, R.I., Fitzgibbon, A.W.: Bundle adjustment–a modern synthesis. In: International Workshop on Vision Algorithms (1999)
68. Truong, P., Danelljan, M., Timofte, R.: GLU-Net: global-local universal network for dense flow and correspondences. In: CVPR (2020)
69. Ummenhofer, B., et al.: DeMoN: depth and motion network for learning monocular stereo. In: CVPR (2017)
70. Vijayanarasimhan, S., Ricco, S., Schmid, C., Sukthankar, R., Fragkiadaki, K.: SfM-Net: learning of structure and motion from video. arXiv:1704.07804 (2017)
71. Wang, C., et al.: DenseFusion: 6D object pose estimation by iterative dense fusion. In: CVPR (2019)
72. Wang, Q., Zhou, X., Hariharan, B., Snavely, N.: Learning feature descriptors using camera pose supervision. In: Vedaldi, A., Bischof, H., Brox, T., Frahm, J.-M. (eds.) ECCV 2020. LNCS, vol. 12346, pp. 757–774. Springer, Cham (2020). https://doi.org/10.1007/978-3-030-58452-8_44
73. Wang, S., Clark, R., Wen, H., Trigoni, N.: DeepVO: towards end-to-end visual odometry with deep recurrent convolutional neural networks. In: ICRA (2017)
74. Wang, W., Hu, Y., Scherer, S.: TartanVO: a generalizable learning-based VO. In: CoRL (2020)
75. Wei, X., Zhang, Y., Li, Z., Fu, Y., Xue, X.: DeepSFM: structure from motion via deep bundle adjustment. In: Vedaldi, A., Bischof, H., Brox, T., Frahm, J.-M. (eds.) ECCV 2020. LNCS, vol. 12346, pp. 230–247. Springer, Cham (2020). https://doi.org/10.1007/978-3-030-58452-8_14
76. Wong, J.M., et al.: SegICP: integrated deep semantic segmentation and pose estimation. IROS (2017)
77. Xiang, Y., Schmidt, T., Narayanan, V., Fox, D.: PoseCNN: a convolutional neural network for 6D object pose estimation in cluttered scenes. In: RSS (2018)
78. Xiao, Y., Qiu, X., Langlois, P., Aubry, M., Marlet, R.: Pose from shape: deep pose estimation for arbitrary 3D objects. In: BMVC (2019)
79. Yi, K.M., Trulls, E., Lepetit, V., Fua, P.: LIFT: learned invariant feature transform. In: Leibe, B., Matas, J., Sebe, N., Welling, M. (eds.) ECCV 2016. LNCS, vol. 9910, pp. 467–483. Springer, Cham (2016). https://doi.org/10.1007/978-3-319-46466-4_28
80. Yin, Z., Shi, J.: GeoNet: unsupervised learning of dense depth, optical flow and camera pose. In: CVPR (2018)
81. Zhang, J.Y., Pepose, S., Joo, H., Ramanan, D., Malik, J., Kanazawa, A.: Perceiving 3D human-object spatial arrangements from a single image in the wild. In: Vedaldi, A., Bischof, H., Brox, T., Frahm, J.-M. (eds.) ECCV 2020. LNCS, vol. 12357, pp. 34–51. Springer, Cham (2020). https://doi.org/10.1007/978-3-030-58610-2_3
82. Zhang, J.Y., Yang, G., Tulsiani, S., Ramanan, D.: NeRS: neural reflectance surfaces for sparse-view 3D reconstruction in the wild. In: NeurIPS (2021)
83. Zhang, R.: Making convolutional networks shift-invariant again. In: ICML (2019)
84. Zhou, H., Ummenhofer, B., Brox, T.: DeepTAM: deep tracking and mapping. In: Ferrari, V., Hebert, M., Sminchisescu, C., Weiss, Y. (eds.) ECCV 2018. LNCS,

vol. 11220, pp. 851–868. Springer, Cham (2018). https://doi.org/10.1007/978-3-030-01270-0_50

85. Zhou, T., Brown, M., Snavely, N., Lowe, D.G.: Unsupervised learning of depth and ego-motion from video. In: CVPR (2017)

86. Zhou, Y., Barnes, C., Lu, J., Yang, J., Li, H.: On the continuity of rotation representations in neural networks. In: CVPR (2019)

87. Zubizarreta, J., Aguinaga, I., Montiel, J.M.M.: Direct sparse mapping. T-RO (2020)

R2L: Distilling Neural *Radiance* Field to Neural *Light* Field for Efficient Novel View Synthesis

Huan Wang[1,2], Jian Ren[1(✉)], Zeng Huang[1], Kyle Olszewski[1], Menglei Chai[1], Yun Fu[2], and Sergey Tulyakov[1]

[1] Snap Inc., Santa Monica, USA
jren@snapchat.com
[2] Northeastern University, Boston, USA

Abstract. Recent research explosion on Neural Radiance Field (NeRF) shows the encouraging potential to represent complex scenes with neural networks. One major drawback of NeRF is its prohibitive inference time: Rendering a single pixel requires querying the NeRF network hundreds of times. To resolve it, existing efforts mainly attempt to reduce the number of required sampled points. However, the problem of iterative sampling still exists. On the other hand, Neural *Light* Field (NeLF) presents a more straightforward representation over NeRF in novel view synthesis – the rendering of a pixel amounts to *one single forward pass* without ray-marching. In this work, we present a *deep residual MLP* network (88 layers) to effectively learn the light field. We show the key to successfully learning such a deep NeLF network is to have sufficient data, for which we transfer the knowledge from a pre-trained NeRF model via data distillation. Extensive experiments on both synthetic and real-world scenes show the merits of our method over other counterpart algorithms. On the synthetic scenes, we achieve $26 \sim 35\times$ FLOPs reduction (per camera ray) and $28 \sim 31\times$ runtime speedup, meanwhile delivering *significantly better* ($1.4 \sim 2.8$ dB average PSNR improvement) rendering quality than NeRF without any customized parallelism requirement.

1 Introduction

Inferring the representation of a 3D scene from 2D observations is a fundamental problem in computer graphics and computer vision. Recent research innovations in implicit neural representations [10,32,36,49] and differential neural renders [34] have remarkably advanced the solutions to this problem. Neural radiance field (NeRF) learned by a simple Multi-Layer Perceptron (MLP) network shows a great potential to store a complex scene into a compact neural network [34], thus has inspired plenty of follow-up works [6,11,27,60] (Fig. 1).

Project: https://snap-research.github.io/R2L.
H. Wang—Work done when Huan was an intern at Snap.
Z. Huang—Now at Google.

© The Author(s), under exclusive license to Springer Nature Switzerland AG 2022
S. Avidan et al. (Eds.): ECCV 2022, LNCS 13691, pp. 612–629, 2022.
https://doi.org/10.1007/978-3-031-19821-2_35

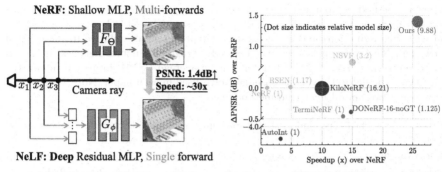

(a) NeRF *vs.* our NeLF method   (b) Speedup-PSNR-Model Size comparison

Fig. 1. (a) Our neural light field (NeLF, bottom) method improves the rendering quality by 1.40 PSNR over neural radiance field (NeRF, top) [34] on the NeRF synthetic dataset, while being around 30× faster. (b) Our method achieves a more favorable speedup-PSNR-model size tradeoff than other efficient novel view synthesis methods on the NeRF synthetic dataset. The number in the parentheses indicates the model size relative to the baseline NeRF model used in each paper (*best viewed in color*).

Despite the success of NeRF and its extensions, the drawback is still apparent. The rendering time even for a single pixel is prolonged since the NeRF framework needs to aggregate the radiance of *hundreds of* sampled points via alpha-composition. It requires hundreds of network forwards, thus is prohibitively slow, especially on resource-constrained devices. One intuitive solution to the problem is to reduce the model size of NeRF MLP. However, apparent quality degradation of rendered images can be observed (*e.g.*, reducing the network width by only half causes around 0.01 SSIM [56] drop in [42]) while the reduction of inference time is only limited. Other research efforts focus on decreasing the number of sampled points [28,35]. However, this does not fundamentally resolve the sampling issue. Some work [35] demands extra depth information for training, which is usually unavailable in most practical cases. Thus, a method that only requires *2D images* as input, represents the scene *compactly*, and enjoys a *fast* rendering speed with *high* image quality is highly desired. This paper aims to present such a method that can achieve all the four goals simultaneously by representing the scene as Neural *Light* Field (NeLF) instead of neural *radiance* field. In the neural light field, ray origin and direction are directly mapped into its associated RGB values, avoiding the need of sampling multiple points along the camera ray. Therefore, rendering a pixel requires only one single query, making it much faster than the radiance scene representation.

The idea of NeLF is attractive; however, realizing it for representing *complex real-world* scenes with better quality than NeRF is still challenging. Our first key technical innovation enabling this is a novel network architecture design for the neural light field network. Specially, we propose a deep (88 layers) residual MLP network with extensive residual MLP blocks. The *deep* network has much greater expressivity than the shallow counterparts, thus can represent the light

Table 1. Method comparison between our R2L approach and recent efficient novel view synthesis methods. Rendering speedup (measured by FLOPs reduction per ray and wall-time reduction) and representation (Repre.) size are relative to the original NeRF [34]. Repre. size measures the required storage of a neural network or cached files to represent a scene. ΔPSNR refers to the average PSNR improvement (on the NeRF synthetic dataset) over the baseline NeRF used in each paper. Note, ours and [4] are the only two neural *light* field methods here

Method	FLOPs speedup↑	Wall-time speedup↑	Repre. size↓	Extra design	ΔPSNR (dB)↑
NeRF [34]	1×	1×	1×	No	0
PlenOctrees [59]	-	3000×	~600×	No	+0.02
DONeRF-8 [35]	27.60×	-	1.125×	Depth data	−0.14
KiloNeRF [43]	~0.6×	692×	16.21×	Parallelism	−0.01
NSVF [30]	-	~15×	~3.2×	No	+0.74
AutoInt [28]	-	3.22×	~1×	No	−4.2
TermiNeRF [41]	-	13.49×	~1×	No	−0.46
RSEN [4]	-	4.86×*	1.17×	No	+0.013
Ours	26 ~ 35×	28 ~ 31×	4 ~ 10×	No	+1.40

field faithfully. Notably, since the debut of NeRF [34], its MLP-based network architecture is inherited with few substantial changes [6,35,42,43]. To our best knowledge, this is the *first* attempt to address the NeRF rendering efficiency issue *from the network design perspective*. Although our network contains more parameters than the original NeRF, we only need *one* single network forward to render the color of a pixel, leading to much faster inference speed than NeRF.

The major technical problem is how to train the proposed deep residual MLP network. It is well-known that large networks hunger for large sample sizes to curb overfitting [23,52]. We can barely train such a large network using only the original 2D images (which are typically less than 100 in real-world applications). To tackle this problem, as the second key technical innovation of this paper, we propose to distill the knowledge [8,18] from a *pretrained* NeRF model to our network, by rendering pseudo data from random views using the pre-trained NeRF model. We name our method as **R2L** since we show distilling neural **R**adiance filed **to** neural **L**ight filed is an effective way to obtain a powerful NeLF network for efficient novel view synthesis. Empirically, we evaluate our method on both synthetic and real-world datasets. On the synthetic scenes, we achieve 26 ~ 35× FLOPs reduction (28 ~ 31× wall-time speedup) over the original NeRF with significantly *higher* rendering quality. Comparison between ours and other efficient novel view synthesis approaches is summarized in Table 1. Overall, our contributions can be summarized into the following aspects:

- Methodologically, we present a brand-new deep residual MLP network aiming for compact neural representation, fast rendering, without extra demand besides 2D images, for efficient novel view synthesis. This is the *first* attempt to improve the rendering efficiency via network architecture optimization.

- Our network represents complex real-world scenes as neural light fields. To resolve the data shortage problem when training the proposed deep MLP network, we propose an effective training strategy by distilling knowledge from a pre-trained NeRF model, which is the key to enabling our method.
- Practically, our approach achieves $26 \sim 35\times$ FLOPs reduction ($28 \sim 31\times$ wall-time speedup) over the original NeRF with even better visual quality, which also performs favorably against existing counterpart approaches.

2   Related Work

Efficient Neural Scene Representation and Rendering. Since the debut of NeRF [34], many follow-up works have been improving its efficiency. One major direction is to skip the empty space and sample more wisely along a camera ray. NSVF [30] defines a set of voxel-bounded implicit fields organized in a sparse voxel octree structure, which enables skipping empty space in novel view synthesis. AutoInt [28] improves the rendering efficiency by reducing the number of evaluations along a ray through learned partial integrals. DeRF [42] spatially decomposes the scene into Voronoi diagrams, each learned by a small network. They achieve 3 times rendering speedup over NeRF with similar quality. Similarly, KiloNeRF [43] also spatially decomposes the scene, but into thousands of *regular* grids. Each of them is tackled by a tiny MLP network. Their work is similar to ours as a pre-trained NeRF model is also used to generate pseudo samples for training. Differently, KiloNeRF is still a *NeRF*-based method while ours is *NeLF*. Point sampling is still needed in KiloNeRF while our method *roots out* this problem. Besides, KiloNeRF results in *thousands of* small networks, making parallelism more challenging and requiring customized parallelism implementation, while our *single* network can get significant speedup simply using the vanilla PyTorch [39]. DONeRF [35] is proposed recently to reduce sampling through a depth oracle network learned with the ground-truth depth as supervision. It decimates the sampled points from hundreds (*i.e.*, 256 in NeRF [34]) to only 4 to 16 while maintaining comparable or even better quality. However, the depth oracle network is learned with *ground-truth depth* as target, which is typically unavailable in practice. Our method does not demand it. Another direction for faster NeRF rendering is to pre-compute and cache the representations per the idea of trading memory for computational efficiency. FastNeRF [12] employs a factorized architecture to independently cache the position-dependent and ray direction-dependent outputs and achieves 3000 times faster than the original NeRF at rendering. Baking [15] precomputes and stores NeRF as sparse neural radiance grid that enables real-time rendering on commodity hardware. We consider this line of works *orthogonal* to ours.

Neural Light Field (NeLF). Light fields enjoy a long history as a scene representation in computer vision and graphics [1,2]. Levoy *et al.* [26] and Gortler *et al.* [13] introduced light fields in computer graphics as 4D scene representation for fast image-based rendering. With them, novel view synthesis can be realized by simply extracting 2D slices in the 4D light field, yet with two major draw-backs. First, they tend to cause considerable storage costs. Second, it is hard to achieve a full 360° representation without concatenating multiple light fields. In the era of deep learning, neural light fields based on convolutional networks have been proposed [7,22,33]. One recent neural light field paper is Sitzmann *et al.* [46]. They employ Plücker coordinates to parameterize 360° light fields. In order to ensure multi-view consistency, they propose to learn a prior over the 4D light fields in a meta-learning framework. Despite intriguing ideas, their method is only evaluated on toy datasets, not as comparable to NeRF [34] in representing complex real-world scenes. Another recent NeLF work is RSEN [4]. To tackle the insufficient training data issue, they propose to learn a voxel grid of subdivided *local* light fields instead of the global light field. In their experiments, they also employ a pre-trained NeRF teacher for regularization. A very recent work [48] proposes a two-stage transformer-based model that can represent view-dependent effects accurately. A concurrent work NeuLF [29] employs a two-plane parameterization of the light field and uses a vanilla MLP network to learn the NeLF mapping. Our NeLF network is different from these in that, **(1)** methodologically, we propose a *deep residual* MLP (88 layers) to learn the light field, while these NeLF works still employ the NeRF-like shallow MLP networks (*e.g.*, 6 layers in [46], 8 layers in [4]); **(2)** we propose to leverage a NeRF model to synthesize extra data for training, making our method a bridge from radiance field to light field; **(3)** thanks to the abundant capacity, our R2L network can achieve better rendering quality (*e.g.*, our method can represent complex real-world scenes against [46]), or can achieve better efficiency while maintaining the rendering quality (*e.g.*, [4] achieves merely around 5× speedup *vs.* our 30× speedup over the baseline NeRF method).

Knowledge Distillation (KD). The general idea of knowledge distillation is to guide the training of a student model through a larger pre-trained teacher model. Pioneered by Buciluǎ *et al.* [8] and later refined by Hinton *et al.* [18] for image classification, knowledge distillation has seen extensive application in vision and language tasks [9,20,54,55]. Many variants have been proposed regarding the central question in knowledge distillation – how to define the *knowledge* that is supposed to be transferred from the teacher to the student, examples including output distance [5,18], internal feature distance [44,54], feature map attention [61], feature distribution [38], activation boundary [17], inter-sample distance relationship [31,37,40,51], and mutual information [50]. The distillation method in this work is to regress the output of the NeRF model with extra data labeled by the teacher (akin to [5,8]), which is the most straightforward way of distillation for the numerical target. Yet we will show this simple scheme can work powerfully to train a deep neural light field network.

3   Methodology

3.1   Background: Neural Radiance Field (NeRF)

In NeRF [34], the 3D scene is implicitly represented by an MLP network, which learns to map the 5D coordinate (spatial location (x, y, z) and viewing direction (θ, ϕ)) to the 1D volume density and 3D view-dependent emitted radiance at that spatial location, $F_\Theta : \mathbb{R}^5 \mapsto \mathbb{R}^4$, where F refers to an MLP neural network (parameterized by Θ) to represent a scene. For rendering, the classic volume rendering technique [21] is adopted in NeRF to obtain the desired color for an oriented ray. Volume rendering is differential thus making NeRF end-to-end trainable by using the captured 2D images as supervision. For novel view synthesis, given an oriented ray, NeRF first samples several locations along the camera ray, predicts their emitted radiance by querying the MLP network F_Θ, and then aggregates the radiance together by alpha composition to output the final color. As sampling at vacuum points contributes nothing to the final color, a sufficient number of sampled points is critical to NeRF's performance so as to cover the worthy locations (such as those near the object surface). However, increased sampling incurs linearly increased query cost of the MLP network.

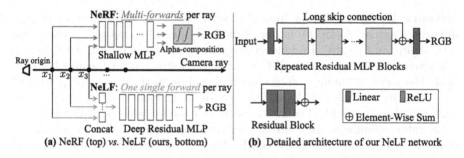

Fig. 2. (a) Comparison between our proposed NeLF network (*Deep Residual MLP*, bottom) and NeRF network (*Shallow MLP*, top). (b) Detailed architecture of the proposed *deep* light field network, which employs extensive repeated residual MLP blocks.

3.2   R2L: Distilling NeRF to NeLF

On the other hand, a scene can also be represented as a *light* field instead of *radiance* field, parameterized by a neural network. The network G_ϕ learns a mapping function directly from a 4D oriented ray to its target 3D RGB, $G_\phi : \mathbb{R}^4 \mapsto \mathbb{R}^3$. NeLF has several attractive advantages over NeRF. **(1)** Methodologically, it is more straightforward for novel view synthesis, in that the output of the NeLF network is already the wanted color, while the output of a NeRF network is the radiance of a sampled point; the desired color has to been obtained through an extra step of ray marching (see Fig. 2(a)). **(2)** Practically, given the same input ray (origin coordinate and direction), rendering in a light field simply amounts to a *single query* of the light field function. It *fundamentally* obviates the need for point sampling along a ray (which is the speed bottleneck in NeRF [34]), thus can be orders-of-magnitude faster than NeRF. Despite these intriguing properties, not many successful attempts have crystallized NeLF *with comparable quality to NeRF* up to date. To our best knowledge, only one recent NeLF method [4] achieves comparable quality to NeRF, but its speedup is relatively limited (around 5×wall-time speedup). In this paper, we propose a novel network architecture to make NeLF as effective as NeRF (meanwhile being much faster). Intuitively, the light field is *harder* to learn than radiance field – radiance at neighbor space locations does not change dramatically given the radiance field in the physical world is typically continuous; while two neighbor rays can point to starkly different colors because of occlusion. That is, the light field is intrinsically *less smooth* (sharply changing) than the radiance field. To capture the inherently more complex light field, we need a more *powerful* network. Per this idea, the 11-layer MLP network used in NeRF can hardly represent a complex light field by our empirical observation (see Table 5). We thereby propose to employ a *deep* MLP network to parameterize the above G function. Then, the foremost technical question is how to design the deep network.

Network Design. Different from the NeRF network, we propose to employ intensive residual blocks [14] in our network. The resulted network architecture is illustrated in Fig. 2(b). Residual connections were shown critical to enable the much greater network depth in [14], which also applies here for learning the light field. The merit of having a *deeper* network will be justified in our experiments (see Fig. 6(b)). We also study an underperformance case in the supplementary material when the residual connections are *not* used in a deep MLP network.

Notably, enabling a deep network for neural radiance/light field parameterization is *non-trivial*. Noted by DeRF [42], *"there are diminishing returns in employing larger (deeper and/or wider) networks"*. As a result, notably, most NeRF follow-up works for improving rendering efficiency (*e.g.*, [35, 42, 43]) actually inherit the MLP architecture in NeRF with *few* substantial innovations. To our best knowledge, we are the *first* to address the efficiency issue of NeRF *through the network architecture optimization perspective*. Despite the residual structure is not new itself (due to ResNets [14]), its necessity and potential have not been fully recognized and exploited in the NVS task. Our paper is meant to make a step forward in this direction.

3.3 Synthesize Pseudo Data

Deep networks hunger for excessive data to be powerful. Unfortunately, this is not the case in novel view synthesis, where a user typically captures fewer than 100 images. To overcome this problem, we propose to employ a pre-trained NeRF model to synthesize extra data for training. This makes our method a bridge from neural *radiance* field to neural *light* field.

We need to decide where to sample to synthesize the pseudo data to avoid unnecessary waste. Specifically, with the original training data (images and their associated camera poses), we know the bounding box of the camera locations and their orientations. Then we *randomly* sample the ray origins (x_o, y_o, z_o) and normalized directions (x_d, y_d, z_d) obeying a uniform distribution U *within the bounding box* to make a 6D input as follows,

$$x_o \sim U(x_o^{\min}, x_o^{\max}), \ y_o \sim U(y_o^{\min}, y_o^{\max}), \ z_o \sim U(z_o^{\min}, z_o^{\max}),$$
$$x_d \sim U(x_d^{\min}, x_d^{\max}), \ y_d \sim U(y_d^{\min}, y_d^{\max}), \ z_d \sim U(z_d^{\min}, z_d^{\max}), \tag{1}$$

where the viewing bounding box can be inferred from the training data. An example illustration of the pseudo data origins and directions in our method is shown in our supplementary material. Note, since we can control the generated data, we explicitly demand the pseudo data completely cover the original training data, implying they are in the same domain, which is critical to the performance.

For a trained NeRF model F_{Θ^*}, the target RGB value can be queried as:

$$(\hat{r}, \hat{g}, \hat{b}) = F_{\Theta^*}(x_o, y_o, z_o, x_d, y_d, z_d), \tag{2}$$

where Θ^* stands for the converged model parameters. Then a slice of training data is simply a vector of these 9 numbers: $(x_o, y_o, z_o, x_d, y_d, z_d, \hat{r}, \hat{g}, \hat{b})$. To have an effective neural light field network F_Θ, we feed abundant pseudo data into the proposed deep R2L network and train it by the MSE loss function,

$$\mathcal{L} = \mathrm{MSE}(G_\phi(x_o, y_o, z_o, x_d, y_d, z_d), (\hat{r}, \hat{g}, \hat{b})). \tag{3}$$

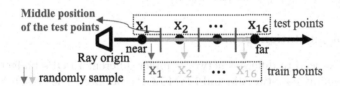

Fig. 3. Illustration of the point sampling in training and testing of our method. The orange and green colors denote the different *segments* of the ray. The blue color marks the *start* and *end* points of each segment. Each sampled train point is colored *based on the corresponding segment color* (Color figure online)

3.4 Ray Representation and Point Sampling

It is critical to have a proper representation of a ray in NeLF. In this work, we propose a new simple and effective representation – we concatenate the spatial coordinates of K sampled points along a ray to form an input vector ($3K$-d), fed into the NeLF network. Mathematically, we need at least two points to define a ray. More points will make the representation more precise. In this paper, we choose $K = 16$ points (see the ablation of K in Fig. 6(a)) along a ray. A critical design here is that we expect the network not to overfit the K points but to capture the underlying ray information. Thus, during training the K points are *randomly* sampled along the ray using the stratified sampling (same as NeRF [34], see Fig. 3). This design is critical to generalization. During testing, the K points are evenly spaced. We also tried changing the input to Plücker coordinates for our R2L network (inspired by [46]). Our representation achieves *better* test quality than Plücker (PSNR: 29.50 *vs.* 29.08, scene Lego, W181D88 network, trained with only pseudo data, $200K$ iters).

3.5   Training with Hard Examples

Given that we randomly sample the camera locations and orientations, the rays are likely to point to the trivial parts of a scene (*e.g.*, the white background of a synthetic scene). Also, during training, some easy-to-regress colors will be well-learned early. Feeding these pixels again to the network barely increases its knowledge. We thus propose to tap into the idea of hard examples [16,45]. That is, we want the network to pay more attention to the rays that are harder to regress (typically corresponding to the high-frequency details) during learning.

Specially, we maintain a *hard example pool*. A *harder* example is defined by a *larger* loss (Eq. (3)). In each iteration, we sort the losses for each sample in a batch in ascending order and add the top r (a pre-defined percentage constant) into the hard example pool. Meanwhile, in each iteration, the same amount r of hard examples are randomly picked out of the pool to augment the training batch. This design can accelerate the network convergence significantly as we will show in the experiments (see Fig. 6).

3.6   Implementation Details

Our R2L can lead to different networks under different FLOPs budgets. In this paper, we mainly have two: 6M and 12M FLOPs (per ray). They result in a bunch of networks: 12M: W256D88, 6M: W181D88, W256D44, W363D22 (W stands for width, D for depth). Obviously, a larger network is expected to perform better, so W256D88 is used for obtaining better quality; ablation studies will be conducted on the 6M-budget networks since they are faster to train. Following NeRF [34], positional encoding [53] is used to enrich the input information.

4   Experiments

Datasets. We show experiments on the following datasets:

- **NeRF datasets** [34]. We evaluate our method on two datasets: synthetic dataset (Realistic Synthetic 360°) and real-world dataset (Real Forward-Facing). Realistic Synthetic 360° contains path-traced images of 8 objects that exhibit complicated geometry and realistic non-Lambertian materials. 100 views of each scene are used for training and 200 for testing, with resolution of 800×800. Real Forward-Facing also contains 8 scenes, captured with a handheld cellphone. There are 20 to 62 images for each scene with 1/8 held out for testing. All images have a resolution of 1008×756.

- **DONeRF dataset** includes their synthetic data. Images are rendered using Blender and their Cycles path tracer to render 300 images for each scene, which are split into train/validation/test sets at a 70%, 10%, 20% ratio.

Training Settings. All images in the synthetic dataset are down-sampled by $2\times$ during training and testing. Due to limited space, we defer the full-resolution (800×800) results to our supplementary material. The original NeRF model is trained with a batch size of $1,024$ and initial learning rate as 5×10^{-4} (decayed during training) for $200k$ iterations. We synthesize $10k$ images using the pre-trained NeRF model. Our proposed R2L model is trained for $1,000k$ iterations with the same learning rate schedule. The rays in a batch (batch size $98,304$ rays) are randomly sampled from different images so that they do not share the same origin. This is found critical to achieving superior performance. Adam optimizer [24] is employed for all training. We use PyTorch 1.9 [39], referring to [58]. Experiments are conducted with 8 NVIDIA V100 GPUs.

Comparison Methods. We compare with the original NeRF [34] to show that we can achieve significantly better rendering quality while being much faster. Meanwhile, we also compare with DONeRF [35], NSVF [30], and NeX [57] since they also target efficient NVS as we do. Other efficient NVS works such as AutoInt [28] and X-Fields [7] have been shown less favorable than RSEN [4]. Therefore, we only compare with RSEN [4]. KiloNeRF [43], another closely related work apart from RSEN, will also be compared to. Similar to [4], we do not compare to baking-based methods [12,15,59]) as they trade memory footprint for speed while our method aims to maintain the compact representation.

Table 2. PSNR↑, SSIM↑, and LPIPS↓ (AlexNet [25] is used for LPIPS) on the NeRF synthetic dataset (Realistic Synthetic 360°) and real-world dataset (Real Forward-Facing). R2L network: W256D88. †KiloNeRF adopts Empty Space Skipping and Early Ray Termination, so the FLOPs is scene-by-scene; we estimate the average FLOPs based on the description in their paper. The best results are in red, second best in blue

Method	Storage (MB)	FLOPs (M)	Synthetic			Real-world		
			PSNR↑	SSIM↑	LPIPS↓	PSNR↑	SSIM↑	LPIPS↓
Teacher NeRF [34]	2.4	303.82	30.47	0.9925	0.0391	27.68	0.9725	0.0733
Ours-1 (Pseudo)	23.7	11.79	30.48 (+0.01)	0.9939	0.0467	27.58 (−0.10)	0.9722	0.0997
Ours-2 (Pseudo+real)	23.7	11.79	31.87 (+1.40)	0.9950	0.0340	27.79 (+0.11)	0.9729	0.0968
Teacher NeRF in [43]	2.4	303.82	31.01	0.95	0.08	-	-	-
KiloNeRF [43]	38.9	∼500†	31.00 (−0.01)	0.95	0.03	-	-	-
Teacher NeRF in [4]	4.6	∼300	-	-	-	27.928	0.9160	0.065
RSEN [4]	5.4	67.2	-	-	-	27.941 (+0.013)	0.9161	0.060

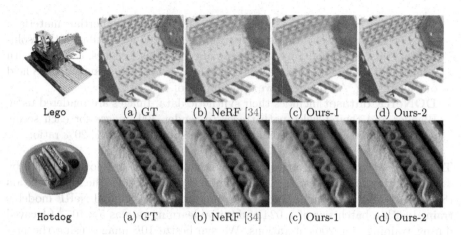

Fig. 4. Visual comparison between our R2L network (W256D88) and NeRF on the synthetic scene Lego and Hotdog. Ours-1 is trained sorely on pseudo data, ours-2 on pseudo + real data. Please refer to our supplementary material for the visual comparison on the real-world dataset

Table 3. PSNR↑ and FLIP↓ comparison on the DONeRF synthetic dataset. All the PSNR and FLIP results except ours and NeRF are directly cited from the DONeRF paper since we are using exactly the same dataset here. Training with pseudo and real data (ours-2) gives us better results. The best results are in red, second best in blue

Method	Storage (MB)	FLOPs (M)	PSNR↑	FLIP↓
Teacher NeRF (log+warp)	3.2	211.42	32.67	0.070
NSVF-large [30]	8.3	187.52	30.01 (-2.66)	0.078
NeX-MLP [57]	89.0	42.71	30.55 (-2.12)	0.076
DONeRF-16-noGT [35]	3.6	14.29	32.25 (-0.42)	0.065
DoNeRF-8 [35]	3.6	7.66	32.50 (-0.17)	0.064
Ours-1 (Pseduo data)	12.1	6.00	32.67 $(+0.00)$	0.071
Ours-2 (Pseduo + real data)	12.1	6.00	35.45 **$(+2.78)$**	0.047

4.1   NeRF Synthetic and Real-World Dataset

The quantitative comparisons (PSNR, SSIM [56], LPIPS [62]) on the NeRF synthetic and real-world dataset are presented in Table 2. Visual comparison is shown in Fig. 4. **(1)** Using the pseudo data alone, our R2L network achieves comparable performance to the original ray-marching NeRF model either quantitatively or qualitatively, with only 1/26 FLOPs. The blurry parts of NeRF results usually also appear on our results, since our model learns from the data generated by the NeRF teacher model. **(2)** With the original data included for training, our R2L network *significantly* improves the test PSNR **by** 1.40 over the teacher NeRF model. This means that the performance of our method is *not* upper-bounded by the teacher model. Two primary reasons answer for this

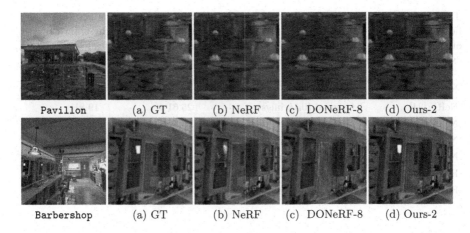

Fig. 5. Visual comparison of ours, NeRF [34], DONeRF [35] on the DONeRF dataset

remarkable performance. First, our R2L network is *much deeper* than the NeRF network, which bestows a much greater capacity to represent scenes with fine-grained details. Second, we propose *hard-example training* (Sect. 3.5), which makes the network focus more on regressing the fine-grained details. **(3)** For the related works KiloNeRF and RSEN, their baseline NeRF models have different PSNRs due to different settings, so the PSNR results cannot be directly compared. Instead, we compare the *PSNR change* over the baseline NeRFs. Kilo-NeRF gets 0.01 dB PSNR drop *vs.* ours 1.40 dB PSNR boost. RSEN improves the PSNR on the much more challenging real-world dataset marginally (by 0.013 dB). In comparison, our improvement is more significant (0.11 dB) with much fewer FLOPs.

4.2 DONeRF Synthetic Dataset

DONeRF [35] achieves fast rendering using *ground-truth depth* for training. However, the ground-truth depth is *not* available in most practical cases. As a remedy, they propose to use a pre-trained NeRF model to estimate depth as a proxy for the ground-truth depth. The approach of DONeRF without ground-truth depth

Table 4. Average time (s) comparison among our R2L network (W181D88), DONeRF, and NeRF. The benchmark is conducted under the *same* hardware and software. The speedup of ours and DONeRF is relative to the running time of NeRF. Results are averaged by 60 frames

Method	FLOPs (M)	GeForce 2080Ti	Tesla V100	CPU
NeRF	211.42	5.9343	4.9902	142.2612
DONeRF-16	14.29 (14.79×)	0.4162 (14.26×)	0.3524 (14.16×)	9.9344 (14.32×)
Ours	**6.00 (35.24×)**	**0.2103 (28.22×)**	**0.1629 (30.63×)**	**5.0198 (28.34×)**

Table 5. Ablation study of different network and data schemes when learning a light field. Scene: Lego. All models are trained for $200k$ iterations. Note, the train PSNR of our method is lower than test PSNR because we use the hard examples (Sect. 3.5) *i.e.*, examples with small PSNR, for training.

Network	Data	Train PSNR (dB)	Test PSNR (dB)
NeRF [34]	Original ($0.1k$ imgs)	25.61	19.81
NeRF+dropout [47]	Original ($0.1k$ imgs)	25.56	19.83
NeRF+BN [19]	Original ($0.1k$ imgs)	25.43	19.76
NeRF [34]	Pseudo ($10k$ imgs)	23.82	26.67
R2L (W181D88)	Pseudo ($10k$ imgs)	28.38	29.50
R2L (W181D88)	Pseudo + Original ($10.1k$ imgs)	29.85	30.09

(*e.g.*, DONeRF-16-noGT) is very relevant to ours. Thus, we compare with it using the synthetic dataset collected by the DONeRF paper. The quantitative results (PSNR and FLIP [3]) are presented in Table 3. **(1)** Trained purely with pseudo data, our method already outperforms DONeRF-16-noGT and DONeRF-8 (which even demands the ground-truth depth as input). **(2)** Similar to the case (Table 2) on the NeRF synthetic dataset, including the original real images for training significantly boosts the performance by 2.78 dB.

Visual results in Fig. 5 show that our method delivers better visual quality than the baseline NeRF. On the scene Pavillon and Barbershop, our R2L network achieves *better* rendering quality than DONeRF-8 despite not using the ground-truth depth. Particularly note the reflection surfaces (*e.g.*, water in Pavillon and mirror in Barbershop), DONeRF cannot learn the reflection surfaces well because the ground-truth depth does not apply to the depth in the reflections, while our method (and the original NeRF) still performs well.

Actual Speed Comparison. We further report the benchmark results of wall-time speed in Table 4 to demonstrate the FLOPs reduction is well-aligned with actual speedup. Our R2L network (W181D88) is $28 \sim 31\times$ faster than NeRF and $2\times$ faster than DONeRF-16-noGT.

4.3   Ablation Study

More **Data and** *Deep* **Network are Critical.** Table 5 shows the results of using the original 11-layer NeRF network to learn a light field on scene Lego. **(1)** Because of the severely insufficient data (only $0.1k$ training images), the network overfits to the training data with only 19.81 test PSNR. Note, this overfitting cannot be resolved by common regularization techniques like dropout [47] and BN [19]. Only when the data size is greatly inflated (with pseudo data) from $0.1k$ to $10k$, can we see a significant test PSNR improvement (from 19.81 to 26.67). This shows the (abundant) pseudo data is indispensable. **(2)** Compare our R2L to NeRF at the same setting of $10k$ pseudo images, our network design improves test PSNR by around 3 (from 26.67 to 29.50), which is a significant boost in

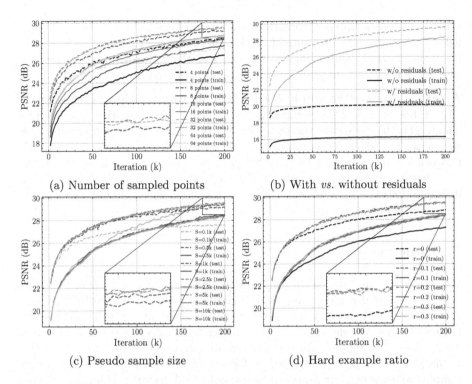

Fig. 6. Ablation studies. All networks are trained for $200k$ iterations, scene: `Lego`. Test PSNRs are plotted with dashed lines; train PSNRs are plotted with solid lines. **(a)** PSNR comparison of different sampled points in our R2L network (W181D88). Default: 16 points (blue lines) **(b)** PSNR comparison between two network designs: using residuals or not for our R2L network. **(c)** PSNR comparison under different pseudo sample sizes. Default: $S = 10k$. **(d)** PSNR comparison under different hard example ratios $r \in \{0, 0.1, 0.2, 0.3\}$. Default: $r = 0.2$ (Color figure online)

terms of rendering quality. This justifies the necessity of our *deep* network design. Another reason encouraging us to use deep networks is that we empirically find trading width for depth under the same FLOPs budget can consistently lead to performance gains (see our supplementary material).

Ablation of Residuals in our R2L Network. Although the original NeRF network also employs skip connections (to add ray directions as input), it can hardly be considered as a typical residual network [14] in fact, as they do not use residuals in the internal layers. In comparison, we promote employing extensive residual blocks in the internal layers. Its necessity is justified by Fig. 6(b). As seen, without residuals, the network is barely trainable.

Ablation of Pseudo Sample Size. The effect of pseudo sample size is of particular interest. As shown in Fig. 6(c), 100 images (see $S = 0.1k$) are not enough to train our deep R2L network – note the test PSNR saturates early at around $50k$ iterations while its train PSNR keeps arising sharply. This is a typical case of overfitting, caused by the over-parameterized model not being fed with enough data. In contrast, with more data (see the cases of $S \geq 0.5k$), the train PSNR is held down and the test PSNR keeps arising. We observe no significant improvement starting from around $5k$ images.

Ablation of Hard Example Ratio. Here we vary the hard example ratio r and see how it affects the performance. To make a fair comparison, we keep the training batch size always the same (98, 304 rays per batch) when varying r. As shown in Fig. 6(d), using hard examples in each batch significantly improves the network learning in either train PSNR (*i.e.*, better optimization) or test PSNR (*i.e.*, better generalization) against the case of $r = 0$. There is no significant difference between hard example ratio $r = 0.1$, 0.2, and 0.3. In our experiments, we simply use a setting as $r = 0.2$.

5   Conclusion

We present the first *deep* neural light field network that can represent complex synthetic and real-world scenes. Starkly different from existing NeRF-like MLP networks, our R2L network is featured by an unprecedented depth and extensive residual blocks. We show the key to training such a deep network is abundant data, while the original captured images are barely sufficient. To resolve this, we propose to adopt a pre-trained NeRF model to synthesize excessive pseudo samples. With them, our proposed neural light field network achieves more than $26 \sim 35\times$ FLOPs reduction and $28 \sim 31\times$ wall-time acceleration on the NeRF synthetic dataset, with rendering quality improved significantly.

References

1. Adelson, E.H., Bergen, J.R., et al.: The Plenoptic Function and the Elements of Early Vision, vol. 2. MIT Press, Cambridge (1991)
2. Adelson, E.H., Wang, J.Y.: Single lens stereo with a plenoptic camera. TPAMI **14**(2), 99–106 (1992)
3. Andersson, P., et al.: Flip: a difference evaluator for alternating images. In: Proceedings of the ACM in Computer Graphics and Interactive Techniques (2020)
4. Attal, B., Huang, J.B., Zollhoefer, M., Kopf, J., Kim, C.: Learning neural light fields with ray-space embedding networks. In: CVPR (2022)
5. Ba, J., Caruana, R.: Do deep nets really need to be deep? In: NeurIPS (2014)
6. Barron, J.T., Mildenhall, B., Tancik, M., Hedman, P., Martin-Brualla, R., Srinivasan, P.P.: Mip-NeRF: a multiscale representation for anti-aliasing neural radiance fields. arXiv preprint arXiv:2103.13415 (2021)
7. Bemana, M., Myszkowski, K., Seidel, H.P., Ritschel, T.: X-fields: implicit neural view-, light-and time-image interpolation. ACMTOG **39**(6), 1–15 (2020)
8. Bucilă, C., Caruana, R., Niculescu-Mizil, A.: Model compression. In: SIGKDD (2006)
9. Chen, G., Choi, W., Yu, X., Han, T., Chandraker, M.: Learning efficient object detection models with knowledge distillation. In: NeurIPS (2017)

10. Chen, Z., Zhang, H.: Learning implicit fields for generative shape modeling. In: CVPR (2019)
11. Dellaert, F., Yen-Chen, L.: Neural volume rendering: nerf and beyond. arXiv preprint arXiv:2101.05204 (2020)
12. Garbin, S.J., Kowalski, M., Johnson, M., Shotton, J., Valentin, J.: FastNeRF: high-fidelity neural rendering at 200FPS. arXiv preprint arXiv:2103.10380 (2021)
13. Gortler, S.J., Grzeszczuk, R., Szeliski, R., Cohen, M.F.: The lumigraph. In: Proceedings of the Annual Conference on Computer Graphics and Interactive Techniques (1996)
14. He, K., Zhang, X., Ren, S., Sun, J.: Deep residual learning for image recognition. In: CVPR (2016)
15. Hedman, P., Srinivasan, P.P., Mildenhall, B., Barron, J.T., Debevec, P.: Baking neural radiance fields for real-time view synthesis. arXiv preprint arXiv:2103.14645 (2021)
16. Henriques, J.F., Carreira, J., Caseiro, R., Batista, J.: Beyond hard negative mining: efficient detector learning via block-circulant decomposition. In: CVPR (2013)
17. Heo, B., Lee, M., Yun, S., Choi, J.Y.: Knowledge transfer via distillation of activation boundaries formed by hidden neurons. In: AAAI (2019)
18. Hinton, G., Vinyals, O., Dean, J.: Distilling the knowledge in a neural network. In: NeurIPS Workshop (2014)
19. Ioffe, S., Szegedy, C.: Batch normalization: accelerating deep network training by reducing internal covariate shift. In: ICML (2015)
20. Jiao, X., et al.: TinyBERT: distilling BERT for natural language understanding. arXiv preprint arXiv:1909.10351 (2019)
21. Kajiya, J.T., Von Herzen, B.P.: Ray tracing volume densities. SIGGRAPH **18**(3), 165–174 (1984)
22. Kalantari, N.K., Wang, T.C., Ramamoorthi, R.: Learning-based view synthesis for light field cameras. ACM Trans. Graph. **35**(6), 1–10 (2016)
23. Kearns, M.J., Vazirani, U.V., Vazirani, U.: An Introduction to Computational Learning Theory. MIT Press, Cambridge (1994)
24. Kingma, D.P., Ba, J.: Adam: a method for stochastic optimization. In: ICLR (2015)
25. Krizhevsky, A., Sutskever, I., Hinton, G.E.: Imagenet classification with deep convolutional neural networks. In: NeurIPS (2012)
26. Levoy, M., Hanrahan, P.: Light field rendering. In: Proceedings of the Annual Conference on Computer Graphics and Interactive Techniques (1996)
27. Li, Z., Niklaus, S., Snavely, N., Wang, O.: Neural scene flow fields for space-time view synthesis of dynamic scenes. In: CVPR (2021)
28. Lindell, D.B., Martel, J.N., Wetzstein, G.: Autoint: automatic integration for fast neural volume rendering. In: CVPR (2021)
29. Liu, C., Li, Z., Yuan, J., Xu, Y.: Neulf: efficient novel view synthesis with neural 4D light field. In: EGSR (2022)
30. Liu, L., Gu, J., Zaw Lin, K., Chua, T.S., Theobalt, C.: Neural sparse voxel fields. In: NeurIPS (2020)
31. Liu, Y., Cao, J., Li, B., Yuan, C., Hu, W., Li, Y., Duan, Y.: Knowledge distillation via instance relationship graph. In: CVPR (2019)
32. Mescheder, L., Oechsle, M., Niemeyer, M., Nowozin, S., Geiger, A.: Occupancy networks: learning 3D reconstruction in function space. In: CVPR (2019)
33. Mildenhall, B., et al.: Local light field fusion: practical view synthesis with prescriptive sampling guidelines. ACM Trans. Graph. **38**(4), 1–14 (2019)

34. Mildenhall, B., Srinivasan, P.P., Tancik, M., Barron, J.T., Ramamoorthi, R., Ng, R.: Nerf: representing scenes as neural radiance fields for view synthesis. In: ECCV (2020)
35. Neff, T., et al.: DONeRF: towards real-time rendering of compact neural radiance fields using depth oracle networks. In: Computer Graphics Forum (2021)
36. Park, J.J., Florence, P., Straub, J., Newcombe, R., Lovegrove, S.: Deepsdf: learning continuous signed distance functions for shape representation. In: CVPR (2019)
37. Park, W., Kim, D., Lu, Y., Cho, M.: Relational knowledge distillation. In: CVPR (2019)
38. Passalis, N., Tefas, A.: Learning deep representations with probabilistic knowledge transfer. In: ECCV (2018)
39. Paszke, A., et al.: Pytorch: an imperative style, high-performance deep learning library. In: NeurIPS (2019)
40. Peng, B., et al.: Correlation congruence for knowledge distillation. In: ICCV (2019)
41. Piala, M., Clark, R.: Terminerf: ray termination prediction for efficient neural rendering. In: 3DV (2021)
42. Rebain, D., Jiang, W., Yazdani, S., Li, K., Yi, K.M., Tagliasacchi, A.: Derf: decomposed radiance fields. In: CVPR (2021)
43. Reiser, C., Peng, S., Liao, Y., Geiger, A.: KiloNeRF: speeding up neural radiance fields with thousands of tiny MLPs. In: ICCV (2021)
44. Romero, A., Ballas, N., Kahou, S.E., Chassang, A., Gatta, C., Bengio, Y.: Fitnets: hints for thin deep nets. In: ICLR (2015)
45. Shrivastava, A., Gupta, A., Girshick, R.: Training region-based object detectors with online hard example mining. In: CVPR (2016)
46. Sitzmann, V., Rezchikov, S., Freeman, W.T., Tenenbaum, J.B., Durand, F.: Light field networks: neural scene representations with single-evaluation rendering. In: NeurIPS (2021)
47. Srivastava, N., Hinton, G., Krizhevsky, A., Sutskever, I., Salakhutdinov, R.: Dropout: a simple way to prevent neural networks from overfitting. JMLR 15(1), 1929–1958 (2014)
48. Suhail, M., Esteves, C., Sigal, L., Makadia, A.: Light field neural rendering. In: CVPR (2022)
49. Takikawa, T., et al.: Neural geometric level of detail: real-time rendering with implicit 3D shapes. In: CVPR (2021)
50. Tian, Y., Krishnan, D., Isola, P.: Contrastive representation distillation. In: ICLR (2020)
51. Tung, F., Mori, G.: Similarity-preserving knowledge distillation. In: CVPR (2019)
52. Vapnik, V.: The Nature of Statistical Learning Theory. Springer, New York (2013)
53. Vaswani, A., et al.: Attention is all you need. In: NeurIPS (2017)
54. Wang, H., Li, Y., Wang, Y., Hu, H., Yang, M.H.: Collaborative distillation for ultra-resolution universal style transfer. In: CVPR (2020)
55. Wang, L., Yoon, K.J.: Knowledge distillation and student-teacher learning for visual intelligence: a review and new outlooks. TPAMI (2021)
56. Wang, Z., Bovik, A.C., Sheikh, H.R., Simoncelli, E.P.: Image quality assessment: from error visibility to structural similarity. TIP 13(4), 600–612 (2004)
57. Wizadwongsa, S., Phongthawee, P., Yenphraphai, J., Suwajanakorn, S.: Nex: real-time view synthesis with neural basis expansion. In: CVPR (2021)
58. Yen-Chen, L.: Nerf-pytorch (2020). https://github.com/yenchenlin/nerf-pytorch/
59. Yu, A., Li, R., Tancik, M., Li, H., Ng, R., Kanazawa, A.: Plenoctrees for real-time rendering of neural radiance fields. In: ICCV (2021)

60. Yu, A., Ye, V., Tancik, M., Kanazawa, A.: pixelNeRF: neural radiance fields from one or few images. In: CVPR (2021)
61. Zagoruyko, S., Komodakis, N.: Paying more attention to attention: improving the performance of convolutional neural networks via attention transfer. In: ICLR (2017)
62. Zhang, R., Isola, P., Efros, A.A., Shechtman, E., Wang, O.: The unreasonable effectiveness of deep features as a perceptual metric. In: CVPR (2018)

KD-MVS: Knowledge Distillation Based Self-supervised Learning for Multi-view Stereo

Yikang Ding[1,2], Qingtian Zhu[1], Xiangyue Liu[1], Wentao Yuan[1],
Haotian Zhang[1(✉)], and Chi Zhang[1]

[1] Megvii Research, Beijing, China
zhanghaotian@megvii.com
[2] Tsinghua University, Beijing, China

Abstract. Supervised multi-view stereo (MVS) methods have achieved remarkable progress in terms of reconstruction quality, but suffer from the challenge of collecting large-scale ground-truth depth. In this paper, we propose a novel self-supervised training pipeline for MVS based on knowledge distillation, termed *KD-MVS*, which mainly consists of self-supervised teacher training and distillation-based student training. Specifically, the teacher model is trained in a self-supervised fashion using both photometric and featuremetric consistency. Then we distill the knowledge of the teacher model to the student model through probabilistic knowledge transferring. With the supervision of validated knowledge, the student model is able to outperform its teacher by a large margin. Extensive experiments performed on multiple datasets show our method can even outperform supervised methods. Code is available at https://github.com/megvii-research/KD-MVS.

1 Introduction

The task of multi-view stereo (MVS) is to reconstruct a dense 3D presentation of the observed scene using a series of calibrated images, which plays an important role in a variety of applications, e.g. augmented and virtual reality, robotics and computer graphics. Recently, learning-based MVS networks [6,7,11,21,44,45] have obtained impressive results. However, supervised methods require dense depth annotations as explicit supervision, the acquisition of which is still an expensive challenge. Subsequent attempts [14,18,38,39,42] have made efforts to train MVS networks in a self-supervised manner by using photometric consistency [4,18], optical flow [39] or reconstructed 3D models [14,42].

This work is done by the first four authors as interns at Megvii Research.

Supplementary Information The online version contains supplementary material available at https://doi.org/10.1007/978-3-031-19821-2_36.

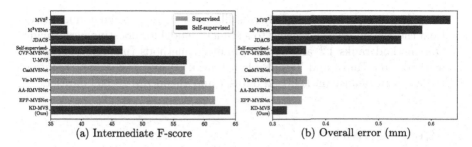

Fig. 1. Visualized performance comparisons of state-of-the-art MVS methods on (a) Tanks and Temples benchmark [19] and (b) DTU dataset [2].

Though great improvement has been made, there is a significant gap in either reconstruction completeness or accuracy compared to supervised methods.

In this paper, we propose a novel self-supervised training pipeline for MVS based on knowledge distillation [13], named *KD-MVS*. The pipeline of KD-MVS mainly consists of (a) self-supervised teacher training and (b) distillation-based student training. In the self-supervised teacher training stage, the teacher model is trained by enforcing both the photometric consistency [18] and featuremetric consistency between the reference view and the reconstructed views, which can be obtained via homography warping according to the estimated depth. Unlike the existing self-supervised MVS methods [4,18,42] that use only photometric consistency, we propose to use the internally extracted features to utilize the featuremetric consistency, which is different from the externally extracted features-based loss, e.g. perceptual loss [16]. We analyze and show that the proposed internal featuremetric loss is more suitable for MVS and is able to help the self-supervised teacher model yield relatively complete and accurate depth maps.

The distillation-based student training stage consists of two main steps: the pseudo probabilistic knowledge generation and the student training. We first use the teacher model to infer raw depth maps on unlabeled training data and perform cross-view check to filter unreliable samples. We then generate the pseudo probability distribution of the teacher model by probabilistic encoding. The probabilistic knowledge can be transferred to the student model by forcing the predicted probability distribution of the student model to be similar to the pseudo probability distribution. As a result, the student model can surpass its teacher and even outperform supervised methods. Extensive experiments on DTU dataset [2], Tanks and Temples benchmark [1] and BlendedMVS dataset [46] show that KD-MVS brings significant improvement to off-the-shelf MVS networks, even outperforming supervised methods, as is shown in Fig. 1. It is worth noting that applying with CasMVSNet [11], KD-MVS ranks 1st among all submitted methods on Tanks and Temples benchmark [1].

Our main contributions are four-fold as follows:

- We propose a novel self-supervised training pipeline named KD-MVS based on knowledge distillation.
- We design an internal featuremetric consistency loss to perform robust self-supervised training of the teacher model.

- We propose to perform knowledge distillation to transfer validated knowledge from the self-supervised teacher to a student model for boosting performance.
- Our method ranks 1st among all submitted methods (including supervised methods) on Tanks and Temples benchmark [1] and also achieves state-of-the-art performance on DTU [2] dataset and BlendedMVS [46] dataset.

2 Related Work

2.1 Learning-based MVS

Supervised MVS. Learning-based methods for MVS have achieved impressive reconstruction quality. MVSNet [44] transforms the MVS task to a per-view depth estimation task and encodes camera parameters via differentiable homography to build 3D cost volumes, which will be regularized by a 3D CNN to obtain a probability volume for pixel-wise depth distribution. However, at cost volume regularization, 3D tensors occupy massive memory for processing. To alleviate this problem, some attempts [36,41,45] replace the 3D CNN by 2D CNNs and a RNN and some other methods [3,11,43,48] use a multi-stage approach and predict depth in a coarse-to-fine manner.

Self-supervised MVS. The key of self-supervised MVS methods is how to make use of prior multi-view information and transform the problem of depth prediction into other forms of problems. Unsup-MVS [18] firstly handles MVS as an image reconstruction problem by warping pixels to neighboring views with estimated depth values. Given multiple images, MVS^2 [4] predicts each view's depth simultaneously and trains the model using cross-view consistency. M^3VSNet [14] makes use of the consistency between the surface normal and depth map to enhance the training pipeline and JDACS [38] proposes a unified framework to improve the robustness of self-supervisory signals against natural color disturbance in multi-view images. U-MVS [39] utilizes the pseudo optical flow generated by off-the-shelf methods to improve the self-supervised model's performance. [42] renders pseudo depth labels from reconstructed mesh models and continues to train the self-supervised model.

2.2 Knowledge Distillation

Knowledge distillation [13] aims to transfer knowledge from a teacher model to a student model, so that a powerful and lightweight student model can be obtained. [25,26,29,34,35] consider knowledge at feature space and transfer it to the student model's feature space. Born-Again Networks (BAN) [8] trains a student model similarly parameterized as the teacher model and makes the trained student be a teacher model in a new round. The self-training scheme [37] generates distillation labels for unlabeled data and trains the student model with these labels. Probabilistic knowledge transfer (PKT) [27,28] trains the student model via matching the probability distribution of the teacher model. Since labeled data are not required to minimize the difference of probability distribution, PKT can also be applied to unsupervised learning. In this work, we are inspired by PKT and offline distillation [15,20,24,30,47] and propose to transfer the response-based knowledge [10] by forcing the predicted probability distribution of the student model to be similar to the probability distribution of the teacher model in an offline manner.

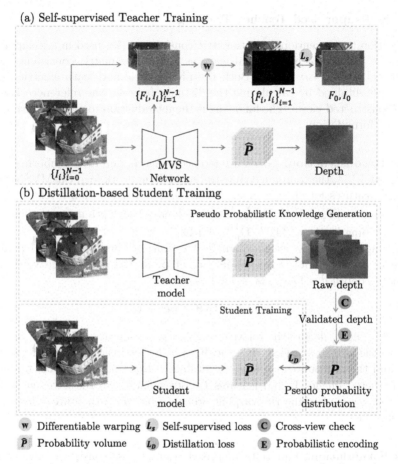

Fig. 2. Overview of KD-MVS. The first stage is self-supervised teacher training. The second stage is distillation-based student training, including pseudo probabilistic knowledge generation and student training.

3   Methodology

In this section, we elaborate the proposed training framework as illustrated in Fig. 2. KD-MVS mainly consists of self-supervised teacher training (Sect. 3.1) and distillation-based student training (Sect. 3.2). Specifically, we first train a teacher model in a self-supervised manner by using both the photometric and featuremetric consistency between the reference view and the reconstructed views.

We then generate the pseudo probability distribution of the teacher model via cross-view check and probabilistic encoding. With the supervision of the pseudo probability, the student model is trained with distillation loss in an offline distillation manner. It is worth noting that the proposed KD-MVS is a general pipeline for training MVS networks, it can be easily adapted to arbitrary learning-based MVS networks. In this paper, we mainly study KD-MVS with CasMVSNet [11].

3.1   Self-supervised Teacher Training

In addition to conventional photometric consistency [18] used in self-supervised MVS, we propose to use internal features and featuremetric consistency as an additional supervisory signal. Both the photometric and featuremetric consistency are obtained by calculating the distance between the reference view and the reconstructed views. The following is the introduction to view reconstruction and loss formulation.

View Reconstruction. Given a reference image $\mathbf{I}_0$ and its neighboring source images $\{\mathbf{I}_i\}_{i=1}^{N-1}$, the common coarse-to-fine MVS network (e.g. CasMVSNet [11]) extracts features for all N images at three different resolution levels (1/4, 1/2, 1), denoted as $\{\mathbf{F}_i^{1/4}, \mathbf{F}_i^{1/2}, \mathbf{F}_i\}_{i=0}^{N-1}$, and estimates the depth maps at these three corresponding levels, as $\mathbf{D}_0^{1/4}$, $\mathbf{D}_0^{1/2}$ and $\mathbf{D}_0$.

Taking $\mathbf{F}_0$ and $\mathbf{D}_0$ as an example, the warping between a pixel $\mathbf{p}$ at the reference view and its corresponding pixel $\hat{\mathbf{p}}_i$ at the i-th source view under estimated depth $d = \mathbf{D}_0(\mathbf{p})$ is defined as:

$$\hat{\mathbf{p}}_i = \mathbf{K}_i[\mathbf{R_i}(\mathbf{K}_0^{-1}\mathbf{p}d) + \mathbf{t_i}], \tag{1}$$

where $\mathbf{R}_i$ and $\mathbf{t}_i$ denote the relative rotation and translation from the reference view to the i-th source view. $\mathbf{K}_0$ and $\mathbf{K}_i$ are the intrinsic matrices of the reference and the i-th source camera. According to Eq. (1), we are able to get the reconstructed images $\hat{\mathbf{I}}_i$ and features $\hat{\mathbf{I}}_i$ corresponding to the i-th source view. Fig. 4 shows a photometric warping process from the i-th source view to the reference view.

Loss Formulation. Our self-supervised training loss consists of two components: photometric loss $\mathcal{L}_{\text{photo}}$ and featuremetric loss $\mathcal{L}_{\text{fea}}$. Following [18], the $\mathcal{L}_{\text{photo}}$ is based on the ℓ-1 distance between the raw RGB reference image and the reconstructed images. However, we find that the photometric loss is sensitive to lighting conditions and shooting angles, resulting in poor completeness of predictions. To overcome this problem, we use the featuremetric loss to construct a more robust loss function. Given the extracted features $\{\mathbf{F}_i\}_{i=0}^{N-1}$ from the feature net of MVS network, and the reconstructed feature maps $\hat{\mathbf{F}}_i$ generated from the i-th view, our featuremetric loss between $\hat{\mathbf{F}}_i$ and $\mathbf{F}_0$ is obtained by:

$$\mathcal{L}_{\text{fea}}^{(i)} = \|\hat{\mathbf{F}}_i - \mathbf{F}_0\|. \tag{2}$$

Fig. 3. Visualized examples of RGB colors (photometric) and extracted features (featuremetric). Dimension reduction of features is done by PCA. Features in (b) are extracted by a pre-trained ResNet-18 [12] and those in (c) are the features of the online training MVS network. Pretrained backbones tend to neglect the pixel-wise differences within intra-class regions while the online training MVS network is able to extract locally distinguishable features, which are more beneficial to downstream feature matching.

It is worth noting that we put forward to use the internal features extracted by the internal feature net of the online training MVS network instead of the external features (e.g. extracted by a pre-trained backbone network [16]) to compute featuremetric loss. Our insight is that the nature of MVS is multi-view feature matching along epipolar lines, so the features are supposed to be locally discriminative. The pre-trained backbone networks, e.g. ResNet [12] and VGG-Net [32], are usually trained with image classification loss, so that their features are not locally discriminative. As shown in Fig. 3, we compare the features extracted by an external pre-trained backbone (ResNet [12]) and by the internal encoder of the MVS network during online self-supervised training. These two options lead to completely different feature representation and we study it in Sect. 4.4 with experiments.

To summarize, the final loss function for self-supervised teacher training is

$$\mathcal{L}_S = \frac{1}{|\mathbf{V}|} \sum_{\mathbf{p} \in \mathbf{V}} \sum_{i=1}^{N-1} (\lambda_{\text{fea}} \mathcal{L}_{\text{fea}}^{(i)} + \lambda_{\text{photo}} \mathcal{L}_{\text{photo}}^{(i)}), \quad (3)$$

where $\mathbf{V}$ is the valid subset of image pixels. λ_{fea} and λ_{photo} are the two manually tuned weights, and in our experiments, we set them as 4 and 1 respectively. For coarse-to-fine networks, e.g. CasMVSNet, the loss function is applied to each of the regularization steps.

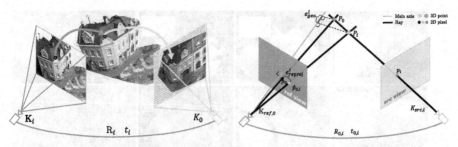

Fig. 4. Photometric warping.   **Fig. 5.** Cross-view check.

3.2   Distillation-Based Student Training

To further stimulate the potential of the self-supervised MVS network, we adopt the idea of knowledge distillation and transfer the probabilistic knowledge of the teacher to a student model. This process mainly consists of two steps, namely pseudo probabilistic knowledge generation and student training.

Pseudo Probabilistic Knowledge Generation. We consider the knowledge transfer is done through the probability distribution as is done in [15,30,35]. However, we face two main problems when applying distillation in MVS. (a) The raw per-view depth generated from the teacher model contains a lot of outliers, which is harmful to training student model. Thus we perform cross-view check to filter outliers. (b) The real probabilistic knowledge of the teacher model cannot be used directly to train the student model. That is because the depth hypotheses in the coarse-to-fine MVS network need to be dynamically sampled according to the results of the previous stage, and we cannot guarantee that the teacher model and student model always share the same depth hypotheses. To solve this problem, we propose to generate the pseudo probability distribution by probabilistic encoding.

Cross-view Check is used to filter outliers in the raw depth maps, which are inferred by the self-supervised teacher model on the unlabeled training data. Naturally, the outputs of the teacher model are per-view depth maps and the corresponding confidence maps. For coarse-to-fine methods, e.g. CasMVSNet [11], we multiply confidence maps of all three stages to obtain the final confidence map and take the depth map in the finest resolution as the final depth prediction.

We denote the final confidence map of reference view as $\mathbf{C}_0$ and the final depth prediction as $\mathbf{D}_0$, the depth maps of source views as $\{\mathbf{D}_i\}_{i=1}^{N-1}$. As is illustrated in Fig. 5, considering an arbitrary pixel $\mathbf{p}_0$ in the reference image coordinate, we cast the 2D point $\mathbf{p}_0$ to a 3D point $\mathbf{P}_0$ with the depth value $\mathbf{D}_0(\mathbf{p}_0)$. We then back-project $\mathbf{P}_0$ to i-th source view and obtain the point $\mathbf{p}_i$ in the source view. Using its estimated depth $\mathbf{D}_i(\mathbf{p}_i)$, we can cast the $\mathbf{p}_i$ to the 3D point $\mathbf{P}_i$. Finally, we back project $\mathbf{P}_i$ to the reference view and get $\hat{\mathbf{p}}_{0,i}$. Then the reprojection error at $\mathbf{p}_0$ can be written as $e_{\text{reproj}}^i = \|\mathbf{p}_0 - \hat{\mathbf{p}}_{0,i}\|$. A geometric error

e_{geo}^i is also defined to measure the relative depth error of $\mathbf{P}_0$ and $\mathbf{P}_i$ observed from the reference camera as $e_{\text{geo}}^i = \|\tilde{D}_0(\mathbf{P}_0) - \tilde{D}_0(\mathbf{P}_i)\|/\tilde{D}_0(\mathbf{P}_0)$, where the $\tilde{D}_0(\mathbf{P}_0)$ and $\tilde{D}_0(\mathbf{P}_i)$ are the projected depth of $\mathbf{P}_0$ and $\mathbf{P}_i$ in the reference view. Accordingly, the validated subset of pixels with regard to the i-th source view is defined as

$$\{\mathbf{p}_0\}_i = \{\mathbf{p}_0 | C_0(\mathbf{p}_0) > \tau_{\text{conf}}, e_{\text{reproj}}^i < \tau_{\text{reproj}}, e_{\text{geo}}^i < \tau_{\text{geo}}\}, \qquad (4)$$

where τ represents threshold values, we set τ_{conf}, τ_{reproj} and τ_{geo} to 0.15, 1.0 and 0.01 respectively. The final validated mask is the intersection of all $\{\mathbf{p}_0\}_i$ across N-1 source views. The obtained $\{\tilde{D}_0(\mathbf{P}_i)\}_{i=0}^{N-1}$ and validated mask will be further used to generate the pseudo probability distribution.

Probabilistic Encoding uses the $\{\tilde{D}_0(\mathbf{P}_i)\}_{i=0}^{N-1}$ to generate the pseudo probability distribution $P_{\mathbf{p}_0}(d)$ of depth value d for each validated pixel $\mathbf{p}_0$ in reference view. We model $P_{\mathbf{p}_0}$ as a Gaussian distribution with a mean depth value of $\mu(\mathbf{p}_0)$ and a variance of $\sigma^2(\mathbf{p}_0)$, which can be obtained by maximum likelihood estimation (MLE):

$$\mu(\mathbf{p}_0) = \frac{1}{N} \sum_{i=0}^{N-1} \tilde{D}_0(\mathbf{P}_i), \quad \sigma^2(\mathbf{p}_0) = \frac{1}{N} \sum_{i=0}^{N-1} \left(\tilde{D}_0(\mathbf{P}_i) - \mu(\mathbf{p}_0)\right)^2. \qquad (5)$$

The $\mu(\mathbf{p}_0)$ fuses the depth information from multiple views, while the $\sigma^2(\mathbf{p}_0)$ reflects the uncertainty of the teacher model at $\mathbf{p}_0$, which will provide probabilistic knowledge for the student model during distillation training.

Student Training. With the pseudo probability distribution P, we are able to train a student model from scratch via forcing its predicted probability distribution $\hat{P}$ to be similar with P. For the discrete depth hypotheses $\{d_k\}_{k=0}^D$, we obtain their pseudo probability $\{P(d_k)\}_{k=0}^D$ on the continuous probability distribution P and normalize $\{P(d_k)\}_{k=0}^D$ using SoftMax, taking the result as the final discrete pseudo probability value. We use Kullback-Leibler divergence to measure the distance between the student model's predicted probability and the pseudo probability. The distillation loss $\mathcal{L}_D$ is defined as

$$\mathcal{L}_D = \mathcal{L}_{KL}(P||\hat{P}) = \sum_{\mathbf{p} \in \{\mathbf{p}_v\}} \left(P_{\mathbf{p}} - \hat{P}_{\mathbf{p}}\right) log \left(\frac{P_{\mathbf{p}}}{\hat{P}_{\mathbf{p}}}\right), \qquad (6)$$

where $\{\mathbf{p}_v\}$ represents the subset of valid pixels after cross-view check.

In experiments, we find that the trained student model also has the potential of becoming a teacher and further distilling its knowledge to another student model. As a trade-off between training time and performance, we perform the process of knowledge distillation once more. More details can be found in Sect. 4.4.

Table 1. Quantitative results on DTU evaluation set [2] (**lower is better**). Sup. indicates whether the method is supervised or not.

Method	Sup.	Acc.	Comp.	Overall
Gipuma [9]	–	0.283	0.873	0.578
COLMAP [31]	–	0.400	0.664	0.532
MVSNet [44]	✓	0.396	0.527	0.462
AA-RMVSNet [36]	✓	0.376	0.339	0.357
CasMVSNet [11]	✓	0.325	0.385	0.355
UCS-Net [3]	✓	0.338	0.349	0.344
Unsup_MVS [18]	✗	0.881	1.073	0.977
MVS^2 [4]	✗	0.760	0.515	0.637
M^{3}VSNet [14]	✗	0.636	0.531	0.583
JDACS [38]	✗	0.571	0.515	0.543
Self-supervised-CVP-MVSNet [42]	✗	**0.308**	0.418	0.363
U-MVS+MVSNet [39]	✗	0.470	0.430	0.450
U-MVS+CasMVSNet [39]	✗	0.354	0.354	0.354
Ours+MVSNet	✗	0.424	0.426	0.425
Ours+CasMVSNet	✗	0.359	**0.295**	**0.327**

4   Experiments

4.1   Datasets

DTU dataset [2] is captured under well-controlled laboratory conditions with a fixed camera rig, containing 128 scans with 49 views under 7 different lighting conditions. We split the dataset into 79 training scans, 18 validation scans, and 22 evaluation scans by following the practice of MVSNet [44]. BlendedMVS dataset [46] is a large-scale dataset for multi-view stereo and contains objects and scenes of varying complexity and scale. This dataset is split into 106 training scans and 7 validation scans. Tanks and Temples benchmark [19] is a public benchmark acquired in realistic conditions, which contains 8 scenes for the intermediate subset and 6 for the advanced subset.

4.2   Implementation Details

At the phase of self-supervised teacher training on DTU dataset [2], we set the number of input images $N = 5$ and image resolution as 512×640. For coarse-to-fine regularization of CasMVSNet [11], the settings of depth range and the number of depth hypotheses are consistent with [11]; the depth interval decays by 0.25 and 0.5 from the coarsest stage to the finest stage. The teacher model is trained with Adam for 5 epochs with a learning rate of 0.001. At the phase of distillation-based student training, we train the student model with the pseudo probability distribution for 10 epochs. Model training of all experiments is carried out on 8 NVIDIA RTX 2080 GPUs.

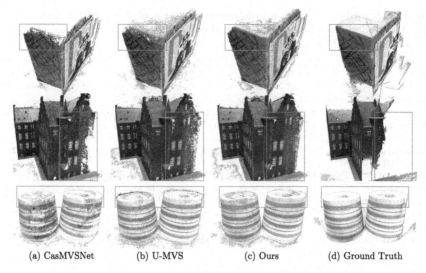

(a) CasMVSNet   (b) U-MVS   (c) Ours   (d) Ground Truth

Fig. 6. Comparison of reconstructed results with the supervised baseline [11] and the state-of-the-art self-supervised method U-MVS [39] on DTU test set [2].

4.3 Experimental Results

DTU Dataset. We evaluate KD-MVS, applied to MVSNet [44] and CasMVS-Net [11] on DTU dataset [2]. We set $N = 5$ and input resolution as 864×1152 at evaluation. Quantitative comparisons are shown in Table 1. Accuracy, Completeness and Overall are the three official metrics from [2]. Our method outperforms all self-supervised methods by a large margin and even the supervised ones. Fig. 6 shows a visualization comparison of reconstructed point clouds. Our method achieves much better reconstruction quality when compared with the baseline network and the state-of-the-art self-supervised method.

Tanks and Temples Benchmark. We test our method on Tanks and Temples benchmark [19] to demonstrate the ability to generalize on varying data. For a fair comparison with state-of-the-art methods, we fine-tune our model on the training set of the BlendedMVS dataset [46] using the original image resolution (576×768) and $N = 5$. More details about the fine-tuning process can be found in supp. materials. Similar to other methods [11,39], the camera parameters, depth ranges, and neighboring view selection are aligned with [45]. We use images of the original resolution for inference. Quantitative results are shown in Table 2 and Table 3, and the qualitative comparisons ares shown in Fig. 7. When applied on CasMVSNet [11], our method ranks 1st among all submitted methods (including supervised methods) on intermediate set of Tanks and Temples online benchmark [19] by Mar. 5, 2022.

Table 2. Quantitative results on the intermediate set of Tanks and Temples benchmark [1]. Sup. indicates whether the method is supervised or not. **Bold** and underlined figures indicate the best and the second best results.

Method	Sup.	Mean	Family	Francis	Horse	L.H.	M60	Panther	P.G.	Train
COLMAP [31]	-	42.14	50.41	22.25	26.63	56.43	44.83	46.97	48.53	42.04
ACMM [40]	-	57.27	69.24	51.45	46.97	63.20	55.07	57.64	60.08	54.48
AttMVS [22]	-	60.05	73.90	62.58	44.08	**64.88**	56.08	59.39	**63.42**	56.06
MVS^2 [4]	✗	37.21	47.74	21.55	19.50	44.54	44.86	46.32	43.38	29.72
M^{3}VSNet [14]	✗	37.67	47.74	24.38	18.74	44.42	43.45	44.95	47.39	30.31
JDACS [38]	✗	45.48	66.62	38.25	36.11	46.12	46.66	45.25	47.69	37.16
Self-supervised-CVP-MVSNet [42]	✗	46.71	64.95	38.79	24.98	49.73	52.57	51.53	50.66	40.52
U-MVS+CasMVSNet [39]	✗	57.15	76.49	60.04	49.20	55.52	55.33	51.22	56.77	52.63
CasMVSNet [11]	✓	56.84	76.37	58.45	46.26	55.81	56.11	54.06	58.18	49.51
Vis-MVSNet [48]	✓	60.03	77.40	60.23	47.07	63.44	62.21	57.28	60.54	52.07
AA-RMVSNet [36]	✓	61.51	77.77	59.53	51.53	64.02	64.05	59.47	60.85	54.90
EPP-MVSNet [23]	✓	61.68	77.86	60.54	52.96	62.33	61.69	60.34	62.44	55.30
Ours+CasMVSNet	✗	**64.14**	**80.42**	**67.42**	**54.02**	64.52	64.18	61.60	62.37	**58.59**

Table 3. Quantitative results on the advanced set of Tanks and Temples benchmark [1].

Method	Sup.	Mean	Auditorium	Ballroom	Courtroom	Museum	Palace	Temple
COLMAP [31]	–	27.24	16.02	25.23	34.70	41.51	18.05	27.94
ACMM [40]	–	34.02	23.41	32.91	**41.17**	48.13	23.87	34.60
CasMVSNet [11]	✓	31.12	19.81	38.46	29.10	43.87	27.36	28.11
AA-RMVSNet [36]	✓	33.53	20.96	40.15	32.05	46.01	29.28	32.71
Vis-MVSNet [48]	✓	33.78	20.79	38.77	32.45	44.20	28.73	37.70
EPP-MVSNet [23]	✓	35.72	21.28	39.74	35.34	**49.21**	30.00	**38.75**
Ours+CasMVSNet	✗	**37.96**	**27.22**	**44.10**	35.53	49.16	**34.67**	37.11

BlendedMVS Dataset. We further demonstrate the quality of depth maps on the validation set of BlendedMVS dataset [46]. The details of the training process can be found in supp. materials. We set $N = 5$, image resolution as 512×640, and apply the evaluation metrics described in [5] where depth values are normalized to make depth maps with different depth ranges comparable. Quantitative results are illustrated in Table 4. EPE stands for the endpoint error, which is the average ℓ-1 distance between the prediction and the ground truth depth; e_1 and e_3 represent the percentage of pixels with depth error larger than 1 and larger than 3.

4.4   Ablation Study

Implementation of Featuremetric Loss. As analyzed in Sect. 3.1, we consider the nature of the MVS is multi-view feature matching along epipolar lines, where the features are supposed to be relatively locally discriminative. Table 5 shows the quantitative results of different settings. Compared with using photometric loss only, both internal featuremetric and external featuremetric loss can

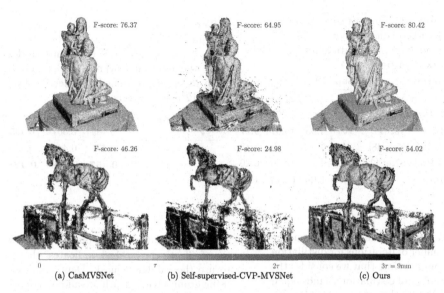

Fig. 7. Comparison of reconstructed results with the supervised baseline CasMVS-Net [11] and the state-of-the-art self-supervised method [42] on Tanks and Temples benchmark [19]. $\tau = 3mm$ is the distance threshold determined officially and darker regions indicate larger error encountered with regard to τ.

boost the performance. And our proposed internal featuremetric loss shows superiority over the external featuremetric loss with external features by a pre-trained ResNet. It is worth noting that it is not feasible to adopt our featuremetric loss alone. The reason is that the feature network is online trained within the MVS network and thus applying featuremetric loss alone will lead to failure of training where features tend to be a constant (typically 0).

Number of Self-training Iterations. Given the scheme of knowledge distillation via generating pseudo probability, we can iterate the distillation-based student training for an arbitrary number of loops. Here we study the performance gain when the number of iterations increases in Table 6. As a trade-off of efficiency and accuracy, we set the number of iterations to be 2.

5   Discussion

5.1   Insights of Effectiveness

We attribute the effectiveness of KD-MVS to the following four parts. (a) The first one is multi-view consistency as introduced in Sect. 3.2, which can be used to filter the outliers in noisy raw depth maps. The remaining inliers are relatively accurate and are equivalent to ground-truth depth to a certain extent. (b) The probabilistic knowledge brings performance gain to the student model.

Table 4. Quantitative results towards predicted depth maps on BlendedMVS validation set [46] (**lower is better**).

Method	Sup.	EPE	e_1	e_3
MVSNet [44]	✓	1.49	21.98	8.32
CVP-MVSNet [43]	✓	1.90	19.73	10.24
CasMVSNet [11]	✓	1.43	19.01	9.77
Vis-MVSNet [48]	✓	1.47	15.14	5.13
EPP-MVSNet [23]	✓	1.17	12.66	6.20
Ours	✗	**1.04**	**10.17**	**4.94**

Table 5. Ablation study on loss for self-supervised training stage (teacher model). $\mathcal{L}_{fea}$ and $\mathcal{L}_{fea}^*$ denotes featuremetric loss by the internal feature encoder and by an external pretrained encoder (ResNet-18 [12]) respectively.

$\mathcal{L}_{photo}$	$\mathcal{L}_{fea}^*$	$\mathcal{L}_{fea}$	Acc.	Comp.	Overall
✓			0.489	0.501	0.495
✓	✓		0.477	0.441	0.459
✓		✓	**0.457**	**0.399**	**0.428**

Table 6. Ablation study on the number of iterations for distillation training. Note that we consider the number of distillation rounds equal to the number of times fused depth is generated and verified.

#round(s)	Acc.	Comp.	Overall
1	0.387	0.334	0.361
2	0.359	**0.295**	**0.327**
3	**0.357**	0.298	**0.327**
4	0.358	0.297	0.328

Table 7. Ablation study on the main factor of effectiveness. Mask indicates whether to use the validated mask. Depth indicates using ground truth depth or validated depth. Loss indicates which loss is used.

	Mask	Depth	Loss	Acc.	Comp.	Over
(1)	✗	GT	ℓ-1	0.358	0.346	0.352
(2)	✓	GT	ℓ-1	**0.352**	0.334	0.343
(3)	✓	vali	ℓ-1	0.361	0.331	0.346
(4)	✓	vali	Distill	0.359	**0.295**	**0.327**

Compared with using hard labels such as ℓ-1 loss and depth labels, applying soft probability distribution to student model brings additional inter-depth relationships and thus reduces the ambiguity of noisy 3D points. (c) The validated depth contains less perspective error than rendered ground truth labels. As shown in the last row of Fig. 8 (marked with a red box), there are some incorrect values in the ground-truth depth maps of DTU dataset [2] caused by perspective error, which is harmful to training MVS models. (d) The validated masks of the teacher model reduce the ambiguity of prediction by filtering the samples which are hard to learn, benefiting the convergence of the model. We perform an ablation study on these parts as shown in Table 7. (1) and (2) show that the validated mask is helpful, (3) and (4) show that enforcing the probability distribution can bring significant improvement. More details can be found in supp. materials.

5.2   Comparisons to SOTA Methods

U-MVS [39] leverages optical flow to compute a depth-flow consistency loss. To get reliable optical flow labels, U-MVS trains a PWC-Net [33] on DTU dataset [2] in a self-supervised manner, which costs additional training time and needs storage space for the pseudo optical flow labels (more than $120GB$).

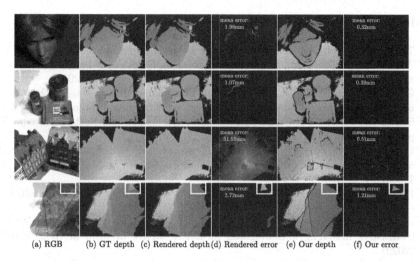

(a) RGB   (b) GT depth (c) Rendered depth(d) Rendered error   (e) Our depth   (f) Our error

Fig. 8. Visualization of depth maps and errors. (a) RGB reference images; (b) ground-truth depth maps; (c) rendered depth maps by [42]; (d) errors between (b) and (c); (e) pseudo labels in KD-MVS; (f) errors between (b) and (e). We apply the same mask on (b)(c)(e) for better visualization.

Self-supervised-CVP-MVSNet [42] renders depth maps from the reconstructed meshes, which brings in error during Poisson reconstruction [17]. We compare the rendered depth maps [42] and our validated depth maps in Fig. 8.

5.3   Limitations

- The quality of pseudo probability distribution highly depends on the cross-view check stage and relevant hyperparameters need to be tuned carefully.
- Knowledge distillation is known as data-hungry and it may not work as expected with a relatively small-scale dataset.

6   Conclusion

In this paper, we propose KD-MVS, which is a general self-supervised pipeline for MVS networks without any ground-truth depth as supervision. In the self-supervised teacher training stage, we leverage a featuremetric loss term, which is more robust than photometric loss alone. The features are yielded internally by the MVS network itself, which is end-to-end trained under implicit supervision. To explore the potential of self-supervised MVS, we adopt the idea of knowledge distillation and distills the teacher's knowledge to a student model by generating pseudo probability distribution. Experimental results indicate that the self-supervised training pipeline has the potential to obtain reconstruction quality equivalent to supervised ones.

References

1. Tanks and temples benchmark. https://www.tanksandtemples.org
2. Aanæs, H., Jensen, R.R., Vogiatzis, G., Tola, E., Dahl, A.B.: Large-scale data for multiple-view stereopsis. Int. J. Comput. Vis. **120**(2), 153–168 (2016)
3. Cheng, S., Xu, Z., Zhu, S., Li, Z., Li, L.E., Ramamoorthi, R., Su, H.: Deep stereo using adaptive thin volume representation with uncertainty awareness. In: Proceedings of the IEEE/CVF Conference on Computer Vision and Pattern Recognition, pp. 2524–2534 (2020)
4. Dai, Y., Zhu, Z., Rao, Z., Li, B.: Mvs2: Deep unsupervised multi-view stereo with multi-view symmetry. In: 2019 International Conference on 3D Vision (3DV), pp. 1–8. IEEE (2019)
5. Darmon, F., Bascle, B., Devaux, J.C., Monasse, P., Aubry, M.: Deep multi-view stereo gone wild. arXiv preprint arXiv:2104.15119 (2021)
6. Ding, Y., Li, Z., Huang, D., Li, Z., Zhang, K.: Enhancing multi-view stereo with contrastive matching and weighted focal loss. arXiv preprint arXiv:2206.10360 (2022)
7. Ding, Y., Yuan, W., Zhu, Q., Zhang, H., Liu, X., Wang, Y., Liu, X.: Transmvsnet: global context-aware multi-view stereo network with transformers. In: Proceedings of the IEEE/CVF Conference on Computer Vision and Pattern Recognition, pp. 8585–8594 (2022)
8. Furlanello, T., Lipton, Z., Tschannen, M., Itti, L., Anandkumar, A.: Born again neural networks. In: International Conference on Machine Learning, pp. 1607–1616. PMLR (2018)
9. Galliani, S., Lasinger, K., Schindler, K.: Massively parallel multiview stereopsis by surface normal diffusion. In: Proceedings of the IEEE International Conference on Computer Vision, pp. 873–881 (2015)
10. Gou, J., Yu, B., Maybank, S.J., Tao, D.: Knowledge distillation: a survey. Int. J. Comput. Vis. **129**(6), 1789–1819 (2021)
11. Gu, X., Fan, Z., Zhu, S., Dai, Z., Tan, F., Tan, P.: Cascade cost volume for high-resolution multi-view stereo and stereo matching. In: Proceedings of the IEEE/CVF Conference on Computer Vision and Pattern Recognition, pp. 2495–2504 (2020)
12. He, K., Zhang, X., Ren, S., Sun, J.: Deep residual learning for image recognition. In: Proceedings of the IEEE/CVF International Conference on Computer Vision (2016)
13. Hinton, G., Vinyals, O., Dean, J., et al.: Distilling the knowledge in a neural network. arXiv preprint arXiv:1503.02531 2(7) (2015)
14. Huang, B., Yi, H., Huang, C., He, Y., Liu, J., Liu, X.: M3vsnet: unsupervised multi-metric multi-view stereo network. arXiv preprint arXiv:2004.09722 (2020)
15. Huang, Z., Wang, N.: Like what you like: knowledge distill via neuron selectivity transfer. arXiv preprint arXiv:1707.01219 (2017)
16. Johnson, J., Alahi, A., Fei-Fei, L.: Perceptual losses for real-time style transfer and super-resolution. In: Leibe, B., Matas, J., Sebe, N., Welling, M. (eds.) ECCV 2016. LNCS, vol. 9906, pp. 694–711. Springer, Cham (2016). https://doi.org/10.1007/978-3-319-46475-6_43
17. Kazhdan, M., Hoppe, H.: Screened poisson surface reconstruction. ACM Trans. Graph. (ToG) **32**(3), 1–13 (2013)
18. Khot, T., Agrawal, S., Tulsiani, S., Mertz, C., Lucey, S., Hebert, M.: Learning unsupervised multi-view stereopsis via robust photometric consistency. arXiv preprint arXiv:1905.02706 (2019)

19. Knapitsch, A., Park, J., Zhou, Q.Y., Koltun, V.: Tanks and temples: benchmarking large-scale scene reconstruction. ACM Trans. Graph. (ToG) **36**(4), 1–13 (2017)
20. Li, T., Li, J., Liu, Z., Zhang, C.: Few sample knowledge distillation for efficient network compression. In: Proceedings of the IEEE/CVF Conference on Computer Vision and Pattern Recognition, pp. 14639–14647 (2020)
21. Liao, J., et al.: Wt-mvsnet: window-based transformers for multi-view stereo. arXiv preprint arXiv:2205.14319 (2022)
22. Luo, K., Guan, T., Ju, L., Wang, Y., Chen, Z., Luo, Y.: Attention-aware multi-view stereo. In: Proceedings of the IEEE/CVF Conference on Computer Vision and Pattern Recognition, pp. 1590–1599 (2020)
23. Ma, X., Gong, Y., Wang, Q., Huang, J., Chen, L., Yu, F.: Epp-mvsnet: epipolar-assembling based depth prediction for multi-view stereo. In: Proceedings of the IEEE/CVF International Conference on Computer Vision, pp. 5732–5740 (2021)
24. Mirzadeh, S.I., Farajtabar, M., Li, A., Levine, N., Matsukawa, A., Ghasemzadeh, H.: Improved knowledge distillation via teacher assistant. In: Proceedings of the AAAI Conference on Artificial Intelligence, vol. 34, pp. 5191–5198 (2020)
25. Park, W., Kim, D., Lu, Y., Cho, M.: Relational knowledge distillation. In: Proceedings of the IEEE/CVF Conference on Computer Vision and Pattern Recognition, pp. 3967–3976 (2019)
26. Passalis, N., Tefas, A.: Learning deep representations with probabilistic knowledge transfer. In: Proceedings of the European Conference on Computer Vision (ECCV), pp. 268–284 (2018)
27. Passalis, N., Tefas, A.: Learning deep representations with probabilistic knowledge transfer. In: Proceedings of the European Conference on Computer Vision (ECCV), pp. 268–284 (2018)
28. Passalis, N., Tzelepi, M., Tefas, A.: Probabilistic knowledge transfer for lightweight deep representation learning. IEEE Trans. Neural Netw. Learn. Syst. **32**(5), 2030–2039 (2020)
29. Peng, B., et al.: Correlation congruence for knowledge distillation. In: Proceedings of the IEEE/CVF International Conference on Computer Vision, pp. 5007–5016 (2019)
30. Romero, A., Ballas, N., Kahou, S.E., Chassang, A., Gatta, C., Bengio, Y.: Fitnets: hints for thin deep nets. arXiv preprint arXiv:1412.6550 (2014)
31. Schönberger, J.L., Zheng, E., Frahm, J.-M., Pollefeys, M.: Pixelwise view selection for unstructured multi-view stereo. In: Leibe, B., Matas, J., Sebe, N., Welling, M. (eds.) ECCV 2016. LNCS, vol. 9907, pp. 501–518. Springer, Cham (2016). https://doi.org/10.1007/978-3-319-46487-9_31
32. Simonyan, K., Zisserman, A.: Very deep convolutional networks for large-scale image recognition. arXiv preprint arXiv:1409.1556 (2014)
33. Sun, D., Yang, X., Liu, M.Y., Kautz, J.: Pwc-net: Cnns for optical flow using pyramid, warping, and cost volume. In: Proceedings of the IEEE Conference on Computer Vision and Pattern Recognition, pp. 8934–8943 (2018)
34. Tian, Y., Krishnan, D., Isola, P.: Contrastive representation distillation. arXiv preprint arXiv:1910.10699 (2019)
35. Tung, F., Mori, G.: Similarity-preserving knowledge distillation. In: Proceedings of the IEEE/CVF International Conference on Computer Vision, pp. 1365–1374 (2019)
36. Wei, Z., Zhu, Q., Min, C., Chen, Y., Wang, G.: Aa-rmvsnet: adaptive aggregation recurrent multi-view stereo network. In: Proceedings of the IEEE/CVF International Conference on Computer Vision, pp. 6187–6196 (2021)

37. Xie, Q., Luong, M.T., Hovy, E., Le, Q.V.: Self-training with noisy student improves imagenet classification. In: Proceedings of the IEEE/CVF Conference on Computer Vision and Pattern Recognition, pp. 10687–10698 (2020)

38. Xu, H., Zhou, Z., Qiao, Y., Kang, W., Wu, Q.: Self-supervised multi-view stereo via effective co-segmentation and data-augmentation. In: Proceedings of the AAAI Conference on Artificial Intelligence, vol. 2, p. 6 (2021)

39. Xu, H., Zhou, Z., Wang, Y., Kang, W., Sun, B., Li, H., Qiao, Y.: Digging into uncertainty in self-supervised multi-view stereo. In: Proceedings of the IEEE/CVF International Conference on Computer Vision, pp. 6078–6087 (2021)

40. Xu, Q., Tao, W.: Multi-scale geometric consistency guided multi-view stereo. In: Proceedings of the IEEE/CVF Conference on Computer Vision and Pattern Recognition, pp. 5483–5492 (2019)

41. Yan, J., Wei, Z., Yi, H., Ding, M., Zhang, R., Chen, Y., Wang, G., Tai, Y.-W.: Dense hybrid recurrent multi-view stereo net with dynamic consistency checking. In: Vedaldi, A., Bischof, H., Brox, T., Frahm, J.-M. (eds.) ECCV 2020. LNCS, vol. 12349, pp. 674–689. Springer, Cham (2020). https://doi.org/10.1007/978-3-030-58548-8_39

42. Yang, J., Alvarez, J.M., Liu, M.: Self-supervised learning of depth inference for multi-view stereo. In: Proceedings of the IEEE/CVF Conference on Computer Vision and Pattern Recognition, pp. 7526–7534 (2021)

43. Yang, J., Mao, W., Alvarez, J.M., Liu, M.: Cost volume pyramid based depth inference for multi-view stereo. In: Proceedings of the IEEE/CVF Conference on Computer Vision and Pattern Recognition, pp. 4877–4886 (2020)

44. Yao, Y., Luo, Z., Li, S., Fang, T., Quan, L.: Mvsnet: depth inference for unstructured multi-view stereo. In: Proceedings of the European Conference on Computer Vision (ECCV), pp. 767–783 (2018)

45. Yao, Y., Luo, Z., Li, S., Shen, T., Fang, T., Quan, L.: Recurrent mvsnet for high-resolution multi-view stereo depth inference. In: Proceedings of the IEEE/CVF Conference on Computer Vision and Pattern Recognition, pp. 5525–5534 (2019)

46. Yao, Y., Luo, Z., Li, S., Zhang, J., Ren, Y., Zhou, L., Fang, T., Quan, L.: Blended-mvs: a large-scale dataset for generalized multi-view stereo networks. In: Proceedings of the IEEE/CVF Conference on Computer Vision and Pattern Recognition, pp. 1790–1799 (2020)

47. Zagoruyko, S., Komodakis, N.: Paying more attention to attention: improving the performance of convolutional neural networks via attention transfer. arXiv preprint arXiv:1612.03928 (2016)

48. Zhang, J., Yao, Y., Li, S., Luo, Z., Fang, T.: Visibility-aware multi-view stereo network. British Machine Vision Conference (BMVC) (2020)

SALVe: Semantic Alignment Verification for Floorplan Reconstruction from Sparse Panoramas

John Lambert[2(✉)], Yuguang Li[1], Ivaylo Boyadzhiev[1], Lambert Wixson[1],
Manjunath Narayana[1], Will Hutchcroft[1], James Hays[2], Frank Dellaert[2],
and Sing Bing Kang[1]

[1] Zillow Group, Seattle, USA
[2] Georgia Institute of Technology, Atlanta, USA
johnwlambert@gmail.com

Abstract. We propose a new system for automatic 2D floorplan reconstruction that is enabled by *SALVe*, our novel pairwise learned alignment verifier. The inputs to our system are sparsely located 360° panoramas, whose semantic features (windows, doors, and openings) are inferred and used to hypothesize pairwise room adjacency or overlap. SALVe initializes a pose graph, which is subsequently optimized using GTSAM [16]. Once the room poses are computed, room layouts are inferred using HorizonNet [50], and the floorplan is constructed by stitching the most confident layout boundaries. We validate our system qualitatively and quantitatively as well as through ablation studies, showing that it outperforms state-of-the-art SfM systems in completeness by over 200%, without sacrificing accuracy. Our results point to the significance of our work: poses of 81% of panoramas are localized in the first 2 connected components (CCs), and 89% in the first 3 CCs.

Keywords: Floorplan reconstruction · 3D reconstruction · Structure from motion · Extreme pose estimation

1 Introduction

Indoor geometry reconstruction enables a variety of applications that include virtual tours, architectural analysis, virtual staging, and autonomous navigation. There are solutions for image-based reconstruction based on inputs ranging from dense image capture to sparser capture using specialized imaging equipment (e.g., Matterport Pro2). For scalability of adoption, however, data bandwidth, equipment costs, and amount of labor must be considered.

We reconstruct floorplans from sparsely captured 360° panoramas, as provided by ZInD [14]. Currently, this problem is far from solved. Traditional Structure-from-Motion (SfM) [25,35] suffers from very limited reconstruction completeness [14,45].

J. Lambert—Work completed during an internship at Zillow Group.

Supplementary Information The online version contains supplementary material available at https://doi.org/10.1007/978-3-031-19821-2_37.

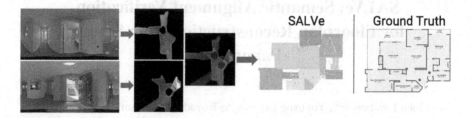

Fig. 1. A challenging wide-baseline scenario where traditional SfM systems that rely upon key-point feature matches struggle, but where we succeed by exploiting semantic features such as doors, windows, and openings, or W/D/O). We infer layout and hypothesize plausible pairwise relative poses, which are then accepted or rejected, by feeding top-down aligned renderings into our learned *SALVe* verifier. Our global pose estimation has high completeness, leading to dramatic improvements in floorplan reconstruction (indicated by colored regions) vs. state-of-the-art systems such as OpenMVG [35] and OpenSfM [25]. For this hallway/entryway pano pair, SALVe easily validates a relative pose that was generated by grounding on a hallway opening feature.

Semantic SfM has been proposed [4,12,13], but accuracy is still limited, typically requiring a human in the loop [14] (Fig. 1).

Indoor floorplan reconstruction from unordered panoramas is a *discrete* instance of the wide-baseline SfM problem. Unlike traditional SfM, which is associated with a continuous estimation problem, for indoor residential floorplan reconstruction, discrete room pieces must align at specific junction points (such as doors and walls), similar to solving a jigsaw puzzle [30]. We show how objects with repetitive structure, such as windows and doors, can be used to hypothesize room adjacency or overlap. Each hypothesis, i.e. a matched semantic element, provides a relative 2D room pose. The main innovation of our work is *SALVe*, a learned pairwise room alignment verifier. Given a room pair alignment hypothesis, *SALVe* uses the bird's eye view (BEV) of floors and ceilings to predict the likelihood score of adjacency or overlap. Our use of a discrete combinatorial proposal step, followed by a learned deep verifier, is akin to recent trends in language models, for tasks requiring multi-step reasoning [11,46], as *"Verifiers benefit both from their inherent optionality and from verification being a simpler task than generation in general."* [11].

Once the relative poses are computed and verified, we perform global pose graph optimization using GTSAM [16]. Using the estimated poses and room layouts generated using HorizonNet [50], we construct the floorplan by stitching these layouts.

Our contributions are:

- To our knowledge, the first system for creating floorplans from unaligned panoramas with small to extremely wide baselines. These baselines can be so large that traditional SfM techniques fail.
- SALVe, a novel learning-based approach for validating discrete pairwise alignment proposals between panoramas in polynomial time.
- We show how our network verifies measurements with a high enough signal-to-noise ratio to directly apply global aggregation and optimization techniques.

2 Related Work

We briefly review approaches in floorplan reconstruction, SfM, and pose estimation under extreme baselines. While single-room layout estimation and depth estimation are also relevant, we do not claim novelty in these areas. Good surveys of such methods can be found in [1,41].

Floorplan Reconstruction. Early systems require a human in the loop [15,22]. One notable manual approach is that of Farin *et al.* [22], which uses sparsely located 360° panoramas for joint floorplan and camera pose estimation.

For more automated solutions, SfM is used on densely captured perspective images [24] or 360° panoramas [5]. Both use SfM and MVS output to formulate graph optimization problems on a regular grid, through either graph cuts [24] or shortest-path problems [5], from which a rough 2D floorplan can be extracted. For sparser image inputs, semantic information such as floors, ceilings, and walls are used as additional cues [39]. Pintore *et al.* [40] cluster panoramas by room using photo-consistency at the central horizon line and plane sweeping with superpixel object masks to model clutter and floorplans in 3D. There are also methods on floorplan reconstruction from known camera poses [7,30,31,42,49] or RGBD data [7,20,21,28,30,31,36,42,49].

Structure from Motion (SfM). Much work has been done on SfM, and we refer readers to surveys such as [38]. Recently, deep learning with graph-based attention [44] or transformers [52] for deep, differentiable key point matching has been exploited to learn and match features from data. These "deep front-ends" offer a promise of less noisy input to back-end optimization [44]. Our system can be viewed as a deep verifier network (a deep front-end) that feeds measurements to global SfM [34,53]; however, instead of requiring complex outlier rejection schemes typical of global SfM [19,34,35,53,54,57], we show that outlier rejection can simply be based on predicted scores.

Semantic information has been used to overcome the limitation of keypoint matching for large baselines or scenes with little detail or repetitive textures [4,10]. Cohen *et al.* [12] first introduced a combinatorial approach for 3D model registration by aligning semantic objects such as windows [13]. More recent work [14,45] exploits this same idea to assemble floorplans from room layouts.

Extreme Pose Estimation. This refers to computing relative pose with little to no visual overlap. On localizing RGBD images, Yang *et al.* [55,56] demonstrate scan completion to a 360° image, followed by feature-based registration can be useful. Chen *et al.* [8] introduce DirectionNet to estimate a distribution of relative poses in 5 DOF space, i.e., when scale is unknown. SparsePlanes [27] uses planar surface estimation from perspective views within a single room for relative pose estimation. Other CNN-based approaches on perspective image re-localization include [3,18,29].

In concurrent work, Shabani *et al.* [45] use semantic information to generate global pose hypotheses by synthesizing Manhattan-only floorplans. The hypotheses are then scored by ConvMPN [58] and used to produce plausible room layout arrangements along with camera poses. They assume each panorama is captured in separate but connected rooms. Another key difference from our work is that their learning-based verifier is trained to evaluate the *final floorplan arrangements*, after using heuristics to enumerate many possible solutions. This is *exponential* in the number of input panoramas.

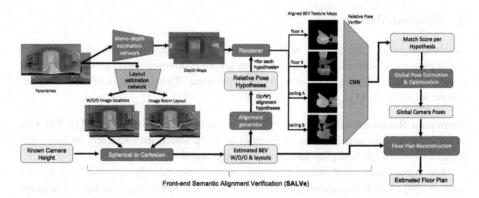

Fig. 2. Overview of our floorplan reconstruction system. "BEV" = "bird's eye view". Blue boxes are processing components, gray boxes are data. Trapezoids denote components based on deep networks; lighter blue networks are trained by us. 'Image Room Layout' represents the image coordinates of the floor-wall boundary (at each panorama column). n is the number of panoramas and k is the average number of detected windows/doors/openings per panorama. We show rendered floor and ceiling texture maps for a consistently-aligned pair of panoramas. (Color figure online)

Their approach is expected to produce several layout arrangements. In contrast, *SALVe* matches semantic elements between pairs of panoramas in polynomial time. Our model is then trained to verify the individual pairwise arrangements, allowing our approach to be substituted as a front-end in any pose-graph optimization and producing a single reconstruction with higher reliability.

3   System Overview

We address the problem of global pose estimation of sparsely located panoramas, for the purpose of floorplan reconstruction. Formally, we define the global pose estimation problem as, given an unordered collection of n panoramas $\{\mathbf{I}_i\}$, determine poses $\{{}^w\mathbf{T}_i\}_{i=1}^n \in SE(2)$ of each panorama in global coordinate frame w. Similar to [42], we define the floorplan reconstruction problem as generating a *raster* (1) floor occupancy and (2) per-room masks.

Global pose estimation inherently relies on methods that build up global information from local signals. In our work, these local signals are estimated relative poses between pairs of panoramas. Our system for generating the floorplan from sparsely located panoramas is shown in Fig. 2. The system consists of a front-end designed to hypothesize and compute relative pairwise poses, and a back-end designed to optimize global poses using these measurements.

The front-end (*SALVe*, or Semantic Alignment Verifier) first generates hypotheses of relative pose between the input pair of panoramas using their estimated room layout and detected semantic objects (specifically windows, doors, and openings, or W/D/O).[1] A hypothesis consists of pairing the same type of object across the two panoramas. Each pair of hypothesized corresponding W/D/O detections generates two relative pose

---

[1] Openings are constructs that divide a large room into multiple parts [14].

hypotheses, by solving for the 2D translation that aligns their centers (on the ground plane), and the two possible rotation angles $\alpha, 180° + \alpha$ that align their extents. Each pairing allows us to compute the relative SE(2) pose.

A main novelty in this paper is how we test whether a hypothesis is plausible with *SALVe*. For a hypothesized relative pose, the system renders bird's-eye views of the floor and ceiling for both panoramas in the same BEV coordinate system, which produces overlapped top-down renderings. The rendering is computed with per-panorama depth distribution estimation using HoHoNet [51]. Then we use a deep CNN with a ResNet [26] backbone to generate a likelihood score that the overlapped images are a plausible match. Implausible matches are discarded, and from the remaining plausible matches we construct a pose graph. The back-end then globally optimizes the constructed pose graph using GTSAM [16]. Finally, floorplans are created by clustering the panoramas by room, extracting the most confident room layout given predicted panorama poses, and finally stitching these room layouts.

4   Approach

In this section, we detail the steps taken to generate a 2D floorplan from sparsely distributed 360° panoramas. The first step is to generate alignment hypotheses between pairs of panoramas.

4.1   Assumptions

We assume the inputs are a set of unordered 360° panoramas, captured from an indoor space. The images cover the entire space and the connecting doors between different rooms. Neighboring images may or may not have visual overlap. We assume the panoramas are in equirectangular form, i.e., their fields of view are 360° (horizontal) and 180° (vertical). The camera is assumed to be of known height and fixed orientation parallel to the floor[2], so pose is estimated in a 2D bird's-eye view (BEV) coordinate system.

4.2   Generating Alignment Hypotheses

Since our floorplan is 2D, alignment between pairs of panoramas has 3 DOFs (horizontal position and rotation). Scale is not a free parameter, assuming known, fixed camera height and a single floor plane (see [2] or our supplementary material for a derivation). To handle wide baselines, we use semantic objects (windows, doors, and openings, or W/D/O) to generate alignment hypotheses. While this is similar to the W/D/O-based room merge process in [14], we additionally make use of estimated room layout. Each room layout is estimated using a modified HorizonNet model [50]; it is trained with partial room shape geometry to predict both the floor-wall boundary with an uncertainty score and locations of W/D/O.

Each alignment hypothesis is generated with the assumption that W/D/O being aligned are in either the same room or different rooms. The outward surface normals of W/D/O are either in the same or opposite directions; we assume a window can only be

---

[2] We achieve this orientation assumption via pre-processing that straightens the panoramas using vanishing points [59].

Fig. 3. Generating training samples. Orthographic BEVs of given panoramas, after semantic alignment proposal. Red arrows indicate the W/D/O, used to generate the pose proposals. *Column 1:* Example of extreme baseline pair. *Column 2:* overlaid floor (**top**) and ceiling (**bottom**). *Column 3:* Example of a wide baseline pair. *Column 4:* overlaid floor (**top**) and ceiling (**bottom**). (Color figure online)

aligned in the direction of its interior normal, while a door or opening could be aligned in either direction. The hypothesis for rotation is refined using dominant axes of the two predicted room layouts.

Exhaustively listing pairs of W/D/O can produce many hypotheses for alignment verification. We halve the combinatorial complexity by ensuring that each pair of matched W/D/O have widths with a ratio within $[0.65, 1.0]$, i.e. a door that is 2 units wide cannot match to a door that is 1 units wide. Once the alignment hypotheses are found, they need to be verified.

4.3 SALVe: Semantic Alignment Verifier

While domain knowledge of indoor space such as room intersections and loop closure can be helpful in constructing the floorplan [14], visual cues can also be used to verify pairwise panorama overlap [17]. We use bird's eye views (BEVs, which are orthographic) of the floor and ceiling as visual cues for alignment verification. Given the significant variation in lighting and image quality across panoramas, traditional photometric matching techniques may not be very effective. Instead, we train a model to implicitly verify spatial overlap based on these aligned texture signals.

We extract depth using HoHoNet [51], which is used to render the BEVs. Example views can be found in Fig. 3. Given an alignment hypothesis, we map the BEVs of the floor and ceiling for both panoramas to a common image coordinate system. The four stacked views are then fed into our deep-learning based pairwise alignment verification model to classify 2-view alignment. Given n panoramas, each with k W/D/O, $\mathcal{O}(n^2k^2)$ alignments are possible and thus need to be verified.

SALVe uses a ResNet [26] ConvNet architecture as the backbone for verification. Its input is a stack of 4 aligned views (2 from each panorama), with a total of 12 channels. It is trained with softmax-cross entropy over 2 classes, representing the "mismatch" and "match" classes. We generate these classes by measuring the deviation of generated relative poses (alignments from window-window, opening-opening, or door-door pairs) against the ground truth poses. Those below a certain amount of deviation are considered "matches", and all others are considered "mismatches".

Fig. 4. An example of different stages of floorplan reconstruction: *Left*: Estimated positions of panorama centers. *Center*: Grouped panoramas with estimated dense room layouts. Panorama centers with the same color are part of the same group. Notice that each open space is grouped together. Distinct groups correspond largely to physical rooms separated by doors. *Right*: The final floorplan after highest-confidence contour extraction is applied to each group. Each contour is filled with a unique color.

4.4   Global Pose Estimation and Optimization

SALVe is used to generate a set of pairwise alignments, which are used to construct a pose graph; its nodes are panoramas and edges are estimated relative poses. The pose graph has an edge between any two panoramas $\mathbf{I}_{i_1}$ and $\mathbf{I}_{i_2}$ where pairing a detection $\mathbf{d}_{k_1}^{i_1}$ with detection $\mathbf{d}_{k_2}^{i_2}$ yields a plausible (according to SALVe) alignment. A detection may participate in multiple edges e.g., pairing $(\mathbf{d}_{k_1}^{i_1}, \mathbf{d}_{k_2}^{i_2})$ may add an edge between i_1 and i_2, and pairing $(\mathbf{d}_{k_1}^{i_1}, \mathbf{d}_{k_3}^{i_3})$ may add an edge between panos i_1 and i_3. Although conflicting relative pose hypotheses are possible, in practice SALVe is a sufficiently accurate verifier that they are quite rare.

When multiple disjoint graphs result, we only consider the largest connected component. We experiment with two algorithms for global localization: spanning tree pose aggregation and pose graph optimization (PGO) with a robust noise model, detailed in the supplementary material.

4.5   Floorplan Reconstruction

Figure 4 shows the progression of floorplan reconstruction, from estimated panorama poses and room layouts to the output. There are three steps: panorama room grouping, highest confidence room contour extraction, and floorplan stitching. To refine a room layout, we first identify all the panoramas within that room; this is done using 2D IoU. Since each panorama has its own layout with local shape confidence (Sect. 4.2) within a room, we extract a single global layout by searching for the most confident contour points. The search is done by raycasting from panorama centers and voting for the most confident contour point along each ray. The final floorplan is found by taking the union of (stitching) all room layouts. Details are in the supplementary material.

5   Experimental Results

In this section, we explain why we use ZInD [14], provide implementation details, and describe our metrics before showing results for different global pose estimation techniques. We also describe ablation studies that show how different types of inputs affect the results.

5.1   Use of ZInD [14]

In order to evaluate every part of our approach, as well as the entire system, we use the recently released Zillow Indoor Dataset (ZInD) [14]. ZInD has all the required components: (1) *large scale* with $67,448$ panoramas taken in $1,575$ real homes; (2) *multiple localized panoramas per-room* with 42 panoramas over 15 rooms per-home on average; (3) *layout and W/D/O* annotations including complex, non-Manhattan layouts and (4) *2D floor-plans* with 1.8 number of floors per-home on average. We use the official train, val, and test splits that contain 1260, 157, and 158 homes, and 2168, 278, 291 floors respectively. We acknowledge that in ZInD most rooms are unfurnished, but this is a frequent scenario in the domain of real estate floor plan reconstruction. While there are other real [6,45,61] and synthetic [48,60] indoor datasets, none of them have all the required components. Structured3D [60] is a synthetic dataset with only one panorama per room and doors in almost all rooms are closed (uncommon in real estate capture scenarios); these factors result in a significant change of modality.

5.2   Implementation Details

Layout and W/D/O Estimation. We use a modified version of HorizonNet [50], trained to jointly predict room layout as well as 1D extents of W/D/O. We trained the joint model on ZInD and make the predictions publicly available.

Verifier Supervision. We consider a pair-wise alignment to be a "match" if ground truth relative pose $(x, y, \theta) \in SE(2)$ and generated relative pose $(\hat{x}, \hat{y}, \hat{\theta}) \in SE(2)$ differ by less than $7°$ (θ) for doors and windows, and less than $9°$ for openings. A larger threshold is used for openings because there is more variation in their endpoints. We also require that $\left\| [x, y]^\top - [\hat{x}, \hat{y}]^\top \right\|_\infty < 0.35$ in normalized room coordinates (i.e., when camera height is scaled to 1).

Texture Mapping, Verifier Data Augmentation and Verifier Training. Details are provided in the supplementary material.

5.3   Evaluation Metrics

In order to evaluate our entire system, we measure increasing subsets of components.

Layout Estimation and W/D/O Detection Accuracy. To evaluate the quality of the layout estimation, we report 2D IoU between the predicted and ground truth room layouts per panorama. Because we project 1D W/D/O on the predicted layout, we use 1D IoU to measure the accuracy of those semantic elements, with F1 score evaluated at a true positive 1D IoU threshold of 70%.

Relative Pose Classification Accuracy. We report intermediate system metrics that measure the model's accuracy at discerning between correct and inaccurate alignments. We use mean accuracy over two classes, as well as precision, recall, and F1 score.

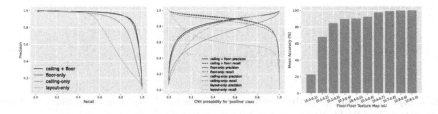

Fig. 5. Precision-recall analysis of SALVe. *Left*: curve for SALVe under different inputs ('layout-only' refers to a model with access only to estimated room geometry, but no floor or ceiling texture). *Center*: Comparison of confidence thresholds versus their effect on precision and recall. The purple line indicates our operating point (93% confidence). *Right*: Classification accuracy vs. visual overlap for the GT **positive** class only from SE(2) alignments generated from predicted W/D/O's. Small visual overlap often corresponds to "extreme" baselines. (Color figure online)

Global Pose Estimation Accuracy and Completeness. We first align an estimated pose graph $\{\hat{\mathbf{T}}_i\}_{i=1}^{M}$ to a ground truth pose graph $\{\mathbf{T}_i\}_{i=1}^{N}$ where $\mathbf{T}_i \in SE(2)$ $\forall i \in 1, \ldots, N$, by estimating a Sim(2) transformation between them, where $M \leq N$, since not all poses may be estimated. To reduce the influence of outliers for mostly-correct global pose estimates, we perform pose graph alignment in a RANSAC loop, with a randomly selected subset (2/3 of the M estimated poses) used to fit each alignment hypothesis, over 1000 hypotheses. We then measure the distance between the predicted and true i'th camera location $\|t_i - \hat{t}_i\|_2$, and difference between true and predicted i'th camera orientation $|\theta_i - \hat{\theta}_i|$. Completeness is essential to floorplan reconstruction, so we also report the percent of panoramas localized in the largest connected component.

Floorplan Reconstruction Accuracy and Completeness. We measure the 2D IoU between a rasterized binary occupancy map of the ground truth and the predicted floorplans. This metric measures the quality of our end-to-end system, as it encapsulates the *accuracy* of our *pair-wise relative pose proposal* in combination with the *accuracy* and *completeness* of the global pose estimation and the fusion of the room layouts (see supplementary for more details).

5.4   Layout and W/D/O Estimation Accuracy

The layout estimation module used in the system yields an average of 85% IoU with ground truth shape. W/D/O detection is accurate; at a 70% 1D IoU threshold, we correctly identify W/D/O with F1 scores of 0.91, 0.89, and 0.67, respectively. Our model is the least accurate in predicting openings. As discussed in [14], there are issues with annotator error and possibly ambiguous tagging of rooms in open spaces that cover different room types, making locations of openings less clear. We speculate that these contribute to the errors, especially for openings. In the Supplement, we provide qualitative examples of the various types of failure modes of the model.

5.5   Relative Pose Classification

We first measure the performance of the SALVe "front-end". These trained models achieve 92–95% accuracy on the test split (see Supplement). We show that a larger

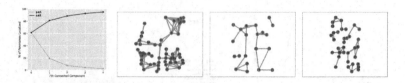

Fig. 6. *Left:* Distribution of localization percentage in the first 5 connected components, averaged over all test tours. *Right:* Topology of global pose graphs for various different homes.

capacity model than ResNet-50 (i.e. ResNet-152) further improves performance. We also note that the accuracy is limited by noisily-generated 'ground truth'. We train on 587 number of tours from ZInD, and use the official train/val/test splits.

In Fig. 5, we show a PR curve, indicating the precision of the model at different recall thresholds. We choose a 93% confidence threshold as our operating point, as it maximizes precision just before a precipitous drop in recall.

How Does the Amount of Visual Overlap Affect Relative Pose Classification Accuracy? More overlap yields higher accuracy for the ground truth positive class, but lower accuracy for the ground truth negative class. In Fig. 5, we analyze the performance of our relative pose classification method under varying amounts of visual overlap. 100% overlap would indicate that two panoramas were captured in exactly the same position, with the scene unchanged between the two captures. On the other hand, 0% overlap would indicate that the panoramas were captured in completely different locations, i.e. in two rooms, on opposite sides of a closed door (an example of an "extreme" baseline). We use a proxy metric, IoU of the texture map generated using HoHoNet-estimated [51] monocular depth, which introduces some amount of noise.

5.6   Global Pose Estimation Results

Next, we measure performance of both the "front-end" along with some form of global aggregation ("back-end"). We compare with two baselines from state-of-the-art structure from motion systems that support optimization from 360° images.

OpenMVG [34,35]. We use the recommended setting for 360° image input, with incremental SfM using an upright SIFT feature orientation, an upright 3-point Essential matrix solver with A-Contrario RANSAC, following the planar motion model described by [2,9,37], with an angular constraint for matching.

OpenSfM [25]. Incremental SfM system that uses the Hessian-Affine interest point detector [33], SIFT feature descriptor [32], and RANSAC [23].

In Table 1, we show the results of global pose estimation on the ZInD test set. We outperform OpenMVG by 656% and OpenSfM by 257% in the median percentage of panoramas localized (their 8.7% and 22.2% vs. our 57.1%), with even lower median rotation error (our 0.17° vs. their 0.37° and 0.36°). Our median translation error is comparable (our 25 cm vs. their 12 cm and 10 cm). PGO is significantly more accurate than spanning tree when VP estimation is not employed (see Table 3). However, when using vanishing point-based dominant axis-alignment, both spanning trees and pose

Table 1. Results of global pose estimation on the ZinD test set. Two global aggregation methods are evaluated: spanning tree ('ST'), and pose graph optimization ('PGO'), with axis-alignment ('AA'). ST and PGO both use the same largest connected component of $\mathcal{G}$ as input, and thus localize an equal number of panoramas.

Method	Localization %		Tour avg. rotation error (deg.)		Tour avg. translation error (meters)	
	MEAN	MEDIAN	MEAN	MEDIAN	MEAN	MEDIAN
OPENSFM [25]	27.62	22.22	9.52	0.36	1.88	0.12
OPENMVG [34,35]	13.94	8.70	3.84	0.37	**0.41**	**0.10**
OURS (W/ ST + AA)	**60.70**	**57.10**	**3.69**	**0.03**	0.81	0.26
OURS (W/ PGO + AA)	**60.70**	**57.10**	3.73	0.17	0.80	0.25

graph optimization on SALVe-verified measurements produce similar global aggregation results. In the left column of Fig. 7, we show the topological structure of the largest component of the pose graph for a few homes.

6   Discussion

Is Deep Learning Necessary for Verification, or Can Heuristics be Used? To verify pairwise alignment, matching texture is necessary but hard to feature engineer. Using geometry alone is insufficient (See Fig. 5(a-b) and Table 2), motivating others to explore graph neural networks for the task [45]. We implemented rule-based baselines that classify BEV image pairs via FFT cross-correlation scores [43], and found they do not work well due in part to difficulty in choosing thresholds. Previous works such as Layout-Loc [14] have explored rule-based checking, but found that it only can be successful when given access to *oracle* within-room pano grouping information; estimation of such within-room grouping (i.e. adjacency) is itself one of the fundamental challenges of global pose estimation in an indoor environment.

What Type of Semantic Object is Most Useful for Alignment in this Semantic SfM Problem? Doors, but all are essential. Openings are the second-most effective object type to achieve complete localization, and windows are least effective. Among the alignments that the model predicts to be positives with confidence $\geq 97\%$, we find that 63% originate from door-door hypotheses, 24% originate from opening-opening hypotheses, and 20% originate from window-window hypotheses. While rooms in residential homes are rarely connected by a window, these window alignments can provide additional redundancy, or ground alignments in very large open spaces when doors are not visible as in Fig. 3, pair 2. In Table 2, we report global pose estimation results when only one type of semantic object is used to create the edges $\mathcal{E}$ of the relative pose graph $\mathcal{G}$.

To What Extent is the Pose Graph Shattered into Multiple Clusters? Typically, the first three connected components contain 61%, 20%, and 7% of all panoramas (See Fig. 6a). We measure the distribution of connected components (CCs), as global pose estimation relies upon a single CC (we use the largest), and we find that often the

Table 2. Results of ablation experiments on how inputs to SALVe affect global pose estimation accuracy and completeness. Pose graph optimization and vanishing point-based axis alignment ('PGO + AA') are utilized for all entries below.

W/D/O Inputs			Raster inputs			Localization %		Tour avg. rotation error (deg.)		Tour avg. translation error (meters)	
Doors	Windows	Openings	Floor texture	Ceiling texture	Layout	MEAN	MEDIAN	MEAN	MEDIAN	MEAN	MEDIAN
✓	✓	✓	✓	✓		60.70	57.14	3.73	0.17	0.80	0.25
✓			✓	✓		43.30	40.00	2.41	0.07	0.59	0.20
	✓		✓	✓		15.57	13.33	2.20	**0.00**	0.74	**0.11**
		✓	✓	✓		23.87	23.08	**0.66**	0.05	**0.34**	0.18
✓	✓	✓	✓			60.64	58.33	3.75	0.15	0.91	0.25
✓	✓	✓		✓		**60.93**	**64.58**	10.94	0.28	2.12	0.35
✓	✓	✓			✓	19.19	16.67	3.43	0.03	0.53	**0.11**

second and third largest CCs are also large, indicating the potential for merging, e.g. combining ideas from [45] or [47]. We compute an average probability density function and cumulative density function by averaging per-floor distributions across the test set.

Is the RGB Photometric Signal from Panoramas Actually Necessary, as Opposed to Solely Using Geometric Context? Yes, the RGB texture is essential. In Table 2, we show that using a layout-only rasterization as input to the CNN, instead of a photometric texture map, leads to severe performance degradation.

Does Floor or Ceiling Texture Provide a more Useful Signal for Alignment Classification? Floor texture. However, using both signals jointly improves performance. In Table 2, we show the results of using as input to the network only the floor texture maps, or only the ceiling texture maps, as opposed to reasoning about both jointly.

Is a Manhattan World Assumption Helpful? For pose estimation, yes, but for shape estimation, no. Many rooms at critical junctures in the floorplan are non-Manhattan in shape, and 'Manhattanizing' them would be destructive when chaining together. However, room organization in a home is usually tied to three dominant, orthogonal directions. In Table 3, we show that using vanishing point estimation to align relative poses

Table 3. Comparison of results with and without axis-alignment ('AA') of relative poses (via vanishing angles) before global aggregation. The amount of panoramas localized is unaffected, as adjacency is maintained during the correction. For this comparison, 'oracle' layouts are used to isolate the effect of pose error. With vanishing point (VP) information, the difference between PGO and Spanning Tree is not statistically significant (1 cm and 0.04° error on average).

Method	Tour avg. rotation error (deg.)		Tour avg. translation error (meters)		Floorplan IoU	
	MEAN	MEDIAN	MEAN	MEDIAN	MEAN	MEDIAN
Spanning Tree	5.41	1.92	0.86	0.33	0.55	0.52
Spanning Tree + AA	**3.69**	**0.03**	0.81	0.26	**0.56**	0.52
PGO	4.93	1.53	0.81	0.29	**0.56**	0.52
PGO + AA	3.73	0.17	**0.80**	**0.25**	**0.56**	**0.53**

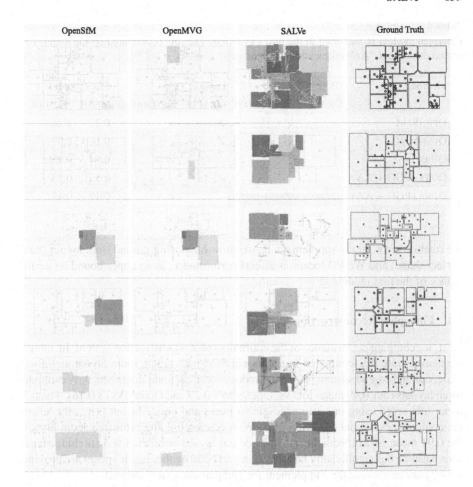

Fig. 7. Qualitative comparison of floorplan results. *Column 1:* OpenSfM. *Column 2:* OpenMVG. *Column 3:* Ours. *Column 4:* Ground truth floorplan. All results are superimposed on the ground truth floorplan. Colored regions indicated the reconstruction result; at times, the baselines localize no panos. Our floorplan recall is significantly better than the state-of-the-art. Each row corresponds to a single floor of a different home. Colored lines represent W/D/O objects – doors, openings and windows. The multiple cyan edges in the overlaid graph correspond to verified W/D/O alignment hypotheses. For an open layout, a successful case often involves edges from panoramas in many different rooms to a single pano. These examples are intended to offer an even-handed selection of reconstructions that indicate both good performance as well as areas for improvements. Rows 1 and 6 illustrate good reconstructions. Row 2 illustrates a more challenging case with only 1–2 panos in most rooms. Rows 3–5 are more challenging as they include bottlenecks in the actual physical layout, which is critical in joining connected components. (Color figure online)

up to a 15° correction significantly improves both global pose estimation accuracy and slightly improves floorplan reconstruction accuracy. Both vanishing point relative rotation angle correction and pose graph optimization are effective means of decreasing

Table 4. Floorplan reconstruction results against the ground truth manually annotated floorplan. Floorplan 2D IoU is measured in the bird's eye view. The IoU is measured on the largest connected component. 'AA' represents axis-alignment.

Method	Global poses		Layout		Floorplan IoU	
	ORACLE	ESTIMATED	ORACLE	ESTIMATED	MEAN	MEDIAN
OPENSFM		✓	✓		0.29	0.26
OPENMVG		✓	✓		0.16	0.07
OURS	✓			✓	**0.94**	**0.95**
OURS (PGO + AA)		✓	✓		0.56	0.53
OURS (PGO + AA)		✓		✓	0.49	0.45

the rotation error. In the supplementary we show how using ground truth layout (near-perfect shape) and W/D/O locations affects performance, as an upper-bound on performance of the first module in our system.

6.1 Floorplan Reconstruction Results

Next, we compare performance of the entire floorplan reconstruction system. In Table 4, we demonstrate that compared to traditional SfM with oracle room layout and oracle scale, our end-to-end system is able to produce more accurate floorplans with estimated room layouts (our 0.49 mean IoU vs. OpenSfM's 0.29 and OpenMVG's 0.16). The 0.56 mean IoU score using our estimated global poses and oracle layout primarily reflects the completeness of our final floorplan. With oracle pose and estimated room layouts, the 0.94 mean IoU reflects the accuracy of our layout estimation and stitching stages. This baseline has significantly larger IoU in part because the 'oracle' poses are provided for *all* panoramas (see the Supplement for comparison visualizations).

Qualitative Results. Figure 7 provides qualitative results for a number of different homes. For floors of some homes, our method produces nearly complete reconstructions, while for others, the results are more sparse. As shown by the third column of Fig. 7, the topology of the pose graph directly affects the completeness of the reconstruction; when multiple large connected components appear, the reconstruction is shattered apart. For several homes, OpenMVG and OpenSfM fail to converge, localizing no panoramas.

7 Conclusion

We present a new system for automatic 2D floorplan reconstruction from sparse, unordered panoramas. This work represents a breakthrough in the completeness of reconstructed floorplans, with over two times more coverage than previous systems [25,35], without sacrificing accuracy. We demonstrate how *SALVe*, our novel pairwise learned alignment verifier, capitalizes on the mature field of semantic detection of features (W/D/O) to handle a tractable number of alignment hypotheses and generate high-quality results. A human annotator may use it to accelerate labeling by automatically generating the majority of necessary decisions before making the final choices about glueing connected components. Figure 7 only illustrates the largest CC; other CCs are also generated, but not shown (Fig. 6, a CDF of 89% for the first 3 CCs).

Limitations. Because the number of pairwise alignments is combinatorial in the number of W/D/O, the runtime of the current system is limited, although we have not heavily optimized it. As ZInD [14] contains only unfurnished homes, our system has not yet been evaluated in a furnished home regime, due to dataset availability. Camera localization completeness is still in the 55–60% range. With future improvements to each part of the system, especially omnidirectional depth estimation and layout estimation, we expect floorplan reconstruction performance to continue to improve.

References

1. Albanis, G., et al.: Pano3D: a holistic benchmark and a solid baseline for 360° depth estimation. CVPR Workshops (2021)
2. Aly, M., Bouguet, J.Y.: Street view goes indoors: automatic pose estimation from uncalibrated unordered spherical panoramas. In: 2012 IEEE Workshop on the Applications of Computer Vision (WACV), pp. 1–8 (2012)
3. Balntas, V., Li, S., Prisacariu, V.: RelocNet: continuous metric learning relocalisation using neural nets. In: Ferrari, V., Hebert, M., Sminchisescu, C., Weiss, Y. (eds.) Computer Vision – ECCV 2018. LNCS, vol. 11218, pp. 782–799. Springer, Cham (2018). https://doi.org/10.1007/978-3-030-01264-9_46
4. Bao, S.Y., Savarese, S.: Semantic structure from motion. In: CVPR (2011)
5. Cabral, R., Furukawa, Y.: Piecewise planar and compact floorplan reconstruction from images. In: CVPR (2014)
6. Chang, A., et al.: Matterport3d: learning from RGB-D data in indoor environments. In: International Conference on 3D Vision (3DV) (2017)
7. Chen, J., Liu, C., Wu, J., Furukawa, Y.: Floor-SP: inverse CAD for floorplans by sequential room-wise shortest path. In: ICCV (2019)
8. Chen, K., Snavely, N., Makadia, A.: Wide-baseline relative camera pose estimation with directional learning. In: CVPR (2021)
9. Choi, S., Kim, J.H.: Fast and reliable minimal relative pose estimation under planar motion. Image Vis. Comput. **69**, 103–112 (2018)
10. Choudhary, S., Trevor, A.J., Christensen, H.I., Dellaert, F.: SLAM with object discovery, modeling and mapping. In: 2014 IEEE/RSJ International Conference on Intelligent Robots and Systems, pp. 1018–1025. IEEE (2014)
11. Cobbe, K., et al.: Training verifiers to solve math word problems. ArXiv:2110.14168 (2021)
12. Cohen, A., Sattler, T., Pollefeys, M.: Merging the unmatchable: stitching visually disconnected SfM models. In: ICCV (2015)
13. Cohen, A., Schönberger, J.L., Speciale, P., Sattler, T., Frahm, J.-M., Pollefeys, M.: Indoor-outdoor 3D reconstruction alignment. In: Leibe, B., Matas, J., Sebe, N., Welling, M. (eds.) ECCV 2016. LNCS, vol. 9907, pp. 285–300. Springer, Cham (2016). https://doi.org/10.1007/978-3-319-46487-9_18

14. Cruz, S., Hutchcroft, W., Li, Y., Khosravan, N., Boyadzhiev, I., Kang, S.B.: Zillow indoor dataset: annotated floor plans with 360deg panoramas and 3D room layouts. In: CVPR (2021)
15. Debevec, P.E., Taylor, C.J., Malik, J.: Modeling and rendering architecture from photographs: a hybrid geometry- and image-based approach. In: Proceedings of the 23rd Annual Conference on Computer Graphics and Interactive Techniques, SIGGRAPH 1996 (1996)
16. Dellaert, F.: Factor graphs and GTSAM: a hands-on introduction. Technical report, Georgia Institute of Technology (2012)
17. Dellaert, F., Burgard, W., Fox, D., Thrun, S.: Using the condensation algorithm for robust, vision-based mobile robot localization. In: CVPR (1999)
18. Ding, M., Wang, Z., Sun, J., Shi, J., Luo, P.: CamNet: coarse-to-fine retrieval for camera re-localization. In: ICCV (2019)
19. Enqvist, O., Kahl, F., Olsson, C.: Non-sequential structure from motion. In: ICCV Workshops (2011)
20. Fang, H., Lafarge, F., Pan, C., Huang, H.: Floorplan generation from 3D point clouds: a space partitioning approach. ISPRS J. Photogram. Remote Sens. **175**, 44–55 (2021)
21. Fang, H., Pan, C., Huang, H.: Structure-aware indoor scene reconstruction via two levels of abstraction. ISPRS J. Photogram. Remote Sens. **178**, 155–170 (2021)
22. Farin, D., Effelsberg, W., de With, P.H.: Floor-plan reconstruction from panoramic images. In: Proceedings of the 15th ACM International Conference on Multimedia (2007)
23. Fischler, M.A., Bolles, R.C.: Random sample consensus: a paradigm for model fitting with applications to image analysis and automated cartography. Commun. ACM **24**(6), 381–395 (1981)
24. Furukawa, Y., Curless, B., Seitz, S.M., Szeliski, R.: Reconstructing building interiors from images. In: ICCV (2009)
25. Gargallo, P., Kuang, Y., et al.: OpenSfM (2016)
26. He, K., Zhang, X., Ren, S., Sun, J.: Deep residual learning for image recognition. In: CVPR (2016)
27. Jin, L., Qian, S., Owens, A., Fouhey, D.F.: Planar surface reconstruction from sparse views. In: ICCV (2021)
28. Kim, Y.M., Dolson, J., Sokolsky, M., Koltun, V., Thrun, S.: Interactive acquisition of residential floor plans. In: ICRA (2012)
29. Laskar, Z., Melekhov, I., Kalia, S., Kannala, J.: Camera relocalization by computing pairwise relative poses using convolutional neural network. In: ICCV Workshops (2017)
30. Lin, C., Li, C., Wang, W.: Floorplan-jigsaw: jointly estimating scene layout and aligning partial scans. In: ICCV (2019)
31. Liu, C., Wu, J., Furukawa, Y.: FloorNet: a unified framework for floorplan reconstruction from 3D scans. In: Ferrari, V., Hebert, M., Sminchisescu, C., Weiss, Y. (eds.) ECCV 2018. LNCS, vol. 11210, pp. 203–219. Springer, Cham (2018). https://doi.org/10.1007/978-3-030-01231-1_13
32. Lowe, D.G.: Distinctive image features from scale-invariant keypoints. Int. J. Comput. Vis. **60**, 91–110 (2004)
33. Mikolajczyk, K., Schmid, C.: Scale & affine invariant interest point detectors. Int. J. Comput. Vision **60**(1), 63–86 (2004)
34. Moulon, P., Monasse, P., Marlet, R.: Global fusion of relative motions for robust, accurate and scalable structure from motion. In: ICCV (2013)
35. Moulon, P., Monasse, P., Perrot, R., Marlet, R.: OpenMVG: open multiple view geometry. In: Kerautret, B., Colom, M., Monasse, P. (eds.) RRPR 2016. LNCS, vol. 10214, pp. 60–74. Springer, Cham (2017). https://doi.org/10.1007/978-3-319-56414-2_5
36. Okorn, B., Xiong, X., Akinci, B., Huber, D.: Toward automated modeling of floor plans. In: 3D DPVT (2010)

37. Oskarsson, M.: Two-view orthographic epipolar geometry: minimal and optimal solvers. J. Math. Imaging Vis. **60**(2), 163–173 (2018)

38. Ozyesil, O., Voroninski, V., Basri, R., Singer, A.: A survey of structure from motion. Acta Numerica **26**, 305–364 (2017)

39. Pintore, G., Ganovelli, F., Pintus, R., Scopigno, R., Gobbetti, E.: 3D floor plan recovery from overlapping spherical images. Comput. Visual Media **4**(4), 367–383 (2018)

40. Pintore, G., Ganovelli, F., Villanueva, A.J., Gobbetti, E.: Automatic modeling of cluttered multi-room floor plans from panoramic images. Comput. Graph. Forum **38**(7) (2019)

41. Pintore, G., Mura, C., Ganovelli, F., Fuentes-Perez, L., Pajarola, R., Gobbetti, E.: State-of-the-art in automatic 3D reconstruction of structured indoor environments. Comput. Graphics Forum **39**(2) (2020)

42. Purushwalkam, S., et al.: Audio-visual floorplan reconstruction. In: ICCV (2021)

43. Reddy, B., Chatterji, B.: An FFT-based technique for translation, rotation, and scale-invariant image registration. IEEE Trans. Image Process. **5**(8), 1266–1271 (1996)

44. Sarlin, P.E., DeTone, D., Malisiewicz, T., Rabinovich, A.: SuperGlue: learning feature matching with graph neural networks. In: CVPR (2020)

45. Shabani, M.A., Song, W., Odamaki, M., Fujiki, H., Furukawa, Y.: Extreme structure from motion for indoor panoramas without visual overlaps. In: ICCV (2021)

46. Shen, J., Yin, Y., Li, L., Shang, L., Zhang, M., Liu, Q.: Generate & Rank: a multi-task framework for math word problems. In: Findings of the Association for Computational Linguistics: EMNLP 2021. Association for Computational Linguistics (2021)

47. Son, K., Moreno, D., Hays, J., Cooper, D.B.: Solving small-piece jigsaw puzzles by growing consensus. In: CVPR (2016)

48. Song, S., Yu, F., Zeng, A., Chang, A.X., Savva, M., Funkhouser, T.: Semantic scene completion from a single depth image. In: CVPR (2017)

49. Stekovic, S., Rad, M., Fraundorfer, F., Lepetit, V.: Montefloor: extending MCTS for reconstructing accurate large-scale floor plans. In: ICCV (2021)

50. Sun, C., Hsiao, C.W., Sun, M., Chen, H.T.: Horizonnet: learning room layout with 1D representation and PANO stretch data augmentation. In: CVPR (2019)

51. Sun, C., Sun, M., Chen, H.T.: HohoNet: 360 indoor holistic understanding with latent horizontal features. In: CVPR (2021)

52. Sun, J., Shen, Z., Wang, Y., Bao, H., Zhou, X.: LOFTR: detector-free local feature matching with transformers. In: CVPR (2021)

53. Sweeney, C., Hollerer, T., Turk, M.: Theia: a fast and scalable structure-from-motion library. In: Proceedings of the 23rd ACM International Conference on Multimedia (2015)

54. Wilson, K., Snavely, N.: Robust global translations with 1DSfM. In: Fleet, D., Pajdla, T., Schiele, B., Tuytelaars, T. (eds.) ECCV 2014. LNCS, vol. 8691, pp. 61–75. Springer, Cham (2014). https://doi.org/10.1007/978-3-319-10578-9_5

55. Yang, Z., Pan, J.Z., Luo, L., Zhou, X., Grauman, K., Huang, Q.: Extreme relative pose estimation for RGB-D scans via scene completion. In: CVPR (2019)

56. Yang, Z., Yan, S., Huang, Q.: Extreme relative pose network under hybrid representations. In: CVPR (2020)

57. Zach, C., Klopschitz, M., Pollefeys, M.: Disambiguating visual relations using loop constraints. In: CVPR (2010)

58. Zhang, F., Nauata, N., Furukawa, Y.: Conv-MPN: convolutional message passing neural network for structured outdoor architecture reconstruction. In: CVPR (2020)

59. Zhang, Y., Song, S., Tan, P., Xiao, J.: PanoContext: a whole-room 3D context model for panoramic scene understanding. In: Fleet, D., Pajdla, T., Schiele, B., Tuytelaars, T. (eds.) ECCV 2014. LNCS, vol. 8694, pp. 668–686. Springer, Cham (2014). https://doi.org/10.1007/978-3-319-10599-4_43

60. Zheng, J., Zhang, J., Li, J., Tang, R., Gao, S., Zhou, Z.: Structured3D: a large photo-realistic dataset for structured 3D modeling. In: Vedaldi, A., Bischof, H., Brox, T., Frahm, J.-M. (eds.) ECCV 2020. LNCS, vol. 12354, pp. 519–535. Springer, Cham (2020). https://doi.org/10.1007/978-3-030-58545-7_30
61. Zou, C., et al.: Manhattan room layout reconstruction from a single 360° image: a comparative study of state-of-the-art methods. Int. J. Comput. Vis. **129**(5), 1410–1431 (2021)

RC-MVSNet: Unsupervised Multi-View Stereo with Neural Rendering

Di Chang[1]([✉]), Aljaž Božič[1], Tong Zhang[2], Qingsong Yan[3], Yingcong Chen[3], Sabine Süsstrunk[2], and Matthias Nießner[1]

[1] Technical University of Munich, Munich, Germany
di.chang@tum.de
[2] École Polytechnique Fédérale de Lausanne, Canton of Vaud, Switzerland
[3] Hong Kong University of Science and Technology, Hong Kong, China

Abstract. Finding accurate correspondences among different views is the Achilles' heel of unsupervised Multi-View Stereo (MVS). Existing methods are built upon the assumption that corresponding pixels share similar photometric features. However, multi-view images in real scenarios observe non-Lambertian surfaces and experience occlusions. In this work, we propose a novel approach with neural rendering (RC-MVSNet) to solve such ambiguity issues of correspondences among views. Specifically, we impose a depth rendering consistency loss to constrain the geometry features close to the object surface to alleviate occlusions. Concurrently, we introduce a reference view synthesis loss to generate consistent supervision, even for non-Lambertian surfaces. Extensive experiments on DTU and Tanks&Temples benchmarks demonstrate that our RC-MVSNet approach achieves state-of-the-art performance over unsupervised MVS frameworks and competitive performance to many supervised methods. The code is released at https://github.com/Boese0601/RC-MVSNet.

Keywords: End-to-end Unsupervised Multi-View Stereo · Neural rendering · Depth estimation

1 Introduction

Multi-View Stereo (MVS) [19] is a long-standing and fundamental task in 3D computer vision. MVS aims to recover a 3D point cloud of real scenes from multi-view images and corresponding calibrated cameras. The widespread application of deep learning in recent years has lead to the emergence of end-to-end MVS depth estimation networks. A popular learning-based pipeline MVS-Net [33] proposes to encode RGB information from different camera views into a cost volume and predict depth maps for point cloud reconstruction. Follow-up

---

Supplementary Information The online version contains supplementary material available at https://doi.org/10.1007/978-3-031-19821-2_38.

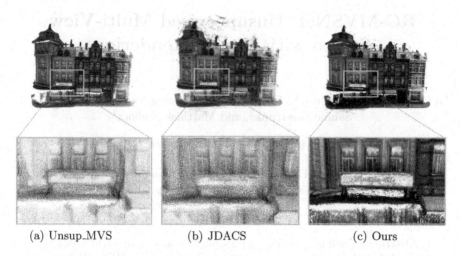

(a) Unsup_MVS   (b) JDACS   (c) Ours

Fig. 1. Qualitative comparison of 3D reconstruction of our RC-MVSNet and previous unsupervised methods [11,26].

fully-supervised methods [8,14,21,29] further improved the neural network architecture, lowering memory usage and achieving state-of-the-art depth estimation performance on several benchmarks [2,12]. However, these methods heavily rely on ground truth depth for supervision, which requires a depth sensor to collect the training data. It restricts these methods to limited datasets and largely indoor settings. To make MVS practical in more general real-world scenarios, it is vital to consider alternative unsupervised learning-based methods that can provide competitive accuracy compared to the supervised ones, while not requiring any ground truth depth.

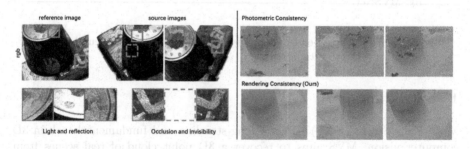

Fig. 2. (left) Real-world photometric conditions and occlusions. (right) Top: Failure cases of a photometric consistency assumption. Bottom: The results of our proposed rendering consistency approach.

Existing unsupervised MVS methods [6,9,11,26] are based on a *photometric consistency hypothesis*, which states that pixels belonging to the same 3D point have identical color properties under different view directions. However, in a real-world environment, as shown in Fig. 2, occlusions, reflecting, non-Lambertian surfaces, varying camera exposure, and other variables will make such a hypothesis invalid. Thus, inaccurately matched points lead to false geometric reconstruction. Although Xu et al. [26] proposes to use semantic clues to remove the ambiguity in stereo matching, the improvement is very marginal due to its high dependency on the accuracy of a pretrained semantic features extraction model (with supervision). To remove inconsistencies with supervision, in this paper, we propose to use neural rendering to solve ambiguity in the case of view-dependent photometric effects and occlusions.

Recently, there has been an increasing interest in novel view synthesis, particularly with the introduction of Neural Radiance Fields [15] that can model view-dependent photometric effects based on differentiable volumetric rendering. While initially focused on per-scene optimization with densely sampled input views, follow-up approaches [4,18,22] propose to use a 2D CNN encoder that can be trained to predict novel views even with very few input images. Aside from the view-dependent radiance that defines the color along the viewing ray, these methods also learn a volume density, which can be interpreted as depth when integrated over the viewing ray. It is worth noting that the depth is learned in a purely unsupervised fashion. However, since the main goal is novel view synthesis, the depth obtained from volume density is often inaccurate. In our method, we build from the volumetric rendering approach proposed in [15] with novel loss functions that can resolve view-dependent effects and occlusions, while keeping the depth representation used in MVS approaches to ensure locally accurate and smooth depth predictions.

To this end, we introduce RC-MVSNet, a novel end-to-end differentiable network for *unsupervised multi-view stereo*. Combining the benefits of view-dependent rendering and structured depth representation, our method achieves state-of-the-art depth prediction results in the competitive DTU benchmark [2], and also demonstrates robust performance on out-of-distribution samples in the Tanks and Temples dataset [12]. In summary, our contributions are the following:

- We propose a reference view synthesis loss based on neural volumetric rendering to generate RGB supervision that is able to account for view-dependent photometric effects.
- We introduce Gaussian-Uniform mixture sampling to learn the geometry features close to the object surface to overcome occlusion artefacts present in existing unsupervised MVS approaches.
- We introduce a depth rendering consistency loss to refine the initial depth map by depth priors and ensure the robustness and smoothness of the prediction.

2   Related Work

2.1   Supervised Multi-View Stereo

Many *supervised* approaches have proposed to use CNNs to interpret 3D scenes by predicting depth maps of the RGB inputs and reconstructing the point cloud using depth map filtering. Most state-of-the-art methods employ 3D cost volumes. As a representative work, MVSNet [33] encodes camera parameters and features into cost volumes through homography warping and regularizes the volume by 3D CNNs to generate depth prediction. Following works, e.g., [8,21,32] improve the performance of MVSNet and reduce the memory cost by introducing a multi-stage architecture and learn depth prediction in a coarse-to-fine manner. Furthermore, [25,30,34] replace dense 3D convolution with convolutional recurrent GRU or LSTM units. However, the reliance on ground truth depth limits their application to specific datasets as discussed in Sect. 1. Therefore, it is necessary to explore alternative unsupervised methods.

2.2 Unsupervised and Self-supervised Multi-View Stereo

End-to-end unsupervised and pseudo-label-based multi-stage self-supervised learning play pivotal roles in 3D vision, especially in multi-view reconstruction systems. The fundamental assumption of photometric consistency provides feasibility for unsupervised MVS. For instance, Unsup_MVS [11] proposed the first end-to-end learning-based unsupervised MVS framework: the images of source views are inversely warped to the reference view with its predicted depth map, and photometric consistency and SSIM [23] are enforced to minimize the discrepancy between the reference image and warped image. JDACS [26] proposes cross-view consistency of extracted semantic features and provides supervision of the segmentation map by non-negative matrix factorization. However, it still requires a pretrained semantic feature extraction backbone, and suffers from unstable convergence of cross-view semantic consistency that fails to provide reliable supervision. U-MVSNet [27] employs a flow-depth consistency loss to resolve ambiguous supervision. The dense 2D optical flow correspondences are used to generate pseudo labels for uncertainty-aware consistency, which improves the supervision to some extent. However, this method cannot be trained in an end-to-end fashion, as it requires complex pre-training and fine-tuning. Self-supervised CVP-MVSNet [31] also proposes to learn depth pseudo labels with unsupervised pre-training, followed with the iterative self-supervised training to refine the pseudo label; however, it is still affected by ambiguous supervision. Furthermore, these unsupervised and self-supervised methods lack an occlusion-aware module to learn features from different viewing directions, leading to incomplete reconstruction of point clouds.

In contrast, our simple but effective model directly learns the geometric features of the scene by a reference view synthesis loss. This significantly reduces the training complexity and alleviates ambiguous photometric supervision. It also avoids the problems caused by occlusions through NeRF-like rendering.

2.3 Multi-view Neural Rendering

Recently, various neural rendering methods [3,13,15,20,38] have been presented, focusing on task of novel view synthesis. In particular, Neural Radiance Fields [15] represent scenes with a continuous implicit function of positions and orientations for high quality view synthesis; several following up

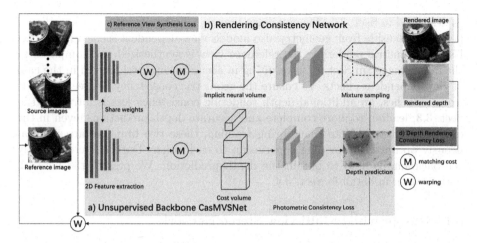

Fig. 3. Overview of our unsupervised MVS approach (RC-MVSNet). a) Unsupervised Backbone CasMVSNet predicts initial depth map by photometric consistency and provides depth priors for rendering consistency network. b) Rendering Consistency Network generates image and depth by neural rendering under the guidance of depth priors. c) The rendered image is supervised by the reference view synthesis loss. d) The rendered depth is supervised by the depth rendering consistency loss.

works [16,35–37] improve both its efficiency and performance. There are also a few extensions [4,18,24] of NeRF which introduce multi-view information to enhance the generalization ability of view synthesis. MVSNeRF [4] proposes to leverage plane-swept cost volumes, which have been widely used in multi-view stereo, for geometry-aware scene understanding, and combines this with volumetric rendering for neural radiance field reconstruction; however, it fails to generate high-quality depth prediction in an unsupervised manner. Nerfing-MVS [24] uses sparse depth points from SfM for learning depth completion to guide the optimization process of NeRF. Our method takes advantage of both precise neural rendering and strong generalization of cost volumes and provides accurate depth estimation based on end-to-end unsupervised learning, which surpasses all previous unsupervised multi-view-stereo approaches and demonstrates accurate reconstruction of both indoor objects and out-of-distribution outdoor scenes.

3   Method

In this section, we describe RC-MVSNet, our proposed method for unsupervised multi-view stereo. Given N images as input, with their corresponding cameras' intrinsic and extrinsic parameters, our method predicts a depth map in the reference camera view. The overall pipeline is illustrated in Fig. 3. It consists of a backbone branch and an auxiliary branch. The backbone is built upon CasMVSNet [8], which predicts a depth map in a coarse-to-fine manner, as described in Sect. 3.1. The auxiliary branch is built upon the neural radiance fields, which aside from geometry also models view-dependent scene appearance. Using volumetric rendering, the reference view is synthesized and compared to the input image (in Sect. 3.2), resulting in accurate supervision even in the case of view-dependent effects. To ensure the geometric consistency between the network branches, an additional depth rendering consistency loss is introduced in Sect. 3.3, leading to more complete and accurate depth predictions, even in the case of occlusions. Note that during training, these two branches are simultaneously optimized, providing supervision to each other. During inference, only the backbone is used to obtain the depth prediction. We present the network optimization in detail in Sect. 3.4.

3.1 Unsupervised Multi-view Stereo Network

The backbone network closely follows the CasMVSNet [8] architecture. Input images $\{I_j\}_{j=1}^{N}$ are initially encoded with a shared 2D U-Net that generates pixelwise features. Afterwards, a feature cost volume is constructed in the reference camera frustum. Each volume voxel's position is projected into every input image using cameras' intrinsic and extrinsic parameters, and pixel features are queried via bilinear interpolation. This results in warped feature volumes $\{V_j\}_{j=1}^{N}$ that are fused across views into a common feature volume C by computing feature variance:

$$C = Var\left(V_1, \cdots, V_N\right) = \frac{\sum_{j=1}^{N} \left(V_j - \overline{V}_j\right)^2}{N}. \tag{1}$$

The feature cost volume C is further refined with a 3D U-Net and finally outputs a depth map in the reference view in a coarse-to-fine manner. Further details can be found in the supplementary material.

Photometric Consistency. To supervise depth map prediction without any ground truth depth, existing methods [6,9,11,27,31] enforce photometric consistency between reference and other source input views. The key idea is to maximize the similarity between the reference image I_1 and any source image I_j after being warped to the reference view. Given corresponding intrinsics K, the relative transformation from reference to source view T, and predicted depth map D in the reference view, we warp any pixel p_i in the reference image (in a homogeneous notation) to the source image via inverse warping:

$$\hat{p}_i = KT\left(D(p_i) \cdot K^{-1}p_i\right). \tag{2}$$

The warped source image $\hat{I}_1^j$ is synthesized by bilinearly sampling the source image's color values at the warped pixel location $\hat{p}_i$, i.e. $\hat{I}_1^j(p_i) = I_j(\hat{p}_i)$. In additon to the warped image $\hat{I}_1^j$, a binary mask M_j is also generated, masking out invalid pixels that are projected outside the source image bounds. In the unsupervised MVS system, all $N-1$ source views are warped into the reference view to compute the photometric consistency loss:

$$\mathcal{L}_{PC} = \sum_{j=2}^{N} \frac{1}{\|M_j\|_1} \left(\left\| \left(\hat{I}_1^j - I_1 \right) \odot M_j \right\|_2 + \left\| \left(\nabla \hat{I}_1^j - \nabla I_1 \right) \odot M_j \right\|_2 \right). \quad (3)$$

Here, ∇ refers to a pixel-wise gradient and $\odot$ represents pixel-wise product.

3.2   Reference View Synthesis

Photometric consistency assumes consistent pixel colors across different input views, which does not hold in the case of view-dependent effects that are common with reflective materials. Furthermore, if certain pixels in the reference view are occluded in the matched source view, incorrect color similarity is enforced. To cope with these shortcomings, instead of using error-prone image warping of source images, we propose to learn the synthesis of reference views from source images using neural radiance fields [15], with the network learning how to take care of view-dependent effects and occlusions.

Implicit Neural Volume Construction. Similar to the cost volume C for the backbone branch, an implicit neural volume C' is also constructed via computation of feature variance, as defined in Eq. (1). However, since we want to synthesize the reference view image using *only* the information from the source views, we calculate the variance volume C' from warped volumes $\{V_j\}_{j=2}^{N}$, without the reference feature volume V_1. We thus gather features across $N-1$ source views, and apply a 3D U-Net $U(\cdot)$ to learn an implicit neural volume F that we denote as $F = U(C')$.

Point Feature Aggregation. To restore the scene geometry and appearance, rays are emitted from the reference camera center in the viewing direction of ϕ. For each point $q \in \mathbb{R}^3$ along the ray we query RGB values $\ell = \{I_j[x_j, y_j]\}_{j=2}^{N}$ by bilinearly sampling source images, where x_j and y_j represent the 2D location of point q, when it is projected to the image coordinate system of jth view. In addition to these properties, we also obtain a neural feature $f = F(q)$ from the implicit neural volume F by trilinear interpolation at the location q. These neural features overcome the poor generalization of traditional neural radiance field approaches that require per-scene training or fine-tuning, by regressing properties from the geometric-aware cost volume (e.g. implicit neural volume in our case). This improves our method's robustness on datasets that are very different from the training set. These input features are concatenated into point features and we use an MLP $M(\cdot)$ to convert these features into predicted volume density σ and color $c = [r, g, b]$. The whole process can be summarized as:

$$\sigma, c = M(q, \phi, f, \ell). \quad (4)$$

Following previous works [4,15,17], we encode the location q and direction d using positional encoding.

Reference View Synthesis Loss. As in NeRF [15], we sample K point candidates along the camera ray $\mathbf{r}(t) = \mathbf{o} + t\phi$, where $\mathbf{o}$ origin is the camera and ϕ is the pixel's viewing direction. For the sample distance t_k in the range from near to far plane $(t_n \leq t_k \leq t_f)$, we query the corresponding density σ_k and color c_k. To compute pixel-wise color $\hat{\mathbf{C}}(\mathbf{r})$, color values are integrated along the ray $\mathbf{r}(t)$:

$$\hat{\mathbf{C}}(\mathbf{r}) = \sum_{k=1}^{K} w_k c_k. \tag{5}$$

Here $w_k = T_k \left(1 - \exp\left(-\sigma_k \delta_k\right)\right)$ is the integration weight, where $\delta_k = t_{k+1} - t_k$ refers to the interval between adjacent sampling locations and T_k indicates the accumulation of transmittance from t_n to t_f:

$$T_k = \exp\left(-\sum_{k'=1}^{k} \sigma_{k'} \delta_{k'}\right). \tag{6}$$

To optimize the radiance field color output $\hat{\mathbf{C}}(\mathbf{r})$ in Eq. (5), i.e. the synthesized RGB value of a pixel (x, y) in the reference view, the rendering consistency loss L_{RC} composed of a mean squared error is applied:

$$\mathcal{L}_{RC} = \|\hat{\mathbf{C}}(\mathbf{r}) - \mathbf{C}(\mathbf{r})\|_2^2. \tag{7}$$

Here $\mathbf{C}(\mathbf{r})$ refers to pixel color in the reference image $I_1[x, y]$.

3.3   Depth Rendering Consistency

Using an auxiliary rendering branch and applying rendering consistency loss significantly improves the quality of unsupervised depth predictions, as can be seen in our ablations in Sect. 4.4. This results from joint training of both branches and optimizing a shared 2D image encoder. To further benefit from rendering consistency and additionally improve unsupervised depth prediction, we also apply Gaussian-Uniform mixture sampling and a depth rendering consistency loss, which increase the beneficial coupling of both network branches.

Gaussian-Uniform Mixture Sampling. To sample points along the ray for volumetric rendering in Eq. (5), existing methods [4,15,18,24,36] partition $[t_n, t_f]$ into K bins following a uniform distribution:

$$t_k \sim \mathcal{U}\left[t_n + \frac{k-1}{K}\left(t_f - t_n\right), t_n + \frac{k}{K}\left(t_f - t_n\right)\right]. \tag{8}$$

This sampling strategy is inefficient and also independent of depth predictions of the backbone branch. We propose to sample the point candidates following a Gaussian distribution with the guidance of the depth prior from predicted depth map D, as illustrated in Fig. 4. Assuming the predicted depth for a pixel

$\mathbf{p} = (x, y)$ to be $z_\mathbf{p} = D(x, y)$, we sample the candidates using the following distribution:

$$t_k \sim \mathcal{N}\left(z_\mathbf{p}, s_\mathbf{p}^2\right). \tag{9}$$

$$\text{where } s_\mathbf{p} = \frac{\min\left(|z_\mathbf{p} - t_f|, |z_\mathbf{p} - t_n|\right)}{3}. \tag{10}$$

Here $z_\mathbf{p}$ and $s_\mathbf{p}$ are the mean and standard deviation of the proposed normal distribution, respectively. This enables geometry features for rendering to be more efficiently optimized, since we sample more point candidates close to the object surface. Furthermore, since we employ differentiable Gaussian sampling, the depth predictions from the backbone branch obtain useful cues on how to improve depth, also in the case of occlusions. In order to make the training stable and help the network to converge, particularly during the beginning stage of the end-to-end training, half of the samples are drawn from the Gaussian distribution from Eq. (9) and the other half is uniformly distributed between the near and far planes.

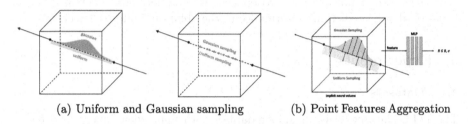

(a) Uniform and Gaussian sampling   (b) Point Features Aggregation

Fig. 4. Demonstration of our proposed Gaussian-Uniform mixture sampling. (a) Uniform and Gaussian sampling. (b) Point Features Aggregation.

Depth Rendering Consistency Loss. Our rendering consistency network encodes geometry through density estimation. We can convert the density estimate to a depth map in reference view through density integration along the ray:

$$\hat{z}(\mathbf{r}) = \sum_{k=1}^{K} w_k t_k. \tag{11}$$

We use the same rendering weights w_k as in Eq. (5), and t_k is a sampled point candidate as introduced in Sect. 3.2, following the normal distribution. To enforce that geometry estimated by the backbone branch and by the auxiliary rendering branch match, we minimize the difference between the depth maps with an additional depth rendering consistency loss L_{DC}, defined as a Smooth-L1 loss [7]:

$$\mathcal{L}_{DC} = \text{smooth}_{L_1}\left(\hat{z}(\mathbf{r}) - z_\mathbf{p}\right). \tag{12}$$

Here, $\hat{z}(\mathbf{r})$ is the integrated depth value from the rendering consistency network and $z_\mathbf{p}$ the corresponding pixel depth value from the backbone network.

3.4 End-to-end Network Optimization

Unlike pseudo-label-based multi-stage self-supervised methods [27,31], our model is trained from scratch in an end-to-end fashion, without any pre-processing or pre-training. The two parts indicated in Sect. 3, the backbone and auxiliary network branches, are jointly trained on the whole dataset by minimizing the following overall loss:

$$\mathcal{L} = \lambda_1\mathcal{L}_{PC} + \lambda_2\mathcal{L}_{RC} + \lambda_3\mathcal{L}_{DC}$$
$$+\lambda_4\mathcal{L}_{SSIM} + \lambda_5\mathcal{L}_{Smooth} + \lambda_6\mathcal{L}_{DA}. \tag{13}$$

Losses $\mathcal{L}_{SSIM}$ and $\mathcal{L}_{Smooth}$, commonly used in previous works [6,9,11,26], ensure structural similarity and smoothness of predicted depth maps. As proposed by [26], we also apply color fluctuation augmentation to input images and calculate the L1 loss between depth maps predicted under different color augmentations, resulting in L_{DA}. We use fixed weights $\lambda_1 = 0.8$, $\lambda_2 = 1.0$, $\lambda_3 = 1.0$, $\lambda_4 = 0.2$ and $\lambda_5 = 0.0067$. The weight for data augmentation is initialized with $\lambda_6 = 0.01$ and doubled every two epochs. We evaluate the effect of different losses on depth prediction performance in the ablation study (see Sect. 4.4).

4 Experiments

4.1 Datasets

The **DTU** dataset [2] is an indoor dataset with multi-view images and corresponding camera parameters. We follow the settings of MVSNet [33] for dividing training, validation and evaluation sets. There are 124 scenes that are scanned from 49 or 64 views under 7 different light conditions. In the DTU benchmark, models are trained on training set and tested on the evaluation set. We use the official error metrics in DTU to evaluate the *Accuracy*, which is measured as the distance from the result to the structured light reference, indicating the quality of the reconstruction, and *Completeness*, which is measured as the distance from the ground truth reference to the reconstructed result, indicating the proportion of the reconstructed part in the entire point cloud. *Overall* is the average of *Accuracy* and *Completeness* and it reflects the overall quality of the reconstruction. **Tanks and Temples** [12] is a large-scale dataset with various outdoor scenes. It contains an intermediate subset and an advanced subset. The evaluation on this benchmark is conducted online by submitting generated point clouds to the official website. In this benchmark, F-score is calculated for each scene and we compare the mean F-score of intermediate and advanced subset respectively.

4.2 Implementation Details

Training Details. The proposed RC-MVSNet is trained on the DTU dataset. Following [6,9,11,26], we use the high-resolution DTU data provided by the open source code of MVSNet [33]. We first resize the input images to 600×800,

Table 1. Point cloud evaluation results on DTU [2]. The lower is better for Accuracy (Acc.), Completeness (Comp.), and Overall. The sections are partitioned into supervised, multi-stage self-supervised and end-to-end (E2E) unsupervised, respectively. The best result is highlighted in bold for each category. All the results other than ours are from previously published literature.

	Method	Acc.↓	Comp.↓	Overall.↓
	SurfaceNet [10]	0.450	1.040	0.745
	MVSNet [33]	0.396	0.527	0.462
	Cas-MVSNet [8]	0.325	0.385	0.355
Supervised	PatchmatchNet [21]	0.427	0.277	0.352
	CVP-MVSNet [32]	**0.296**	0.406	0.351
	UCSNet [5]	0.338	0.349	0.344
	GBi-Net [14]	0.315	**0.262**	**0.289**
Multi-Stage	Self_sup CVP-MVSNet [31]	**0.308**	0.418	0.363
Self-Sup.	U-MVSNet [27]	0.354	**0.3535**	**0.3537**
	Unsup_MVSNet [11]	0.881	1.073	0.977
	MVS2 [6]	0.760	0.515	0.637
E2E UnSup.	M3VSNet [9]	0.636	0.531	0.583
	JDACS-MS [26]	0.398	0.318	0.358
	RC-MVSNet	**0.396**	**0.295**	**0.345**

following previous methods. Then we crop resized images into 512×640 patches. We adopt the backbone of Cas-MVSNet [8] to construct our multi-scale pipeline with 3 stages. For each stage, we use different feature maps and the 3D-CNN network parameters. The whole network is optimized by an Adam optimizer in Pytorch for 15 epochs with an initial learning rate of 0.0001, which is down-scaled by a factor of 2 after 10, 12, and 14 epochs. We train with a batch size of 4 using four NVIDIA RTX 3090 GPUs.

Testing Details. The model trained on DTU training set is used for testing on DTU testing set. The input image number N is set to 5, each with a resolution of 1152×1600. It takes 0.475 seconds to test each sample. The model trained on DTU training dataset is directly used for testing on Tanks and Temples intermediate and advanced datasets without finetuning. The image sizes are set to 1024×1920 or 1024×2048 and the input image number N is set to 7. We then filter predicted depth maps of a scene using photometric and geometric consistencies and fuse then into one point cloud. We define geometric and photometric consistencies similarly to the ones used in MVSNet [33], a detailed description can be found in supplemental material. Fig. 1 shows visualizations of point clouds of RC-MVSNet and previous unsupervised methods, and Fig. 5 shows reconstructions of our method on the test dataset.

4.3 Benchmark Performance

Evaluation on DTU Dataset. We evaluate the depth prediction performance on the DTU test set, and compare with previous state-of-the-art methods in Table 1. Our RC-MVSNet architecture achieves the best accuracy, completeness and overall score (lower is better for all metrics) among all end-to-end unsupervised methods. Our model improves the overall score from **0.358** of JDACS [26] to **0.345**. The completeness is improved by **0.023**, demonstrating the effectiveness of our method to resolve incomplete predictions caused by occlusions. The overall score is also better than the multi-stage self-supervised approaches, and even most supervised methods. In addition to the performance of point cloud reconstruction, we also provide evaluations of predicted depth maps. We compare them with supervised MVSNet [33] and previous unsupervised approaches [6,9,11,26], the results are summarized in Table 3. Our method again achieves state-of-the-art accuracy. Visualizations of our depth predictions can be found in the supplementary material.

Table 2. Point cloud evaluation results on the intermediate subsets of Tanks and Temples dataset [12]. Higher scores are better. The Mean is the average score of all scenes. The sections are partitioned into supervised, multi-stage self-supervised and end-to-end (E2E) unsupervised, respectively. The best result is highlighted in bold for every section.

| | Method | Tanks & Temples intermediate | | | | | | | | |
		Mean↑	Family↑	Francis↑	Horse↑	Lighthouse↑	M60↑	Panther↑	Playground↑	Train↑
Supervised	MVSNet [33]	43.48	55.99	28.55	25.07	50.79	53.96	50.86	47.90	34.69
	CIDER [28]	46.76	56.79	32.39	29.89	54.67	53.46	53.51	50.48	42.85
	PatchmatchNet [21]	53.15	66.99	52.64	43.24	54.87	52.87	49.54	54.21	**50.81**
	CVP-MVSNet [32]	54.03	**76.50**	47.74	36.34	55.12	**57.28**	**54.28**	57.43	47.54
	UCSNet [5]	54.83	76.09	53.16	43.03	54.00	55.60	51.49	57.38	47.89
	Cas-MVSNet [8]	**56.42**	76.36	**58.45**	**46.20**	**55.53**	56.11	54.02	**58.17**	46.56
Multi-Stage Self-Sup.	Self_sup CVP-MVSNet [31]	46.71	64.95	38.79	24.98	49.73	52.57	**51.53**	50.66	40.45
	U-MVSNet [27]	**57.15**	**76.49**	**60.04**	**49.20**	**55.52**	**55.33**	51.22	**56.77**	**52.63**
E2E Unsup.	MVS2 [6]	37.21	47.74	21.55	19.50	44.54	44.86	46.32	43.38	29.72
	M3VSNet [9]	37.67	47.74	24.38	18.74	44.42	43.45	44.95	47.39	30.31
	JDACS-MS [26]	45.48	66.62	38.25	36.11	46.12	46.66	45.25	47.69	37.16
	RC-MVSNet	**55.04**	**75.26**	**53.50**	**45.52**	**53.49**	**54.85**	**52.30**	**56.06**	**49.37**

(a) Qualitative results of proposed RC-MVSNet on DTU Benchmark   (b) Qualitative results on Tanks and Temples Benchmark, including Advanced and Intermediate subset

Fig. 5. Point cloud visualization of our method on DTU [2] and Tanks and Temples [12].

Evaluation on Tanks and Temples. We train the proposed RC-MVSNet on the DTU train set, and test on the Tanks and Temples dataset without fine-

Table 3. Depth map evaluation results in terms of accuracy on DTU evaluation set [2] (higher is better). All thresholds are given in millimeters.

Method	<2↑	<4↑	<8↑
MVSNet [33]	0.704	0.778	0.815
MVSNeRF [21]	0.510	0.645	0.734
Unsup_MVSNet [11]	0.317	0.384	0.402
M3VSNet [9]	0.603	0.769	0.857
JDACS-MS [26]	0.553	0.705	0.786
RC-MVSNet	**0.730**	**0.795**	**0.863**

tuning. We compare our method to state-of-the-art supervised, pseudo-label-based multi-stage self-supervised methods and end-to-end unsupervised methods. Table 2 shows the evaluation results on the intermediate subset. Our RC-MVSNet achieves the best performance among unsupervised methods. In particular, our mean score achieves significant improvement of **+17.37** over M3VSNet [9] and **+9.56** over JDACS [26]. Moreover, we also obtain state-of-the-art performance in all sub-scenes, which fully confirms the effectiveness of our method. Our **anonymous** evaluation on the leaderboard [1] is named as RC-MVSNet. The results of advanced subset can be found in the supplementary material, along with additional qualitative results and discussion.

4.4 Ablation Study

We provide an ablation analysis, demonstrating the point cloud reconstruction performance gain of each component of our proposed method. We also evaluate

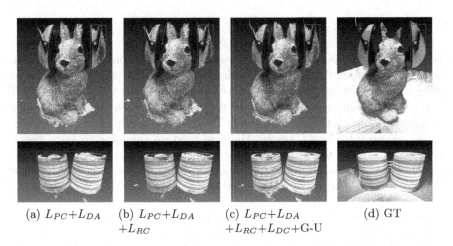

(a) $L_{PC}+L_{DA}$ (b) $L_{PC}+L_{DA}$ (c) $L_{PC}+L_{DA}$ (d) GT
                              $+L_{RC}$ $+L_{RC}+L_{DC}+$G-U

Fig. 6. Qualitative results of RC-MVSNet on scan33 (top) and scan48 (bottom) of the DTU dataset.

performance when sampling different number of rays during rendering in the supplementary material.

Effect of Each Component of the Unsupervised Approach. To evaluate the performance gain of each part in our method, we provide qualitative comparison of models trained using different combinations of core contributions in Fig. 6. We can easily observer that both reference view synthesis and depth rendering consistency yield better reconstruction results, especially when considering completeness. Quantitative results are listed in Table 4, further confirming the importance of all proposed network components.

Table 4. Ablation study of different components of our proposed unsupervised approach (the lower is better). L_{PC}: Photometric Consistency Loss. L_{DA}: Data Augmentation Loss. L_{RC}: Reference View Synthesis Loss. G-U: Gaussian-Uniform Mixture Sampling. L_{DC}: Depth Rendering Consistency Loss. The last three are contributions in this work.

L_{PC}	L_{DA}	L_{RC}	G-U	L_{DC}	Acc↓	Comp↓	Overall↓
✓					0.462	0.328	0.395
✓	✓				0.419	0.346	0.383
✓	✓	✓			0.415	0.300	0.357
✓	✓	✓	✓		0.404	0.299	0.352
✓	✓	✓		✓	0.397	0.299	0.348
✓	✓	✓	✓	✓	**0.396**	**0.295**	**0.345**

5   Conclusions

We show that unsupervised multi-view-stereo can be improved by challenging the previous assumption of photometric consistency. We thus propose a novel unsupervised MVS approach based on rendering consistency (RC-MVSNet). To handle the ambiguous supervision, we propose a reference view synthesis loss via differentiable volumetric rendering. To solve the incompleteness caused by occlusions, we introduce Gaussian-Uniform mixture sampling to learn geometry features close to the object surface. To further improve the robustness and smoothness of the depth map, we propose a depth rendering consistency loss. The experiments demonstrate the effectiveness of our RC-MVSNet approach.

Acknowledgment. This project is funded by the ERC Starting Grant Scan2CAD (804724), a TUM-IAS Rudolf Mößbauer Fellowship, and the German Research Foundation (DFG) Grant Making Machine Learning on Static and Dynamic 3D Data Practical.

References

1. Tanks and temples leaderboard. https://www.tanksandtemples.org/leaderboard
2. Aanæs, H., Jensen, R.R., Vogiatzis, G., Tola, E., Dahl, A.B.: Large-scale data for multiple-view stereopsis. Int. J. Comput. Vis. **120**(2), 153–168 (2016)
3. Bi, S., Xu, Z., Sunkavalli, K., Hašan, M., Hold-Geoffroy, Y., Kriegman, D., Ramamoorthi, R.: Deep reflectance volumes: relightable reconstructions from multi-view photometric images. In: Vedaldi, A., Bischof, H., Brox, T., Frahm, J.-M. (eds.) ECCV 2020. LNCS, vol. 12348, pp. 294–311. Springer, Cham (2020). https://doi.org/10.1007/978-3-030-58580-8_18
4. Chen, A., et al.: Mvsnerf: fast generalizable radiance field reconstruction from multi-view stereo. arXiv preprint arXiv:2103.15595 (2021)
5. Cheng, S., Xu, Z., Zhu, S., Li, Z., Li, L.E., Ramamoorthi, R., Su, H.: Deep stereo using adaptive thin volume representation with uncertainty awareness. In: Proceedings of the IEEE/CVF Conference on Computer Vision and Pattern Recognition, pp. 2524–2534 (2020)
6. Dai, Y., Zhu, Z., Rao, Z., Li, B.: Mvs2: deep unsupervised multi-view stereo with multi-view symmetry. In: 2019 International Conference on 3D Vision (3DV), pp. 1–8. IEEE (2019)
7. Girshick, R.: Fast r-cnn. In: Proceedings of the IEEE International Conference on Computer Vision, pp. 1440–1448 (2015)
8. Gu, X., Fan, Z., Zhu, S., Dai, Z., Tan, F., Tan, P.: Cascade cost volume for high-resolution multi-view stereo and stereo matching. In: CVPR (2020)
9. Huang, B., Yi, H., Huang, C., He, Y., Liu, J., Liu, X.: M3vsnet: unsupervised multi-metric multi-view stereo network. In: 2021 IEEE International Conference on Image Processing (ICIP), pp. 3163–3167. IEEE (2021)
10. Ji, M., Gall, J., Zheng, H., Liu, Y., Fang, L.: Surfacenet: an end-to-end 3D neural network for multiview stereopsis. In: ICCV (2017)
11. Khot, T., Agrawal, S., Tulsiani, S., Mertz, C., Lucey, S., Hebert, M.: Learning unsupervised multi-view stereopsis via robust photometric consistency. arXiv preprint arXiv:1905.02706 (2019)
12. Knapitsch, A., Park, J., Zhou, Q.Y., Koltun, V.: Tanks and temples: benchmarking large-scale scene reconstruction. ACM ToG **36**(4), 1–13 (2017)
13. Lombardi, S., Simon, T., Saragih, J., Schwartz, G., Lehrmann, A., Sheikh, Y.: Neural volumes: learning dynamic renderable volumes from images. arXiv preprint arXiv:1906.07751 (2019)
14. Mi, Z., Chang, D., Xu, D.: Generalized binary search network for highly-efficient multi-view stereo (2021)
15. Mildenhall, B., Srinivasan, P.P., Tancik, M., Barron, J.T., Ramamoorthi, R., Ng, R.: NeRF: representing scenes as neural radiance fields for view synthesis. In: Vedaldi, A., Bischof, H., Brox, T., Frahm, J.-M. (eds.) ECCV 2020. LNCS, vol. 12346, pp. 405–421. Springer, Cham (2020). https://doi.org/10.1007/978-3-030-58452-8_24
16. Rebain, D., Jiang, W., Yazdani, S., Li, K., Yi, K.M., Tagliasacchi, A.: DeRF: decomposed radiance fields. In: Proceedings of the IEEE/CVF Conference on Computer Vision and Pattern Recognition, pp. 14153–14161 (2021)
17. Roessle, B., Barron, J.T., Mildenhall, B., Srinivasan, P.P., Nießner, M.: Dense depth priors for neural radiance fields from sparse input views. arXiv preprint arXiv:2112.03288 (2021)

18. Rosu, R.A., Behnke, S.: NeuralMVS: bridging multi-view stereo and novel view synthesis. arXiv preprint arXiv:2108.03880 (2021)
19. Seitz, S.M., Curless, B., Diebel, J., Scharstein, D., Szeliski, R.: A comparison and evaluation of multi-view stereo reconstruction algorithms. In: 2006 IEEE Computer Society Conference on Computer Vision and Pattern Recognition (CVPR 2006), vol. 1, pp. 519–528. IEEE (2006)
20. Thies, J., Zollhöfer, M., Nießner, M.: Deferred neural rendering: image synthesis using neural textures. ACM Trans. Graph. (TOG) **38**(4), 1–12 (2019)
21. Wang, F., Galliani, S., Vogel, C., Speciale, P., Pollefeys, M.: Patchmatchnet: learned multi-view patchmatch stereo. In: CVPR (2021)
22. Wang, Q., et al.: IBRNet: learning multi-view image-based rendering. In: Proceedings of the IEEE/CVF Conference on Computer Vision and Pattern Recognition, pp. 4690–4699 (2021)
23. Wang, Z., Bovik, A.C., Sheikh, H.R., Simoncelli, E.P.: Image quality assessment: from error visibility to structural similarity. IEEE Trans. Image Process. **13**(4), 600–612 (2004)
24. Wei, Y., Liu, S., Rao, Y., Zhao, W., Lu, J., Zhou, J.: Nerfingmvs: guided optimization of neural radiance fields for indoor multi-view stereo. In: Proceedings of the IEEE/CVF International Conference on Computer Vision, pp. 5610–5619 (2021)
25. Wei, Z., Zhu, Q., Min, C., Chen, Y., Wang, G.: Aa-rmvsnet: adaptive aggregation recurrent multi-view stereo network. In: ICCV (2021)
26. Xu, H., Zhou, Z., Qiao, Y., Kang, W., Wu, Q.: Self-supervised multi-view stereo via effective co-segmentation and data-augmentation. In: Proceedings of the AAAI Conference on Artificial Intelligence, vol. 2, p. 6 (2021)
27. Xu, H., Zhou, Z., Wang, Y., Kang, W., Sun, B., Li, H., Qiao, Y.: Digging into uncertainty in self-supervised multi-view stereo. In: Proceedings of the IEEE/CVF International Conference on Computer Vision, pp. 6078–6087 (2021)
28. Xu, Q., Tao, W.: Learning inverse depth regression for multi-view stereo with correlation cost volume. In: AAAI, vol. 34 (2020)
29. Xu, Q., Tao, W.: Pvsnet: pixelwise visibility-aware multi-view stereo network (2020)
30. Yan, J., et al.: Dense hybrid recurrent multi-view stereo net with dynamic consistency checking. In: ECCV (2020)
31. Yang, J., Alvarez, J.M., Liu, M.: Self-supervised learning of depth inference for multi-view stereo. In: Proceedings of the IEEE/CVF Conference on Computer Vision and Pattern Recognition, pp. 7526–7534 (2021)
32. Yang, J., Mao, W., Alvarez, J.M., Liu, M.: Cost volume pyramid based depth inference for multi-view stereo. In: CVPR (2020)
33. Yao, Y., Luo, Z., Li, S., Fang, T., Quan, L.: Mvsnet: depth inference for unstructured multi-view stereo. In: ECCV (2018)
34. Yao, Y., Luo, Z., Li, S., Shen, T., Fang, T., Quan, L.: Recurrent mvsnet for high-resolution multi-view stereo depth inference. In: CVPR (2019)
35. Yu, A., Fridovich-Keil, S., Tancik, M., Chen, Q., Recht, B., Kanazawa, A.: Plenoxels: radiance fields without neural networks. arXiv preprint arXiv:2112.05131 (2021)
36. Yu, A., Ye, V., Tancik, M., Kanazawa, A.: pixelnerf: neural radiance fields from one or few images. In: Proceedings of the IEEE/CVF Conference on Computer Vision and Pattern Recognition, pp. 4578–4587 (2021)
37. Zhang, K., Riegler, G., Snavely, N., Koltun, V.: Nerf++: analyzing and improving neural radiance fields. arXiv preprint arXiv:2010.07492 (2020)
38. Zhou, T., Tucker, R., Flynn, J., Fyffe, G., Snavely, N.: Stereo magnification: learning view synthesis using multiplane images. arXiv preprint arXiv:1805.09817 (2018)

Box2Mask: Weakly Supervised 3D Semantic Instance Segmentation using Bounding Boxes

Julian Chibane[1,2]([envelope]), Francis Engelmann[3], Tuan Anh Tran[2],
and Gerard Pons-Moll[1,2]

[1] University of Tübingen, Tübingen, Germany
[2] Max Planck Institute for Informatics, Saarland Informatics Campus, Saarbrücken,
Germany
`jchibane@mpi-inf.mpg.de`
[3] ETH Zürich, AI Center, Zürich, Switzerland
`https://virtualhumans.mpi-inf.mpg.de/box2mask`

Abstract. Current 3D segmentation methods heavily rely on large-scale point-cloud datasets, which are notoriously laborious to annotate. Few attempts have been made to circumvent the need for dense per-point annotations. In this work, we look at weakly-supervised 3D semantic instance segmentation. The key idea is to leverage 3D bounding box labels which are easier and faster to annotate. Indeed, we show that it is possible to train dense segmentation models using only bounding box labels. At the core of our method, Box2Mask, lies a deep model, inspired by classical Hough voting, that directly votes for bounding box parameters, and a clustering method specifically tailored to bounding box votes. This goes beyond commonly used center votes, which would not fully exploit the bounding box annotations. On ScanNet test, our weakly supervised model attains leading performance among other weakly supervised approaches ($+18\,\text{mAP}_{50}$). Remarkably, it also achieves 97% of the mAP_{50} score of current fully supervised models. To further illustrate the practicality of our work, we train Box2Mask on the recently released ARKitScenes dataset which is annotated with 3D bounding boxes only, and show, for the first time, compelling 3D instance segmentation masks.

Keywords: 3D semantic instance segmentation · Weakly supervised learning · 3D scene understanding

1 Introduction

Semantic instance segmentation of 3D scenes is one of the fundamental challenges in computer vision and robotics. The goal is to predict a foreground-background

Supplementary Information The online version contains supplementary material available at https://doi.org/10.1007/978-3-031-19821-2_39.

S. Avidan et al. (Eds.): ECCV 2022, LNCS 13691, pp. 681–699, 2022.
https://doi.org/10.1007/978-3-031-19821-2_39

mask and a semantic class (*e.g.*, 'chair', 'fireplace') for each object in a 3D scene (point cloud or mesh). Over the last years, the research community has contributed numerous methods [6,11,12,17,19,25,29,33,53]. This rapid development was made possible, not only by substantial advances in 3D deep learning backbones [8,16,39,40,43,45], but also by large-scale 3D datasets [2,9,36,44] crucial to train data-hungry deep models. While the acquisition of large datasets has become easier with commodity 3D scanners [3], per-point annotations (Fig. 2, left) – largely required by current methods – are still very labour-intensive. For example, labeling an average scene in ScanNet takes ∼22.3 min [9]. It is therefore highly desirable to alleviate the need for dense point labels. Only few works have addressed this challenge. Hou *et al.* [21] build on self-supervised pre-training [51] and propose contrastive learning techniques using sparse point annotations (Fig. 2, middle) which, however, depend on carefully selected points during the annotation process.

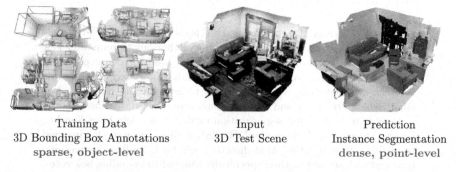

Training Data	Input	Prediction
3D Bounding Box Annotations	3D Test Scene	Instance Segmentation
sparse, object-level		dense, point-level

Fig. 1. Can we use 3D bounding box annotations alone to train dense 3D semantic instance segmentation models? We find that this is the case and propose a Deep Hough Voting based method that fully exploits bounding box annotations.

The key idea of this work is to use 3D bounding box annotations as weak supervision signal for dense 3D semantic instance segmentation (Fig. 1). Despite promising results on image understanding tasks [28], bounding boxes have so far been overlooked for dense 3D instance segmentation. We find that obtaining dense segmentation masks from object detection models (predicting one box per object) is non-trivial and leads to unsatisfying results (see Sect. 6.2). We present Box2Mask, the first method for dense instance segmentation trained solely on coarse bounding box annotations. The main result of this paper is that our weakly supervised method outperforms previous weakly supervised works [23, 51] by a large margin, and is even competitive with fully-supervised state-of-the-art methods [6,33] (Fig. 2, right). To achieve this goal, we face two key challenges. First, we lack dense per-point instance annotation. Second, there is no obvious representation for instance segmentation, because in contrast to semantic segmentation we cannot assign a single categorical label to points.

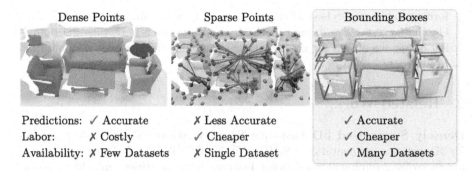

| Dense Points | Sparse Points | Bounding Boxes |

Predictions: ✓ Accurate   ✗ Less Accurate   ✓ Accurate
Labor: ✗ Costly   ✓ Cheaper   ✓ Cheaper
Availability: ✗ Few Datasets ✗ Single Dataset ✓ Many Datasets

Fig. 2. Annotation types. Our key finding is that bounding box annotations serve as a surprisingly valuable annotation type for learning dense 3D instance masks. Prior work either requires per-point annotations *(left)* with instance ids and semantic classes for millions of points, or initial weak supervision methods [21] use sparse point annotations *(middle)*, where a subset of points is annotated with instance centers and semantic classes. We propose to use bounding box annotations *(right)*, where each object is annotated with its tight fitting box and a semantic label. We find boxes combine desirable properties: they allow for results on par with full supervision, reduce annotation effort to the object-level and are readily available in several large-scale 3D datasets [3,5,14,33].

To address these challenges, we represent instances with the six parameters of an axis-aligned bounding box, fully exploiting the given labels. Since bounding boxes cover the full extent of the object, they are naturally a richer instance representation than the commonly used centers. Moreover, leveraging this representation leads to novel algorithms for voting, instance clustering, and a new training strategy to cope with weak labels. Specifically, we train a model where each point in the scene votes for the bounding box to which it belongs. We devise a new algorithm to cluster votes based on box volumetric overlap. Such overlap can be back-projected to the original scene points to obtain a probabilistic instance mask. Since we lack dense labels, we propose a training strategy where point to instance associations are approximated on the fly based on bounding boxes. An overview of Box2Mask is presented in Fig. 3. We evaluate our approach on three challenging indoor 3D datasets: ScanNet [9], S3DIS [2] and ARKitScenes [3].

In summary, our contributions are as follows:

- We propose a principled method leveraging bounding boxes both as a representation and to guide the training scheme. This comprises a novel method for voting, instance clustering and training with weak labels. Code, models and annotations are available at https://virtualhumans.mpi-inf.mpg.de/box2mask.
- We present the first dense 3D instance semantic segmentation method trained with only bounding boxes. It is competitive with the best fully supervised baselines (97% of HAIS [6] on ScanNet test, mAP_{50}) and it largely outper-

forms weakly supervised alternatives ($+18\,\text{mAP}_{50}$ compared to CSC [21]). On the largest scene dataset ARKitScenes annotated only with 3D bounding boxes, we obtain for the first time compelling 3D instance segmentation results.

2   Related Work

Densely Supervised 3D Instance Segmentation. The first deep models for 3D instance segmentation] (SGPN [47], 3D-BEVIS [11], ASIS [48]) estimated instances by grouping learned point features in an abstract embedding space. Extending this, MTML [29] proposes an additional learned directional embedding space. All these methods require non-learned, computationally expensive point-feature clustering. Similar to the popular MaskRCNN [18] for 2D instance segmentation, 3D-SIS [20] extracts bounding box proposals and extracts the per-voxel masks via a 3D-RoI layer. An interesting alternative is proposed in 3D-BoNet [53] which, from a single global scene descriptor, directly predicts all object bounding boxes which are then segmented into foreground and background. Both previous methods are sensitive to missed object detections since they cannot be recovered at later stages in the model. More recently, several works group points based on predicted semantics and object centers [6,12,17,25,33]. 3D-MPA [12] first combines points into sets of points and then groups these into objects based on features learned via a graph convolutional network. PointGroup [25] combines sets of points based on both the original point positions and learned center positions. OccuSeg [17] additionally predicts instance occupancy as a proxy for the physical size of an instance. Similar in spirit to [12], HAIS [6] groups points into sets of points, and performs additional set refinement steps as well as scoring as in [25]. SSTNet [33] generalizes the over-segmentation idea from [17] using a super-point semantic tree network which hierarchically merges segments into object instances. Different from the above methods, our Box2Mask does not estimate object centers but votes for object bounding boxes. By doing so, the voting mechanism is robust towards varying object sizes (see Fig. 4).

Weak Supervision for 3D Segmentation. Many efforts have been made to reduce the labeling cost of dense annotation for 2D images, with models learning from only weak annotations such as bounding boxes [10,22,28], scribbles [34,46,54], points [4] and image-level labels [1,26,41,59].

In 3D, mostly semantic segmentation on point clouds was addressed with weak labels, where only sparsely labeled points are given [7,21,24,35,52,52,55, 56]. SSPC-Net [7] and Liu *et al.* [35] assign sparse labels to super-points, construct graphs over super-points and learn to propagate semantic labels between nodes in the graph from labeled super-points to the unlabeled super-points. In this fashion, and with only 10% of labeled points, Xu *et al.* [52] achieve a performance close to fully supervised semantic segmentation methods. Another line of work explores scene-level annotations or subcloud-level annotations for semantic segmentation [42,49,58]. Here, only a list of semantic classes contained in a scene (or part of it) are assumed, without precise localization. However, since scene and sub-scene labels are the coarsest annotations assumed, results typically lack details.

Only recently, the first work on weak supervision for 3D semantic instance segmentation was proposed, assuming a sparse number of points is annotated with their instance centers [21]. To reduce data hungriness, unsupervised pre-training on 3D point clouds [15,32,51] is used. PointContrast [51] improves supervised down-stream tasks significantly via contrastive pre-training on point clouds. CSC [21] additionally incorporates point-level correspondences and spatial contexts in a scene. CSC achieves encouraging initial results, but still leaves a significant gap to fully supervised methods.

3   Hough Voting for Bounding Boxes

Our model votes for instances represented as bounding boxes (Fig. 3). This is unlike prior work, which represents instances as centers. Our experiments show that the proposed box representation has several advantages over centers.

Encoding. Input are scene points $\mathcal{S} \in \mathbb{R}^{N \times F}$, where N is the number of scene points and F the number of per-point input features ($F = 9$ in our experiments, for position, color and estimated surface normal). We use the popular sparse convolutional U-Nets [8,16] as backbone, to obtain per scene point features. Those require discretization of point positions into regular grids, but allow for high resolution (we use 2 cm). In case multiple points fall into the same grid location, instead of averaging features and associated ground truth annotations leading to a blurry combination, we pick the features of the nearest neighboring scene point. We retain this mapping to allow reversing the discretization later.

| Input: | Bounding | Clustered Bounding | Output: |
| 3D Point Cloud | Box Votes | Box Votes | 3D Semantic Instances |

Fig. 3. Box2Mask overview. Input to Box2Mask is a colored 3D point cloud of a scene. **Bounding box voting:** For each point in the input scene, our model predicts the points instance, parameterized as 6-DoF bounding box. The key contribution is the training procedure with only coarse bounding box labels (requiring no per-point labels) by associating points to bounding box labels. **Non-maximum clustering:** Votes are clustered using our Non-Maximum Clustering (NMC) that is specifically tailored to the bounding box representation. **Back-projection:** A point is associated with the cluster of the box it predicted. Doing this for each point yields the final instance masks.

Decoding. Based on the point features, we predict a bounding box, a score, and a semantic label per scene point. We branch out decoding with separate (3 layers) MLP networks. We predict axis-aligned bounding boxes, parameterized using their centers, and sizes (width, height, depth), with one MLP for center and one for size. Similarly, another MLP predicts a scalar score, estimating the intersection-over-union of the predicted bounding box with the ground truth, and a fourth branch predicts the semantic label ("chair", "table", ...).

4   Clustering and Back-projection

Next, we want to turn our model predictions into instance masks. Since, scene points vote for the bounding box of their instance, all points voting for the same box define an instance and points voting for a different box define a different instance. However, due to noisy predictions, box votes from points of the same instance will not be perfectly aligned which demands a clustering strategy.

In contrast to clustering based on centers with Euclidean distance metrics (as commonly employed in 3D instance segmentation), we make full use of our bounding box votes, by defining a novel 3D clustering method based on volumetric similarity (Fig. 4 A, B). Specifically, we define our clustering similarity-metric over two bounding box votes, $\mathbf{b}_a$ and $\mathbf{b}_b$, as the intersection-over-union (IoU):

$$\text{vote-space similarity: IoU}(\mathbf{b}_a, \mathbf{b}_b) = \frac{\text{area of overlap}}{\text{area of union}}. \tag{1}$$

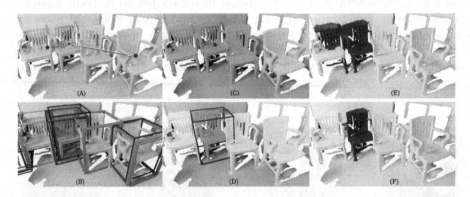

Fig. 4. Center clustering (top row) *v.s.* our box clustering (bottom row). **(A)** Scene points predict their instance centers (yellow). For clustering, the Euclidean metric between votes is used (arrows between highlighted votes). **(B)** In contrast, we propose to use IoU (Eq. 1) on bounding box votes. Intersection of blue and red votes visualized in green. Since boxes define the extend of objects, this metric can discriminate distinctively when overlap is not present, as with the violet box vote. This is key for obtaining sharp similarity decay of the scene points **(D)**, instead of smooth decay with distance **(C)**. The latter is sensitive to errors in binarization thresholds (handcrafted and dataset specific) when converting to instance masks **(E)**. In contrast, our method naturally encodes this threshold via box sizes, *i.e.*, converting from **(D)** to **(F)** is robust.

Voting and clustering of bounding boxes has two key benefits: First, IoU allows to separate two instances when no box overlap is present, which requires careful handcrafted thresholds for center voting (see Fig. 4). Second, while center clustering will fail when two instances have the same center (*e.g.*, an apple in a bowl), boxes additionally distinguish instance size.

Clustering Volumetrically. First, all bounding box votes are sorted in descending order according to the predicted scores. Then, the highest-scoring box is picked and serves as the representative, $\mathbf{b}_r$, of the first cluster. All boxes, $\mathbf{b}$, that are sufficiently similar to the representative, $\text{IoU}(\mathbf{b}, \mathbf{b}_r) > \tau$, are assigned to this cluster. Higher values of $\tau \in (0, 1)$ will result in numerous smaller clusters and lower values will result in fewer larger clusters. The next step is to take the next highest scoring box that has not yet been clustered: it will serve as next representative. This process is repeated until all boxes are assigned to a representative or are chosen as representative themselves. We call this clustering *non-maximum clustering* (NMC). A pseudo-code description is given in the appendix.

Back-projection to Instance Masks. Ultimately, we are interested in clusters in the original point cloud. Therefore, we *back-project* each clustered bounding box to the point that voted for it. All points that voted for boxes within the same cluster form an instance mask. For semantic instance segmentation, each instance mask should be accompanied with a semantic class and a score. Since our model predicts semantics for each scene point, we obtain instance labels by performing a majority-vote per mask. For the score, we rely on the predicted IoU score of the point that voted for the instance's cluster representative $\mathbf{b}_r$.

5   Training with Weak Bounding Box Labels

Fully supervised 3D instance segmentation methods rely on densely annotated point clouds and learn to predict at each scene point $\mathbf{p}$ some ground truth value, $gt(\mathbf{p})$ (*e.g.* instance center). However, this strategy cannot be applied when a scene is annotated only with a set of bounding boxes. More specifically, boxes do not define instance ground truth on a point-level, such that $gt(\mathbf{p})$ is unclear. We address this issue by finding a strategy to approximate point-to-bounding box associations. More formally, let $\mathcal{B} = \{\mathbf{b}_1, ..., \mathbf{b}_B\}$, $\mathbf{b}_i = [\text{center}, \text{size}, \text{label}] \in \mathbb{R}^6 \times \mathbb{N}$ be the set of annotated boxes in a scene, we define a function $a : \mathcal{P} \to \mathcal{B}$ which maps a 3D scene point $\mathbf{p} \in \mathcal{P}$ to a ground truth bounding box $a(\mathbf{p}) \in \mathcal{B}$. Once such a function is found, the model can be trained in a similar fashion as fully supervised models, replacing the exact point-to-point ground truth $gt(\mathbf{p})$ with our approximate point-to-box ground truth $gt(a(\mathbf{p}))$.

How Should the Mapping Function a Be Defined? Since ideally, an object bounding box contains all the points of its instance, the possible box associations of a point are reduced to only those boxes containing it. In turn, if a point is contained in no bounding box, it can only be part of the background (*e.g.*,

wall, ceiling, floor). This simple observation has an important effect: with high
certainty, we can learn to segment (or discard) non-instance points, a crucial part
of instance segmentation. We can specify our approximate associations further
for points contained in only a single box: all those points will actually belong
to the instance of the box, up to points from non-annotated background points.
If a point, however, is located in multiple bounding boxes, we cannot get exact
point-to-box association. These observations can be formulated into our initial
approximate association function:

$$a(\mathbf{p}) = \begin{cases} \text{background}, & \text{if } \mathbf{p} \text{ is not contained in any } \mathbf{b} \in \mathcal{B} \\ \mathbf{b}, & \text{if } \mathbf{p} \text{ is only contained in a single } \mathbf{b} \in \mathcal{B} \\ \text{undecided} & \text{else} \end{cases} \qquad (2)$$

and updates the co-domain of a to $\mathcal{B} \cup \{\text{background}, \text{undecided}\}$. These associations are already surprisingly useful for supervising on *decided* points only (i.e.
none or single box points): in experiments, this initial strategy achieves 87% of
current fully-supervised methods with dense per-point labels.

A key remaining question however is: can we increase prediction quality by
integrating approximate associations for points in multiple boxes? In our analysis (Table 5), we find that choosing the smallest of multiple available boxes
improves over other strategies. This makes sense since smaller objects are often
fully contained in bounding boxes of larger objects (a pillow on a sofa, a sink in a
cabinet). Using this strategy, and only relying on bounding box annotations, we
achieve 97% of the performance of fully-supervised methods trained with dense
per-point labels.

Losses. Let $\mathcal{P}$ be the set of scene points and $\mathcal{B}$ the set of annotated bounding
boxes. Using our association function, a, we define our losses, only given the
box annotations. We define our instance losses only for points associated with
the scene foreground $\mathcal{F} := \{\mathbf{p} \in \mathcal{P} | a(\mathbf{p}) \in \mathcal{B}\}$, excluding "background" and
"undecided" points. Our instance prediction losses are defined as:

$$\mathcal{L}_{\text{offset}} := \frac{1}{|\mathcal{F}|} \sum_{\mathbf{p} \in \mathcal{F}} \| o(\mathbf{p}, a(\mathbf{p})) - \hat{o}(\mathbf{p}) \|_1,$$

$$\mathcal{L}_{\text{size}} := \frac{1}{|\mathcal{F}|} \sum_{\mathbf{p} \in \mathcal{F}} \| s(a(\mathbf{p})) - \hat{s}(\mathbf{p}) \|_1, \qquad (3)$$

$$\mathcal{L}_{\text{score}} := \frac{1}{|\mathcal{F}|} \sum_{\mathbf{p} \in \mathcal{F}} \text{CE}\left(iou(a(\mathbf{p})), \widehat{iou}(\mathbf{p}) \right),$$

where o is the offset from $\mathbf{p}$ to the center of its associated bounding box, $a(\mathbf{p})$;
s is the size (width, height, depth) and iou is the IoU of the predicted bounding
box with the associated box, $a(\mathbf{p})$. We denote the predicted values with a hat
and the cross-entropy loss with CE. Similarly, the dense semantic segmentation
is learned from only bounding boxes, relying on their semantic label. In contrast

to above instance losses, the semantic loss, $\mathcal{L}_{\text{sem}}$, includes the points associated with the background $\mathcal{D} := \{\mathbf{p} \in \mathcal{P} | a(\mathbf{p}) \neq \text{undecided}\}$:

$$\mathcal{L}_{\text{sem}} := \frac{1}{|\mathcal{D}|} \sum_{\mathbf{p} \in \mathcal{D}} \text{CE}\Big(sem\big(a(\mathbf{p})\big), \widehat{sem}(\mathbf{p})\Big). \tag{4}$$

where sem defines the ground truth, including a generic semantic class "background" for all points associated with it:

$$sem(\mathbf{p}) := \begin{cases} \text{background\_class}, & \text{if } \mathbf{p} \text{ in no box} \\ \text{label}\big(a(\mathbf{p})\big), & \text{else} \end{cases} \tag{5}$$

Importantly, this allows us at inference time, to predict and filter background points, not defining any instances. Our network prediction consists of a forward pass, fully implemented with convolutions and trained end-to-end with the combined, multi-task loss defined as $\mathcal{L} := \mathcal{L}_{\text{offset}} + \mathcal{L}_{\text{size}} + \mathcal{L}_{\text{score}} + \mathcal{L}_{\text{sem}}$.

5.1   Implementation and Training Details

We train our network end-to-end and from scratch with the Adam optimizer, using an initial learning rate of 0.001, a batch size of 8 entire scenes, and train for 500 epochs on a single NVIDIA Quadro RTX 8000. For data augmentation, scenes are randomly rotated around height, flipped, and scaled in Uniform[0.9, 1.1]. Our backbone is a 6-layer sparse-convolutional encoder-decoder including skip connections based on [6]. The MLP heads are implemented using 3 layers with 96 hidden units. Similar to other current segmentation methods [17,33,37], we perform point over-segmentation [13,27] on ScanNet and ARKitScenes, and similarly employ [30,31] on S3DIS. This reduces the number of votes by averaging over segments before clustering, alleviating the computational load. Empirically, we set the NMC clustering threshold $\tau = 0.3$. More details are in the appendix.

6   Experiments

6.1   Comparing with State-of-the-art Methods

Datasets. S3DIS [2] consists of 272 scans of 6 large-scale indoor areas collected from three different buildings. Scans are represented as point clouds and points are annotated with instance- and semantic-labels out of 13 object classes. To obtain bounding box annotations from masks, we use the standard approach of [12,19–21,38,50,53,57], *i.e.*, we obtain axis-aligned bounding boxes from the instance point annotations. We report scores on Area-5 and 6-fold cross-validation.

ScanNet [9] is a richly annotated dataset of 3D reconstructed indoor scenes represented as meshes. Similar to S3DIS, each scene is annotated with semantic- and instance-segmentations of 18 object categories. It consists of 1201 training scenes, 312 validation scenes, and 100 hidden test scenes. Bounding box annotations are obtained the same way as for S3DIS.

ARKitScenes [3] is the largest of these datasets with 4499 training scenes and 550 validation scenes. The scenes are represented as reconstructed meshes and are recorded in real-world homes. The dataset is annotated with oriented object bounding boxes across 17 semantic classes. Importantly, per-point labels are not available. Nevertheless, our approach is able to leverage the bounding box annotations as weak supervision signal, which is an *immense practical advantage* over existing 3D instance segmentation methods which require dense per-point annotations and can therefore not be trained on this dataset.

Methods in Comparison. We compare to both fully-supervised and weakly-supervised SOTA prior methods. Fully-supervision methods are the majority: we compare top-down segmentation methods 3D-BoNet [53], 3D-SIS [20] and bottom-up methods MTML [29], PointGroup [25], 3D-MPA [12], OccuSeg [17], HAIS [6] and SSTNet [33]. See Sect. 2 for more details.

Weakly-supervised methods are much less, and only recently explored. Point-Contrast [51] and CSC [21] both make use of unsupervised pre-training via contrastive-learning. Compared to PointContrast, CSC follows a more sophisticated approach by taking spatial scene context into account. For 3D instance segmentation, the pre-trained models are supervised with a limited number of sparsely annotated points (20, 50, 100 or 200 Points), for which the ground truth object centers and semantic classes are known during training.

Results on S3DIS and ScanNet are summarized in Table 1. Our approach improves upon prior (point-based) weakly-supervised methods [21,51] by more than **10 mAP**. While sparse point labels and bounding box labels might not be directly comparable, it is noteworthy that this improvement is achieved without pre-training as used by [21,51]. Compared to fully-supervised approaches, our weakly-supervised method achieves 92% and 94% of the performance of leading methods on ScanNet (SSTNet, val, mAP_{50}) and S3DIS (HAIS, A5, mPrec) respectively. This is extremely encouraging, as it indicates that densely labeled points might not be entirely necessary. Qualitative ScanNet results are shown in Fig. 6. Our method predicts clear masks in heavily cluttered environments and accurately segments even very large objects like tables. The difference between weak- and full-supervision is marginal, however, bounding boxes need only be annotated on object-level in contrast to per-point annotations. Additional qualitative results and analysis, including S3DIS, are in the appendix.

Quantitative results on ARKitScenes are shown in Table 2, visual results in Fig. 5. As per-point instance labels are not available, we cannot report segmentation scores. Instead, as a proxy, we compare to recent object detection methods [38,50,57] by fitting oriented bounding boxes to our predicted masks. This indirectly measures mask quality. However, high detection scores are only obtained if the predicted point masks are accurate. Therefore, the correctness of position

Table 1. State-of-the-art 3D semantic instance segmentation. We show fully-supervised methods (dense point annotations) and weakly-supervised methods (sparse points and bounding boxes) on ScanNet [9] and S3DIS [2]. [51] is as reported in [21].

	Method	Supervision	ScanNet Validation mAP @50%	mAP @25%	ScanNet Hidden Test @50%	mAP @25%	S3DIS Area 5 mAP mPrec	mRec	S3DIS 6-fold CV mPrec	mRec
	CSC [21]	20 Points	26.3	–	28.9	49.6				
	PointContrast [51]	20 Points	–	–	25.9	47.4				
	CSC [21]	50 Points	32.6	–	41.4	62.0				
	PointContrast [51]	50 Points	–	–	40.0	60.3				
	CSC [21]	100 Points	39.9	–	46.0	65.4				
Weakly Supervised	PointContrast [51]	100 Points	–	–	45.6	63.7				
	CSC [21]	200 Points	48.9	–	49.4	70.2				
	PointContrast [51]	200 Points	44.5	–	47.1	66.2				
	Box2Mask (Ours)	Boxes	**59.7**	**71.8**	**67.7**	**80.3**	66.7	65.5	72.2	70.5
	Relative to SOTA		92.8%	95.0%	96.9%	100%	93.8%	99.8%	98.2%	96.0%
	3D-SIS [20]	All Points	18.7	35.7	38.2	55.8				
	3D-BoNet [53]	All Points	–	–	48.8	68.7	–	–	65.6	47.6
	MTML [29]	All Points	40.2	55.4	54.9	73.1				
	PointGroup [25]	All Points	56.9	71.3	63.6	77.8	61.9	62.1	69.6	69.2
Fully Supervised	3D-MPA [12]	All Points	59.1	72.4	61.1	73.7	46.7	**65.6**	66.7	64.1
	OccuSeg [17]	All Points	60.7	71.9	63.4	73.9	–	–	72.8	60.3
	HAIS [6]	All Points	64.1	**75.6**	**69.9**	**80.3**	**71.1**	65.0	73.2	69.4
	SSTNet [33]	All Points	**64.3**	74.0	69.8	78.9	65.5	64.2	**73.5**	**73.4**

and size of the masks are measured. Our approach achieves leading performance among all methods (**+4 mAP**) suggesting good quality masks.

Limited Annotations 3D Semantic Instance Benchmark. On this benchmark, the ground truth labels are given for only a limited number of annotated points per scene. We compare to the baseline methods introduced in [21]. These methods perform instance segmentation by predicting centers, which means that they rely on annotated centers (see Fig. 2, middle). Instead, our approach relies on bounding box annotations. We believe that bounding boxes are more realistic and easier to annotate than 3D object centers, which are usually located somewhere in empty space and can be hard for an annotator to precisely locate. Results are shown in Table 3. Our approach consistently outperforms prior work with a large margin, even without relying on any pre-training.

Table 2. Whole-scene 3D object detection scores on ARKitScenes [3]. The ground truth includes only oriented bounding box annotations, no point-level instance masks. Therefore, we cannot directly compute instance segmentation scores. Instead, as a proxy, we compare to recent object detection methods by fitting an oriented bounding box containing our predicted masks. We report the average precision on the validation set with an IoU threshold of 50% as in [38]. All other scores are as reported in [3].

	Cabinet	Refrig	Shelf	Stove	Bed	Sink	Washer	Toilet	Bathtub
VoteNet [38]	37.1	62.7	12.4	0.3	85.0	31.1	45.3	75.5	93.3
H3DNet [57]	40.2	59.4	10.0	1.6	**88.2**	40.1	49.0	83.8	93.0
MLCVNet [50]	45.1	**70.0**	16.9	2.4	88.0	**40.2**	51.5	85.9	**94.1**
Box2Mask(ours)	**45.9**	62.6	**28.0**	**5.2**	87.1	30.6	**53.8**	**89.4**	92.9
	Oven	Dishw	Fireplace	Stool	Chair	Table	Monitor	Sofa	**mAP**
VoteNet [38]	18.3	2.9	22.1	3.0	20.1	31.0	0.6	68.3	35.8
H3DNet [57]	24.1	**3.9**	19.5	8.8	25.2	32.2	1.5	70.4	38.3
MLCVNet [50]	24.2	3.0	38.5	8.0	31.5	36.6	4.1	71.9	41.9
Box2Mask (ours)	**28.1**	3.8	**59.9**	**20.8**	**35.2**	**60.3**	**7.3**	**82.8**	**46.7**

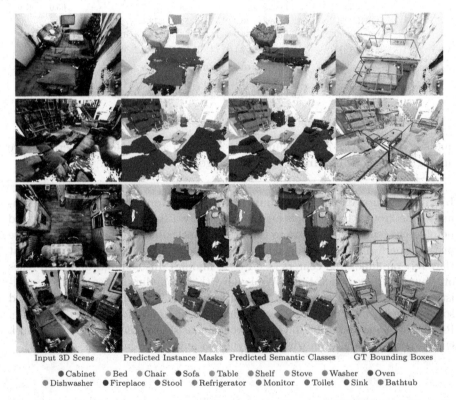

Input 3D Scene   Predicted Instance Masks Predicted Semantic Classes   GT Bounding Boxes

● Cabinet ● Bed ● Chair ● Sofa ● Table ● Shelf ● Stove ● Washer ● Oven
● Dishwasher ● Fireplace ● Stool ● Refrigerator ● Monitor ● Toilet ● Sink ● Bathtub

Fig. 5. Qualitative instance segmentation results on ARKitScenes [3]. Individual instance masks are colored randomly. Semantic classes are colored as indicated. Ground truth boxes are shown for reference only and are not used during inference.

Table 3. ScanNet data efficient benchmark test. Instance segmentation on limited annotations (LA). Scores as in [21]. Star (*) indicates usage of pre-training.

mAP_{50}	200 points	100 Points	50 Points	20 Points
CSC trained from scratch [21]	46.4	41.8	31.1	20.0
PointContrast*[51]	47.1	45.6	40.0	25.9
CSC*[21]	49.4	46.0	41.4	28.9
Ours	**59.2** (+9.8)	**56.5** (+10.5)	**49.8** (+8.4)	**46.5** (+17.6)

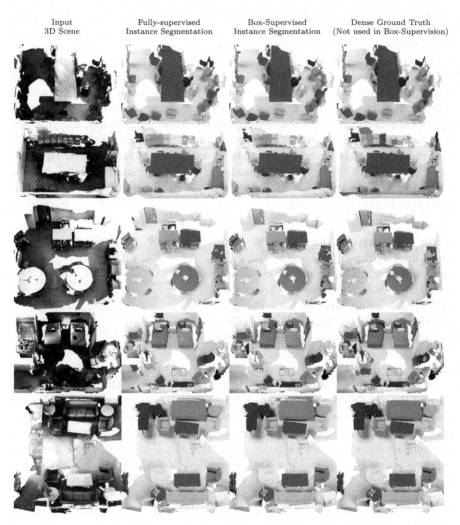

Input 3D Scene   Fully-supervised Instance Segmentation   Box-Supervised Instance Segmentation   Dense Ground Truth (Not used in Box-Supervision)

Fig. 6. Qualitative instance segmentation results (validation) on ScanNet [9]. Results trained only on bounding boxes well resemble the fully supervised model, and both are close to densely annotated ground truth. Instance masks have the same random color as the corresponding ground truth mask.

6.2 Analysis

Boxes or Centers? An important baseline to the proposed *bounding-box* representation is the popular *center* representation [6,21,25,33,41]. We also analyse different techniques for clustering the voting space and compare to the proposed *non-maximum clustering* (NMC). Spatial clustering (SC), such as breadth-first search as in [25] or DBScan as in [12], groups votes based on their pairwise Euclidean distance. Further, it is common practice to cluster votes separately *per semantic class*, which ensures that

Table 4. Non-maximum clustering (NMC) and spatial clustering (SC) on center- and bounding box-votes.

	mAP_{50}	mAP_{25}
Centers + SC	51.4	63.8
Centers + SC (per Sem.)	52.0	67.7
Boxes + SC (per Sem.)	53.1	67.9
Boxes + NMC (per Sem.)	55.1	68.3
Boxes + SC	53.5	65.2
Boxes + NMC	**59.7**	**71.8**

points of disagreeing semantics are in different instances. Table 4 shows that clustering conditioned on the semantic class is beneficial only for centers. This indicates that box votes already encode sufficient semantics (via the size) increasing robustness to wrongly predicted semantics. More importantly, the proposed bounding boxes consistently outperform centers, suggesting that object size is important for vote clustering. The largest improvement is observed by NMC over SC. While SC treats all dimensions in the voting space equally, NMS is tailored to bounding boxes, using the actual geometric meaning of each feature dimension in the voting space.

Weak Supervision Analysis. We introduced *undecided points* as points inside multiple ground truth bounding boxes. *Decided* points are either supervised as background (if they are in no box) or with the single box they are in (*c.f.* Eq. 2). For all others, the undecided points, we compare multiple heuristics, as summarized in Table 5. The

Table 5. Analysis of association strategies

Supervision	mAP_{50}	mAP_{25}
(1) Decided Only	56.0	70.8
(2) Decided + Closest Box	58.7	71.7
(3) Decided + Smallest Box	**59.7**	**71.8**

simplest baseline (1) does not supervise undecided points at all, which results in 56 mAP_{50}. This is already 87% of the performance of the fully-supervised state-of-the-art SSTNet [33] (64.3 mAP_{50}). We then compare two additional heuristics: points that are in multiple ground truth bounding boxes are supervised with the closest bounding box in terms of distance to the center (2), and the smallest bounding box in terms of volume (3). The additional supervision improves scores by +3.7 mAP while the smallest box performs a bit better than the closest. Importantly, using these associations, our weakly supervised model obtains 97% of the performance of a comparable fully supervised model which shows that coarse bounding box annotations are surprisingly strong supervision signal compared to dense per-point annotations.

Effect of Noisy Box Labels. Since training bounding boxes on ScanNet are obtained from point masks, they are perfectly aligned to the points – an accu-

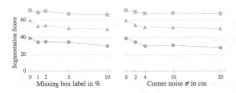

Fig. 7. Reduced annotation quality. Semantic instance segmentation scores on ScanNet val. trained with missing box labels *(left)* and noisy box labels *(right)*.

Table 6. Fully supervised setting. Our model achieves competitive instance segmentation scores on ScanNet validation and S3DIS 6-fold cross validation.

Fully Supervised	ScanNet		S3DIS	
	mAP$_{50}$	mAP$_{25}$	mPrec	mRec
PointGroup [25]	56.9	71.3	69.6	69.2
3D-MPA [12]	59.1	72.4	66.7	64.1
OccuSeg [17]	–	–	72.8	60.3
HAIS [6]	64.1	**75.6**	73.2	69.4
SSTNet [33]	64.3	74.0	73.5	**73.4**
Box2Mask (Ours)	**64.7**	74.5	**75.4**	69.3

racy a human annotation might not achieve. This motivates an experiment on the robustness towards more incorrect labels. We trained separate models on annotation with missing labels (levels 0 to 10%) and inaccurate placement (0 to 20 cm error in box corners). See Fig. 7 for the results. We observe good robustness, with only around 4 mAP differences.

Fully Supervised Setting. Our model can also be adapted to the fully supervised setting, where dense per-point labels are available. The association function a returns the corresponding ground truth point label. Our model compares favorably to recent state-of-the-art approaches, as summarized in Table 6.

Is a Detection Model Enough? As a simple baseline, instead of using the box annotations for directly training instance segmentation, we train a detection model that predicts one box per object. We obtain an instance mask via postprocessing with the best performing box-to-point association strategy (Table 5), which was also used for weak supervision of our model. Our proposed approach largely outperforms this baseline quantitatively (+11.8 mAP$_{50}$ on ScanNet) as well as qualitatively, see appendix (Sect. A) for details. This suggests that our model generalizes beyond the weak point associations, to complete object priors.

7 Conclusion

In this work, we show that 3D bounding box annotations serve surprisingly well as weak supervision for training dense instance segmentation models. Prior works either use dense supervision on all points (which is costly to label), or weak supervision from only a few annotated points (which performs less well). Bounding boxes provide an attractive alternative: the annotation effort is drastically reduced compared to dense point labeling, and they perform notably better than prior sparse labels and are even close to fully-supervised methods. We demonstrate the effectiveness of our instance segmentation approach on several benchmarks, and in particular on the recent, largest scene dataset, ARKitScenes. Although annotated with 3D bounding boxes only, we obtain for the first time compelling 3D instance segmentation results. This unlocks a large body of 3D detection datasets to be viable for learning instance segmentation.

Acknowledgment. We thank Alexey Nekrasov and Jonas Schult for their feedback. This work is funded by the Deutsche Forschungsgemeinschaft (DFG, German Research Foundation) - 409792180 (Emmy Noether Programme, project: Real Virtual Humans) and the German Federal Ministry of Education and Research (BMBF): Tübingen AI Center, FKZ: 01IS18039A. G. Pons-Moll is a member of the Machine Learning Cluster of Excellence, EXC number 2064/1, Project number 390727645. J. Chibane is a fellow of the Meta Research PhD Fellowship Program - area: AR/VR Human Understanding. F. Engelmann is a post-doctoral research fellow at the ETH Zürich AI Center.

References

1. Ahn, J., Kwak, S.: Learning pixel-level semantic affinity with image-level supervision for weakly supervised semantic segmentation. In: Conference on Computer Vision and Pattern Recognition (CVPR) (2018)
2. Armeni, I., et al.: 3D semantic parsing of large-scale indoor spaces. In: Conference on Computer Vision and Pattern Recognition (CVPR) (2016)
3. Baruch, G., et al.: ARKitScenes: a diverse real-world dataset for 3D indoor scene understanding using mobile RGB-D data. In: Neural Information Processing Systems (NIPS) (2021)
4. Bearman, A., Russakovsky, O., Ferrari, V., Fei-Fei, L.: What's the point: semantic segmentation with point supervision. In: Leibe, B., Matas, J., Sebe, N., Welling, M. (eds.) ECCV 2016. LNCS, vol. 9911, pp. 549–565. Springer, Cham (2016). https://doi.org/10.1007/978-3-319-46478-7_34
5. Caesar, H., et al.: nuScenes: a multimodal dataset for autonomous driving. In: Conference on Computer Vision and Pattern Recognition (CVPR) (2020)
6. Chen, S., Fang, J., Zhang, Q., Liu, W., Wang, X.: Hierarchical aggregation for 3D instance segmentation. In: International Conference on Computer Vision (ICCV) (2021)
7. Cheng, M., Hui, L., Xie, J., Yang, J.: SSPC-Net: semi-supervised semantic 3D point cloud segmentation network. In: Conference on Artificial Intelligence (AAAI) (2021)
8. Choy, C., Gwak, J., Savarese, S.: 4D spatio-temporal ConvNets: minkowski convolutional neural networks. In: Conference on Computer Vision and Pattern Recognition (CVPR) (2019)
9. Dai, A., Chang, A.X., Savva, M., Halber, M., Funkhouser, T., Nießner, M.: ScanNet: richly-annotated 3D reconstructions of indoor scenes. In: Conference on Computer Vision and Pattern Recognition (CVPR) (2017)
10. Dai, J., He, K., Sun, J.: Boxsup: exploiting bounding boxes to supervise convolutional networks for semantic segmentation. In: International Conference on Computer Vision (ICCV) (2015)
11. Elich, C., Engelmann, F., Kontogianni, T., Leibe, B.: 3D bird's-eye-view instance segmentation. In: Fink, G.A., Frintrop, S., Jiang, X. (eds.) DAGM GCPR 2019. LNCS, vol. 11824, pp. 48–61. Springer, Cham (2019). https://doi.org/10.1007/978-3-030-33676-9_4

12. Engelmann, F., Bokeloh, M., Fathi, A., Leibe, B., Nießner, M.: 3D-MPA: multi proposal aggregation for 3D semantic instance segmentation. In: IEEE Conference on Computer Vision and Pattern Recognition (CVPR) (2020)
13. Felzenszwalb, P.F., Huttenlocher, D.P.: Efficient graph-based image segmentation. Int. J. Comput. Vis. **59**, 167–181 (2018). https://doi.org/10.1023/B:VISI. 0000022288.19776.77
14. Gählert, N., Jourdan, N., Cordts, M., Franke, U., Denzler, J.: Cityscapes 3D: dataset and benchmark for 9 DoF vehicle detection. arXiv preprint arXiv:2006.07864 (2020)
15. Gidaris, S., Singh, P., Komodakis, N.: Unsupervised representation learning by predicting image rotations. In: International Conference on Learning Representations (ICLR) (2018)
16. Graham, B., Engelcke, M., Van Der Maaten, L.: 3D semantic segmentation with submanifold sparse convolutional networks. In: Conference on Computer Vision and Pattern Recognition (CVPR) (2018)
17. Han, L., Zheng, T., Xu, L., Fang, L.: OccuSeg: occupancy-aware 3D instance segmentation. In: Conference on Computer Vision and Pattern Recognition (CVPR) (2020)
18. He, K., Gkioxari, G., Dollár, P., Girshick, R.: Mask R-CNN. In: Conference on Computer Vision and Pattern Recognition (CVPR) (2017)
19. He, T., Shen, C., van den Hengel, A.: DyCo3d: robust instance segmentation of 3D point clouds through dynamic convolution. In: Conference on Computer Vision and Pattern Recognition (CVPR) (2021)
20. Hou, J., Dai, A., Nießner, M.: 3D-SIS: 3D semantic instance segmentation of RGB-D scans. In: Conference on Computer Vision and Pattern Recognition (CVPR) (2019)
21. Hou, J., Graham, B., Nießner, M., Xie, S.: Exploring data-efficient 3D scene understanding with contrastive scene contexts. In: Conference on Computer Vision and Pattern Recognition (CVPR) (2021)
22. Hsu, C.C., Hsu, K.J., Tsai, C.C., Lin, Y.Y., Chuang, Y.Y.: Weakly supervised instance segmentation using the bounding box tightness prior. In: Advances in Neural Information Processing Systems (2019)
23. Hu, W., Zhao, H., Jiang, L., Jia, J., Wong, T.T.: Bidirectional projection network for cross dimensional scene understanding. In: Conference on Computer Vision and Pattern Recognition (CVPR) (2021)
24. Jiang, L., et al.: Guided point contrastive learning for semi-supervised point cloud semantic segmentation. In: Conference on Computer Vision and Pattern Recognition (CVPR) (2021)
25. Jiang, L., Zhao, H., Shi, S., Liu, S., Fu, C.W., Jia, J.: PointGroup: dual-set Point grouping for 3D instance segmentation. In: Conference on Computer Vision and Pattern Recognition (CVPR) (2020)
26. Joon Oh, S., Benenson, R., Khoreva, A., Akata, Z., Fritz, M., Schiele, B.: Exploiting saliency for object segmentation from image level labels. In: Conference on Computer Vision and Pattern Recognition (CVPR) (2017)
27. Karpathy, A., Miller, S., Fei-Fei, L.: Object discovery in 3D scenes via shape analysis. In: Robotics and Automation (ICRA) (2013)
28. Khoreva, A., Benenson, R., Hosang, J., Hein, M., Schiele, B.: Simple does it: weakly supervised instance and semantic segmentation. In: Conference on Computer Vision and Pattern Recognition (CVPR) (2017)

29. Lahoud, J., Ghanem, B., Pollefeys, M., Oswald, M.R.: 3D instance segmentation via multi-task metric learning. In: International Conference on Computer Vision (ICCV) (2019)

30. Landrieu, L., Boussaha, M.: Large-scale point cloud semantic segmentation with superpoint graphs. In: Conference on Computer Vision and Pattern Recognition (CVPR) (2018)

31. Landrieu, L., Boussaha, M.: Point cloud over-segmentation with graph-structured deep metric learning. In: Conference on Computer Vision and Pattern Recognition (CVPR) (2019)

32. Li, J., Chen, B.M., Lee, G.H.: SO-Net: self-organizing network for point cloud analysis. In: Conference on Computer Vision and Pattern Recognition (CVPR) (2018)

33. Liang, Z., Li, Z., Xu, S., Tan, M., Jia, K.: Instance segmentation in 3D scenes using semantic superpoint tree networks. In: Conference on Computer Vision and Pattern Recognition (CVPR) (2021)

34. Lin, D., Dai, J., Jia, J., He, K., Sun, J.: ScribbleSup: scribble-supervised convolutional networks for semantic segmentation. In: Conference on Computer Vision and Pattern Recognition (CVPR) (2016)

35. Liu, Z., Qi, X., Fu, C.W.: One thing one click: a self-training approach for weakly supervised 3D semantic segmentation. In: Conference on Computer Vision and Pattern Recognition (CVPR) (2021)

36. Mo, K., et al.: PartNet: a large-scale benchmark for fine-grained and hierarchical part-level 3D object understanding. In: Conference on Computer Vision and Pattern Recognition (CVPR) (2019)

37. Nekrasov, A., Schult, J., Litany, O., Leibe, B., Engelmann, F.: Mix3D: out-of-context data augmentation for 3D scenes. In: 3DV (2021)

38. Qi, C.R., Litany, O., He, K., Guibas, L.J.: Deep hough voting for 3D object detection in point clouds. In: Conference on Computer Vision and Pattern Recognition (CVPR) (2019)

39. Qi, C.R., Su, H., Mo, K., Guibas, L.J.: PointNet: deep learning on point sets for 3D classification and segmentation. In: Conference on Computer Vision and Pattern Recognition (CVPR) (2017)

40. Qi, C.R., Yi, L., Su, H., Guibas, L.J.: PointNet++: deep hierarchical feature learning on point sets in a metric space. In: Neural Information Processing Systems (NIPS) (2017)

41. Qi, X., Liu, Z., Shi, J., Zhao, H., Jia, J.: Augmented feedback in semantic segmentation under image level supervision. In: Leibe, B., Matas, J., Sebe, N., Welling, M. (eds.) ECCV 2016. LNCS, vol. 9912, pp. 90–105. Springer, Cham (2016). https://doi.org/10.1007/978-3-319-46484-8_6

42. Ren, Z., Misra, I., Schwing, A.G., Girdhar, R.: 3D spatial recognition without spatially labeled 3D. In: Conference on Computer Vision and Pattern Recognition (CVPR) (2021)

43. Schult, J., Engelmann, F., Kontogianni, T., Leibe, B.: DualConvMesh-Net: joint geodesic and Euclidean convolutions on 3D meshes. In: Conference on Computer Vision and Pattern Recognition (CVPR) (2020)

44. Song, S., Yu, F., Zeng, A., Chang, A.X., Savva, M., Funkhouser, T.: Semantic scene completion from a single depth image. In: Conference on Computer Vision and Pattern Recognition (CVPR) (2017)

45. Thomas, H., Qi, C.R., Deschaud, J.E., Marcotegui, B., Goulette, F., Guibas, L.J.: KPConv: flexible and deformable convolution for point clouds. In: Conference on Computer Vision and Pattern Recognition (CVPR) (2019)

46. Wang, B., et al.: Boundary perception guidance: a scribble-supervised semantic segmentation approach. In: IJCAI International Joint Conference on Artificial Intelligence (2019)

47. Wang, W., Yu, R., Huang, Q., Neumann, U.: SGPN: similarity group proposal network for 3D point cloud instance segmentation. In: Conference on Computer Vision and Pattern Recognition (CVPR) (2018)

48. Wang, X., Liu, S., Shen, X., Shen, C., Jia, J.: Associatively segmenting instances and semantics in point clouds. In: Conference on Computer Vision and Pattern Recognition (CVPR) (2019)

49. Wei, J., Lin, G., Yap, K.H., Hung, T.Y., Xie, L.: Multi-path region mining for weakly supervised 3D semantic segmentation on point clouds. In: Conference on Computer Vision and Pattern Recognition (CVPR) (2020)

50. Xie, Q., et al.: MLCVNet: multi-level context VoteNet for 3D object detection. In: Conference on Computer Vision and Pattern Recognition (CVPR) (2020)

51. Xie, S., Gu, J., Guo, D., Qi, C.R., Guibas, L., Litany, O.: PointContrast: unsupervised pre-training for 3D point cloud understanding. In: Vedaldi, A., Bischof, H., Brox, T., Frahm, J.-M. (eds.) ECCV 2020. LNCS, vol. 12348, pp. 574–591. Springer, Cham (2020). https://doi.org/10.1007/978-3-030-58580-8_34

52. Xu, X., Lee, G.H.: Weakly supervised semantic point cloud segmentation: towards 10x fewer labels. In: Conference on Computer Vision and Pattern Recognition (CVPR) (2020)

53. Yang, B., et al.: Learning object bounding boxes for 3D instance segmentation on point clouds. In: Neural Information Processing Systems (NIPS) (2019)

54. Zhang, J., Yu, X., Li, A., Song, P., Liu, B., Dai, Y.: Weakly-supervised salient object detection via scribble annotations. In: Conference on Computer Vision and Pattern Recognition (CVPR) (2020)

55. Zhang, Y., Li, Z., Xie, Y., Qu, Y., Li, C., Mei, T.: Weakly supervised semantic segmentation for large-scale point cloud. In: Conference on Artificial Intelligence (AAAI) (2021)

56. Zhang, Y., Qu, Y., Xie, Y., Li, Z., Zheng, S., Li, C.: Perturbed self-distillation: weakly supervised large-scale point cloud semantic segmentation. In: International Conference on Computer Vision (ICCV) (2021)

57. Zhang, Z., Sun, B., Yang, H., Huang, Q.: H3DNet: 3D object detection using hybrid geometric primitives. In: European Conference on Computer Vision (ECCV) (2020)

58. Zhou, B., Khosla, A., Lapedriza, A., Oliva, A., Torralba, A.: Learning deep features for discriminative localization. In: Conference on Computer Vision and Pattern Recognition (CVPR) (2016)

59. Zhou, Y., Zhu, Y., Ye, Q., Qiu, Q., Jiao, J.: Weakly supervised instance segmentation using class peak response. In: Conference on Computer Vision and Pattern Recognition (CVPR) (2018)

NeILF: Neural Incident Light Field for Physically-based Material Estimation

Yao Yao[1], Jingyang Zhang[2]([✉]), Jingbo Liu[1], Yihang Qu[1], Tian Fang[1],
David McKinnon[1], Yanghai Tsin[1], and Long Quan[1]

[1] Apple,Cupertino, USA
{yaoyao,jingbo,yihang,fangtian,dmckinnon,quan_long}@apple.com
[2] HKUST,Clear Water Bay, Hong Kong
jzhangbs@cse.ust.hk

Abstract. We present a differentiable rendering framework for material and lighting estimation from multi-view images and a reconstructed geometry. In the framework, we represent scene lightings as the Neural Incident Light Field (NeILF) and material properties as the surface BRDF modelled by multi-layer perceptrons. Compared with recent approaches that approximate scene lightings as the 2D environment map, NeILF is a fully 5D light field that is capable of modelling illuminations of any static scenes. In addition, occlusions and indirect lights can be handled naturally by the NeILF representation without requiring multiple bounces of ray tracing, making it possible to estimate material properties even for scenes with complex lightings and geometries. We also propose a smoothness regularization and a Lambertian assumption to reduce the material-lighting ambiguity during the optimization. Our method strictly follows the physically-based rendering equation, and jointly optimizes material and lighting through the differentiable rendering process. We have intensively evaluated the proposed method on our in-house synthetic dataset, the DTU MVS dataset, and real-world BlendedMVS scenes. Our method outperforms previous methods by a significant margin in terms of novel view rendering quality, setting a new state-of-the-art for image-based material and lighting estimation.

Keywords: Differentiable rendering · Physically-based rendering · BRDF estimation · Incident light field

1 Introduction

Material estimation from a set of sparse images is a challenging task in both computer vision and computer graphics. The problem is usually approached by inverse rendering, where the spatially-varying bidirectional reflectance distribution functions (SV-BRDFs) and lightings of the scene are jointly optimized by minimizing the rendering loss. However, the problem is hard to solve due to

Supplementary Information The online version contains supplementary material available at https://doi.org/10.1007/978-3-031-19821-2_40.

the complex form of the BRDF and the high-dimensional nature of scene illuminations. To mitigate the problem, previous methods usually apply simplified material and lighting models. For example, non-spatially varying BRDF [46] is applied for certain types of objects; approximated illuminations, such as co-located flash lights [3,4,25,31] and environment maps [5,6,24,46,48], are applied to reduce the complexity of the scene lighting. In most scenarios, special capturing devices or environments are required to assist the estimation, limiting these methods to real-world applications. As the result, a practical material estimator is still missing.

On the other hand, recent progress on neural representation has shown promising results for lighting modelling. NeRF [22] jointly optimizes a neural radiance field and a density field, which has demonstrated great success for novel view synthesis. The surface light field is applied to model the outgoing light from the surface, which has been widely applied to neural surface reconstructions [41,45]. Other methods further decompose observed lights into neural material properties and environmental lightings. However, similar to classical methods, they either use simplified lighting representations [3,5,6,24], or apply approximated occlusion and indirect light handling [33,48]. Until now, lighting modelling is still an open problem in image-based material estimation.

In this work, we address this long-standing problem by representing scene lightings as the neural incident light field. Without losing generality, the proposed NeILF is capable of modelling lighting conditions of any static scenes. Also, occlusions and indirect lights could be naturally handled in the proposed framework without tracing multiple bounces of rays. For material properties, we consider a simplified Disney BRDF model [7] consisting of base color, roughness and metallic. Implementation-wise, we use multi-layer perceptrons (MLPs) to represent both the incident light field and the BRDF. The NeILF network takes a 5D vector of location and incident direction as inputs, and returns as output a RGB value of the incident light; the material network takes a 3D location as input, and outputs a 5D vector of surface BRDF properties. Meanwhile, to reduce the ambiguity between the material and the scene lighting, we propose two regularization terms, namely the bilateral smoothness and the Lambertian assumption, to constrain the optimization of roughness and metallic. Finally, we analyze similarities between NeILF for material estimation and NeRF for novel view synthesis [22], providing readers an intuitive explanation of the complexity and solvability of the problem.

We demonstrate in several datasets that our method significantly outperforms previous SOTA methods in terms of novel view rendering accuracy. Our method is able to recover the surface BRDF even for scenes with complex lightings and geometries, which cannot be handled by previous environment map based methods. To summarize, main contributions of the paper include:

- Representing scene lightings by the neural incident light field, where occlusions and indirect lights of the scene can be naturally handled.
- A differentiable framework for joint material and lighting estimation, which significantly outperforms previous state-of-the-art methods in various datasets.

- A bilateral smoothness and a Lambertian assumption to constrain the roughness and the metallic, reducing the material-lighting ambiguity during the
  network optimization.

2 Related Works

2.1 The Rendering Equation

The rendering equation [13] computes the emitted radiance from a surface point
$\mathbf{x}$ along a viewing direction $\boldsymbol{\omega}_o$:

$$L_o(\boldsymbol{\omega}_o, \mathbf{x}) = \int_\Omega f(\boldsymbol{\omega}_o, \boldsymbol{\omega}_i, \mathbf{x}) L_i(\boldsymbol{\omega}_i, \mathbf{x})(\boldsymbol{\omega}_i \cdot \mathbf{n}) d\boldsymbol{\omega}_i, \tag{1}$$

where $\mathbf{n}$ is the normal of the surface, L_i is the incoming light from direction $\boldsymbol{\omega}_i$,
and f is the BRDF function to describe the reflectance property, which is usually
decomposed into a diffuse term and a specular term $f = f_d + f_s$. The integration
is performed over all incident direction $\boldsymbol{\omega}_i$ on the hemisphere Ω where $\boldsymbol{\omega}_i \cdot \mathbf{n} > 0$.

The goal of material estimation is to recover continuous functions of the
scene lighting L_i and the BRDF property f in the above equation. Due to the
complex form of the scene lighting and the material property, it is crucial to
select suitable representations for L_i and f. In this paper, we propose to use a
neural incident light field to model L_i (Sect. 3.1), and apply a simplified Disney
BRDF [7] model to approach the BRDF f (Sect. 3.2). Below we give a brief
review on the physically-based material estimation from multi-view images.

2.2 Differentiable Rendering

Unlike classical approaches that recover 3D scene parameters in a forward reconstruction manner, differentiable rendering [2,14] inverses the rendering process
in graphics, and optimizes all parameters by minimizing the difference between
rendered and input images.

Recently, the technique has been combined with neural representations and
has shown promising results for image-based 3D problems. NeRF [22] and follow-
up works [18,21,47] decouple a 3D scene into a density field and a radiance field.
Other methods also apply implicit functions to model different geometry [19,20,
45] and appearance representations [26,41]. In another line of works, the received
radiance is further decomposed into BRDF properties and input light sources [5,
33,46,48]. Our method follows this practice and applies a neural BRDF model
to approach the material property of the surface.

2.3 Material and Lighting Estimation

Due to the difficulty of joint material and lighting estimation, previous methods
usually apply additional sensors or controlled lightings to facilitate the optimization process. For example, additional sensors [2,11,29], co-located flash

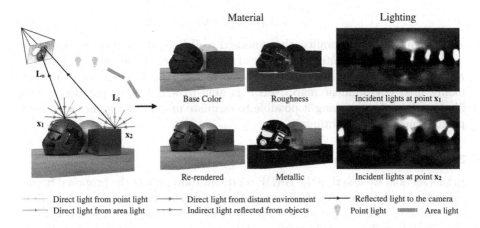

Material   Lighting

Base Color   Roughness   Incident lights at point x₁

Re-rendered   Metallic   Incident lights at point x₂

---- Direct light from point light ——→— Direct light from distant environment ——→— Reflected light to the camera
---- Direct light from area light   ——•→— Indirect light reflected from objects   💡 Point light   ▬▬▬ Area light

Fig. 1. Illustrations of the proposed method and our material and lighting estimation results. NeILF is capable of modelling the joint illumination of direct/indirect lights from different sources. Estimated incident lights at point x_1 and point x_2 well explain the mixed lighting of the scene, including an environment map with high-radiance sun light, two near-range point lights, and two near-range area lights.

lights [3,4,25,31], or turn-table settings [10,38] are applied to capture images or scene lightings. Moreover, simplified material and lighting models, e.g., the non-spatially varying BRDF [46] or approximated illuminations of environment maps [5,8,46,48], are applied to reduce the complexity of the problem. NeRV [33] introduces the visibility field to model indirect lights. However, it requires environmental lightings to be known in advance. Nevertheless, such mitigations will inevitably limit these methods to real-world applications. Nimier-David et al. proposed a method [27] for joint illumination and material estimation. However, the method requires to trace the ray of multiple bounces. In contrast, our method applies a unified incident light field to represent different light sources in the scene, and is capable of estimating material under any lighting conditions without the need of multi-bounce raytracing.

3   Method

3.1   Neural Incident Light Field

One of the keys to invert the rendering equation is to model the incoming light L_i in a correct way. Ideally, L_i should take into account 1) *direct lights* from light sources in the scene, 2) *occlusions* that block the surface point from receiving direct lights, and 3) *indirect lights* that are reflected from other surface points. However, each of the three components is hard to model. Previous methods [5, 17,46,48] usually approximate direct lights as an environment map and hardly handle indirect lights as they require multi-bounce raytracing.

In contrast, we formulate incoming lights in the scene directly as a neural incident light field, where an MLP takes a point location $\mathbf{x}$ and an incident direction $\boldsymbol{\omega}$ as inputs, and returns an incident light radiance L as output:

$$\mathbb{L} : \{\mathbf{x}, \boldsymbol{\omega}\} \to \mathbf{L}. \tag{2}$$

Without losing generality, the proposed NeILF representation is capable of modelling the joint illumination effect of direct/indirect lights and occlusions of *any static scenes*. An illustration is shown in Fig. 1. Compared with the commonly used environment map, NeILF is able to handle the spatially-varying illumination effect, making it possible to estimate material for scenes with complex geometries and lightings.

3.2   Simplified Disney BRDF

In this section, we describe the BRDF representation used in the proposed framework. We apply a simplified Disney principled BRDF model, where the BRDF of a surface point $\mathbf{x}$ is parameterized by a base color $\mathbf{b}(\mathbf{x}) \in [0,1]^3$, a roughness $r(\mathbf{x}) \in [0,1]$ and a metallic $m(\mathbf{x}) \in [0,1]$, which is a subset of the full Disney model [7]. Similar to the neural incident lighting field, BRDF parameters are also stored using multi-layer perceptrons:

$$\mathbb{B} : \mathbf{x} \to \{\mathbf{b}, r, m\}, \tag{3}$$

where the MLP takes a 3D surface point $\mathbf{x}$ as input, and returns the 5-channel BRDF parameters as output. Note that other representations, e.g. UV atlas or per-vertex BRDF parameters, can also be applied. Here we choose the neural representation because it has been proven to be effective for modelling continuous functions in 3D space [22,46], and its derivative can be easily and analytically derived for our regularization computation (Sect. 3.3).

The Rendering Equation. Given the BRDF parameterization, we now describe the concrete formulation of f in Eq. 1. In the following equations, we omit notations of surface point $\mathbf{x}$ and normal $\mathbf{n}$ as the geometry of the scene is assumed to be given. The diffuse term can be calculated as $f_d = \frac{1-m}{\pi} \cdot \mathbf{b}$, and the specular term as:

$$f_s(\boldsymbol{\omega}_o, \boldsymbol{\omega}_i) = \frac{D(\mathbf{h}; r) \cdot F(\boldsymbol{\omega}_o, \mathbf{h}; \mathbf{b}, m) \cdot G(\boldsymbol{\omega}_i, \boldsymbol{\omega}_o, \mathbf{h}; r)}{4 \cdot (\mathbf{n} \cdot \boldsymbol{\omega}_i) \cdot (\mathbf{n} \cdot \boldsymbol{\omega}_o)}, \tag{4}$$

where $\mathbf{h}$ is the half vector between the incident direction $\boldsymbol{\omega}_i$ and the viewing direction $\boldsymbol{\omega}_o$. The first term D is the normal distribution function of the microfacets in the surface. It is related to the roughness r and we use Spherical Gaussians to model this function as in previous methods [35,46]. The second Fresnel term F models the portion of light that can be reflected from the surface, which is determined by the surface metallic m and the base color $\mathbf{b}$. The final geometry term G handles the shadow and occlusion of the microfacets, which is parameterized on the roughness r and is approximated using the GGX distribution [34]. Details of D, F and G are provided in the supplementary material.

3.3   Material-Lighting Ambiguity and Regularizations

While the Disney BRDF and incident light field are capable of representing materials and lightings of different scenes, jointly optimizing both would inevitably lead to ambiguous solutions between them. One degenerate case could be that we can force a pure reflective BRDF to all surface points, and then only optimize the incident lights to adjust the input image. Theoretically, we can still find a perfect solution that fits the given BRDF and input images: for each 3D point, whenever there is a visible camera, we set its mirror symmetric incident light equal to the viewing out-going light, and set other incident lights equal to zero. It is also reported in previous work [30] that even human observers cannot distinguish the two confounded components from only image observations.

In the proposed framework, we can still manage to recover reasonable material and lighting results as MLPs can implicitly enforce a spatial smoothness constraint [47] on the two components. However, for robust material and lighting estimation, additional regularizations are desired. In this paper, we propose two regularizations for roughness r and metallic m:

Bilateral Smoothness. We encourage r and m not to change rapidly in space, and the gradient of the input image $\mathbf{I}$ can be used as a hint to guide the smoothing process. Thus, we define the bilateral smoothness cost of r and m as:

$$l_{smooth} = \frac{1}{|S_I|} \sum_{\mathbf{p} \in S_I} (\|\nabla_{\mathbf{x}} r(\mathbf{x_p})\| + \|\nabla_{\mathbf{x}} m(\mathbf{x_p})\|) e^{-\|\nabla_{\mathbf{p}} \mathbf{I}(\mathbf{p})\|}, \quad (5)$$

where S_I is the set of all sampled pixels and $\mathbf{x_p}$ is the corresponding 3D point of the sampled pixel $\mathbf{p}$. The image gradient $\nabla_{\mathbf{p}} \mathbf{I}(\mathbf{p})$ can be pre-calculated from the input image, and the roughness gradient $\nabla_{\mathbf{x}} r(\mathbf{x_p})$ and metallic gradient $\nabla_{\mathbf{x}} m(\mathbf{x_p})$ can be derived analytically by back-propagating the neural network.

Lambertian Assumption. We also assume that all surfaces tend to be Lambertian if no view-dependent lighting is observed, which leads to high roughness and low metallic, and we define the Lambertian cost as:

$$l_{lambertian} = \frac{1}{|S_I|} \sum_{\mathbf{p} \in S_I} (|r(\mathbf{x_p}) - 1| + |m(\mathbf{p})|). \quad (6)$$

The proposed two regularizations will be minimized during network training. It is noteworthy that the two losses may not necessarily improve quantitative results as they are heuristically defined for robust material and lighting estimation. We show in a later ablation study that the bilateral smoothness will lead to visually much more pleasing results for real-world reconstructions.

3.4   Loss

Similar to other differentiable rendering frameworks, we compute the L1 loss between the rendered image and the input image:

$$l_{image} = \frac{1}{|S_I|} \sum_{\mathbf{p} \in S_I} \|\mathbf{I}(\mathbf{p}) - L_o(\mathbf{x_p}, \boldsymbol{\omega}_o)\|_1. \quad (7)$$

The final loss of the proposed system is a weighted sum of the image loss and the two regularization losses: $l = l_{image} + w_s l_{smooth} + w_l l_{lambertian}$, where the two weights are empirically set to $w_s = 10^{-4}$ and $w_l = 10^{-3}$ in all our experiments.

4   Implementations

4.1   Sphere Sampling

To compute L_o using a finite number of incident lights, we need to discretize Eq. 1 as: $L_o(\boldsymbol{\omega}_o, \mathbf{x}) = \sum_{i \in S_L} f(\boldsymbol{\omega}_o, \boldsymbol{\omega}_i, \mathbf{x}) L_i(\boldsymbol{\omega}_i, \mathbf{x})(\boldsymbol{\omega}_i \cdot \mathbf{n}) \cdot A(\boldsymbol{\omega}_i)$, where S_L is the set of incident lights sampled for point $\mathbf{x}$ and $A(\boldsymbol{\omega}_i)$ is the solid angle that corresponds to the incident light. In computer graphics, randomized Monto-Carlo Samplings are usually applied in ray-tracing, and the solid angle $A(\boldsymbol{\omega}_i)$ is approximated by the probability distribution $P(\boldsymbol{\omega}_i)$ of ray samples.

However, in differentiable rendering, it is critical to accurately compute the solid angle $A(\boldsymbol{\omega}_i)$ for each light sample as we need to correctly pass loss gradients to network parameters. We found that using random sampling and approximating $A(\boldsymbol{\omega}_i)$ as the probability distribution $P(\boldsymbol{\omega}_i)$ will lead to erroneous BRDF results. Thus, we apply a fixed Fibonacci sampling over the half sphere to get all samples. In this case, $A(\boldsymbol{\omega}_i) = \frac{2\pi}{|S_L|}$ and the rendering equation becomes:

$$L_o(\boldsymbol{\omega}_o, \mathbf{x}) = \frac{2\pi}{|S_L|} \sum_{i \in S_L} f(\boldsymbol{\omega}_o, \boldsymbol{\omega}_i, \mathbf{x}) L_i(\boldsymbol{\omega}_i, \mathbf{x})(\boldsymbol{\omega}_i \cdot \mathbf{n}). \tag{8}$$

4.2   Learned HDR-LDR Mapping

For real-world datasets with low dynamic range (LDR) images, we need to convert the high dynamic range (HDR) output from our renderer to LDR before computing the image loss. As such transformation is unavailable in previous MVS datasets, we apply a learned HDR-LDR mapping to mimic the conversion in our network. Note that linear transformations, including exposure and white balance, can be embedded into the incident light. Thus, we only explicitly model the gamma correction with a learnable parameter:

$$L_o^{LDR} = (L_o^{HDR})^\gamma. \tag{9}$$

4.3   Training Details

We use an 8-layer Siren [32] with feature size of 512 and a skip connection in the middle to represent the BRDF MLP. Also, the positional encoding [21] is applied to further strengthen the network. The NeILF MLP shares the same implementation as BRDF, except that 1) the feature size is downsized to 128 to reduce the VRAM usage and 2) the last layer activation function is changed from *tanh* to *exp* in order to guarantee non-negative and unbounded light intensities.

In the experiment, we use $|S_L| = 128$ incident lights to compute the output radiance during training, and use $|S_L| = 256$ incident lights to evaluate the rendered image during testing. For each training iteration, we randomly sample 16000 pixels from all images, and the network is optimized for a total of 15000 iterations. The Adam optimizer [16] with an initial learning rate of 10^{-3} is applied in our network, and the learning rate is scaled down by $\sqrt{0.1}$ at 5000 and 10000 iterations. The training process takes around 1.5 h to finish on a Tesla V100 GPU and the VRAM consumption is around 30 GB.

5   Experiments

5.1   Baseline Methods

We compare our method with the following baselines:

PhySG * Firstly, we consider the recent PhySG [46] for material estimation. The original PhySG jointly optimizes the non-spatially varying BRDF, the environment map, and the geometry of the object. To fairly compare with the method, we fix the given geometry and optimize only the uniform BRDF and the environment map.

SG-Env This baseline is another variant of PhySG [46]. Compared with PhySG*, SG-Env applies a SV-BRDF model and a slightly different rendering formulation (the same f_d, D and G as ours). We use this baseline to directly compare NeILF with the SG environment map representation.

NeRFactor * This baseline is a variant of NeRFactor [48] with the ground truth geometry input. In the setting, we follow NeRFactor to represent the scene lighting as a 2D environment map of resolution 32×16. The ground truth geometry are fixed during the training and we use the online raytracing to compute the ground truth visibilities of each ray.

Ne-Env Lastly, we compare our method with the neural environment map representation. This baseline shares the same implementation of the proposed NeILF, except that the positional input in the incident light field is omitted such that the incident light is only related to the incoming direction: $\{\boldsymbol{\omega}\} \rightarrow \mathbf{L}$.

5.2   Benchmark on Synthetic Scenes

To quantitatively evaluate our method under different lighting conditions, we generate a set of synthetic data and compare our method with the above baselines.

Data Preparation. The synthetic dataset contains three objects and their combinations: a single rough metallic sphere, a single rough metallic cube, and a helmet with spatially variant materials. The objects are placed on a plane to model the real-world object capture. We also create six lighting conditions to lit the objects, including three environment maps and three mixed lightings:

- *Env-city*: an environment map of a city;
- *Env-studio*: an environment map of a studio;

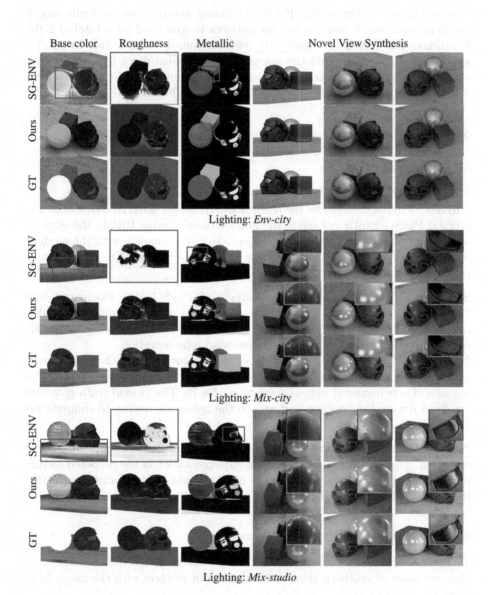

Fig. 2. Comparative results on BRDF estimation and novel view synthesis on the synthetic dataset. From left to right are images of *base color*, *roughness*, *metallic* and synthesized testing views. Our method is able to generate high-quality BRDF and novel view synthesis results under different lighting conditions. In contrast, the environment map based SG-ENV [46] produces noisy BRDF outputs especially in occluded regions. And also, highlights are wrongly recovered in novel view renderings if mixed lightings occur.

Table 1. Quantitative results on Synthetic scenes. We compare the proposed NeILF with four baseline methods described in Sect. 5.1 using PSNR scores. Our method generates consistently the best novel view rendering for all scenes. Also, our method produces significantly better BRDF results than other methods if multiple objects and mixed lightings are given.

Scene Geometry		Single-helmet			Combined-objects					
Scene Lighting		Env-city	Env-studio	Env-castel	Env-city	Env-studio	Env-castel	Mix-city	Mix-studio	Mix-castel
Base Color	PhySG* [46]	13.43	14.87	13.95	15.01	16.96	16.13	14.16	12.43	14.29
	SG-ENV [46]	**20.61**	**18.45**	15.99	**22.38**	**20.74**	**22.21**	16.92	13.16	16.69
	NeRFactor* [48]	13.02	11.73	11.98	8.09	13.60	7.37	8.64	11.63	8.03
	Ne-ENV	13.43	12.65	12.45	11.68	11.98	7.66	11.87	10.90	9.54
	Ours	16.36	16.36	**18.28**	15.59	15.48	12.95	**17.39**	**16.88**	**17.37**
Metallic	PhySG* [46]	7.57	7.48	7.83	8.72	7.97	8.35	8.67	8.95	8.76
	SG-ENV [46]	**21.19**	**21.31**	**21.79**	17.01	16.40	**16.39**	15.44	14.25	14.49
	NeRFactor* [48]	12.88	17.39	16.78	12.38	13.43	11.98	11.77	11.88	11.95
	Ne-ENV	9.31	17.40	6.15	15.86	16.10	11.42	15.43	15.35	15.49
	Ours	17.79	18.52	16.82	**18.22**	**19.11**	10.29	**18.42**	**18.43**	**17.34**
Roughness	PhySG* [46]	6.91	11.88	6.75	6.62	11.29	6.22	6.27	6.83	6.14
	SG-ENV [46]	14.77	15.87	9.64	9.61	17.64	9.74	8.77	12.58	9.14
	NeRFactor* [48]	12.84	11.59	12.89	9.21	17.95	9.02	9.12	12.62	8.54
	Ne-ENV	11.95	14.84	9.26	15.56	14.48	12.94	16.20	14.43	14.14
	Ours	**16.13**	**16.19**	**17.16**	**17.48**	**18.30**	**13.40**	**17.05**	**16.27**	**16.44**
Rendering	PhySG* [46]	24.59	24.77	26.52	24.82	25.65	27.24	24.38	24.04	25.81
	SG-ENV [46]	29.73	29.86	32.13	31.01	29.46	32.34	27.20	25.88	27.70
	NeRFactor* [48]	29.30	28.78	30.58	29.31	30.10	30.66	27.50	27.00	28.11
	Ne-ENV	28.60	29.56	29.76	30.75	29.07	32.05	28.07	26.01	28.33
	Ours	**31.57**	**30.84**	**34.43**	**33.77**	**31.07**	**35.28**	**31.11**	**28.59**	**32.11**

- *Env-castel*: an environment map of a castel;
- *Mix-city*: Env-city plus two point lights and two area lights;
- *Mix-studio*: Env-studio plus two point lights and two area lights;
- *Mix-castel*: Env-castel plus two point lights and two area lights.

Each scene contains 96 images, where images $\{9, 18, 30, 41, 50, 62, 73, 82, 94\}$ are used for evaluation and the remaining 87 images are used for training. The image resolution is set to 1600×1200. We use Blender [9] to render the HDR images by ray tracing. Position maps and normal maps at all viewpoints are rendered to serve as the geometry input for the system. Meanwhile, per-view ground truth base color, metallic and roughness maps are provided for quantitative evaluation.

Results. We use the PSNR score as our evaluation metric. Quantitative comparisons on 1) base color, 2) metallic, 3) roughness and 4) novel view synthesis are shown in Table 1. Our method consistently outperforms other methods with a large margin in terms of the novel view rendering quality. For material estimation, we found that if single objects and environment map light sources are given, SG-Env [46] is able to generate comparable results with ours. However, in the case of multiple objects or mixed light sources, the estimation quality of SG-Env will drop significantly. This is because the environment map representation cannot model mixed light sources of point and area lights. Also, indirect lights and occlusions within multiple objects are not handled by SG-Env. In contrast,

Table 2. Quantitative results on DTU [12] and BlendedMVS [39] Datasets. The table shows PSNR scores of novel view renderings of test images. Our method consistently outperforms the other methods in terms of the rendering quality.

	DTU [12]					BlendedMVS [39]					
	scan-1	scan-11	scan-37	scan-75	scan-97	bull	cam	dog	gold	statue	stone
PhySG* [46]	20.40	20.78	20.30	16.03	19.86	21.64	18.11	20.70	19.06	19.74	21.22
SG-ENV [46]	22.18	21.56	21.71	18.06	21.09	22.51	20.14	22.06	19.44	20.79	22.31
NeRFactor* [48]	23.68	23.43	23.86	19.89	22.10	21.87	20.03	21.54	19.47	20.51	22.98
Ne-ENV	23.77	23.79	22.87	19.52	21.51	22.17	20.17	21.73	19.66	20.55	23.08
NeILF (Ours)	**24.79**	**24.33**	**24.44**	**23.46**	**23.96**	**24.93**	**22.10**	**22.36**	**20.80**	**21.51**	**24.22**

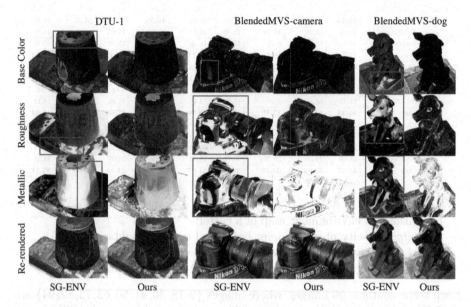

Fig. 3. Qualitative results on the real-world DTU and BlendedMVS datasets. Our method successfully removes high lights in the base color and produces visually plausible results of roughness and metallic.

our NeILF representation can robustly deal with mixed lightings and complex scene geometries. Qualitative results are shown in Fig. 2.

5.3 Test on Real-world Scenes

We then test our method on two real-world datasets, namely DTU [12] and BlendedMVS [39] datasets. DTU dataset is captured in a lab setting with a fixed lighting and camera trajectory, while BlendedMVS contains a variety of indoor and outdoor scenes captured by different users. As the two datasets provide only LDR images, the learned HDR-LDR mapping described in Sect. 4.2 is applied for the loss computation. For each scene, we select 5 images {2, 12, 17, 30, 34} for testing and the rest of the images for training.

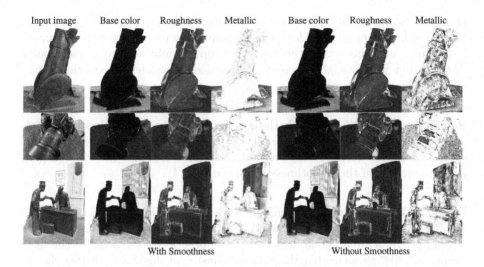

Fig. 4. Qualitative comparisons on with and without the proposed bilateral smoothness regularization.

It is noteworthy that unlike in the synthetic dataset, here we use multi-view stereo methods to generate the geometry input rather than directly using the ground truth. For DTU datatset, we use Vis-MVSNet [44] to generate the dense 3D point cloud and SPSR [15] to recover the mesh surface. For BlendedMVS dataset, we use original images and the provided reference mesh geometry as our inputs. By doing so, our method can be viewed as an extension to nowadays 3D reconstruction pipelines.

Quantitative results are shown in Table 2 and qualitative results compared with SG-ENV are shown in Fig. 3. The proposed method produces both the best rendering PSNR and the most visually pleasing BRDF in all selected scenes. We believe the proposed method can be integrated into traditional 3D reconstruction pipelines for relightable mesh model reconstruction.

5.4   Ablation Study

In this section, we analyze several design choices of the proposed framework. The ablation studies are conducted on the synthetic dataset, and we report the average scores over all scenes to compare different settings.

Ray Sample Number. We first study the influence of the ray sample number for material estimation quality. The ray sample number is decreased from $S_L = 128$ to $S_L = 64$ and $S_L = 32$. As shown in Table 3, higher sampling number will lead to better reconstruction results. In our default setting, we choose $S_L = 128$ to better balance the quality and the VRAM/runtime consumption.

Random Sample. Next, we compare the fixed Fibonacci sample described in Sect. 4.1 with the random uniform sample commonly used in computer graphics. It is shown in Table 3 that the random sample would lead to worse results, showing that it is crucial to precisely discretize the rendering equation in the differentiable rendering.

Regularizations. We also study the effectiveness of the two regularizations proposed in Sect. 3.3. We find that the bilateral smoothness is essential for material estimation of real-world scenes, where the roughness and metallic will be significantly improved if the smoothness is applied (Fig. 4).

Learned Gamma. Lastly, we compare the proposed learned gamma in Sect. 4.2 with the fixed $\gamma = \frac{1}{2.2}$. In BlendedMVS dataset, the learned gamma produces a mean PSNR score of 22.65, which slightly outperforms the score of the fixed gamma (22.51), showing that the learned adjustment might be a better choice.

On the other hand, we also find that the two heuristics have limited influence to quantitative results of the synthetic dataset. We believe this is because the vanilla NeILF already produces high-quality estimations for synthetic scenes. In our default setting, we keep the two regularizations for all scenes but we encourage

Table 3. Ablation studies. Average scores among all synthetic scenes are reported.

	Base	Meta	Roug	Rend
S = 128	**16.30**	**17.22**	16.49	**32.09**
S = 64	15.20	16.47	18.88	31.40
S = 32	13.40	16.27	**19.49**	30.57
Rand. Samp	12.45	15.11	18.10	29.73

users to selectively apply the two terms depending on different characteristics of input scenes.

6   Discussions

6.1   Comparison with NeRF Optimization

In this section, we compare the proposed NeILF with the neural radiance field [21]. We show that the two frameworks share similarities in many aspects, and thus provide readers an intuitive explanation of why NeILF can successfully disentangle the complex material and lighting in the joint optimization.

Lighting Representations. NeRF [21] represents the scene appearance as the neural radiance field. While the radiance is physically different with the incident light, their complexities are completely the same: both NeILF and NeRF take a 3D position $\mathbf{x}$ and a direction $\boldsymbol{\omega}$ as inputs, and returns a RGB value as output.

Spatially-varying Properties. NeILF aims to recover surface materials as BRDF properties, while NeRF jointly optimizes the scene geometry as a density field. Both our BRDF and NeRF's density MLPs take only a 3D position $\mathbf{x}$

as input, and return different spatial properties as outputs. Implementation-wise, the only difference is that our BRDF is consist of a 5D parameter vector, while the density value is a 1D scalar. Nevertheless, the two spatially-varying properties are very similar and their complexities are comparable.

Rendering Formulations. Our method applies the surface rendering to compute the reflected light from a surface point, while NeRF adopts the volume rendering to get the accumulated color along a viewing ray. On the one hand, NeILF requires the incident light integration over the hemisphere; on the other hand, NeRF requires alpha composition along the ray. To render a pixel, NeILF needs to sample the BRDF MLP once and the incident light MLP for multiple times, while NeRF does the same on the density and radiance MLPs.

Reconstruction Ambiguities. The geometry-appearance ambiguity is addressed in NeRF++ [47]. Similarly, we analyze the material-lighting ambiguity in the NeILF optimization. It has been reported that with proper geometry regularizations [28,36,40], NeRF is able to produce high-quality geometry outputs. In contrast, we also show that the proposed bilateral smoothness can significantly improve the roughness and metallic quality for real-world scenes (Fig. 4).

6.2 Limitations and Future Works

While the proposed method has already shown promising results for material estimation, the current pipeline still contains several limitations that could be further addressed in future works.

Geometry Optimization. The major limitation of our method is that the geometry is required to be given in advance. Although we have shown that meshes from 3D reconstruction pipelines are qualified for real-world DTU and BlendedMVS scenes, it is still desired that we can jointly optimize the scene geometry during training. Possible directions include displacement/normal map estimation and the differentiable surface refinement [41,43,45,46].

High-intensity Singularities in Light Sources. Rippled noises would sometimes occur in our estimation if direct lights contain high-intensity singularities. One example is the metallic result of *Mix-studio* in Fig. 2. It is worth investigating better training losses/strategies to mitigate this problem in the future.

Running Speed. Similar to NeRF, our method requires frequent MLP samplings and the training process is time consuming. Our current implementation takes around 1.5 h to estimate the BRDF of a given scene (details in Sect. 4.3). We hope that in the future, explicit Octree [42], spherical harmonics [1,37] or neural hashing [23] can be applied to speed up the NeILF optimization.

7 Conclusions

We have presented a differentiable rendering framework for material and lighting estimation. Compared with the environment map approximation, the proposed neural incident light field is capable of modelling the lighting condition of any static scenes, making it possible to estimate qualified material properties even for scenes with complex lightings and geometries. The proposed method strictly follows the physically-based rendering equation, and jointly optimizes material and lighting through the differentiable rendering process. We have intensively evaluated our method on our in-house synthetic dataset, the DTU MVS dataset, and the real-world BlendedMVS scenes. Our method is able to outperform previous methods by a significant margin in terms of the novel view rendering quality, setting a new state-of-the-art for image-based material and lighting estimation.

References

1. Yu, A., Fridovich-Keil, S., Tancik, M., Chen, Q., Recht, B., Kanazawa, A.: Plenoxels: radiance fields without neural networks. arXiv:2112.05131 (2021)
2. Azinovic, D., Li, T.M., Kaplanyan, A., Niessner, M.: Inverse path tracing for joint material and lighting estimation. In: CVPR (2019)
3. Bi, S., et al.: Deep reflectance volumes: relightable reconstructions from multi-view photometric images. In: ECCV (2020)
4. Bi, S., Xu, Z., Sunkavalli, K., Kriegman, D., Ramamoorthi, R.: Deep 3D capture: geometry and reflectance from sparse multi-view images. In: CVPR (2020)
5. Boss, M., Braun, R., Jampani, V., Barron, J.T., Liu, C., Lensch, H.: Nerd: neural reflectance decomposition from image collections. In: ICCV (2021)
6. Boss, M., Jampani, V., Braun, R., Liu, C., Barron, J., Lensch, H.P.: Neural-pil: neural pre-integrated lighting for reflectance decomposition. In: NeurIPS (2021)
7. Burley, B., Studios, W.D.A.: Physically-based shading at disney. In: ACM SIGGRAPH (2012)
8. Chen, W., et al.: DIB-R++: learning to predict lighting and material with a hybrid differentiable renderer. In: NeurIPS (2021)
9. Community, B.O.: Blender - a 3D modelling and rendering package. Blender Foundation, Stichting Blender Foundation, Amsterdam (2018). http://www.blender.org
10. Dong, Y., Chen, G., Peers, P., Zhang, J., Tong, X.: Appearance-from-motion: recovering spatially varying surface reflectance under unknown lighting. ACM Trans. Graph. 33(6), 1–12 (2014)
11. Guo, K., et al.: The relightables: volumetric performance capture of humans with realistic relighting. ACM Trans. Graph. 38(6), 1–19 (2019)
12. Jensen, R., Dahl, A., Vogiatzis, G., Tola, E., Aanæs, H.: Large scale multi-view stereopsis evaluation. In: CVPR (2014)
13. Kajiya, J.T.: The rendering equation. In: Proceedings of the 13th Annual Conference on Computer Graphics and Interactive Techniques (1986)
14. Kato, H., et al.: Differentiable rendering: a survey. arXiv preprint arXiv:2006.12057 (2020)
15. Kazhdan, M., Hoppe, H.: Screened poisson surface reconstruction. ACM Trans. Graph. 32(3), 1–13 (2013)
16. Kingma, D.P., Ba, J.: Adam: a method for stochastic optimization. In: ICLR (2015)

17. Li, Z., Xu, Z., Ramamoorthi, R., Sunkavalli, K., Chandraker, M.: Learning to reconstruct shape and spatially-varying reflectance from a single image. ACM Trans. Graph. **37**(6), 1–11 (2018)

18. Liu, L., Gu, J., Lin, K.Z., Chua, T.S., Theobalt, C.: Neural sparse voxel fields. In: NeurIPS (2020)

19. Liu, S., Zhang, Y., Peng, S., Shi, B., Pollefeys, M., Cui, Z.: Dist: rendering deep implicit signed distance function with differentiable sphere tracing. In: CVPR (2020)

20. Liu, S., Saito, S., Chen, W., Li, H.: Learning to infer implicit surfaces without 3D supervision. arXiv preprint arXiv:1911.00767 (2019)

21. Martin-Brualla, R., Radwan, N., Sajjadi, M.S., Barron, J.T., Dosovitskiy, A., Duckworth, D.: Nerf in the wild: neural radiance fields for unconstrained photo collections. In: CVPR (2021)

22. Mildenhall, B., Srinivasan, P.P., Tancik, M., Barron, J.T., Ramamoorthi, R., Ng, R.: Nerf: representing scenes as neural radiance fields for view synthesis. In: ECCV (2020)

23. Müller, T., Evans, A., Schied, C., Keller, A.: Instant neural graphics primitives with a multiresolution hash encoding. arXiv preprint arXiv:2201.05989 (2022)

24. Munkberg, J., et al.: Extracting triangular 3D models, materials, and lighting from images. arXiv preprint arXiv:2111.12503 (2021)

25. Nam, G., Lee, J.H., Gutierrez, D., Kim, M.H.: Practical svbrdf acquisition of 3D objects with unstructured flash photography. ACM Trans. Graph. **37**(6), 1–12 (2018)

26. Niemeyer, M., Mescheder, L., Oechsle, M., Geiger, A.: Differentiable volumetric rendering: learning implicit 3D representations without 3D supervision. In: CVPR (2020)

27. Nimier-David, M., Dong, Z., Jakob, W., Kaplanyan, A.: Material and lighting reconstruction for complex indoor scenes with texture-space differentiable rendering (2021)

28. Oechsle, M., Peng, S., Geiger, A.: Unisurf: unifying neural implicit surfaces and radiance fields for multi-view reconstruction. In: ICCV (2021)

29. Park, J.J., Holynski, A., Seitz, S.M.: Seeing the world in a bag of chips. In: CVPR (2020)

30. Pont, S.C., Te Pas, S.F.: Material-illumination ambiguities and the perception of solid objects. Perception **35**(10), 1331–1350 (2006)

31. Schmitt, C., Donne, S., Riegler, G., Koltun, V., Geiger, A.: On joint estimation of pose, geometry and svbrdf from a handheld scanner. In: CVPR (2020)

32. Sitzmann, V., Martel, J., Bergman, A., Lindell, D., Wetzstein, G.: Implicit neural representations with periodic activation functions. In: NeurIPS (2020)

33. Srinivasan, P.P., Deng, B., Zhang, X., Tancik, M., Mildenhall, B., Barron, J.T.: Nerv: neural reflectance and visibility fields for relighting and view synthesis. In: CVPR (2021)

34. Walter, B., Marschner, S., Li, H., Torrance, K.: Microfacet models for refraction through rough surfaces. In: EGSR (2007)

35. Wang, J., Ren, P., Gong, M., Snyder, J., Guo, B.: All-frequency rendering of dynamic, spatially-varying reflectance. In: ACM SIGGRAPH Asia (2009)

36. Wang, P., Liu, L., Liu, Y., Theobalt, C., Komura, T., Wang, W.: Neus: learning neural implicit surfaces by volume rendering for multi-view reconstruction (2021)

37. Wizadwongsa, S., Phongthawee, P., Yenphraphai, J., Suwajanakorn, S.: Nex: real-time view synthesis with neural basis expansion. In: CVPR (2021)

38. Xia, R., Dong, Y., Peers, P., Tong, X.: Recovering shape and spatially-varying surface reflectance under unknown illumination. ACM Trans. Graph. **35**(6), 1–12 (2016)

39. Yao, Y., et al.: Blendedmvs: a large-scale dataset for generalized multi-view stereo networks. In: CVPR (2020)

40. Yariv, L., Gu, J., Kasten, Y., Lipman, Y.: Volume rendering of neural implicit surfaces. arXiv preprint arXiv:2106.12052 (2021)

41. Yariv, L., et al.: Multiview neural surface reconstruction by disentangling geometry and appearance. In: NeurIPS (2020)

42. Yu, A., Li, R., Tancik, M., Li, H., Ng, R., Kanazawa, A.: PlenOctrees for real-time rendering of neural radiance fields. In: ICCV (2021)

43. Zhang, J., et al.: Critical regularizations for neural surface reconstruction in the wild. In: CVPR (2022)

44. Zhang, J., Yao, Y., Li, S., Luo, Z., Fang, T.: Visibility-aware multi-view stereo network. In: BMVC (2020)

45. Zhang, J., Yao, Y., Quan, L.: Learning signed distance field for multi-view surface reconstruction. In: ICCV (2021)

46. Zhang, K., Luan, F., Wang, Q., Bala, K., Snavely, N.: Physg: inverse rendering with spherical gaussians for physics-based material editing and relighting. In: CVPR (2021)

47. Zhang, K., Riegler, G., Snavely, N., Koltun, V.: Nerf++: analyzing and improving neural radiance fields. arXiv preprint arXiv:2010.07492 (2020)

48. Zhang, X., Srinivasan, P.P., Deng, B., Debevec, P., Freeman, W.T., Barron, J.T.: NeRFactor: neural factorization of shape and reflectance under an unknown illumination. ACM Trans. Graph. **40**(6), 1–18 (2021)

ARF: Artistic Radiance Fields

Kai Zhang[1]([✉]), Nick Kolkin[2], Sai Bi[2], Fujun Luan[2], Zexiang Xu[2],
Eli Shechtman[2], and Noah Snavely[1]

[1] Cornell University, Ithaca, USA
kz298@cornell.edu
[2] Adobe Research, San Jose, USA

Abstract. We present a method for transferring the artistic features
of an arbitrary style image to a 3D scene. Previous methods that perform 3D stylization on point clouds or meshes are sensitive to geometric
reconstruction errors for complex real-world scenes. Instead, we propose
to stylize the more robust radiance field representation. We find that the
commonly used Gram matrix-based loss tends to produce blurry results
lacking in faithful style detail. We instead utilize a nearest neighbor-
based loss that is highly effective at capturing style details while maintaining multi-view consistency. We also propose a novel deferred back-
propagation method to enable optimization of memory-intensive radiance fields using style losses defined on full-resolution rendered images.
Our evaluation demonstrates that, compared to baselines, our method
transfers artistic appearance in a way that more closely resembles the
style image. Please see our project webpage for video results and an
open-source implementation: https://www.cs.cornell.edu/projects/arf/.

Keywords: Style transfer · Neural radiance fields · 3D content
creation

1 Introduction

Creating art in a specific style can require significant time and expertise. Extending an artwork to dimensions beyond the 2D image plane, such as time (in the
case of animation), or 3D space (in the case of sculptures or virtual environments), involves further constraints and challenges. Hence, the styles employed
by artists when moving their work beyond a static 2D canvas are constrained by
the effort required to create a consistent visual experience.

We propose Artistic Radiance Fields (ARF), a new approach to transferring
the artistic features from a single 2D image to a full, real-world 3D scene that
yields high-quality, artistic free-viewpoint renderings. Our method converts a
photorealistic radiance field [1,4,32] reconstructed from multiple images of complex, real-world scenes into a new, stylized radiance field that can be consistently

---

Supplementary Information The online version contains supplementary material
available at https://doi.org/10.1007/978-3-031-19821-2_41.

rendered from different viewpoints, as shown in Fig. 1. The quality of these renderings is in contrast to that of prior 3D stylization work [14, 16, 33] that often suffers from geometrically inaccurate reconstructions of point clouds or triangle meshes and can lack style detail.

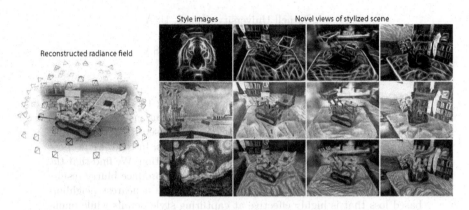

Fig. 1. We propose ARF, a new approach to 3D stylization. ARF takes a reconstructed radiance field of a real scene (1st column) and converts it into an artistic radiance field by matching features extracted from an input 2D style image (2nd column), leading to high-quality stylized novel views (3rd–5th columns). Our approach produces consistent results across viewpoints, as can be seen more clearly in the supplementary video.

We formulate the stylization of radiance fields as an optimization problem: we render images of the radiance fields from multiple viewpoints in a differentiable manner, and minimize a content loss between the rendered stylized images and the original captured images, and a style loss between the rendered images and the style image. While prior methods [14, 16, 33] apply the commonly-used Gram matrix–based style loss for 3D stylization, we observe that this type of loss leads to averaged-out style details that degrade the quality of the stylized renderings.

This limitation motivates us to apply a novel style loss based on Nearest Neighbor Feature Matching (NNFM) that is better suited to the creation of high-quality 3D artistic radiance fields. In particular, for each feature vector in the VGG feature map of a rendered image, we find its nearest neighbor (NN) feature vector in the style image's VGG feature map, and seek to minimize the distance between these two feature vectors. In contrast to a Gram matrix describing global feature statistics across the entire image, NN feature matching focuses on local image descriptions, better capturing distinctive local details. Coupled with our style loss, we also enforce a VGG feature-based content loss – which balances stylization and content preservation – as well as a color transfer technique that improves the color match between our final renderings and the input style image.

One challenge is that volumetric radiance field rendering consumes significant memory. Such rendering can often only regress sparsely sampled pixels during training, and not the full images needed to compute VGG features used in many style losses. We propose a practical innovation called *deferred back-propagation* that allows us to perform optimization on high-resolution images. Deferred back-propagation enables memory-efficient auto-differentiation of scene parameters with image losses computed on full-resolution images (e.g., VGG-based style losses) by accumulating cached gradients in a patch-wise fashion.

We demonstrate that ARF can robustly transfer detailed artistic features from diverse 2D style exemplars to a variety of complex 3D scenes, yielding significantly better visual quality compared to prior methods, which tend to yield over-smoothed and blurry stylized novel views (see Figs. 4, 5, and 6). In our user studies, our method is also consistently preferred over baselines.

In summary, our contributions are:

- A new radiance field-based approach to 3D scene stylization that can faithfully transfer detailed style features from a 2D image to a 3D scene, and which produces consistent stylized novel views of high visual quality.
- A finding that Nearest Neighbor Feature Matching (NNFM) loss better preserves details in the style images than the Gram matrix–based loss commonly used in prior 3D stylization work.
- A deferred back-propagation method for differentiable volumetric rendering, allowing for computation of losses on full-resolution images while significantly reducing the GPU memory footprint.

2   Related Work

In this section, we review related work to provide context for our work.

Image Style Transfer. Since Gatys et al. [11] introduced neural style transfer, significant progress has been made towards image stylization [22,25], image harmonization [29,40,49], color matching [28,42,43], texture synthesis [13,23,36] and beyond [18]. These style transfer approaches leverage features extracted by a pre-trained convolutional neural network (e.g., VGG-19 [39]) and optimize for a set of loss functions (typically a content loss capturing an input photo's features and a style loss matching a style image's feature statistics, e.g., as captured by a Gram matrix). Depending on whether the style transfer is achieved via iterative optimization or a single forward pass of a deep network, existing methods can be categorized as optimization-based and feed-forward-based:

Optimization-Based Style Transfer. Gatys et al. [11] perform style transfer via iterative optimization to minimize content and style losses. Many follow-up works [7,12,21,22,25,30,30,36] have investigated alternative style loss formulations to further improve semantic consistency and high-frequency style details like brushstrokes. Unlike style transfer methods that encode the statistics of style features with a single Gram matrix, Chen and Schmidt [7], CNNMRF [22], Deep Image Analogy [25] and NNST [20] propose to search for nearest neighbors and minimize distances between features extracted from corresponding content and style patches in a coarse-to-fine fashion. These methods achieve impressive 2D stylization quality when provided with source and target images that share similar semantics. Our approach draws inspiration from this line of work and is the first to introduce nearest neighbor feature matching (NNFM) for 3D stylization. Our NNFM loss is most similar to that proposed in [20] for 2D style transfer. However, when stylizing 3D radiance fields, we find that we can achieve the same level of stylistic detail more efficiently by only applying stylization at a single coarse scale (as opposed to coarse-to-fine) and by skipping the style image augmentations (rotation and/or scaling) used in [20,22]. Compared with the contextual loss [30], our NNFM loss is simpler and avoids the need for distance and similarity normalizations.

Feed-Forward Style Transfer. Rather than performing iterative optimization, feed-forward approaches [2,9,17,24,35,38,44] train neural networks that can transfer the style of an exemplar image to an input image using a single forward pass. While fast, these methods often struggle to faithfully reproduce style details like brushstrokes, and yield lower visual quality compared to optimization-based techniques. In the pursuit of high-quality results, we did not pursue this direction in our work.

Video Style Transfer. Stylizing a video by separately processing each frame with a 2D style transfer method often leads to flickering artifacts in the resulting stylized video. Video style transfer [37] methods address this problem by enforcing an additional temporal coherency loss across frames [6,15,37,41]. Alternative approaches rely on aligning and fusing style features according to their similarity to content features [10,27] to maintain temporal consistency. Despite sharing the similar challenge of consistency across views, stylizing a 3D scene is a distinct problem from video stylization, because it requires synthesizing novel views while maintaining style consistency, which is best achieved through stylization in 3D world space rather than in 2D image space.

3D Style Transfer. 3D style transfer aims to transform the appearance of a 3D scene so that its renderings from different viewpoints match the style of a desired image. Prior methods represent real world scenes using point clouds [16,33] or triangle meshes [31,45]. For example, Huang et al. [16] and Mu et al. [33] use featurized 3D point clouds modulated with the style image, followed by a 2D CNN renderer to produce stylized renderings. Yin et al. [45] create novel geometric and texture variations of 3D meshes by transferring the shape and texture style from one textured mesh to another. The performance of such methods is limited by the quality of these point clouds or meshes, which frequently contain noticeable artifacts when reconstructed from complex real-world scenes. In contrast, we perform style transfer on radiance fields [5,26,32,47,48] which can more faithfully reproduce the appearance of real world scenes. Work closely relevant to ours is that of Chiang et al. [8], who use neural radiance fields as a scene representation and apply pre-trained style hypernetworks for appearance stylization. However, their method produces over-smoothed and blurry stylization results, and cannot capture detailed structures in the style image such as brushstrokes, due to the limitations of pre-trained feed-forward models. Our approach can more faithfully capture distinctive details in the style exemplar while preserving recognizable scene content.

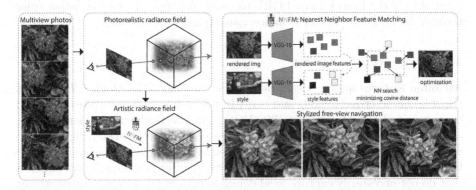

Fig. 2. Overview of our method. We first reconstruct a photo-realistic radiance field from multiple photos. We then stylize this reconstruction using an exemplar style image through the use of a nearest neighbor feature matching (NNFM) style loss. Once this stylization is done, we can obtain consistent free-viewpoint stylized renderings. We invite readers to watch the videos on our project page to better appreciate our results.

3   Background on Radiance Fields

NeRF [32] proposes neural radiance fields to model and reconstruct real scenes, achieving photo-realistic novel view synthesis results. In general, the radiance field representation can be seen as a 5D function that maps any 3D location **x** and viewing direction **d** to volume density σ and RGB color **c**:

$$\sigma, \mathbf{c} = \mathrm{RADIANCEFIELD}(\mathbf{x}, \mathbf{d}). \tag{1}$$

This representation can be rendered from any viewpoint via differentiable volume rendering, and hence can be optimized to fit a collection of photos capture from multiple viewpoints, then later used to synthesize photo-realistic novel views. We move beyond photo-realism and add an artistic feel to the radiance field by stylizing it using an exemplar style image, such as a painting or sketch.

4   Stylizing Radiance Fields

Given a photo-realistic radiance field reconstructed from photos of a real scene, our approach transforms it into an artistic one by stylizing the 3D scene appearance with a 2D style image. We achieve this by fine-tuning the radiance field using a novel nearest neighbor feature matching style loss (Sect. 4.1) that can transfer detailed local style structures. We also introduce a deferred back-propagation technique that enables radiance field optimization with full-resolution images (Sect. 4.2) in the face of limited GPU memory. We apply a view-consistent color transfer technique to further enhance visual quality (Sect. 4.3).

4.1   Style Transfer Losses

Art often features unique visual details. For instance, Van Gogh's *The Starry Night* is characterized by long and curvy brushstrokes. Neural features produced by pre-trained neural networks (like VGG) can effectively capture such details and have been widely used for 2D style transfer. However, transferring such rich visual details to 3D scenes using prior VGG-based style losses is a challenge, since the style information measured by such losses are often based on global statistics that do not necessarily capture local details accurately in a view-consistent way.

To address this issue, we propose to use the N*earest* N*eighbor* F*eature* M*atching* (NNFM) loss to transfer complex high-frequency visual details from a 2D style image to a 3D scene (parameterized by a radiance field) in a way that yields consistency across multiple viewpoints. In particular, let I_{style} denote the style image, and I_{render} denote an image rendered from the radiance field at a selected viewpoint. We extract VGG feature maps F_{style} and F_{render} from I_{style} and I_{render}, respectively. Let $F_{\text{render}}(i,j)$ denote the feature vector at pixel location (i,j) of the feature map F_{render}. Our NNFM loss can be written as:

$$\ell_{\text{nnfm}}(F_{\text{render}}, F_{\text{style}}) = \frac{1}{N} \sum_{i,j} \min_{i',j'} D\big(F_{\text{render}}(i,j), F_{\text{style}}(i',j')\big), \qquad (2)$$

where N is the number of pixels in F_{render}, and $D(v_1, v_2)$ computes the cosine distance between two vectors v_1, v_2:

$$D(v_1, v_2) = 1 - \frac{< v_1, v_2 >}{\|v_1\|_2 \|v_2\|_2}. \qquad (3)$$

In short, for each feature in F_{render}, ℓ_{nnfm} minimizes its cosine distance (Eq. (3)) to its nearest neighbor in the style image's VGG feature space (F_{style}). The NNFM loss can also be viewed as a variant of the Chamfer distance for comparing high-dimensional feature sets, similar to the Chamfer L1 distance widely used for comparing 2D images and 3D point clouds.

Note that our loss does not rely on per-view global statistics. This grants more flexibility to the optimization process and focuses it on adjusting local 3D scene appearance to perceptually match patches of the style exemplar.

Controlling Stylization Strength. Using our NNFM loss alone can sometimes lead to overly strong stylization, making the content harder to recognize. To address this issue, we add an additional content-preserving loss penalizing the ℓ_2 difference between the feature maps of rendered and content images:

$$\ell = \ell_{\text{nnfm}}(\boldsymbol{F}_{\text{render}}, \boldsymbol{F}_{\text{style}}) + \lambda \cdot \ell_2(\boldsymbol{F}_{\text{render}}, \boldsymbol{F}_{\text{content}}), \qquad (4)$$

where λ is a weight controlling stylization strength: a larger λ better preserves content, while a smaller λ leads to stronger stylization. $\boldsymbol{F}_{\text{render}}$, $\boldsymbol{F}_{\text{style}}$ and $\boldsymbol{F}_{\text{content}}$ are feature maps of a rendered image, the style image and a content image, respectively; they are all extracted using exactly the same VGG feature extractor. (See Sect. 4.4 for more detail.)

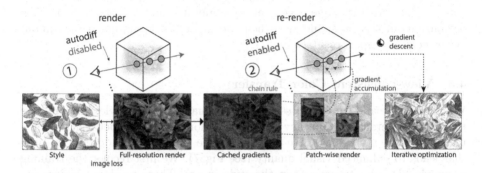

Fig. 3. Illustration of deferred back-propagation. We first disable auto-differentiation to render a full-resolution image, then compute the image loss (e.g., a style loss defined by NNFM or by a Gram matrix), and cache its gradients with respect to pixel values of the full-resolution image. Next, we back-propagate the cached gradients to scene parameters and accumulate in a patch-wise manner: For each patch, we re-render it with auto-differentiation enabled, and apply the chain rule to back-propagate the corresponding cached patch gradients to scene parameters for accumulation. This way, we correctly compute the gradients of a loss imposed on the full-resolution rendered image with respect to the scene parameters, with the same GPU memory footprint of rendering a single small patch differentiably.

4.2   Deferred Back-Propagation

We stylize a radiance field by minimizing our loss (Eq. 4) imposed on images rendered using differentiable volume rendering. Such rendering is very memory-inefficient in practice, because the color of each pixel is composited from a large number of samples along the corresponding ray. As a result, rather than rendering a full-resolution image at each optimization step, many methods randomly sample a sparse set of pixels for rendering. While such sparse pixel sampling is a reasonable strategy when minimizing a loss computed independently per-pixel, such as an ℓ_1/ℓ_2 loss, it does not work for complex CNN-based losses, such as our NNFM loss or a Gram-matrix style loss, which require full-resolution renderings.

We propose a simple technique we call *deferred back-propagation* that can directly optimize on full-resolution images, allowing for more sophisticated and powerful image losses to be used in conjunction with radiance fields. As shown by Fig. 3, we first render a full-resolution image with auto-differentiation disabled, then compute the image loss and its gradient with respect to the rendered image's pixel colors, which produces a cached gradient image. Finally, in a *patch-wise* manner, we re-render the pixel colors with auto-differentiation enabled, and back-propagate the cached gradients to the scene parameters for accumulation. In this way, gradient back-propagation is deferred from the full-resolution image rendering stage to the patch-wise re-rendering stage, reducing the GPU memory cost from that of rendering a full-resolution image to that of rendering a small patch. While this technique is general, we apply it to our stylization task when optimizing our style loss, and also when optimizing the Gram-matrix loss in our experimental comparisons (see Fig. 7).

4.3   View-consistent Color Transfer

While our style and content losses can perceptually transfer styles and preserve the original content, we find they can lead to color mismatches between rendered images and the style image. We devise a simple technique to address this issue that leads to enhanced visual quality (see Fig. 7). We first recolor the training views via 2D color transfer from the style image. These recolored images are used to pre-optimize our artistic radiance field as initialization for our stylization optimization; they are also used for our content preservation loss (Eq. 4). Additionally, after the 3D stylization process, we compute another color transfer transform on images rendered to the training viewpoints, and apply this same color transform to the color values produced from rendering the radiance fields.

For color transfer we adopt a simple affine transformation of colors in RGB space, the parameters of which are estimated by matching color statistics of an image set to those of an image. Specifically, let $\{c_i\}_{i=1}^{m}$ be the set of all pixel colors in an image set to be recolored, and let $\{s_i\}_{i=1}^{n}$ be the set of all pixel colors of the style image. We analytically solve for an affine transformation A such that $E[Ac] = E[s]$ and $\text{Cov}[Ac] = \text{Cov}[s]$, i.e., the mean and covariance of the color-transformed image set should match those of the style image. We refer the readers to our supplemental document for derivation of A.

4.4   Implementation Details

To represent a radiance field, our work primarily uses Plenoxels [46] for its fast reconstruction and rendering speed. However, our framework is agnostic to the radiance field representation. To demonstrate this flexibility, we also apply ARF to stylize NeRF [32] and TensoRF [46] representations, and in each case achieve high visual quality with faithful style transfer, as shown in Fig. 8.

During stylization, we fix the density component of the initial photorealistic radiance field, and only optimize the appearance component when converting to an artistic radiance field. We also discard any view-dependent appearance modelling. To extract the feature maps F_{render}, F_{style}, and $F_{content}$ in Eq. 4, we use a pretrained VGG-16 network that consists of 5 layer blocks: conv1, conv2, conv3, conv4, conv5. We use the conv3 block as the feature extractor, because we empirically find that it captures style details better than the other blocks. We set the content-preserving weight $\lambda = 0.001$ in Eq. 4 for all forward-facing captures, and $\lambda = 0.005$ for all 360° captures. We refer the readers to our supplemental document for more implementation details.

5 Experiments

We evaluate our method by performing both qualitative and quantitative comparisons to baseline methods. We show stylization results for various real-world scenes guided by different style images. Our experimental results show that our method significantly outperforms baseline methods by generating stylized renderings that are more faithful to the input style image, while maintaining the recognizable semantic and geometric features of the original scene. We invite readers to our project page for better assessment of 3D stylization quality.

Datasets. We conduct extensive experiments on multiple real-world scenes including four forward-facing captures: *Flower*, *Orchids*, *Horns*, and *Trex*, from [32], and seven 360° captures: *Family*, *Horse*, *Playground*, *Truck*, *M60*, and *Train* from the Tanks and Temples dataset [19], as well as the *Real Lego* dataset from [1]. All scenes contain complex structures and intricate details that are difficult to reconstruct with prior triangle mesh or point cloud-based methods. We also experiment with a diverse set of style images including a neon tiger, Van Gogh's *The Starry Night*, sketches, etc., to test our method's ability to handle a diverse range of style exemplars.

Baselines. We compare our method to state-of-the-art methods [8,16] for 3D style transfer quality. Specifically, Huang et al. [16] adopt point clouds featurized by VGG features averaged across views as a scene representation, and transform the pointwise features by modulating them with the encoding vector of a style image for stylization. Chiang et al. [8] use implicit MLPs as in NeRF++ [48] to reconstruct a radiance field for a scene, then update the weights of the radiance prediction branch using a hypernetwork that takes a style image as input. For both methods, we use their released code and pre-trained models. We did not compare to off-the-shelf video stylization methods, because prior work has demonstrated that they are less competitive compared to 3D style transfer approaches [8,16].

Qualitative Comparisons. We show visual comparisons between methods in Fig. 4 (forward-facing captures) and Fig. 5 (360° captures). Visually, we see that our results exhibit a better style match to the exemplar image compared to the baselines. For instance, in the *Flower* scene in Fig. 4, our method faithfully captures both the color tone and the brushstrokes of *The Starry Night*, while the baseline method of Huang et al. [16] generates over-smoothed results without detailed structures. Moreover, Huang et al. also fails to recover complex geometric structures such as plant leaves due to inaccuracies in the reconstructed meshes. In comparison, our method effectively reconstructs and preserves the geometric and semantic content of the original scene, thanks to the more robust radiance fields representation.

Chiang et al. [8] only transfers the overall color tone of the style image to the scene and fails to recover the rich details that our method does. For example, in the *Family* statue scene in Fig. 5, our method captures the subtle textural details of the watercolor feather style image, and reproduces them in the stylized renderings. In contrast, the method of Chiang et al. [8] generates blurry results without such intricate structures, because their hypernetwork is trained on a fixed dataset of style images and can fail to capture the details of an unseen style input. Our method benefits from both the optimization-based framework as well as our NNFM style loss, which greatly boost 3D stylization quality.

We show additional results from our method in Fig. 6. Our method is robust to different scenes with varying levels of complexity and generates consistently superior results under a variety of styles.

User Study. We also perform a user study to compare our method to prior work. A user is presented with a sequence of stylization results, where for each result the user is shown a style image, a video of the original scene, and two corresponding stylized videos, one produced with our method and one by a baseline. The user is then asked to select the result whose style better matches that of the given style image. In total, we collected ratings covering 25 randomly selected (scene, style) pairs. We divided the questions into 5 batches, each with 5 questions, and asked a group of users to rate a randomly selected batch. We collected an average of ~12 ratings for each individual pair. We found that users preferred our method over the method of Huang et al. [16] 86.8% of the time, and over that of Chiang et al. [8] 94.1% of the time. These results show a clear preference for our method.

Ablations. We perform ablation studies to justify our design choices. We first compare our NNFM loss to the prior Gram matrix–based and CNNMRF losses. As we can see from Fig. 7, our NNFM loss generates significantly better results and more faithfully preserves the style details of the example images compared to the other two losses. In Fig. 7, we also validate the necessity of the color transfer stage. Without color transfer, the generated results tend to have different color tones compared to the style image, leading to a degraded style match. Our color transfer method effectively addresses this issue. Finally, we perform an

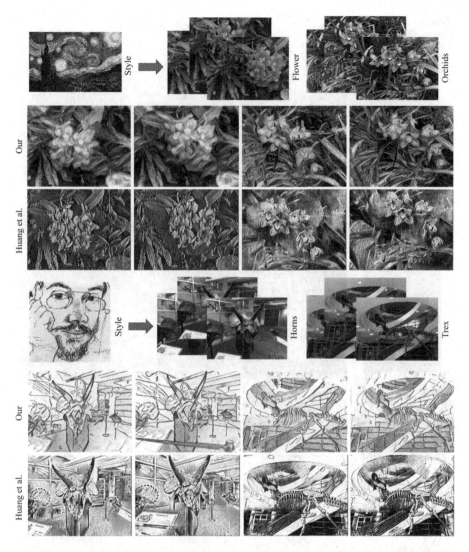

Fig. 4. Comparison with the baseline method Huang et al. [16] on real-world forward-facing data. Our stylized novel views contain significantly more faithful style details. Additionally, Huang et al. [16] requires reconstructing meshes from images, an error-prone process. Such errors can impact the quality of stylized novel views, as can be seen in the leaves in the *Flower* and *Orchids* scenes, and in ceiling of *Trex*. In contrast, our method, based on radiance fields, exhibits many fewer geometric artifacts.

ablation of using the feature map at different layers of the VGG-16 network for computing the NNFM loss. We find that our choice of the `conv3` layer block preserves stylistic details better than other layers. We refer the readers to our

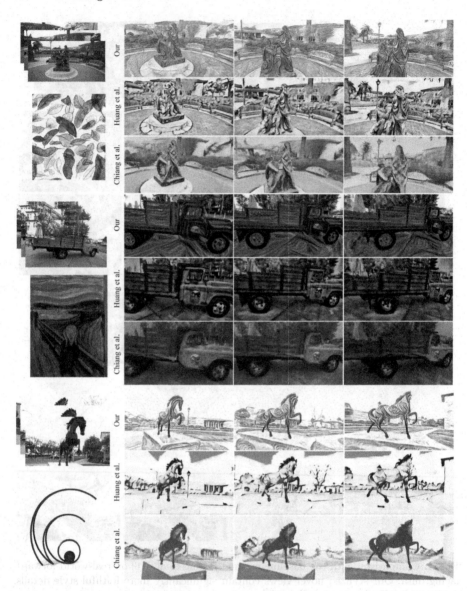

Fig. 5. Comparison with the baseline methods Huang et al. [16] and Chiang et al. [8] on real-world Tanks and Temples data. Our results match both the colors and details of the style image most faithfully, while preserving sharp and recognizable content.

supplemental document for the results of this ablation experiment, as well as an ablation of using different color spaces for the color transfer method in Sect. 4.3.

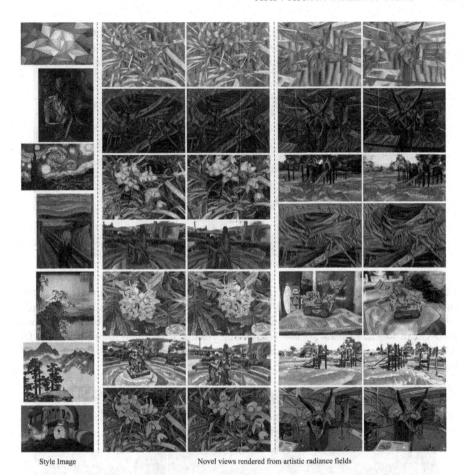

Style Image   Novel views rendered from artistic radiance fields

Fig. 6. Our method can generate compelling results for a wide range of (real-world scene, style image) pairs. The leftmost image in each row is the style image, and the rest are stylized novel views rendered from corresponding artistic radiance fields (two novel views are shown for each artistic radiance field).

Limitations. Our method has a few limitations. First, geometric artifacts, e.g., floaters, in the radiance fields can cause artifacts in both the photorealistic and our stylized renderings. Such floaters can be removed by adding additional regularizers on volume density to the loss during optimization [3,34]. Second, although our artistic radiance fields can be rendered in real time once optimized, a relatively time-consuming optimization procedure is still required for every style image (~3 mins for forward-facing captures, and ~20 mins for 360 captures on a single NVIDIA RTX 3090 GPU). Third, our reconstructed artistic radiance fields do not support manual editing. Enabling artists to interactively edit them is highly desirable for the sake of facilitating creativity.

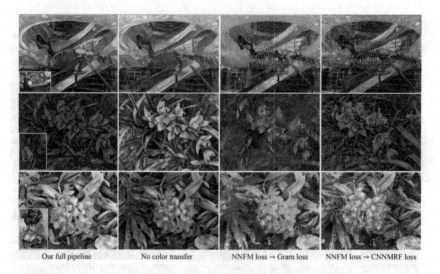

Our full pipeline   No color transfer   NNFM loss → Gram loss   NNFM loss → CNNMRF loss

Fig. 7. Ablation studies of color transfer and NNFM loss. Without color transfer, there is a noticeable color mismatch between the synthesized views and the style image (shown as insets in the first column). Replacing the NNFM loss with the commonly-used Gram loss [11] leads to less compelling results with many more artifacts. Our NNFM loss also generates more faithful 3D stylization results than the prior CNNMRF loss [22].

(a) ARF + Plenoxels   (b) ARF + NeRF   (c) ARF + TensoRF

Fig. 8. Applicability across different radiance field representations. Our ARF method is applicable to a variety of radiance fields representations, including Plenoxels [46], NeRF [32] and TensoRF [4], in each case producing high-quality 3D stylization results.

6   Conclusion

We have presented a method to create artistic radiance fields from photorealistic radiance fields given user-specified style exemplars. The reconstructed artistic radiance fields can then be used to render high-quality stylized novel views that faithfully mimic the input style image in terms of color tone and style details like brushstrokes. This enables an immersive experience of artistic 3D scenes. Key to our method's success is the proposed coupling of the nearest neighbor featuring matching loss and view-consistent color transfer, rather than the commonly-used

Gram loss. We demonstrate that our method achieves superior 3D stylization quality over baselines through evaluations across various 3D scenes and 2D styles.

Acknowledgment. We would like to thank Adobe artist Daichi Ito for helpful discussions about 3D artistic styles.

References

1. Yu, A., Fridovich-Keil, S., Tancik, M., Chen, Q., Recht, B., Kanazawa, A.: Plenoxels: radiance fields without neural networks (2021)
2. An, J., Huang, S., Song, Y., Dou, D., Liu, W., Luo, J.: ArtFlow: unbiased image style transfer via reversible neural flows. In: Proceedings of the IEEE/CVF Conference on Computer Vision and Pattern Recognition, pp. 862–871 (2021)
3. Barron, J.T., Mildenhall, B., Verbin, D., Srinivasan, P.P., Hedman, P.: Mip-NeRF 360: unbounded anti-aliased neural radiance fields. In: CVPR (2022)
4. Chen, A., Xu, Z., Geiger, A., Yu, J., Su, H.: TensoRF: tensorial radiance fields. arXiv preprint arXiv:2203.09517 (2022)
5. Chen, A., et al.: MVSNeRF: fast generalizable radiance field reconstruction from multi-view stereo. In: Proceedings of the IEEE/CVF International Conference on Computer Vision, pp. 14124–14133 (2021)
6. Chen, D., Liao, J., Yuan, L., Yu, N., Hua, G.: Coherent online video style transfer. In: Proceedings of the IEEE International Conference on Computer Vision, pp. 1105–1114 (2017)
7. Chen, T.Q., Schmidt, M.: Fast patch-based style transfer of arbitrary style. arXiv preprint arXiv:1612.04337 (2016)
8. Chiang, P.Z., Tsai, M.S., Tseng, H.Y., Lai, W.S., Chiu, W.C.: Stylizing 3D scene via implicit representation and hypernetwork. In: Proceedings of the IEEE/CVF Winter Conference on Applications of Computer Vision, pp. 1475–1484 (2022)
9. Chiu, T.-Y., Gurari, D.: Iterative feature transformation for fast and versatile universal style transfer. In: Vedaldi, A., Bischof, H., Brox, T., Frahm, J.-M. (eds.) ECCV 2020. LNCS, vol. 12364, pp. 169–184. Springer, Cham (2020). https://doi.org/10.1007/978-3-030-58529-7_11
10. Deng, Y., Tang, F., Dong, W., Huang, H., Ma, C., Xu, C.: Arbitrary video style transfer via multi-channel correlation. arXiv preprint arXiv:2009.08003 (2020)
11. Gatys, L.A., Ecker, A.S., Bethge, M.: Image style transfer using convolutional neural networks. In: Proceedings of the IEEE Conference on Computer Vision and Pattern Recognition, pp. 2414–2423 (2016)
12. Gu, S., Chen, C., Liao, J., Yuan, L.: Arbitrary style transfer with deep feature reshuffle. In: Proceedings of the IEEE Conference on Computer Vision and Pattern Recognition, pp. 8222–8231 (2018)
13. Heitz, E., Vanhoey, K., Chambon, T., Belcour, L.: A sliced wasserstein loss for neural texture synthesis. In: Proceedings of the IEEE/CVF Conference on Computer Vision and Pattern Recognition, pp. 9412–9420 (2021)
14. Höllein, L., Johnson, J., Niessner, M.: StyleMesh: style transfer for indoor 3D scene reconstructions. arXiv preprint arXiv:2112.01530 (2021)
15. Huang, H., et al.: Real-time neural style transfer for videos. In: Proceedings of the IEEE Conference on Computer Vision and Pattern Recognition, pp. 783–791 (2017)

16. Huang, H.P., Tseng, H.Y., Saini, S., Singh, M., Yang, M.H.: Learning to stylize novel views. In: Proceedings of the IEEE/CVF International Conference on Computer Vision, pp. 13869–13878 (2021)

17. Huang, X., Belongie, S.: Arbitrary style transfer in real-time with adaptive instance normalization. In: Proceedings of the IEEE International Conference on Computer Vision, pp. 1501–1510 (2017)

18. Jing, Y., Yang, Y., Feng, Z., Ye, J., Yu, Y., Song, M.: Neural style transfer: a review. IEEE Trans. Vis. Comput. Graph. **26**(11), 3365–3385 (2019)

19. Knapitsch, A., Park, J., Zhou, Q.Y., Koltun, V.: Tanks and temples: benchmarking large-scale scene reconstruction. ACM Trans. Graph. **36**(4), 1–13 (2017)

20. Kolkin, N., Kucera, M., Paris, S., Sykora, D., Shechtman, E., Shakhnarovich, G.: Neural neighbor style transfer. arXiv e-prints pp. arXiv-2203 (2022)

21. Kolkin, N., Salavon, J., Shakhnarovich, G.: Style transfer by relaxed optimal transport and self-similarity. In: Proceedings of the IEEE/CVF Conference on Computer Vision and Pattern Recognition, pp. 10051–10060 (2019)

22. Li, C., Wand, M.: Combining Markov random fields and convolutional neural networks for image synthesis. In: Proceedings of the IEEE Conference on Computer Vision and Pattern Recognition, pp. 2479–2486 (2016)

23. Li, Y., Fang, C., Yang, J., Wang, Z., Lu, X., Yang, M.H.: Diversified texture synthesis with feed-forward networks. In: Proceedings of the IEEE Conference on Computer Vision and Pattern Recognition, pp. 3920–3928 (2017)

24. Li, Y., Fang, C., Yang, J., Wang, Z., Lu, X., Yang, M.H.: Universal style transfer via feature transforms. In: Advances in Neural Information Processing Systems 30 (2017)

25. Liao, J., Yao, Y., Yuan, L., Hua, G., Kang, S.B.: Visual attribute transfer through deep image analogy. ACM Trans. Graph **36**(4), 1–15 (2017)

26. Liu, L., Gu, J., Zaw Lin, K., Chua, T.S., Theobalt, C.: Neural sparse voxel fields. In: Advances in Neural Information Processing Systems, vol. 33, pp. 15651–15663 (2020)

27. Liu, S., et al.: AdaAttN: revisit attention mechanism in arbitrary neural style transfer. In: Proceedings of the IEEE/CVF International Conference on Computer Vision, pp. 6649–6658 (2021)

28. Luan, F., Paris, S., Shechtman, E., Bala, K.: Deep photo style transfer. In: Proceedings of the IEEE Conference on Computer Vision and Pattern Recognition, pp. 4990–4998 (2017)

29. Luan, F., Paris, S., Shechtman, E., Bala, K.: Deep painterly harmonization. Comput. Graph. Forum **37**(4), 95–106 (2018)

30. Mechrez, R., Talmi, I., Zelnik-Manor, L.: The contextual loss for image transformation with non-aligned data. In: Ferrari, V., Hebert, M., Sminchisescu, C., Weiss, Y. (eds.) Computer Vision – ECCV 2018. LNCS, vol. 11218, pp. 800–815. Springer, Cham (2018). https://doi.org/10.1007/978-3-030-01264-9_47

31. Michel, O., Bar-On, R., Liu, R., Benaim, S., Hanocka, R.: Text2Mesh: text-driven neural stylization for meshes. arXiv preprint arXiv:2112.03221 (2021)

32. Mildenhall, B., Srinivasan, P.P., Tancik, M., Barron, J.T., Ramamoorthi, R., Ng, R.: NeRF: representing scenes as neural radiance fields for view synthesis. In: Vedaldi, A., Bischof, H., Brox, T., Frahm, J.-M. (eds.) ECCV 2020. LNCS, vol. 12346, pp. 405–421. Springer, Cham (2020). https://doi.org/10.1007/978-3-030-58452-8_24

33. Mu, F., Wang, J., Wu, Y., Li, Y.: 3D photo stylization: learning to generate stylized novel views from a single image. arXiv preprint arXiv:2112.00169 (2021)

34. Niemeyer, M., Barron, J.T., Mildenhall, B., Sajjadi, M.S.M., Geiger, A., Radwan, N.: RegNeRF: regularizing neural radiance fields for view synthesis from sparse inputs. In: Proceedings IEEE Conference on Computer Vision and Pattern Recognition (CVPR) (2022)

35. Park, D.Y., Lee, K.H.: Arbitrary style transfer with style-attentional networks. In: Proceedings of the IEEE/CVF Conference on Computer Vision and Pattern Recognition, pp. 5880–5888 (2019)

36. Risser, E., Wilmot, P., Barnes, C.: Stable and controllable neural texture synthesis and style transfer using histogram losses. arXiv preprint arXiv:1701.08893 (2017)

37. Ruder, M., Dosovitskiy, A., Brox, T.: Artistic style transfer for videos and spherical images. Int. J. Comput. Vis. **126**(11), 1199–1219 (2018)

38. Sheng, L., Lin, Z., Shao, J., Wang, X.: Avatar-Net: multi-scale zero-shot style transfer by feature decoration. In: Proceedings of the IEEE Conference on Computer Vision and Pattern Recognition, pp. 8242–8250 (2018)

39. Simonyan, K., Zisserman, A.: Very deep convolutional networks for large-scale image recognition. arXiv preprint arXiv:1409.1556 (2014)

40. Tsai, Y.H., Shen, X., Lin, Z., Sunkavalli, K., Lu, X., Yang, M.H.: Deep image harmonization. In: Proceedings of the IEEE Conference on Computer Vision and Pattern Recognition, pp. 3789–3797 (2017)

41. Wang, W., Xu, J., Zhang, L., Wang, Y., Liu, J.: Consistent video style transfer via compound regularization. In: Proceedings of the AAAI Conference on Artificial Intelligence, vol. 34, pp. 12233–12240 (2020)

42. Xia, X., et al.: Real-time localized photorealistic video style transfer. In: Proceedings of the IEEE/CVF Winter Conference on Applications of Computer Vision, pp. 1089–1098 (2021)

43. Xia, X., et al.: Joint bilateral learning for real-time universal photorealistic style transfer. In: Vedaldi, A., Bischof, H., Brox, T., Frahm, J.-M. (eds.) ECCV 2020. LNCS, vol. 12353, pp. 327–342. Springer, Cham (2020). https://doi.org/10.1007/978-3-030-58598-3_20

44. Yao, Y., Ren, J., Xie, X., Liu, W., Liu, Y.J., Wang, J.: Attention-aware multi-stroke style transfer. In: Proceedings of the IEEE/CVF Conference on Computer Vision and Pattern Recognition, pp. 1467–1475 (2019)

45. Yin, K., Gao, J., Shugrina, M., Khamis, S., Fidler, S.: 3DStyleNet: creating 3D shapes with geometric and texture style variations. In: Proceedings of the IEEE/CVF International Conference on Computer Vision, pp. 12456–12465 (2021)

46. Yu, A., Li, R., Tancik, M., Li, H., Ng, R., Kanazawa, A.: PlenOctrees for real-time rendering of neural radiance fields. In: Proceedings of the IEEE/CVF International Conference on Computer Vision, pp. 5752–5761 (2021)

47. Yu, A., Ye, V., Tancik, M., Kanazawa, A.: pixelNeRF: neural radiance fields from one or few images. In: Proceedings of the IEEE/CVF Conference on Computer Vision and Pattern Recognition, pp. 4578–4587 (2021)

48. Zhang, K., Riegler, G., Snavely, N., Koltun, V.: Nerf++: analyzing and improving neural radiance fields. arXiv preprint arXiv:2010.07492 (2020)

49. Zhang, L., Wen, T., Shi, J.: Deep image blending. In: Proceedings of the IEEE/CVF Winter Conference on Applications of Computer Vision, pp. 231–240 (2020)

Multiview Stereo with Cascaded Epipolar RAFT

Zeyu Ma$^{(\boxtimes)}$, Zachary Teed, and Jia Deng

Princeton University, Princeton, NJ 08544, USA
{zeyum,zteed,jiadeng}@princeton.edu

Abstract. We address multiview stereo (MVS), an important 3D vision task that reconstructs a 3D model such as a dense point cloud from multiple calibrated images. We propose CER-MVS (Cascaded Epipolar RAFT Multiview Stereo), a new approach based on the RAFT (Recurrent All-Pairs Field Transforms) architecture developed for optical flow. CER-MVS introduces five new changes to RAFT: epipolar cost volumes, cost volume cascading, multiview fusion of cost volumes, dynamic supervision, and multiresolution fusion of depth maps. CER-MVS is significantly different from prior work in multiview stereo. Unlike prior work, which operates by updating a 3D cost volume, CER-MVS operates by updating a disparity field. Furthermore, we propose an adaptive thresholding method to balance the completeness and accuracy of the reconstructed point clouds. Experiments show that our approach achieves state-of-the-art performance on the DTU and Tanks-and-Temples benchmarks (both intermediate and advanced set). Code is available at   https://github. com/princeton-vl/CER-MVS.

Keyword: Multiview stereo

1 Introduction

Multiview stereo (MVS) is an important task in 3D computer vision. It seeks to reconstruct a full 3D model, typically in the form of a dense 3D point cloud, from multiple RGB images with known camera intrinsics and poses. It is a difficult task that remains unsolved; the main challenge is producing a 3D model that is not only accurate but also complete, that is, no parts should be missing and all fine details should be recovered.

Many of the latest results of multiview stereo are achieved by deep networks. In particular, many recent leading methods [32,42] are variants of MVSNet [34], a deep architecture that consists of two main steps: (1) constructing a 3D cost volume in the frustum of a reference view, by warping features from other views, and (2) using 3D convolutional layers to transform, or "regularize", the cost

Supplementary Information The online version contains supplementary material available at https://doi.org/10.1007/978-3-031-19821-2_42.

volume before using it to predict a depth map. The resulting depth maps, one from each reference view, are then combined to form a single 3D point cloud through a heuristic procedure.

However, a drawback of MVSNet is that regularizing the 3D plane-sweeping cost volume using 3D convolutions can be costly in terms of computation and memory, potentially limiting the quality of reconstruction under finite resources. Subsequent variants [35] of MVSNet have attempted to address this issue by replacing 3D convolutions with recurrent sequential processing of 2D slices. Despite significant empirical improvements, however, such sequential processing can be suboptimal because the 3D cost volume does not have a natural sequential structure.

In this work, we propose CER-MVS, a new deep-learning multiview stereo approach that is significantly different from existing methods. Like prior deep-learning work on multiview stereo, CER-MVS predicts individual depth maps and then fuses them, but differs significantly in how it predicts each depth map. Given a reference view and multiple neighbor views, CER-MVS constructs a 3D cost volume for each neighbor view by computing the similarity between each pixel in the reference view and pixels along the epipolar line, indexed by increments of inverse depth (i.e. disparity) in the reference view. Then, the cost volumes from all neighbor views are aggregated into a single cost volume. CER-MVS uses a GRU to iteratively update a disparity field—the field that represents pixel correspondence. Each update is generated by the GRU by sampling from the aggregated cost volume using the current disparity field.

The key difference of CER-MVS from MVSNet and its variants lies in how depth is predicted from the 3D cost volume. MVSNet updates (i.e. regularizes) the 3D cost volume and predicts depth through a soft argmax on the updated cost volume. In contrast, CER-MVS does not update the cost volume at all; instead it iteratively updates a disparity field, which is used to retrieve values from the cost volume. The final depth prediction is simply the inverted disparity field. Updating a disparity field, which is less expensive than updating the cost volume, can allow more effective use of finite computing resources.

CER-MVS builds upon RAFT [25], an architecture that estimates optical flow between two video frames. Compared to RAFT, which cannot be directly applied to multiview stereo, CER-MVS introduces five novel changes:

- *Epipolar cost volume:* RAFT constructs a 4D cost volume that compares all pairs of pixels from two views, whereas we construct a 3D cost volume comparing each pixel in the reference view with pixels which are on the epipolar line in a neighbor view and spaced by uniform increments of disparity.
- *Cost volume cascading:* Unlike RAFT, the size of our epipolar cost volumes depends not only on the image resolution but also the number of disparity increments. To reconstruct fine details, a large number of disparity increments is necessary, but can blow up GPU memory. To address this issue, we introduce cascaded epipolar cost volumes, a novel design in the context of RAFT. In particular, after a fixed number of RAFT iterations, we construct additional finer-grained epipolar cost volumes centered around current disparity predictions with finer increments of disparity, allowing reconstruction of fine details with less memory.

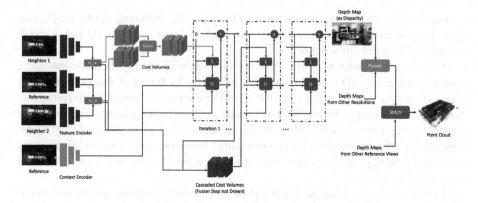

Fig. 1. Overview of CER-MVS, which includes an architecture that constructs cascaded epipolar cost volumes and performs recurrent iterative updates of disparity (inverse depth) maps, with fusion of cost volumes from multiple views as well as fusion of disparity maps of multiple resolutions.

- *Multiview fusion of cost volumes:* RAFT constructs a single cost volume from two views, whereas CER-MVS constructs multiple cost volumes, one for each neighbor of a reference view. The cost volumes are then aggregated into a single volume through a simple averaging operator.
- *Dynamic supervision:* RAFT uses exponentially decaying weights to add up flow errors in each iteration. We also use such weights, but supervise a dynamic combination of depth errors and disparity errors.
- *Multiresolution fusion of depth maps:* RAFT operates on a single resolution of the input images, whereas CER-MVS applies the same network to predict depth maps on multiple resolutions, and aggregate the depth maps into a single high-resolution depth map through a simple but novel heuristic.

When stitching the depth maps into point clouds, a filtering algorithm is often used, e.g., Dynamic Consistency Checking proposed in D2HC-RMVSNet [32]. However, a good balance of accuracy and completeness is required for high scores on the evaluation metric, which is ignored by these algorithms. Therefore, we propose an adaptive thresholding method built on top of [32].

We evaluate CER-MVS on two challenging benchmarks, DTU [2] and Tanks-and-Temples [15]. On both benchmarks, CER-MVS achieves significant improvements over the previous state of the art. On DTU, CER-MVS improves error metric from 0.344 to 0.332. On Tanks-and-Temples, CER-MVS advances the state of the art of the intermediate set from a mean F1 score of 61.68 to 64.82, and the advanced set from 37.44 to 40.19.

2   Related Work

Classical MVS. Classical methods [4,8,9,12,23,26] essentially formulate multiview stereo as an optimization problem, which seeks to find a 3D model that is most compatible with the observed images. The compatibility is typically based on some hand-designed notion of photo-consistency, assuming that pixels that are projections of the same 3D point should have similar appearance. Often photo-consistency alone does not sufficiently constrain the solution space, and the optimization objective can also include shape priors, which make additional assumptions about what shapes are likely. To solve the optimization problem, a concrete classical algorithm usually consists of a particular 3D representation (e.g. polygon meshes, voxels, or depth maps) and a optimization procedure to compute the best model under that representation. The different combinations of photo-consistency measures, shape priors, 3D representations, and optimization procedures give rise to a large variety of algorithms. For more details, we refer the reader to excellent surveys of these algorithms by Seitz et al. [24] and by Furukawa and Hernández [7].

One family of classical MVS methods [9,22,23,28,30,44] is based on the PatchMatch [3] algorithm, which enables efficient dense matching of pixels across views. PatchMatch methods have proved very effective and have demonstrated highly competitive performance. In particular, Xu and Tao [30] introduced the ACMP algorithm, which, among other enhancements, incorporates planar priors and has achieved competitive results on Tanks-and-Temples.

Learning-Based MVS. Unlike classical algorithms, our approach is learning-based. Existing learning-based MVS methods either use learning to improve parts of a classical pipeline such as PatchMatch [11,39–41], or develop end-to-end architectures [5,6,10,13,14,19,29,31–35,37,38,42]. A common step in existing end-to-end architectures is the construction of a 3D cost volume (or feature grid) through some differentiable geometric operations. Then, this 3D cost volume undergoes further updates, often through 3D convolutions, before being transformed into the final 3D model in some particular representation such as voxels [13,14], depth maps [6,10,19,21,27,29,31–35,37,38,42], or point clouds [5].

The main difference between our approach and existing works is that although we also construct a 3D cost volume, we do not update it. Instead, we update an inverse-depth field that is used to iteratively index from the 3D cost volume to produce 2D feature maps. Our approach thus avoids the costly operations of updating a 3D volume and focuses limited computing resources on refining the depth maps directly.

Difference from RAFT-Stereo. RAFT-Stereo [18] is a deep architecture for rectified stereo which is also based on the optical flow network RAFT. Our work differs significantly from RAFT-Stereo. RAFT-Stereo cannot be used for multiview stereo, because it only works with 2 rectified views whereas we need to handle an arbitrary number of unrectified views. RAFT-Stereo only needs to produce a single depth map, whereas we need to produce a point cloud fused from many views. Although both are based on RAFT, we extend RAFT in very different ways due to the different task setup: e.g. epipolar cost volumes, multiview cost volume aggregation, adaptive point cloud fusion are all unique to our method, and not present in RAFT-Stereo.

3   Approach

This section describes the detailed architecture and pipeline of CER-MVS, as shown in Fig. 1. Given a reference view and a set of neighbor views, we first extract features using a set of convolutional networks. Features are then used to build a collection of cost volumes. We then predict a depth map through recurrent iterative updates, followed by the fusion of multiresolution depths. Finally, depth maps from all references views are fused and stitched to produce a final point cloud.

3.1   Cost Volume Construction

Image Features. We need to extract image features from both reference views and neighbor views before using them to construct the cost volumes. In addition, the iterative update unit, to be introduced later, needs context features from reference views. We extract these image features using convolutional encoders following RAFT: $\mathbb{R}^{H \times W \times 3} \to \mathbb{R}^{H/2^k \times W/2^k \times D_f}$, where k and D_f are hyperparameters that control the feature resolution and dimension (See Sect. 4.1 and the supplemental material for more details).

Epipolar Cost Volume. After extracting feature maps $\{\mathbf{f}_i, i = 0, ..., N+1\}$, where $\mathbf{f}_0$ is the reference view and others are neighbor views, each with resolution $(D_f, H_f, W_f) = (D_f, H/2^k, W/2^k)$, we construct a 3D cost volume by computing the correlation of each pixel in the reference view with pixels along its epipolar line in a neighbor view. Specifically, for a pixel in the reference view, we back-project it to D 3D points with disparity (inverse depth) uniformly spaced in the range from 0 to $d_{\max}$ (after proper scaling as described in Sect. 4.1), reproject the 3D points to the epipolar line in the neighbor view, and use differentiable bilinear sampling to retrieve the features from the neighbor view. This procedure outputs a volume $\mathbf{C} \in \mathbb{R}^{N \times H_f \times W_f \times D}$.

Like RAFT, we compute a stack of $\mathbf{C}_P$ of multiscale cost volumes by repeated average-pooling, i.e., $\mathbf{C}_P = \{\mathbf{C}_0, \mathbf{C}_1, ..., \mathbf{C}_{L-1}\}$ where $\mathbf{C}_l \in \mathbb{R}^{N \times H_f \times W_f \times D/2^l}$, for $l = 0, ..., L-1$.

Cost Volume Cascading. Unlike RAFT, the size of an epipolar cost volume depends on not only the image resolution but also the number of disparity values sampled. A dense sampling of a large number of disparity values effectively increases the resolution of the cost volume along the depth dimension and can help reconstruct fine details. However, using a large number of disparity values can take too much GPU memory. To address this issue, we introduce a cascade design. The basic idea is to construct additional cost volumes that are finer-grained along the disparity dimension and centered around the current disparity predictions.

Concretely, after T_1 iterative updates, we create a new stack of cost volumes $\mathbf{C}_P^f = \{\mathbf{C}_0^f, \mathbf{C}_1^f, ..., \mathbf{C}_{L-1}^f\}$, $\mathbf{C}_l^f \in \mathbb{R}^{N \times H_f \times W_f \times D^f/2^l}$, $l = 0, ..., L-1$, where D^f is the number of disparity values uniformly sampled centered around the current prediction of disparities with smaller increments than those used in the initial stack of cost volumes. Specifically, the value of D^f is determined by $2^{L-1} * R$, where R is a hyperparameter that controls the size of the neighborhood described in Sect. 3.2. The factor 2^{L-1} is needed to allow repeated pooling. In this work we use up to 2 stages in our experiments, but the design can be trivially extended to more stages.

It is worth noting that cost volume cascading has been used in prior MVS work [10,33], but it is a novel design in the context of a RAFT-like architecture, which differs significantly from prior MVS work in that the cost volumes are not updated and are only used as static lookup tables.

3.2 Iterative Updates

The iterative updates follow RAFT in overall structure. We iteratively update a disparity field $\mathbf{d} \in \mathbb{R}^{H_f \times W_f}$ initialized to zero. In each iteration, the input to the update operator includes a hidden state $\mathbf{h} \in \mathbb{R}^{H_f \times W_f \times D_h}$, the current disparity field, the context features $\mathbf{i} \in \mathbb{R}^{H_f \times W_f \times D_h}$ from the reference view, as well as per-pixel features retrieved from the cost volumes using the current disparity field. The output of the update operator includes a new hidden state and an increment to the disparity field.

Multiview Fusion of Cost Volumes. Different from RAFT, in multiview stereo we need to consider multiple neighbor views. For each pixel in the reference view, we generate one correlation feature vector against each neighbor view. Given such feature vectors from multiple neighbor views, we take the element-wise mean as the final vector. The intuition behind this operator is that mean value is more robust as the number of neighbor views can vary in test time.

To generate the correlation feature vector for each pixel against a single neighbor view, we perform the same lookup procedure as RAFT. Given the current disparity estimate for the pixel and the stack of cost volumes $\mathbf{C}_P = \{\mathbf{C}_0, \mathbf{C}_1, ..., \mathbf{C}_{L-1}\}$ against the neighbor views, we retrieve, from each cost volume, correlation values corresponding to a local 1D integer grid of length R centered around the current disparity. This is repeated for each level of the stack, and the values from all levels are concatenated to form a single feature vector.

Update Operator. We use a GRU-based update operator to propose a sequence of incremental updates to the disparity field.

First, we extract features from the current disparity estimate $\mathbf{d}_t$. The feature vector is formed by subtracting the disparity of each pixel by its 7×7 neighborhood, then reshaping the result into a 49-dimensional vector. This operation has the effect of making the feature vector invariant to the disparity field up to a shift factor, since the retrieved vector only depends on relative disparity between neighboring pixels.

Second, because we have a cascade of cost volumes and our update operator accesses different cost volumes at different stages of the cascade, the operator, while still recurrent, should be given the flexibility to behave somewhat differently for different stages of the cascade. Thus, we modify the weight tying scheme of RAFT such that some weights are tied across all iterations while others are tied only within a single stage of the cascade. Specially, we tie all weights across iterations except the decoder layer that decodes a disparity update from the hidden state of the GRU. The weights of the decoder layer are tied only within each stage of the cascade.

Third, RAFT uses upsampling layers for final predictions of flow field, whereas we do not use any upsampling layer.

The update equations are as follows, with a 2-stage cascade with T_1 iterations for stage 1.

$$\mathbf{x}_t = [\text{Encoder}_d(\mathbf{d}_t), \text{Encoder}_c(\mathbf{c}), \mathbf{i}] \tag{1}$$

$$\mathbf{z}_t = \sigma\left(\text{Conv}_{3\times3}\left([\mathbf{h}_{t-1}, \mathbf{x}_t], W_z\right)\right) \tag{2}$$

$$\mathbf{r}_t = \sigma\left(\text{Conv}_{3\times3}\left([\mathbf{h}_{t-1}, \mathbf{x}_t], W_r\right)\right) \tag{3}$$

$$\tilde{\mathbf{h}}_t = \tanh\left(\text{Conv}_{3\times3}\left([\mathbf{r}_t \odot \mathbf{h}_{t-1}, \mathbf{x}_t], W_h\right)\right) \tag{4}$$

$$\mathbf{h}_t = (1 - \mathbf{z}_t) \odot \mathbf{h}_{t-1} + \mathbf{z}_t \odot \tilde{\mathbf{h}}_t \tag{5}$$

$$\Delta\mathbf{d}_t = \begin{cases} \text{Decoder}_1(\mathbf{h}_t), t \leq T_1 \\ \text{Decoder}_2(\mathbf{h}_t), t > T_1 \end{cases} \tag{6}$$

Here $\mathbf{i}$ is the context features, and Encoder_c is an encoder the transforms the correlation features using two convolution layers (see the supplemental material for details).

3.3   Multiresolution Depth Fusion

To construct fine details, it generally helps to operate at high resolution, but the available GPU memory limits the highest resolution the network can access, especially during training with large mini-batches. One approach to get around this limit is to apply the network to a higher resolution during inference, which is the common approach adopted in prior works.

However, we find that while using a higher resolution during inference can help, an even better approach is to apply the same network on two input resolutions, the "low" resolution $W \times H$ used to train the network and the higher resolution $2W \times 2H$, and combine the two disparity maps LR and HR to form a fused disparity map MR with a control parameter t:

$$\mathbf{d}_{\text{MR}} = \begin{cases} \mathbf{d}_{\text{HR}}, \text{if} |\mathbf{d}_{\text{LR}}^{-1} - \mathbf{d}_{\text{HR}}^{-1}| < t * \mathbf{d}_{\text{LR}}^{-1} \\ \mathbf{d}_{\text{LR}}, \qquad\qquad \text{otherwise} \end{cases} \tag{7}$$

That is, if the low resolution prediction and high resolution prediction are similar at a pixel, we use the high resolution prediction; otherwise we use the low resolution prediction. This is motivated by the observation that low resolution predictions are more reliable in term of texture-less large structures such as planes, whereas high resolution predictions are more reliable in terms of fine details, which do not tend to deviate drastically from low resolution predictions. Note that as the control parameter t varies from 0 to infinity, $\mathbf{d}_{\mathrm{MR}}$ varies from $\mathbf{d}_{\mathrm{LR}}$ to $\mathbf{d}_{\mathrm{HR}}$.

3.4 Adaptive Point Cloud Stitching

As a last step, the depth maps from the reference views are stitched together to form a single point cloud. We use an adaptive thresholding approach based on Dynamic Consistency Checking (DCC) proposed in D2HC-RMVSNet [32]. DCC hard-codes two thresholds t_1 and t_2 for reprojection errors, however, we use the thresholds kt_1 and kt_2 where k is different for each scene to ensure a fixed percentage, $p\%$ of all pixels pass through consistency test. And p is optimized through the validation set.

3.5 Supervision

We supervise our network with a loss consisting of two parts. The first part measures the L1 error of the predicted disparity against the ground truth at each iteration, with exponentially increasing weights for later iterations. This part enables faster training of all disparity ranges regardless of outliers at the beginning. The second part of the loss is similar to the first part except that (1) it measures the error of depth (i.e. inverted disparity) so as to be more aligned with point cloud evaluation, and that (2) the error is capped at a constant κ so as to prevent outliers from dominating the loss.

Given the predicted disparity in each iteration be $\mathbf{d}_t, t = 1, ..., T_1 + T_2$ and ground truth disparity $\mathbf{d}_{\mathrm{gt}}$, the combined loss is defined as follows:

$$\mathcal{L}_1 = \sum_{t=1}^{T_1+T_2} \gamma^{T_1+T_2-t} \left\| \mathbf{d}_{\mathrm{gt}} - \mathbf{d}_t \right\|_1 \tag{8}$$

$$\mathcal{L}_2 = \sum_{t=1}^{T_1+T_2} \gamma^{T_1+T_2-t} \min(\left\| \mathbf{d}_{\mathrm{gt}}^{-1} - \mathbf{d}_t^{-1} \right\|_1, \kappa) \tag{9}$$

$$\mathcal{L} = (1 - w) \cdot \mathcal{L}_1 + w \cdot \mathcal{L}_2 \cdot \lambda \tag{10}$$

where γ controls the weights across iterations and λ makes the two parts have roughly the same range. The parameter w balances the two parts and changes from 0 to 1 linearly as training progresses to focus more on the depth error, e.g. for a total number of 16 training epochs, w would be 0.5 when 8 epochs are finished.

Table 1. Implementation hyperparameters

Training dataset	DTU	BlendedMVS
Native resolution (H, W)	(1200, 1600)	(1536, 2048)
# neighbor views	10	8
# training epochs	15	16
Feature map downsize ratio	4	
Feature map dimension	64	
Cost volume stack size L	3	
Retrieved neighborhood size R	11	
Cascaded stages	2	
Max disparity d_{max}	0.0025	
Disparity increment in stage 1	$d_{max}/64$	
Disparity increment in stage 2	$d_{max}/320$	
# GRU iterations in each stage	8	
Batch size	2	
Loss parameter	$\lambda = 2.8 \times 10^{-6}, \kappa = 100, \gamma = 0.9$	
Test dataset	DTU	Tanks-and-Temples
Native resolution (H, W)	(1200, 1600)	(1080, 1920) or (1080, 2048)
# Neighbor views for native resolution input	10	15
# Neighbor views for 2 × native resolution input	10	25
Multires fusion threshold t	0.02	0.02
Resolution for point cloud stitching	Native resolution	1/2 native resolution
Adaptive thresholding parameter p	0.25	0.25

Table 2. Results on DTU test set

	DTU mean distance (mm)		
	Acc.	Comp.	Overall
COLMAP [23]	0.400	0.664	0.532
MVSNet [34]	0.396	0.527	0.462
D2HC-MVSNet [32]	0.395	0.378	0.386
Point-MVSNet [5]	0.342	0.411	0.376
Vis-MVSNet [42]	0.369	0.361	0.365
AA-RMVSNet [27]	0.376	0.339	0.357
CasMVSNet [10]	0.325	0.385	0.355
EPP-MVSNet [21]	0.413	**0.296**	0.355
CVP-MVSNet [33]	**0.296**	0.406	0.351
UCSNet [6]	0.338	0.349	0.344
LANet [43]	0.320	0.349	0.335
Ours	0.359	0.305	**0.332**

4   Experiments

4.1   Implementation Details

We evaluate our models on two datasets, DTU and Tanks-and-Temples. On DTU, we train on its training split of DTU and evaluate on its test split, which was suggested by Yao et al. [34] and followed by most authors. On Tanks-and-Temples, we train on the BlendedMVS dataset [36], following the practice of prior work [21,32,34]. For all datasets, during training we use the native image resolutions after some random cropping and scaling as input to the network and other details on the hyperparameters are given in Table 1.

To pair neighbor views with reference views, we use the same method as MVS-Net [34]. In BlendedMVS, which is used for training only, the scenes have large variations in the range of depth values, we scale each reference view, along with its neighbor views, so that its ground-truth depth has a median value 600 mm. When we evaluate on Tanks-and-Temples, due to lack of ground-truth and noisy background, we scale each reference view, along with its neighbor views, so that its minimum depth of a set of reliable feature points (computed by COLMAP [23] as in MVSNet [34]) is 400 mm. To stitch the predicted depth maps from multiple reference views, we simply scale back each depth map to its original scale.

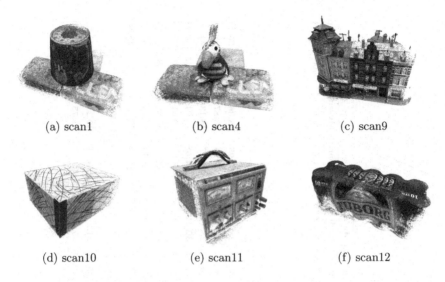

(a) scan1   (b) scan4   (c) scan9

(d) scan10   (e) scan11   (f) scan12

Fig. 2. Visualization of results on DTU (test set).

(a) Family (Intermediate) (b) Francis (Intermediate) (c) Horse (Intermediate)

(d) Lighthouse (Intermediate) (e) M60 (Intermediate) (f) Auditorium (Advanced)

(g) Ballroom (Advanced) (h) Courtroom (Advanced) (i) Museum (Advanced)

Fig. 3. Visualization of results on Tanks-and-Temples.

Table 3. Results on Tanks-and-Temples

Method	Intermediate									Advanced						
	mean	Fam.	Franc.	Horse	Light.	M60	Pan.	Play.	Train	mean	Audi.	Ballr.	Courtr.	Museum	Palace	Temple
COLMAP [23]	42.14	50.41	22.25	25.63	56.43	44.83	46.97	48.53	42.04	27.24	16.02	25.23	34.7	41.51	18.05	27.94
MVSNet [34]	43.48	55.99	28.55	25.07	50.79	53.96	50.86	47.90	34.69	–	–	–	–	–	–	–
Point-MVSNet [5]	48.27	61.79	41.15	34.20	50.79	51.97	50.85	52.38	43.06	–	–	–	–	–	–	–
CVP-MVSNet [33]	54.03	76.50	47.74	36.34	55.12	57.28	54.28	57.43	47.54	–	–	–	–	–	–	–
UCSNet [6]	54.83	76.09	53.16	43.03	54.00	55.60	51.49	57.38	47.89	–	–	–	–	–	–	–
LANet [43]	55.70	76.24	54.32	49.85	54.03	56.08	50.82	53.71	50.57	–	–	–	–	–	–	–
Altizure-SFM, PCF-MVS [16]	55.88	70.99	49.60	40.34	63.44	57.79	58.91	56.59	49.40	35.69	28.33	38.64	35.95	48.36	26.17	36.69
CasMVSNet [10]	56.84	76.37	58.45	46.26	55.81	56.11	54.06	58.18	49.51	31.12	19.81	38.46	29.10	43.87	27.36	28.11
ACMM [28]	57.27	69.24	51.45	46.97	63.20	55.07	57.64	60.08	54.48	34.02	23.41	32.91	41.17	48.13	23.87	34.60
ACMP [30]	58.41	70.30	54.06	**54.11**	61.65	54.16	57.60	58.12	57.25	37.44	**30.12**	34.68	**44.58**	50.64	27.20	37.43
Altizure-HKUST-2019 [1]	59.03	77.19	61.52	42.09	63.50	59.36	58.20	57.05	53.3	37.34	24.04	44.52	36.64	49.51	30.23	39.09
DeepC-MVS [17]	59.79	71.91	54.08	42.29	66.54	55.77	**67.47**	60.47	**59.83**	34.54	26.30	34.66	43.50	45.66	23.09	34.00
Vis-MVSNet [42]	60.03	77.40	60.23	47.07	63.44	62.21	57.28	60.54	52.07	33.78	20.79	38.77	32.45	44.20	28.73	37.70
AttMVS [20]	60.05	73.90	62.58	44.08	64.88	56.08	59.39	63.42	56.06	31.93	15.96	27.71	37.99	**52.01**	29.07	28.84
D2HC-MVSNet [32]	60.13	77.36	57.74	45.74	63.39	63.30	57.82	60.71	54.99	–	–	–	–	–	–	–
AA-RMVSNet [27]	61.51	77.77	59.53	51.53	64.02	**64.05**	59.47	60.85	54.90	–	–	–	–	–	–	–
EPP-MVSNet [21]	61.68	77.86	60.54	52.96	62.33	61.69	60.34	62.44	55.30	35.72	21.28	39.74	35.34	49.21	30.00	38.75
Ours	**64.82**	**81.16**	**64.21**	50.43	**70.73**	63.85	63.99	**65.90**	58.25	**40.19**	25.95	**45.75**	39.65	51.75	**35.08**	**42.97**

4.2   Main Results

DTU. The results on the DTU benchmark are presented in Table 2. Our method achieves the best overall score, which is an average completeness and accuracy [2]. Visualizations of sample reconstructions on DTU are shown in Fig. 2.

Tanks-and-Temples. On the Tanks-and-Temples intermediate set, we achieve state of the art performance, as shown in Table 3. Notably, the model is trained on the BlendedMVS dataset without finetuning on Tanks-and-Temples except for some test-time hyperparameter selection using the validation set, as described in Table 1. This indicates a good generalization ability of our approach. A visualization of some results is shown in Fig. 3, from which we can see that many reconstructed scenes look reasonably accurate, detailed, and complete, but there is still substantial room for improvement, especially on low-texture planar regions.

4.3   Ablations

We show our ablation experiments on Tanks-and-Temples official training set (used as validation set) in a restricted setting where we only train the model on BlendedMVS for 2 epochs but keep everything else the same as in Table 1.

Cost Volume Cascading. We study the effect of cost volume cascading on memory consumption. In Fig. 4, we plot the GPU memory usage versus F_1-score on Tanks-and-Temples validation set for (1) a series of cascaded model (with different disparity increments in the first stage), annotated by a single number (2) its non-cascaded counterpart, which matches the first-stage disparity resolution used in the cascaded model and has equal total GRU iterations, annotated by a 2-tuple. We train all models as described in Sect. 4.1 and finally chose the

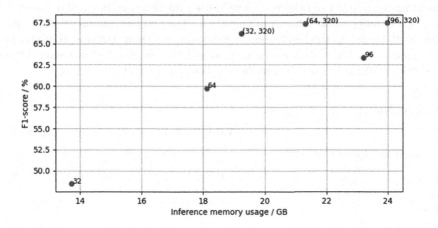

Fig. 4. Memory usage of cascaded v.s. non-cascaded model. The label for cascaded models means coarse and fine disparity increments (larger number means smaller increments), and the label for non-cascaded models means the single disparity increment.

cascaded model (64, 320) for long-time training and benchmarking. It uses 44 disparity values with an increment of $d_{max}/320$ in the second stage, and uses 64 values with a coarser increment $d_{max}/64$ in the first stage to cover the entire disparity range from 0 to d_{max}. For the non-cascaded model, because it needs to fill the entire disparity range from 0 to d_{max}, it needs significantly more memory as the disparity resolution increases. We see from Fig. 4 that cascading produces significant savings of memory. Note the reported memory is the peak memory reported by the command"nvidia-smi".

Table 4. Ablation on supervision

Method	F_1-score
(1) Truncated L_1 depth loss	N/A
(2) L_1 disparity loss	66.79
(3) Average of (1) and (2)	67.32
(4) Proposed dynamic loss	**67.36**

Table 5. Ablation of neighbor view number

Mean F_1-score (%)		# Neighbor views in 2 × native resolution		
		5	15	25
# Neighbor views in native resolution	5	62.62	66.42	67.27
	15	62.73	66.48	**67.36**
	25	62.66	66.37	67.27

Dynamic Supervision. In Table 4, we show our model trained with different loss supervision. Among them, the truncated L_1 depth loss does not help the model to start up; and L_1 disparity loss has inferior performance; while the proposed dynamic loss is marginally better than the direct average of L_1 depth loss and L_1 disparity loss.

Number of Neighbor Views. During inference, our network can use a different number of neighbor views than in training. In Table 5, we study the effect of changing the number of neighbor views during inference. In particular, we study how this number can be chosen differently for the two resolutions we use to predict depth maps. As the results on the validation set show, the best combination is 15 views for native resolution prediction and 25 views for 2 × native resolution prediction. And these are the numbers we use on the test set.

Table 6. Ablation of aggregation options

Aggergation option	Mean F_1-score (%)
max	57.77
max + mean	65.37
std	59.90
std + mean	66.85
mean	**67.36**

Table 7. Ablation of adaptive thresholding

Controlled percentage p%	15%	20%	25%	30%	35%
Mean F_1-score (%)	66.83	67.31	**67.36**	67.11	66.60
Fixed threshold k	1	1.5	2	2.5	3
Mean F_1-score (%)	65.33	66.10	66.33	66.32	66.13

Aggregation of Cost Volumes. Here in Table 6 we study the effect of aggregation options different from our simple averaging including both one-channel and two-channel ones. It shows that taking the mean is the best.

Adaptive Thresholding. To strike a balance between accuracy and completeness scores, we use adaptive thresholding method and search for the best parameter p. The results are in Table 7 in comparison with results from fixed thresholds. We see that our adaptive thresholding approach is significantly better than fixed thresholding.

Table 8. Ablation of multiresolution fusion

Multi-resolution with control threshold t	0 = native input	0.01	0.02	0.04	∞ = 2 × native input
Mean F_1-score (%)	64.38	68.47	**68.49**	68.39	68.08
Weighted average with w	0 = native input	0.25	0.5	0.75	1 =2 × native input
Mean F1-score (%)	64.38	65.30	66.55	67.51	68.08

Multiresolution Fusion of Depth Maps. An important part of CER-MVS is the multiresolution fusion of depth maps. Different from previous components, its effect is most obvious on our final model trained for 16 epochs. We report the following results on the validation sets of Tanks-and-Temples: (1) Different control parameter t, and (2) simple weighted average of native input results and 2 × native input results with weight w. We see from Table 8 that our novel fusion approach is significantly better than all the other approaches.

4.4   Memory and Runtime

The computational cost of CER-MVS is compared with other methods in Table 9. When using similar resolution and numbers of views, the time and memory cost of our method is comparable to others.

Table 9. Comparison of running time and memory cost

Method	# Neighbor views	Input resolution	Output resolution	Times per view (ms)	Mem. (GB)
CasMVSNet	4	(1056, 1920)	(1056, 1920)	792.2	9.5
Vis-MVSNet			(528, 960)	864.2	4.5
PatchmatchNet			(1056, 1920)	317.7	3.2
EPP-MVSNet			(528, 960)	522.2	8.2
Ours			(264, 480)	664.4	3.0
Ours		(2112, 3840)	(528, 960)	1754.5	7.0
Ours	25			7611.3	22.6

5   Conclusion

We have proposed CER-MVS, a new approach based on the RAFT architecture developed for optical flow. CER-MVS introduces five new changes to RAFT: epipolar cost volumes, cost volume cascading, multiview fusion of cost volumes, dynamic supervision, and multiresolution fusion of depth maps, as well as adaptive thresholding to construct point clouds. Experiments show that our approach achieves state-of-the-art performance on challenging benchmarks.

Acknowledgments. This work is partially supported by the National Science Foundation under Award IIS-1942981.

References

1. https://www.altizure.com
2. Aanæs, H., Jensen, R.R., Vogiatzis, G., Tola, E., Dahl, A.B.: Large-scale data for multiple-view stereopsis. Int. J. Comput. Vision **120**(2), 153–168 (2016)
3. Barnes, C., Shechtman, E., Finkelstein, A., Goldman, D.B.: PatchMatch: a randomized correspondence algorithm for structural image editing. ACM Trans. Graph. **28**(3), 24 (2009)
4. Campbell, N.D.F., Vogiatzis, G., Hernández, C., Cipolla, R.: Using multiple hypotheses to improve depth-maps for multi-view stereo. In: Forsyth, D., Torr, P., Zisserman, A. (eds.) ECCV 2008. LNCS, vol. 5302, pp. 766–779. Springer, Heidelberg (2008). https://doi.org/10.1007/978-3-540-88682-2_58
5. Chen, R., Han, S., Xu, J., Su, H.: Point-based multi-view stereo network. In: Proceedings of the IEEE/CVF International Conference on Computer Vision, pp. 1538–1547 (2019)
6. Cheng, S., et al.: Deep stereo using adaptive thin volume representation with uncertainty awareness. In: Proceedings of the IEEE/CVF Conference on Computer Vision and Pattern Recognition, pp. 2524–2534 (2020)
7. Furukawa, Y., Hernández, C.: Multi-view stereo: a tutorial. Found. Trends. Comput. Graph. Vis. **9**(1–2), 1–148 (2015)
8. Furukawa, Y., Ponce, J.: Accurate, dense, and robust multiview stereopsis. IEEE Trans. Pattern Anal. Mach. Intell. **32**(8), 1362–1376 (2009)
9. Galliani, S., Lasinger, K., Schindler, K.: Massively parallel multiview stereopsis by surface normal diffusion. In: Proceedings of the IEEE International Conference on Computer Vision, pp. 873–881 (2015)
10. Gu, X., Fan, Z., Zhu, S., Dai, Z., Tan, F., Tan, P.: Cascade cost volume for high-resolution multi-view stereo and stereo matching. In: Proceedings of the IEEE/CVF Conference on Computer Vision and Pattern Recognition, pp. 2495–2504 (2020)
11. Han, X., Leung, T., Jia, Y., Sukthankar, R., Berg, A.C.: MatchNet: unifying feature and metric learning for patch-based matching. In: Proceedings of the IEEE Conference on Computer Vision and Pattern Recognition, pp. 3279–3286 (2015)
12. Hirschmuller, H.: Stereo processing by semiglobal matching and mutual information. IEEE Trans. Pattern Anal. Mach. Intell. **30**(2), 328–341 (2007)
13. Ji, M., Gall, J., Zheng, H., Liu, Y., Fang, L.: SurfaceNet: an end-to-end 3D neural network for multiview stereopsis. In: Proceedings of the IEEE International Conference on Computer Vision, pp. 2307–2315 (2017)

14. Kar, A., Häne, C., Malik, J.: Learning a multi-view stereo machine. arXiv preprint arXiv:1708.05375 (2017)
15. Knapitsch, A., Park, J., Zhou, Q.Y., Koltun, V.: Tanks and temples: benchmarking large-scale scene reconstruction. ACM Trans. Graph. (ToG) **36**(4), 1–13 (2017)
16. Kuhn, A., Lin, S., Erdler, O.: Plane completion and filtering for multi-view stereo reconstruction. In: Fink, G.A., Frintrop, S., Jiang, X. (eds.) DAGM GCPR 2019. LNCS, vol. 11824, pp. 18–32. Springer, Cham (2019). https://doi.org/10.1007/978-3-030-33676-9_2
17. Kuhn, A., Sormann, C., Rossi, M., Erdler, O., Fraundorfer, F.: DeepC-MVS: deep confidence prediction for multi-view stereo reconstruction. In: 2020 International Conference on 3D Vision (3DV), pp. 404–413. IEEE (2020)
18. Lipson, L., Teed, Z., Deng, J.: Raft-stereo: multilevel recurrent field transforms for stereo matching. In: 2021 International Conference on 3D Vision (3DV), pp. 218–227. IEEE (2021)
19. Luo, K., Guan, T., Ju, L., Huang, H., Luo, Y.: P-MVSNet: learning patch-wise matching confidence aggregation for multi-view stereo. In: Proceedings of the IEEE/CVF International Conference on Computer Vision, pp. 10452–10461 (2019)
20. Luo, K., Guan, T., Ju, L., Wang, Y., Chen, Z., Luo, Y.: Attention-aware multi-view stereo. In: Proceedings of the IEEE/CVF Conference on Computer Vision and Pattern Recognition, pp. 1590–1599 (2020)
21. Ma, X., Gong, Y., Wang, Q., Huang, J., Chen, L., Yu, F.: EPP-MVSnet: epipolar-assembling based depth prediction for multi-view stereo. In: Proceedings of the IEEE/CVF International Conference on Computer Vision, pp. 5732–5740 (2021)
22. Romanoni, A., Matteucci, M.: TAPA-MVS: textureless-aware patchmatch multi-view stereo. In: Proceedings of the IEEE/CVF International Conference on Computer Vision, pp. 10413–10422 (2019)
23. Schönberger, J.L., Zheng, E., Frahm, J.-M., Pollefeys, M.: Pixelwise view selection for unstructured multi-view stereo. In: Leibe, B., Matas, J., Sebe, N., Welling, M. (eds.) ECCV 2016. LNCS, vol. 9907, pp. 501–518. Springer, Cham (2016). https://doi.org/10.1007/978-3-319-46487-9_31
24. Seitz, S.M., Curless, B., Diebel, J., Scharstein, D., Szeliski, R.: A comparison and evaluation of multi-view stereo reconstruction algorithms. In: 2006 IEEE Computer Society Conference on Computer Vision and Pattern Recognition (CVPR 2006), vol. 1, pp. 519–528. IEEE (2006)
25. Teed, Z., Deng, J.: RAFT: recurrent all-pairs field transforms for optical flow. In: Vedaldi, A., Bischof, H., Brox, T., Frahm, J.-M. (eds.) ECCV 2020. LNCS, vol. 12347, pp. 402–419. Springer, Cham (2020). https://doi.org/10.1007/978-3-030-58536-5_24
26. Tola, E., Strecha, C., Fua, P.: Efficient large-scale multi-view stereo for ultra high-resolution image sets. Mach. Vis. Appl. **23**(5), 903–920 (2012)
27. Wei, Z., Zhu, Q., Min, C., Chen, Y., Wang, G.: AA-RMVSNet: adaptive aggregation recurrent multi-view stereo network. In: Proceedings of the IEEE/CVF International Conference on Computer Vision, pp. 6187–6196 (2021)
28. Xu, Q., Tao, W.: Multi-scale geometric consistency guided multi-view stereo. In: Proceedings of the IEEE/CVF Conference on Computer Vision and Pattern Recognition, pp. 5483–5492 (2019)
29. Xu, Q., Tao, W.: Learning inverse depth regression for multi-view stereo with correlation cost volume. In: Proceedings of the AAAI Conference on Artificial Intelligence, vol. 34, pp. 12508–12515 (2020)

30. Xu, Q., Tao, W.: Planar prior assisted patchmatch multi-view stereo. In: Proceedings of the AAAI Conference on Artificial Intelligence, vol. 34, pp. 12516–12523 (2020)

31. Xue, Y., et al.: MVSCRF: learning multi-view stereo with conditional random fields. In: Proceedings of the IEEE/CVF International Conference on Computer Vision, pp. 4312–4321 (2019)

32. Yan, J., et al.: Dense hybrid recurrent multi-view stereo net with dynamic consistency checking. In: Vedaldi, A., Bischof, H., Brox, T., Frahm, J.-M. (eds.) ECCV 2020. LNCS, vol. 12349, pp. 674–689. Springer, Cham (2020). https://doi.org/10.1007/978-3-030-58548-8_39

33. Yang, J., Mao, W., Alvarez, J.M., Liu, M.: Cost volume pyramid based depth inference for multi-view stereo. In: Proceedings of the IEEE/CVF Conference on Computer Vision and Pattern Recognition, pp. 4877–4886 (2020)

34. Yao, Y., Luo, Z., Li, S., Fang, T., Quan, L.: MVSNet: depth inference for unstructured multi-view stereo. In: Ferrari, V., Hebert, M., Sminchisescu, C., Weiss, Y. (eds.) ECCV 2018. LNCS, vol. 11212, pp. 785–801. Springer, Cham (2018). https://doi.org/10.1007/978-3-030-01237-3_47

35. Yao, Y., Luo, Z., Li, S., Shen, T., Fang, T., Quan, L.: Recurrent MVSNet for high-resolution multi-view stereo depth inference. In: Proceedings of the IEEE/CVF Conference on Computer Vision and Pattern Recognition, pp. 5525–5534 (2019)

36. Yao, Y., et al.: BlendedMVS: a large-scale dataset for generalized multi-view stereo networks. In: Proceedings of the IEEE/CVF Conference on Computer Vision and Pattern Recognition, pp. 1790–1799 (2020)

37. Yi, H., et al.: Pyramid multi-view stereo net with self-adaptive view aggregation. In: Vedaldi, A., Bischof, H., Brox, T., Frahm, J.-M. (eds.) ECCV 2020. LNCS, vol. 12354, pp. 766–782. Springer, Cham (2020). https://doi.org/10.1007/978-3-030-58545-7_44

38. Yu, Z., Gao, S.: Fast-MVSNet: sparse-to-dense multi-view stereo with learned propagation and gauss-newton refinement. In: Proceedings of the IEEE/CVF Conference on Computer Vision and Pattern Recognition, pp. 1949–1958 (2020)

39. Zagoruyko, S., Komodakis, N.: Learning to compare image patches via convolutional neural networks. In: Proceedings of the IEEE Conference on Computer Vision and Pattern Recognition, pp. 4353–4361 (2015)

40. Zbontar, J., LeCun, Y.: Computing the stereo matching cost with a convolutional neural network. In: Proceedings of the IEEE Conference on Computer Vision and Pattern Recognition, pp. 1592–1599 (2015)

41. Zbontar, J., LeCun, Y.: Stereo matching by training a convolutional neural network to compare image patches. J. Mach. Learn. Res. 17(1), 2287–2318 (2016)

42. Zhang, J., Yao, Y., Li, S., Luo, Z., Fang, T.: Visibility-aware multi-view stereo network. arXiv preprint arXiv:2008.07928 (2020)

43. Zhang, X., Hu, Y., Wang, H., Cao, X., Zhang, B.: Long-range attention network for multi-view stereo. In: Proceedings of the IEEE/CVF Winter Conference on Applications of Computer Vision, pp. 3782–3791 (2021)

44. Zheng, E., Dunn, E., Jojic, V., Frahm, J.M.: Patchmatch based joint view selection and depthmap estimation. In: Proceedings of the IEEE Conference on Computer Vision and Pattern Recognition, pp. 1510–1517 (2014)

Author Index

Printed in the United States
by Baker & Taylor Publisher Services